Ecosystems of Florida

Merritt Island National Wildlife Refuge. Photo by Robert Thompson.

Ecosystems of Florida

Edited by
Ronald L. Myers
and John J. Ewel

Foreword by Marjorie H. Carr

University of Central Florida Press/Orlando

Copyright 1990 by the Board of Regents of the State of Florida and the State of Florida, Department of State, for the Game and Fresh Water Fish Commission

06 05 11 10 9 8 7

Library of Congress Cataloging-in-Publication Data
Ecosystems of Florida / edited by Ronald L. Myers and John J. Ewel.
p. cm.
Includes bibliographical references.
ISBN 0–8130–1012–8 (alk. paper). — ISBN 0–8130–1022–5 (pbk.: alk. paper)
1. Biotic communities—Florida. 2. Ecology—Florida. 3. Natural history—Florida. I. Myers, Ronald L. II. Ewel, John J.
QH105.F6E26 1990 90–10882
574.5'09759—dc20 CIP

The University of Central Florida Press is a member of University Presses of Florida, the scholarly publishing agency of the State University System of Florida. Books are selected for publication by faculty editorial committees at each of Florida's nine public universities: Florida A&M University (Tallahassee), Florida Atlantic University (Boca Raton), Florida International University (Miami), Florida State University (Tallahassee), University of Central Florida (Orlando), University of Florida (Gainesville), University of North Florida (Jacksonville), University of South Florida (Tampa), University of West Florida (Pensacola).

Orders for books published by all member presses should be addressed to: University Presses of Florida, 15 NW 15th St., Gainesville, FL 32611
http://www.upf.com

Contents

Acknowledgments

We owe a special debt to Louise Robbins of The Nature Conservancy. Had she been with the project at its inception, she would have been both coeditor and coauthor. She contributed to every chapter, and *Ecosystems of Florida* would not have come to fruition without her efforts.

Each chapter was reviewed by at least two referrees. For these reviews, we thank Warren Abrahamson, Mark Benedict, Karla Brandt, Russell Burke, Steven Christman, Andre Clewell, Robert Craig, Michael Duever, Katherine Ewel, Richard Fisher, Gordon Godshalk, Thomas Gleeson, Henry Gholz, Pamela Hallock, Dennis Hardin, Gary Hendricks, Walter Jaap, Ann Johnson, Wiley Kitchens, Robert Livingston, Fred Lohrer, Lloyd Loope, Ariel Lugo, Ian Macintyre, William Platt, Francis Putz, John Reed, A. Christine Robbins, Louise Robbins, William Robertson, Daniel Simberloff, Samuel Snedaker, James Snyder, Robert Twilley, Susan Vince, and Charles Wharton.

We found that black and white photography is becoming a lost art. We thank Lawrence Battoe, David Boughton, Allan Horton, Jan Knoblock, Paige Martin, Walter Thomson, and Holly Tuck for their photography and Pam Wallheiser for her developing and printing.

We are grateful to Diane Hudgins of Archbold Biological Station, Karla Brandt, and Beatriz Pace of the University of Florida, and Susan Boettcher and Holly Tuck of The Nature Conservancy for their help with many aspects of the project: editorial, photograph-seeking, bibliographic, and many other tasks.

The Florida Game and Fresh Water Fish Commission provided funds to support this project through its Nongame Wildlife Section. We extend special thanks to Brad Gruver, David Cook, Susan Cerulean, and Brian Milsap of that agency. Archbold Biological Station encouraged us to undertake the project, hosted a workshop for the authors, and administered the funds. We are especially grateful for the advice and encouragement of Archbold staff members James Wolfe, David Johnston, Fred Lohrer, and James Layne and the members of the Archbold Scientific Advisory Board. For the past three years, The Nature Conservancy, with the support of Willard Rose, stewardship director for the Conservancy's Southeast Region, has generously provided Myers and, more recently, Louise Robbins with the time to complete this project. Tall Timbers Research Station, which houses The Nature Conservancy's Fire Management and Research Program, graciously made its facilities and staff available to us. We thank Jean E. Thomson Black, John Thomas, and Chuck Arthur of Academic Press, Inc. for their advice and assistance. We are grateful to the staff of the University Presses of Florida and to the Executive Board of the University of Central Florida Press.

Our authors acknowledge the following individuals for their advice and assistance: chapter 4—G. Morgan, W. Judd, and D. Jones; chapter 5—A. Clewell, D. Hardin, H. Gholz, A. Johnson, L. Robbins, J. Layne, K. McCrea, I. Kralick, and F. Lohrer; chapter 6—L. Robbins, S. Christman, F. Putz, F. Lohrer, S. Denton, M. Deyrup, and R. Burke; chapter 7—A. Clewell, H. Delcourt, P. Delcourt, G. Evans, K. Ewel, J. Glitzenstein, A. Greller, P. Harcombe, B. Means, C. Monk, M. Platt, S. Rathbun, D. Streng, T. Boline, K. Gainey, and S. Moroshok; chapter 10—T. Alexander, D. Black, the late F. Craighead, Sr., G. Davis, W. Dineen, K. Ewel, P. Frohring, the late W. Gillis, J. Hefner, A. Higer, R. Hofstetter, B. Hunt, T. Jacobsen, H. Klein, M. Kolipinski, J. Lincer, E. Lowe, H. Odum, O. Owre, L. Perrin, W. Robertson, Jr., P. Sykes, D. Tabb, and B. Winchester; chapter 11—M. Flannery and F. Nordlie; chapter 12—G. Kiltie, C. Binello, D. Vallejos-Nichols, S. Walsh, G. Bass, G. Godshalk, P. Moler, T. Swihart, and S. Flannery; chapter 13—D. Addison, M. Benedict, W. Bidlingmeyer, W. Campbell, D. Crewz, L. Duever, H. Gilfond, D. Hall, D. Hardin, A. Herndon, A. Hine, J. Layne, R. Roberts, B. Robertson, P. Schmalzer, H. Tuck, J. Wolfe, G. Woolfenden, and R. Wunderlin; chapter 14—M. Summers and E. Rivera.

Several authors were partially supported by research grants. S. D. Webb received support from NSF grant EAR 8708045, and his chapter is University of Florida Contribution to Paleobiology Number 341. W. J. Platt received support from the Nongame Wildlife Program of the Florida Game and Fresh Water Fish Commission and NSF grants DEB8012090 and BSR8605318. The authors of chapter 11 were supported in part by NSF grant EAR8419506 and a grant from The Whitehall Foundation, Inc.

Foreword

Marjorie Harris Carr

When I first looked over this excellent book, *Ecosystems of Florida*, I realized that my life in Florida has spanned the development of ecology as a concept essential to an understanding and appreciation of our natural environment. The urge to recognize and understand the physical characteristics of the various landscapes of Florida has been evident since humans came into the peninsula. An appreciation of the complex interactions among life forms, their vulnerability to careless use, and their importance to the quality of life in Florida has burgeoned in the past twenty years. This book has come just in time to save the landscapes of Florida. With a population in 1990 of nearly 13 million and growing, Florida needs a large cadre of well-informed citizens if the landscapes we admire today are to be part of our environment in the twenty-first century.

When I was growing up in south Florida, the words "ecologist" and "ecosystem" were not abroad in the land. However, there was a recognition of different and distinct associations of plants—flatwoods, bayheads, cypress swamps, scrub, and marsh. Settlers of that era needed to identify these ecosystems in order to determine the most profitable uses of their lands.

These pioneers were looking for timberlands, hunting and trapping areas, lands for citrus groves and truck crops, and, of course, homesites. The landscape was described and catalogued according to its potential for exploitation. Today a relic of this early system for describing the land is still evident in the category "waste land" for marshes and swamps on the tax assessors' rolls.

In the early part of this century, my father, a Boston schoolteacher, dreamed of retiring to a small citrus grove and vegetable garden, surrounded by wilderness, near a river and close to the Gulf of Mexico. He first moved to Fort Myers in Lee County, where an old experienced grove man told him how to find the site for his new venture. The best citrus land, he said, could be recognized by the types of forest it supported. In 1920 my father found his homesite in the pine woods bordering the Imperial River west of Bonita Springs, three miles from the Gulf of Mexico. He chose land with a heavy stand of Caribbean pine and saw palmetto—indicators of good citrus land, according to the wisdom of the day.

Florida landscapes were examined and described by the early naturalist-explorers. Their enthusiastic discourses tantalize the modern reader with images of a Florida Eden—although even in those early days the more perceptive naturalists deplored the destruction of the wilderness.

Along with tales of adventure and exploration came the lists and descriptions of the plants and animals of Florida. Dr. John Kunkel Small published his *Trees of Florida* in 1913. I well remember the excitement in our home when *Florida Wild Flowers* by Mary Francis Baker appeared in 1926. By the 1930s the different plant associations in Florida had been described, and checklists of the major groups of plants and animals were available. It was time to find out how and why these plant associations came about and time to describe the life histories of plants and animals.

I entered Florida State College for Women in Tallahassee in 1932. My aim was to become a zoologist. I wanted to work with whole, live animals, preferably birds, in their natural surroundings. Fortunately, I came under the direction of an outstanding teacher, Dr. Edza Mae Deviney, who guided and advised me during my undergraduate years. The zoology department offered only a few field courses, such as ornithology and marine invertebrates, but the botany department under the direction of Dr. Herman Kurz provided a stimulating, even exciting, experience.

At that time, Dr. Kurz was perfecting his theories on the formation of various plant associations of Florida. Nearly every Saturday found us out in some type of woods, rushing to keep up with Dr. Kurz as he strode rapidly along, lecturing vigorously as he went. Each of us was encumbered with our own vasculum, notebooks, lunch, water bottle, and knife. We also carried Dr. Kurz's paraphernalia because he needed both hands to demonstrate his points. We not only learned the characteristics of the different hardwood forests, but we heard Dr. Kurz's arguments about how they had evolved and to what type of climax forest they were headed. We saw how climate and fire could modify the process by holding a given plant association at a subclimax level or by returning it to an earlier level of development.

Dr. Herbert Stoddard, on his plantation north of Tallahassee, was then at the peak of his career. His experimental plots visually demonstrated the impact of fire on the southern pine forest. His results were so unequivocal that it is incomprehensible to me why it took so long for official forestry people to accept what today is so obvious: that fire, like rain and wind, is a natural sculptor of landscape in our environment.

Absorbing all this information was enormously satisfying. What a pleasure it was to go into the woods and fields and, by recognizing a set of characteristic key plants, be able to put a name to a particular association of plants. It was thrilling to look at a landscape and think perhaps you knew its past history and its future. The ability to "read" a landscape provides the kind of pleasure that comes from a knowledge of Bach or Shakespeare or Van Gogh. It is a pleasure that increases with your knowledge and understanding of the ecology of Florida, and it lasts an entire lifetime.

I came to the University of Florida in 1937 as the wife of Archie Carr and as a graduate student in zoology. Dr. J. Speed Rogers was the head of the department and Dr. Theodore H. Hubbell his first lieutenant. Dr. C. Francis Byers and Dr. Harley B. Sherman completed the senior staff. Ecology in Florida owes an enormous debt to them.

Florida was a zoologist's paradise in those days. A graduate student could select a set of animals to work on and realize that he or she was the first to focus on that particular group in Florida. For example, H. K. Wallace studied spiders, Archie focused on herps and fishes, Frank Young selected water beetles, Horton Hobbs studied crayfish, and Louis Berner specialized in mayflies. The plan of study for any group of animals was rigorous. First, one needed a sound grounding in geology and soils. Next, one needed a knowledge of the different plant associations of Florida and the diagnostic animals associated with them. With this knowledge in place, one could place the different species of one's special group of animals in their proper niches. Before long one would be describing subspecies and races and other subsets in the heady but confusing world of taxonomy.

In these early years Al Laessle was thoughtfully stalking around in the Big Scrub east of Ocala. His studies provided us with an understanding of the formation and evolution of the scrub ecosystem. Erdmon West and Lillian Arnold were working on their book, *The Trees of Florida,* and were ever ready to assist the zoologists in their quest to understand plant and animal relationships.

These are some of the Florida pioneers in the field of ecology. They provided the groundwork—the data base—for the ecological research that has grown and flourished in the last fifty years.

Ecosystems of Florida has a proud heritage. Its authors have the same skill and enthusiasm that characterized the early Florida ecologists. The descriptions in this book will encourage and delight a multitude of men and women who are enamored of Florida's landscapes. The salvation of the Florida scene will come about only if the public savors its beauty, understands its limitations, and speaks up for its preservation.

Preface

In 1984, the scientific advisory committee of the fledgling Nongame Program of Florida's Game and Fresh Water Fish Commission determined that the lack of basic descriptions of the state's habitats was a major impediment to the management of nongame species. As ecologists who had taught and done research both in Florida and in the tropics for a number of years, Ron Myers and I recognized the state's unique ecological status and we wanted to make it better known to a broader community of scholars: Florida bridges the tropics and the temperate zone; its geologically ancient and recent formations result in mosaics of habitats and organisms of worldwide importance; its humid climate is an anomaly at a latitude characterized by deserts; and, as a peninsula, it combines island and continental biogeographies. And despite the fact that many people are attracted to Florida because of its natural features, there was no single reference that tourists and residents could use to help them sort out the complexity of Florida's environment.

This combination of needs led to a workshop at the Archbold Biological Station in February 1986. During that lively meeting we honed our plans for this book, and at the end of the session we gave our ambitious charge to authors: write a technically sound, state-of-the-art chapter on your subject, but write so that your prose will be accessible to the lay reader. Our intended audience is broad: students of Florida's ecosystems, resource managers, scholars outside the region, environmental consultants, and members of the general public interested in the environments of Florida.

The objective of this book is to introduce the reader to the ecology of Florida's landscape: its forests, fresh waters, marshes, and marine life. Chapter 1 introduces Florida and the book, and chapters 2, 3, and 4 deal with topics that are fundamental to all ecosystems: climate, soil, and biogeography. Each of the next thirteen chapters explores a particular type of community, and we end with a brief overview of some important conservation and environmental issues. The ecosystem chapters are arranged from high ground to low ground, from terrestrial to aquatic, and from fresh water to salt water. We hope that our readers can visualize the continua that exist among these categories. If we have done our job, the glimmer of Florida past, the reality of Florida today, and the prospect of Florida tomorrow will be apparent.

John J. Ewel

Contributors

Warren G. Abrahamson
Department of Biology, Bucknell University, Lewisburg, PA 17837

Michael G. Barbour
Department of Botany, University of California, Davis, CA 95616

Michael W. Binford
Graduate School of Design, Harvard University, 48 Quincy Street, Cambridge, MA 02138

Mark Brenner
Department of Fisheries and Aquaculture, University of Florida, 7922 NW 71st Street, Gainesville, FL 32606

Randall B. Brown
Soil Science Department, University of Florida, Gainesville, FL 32611

Victor Carlisle
Soil Science Department, University of Florida, Gainesville, FL 32611

Ellen Chen
1620 NW 65th Street, Gainesville, FL 32605

Edward S. Deevey (deceased)

John J. Ewel
Department of Botany, University of Florida, Gainesville, FL 32611

Katherine C. Ewel
School of Forest Resources and Conservation, Department of Forestry, University of Florida, Gainesville, FL 32611

John F. Gerber
Institute of Food and Agricultural Sciences, University of Florida, Gainesville, FL 32611

Pamela Hallock
Department of Marine Science, University of South Florida, St. Petersburg, FL 33701

David C. Hartnett
Division of Biology, Kansas State University, Manhattan, KS 66506

Alan Herndon
Department of Botany, Louisiana State University, Baton Rouge, LA 70803

Walter C. Jaap
Bureau of Marine Research, Department of Natural Resources, 100 Eighth Avenue, S.E., St. Petersburg, FL 33701

Ann Johnson
Florida Natural Areas Inventory, 1018 Thomasville Road # 200-C, Tallahassee, FL 32303

James A. Kushlan
Department of Biology, University of Mississippi, University, MS 38677

Robert J. Livingston
Center for Aquatic Research and Resource Management, Department of Biological Sciences, Florida State University, Tallahassee, FL 32306

Carole C. McIvor
Cooperative Fish & Wildlife Research Division, University of Florida, Gainesville, FL 32611

Clay L. Montague
Department of Environmental Engineering Sciences, University of Florida, Gainesville, FL 32611

Ronald L. Myers
The Nature Conservancy, Tall Timbers Research Station, Route 1, Box 678, Tallahassee, FL 32312

Frank G. Nordlie
Department of Zoology, University of Florida, Gainesville, FL 32611

William E. Odum
Department of Environmental Sciences, University of Virginia, Charlottesville, VA 22903

William J. Platt
Department of Botany, Louisiana State University, Baton Rouge, LA 70803

William B. Robertson, Jr.
South Florida Research Center, Everglades National Park, P.O. Box 279, Homestead, FL 33030

Mark W. Schwartz
Department of Biology, Florida State University, Tallahassee, FL 32306

James R. Snyder
National Park Service, Big Cypress National Preserve, S.R. Box 110, Ochopee, FL 33943

Earl L. Stone
Soil Science Department, University of Florida, Gainesville, FL 32611

S. David Webb
Florida Museum of Natural History, University of Florida, Gainesville, FL 32611

Richard G. Wiegert
Department of Zoology, University of Georgia, Athens, GA 30602

Part I

Introduction

1

Introduction

John J. Ewel

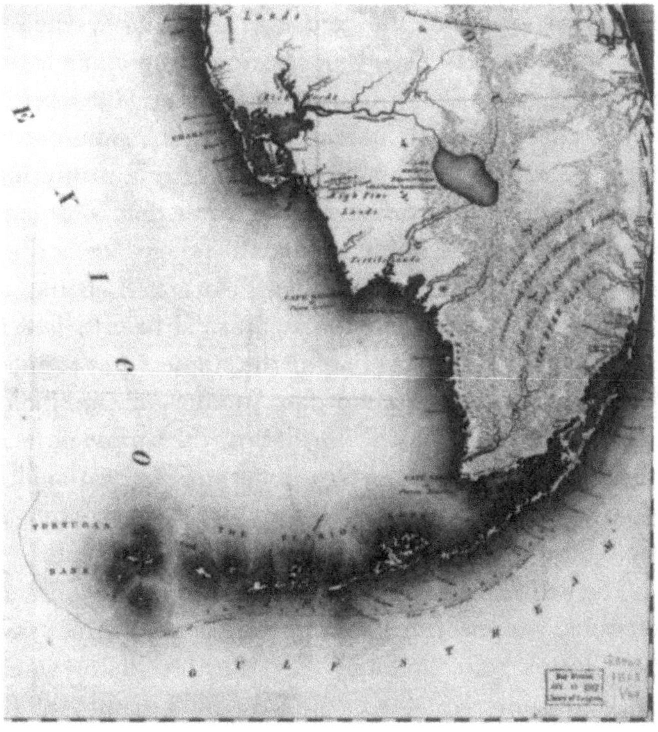

In one very long day, a southbound visitor can cross the Florida state line on Interstate Highway 75 and drive to tropical Key West. A drive like that will not give a tourist much insight into the biology of Florida, yet all but the most myopic passerby would have to note at least three things.

First, Florida is remarkably flat. That transect down the peninsula would never have elevated our visitor more than 70 m above sea level, less than the height of a twelve-story building. Nevertheless, in Florida, a little topography exerts a remarkable effect on the biota: high ground supports semiarid scrubs, and low ground is covered with swamps and marshes.

Second, from the perspective of most farmers, Florida has sand, not soil. Furthermore, its sands are relatively impoverished—infertile and porous. That some of them support magnificent forests attests to the power of the biota to scavenge nutrients and tap subsurface water. Many of the rivers and creeks that drain the forests are tea-colored, stained by tannic acid from the leaves, twigs, and other organic matter in their water. Where the streams

Portion of "Map of Florida Compiled and Drawn from Various Actual Surveys & Observations: by Charles Vignoles, 1823." Courtesy Map Division, Library of Congress.

meet the sea, this organic detritus feeds the inhabitants of salt marshes, mangroves, and estuaries—the sources of Florida's prized seafoods, whose harvest generates $155 million each year. Forest, sand, and seafood: the links are direct and obvious.

Third, the visitor would notice that an underlying platform of limestone is evident wherever the veneer of sand has washed away. In some places, this limestone has dissolved, creating dimple-like lakes and sinkholes where it is overlaid by sand. Florida has some 7800 lakes, more than any other state south of glacially pocked Wisconsin. Porous sands on porous substrates mean that water has a short residence time in the soil, so Florida's ecosystems rely on a thin surface film of water that is replenished with each year's rains. In the limestone far beneath the surface is the Floridan Aquifer, recharged primarily by rainfall in Georgia, Alabama, and northern Florida. "Florida's rain barrel," as the aquifer has been called (Parker, 1951), enables Floridians to engage in one of the highest per capita rates of water use in the United States. The Floridan Aquifer and the shallower Biscayne Aquifer underlying southeastern Florida together provide nearly 90 percent of the state's drinking water, irrigation water, recreational water, and waste disposal water (Heath and Conover, 1981). Ultimately, Florida's aquifers will likely limit the human carrying capacity of the state.

One would think that flat topography, poor soils, and limited surface water would support only an impoverished biota. Not so. On that trip between the Georgia state line and Key West, a visitor would have traversed the ranges of some 425 species of birds, 3500 plants, and 65 snakes—a degree of diversity unmatched by any other state east of the Mississippi. Several factors combine to account for Florida's remarkable biotic diversity, and many of them are explored in detail in this book.

One important factor is the state's latitudinal position. Florida spans 6.5° latitude, protruding southward from a temperate zone continent into warm tropical seas. It is unique among the states in the way it bridges temperate zone and tropics.

Another factor is Florida's humid climate. The same humidity that supports the fungi colonizing shoes forgotten in a closet is also responsible for Florida's luxuriant vegetation. Examining a world vegetation map reveals that most of the land at Florida's latitude is desert. The fact that Florida is a peninsula, surrounded by warm oceans, saves it from a similar fate.

Finally, Florida's sand-covered limestone looks deceptively more uniform and static than it is. The parts of Florida that are above sea level today encompass a tremendous range of landscape ages. On the one hand, some of Florida has been continuously occupied by plants and animals for 25 million years. On the other hand, the flat terrace of extreme southwest Florida is one of the youngest landscapes in North America—land that has been above sea level for only a few thousand years.

The Imprint of Human Settlement

People have inhabited Florida for 10,000 years, perhaps longer. Paleo-Indians, the earliest Floridians, were nomadic hunters of mammoths, bison, camels, and giant tortoises. After the extinction of the megafauna, humans diversified their economy. The contents of middens reveal that they exploited fish, game, shellfish, and plants; their other effects on the environment are less clear. Florida's aborigines did not engage in agriculture until about 800 years ago, but it seems likely that they changed the face of the landscape, especially through their use of fire.

The impact of Native Americans, however, was slight compared to what would happen in the four centuries following European colonization. Florida has been continuously occupied by Europeans and their descendants since 1565. As historian Michael Gannon put it, "When the Pilgrims landed at Plymouth Rock, St. Augustine was up for urban renewal." It was not until Florida was ceded to England in 1763, however, that colonization of the interior began in earnest. In the past 227 years, the state's landscape has been profoundly changed. Three examples of human impact seem especially important because of the magnitude of change involved. Each covers an area huge enough to be prominent on satellite imagery.

First, colonization caused the gradual deforestation of a great swath of land that arches northeast from the Tampa Bay area, curves north and west up the Suwannee River Basin, then cuts west into the Panhandle, parallel to the Georgia border (fig. 1.1). Forests were cleared for agriculture, for

Fig. 1.1. Virgin longleaf pine logging operation, Gilburn Estate, Gadsden County. Photo taken in 1936 by H. E. Whitehead. From Florida State Archives.

lumber, and for fuel for phosphate processing. Some fertile soils (probably once occupied by mixed hardwood forests) were cleared, along with some very infertile, droughty sands. We may never be able to assess the ecological impact of this episode of deforestation. It probably cost most of a once-extensive community type: the red oak/longleaf pine/mockernut hickory/fox squirrel community that exists today only on small islands in a sea of agricultural fields and pine plantations.

Second, the growth of citrus cultivation entailed the conversion of the central ridge to citrus plantations (fig. 1.2). John McPhee describes the ridge this way:

> The Ridge is the Florida Divide, the peninsular watershed, and, to hear Floridians describe it, the world's most stupendous mountain range after the Himalayas and the Andes. Soaring two hundred and forty feet into the sub-tropical sky, the Ridge is difficult to distinguish from the surrounding lowlands, but it differs more in soil conditions than in altitude, and citrus trees cover it like a long streamer, sometimes as little as a mile and never more than twenty-five miles wide, running south, from Leesburg to Sebring, for roughly a hundred miles. It is the most intense concentration of citrus in the world. (McPhee, 1966, p. 18)

Citrus cultivation is constrained by frost to the north and the absence of deep sandy soils to the east, west, and south. Citrus experts seem determined to alter soils through drainage and the use of fertilizers and pesti-

Fig. 1.2. Early citrus operation near Lake Placid, Highlands County, c. 1920. Photo by Burgert Bros., Tampa. Courtesy of M. Jackson, Lake Placid.

cides. The pre-citrus ridge was covered with two main kinds of plant communities, the most extensive one a mixture of longleaf pine, turkey oak, and wiregrass. We do not know the ecological cost of losing that longleaf pine community; it might have been no more severe than would be expected anywhere else from such extensive deforestation. Intermixed with the longleaf pine stands were patches of scrub, the oldest kind of plant community unique to Florida. The loss of these pockets of endemism was quite another matter. Surely some species found nowhere else on earth succumbed to the land-clearing operations of the 1800s and early 1900s.

Meanwhile, in the southern quarter of the peninsula, the dewatering of the landscape was under way (Tebeau, 1971; Carter, 1974). Construction of the network of canals and dikes that radiate from Lake Okeechobee and slice across the Everglades was begun in the 1880s as a private enterprise financed by Hamilton Disston. His objective was to convert marshes into land suitable for agriculture, and dredges were his tools. He dug canals to connect lakes in the Kissimmee Basin and, by blasting out the waterfall at Fort Thompson, connected the Caloosahatchee River to Lake Okeechobee.

The state got into the act in the early 1900s by dredging canals and by constructing the Tamiami Trail, a project that created the longest dike outside of the Netherlands (fig. 1.3). Today, the highway still impedes the free flow of surface water through the Everglades, despite its occasional perforation by culverts.

The main impediment to the free flow of south Florida's water was built following the terrible hurricanes of 1926 and 1928, which pushed water out of Lake Okeechobee and drowned more than 2500 people. The "Hoover Dike," a levee 10 m tall that extends 140 miles (224 km) around the south rim of the lake, obliterated Okeechobee's natural spillway.

In a place like south Florida, where almost everything between Orlando and Florida Bay is in the same watershed, the ecological impact of structures that either accelerate or impede sheet flow extends very far, both upstream and down. The dewatering of south Florida was a giant, uncontrolled experiment. Although it is unlikely that we will ever understand its consequences

Fig. 1.3. Construction of the Tamiami Trail (U.S. 41) through the Big Cypress Swamp. From Florida State Archives.

completely, we do know that changed hydrology has greatly affected fire regimens, vegetation patterns, salinization, and invasions of exotic species.

Classification of Florida's Ecosystems

Communities of plants and animals occur as continua, some species becoming more abundant as others decrease in importance along environmental gradients. Nevertheless, ecologists find it useful to classify clusters of organisms into communities and ecosystems. Sometimes, in fact, the boundaries between certain clusters or groups of species are well demarcated. This demarcation is especially evident in Florida, where striking changes in moisture, soil fertility, fire frequency, and land-use history occur over very short distances. For example, abrupt changes in soil moisture and depth to water table can result in a scrub community adjoining a cypress pond, and a low-fire-frequency island nestled within a fire-prone landscape can lead to a tropical hammock sharply demarcated from the surrounding pineland.

Ecologists do not agree, however, on the way that communities should be classified. A variety of ways exist to delineate ecosystems, and at one time or another almost all major approaches have been applied in Florida. Each approach has its purposes and proponents, and scientists in different fields—foresters, hydrologists, botanists, fisheries biologists, agronomists, conservationists, and archaeologists—naturally select the approach best suited to their particular needs. Most classification schemes are amalgamations of floristics, physiognomy, environmental factors, and successional status.

One approach widely used by plant ecologists is to classify potential natural vegetation. The map units represent the communities that would be found if the land were to revert to its "natural" state, so farms, cities, and roads are all included within the vegetation type they originally supported. Miami is shown as south Florida pineland and tropical hammocks, and the muck farms south of Lake Okeechobee are mapped as marshes and custard apple swamps. One of the earliest such maps in Florida was produced as a result of land surveys conducted in East Florida from 1766 to 1770 by William Gerard DeBrahm (DeBrahm, 1773), just after William Bartram's explorations of the same area. A favorite unit on DeBrahm's map corresponds to what is today most of Volusia County: "Great Swamp whose Inside as yet unknown."

It was not until this century that vegetation maps were drawn accurately enough to be useful in interpreting the Florida landscape. Consider the history of vegetation mapping in Florida south of a line connecting Sarasota with Fort Pierce. One of the earliest efforts was the "Phytogeographic Map of South Florida" prepared in 1913 by John W. Harshberger (Harshberger, 1914). You would not want to try to navigate across the Everglades using

Harshberger's map, but considering how inaccessible the area must have been at that time, the detail and general accuracy of his map showing eleven vegetation types are remarkable.

In 1927, Roland M. Harper (who called Harshberger's work "pretentious") published descriptions of twenty-four vegetation types in south Florida, including several variants of tropical hammocks and submarine communities. Harper—who also contributed detailed vegetation descriptions of northern and central Florida (Harper, 1914a, 1921, respectively) that are cited repeatedly in this book—recognized the urgency and importance of his task. In his prophetic south Florida report, he wrote:

> In an area with . . . so little land cultivated yet, the native vegetation is . . . the most conspicuous feature of the landscape. . . . Furthermore, the 'developers' are trying to destroy the vegetation . . . to make room for cities and farms, . . . and some that was studied by the writer in 1909, 1910, or even later, is already gone forever. All these circumstances make it desirable to put on record a pretty full account of the vegetation, for the benefit of future generations, who will not have such good opportunities to study it as there are at present. (Harper, 1927, pp. 75–76)

The same area mapped by Harshberger was remapped in much greater detail by John H. Davis, Jr., in 1943 (Davis, 1943). Davis delineated nineteen vegetation types based on fieldwork and aerial photographs. His map served as a standard reference for decades, until research facilitated by helicopters, airboats, and high quality remote-sensing imagery made the production of even more detailed vegetation maps possible (e.g., McPherson, 1973, a, b; Gunderson and Loope, 1982a–d; Gunderson et al., 1982, 1986; Olmsted et al., 1981, 1983; Pesnell and Brown, 1977). Nonetheless, the monograph that accompanied Davis's map is still a basic reference on south Florida vegetation.

The level of detail used by ecologists to describe ecosystems depends in part on the scale being considered. For example, Davis's nineteen south Florida vegetation types (1943) were reduced to ten on his later vegetation map of the entire state (Davis, 1967). Küchler (1964), in turn, traced a prepublication version of Davis's 1967 map when making his map of the vegetation of the United States, but he combined many of the units, reducing Davis's seventeen vegetation types for the entire state to ten. For example, Küchler retained the pine-dominated rocklands of south Florida, but he lumped together all the pine flatwoods, which cover half the state, with southern mixed hardwood forest. At the other extreme, researchers with The Nature Conservancy and the Florida Natural Areas Inventory, who are interested in the uniqueness and value of specific ecological elements, operate at a very fine level of resolution. They distinguish sixty-nine community types in Florida (Florida Natural Areas Inventory, 1988).

In deciding upon suitable classification of ecosystems for this book, the editors elected to identify a few broadly defined units. Having invited scholars possessing broad vision and detailed expertise to write the chapters describing these units, we hope that the breadth and depth of treatment provided will be useful to those seeking technical details as well as to Floridians and visitors interested in general information about the environment.

The units we chose are not too dissimilar from those of Vignoles (1823), who published one of the earliest descriptions of Florida's vegetation, divided as follows: scrub lands and undulating pine lands; oak and hickory lands and high hummock; flat pine lands and pine land savannas; low hummock, river swamps, and cypress swamps; fresh marshes and hummock savannas; and salt marshes. We have added chapters on some coastal communities and aquatic ecosystems that Vignoles did not cover, but otherwise his classification rests reasonably comfortably within ours. Our perceptions of the broad units of Florida's landscape may not have changed much in 165 years, but surely we know a great deal more about the organisms that inhabit the ecosystems, the forces that maintain them, and the agents that threaten them.

2
Climate

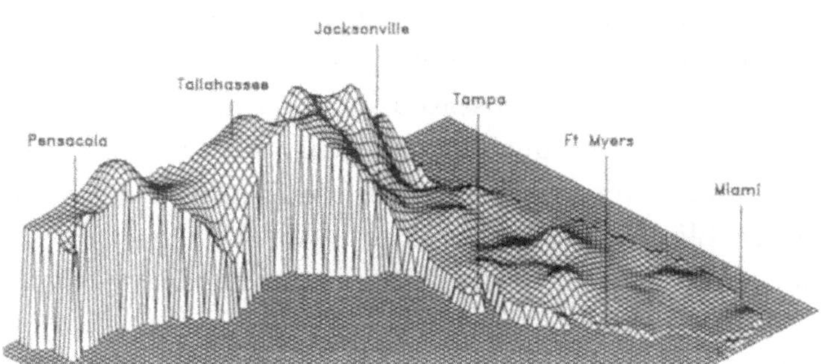

Ellen Chen
John F. Gerber

Climate can be defined as the year-to-year persistence of weather patterns over time at a particular place. In this chapter, we summarize the physical processes responsible for these climatic patterns and the maritime influence that creates specific, unique characteristics in the Florida climate. Florida's weather and the forces that control it are described in a very readable book by Winsberg (1990).

Florida has a humid, subtropical climate. From its location on the eastern shore of a large landmass, one would expect a subhumid or arid climate, but the maritime influence of the Caribbean Sea and the Gulf of Mexico transforms Florida's climate.

The Bermuda high pressure cell keeps Florida from being continuously awash in rain. The subsidence from this high, rather than a shortage of water vapor, keeps convective clouds from building into thunderstorms in the fall and winter. As the Bermuda high weakens in late spring and summer, convective rains—i.e., thunderstorms—occur in late afternoon over the land and at night over the Gulf of Mexico and the Atlantic Ocean. More lightning occurs in Florida than in any other place in the United States.

Tropical low pressure storms from the Atlantic and Caribbean sweep

Map: mean annual frost occurrence.

over Florida, bringing hours of heavy rain in late summer and early autumn. Fronts from the North American continent also sweep over the state in late fall, winter, and early spring. These fronts bring on radical swings in temperature and humidity, causing the weather to oscillate between maritime tropical and continental winter weather. Winters in Florida are literally "here today and gone tomorrow."

In Florida, a cool dry season and a warm, rainy season constitute a strong climatic cycle. Seasonal climatic changes are often slight, but the daily temperature ranges at some times and places may exceed the average annual ranges. Climatic differences also occur over short distances. Variations in the topography and in the daily weather produce a finely structured mosaic of microclimates.

Superimposed upon the generally mild climate of Florida are more extreme climatic events. During the dry season, fronts mitigate the dryness but may also cause severe low temperature stresses. During the wet season, tropical storms and hurricanes help replenish the water supply but may also cause flooding. These mostly random, and sometimes very large, deviations produce temperature and rainfall extremes that can severely damage plants. For example, freezes occasionally kill extensive areas of mangrove forests and, since 1835, have forced the abandonment of some areas for citrus growing (Davis, 1937; Sanders, 1980).

Because daily, annual, and extra-annual extreme events are an important part of Florida's climatic pattern, it is necessary to understand them and their causes to appreciate their role in the state's climate. Extreme events exert a large influence upon the plant community because, although plants can adjust to gradual or seasonal changes, they cannot always adjust to sudden, abnormally large changes.

Gross climatic trends are shown in figure 2.1, which presents temperature and rainfall data in the form of climographs for ten weather stations. The annual temperature and rainfall ranges for each station are represented by the vertical thickness and by the horizontal width of the climographs, respectively. The similarly shaped climographs show that climatic patterns are similar throughout Florida. The seven to eight months of the dry season (usually from October or November to May) show changing temperatures and low monthly rainfall. The four to five months of the wet season (June through September or October) show relatively uniform temperatures and high monthly rainfall.

The progressive change from temperate to tropical climate is shown by the north-to-south decrease of the annual temperature range. At the same time, variations in seasonal rainfall become more pronounced. In south Florida, the dry season is drier and the wet season wetter than in north Florida.

The climate of Key West is distinct from that of the rest of Florida. The distinction between wet and dry seasons largely disappears. Key West is the driest of the stations presented.

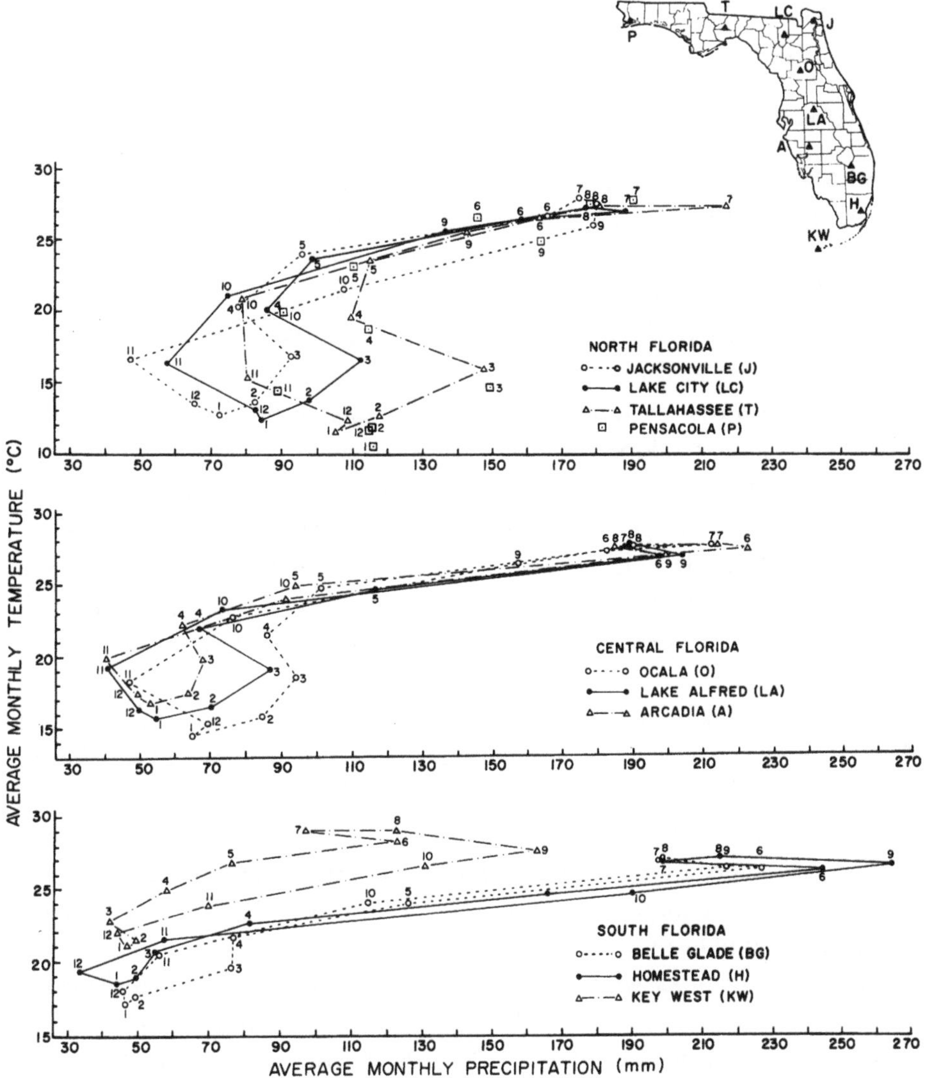

Fig. 2.1. The climate of Florida depicted by average monthly temperature and average monthly precipitation (1930–85) at Pensacola, Tallahassee, Lake City, Jacksonville, Ocala, Lake Alfred, Arcadia, Belle Glade, Homestead, and Key West. Numbers refer to months (1 - January, 2 - February). From NOAA, 1930–85.

The diagram shows that the temperature trends are quite strongly linked to latitude and to proximity to bodies of water, but the rainfall trends are less well defined (MacVicar, 1981; Palmer and Nguyen, 1986). Winter temperatures are progressively warmer toward southern latitudes, where the mitigating effects from the water also become more prominent. Regionally, Arcadia in March is warmer and drier than Lake Alfred, which in turn is warmer and drier than Ocala. Jacksonville has slightly warmer winters than Lake City. The clustering of the monthly means for December, January, and February indicates that the winter months are similar to each other in rainfall and temperature. January is generally the coldest month at all of these stations.

Spring (March–May)

Around March 21, the spring equinox, the sun has reached the equator on its apparent northward track to the northern hemisphere. The span of sunlight per day increases from about 11 hours in February to about 13.5 hours in May. The direction from which the sun rises changes by almost 45°, from near east-southeast in February to near east-northeast in May. The change in direction over the three-month period gives rise to changes in the patterns of shadows cast by trees and landforms. Generally speaking, the casting of shadows due to slope and exposure is not as important in the flat terrain of Florida as in hilly regions. However, numerous limestone depressons in the north Florida ridge (60 m to 90 m elevation), and to a lesser degree in the central Florida ridge (30 m to 45 m elevation), have slopes steep enough to provide shaded microclimates. Since many Florida soils are well drained and naturally droughty, shading may lessen water stress during the spring growing season.

The increased exposure to the sun's rays, or insolation, warms the land and water surfaces, but water temperature does not increase as quickly as land temperature. This creates a temperature difference between the land and the surrounding water that causes air to circulate along the shores of lakes and seas. Since Florida has a long coastline, these sea breezes influence a large area and are important influences on local weather. The sea breeze effect is year-round but is greatest during summer (fig. 2.2).

Because spring links winter and summer, it has some characteristics of both. Temperatures as low as −5°C (23°F) and as high as 39°C (102°F) have been recorded in interior north Florida. Spring has a wider temperature span (about 44°C [79°F]) than any of the other seasons.

Drought is often a threat during spring in Florida because this season follows four months of low rainfall, but Florida frequently escapes the serious and long-lasting droughts that characterize other southern states. However, agriculturally significant droughts can easily develop, especially when dry spells occur together with warm spells. Water deficit generally shows up during spring (Jones et al., 1984; Smajstrla et al., 1985; Allen et al., 1982; Rogers et al., 1983). Hence the threat of dry spells and agricultural droughts is a major climatic characteristic of the Florida spring.

The Bermuda High

The dominant weather pattern in the spring months that produces the large deviations in temperature and rainfall is the semipermanent high pressure system commonly referred to as the Bermuda high (Nieuwolt, 1977; Riehl,

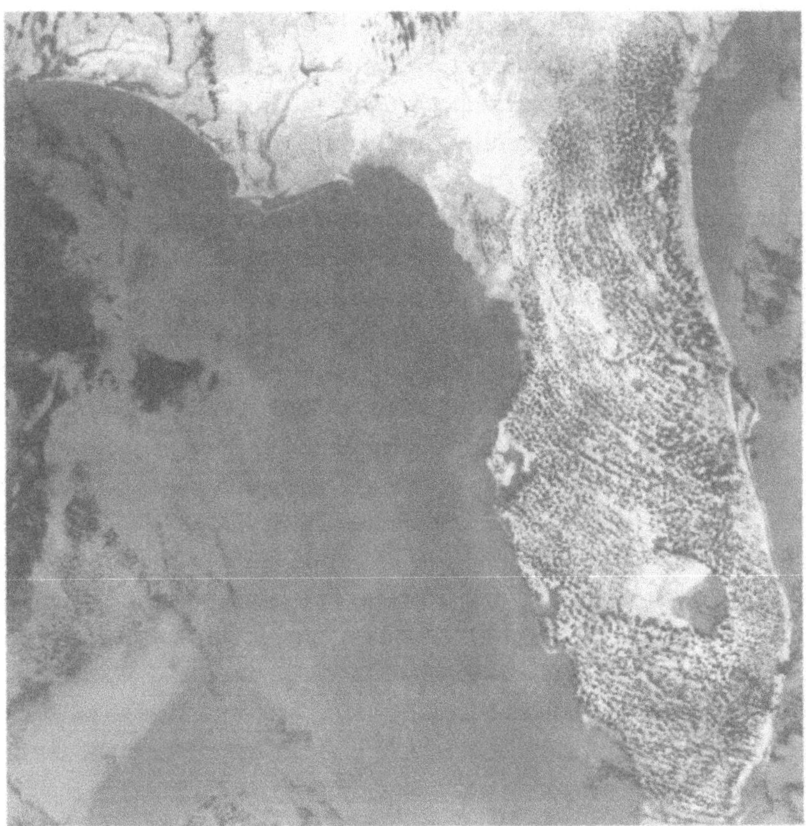

Fig. 2.2. Bands of clouds over the Florida peninsula are indicative of differential heating of land surfaces and water bodies. Note cloud-free area west of Lake Okeechobee.

1954). Its center is generally located over the north Atlantic Ocean in the Bermuda-Azores area (fig. 2.3).

A normal spring in Florida brings increasing warmth, abundant sunshine, and clear blue skies. Days are breezy, and afternoon showers occur more regularly as the season progresses. However, spring can be cold, with

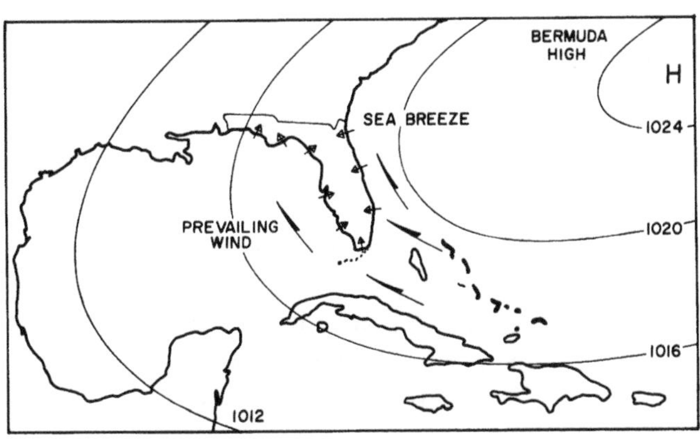

Fig. 2.3. A common weather pattern for spring and summer illustrating effects of the Bermuda high, the prevailing wind, and the sea breeze. The pressure is in millibars. If the Bermuda high is farther south, the prevailing wind over Florida is southwesterly.

episodes of nighttime temperatures below 0°C (32°F); or it may be hot and dry when the expected light rain does not materialize. Weather in spring depends to a large extent on the position of the Bermuda high. During winter, the Bermuda high is generally small and is located to the south and east of the north Atlantic Ocean. As winter turns to spring, the pressure cell expands and migrates north and west (Riehl, 1954), exerting more and more influence on the east coast of the United States and, of course, on Florida.

The expanded Bermuda high can diminish the chance for rain by hindering cloud development (Lockwood, 1979; Namias, 1978). Air motion in a high pressure system generally subsides, and sinking air warms at the rate of 10°C (18°F) per kilometer of descent. Warmer air can hold more moisture; hence, clouds evaporate and disappear, and air temperature rises quickly under the cloudless skies. If the westward extension of the Bermuda high persists, dry spells or droughts can quickly develop.

In March, and to a lesser degree in April, winter storms and frontal weather are still frequent in north Florida. The timely expansion and migration of the Bermuda high to the northwest can slow or block the southerly penetration of cold air masses into the Florida peninsula, diminishing chances of below-freezing and near-freezing temperatures. However, if the influence of the Bermuda high is absent because it has moved, the chance for frost episodes in the peninsula increases.

An example of how the location of the Bermuda high affects regional weather is shown by the weather in the spring and summer of 1986. In March and April of that year, the influence of the Bermuda high was absent from the latitude of Florida. The monthly mean temperature in Gainesville during that March was 3°C (5°F) below its seventy-year average, and again in April it was below that average. Such episodes of low temperatures and late frosts can delay spring planting or slow early plant growth and can cause the water needs of plants to be out of step with the onset of summer rain. The delayed expansion of the Bermuda high and its persistence during late spring and early summer of 1986 influenced Florida's weather well into the summer months. Thus, the Bermuda high was partly responsible for one of the worst droughts ever recorded in the southeastern United States.

Spring Frosts

One way to identify the gradual and sometimes imperceptible change from the temperate climate of north Florida to the tropical climate of south Florida is to look at regional increases in mean monthly temperatures. (Geographically, the tropical zone extends to latitude 23.5°N, but the climatic tropical zone is generally different [Nieuwolt, 1977]. The climate of extreme southern Florida, latitude 25.5°N, is considered tropical.) The greatest increases in the mean monthly temperature in the three spring months are 11°C (20°F) in the maritime temperate climate of north Florida, 8°C

(14°F) in central Florida, and only 6°C (11°F) in south Florida. The temperature differences separating adjacent regions are minor, normal, day-to-day variations; microclimatic differences can overcome regional climatic differences. Within a rather short period of time, the natural climatic zones may be reversed or interchanged.

Winter-like conditions in spring can be described by the number of times the temperature drops below a certain value, such as below 0°C (32°F). The gradual moderation between coastal and interior regions and between maritime temperate and tropical climate is illustrated by changes in the number of occurrences of 0°C (32°F) (fig. 2.4). The difference between coastal and interior regions is illustrated in north Florida. Between 1930 and 1979, below-freezing temperatures occurred fifteen times at Pensacola and thirteen times at Jacksonville along the coast, compared to thirty-one times at Tallahassee and twenty-seven times at Lake City in the interior. It appears that even a short distance inland may double the chances of below-freezing temperatures. Farther south, peninsular cities (Ocala, Lake Alfred, Arcadia, and Belle Glade) registered freezing temperatures only five to eight times, and Homestead only twice. The lowest temperatures registered for the ten cities surveyed during the spring months were about −5°C (23°F) in north Florida and about −3°C (27°F) in central and south Florida. These temperatures generally lasted for only a few hours. In April, only Tallahassee has ever recorded freezing temperatures (three times between 1930 and 1985).

The mean monthly maximum temperature for May is around 31°C (89°F). If the onset of rainfall is delayed, the daily temperature can climb even higher. This situation can generate extremely high temperatures and significantly increase the chances of dry spells or drought. Temperatures of 38°C (100°F) and higher have been recorded in May for many stations, with the exception of those in south Florida (Belle Glade, Homestead, and Key West). Temperatures greater than 38°C occurred about five or six

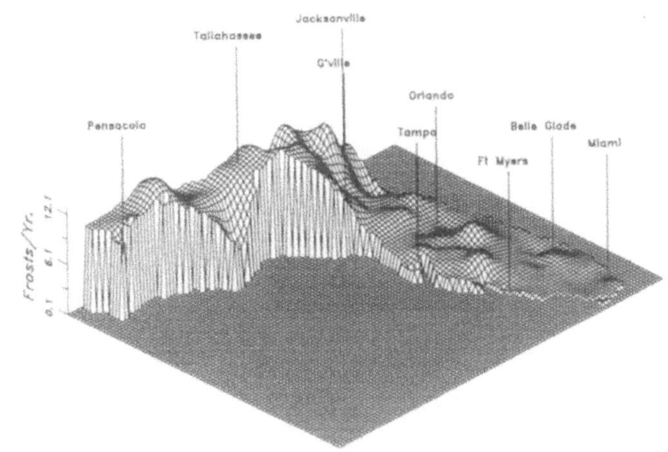

Fig. 2.4. Mean annual frost occurrences for Florida, showing the moderating influence of decrease in latitude and proximity to the coast.

times in Lake City, Ocala, and Arcadia but only once or twice in the coastal cities. The highest May temperature recorded between 1930 and 1985 in the cities in figure 2.1 was 39°C (103°F) in Lake City. On windless days or in sheltered, sunny areas, the temperature near the ground is frequently higher than the standard air temperature (which is measured 1.5 m above the ground), often by as much as 4°C to 5°C (7°F to 9°F).

Rainfall Patterns and Dry Spells

In general, spring rainfall decreases from northwest Florida eastward and southward (figs. 2.1 and 2.5). The rainfall peaks in March in north Florida are due to the region's proximity to winter storm tracks, which generally originate in the north and west and travel eastward (Trewartha, 1981). Peaks for Pensacola and Tallahassee are particularly prominent. The fronts associated with late winter storms often become stationary over north Florida or oscillate over the region, sometimes producing rain. Although the fronts themselves are frequently dry, many of them are preceded by squall lines that produce most of the rain. The squall lines and fronts have a

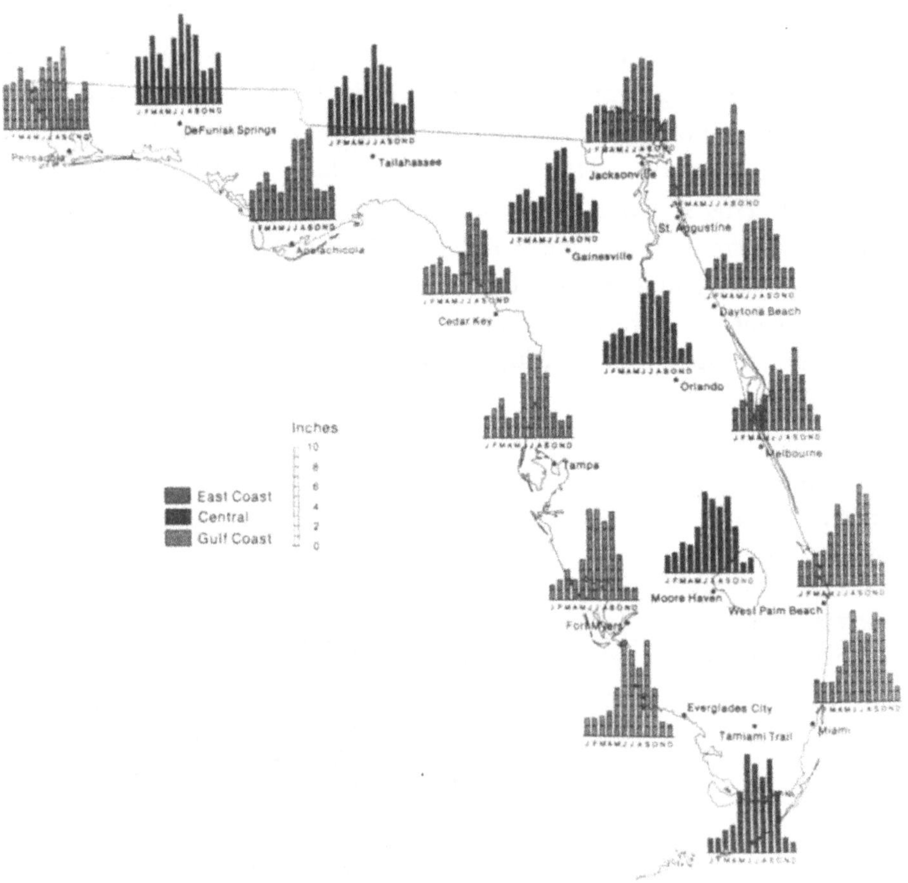

Fig. 2.5. Seasonal variation of rainfall, 1941–70 average. From Jordan, 1984.

strong tendency to diminish as they move southward. As a result, central and south Florida do not receive as much frontal rainfall and are quite dry.

In central Florida the March peak is weak, and April and May frequently bring even less rain; central Florida often has more severe and extended dry periods than either north or south Florida (fig. 2.6). In south Florida, where the March peak is generally absent, the start of summer rain is well defined, as rainfall from afternoon showers begins to increase in April and May (fig. 2.5).

Following the four to five months of dry weather during fall and winter, even a small monthly rainfall deficit during early spring can result in severe dry spells. The strong insolation during this period only increases the demand for water and adds to the stress on vegetation. Often it is a question not of how much rain has fallen but of how the rain is distributed through time. One or more dry periods during an otherwise normal spring may cause severe damage to plant communities, even if the total rainfall for that spring equals the long-term average. Tropical depressions, which frequently form off the Gulf and Atlantic coasts of Florida, can produce enough rain to equal normal seasonal rainfall totals, but little or no rain might fall in the

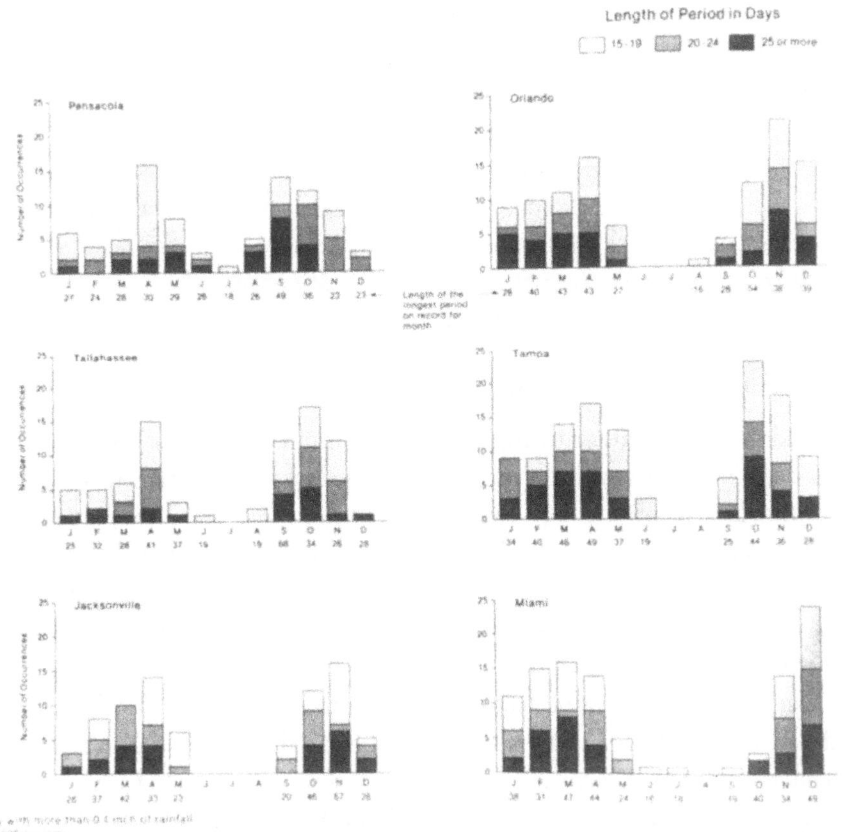

Fig. 2.6. Occurrence of extended dry periods (no day with more than 0.1 inch of rainfall), 1951–80 average. From Jordan, 1984.

remainder of the season. The driest periods in recent times in Florida were in 1950–51, 1960–61, 1970–71, and mid–1980 to mid–1981 (Jordan, 1984; Palmer and Nguyen, 1986). The lowest monthly rainfall for spring in north Florida (Pensacola, Tallahassee, and Lake City) was about 17 to 27 mm. But in peninsular Florida, the lowest monthly rainfall has ranged from trace amounts to approximately 13 mm. Peninsular Florida (Orlando, Tampa, and Miami) also experiences more days without rain and more periods of low rainfall than north Florida (Pensacola, Tallahassee, and Jacksonville) (fig. 2.6).

Toward the end of May the daily temperatures in many parts of the state are summer-like, and afternoon showers and thunderstorms have increased. These changes signal the onset of the four-month-long summer wet season.

Summer (June–September)

The sun appears farthest north in the northern hemisphere around June 21 (summer solstice, latitude 23.5° N). Since the sun's position at noon is nearest zenith, daily insolation is strongest except in cases of persistent heavy cloud cover. Day length, about fourteen hours, is the longest of the year. Sunrise hovers near east-northeast, unlike in spring, when the direction of sunrise moves through almost 23 degrees. In August the sun does not appear as high in the sky, days are shorter, and the direction of sunrise has shifted farther to the east.

Mean monthly temperature reaches a plateau of about 33° C (91° F) in June and is maintained through September. With respect to monthly temperature and rainfall, September is more like the summer months of June, July, and August than the fall months of October and November (fig. 2.5), so September is included in the summer season.

Temperature and Rainfall Patterns

In Florida's environment of high humidity and temperature, some differences in regional temperatures are present, primarily among coastal, inland, and peninsular locations. For example, between 1930 and 1985, air temperatures greater than 38° C (100° F) occurred much more frequently in northern and central interior regions (twenty-five times in Tallahassee, twenty-eight times in Lake City, and twenty times in Ocala) than in two northern coastal cities (fourteen times in Pensacola and sixteen times in Jacksonville). However, temperatures greater than 38° C occurred only two to five times in southern Florida (Lake Alfred, Arcadia, Belle Glade, and Homestead). The highest temperature recorded in Lake City was 41° C (105° F) in July 1954. The highest temperature registered in Key West was 35° C (95° F) in July 1948. The maximum temperature range in summer is about 32° C (58° F).

The higher mean monthly temperature of Key West is a result of higher minimum temperatures rather than higher maximum temperatures.

The broad summer rainfall peak from June through September is more pronounced in south Florida, where summer rainfall accounts for 50 to 60 percent of the annual total. At several locations, mostly along the east coast (Daytona Beach, West Palm Beach, Miami), monthly rainfall is almost as high in October as in September. Most of this rainfall comes from afternoon showers and thunderstorms and from tropical storms and hurricanes. Over a period of fifteen years, Florida experienced a total of forty tropical lows and hurricanes in September, while the northern Gulf coast was affected by only eleven (Trewartha, 1981). Summer rainfall is generally highest along the coastal areas, decreasing inland as the sea breeze weakens. However, MacVicar (1981) noted that within about a mile of the coast the rainfall is 15 to 20 percent less than slightly farther inland; he also indicated that the coastal barrier islands from Miami Beach to Key West probably have a different precipitation regime. Because Lake Okeechobee generates its own lake breezes, the air over the lake generally subsides and produces less rain. Aircraft and satellite photographs of the peninsula frequently show clouds organized along the coast of Florida and the absence of clouds over Lake Okeechobee. Summer rainfall over Lake Okeechobee, estimated from radar, is about 0.7 times that of the surrounding area (Riebsame and Woodley, 1974).

Mechanism of Summer Rainfall

The causes of precipitation in Florida are convective clouds, the sea breeze, and tropical storms and hurricanes. The sea breeze produces rain both by its convective action and by organizing the convective clouds and aligning them parallel to the coast. The organized lines of clouds may produce front-like activities and are sometimes called the "sea breeze front." The summertime prevailing wind is generally southeasterly for the peninsula and southwesterly for the Panhandle and northern Florida. Lake Okeechobee generates a lake breeze that interacts with the sea breeze and the prevailing wind to affect local convective rains. The prevailing wind is superimposed on the sea breeze and the local winds, and it exerts a strong influence on local weather and rainfall (Trewartha, 1981). Miami, for example, receives much of its summer rainfall when the wind is from the southwest; these southwest winds keep the onshore sea breeze near the coast (Pielke, 1974). This situation frequently produces heavy rain and lightning. In contrast, if the prevailing wind is from the southeast, its direction is the same as the onshore sea breeze, helping to push the zone of rainfall (convergence) farther inland. Showers are then more apt to develop west of the city, leaving Miami generally cloudless.

Convective Rain and the Sea Breeze

Convective rain is the result of diurnal heating of the land surface, which causes air to rise. Upon rising, air encounters lower atmospheric pressure and expands. Expansion causes the air to cool; the moisture in the air then condenses and forms clouds, which organize to produce rain, though the clouds may evaporate and disappear if the atmosphere is dry. This mechanism is mainly responsible for Florida's daily summer showers. Convective storms are usually small and slow moving, frequently building and dissipating within a limited area. Surface temperature differences between large urban areas and surrounding rural land may be large enough to produce updrafts that influence convection. Land use may thus influence local weather.

The daily convective rains and thunderstorms are controlled by both the prevailing wind and the sea breeze on each side of the peninsula (Byers and Rodebush, 1948; Trewartha, 1981). The triggering mechanism for the sea breeze is the difference in temperature between the water surface and the land mass (Munn, 1966). On sunny days the circulation is generally evident by midmorning and dies down when the sun sets. At night the process is reversed, and a land breeze is produced. But because there is generally less difference between land and sea temperatures at night, the land breeze is usually weaker than the sea breeze. The offshore land breeze can cause upwelling of local coastal water, bringing cooler water to the surface (Munn, 1966). In areas where coastline curvature causes the land to jut out (e.g., Apalachicola, Merritt Island, Cape Canaveral, and the southern tip of Florida), the sea breezes converge and can produce stronger vertical motion, resulting in more rain than at nearby, less curved areas.

The sea breeze builds near the coast and by midmorning may be as much as 25 km inland (Frank et al., 1967). It is better organized and more prominent when coupled with the prevailing wind. For example, the east coast line of the sea breeze is more prominent on days when the prevailing wind is from the southeast. In south Florida, the two sea breezes tend to converge in late afternoon. The area of convergence between the east coast and west coast sea breezes tends to migrate according to prevailing conditions and tends to be found near the leeward coast. Thunderstorm activity associated with sea breeze convergence reaches a maximum in the afternoon.

While the sea breeze serves to cool the coastal zone, it is also a vehicle for transporting pollutants. In Florida, where most of the metropolitan areas are along the coast, the main pollutant is automobile exhaust. Emissions from coastal power plants and automobiles are carried inland by the sea breeze and the prevailing wind, where the pollutants may be transported upward and deposited back on land by showers. The prevailing wind in the summer is predominantly southerly and, together with the coastal sea breeze, has the effect of channeling pollutants to the middle of the state and northward.

Tropical Storms and Hurricanes

Superimposed on the pattern of daily showers and thunderstorms is precipitation resulting from large-scale (synoptic) circulation, such as easterly waves, tropical storms, and hurricanes. Easterly waves are regions of ill-defined, weak, low pressure that are found in the trade wind belt in the tropics (Critchfield, 1966; Nieuwolt, 1977). The waves move from east to west and may originate as far away as Africa. Sometimes they move northward and acquire curvature in their circulation; then they may become tropical storms and even hurricanes. Since easterly waves originate in the trade wind belt, their occurrence in Florida is generally confined to the southern part of the state.

Tropical storms and hurricanes that affect Florida originate in the Atlantic tropical cyclone basin, which includes the North Atlantic Ocean, the Caribbean Sea, and the Gulf of Mexico (Simpson and Riehl, 1981; Nieuwolt, 1977). The peak time for hurricanes is September and October, when the ocean temperature is warmest and the humidity highest. In a typical year more than a hundred disturbances in the Atlantic, Caribbean, and Gulf have the potential to form hurricanes. However, on average, fewer than ten develop into tropical storms (wind speeds greater than 34 knots), and only about five mature to full hurricanes (winds greater than 64 knots) (Neumann et al., 1985). About half of these hurricanes reach the coast of the United States, from Texas to New England. Hurricanes that have hit the Florida coast during most of the last century are shown in figure 2.7. The coasts from Florida Bay to Melbourne and from Pensacola to Panama City have the highest risk of hurricanes, with an expected return rate of one hurricane every six to eight years (Simpson and Riehl, 1981). The risk drops to one hurricane per twelve to seventeen years for the Gulf coast from Apalachicola to Tampa Bay and for the Atlantic coast from Fort Pierce to Cape Canaveral.

Major effects of hurricanes are wind damage and flooding (fig. 2.8). Flooding results both from rainfall associated with the storm and from wind-generated waves and tides (Harris, 1982). Flooding is also caused by the rise in water level, known as storm surge (fig. 2.9), which is produced by falling pressure at the center of the storm. Wind-generated currents and waves also cause flooding.

Hurricane wind is strongest in the right front quadrant of the advancing storm. Therefore, the region of landfall nearest the right front quadrant of the hurricane should in general experience the greatest sustained wind pressure and corresponding damage. The stronger wind of that quadrant results

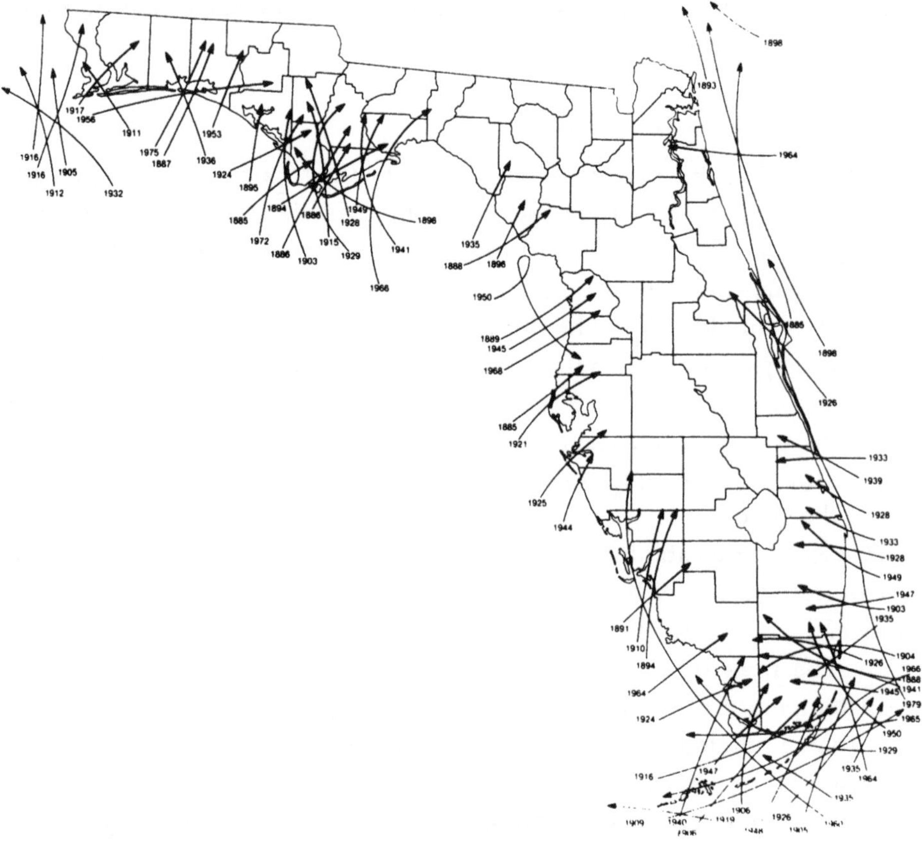

Fig. 2.7. Hurricanes from 1885 to 1980. From Jordan, 1984.

from a combination of the sustained wind of the hurricane and its forward speed (Simpson and Riehl, 1981). For example, if a hurricane has a maximum sustained wind of 80 miles per hour (mph) and approaches landfall with a forward speed of 10 mph, a point facing the right front quadrant will experience wind of 90 mph while a point facing the left front quadrant should experience wind of 70 mph. When the hurricane is near landfall, the wind in the right front quadrant moves over the water surface and encounters less surface friction than does the wind in the left front quadrant, which passes over land. The greater friction encountered over land reduces the wind speed. Hurricane winds often have a gusty component, and tornadoes are often generated in the cloud bands of the right front quadrant. But in the so-called eye, winds are calm. Thus wind damage depends on the observer's position relative to the eye of the hurricane at landfall.

The average minimum pressure in hurricanes that have struck Florida's coast is 50 mm less than the average atmospheric pressure (Simpson and Riehl, 1981). This amounts to a lifting of 0.5 m of water. But near shore, in shoal water, the uplift can translate into a mound of water as high as 4 m. Because of the action of waves, the surge of water is generally higher if the

Fig. 2.8. Damage in hardwood swamp caused by hurricane of September 4, 1935, Taylor County, Fla. Photo by W. F. Jacobs. From Florida State Archives.

Fig. 2.9. Hurricane storm surge. From NOAA.

hurricane approaches shore rapidly than if it approaches slowly. Furthermore, coastal areas with a greater extent of shoal water will generally experience a higher storm surge. Thus, in hurricanes of equal size and strength, the Gulf coast of Florida should expect greater storm surges than the Atlantic coast.

Hurricane-generated waves also transport water shoreward, piling it up along the coast and causing flooding. The shapes of bays and estuaries can cause storm surge levels to differ even in contiguous parts of the coastline. Storm surge levels will be higher if the storm coincides with high tide. Storm surges can also cause saltwater contamination and produce currents along the shore that affect beach and coastal areas. The wave action of hurricanes can also bring colder water to the surface through upwelling and mixing, particularly when the forward speed of the hurricane is slow (4 to 8 knots). This water can be as much as 5°C colder than the normal surface water (Simpson and Riehl, 1981), and the pool of cool water can remain for days.

Thunderstorms and Lightning

Warm, moist, unstable air is the basic factor in thunderstorm development. The unstable air may rise rapidly to heights of 12 to 18 km, where the top of the column of rising air usually spreads out in the familiar anvil shape of a thunderstorm (fig. 2.10). Heavy rain, gusty winds, and violent up-and-down air movements are characteristic of thunderstorm weather, sometimes accompanied by hail. The duration of rain in a thunderstorm generally is about half an hour, with the heaviest rain lasting from five to fifteen minutes. A thunderstorm is actually an electrical storm because thunder is the result of lightning and cannot occur without it (Uman, 1971). Thunder is heard when the air pressure along the lightning path is increased suddenly by the electrical energy of the lightning bolt. The propagation and dissipation of the compressed air produce the sound. The heat and pressure also cause ionization of molecules, producing the light associated with lightning.

Thunderstorms that are caused by the rising air of a strongly heated surface generally occur in the afternoon, but over the ocean they are more apt to occur between midnight and dawn. Thunderstorms during spring and winter are most frequently produced by passage of fronts and squall lines; these can occur at any time of the day. Hurricanes and tropical storms also produce thunderstorms. But it is the summertime convective thunderstorms, which are sometimes organized by the sea breeze, that give Florida the distinction of having the most "thunderstorm days" in the United States. A thunderstorm day is defined as a day when thunder is heard at a given station. Thunder usually cannot be heard more than fifteen miles away; thus a thunderstorm day usually includes storms occurring within a fifteen-mile radius of the station. Florida and the northern Gulf coast regions have the highest number of thunderstorm days in the continental United States (from 70 to more than 90 days). Central Florida has the highest, with more than 90 days annually. The mean number of thunderstorm days in Florida

Fig. 2.10. Thunderstorm activity in Florida peaks in August, but lightning-ignited fires occur more frequently in May and June, marking the beginning of warm-season convective storms. From NOAA.

increases from about 6.6 days in May to about 12 days in June, 17 days in July, and 16 days in August, decreasing to about 10 days in September (Davis and Sakamoto, 1976). During winter there are, on average, only one or two thunderstorm days each month. The highest average number of thunderstorm days—20 to 23 days—occurs in July and August in central Florida around Tampa, Lakeland, and Fort Myers.

The decrease in thunderstorm days and the leveling off of afternoon showers are the main indications that summer is gradually giving way to fall.

Autumn (October, November)

Fall is a season of change. Many climatic processes that operate during the spring months are now reversed to complete the annual cycle of the seasons. Having crossed the equator around September 22 (the autumn equinox), the sun continues on its apparent southward course in the southern hemisphere. The direction of sunrise moves toward the east-southeast. The altitude of the midday sun continues to decrease from about 60° C to about 45° C by the end of November. Day length is about eleven hours.

The uniformly high temperatures and rainfall that have been sustained since June begin their decline in October for most of Florida except the east coast and southeast Florida. The daily decrease in air temperature is most obvious in northern Florida, less so in southern Florida. The daily maximum temperatures in north Florida are around 30°C (86°F), which is only about 5°C (9°F) lower than the maximum summer temperatures. However, the nighttime temperature can be as low as −5° to 0°C (23°F to 32°F), or about 10°C to 15°C (18°F to 27°F) lower than the nighttime low of the four previous months. The nighttime low temperatures generally last no more than a few hours.

In conjunction with the gradual temperature decrease, the rainfall also decreases by about half, except along the east coast and southeast Florida where it decreases only slightly (fig. 2.5). Rainfall in November is commonly the lowest of the twelve months for most of north and central Florida (fig. 2.1). Monthly rainfall in November decreases from west to east and from north to south because the cold fronts that have returned to north Florida stall there and do not reach central or south Florida. The decrease in rainfall in south Florida is partly due to the decline in the number of tropical storms and depressions. The annual dry season begins during fall and commonly lasts until March, April, or May. A slight or insignificant rainfall deficit accumulated during this time may turn into a severe water deficit in late spring unless enough additional rainfall is accumulated during the winter months.

The declining day length, the repeated mild frosts, the steadily declining nighttime temperatures, and the onset of the dry season are normal climatic events that occur in the fall and signal the onset of winter. If this rhythm is upset, as is common in a mild climate, plants may lose their hardiness and emerge prematurely from dormancy, thus becoming more vulnerable to damage by the low temperatures of winter.

Winter (December–February)

Sunrise is near east-southeast and remains near this direction for most of the winter. The day length is now less than eleven hours, and the highest point reached by the sun at noon increases from a low of about 40° C in December to about 55° C by the end of February for the middle latitude of the state. Between 1930 and 1979, no place in Florida escaped below-freezing temperatures except Key West.

The distinctive feature of Florida's winter is the frequent intrusion of cold air, sometimes as low as −10°C (14°F) (fig. 2.11), into spells of spring-like temperatures. Natural and agricultural vegetation must be adapted to a three-month temperature environment spanning 40°C (72°F). The spells of warm temperature may cause some native and agricultural plants to break dormancy or to increase active growth at a time when they can become more vulnerable to stress or damage by subsequent low temperatures.

The highest daily temperature during winter tends to occur in February rather than in December. The mean daily maximum temperatures for the winter months are 17°C to 19°C (63°F to 66°F) for north Florida, 21°C to 23°C (70°F to 73°F) for central Florida, and 24°C to 26°C (75°F to 79°F) for south Florida. Unlike spring and summer, when temperatures throughout the peninsula are almost uniform, during winter there is an increase of about 6°C (11°F) from north Florida to south Florida (excluding Key West), or an increase of approximately 1.2°C (2°F) per degree of latitude.

Rainfall is usually associated with frontal passage and with the infrequent low pressures that sometimes may form in the Gulf of Mexico close to the Florida coast.

Winter Temperature and Rainfall Trends

The highest temperatures recorded from 1930 to 1985 were between 28°C and 31°C (82°F and 88°F) in Pensacola, Tallahassee, Jacksonville, and Key West and between 32°C and 37°C (90°F and 99°F) in the peninsula (Lake City, Ocala, Lake Alfred, Arcadia, Belle Glade, and Homestead). The surrounding water moderates daily maximum temperatures in Key West so that they are more like those of northern coastal cities. The greatest possible winter temperature range for Florida is about 40°C (72°F), from lower than −10°C (14°F) to over 32°C (90°F) in the northern interior Florida.

Winter in Florida is dry. As in the spring, rainfall decreases from west to east across north Florida and from north to south down the peninsula (figures 2.1 and 2.5). This trend reflects the facts that squall lines produce most of the rain and that fronts are frequently dry. The squall lines and fronts weaken as they move south. Also, as cold air masses move southeast through the peninsula, they gradually lose their identity through mixing and warming from the surface and therefore produce less rain. Jacksonville experiences more frontal passages than many other reporting stations in the nation because warm and cold fronts frequently "hang up" over the northern peninsula, oscillating back and forth over Jacksonville, while every little ripple in the front moves eastward (J. G. Georg, personal communication). The mean monthly rainfall is 70 to 110 mm in north Florida, 50 to 90 mm in central Florida, and 40 to 50 mm in south Florida. However,a local rainfall maximum is located along the southeast coast centered on Palm Beach and Boca Raton (MacVicar, 1981). Rainfall gradually decreases westward.

Winter Freezes

The jet stream, a region of concentrated west-to-east air motion that appears as a narrow band of strong winds in the middle and upper levels of the atmosphere, steers the movement of cold air masses. It tends to wander as the Gulf Stream does, and its meandering directly affects the winter cli-

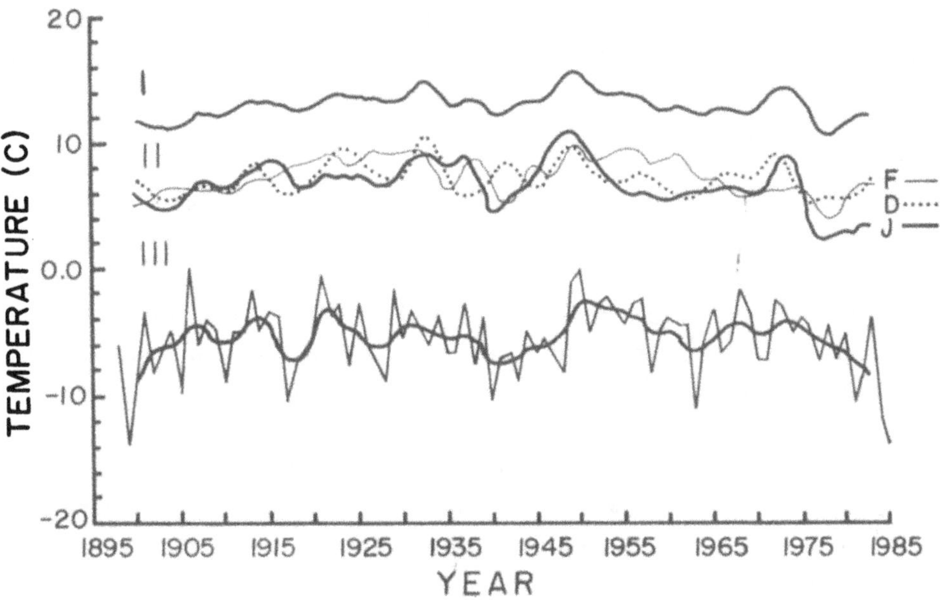

Fig. 2.11. The winter climate of Jacksonville (1897–1985). I. Smoothed average winter temperature (near 12°C [54°F]). II. Smoothed mean monthly (December, January, February) minimum temperatures (near 6°C [43°F]). III. Lowest seasonal temperatures and the smoothed trend line (near −6°C [21°F]). From Chen and Gerber, 1986.

mate of Florida. When the jet stream is positioned far to the north, it steers the cold air north of Florida, and the peninsula escapes the brunt of the cold weather. But when it loops southward, cold air masses are steered into Florida. As a result, the temperature may plunge overnight. The position of the southern loop of the jet stream helps to determine how cold Florida will be. It is most damaging when the southern loop is directly over Florida. If the jet stream is to the west (over Texas, for example), the coldest air is likely to skirt the Panhandle and southern Georgia in an easterly track, protecting the peninsula from the worst conditions. The cold air also loses part of its punch if it passes over the Gulf of Mexico, where it takes up moisture and warmer air.

Recent examples of what happens when the southern loop of the jet stream is near Florida are the freezes of December 25, 1983, and January 21, 1985, when mature citrus trees were killed or damaged extensively in central Florida (fig. 2.12). December 1983 was one of the coldest Decembers on record (Quiroz, 1984). The Christmas freeze of 1983 was especially damaging to Florida both because it came on unusually rapidly and because there was extended snow cover farther to the north (Mogil et al., 1984). Perhaps its worst feature was that it came after two weeks when the nighttime minimum temperatures had been in the high range (10°C to 16°C [50°F to 61°F]) throughout central and southern Florida, and many crops had become quite tender.

The frequency and duration of cold air intrusions vary considerably from season to season and from year to year. Both the severity and the duration of critical temperatures are important because of Florida's wide variety of plant species, each having its own critical threshold temperature. Not all changes from warm to cold periods are harmful at all latitudes and to all plants.

Counting the number of intruding cold air masses may lead to a better understanding of this feature, one of the most significant weather hazards to plants. Georg (1977) identified seventy-two freeze episodes severe enough to damage citrus over a forty-four-year period (1934–77) in central Florida near Lake Apopka. He found that these freeze episodes lasted from one to five nights, with shorter durations more common. The records for this period show that in 70 percent of the freezes, winds were from the north to northwest, in 15 percent from the west or west-northwest, and in 6 percent winds were calm. Sometimes two or three cold fronts may enter the peninsula in rapid succession, without the associated changes in temperature, rain, and wind direction. This is because the leading air mass does not have time to warm before the arrival of the second air mass, so the difference between the two air masses is small and changes in weather are less noticeable.

The lowest temperatures experienced in Florida vary greatly from year to year but exhibit some recurring patterns. Examples of this variation are

Fig. 2.12. Freeze-damaged citrus grove in central Florida. Courtesy of D.P.H. Tucker, IFAS.

shown in the data for Jacksonville between 1897 and 1985 (fig. 2.11). The absolute minimum temperature patterns for other cities in Florida are similar, but minimum temperatures are higher at more southerly latitudes (Chen and Gerber, 1985). The five-year running average shows warmer and colder intervals in the time series and suggests recurrences of cold periods in seven to twelve years and twenty-five to forty years. (A five-year running average is a series of points obtained by averaging the first five numbers of the series, then moving one position to the right and averaging the next five numbers, and so on until the last five numbers in the series are reached.) The lowest temperatures in the ninety-year record occurred in the winter of 1894–95 and again in the winters of 1983 and 1985. The epochal advective freeze of 1835 killed many mature, fifty- to one hundred-year-old citrus trees in the St. Augustine and St. Johns River areas (Davis, 1910, 1937). Taken together, these freeze records suggest that the worst conditions occur about sixty to ninety years apart. These severe freezes were undoubtedly instrumental in the southward movement of citrus culture. Freezes in 1835 and in 1962 damaged citrus extensively (Johnson, 1963); they were, fortunately, isolated events. Even though the negative impact on plants and ecosystems from a single occurrence of low temperature is sometimes severe—as in the freezes of 1835 and 1962—it is not nearly as severe as the cumulative negative impact from a series of freezes, such as those that occurred between 1894 and 1899 (Sanders, 1980) and between 1980 and 1985 (Chen and Gerber, 1986). During the latter period, the only winter without a severe freeze was the 1982–83 season. These two series of freezes, viewed as a long-term climatic trend, forced the southward movement of citrus cultivation (Bein, 1971). The damage to native plants as a result of freezes is summarized by Myers (1986).

Winter Microclimate

Agriculturists generally recognize two cooling processes: cooling by advection (advective freeze) and cooling by radiation (radiative frost). Advective freezes result from the active transport of cold air and are usually accompanied by moderate to strong winds; they result from large-scale weather patterns. In contrast, radiative frosts, which occur only at night, result from loss of heat from the land surface (Geiger, 1980) and depend on local conditions such as terrain, land use, soil type, and soil moisture. The greatest radiative cooling rates—and hence the lowest temperatures to be expected—are associated with calm conditions or low wind speeds, clear skies, low humidity, and low soil moisture. While the two processes frequently operate together, in Florida it is usually radiative frosts that bring temperatures below the critical level. Agriculturists also differentiate black frost from white frost. White frost occurs when moisture in the air is high and leaves a layer of ice particles on plants or on the ground; black frost occurs when the air does not contain enough moisture for a layer of ice particles to form.

During radiative frosts, air layers in contact with cold land surfaces are cooled, and these air layers cool the air above them by conduction. This process progresses upward throughout the night if other conditions remain unchanged, resulting in an inversion near the ground—i.e., an increase in air temperature with height above ground. Sunrise heats the ground and generally breaks up inversion layers.

In Florida, light frosts generally occur near ground level when the temperature at 1.5 m above ground is about 2°C (36°F) over rangeland in central Florida (McCaleb and Hodges, 1960) and over farmlands in south Florida (Mincey et al., 1967). Thus temperature near the ground surface is about 2°C (4°F) colder than the air temperature at 1.5 m. For 134 nights from 1966 to 1972, Georg (1974) measured the strengths of inversions from a 19.5 m tower located in an orange grove south of Lakeland. He found that in an average inversion the temperature difference between the surface and the 19 m level was 3°C (5°F). On about 60 percent of the nights, the inversions were greater than 5.5°C (10°F) for at least part of the night. Low-growing plants experience temperatures much colder than taller species do, especially if they are unprotected by plant canopies or if the weather is dry.

Data on minimum temperatures in rural agricultural areas show that, in general, the western portion of central Florida experienced lower temperatures than did the eastern portion during freeze nights (Johnson, 1970). Remotely sensed thermal radiation from the surface (detected by the Geostationary Satellite) indicates that this difference can be as great as 5°C (9°F) (Chen and Martsolf, 1982). During periods of nocturnal radiative cooling, the dry, sandy soils of the Florida ridge in Alachua and Marion counties can be 1°C to 2°C (2°F to 4°F) colder than soils with higher water contents (Chen et al., 1982). Surface temperatures of drained organic soils in the Everglades Agricultural Area south of Lake Okeechobee are colder at night by 2°C to 4°C (4°F to 7°F) and warmer during the day by 3°C to 4°C (5°F to 7°F) than the surrounding water conservation areas (Shih and Chen, 1984). Air temperatures at 1.5 m above ground measured during selected winter nights from 1979 to 1981 along rural highways in Florida showed increases of 3°C to 4°C (5°F to 7°F) from the center of the state to the coast (Chen et al., 1983).

Climatologists and agriculturists have known for some time that the lee shore of a body of water offers some protection for crops. The protection is provided by a plume of warmer air advected from the lake to the lee shore by the wind. Studies conducted south of Lake Apopka showed a temperature increase of 1°C to 2°C (2°F to 4°F) at the lee shore of the lake (Bill et al., 1979). The area of elevated temperature extended about 6 km inland. Aerial infrared photography shows that the plume changes shape and position with changes in wind speed and wind direction. The plume disappears under calm conditions. The larger the lake and the greater the depth of the water, the greater the plume and the attendant warming it provides. For example, Lake Santa Fe in north Florida provided a warming of about 1°C (2°F) for all nights during the winter of 1962–63, with greater protection (2°C [4°F]) during cold nights (Davis, 1963), and there was a difference of 7°C (13°F) between a station near Lake Okeechobee and one well away from the lake.

By late February, the days are warmer. Weather in the peninsula—especially in south Florida—is often spring-like. Spells of winter-like conditions still occur but are often short lived and are frequently mitigated by midday sunshine. The coldest month of the year is well over, and daily temperatures are slowly rising. However, at the northern edge of the peninsula, late frosts are not unusual; for example, in the Gainesville area (latitude 29.5° N), the last severe winter frost that can cause bud loss tends to occur between March 7 and March 15.

As winter melts into spring, another year of the climatic cycle begins. Low rainfall in winter can lead to drought in the spring, depending on the position of the Bermuda high and the frequency of rain. This illustrates the influence of climatic conditions in one season on plant growth in the next. Dividing the year into seasons provides a framework for examining climatic conditions and determinants. However, Florida's climate is truly cyclical in nature, as can be seen in the way that events in one part of the year affect those that come later.

3

Soils

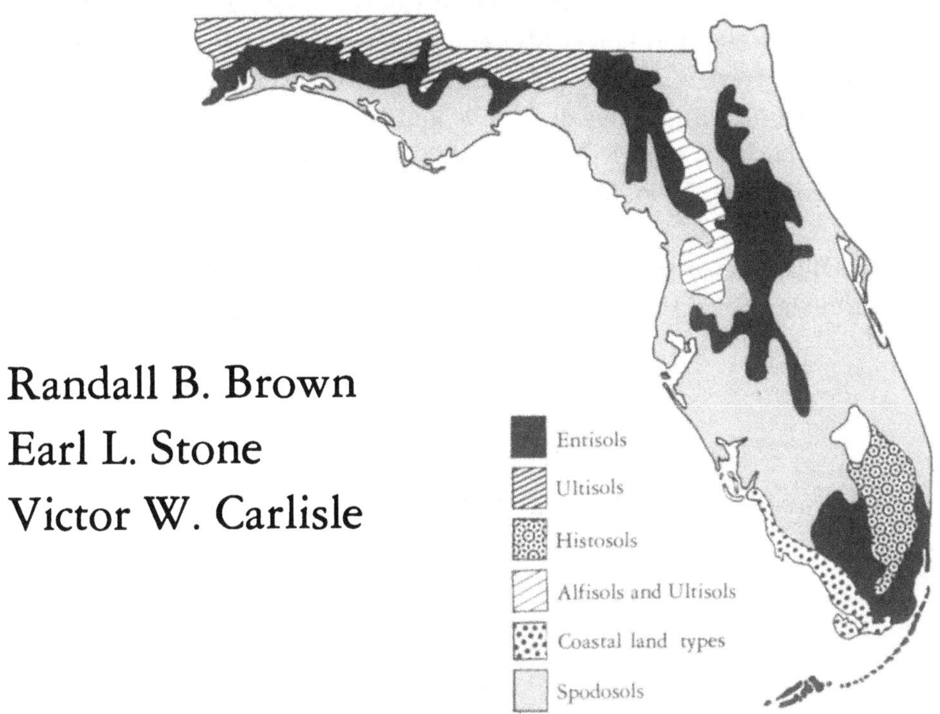

Randall B. Brown
Earl L. Stone
Victor W. Carlisle

Florida is endowed with a wide variety of soils and landscapes, ranging from the red, loamy soils of the upper Florida Panhandle to the deep, droughty sands of central Florida, to the poorly drained, sandy soils of the flatwoods, the peat soils of the northern Everglades and the shallow, limerock-influenced soils of extreme south Florida. Seven of the eleven soil orders recognized at the highest categorical level in the U.S. soil classification system are found in Florida. This range is the result of variations in types, layering, and ages of soil parent materials; landscape position; natural drainage conditions of soils; and other factors.

Origins of Florida's Soil Materials

Geology

The Floridan plateau consists of the present peninsula plus a submerged shelf in the Gulf of Mexico that extends the length of the state. In late Cretaceous and early Tertiary times (from about 100 to about 20 MYBP), the Florida peninsula existed in an environment similar to today's Bahama

Banks, where pure calcium and magnesium carbonates with associated evaporites were deposited. Thus the Eocene and Oligocene rocks contain little or no quartz sand or clay minerals, except in the Panhandle where some clastics (fragments of pre-existing rocks) were brought in by rivers from the north (fig. 3.1) (Vernon and Puri, 1964; Cooke, 1945). The early Tertiary (Eocene, Oligocene, and Lower Miocene) limestones and dolomites serve as the Floridan artesian aquifer and transmit enormous amounts of water to wells and springs. Impermeable Middle and Upper Miocene beds form the principal aquiclude (overlying, confining layer) to the Floridan aquifer (Vernon and Puri, 1964; Roseneau and Faulkner, 1975; Roseneau et al., 1977).

Post-Oligocene orogeny (crustal changes associated with mountain-making) throughout the Gulf coast caused streams from the mainland, begin-

Fig. 3.1. Generalized geologic map of Florida. Adapted from Vernon and Puri, 1964.

Recent and Pleistocene:

Qt: Lower marine and estuarine terrace deposits (alluvium, marl, peat)

ning about 25 to 20 MYBP, to bring clastic sediments that eventually nearly covered the carbonate plateau. This transgression of clastic sediments marked the start of the Miocene epoch in Florida (Vernon and Puri, 1964; Cooke, 1945). Some of the Miocene and younger sediments contained large amounts of phosphorite, attapulgite (Fuller's earth), kaolin, and heavy minerals (Vernon and Puri, 1964; Riggs, 1984; Pirkle et al., 1977).

Post-Oligocene orogeny also produced two areas of pronounced uplift: the Ocala Uplift and the Marianna Structural High (also known as the Chattahoochee Arch). These two areas—associated respectively with the Ocala Uplift and Dougherty Karst physiographic districts (fig. 3.2)—have little or no Miocene sediment and today are areas of outcrop of Eocene and Oligocene carbonates (Vernon and Puri, 1964; Brooks, 1982).

Due to the dominance of carbonate-rich rocks in Florida's geology, karst topography is widespread. Karst is defined as "a landscape, generally lacking

---

Fig 3.1 (*continued*)

Pleistocene:

- Qa: Anastasia Formation (limestone, sand, clay)
- Qc: Caloosahatchee Formation (sand, shell marl)
- Qf: Fort Thompson Formation (shell, marl, clay, sand)
- Qk: Key Largo Limestone (coral reef limestone)
- Qm: Miami Oolite (oolitic limestone)

Plio-Pleistocene:

- Pc: Citronelle Formation (sand, gravel, clay)

Miocene:

- Ma: Alachua Formation (clay, sand, sandy clay)
- Mb: Bone Valley Formation (phosphatic boulders, pebbles, sandy clay)
- Mc: Chipola Formation (marl, sandy limestone, sand, clay)
- Mf: Fort Preston Formation (sand)
- Mh: Hawthorn Formation (phosphatic sand, clay, marl, sandy limestone)
- Mj: Jackson Bluff Formation (sand, marl)
- Mm: Miccosukee Formation (silty, clayey sand)
- Mr: Red Bay Formation (sandy and clayey marl)
- Ms: Shoal River Formation (sand)
- Mt: Tamiami Formation (limestone, marl, sand, clay)
- Mu: Miocene Undifferentiated (includes small areas of Mc, Mf, Mh, Mj, and Ms)

Oligocene:

- Os: Suwannee Limestone (limestone, dolomitized limestone)
- Ou: Oligocene Undifferentiated (limestone, fossiliferous sediment)

Eocene:

- Ea: Avon Park Limestone (limestone, dolomite)
- Ec: Crystal River Formation (limestone)
- Ei: Inglis Formation (limestone, dolomite)
- Ew: Williston Formation (limestone, dolomite)

SCALE

0 50 100 MILES

0 80 160 KILOMETERS

Fig. 3.2. Generalized physiographic map of Florida. Adapted from Brooks, 1982.

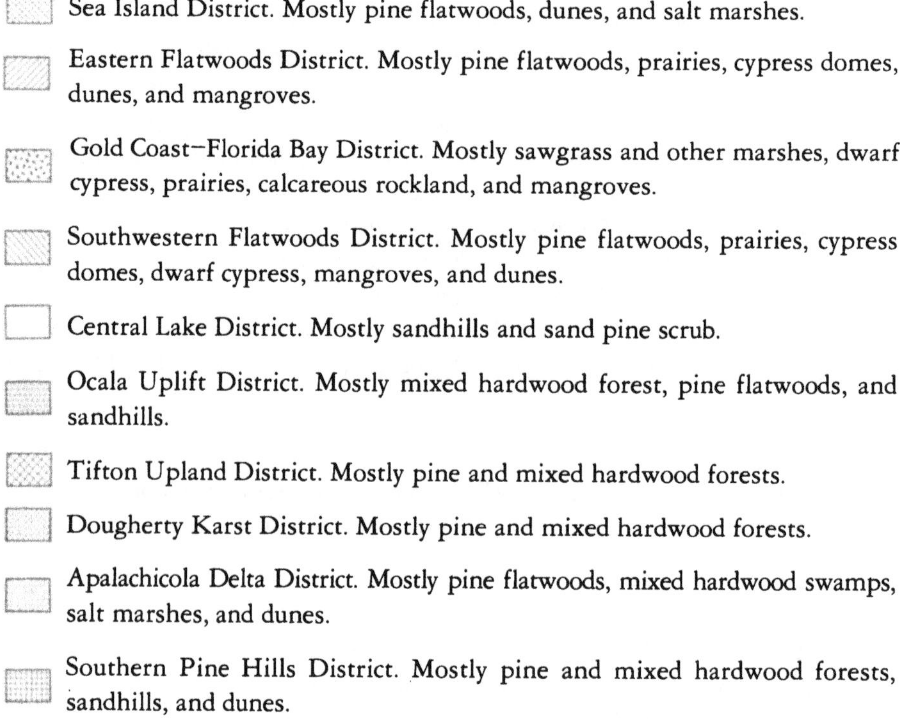

Sea Island District. Mostly pine flatwoods, dunes, and salt marshes.

Eastern Flatwoods District. Mostly pine flatwoods, prairies, cypress domes, dunes, and mangroves.

Gold Coast–Florida Bay District. Mostly sawgrass and other marshes, dwarf cypress, prairies, calcareous rockland, and mangroves.

Southwestern Flatwoods District. Mostly pine flatwoods, prairies, cypress domes, dwarf cypress, mangroves, and dunes.

Central Lake District. Mostly sandhills and sand pine scrub.

Ocala Uplift District. Mostly mixed hardwood forest, pine flatwoods, and sandhills.

Tifton Upland District. Mostly pine and mixed hardwood forests.

Dougherty Karst District. Mostly pine and mixed hardwood forests.

Apalachicola Delta District. Mostly pine flatwoods, mixed hardwood swamps, salt marshes, and dunes.

Southern Pine Hills District. Mostly pine and mixed hardwood forests, sandhills, and dunes.

in rivers, marked by sinkholes and caves; formed because the underlying rock dissolves more easily than most rocks" (Beck and Sinclair, 1986). Sinkhole formation is part of the natural process of landscape evolution in Florida, which has led to the many lakes and closed depressions so characteristic of the state. Sinkholes are formed by solution of near-surface limestone or limy materials and consequent subsidence or collapse of overlying material into the solution cavities.

Solution sinkholes are the dominant type in terrain having bare or thinly covered limestone, as in much of the Dougherty Karst District, Ocala Uplift District, the south and west parts of the Gold Coast–Florida Bay District, and the extreme southern Southwestern Flatwoods District (fig. 3.2). Solution is most active at the surface of the limestone and is concentrated where cracks in the rock permit water to drain easily to the subsurface. Rather than forming large voids, the cover material gradually subsides as the limestone surface dissolves, leaving a bowl-shaped depression. If surface runoff carries clayey sediment into the depression, a lake or marsh may form. Thus are formed the gently rolling hills and shallow depressions typical of these thinly covered limestone areas (Beck and Sinclair, 1986; Sinclair and Stewart, 1985).

Where the sedimentary cover over limestone is 10 to 60 m thick and consists of relatively incohesive, permeable materials, cover subsidence sinkholes tend to predominate. This kind of sinkhole is found in the central and southern Eastern Flatwoods District, the northeastern Gold Coast–Florida Bay District, and the south-central part of the Southwestern Flatwoods District (fig. 3.2), though sinkholes of any type are comparatively rare in these regions. Solution cavities that develop initially along cracks in the limestone are propagated upward as overlying sands move downward to fill the voids. Sinkholes formed in this way often are only a few meters in diameter and depth, because the limestone cavities quickly fill with sand (Beck and Sinclair, 1986; Sinclair and Stewart, 1985).

Where the sedimentary cover is 10 to 60 m thick but a dense layer of impermeable clay—such as the Hawthorn formation (fig. 3.1)—occurs between the overlying sandy material and the underlying limestone, cover collapse sinkholes dominate. This situation occurs in much of the Central Lake District, on the fringes of the Ocala Uplift District, in the northern part of the Eastern Flatwoods District, and in the northern part of the Southwestern Flatwoods District (fig. 3.2). Here sinkholes are numerous and of varying size and develop abruptly. The clay forms a bridge over a developing cavity in the limestone. Eventual failure of the bridge results in a cover collapse sinkhole that may be small or very large (Beck and Sinclair, 1986; Sinclair and Stewart, 1985).

Sinkholes are rare where the cover is more than about 60 m thick, as in the north-central Southwestern Flatwoods District, the Sea Islands District, the Tifton Upland District, the Apalachicola Delta District, and the Southern Pine Hills District. A dearth of sinkholes is reflected in the better defined stream patterns that can be seen on topographic maps, air photos, and satellite images of these areas, in contrast to most other parts of the state where closed depressions are common. A few large, deep, cover collapse sinkholes do occur in these areas of thick cover, however, as does small-scale subsidence where shell beds or limestone lenses are buried at shallow depths (Beck and Sinclair, 1986; Sinclair and Stewart, 1985; Brooks, 1982).

Physiography

The topography of Florida is the result of erosional, depositional, and solution-related processes that have sculptured the land over time. Step-like surfaces or terraces, variously dissected by erosional processes, are thought to range in age from Recent (less than about 10,000 YBP) in the case of the lowest coastal terraces to possibly as old as Miocene (about 5 to 25 MYBP) in the case of the highest surfaces of Panhandle, north-central, and central Florida (Healey, 1975). Ten major physiographic subdivisions of Florida are outlined here (Brooks, 1982; Caldwell and Johnson, 1982).

Sea Island District

The Sea Island District of northeastern Florida is the only Florida portion of what Brooks (1982) calls the Atlantic Coastal Plain Section of the Coastal Plain Physiographic Province. In most parts of this district, the underlying limestone is too thickly covered by overburden to influence the landscape or drainage. The landscape ranges from upland terraces, with variable or no dissection, to plains and ridges. Surficial materials are dominantly sandy, but significant expanses of relatively clayey deposits exist.

Eastern Flatwoods District

This generally low, flat district originated as a sequence of barrier islands and lagoons in Plio-Pleistocene and Recent times. The resulting landscape consists of broad expanses of flatwoods with prairies, ridges, and a variety of coastal features. Surficial materials are primarily sandy with significant areas of peaty deposits.

Gold Coast–Florida Bay District

This uniformly low-lying district includes the area of sluggish south and southeastward drainage from Lake Okeechobee (i.e., the Everglades), together with coastal ridges, mangrove swamps, and the Florida Keys. Rocks are Pleistocene and largely limestones (fig. 3.3). The covering materials are dominantly sand, marl, organic material, and limestone.

Fig. 3.3. This wellhole shows the porous Miami oolite limestone, which underlies the soil at very shallow depths in much of the Gold Coast–Florida Bay physiographic district. Photo by R. B. Brown.

Southwestern Flatwoods District

This largely low, flat district was developed on rocks and sediments that range mainly from Miocene to Pleistocene in age. The landscapes include low plateaus and ridges, flatwoods, prairies, rockland/marl plains, and a variety of coastal features. Surficial materials are dominantly sand (often with relatively clayey substrata), limestone, and organic deposits.

Central Lake District

In this district, with its sandhills and lakes so typical of the central Florida ridge, the uplifted limestones of the Floridan Aquifer lie beneath surficial sands. This is a sandhill karst terrain with innumerable solution basins. Because of the permeable sands and rapid internal drainage, this region is the principal recharge area of the Floridan Aquifer (Stewart, 1980). Surficial materials are dominantly sandy, occasionally with relatively clayey substrata, and with significant organic deposits.

Ocala Uplift District

This highly diverse region has a wide range of elevations, landscapes, and surficial materials. Tertiary (chiefly Eocene, Oligocene, and Miocene) limestones are at or near the surface, though Miocene limestones are absent in the central part of the district. Low, rolling karst plains are distinctive, but the landscape is varied and also includes stream-sculptured hills, flats and swamps, and sandhills. The karst plain in the central portion of the district grades to sandy flatwoods toward the west and south. The extreme northern part of the district is upland, with medium to high clay contents in soils. The northeastern portion of the district is a sandhill terrain, whereas the eastern part is upland influenced by clayey, phosphatic Miocene deposits.

Tifton Upland District

This high upland's topography is controlled by thick deposits of lower Miocene clastic sediments that have been sculptured by surface drainage. Surficial materials are dominantly clayey or loamy, but these may be capped by varying thicknesses of sand.

Dougherty Karst District

In this area of the Marianna Structural High, Tertiary (chiefly Eocene, Oligocene, and Miocene) limestones are close to the surface and have influenced landscape development, with karst dominating. Elevations are low compared to the Tifton Upland and Southern Pine Hills Districts to the east and west, where thick deposits of younger sediments control topography. Surficial materials consist primarily of loamy or clayey materials, but a sandy cap may exceed 2 m in thickness in the southern and eastern parts of the district.

Apalachicola Delta District

This district is a clastic terrain built with Apalachicola River sediments. Landscape features range from relic deltas, ridges, and lagoons to river terraces, delta plains, and barrier islands. Karst is absent. Surficial materials range from sandy to clayey.

Southern Pine Hills District

Part of the Gulf Coastal Plain Section of the Coastal Plain Province, this district, like the Tifton Upland District, is an area of thick, clastic sediments. The northernmost, highest parts are stream-sculptured from an alluvial plain underlain by sand, gravel, silt, and clay. Intermediate elevations include ridges formed of coastal sediments. The coastal strip consists of relic lagoon and barrier island features. Surficial materials are largely loamy or clayey to the north, with increasing thicknesses of sand toward the southern parts of the district.

Major Kinds of Soils in Florida

How Soils Are Classified in the United States

In 1951, a decision was made in the United States to develop a soil classification system based entirely on observable, measurable soil properties rather than on presumed origins or pathways of formation of soils, as was the case at higher categorical levels of the system then in use (Buol et al., 1980). After numerous revisions, the new classification was published as a book, *Soil Taxonomy* (Soil Survey Staff, 1975), which outlines the current system used in the United States.

Soil Taxonomy is used as a key to classify a soil at one or more of six categorical levels: *order* (highest), *suborder, great group, subgroup, family,* and *series* (lowest). To key out or classify a soil, one must know the soil's morphology (features such as color, particle size distribution, moisture regime, presence or absence of various kinds of hardpans and other horizons, depth to bedrock and so forth) and numerous physical and chemical properties (e.g., soil temperature regime, organic carbon content, sulfide content, mineralogy, shrinking and swelling characteristics, and so forth) that require field measurements and/or sampling and laboratory analysis.

An unknown soil is keyed out by first determining the soil order (highest categorical level). To do this, one initially establishes whether the soil is in the Histosol soil order. If not, one then determines whether the soil is in the Spodosols, then the next soil order, and so on (see table 3.1).

Having determined the soil order, one continues in sequence through the taxonomic criteria within that order to classify the soil at one or more of the lower categorical levels. A soil in the Spodosol order, for example, might be in the Aquod or Humod suborder, depending on the wetness of the soil, one in the Aquods might fit into either the Haplaquod or Sideraquod great group, depending on the level of free iron in the stained subsoil layer, and so on down to the level of soil series. More than 300 soil series have been

Table 3.1 Abbreviated key to the seven soil orders that occur in Florida

A.	Soils that consist of organic materials (muck or peat) in at least half of the upper 80 cm of soil, or that have organic materials extending from the surface to within 10 cm of bedrock, provided the organic material is more than twice as thick as any mineral soil above the bedrock (occur extensively in Florida)	HISTOSOLS
B.	Other soils that have a *spodic horizon* (a subsurface horizon in which organic matter in combination with aluminum and/or iron has accumulated) whose upper boundary is within 2 m of the soil surface (occur extensively in Florida)	SPODOSOLS
C.	Other soils that have an argillic horizon and a base saturation of less than 35 percent. (An *argillic horizon* is a subsurface zone of accumulation of clay-size particles at the expense of horizons above, which as a result are less clayey. *Base saturation* is the proportion of chemical exchange sites on soil particles that are occupied by basic cations [Ca^{2+}, Mg^{2+}, K^{+}, Na^{+}] as opposed to acid cations [H_3O^{+}, Al^{3+}].) (occur extensively in Florida)	ULTISOLS
D.	Other soils that have a thick (usually more than 25 cm), dark, mineral surface horizon having a base saturation of 50 percent or more (occur to minor extent in Florida)	MOLLISOLS
E.	Other soils that have an argillic horizon and base saturation of 35 percent or more (occur to moderate extent in Florida)	ALFISOLS
F.	Other soils that have significant but minor horizon development (occur to minor extent in Florida)	INCEPTISOLS
G.	Other soils (occur extensively in Florida)	ENTISOLS

Sources: Soil Management Support Services (1984); Soil Survey Staff (1975); Collins (1985).

identified and mapped in Florida, but discussion here is confined to the two highest categorical levels: order and suborder.

Soils of Florida

Of the seven soil orders found in Florida, four (the Histosols, Spodosols, Ultisols, and Entisols) occur extensively. Of the remaining three, one (the Alfisols) occurs to a moderate extent and two (the Mollisols and Inceptisols) only to a minor extent (table 3.1; fig. 3.4). The following paragraphs briefly

Fig. 3.4. Generalized soil map of Florida. Adapted from contribution by V. W. Carlisle to *Atlas of Florida*, Fernald, ed., 1981.

Soils of the western highlands

Mostly Ultisols. Dominated by level to sloping, well-drained loamy soils and sandy soils with loamy subsoils. Natural ecosystems are generally mixed hardwood and pine forests. Primarily used for field crops, pastures, and forest products. Excellent for homesites and urban development.

Mostly Entisols. Dominated by nearly level to sloping, excessively drained thick sands. Ecosystems are generally sandhill and sand pine scrub. Primarily used for field crops, tobacco, watermelons, and forest products. Very good for homesites and urban development.

Soils of the central ridge

Mostly Entisols. Dominated by nearly level to sloping, excessively drained thick sands. Ecosystems generally are sandhill and sand pine scrub. Primarily used for field crops, tobacco, watermelons, and forest products. Citrus in the south. Very good for homesites and urban development.

Mostly Alfisols and Ultisols. Dominated by gently sloping, well-drained sandy soils with loamy subsoils underlain by phosphatic limestone. Natural ecosystems are largely mixed hardwood forests. Primarily used for field crops, tobacco, vegetables, and pastures. Excellent to good for homesites and urban development.

Soils of the flatwoods

Mostly Spodosols. Dominated by nearly level, somewhat poorly to poorly drained sandy soils with dark sandy subsoil layers. Ecosystems generally are flatwoods and wet to dry prairies with ponds and cypress domes interspersed. Primarily used for pastures, vegetables, flowers, and forest products. Citrus in the south. Good to poor for homesites and urban development.

Soils of organic origin

Mostly Histosols. Dominated by level, very poorly drained organic soils underlain by marl and/or limestone. Ecosystems are dominantly swamps and marshes. Primarily used for sugarcane, vegetables, pastures, and sod. Very poor for homesites and urban development.

Soils of recent limestone origin

Mostly Entisols. Dominated by level, very poorly drained marly and thin sandy soils underlain by limestone. Ecosystems are largely south Florida rockland communities. Used for winter vegetables in localized areas. Usually very poor for homesites and urban development.

Miscellaneous coastal land types

Mostly Entisols and Histosols. Dominated by nearly level to sloping sandy beaches and adjacent sand dunes; also level, very poorly drained coastal marshes and swamps of variable-textured mineral and organic materials subject to frequent tidal flooding. Ecosystems include dunes, maritime forests, salt marshes, and mangroves. Primarily used for recreation and wildlife. Highly variable for homesites and urban development.

--- Soils occurring north of the boundary are considered in the thermic temperature regime (mean annual temperature 20 inches below soil surface is 59° F to 72° F with 9° F or more variability between mean summer and winter temperatures), and soils occurring south of this boundary are considered to be in the hyperthermic temperature regime (mean annual temperature 20 inches below soil surface is higher than 72° F with 9° F or more variability between mean summer and winter temperatures).

characterize these seven soil orders and their major taxonomic subdivisions (suborders). The ecosystems with which they are most often associated are tabulated in table 3.2 (Soil Survey Staff, 1975; Caldwell and Johnson, 1982; Brooks, 1982).

Histosols

Histosols are dominantly organic, consisting of peat and muck deposits of varying thickness over sand, marl, limestone, or other material (table 3.1; figs. 3.4 and 3.5). The organic material usually has accumulated in an extremely wet environment and can vary in consistency from a "fibrous, matted, turf-like material to a mud-like, plastic, slime or ooze" (Davis, 1946).

Different kinds of peat have been distinguished on the basis of the plants that formed them, of the peat's texture and composition, and of mode of origin (Davis, 1946; Cohen and Spackman, 1984). The term *muck* can have various meanings, ranging from highly disintegrated peat, as might occur in the surface layers of peat that has been drained and farmed, to soils that are composed of more mineral than organic matter, as might occur in lands bordering deeper areas of peat (Davis, 1946; Griffin et al., 1982; Gallatin and Henderson, 1943).

Florida's peat deposits are generally thought to be Recent in age. Gleason et al. (1984) and Stephens (1984) cite McDowell et al. (1969) and other sources that show an average rate of peat accumulation of about 8 cm per 100 years.

When drained for agriculture or other purposes, peat is subject to subsidence or thinning due to biological oxidation and settling (fig. 3.6). Estimated rates of subsidence are on the order of 2.5 cm/yr. As a result of this rapid rate of subsidence, peats in drained areas are becoming thinner, their extent is declining, and in many cases the classification of the soils is changing (Collins et al., 1986; Griffin et al., 1982; Stephens et al., 1984; Snyder et al., 1978).

Folists. Folists are the Histosols (note the formative word element *ist* from Histosol appearing in the suborder name) that, unlike most Histosols, are never saturated with water in their upper profile for more than a few days after heavy rains. These soils tend to be thin (<1 m) over bedrock and are formed where leaf litter, twigs, and branches have accumulated beneath tropical hammocks.

Hemists. Hemists are the Histosols in which organic materials are largely but not entirely decayed beyond recognition. These soils are naturally wet, although like any wet soils they may be drained artificially for agricultural or other purposes.

Saprists. Saprists are the Histosols consisting of almost completely disintegrated plant remains. They are naturally wet, and they are the most widespread Histosols in Florida.

Table 3.2 Orders and suborders of Florida's soils, and associated ecosystems

Soil taxonomic unit		Ecosystem								
Order	Suborder	Flatwoods and dry prairies	Sandhill and sand pine scrub	Mixed hardwood forests	South Florida rockland	Swamps	Marshes	Dunes and maritime forests	Salt marshes	Mangroves
Histosols	Folists				X					
	Hemists					XX	XX		XXX	XX
	Saprists				X	XXX	XXX		XX	XX
Spodosols	Aquods	XXX		X		XX	XXX		X	X
	Humods	XXX	XX	XX		XX	X			
Ultisols	Aquults	XX		XXX		XXX	XX			
	Udults	XX	XX	XXX						
Mollisols	Aquolls			X		XXX	XXX		X	
	Rendolls				XX					
Alfisols	Aqualfs	XX		XX	XX	XX	XX		X	X
	Udalfs	XX	XX	XXX		XX				
Inceptisols	Aquepts	XX				XX	XX			
	Ochrepts			X		XX				
	Umbrepts		X	XX		X				
Entisols	Aquents	XX		X	XX	XX	XX	X	XX	XX
	Psamments	XX	XXX	XX	X			XX		
	Fluvents			XX						

Sources: Primary source was U.S. Soil Conservation Service (1985). Additional insight came from official series descriptions, soil survey reports, other information generated by the National Cooperative Soil Survey, and the experiences and observations of the authors.

Note: Ecosystems shown as column headings were chosen to correspond approximately with the broad groupings used in organizing this book. XXX = frequent association; XX = common association; X = infrequent association; blank = rare or no association. These relationships are highly qualitative, and exceptions may be expected.

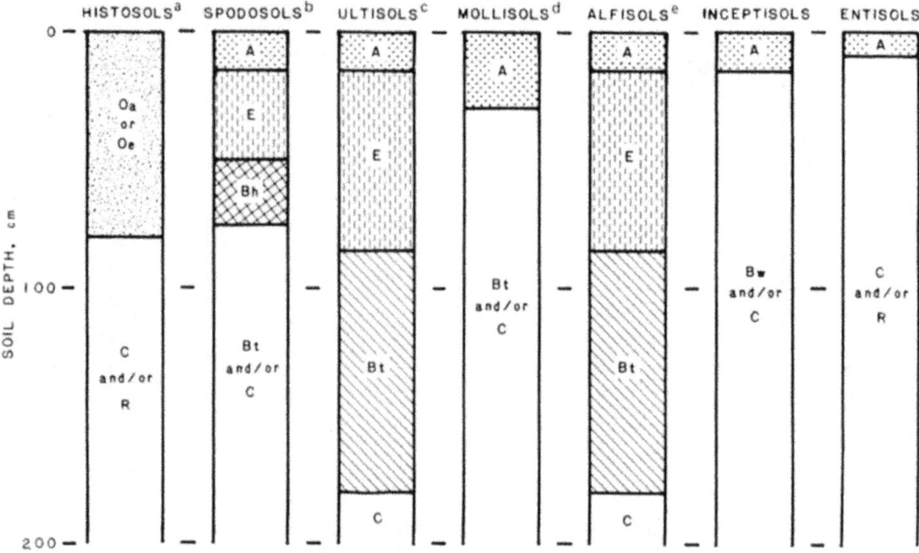

Fig. 3.5. Idealized profiles of the seven soil orders found in Florida, with major differentiating characteristics. Horizon designations (Collins and Carlisle, 1984): Oa = highly decomposed organic material; Oe = moderately decomposed organic material; A = mineral topsoil with accumulation of humified organic material; E = eluvial (leached) horizon, primarily quartz sand; Bh = horizon with illuvial accumulation of organic matter (i.e., a spodic horizon); Bt = horizon with illuvial accumulation of clay (i.e., an argillic horizon); Bw = horizon having slight color change or other minor evidence of subsoil development; C = horizon with little or no evidence of alteration from original parent material; R = hard bedrock. a. Histosols, depth to C or R is variable. b. Spodosols, depth to Bh is variable. c. Ultisols, depth to Bt is variable; base saturation of Bt is low. d. Mollisols, A is thick and dark; base saturation of A is high. e. Alfisols, depth to Bt is variable; base saturation of Bt is high.

Spodosols

Spodosols have a spodic horizon, a subsurface zone in which organic matter in combination with aluminum and/or iron has accumulated due to downward leaching (table 3.1; figs. 3.4 and 3.5). Soil textures are sandy, except that an argillic horizon (a zone of accumulation of clay-size particles) may occur beneath the spodic horizon.

Aquods. Aquods are the Spodosols (note the formative word element *od* from Spodosol) that are wet for extended periods in most years or have been artificially drained to control the water table. The Myakka soil shown in figure 3.7 is an Aquod.

Humods. Humods are Spodosols that are naturally drier than Aquods.

Ultisols

Ultisols have an argillic horizon, a subsurface horizon enriched by clay-size particles that have moved downward in the profile from overlying horizons.

Fig. 3.6. Subsidence of an organic soil (in this case a Saprist) has lowered the ground surface around the pilings and around the septic tank of this house at the Everglades Research and Education Center, Belle Glade (Gold Coast–Florida Bay physiographic district). The ground surface originally was just below the floor of the house. Photo by R. B. Brown.

Fig. 3.7. A white, strongly leached horizon contrasts sharply with the underlying zone of accumulation of organic materials and iron/aluminum oxides (the spodic horizon) in Myakka soil (an Aquod), found extensively in the flatwoods of peninsular Florida. Photo by V.W. Carlisle.

Thus the profile usually consists of sandy material overlying a loamy (medium-textured or moderate in clay content) or a clayey subsoil. Thickness of the overlying sand ranges from less than 0.5 to 2 m. The base saturation (the proportion of chemical exchange sites in the soil occupied by basic cations) is less than 35 percent in Ultisols (table 3.1; figs. 3.4 and 3.5).

Aquults. Aquults are the Ultisols (note the formative element *ult*) that occur in wet places where groundwater approaches the soil surface for large parts of most years, unless the land has been drained.

Udults. Udults (fig. 3.8) are naturally drier than Aquults, although the natural ability of the Udults to retain plant-available water ranges widely, depending largely on the thickness of the sandy (i.e., more droughty) surface soil over loamy or clayey subsoil.

Mollisols

Mollisols have a thick, dark surface horizon and a base saturation of 50 percent or more. Limestone bedrock, an argillic horizon, and marl may be present or absent (table 3.1; fig. 3.5). Mollisols do not occur extensively in Florida; they are found only in relatively small, scattered areas.

Aquolls. Aquolls (note the formative element *oll*) are naturally wet Mollisols.

Rendolls. Rendolls are Mollisols that are somewhat drier than Aquolls. They are rich in calcium carbonates either in or immediately below the surface.

Alfisols

Alfisols are like Ultisols in that they have an argillic horizon. As with Ultisols, thickness of sandy soil over the loamy or clayey argillic horizon may range from less than 0.5 to 2 m. Unlike Ultisols, however, Alfisols have a percent base saturation of 35 percent or more (table 3.1; figs. 3.4 and 3.5). The higher base status of Alfisols generally derives from wet conditions that prevent or retard downward leaching of bases or from a high content of Ca and Mg carbonates in the soil parent materials, providing a continuous source of basic cations.

Aqualfs. Aqualfs are the Alfisols (note the formative element *alf*) that are wet for extended periods in most years unless they are artificially drained.

Udalfs. Udalfs are drier than Aqualfs and occur with a somewhat more restricted variety of ecosystems.

Inceptisols

Inceptisols have had some development and differentiation of horizons from the original parent materials but not enough to cause them to be classified as Spodosols, Ultisols, or any other orders already described. The mi-

Fig. 3.8. Sandy topsoil overlies a relatively clayey subsoil in this profile of Kendrick soil (a Udult) from Alachua County. Photo by V.W. Carlisle.

nor but significant degree of horizon development may take the form of some chemical alterations and color change in the subsoil, darkening and thickening of the topsoil, or other limited expression of profile development (table 3.1; fig. 3.5). Inceptisols are found only in small, scattered areas in Florida.

Aquepts. Aquepts (formative element *ept*) are Inceptisols that are wet for extended periods in most years, unless they have been drained.

Ochrepts. Ochrepts are drier than Aquepts. In Florida they are most likely to occur on floodplains and low terraces along alluvial streams, where soils are young due to repeated addition of sediment during floods, primarily in north Florida.

Umbrepts. Umbrepts have a thick, dark surface horizon, but base saturation is too low for them to qualify as Mollisols.

Entisols

Soil profile development is either minor or lacking altogether in the Entisols. They lack thick, dark surfaces, argillic horizons, and any other diagnostic features that would qualify them for placement in one of the other soil orders (table 3.1; fig. 3.5). Entisols in Florida range widely not only in geographic extent but also in natural degree of wetness or dryness, depth to bedrock, nature of parent materials, and landscape position (fig. 3.4).

Aquents. Aquents are wet Entisols (formative element *ent*), unless they have been artificially drained. Aquents are the dominant Entisols in south Florida but are found elsewhere, especially in coastal and/or alluvial environments.

Psamments. Psamments are sandy Entisols that are better drained than the Aquents. They generally occur as deep (>2 m) deposits of sand.

Fluvents. Fluvents are flood-prone Entisols occasionally found on medium to high terraces along alluvial streams, primarily in North Florida.

Chemical and Physical Characteristics of Soils

Florida's soils range widely in chemical and physical characteristics. Sand and clay contents exert major influence on the behavior of chemicals and water in soils. The Orangeburg and Felda soils (table 3.3), for example, are classified as Ultisols and Alfisols, respectively, due in part to their relatively high subsoil clay contents. Chemical characteristics also may determine the classification of soils. Orangeburg soils are Ultisols, in part because they have base saturation of less than 35 percent, in contrast with Felda soils, which have a higher base saturation and are therefore Alfisols.

Depth from the soil surface to the water table is another attribute that may distinguish one soil from others. Leon soils, for example, have a water table that rises to within 0 to 30 cm during wet seasons of most years (table 3.3). They are classified in the Aquods at the suborder level to reflect this wetness.

Available water capacity (table 3.3) is that portion of the water retained in a soil after a thorough wetting and subsequent drainage that can be used by plants. This term assumes that the soil is freely drained, either naturally or by an artificially lowered water table. This assumption is important: the concept of available water capacity has no meaning when the water table is in or above the soil horizon of concern. Available water capacity is meaningless for the wet Lauderhill, Leon, and Felda soils when the water table is high. During times of drawdown, however, available water capacity reflects availability of water to plant roots in the zones well above the water table.

Availability of Soil Surveys

Soil survey reports prepared by the U.S. Department of Agriculture (USDA) Soil Conservation Service and cooperating agencies are available for most counties in Florida. Through the state's Accelerated Soil Survey Program, reports for the remaining counties will be completed by the mid-1990s.

These reports contain photo-based soil maps at scales ranging from 1:15,840 (6.3 cm/km) to 1:24,000 (4.2 cm/km). The reports and assistance in their use are available from local offices of the USDA Soil Conservation Service, from local Soil and Water Conservation Districts, and from county Extension Service offices.

Use and Misuse of Soil Maps and Related Information

The land area represented by a given area of a map increases as the scale decreases; hence, less detail can be shown on smaller scale maps. The map units on generalized maps of states or counties rarely consist of phases of single soil series; more often, the mapping units are associations of more than one soil series or other taxonomic unit (e.g., soil family, subgroup, or great group). The General Soil Map of Florida (Caldwell and Johnson, 1982) (fig. 3.9a), for example, depicts four soil mapping units, each a soil association, in a 1650 km^2 portion of Pasco County. On the larger scale General Soil Map of Pasco County (Stankey, 1982) (fig. 3.9b), however, we see that a 106 km^2 segment of that 1650 km^2 area comprises six soil associations. Similarly, on the still larger scale, detailed soil map (fig. 3.9c) of Pasco County (Stankey, 1982), nine mapping units (each a phase of a soil series) are used, revealing that a 65 ha portion of this landscape is actually far more complicated than can be shown on smaller scale maps.

Users of soil maps must also realize that even at the scales and levels of detail of county soil maps, the map units are necessarily generalized to some degree. Soils are highly variable across the landscape. Limitations of map scale, of time and other available resources, and of knowledge regarding random spatial variations of soil properties cause considerable imprecision in most soil maps. Thus, a highly detailed soil survey of the area in figure 3.9c, at a scale of 1:10,000 or larger, for purposes of irrigation design, urban development, or research on soil-vegetation relationships, would reveal that the landscape and soils are, in fact, even more complex than depicted in the county soil survey report.

Soil as Habitat

Every naturalist has noted abrupt changes in vegetation across major soil boundaries—between upland and swamp, sandhills and their surroundings, or perhaps between higher and lower terrace levels along rivers. Reasons for such changes are usually apparent in contrasting water or nutrient supply regimes across the boundaries. These observations may suggest that other vegetational changes over the landscape should be associated with differences in soils, or, conversely, that the same soil series or phase should always be associated with similar kinds of vegetation, barring recent disturbance. Unfortunately, such assumptions do not provide useful field guides

Table 3.3 Selected characterization data (dry weight basis) for pedons representing five of the soil orders found in Florida

Order/suborder/series County/land use Depth to wet season water table	Depth (cm)	Horizon designation	Sand (%)	Silt (%)	Clay (%)	Organic C[a] (%)	pH	Exchangeable cations[b] (meq/100g) Ca^{2+}	Mg^{2+}	Na^{+}	K^{+}	Extract-able acidity (meq/100g)	Base saturation (%)	Bulk density (g/cm³)	Available water capacity[c] (cm/cm)
Histosols/Saprists/*Lauderhill*	0–20	Oap	—	—	—	45	6.2	138	18	0.8	2.1	52	76	0.29	0.40
Palm Beach/Sugar cane	20–46	Oa1	—	—	—	46	6.3	138	22	0.8	0.9	48	77	0.26	0.40
−30 (ponded) to 30 cm	46–66	Oa2	—	—	—	39	6.6	86	18	1.2	0.5	34	76	0.12	0.54
	66	2R	—	—	—	—	—	—	—	—	—	—	—	—	—
Spodosols/Aquods/*Leon*	0–5	A	92	3	2	2.0	3.8	0.05	0.14	0.09	0.03	8.3	4	—	—
Santa Rosa/Pine plantation	5–40	E	96	4	1	0.3	4.6	0.05	0.03	0.01	<0.005	1.6	5	1.52	0.07
0 to 30 cm	40–53	Bh1	87	8	5	1.7	4.4	0.03	0.04	0.03	0.01	10.8	1	1.34	0.31
	53–64	Bh2	89	6	5	1.7	4.8	0.03	0.02	0.02	<0.005	10.0	1	1.47	0.16
	64–81	BC	92	5	3	0.4	4.9	0.03	0.02	0.02	<0.005	3.7	2	1.61	0.11
	81–112	C	96	3	1	0.1	4.8	0.02	0.01	<0.005	<0.005	1.0	3	1.57	0.05
Ultisols/Udults/*Orangeburg*	0–13	A	75	11	14	2.5	5.3	2.7	0.7	0.03	0.14	12.6	22	1.42	0.12
Leon/Mixed hardwood and pine	13–25	Bt1	75	8	17	0.7	5.6	1.3	0.5	0.03	0.06	8.6	17	1.58	0.12
>150 cm	25–41	Bt2	68	6	26	0.4	5.5	1.2	0.6	0.03	0.05	8.7	18	1.50	0.21
	41–102	Bt3	63	8	29	0.1	5.3	1.0	0.5	0.03	0.04	9.2	15	1.53	0.16
	102–155	Bt4	60	3	37	0.1	5.4	1.6	0.5	0.03	0.04	9.2	19	1.71	0.13
	155–203	Bt4	63	2	35	0.1	5.5	1.6	0.6	0.03	0.03	8.0	22	1.71	0.13
Alfisols/Aqualfs/*Felda*	0–10	A	96	1	2	1.2	7.5	7.3	0.4	0.04	0.07	0.7	92	—	—
Pasco/Pasture	10–25	E1	97	3	1	0.3	8.2	2.5	0.1	0.02	<0.005	<0.005	100	1.55	0.16
0 to 30 cm	25–58	E2	92	5	2	0.2	8.8	16.6	0.2	0.03	<0.005	<0.005	100	1.60	0.17
	58–68	Btg1	73	6	22	0.1	8.2	25.9	2.5	0.17	0.10	3.5	89	1.36	0.21
	68–89	Btg2	66	17	17	0.1	8.2	25.4	2.3	0.18	0.06	3.1	90	1.50	0.20
	89–104	Btg3	84	3	13	0.0	8.3	15.6	1.2	0.10	0.03	2.0	89	1.70	0.22
	104–119	BCg	87	2	11	0.1	8.5	7.4	0.8	0.06	0.05	2.0	81	—	—
	119–203	C	99	0	1	0.0	8.6	0.2	0.02	<0.005	<0.005	<0.005	100	—	—
Entisols/Psamments/*Astatula*	0–15	Ap	96	2	2	0.6	5.7	0.70	0.10	<0.005	<0.005	2.70	23	1.49	0.13
Osceola/Former citrus grove	15–51	C1	96	1	3	0.2	5.5	0.10	<0.005	<0.005	<0.005	1.60	6	1.59	0.04
>180 cm	51–102	C2	96	1	3	0.1	5.3	<0.005	<0.005	<0.005	<0.005	1.30	0	1.50	0.03
	102–152	C3	96	1	3	0.1	5.3	0.10	<0.005	<0.005	<0.005	1.20	8	1.51	0.03
	152–208	C4	97	1	3	0.1	5.2	<0.005	<0.005	<0.005	<0.005	1.30	0	1.56	0.04

Note: These data are from Carlisle et al. (1978) and Carlisle et al. (1981), except that water table data were taken from Soil Interpretation Records generated by the National Cooperative Soil Survey for the series wherever mapped. These are the ranges within which the water table may be found during wet seasons of most years. These tables are in the form used in soil survey reports and other soil science publications. The values are readily converted to weight of constituent per horizon per unit area (hectare or acre), by the equations given in the notes that follow.

a. Organic carbon (O.C.) (%). *Multiply* percent × horizon depth (cm) × bulk density to give weight in metric tons per hectare (× 890 = lbs/acre). Examples:
Lauderhill soil, 0–20 cm: 45% × 20 cm × 0.29 = 261 metric tons/ hectare (mt/ha) = 232,000 lbs/a
Leon soil, 5–40 cm: 0.3% × 35 cm × 1.52 = 16 mt/ha = 14,000 lbs/a
(O.C. × 1.72 = approximate organic matter percentage.)

b. Exchangeable cations (meq/100g). The equivalent weights (grams) required for conversion are: calcium (Ca), 20; magnesium (Mg), 12; sodium (Na), 23; potassium (K), 39. (Note that the equation uses not only number of milliequivalents as listed in the tables, but also equivalent weight.) *Multiply* number milliequivalents × equivalent weight × depth (cm) × bulk density to give weight in kg/ha (× 0.9 = lbs/a). Examples:
Calcium in Leon soil, 5–40 cm: 0.05 × 20 × 35 cm × 1.52 = 53 kg/ha = 48 lbs/a
Calcium in Felda soil, 25–58 cm: 16.6 × 20 × 33 cm × 1.60 = 17,500 kg/ha = 15,600 lbs/a
Potassium in Orangeburg soil, 0–13 cm: 0.14 × 39 × 13 cm × 1.42 = 101 kg/ha = 90 lbs/a
Summing values for successive horizons gives the profile total. Note the enormous difference in calcium contents in the upper meter or so of the Leon and Felda soils.

c. Available water storage capacity (cm/cm). Like rainfall or evaporation, available water is expressed in terms of depth. In this case, the unit is the depth of water that can be retained in a centimeter depth of soil. Hence, storage capacity (cm/cm) × horizon thickness = storage capacity of the horizon. Summing amounts in successive horizons yields total storage in the profile. Example:
Astatula soil, 0–208 cm: 15 cm × 0.13 + 36 cm × 0.04 + 51 cm × 0.03 + 50 cm × 0.03 + 56 cm × 0.04 = 8.7 cm = 3.4 in.
As noted in the text, such calculation is meaningless for soils having a water table within the rooting zone.

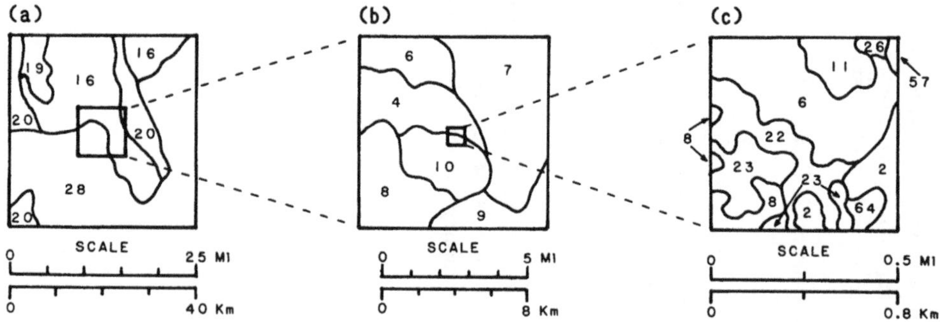

Fig. 3.9. Three soil maps encompassing a quarter section (65 ha) in Pasco County, Florida, showing differences in amount of detail that can be represented, depending on map scale. Note that the symbols (numbers) in the map legends have different meanings on the three different maps.

a. General soil map of Florida (Caldwell and Johnson, 1982). 16: Arredondo-Kendrick-Millhopper association; minor soils: Blichton, Lake, Sparr.
19: Blichton-Flemington-Kanapaha association; minor soils: Bivans, Lochloosa, Micanopy.
20: Candler-Apopka-Astatula association; minor soils: Arredondo, Tavares.
28: Myakka-Immokalee-Waveland association; minor soils: Basinger, Pomello, Pomona.

b. General soil map of Pasco County, Florida (Stankey, 1982). *4:* Tavares-Sparr-Adamsville.
6: Millhopper-Candler Variant.
7: Nobleton-Blichton-Flemington Variant.
8: Smyrna-Sellers-Myakka.
9: Pomona-EauGallie-Sellers.
10: Basinger-Wauchula.

c. Detailed soil map of SW¼, Sec. 23, T24S, R19E, Pasco County, Florida (Stankey, 1982).
2: Pomona.
6: Tavares.
8: Sellers.
11: Adamsville.
22: Basinger.
23: Basinger, depressional.
26: Narcoossee.
57: Vero Variant.
64: Nobleton.

except as tempered with substantial knowledge of both soil series and vegetation history.

Specific reasons why soil and vegetation can vary either coincidentally or independently are too numerous for exposition here. One set of reasons has to do with the nature of soil classification and mapping, as has been suggested. The criteria used in distinguishing one soil series from another may not separate factors critical to the establishment and dominance of some major plant species. In Florida, soil surveyors examine the top 2 m of soil, which is difficult enough. In some porous soils, however, roots of pines, some oaks, and magnolia may absorb water and nutrients from even greater depths and so respond to soil differences that are "invisible" to soil surveyors—and to almost all other observers.

Other reasons for noncoincidence of present-day vegetation and soil boundaries arise from the profound impact of past events, such as millennia of hurricanes, periodic great droughts, and human-generated and lightning-caused fires, followed by the impacts of European settlement. Little if any of the present-day forest has escaped logging, turpentining, grazing and, sometimes, a period of cultivation or open pasture. Few of the open prairies have been free of grazing since the time of Spanish settlement. Great expanses of longleaf pine were converted to open range, to scrub, or to other forest types by logging, followed by persistent destruction of the thick-rooted seedlings by hogs. Similarly, residual stumps testify that many present-day gum swamps were formerly cypress stands.

Few natural or human-caused events fall uniformly on the landscape. The barriers created by myriad lakes and swamps, for example, ensure unequal frequency and intensity of fire, regardless of soil characteristics. Likewise variable are the paths of hurricanes and the tornadoes and floods that accompany them. So it is unlikely that any two separate areas of seemingly identical soil have had identical ecological histories. It is much more probable that any two adjacent areas, although dissimilar in soil, may have suffered similarly from some past catastrophes and perhaps also have shared common seed sources during the early stages of recovery. For example, after severe fire a sand pine stand not only reestablishes itself from seed stored in closed cones but also may spread aggressively into adjacent newly burned areas. Although it will die prematurely where these soils are wet or otherwise unsuitable, its brief tenure will affect the successional development of other species compared with burns where sand pine did not invade.

It is convenient to picture any particular soil area as a stage on which many, some, or only a few dramas are possible. The stage itself is by no means passive; its collective properties can be favorable, neutral, or unfavorable toward some plays and players. But control over what actually takes place on the stage is shared with and often dominated by nonsoil factors and events. Over time, of course, similarities in the stage, and recurrent assemblages of the same players, inevitably produce many similarities in the resulting dramas. This view is expressed, in part, by present concepts of "multiple pathways of succession" (Cattelino et al., 1979).

A concern for soil as habitat thus involves attention to (1) the major soil features and process variables and (2) how plants, animals, and ecosystems respond to the intensities and interactions of these variables. We are far from fully understanding either, but because many of these features and variables are incorporated in the soil classification, soil classes at one level or another often do delimit major vegetation strata. Discussion of some major variables affecting plants and animals follows.

Water Tables

Swamp and marsh soils, together with other soils having water tables within reach of plant roots for at least part of the year, make up a large proportion of the Florida landscape still in natural or seminatural vegetation. Characterization of water table regimes is thus a primary consideration when assessing landscapes, soils, or ecosystems. In swamps and marshes, obviously, the water table is usually at or above the soil surface for much of the year. This fact and its associated effects are the only features common to all swamp and marsh soils, which vary widely in all other properties affecting plant growth. The normal ranges in water level may be limited and controlled, as in tidal marshes or those adjacent to large lakes. Elsewhere, most Florida swamps and marshes are subject to wide fluctuations in water level in accord with cumulative rainfall. In many instances, such fluctuation is now either increased or decreased by artificial drainage and, occasionally, by excessive pumping of groundwater.

The boundaries between wet prairies and grassy lakes vary with rainfall. Likewise, wooded swamps and cypress ponds that are saturated or flooded in most years are nevertheless subject to drying and even to fire during occasional droughts. Perhaps as a result, surface organic accumulation in many wet areas is less than might be expected.

Outside of recognizable marshes, swamps, and wet river bottoms, however, are large areas of almost imperceptibly sloping soils that have water tables within rooting depth for at least several months of most years. In some, the water surfaces are continuous with those of nearby lakes and swamps. Such water tables fluctuate with rainfall but are usually present at some depth. In others, however, the water tables are perched above nearly impervious clay layers and endure only as long as rainfall exceeds losses due to evapotranspiration and slow lateral or downward seepage. Such water tables often disappear entirely during dry periods. Since transpiration is a major avenue of water loss, destruction of the green canopy by fire, wind, or logging often temporarily increases the height and duration of both types of water tables.

There is little exact information about the adaptations of most plant species to high or variable water tables, although much can be inferred from their distribution and root anatomy. Cypress (*Taxodium*), slash pine (*Pinus elliottii*), and gums (*Nyssa*) have an internal porosity that allows ventilation of at least portions of root systems below the water table. Pond pine (*Pinus serotina*), bays (*Persea*), and loblolly bay (*Gordonia lasianthus*) presumably have similar arrangements.

Some wet-site oaks depend on a very shallow main root system with numerous small-diameter "sinkers" that appear to grow downward rapidly in dry periods and die off during prolonged high stands of the water table. Roots of saw palmetto (*Serenoa repens*) have continuous open cavities, unequaled in diameter by any of the woody dicotyledons. Roots of this widely adapted species are often found a meter or more below groundwater levels as well as in dry sands remote from any water table. Palmetto often forms a conspicuous ring around margins of cypress ponds and similar wet areas, with its inner edge just above the presumed high water mark. A plausible explanation is that although the roots conduct air, the prostrate stems must be above the water surface to allow air to enter. The upright cabbage palm (*Sabal palmetto*), which has a similar root structure, is far more tolerant of flooding. Sedges, rushes, wet-site grasses, and many other monocots have conspicuous gas transport structures. Doubtless many herbaceous and shrubby dicots that succeed in soils with high water tables also have effective air-conducting tissues, but there has been little study of them.

Soil water levels obviously influence the distribution of soil-dwelling animals. The gopher tortoise (*Gopherus polyphemus*), pocket gopher (*Geomys pinetis*) (fig. 3.10), harvest mouse (*Peromyscus polionotus*), and harvest ant (*Pogonomyrmex badius*) all confine their burrowing to well-drained soils, although they have additional requirements as well. The "push up" mounds of a scarab beetle (*Peltotrupes youngi*), which excavates its brood chambers from 1 to more than 3 m below the soil surface in sandy soils, define the absence of high water tables as accurately as any soil surveyor. Its less ambitious relative, *Mycotrupes*, appears equally perceptive.

Conversely, several species of crayfish that have evolved to live in wet soils reveal the presence of water tables within depths to which they can burrow. The burrows may be shallow or deep, scarce or numerous, and large or small in diameter, depending on species and soil. *Procambarus rogersi*, for example, excavates successively deeper tunnels and chambers as the wa-

Fig. 3.10. Pocket gopher (*Geomys pinetus*) mounds are abundant only in better-drained sites, as in this landscape of dry, sandy soils (Psamments) in the Central Lakes physiographic district. The striking number of mounds shows up well in this freshly burned area. Photo by E.L. Stone.

ter table falls. These form an interconnecting network in the upper 40 to 60 cm layer, allowing rapid lateral water flow when water tables are above this depth. These large galleries also provide numerous refuges for frogs, toads, and snakes during dry periods.

Clay layers and morphological evidence of water tables are major features in soil classification. Thus their occurrences within the upper 2 m depth are well described by soil maps, and occurrences below 2 m often can be inferred.

Seasonal Water Availability

With few exceptions, plants in full sun are exposed to inexorable transpiration demands that they must meet or suspend photosynthetic activity. Although Florida is exceptional in the proportion of soils with water tables within rooting depth, there are also large areas of natural vegetation that lack contact with water tables, either entirely or except for brief periods after exceptional rains. Here the quantity of available water stored within the reach of roots determines how effectively plants grow in the intervals between rains. The same is true for soils with water tables whenever the free water disappears or sinks beyond maximum rooting depth.

Available water storage is the product of the amount of available water per unit volume (or depth) of soil and the total volume (or depth) of soil exploited by roots (table 3.3). The amounts per unit depth (inches per foot or centimeters per meter) vary downward, depending not only upon properties of the individual layers but also upon those features of underlying layers that retard free drainage. A sand with a clayey layer or lamellae (thin bands of relatively clayey soil) below 2 m is not the same environment for deep-rooted plants as one without, although it would be mapped the same and shallow-rooted plants might reflect no difference.

Depth of effective root exploitation varies greatly with both soil and species and is difficult to establish except by special studies (Schultz, 1972; Oliver, 1978). Hence its role in accounting for habitat differences is commonly neglected.

Aeration

Most terrestial plants require a reasonably well-aerated soil for normal root activity. The exceptions, which are numerous in Florida flatwoods and wetlands, have an internal mechanism for ventilating deep roots or some other special adaptation. The remainder can tolerate submersion of their roots by flooding or a rising water table for variable but usually brief periods before some degree of damage occurs. Low soil temperatures reduce oxygen consumption by both roots and soil microbes, however, and so allow longer submersion without damage. Flowing water is more tolerable than standing water because the water remains oxygenated and perhaps also because high concentrations of carbon dioxide and other adverse products are less likely to occur.

To a considerable degree, the depth of well-aerated soil is directly related to depth to water table or saturated zone, though exceptions occur. In highly porous surface soils, for example, oxygen can diffuse rapidly through large pores even though the soil surrounding the large pores appears saturated, with a water table only a few centimeters below. Some dense subsoils and compacted surfaces, however, may have so few macropores that drainage of excess water and the ventilation that follows take place slowly after saturation.

Since water tables and saturation episodes vary seasonally and with wet and dry years, aeration likewise varies. The range of plant adaptations for avoiding, mitigating, and recovering from the effects of poor aeration is large and obviously influences which plants succeed in flooded or ill-drained soils.

Penetrability

Poor aeration is not the only restriction to root development. Even in well-aerated soils, roots cannot enter very small pores and, after entering somewhat larger pores, may not be able to exert sufficient force to overcome soil resistance to expansion. Layers of high soil strength hinder downward growth of roots, limit exploitation by fine roots, and result in a variety of deformations that are visible on excavated stumps and windthrown trees.

Resistance, or the degree of mechanical impedance, often varies seasonally with soil moisture status. Some ill-drained sands that are almost impenetrable when dry become soft or fluid when saturated by a rising water table. On the other hand, some (but not all) sandy clays and clay loams shrink as they dry, opening a network of cracks that improves aeration and facilitates root development. The ranges of clay mineral types and proportions of sand and clay are too great, however, for easy generalization about root development in clayey soils. Many clayey substrates combine high soil strength with poor aeration, making it uncertain which is the primary restriction.

The black (spodic) horizons of acid flatwood Spodosols are saturated for long periods and thus limit penetration by nonadapted species. Most of these spodic horizons are soft when moist. A few, however, are hard enough to prevent development of taproots and sinkers and so deny anchorage to large trees (Schultz, 1973).

Apart from affecting anchorage for tall trees, differences in degree of aeration and penetrability affect vegetation only as they influence uptake of water and nutrients. Nutrient-rich soils with high moisture-storage capacities or permanent water tables below a well-aerated surface are likely to be highly productive and to support many species, regardless of rooting depth. The productivity of an infertile well-drained sand, however, may depend entirely on deep root penetration, including possible access to supplies of water or nutrients that are below the upper meter or two.

Acidity and Base Content

Surface soils in Florida range from extremely acid (near pH 4 in most pine flatwoods) to neutral or moderately alkaline (pH 7 to 8.3) where limestone outcrops. Acidity of individual layers, expressed on the pH scale, is correlated with the amount of plant-available calcium and magnesium. Development of a strongly acid surface does not necessarily preclude higher pH and appreciable supplies of calcium and magnesium at greater depth in the rooting profile.

Various types of limestone underlie all of peninsular Florida, and some overlying deposits are also calcareous. Both soil development and vegetative composition are greatly affected by the proximity of such limy materials to the present surface. Over much of the state, the depth of overlying sands and clays is too great for these materials to influence the surface soil. In contrast, outcropping and near-surface limestones dominate the soils of southernmost Florida and underlie the Everglades at shallow depths. Thinly mantled limestones or other calcareous materials approach the surface at numerous other points in the state.

As might be expected, however, there are also varied combinations of acid surface soils overlying limy substrates at intermediate depths. When such substrates are below 2 m in depth, they are likely to go unnoted in soil surveys and yet may influence deep-rooted species. The presence of occasional cabbage palms in otherwise typical acid pine flatwoods near both coasts of the Peninsula usually indicates lime at some depth. Neither the surface soils, which are strongly acid Spodosols, nor most plant species give any hint of the deep limy layers, although some observers believe that the vegetation is more vigorous than elsewhere.

As has long been known, the vegetation characteristic of limy and acid soils—that is, base-rich and base-poor soils—usually differs markedly. Some species extend over a wide range of surface soil pH, although they are not necessarily present in equal abundance throughout the range. Others are confined to some fraction of the total range (about pH 3.8 to 8.3). The so-called acid loving species tolerate the high levels of soluble aluminum and manganese characteristic of most acid soils, whereas many other species do not. Numerous acid-soil species, including many in the family Ericaceae, are unable to absorb sufficient iron and manganese from near-neutral or alkaline soils. A number of herbaceous species compete well only when supplied with the nitrate form of nitrogen. Nitrate is usually more abundant in near-neutral to alkaline soils, though not necessarily limited to these. In contrast, many other shrubs and herbs grow best when supplied with ammonium nitrogen, which is the dominant form in most acid soils. Apart from these and similar generalizations, little is known about the actual requirements of individual species.

Nutrient Supplies

Water excess or deficiency, pH, and fire exert such large effects on Florida vegetation that other influences are easily overlooked. One of these is soil nutrient supply. Essential plant nutrients vary in availability independently of one another, except as linked by soil development or organic content. Thus, one obviously infertile soil may fail to provide adequate amounts of only a single element, whereas another may lack several. Furthermore, some deep sands lack the capacity to retain nutrients even when these are added. Curiously, low fertility and low moisture supplies often have grossly similar effects on the growth and appearance of vegetation, so that appearance alone is no certain indication of which factor is limiting.

The materials of many Florida soils were well weathered before deposition or emergence at the present land surface above the sea, and they have been weathered even further since that time. Thus it is not surprising that the supplies of most mineral nutrients available to plants are very low in such soils and are retained chiefly in organic matter. Nitrogen is likewise low because of low fixation rates in strongly acid soils and high rates of leaching. On the other hand, limestone occurring near the surface often gives rise to more fertile soils and productive vegetation, such as the formerly extensive upland hardwood communities along the eastern fringe of the Ocala Uplift District. Moreover, phosphate-bearing clays are close enough to the surface to influence plant growth in several areas. Probably no other state presents such extreme contrasts of acute phosphorus deficiency and superabundant availability for plant growth.

Interest in fertilizing forests has produced substantial evidence of the limiting role of nutrients. A striking example is phosphorus deficiency and response in coastal savannas—level, poorly drained old deltaic deposits bearing slow-growing, open slash pine stands above a cover of wiregrass and shrubs. In experiments north of Port St. Joe, single applications of phosphates at the time of planting young slash pine increased total stem volume as much as thirtyfold by age seventeen (Pritchett and Comerford, 1982). Moreover, the whole physiognomy of the vegetation on the fertilized plots changed. Needle fall from the dense canopy largely suppressed the wiregrass sod with its intermingled herbs and other grass species. Some shrubs, such as St. John's-wort (*Hypericum* spp.), diminished, whereas gallberry (*Ilex glabra*) and other hollies became more vigorous. Wax myrtle (*Myrica cerifera*) flourished on the most heavily fertilized plots, reaching large dimensions. In effect, overcoming acute deficiency of a single nutrient initiated a series of consequences. Development of a dense forest canopy increased both litter deposition and shade on the forest floor. It also increased evapotranspiration, which in turn lowered water tables during rainless periods and so allowed greater root exploitation of the surface soil.

Previously, before phosphorus deficiency of natural vegetation was even considered, Kurz and Godfrey (1962) attributed depauperate forms of black-gum (*Nyssa biflora*), magnolia (*Magnolia virginiana*), red maple (*Acer rubrum*), and cypress (*Taxodium ascendans*), in the wetter portions of the area already described, to periodic burning. They favored this explanation for the dwarf habit of *Nyssa* in preference to Small's establishment of a separate species, *Nyssa ursina.* As in other areas of stunted vegetation, the possibility of genotypic dwarfs must be admitted until experiment demonstrates otherwise. It is now clear, however, that severe phosphorus deficiency is the overriding factor controlling plant growth here and in similar areas, such as the pitcher plant flats of northwest Florida.

Numerous forest fertilization experiments in north Florida demonstrate that such extreme deficiency is rare. Nevertheless, growth of slash pine and, to a greater extent, loblolly pine (*Pinus taeda*) is often increased by additions of either phosphorus or nitrogen alone or the two in combination. Such responses imply that abundance and growth of other species on the same soils are similarly limited. For example, preliminary foliar analyses reveal that some shrubs and trees characteristic of wet bays and cypress ponds have extremely low phosphorus concentrations—.03 to .04 percent dry weight. Such low values are matched only by those of the Australian heath vegetation, suggesting that soil phosphorus levels influence species composition on many wet acid soils.

Salinity

Salt concentration in water and underlying soil is an important variable in tidal marshes, but its role in adjacent swamps and wet forests is little known. Lateral outflow of fresh water prevents encroachment of brackish waters except after long droughts. Even then, slowly permeable clayey subsoils greatly restrict inward movement, whereas open sandy substrates are more vulnerable to encroachment.

Occasional hurricanes or other great storms may drive salt water inland along coastal fringes. The resulting salt concentrations in soils may persist for at least a year, with reported damage to young slash pine. Doubtless other species are also affected, thus influencing the course of plant succession. It seems likely that swamps and riverine forests already flooded with fresh water may suffer less from such storm-driven encroachment.

Root Pathogens

Root pathogens—chiefly fungi and nematodes—exert unknown but perhaps large influences on competition among plants, the course of secondary succession, and soil-plant interactions. In the main, however, few noncultivated plants other than major timber and ornamental species have been studied. Even then, the ecological relationships are often not well understood. Thus the probable roles of root pathogens are suggested by a few case histories rather than by firm generalizations.

The short life span and increasingly open canopy of sand pine after about three decades of growth seem due to *Inonotus circinatus* (*Polyporus circinatus*), a widespread root rot that is also important in slash pine and Canadian spruce forests (Barnard et al., 1985). It may be that the dense shrub and dwarf palm understory so characteristic of some older peninsular sand pine stands reflects a continuous erosion of the pine canopy as the root system is impaired.

Another widespread root rot, *Heterobasidion annosum* (*Fomes annosus*), infects many tree species but is lethal to pines and juniper. Most reports of damage are from pine plantations or old-field stands where the fungus enters wounds or the freshly cut stumps left by thinning. It then spreads through root contact, causing slowly widening circles of overstory decline and death. Understory hardwood saplings, shrubs, and herbs respond quickly to the reduced overstory competition, hastening the appearance of a pine-to-hardwood succession. Various associations of the fungus with soil properties and prescribed fire have been reported but mostly do not allow firm generalizations. The disease is, however, favored by near-neutral to alkaline soils and by some unknown condition in old fields as opposed to natural forest.

Slash pine is widespread on ill-drained soils. When planted on excessively drained sandhills, however, or on similar sands lacking clayey layers or water tables within rooting depth, it often grows poorly, either from the outset or after a brief period of seemingly favorable growth. Such soils are now recognized as "off site" for this species and suitable only for the sand pine (*Pinus clausa*) or longleaf pine (*Pinus palustris*) that grew there in the native forest. The reasons for slash pine failure or decline have remained a mystery. In one well-studied occurrence on an Astatula soil, however, the pine cystoid nematode, *Meloidodera floridensis*, was abundant on the fine roots of slash pine (Bengtson and Smart, 1981). Seedlings planted in soil that had been treated with a nematicide grew much better and had better potassium nutrition than the controls. It appears probable that this nematode limits this tree on this particular soil. Many other native plant species may well be found limited in distribution, not uniquely by soil or by some pest but by some parallel kind of soil-pest interaction.

Changing Soils

Under natural conditions the soils of weathered landscapes change only slowly, barring major climatic or geological disruptions. The arrival of aboriginal humans in Florida some 10,000 to 12,000 YBP instituted more rapid changes, most of which were ephemeral or affected only small areas. The widespread burning noted by early Europeans was superimposed upon, and in part substituted for, a natural regime of lightning-caused fire (Komarek, 1964). Thus the consequences of Indian fire cannot be readily separated except in a few areas where lightning fires would have been too infrequent to have produced the observed results (Kalisz et al., 1986). The eventual development of agriculture and growth of Indian populations (Milanich and Fairbanks, 1980) certainly entailed progressive land clearing in localized areas. The fields were cultivated for only a few years, however, and any input, improvement, or erosion would have been trivial. In contrast, sites of long-occupied villages and middens were decidely affected, as exemplified by the shell mounds along the St. Johns River. Lesser quantities of shell and bone have disappeared from acid soils, but soil phosphorus accumulations usually remain as markers of human occupancy.

In contrast, human activities from colonial times onward have had profound and widespread effects on soil and so on the environment of present-day vegetation. Many such activities and their consequences—such as atmospheric deposition, surface mining, lowering of aquifers by pumping, eutrophication of marshes and estuaries by sewage effluent and land runoff, and deposition of lead, zinc, and cadmium in soils adjacent to highways—are now matters of public knowledge. Other effects, such as those associated with past cultivation and drainage, or with artificial impoundments and floodplain barriers, either are often not recognized at all or are not perceived as creating new soil-plant relationships.

Some large part of Florida's forests now accepted as natural or quasi-natural actually occur on soils that were once cultivated or cleared for pasturage. After these uses were discontinued, the land, changed in some degree, reverted to secondary forest either naturally or by reforestation. Tillage or prolonged grazing eliminated the forest microtopography that influences seedling establishment and surface drainage patterns on wet soils. It also lowered the organic matter and nitrogen contents of soils, and it usually reduced macroporosity and friability of the surface layers. All of these reductions are restorable over time after reversion to natural vegetation.

More profound and essentially nonrestorable changes resulted from accelerated erosion and deposition. Over much of Florida such effects were localized; soil washed from the slightly steeper portions of gently sloping fields was deposited on the lower portions, accentuating any preexisting differences in surface soil depth and fertility. In hilly regions, however, such erosion removed or thinned the sandy surface soil, especially on upper slopes and hill crests, often leaving a clayey subsoil as the new surface. Sometimes networks of rills or small gullies created channelized drainage patterns that are now obscured by slumping and forest litter. The net effect of erosion was reduced fertility and lessened opportunities for trees, shrubs, and herbs with high nutrient requirements to compete in the long process of secondary succession. Less demanding species, such as pines and oaks, often grew well, provided that the newly exposed subsoils were friable enough for good root penetration.

In many watersheds the area of present or formerly cultivated fields is large relative to the area in stream terraces and bottoms. Thus erosion of only a few centimeters of soil from the fields provides a potential for several or many centimeters of deposition along stream courses. Some of the eroded soil may be trapped before reaching the stream course, and an additional fraction is transported further downstream into successively larger watersheds. The remainder is deposited on bottomlands and terraces.

Studies of north Florida rivers are lacking, but elsewhere deposition has altered stream hydraulics and raised the elevation of some bottomlands since European settlement began (Trimble, 1970, 1974). Streams flowing from lakes or swamps, or without appreciable agriculture in the headwaters, are unaffected. In other cases, it is likely that apparently pristine bottomland vegetation actually is growing on some depth of new sediments veneered over precolonial surfaces. The deepest of the new sediments, representing original topsoil of the uplands, may be the most fertile, but many other combinations of alternating or mixed surface and subsoil are possible. Thus units of recent alluvium delineated on soil maps are often highly variable. Soil moisture regimes of bottomlands may be altered where stream channels have been choked by recent sediment, thus retarding drainage (fig. 3.11) (Trimble, 1970). Clearing of land next to streams also can remove the source of woody debris, reducing availability of woody habitat in the streams and on adjacent lands (Triska, 1984).

Although only a small fraction of the soil eroded from cultivated uplands since first settlement has yet reached sea level, that amount obviously influences deposition in deltas, marshes, and estuaries. Specific information about effects on vegetation is slight, but some marsh soil surfaces have been veneered with new sediment, raising the elevation and altering nutrient supply and salinity.

Yet another frequent consequence of past agricultural use is an enhanced level of available phosphorus residual from fertilizer applications. Phosphates were widely available in Florida beginning late in the last century, though not all farmers used them. Firm evidence is lacking, but it appears that superior growth of planted pines in old fields is commonly associated with higher levels of extractable soil phosphorus (Carlisle, 1953). Presumably many other species benefit similarly.

For much of Florida the histories of both agriculture and real estate development involve a history of extensive land drainage (fig. 3.12) (Blake, 1980). The effects of canals and ditches commonly reached beyond the area of intentional drainage, lowering the maximum height or duration of soil water tables in adjacent wild lands. Some drained areas have since reverted

Fig. 3.11. This graded road across a bottomland in northwest Florida retards stream flow that ordinarily would pass readily from left to right. In addition, both road ditches are completely choked by sediment from the road and from upslope erosion beyond the curve. Such sediment accumulation in ditches, culverts, and stream channels, as well as on surfaces of floodplains, further hinders stream flow and can make bottomland soils wetter than they otherwise would be. Photo by R.B. Brown.

to uncultivated vegetation, which may be growing on a soil that is actually better drained than an unqualified soil map would indicate.

Another great but generally unrecognized impact on near-surface water tables results from the network of developed roads. Subdrainage by shallow roadside ditches is usually effective for only short distances, perhaps 10 to 30 m, that is, some 2 to 6 ha per km of road if both sides are affected. The

Fig. 3.12. Artificial drainage for agricultural and urban purposes has been used to control the water table in many areas, as in this example from south Florida. Photo by R.B. Brown.

consequences for plant growth range from trivial to large. Growth of planted slash pine on wet, phosphorus-deficient soils may be twice as great or more in the vicinity of such ditches compared to others only 30 m distant, and at least some understory shrubs are similarly affected. Enhanced growth of trees and tall shrubs leads to elimination or reduced density of species characteristic of open swamps and bogs, but some of these prosper along the permanently wet ditches. Thus ditching alone on some wet soils may induce strong contrasts in vegetation within very short distances. A car-window observer, viewing only growth along the road margin, might easily misjudge the natural vegetation characteristic of such soils.

Roadside ditches affect much greater areas, however, when prolonged rains, such as those accompanying hurricanes, flood the surface of flatwoods and other level lands. Then, the ditches serve as an extended drainage net, hastening the off-flow of surface water by some days or weeks. Concomitantly, the streams and lowlands into which the ditches discharge are subject to greater peak flows but shorter flow durations than previously. The effects of these several alterations on soils and vegetation are probably large but are unlikely ever to be shown by experiment.

Construction of road and railroad grades across wet areas (fig. 3.11) often retards surface and subsurface drainage, resulting in greater saturation or ponding on the upslope side and sometimes better drainage downslope. These effects are seldom prevented by culverts, which serve only to limit depth of surface water accumulation. Death of trees in ponded areas makes some such occurrences highly visible until concealed by regrowth. Thereafter, these areas, as well as large, less affected ones, usually go unnoticed. In effect, this is the converse of response to drainage. In both cases, soil morphology and soil mapping units are no longer indicators of the present-day soil moisture regimes affecting vegetation.

Thus, like the ecosystems of which they are a part, Florida's soils are variable, dynamic, and responsive to human activities as well as natural events.

4
Historical Biogeography

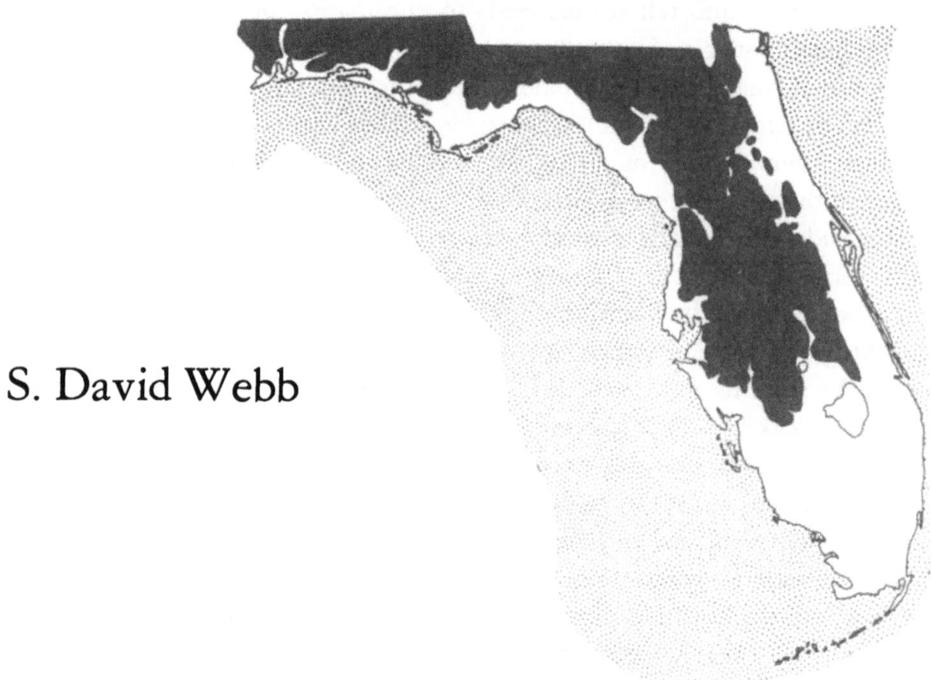

S. David Webb

Of all the states and provinces in North America, Florida is most intimately linked with the sea. The entire state lies within the coastal plain, with maximum elevation of about 120 m, and no part is more than 100 km from the Atlantic Ocean or the Gulf of Mexico. Its highest ridges were formed as coastal dunes, and all major rock formations anywhere near its surface are blankets of marine sediments. Florida's oldest terrestrial sediments are only 25 million years old; most of its earlier history took place beneath the ocean.

One might expect Florida's biogeographic history to be simple in view of its low relief, recent emergence, and proximity to the sea. That clearly is not the case, as this volume reflects in many ways. Five factors complicate Florida's biogeography: (1) Its latitudinal position, astride the northern edge of the tropics, fosters mingling of, and competition between, temperate and tropical biotas. (2) Its long, narrow shape spanning more than 700 km in an east-west direction and an equal distance down the peninsula—the axis of

Map: *dotted area*, extent of land surface of Florida in the last full glacial interval ca. 18,000 years ago; *black area*, last interglacial shoreline ca. 110,000 years ago.

which runs about 20° east of south—attenuates the distribution of many species. (3) Its relatively humid climate makes the land quite productive and greatly enriches the variety of the state's aquatic and semiaquatic habitats. (4) Its long peninsula, open to the north and closed to the south, raises the question of whether there is a "peninsular effect" (i.e., decreasing species richness from north to south) and, if so, how it works. (5) Its complex history of changes in size and shape, as a result of late Cenozoic sea-level cycles, has frequently shaken up its entire biota. A subsidiary question is whether (and when) the central peninsula and its biota were isolated by the "Suwannee Strait."

Thus, Florida's present configuration is deceptively simple. Its present geography does not adequately explain its present biogeography. Current distribution of each taxon represents a single snapshot of a complex trajectory through time and space.

The account of Florida's biogeography that follows takes a historical viewpoint. The framework is a synopsis of Florida's geological history. This account begins with Florida's early separation from Africa and its long marine record. It develops in more detail Florida's terrestrial history, which began in the Oligocene (about 30 million years before present [MYBP]) and represents only the last 5 percent of the Phanerozoic record (Cambrian through Quaternary). Direct evidence of the state's terrestrial history consists primarily of fossil vertebrates; leaf and pollen floras will be cited where available. It is also possible to assess Florida's paleogeography by compiling the distribution of marine and terrestrial sediments of known ages. From these data it is possible to conclude when and under what circumstances Florida's major ecosystems were established.

Early Marine Geologic History

This section briefly recounts the geologic history of Florida while it was under the sea. This marine interval accounts for 95 percent of Florida's known history, and spans the Paleozoic and Mesozoic eras and more than half of the Cenozoic era.

The Paleozoic Era (fig. 4.1)

Florida's basement rocks occur at depths of 1 to 3 km below the northern peninsula. They consist principally of the Osceola granite and various high-feldspar volcanic rocks. They yield radiometric dates of about 600 MYBP and therefore probably represent the Cambrian period.

This Cambrian basement is overlain by a sequence of early Paleozoic sediments that reaches a thickness of several kilometers. The oldest beds, consisting of quartz sandstones and interbedded shales, contain marine fossils of Ordovician age. They are succeeded by dark shales, interrupted occasionally by thin sandstones, with ages ranging from Silurian through middle Devonian.

Three lines of evidence show convincingly that during the Paleozoic era, Florida was part of Gondwanaland and specifically part of Africa. First, Florida's Paleozoic fossils—including conodonts, graptolites, crinoids, trilobites, brachiopods, and mollusks, as well as a pollen flora—more closely resemble the Gondwanan biota than that of North America (Pojeta et al., 1976). Second, paleomagnetic inclinations recorded in Paleozoic sediments from a well core in Alachua County indicate a paleolatitude of 49°. This measurement corresponds with a Gondwanan reconstruction, whereas if Florida had been attached to North America in the early Paleozoic its expected paleolatitude should have been about 28° (Opdyke et al., 1987). Third, the ages of some detrital minerals derived from Florida's Paleozoic sediments correspond closely with metamorphic and igneous rocks in northwestern Africa but not with any known sources in the Appalachian region (Opdyke et al., 1987; Dallmayer, 1987). Presumably Florida remained part of Gondwanaland through most if not all of the Paleozoic era.

The Mesozoic Era (fig. 4.2)

When Gondwanaland broke up, Florida was one of several terranes that dispersed as the Atlantic Ocean basin formed. In the Panhandle, the Eagle Mills Formation of Triassic age includes continental red beds interbedded with igneous rock formed along the rifting edge of Africa. The Tallahassee graben, a basement structure of about Triassic age, is thought to have originated at the time that Florida separated from Africa. Subsequently, during the Alleghenian orogeny, Florida was sutured onto North America along a zone now indicated by the Brunswick gravity anomaly in Georgia.

During the early Mesozoic, south Florida became the focus of new intrusive and extrusive volcanic activity generated by an oceanic hot spot situated where the Bahamas are now. Later, during the middle Jurassic, Florida became the deposition center for shallow marine carbonate sediments. Some of these sediments, for example, the Louann Formation in the Panhandle, were accompanied by evaporites, which indicate high salinity and restricted circulation. Doming of these Jurassic salt deposits produces traps for oil and gas reserves, especially in the overlying Smackover Formation of late Jurassic limestone. The predominantly carbonate sequence of the peninsula interfingers in north Florida with marine clays and sands presumably derived from terrestrial sources in the Appalachian region.

The principal deposits of the Cretaceous period were fossiliferous chalky limestones characteristic of that period in many parts of the world. The Sunniland Limestone north of the Everglades reaches a thickness of over 3,000 m. To the west, around the Gulf of Mexico, sand and shale accumulated. A major barrier reef, the Rebecca Shoal, developed along the southeastern margin of the Florida platform. At about the same time, however, rhyolitic (continentally derived) volcanic rocks were extruded in south Florida adjacent to the newly opened Florida Straits.

The Early Cenozoic Era (fig. 4.3)

Shallow marine conditions continued to prevail over Florida during the early Cenozoic. Extensive carbonate sequences rich in marine fossils were deposited more or less continuously from the Paleocene into the Oligocene. Major reef deposits are notably absent. Several episodes of marine transgressions are represented by thicker strata and sedimentary wedges that coarsen to the north (Randazzo and Saroop, 1976). The middle Eocene Avon Park formation in west-central Florida includes shallow marine, clayey deposits that yield impressions of sea grasses and (very rarely) of land plant leaves. The latter provide the earliest evidence that some part of Florida had emerged from the sea. By the late Eocene, however, the state was once more fully inundated and accumulating thick carbonate sediments.

From the Paleocene through middle Eocene, Florida's rich marine faunas reflect strong geographic affinities with north Africa and the Paris basin. This affiliation was maintained by the Tethys Seaway, with major equatorial currents that closely joined the oceans now distinguished as the Caribbean and Mediterranean. Florida's rich middle Eocene faunas particularly register this trans-Atlantic continuity. Eocene shells in the pyramids of Egypt bear a remarkable resemblance to those found in central Florida limestones. Richards and Palmer (1953) have detailed such relationships for a number of genera of mollusks from the Inglis formation. Likewise the earliest known

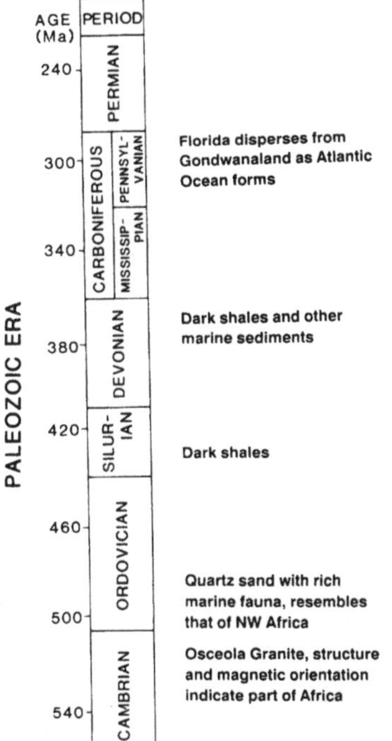

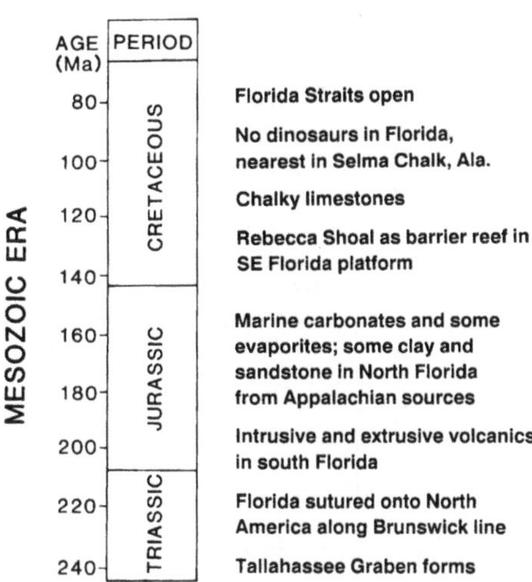

Fig. 4.2. Geological time scale for Mesozoic Era with a synopsis of Florida's biogeographic history.

Fig. 4.1 Geological time scale for Paleozoic Era with a synopsis of Florida's biogeographic history.

sea cow, *Protosiren*, ranges from mid-Eocene carbonate deposits in Florida to similar sites in the Fayum formation of Egypt and elsewhere along the eastern margins of the Tethys Sea (Domning et al., 1982). In the late Eocene Crystal River formation, however, one starts to see the development of a characteristic North American marine biota, reflecting increased separation across the Atlantic Ocean.

Oligocene sediments, mainly the Suwannee Formation, generally contain more clastic (sand, silt, and clay) sediments than the earlier carbonate sequences. During that epoch the Appalachian Range experienced renewed uplift, thus accounting for the increased load of clastic sediments that were carried southward. At last, in the late Oligocene, direct evidence of a land biota appears.

Terrestrial Geologic History

During the past 25 million years, Florida has accumulated a rich record of terrestrial vertebrate life (fig. 4.4). No state east of the Mississippi River, and few to the west, can rival the abundance and variety of Florida's Ceno-

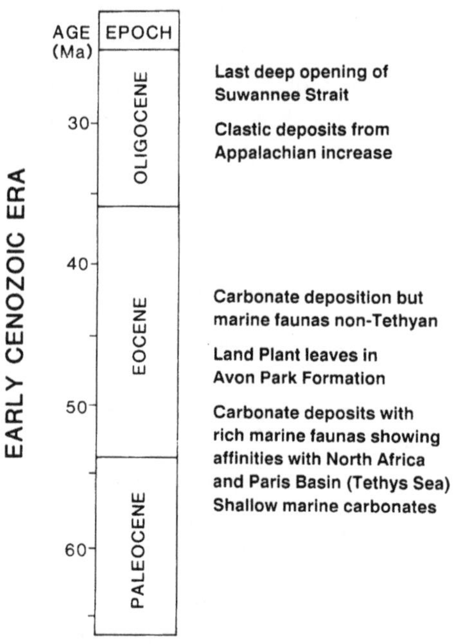

Fig. 4.3 Geological time scale for Early Cenozoic Era with a synopsis of Florida's biogeographic history.

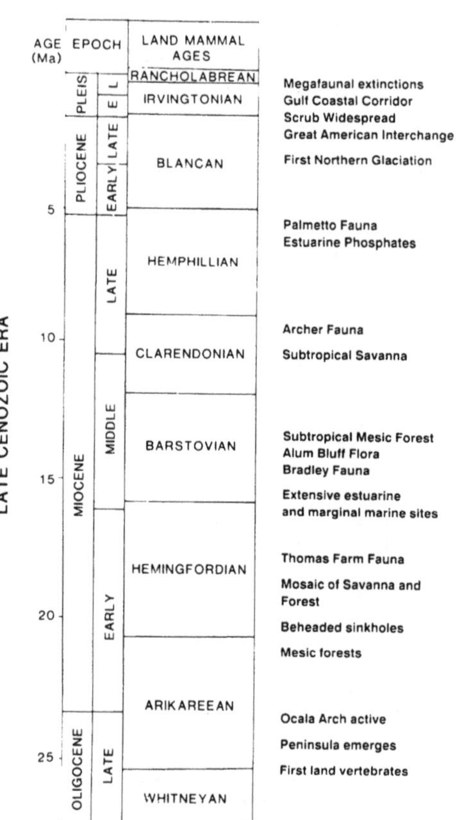

Fig. 4.4 Geologic time scale for Late Cenozoic Era with a synopsis of Florida's biogeographic history.

zoic fossil heritage. This record provides one or more rich samples for each stage since the late Oligocene, including many sites for the late Miocene and especially for the Pleistocene. Figure 4.5 indicates the geographic location of the most important pre-Pleistocene vertebrate sites.

The fossil record of plant life in Florida is less complete but nevertheless significant for understanding the state's biogeographic history. The two landmarks in Florida paleobotany are the Alum Bluff flora of late Miocene age and the excellent pollen record of the late Pleistocene. Other floras, such as the petrified wood flora of the Bone Valley late Miocene, are potentially important but greatly in need of detailed study.

Florida's terrestrial fossil record offers several important clues to the state's biogeographic history. Not only does it indicate the presence of various taxa but it also gives evidence of the time of origin and subsequent development of various ecosystems. Also, the floras and vertebrate faunas indicate former climatic patterns. Finally, Florida's terrestrial fossil sites provide an indication of the changing relationships between land and sea.

Despite its several advantages, Florida's fossil record, as presently known, has many limitations. The record of fossil leaves and wood is extremely sparse. Even the vertebrate record contains three long chronological gaps: in the earliest Miocene (between 23 and 20 MYBP); in the middle Miocene (between 15 and 11 MYBP); and in the early Pliocene (between 5 and 2.5 MYBP). Furthermore, terrestrial geographic coverage is sparse for many time intervals, often consisting of only one or two points for the whole peninsula. And taxonomic coverage is uneven, so it is difficult to know how completely the variable collections of vertebrates at hand sample the real Florida faunas of various ages during the middle and late Cenozoic. In gen-

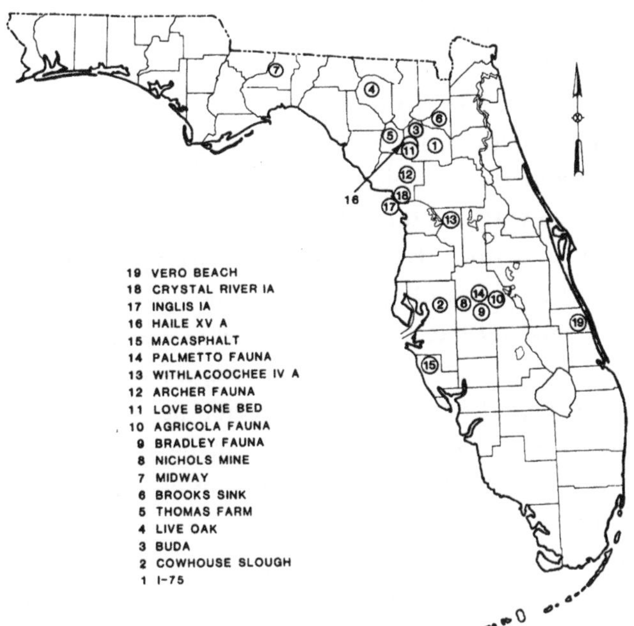

Fig. 4.5. Key fossil vertebrate sites in peninsular Florida.

eral, the adequacy of terrestrial vertebrate coverage increases approaching the present. Thus the Pleistocene provides a more detailed record than the Pliocene. With these limitations in mind, we can proceed to sketch the history of terrestrial life in Florida.

The Late Oligocene

Two fossil vertebrate localities in central Florida record all we know of the first 5 million years of terrestrial life in Florida. The oldest site, known as "I-75," was discovered by Mervin Kontrovitz on the outskirts of Gainesville at the intersection of State Road 121 and Interstate Highway 75. It consisted of fossiliferous sands and clays deposited in a small fissure (about 5 m in diameter and about 2 m deep) within the Williston limestone of late Eocene age. Patton (1969) produced a preliminary report on the fauna. The small mammals consist of an opossum, five species of bats, an insectivore known as *Centetodon* (G. Morgan, personal communication), and at least five species of rodents, including a beaver, a pocket mouse, and two taxa of the extinct family Eutypomyidae. The large mammals include at least two medium-sized carnivores, the Oligocene horse (*Mesohippus*), a small pig-like peccary, and two kinds of extinct goat-sized oreodonts. There are also two small, deer-like ungulates, *Leptomeryx* and *Hypisodus*, and several species each of frogs, snakes, and lizards, as well as a small tortoise and a box turtle. Despite its limited diversity (presumably attributable to the small size of the sample), the I-75 collection apparently represents a balanced terrestrial vertebrate fauna. It consists entirely of small isolated teeth and fragmented bones. The land fossils may have accumulated as owl pellets or other predator scat. This would explain the absence of really large forms such as rhinocerotids, although the nature of the site—a small sinkhole—also could have excluded them.

About ten species of marine vertebrates are represented by abundant teeth and spines from the I-75 locality. These include seven species of sharks (Tessman, 1969), as well as various sting ray and bony fish taxa. It is clear from their similar preservation that these marine vertebrates were deposited with the terrestrial vertebrates and are not derived from the older Eocene limestone. Evidently, the entire vertebrate sample accumulated at or very near the late Oligocene shoreline.

The second late Oligocene vertebrate site is Cowhouse Slough, a minute pocket of sediments (a few cm in diameter) cut into the Tampa limestone in Hillsborough County. The tiny vertebrate sample taken from this site is still under study (Jackson, n.d.) but can be reported briefly here. Among the small mammals are five different families of rodents, as well as a rabbit and an insectivore. The only carnivore is a sabercat of the genus *Nimravus*. Ungulates include a small horse, *Miohippus*; an oreodont; and the small deer-like genus, *Leptomeryx*. The herpetofauna includes a small primitive tortoise, an anguid lizard, and several boid snakes, appearing far more primitive than the Thomas Farm herpetofauna discussed below. No remains of marine or aquatic taxa, other than one water-worn shark tooth, have been found in the sample.

These two terrestrial sites do not provide enough evidence to reconstruct Florida's outline during the late Oligocene. Nonetheless, three conclusions are secure: that a significant landmass existed in central Florida; that it supported a varied vertebrate fauna; and that the mainly arboreal and browsing species indicate mesic forest as the predominant habitat.

The Early Miocene

As defined here, Florida's early Miocene vertebrate sites range up to late Hemingfordian time; they thus include the Thomas Farm and other purely terrestrial sites. The marine and estuarine sites of the late Hemingfordian are grouped in the middle Miocene with Barstovian sites of generally similar character. Two formations make up Florida's early Miocene marginal marine deposits: in the northern peninsula, the St. Marks formation, consisting of quiet-water deltaic and estuarine deposits; in the west-central peninsula, an upper member of the Tampa formation, appearing in the form of mixed clastic and carbonate sediments. Of the several sites representing early Miocene land life in Florida, none includes any marine or estuarine species. I have selected three of these sites to illustrate the present state of our knowledge.

In northern Alachua County is the Buda site, named after the limestone mine in which it occurs. Several contiguous small sinkholes filled with fossiliferous sandy clay produced, among small mammals, a hedgehog (Rich and Patton, 1975) and at least five kinds of rodents, including two kinds of pocket mice (A. Pratt, personal communication). The large mammals, described by Frailey (1979), include five genera of carnivores: two omnivorous canids, a member of the extinct bear-like family Amphicyonidae, a sabercat, and a weasel-like form. The odd-toed ungulates consist of a browsing horse and a small species of the extinct, claw-bearing, ungulate family, Chalicotheriidae (Coombs, 1978). Five species of even-toed ungulates are present: two omnivorous pig-like taxa, one a peccary and one representing the extinct oreodonts; a tiny deer-like browser; and two kinds of primitive camelids. The Buda collection evidently represents a well-balanced mammalian fauna, one that might be expected from a mesic forest.

The Live Oak site (also known as SB IA) occurs near the Suwannee River on the outskirts of the town of Live Oak. The fauna, described in part by Frailey (1978), is an oddly imbalanced sample—five of the eight described mammal species are carnivores. The horse is known from only one bone. The most abundant species by far is the small camelid, *Nothokemas*, which is not represented at Buda. Small mammals include an extinct squirrel, an opossum, a bat, and other rodents, including several species of pocket mice (G. Morgan, personal communication). Possibly the Live Oak vertebrates accumulated in a carnivore den. The sediments are poorly bedded or slumped sands, clays, and limestone conglomerates deposited in a karst depression in the Suwannee limestone of Oligocene age.

By far the richest early Miocene site in eastern North America is Thomas Farm in Gilchrist County near the confluence of the Santa Fe and Suwannee rivers. It has been extensively studied for more than half a century by field parties from Harvard University, the Florida Geological Survey, and the University of Florida. Originally thought to be a stream deposit, the site has been rcognized more recently as a major sinkhole accumulation, analogous to the Devil's Millhopper north of Gainesville. Webb (1981b) includes a recent faunal list that includes about seventy-five species. That is far from the final tally; knowledge of small vertebrates—notably bats, birds, and rodents—is now being greatly extended by intensive screen-washing efforts by Florida Museum of Natural History parties under the direction of A. Pratt (1990). It includes one of the earliest samples of diverse songbirds. The odd-toed ungulates include two kinds of rhinoceroses and three kinds of horses (two species of which are browsers, the third being the abundant grazer, *Parahippus*). Among the even-toed ungulates are several camelids and deer-like ruminants, a peccary, an oreodont, and *Prosynthetoceras*, an extinct horned cameloid. These diverse ungulate species all have low- to medium-crowned dentitions and presumably represent browsers or mixed feeders. And there are at least ten species of large, medium, and small-sized carnivores that evidently fed on the diverse herbivore fauna.

The herpetofauna is diverse (about twenty-five genera) and remarkably modern, as pointed out by Meylan (1984). One of the commonest reptiles is a large species of tortoise. Among snakes there are four boids and two colubrids. Most, including a racer and three boids, are ground-dwelling forms; arboreal types include a tree boa and a vine snake. The lizards include a skink, a gekko, a "Gila monster," a curly-tailed lizard, an anole, and a large iguanid. The amphibians are exceedingly diverse and are generally referable to modern Florida genera (Meylan, 1984).

Thomas Farm is the oldest Cenozoic site that offers a full view of a large and diverse terrestrial fauna in Florida—or for that matter, in eastern North America. Preliminary efforts to obtain pollen from the site have been unrewarding; therefore, ecological interpretations depend on analysis of the vertebrate fauna.

The Thomas Farm vertebrates fall into four habitat groups. Two relatively minor components lived in the karst cave system rather than at the land surface. One of these, the pond dwellers, consisted of the turtles and most of the amphibians. The principal cave dwellers were the diverse bat species.

The vast majority of the vertebrate fauna lived on the land surface and secondarily accumulated in the Thomas Farm sinkhole. This third habitat group may be divided somewhat arbitrarily into grazers and granivores, and browsers and arboreal species. By far the most abundant large vertebrate is the three-toed grazing horse, *Parahippus*, which accounts for about 80 percent of the megafaunal remains. The most abundant small vertebrate is the granivorous pocket mouse, *Proheteromys*. Both of these common taxa are terrestrial herbivores—the horse a mixed feeder or precocious grazer, and the pocket mouse a seed harvester. Tortoises are another important group of grazing and forb-eating vertebrates. These taxa, because of their abundance, indicate a fairly extensive open habitat.

The fourth faunal component consists of arboreal forms and browsing or mast-eating species, including hylid frogs, tree squirrels, oppossums, peccaries, and turkeys. A majority of the ungulates were also browsing types.

Taking into account all of these ecological components, Thomas Farm may be viewed as a mosaic of deciduous forest with patches of grassy woodland savanna. Presumably the distribution of these ecosystems in the landscape was determined by subtle variation in the depth of the sandy soils covering the older limestone; they probably ranged from well drained to excessively well drained. There were no freezing winters. Rainfall was seasonally distributed, and the annual total was probably somewhat greater than at present. Fires periodically raged through these habitats. Perhaps the primary difference between this reconstructed landscape of the early Miocene and the present central Florida landscape of alternating hammock and turkey-oak savanna was a greater diversity of tropical genera in the early Miocene (Pratt, 1990).

The rich Thomas Farm sample permits assessment of the geographic relationships of Florida's early Miocene fauna to those elsewhere in North America. Thomas Farm shares a number of taxa with the Garvin Gulley fauna of Texas that are not known in rich contemporaneous faunas of the Great Plains, such as the Runningwater fauna of Nebraska. Among the Gulf coast endemics are the cameloids, *Nothokemas*, *Floridatragulus*, and *Prosynthetoceras*, and also the rhinocerotid, *Floridaceros*. Presumably, the endemism of these Gulf coastal genera was the result of an ecological and climatic filter, rather than any major physical barrier.

Early Miocene Paleogeography

A striking feature of Florida's earliest land vertebrate sites is that they fall many meters below the widely accepted eustatic sea-level curve (Haq et al., 1987), as illustrated in figure 4.6. This observation extends to the Thomas Farm site and every older site, i.e., to all sites of early Miocene and late Oligocene age. Thomas Farm is perhaps the best-understood example. This site holds no hint of marine influence; rather its rich terrestrial fauna was deposited, along with a few freshwater species, in a sizable sinkhole (Auf-

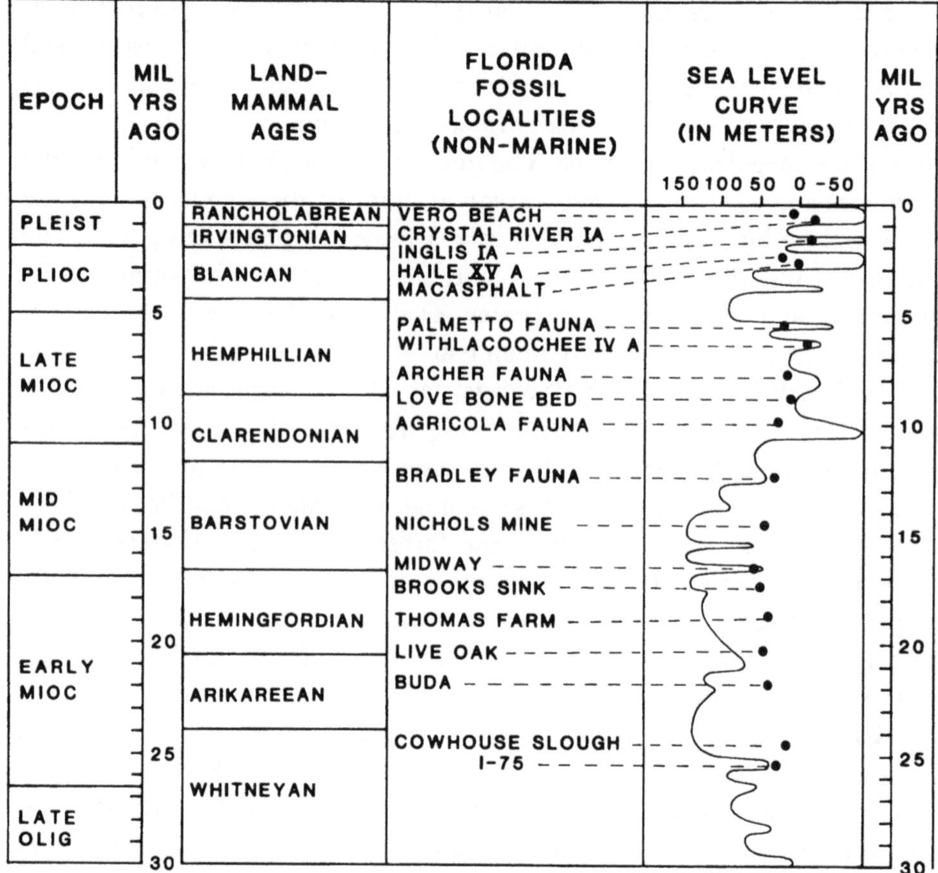

Fig. 4.6. Florida fossil vertebrate sites in relation to eustatic sea levels. Fossil sites range from terrestrial to estuarine but are essentially nonmarine. Note that sites older than 17 million years fall 10 to 100 m below widely accepted sea levels. Sea-level curve after Haq et al., 1987.

fenberg, 1963; Webb, 1981b; Pratt, 1990). The present elevation of the site ranges from about 18 m above sea level to 10 m or less—some 100 m below the presumed level of the sea at the time it accumulated about 18 million years ago. All other early Miocene vertebrate sites (see fig. 4.3) also occurred as sinkhole fillings with no evidence of marine influence.

There seems to be only one reasonable explanation for the anomalously low elevations of these early land sites in Florida: Their surface openings must have reached much higher than they do at present. Since they are sinkhole accumulations, it is possible to postulate such an upward extension in the past. Subsequent surface erosion must have been extensive. At Thomas Farm, eroded blocks of Suwannee limestone accumulated along with other sediments filling the sinkhole; today that formation lies some 20 km to the west. If the Suwannee formation is projected back over the site, it would lie about 40 m above the present land surface (Pratt, 1990). That gives an approximation of the surface erosion at the Thomas Farm site, but it is a minimum estimate. In fact it would require at least 60 m to restore the surface of the Thomas Farm site to a level somewhat above the presumed sea level for that time.

The oldest terrestrial vertebrate site in Florida, the late Oligocene I-75 site, includes some marine species along with its predominantly terrestrial fauna. Comparison of its present elevation (28 m) with the presumed global sea-level height (about 50 m) indicates that it too is a "beheaded" sinkhole site. The discrepancy of about 22 m can be reconciled if one assumes that much has been stripped from its surface and that the site correlates with the principal sea-level regression about 25 MYBP. If correct, this correlation suggests that the site formed as a deep sinkhole during low sea level and that the fossils accumulated as it subsequently backfilled with sediment. On the other hand, the I-75 site could be as much as a million years older or younger than its presumed age, without violating its late Whitneyan biostratigraphic age determination. In either of these cases it could be over 100 m below the presumed global sea-level height. Such a discrepancy seems incredibly large and considerably exceeds the other differences in figure 4.3. The important point is that the I-75 site, like all other vertebrate sites of late Oligocene and early Miocene age in Florida, appears to represent a beheaded sinkhole accumulation.

This pattern of beheaded sinkhole accumulations in the late Oligocene and early Miocene indicates a regional pattern of extensive surface erosion subsequent to the early Miocene. Known sites of these ages range from the present area of the Suwannee River to Tampa Bay along the Gulf coastal side of the peninsula. They coincide with the region of Florida that is now predominantly surface limestone and largely lacking a mantle of clastic deposits. Evidently this region had roughly 50 m of early Miocene and older sediments removed by surface erosion. This erosion exposed the thick Eocene limestones and created the central karst region of Florida.

The Middle Miocene

Florida's middle Miocene history is represented by a considerable mantle of terrigenous and marginal marine sediments over much of the northern and central peninsula. Phosphatic sands, clays, and lignitic deposits interfinger with carbonate facies and range from fluvial through estuarine to shallow marine environments. Such deposits are widely referred to the Hawthorn formation (Scott, 1988). In the area of the Suwannee River valley and the eastern part of the Panhandle, equivalent beds are usually assigned to the Torreya formation (Tedford and Hunter, 1984). These deposits reflect a steepened gradient across which clastic sediments were transported from the Appalachians across the coastal plain. Deposition was further governed by generally high, but strikingly varied, sea levels that repeatedly deposited marine and estuarine sediments on the peninsula.

Virtually all of Florida's middle Miocene (late Hemingfordian and Barstovian land mammal age) terrestrial fossils occur in fluvio-estuarine depositional environments. Vertebrate remains are found in many different formations, including the Hawthorn, upper part of the Torreya, Alachua, and the lower part of the Bone Valley formation. The Alum Bluff flora, also Barstovian in age, occurs in the Alum Bluff formation in the Apalachicola embayment.

Several late Hemingfordian vertebrate sites are associated with deltaic sediments of the early middle Miocene. These include the Midway and Quincy local faunas from the upper part of the Torreya formation in the eastern part of the Panhandle, reviewed by Tedford and Hunter (1984). Recent work by Morgan and Pratt (1988) at Brooks Sink in the Hawthorn formation of north peninsular Florida has shown it to be the richest known vertebrate site (fifty-six species) in the middle Miocene of eastern North America. The marine and estuarine species include seventeen species of sharks and bony fishes, as well as the extinct saltwater crocodilian, *Gavialosuchus*, an extinct sea cow, and a narrow-beaked dolphin. The herpetofauna consists of three genera of frogs, three kinds of snakes including *Typhlops*, six kinds of lizards, including *Heloderma* ("Gila monster"), as well as *Alligator* and *Geochelone* (giant tortoise). Two kinds of horses provide the best present basis for determining the age of the Brooks Sink local fauna. They are *Archaeohippus blackbergi*, indistinguishable from the larger sample at Thomas Farm, and *Merychippus gunteri*, which is more progressive than the possibly ancestral *Parahippus leonensis* from Thomas Farm. Even-toed ungulates include two small deer-like forms also known from Thomas Farm, and an unidentified camelid. Carnivores are rare, and consist of a few elements of small canids and mustelids but no larger forms. Most important, there are at least nine kinds of rodents, including three kinds of squirrels, the extinct burrowing genus *Mesogaulus*, two geomyoids, the same two species of pocket mice that occur at Thomas Farm, and a primitive field mouse comparable to *Leidymys*. There are also shrews, moles and bats, and an excellent sample of the extinct marsupial, *Peratherium*. The terrestrial component of the fauna is suggestive of a well-wooded habitat near a small (microtidal) estuary (Morgan and Pratt, 1988).

A number of Barstovian fossil vertebrate sites occur in the lower part of the Bone Valley formation of Polk and adjacent counties. These deposits and their faunas have been described in preliminary fashion by Webb and Crissinger (1983) and by Webb and Hulbert (1986). They are grouped conveniently into a threefold succession including the Nichols Mine (about 15 MYBP), the Bradley fauna (about 13 MYBP), and the Agricola fauna (about 11 MYBP).

The Nichols Mine local fauna occurs in a dark organic clay in the base of the exposed section at a phosphate mine in Hillsborough County. The microvertebrate sample includes a varied herpetofauna, an opossum, a bat, two insectivores, and diverse rodents, including two kinds of pocket mice and two kinds of field mice (G. Morgan and A. Pratt, personal communication). The larger vertebrates include a large rhinocerotid near *Floridaceros*, a camelid, and three horse species, including one of *Parahippus* and two of early *Merychippus*.

The Bradley fauna is known from a limited set of localities in the lowest pebble-phosphate channels of the Bone Valley formation. The horses are the best-known taxa and include the large browsing horse, *Megahippus*, as well as five grazing species—*Merychippus*, *Protohippus*, *Pliohippus*, *Calippus*, and a new species of *Pseudhipparion* (Webb and Hulbert, 1986). The largest vertebrates present are two elephant-like genera, *Gomphotherium* and *Miomastodon*. A camelid, a medium-sized giraffoid, and a rhinocerotid complete the known sample (Webb and Crissinger, 1983).

The Agricola fauna has a more varied vertebrate fauna, some of which has been reported by Webb and Crissinger (1983). The most abundant material consists of varied sharks, bony fishes, whales, and—most abundantly—extinct sea cows of the genus *Metaxytherium*. The terrestrial mammals include a small beaver (*Eucastor*), a medium-sized carnivore (*Aelurodon*), and a varied assemblage of grazing and browsing ungulates. Among the browsers are the horse *Hypohippus* and the extinct three-horned genus *Synthetoceras*. The many probable grazers include another short-legged rhino and seven species of horses with high-crowned dentitions, including *Pseudhipparion curtivallum* (Webb and Hulbert, 1986).

An important botanical record of middle Miocene habitats in north Florida comes from the Alum Bluff flora. Berry (1916) studied this flora on the basis of leaf impressions collected near the top of Alum Bluff on the east bank of the Apalachicola River in Liberty County. Although deposited in littoral sands, the leaves were moderately well preserved. The most abundant species by far is a fan palm of the genus *Sabalites*. Berry described and illustrated eleven species of dicots and noted three others that were impossible to collect. He distinguished within this assemblage three plant associations: "semiswamp palmetto-brake"; "sandy strand . . . with forms such as *Pisonia*, *Caesalpinia* and *Fagara* (= *Zanthoxylon*)"; and, most important, one that "corresponds in a general way to the 'low hammock' of present-day peninsular Florida" (Berry, 1916, p. 44). The hammock group included *Ficus*, *Carpinus*, *Diospyros*, *Cinnamomum*, *Rhamnus*, *Nectandra*, *Bumelia*, *Sapotacites*, and *Ulmus*. According to Graham (1964), the "exotic" (mainly ancient tropical) component of the Alum Bluff flora accounts for 42 percent of the known species from this site. Similarly Berry (1916, p. 44), impressed by the presence of such tropical species as *Artocarpus* (breadfruit) and predominantly tropical species such as *Cinnamomum* (camphor), considered the Alum Bluff flora "to be the result of a reversal of the history of the present flora of peninsular Florida. That is to say, the present flora represents primarily a temperate flora receiving additions from the Tropics, whereas the Alum Bluff flora represents an endemic tropical flora gradually becoming invaded by members of a temperate flora as a result of changing climatic conditions." Graham (1964, p. 578) reaffirmed this view that during most of the Tertiary, floras of the southeastern United States progressively lost tropical species and gained temperate ones and that the Alum Bluff flora lay somewhere near the middle of the known progression.

The "Suwannee Strait"

During most of its terrestrial history Florida has had the form of a peninsula, connected at its northern base to the mainland (now the southeastern United States) with its southern tip widely separated from any other terrestrial landmass. On the other hand, a contrary idea frequently has been suggested for certain intervals of Florida's history. If the sea stood sufficiently high, Florida's present topography would produce an "Ocala Island" separated from the mainland by a "Suwannee Strait." Various authors have proposed various times in Florida's history when such a break might have existed. An important aspect of understanding Florida's biogeographic history is to determine when, if ever, such a barrier existed.

Dall and Harris (1892, pp. 121–122) proposed that peninsular Florida was isolated in the Eocene and again in the Miocene by a seaway passing through "Okefenokee and Suwannee Swamps and the trough of the Suwannee River." A number of subsequent geologists postulated a seaway in the same area to explain a major break in sedimentary regimes—the coarser clastics accumulating to the north and west but the chemical deposits (mainly limestones) lying to the south and east, i.e., down the Florida peninsula. Many geologists considered that this trough was erosionally produced, some suggesting that it was due to the Gulf Stream current passing northeastward. There has been a trend among geologists to shift the trough about 60 km westward of the Suwannee River; for example Puri and Vernon (1964, p. 4) illustrate its axis passing up the Aucilla River through Wakulla and Jefferson counties.

Most geologists tend to place the time of existence of the Suwannee Strait in the Eocene and earlier, before there was much evidence of a persistent landmass in the area of the present peninsula. In his review of Florida paleogeography, Chen (1965) recognized the Suwannee Strait from late Cretaceous through late Eocene. In their discussion of Miocene correlations, Tedford and Hunter (1984) figure a broad "Gulf Trough," but their discussion (p. 141) suggests that it was principally an older feature that had become filled by Miocene time. On the other hand, Husted (1972) recognized the Suwannee Strait in the Miocene and believed that the current flowed in the opposite direction (into the Gulf of Mexico) from its earlier course.

Biogeographers have seized upon the geological concept of the Suwannee

Strait to explain many biological distributions, at the same time taking a few extra liberties with its time and place. For example, Neill (1957, p. 188) postulated that central Florida was "in the Oligocene an island . . . separate from the mainland but . . . connected with Cuba." He reactivated the Suwannee Strait again during the Miocene and again during the highest interglacial sea levels of the early Pleistocene (e.g., the Brandywine sea at 82 m above present sea level). At that time, presumably there existed "a fair-sized island in Polk County and several smaller islands just north of there" (Neill, 1957, p. 187). Clench and Turner (1956, p. 105) found "good evidence among the freshwater mollusks for the existence of an island in what is now central Florida during the period of fluctuation of the epicontinental Pliocene and Pleistocene seas." Presumably such biological arguments, based on various degrees of endemism in the biota of the central peninsula, would be just as well satisfied by the existence of habitat islands as by the existence of a hypothetical seaway to produce "real" islands.

The biogeographic literature offers a wide range of options for the location of the supposed Suwannee Straits. A few of the postulated positions are indicated in figure 4.7. Frailey (1980, p. 9) placed "the hypothetical Suwannee Strait" north of the present Suwannee River. Chronologically, he placed it in the late Oligocene and early Miocene. At this time, as he noted, the course of the seaway is geographically constrained by the presence of a wholly terrestrial early Miocene fossil site at Live Oak. For this reason Frailey (1980) illustrated the midpoint of the strait about 25 km northwest of

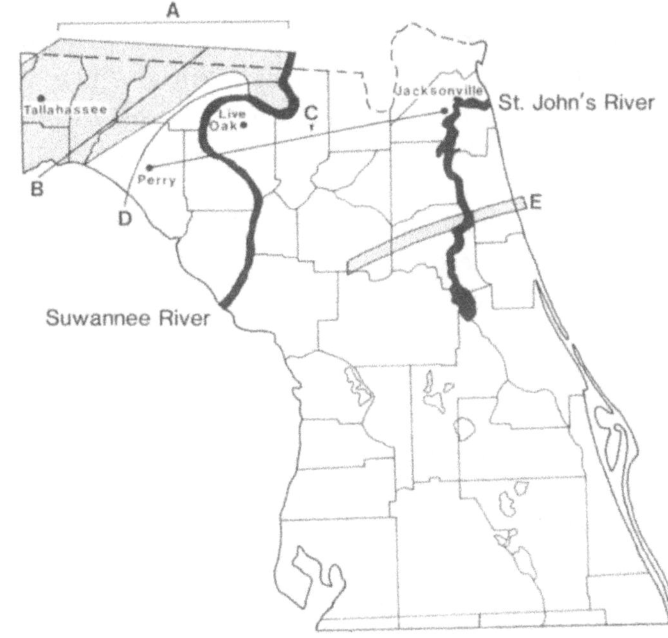

Fig. 4.7. Locations of hypothetical "Suwannee Strait" and related concepts in north peninsular Florida. *A.* Shaded area, "Gulf Trough" (Tedford and Hunter, 1984). *B.* "Shaler's Line" (Husted, 1972). *C.* "Suwannee Strait" as described in text (Frailey, 1980). *D.* "Suwannee Straits" as figured (Frailey, 1980). *E.* "Suwannee Straits" as related to gap in Wicomico shoreline (Gilbert, 1987).

the town of Live Oak. On the other hand the text (Frailey, 1980, p. 11) described "a strong current through the trough . . . which extended across northern Florida in a line running roughly through Jacksonville and Perry," about 15 km south of the town of Live Oak.

In his thorough discussion of freshwater fish zoogeography, Gilbert (1987) placed the Suwannee Strait far southeast of the Suwannee River. He illustrated the Wicomico shoreline ("Cody Scarp") with a narrow gap near Palatka, about 100 km east-southeast of the Suwannee River and identified that gap as the "position of the Suwannee Straits." While the strait was open, according to Gilbert (1987, p. 47), there had been "many freshwater springs" throughout the Suwannee River valley itself. Based on the timing of the eustatic sea-level curves, Gilbert (1987, p. 36) postulated that the strait had existed at two different times: the first "partial, or possibly complete" establishment of the Suwannee Strait occurred in the mid-Miocene; the second came "in the latest Miocene" and "persisted throughout the Pliocene." Furthermore Gilbert (1987, p. 37) attributed species-level endemism in modern peninsular fishes to the first (mid-Miocene) isolation, whereas he regarded subspecifically or racially distinct populations as products of the second (Pliocene) isolation. The presumed older group consisted mainly of secondary division (partly saltwater tolerant) species in the family Cyprinodontidae, while the presumed younger group was made up entirely of primary division (purely freshwater) populations.

Four lines of evidence reduce the likelihood that the "Suwannee Strait" existed during the Miocene. First, as observed above, at least 50 m more of surface sediments evidently existed over much of the peninsula in the early Miocene. Certainly it is naive to restore former hypothetical shorelines by simply tracing present-day topography. Second, the presence of mid-Miocene terrestrial sites such as Thomas Farm and Live Oak near the supposed course of the seaway argues forcefully against its presence in the usual place (see fig. 4.5, locality 4). Tedford and Hunter (1984, p. 133) correctly locate six terrestrial to estuarine vertebrate sites, of early to middle Miocene age, in the area previously occupied by the "Gulf Trough." Third, middle and late Miocene fluvio-estuarine complexes in the Suwannee River valley and in Bone Valley indicate nearly continuous presence of a source of terrigenous sediments in approximately the position of the present peninsula (see Scott, 1988). Fourth, the known record of eustatic sea levels makes it unlikely that the late Miocene could have produced any sea sufficiently elevated to have flooded the Suwannee region (Haq et al., 1987). These arguments do not affect the possibility that in the Eocene and earlier, when Florida was largely a carbonate bank, a deep seaway flowed approximately through the present route of the Suwannee River. They make it clear, however, that during Miocene time such a seaway probably did not exist. During most, if not all, of its terrestrial history, the Florida peninsula has been connected to the mainland.

The Late Miocene

The late Miocene is one of the best-known intervals in Florida's sequence of terrestrial faunas. Fluvial and estuarine deposits accumulated in the north and central peninsula about as in the middle Miocene. Although the Bone Valley district supplies some of the sites, several richer samples come from the Alachua formation in Alachua and Levy counties.

The Love bone bed from the Alachua formation in Alachua County was extensively excavated in the 1970s and reported by Webb et al. (1981). Much like the middle Miocene sites, the Love bone bed occupies fluvial sediments within the range of tidal influence. With about one hundred species, it is the richest late Miocene vertebrate site in eastern North America. It is impossible to review its diverse fauna here; it will suffice to indicate briefly its principal ecological components.

The most abundant vertebrate component at the Love bone bed consists of varied freshwater aquatic species, especially lentic taxa, including chicken-turtles, softshell turtles, garfishes, and alligators. There are limited remains of sharks, whales, and estuarine to marine species. The three terrestrial habitats sampled by the Love bone bed are evidently stream-bank, riverine forest, and grassland savanna. The forest taxa include a number of birds and a considerable diversity of browsing ungulates, such as peccaries, tapirs, giraffe-camels, and a new species of the giraffoid, *Pediomeryx*. The savanna indicators include an abundance of cranes, tortoises, one kind of extinct pronghorn antelope, two kinds each of camelids and rhinocerotids, and ten species of grazing horses. Hulbert (1982) finds evidence from the pulsed age structure of its large population sample that the horse, *Cormohipparion*, underwent seasonal migrations to and from the Love bone bed site. Small mammals include the extinct grazing rodent, *Mylagaulus*, and a number of cricetid rodents.

In many respects the Love bone bed is closely comparable to contemporaneous vertebrate sites from the Great Plains. Nevertheless, it differs not only in the presence of marine species but also in the much greater abundance of aquatic and forest-dwelling species. The low endemism and high diversity of the vertebrate fauna from the Love bone bed militate against any suggestion of insularity for north-central Florida during the middle Miocene.

The end of the late Miocene is characterized by eustatically lowered sea levels worldwide. This interval is represented in Florida by the Withlacoochee 4A site in Citrus County and the Manatee County dam site farther south near Bradenton. Neither site is very rich, but together they suffice to indicate that the same general late Miocene fauna persisted in Florida, with a few evolutionary changes within lineages as well as a few extinctions.

In most respects the late Miocene fauna resembles that of the middle

Miocene. Even more striking is the predominance of large herds of savanna-adapted ungulates. There are at least ten kinds of horses, three kinds of camelids, two kinds of horned ruminants, a large and abundant proboscidean, and at least one kind of peccary. The grazing rodent, *Mylagaulus*, persists. New immigrants include two kinds of ground sloths from South America, as well as sabercats and primitive bears from the Old World.

Late Miocene Paleogeography

The eustatic curve of figure 4.6 strongly indicates two major sea-level drops during the late Miocene. The sea-level drop about 5 million years ago is correlated with the Messinian episode in which the Mediterranean Sea, cut off from the ocean once it began to drop, evaporated to abyssal depths. In the eastern United States, extreme low shorelines extended almost to the base of the continental shelf and led to dumping of phosphatic gravel and other continental debris into unstable marine canyons (Wise and van Hinte, 1987). Florida's land area probably reached its greatest extent during the late Miocene, and the climate was probably semiarid. Terrestrial sites are known as far south as the Kissimmee Prairie, and others occur along Florida's west coast below present sea level (Webb and Tessman, 1968; Webb and Crissinger, 1983).

Several late Miocene eustatic cycles were roughly comparable to those of the Pleistocene, but the oscillations were apparently much slower so the elapsed time may have been much greater. It seems plausible that during the late Miocene the central karst region of Florida experienced about twice as much karst erosion and uplift as it did during the Pleistocene. This was the time when the Ocala Arch experienced most of its uplift.

As indicated in figure 4.6, middle and late Miocene land sites fall close to but above the eustatic sea-level curve. For example, the Love bone bed includes some estuarine species, is very late Clarendonian in age (about 9 MYBP), and occurs at an elevation of 20 m. That places it about 20 m above the sea level proposed by Haq et al. (1987) for that time interval. The difference presumably represents subsequent uplift in that part of the central karst region. Fossils at the Love bone bed were deposited in a high-energy stream system (Webb et al., 1981); today, however, they occupy a limestone plain of karst drainage where no streams flow. This contrast dramatizes the subsequent erosion and uplift that have affected Florida's central karst region.

The Early Pliocene

The early Pliocene is well represented by the classic Bone Valley fauna, now formally distinguished as the Palmetto fauna (Webb and Hulbert, 1986). The early Pliocene vertebrates maintain general continuity with faunal elements of the late Miocene, most notably with the diverse savanna ungulates.

More than any other time interval recorded in Florida, the early Pliocene supported several relicts that had already become extinct in well-documented contemporaneous faunas of the Great Plains. Among the largest relict genera are the horses, *Cormohipparion*, *Nannippus*, and *Pseudhipparion*, and the large, horned cameloid *Kyptoceras* (Webb, 1981a). The most probable explanation is that relatively well-watered subtropical savannas persisted in Florida, whereas a secular trend toward increased aridity had converted the Great Plains predominantly to grasslands, thereby exterminating the browsers and mixed-feeders and decimating even the grazers (Webb, 1984).

In Florida, several unique faunal elements of the early Pliocene further testify to the persistence of forested conditions. Most notable are a large flying squirrel, an early odocoileine deer, and the oldest record of the long-nosed peccary *Mylohyus*. Thus, Florida maintained a rich fauna of grazers and browsers in a mosaic of subtropical forests and savannas even as the Great Plains faunas experienced severe aridifcation and vertebrate extinction.

The Late Pliocene

A gap of more than 2 million years separates Florida's late Pliocene terrestrial vertebrate records from those of the early Pliocene, and in that interval there was an immense turnover in mammalian groups. Many of the characteristic late Miocene ungulate groups had vanished from all of North America, and many new immigrant groups had entered the continent.

Florida provides a particularly rich record of such new faunas, most notably the wave of immigrant land vertebrates that came about 2.5 million years ago from South America. The giant, flightless, predatory bird *Titanis* was surely the most impressive, standing more than 3 m tall. The large, semiaquatic, grazing rodent *Neochoerus*, related to present-day South American capybaras, was also a notable arrival. Four kinds of edentate mammals came, including great bear-like mylodont sloths and three sizes of shelled armadilloids, the largest of which were the glyptodonts with solidly fused shells more than 1 m in diameter (Webb, 1985).

Three Florida sites best record these late Blancan immigrants along with native forms: Haile 15A, Santa Fe River 1A in north central Florida, and Macasphalt Pit near Sarasota. Together these sites produce a combination of many grazing and some browsing species, suggesting that the predominant habitat was a subtropical savanna. At Macasphalt I A the persistance of the relict grazing horse *Cormohipparion emsliei*—along with two other kinds of horses, two genera of peccaries, a llama, an ox-like animal, a short-jawed proboscidean near *Cuvieronius*, capybaras, and cotton rats—indicates coastal scrub and grassland savanna. These mammals are associated with a rich variety of freshwater and coastal birds, reptiles, and amphibians (Morgan and Ridgeway, 1987; Hulbert, 1987).

Late Pliocene sites in the Santa Fe River also produce a predominance of grazers, including two kinds of horses, a proboscidean, a great abundance of pronghorn antelopes, and the armadilloid *Glyptotherium.* Haile 15A is a spring site that produces a relatively great abundance of forest dwellers, including a rare flying squirrel (Robertson, 1976).

Pliocene Paleogeography

An approximate outline of Florida in the early Pliocene may be determined from the distribution of phosphatic estuarine deposits around the margins of the central karst region. These deposits consist mainly of the Bone Valley formation in south-central Florida. In the northern peninsula the youngest phosphatic beds in the Suwannee River district may be partly correlative with the Bone Valley formation to the south (e.g., Webb and Tessman, 1968), but for the most part they are Clarendonian (late Miocene) and older. In general the Mio-Pliocene sediments from the Suwannee River district are fluvio-estuarine. There is little positive evidence for a deep marine seaway, or Suwannee Strait, in that area, although during the maximum high sea level of the early Pliocene (about 4 MYBP) a brief passage cannot be ruled out. (See discussion of the "Suwannee Strait" concept earlier in this chapter.) More probably Florida's early Pliocene outline approximated that of the early Pleistocene.

The Early Pleistocene

The two most impressive biogeographic features of the early Pleistocene in Florida are continuation of the "great American interchange" with South America and extensive development of longleaf pine habitats. The early Pleistocene (formally known as the Irvingtonian land mammal age) lasted over a million years. It is represented by six major sites set in various environments, including a coastal slough, an inland stream, and four rich sinkhole sites of subtly different ages and environments. More than 300 mammal species are known from Florida's Pleistocene sites (Webb, 1974), as well as about an equal number of other vertebrate species. It is thus possible to give only a brief summary of Florida's rich history of terrestrial vertebrate faunas during the ice ages.

No site more clearly epitomizes the great American interchange than the Inglis site, a sinkhole representing a coastal longleaf pine environment during an early glacial interval. This site was exposed in about 1968 by excavation for the intended Cross-Florida Barge Canal and was possibly the most useful result of that ill-starred project. Nearly half of the fifty or so mammalian genera were distributed from Florida to Argentina and were thus part of the great American faunal interchange, which was then at its peak.

Newly recorded (and therefore presumably newly arrived from South America) were the giant ground sloth (*Eremotherium*), a capybara (*Hydrochoerus*), and an extinct species of porcupine (*Erethizon*). The same five species of edentates known earlier were also present, as was *Titanis*, the "big bird." In the other direction a score of northern genera, including tapirs, peccaries, llamas, horses, gomphotheriid proboscideans, sabercats, raccoons, spectacled bears, and jaguars, extended their ranges into South America (Webb, 1985). Other Florida sites of Irvingtonian age record the northward arrival of manatees, a small glyptodont, the small ground sloth *Nothrotheriops*, and the vampire bat *Desmodus*. Three snake genera that appear at Inglis—*Drymarchon*, *Rhadinea*, and *Tantilla*— probably came from Central America at this time (Meylan, 1982). The inter-American continuity of the interchanged fauna presumably was established by means of an extensive subtropical savanna corridor (Webb and Wilkins, 1984). In Florida it extended broadly around the Gulf of Mexico, especially during intervals of low sea level.

During the late Pliocene and early Pleistocene, continuity of a rich semiarid biota was established between Florida and western North America. Among mammals the small pronghorn *Capromeryx* appears in the late Pliocene, whereas jackrabbits of the genus *Lepus* and western pocket gophers (*Thomomys*) reach Florida from the west in the early Pleistocene. *Nothrotheriops*, the smallest of the ground sloths that reached North America, is best known in semiarid habitats in the Great Basin, but it appears in the early Pleistocene Leisey Shell Pit on Tampa Bay (Webb et al., 1989). Florida's western connection is most strikingly evinced by the early Pleistocene herpetofauna from Inglis, which is the richest assemblage of fossil reptiles and amphibians in eastern North America. The vast majority of its thirty-one squamate species represent a longleaf pine habitat and have clear affinities with the western semiarid herpetofauna. Direct evidence places eight xeric lizard and snake species in Florida during the Pliocene, but Inglis strongly suggests that the acme of the herpetofaunal affiliation with the arid west came in the earliest Pleistocene (Meylan, 1982).

By about mid-Pleistocene time, the strength of Florida's vertebrate affiliation with the semiarid west had been considerably weakened. It is most evident among the mammals: the pronghorns, jackrabbits, and relatively small nothrothere sloths, all previously abundant in at least one site, wholly disappeared. The reptiles, birds, and plants, on the other hand, became Florida relicts but did not become extinct. Wetlands associated with the Mississippi River delta separated many Florida species of xeric lizards and snakes from their western relatives; such disjunct genera include *Cemophora*, *Cnemidophorus*, *Eumeces*, *Lampropeltis*, *Masticophis*, *Micrurus*, *Pituophis*, and *Sceloporus*. The scrub jay, among birds, and the cactuses, among plants, represent similar disjunct patterns in arid-adapted biota. The paleontological evidence from scrub-adapted mammals and xeric reptiles indicates that the semiarid circum-Gulf corridor was broken in the mid-Pleistocene.

Pleistocene Paleogeography

Florida's most obvious paleogeographic features are the several former shorelines that encircle the peninsula above present sea level. Six such shorelines are confidently recognized in Florida and northward along the Atlantic coastal plain. Table 4.1 lists their names and approximate elevations, from the oldest (at the top) to the youngest (at the bottom). This system of former shorelines has been widely recognized for more than fifty years (e.g., Cooke, 1939, 1945; MacNeil, 1950; Jones et al., 1973). Successively higher sets of shoreline features are thought to represent successively older interglacial (high sea level) stillstands. Still higher shorelines are known, but they are far more difficult to recognize consistently. The low shorelines are confidently referred to the Pleistocene, but the ages of the higher shorelines have been debated for several decades.

Generally the most prominent of these higher shorelines is the Wicomico, illustrated in figure 4.8. The age of the Wicomico is a critical question. The most recent estimates, based on marine fossils from the west flank of Trail Ridge in northern Florida, suggest an age "no older than late Pliocene and almost certainly Pleistocene in age" (Opdyke et al., 1984, p. 227). Support for an early Pleistocene age comes indirectly from Haile 15A, a fossil vertebrate site in western Alachua County. It is late Pliocene (Blancan) in age, includes sharks and other marine species, and lies at a present elevation of about 30 m (Robertson, 1976). It lies about 15 km inland from the west-facing scarp of the Wicomico shoreline in Levy County, and its elevation is only slightly higher than the toe of that shoreline. The physical relationship between Haile 15A and the Wicomico shoreline indicates that the shoreline is younger than the site; if it were otherwise, the sea that reached the site would have destroyed the Wicomico shoreline features. Thus the Wicomico shoreline is thought to provide an outline of Florida during an interglacial interval in the early Pleistocene.

Table 4.1. Names, elevations, and approximate ages of seven Plio-Pleistocene shorelines in Florida

Shoreline Name	Elevation (m)	Age (est.)
Okefenokee	ca. 50	Late Pliocene
Wicomico	32–35	Early Pleistocene
Penholoway	19–24	Mid Pleistocene
Talbot	10–13	Late Pleistocene
Pamlico	8–10	Last interglacial
Princess Anne	4–5	Last interglacial
Silver Bluff	2–3	Last interglacial

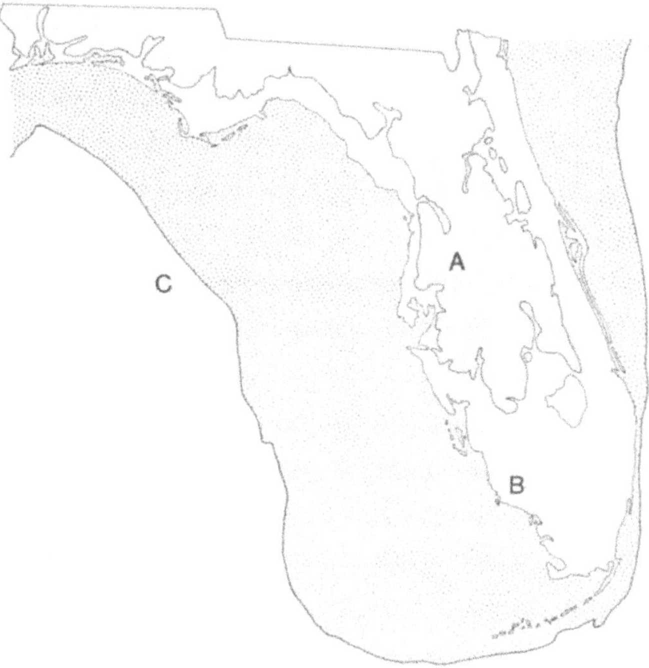

Fig. 4.8. Three outlines of Florida during the Quaternary Era. *A.* Wicomico shoreline (probably early) Pleistocene interglacial interval). *B.* Present coastline. *C.* Estimated Wisconsinan glacial shoreline (about 20,000 YBP). Outlines after Fernald, 1981.

The Wicomico shoreline reaches its southernmost extent in the Lake Wales Ridge in Highlands County, where extensive fossil dunes represent the uppermost feature of a high-energy shoreline complex. In many respects the features of the Lake Wales Ridge resemble those of Trail Ridge in Putnam and Clay counties, although the southern ridge may represent a younger shoreline (Pirkle et al., 1977).

As one traces the Wicomico shoreline up the Atlantic coastline, its irregular elevation offers an important clue to Florida's paleogeography. From its maximum height near Starke in northern Florida, the shoreline warps downward by as much as 22 m, reaching its presumed "true" height in southern Georgia (Hoyt, 1969; Winker and Howard, 1977). Shoreline elevations are determined from brackish sediments, especially indicated by fossil burrows (*Skolithus*) of the decapod crustacean, *Callianassa*, and not from associated but higher barrier island sediments that lie inland.

The next lower shoreline facing the Atlantic coast is the Penholoway. In northeastern Florida it lies some 10 km east of the Wicomico and warps upward only about 6 m between southern Georgia and northern Florida. These physical data raise the question as to why the Wicomico shoreline in northern Florida is elevated three or four times more than the nearby Penholoway shoreline. Subsequent upwarp of these shorelines in north Florida can be accounted for by isostatic adjustment following karst erosion. Such erosion and uplift were greatly accelerated during times of low sea level (Opdyke et al., 1984; Winker and Howard, 1977). If upwarping occurred at a steady rate during glacial intervals of the Pleistocene, then the Wicomico is at least three times as old as the Penholoway shoreline. Presumably, the

Wicomico represents an early part of the Pleistocene, while the Penholoway is the oldest of the late Pleistocene shorelines. The other lower terraces show little or no warping, and the youngest two have yielded dates around 12,000 YBP (Cronin, 1982). If this scheme is correct, it implies that no interglacial sea levels that fell chronologically between the Wicomico and the Penholoway reached higher than the Penholoway: otherwise they would be evident.

It is more difficult to map Florida's outline during low sea levels, both because the former low shorelines lie under the sea and because they have been extensively altered by currents. Buried forests and former stream channels are known in many sites on Florida's submerged Gulf coastal plain (Jones et al., 1973, p. II-E-7). Full-glacial Florida can be envisioned most readily by projecting the probable minimum eustatic sea level onto present bottom topography. That level—exceeding 100 m below that of the present—is determined in various ways in many parts of the world (Bloom, 1983; Cronin, 1982). The approximate maximum area of Florida during the last glacial (Wisconsinan stage) is illustrated in figures 4.8 and 4.9. Florida's outline during earlier glacial intervals is virtually unknown, since all traces evidently were covered or destroyed. It is perhaps a reasonable working assumption that most of the two dozen glacial episodes of the Pleistocene produced roughly similar paleogeographic results.

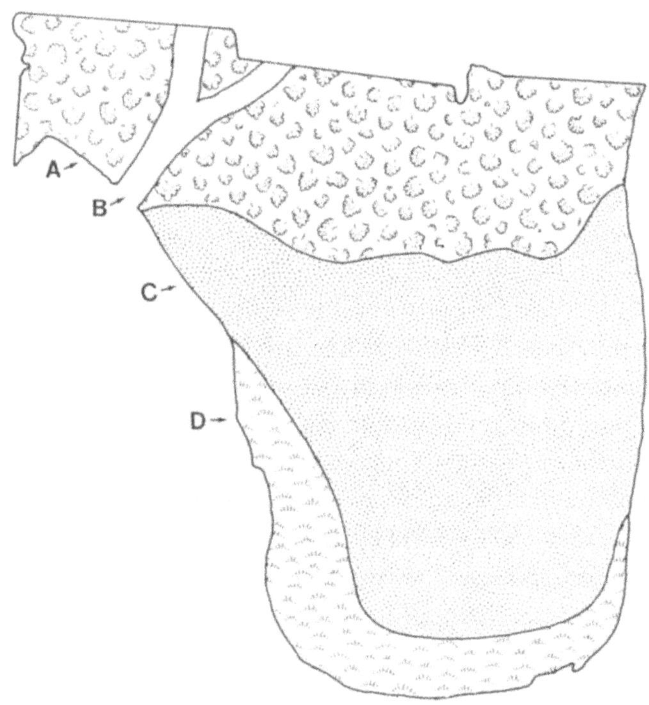

Fig. 4.9. Wisconsinan (full glacial) vegetation map of peninsular Florida (after Delcourt et al., 1983a). *A.* Mesophytic forest. *B.* Riparian forest. *C.* Scrub. *D.* Swamp and mangrove.

The Late Pleistocene

Late Pleistocene evidence of vertebrate life in Florida is vastly more extensive than for any preceding time intervals. The late Pleistocene is also of utmost relevance because of its proximity to the present. Late Pleistocene fossil vertebrates occur in virtually every county in Florida and represent a great variety of habitats. The richest sites of deposition are in coastal lagoons, intercoastal waterways, streams, ponds, and sinkholes. Glacial and interglacial intervals are somewhat unevenly represented; the most likely times for extensive deposition are toward the ends of glacial intervals when sea level and water tables rise, backfilling potential sites of deposition. The fullest record in the late Pleistocene, as earlier, comes from terrestrial vertebrates, especially mammals (Webb, 1974; Robertson, 1976; Webb and Wilkins, 1984).

There are few large-scale changes in the vertebrate fauna after the mid-Pleistocene loss of the xeric component already discussed. One notable faunal event is the immigration of long-horned *Bison* from Asia. Its arrival is clearly recorded in Florida as elsewhere in North America. Its subsequent evolution features reduction of the horns to the relatively modest length of the living American *Bison*.

The most dramatic faunal event of the late Pleistocene is the extinction of numerous large vertebrates at the end of the epoch. In Florida about two dozen large mammals became extinct; these same taxa were widely distributed across North America and became extinct throughout their ranges at about the same time. Nonmammalian extinctions in Florida during this period included the large birds *Gymnogyps* and *Teratornis* and the giant tortoise *Geochelone*. At the same time, several small mammals disappeared from Florida, including the bog lemming (*Synaptomys*), the porcupine (*Erethizon*), and the muskrat (*Ondatra*). All of these still exist at more northern latitudes.

The causes of the late Pleistocene extinctions remain controversial, although there is a general consensus that rapid environmental changes may have been the primary cause (Webb, 1984). Immigration of human hunters may have been equally important, and their excessive predation is often cited as the final blow for the large herbivore species. Both possible causal mechanisms occurred at the end of the Pleistocene. In Florida, three major environmental changes negatively affected the megafauna during the latest Pleistocene: reduction of land area by about half; reduction of topographic relief by at least half and probably much more; and vast reduction of xeric and open habitats.

Late Pleistocene Pollen

The distribution of late Pleistocene environments in Florida can be considerably clarified by an excellent pollen record. It was long suspected that with lowered sea levels during glacial intervals, Florida's interior would have been more arid than at present. It was presumed that the water table would drop, tracking sea level at least to some degree. Since much of peninsular Florida consists of porous karstic limestone blanketed by ridges of well-drained sand, it was hypothesized that xeric conditions would prevail once surface waters had disappeared. Even so, the force and extent of late Pleistocene aridity, now confirmed by pollen samples, is quite remarkable.

Most of the fundamental contributions, as well as several comprehensive reviews, have been provided by W. A. Watts (e.g., 1975, 1980, 1983; Watts and Hansen, 1988). Another major review is by Delcourt and Delcourt (1985). These studies permit one to infer the approximate distribution of the major vegetational formations in Florida during the last glacial interval (Wisconsinan) as illustrated in figure 4.9. Key sites are Sheelar Lake in north-central Florida and Lake Annie and Tulane Lake in south-central Florida. Boreal spruce/pine vegetation did not enter Florida, although it was widespread in the southeast, including central Georgia and eastern Louisiana. The vegetation of the northern half of Florida was dominated by a two-needle pine, probably sand pine (*Pinus clausa*). This type of pine probably became endemic to Florida during a late Pleistocene glacial interval when boreal forest, encircling the northern edge of its range, confined it to the peninsula. Oak and hickory were also common trees. Herbs provide a significant input to the pollen record and evidently represent extensive prairie and sandhill communities. At Sheelar Lake in Putnam County the abundance of wind-blown sand in the sediments of full glacial age reinforces this impression (Watts and Stuiver, 1980). Most lake cores in peninsular Florida simply represent the glacial interval by a hiatus of erosion or nondeposition.

Sheelar Lake also records the late glacial transition to the Holocene (Watts and Stuiver, 1980). At about 14,000 YBP, pine became less important than earlier. At the same time oak, hickory, and juniper, as well as various upland herbs, especially *Ambrosia*, became abundant. The hickory species may have been the Florida endemic scrub hickory. For the latest Pleistocene, as summarized by Watts (1983, p. 305), "the inferred vegetation is drought-adapted forest or woodland with some prairie." Within another 500 years warmer conditions and increased moisture (through increased precipitation, rising water tables, or both) led to a predominance of oaks and a considerable variety of mesic broadleaved trees, especially beech (which provided 7 percent of the total pollen). By 11,000 YBP, the mesic trees had been replaced by pine, oak, and upland herbs. Periodic increases in pine abundance during that interval probably reflect a corresponding increase in the importance of fire. Thus, by the early Holocene the well-drained regions of north-central Florida had established an ecosystem much like that in existence today.

In south-central Florida the late glacial setting was more severely xeric. At Lakes Annie and Tulane in Highlands County oak and a two-needled pine were the only trees, whereas grasses, composites (*Ambrosia*), and a shrub, Florida rosemary (*Ceratiola*), were abundant. This scrub vegetation persisted until the mid-Holocene (about 5,000 YBP) when some more mesic forms appeared in the pollen record (Watts, 1983; Watts and Hansen, 1988). The Everglades plant communities were evidently not established until about that time.

Submerged lands were exposed during the late Pleistocene along the Gulf of Mexico, greatly extending the area of peninsular floras (fig. 4.9). Along the margins were limited tracts of wetlands, including mangroves and other swampy formations. Major stream systems also interdigitated inland, providing refuges for *Taxodium*, *Nyssa*, and other mesic and bayhead species.

Biogeography of Modern Flora and Fauna

Despite many variations in size, shape, and topography, Florida probably has persisted as a peninsula throughout its terrestrial history. Webb and Wilkins (1984, p. 370) proposed that during its most expanded phases when sea level was very low, as during late Miocene or Pleistocene glacial stages, "non-volant biota could enter the peninsula by any one of three more or less distinct routes: the Gulf Coastal, the Northern, and the Atlantic Coastal." During the Pleistocene about 10 percent of the species in successive mammalian faunas entered the peninsula by the northern route. The Gulf coastal corridor transmitted about 20 percent to 30 percent of the species in successive mammalian faunas of the Pleistocene and was especially effective during interglacial intervals, when the width of the corridor was greatly expanded into the Gulf of Mexico. The Atlantic coastal route appeared relatively unimportant in the Pleistocene analysis of Webb and Wilkins (1984). These data apply only to Pleistocene land mammals, but perhaps they may be taken as representative for other terrestrial species that do not easily disperse over water.

The thirty-one species in the early Pleistocene herpetofauna from Inglis 1A "document an important late Tertiary link between the savannas of Florida and those of the American West" (Meylan, 1982, p. 69). That link was almost surely the Gulf coastal corridor at a time of low sea level. Twenty-four of the species and twenty-seven of the genera known at Inglis survive in Florida's xeric habitats today. Most of Florida's other xeric elements, such as the "cactus gardens" of southwest Florida, presumably followed the Gulf coastal corridor.

The northern corridor, on the other hand, served to transmit mesic taxa southward down Florida's central axis. It probably functioned most effectively during intervals of higher sea level like the present, especially when summers were cooler than now. Neill (1957) provides an excellent discussion of the "northern element" in Florida, especially around the Apalachicola River bluffs. The common feature of taxa that have followed this corridor is that they do not enter Florida's xeric habitats.

The Peninsula Effect

The term *peninsula effect* was introduced by Simpson (1964) in his study of mammalian species densities across North America. He used it to describe the pattern in which a peninsula held fewer species than did an equal area of the mainland. Others subsequently altered (refined?) the meaning to denote a gradient of decreasing species richness along a peninsula from base to tip. Both of these meanings evidently apply to the Florida peninsula with respect to many groups of organisms.

By thorough analysis of the ranges and habitats occupied by Florida's peninsular herpetofauna, Means and Simberloff (1987) suggested that the major southward decrease in species numbers coincided with the loss of topographic and habitat variety. They found that a central block of counties with relatively uneven topography and diverse habitats, extending from Alachua and Marion on the northern edge to Polk and Highlands on the south, included the southernmost records of many species. The most striking impoverishment came in the southern third of the peninsula, the Everglades–Big Cypress region, where they attributed the steep loss of species diversity to low habitat diversity reflecting low topography and absence of major streams.

The explanation offered by Simpson (1964) and others for the peninsula effect was a winnowing out of immigrant species over distance. As the word "peninsula" suggests, the land becomes more insular as one moves from the base to the tip, and the potential source area for immigrants becomes increasingly narrower and more distant. The proposed process of winnowing out diversity could become operational in some groups that dispersed slowly enough down the peninsula. If such examples ever existed, however, now would be one of the least probable times to observe them. The present represents approximately the end of a glacial stage, so that not long ago the peninsula was wide. The best time to observe the proposed peninsular winnowing process would be toward the end of an interglacial stage, when the peninsula had remained long and narrow for about 100,000 years.

Another biogeographic pattern similar to the proposed peninsular pattern has been called an *umbilicus* by Diamond and Gilpin (1983). It differs from a peninsula in having a relatively large expanse of habitable area at the end of a relatively narrow corridor. The expanse of marshes in south Florida, accessible via a narrow chain of coastal swamplands along the peninsula, may exemplify a biogeographic umbilicus in Florida. The consequence, in terms of species richness, approaches that of an island of similar area at a similar distance from a large source. This concept may have some utility in Florida biogeography, but it has not yet been demonstrated in any detailed studies.

Habitat Islands

Various parts of Florida may be studied biogeographically as habitat islands. Florida scrublands, for example, have been dramatically reduced and dissected since their maximum expanse during the Wisconsinan glacial stage. In a little over 10,000 years rising water tables have fostered mesic habitats and even cypress ponds where xeric habitats previously held sway. Insular relationships between species numbers and habitat areas can be observed but have not been studied in detail. Such relationships would be useful for predicting the biogeographic results of further habitat subdivision by human development (Harris, 1984).

Most of Florida's major lakes, bayheads, and swamps are newly formed since the Wisconsinan glacial stage. Watts (1983) showed that lake sedimentation was broken in most instances during that interval by large-scale depression of the piezometric surface. In the case of Okefenokee Swamp, for example, Parrish and Rykiel (1979) reviewed extensive evidence for its formation in about the last 6,000 years by rising water tables over a previously semiarid terrain characterized by sand dune ridges. Presumably therefore, lakes, bayheads, and swamps have been repopulated during the last several thousand years in a manner comparable to island colonization.

The tropical hammocks and coastal scrubs of southern Florida also may be viewed as habitat islands with respect to vagile tropical organisms. The major source area is probably the West Indies. The flora of southern Florida has numerous striking affinities with West Indian floras. Likewise, birds and insects of the southern tip reflect a substantial influence from Cuba, the Bahamas, and other West Indian faunas.

Conclusions

One of the most valuable results that historical biogeography can offer is to estimate the antiquity and scope of Florida's principal habitats. Among terrestrial habitats the oldest and most persistent is surely mesic forest. Indirect evidence comes in the late Oligocene and early Miocene from a number of small arboreal and scansorial species along with others that occupied deep litter. The first direct evidence, however, comes from the Alum Bluff flora from north peninsular deposits about 15 million years old. The evidence, though scattered, suggests that Florida's mixed hardwood forests have persisted from the very beginning of the state's terrestrial history more than 25 MYBP.

The first evidence of sandhill and scrub habitats appeared nearly 20 million years ago. The Thomas Farm site offers the most convincing indirect evidence of such habitats, along with more mesic settings. The first extensive influx of clastic sediments into the Florida peninsula arrived in the middle and late Miocene and initiated the buildup of extensive coastal dune systems. This trend was further elaborated in the late Miocene by the occurrence of two very low sea-level excursions, which carried sands and gravels far across the peninsula and built them into various ancient shorelines. Rich phosphate deposits also accumulated in Florida estuarine settings during the middle and late Miocene.

The most complete record of Florida's former terrestrial habitats is that of the last glacial (Wisconsinan) stage, when extensive pollen floras and vertebrate faunas are known. The area of the peninsula was nearly doubled. The extent of semiarid habitats and the near absence of suface water are remarkable. The northern half of the peninsula was evidently dominated by savanna vegetation, with mesic forests occupying favorable sites, while the southern half of the peninsula was limited to semiarid sandhill scrub vegetation. Pleistocene sea-level cycles again led to the construction of extensive sandhill systems, evident in the coast-parallel terrace deposits.

The most striking conclusion that historical research conveys about Florida and its ecosystems is that in any one area there have been immense changes. Although Florida has sustained terrestrial ecosystems for some 25 million years, many of its present features have only recently been emplaced. Probably the most ancient terrestrial habitats consist of mesic forests. Almost as old are the xeric hammock and sandhill scrub ecosystems, although most evidence for their existence comes indirectly from vertebrate faunas. These formations have persisted despite many changes in land area, climate, and local topography. Since the late Oligocene, Florida has probably consisted of a continuous peninsula, unbroken by the "Suwannee Strait." The peninsula has experienced much erosion in the Miocene and later, with consequent upward arching in the central areas of limestone exposure. During glacial cycles, wetland systems virtually disappeared, while semiarid formations expanded greatly, as did the total land area. Present swamps, bayheads, and lakes are no more than several thousand years old.

Since its definitive emergence some 25 million years ago, Florida has changed substantially and variously in both size and shape. At times Florida's land area has been much smaller than at present; at other times, for example during the last glacial interval, it has reached more than twice its present size. Such prior configurations of the land affected Florida's ancient biota in at least two fundamental ways. First, establishment of physical barriers or filters governed the degree of its isolation. Corridors, peninsulas, and habitat islands affected colonization by various groups of plants and animals. Many vagile groups came across seaways, but access by many terrestrial groups was constrained by the width of the peninsula. Second, paleogeography controlled the area available for occupation by each of Florida's ecosystems. The interplay between marshy mesic and xeric environments has repeatedly and dramatically altered the record of the state's rich biota.

Part II

Upland Ecosystems

5

Pine Flatwoods and Dry Prairies

Warren G. Abrahamson
David C. Hartnett

The most extensive type of terrestrial ecosystem in Florida, and perhaps the one historically most influenced by humans, is the pine flatwoods. This ecosystem is characterized by low, flat topography, and relatively poorly drained, acidic, sandy soil sometimes underlain by an organic horizon. In the past, this ecosystem was characterized by open pine woodlands and supported frequent fires (Laessle, 1942; Ober, 1954; Edmisten, 1963). The early European settlers coined the term *flatwoods*, emphasizing its characteristic lack of topographical relief (Ober, 1954). Early writers referred to this ecosystem variously as "barrens" (Bartram, 1791), "pine flats" (Penfound and Watkins, 1937), "low pineland", or "pine flatwoods" (Laessle, 1942). Harper (1914a) described the flatwoods forests of northern Florida as "open forests of longleaf pine with an undergrowth of saw palmetto (*Serenoa repens*), gallberry (*Ilex glabra*), wiregrass (*Aristida stricta*), and bearing marks of frequent fires." Weaver and Clements (1938) classified the flatwoods, along with the rest of the southeastern pine forests, as a fire subclimax within the deciduous forest region (fig. 5.1). Dry prairies in Florida

Map: Shaded areas, flatwoods; *cross-hatched areas*, dry prairies.

Fig. 5.1. Virgin longleaf pine flatwoods in the Choctawatchee National Forest (now Eglin Air Force Base). Photo by E. S. Shipp, 1928. Forest Service Photo Collection, National Agricultural Library.

have essentially the same features as pine flatwoods except that they lack a pine overstory. Another variant of the flatwoods association, the "scrubby flatwoods," is often ecotonal between flatwoods and scrub, occurring at slightly higher elevations than pine flatwoods or dry prairies. The tree stratum is variable, and the shrub layer differs from that of pine flatwoods in having a higher frequency of shrub oak species and a sparser herb layer. Pine savannas, in contrast, are nearly shrub-free and support a diverse herbaceous flora in poorly drained flatlands.

Many of the characteristics of flatwoods ecosystems changed markedly following human settlement. Early Spanish settlers attempted agriculture and introduced livestock. Extensive areas of virgin pine were cleared during the Civil War. With continued population growth came the construction of roads and other fire barriers and concomitant decreases in the extent and frequency of natural fires. Recently, flatwoods have been diverted to numerous other land uses. In some areas, nonnative species have become established. These changes have resulted in such appreciable departures from the characteristics of a "natural"—i.e., presettlement—flatwoods ecosystem that probably only a few stands closely resemble those of the past. Although certain features of the presettlement flatwoods are not fully understood and are still debated, the consensus is that present stands differ from presettlement stands by having lower fire frequencies, more even age structure, and a denser understory with greater shrub cover and less herb cover. Some early writers described the natural pine flatwoods as open enough to drive wagons through easily (Platt et al., 1988a, and references therein).

It has been suggested that changes in the occurrence of fire—particularly reductions in fire frequencies and average area burned per fire event—are primarily responsible for the differences we see between "natural" and present flatwoods ecosystems. Land drainage and other factors may also have contributed to changes in the characteristics of flatwoods and their distribution (Richardson, 1977). Dry prairies have also been subjected to numerous human influences, and it has been argued that many dry prairies may be artifacts of altered drainage or burning patterns of other human influences.

Fire strongly influences community structure and composition and has always been an important factor in the maintenance of flatwoods. Tremendous seasonal variation in water availability, created by a combination of seasonal precipitation, low and flat topography, and sandy soils, is another characteristic feature of the flatwoods ecosystems that influences their community structure (Ober, 1954; Golkin and Ewel, 1984).

Structure and Species Composition

The term *flatwoods* includes several vegetationally distinct communities found on a variety of soil types (Laessle, 1942). In general, present-day flatwoods stands are characterized by a relatively open overstory of pines, an extensive low shrub stratum, and a variable and often sparse herbaceous layer. Each of these components shows marked xerophytic (i.e., adapted to a dry environment) and pyrophytic (i.e., adapted to withstand fire) physiognomy (Harper, 1914a; Gunter, 1921; Laessle, 1942; Edmisten, 1963).

The four dominant trees characteristic of the flatwoods are *Pinus palustris* (longleaf pine), *P. elliottii* var. *elliottii* (typical slash pine), *P. elliottii* var. *densa* (south Florida slash pine), and *P. serotina* (pond pine). They occur either in pure stands or in various combinations with densities and proportions dependent on geographical location, climate, edaphic conditions, fire history, and history of human influences (Heyward, 1937; Laessle, 1942; Ober, 1954; Bethune, 1960; Edmisten, 1963, 1965; Grelen, 1983; Abrahamson et al., 1984). Some minor or infrequent trees, such as live oak (*Quercus virginiana*), water oak (*Q. nigra*), sweet gum (*Liquidambar styraciflua*), red maple (*Acer rubrum*), and ash (*Fraxinus* spp.), occur in the flatwoods of central and northern Florida (Gunter, 1921; Edmisten, 1963).

Tree densities in the flatwoods vary considerably, from high with dense, almost closed canopies to low with widely spaced trees giving an open savanna-like aspect. However, even the densest stands (greater than 5400 trees/ha) have discontinuous canopies, allowing considerable light to penetrate to the forest floor (Laessle, 1942). A typical pine canopy may reach up to 30 m in height; however, in a few areas the pines are stunted because of a clay hardpan beneath the surface or waterlogging that impedes root growth.

The understory shrub layer includes species such as saw palmetto, gallberry, fetterbush (*Lyonia lucida*), staggerbush (*L. fruticosa*), dwarf huckleberry (*Gaylussacia dumosa*), wax myrtle (*Myrica cerifera*), dwarf live oak (*Q. minima*), and tarflower (*Befaria racemosa*) and is typically quite dense in present stands (Harper, 1914a, 1927; Laessle, 1942; Ober, 1954; Hubbell et al., 1956; Edmisten, 1963; Richardson, 1977; Mytinger, 1979; Abrahamson et al., 1984). The shrubs also vary in species composition, relative abundance, and physiognomy due to a variety of edaphic and historical factors. The shrub layer may vary from almost pure stands of saw palmetto only 0.5 m in height to dense thickets up to 2 m or more. It may sometimes have a distinct two-layered structure composed of a low cover of saw palmetto and a sparse upper layer consisting of the canopies of taller shrubs such as gallberry or fetterbush. The pines self-prune their lower branches, leaving a large gap between their canopy and the shrub layer (Abrahamson, 1984b). As a result of these growth patterns, the flatwoods often appear distinctly stratified.

An appreciable herbaceous ground cover typically exists only in stands where the tree canopy and shrub layer are relatively open—i.e., where fire is frequent. Grasses usually make up a larger percentage of total cover than forbs; wiregrass (*Aristida stricta*) is the most characteristic species. Herb abundance usually decreases with the age of the stand (Ball et al., 1979; Abrahamson, 1984a,b).

The flatwoods habitat supports various populations of birds, small mammals—the cotton rat (*Sigmodon hispidus*), cotton mouse (*Peromyscus gossypinus*), and short-tailed shrew (*Blarina carolinensis*)—twenty to thirty species of amphibians and reptiles, and large mammals including white-tailed deer (*Odocoileus virginianus*). Avian densities are typically low throughout the year, with some increase in winter due to the influx of migratory winter residents. Birds use all three vegetation strata and are particularly heavy users of forest edges.

Area Coverage and Distribution

Flatwoods occur throughout the southeastern coastal plain and cover approximately 50 percent of the land area of Florida (Edmisten, 1963; Davis, 1967). They are particularly extensive in the southwestern lowlands (Hendry, Lee, Charlotte, Sarasota, Manatee, Hardee, Hillsborough, and Pasco counties), the east coast lowlands (eastern Palm Beach county northward), the northern Gulf coast region (Dixie, Lafayette, Taylor, Wakulla, Liberty, Franklin, Gulf, and Bay counties), and the north-central peninsular region (Alachua, Bradford, Union, Baker, and Columbia counties). Individual stands may comprise thousands of hectares, often forming an extensive matrix interspersed with smaller, often isolated, cypress heads, bayheads, hammocks, marshes, or wet prairies, or regions of upland sandhill or sand pine scrub.

The present distribution of the flatwoods associations in Florida can be explained in part by past changes in sea level during repeated glaciations, as well as existing soil and topographic patterns. During the Plio-Pleistocene or perhaps as early as the Miocene period, different advances and recessions of the north polar ice cap—each of many thousands of years' duration—resulted in concomitant changes in sea level (Healey, 1975; Brooks, 1982).

Each drop in the sea level exposed extensive areas of continental shelf. During each period of glacial recession the sea levels rose, and these newly exposed lands were inundated. The beds of sand deposited on these shallow sea floors formed the parent material of the flatwoods soils. These fine sandy soils, along with low relief, resulted in the low rates of runoff and percolation to deeper soil layers that created the edaphic conditions characteristic of the present flatwoods ecosystem.

Physical Environment

Because flatwoods and dry prairies are widely distributed throughout Florida and the southeastern coastal plain, they exhibit appreciable geographical and seasonal variation in climate, hydrology, and soils. Additional local variation in the physical environment occurs as a result of differences in fire regime, drainage alterations, other human activities, or other aspects of site history.

Climate

The climate of flatwoods varies from warm temperate in the northern part of the state to subtropical in south Florida. Scrubby flatwoods and dry prairies, typically more frequent in the southern part of the state, are influenced by a subtropical climate.

Seasonal change in the frequency and amount of precipitation is the most important of the climatic variables influencing the flatwoods ecosystems. It results in alternate seasons of flooding and droughty conditions, as well as related changes in hydrology, soils, and vegetation. Occasional climatic extremes such as freezes and hurricanes are also important agents of physical disturbance that influence the population biology of individual species as well as ecosystem structure and function.

Soils

A variety of soil types support pine flatwoods and dry prairies and influence the distribution of their various floristic phases (Abrahamson et al., 1984; Huck, 1987). Typical flatwoods soils are imperfectly drained to poorly drained, lightly textured fine sands (Heyward, 1937; McCulley, 1950). They are generally acidic and have low reserves of extractable nutrients, low clay content (often less than 2 percent), low organic matter content, and low cation exchange capacity (Heyward, 1939b; Ober, 1954; Edmisten, 1963; Morris, 1981; Gholz and Fisher, 1982; Gholz et al., 1985a).

A complex of interacting factors influences soil characteristics in the flatwoods. Frequent fires, a warm humid climate, low clay content, and low soil retention contribute in varying degrees to the low organic matter content. Because there is so little clay, the soil cation exchange capacity and moisture-holding capacity and the kinds and numbers of soil organisms present are determined by the small amount of organic matter (Edmisten, 1963). The organics typically accumulate directly within the soil from plant roots rather than accumulating from litterfall on the surface, although fine surface organics not consumed by fires may percolate into the soil (Heyward, 1937).

Many flatwoods soils contain a spodic (organic) horizon, occasionally underlain by a clay hardpan (Ober, 1954; Bastos and Smith, 1979). The spodic horizon is formed when organics are translocated downward by water percolation. Water loss through capillary rise and evaporation causes material to accumulate at the lower levels of capillary action and root penetration. Clay hardpans may result from the transport and accumulation of clays in a similar fashion, or they may be depositional in origin. Flatwoods soils vary considerably with respect to the presence of a hardpan and its thickness and depth (up to 1.5 m below the surface). When present, the hardpan may reduce already poor drainage, thus contributing to the development of the overlying spodic horizon and in extreme cases restricting root growth. Translocation of material to deeper soil layers, along with cation exchange, concentrates hydrogen ions in the upper horizons and contributes to the low pH of the soil. Each of these processes and soil profile characteristics is variable both among and within sites. The establishment of the modern pine flora in Florida around 5000 YBP may have been an important factor in the development of spodosols in flatwoods ecosystems. Acid released from the litter of pines and other plants, along with the fluctuating water table, facilitates the flushing of exchangeable bases from the upper soil layers (Huck, 1987).

Many of the soils supporting flatwoods are typical Florida spodosols (haplaquods, the dominant soil type in Florida [Smith et al., 1967; Huck, 1987]). They are intermediate in drainage between the well-drained sandy soils of the upland sandhill or scrub communities and the poorly drained organic soils of the flatwoods ponds and other adjacent wetlands. Again, however, much variation exists, and large areas of flatwoods include other soil types.

A number of different specific soil types, with these general characteristics or with some variations, support flatwoods. For example, in flatwoods dominated by cabbage palm, soils with a pH range of 6.0 to 7.5 are typical. These soils are derived from beds of sand over alkaline material such as marl or shell beds. Soils of scrubby flatwoods are typically well-drained white sands but with some topographic relief; thus they are similar to soils of scrub. Soils of dry prairies are usually acidic sands similar to those supporting pine flatwoods but often without a hardpan.

Edmisten (1963) documented appreciable variation in soil characteristics among numerous flatwoods sites in central Florida. He found that sites varied in the presence or absence of a hardpan, in soil pH (from 3.1 to 7.8), and in drainage. Most sites had soils with low clay content, but clay contents of up to 37 percent were found in one or more soil horizons on certain sites.

Abrahamson et al. (1984) showed that soil characteristics in flatwoods and adjacent associations on the southern Lake Wales Ridge varied in pH, nutrient content, and other characteristics, and that flatwoods soils tended to show greater site-to-site variation than did soils of other associations. They found that flatwoods soils showed the greatest range of pH of all associations in the area and that palmetto flatwoods exhibited the highest nutrient levels of all sites.

Hydrology

Flat topography, sandy soils, and seasonal precipitation strongly influence hydrological processes in flatwoods. For example, minimal water runoff owing to the flat topography results in very poorly defined first-order streams. Where a hardpan is present, water may move through it slowly relative to movement through horizons above or below it. Hence, flatwoods soils become waterlogged and poorly aerated during the rainy season, and there may be standing water for varying periods of time. During the dry season, however, high evapotranspiration draws much water from the upper horizons. Water cannot move upward from lower horizons because of the impermeable hardpan; thus, soil moisture becomes rapidly depleted in the upper horizons, and persistent droughty conditions result.

Soil moisture is also influenced by organic matter content, the total amount of foliage, evapotranspiration, and the litter layer. Litter has a mulching effect, retaining water above the mineral horizon and ameliorating soil surface temperatures (Heyward, 1937, 1939b; Bastos and Smith, 1979). Fire alters plant biomass, litter, and organics and thus indirectly influences these edaphic conditions. For example, Heyward (1939b) found that soil moisture was 52 percent higher in unburned than in burned flatwoods, primarily owing to accumulated litter.

The hydrology of flatwoods varies with elevation and topography. In general, mesic flatwoods are infrequently and briefly inundated only during extreme high water periods in the rainy season. Flatwoods on lower elevations may contain standing water for one or two months every year. The water table in dry prairies is typically a meter or so below the surface during the dry season and many centimeters deep during the wet season but may reach several centimeters above the surface for brief periods. In scrubby flatwoods the upper meter or so of soil is well drained and the water table, although not as deep as in the sandhills or scrub, is rarely near the surface.

Major Associations

Although different flatwoods associations have markedly similar vegetation, they vary considerably in community structure. Pine flatwoods and dry prairies are the two most readily distinguishable associations, although some authors also identify a third transitional association, scrubby flatwoods.

Pine Flatwoods

Pine flatwoods associations occur in areas of more level topography and on more poorly drained sands (Monk, 1968) than do the sand pine scrub or sandhill associations. Flatwoods range from open forests of scattered pines with little understory to dense pine stands with a rather dense undergrowth of grasses (particularly wiregrass), saw palmettos, and other low shrubs.

Some pine flatwoods associations, at least in the peninsula, may be even more extensive today than they were 100 years ago because flatwoods have invaded some wet prairie habitats subjected to drainage (Richardson, 1977). In more recent times, flatwoods have become established on some areas formerly cleared for agriculture. However, flatwoods have decreased in area where a reduction of fire frequency has enabled hammocks, bayheads (Peroni and Abrahamson, 1986), riverine forests (A. F. Clewell, personal communication), or titi thickets to expand into them or where agricultural and urban development has destroyed them (Peroni and Abrahamson, 1985).

Vegetation

Edmisten (1963) aptly described flatwoods as representing the matrix that ties together and merges with other Florida vegetation types, such as wet prairies, marshes, sandhills, hammocks, scrubs, bayheads, and swamps. Throughout most of Florida, imperceptible changes in elevation—as little as several centimeters—can result in marked alteration of the flora. For example, Abrahamson et al. (1984) documented a transition involving many associations, the extremes being sand pine scrub and flatwoods, over an approximately 2 m change in elevation (fig. 5.2).

Many authors have noted strong relationships among soils, drainage, hydroperiod, and plant associations in Florida (Harshberger, 1914; Harper, 1914a; Laessle, 1942; Davis, 1943; Abrahamson et al., 1984) and have used these to classify associations and to attempt to clarify the mosaic patterns of vegetation (Laessle, 1942; Abrahamson et al., 1984). Some treatments have described Florida flatwoods on the basis of their hydrology and understory components (Duever, 1984–1985). Wet flatwoods, for example, occur in seasonally inundated flatlands with sand substrates and have canopies of slash pine, pond pine, and/or cabbage palm. They have an understory of mixed hydrophytic shrubs, such as wax myrtle and gallberry, grasses, and forbs that varies with fire frequency. In contrast, mesic flatwoods occupy sandy, seldom inundated flatlands and typically have canopies of slash or longleaf pine with a dense understory of saw palmetto. Gallberry, rusty lyonia (*Lyonia ferruginea*), wax myrtle, and wiregrass are also usually abundant.

Unfortunately, most classifications have two major problems. First, they

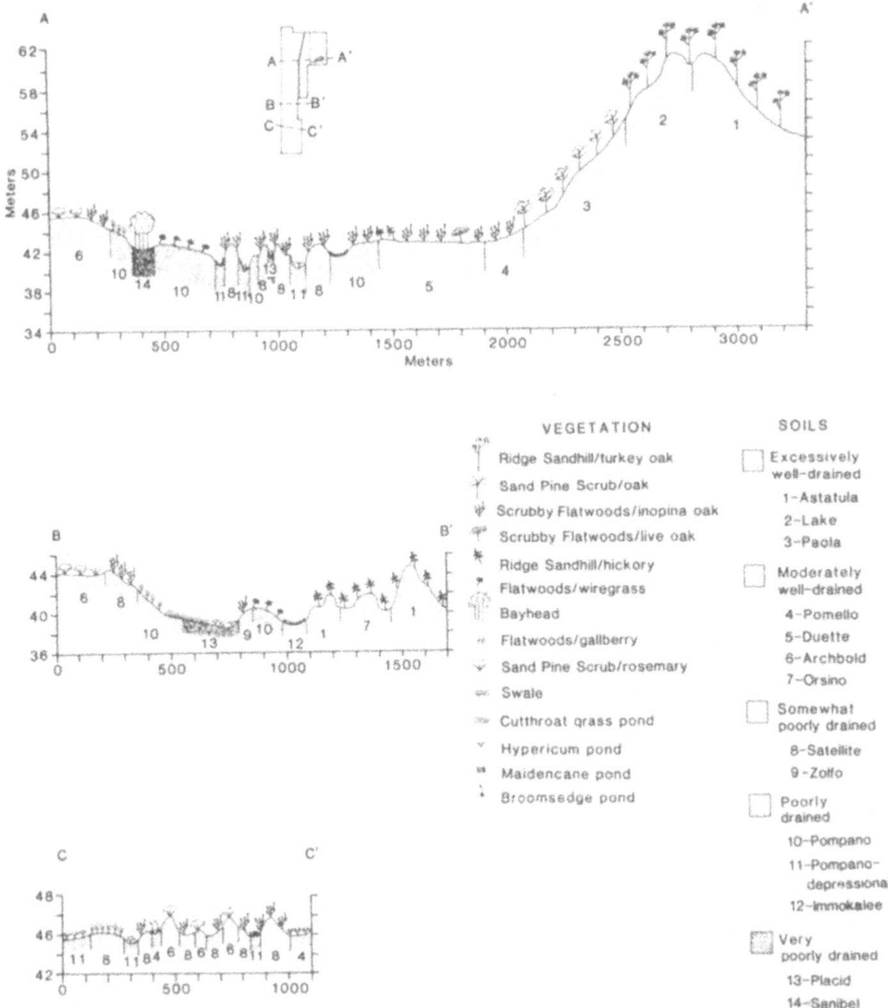

Fig. 5.2. Three east-west profiles across the Archbold Biological Station, Highlands County, showing the relation of soils and vegetation to topography. The vertical exaggeration is 40X. From Abrahamson et al., 1984. Used with permission of the Florida Academy of Sciences, Inc.

are based on patterns observed within a local geographical area (Harper, 1914a; Laessle, 1942; Abrahamson et al., 1984) and thus are not generally applicable throughout the state or the southeastern United States (Christensen, 1988). Second—and this is a problem of classification itself—the variation from one association to another is continuous. Thus, classification schemes fail to emphasize adequately the gradations along a vegetation continuum. The approach we take is to provide an overview of flatwoods by describing, without attempting to classify, some of the variations in the components and structure of flatwoods communities throughout the state.

The tree canopy of flatwoods differs depending upon latitude, soils, and hydroperiod. In north and central Florida, longleaf pine typically dominates on better-drained and frequently burned sites (Monk, 1968; Platt et al., 1988a). These sites are often transitional between sandhills and slash pine flatwoods. Laessle (1942) described a pattern of longleaf pine dominance on higher ground and pond pine (fig. 5.3) and slash pine (fig. 5.4) on lower sites with a longer hydroperiod. Slash pine, being less fire-tolerant than longleaf pine, may be naturally restricted to the wetter and less frequently burned sites, while pond pine occurs in the more acidic, poorly drained locations (Hubbell et al., 1956; Monk, 1968). In the Ocala National Forest, longleaf pine occupies the drier flatwoods sites, with slash pine on less well-drained sites, and pond pine on the wettest sites (Snedaker and Lugo, 1972). However, with fire suppression and the harvest of virgin longleaf pine forests in this century, mixed slash pine–longleaf pine stands began to dominate a large portion of the landscape. The extent of slash pine forests has increased appreciably since the early 1960s due to the development of extensive pine plantations, primarily for pulpwood production (Stone, 1983). Estimates suggest that slash pine now occupies 41 percent of Florida's commercial forest land (Sheffield et al., 1983).

Interpreting slash pine distribution is complicated because of the two varieties of slash pine that occur within Florida. Typical slash pine (*Pinus elliottii* var. *elliottii*) ranges along the southeastern coastal plain from South Carolina to central Florida (fig. 5.5) and eastern Louisiana. Its seedlings grow with a characteristic pencil-like shape on mesic sites with infrequent fires (Little and Dorman, 1954a, b). South Florida slash pine (*P. elliottii* var. *densa*) occurs in the central and southern portions of the Florida peninsula as well as in the Keys. In southern Florida, it is the only common pine and occurs throughout the sandy flatwoods and rocklands. Its seedlings have a grass-like, almost stemless stage and possess a thick taproot and heavy wood (Little and Dorman, 1954a; Saucier and Dorman, 1969). South Florida slash pine is more fire-tolerant and drought-resistant than typical slash pine (Ketcham and Bethune, 1963; Bethune, 1966; McMinn and McNab, 1971) but less fire-tolerant than longleaf pine (Wade, 1983). Although Mirov (1967) concluded that the two varieties were distinct, Squillace (1966) found that the variation in several morphological traits was clinal, indicating a gradual transition from one variety to the other.

Considerable overlap in understory plants exists among flatwoods associations. Generally, saw palmetto and gallberry dominate the understory in slash pine flatwoods, wiregrass and running oak (*Quercus pumila*) are frequently abundant in longleaf pine flatwoods, and fetterbush and several of the bay trees are characteristic of pond pine areas (Ward, 1978).

Other authors, dealing with vegetation classification at a site-by-site level, have described flatwoods in sufficient detail to allow us the opportunity to explore patterns of variation in flatwoods flora throughout the state. In the Apalachicola, St. Marks, and Tarpon Springs regions along the northern Gulf coast, flatwoods canopies were predominantly longleaf pine.

Fig. 5.3. Pond pine flatwoods in Paynes Prairie State Preserve near Gainesville, Alachua County. Photo by R. Myers.

Fig. 5.4. Slash pine flatwoods in Franklin County. Photo by R. Myers.

Fig. 5.5. Natural ranges of (*A*) *Pinus elliottii* var. *elliottii* and *P. elliottii* var. *densa* and (*B*) *P. palustris* and *P. serotina*. Adapted from Little, 1971.

The understories were uniform in species composition and include saw palmetto, ericaceous shrubs, wiregrass, and herbaceous undergrowth with many legumes (Harper, 1914a). The degree of dominance of any species depends, to a large extent, on the length of time since fire.

In northeastern Florida, considerable variation occurred in flatwoods vegetation (Harper, 1914a). For example, ericaceous shrubs—such as sparkleberry, *Vaccinium arboreum*—were frequent west of the Trail Ridge (Baker and Bradford counties) while few occur east of the ridge (Clay and Duval counties). Harper (1914a) correlated this difference with the presence of clayey, calcareous, or phosphatic soils to the west of the ridge.

The predominant pine of flatwoods changes in the central to south Florida region. To the north (Levy, Marion, Putnam, and Flagler counties [Harper 1921]), longleaf pine is typical in better-drained flatwoods, typical slash pine in swamps and near ponds, and pond pine in poorly drained flatwoods. To the south (Lee, Desoto, Highlands, and Okeechobee counties), south Florida slash pine becomes the only flatwoods pine; pond pine extends only to about Orange County (Harshberger, 1914; Harper, 1927) (fig. 5.5).

On the east coast in Broward County, south Florida slash pine flatwoods occur on moderately to well-drained sandy soils (Steinberg, 1980), but farther south (Dade County) this association occurs on outcrops and low ridges of oolitic limestone (Harshberger, 1914). The flatwoods understories vary considerably from east to west within south Florida. In the southeast, silver palm (*Coccothrinax argentata*), coontie (*Zamia floridana*), and running oak are common. Toward the west coast, where the limestone is mantled by sand, herbs are more evenly distributed and dwarf live oak and myrtle oak (*Q. myrtifolia*) are more abundant (Harshberger, 1914).

In many areas, numerous seasonal ponds, wet depressions, bayheads, cypress ponds, bogs, titi swamps, and cabbage palm hammocks are embedded within the flatwoods matrix. The sizes of these "contained" associations vary greatly, but collectively they can provide considerable coverage (fig. 5.6). The vegetation of these islands within the flatwoods matrix varies with edaphic conditions, hydroperiod, and basin characteristics.

This matrix of flatwoods merging with other plant associations produces various ecotones. For example, a dense, vigorous thicket of saw palmettos with some gallberry and fetterbush frequently rings flatwoods seasonal ponds, making an abrupt transition to the vegetation of the pond (Laessle, 1942; Abrahamson et al., 1984). These palmetto thickets are rarely inundated, but they probably receive substantial seepage water from the higher flatwoods areas (Laessle, 1942).

Fig. 5.6. Longleaf–slash pine flatwoods and a seasonal pond with a saw grass fringe, Ochlockonee River State Park, Wakulla County. Photo by R. Myers.

One extreme variant of flatwoods that occurs on somewhat alkaline sands is the cabbage palm savanna. This association is particularly common on the Indian Prairie, northwest of Lake Okeechobee. Here, the level flatlands are dotted with cabbage palms, either singly or in groves. Cabbage palm flatwoods are also found on Merritt Island, near the Gulf coast from Lee to Franklin counties, and in the upper St. Johns River basin east of Orlando.

Fauna

The flatwoods variants are inhabited by a number of vertebrates. Depending on the association, these include the following: pine woods tree frog (*Hyla femoralis*), oak toad (*Bufo quercicus*), box turtle (*Terrapene carolina*), pine woods snake (*Rhadinaea flavilata*), eastern diamondback rattlesnake (*Crotalus adamanteus*), black racer (*Coluber constrictor*), brown-headed nuthatch (*Sitta pusilla*), the threatened red-cockaded woodpecker (*Picoides borealis*), Bachman's sparrow (*Aimophila aestivalis*), pine warbler (*Dendroica pinus*), great horned owl (*Bubo virginianus*), least shrew (*Cryptotis parva*), cotton mouse, cotton rat, and gray fox (*Urocyon cinereoargenteus*) (Snedaker and Lugo, 1972; Layne, 1974; Layne et al., 1977). No mammal is exclusive to flatwoods (Layne, 1974), although the fox squirrel (*Sciurus niger*) is highly characteristic of flatwoods with open understory. Three large mammals native to Florida use flatwoods: the white-tailed deer, black bear (*Ursus americanus*), and the endangered Florida panther (*Felis concolor coryi*) (Layne, 1974).

Dry Prairies

The term *prairie* has a different usage in Florida than in the central or western United States. The common feature is their treeless or nearly treeless, grass-covered nature (Harshberger, 1914). Florida dry prairies are open, grassy expanses—including wiregrass, bottlebrush three-awn (*Aristida spiciformis*), arrowfeather (*A. purpurascens*), broomsedge (*Andropogon virginicus*), and love grasses (*Eragrostis* spp.)—with sparse saw palmettos and scattered patches of low shrubs, such as fetterbush, rusty lyonia, dwarf blueberry (*Vaccinium myrsinites*), and wax myrtle. They merge with open pine flatwoods in some cases and with open hammock-dotted savannas in other situations (fig. 5.7).

A number of authors (e.g., Harper, 1921, 1927; Davis, 1943; Ward, 1978; Steinberg, 1980) have noted that dry prairies hardly differ from pine flatwoods except in the absence of pine trees. They occur on acid sands similar to those that support pine flatwoods. Although these soils may flood with several centimeters of water for short periods after heavy summer rains, the normal water table is below ground surface during most of the year. Davis

Fig. 5.7. Dry prairie with oak–cabbage palm hammock in the background, Brighton Indian Reservation, Highlands County. Photo by M. McMillan.

(1943) suggested that dry prairies have a shorter hydroperiod than wiregrass flatwoods. The reason for their treelessness is unclear, but in some area dry prairies are known to be an artifact of clear-cutting, unnaturally frequent burning, and livestock grazing.

Vegetation

Davis (1943) noted considerable variation in the dominant species in dry prairies. For instance, in the south Florida rocklands, switch grass (*Panicum virgatum*) and short grasses in general are common, while on acidic sands wiregrass is abundant. In addition, the coverage of saw palmetto varies from a few scattered individuals to dense stands. In extreme northwestern Florida, slender bluestem (*Schizachyrium tenerum*) replaces wiregrass (A.F. Clewell, personal communication).

The most extensive dry prairies in Florida occur north and west of Lake Okeechobee along the Kissimmee River (Ward, 1978), but this association is also common farther west through Desoto County. Smaller patches of dry prairie occur as far north as Volusia and Wakulla counties (Harper, 1927). Dry prairies are dotted with cabbage palm flatwoods in some areas and often grade into wet flatwoods, savannas, or pine flatwoods in others.

Fauna

Dry prairies provide the primary habitat for several distinctive bird species, including the threatened crested caracara (*Polyborus plancus*), burrowing owl (*Athene cunicularia*), and the threatened Florida sandhill crane (*Grus canadensis*). Other dry prairie species with greater numbers include the box turtle, black racer, turkey vulture (*Cathartes aura*), black vulture (*Coragyps atratus*), common nighthawk (*Chordeiles minor*), eastern meadowlark (*Sturnella magna*), least shrew, cotton rat, eastern harvest mouse (*Reithrodontomys humulis*), and eastern spotted skunk (*Spilogale putorius*) (Layne et al., 1977).

Scrubby Flatwoods

The scrubby flatwoods association occurs on sites that are slightly higher and relatively better drained than flatwoods or dry prairies but lower than scrub or sandhills (Laessle, 1942). In contrast to flatwoods, the soils of scrubby flatwoods are sufficiently well drained that there is no standing water even under extremely wet conditions, yet they have a higher water table than scrub and sandhills (Abrahamson et al., 1984). Scrubby flatwoods represent an ecotone between flatwoods and scrub habitats, but because this association covers large areas in parts of Florida, we recognize it as a separate association.

Vegetation

This association is predominantly evergreen with xeromorphic physiognomy—i.e., small, sclerophyllous (tough, leathery) leaves that often have leaf margins rolled under and pubescent undersides. Tree presence is variable and consists of scattered pines, such as south Florida slash pine, sand pine, or longleaf pine, over a shrubby understory of moderate to high density. Shrub oak species, such as scrub oak (*Quercus inopina*), Chapman's oak (*Q. chapmanii*), and sand live oak (*Q. geminata*), form a shrub canopy averaging 1–2 m tall, but height varies with local soil moisture (and perhaps nutrient) conditions and time elapsed since the last fire (Abrahamson et al., 1984) (fig. 5.8). Saw palmetto and, through the Lakes region of Florida, scrub palmetto (*Sabal etonia*) provide substantial coverage at most sites. Herbaceous vegetation is sparse, consisting primarily of wiregrass and forbs, but cover of lichens (*Cladonia* spp.) and spike moss (*Selaginella arenicola*) can be considerable in all but recently burned areas (Abrahamson et al., 1984).

Floristically, the scrubby flatwoods are intermediate between scrub and mesic flatwoods associations, seeming to be just a combination of species from these associations. However, *Q. inopina*, the most characteristic species of this association within this oak's range, is rare in flatwoods or typical scrub (Abrahamson et al., 1984). In north Florida, Chapman's oak, myrtle oak, and sand live oak predominate. Even though the scrubby flatwoods association appears to be natural throughout much of its range, in some areas it may be an artifact of logging and fire exclusion. Some interpret the scrubby flatwoods as nothing more than flatwoods (often with pine logged out) from which fire has been excluded. Fire exclusion results in the subsequent invasion of sand pine and various scrub shrubs (A. F. Clewell, personal communication).

Although nearly endemic to Florida, the scrubby flatwoods association has received little study. This association occurs in varying forms in coastal areas along the Gulf of Mexico into Alabama and Mississippi and north

Fig. 5.8. Scrubby flatwoods (in foreground) one year following a burn, Archbold Biological Station, Highlands County. Photo by Paige Martin.

along the Atlantic coast into Georgia and South Carolina (Florida Natural Areas Inventory, 1988). Although scrubby flatwoods are fairly widespread geographically, the total area of this association is quite limited. Unfortunately, the occurrence of scrubby flatwoods in Florida is poorly documented, and they are rapidly disappearing due to agricultural and urban development.

There is considerable gradation in the predominant species of scrubby flatwoods. In south-central Florida, sand live oak forms dense stands in the slightly lower portions of scrubby flatwoods, while scrub oak and Chapman's oak dominate elsewhere. Both saw and scrub palmetto are common, with saw palmetto reaching its highest densities in less elevated sites and scrub palmetto in more elevated sites.

Fauna

Scrubby flatwoods provide habitat for a number of animal species, including the oak toad, pine woods tree frog, gopher tortoise (*Gopherus polyphemus*), six-lined race runner (*Cnemidophorus sexlineatus*), eastern diamondback rattlesnake, bobwhite (*Colinus virginianus*), ground dove (*Columbigallina passerina*), Florida scrub jay (*Aphelocoma c. coerulescens*), rufous-sided towhee (*Pipilo erythrophthalmus*), southeastern pocket gopher (*Geomys pinetis*), and Florida mouse (*Podomys floridanus*).

Endemics, Exotics, and Species of Special Status

Endemics

Approximately 3500 native or naturalized vascular plant species constitute the Florida flora (Ward, 1978). Long (1974) estimates that, of these, perhaps as many as 385 species (approximately 11 percent) are endemic to Florida, although most other estimates are more conservative. The largest share of these endemics is associated with xeric habitats such as sand pine scrub, sandhills, pine rocklands, and scrubby flatwoods. The latter association accounts for a relatively high number of endemics, including *Asclepias feayi*, scrub oak, pennyroyal (*Piloblephis rigida*), and scrub palmetto (Abrahamson et al., 1984). A number of endemic Florida vertebrates, including the scrub lizard (*Sceloporus woodi*), blue-tailed mole skink (*Eumeces egregius lividus*), sand skink (*Neoseps reynoldsi*), Florida scrub jay, and Florida mouse, are also characteristic of scrubby flatwoods associations.

Because flatwoods are extensive and range into neighboring states, they often possess proportionally fewer endemic plant species than do the less extensive scrub associations. An exception to this rule is the Apalachicola lowlands flatwoods (fig. 5.9), which have as many endemic plant species as scrub, if not more (D. Hardin, personal communication). Several notable Florida endemics inhabit flatwoods, including cutthroat grass (*Panicum abscissum*) (fig. 5.10), yellow bachelor's button (*Polygala rugelii*), fall-flowering ixia, (*Nemastylis floridana*), scare-weed (*Baptisia simplicifolia*), *Euphorbia telephioides*, and Edison's ascyrum (*Hypericum edisonianum*). More than a half dozen Florida endemics common to flatwoods are classified as endangered (Ward, 1978; Kral, 1983). These include yellow squirrel-banana (*Deeringothamnus rugelii*), Florida bear grass (*Nolina atopocarpa*), wiregrass gentian (*Gentiana pennelliana*), mock pennyroyal (*Hedeoma graveolens*), Edison's ascyrum, fall-flowering ixia, and Bartram's ixia (*Sphenostigma coelestinum*).

Exotics

Undisturbed flatwoods and scrubby flatwoods are not easily invaded by exotic plant species. Notable exceptions in south Florida include undisturbed moist flatwoods that have been extensively invaded in some areas by the Australian cajeput (*Melaleuca quinquenervia*), Brazilian pepper (*Schinus terebinthifolius*), or downy myrtle (*Rhodomyrtus tomentosus*). Drier and more northern Florida flatwoods appear less vulnerable to invasion by exotics.

Activities that disturb the soil (especially bulldozing of roads and fire lanes) or alter hydrologic patterns make flatwoods, dry prairies, and scrubby flatwoods more susceptible to invasion. Exotics such as Australian pine (*Casuarina litorea*), chinaberry (*Melia azedarach*), Brazilian pepper, and cajeput

Fig. 5.9. Longleaf pine savanna near Post Office Bay, Apalachicola National Forest. Savanna-like flatwoods were once prevalent in the Florida Panhandle. Today, most have been converted to slash pine plantations or have developed into titi thickets after decades of fire exclusion. Photo by R. Myers.

Fig. 5.10. Cutthroat grass (*Panicum abscissum*), a species restricted to seepage slopes and swales of south-central Florida, carpets fire-maintained glades in flatwoods. With fire exclusion, the glades convert to slash pine–bayhead vegetation. Photo by R. Myers.

have successfully invaded such disturbed sites in south Florida (Harper, 1927; Austin, 1976; Steinberg, 1980). Elsewhere, old field weed floras invade and persist, thus changing the character—for example, by reducing fire frequency—of flatwoods, and facilitating hardwood invasion.

A number of exotic vertebrates have established themselves in these associations. The greenhouse frog (*Eleutherodactylus planirostris*) is found occasionally in scrubby flatwoods and flatwoods. The black rat (*Rattus rattus*) and house mouse have been reported in flatwoods, while the red fox (*Vulpes fulva*) occurs uncommonly in dry prairies. The two most common exotic vertebrates of flatwoods and dry prairies are the nine-banded armadillo (*Dasypus novemcinctus*) and the wild hog (*Sus scrofa*). The latter species can destroy vegetation, particularly herbaceous species in seasonal ponds.

Species of Special Status

Pine flatwoods provide important habitat for a number of endangered (E), threatened (T), and rare (R) vertebrate species. Some of the amphibians and reptiles listed for this habitat by McDiarmid (1978) are striped newt (*Notophthalmus perstriatus*) (R), Miami black-headed snake (*Tantilla oolitica*) (T), and mole snake (*Lampropeltis calligaster rhombomaculata*) (R). Kale's (1978) bird list included both the red-cockaded woodpecker (E; T in Florida Game and Fresh Water Fish Commission 1986 listing [Wood, 1986]) and the southeastern kestrel (*Falco sparverius*) (T). Layne (1978) listed, among others, the Florida panther (E), fox squirrel (T; species of special concern in FGFWFC 1986 listing [Wood, 1986]), and black bear (T).

Dry prairies are home to still other vertebrates with limited numbers. Kale (1978) noted, among other bird species, the grasshopper sparrow (*Ammodramus savannarum*) (E), crested caracara (T), Florida sandhill crane (T), and white-tailed kite (*Elanus caeruleus*) (R). Both the endangered Florida panther and threatened Florida black bear are reported to use dry prairies (Layne, 1978). Scrubby flatwoods provide critical habitat for the Florida mouse (T, species of special concern in FGFWFC 1986 listing [Wood, 1986]) (Layne, 1978).

Community Attributes

Seasonal Changes

At low flatwoods sites, the flowering of some herbaceous species with short stature is keyed to hydroperiod. These species—such as bantam buttons (*Syngonanthus flavidulus*) and yellow-eyed grasses (*Xyris* spp.)—flower in spring before the water level rises. Taller herbaceous species, such as blackroot (*Pterocaulon pycnostachyum*) and false foxglove (*Gerardia fasciculata*), flower in summer and autumn when standing water may be present.

Flatwoods soils are generally well drained and arid during the dry season but waterlogged and poorly aerated during the rainy season; both conditions result in physiological drought and influence the physiognomy of the plants. The trees and shrubs are evergreen and often possess other adaptations such as heavy cutinization, hairiness, and reduced or revolute leaves. Adaptations such as extensive underground perennating organs among the herbs and shrubs and the fire-resistant bark of the pines are evidence of the importance of fire. In general, the overall appearance of the flatwoods association shows little seasonal variation.

Scrubby flatwoods show only slight seasonal change. The phenology of the abundant oaks varies, with myrtle oak flowering and leafing first, followed by Chapman's oak and sand live oak, and lastly scrub oak (Johnson and Abrahamson, 1982). There are never extended periods of leaflessness (although spring drought increases the duration of leaf turnover), since each of these species drops its leaves, flowers, and produces new leaves within several weeks during the period from March to May. Flowering of other scrubby flatwoods species occurs throughout spring, summer, and autumn, although the spring bloomers—such as blueberries, huckleberries, staggerbush, tarflower, and gallberry—and autumn bloomers, including garberia (*Garberia heterophylla*) and jointweeds (*Polygonella* spp.), are most conspicuous.

Species Richness and Diversity

Few studies have quantitatively determined these indices for flatwoods associations. However, H. R. Delcourt and P. A. Delcourt (1977) found that flatwoods had the lowest tree species richness of the communities they studied in the Apalachicola River region, which included floodplain forest, tributary bottomland hardwood forest, upland pine-oak forest, and *Magnolia-Fagus* climax forest. In contrast, Monk (1968), working in north-central Florida, showed that flatwoods stands had a relatively high but variable number of tree species. In this study, flatwoods (42 tree species) ranked second to southern mixed hardwoods forests (71) but higher than mixed hardwood swamps (30), bayheads (27), sandhills (26), or cypress domes (18). In south-central Florida, Abrahamson et al. (1984) found considerable variation in tree, shrub, and herb richness and diversity for flatwoods and scrubby flatwoods stands. When compared to adjacent associations, these communities ranked from intermediate to relatively high in richness and diversity of plant species, with bayhead, rosemary scrub, and a mesic swale ranking lower.

Edmisten's (1963) comparison of stands in north and central Florida indicated that, among flatwoods, those dominated by slash pine were botanically the richest, followed by those dominated by longleaf pine, and finally pond pine. Both Edmisten (1963) and Ward (1978) attributed this decline in species richness to hydroperiod differences. They suggested that slash pine flatwoods are subject to the least moisture stress of the three canopy types, while longleaf pine flatwoods are periodically stressed by lack of available water, and pond pine flatwoods by excess water and acidic soil conditions. (fig. 5.11).

We conducted an analysis of a wildlife inventory prepared for a seven-county area in west-central Florida by Layne et al. (1977). Our analysis revealed that pine flatwoods have greater vertebrate species richness (160 species) than either scrubby flatwoods (100 species) or dry prairies (81 species). The inventory also suggests that scrubby flatwoods typically have more amphibian, reptile, and bird species than do dry prairies. This pattern may result in part from the greater structural diversity provided wildlife in scrubby flatwoods as compared to dry prairies. Layne et al. (1977) list slightly more mammal species for dry prairies than for scrubby flatwoods.

Community Similarities

Many species with low coverage in flatwoods are dominants in adjacent communities. Monk (1968) determined that of all forest types he examined, flatwoods had the highest mean percentage similarity to other community types. This may be, in part, because species of adjacent communities invade flatwoods when fire is suppressed.

An analysis of plant community similarity for southern Lake Wales Ridge communities indicated that there were two principal clusters of vegetation associations: communities of well-drained soils and communities of poorly drained soils (Abrahamson et al., 1984). Scrubby flatwoods and flatwoods

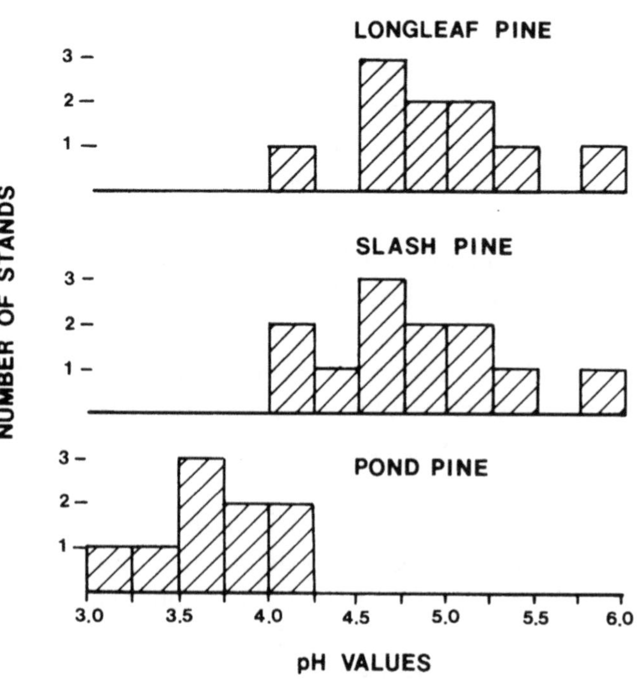

Fig. 5.11. The number of flatwoods stands dominated by longleaf pine, slash pine, and pond pine, arranged according to the pH of the A1 soil horizon. Adapted from Edmisten, 1963.

bridged the two main clusters, probably reflecting the intermediate elevational position of these associations between the better-drained scrubs and sandhills and the more poorly drained swales and bayheads.

The patterns of similarity of vertebrate species composition among flatwoods, dry prairies, and scrubby flatwoods support the notion that flatwoods represent a matrix embedded with smaller stands of other forest types. We performed a community similarity analysis of the seven-county wildlife inventory prepared by Layne et al. (1977). This analysis revealed that flatwoods share many vertebrate species with both dry prairies and scrubby flatwoods. Horne's indices of community similarity for amphibian, reptile, and bird species were greatest between flatwoods and scrubby flatwoods (0.85, 0.72, and 0.81, respectively), intermediate between flatwoods and dry prairies (0.0, 0.55, and 0.56, respectively), and lowest between scrubby flatwoods and dry prairies (0.0, 0.37, and 0.41, respectively). A value of 0.0 represents no community similarity; a value of 1.0 indicates that communities are identical. This pattern is likely to be the result of the similarity in physical structure between flatwoods and scrubby flatwoods and the similarity in plant species composition between flatwoods and dry prairies, whereas both structure and plant species composition are dissimilar between scrubby flatwoods and dry prairies.

As in the case of species richness, the pattern of community similarity for mammals differed from that of herptiles and birds (based on an analysis of the data of Layne et al., 1977). Flatwoods and dry prairies exhibited the greatest community similarity (0.71), while flatwoods and scrubby flatwoods had intermediate similarity (0.55), and scrubby flatwoods and dry prairies had the least in common (0.47).

Ecosystem Processes

Nutrient Availability

The soils of scrubby flatwoods, flatwoods, and dry prairies are typically acidic, nutrient-poor quartz sands. These soils contain few weatherable minerals and have low clay nutrients in the surface soil. Thus, nutrient storage and availability depend on the amount and type of dead organic matter. However, except for often thick litter layers in long-unburned stands, the organic contents of these soils are low because of the low clay content and low retention, which result in a high degree of leaching (Gholz and Fisher, 1982). Therefore, it comes as no surprise that plantations established on these soils are often deficient in nutrients, particularly phosphorus and nitrogen (Pritchett, 1968; Pritchett and Smith, 1975; Pritchett and Comerford, 1983).

An additional complication for nutrient uptake results from the extreme fluctuations of the water table in these associations. Root growth is inhibited by the oscillations between saturated and droughty soil conditions. In some flatwoods, a clay hardpan retards subsurface drainage and prevents the roots of pines from penetrating deeply into the soil. Nutrients may leach downward and become largely unavailable as part of the hardpan (Snedaker and Lugo, 1972). It is also likely that the acidic soil conditions have a detrimental effect on the mycorrhizal symbionts of flatwoods species (Pritchett and Comerford, 1983), thus possibly reducing the nutrient uptake efficiency of higher plants. However, the pines and palmettos may produce very deep roots, even in areas that are often flooded. How these deep roots are metabolically supported and what their ecological importance may be are still largely unknown.

Studies of slash pine plantations indicate that decay occurs primarily due to fungal and mite activities and proceeds at a linear rate of approximately 15 percent each year (Gholz and Fisher, 1984). Slow decomposition rates may result from the acidic soil conditions, which inhibit the activity of bacteria and many micro-invertebrate consumers; from the fluctuating water table; or from nutrient imbalance (Swift et al., 1979; Gholz et al., 1985a). Golkin and Ewel (1984) estimated that the litter in a north Florida flatwoods had an estimated mean turnover time of 11.2 years, a slow rate when compared to other temperate forests and other pine forests. However, wood decay of nonlightered sapwood is relatively rapid, due to the activity of termites (H. Gholz, personal communication); lightered wood is rich in resins and is therefore slow to decompose. The dominance of southern pines on these nutrient-poor soils results at least in part from the fact that conifers have lower nutrient requirements than most hardwoods. Further, the pines are among the least nutrient-demanding of all conifers (Pritchett and Comerford, 1983; Gholz et al., 1985a).

Nutrient Cycling

The preceding discussion indicates that ecosystem processes are slow and that nutrient cycling is likely to be almost imperceptible in flatwoods associations. Unfortunately, there have been few studies examining nutrient movements in naturally occurring, frequently burned flatwoods. However, the studies from managed flatwoods and plantations provide some insight into the probable nutrient dynamics in natural stands.

Nutrient cycles in managed flatwoods are relatively closed, meaning that nutrients are effectively retained (Gholz et al., 1985a). This retention results partly because woody plants quickly accumulate essential nutrients, particularly phosphorus, after a disturbance such as forest cutting (Golkin and Ewel, 1984; Gholz et al., 1985a,b) (fig. 5.12). The growth of slash pine in plantations is initially rapid but slows quickly, probably due to the accumulation of essential elements in the vegetation and litter (Gholz et al., 1985a). Apparently the mineralization processes and the small atmospheric inputs

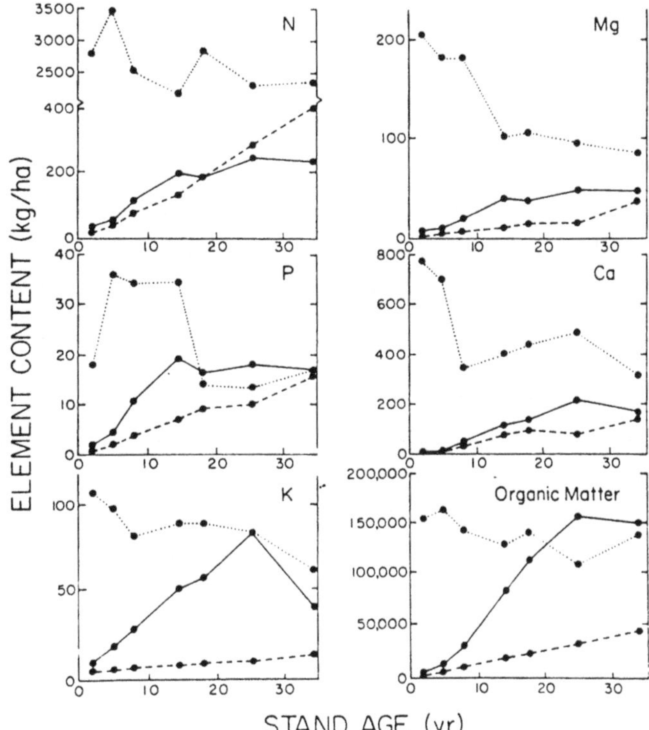

Fig. 5.12. Mean nutrient contents and organic matter in the vegetation (*solid lines*), forest floor (*dashed lines*), and soil (*dotted lines*) for a stand age sequence. Adapted from Gholz et al., 1985a. Used with permission of the Ecological Society of America.

of nutrients are only sufficient to supply the annual nutrient requirements, such as phosphorus, for maintenance of mature stands. In pine plantations, this ultimately leads to the cessation of vegetative biomass accumulation after approximately twenty-five years (Gholz and Fisher, 1982; Gholz et al., 1985a).

When soil supplies of phosphorus and nitrogen decrease, the pines internally reallocate nutrients to sustain growth (Gholz and Fisher, 1984; Gholz et al., 1985a). The vast majority of essential nutrients become tied up in crown components. Needles, for example, make up approximately 7 percent of the biomass of a slash pine but contain 30–37 percent of the forest's complement of nitrogen, phosphorus, and potassium (Pritchett and Smith, 1974). The understory component of pine plantations also shows substantial biomass nutrient accumulations after planting, holding a considerable fraction of the essential elements (Golkin and Ewel, 1984). Gholz and Fisher (1984) suggest that, over the life of a pine plantation, available soil nutrients decline, vegetation nutrient stocks increase to some maximum, and the forest floor continues to accumulate both mass and mineral elements.

It is known that certain species of flatwoods, dry prairies, and scrubby flatwoods play specific roles in the cycling of mineral elements. For example, saw palmetto readily takes up calcium from the soil and returns it as litterfall. This litter calcium can then be taken up by surface feeder roots of other species (Edmisten, 1963; Snedaker and Lugo, 1972). Appreciable amounts of nitrogen can be added to flatwoods soils through nitrogen fixation by wax myrtle symbionts (Edmisten, 1963; Gholz and Fisher, 1984).

The available data suggest that nutrient cycles in dry prairies, flatwoods, and scrubby flatwoods are likely to follow the typical pattern of conserving more nutrients as stands develop (Bormann and Likens, 1979b). Vitousek (1982) noted that stands on nutrient-poor sites typically use nutrients efficiently. It appears that efficient nutrient utilization and closed nutrient cycling are the rule for flatwoods and their associated stands (Gholz et al., 1985a)

Water Effects and Transpiration

The rate of slash pine growth in flatwoods generally increases in proportion to depth to the water table, indicating the inhibitory effect of excessive moisture (Duncan and Terry, 1983). At the other extreme, tree growth can be limited by a lack of available moisture during the dry season (Haines and Gooding, 1983). Pines themselves moderate excessive moisture conditions to a degree, since they can improve drainage through transpiration (Pritchett and Morris, 1982; Duncan and Terry, 1983). In a simulation of the hydrologic cycle of a pine flatwoods, Golkin and Ewel (1984) estimated that pine trees accounted for 83 percent of the ecosystem transpiration of 990 mm/yr. This suggests that markedly less water loss occurs from transpiration in the nearly treeless dry prairies than in pine flatwoods.

Productivity

Golkin and Ewel's (1984) computer simulation model for a north Florida pine flatwoods ecosystem estimated an annual gross primary productivity of 2100 g C m^{-2} yr^{-1}, a community respiration rate of 1300 g C m^{-2} yr^{-1}, and a net community productivity of 860 g C m^{-2} yr^{-1}. The last figure is similar to the average figure for twenty-two pine forests at other latitudes, which had a relatively unproductive mean net primary productivity of 822 g C m^{-2} yr^{-1} (Art and Marks, 1971). A comparison of the gross productivity of several Florida forests suggests that slash pine flatwoods are among the least productive of all forested ecosystems in north Florida (S. Brown, 1981; Golkin and Ewel, 1984).

Gholz and Fisher (1984) argued that the characteristic extremes in soil moisture and limited nutrient availability are responsible for the low productivity of flatwoods ecosystems. It is likely that the accumulation of nutrients in the vegetation and forest floor and the slow rate of decomposition contribute to the low productivity (Gholz and Fisher, 1984; Gholz et al., 1985a). We predict that dry prairies will be found to have markedly lower productivities than flatwoods, given Golkin and Ewel's (1984) finding that understory productivity was only 21 percent of tree productivity in a simulated pine flatwoods ecosystem. Gholz et al. (1985a) have demonstrated that aboveground net primary production as a function of nutrient uptake is relatively efficient in slash pine stands, especially for phosphorus.

Based on studies of managed flatwoods ecosystems, we can conclude that growth and productivity of flatwoods and related associations are strongly limited by both water and nutrient availability. In natural ecosystems, fire was undoubtedly the important mechanism that mineralized nutrients and increased rates of nutrient cycling (Gholz and Fisher, 1984; Gholz et al., 1985a,b).

Successional Relationships and the Role of Fire

Fire, under natural conditions, maintains flatwoods as a stable and essentially nonsuccessional association. However, when the natural frequency or seasonality of fire is altered, flatwoods can succeed to a variety of vegetation types depending on climate, available seed sources, and edaphic conditions (such as soil pH, nutrient availability, and presence or absence of a spodic horizon). Likewise, human modifications to the landscape, such as drainage and logging, can disrupt the stability of flatwoods and initiate succession.

It is dangerous to generalize about successional development for these communities because it occurs primarily as a result of human interference. However, we will attempt to provide insight into some possible outcomes of the interactions of these factors with human intervention.

Fire

Most authors suggest that human alteration of the natural fire frequency is the most common cause of successional change in flatwoods and dry prairies (e.g., Monk, 1968; Richardson, 1977; Peroni and Abrahamson, 1986). Florida has one of the highest frequencies of lightning strikes of any region in the United States (Abrahamson et al., 1984) and more thunderstorm days per year than anywhere else in the country (Wade, 1983). Fire plays a number of roles in flatwoods ecosystems, including reduction of competition from hardwoods; creation of soil conditions suitable for germination of seeds of some species; turnover of litter, humus, and nutrients; and increased vigor of populations of some species (fig. 5.13).

Flatwoods and dry prairies typically burn vigorously and completely (excepting the pines) leaving few unburned patches. The vegetation of both associations has great tolerance to fire, and many species are maintained by its periodic occurrence (Laessle, 1942; Wade, 1983; Abrahamson, 1984a,b). Most species rapidly send up new shoots from underground stems or roots after a burn (Abrahamson, 1984a,b), and many, such as wiregrass and saw palmetto, are highly flammable, thus promoting the spread of the fire. Mutch (1970) suggested that some plant species may possess inherent flammable properties that contribute to the perpetuation of fire-maintained

Fig. 5.13. Forest fire in longleaf pine flatwoods. Photo by C. Mesavage. Forest Service Collection, National Agricultural Library.

plant communities. Mutch's fire facilitation hypothesis states that fire-dependent plant communities burn more readily than communities that are not fire-dependent because natural selection has favored the develpment of characteristics that make the species of fire-dependent communities more flammable. Williamson and Black (1981) examined maximum fire temperatures and tree survival in a Florida sandhill community and concluded that because of litter differences, fire temperatures were sufficiently higher under longleaf pine than under turkey or sand live oaks to ensure elimination of the oaks in the vicinity of adult pines. Platt et al. (1988b) suggested that longleaf pine maintains an environment suitable for its own regeneration by transforming localized disturbances (lightning) into widespread disturbances (ground fires). This fire facilitation creates conditions favorable for longleaf pine but not for other tree species.

Scrubby flatwoods, in contrast to flatwoods and dry prairies, lack easily burned vegetation due to low biomass and patches of bare sand. When fire does occur, it frequently passes through scrubby flatwoods in a spotty manner, leaving a mosaic of lightly burned, intensely burned, and unburned areas (Abrahamson et al., 1984). Strong winds appreciably increase burn coverage and intensity. Even hot fires do little to alter the vegetation pattern, however, because the shrubs readily sprout from underground organs, rapidly restoring the community to its preburn composition (Abrahamson, 1984a,b).

Instead of resprouting, as do many flatwoods species, the pines either resist periodic fires or regenerate from seeds. The pines of flatwoods vary markedly in their tolerance of fire. Longleaf pine, the most resistant, is well known for its ability to tolerate fire even in the seedling "grass" stage (Wade, 1983). Fire is apparently a prerequisite for longleaf pine regeneration, as it creates the necessary mineral surface for germination (Heyward, 1939b). South Florida slash pine, although less fire-tolerant than longleaf pine, also exhibits an appreciable resistance to fire (Ketcham and Bethune, 1963; Abrahamson, 1984b). Typical slash pine and its seedlings, on the other hand, are not particularly fire-resistant (Ketcham and Bethune, 1963). However, fire may nevertheless be important to slash pine regeneration (Hebb and Clewell, 1976). Pond pine, with its closed cones, is dependent on less frequent but more intense fire to release seed and expose mineral soil for seed germination (Edmisten, 1963).

Fire is also important to both grasses and forbs (fig. 5.14). Many authors have reported that frequently burned flatwoods are open and grassy, lacking appreciable oak and saw palmetto cover (Harper, 1914a; Heyward, 1939b; Edmisten, 1963; Moore et al., 1982). Flowering of some herbaceous species can be initiated or enhanced when fire occurs in a particular season (W. J. Platt, personal communication; Platt et al., 1988b). For example, cutthroat grass, beard grasses (*Andropogon* spp.), and wiregrass normally do not flower unless they are burned in spring or summer, and Catesby's lily (*Lilium catesbaei*), yellow bachelor's button, deer tongue (*Carphephorus paniculatus*), and white-topped aster (*Aster tortifolius*) flower more conspicuously following fire (Abrahamson, 1984b).

Several authors have noted that the abundance of some species declines following fire exclusion (Edmisten, 1963; Abrahamson, 1984b). For example, sprouters such as dwarf huckleberry and dwarf blueberry quickly increase in shoot density and dominance after fire by rapid sprouting from existing underground parts (fig. 5.15). Equally dramatic is the rapid decline in density of these dwarf species as they are overtopped by taller species, such as saw palmetto, staggerbush, and gallberry, during intervals without fire (Abrahamson, 1984b). These species exhibit a "sit and wait" strategy, apparently surviving with little aboveground biomass for long periods of time before fire releases them from limitations of nutrients, moisture, and shading (Abrahamson, 1980). In these associations, fire should be viewed as a normal environmental feature that, depending upon its frequency and intensity, creates the particular mixture of species present on a given site.

Fire was probably common before the twentieth century. Originally,

Fig. 5.14. Declines in the frequency of three herbaceous flatwoods plants with degree of protection from fire: (*A*) wiregrass (*Aristida stricta*), (B) deer tongue (*Carphephorus paniculatus*), and (*C*) black root (*Pterocaulon pycnostachyum*). Adapted from Edmisten, 1963.

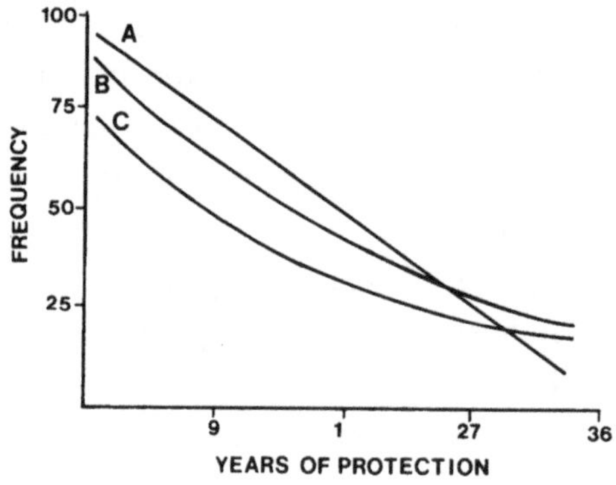

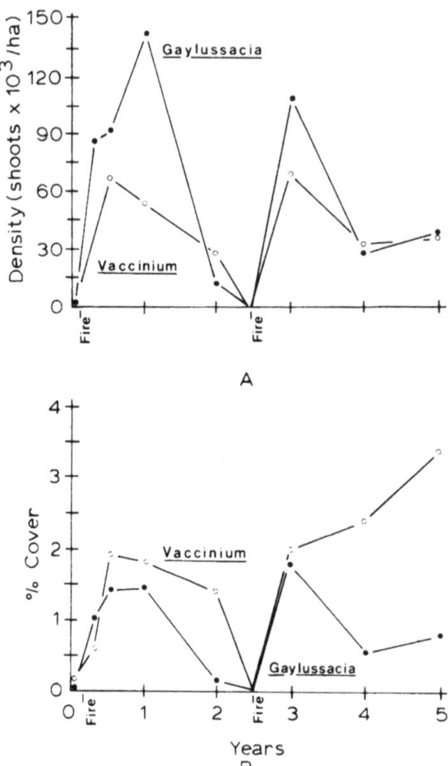

Fig. 5.15. Density (*A*) and percentage cover or dominance (*B*) of *Gaylussacia dumosa* and *Vaccinium myrsinites* at a flatwoods site in a preburn sample and several postburn samples. From Abrahamson, 1984b. Used with permission of the Botanical Society of America.

lightning-originated fires were not limited by human-made barriers, such as roads, cultivated areas, and urban development, and probably burned over extensive areas (Laessle, 1942, Abrahamson, 1984a). In north and central Florida, for example, it is likely that frequent extensive fires prevented slash pine seedlings from colonizing longleaf pine flatwoods, thus controlling composition of these stands (Heyward, 1939b; Laessle, 1942; Edmisten, 1963).

Increased human settlement has drastically altered fire regimes in Florida in at least two ways. First, human-caused fires have created a second fire season during the state's winter dry season, in addition to the natural spring-summer season of lightning-originated fires (Abrahamson, 1984a). Second, land development has limited the area burned per fire, particularly for lightning-originated fires. The result is that undeveloped land probably burns less frequently now than during past centuries (Peroni and Abrahamson, 1986).

The available data suggest that the reduction of frequent, low-intensity fires in flatwoods and dry prairies has had important consequences for the nutrient balances of these associations. Fire consumes much aboveground biomass and litter, appreciably increasing the rate of nutrient turnover. Phosphorus and cations in biomass are mineralized (Gholz et al., 1985b). Fires appreciably increase nutrient cycling rates (especially for phosphorus and molybdenum), raise soil pH, and stimulate nitrogen fixation (Gholz and Fisher, 1984). On the other hand, some loss of nitrogen occurs because of volatilization by fire; the amount varies with fire intensity. Gholz and Fisher (1984) argue that frequent light fires release small pulses of nutrients and volatilize only 20 to 40 percent of the forest floor nitrogen. They note that accumulation from the atmosphere through precipitation alone, even without accounting for the accumulation from biological nitrogen fixation, would replace this loss over a five-year period.

Soil Conditions

Another determinant of successional patterns in flatwoods, dry prairies, and scrubby flatwoods is water availability. Because flatwoods and dry prairies are flat, variation in soil water conditions—in addition to soil texture and chemistry—and the presence or absence of a clay and/or organic hardpan can affect productivity and alter successional development (Laessle, 1942).

Edmisten (1963) noted that successional rates were slower where soil pH was low (3–5) than where pH and soil clay content were higher. Monk (1968) suggested that soil fertility, in addition to soil pH and hydroperiod, was an important determinant of the direction of succession of these associations to different climax communities.

Many authors have noted a close correlation in Florida between soils and vegetation (e.g., Harper, 1914a; Laessle, 1942; Kurz, 1942; Davis, 1943). It is important, however, to recognize the dynamic nature of both soil and vegetation and the interplay between them. Soil characteristics change as vegetation changes, but the two do not necessarily develop contemporaneously (Laessle, 1942). Recent studies of sandhills and scrub clearly indicate that soil characteristics of these associations are determined by the vegetation rather than the reverse (Kalisz and Stone, 1984a). Fire regimes, not soil differences, may account for the particular vegetation association on a given site (Myers, 1985).

Succession

While no change in species composition is expected during a human lifetime under undisturbed conditions, the floras of flatwood and dry prairies can be altered by human modification of the environment. The direction of any successional alteration is influenced by a variety of abiotic factors, but the species involved in the sere (the series of stages of community succession) are determined by the availability of seed sources.

Hardwoods usually invade flatwoods in the absence of fire, but the rate is dependent on seed sources and pine canopy structure. Heyward (1939b), for example, observed that hardwood invasion of naturally burned, dense stands of either longleaf or slash pine is slow until the pine canopy begins to open up. However, rapid hardwood invasion occurred on original-growth pine sites following clear-cutting. At the same time, once established in flatwoods, hardwoods such as myrtle oak are less affected by fire because they respond to it by rapidly resprouting from underground stores of resources.

It seems clear that, regardless of the association, altered fire regimes have brought about major changes in Florida's flatwoods and dry prairies. Further, the rate of change at a given site appears to be appreciably affected by soil moisture relations. Mesic sites tend to change more rapidly than xeric ones. For example, unburned flatwoods adjacent to bayheads, titi swamps, or hardwood swamps have been quickly invaded by species from these stands (Edmisten, 1963; Layne, 1974; Coultas et al., 1979; Peroni and Abrahamson, 1986). Scrubby flatwoods—the most xeric of the associations discussed in this chapter—exhibit slow successional change even over time intervals of fifty or more years (Givens et al., 1984; Peroni and Abrahamson, 1986).

Longleaf pine flatwoods apparently succeed to a southern mixed hardwoods association in the absence of periodic fire (Monk, 1968; H. R. Delcourt and P. A. Delcourt, 1977). The nature of this hardwoods association varies according to moisture conditions. On drier sites, xeric hammocks dominated by live oak and other hardwoods develop (Veno, 1976), while on wetter sites the hardwood composition exhibits a more mesophytic nature (Snedaker and Lugo, 1972).

Slash pine flatwoods can develop in a variety of directions in the absence of fire. Edmisten (1963) suggested that wetter sites with soils of moderately high clay content would tend toward cypress and finally swamp hardwoods, while sites with calcareous soils would develop toward cabbage palm hammocks. Several authors have observed that slash pine flatwoods succeed to mesic southern mixed hardwoods (Monk, 1968; Snedaker and Lugo, 1972) on better drained sites or to bayheads (Monk, 1968; Snedaker and Lugo, 1972; Peroni and Abrahamson, 1986) on more poorly drained sites. The climatic variation from temperate north to subtropical south Florida further complicates these patterns.

Pond pine flatwoods, if unburned, can develop either to bayheads (Monk, 1968) or to mixed hardwood swamps (Edmisten, 1963; Monk, 1968; Snedaker and Lugo, 1972). In fact, some view pond pine flatwoods as burned-out bay swamps, not flatwoods (A. F. Clewell, personal communication).

There has been less speculation about the successional characteristics of dry prairies in the absence of fire. Richardson (1977) suggested that this association will develop to low hammock or pine flatwoods if unburned. In some cases, dry prairies are simply an artifact of previous logging or grazing practices. Steinberg (1980) suggested that the overburning of either scrub or pine flatwoods may create dry prairie. We have a poor understanding of this association, as we have little idea of the conditions that create dry prairies rather than flatwoods in the first place.

Scrubby flatwoods, if unburned, are slow to change (Laessle, 1942; Givens et al., 1984; Abrahamson et al., 1984). However, Laessle (1942) suggested that, given sufficient time, they would develop toward scrub on drier sites or toward xeric live oak hammock and finally mesic hammock on less dry sites. Again our insights are limited for this association, in large part due to the slowness of the changes (Givens et al., 1984).

It is important to bear in mind that along with vegetative changes come alterations of the soil and its moisture relations. As flatwoods develop to hardwood hammocks in the absence of fire, the hardpan—if it exists at all—may break down. Laessle (1942) and others have remarked that broad-leaved associations do not occur on hardpan soils. Hardwoods such as oaks are noted for their ability to penetrate hardpan and increase its permeability (Snedaker and Lugo, 1972). The gradual invasion of bayhead species in poorly drained flatwoods can increase the organic deposits on the soil. This, in turn, can raise the water table in adjacent hardpan flatwoods, leading to the retention of organic matter at the surface rather than its loss to the hardpan. Eventually, these shifts can result in the dissolution of the hardpan and the further invasion of additional flatwoods by bayhead species (Laessle, 1942).

Human Influences and Alterations

Human influence on flatwoods ecosystems dates back at least to the early aborigines, who likely used fire as an important tool in their hunting practices (Bartram, 1791). In the eighteenth and nineteenth centuries and the early part of the twentieth, the leading industries in Florida—lumber, pulpwood, and naval stores—had varying effects on the flatwoods forests (Harper, 1914a). The inherent nutritional poverty, low topographical relief, and resulting poor drainage protected flatwoods from extensive exploitation for agricultural or urban development up until the 1950s. However, with the recent development of improved soil drainage and fertilization methods, flatwoods are now being replaced with truck crops, improved pastures, and citrus. The accelerating population growth and urban development in Florida are resulting in additional losses of flatwoods and alteration of natural fire regimes (Miller et al., 1983; Peroni and Abrahamson, 1985, 1986). Brown and Thompson (1988) report that timberland area in Florida decreased by 4 percent since 1980 while the area in pine plantations increased by 23 percent.

Today, humans are influencing flatwoods ecosystems in two major ways: the destruction of flatwoods for alternative land uses, as described above, and alterations associated with forest and range management practices. The complete destruction of flatwoods has become significant rather recently, within the past few decades, but is expected to increase as urban and agricultural development accelerate. We predict that the most extensive alterations in Florida ecosystems will occur in flatwoods, due to the recently increased protection of the more poorly drained wetland ecosystems coupled with the decreasing availability of upland ecosystems such as sandhill and scrub. Unfortunately, there is a general attitude that, because of their extensive total area in Florida, flatwoods can be exploited with little threat to the future of this ecosystem.

Flatwoods and dry prairies that are not destroyed outright may be altered by forest or rangeland management. Flatwoods are also affected indirectly by human alterations to the surrounding landscape, such as land drainage and alteration of hydrological regimes.

Timber and Pulpwood Production

The pine flatwoods, which make up more than 40 percent of the lower eastern coastal plain, are among the most intensively managed forests in the United States (Swindel et al., 1983). Flatwoods and dry prairies are also the only extensively managed ecosystems in Florida. Thus, the ecological consequences of flatwoods forest management warrant considerable attention.

The different practices used to manage flatwoods sites for timber and pulpwood production vary greatly in the intensity of disturbance and the extent of ecosystem alterations they cause. The primary objectives of these forest management practices are to increase pine seedling establishment, to increase pine growth and total wood yields, and to reduce the abundance of other plant species in favor of the pines (Ball et al., 1979; Moore and Swindel, 1981; Morris, 1981; Swindel et al., 1982) (fig. 5.16). Numerous studies—many sponsored by the Intensive Management Practices Assessment Center (IMPAC) at the University of Florida in Gainesville—have documented some of the effects of different harvesting methods, low- and high-intensity methods of mechanical site preparation, prescribed burning, and other practices on the vegetation, soils, animals, hydrological regimes, and nutrient cycling patterns in flatwoods ecosystems. A discussion of some of these practices and their effects follows.

It should first be noted, however, that our knowledge of the impact of these activities is still limited because most of these are short-term studies.

Fig. 5.16. Fifteen-year-old slash pine plantation. Photo by D. O. Todd. Forest Service Photo Collection, National Agricultural Library.

There is concern that the short-term benefits of some intensive management practices may lead to significant longer-term ecosystem alterations and gradual long-term declines in productivity (Pritchett and Wells, 1978). In addition, the decline in total area of forest land in the Southeast since 1970 is expected to continue (Forest Industries Council, 1980). Therefore, future timber yield increases will be achieved only through more intensive management of the remaining available pine forest lands. As a result, both the loss of existing flatwood forests and greater impact on the remaining flatwoods can be expected if present trends continue.

Prescribed Fire

Following the harvest of mature pines, flatwoods sites are often prepared for pine regeneration by the use of prescribed fires. The objective of this burning is to consume as much surface litter and remaining understory biomass as possible, creating a site easy to plant by machine and removing potential competing vegetation. Burning is also often used in established stands to reduce the potential for hazardous fires in young stands and to control disease and insect pests (Wade, 1983).

Prescribed fires effectively reduce the cover of woody understory species, reduce surface litter cover by as much as 50 percent, and increase the frequency, biomass, and diversity of herbaceous species (Moore and Terry, 1980; Swindel et al., 1982) (fig. 5.17). Although woody species cover is significantly reduced by burning, the species composition generally changes only slightly, and woody species diversity is generally unaffected (Moore et al., 1982; Swindel et al., 1982) (fig. 5.18). Overall, prescribed burning is not appreciably different from the natural disturbance regime and causes little alteration in flatwoods ecosystems.

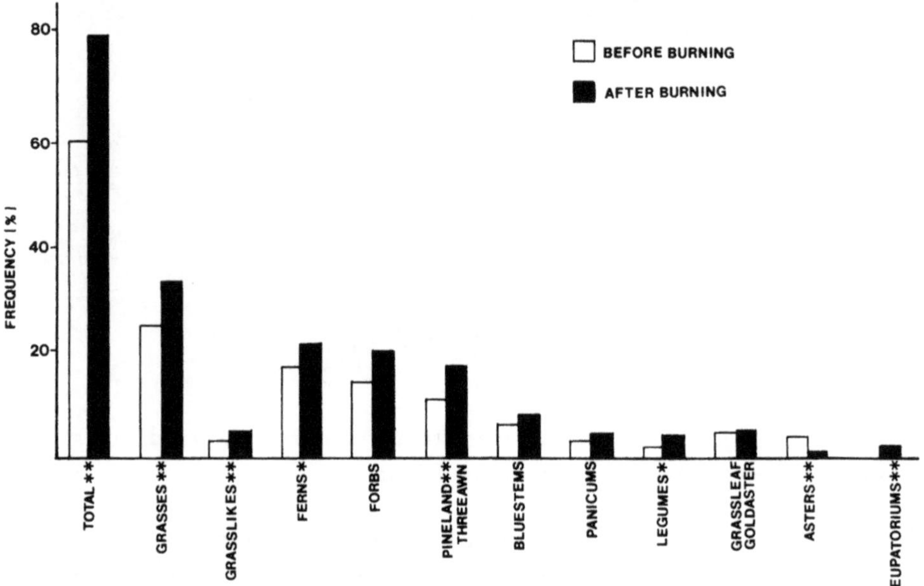

Fig. 5.17. Frequency of herbaceous vegetation before and after prescribed fire in a north Florida flatwoods. Asterisks indicate significant changes: * = p<0.05; ** = p<0.01. From Moore and Terry, 1980.

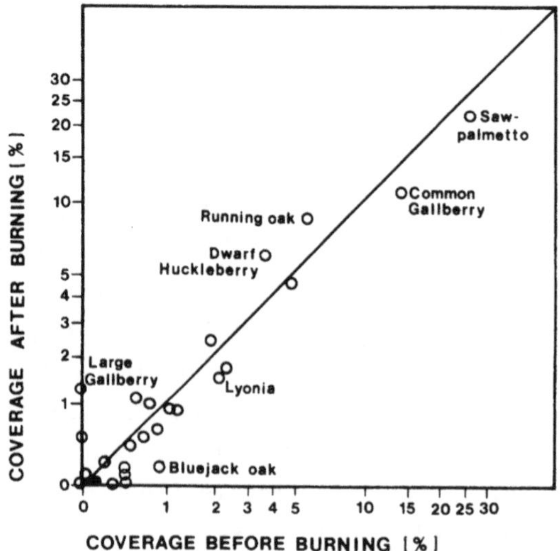

Fig. 5.18. Coverage of woody species below 1.5 m before and after prescribed fire in a north Florida flatwoods. *Plotted straight line* indicates no change. *Open circles* indicate responses of single species; *shaded circles*, more than one species. Named species responded significantly (p<0.01) to burning. From Moore et al., 1982.

Mechanical Site Preparation

Mechanical site preparation methods are almost universally used, with or without fire. Following harvest, residual vegetation is often mechanically chopped to reduce competing vegetation, particularly perennial shrubs, and to increase nutrient availability through increased organic debris decomposition. The site may be bedded with a plow to control spacing and to aid in the early survival of pine seedlings on wet sites by planting on tops of raised beds. Intensive management practices, such as stump removal, windrowing, and harrowing, cause even greater disturbance to both soil and vegetation. These intensive management practices involving the use of heavy equipment to harvest and prepare sites mechanically have a much greater impact than fire and have been accepted practices in southern pine forest management for more than twenty-five years. Approximately 55 percent of all industrially owned forests in the Southeast are prepared by windrowing, 40 percent are chopped, 35 percent are bedded, and 18 percent are disked (Broerman, 1978). Similar site preparation practices are used in dry prairies in south Florida in efforts to establish commercial forests on these sites (Moore and Swindel, 1981).

Effect on Community Structure

Mechanical site preparation methods result in appreciable changes in plant community structure. IMPAC-sponsored studies have shown that chopping appreciably changes woody shrub species composition and relative abundances and may reduce shrub cover by an order of magnitude (Moore and Terry, 1980; Swindel et al., 1982). Herbaceous plant frequencies and species richness increase following chopping. Grasses such as bluestems (*Andropogon* spp.) and panic grasses (*Panicum* spp.) become ubiquitous after site preparation, and other grass-like plants and dicot herbs may increase several-fold (Moore and Terry, 1980; Swindel et al., 1982, 1983). However, the dominant native grass of the flatwoods, wiregrass, decreases significantly in cover and frequency following chopping—an effect opposite that of prescribed burning (Moore and Terry, 1980; Swindel et al., 1982). These differential responses of herbs to mechanical site preparation result in changes in herb species composition and relative abundances. The short-term increase in herb species richness is a result of the addition of undesirable weedy colonizers of disturbed sites that co-occur for a time with the remaining residents, an effect characteristic of many forestry practices and other agents of disturbance. The long-term effects on plant species composition and diversity may be more significant but have not been assessed.

More intensive mechanical site treatment has a quantitatively greater effect on flatwoods, appreciably reducing both woody plant cover and species richness (Swindel et al., 1983). The use of bedding plows in flatwoods introduces environmental heterogeneity by producing distinct microsites such as flats, beds, and furrows. The coverages of different grasses are significantly affected by these microsite differences, resulting in greater spatial variability in the herbaceous vegetation in bedded sites (Schultz and Wilhite, 1975; Ball et al., 1979; Swindel et al., 1982). Shrubs, forbs, and sedges do not appear to respond to these microsite differences. Practices such as stump removal, windrowing, and disking cause greater disturbance and exposure of mineral soil, which in turn cause severe reductions in woody species coverage and richness, and much greater variation in herbaceous species responses (figs. 5.19 and 5.20). Many herb species decrease drastically, while others increase, because of the disturbance and unevenness created by shearing blades and other mechanical equipment (Swindel et al., 1982, 1983). Plant species composition is markedly altered by these activities.

Various management practices have been initiated in dry prairies as well in attempts to establish commercial forests on these sites. In Glades County, dry prairie sites have been managed for the establishment of commercial stands of *Eucalyptus* spp., a genus that may potentially produce high pulpwood yields (Moore and Swindel, 1981). However, *Eucalyptus* is highly sensitive to the effects of competing vegetation and therefore requires the intensive site preparation techniques that have a greater impact on the ecosystem. Mechanical site preparation in dry prairies has been shown to eliminate shrubs, increase herb production (except when bedding is employed), and greatly alter the herb species composition (Swindel et al., 1982).

In summary, the IMPAC-sponsored research, as well as other studies, shows that, for those practices that stop short of significant litter and mineral soil displacement, the woody component of the flatwoods vegetation decreases and the herbaceous species abundances increase in proportion to the intensity of disturbance. Mechanical site preparation methods cause greater vegetation changes than prescribed burning. The effects of these two management approaches are similar in that they both generally increase herb abundance and decrease woody plant abundance, but they are qualitatively different in that they result in very different patterns of species composition and relative abundances. Practices that displace litter and mineral soil, such as windrowing and disking, may potentially eliminate some species, allow the establishment of numerous weed species, and significantly alter species composition and vegetation structure. In addition, the season of the year when flatwoods sites are prepared also affects the species composition of the understory; fewer woody species are killed when sites are prepared in winter than in summer (Lewis, 1972).

Effect on Soils, Nutrient Cycling, and Hydrology

Commercial forest management practices also influence the soils, nutrient cycling, and hydrology in flatwoods ecosystems. Because of the flat topog-

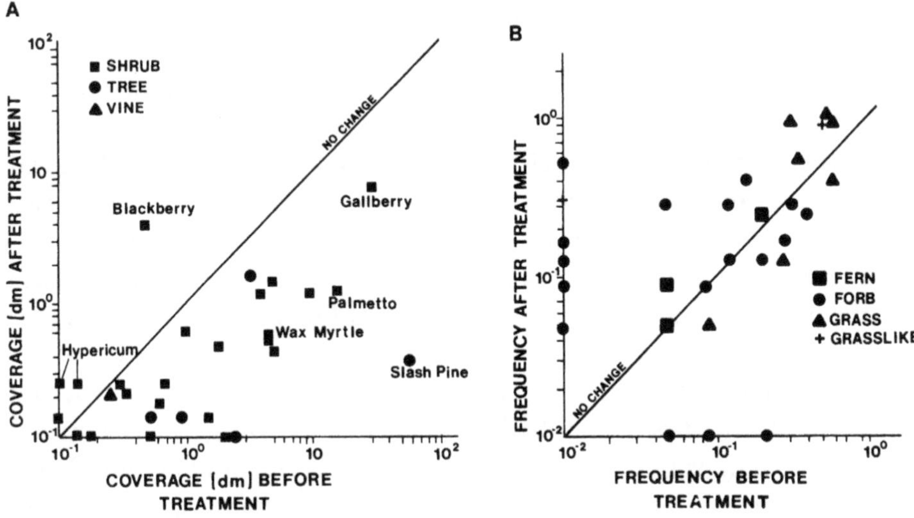

Fig. 5.19. *A*. Crown cover of woody species before and after clear-cutting, chopping, and bedding in a north Florida flatwoods. *B*. Frequency of herbaceous vegetation before and after clear-cutting, chopping, and bedding in a north Florida flatwoods. From Swindel et al., 1982.

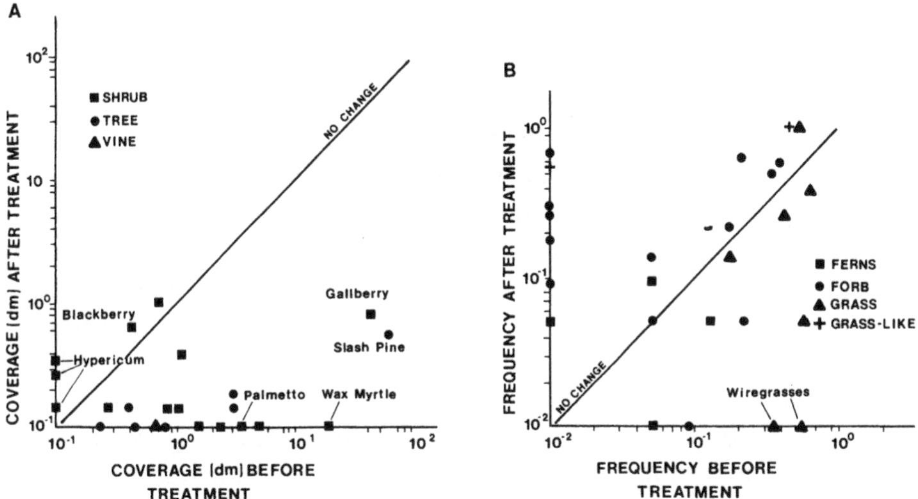

Fig. 5.20. *A*. Crown cover of woody species before and after clear-cutting, stump removal, burning, windrowing, disking, and bedding in a north Florida flatwoods. *B*. Frequency of herbaceous vegetation before and after clear-cutting, stump removal, burning, windrowing, disking, and bedding in a north Florida flatwoods. From Swindel et al., 1982.

raphy and sandy soils, soil loss from managed flatwoods is generally negligible regardless of the intensity of site treatment (Riekerk et al., 1980; Swindel et al., 1983). However, practices such as windrowing cause substantial soil and nutrient relocation, resulting in effective nutrient losses from local sites (Morris, 1981; Pritchett and Morris, 1982). Because flatwoods soils have few weatherable minerals to replace those removed, these losses can contribute to gradually declining productivity (White and Harvey, 1979; Pritchett, 1981). In general, these forest management practices alter physical, chemical, and biological properties directly through soil disturbance.

The harvest and removal of pines also result in nutrient removal from flatwoods ecosystems (Morris, 1981; Pritchett and Morris, 1982). Removal of whole trees removes two to four times as many nutrients per unit biomass as does stemwood and bark removal, owing to the greater concentrations of nutrients in foliage and branches. Removal of whole trees also takes away the mulching and nutrient input potential of decaying branches and foliage. The loss of canopy vegetation by harvesting and the reduction in understory vegetation by site preparation alter nutrient dynamics by reducing total litterfall—needles, wood, bark, and understory foliage—and nutrient return via decomposition (Perry, 1983). The displacement of organic debris by windrowing not only removes nutrients from the planting area but also disturbs the forest floor and increases biological activity, thus increasing potential leaching and runoff losses. Bedding creates heterogeneity, resulting in significantly lower concentrations of many nutrients on furrows and flats relative to the adjacent beds (Morris, 1981). These nutrient losses may result in gradual declines in productivity of flatwoods forests over long periods, although stem-only harvests appear not to threaten productivity (Morris, 1981; Pritchett and Morris, 1982; Gholz and Fisher, 1982).

Atmospheric inputs may balance some of these nutrient losses. With the exception of calcium, estimated nutrient additions from precipitation exceed estimated losses associated with harvests that remove pulpwood only (table 5.1). This suggests that some pulpwood harvesting practices are within the resiliency range of the flatwoods ecosystem and some are not, at least with respect to the cycling of limited nutrients (Pritchett, 1981; Swindel et al., 1983). Some of these potential nutrient losses may also be mitigated as a result of uptake by the increasing understory growth over several years following disturbance (Ewel and Golkin, 1982).

Forest management practices also alter hydrological cycling in flatwoods ecosystems. Harvesting and site preparation cause short-term (two- to

Table 5.1. Nutrient balances (kg/ha/25 yrs.) for a 25-year rotation managed flatwoods forest

Nutrient	N	P	K	Ca	Mg
Rainfall input	162.9	21.8	46.2	99.2	61.9
Runoff—years 1–3	3.2	0.1	1.9	2.9	2.9
Runoff—years 4–25	33.1	1.4	7.1	57.3	40.6
Pulpwood export	52.5	10.0	15.0	65.0	11.9
Net balance	+74.1	+10.3	+21.5	−25.2	+6.5

Source: Swindel et al. (1983).

three-year) increases in water runoff that vary directly with the intensity of site treatment (Ewel and Golkin, 1982; Swindel et al., 1983; Pritchett and Morris, 1982; Riekerk et al., 1980). Areas with wet or fine-textured soils are exceptions and can experience longer-term water losses (Pritchett and Morris, 1982). The increases in water runoff in managed flatwoods are similar in magnitude to, but much shorter in duration than, the runoff increases in more northern forest ecosystems; this is most likely a result of the more rapid revegetation in southern pine forests.

These patterns of water loss in flatwoods ecosystems are caused by alterations in several processes. Harvesting pines reduces both canopy interception and transpirational water losses, resulting in a higher water table and increased surface soil moisture (Bastos and Smith, 1979). Consequently water tables are often near or at the surface, and surface flow may be appreciable during wet periods. Pritchett and Morris (1982) showed that surface soil moisture was greater in less intensively managed flatwoods than in more intensively managed sites. They suggested that the mulching effect of residual slash and litter conserved surface soil moisture. Although water loss from flatwoods is dominated by runoff for the first few years following site disturbance, evapotranspiration becomes increasingly important as vegetation grows back (Ewel and Golkin, 1982).

Increased water runoff in managed flatwoods accounts for some of the observed losses of nutrients (especially cations) and suspended sediments (Ewel and Golkin, 1982; Swindel et al., 1983). In general, water quality in flatwoods watershed streams is positively correlated with the proportion of the landscape in undisturbed forest and inversely correlated with the intensity of forest site management (Hollis et al., 1978; Fisher, 1982).

Effect on Microclimate

In addition to the direct effects already outlined, forest management practices alter soils, vegetation, and animal life indirectly through microclimate changes. Varying intensities of disturbance in flatwoods ecosystems result in differing degrees of alteration in light, temperature, moisture, and wind speeds on a local scale.

The most pronounced microclimate changes associated with site preparation are increases in soil temperatures and soil moisture content (Schultz, 1976; Bastos and Smith, 1979; Pritchett and Morris, 1982). The warmer and wetter conditions on intensively managed sites cause increased biological activity in the soil, contributing to a flushing of nutrients.

In undisturbed flatwoods, as in other forested ecosystems, the canopy vegetation attenuates incoming solar radiation during the day and minimizes reradiation at night, which tends to prevent high diurnal temperature fluctuations at the ground surface. Harvesting and site preparation in flatwoods likely result in much greater incident radiation reaching ground level, much greater nighttime reradiation, and subsequent high temperature fluctuations. The total ground area affected is probably directly related to the intensity of management practices and vegetation and soil disturbance.

The practice of bedding flatwoods sites, as described earlier, alters microtopography and creates distinct microsites that differ in light, soil moisture, soil temperatures, and other microclimatic characteristics. The localized difference in herb species responses on bedded flatwoods sites is most likely a result of these differences.

Microclimatic alterations may influence plant germination, seedling establishment, growth, and dispersal of the understory species and may affect organic matter decomposition, nutrient release, soil metabolic activity, microbial populations, and insect activity. The last two effects are economically and ecologically important because insects and disease are major sources of damage to pine stands (Balmer and Mobley, 1983). Only a few of the indirect effects of microclimatic alterations on managed stands of flatwoods have been studied.

Effect on Animals

Animal populations respond to direct and indirect effects of forest management practices. Both food supply and habitat structural diversity are important determinants of the quality of sites for animal populations, and forest management practices significantly alter both of these. In addition to the alterations in plant species composition discussed above, various management practices, such as harvesting, prescribed burning, and stand thinning, determine vegetation architecture and hence overall habitat structural diversity (Buckner, 1983).

Many of the grasses and forbs of the pine flatwoods and dry prairies are major food sources for numerous small mammals, birds, and reptiles, such as *Gopherus* and *Terrapene*. Thus, changes in vegetation composition or abundance may influence animal populations. For example, the alterations in herb composition and production associated with mechanical site preparation of dry prairies result in large increases in bobwhite food plants and cattle forage species, but also result in decreases in wiregrass cover, which is important for bobwhite nesting (Moore and Swindel, 1981).

Forest management creates altered habitat conditions that are beneficial to some animal species and detrimental to others. Harvesting and site preparation create "open habitats" where rapid vegetation regrowth occurs—conditions favorable for deer, rabbits, small rodents such as cotton rats, and various birds (Perkins, 1974). However, these conditions are detrimental to canopy dwellers, cavity nesters, and other late-successional forest species. Species such as red-cockaded woodpeckers and others with specific habitat requirements experience drastic population reductions following the harvesting of old-growth forests. Rowse (1980) found that approximately 30 percent of avian species in a north Florida flatwoods forest were cavity nesters, species whose nesting habitat is eliminated by harvesting and plantation management.

Marion and O'Meara (1982) found that managed flatwoods in Bradford County, Florida, had low avian densities and species richness in spring and summer but high densities in winter due to migratory winter residents. Cypress and edge habitats supported the greatest diversity and densities of birds, and the cypress domes associated with flatwoods were important refugia for bird species following harvesting of the flatwoods stands. The creation of more extensive forest edge habitats results in increasing abundances of birds such as meadowlarks, wintering robins (*Turdus migratorius*), wintering red-winged blackbirds (*Agelaius phoeniceus*), and sparrows. However, all three vegetation strata (trees, shrubs, and herbs) are used by birds in the interior of flatwoods stands (Marion and O'Meara, 1982) and the reduction or removal of different strata reduces available avian habitat. Minimizing effects of flatwoods management practices on avian populations requires that some understory herb and shrub vegetation be left intact to maintain structural diversity and that adjacent cypress domes be left intact as refugia.

Monitoring of small mammal populations in flatwoods revealed generally low densities both before and after harvesting and site preparation (Marion and O'Meara, 1982). Herpetofauna populations are significantly reduced in flatwoods subjected to clear-cutting and intensive site disturbance, but low intensity site preparation techniques do not appear significantly to alter herptile abundances (Marion and O'Meara, 1982).

The management of flatwood stands typically creates a regional mosaic of cut, regenerating, and mature stands. Because of these vegetational changes and various animal food preferences, the abundances of certain grazer and browser populations, such as white-tailed deer, and the utilization of sites by animals vary with stand age (Skoog and Harris, 1981).

Grazing

The management of flatwoods and dry prairies for domestic livestock and the activity of grazers themselves result in various alterations in soil properties and vegetation structure. Management practices have the objective of reducing the abundance of shrub species such as gallberry and saw palmetto in favor of grasses and other forage plants (Ball et al., 1979) (fig. 5.21).

The original European settlers in Florida were interested primarily in agriculture and cattle, rather than forestry, and fire was their primary management tool (Wade, 1983). Prescribed burning is still the most commonly used method for rangeland management. Prescribed burns are conducted in late winter or early spring to stimulate growth and increase the nutrient content of grasses and forbs, reduce shrub coverage, and increase accessibility

Fig. 5.21. Cattle have grazed Florida's flatwoods for several centuries. Photo from Forest Service Photo Collection, National Agricultural Library.

to forage plants (Wahlenberg et al., 1939; Lemon, 1949; Hilmon and Lewis, 1962; Lewis and Hart, 1972). In the past, the herbicide 2,4,5-t was used to control woody vegetation in grazed flatwoods (Burton and Hughes, 1961).

In a comparative study of the effects of burning and grazing on longleaf pine forests, Duvall and Linnartz (1967) found that the long-term effects of prescribed burning were small relative to the effects of grazers themselves. They found that grazing resulted in increased grass production, changes in floristic composition that varied with the intensity of grazing and with annual precipitation, and decreases in herb production in dry sites. Grazers also caused soil compaction and reduced water infiltration and percolation, but these effects were less pronounced on drier sites where soils are inherently well drained (Duvall and Linnartz, 1967). Campbell (1957) has shown that the soil compaction and trampling associated with heavy grazing also reduce the growth and survival of pine seedlings and thus impair regeneration of pine stands.

Naval Stores Production

Slash and longleaf pine are utilized not only for lumber and pulpwood but also as sources of rosin, turpentine, and other products produced from the gum (sap) of the trees (fig. 5.22). The term *naval stores* originated in the early 1600s when pine tar and pitch were used to caulk seams in the planking and to preserve the ropes of wooden ships. The pine forests of the southeastern United States have been the center of this industry since its early days; slash and longleaf pines are the only gum naval stores species in the United States (McReynolds, 1983). During the early years, the Southeast produced 75 percent of the world's supply of naval stores products (Squillace et al., 1972).

The early naval stores operations extracted gum from mature pines by

Fig. 5.22. Collecting gum and loading barrels for hauling to a turpentine still, Florida National Forest. Date unknown. Photo from Florida State Archives.

periodic wounding and then separated the turpentine from rosin by heating and distillation. After a few years, the trees were sold for timber, pulpwood, or other products.

Today naval stores products are produced by three different methods (Stubbs, 1983). *Gum naval stores* are produced by tapping living pines and collecting resin. *Wood naval stores* are derived from oleoresin obtained by solvent extraction from the stumps of old-growth pines. *Sulfate naval stores* are produced as by-products of the pulping process (Stubbs, 1983). (The pulping process accounts for 73 percent of the current national production of naval stores products.) These pine derivatives are used in the manufacture of paints, varnishes, paper sizing, adhesives, inks, coatings, and other products.

A number of practices associated with naval stores operations influence the flatwoods ecosystems. Like management for timber production, site management for naval stores involves various methods of shrub control, with similar effects on vegetation structure. These woody species compete with pines and also interfere with accessibility and with turpentining operations (Burton and Hughes, 1961). Wounding trees for gum collection weakens them and increases their susceptibility to other sources of mortality, such as fire damage, insect attack, or windthrow. Slash pine is more prone to windthrow than longleaf pine since it often grows on shallow, wet soils

(Balmer and Mobley, 1983). Mechanical equipment such as bark hacks and transportation carts disturb the understory. Because trees with large diameters and crowns are the most desirable for gum production, planting is done at relatively low densities, and stands are thinned; both of these practices alter the canopy vegetation structure.

Other practices associated with the naval stores industry are application of insecticides to wounded trees and application of the herbicide paraquat to bole wood to induce lighterwood formation (resin soaking) within the tree trunk while it continues to grow (Stubbs, 1983). The latter practice may have important effects on the soil, water, and vegetation of the flatwoods ecosystem since paraquat adheres very strongly to soil colloids, wood, and other organic material. The ecological consequences of many of these management practices have not been studied.

Summary

The pine flatwoods and dry prairies constitute the most extensive type of terrestrial ecosystem in Florida. They are characterized by low, flat topography; relatively poorly drained and nutrient-poor, acidic, sandy soils; and an open woodland vegetation with a pine overstory and a variable shrub and herb layer. The dominant pines—*Pinus palustris, P. elliottii* var. *elliottii, P. elliottii* var. *densa*, and *P. serotina*—occur either in pure stands or in various combinations. Common shrubs include saw palmetto, gallberry, fetterbush, staggerbush, dwarf huckleberry, wax myrtle, dwarf live oak, and tarflower. The physiognomy is variable; sites with a history of frequent fires typically have more widely spaced trees, a sparser shrub layer, and a greater cover of herbaceous vegetation than do sites in which fire has been suppressed. Single stands may cover large areas, forming an extensive matrix interspersed with small stands of other forest types such as bayheads, cypress heads, hammocks, sandhill, or scrub.

Although community structure varies among flatwoods associations, several distinct vegetative categories can be recognized, including various pine flatwoods phases, cabbage palm flatwoods, dry prairies, and scrubby flatwoods. Seasonal precipitation, temperature, topography, elevation, drainage pattern, soil type, fire regime, and history of human influence all affect the distribution of these variations on the flatwoods theme.

The flatwoods ecosystem has been influenced by humans at least since the early aborigines included burning in their hunting practices. Attempts at agriculture, the introduction of domestic animals, land clearing and harvest of virgin pine stands, fire suppression, conversion to alternative land uses associated with population growth, and urban development have altered flatwoods in varying ways, such that probably only a few present stands reflect the natural or presettlement conditions.

Today, humans are changing the flatwoods and dry prairie ecosystems in two major ways: the destruction of stands in favor of alternative land uses such as crops, improved pastures, and urban development, and the alteration of various ecosystem and community characteristics by management practices associated with timber, pulpwood, and cattle production. The prognosis for these ecosystems depends primarily on the degree to which these trends and practices are continued or modified. As a result of the minimal available area of remaining upland ecosystems and the recently increased protection of more poorly drained wetland ecosystems, increasing urban and agricultural development will likely come at the expense of the flatwoods and dry prairies. In addition, because of the decreasing total area of southeastern forest lands, continued timber and pulpwood productivity depends on increased yields of individual stands, which will continue to demand more intensive management and will result in more extensive impacts on these ecosystems. As a result of all these factors, we predict that, if present trends continue, the most extensive future alterations and declines in natural Florida ecosystems will occur in the flatwoods and dry prairies.

6
Scrub and High Pine

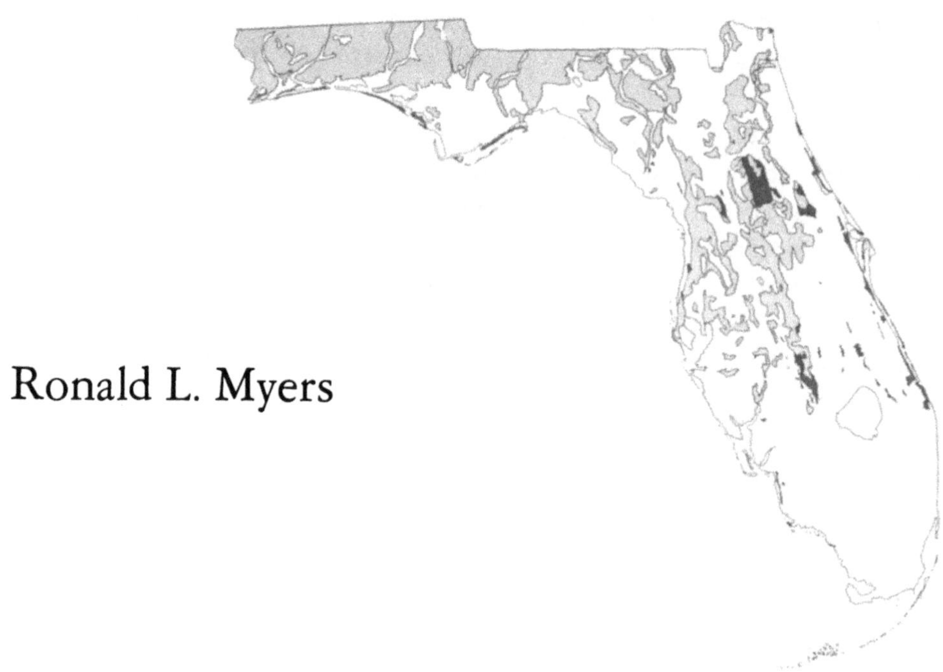

Ronald L. Myers

> The Florida scrub was unique. . . . There was perhaps no similar region anywhere. . . . The soil was a tawny sand, from whose parched infertility there reared, indifferent to water, so dense a growth of scrub pine . . . that the effect of the massed thin trunks was of a limitless, canopied stockade. . . . Wide areas, indeed, admitted of no human passage. . . . A random patch of moisture produced, alien in the dryness, a fine stand of slash pine or long-leaf yellow. These were known as pine islands. To any one standing on a rise, they were visible from a great distance. (Marjorie Kinnan Rawlings, *South Moon Under*)

As well as any scientific definition, Marjorie Kinnan Rawlings's literary description of the lands between the Oklawaha and St. John's rivers—isolated pine islands within a sea of scrub—sets the stage for a discussion of these two contrasting upland ecosystems. Florida scrub is, indeed, unique. Similar habitats composed of many of the same species occur in Georgia (Wharton, 1978), South Carolina (Florida Natural Areas Inventory, 1988),

Map: *black areas* are scrub, *gray areas* are high pine.

and Mississippi (Richmond, 1962); Alabama lays claim to a minuscule piece of truly Floridian sand pine scrub (Harper, 1943). However, nothing elsewhere quite compares to Florida's mature forests of tall, twisted, leaning sand pines (*Pinus clausa*) rising above an impenetrable mass of evergreen scrub oaks; rusty lyonia; rosemary; unusual varieties of holly, bay; and hickory; and an array of inconspicuous species, many with restricted distributions (fig. 6.1).

Scrub, like many of Florida's ecosystems, is pyrogenic—that is, its flora and fauna have developed adaptations to fire. Scrub is maintained by high-intensity fires that recur infrequently, perhaps once every 10 or even 100 years, depending on fuel accumulation and chance ignitions. Much of the variability found among scrubs is a reflection of the varied periodicity of these fires.

Early travelers considered scrub formidable and useless. In describing a traverse of the Big Scrub in north-central Florida in 1822, Simmons wrote that "nothing could be more sterile than the soil; and these tracts are, in fact, concealed deserts, as they are too poor to admit of cultivation, and af-

Fig. 6.1. Sand pine scrub near Carabelle, Franklin County.

ford nothing that is fit, even for the browsing of cattle. The growth upon these places, from its tough and stunted character, forms a complete live fence, which, probably, would never have been penetrated through, but by the Indians, who made the present trail, for the purpose of hunting bear." Even Herman Kurz (1942), one of the original advocates of the biological importance and value of scrub and related dune vegetation, erroneously predicted that "a special plea for the conservation of scrubs seems superfluous. Remoteness from and disrelation to salt water surf as well as undesirability for cultivation constitutes ample protection." Today, unfortunately, scrubs are disappearing at an alarming rate. Some have been converted to citrus groves, but most are falling prey to housing developments, golf courses, and urban encroachment in general.

The pine islands mentioned by Rawlings contrast markedly with the scrub (fig. 6.2). Open and airy, they are inviting and delightful places to explore. Although small pine islands in a sea of scrub were typical of the Ocala area scrubs that Rawlings wrote about, the usual pattern in the state was the converse: islands of scrub in extensive seas of open pinelands. These pinelands, known as high pine, consisted of a rolling park-like woodland of stately longleaf pines (*Pinus palustris*) rising above a continuous cover of wiregrass (*Aristida stricta*) and other grasses and forbs. Interspersed among the pines were occasional clumps, thickets, or scattered individuals of deciduous oaks, most frequently turkey oak (*Quercus laevis*).

Like scrub, high pine is pyric, or fire-controlled. In contrast, high pine requires frequent, low-intensity surface fires that recur every one to ten years, occasionally less often. The abundance and stature of the deciduous oaks may be proportional to the mean length of the fire-return interval: the longer the interval, the more prevalent the oaks.

To Florida's early naturalists the high pine lands, along with the flat-

Fig. 6.2. A high pine landscape reminiscent of pristine conditions, Riverside Island, Ocala National Forest. Wiregrass has bloomed in response to a growing-season burn.

woods, were known collectively as the pine barrens (Romans, 1775). The term *high pine* referred to the hilly portions of the barrens rather than to the stature of the pines themselves. They were also described in early reports as "undulating pine lands" (Vignoles, 1823), "rolling pine lands" (Smith, 1884), and, in the northern Panhandle, "long-leaf pine ridge lands" (Smith, 1884). Xeric sand ridges supporting high pine acquired the name *sandhills*, and the entire community on them is referred to by the same term. More mesic ridges, particularly in the Panhandle, are known to some as *clayhills* (Means and Campbell, 1982; Wolfe et al., 1988).

High pine grades into longleaf pine flatwoods, and many species are common to both. High pine occupies rolling uplands and sand ridges as opposed to the level Pleistocene marine terraces of the flatwoods. Thus, it occurs on well-drained, even droughty soils, rather than substrates characterized by a high water table. High pine possesses diagnostic species, such as the deciduous oaks, that are not found in flatwoods while lacking some typical flatwoods species, such as gallberry (*Ilex glabra*) and fetterbush (*Lyonia lucida*)

Unlike scrub, high pine is not restricted to Florida. Once stretching almost unbroken from Virginia to east Texas, it represented the largest forest type of the southeastern coastal plain (Greene, 1931; Chapman, 1932a; Wahlenberg, 1946; Christensen, 1988, Frost et al., 1986). Whereas passage through scrub was considered formidable, high pine posed few impediments to travel, and the mule-drawn wagons of early European settlers passed with ease through these open forests. The impressive yet monotonous character of high pine was described by Hall (1829): "For five hundred miles, at least, we travelled, in different parts of the South, over a country almost everywhere consisting of sand, feebly held together by a short wiry grass, shaded by the endless forest. I don't know exactly what was the cause, but it was a long time before I got quite tired of the scenery of these pine barrens. There was something, I thought, very graceful in the millions upon millions of tall and slender columns, growing up in solitude, not crowded upon one another, but gradually appearing to come closer and closer, till they formed a compact mass, beyond which nothing was to be seen."

The contemporary disappearance of much of Florida's scrub was heralded more than a century ago by changes taking place in the high pine that have reduced its area by more than 90 percent and in most cases left it highly degraded and fragmented. Little that fits Hall's description exists today in Florida. Scant relics occur elsewhere.

High pine and scrub are so markedly different in general aspect, physiognomy, species composition, fire dynamics, and land use history (see table 6.1) that one may wonder why they are included here in the same chapter. They are closely linked ecologically and historically, however, as well as in other ways. First, both occur on droughty, infertile, upland sites. Second, characteristics of the soils of both ecosystems overlap considerably; in many

Table 6.1. General features of scrub and high pine

	Scrub	High pineland
Pines	*Pinus clausa* (Sand pine)	*Pinus palustris* (Longleaf pine)
Hardwoods	*Quercus myrtifolia* (Myrtle oak)	*Quercus laevis* (Turkey oak)
	Q. geminata (Sand live oak)	*Q. incana* (Bluejack oak)
	Q. chapmanii (Chapman's oak)	*Q. falcata* (Southern red oak)
	Lyonia ferruginea (Rusty lyonia)	*Q. margaretta* (Sand post oak)
	Ceratiola ericoides (Rosemary)	*Q. marilandica* (Blackjack oak)
	Persea humilis (Silk bay)	
Hardwood foliage	Evergreen or persistent	Deciduous
Herbs	Sparse	Abundant
Ground cover	Litter, lichens, bare sand	Grasses, forbs
Aspect	Dense thicket	Open woodland
Fire frequency	Infrequent (15–100 years)	Frequent (1–15 years)
Fire intensity	High	Low
Surface soils	White or light-colored sands	Yellow, buff, or gray sands

Source: Adapted from Kurz (1942).

cases the soils of scrub and high pine, most notably those of xeric sandhills, are derived from the same parent material (Kalisz and Stone, 1984b). Third, both are fire-maintained and fire-dependent ecosystems that are presumably replaced by mixed hardwood forests in the absence of fire (Laessle, 1942, 1958a; Monk, 1968; Veno, 1976; Myers, 1985). Fourth, the integrity of scrub within a natural landscape mosaic probably depends on fires originating in other, more easily ignited, vegetation, particularly high pine. Fifth, at locations where they are contiguous, any extended change in the frequency of fire in one causes a gradual shift to the other (Kalisz and Stone, 1984a; Myers, 1985).

Early naturalists seldom described one of the two ecosystems without mentioning the other. They noted the structural and compositional dissimilarities between the two and puzzled over the close association and abrupt boundary separating them (Nash, 1895; Whitney, 1898; Harper, 1921). Later, a controversy developed over the successional relationship of scrub and high pine: high pine succeeded to scrub (Kurz, 1942); scrub succeeded to high pine (Miller, 1950); or there was no successional relationship between the two (Laessle, 1958a, 1968; Monk, 1968). The question was finally laid to rest as the roles of fire, soils, and allelopathy in the maintenance of the two ecosystems were recognized and better understood (Laessle, 1968; Kalisz and Stone, 1984b; Myers, 1985; Richardson, 1985).

Scrub

In general terms, scrub is a xeromorphic shrub community dominated by a layer of evergreen, or nearly evergreen, oaks (*Quercus geminata, Q. myrti-*

folia, Q. inopina, Q. chapmanii) or Florida rosemary (*Ceratiola ericoides*), or both, with or without a pine overstory, occupying well-drained, infertile, sandy soils. As treated here, it encompasses the following commonly used names: sand pine scrub, oak scrub, rosemary scrub, slash pine scrub, and, in some cases, coastal scrub and scrubby flatwoods. Because this definition of scrub is not limited to sand pine scrub communities, the range of scrub ecosystems extends well beyond the boundaries of Florida. Georgia's "evergreen scrub forest" and "dune oak scrub" (Wharton, 1978), for example, are indistinguishable from the oak/rosemary scrubs found in Florida.

Origin and Distribution

Antecedents of scrub probably appeared during the early Tertiary as part of the sclerophyllous and microphyllous Madro-Tertiary geoflora, which originated in the southern Rocky Mountains and northern Mexico and spread along the Gulf coast to Florida (Axelrod, 1958). Thus, today's scrub is a remnant of an old and formerly extensive ecosystem.

In the late Pleistocene (44,000–10,000 YBP), when Florida's climate was cooler and drier than it is today, scrub-like vegetation was probably widespread in the peninsula. During the latter part of the epoch this vegetation changed from predominantly rosemary scrubs to oak savannas and then to sand pine scrubs (Watts, 1975, 1980; Delcourt and Delcourt, 1983; Watts and Hansen, 1988). Concurrently, the Gulf coast of the United States underwent a succession from oak savanna to oak-hickory-pine lands to southern pine forests (Delcourt and Delcourt, 1983). Throughout these changes, scrub vegetation probably persisted on droughtier soils and on coastal dune ridges of the Florida Panhandle. Contraction of the scrub ecosystem's range likely occurred during the past 5,000–7,000 years as the climate became more moist. Water levels rose, conditions favoring electrical storms developed, and lightning fires, coupled with burning by early human inhabitants, gradually changed the landscape.

The recent distribution of scrub reflects the interplay of soil factors, fire, physiography, landscape patterns, and characteristics of scrub vegetation. Present-day stabilized coastal dunes are composed of essentially the same species found in scrub: Florida rosemary, sand live oak, Chapman's oak, myrtle oak, saw palmetto, sand pine, and so forth. This fact suggests that many of the inland scrubs have probably persisted on fossil dune systems since the early Pleistocene (Laessle, 1968).

A general map of scrub distribution (fig. 6.3) shows three major groupings of the ecosystem in Florida: inland peninsula, coastal peninsula, and coastal Panhandle.

The major concentrations of inland peninsular scrubs occur along a complex of sand ridges and ancient dune fields running north-south from Clay and Putnam counties to Highlands County. These sand ridges, which were derived from a variety of aeolian, alluvial, and marine deposits dating from

Fig. 6.3. General distribution of scrub in Florida with important scrub sites mentioned in the text. Adapted from Davis, 1967.

the Miocene through the early Pleistocene, make up the Florida Central Ridge. During the Pliocene, the highest crests of this ridge system—exemplified by Iron Mountain and Red Hill on the Lake Wales Ridge—formed an archipelago in a shallow sea.

The largest blocks of scrub are inland scrubs. Much of the largest, the Big Scrub complex, lies in and around Ocala National Forest. The southern end of the Lake Wales Ridge in Polk and Highlands counties supported another large expanse of scrub that occurred in a mosaic with xeric high pine. More than 70 percent of the southern Lake Wales Ridge xeric uplands has been lost to citrus cultivation and residential development in the past forty years (Peroni and Abrahamson, 1986). Much of the rest of the central ridge has suffered the same fate.

Peninsular coastal scrubs are found on both the Atlantic and Gulf coasts, occupying the dune systems associated with the two most recent Pleistocene shorelines: the Pamlico and the Silver Bluff. The northernmost examples of these scrubs occur on the east coast in St. John's County near Durbin and on the west coast in Levy County near Cedar Key. The southernmost scrubs were once found on the west coast at Marco Island in Collier County and on the east coast in northern Broward County, but these have been largely lost to development and will soon be extirpated.

Panhandle scrubs are restricted to a narrow strip along the Gulf coast and on barrier islands. They occur not only on the Pamlico and Silver Bluff dune systems but also on dune fields and barrier islands of recent origin (fig. 6.4). They extend from just west of the Ochlockonee River in Franklin County, Florida, to Gulf Bay State Park in Baldwin County, Alabama.

Soils

Practically all scrub soils are entisols (soils with little or no horizon development) that fall under the classification of Quartzipsamments, which are entisols derived from quartz sand. Regardless of their geologic origin, soils supporting scrub vegetation are excessively well drained, siliceous sands practically devoid of silt, clay, and organic matter and thus low in nutrients. Although they represent some of the droughtiest, least fertile soils in the state, scrub soils are by no means uniform. They range from the pure white, excessively leached St. Lucie series (Watts and Stankey, 1980) to moderately leached soils that have a yellowish sandy subsoil, such as the Paola and Orsino series, to the unleached brownish, grayish, or yellowish soils of the Astatula and Tavares series (Thomas et al., 1979).

For years the conventional wisdom maintained that white sand soils supported scrub and darker, yellowish sands supported xeric high pine or sandhill vegetation (Laessle, 1942, 1958a; Monk, 1968). The white sands

Fig. 6.4. Coastal scrub in Franklin County.

were considered to be of Pleistocene origin, having been washed and sorted by waves, while the darker high pine sands were believed to be derived from more ancient residual sources. It was assumed that the latter afforded better nutrient and moisture availability and could, therefore, support sandhill-type high pine vegetation (Laessle, 1958a). However, no consistent physical or chemical differences have been demonstrated between the two types of soils (Whitney, 1898; Harper, 1914a; Mulvania, 1931; Webber, 1935; Laessle, 1968; Kalisz and Stone, 1984b), nor are all soils that support scrub consistently white.

More likely, the color of a particular scrub soil reflects the length of time that the soil has supported scrub vegetation, as some soil characteristics are the result of biotic actions on the soil parent materials. Scrub soils are forest soils and are subject to soil-forming processes associated with forested ecosystems. Organic acids produced in the forest litter remove organic and iron oxide stains from the quartz sand grains as water percolates through the soil column, gradually bleaching the upper soil horizon. The longer a soil has supported scrub, the wider this white horizon is likely to be. The inference is that at a given locale with uniform parent material, deep white sands support the most ancient scrubs, while yellow sands support recently developed scrubs. Scrubs on soils with a layer of whitish sand over yellow are intermediate in age. These features suggest that some scrubs are relatively recent occupants of former high pine sites—a contention further supported by the fact that some yellow sand scrubs, particularly those in the Ocala National Forest, have occasional relict longleaf pines scattered within them (Kalisz, 1982; J. Clutts, District Ranger, Ocala N. F., personal communication). Relatively abundant turkey oak or scrub hickory in scrub also indicates areas where high pine may have formerly occurred.

In contrast to scrub soils, the yellow, brown, or buff sands of the high pine sandhills exhibit characteristics of grassland or savanna soils. Frequent fires prevent accumulation of acid-producing litter. Furthermore, leaching is counteracted by the activities of fossorial, or digging, animals—particularly pocket gophers (*Geomys pinetis*), gopher tortoises (*Gopherus polyphemus*), and ground-dwelling beetles (*Peltotrupes youngi*), which are abundant in these ecosystems. They constantly churn the soil, limiting the development of pronounced soil horizons (Kalisz and Stone, 1984b).

The development of a bleached or eluviated soil horizon under scrub vegetation, however, may be more than a simple function of time. Productivity differences among scrubs may also be a factor. The greater litter accumulation on relatively productive scrub sites would likely result in a faster rate of bleaching relative to less fertile sites. Although data on the variation in nutrient status among different scrub soils are lacking, differences in fertility can be inferred from features of the vegetation. For example, there is a white sand scrub in the Welaka area of Putnam County that supports an even-aged stand of forty-year-old sand pines growing at a density of eighty-six stems per hectare. Their mean diameter (dbh) is 34.2 cm; the shrub layer beneath them is a tall impenetrable mass; and mesic hardwood species are present in the understory. In marked contrast, a sand pine/rosemary scrub grows on white sand at the southern end of the Lake Wales Ridge in a locale known as Hendrie Ranch (fig. 6.5). It supports an uneven-aged stand of sand pines, with the oldest trees approaching 100 years. Tree density is sixty-seven stems per hectare, but the mean diameter of those forty years or older is only 24.1 cm. The shrub layer, dominated by Florida rosemary and scrub oak (*Quercus inopina*), is low and open, and there is no encroachment by adjacent mesic species. Although the soils at the two locations are classed in the same series (St. Lucie), other soil characteristics, likely associated with nutrient status, have produced strikingly different scrubs.

Relative to other soil types in Florida, scrub soils are both droughty and extremely nutrient-poor. The appearance and stature of scrub vegetation seem to be due primarily to the low nutrient supply rather than dry conditions (S. Denton, Archbold Biol. Stn., personal commmunication). The evergreen nature of most of the scrub species is assumed to be an adaptation that helps retain nutrients (Monk, 1966a).

Although scrub soils are excessively well drained, drought stress may not be a common occurrence. Even though the majority of fine roots of scrub species are shallow (probably to facilitate nutrient capture), these species also have deep "sinker" roots that tap soil moisture at considerable depths. In fact, one study has shown that water stress is more frequent in flatwoods vegetation where the water table is closer to the surface—presumably because high water levels restrict rooting depth. When the water table drops, shallowly rooted plants are more likely to experience water stress (S. Denton, Archbold Biol. Stn., personal communication). The greatest effect of droughty conditions in scrub is probably their limitation on regeneration by

Fig. 6.5. Rosemary-dominated scrub with widely scattered sand pines. The oldest pines are over 100 years; all are nonserotinous. Hendrie Ranch, Highlands County.

seed. Extended dry periods following fire have been shown to limit sand pine establishment (Myers et al., 1987). Although scrub is probably desert-like for most seedlings, the ecosystem as a whole may be influenced more by nutrient deficiency than by water deficiency.

Vegetation

Scrub vegetation varies from place to place, yet it possesses a uniformity of aspect that led Vignoles (1823) to state that "they vary but little in general appearance." Indeed, scrub is usually recognizable even to the casual observer. This general uniformity is due to the fact that the woody vegetation is almost always composed of the same relatively few species.

Shrub Layer and Ground Cover

Regardless of the density of the sand pines, more than 90 percent of the shrub layer in Florida scrubs consists of the same six species in approximately the same order of abundance: myrtle oak or scrub oak (*Quercus myrtifolia, Q. inopina*), saw palmetto (*Serenoa repens*), sand live oak (*Q. geminata*), Chapman's oak (*Q. chapmanii*), rusty lyonia (*Lyonia ferruginea*), and Florida rosemary (*Ceratiola ericoides*) (A. M. Laessle, unpublished data). The shrub layer may be dense or open and, though usually dominated by the oaks, may consist of nearly pure stands of rosemary (see fig. 6.5). In the peninsula, saw palmetto is joined by another dwarf palm, *Sabal etonia* (Zona and Judd, 1986).

The ground cover, though always sparse, almost invariably includes gopher apple (*Licania michauxii*), beak rush (*Rhynchospora megalocarpa*), milk peas (*Galactia* spp.), *Andropogon floridanum*, and *Panicum patentifolium*, plus the lichens British soldier moss (*Cladonia leporina*), *C. prostrata*, *Cladina evansii*, and *C. subtenuis*. Usually, the density of this ground cover is inversely proportional to the density of the sand pines and shrubs (A. M. Laessle, unpublished data).

On relatively productive sites that have not burned for several decades, a pronounced layer of litter and duff is usually present. In scrubs with widely spaced shrubs, the interstices may be devoid of vegetation, exposing a pure white "sugar sand," or these openings may be carpeted with mats of lichens. Whole suites of the rarer scrub plants may be altogether lacking on some sites while surprisingly abundant on others.

Scrub has many endemic plant species that occur there and nowhere else. Currently thirteen are federally listed as endangered or threatened, while twenty-two are so listed by the State of Florida. Some of these endemics, although wide-ranging throughout much of the distribution of scrub, occur at low densities. Examples of these are scrub holly (*Ilex opaca* var. *arenicola*), silk bay (*Persea humilis*), garberia (*Garberia heterophylla*), palafoxia (*Pala-*

foxia feayi), and wild olive (*Osmanthus megacarpa*). Others, such as Curtiss' milkweed (*Asclepias curtissii*), are widespread and locally abundant but appear rare only because they are cryptic (Minno, 1987).

Other endemics, such as scrub hickory (*Carya floridana*) and scrub oak, vary from abundant to dominant within restricted ranges. Scrub hickory, although locally abundant, is generally limited to yellow sand scrubs (i.e., young or pioneer scrubs). It also readily invades unburned high pine lands of central Florida, thus serving as a precursor to scrub development on high pine soils. Even more restricted is *Q. inopina*, which for many years was considered a growth form of myrtle oak but now is recognized as a separate species (Johnson and Abrahamson, 1982). It is the dominant oak of many interior peninsular white sand scrubs.

With a few exceptions, the truly rare scrub endemics are restricted to the Lake Wales Ridge. This concentration of endemism is probably due to the antiquity and former island nature of the ridgetops. Two shrubs, the pygmy fringe tree (*Chionanthus pygmaeus*) and scrub plum (*Prunus geniculata*), both federally listed endangered species, are with few exceptions limited to scattered scrub sites in Polk and Highlands counties. An even rarer shrub in the buckthorn family is Garrett's ziziphus (*Ziziphus celata*). Collected only twice in a scrub near Sebring in Highlands County and not seen since 1955, it was presumed extinct (Judd and Hall, 1984) until rediscovered in 1987 (Delaney et al., 1989).

Also restricted to the Lake Wales Ridge are the highlands scrub hypericum (*Hypericum cumulicola*), scrub balm (*Dicerandra frutescens*), wedge-leaved snakeroot (*Eryngium cuneifolium*), Beckner's lupine (*Lupinus aridorum*), hairy jointweed (*Polygonella basiramia*), and Carter's warea (*Warea carteri*), all federally listed endangered species. Other restricted endemics include the Florida gayfeather (*Liatris ohlingerae*), shortleaved rosemary (*Conradina brevifolia*), paper-like nailwort (*Paronychia chartacea*) (federally listed as threatened), and Britton's bear grass (*Nolina brittoniana*). A recently discovered endemic mint (*Dicerandra christmanii*) is known from only five populations in Highlands County (Huck et al., 1989).

Lewton's polygala (*Polygala lewtonii*) and Florida bonamia (*Bonamia grandiflora*), both with slightly larger distributions, are found in scrubs on the Florida Central Ridge from Marion to Highland counties. The latter is federally listed as threatened. Nodding pinweed (*Lechea cernua*) is scattered in scrubs throughout the central third of the peninsula. The longspurred mint (*Dicerandra cornutissima*), federally listed as endangered, is restricted to Big Scrub in Marion County.

Florida golden aster (*Chrysopsis floridana*) is limited to a few coastal scrub sites in Hillsborough County, while the four-petaled pawpaw (*Asimina tetramera*) is endemic to the southeast coastal scrubs of Martin and Palm Beach counties. Lakela's mint (*Dicerandra immaculata*) is known from only nine sites near the Indian River–St. Lucie county line (Robinson, 1981).

Restricted to scrubs and associated xeric habitats in the Panhandle are Godfrey's blazing-star (*Liatris provincialis*), the mint *Conradina canescens*, and large-leaved jointweed (*Polygonella macrophylla*).

Sand Pine

Sand pine has traditionally been the primary diagnostic element of Florida's scrub. In some scrubs it grows in dense stands, in others it is widely scattered or absent. Sometimes it is replaced by slash pine. Sand pine stands may be even- or uneven-aged and may consist of either closed-coned (serotinous) or open-coned (nonserotinous) individuals, or, more commonly, a mixture of the two. In stands with widely spaced trees, low branches that sometimes reach the ground give the trees a bushy appearance, while in dense stands the pruning effect of shade produces limbless trunks below high crowns. From site to site, trees of the same age may vary from tall and robust to stunted and gnarled.

Compared to other pines, sand pine is both precocious and short-lived. Trees as young as five years may produce cones (Cooper et al., 1959). After about fifty to seventy years, stands begin to break up; individuals rarely reach one hundred years. On productive sites the trees reach a height of 20 m and a maximum diameter of 45–50 cm. The champion sand pine, located at Wekiwa Springs State Park in Orange County, north of Orlando, has a height of 26 m, a diameter of 61 cm, and a crown spread of 12 m.

Sand pine seedlings and saplings are relatively shade-tolerant, frequently growing up through a shrub layer that outpaces their growth in the first two to four years following fire. Successful establishment is facilitated by partial shading by other vegetation, which protects the seedlings from lethal temperatures at the soil surface (Cooper et al., 1959). However, seedlings rarely become successfully established in the shade of mature sand pine scrub vegetation.

Sand pine is restricted to well-drained sandy ridges and rises that burn infrequently. Even though individual trees are killed by fire, the species is termed *fire resilient* (McCune, 1988) because it has the capacity to regenerate profusely following fire. Although sand pine may become established on lower, wetter sites, it rarely persists there. In some cases this failure may be due to more frequent fires, but on ill-drained sites sand pine grows poorly and is subject to root disease. It readily invades adjacent high pine in the absence of fire (Snedaker, 1963; Laessle, 1968; Veno, 1976; Myers, 1985; Myers and White, 1987), and it has been successfully introduced as a plantation tree on xeric high pine sites, especially in the Florida Panhandle (Burns, 1973).

There are two major disjunct populations of sand pine, one in the peninsula and the other in the Panhandle and southern Alabama. Between the northwesternmost stands in the peninsula near Cedar Key and the scrubs of Alligator Point in the Panhandle lies an overland gap of about 200 km. Based largely on this geographic discontinuity, two races or varieties of sand pine have been recognized: *Pinus clausa* var. *clausa*, known as the peninsular Ocala variety, and *Pinus clausa* var. *immuginata*, the Choctawhatchee sand pine of the Panhandle (Ward, 1963a). The primary distinguishing characteristic is serotinuous versus nonserotinuous cones. The former's cones remain persistently closed on the tree until their resinous seals are broken, usually by the heat of a passing fire. The latter's cones open each year after they mature in the fall.

Although open-coned sand pines prevail in the Panhandle, the characterization of the two varieties is not as clear-cut as is generally assumed. A small percentage of the trees in Panhandle stands have closed cones, and there are reportedly groves of predominantly closed-coned individuals between East Bay and Ochlockonee Bay in Franklin County (Burns, 1973). In peninsular scrubs, 20 percent or more of the individuals in stands that are predominantly closed-coned may have at least some open cones. Furthermore, open-coned stands are the norm in certain peninsular situations such as coastal scrubs; areas where stands are unlikely to burn within one generation; areas where sand pine has expanded, in the absence of fire, onto sites originally supporting high pine or scrubby flatwoods vegetation; and scrubs lacking dense vegetative cover (Myers and White, 1987; Myers et al., 1987). If open-coned stands burn, reestablishment is dependent on trees located on the periphery of the burn (Myers et al., 1987).

Although provenance tests have demonstrated variation in sand pine—i.e., the Choctawhatchee variety grows best in the Panhandle, while the Ocala variety does better in the peninsula (Hebb and Burns, 1973; Outcalt, 1983)—no consistent morphological differences besides serotiny have been found. The degree of serotiny in a stand is likely a function of fire history. Shifts from populations of mainly open-coned trees to closed-cone ones, and vice versa, could conceivably occur over a single fire cycle. In this light, there seems to be no compelling reason to distinguish two varieties of sand pine.

Fauna

A host of animal species of xeric upland habitats utilize scrub. Vertebrates generally restricted to scrub habitats are the Florida mouse (*Podomys floridanus*), the Florida scrub jay (*Aphelocoma coerulescens coerulescens*), the Florida scrub lizard (*Sceloporus woodi*), the sand skink (*Neoseps reynoldsi*), and the blue-tailed mole skink (*Eumeces egregius lividus*). The scrub jay, sand skink, and mole skink are federally listed as threatened.

The gopher tortoise (*Gopherus polyphemus*), usually considered a sandhill species, frequently burrows in scrub but feeds in nearby herbaceous vegetation (Breininger et al., 1988). A number of large, wide-ranging, or widely distributed mammals utilize scrub, including black bear, white-tailed deer, bobcat, gray fox, spotted skunk, and raccoon.

Any scrub site of a few acres or more is certain to support several thousand species of arthropods. These are directly dependent either on deep, well-drained sands or on hosts with such edaphic requirements. Only a small proportion of the arthropods found in scrub is actually restricted to scrub, most being generally distributed in Florida's upland habitats. For example, of about sixty species of ants found in scrub, only three are restricted to that habitat. Only about forty-five species of scrub-restricted arthropods are now known, but perhaps ten times as many remain undiscovered. Some species of scrub plants, such as Florida rosemary and spike moss (*Selaginella arenicola*), support host-specific herbivores. The Florida scrub jay and Florida mouse each have host-specific parasites (Deyrup, 1989).

The structure and stage of development of the scrub vegetation has a profound effect on wildlife habitat availability. For example, the Florida scrub jay requires a low shrub layer lacking a sand pine canopy (fig. 6.6). If a pine canopy develops, or if the height of the shrub layer reaches critical levels, scrub jays abandon the site (Woolfenden and Fitzpatrick, 1984). Canopy closure also reduces or eliminates habitat for Florida mouse, scrub lizard, sand skink, and many birds, such as common nighthawk (*Chordeiles minor*), common ground dove (*Columbina passerina*), northern bobwhite (*Colinus virginianus*), loggerhead shrike (*Lanius ludovicianus*), and, in winter, palm warbler (*Dendroica palmarum*). All these species prefer low, open vegetation.

Conversely, the development of a sand pine canopy creates habitat for flying squirrel (*Glaucomys volans*), gray squirrel (*Sciurus carolinensis*), golden mouse (*Peromyscus nuttali*) and cotton mouse (*P. gossypinus*), red-bellied woodpecker (*Melanerpes carolinus*), downy and hairy woodpeckers (*Picoides pubescens, P. villosus*), great crested flycatcher (*Myiarchus crini-*

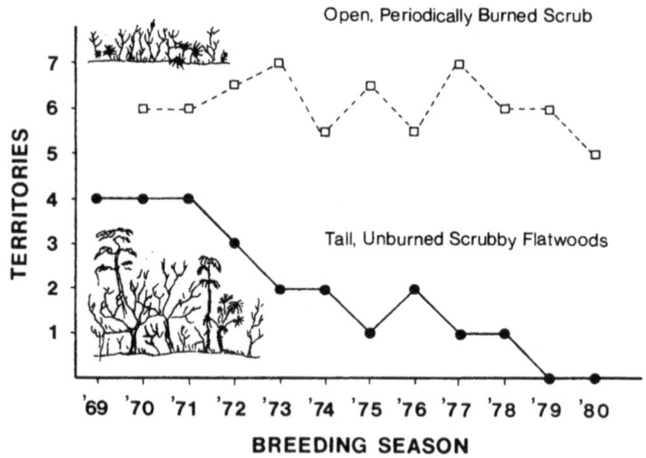

Fig. 6.6. Change in number of scrub jay territories in periodically burned and unburned scrub at Archbold Biological Station. From Woolfenden and Fitzpatrick, 1984. Used with permission of Princeton University Press.

tus), blue jay (*Cyanocitta cristata*), Carolina wren (*Thryothorus ludovicianus*), pine warbler (*Dendroica pinus*), mourning dove (*Zenaida macroura*), eastern screech-owl (*Otus asio*), and Cooper's hawk (*Accipiter cooperii*). Sand pine-dominated scrubs are also utilized by wintering mixed species flocks of wood warblers (*Parulinae*), blue-gray gnatcatchers (*Polioptila caerulea*), and solitary vireos (*Vireo solitarius*).

The best-known scrub endemic is the Florida scrub jay (fig. 6.7) (Westcott, 1970; Breininger, 1981; Cox, 1981; Woolfenden and Fitzpatrick, 1984), a geographically isolated and morphologically and behaviorally distinct race of a widespread western species. The scrub jay populations in Florida probably originated in the late Tertiary or early Quaternary when Florida's scrub was continuous with western xeric scrub and oak woodlands (Neill, 1957). The Pleistocene contraction and fragmentation of scrub habitats along the southeast coastal plain separated the Florida scrub jay from its nearest relative by 1600 km (Woolfenden and Fitzpatrick, 1984). The Florida scrub jay's peculiar behavioral traits—delayed breeding, group living, and cooperation among family members in defending territory and caring for young—probably developed as the extent of its habitat rapidly diminished after the Pleistocene.

Although omnivorous, at some seasons scrub jays feed primarily on acorns, which they gather in the late summer and early fall. Because they cache many acorns by burying them in the sand, the jays may be important dispersal agents of scrub oak species.

Relationships

Scrub is often considered Florida's most distinctive ecosystem. An estimated 40 to 60 percent of its species are endemic. Furthermore, scrub has (or had in the past) unusually discrete boundaries, particularly where it abuts high

Fig. 6.7. Scrub jays on sand live oak, Archbold Biological Station. Photo by Paige Martin.

pine. Historical accounts and descriptions by early naturalists consistently pointed out abrupt transitions between scrub and high pine: "I spoke of the antagonism of these two floras. This is so marked that there is no mistaking it. Wherever they come together the line of division is very distinct" (Nash, 1895); "It is an impressive sight to stand at the border line between the scrub and the high pine land and notice the difference in the character of the vegetation" (Whitney, 1898). (See also Vignoles, 1823; Harper, 1914a, 1915, 1921; Mulvania, 1931; Webber, 1935; Kurz, 1942; Laessle, 1958a.)

Yet other references suggest that the demarcation of scrub and high pine was not always obvious. For example, Harper (1927) observed that the scrub and high pine at the southern end of the Lake Wales Ridge "intergrade in a perplexing pattern."

Apparently the abrupt boundary between scrub and high pine was maintained by the nearly annual fires in the high pine (Myers, 1985), possibly coupled with an allelopathic effect on high pine vegetation by scrub species (Richardson, 1985). Lengthening the interval between fires leads to the breakdown of the boundary, and the two associations homogenize (Myers, 1985). As the pines subsequently die out, this transitional association becomes xeric hardwood forest (Laessle, 1942; Monk, 1968; Veno, 1976). Unfortunately, almost all abrupt boundaries between scrub and high pine have been obliterated, either by the proliferation of woods roads and fire breaks along the boundaries or by vegetation changes resulting from fire suppression. While a hint of such an ecotone can still be seen at Archbold Biological Station in Highlands County, the best remaining example known to the author occurs not in Florida but in the Big Hammock Natural Area in Tattnall County, Georgia. Apparently, a few other distinct ecotones—just as the early naturalists described them—still occur in Florida (S. P. Christman, Fla., Museum of Natural History, personal communication).

In contrast, the gradation from scrub to scrubby flatwoods is so imperceptible that the distinction of the two types as separate ecosystems may not be compelling (but see Chapter 5 for a different interpretation). Both floristically and structurally the two associations are similar. The term *scrubby flatwoods* is usually applied to scrubs that either lack a pine overstory altogether or have slash pine in place of sand pine, or to flatwoods that have not burned for a while and have taken on a scrubby appearance. Clewell (1986) calls Panhandle scrubs lacking a pine overstory "coastal scrub communities" and those with a slash pine overstory "slash pine scrubs." Both are reminiscent of "scrubby flatwoods" located at the southern end of the Lake Wales Ridge. Similar pineless scrubs occur in the Merritt Island–Cape Canaveral area along the Atlantic coast (Schmalzer and Hinkle, 1987; Simon, 1986; Davison and Bratton, 1986) and elsewhere on scattered low sandy rises.

Besides the presence, absence, or character of the pine overstory, the differences between scrub and scrubby flatwoods reflect different fire frequencies and changes that occur along a continuum of depth to water table. Oak scrubs usually appear on isolated sandy rises or low dune ridges within a mosaic of other vegetation types. Slash pines may be widely scattered. Swales and depressions between the rises support flatwoods, dry prairie, cutthroat glades, or flatwoods marsh vegetation. The absence of sand pine on these rises is probably a function of frequent fires originating in the more extensive and easily ignited vegetation surrounding the oak scrubs. On the lower slopes of the rises, the vegetation intergrades with that of the flatwoods; the soils become spodosols; and fetterbush (*Lyonia lucida*), gallberry (*Ilex glabra*), and saw palmetto become abundant.

Fire

Because scrub burns, it is considered a *pyrogenic* ecosystem—one maintained by high intensity, infrequent fires, loosely termed *catastrophic* or *stand-replacing* (fig. 6.8). Fire in scrub follows a reasonably predictable sequence of events. After a lengthy fire-free period of fuel accumulation, an

Fig. 6.8. Aftermath of fire in a 50-year-old sand pine scrub near Astor Park, Ocala National Forest. Burned May 17, 1985; photo taken on November 5, 1985.

intense fire occurs facilitated by severe burning conditions. The overstory sand pines, if present, are killed outright, while the shrub layer is killed back to ground level. The sand pine forest regenerates from fire-induced seed release from individuals with closed cones (or from other sand pine seed sources), while most of the shrubs simply resprout. A few species, notably rosemary, regenerate from seeds stored in the soil (Johnson, 1982). The slow accumulation of fuel reduces the likelihood of a reburn for several decades.

In contrast to structurally analogous vegetation elsewhere, such as chaparral, no significant flush of annuals usually takes place in the first year following fire. A particularly large flush of *Paronychia chartacea* was observed carpeting the ground following a June burn in a rosemary scrub, however, and there have been other reports of three species of *Paronychia* (S. P. Christman, personal communication) and *Lechea deckertii* (A. F. Johnson, FNAI, personal communication) flourishing after fire.

Unlike high pine, flatwoods, and some marsh vegetation (all of which burn at frequent intervals), scrub is not particularly flammable, nor is it easy to ignite. Because it generally lacks fine-textured flashy fuels, such as grasses, pine straw, and dead saw palmetto fronds, scrub has a high heat of ignition. In other words, sustained high temperatures are required for fires to start and spread. As a consequence, fires that burn scrub usually ignite in adjacent ecosystems that do possess flashy fuels. These fires spread into scrub only under severe burning conditions—high wind, low humidity, and low fuel moisture. Because of these pyric properties, Webber (1935) likened scrub to a "fire-fighting association" because it frequently serves as an effective barrier to the spread of fires burning in other vegetation types.

Accumulation of sufficient fuel to sustain a fire in scrub may take from a decade to a century or more, depending on the productivity of the site. In scrubs on excessively well-drained, infertile sites, fuel accumulation may be so slow that fires rarely, if ever, occur. In other situations, the shrub layer may regain its preburn cover in a few years (Abrahamson, 1984a; Schmalzer and Hinkle, 1987), and reburns are possible at short intervals, at least for a few fire cycles (fig. 6.9).

Because ignition is more likely to occur in adjacent ecosystems than in the scrub itself, the nature of the neighboring vegetation influences scrub's propensity to burn. Scrubs imbedded in a matrix of more ignitable vegetation are more apt to burn than those afforded some protection by nonflammable vegetation or by physiographic barriers to fire's spread, such as rivers or swamps. Therefore, scrub fires are mediated not only by the scrub vegetation itself but also by the surrounding landscape.

Although scrubs themselves act as barriers to fire, their presence usually indicates the existence of other barriers that limit fire frequency. For example, Lake Wales Ridge scrubs are found on the periphery of the ridge and on ridge spurs or peninsulas that are partially or entirely bounded by seepage

Fig. 6.9. Aftermath of a lightning fire in a 15-year-old sand pine scrub at Archbold Biological Station. Burned June 7–8, 1986; photo taken June 9, 1986.

swamps, creeks, lakes, or bayheads. Elsewhere, they occur on the upper edges of ravines between frequently burned high pine vegetation and mesic hardwood forests (fig. 6.10). Coastal scrubs are bounded on at least one side by the sea. Additional barriers are formed by inlets, rivers, and coastal

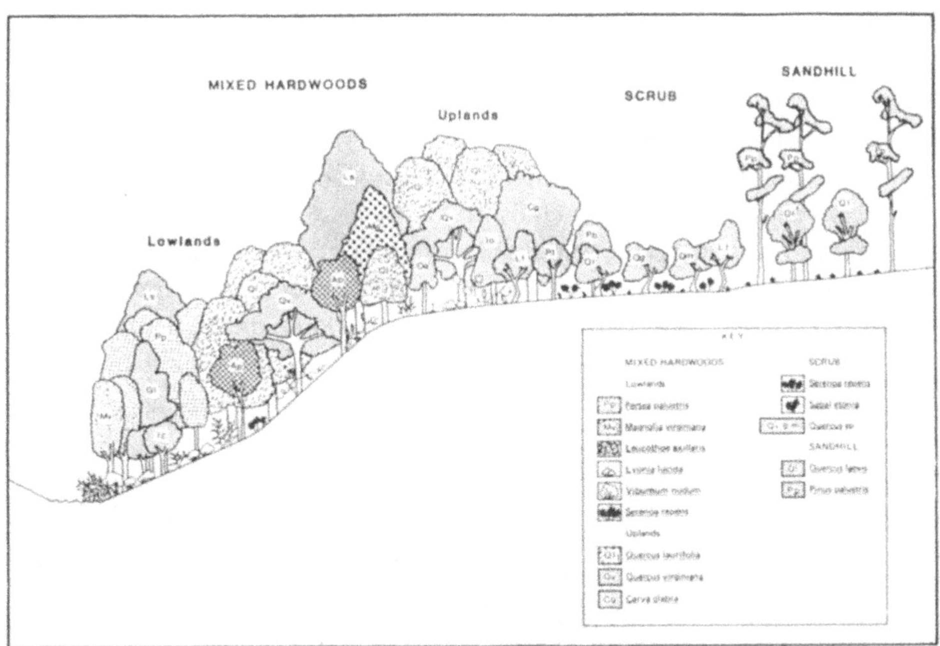

Fig. 6.10. Profile showing scrub as a transition between high pine and mesic slope forest at Goldhead Branch State Park, Clay County. Dominant species listed in key; understory and minor canopy species as follows: AP = *Agarista populifolia*, Gl = *Gordonia lasianthus*, Ic = *Ilex cassine*, Io = *Ilex opaca*, Lf = *Lyonia ferruginea*, Ls = *Liquidambar styraciflua*, Oa = *Osmanthus americana*, Pb = *Persea borbonia*, Pt = *Ptelia trifoliata*. From White and Judd, 1985. Used with permission of the Southern Appalachian Botanical Club.

swamps. The scrubs of the Ocala National Forest are wedged between the St. Johns and Oklawaha rivers.

The role of fire in scrub is far more complicated than usually portrayed, and the patterns created are varied. At one extreme, sites with low productivity may burn only rarely, yet the integrity of the ecosystem persists. In these scrubs, the sand pine stands are uneven-aged and the trees are largely nonserotinous. On more productive sites, scrubs can only persist if fires or other stand-replacing disturbances recur within an appropriate interval. If fires becomes too frequent, the sand pines disappear, and the association becomes oak scrub or changes to high pine; if the fire-free period is too long, xeric hardwood forest develops.

Many Florida rosemary–dominated scrubs, known as rosemary balds, exist on sites so poor that they burn infrequently, if ever (fig. 6.11). As the large rosemaries die, open spaces are created where rosemary or sand pine seedlings may become established. Among the widely spaced rosemary some of the rarer scrub endemics, such as highlands scrub hypericum and the wedge-leaved snakeroot, persist in an abundance not found in scrubs that burn often. Unlike other scrub herbs, such as *Bonamia grandiflora,* that respond favorably to fire (Hartnett and Richardson, 1989), some such as snakeroot appear to lack any propensity for fire (S. P. Vander Kloet, Archbold Biol. Sta., personal communication). Also found in these nonpyric scrubs is the rare lichen *Cladonia perforata,* which, along with the more common lichens, is eliminated from sites that burn and may take a decade or more to reestablish (Buckley and Hendrickson, 1988).

In fire's absence, extrinsic sources of disturbance may serve to maintain scrub. For example, sand pine stands may be at least partially self-perpetuating without fire if they are composed primarily of open-coned individuals. Windthrow during storms may be as important as fire in maintaining coastal sand pine scrubs, particularly those in the Panhandle (fig. 6.12). Little is known about fires and their frequency in scrubs of the Panhandle, but

Fig. 6.11. Rosemary bald (extirpated) south of Josephine Creek, Highlands County, showing patches of bare sand between the shrubs. Photo by A. E. Laessle.

Fig. 6.12. Aftermath of Hurricane Kate (November 21, 1985) in a Franklin County sand pine scrub.

the preponderance of open-coned individuals there, coupled with the frequency of tropical storms relative to some other areas of the state (Bradley, 1972), may mean that fire is less important there than elsewhere, particularly in the scrubs of the inland peninsula.

How fire fits into the life history of most scrub species can only be inferred. Only a handful of life history studies of scrub plants have been undertaken (Johnson, 1982; Minno, 1987; Hartnett and Richardson, 1989), and little is known about the effects of burn frequency, let alone burn season. Field observations strongly suggest that regeneration by seed of most woody scrub species, other than sand pine and rosemary, is rare in intact scrub even after fire. Many of the rarer scrub endemics, however, seem to proliferate after mechanical disturbance of the soil; some of the largest populations occur along fire plow lines, permanent fire breaks, sand roads, and where scrub was cleared in the recent past. In coastal scrubs, storms may serve the same function by creating blow-outs and overwash plains.

Fire in scrub does not initiate widespread changes in species composition but rather creates small localized micro-disturbances. Following fire, most of the extant species either resprout (Abrahamson, 1984a; Schmalzer and Hinkle, 1987) or survive the immediate postburn period as seed. Nevertheless, heterogeneity of fire effects can produce unoccupied sites. Fire-killed rosemary and sand pine will be replaced from seed banks only if conditions are right for both germination and survival. Sand pine may play an important role in scrub by creating the bare sandy patches favored by many of the scrub endemics. Mature sand pines are subject to windthrow, and as old-growth stands become decadent, localized accumulations of fuel develop. When these dead and downed trees burn, they burn longer and hotter than the rest of the vegetation. These "hot spots" kill the root stocks of the sprouting species and create bare areas available for colonization. Although never documented, reburns of scrub with large accumulations of debris derived from fire-killed sand pines may also create such openings. Some bare sand areas in scrubs might possibly be the "ghosts" of former pine stands or rosemary clumps.

Other disturbances in scrub that may create "open" sites include blowouts in coastal scrubs, pits and mounds created by tree falls, clusters of dead trees caused by lightning strikes, and burrows and mounds created by animals, particularly the gopher tortoise. Bare areas may also be created and maintained by some of the species themselves, most notably Florida rosemary, shortleaved rosemary, and Small's jointweed (*Polygonella myriophylla*), either through allelopathic influences (Richardson, 1985; Romeo and Weidenhamer, 1986) or by desiccation of the soil by surficial roots (Kurz, 1942). The death of an individual of one of these species may create a gap larger than had been occupied by the living crown.

Colonization of gaps or openings in scrub appears to be very slow. Many bare areas become filled with a carpet of lichens, which—perhaps via allelopathy (Evans, 1952; Moore, 1968)—preserves the opening until removed by the next fire.

Prognosis and Management

Although scrub is resilient and persistent, its long-term prognosis is not good. Even before the current development boom threatened existing scrubs, the ecosystem was rare. Having steadily contracted over the past several millenia because of changing climatic conditions, it persisted as a natural relic even before the current wave of anthropogenic destruction.

Today, the ancient scrubs of the Lake Wales Ridge are nearly gone. Preserved examples occur at Archbold Biological Station, Saddleblanket Lakes Preserve, Lake Apthorpe Preserve, Catfish Creek Preserve, and Arbuckle Lake State Reserve. Scrubs that are in transition with other ecosystems occur at Highlands Hammock State Park and Tiger Creek Preserve. Virtually all else that remains on the Lake Wales Ridge is for sale and is likely to be developed in the near future (Christman, 1988). Some of the federally listed endangered species have only a single protected site. A few have none.

Unfortunately, current interest in the preservation of scrub may be contributing to more rapid destruction than would have occurred had the ecosystem been ignored. Landowners, fearing government restrictions on the use of their scrublands, have accelerated conversion to citrus, pastureland, and urban development, in some cases clearing the land only to let it lie idle (Kale, 1987). The scrub bordering Josephine Creek in Highlands County (see fig. 6.11) was apparently cleared for this reason.

The southernmost coastal sand pine scrubs are nearly gone. A few sandy rises supporting oak scrub are protected at Rookery Bay National Estuarine Research Reserve near Naples. The best example of protected Atlantic coastal sand pine scrub occurs at Jonathan Dickinson State Park in Martin County. A relatively large oak scrub providing scrub jay habitat lies within the Merritt Island National Wildlife Refuge. Other remnant scrubs of the Atlantic Coastal Ridge are protected at Hobe Sound National Wildlife Refuge and Savannah State Preserve. All other significant scrub tracts are slated for development (Fernald, 1989).

Most of the extensive sand pine scrub in the Ocala National Forest is managed for pulp. The pines are clear-cut in blocks ranging from 50 to 100 ha; the logging equipment mechanically reduces the stature of the shrub layer; and then the sites are reseeded using a "spot scarifier." Although never studied and evaluated except for its effect on the herpetofauna, the method seems to "mimic the natural regeneration process in scrub" by providing a mosaic of vegetation of different ages and densities (Campbell and Christman, 1982). Its long-term effects on individual species, both plant and animal, are unknown.

A few other peninsular scrubs are protected in various state parks and reserves: Lake Louisa, Lake Kissimmee, Blue Springs, Gold Head Branch, and Wekiwa Springs state parks; Little Manatee River State Recreation Area; Rock Springs Run State Reserve; Cedar Keys Scrub State Preserve; portions of the Avon Park Bombing Range; and Lakes Cain and Marsha Park in Orlando. Several examples of barrier island scrubs in the Panhandle are protected (St. Joseph Peninsula, St. George, and St. Andrews state parks; Little St. George Island as part of the Apalachicola National Estuarine Research Reserve; and St. Vincent National Wildlife Refuge), but none are protected on the mainland Panhandle.

Protected scrubs are by no means secure. Because of fragmentation and isolation from other ecosystems, most scrubs are no longer self-maintaining. Fires no longer sweep across the landscape as they once did, and all of Florida's pyric ecosystems must now be burned using prescribed fire. Unfortunately, this management practice is becoming restricted in Florida due to air quality and safety concerns. With scrub, the problem is complicated by the fact that virtually nothing is known about applying and controlling the high intensity fires that are required. Scrub fires can be awe-inspiring. In 1935, a large portion of the scrub within the Ocala National Forest burned in what at the time was the fastest spreading forest fire ever recorded, burning 14,000 ha in four hours. It jumped six firebreaks 91.5 m wide, with spot fires igniting 1.6 km ahead of the main fire front.

Not only do most scrubs have to be burned, but the fires need to be applied in such a way that various stages of development are maintained within isolated fragments. Otherwise, species with special habitat requirements would be adversely affected and perhaps eliminated. Although preliminary steps have been taken to develop techniques to burn scrub (Doren et al., 1987; Myers, 1989), the likelihood of applying them to all situations is remote. Besides liability and fire control considerations, the public may not tolerate the unsightly aftermath of a scrub fire, especially in publicly owned natural areas and parks. In areas that cannot be burned, facsimiles of scrub and scrub species' habitat could possibly be maintained by broad-scale cutting, scraping, and chopping. Implementation of either burning or mechanical techniques will require careful attention to educating the public.

High Pine

Origin and Distribution

High pine is an upland savanna-like ecosystem typified by an open overstory of longleaf pine and a ground cover of perennial grasses (primarily wiregrass) and forbs interspersed with deciduous clonal oaks (fig. 6.12). The oaks may be nearly absent, or they may form dense thickets, groves, or open woodlands. High pine constituted the upland, well-drained portion of the once extensive longleaf pine forests that stretched nearly unbroken from southeastern Virginia to east Texas (fig. 6.13). In Florida, it encompasses the following vegetation categories or community types: sandhill, clayhill, longleaf pine/turkey oak, longleaf pine/wiregrass, turkey oak barrens, and upland pine forest. In terms of potential vegetation, it incorporates Davis's (1967) "forests of longleaf pine and xerophytic oaks" and portions of his "forests of mixed hardwoods and pines," which correspond roughly to sandhill and clayhill vegetation, respectively (fig. 6.14).

The dividing line between sandhills and clayhills is indistinct, falling somewhere along a soil moisture–fertility gradient. Sandhills occupy the dry, infertile part, while clayhills occur along the relatively moist, fertile portion. Sandhill high pine predominates in the peninsula where coarse, excessively drained sands characterize the Plio-Pleistocene sand ridges. The two types cover approximately equal areas in the Panhandle, where they

Fig. 6.13. Presettlement range of the longleaf pine ecosystem. After Frost et al., 1986.

Fig. 6.14. Distribution of high pine (clayhill and sandhill) in Florida. Most forested clayhills now support the latter stages of old field succession rather than high pine. Adapted from Davis, 1967.

form two nearly continuous, parallel tiers stretching westward from the Suwannee River. The tiers are separated by a scarp, which marks the break between clay-rich Miocene and sandy Pleistocene deposits. The most prominent portion of this demarcation is known as the Cody scarp.

Outside Florida, variants of both the sandhill and clayhill types of high pine extend up the coastal plain to the Carolinas and Virginia (Wells and Shunk, 1931; Frost et al., 1986; Frost and Musselman, 1987; Ware et al., 1989) and westward into Alabama (Harper, 1943), Mississippi (Harper, 1914a), and east Texas (Marks and Harcombe, 1981). On the sandhills of Arkansas and Oklahoma, shortleaf pine (*Pinus echinata*) replaces longleaf. Along the westward extension of high pine, wiregrass drops out in Escambia County, Florida; from there to east Texas the understory is dominated by several species of bluestem (*Andropogon* spp.). The southern limit of the ecosystem corresponds to the end of the sand ridges in peninsular Florida, reaching Martin County on the east coast, Lee County on the west coast, and Highlands County in the interior.

The origin of the presettlement longleaf pine forest, which included both high pine land and flatwoods, has been a topic of considerable speculation. We know from palynological evidence that the predominance of southern pines relative to hardwoods has waxed and waned for the past 20,000 years (Watts 1969, 1971; Watts and Stuiver, 1980; Delcourt, 1980; Watts and Hansen, 1988). Unfortunately, the species of pines and oaks involved are unknown. The combination of environmental influences responsible for the shifts between pines and hardwoods is also not known, but it is assumed that changing fire regimes were of primary importance. In the uplands, longleaf pine, deciduous scrub oaks, and evergreen scrub oaks were the likely players on drier sites, while on more mesic sites, mesophytic pine and hardwood species may have intermingled with fire-tolerant longleaf pine and fire-resilient oaks in changing, kaleidoscopic patterns. Although much of the evidence is sketchy, the available data suggest that the longleaf pine/wiregrass/deciduous scrub oak ecosystem expanded during the past several millennia. It displaced mesophytic species, perhaps spreading downslope from ridgetops, and also supplanted scrub vegetation on xeric sites.

While fire is presumed to have been responsible for the expansion of high pine, the relative importance of the two primary sources of fire—lightning and human ignition—will probably never be known. High pine expanded simultaneously with an increase in precipitation (inferred from data on sedimentation rates), presumably coupled with fuel build-up and a higher incidence of thunderstorms, and with human expansion into the coastal plain (according to the most conservative estimates) or possibly changes in human life-styles and population increases brought about by the advent of agriculture. The extent of the longleaf pine forest before European settlement was probably a consequence of an increased number of lightning fires, increased burning by Indians, or some unknown combination of the two. Widespread burning, regardless of origin, induced a gradual retreat of nonpyric vegetation in the advance of a pyric type. Arguments favoring lightning fires over anthropogenic fires, or vice versa, are not convincing (see Robbins and Myers, 1990).

Soils

High pine soils in Florida encompass droughty, coarse sands; fertile, calcareous, phosphatic sandy clays; and loamy sands underlain by clays. They occur on level to strongly sloping terrain. The wide variation in texture, drainage, fertility, and development of high pine soils is evidence that the influence of soils on high pine vegetation is probably secondary to the effects of fire.

Most sandhill soils lack any appreciable profile development and are classed as Entisols. These fall within the same subgroup that supports scrub vegetation, i.e., Typic Quartzipsamments. Primarily derived from marine aeolian or fluvial sand deposits, they are excessively drained, highly permeable, and low in nutrients.

Clayhill soils, on the other hand, are classed as ultisols, the order of soils that exhibit the greatest degree of profile development. Formed primarily from Miocene clastics, they are characterized by a clayey subsoil, known as an argillic horizon, overlain by sand or clayey sand that may range to a meter or more in depth. They are typified by a soil group known as paleudults, literally old, humid, ultisols. Although clayhill soils are well drained, water is more available in the subsoil than in the surface layer. Fertility ranges from good to moderate depending on the parent material. Although exemplified by the soils of the Tallahassee Red Hills (= Tifton Uplands *sensu* Brooks, 1982) and the Western Highlands (= Southern Pinelands District) of the northern Panhandle, variants composed in part of calcitic and phosphatic clays occur in the peninsula, their prevalence decreasing from north to south. These fertile high pine soils are derived from phosphate-rich Miocene marine and fluvial deposits exposed by erosion of the overlying Pleistocene sands.

Intermediate between the extremes of clayhill and sandhill soils are those associated with a geologic formation known as the Citronelle, which probably dates from the Pliocene and is derived from fluvial deposits. The Citronelle consists of sand and clayey sand bound by kaolin, with localized deposits of quartz gravel. The soils may be classed as either entisols or ultisols depending on the depth and extent of the clay horizon. Although no consensus has been reached on the origin, age, or extent of the Citronelle, the formation is most prevalent in the Western Highlands of the Panhandle and in the northern peninsula (Cooke, 1945; Puri and Vernon, 1964).

While eyeing the high pine lands for their agricultural potential, settlers and surveyors of the 1800s grouped them as first, second, or third rate (Smith, 1884). This translates as the better clayhill soils of the Panhandle and phosphate-rich soils of the peninsula, the Citronelle-type and poorer clayhill soils, and sandhill soils, respectively.

Vegetation

Longleaf pine, deciduous oaks, and wiregrass are the primary contributors to the general aspect of Florida's high pine lands. They divide the ecosystem into three distinct strata: pine overstory, deciduous oak underwood, and herbaceous ground cover. "Southern ridge sandhill" is a variant described at the southern end of the Lake Wales Ridge in Highlands County (Abrahamson et al., 1984). Here longleaf pine is replaced by south Florida slash pine (*Pinus elliottii* var. *densa*).

Longleaf Pine

Because of longleaf pine's commercial value, information on its silvics and silviculture is voluminous (Wahlenberg, 1946; Croker, 1968). The role of fire in its perpetuation is well established (Harper, 1911a; Chapman 1932a,b, 1950a,b; Heyward, 1937, 1939a,b), and the use, misuse, and ultimate demise of the once extensive longleaf pine forests have been amply chronicled (Means and Grow, 1985; Tebo, 1985; Croker, 1987; Ware et al., 1989). Of the estimated 25 million hectares of longleaf pine forests that existed in the coastal plain just before European settlement, roughly 3 percent of the uplands support high pine vegetation today. In the late 1800s Florida had an estimated 6.5 billion board feet of virgin longleaf pine (Sargent, 1884). Within four decades virtually none remained.

Unlike sand pine, longleaf pine is long-lived, reaching ages of 500 years or more. Trees generally do not produce cones until they are more than 10 cm in diameter, and significant cone production occurs only after the trees are much larger (Platt et al., 1988a). Although trees produce some cones every year, masts (years with unusually large cone production) occur at intervals of seven to ten years. Complete cone crop failures are not uncommon. Longleaf pine has several adaptations that allow it to survive surface fires and is thus classed within a group of pines called *fire-resistant* (McCune, 1988) rather than *fire-resilient* (like sand pine).

Longleaf pine's tolerance of and need for frequent fire is nearly legendary. Greene (1931) called it "the forest that fire made." The tree's entire life cycle is linked to fire, and it is considered the most fire-tolerant of the southern pines. Seed germination and seedling establishment are enhanced if the seed falls on sparsely vegetated or bare mineral soil. Survival of seedlings, particularly on dry sites, is improved if there is moderate shade from palmettos or oaks (Gaines, 1950; Allen, 1956). Shade protects the seedlings from lethal soil temperatures and desiccating conditions.

There is no special feature of mineral soil per se that improves a seedling's chances of survival; rather, the mineral soil requirement is explained by characteristics of the longleaf pine seed and seedling. Longleaf pine has a large seed (the largest of the southern pines) and persistent wing (other pines have deciduous rather than persistent wings attached to the seeds). Both the large size and persistent wing reduce the likelihood of the seed penetrating the dense cover of unburned grasses and pine straw to reach a moist substrate suitable for germination and establishment. Fire removes these barriers. Recently burned sites offer the added advantage of assuring protection from fire for one or two years before fuels accumulate for the next burn.

During the first couple of years, longleaf pine develops an interim stage between seedling and sapling known as the grass stage, which affords it additional protection from fire. The terminal bud remains near ground level for several years, sometimes a decade or more. While in the grass stage it is protected from low intensity fires by a dense tuft of long, moisture-laden needles. The ability to withstand fire at an early stage of development gives longleaf pine its competitive advantage over other pines on sites that burn frequently. Slash pine and loblolly pine (*Pinus taeda*) have no protection against fire as seedlings or saplings. Shortleaf pine (*P. echinata*) can resprout as a juvenile but still needs an extended fire-free period to advance beyond that stage.

While in the grass stage, longleaf pine builds a long, thick taproot. Then, relying on reserves stored in this root, the tree bolts upward as a single straight stem. Within one growing season it can reach a height of a meter or more. When the next fire occurs, the terminal bud is apt to be above the reach of lethal temperatures (fig. 6.15). As the tree grows from sapling to pole to adult size, its bark thickens into layers of scaly plates. The thickening bark provides insulation while the plates dissipate heat by flaking off as they burn. Longleaf pine's fire tolerance is guaranteed only if the fires remain frequent and of low intensity. Any lengthy period of fuel accumulation not only prevents recruitment but also increases the possibility of burn conditions that can be lethal even to huge trees.

Upland Oaks and Other Hardwoods

Today, because of changes in fire regimes that followed exploitation of longleaf pine, most sandhills are dominated by turkey oak rather than pine (fig. 6.16). These are best classified as turkey oak barrens or turkey oak sandhills rather than high pine. For similar reasons, most of the drier clayhills of today support post or blackjack oak and shortleaf pine rather

Fig. 6.15. Typical low-intensity surface fire in high pine, Ocala National Forest. Both the grass-stage longleaf pines and some individuals that are 1 m or more tall are likely to survive these fires. Photo by L. Battoe.

Fig. 6.16. A turkey oak–dominated sandhill in Clay County. Many but not all oak barrens are the result of past logging and fire suppression.

than longleaf pine, while more fertile, mesic locations, not currently in agriculture, are now forests of mesophytic pines and hardwoods.

The predominant oak of Florida's high pineland is turkey oak (*Quereus laevis*). In places, however, bluejack oak (*Q. incana*) may be codominant with turkey oak, or it may be the sole dominant. The explanation for this pattern has yet to be determined, but Wells and Shunk (1931), Laessle (1942), and Monk (1968) maintained that bluejack oak was either less tolerant than turkey oak of extremely xeric conditions or preferred more fertile soils. Fire may also be a factor in determining which species predominates. On sites where they both occur and where fire has been excluded for several decades, bluejack oak abundance declines more rapidly than that of turkey oak (Myers and White, 1987). Southern red oak (*Q. falcata*), also known as Spanish oak, occurs in place of both bluejack and turkey oak on more mesic, fertile sites in the Panhandle and northern peninsula (Monk, 1968). Blackjack oak (*Q. marilandica*) occurs only in the high pine of the Panhandle, while sand post oak (*Q. stellata* var. *margaretta*) is sparsely scattered throughout the range of the ecosystem, although it is absent from the southern sand ridges of the peninsula. Based on the dominant oak, both Laessle (1942) and Monk (1968) recognized three phases of a "sandhill complex": turkey oak, bluejack oak, and southern red oak.

The oaks of the high pine lands are frequently lumped together with the evergreen oaks of scrublands under the term *scrub oak*. This term refers to the typical habit of these oaks, low stature with multiple stems, and it should not be confused with the scrub ecosystem. In contrast to the evergreen oaks of scrub, those of high pine are deciduous. As the *scrub* label implies, individuals are typically small, stunted, and gnarled, but the term can be misleading, as some specimens of these species are large, single-stemmed trees. For example, the largest turkey oak in Florida has a diameter of 66 cm and a height of 25 m. The Florida champion bluejack oak has a diameter of 63.5 cm and a height of 16 m, while the U.S. champion, which occurs in

Oklahoma, is 135 cm in diameter and 15 m tall. The champion sand post oak is in North Carolina (diameter 107 cm, height 21 m), and the champion southern red oak is in Maryland (diameter 264 cm, height 39 m). Florida's record southern red oak is 229 cm in diameter and 29 m tall. These dimensions illustrate the capacity of scrub oaks to assume tree stature and to form forests in their own right. They reinforce the possibility that forests dominated by these oaks, rather than pines, may have existed in the past and that at least some of today's scrub oak-dominated highlands, generally assumed to be human creations—and undesirable—may not differ too markedly from their presettlement condition.

Sand live oak, which is more typical of scrub, occurs in sandhills as scattered individuals or clumps, in places forming prominent "oak domes" (Guerin, 1988) (fig. 6.17). Live oak (*Q. virginiana*) occupies a similar position in the clayhills. Three other commonly occurring hardwoods, each increasing in abundance as fires become less frequent, are persimmon (*Diospyros virginiana*), black cherry (*Prunus serotina*), and sassafras (*Sassafras albidum*). Several other hardwood species have limited distributions in high pines. Scrub hickory is restricted to the central peninsula and is locally

Fig. 6.17. "Oak dome" formed by a clone of sand live oak in high pine, Ocala National Forest. A relatively nonflammable mat of oak leaf litter on the floor of the dome protects the clone from the frequent fires in high pine and creates a nonpyric refuge for other species. The formation of these domes may be an artifact of former burning practices of the U.S. Forest Service.

abundant there, while mockernut hickory (*Carya tomentosa*) grows in association with southern red oak on more northerly, fertile sites. Sand hickory (*Carya pallida*) and Arkansas oak (*Q. arkansana*) occur only rarely in the high pine of the Panhandle.

Common in the underwood of high pine are sparkleberry (*Vaccinium arboreum*) and pawpaw (*Asimina incarna*). Xeric, infrequently burned sandhills may support scattered to dense stands of Florida rosemary. The evergreen oaks of scrub, particularly myrtle oak, may also occur as scattered clumps or individuals on such sites.

High pine hardwoods reach their greatest size and abundance in the transition zones between high pine and hardwood-dominated forests. Only the deciduous scrub oaks, which exhibit a greater tolerance to fire, are likely to be present in frequently burned areas. None of these oaks, however, tolerates the saturated soils or high water table of flatwoods and bottomlands. Their localized presence in flatwoods indicates a slight topographic rise.

The relative and absolute densities of longleaf pine, oaks, and other hardwoods at any given locale portray the vagaries of the fire regime. Before European settlement, the frequency and regularity of fire were determined by the interplay of chance ignitions; fuel accumulation (related to site productivity); existing topographic and vegetation patterns; the size and shape of natural burn compartments; and proximity to indigenous human habitation, agricultural fields, travel routes, or hunting grounds. The present-day structure, aspect, and composition of remnant high pine sites are, in turn, products of a sequence of overlapping events that began more than 450 years ago with European settlement. Nearly all historical references describing high pine in Florida were made 200 years or more into this sequence (Bartram, 1766; Romans, 1775; Bartram, 1791; Vignoles, 1823; Williams, 1837; Smith, 1884). First, there was cattle grazing and foraging by hogs, followed by turpentining and timbering, and, finally, active and institutionalized fire suppression concomitant with an accelerating rate of landscape fragmentation. Changes in burning practices accompanied each of these events and contributed in untold ways to the character of the landscape that developed.

Just before the era of systematic logging and fire suppression but after several centuries of cattle grazing (Arnade, 1965), longleaf pine forests were described as monospecific stands composed of open groves of scattered large trees and occasional even-aged clumps of younger ones (Schwarz, 1907; Chapman, 1909; Harper, 1911a, 1914b). Across broad expanses of the high pine landscape, oaks were apparently inconspicuous, creating the impression that today's oak-dominated landscapes are in all cases artifacts of human use and neglect (Means and Grow, 1985). Nevertheless, scrub oaks were significant components of parts of the presettlement landscape, and many turkey oak barrens are not recent creations. Their former presence is attested by references in land survey notes to "high pine and blackjack lands" (Randolph, 1849); "blackjack ridges" (Jackson, 1854–1855); and "high rolling blackjack ridges," "rolling pine and blackjack lands," and "rolling blackjack lands" (Daniels, 1855) (blackjack was the former name of turkey oak). Blackjack lands occurred in areas where fires happened irregularly: on dry, sandy rises and ridgetops; on the upper edges of sandy slopes and lips of ravines leading down to seepages areas, stream channels, or swamps; in areas strongly dissected by drainage channels; and on rolling hills interspersed with marshes and ponds.

There are numerous other early references to the prevalence of oaks in high pine. The vegetation on "third-class pine-land soil" was described by Smith (1884) as "consisting of longleaf pine, mostly small and worthless timber, shrubby oaks, occasionally small hickories, sourwood, and whortleberries." Bernard Romans (1775) mentioned that "some high pine hills are so covered with two or three varieties of quercus or oak as to make an underwood to the lofty pines." John Bartram (1766) described a traverse of rolling high pineland that changed in aspect from ridge top to swale: "Rode 35 miles over poor pine barrens which generally is replenished with large lofty pines and good grass and herbs when they grow on red sandy ground mixed with ferruginous, concrete fragments of all shapes and dimensions, some no bigger than bullets, some half a pound weight. But where the hills are high and the sand white with gravel, the trees are poor and scrubby: black oak [turkey oak], broad-leaved willow oak with a hoary leaf [bluejack oak], short pines, and little grass or herbs—only such as is particular to such places—helenium, goldenrod, asters, eupatoriums, shrub dwarf ascyrums, tall poincian, and sensitive acacia." In a similar vein, Charles Vignoles (1823) described "a kind of land . . . covered with the small black or post oak, commonly called black jacks. These are sometimes so thick as to exclude the pines, and when this is the case there is scarcely any grass found on the sand hills."

Although the existence of naturally occurring, turkey oak-dominated barrens is supported by both the historical record and by inferences about probable fire patterns, the present-day dominance of turkey oak on high pine sites that once supported monospecific stands of longleaf pine and carpets of wiregrass is undisputed. Logging during the first four decades of this century removed most of the pine seed source. Hogs had already limited regeneration before logging. Less frequent fires resulting from landscape fragmentation and vigorous fire suppression limited the availability of seed beds for those seed sources that remained. Seedlings that did become established were subject to brown spot disease, a fungus attacking the grass stage that is normally kept in check by frequent fires. More recently, the introduction of low intensity winter fires eliminated any pine seedlings established from the previous fall's seed release but failed to kill the oaks effectively. Eventually, the oak clones attained single-stem dominance, creating many of today's turkey oak woodlands.

Ground Cover

The ground cover in high pine usually consists of a carpet of wiregrasses (usually *Aristida stricta* but also including the vegetatively indistinguishable piney woods dropseed, *Sporobolus junceus*), which provides the matrix for innumerable forbs, low shrubs, and other grasses. The composition of the herb flora varies from one part of the state to another, as well as locally. The richness of the ground cover, in terms of number of species, increases from xeric to mesic sites (Clewell, 1986). Ubiquitous are bracken fern (*Pteridium aquilinum*), gopher apple (*Licania michauxii*), running oak (*Quercus pumila*), dwarf live oak (*Q. minima*), bluestems (*Andropogon* spp.), golden aster (*Pityopsis graminifolia*), low-bush blueberry (*Vaccinium myrsinites*), and blackberry (*Rubus cuneifolius*). Also likely to be present is another wiregrass lookalike, hair grass or hairawn muhly (*Muhlenbergia capillaris*).

Sandhill herb layers generally have a higher species diversity than do those of many other north Florida vegetation types (Monk, 1968). Fifty or more herbaceous species may be encountered within an area of several square meters (Clewell, 1986). The xeric sandhills at Gold Head Branch State Park in Clay County support seventy-two herbaceous (or weakly suffrutescent) species, 76 percent of which are perennial (White and Judd, 1985). The more abundant species, in addition to wiregrass, are golden aster, green eyes (*Berlandiera subacaulis*), summer farewell (*Petalostemon pinnata*), splitbeard bluestem (*Andropogon ternarius*), honeycomb head (*Balduina angustifolia*), blazing star (*Liatris pauciflora*), *Croton argyranthemus*, clammey weed (*Polanisia tenuifolia*), and dog tongue (*Eriogonum tomentosum*).

Unlike scrub, Florida's high pine lands contain only one federally listed endangered species, clasping warea (*Warea amplexifolia*). The State of Florida, however, recognizes pigeon wing (*Clitoria fragrans*) as threatened and bent golden aster (*Pityopsis flexuosa*) as endangered. Both, along with the toothed savory (*Calamintha dentata*), are under consideration for federal listing.

Wiregrass, the object of much speculation, remains poorly understood. Yet it has become an indicator species in the assessment of relative quality among remnant high pine sites. It is a bunch grass that, under appropriate soil conditions and a regimen of frequent fires, occurs as a vigorous dense ground cover. How such swards develop, however, has never been explained. Wiregrass's rate of vegetative spread is so slow that its encroachment into cleared areas has never been observed, and it apparently rarely becomes established from seed. This assumption is based on few observations of seedlings in the field and a presumed but recently discredited notion that the species rarely produces viable seed (see Clewell, 1986, 1989; Seamon et al., 1989).

It is thought that wiregrass, because of its reproductive sluggishness, never returns to a site once it has been extirpated, regardless of the proximity of other populations (Loughridge, 1884; Wells, 1932; Hebb, 1957). Furthermore, it is known to be easily eliminated by intensive forest management practices such as bedding, scraping, and soil scarification (Woods, 1959; Grelen, 1962; Hebb, 1971). Its sensitivity to disturbance and its low reproductive capacity seem at odds with its former abundance and distribution; it was once the nearly uninterrupted ground cover of both the high pine lands and flatwoods from North Carolina to Mississippi. The abrupt termination of its range in the coastal savannas of southeastern Mississippi and in the high pine of west Florida as the rest of the ecosystem proceeds westward has also never been explained.

For years, flowering in wiregrass was rarely observed, at least in Florida. Its flowering response at locations north of Florida is not well established. This paucity of flowering turned out to be an artifact of the practice of burning forested land during the cool winter months. Wiregrass blooms profusely if burned during the growing or warm season, April to mid-August, a period corresponding both to the natural lightning fire season and to the time when fires of any ignition origin would have been most extensive due to the normal spring drought (April, May, and early June)(fig. 6.18).

Wiregrass also blooms following defoliation (by grazing) and after minor soil disturbance (Parrott, 1967), suggesting that other factors besides fire facilitate its spread and may have contributed to its former extensive distribution and general abundance. In fact, because wiregrass is relatively unpalatable, it has been suggested that the nearly 450 years of cattle grazing in the pine barrens may have increased the abundance of wiregrass at the expense of the more palatable bluestems.

The aura of uncertainty that surrounds wiregrass' ability to establish it-

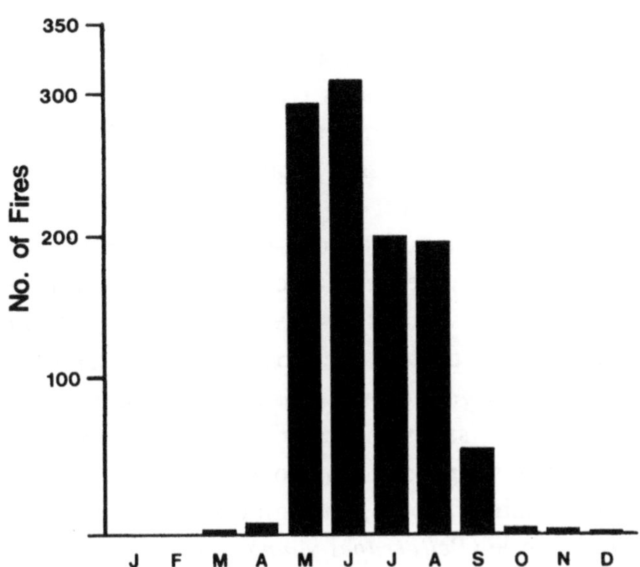

Fig. 6.18. Lightning fire frequency in Florida. From Komarek, 1964.

self is likely a result of both its longevity and its flammability. A long-lived species that provides the fuel for the frequent fires that maintain its habitat may have little need to reproduce readily.

Fauna

High pine supports a host of broadly distributed vertebrates found in a number of Florida's habitats. Only a minority of these, however, depend on xeric habitats, and just a few are largely restricted to high pine habitats. The high pine herpetofauna (reptiles and amphibians), for example, is composed of a small number of xeric-adapted species combined with an array of more widely distributed species (Campbell and Christman, 1982). The truly xeric-adapted species are fossorial—burrowers or "sand swimmers" that require the loose sand medium of open sandhills and scrub. The more wide-ranging species require none of the conditions provided solely by the xerophytic vegetation and sandy soils.

Bird species diversity is relatively high in open high pine, even when compared to more structurally complex mesic hardwood forests (Engstrom et al., 1984). Although no bird species is restricted solely to high pine, several, including the red-cockaded woodpecker (*Picoides borealis*), brown-headed nuthatch (*Sitta pusilla*), and yellow-breasted chat (*Icteria virens*) utilize old-growth longleaf stands. Red-headed woodpecker (*Melanerpes erythrocephalus*), common ground dove (*Columbina passerina*), loggerhead shrike (*Lanius ludovicianus*), eastern kingbird (*Tyrannus tyrannus*), southeastern kestrel (*Falco sparverius paulus*), Bachman's sparrow (*Aimophila aestivalis*), eastern bluebird (*Sialia sialis*), pine warbler (*Dendroica pinus*), and hairy woodpecker (*Picoides villosus*) also prefer open pine land habitats and, of late, their populations have been steadily declining throughout the Southeast (Cox, 1987). In general, population sizes and species richness of birds decline markedly when natural high pine is converted to pine plantations (Repenning and Labisky, 1985).

Five vertebrate species typify high pine habitats: Florida mouse (*Podomys floridanus*), Sherman's fox squirrel (*Sciurus niger shermani*), pocket gopher (*Geomys pinetis*), gopher tortoise (*Gopherus polyphemus*), and red-cockaded woodpecker.

The Florida mouse, a state-listed endangered species, prefers open turkey oak barrens or open evergreen scrub over the pine-wiregrass habitat. The Sherman's fox squirrel, a state species of special concern and a candidate for federal listing, prefers open, park-like pine-oak woodlands. The nearly ubiquitous pocket gopher, which is known colloquially as the "salamander" (corrupted from "sandy mounder"), uses any existing or former sandhill open space that supports herbaceous vegetation, including road shoulders, the edges of citrus groves, and improved pasture. The pocket gopher and the scarab beetle (*Peltotrupes youngi*) are responsible for much of the soil mixing that counteracts horizon-forming processes by homogenizing the upper layer of sandhill soil (Kalisz and Stone, 1984b).

The gopher tortoise (Fig. 6.19) shares its burrow with the crawfish or gopher frog (*Rana areolata*). Both are state species of special concern. For years the tortoise was hunted for food—a practice not prohibited in Florida until 1987—and as a result it has been hunted out of some areas. Today its major threat is loss of habitat, either through outright destruction or lack of fire, which leads to a reduction in its herbaceous food plants (Landers and Speake, 1974; Cox et al., 1987). Fewer tortoises mean fewer burrows for the crawfish frog. The latter is not alone; more than 300 species of obligate and facultative commensals, both vertebrates and arthropods, use gopher tortoise burrows (Jackson and Milstrey, 1988). These include the federally threatened eastern indigo snake (*Drymarchon corais couperi*) and three scarab beetles that are candidates for federal listing (*Aephodius trogloytes*, *Copris gopheri*, and *Onthophagus polyphemi*).

The red-cockaded woodpecker epitomizes old-growth longleaf pine forests of both the highlands and flatwoods. Because it nests in cavities that it creates in large, old pines, its habitat nearly disappeared with the demise of the longleaf pine forests. Today it is not only federally listed as endangered but is also the center of controversy over the management of public forest

Fig. 6.19. Gopher tortoise at mouth of burrow, Archbold Biological Station. Photo by J. N. Layne.

lands in the South. Where it remains, most of its cavity trees are 100 years or older, but in former old-growth stands optimal trees were probably much older (Jackson et al., 1979; Hovis and Labisky, 1985), and current forest practices harvest most trees before they reach 100 years. Noss (1988) pointed out that, like wiregrass, the red-cockaded woodpecker has never been known to colonize a new site or to return to one from which it has been eliminated.

Although attention has been recently focused on the red-cockaded woodpecker as a reason to maintain open, older longleaf pine stands, a more ubiquitous species, the northern bobwhite, was instrumental in preserving the only known examples of intact old-growth high pine, along with some of the best remaining high pine landscape. Interest in maintaining the bobwhite quail populations on private game reserves in south Georgia and north Florida (Stoddard, 1931) led to the acceptance of prescribed burning as a land management tool and ended the policy of total fire suppression (see Pyne [1982] for a history of the controversy over attempts to end woods burning in the South).

Relationships

Unlike the abrupt transition with scrub, which was discussed in detail earlier, high pine's transition with mesic hardwood forest is gradual, particularly on gently sloping land. Species tend to sort out in overlapping zones of abundance based on their respective fire tolerances and on their moisture requirements. One such recognizable pattern along this continuum is a belt of longleaf pine intergrading with the moderately fire-tolerant southern red oak, mockernut hickory, dogwood (*Cornus florida*), and sassafras. Called "red oak woods" by Harper (1915), they apparently were best developed on soils influenced by surficial deposits rich in phosphate (e.g., the Hawthorn formation). Likewise, Vignoles (1823) described "oak hickory lands" that "produce almost exclusively those two kinds of forest trees, with occasionally gigantic pines . . . generally disposed on the exterior edges of the high hammocks, and separate them from the pine lands."

Because the soils were suitable for agriculture, most of these forests were converted long ago, first by the Indians and more extensively after European settlement. Where forested land remains, these transitional woods have been largely obliterated by encroachment of hammock hardwoods, particularly laurel oak (*Quercus hemisphaerica*), water oak (*Q. nigra*), pignut hickory (*Carya glabra*), sweet gum (*Liquidambar styraciflua*), and magnolia (*Magnolia grandiflora*), and by mesophytic pines such as loblolly pine (*Pinus taeda*). This shift stemmed from a combination of fire suppression policies and a general reduction in the frequency and extent of fires as the landscape became fragmented. A portent of their ultimate disappearance is the omission of the categories "red oak woods" and "oak hickory lands" from current vegetation classification systems. The best remaining example of the former occurs at San Felasco Hammock State Preserve in Alachua County (Monk, 1960; Dunn, 1982).

To the casual observer the difference between frequently burned high pine and frequently burned flatwoods is almost imperceptible, as the distinctive shrubs in each are continually suppressed by the fires. Lengthen the interval between fires, however, and the differences become obvious: deciduous scrub oaks proliferate in one, and palmetto, gallberry, titi, and ericaceous shrubs in the other.

On xeric sandhill sites, high pine may intergrade into scrubby flatwoods, scrub, or xeric hammock. Not only is the frequency of fire important in controlling the pattern, aspect, and composition of the vegetation where these ecosystems intermingle, but so is the regularity of fire's return. Areas experiencing a pattern of a few decades of frequent fires followed by a lengthy fire-free period are likely to support mixtures of scrub and high pine species, but may lack certain species from each. They may also contain species uncommon to either dense scrub or open high pine. The "southern ridge sandhills" on the Lake Wales Ridge epitomize this situation, with several plant species reaching their greatest abundance in this association: Carter's warea, scrub buckwheat (*Eriogonum floridanum*), pigeon wing, *Tragia smallii*, *T. urens*, and *Polygala lewtonii* (Christman, 1988).

Fire

Fire is such an overwhelming influence controlling and maintaining high pine that it pervades every aspect of this ecosystem. The elements of high pine, both plant and animal, have evolved in response to frequent, low intensity surface fires. The fuel for these fires is primarily wiregrass, pine straw, and, in the winter, oak leaves. The ignition source throughout most of evolutionary history was lightning, with the pines serving as natural lightning rods. Human-caused fires, however, have been part of the system for millennia. Although Komarek (1964, 1965, 1968, 1974) put together a scenario supporting the contention that lightning fires alone accounted for the former extent of high pine, in certain instances Indians may have been the primary agents of ignition. Kalisz et al. (1986) have marshaled convincing evidence that humans were the primary source of fires in some small, isolated pine islands. Similarly, Ware et al. (1989) point out that the smaller the natural burn compartments, the more likely that Indian burning maintained the high pine vegetation on them.

Frequency, regularity, season, and intensity of burn can have profound, though not fully understood, effects on the structure, species composition, and species abundances in high pine. Fire stimulates seed germination among the herbaceous flora (Whelan, 1985) (fig. 6.20). It can both eliminate and enhance longleaf pine regeneration; it stimulates or alters flower-

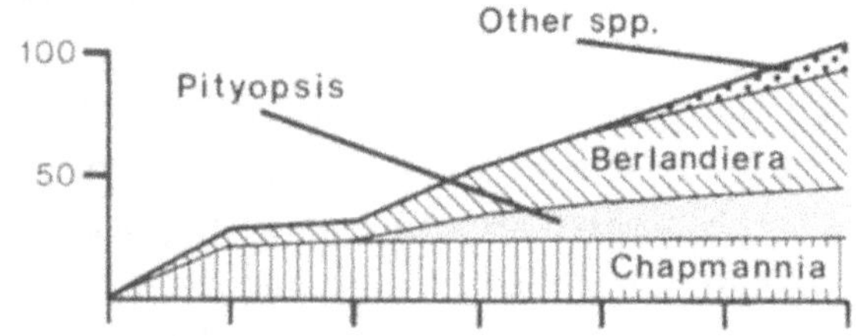

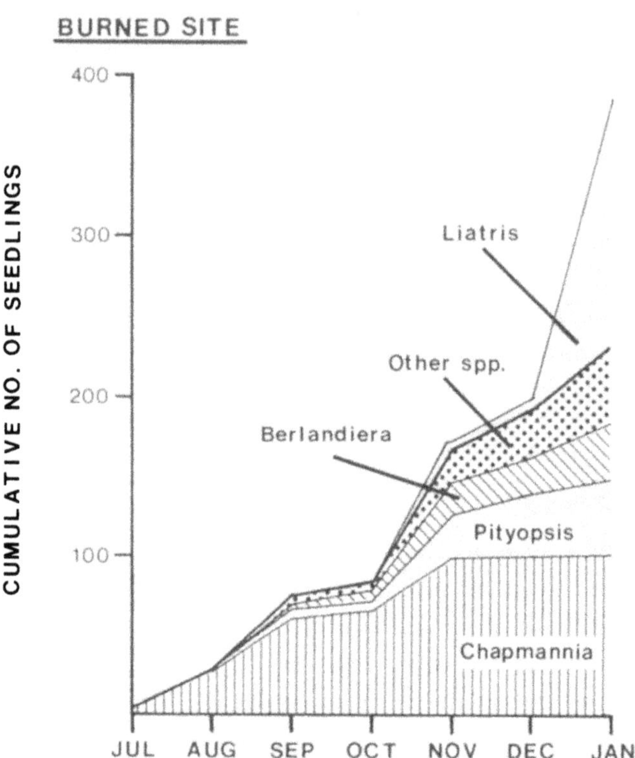

Fig. 6.20. Cumulative numbers of seedlings of high pine forbs appearing on burned and unburned sites. From Whelan, 1985. Used with permission of the Australian Ecological Society.

ing phenologies of a number of species in the herb layer (Platt et al., 1988b); it changes the morphology of flowering stems, particularly in the composites (Platt et al., 1988b; Hartnett, 1987); and it can increase or decrease fruit, browse, and forage for wildlife and domestic livestock (Lemon, 1949; Wood, 1981).

It has been well documented that in the absence of frequent fire, high pine is readily invaded by species from adjacent upland communities, both mesic and xeric (Veno, 1976; Givens et al., 1984; Myers, 1985; Myers and White, 1987; numerous field observations). When fire is excluded, species from surrounding ecosystems invade, the fire-adapted species decline, and the vegetation gradually changes to either xeric or mesic hardwood forest. This led to the labeling of high pine as a fire climax or disclimax. It is not a serial or successional stage of mixed hardwood forest held in check by fire.

Succession following the clearing of upland mixed hardwood forests or high pine for agriculture does not pass through a longleaf pine–wiregrass stage after abandonment. To the contrary, many severely cut-over high pine lands and fallow agricultural fields that once supported high pine vegetation have failed to return to the original vegetation cover even after frequent burning was resumed.

Rather than being a disclimax, high pine is an intricately evolved ecosystem closely linked to the frequent return of fire. The flammability of many of its components—particularly the needles of longleaf pine and the leaves of wiregrass—has given them a competitive advantage over other species (Williamson and Black, 1981; Platt et al., 1988a; Rebertus et al., 1989), and selection may have produced pyrogenic traits that facilitate the spread of fire (Mutch, 1970). High pine is a fire-maintained ecosystem that persists, like scrub, under a regime of fire that is mediated by characteristics of the vegetation itself. High pine, scrub, and hardwood forests are, therefore, mutually exclusive ecosystems composed of species that respond very differently to fire (fig. 6.21).

Prognosis and Management

Unlike scrub, the principal components of high pine are not invasive. Furthermore, if the pine and wiregrass are removed, the primary fuel source disappears. Although structurally similar pine forests can be maintained on former high pine sites, they are artifacts of prescribing fire during brief periods of the year when the fuels are flammable, and they could never be self-maintaining. Under conditions that exist today, once the high pine ground cover is eliminated it is unlikely to recover.

Old-growth longleaf pine sites are a thing of the past. Those that remain are limited to a few hundred hectares in North Carolina and south Georgia. In places, however, old-growth forests could be restored. Probably the best example of longleaf pine–dominated high pine in Florida occurs on the "islands" in the northern half of Ocala National Forest. The 4,000 hectare Riverside Island exhibits many characteristics of pristine high pine, and these could be further enhanced by a combination of uneven-aged forest management using long rotation timber harvests, and varying the season, frequency, and intensity of prescribed burn.

Other reasonably good examples of the high pine ecosystem occur in Blackwater River State Forest; Eglin Air Force Base; a number of Florida state parks, particularly Wekiwa Springs, Torreya, Gold Head Branch, and San Felasco Hammock; the University of Florida's Ordway Preserve in Putnam County; and The Nature Conservancy's Janet Butterfield Brooks Preserve near Brooksville. Sandhill vegetation transitional to scrub occurs at Tiger Creek Preserve and Arbuckle State Reserve, both in Polk County, and at Archbold Biological Station in Highlands County.

Fig. 6.21. (*A*) A view of high pine at Archbold Biological Station taken in 1929, two years after the last burn. (*B*) The same view in 1988 after six decades of fire exclusion. Invasion by species from an adjacent scrub has altered fuel characteristics. A high-intensity fire under current conditions could convert this former high pine site to sand pine scrub.

Burning high pine is not as problematic as burning scrub. High pine fires are generally low intensity, so they are relatively easy to prescribe and control. Four aspects of prescribing fire in high pine, however, are frequently overlooked by the land manager. They must be considered if an array of high pine habitats is to be maintained on the remnants of the ecosystem we still have.

1. There is need for variability in fire regimes (season, frequency, and regularity), both within and among sites. A single regime or burn prescription for high pine favors one suite of species at the expense of others and creates a single landscape image.

2. Recognition is needed of the variability that existed among high pine sites. They ranged from open pine–wiregrass stands to red oak woods and from turkey oak barrens to associations transitional to scrub.

3. It is important to maintain ecotones and transitional communities. These are the central habitats of some species.

4. Appreciation is needed of the fact that many other species and communities were dependent on fires that originated in the high pine lands and flatwoods. Glades of cutthroat grass (*Panicum abscissum*), herb bogs, seepage slopes, and diverse meadows composed of grasses, sedges, and carnivorous plants are nearly forgotten ecosystems. They have changed to bayhead vegetation, gallberry thickets, and titi shrub lands because, like scrub, the connectivity between them and the expansive pinelands has been severed.

7

Temperate Hardwood Forests

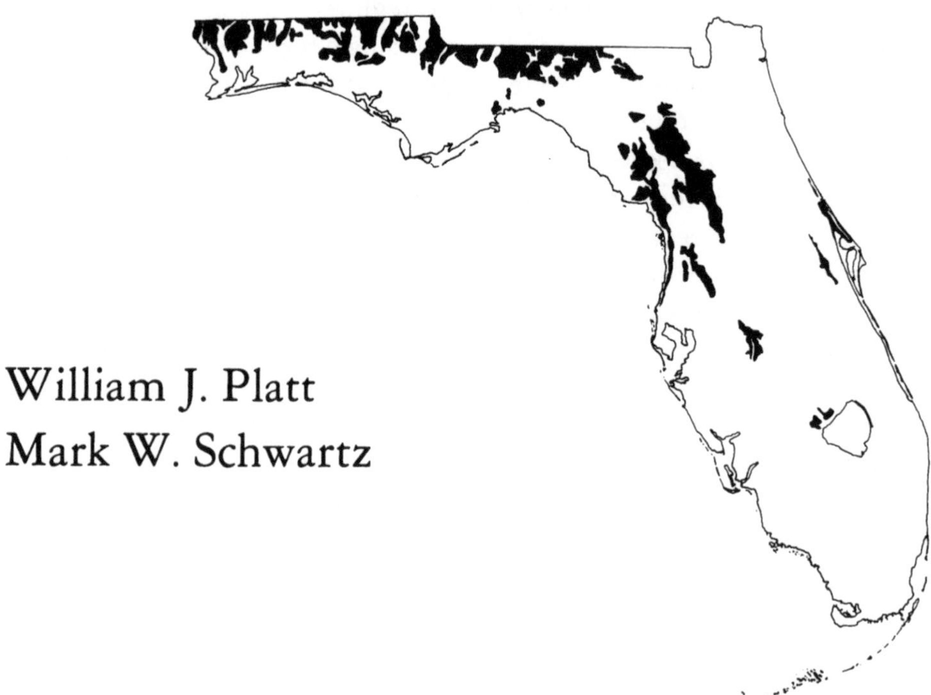

William J. Platt
Mark W. Schwartz

Temperate hardwood forests, or hammocks as they are most often called in Florida (Harper, 1905), occur along the coastal plain of the southeastern United States from the Carolinas to eastern Texas. The diverse flora of the present warm temperate forests of Florida has been present in North America since the late Mesozoic to early Cenozoic eras and in Florida since the Miocene, when portions of northern Florida emerged above sea level. Palynological data indicate continuous presence of hammock species since the Altonian stadial of the early Wisconsinan glaciation (30,000–80,000 YBP) as far south as northern Florida.

Hammocks are currently found throughout Florida, but their composition varies with the transition from a warm temperate forest flora in the north to a tropical flora in the south. In northern Florida, mixed evergreen-deciduous hammocks contain the largest numbers of species of trees and shrubs per unit area in the continental United States. These forests are characterized by a diverse array of overstory and understory species of trees, but few species of herbs. In hammocks located progressively farther south along the central ridge of the peninsula, the overstory and understory become less diverse; there are fewer species but a greater percentage of evergreen trees. However, peninsular hammocks—especially those situated around sinkholes—contain an extraordinarily diverse assemblage of ferns, both temperate and tropical in origin. In southern Florida, there is a marked transition to hammocks that contain primarily tropical species of trees, as well as the largest numbers of epiphytic ferns, bromeliads, and orchids in the continental United States.

Extensive regions of hardwood forest do not occur in Florida. Instead, hammocks typically are narrow bands of vegetation, often only a few hundred meters wide, confined to slopes between upland sand/clayhill pinelands (Chapter 6) and bottomland lake margin or floodplain forests (Chapter 9). The effects of fire and drought, which are pronounced along upper slopes, appear important in the formation and maintenance of high, xeric hammocks. Midslope hammocks tend to be mesic forests into which fires burn less frequently. Along the lower end of the topographic gradient, fire and intermittent flooding may influence the transition from low, hydric hammocks to bottomland forests. Although hammocks are often designated as *xeric, mesic*, or *hydric*, these forests are more frequently defined by their location and vegetation than by measures of soil moisture. Hence, we will describe hammocks by their location along the topographic gradient. In this chapter, we consider hammocks from all three moisture zones. A detailed review of hydric hammocks is provided by Vince et al. (1988).

The large number of tree species found in hammocks has prompted study of the dynamic processes operating in these communities. In the past, hammocks have often been considered the "climax" vegetation of Florida. An alternative hypothesis is that the composition of hammocks is more strongly governed by recurrent natural disturbances such as fire and tropical storms. The mixed species aspects of hammocks has been hypothesized to result from complex disturbance regimes that open space in a variety of ways, enhancing both persistence and sharing of dominance among tree species.

We have divided this chapter into four sections, oriented toward the characteristics of hammocks already outlined. First, we consider how a changing climate has influenced the composition and distribution of hardwood forests in the southeastern United States and produced the mixed hardwood forests that were present along waterways at the time of the European settlement of Florida. Second, we explore the biogeography of hammocks, focusing on latitudinal changes in forest composition along the peninsula, and briefly consider exemplary hammocks throughout the state. Third, we review data on the effects of abiotic environmental conditions upon local distribution of hammocks along topographical gradients. Fourth, we discuss forest dynamics, focusing on the relative importance of interactions among species and disturbance regimes in determining the composition of these species-rich forests. Through the chapter we concentrate on the most prominent element of the biota in this habitat—the trees. The more abundant species of trees in the exemplary hammocks that have provided data used in this review are presented in table 7.1; the locations of these hammocks are presented in figure 7.1. (Nomenclature follows Kurz and Godfrey [1962] and Clewell [1985].)

History of Temperate Mixed Species Hardwood Forests

Cenozoic History

The somewhat fragmentary paleobotanical history indicates that forest vegetation has been continuously present in the southeastern United States for the past 100 million years (Graham, 1964; Axelrod, 1975; Wolfe, 1985, 1986). Taxa characteristic of hardwood forests of the southeastern coastal plain, as well as taxa that are now confined to the southern tip of Florida, have fossil records in North America that date back to the late Mesozoic or early Cenozoic era. Axelrod (1975) and Wolfe (1986) have suggested that bands of tropical-subtropical rain forest and warm temperate, mixed evergreen-deciduous forest extended eastward from Central America to the Appalachians in the early Cenozoic. For example, a diverse tropical to subtropical coastal vegetation (Wilcox flora), including *Coccoloba, Nectandra, Cedrela, Banksia, Cinnamomum, Ficus*, and *Canna*, along with *Magnolia, Nyssa*, and *Liquidambar*, was present along the Mississippi embayment of the Gulf coastal plain during the Eocene epoch (Graham, 1964; Dilcher, 1973). In addition, forests containing mixtures of subtropical and warm temperate broad-leaved evergreens and deciduous species occurred inland and as far north as 60° N latitude (Wolfe, 1986). Nonetheless, temperate genera (e.g., *Quercus, Fagus, Carya, Ulmus, Acer, Tilia, Celtis*, and *Ostrya-Carpinus*) also are known from the Southeast, as, for example, the Eocene Claiborne flora of northern Alabama (Graham, 1964).

Increasingly severe periods of climatic cooling since the middle Eocene epoch have produced pronounced changes in the composition of North American forests. By the early Miocene epoch, warm temperate evergreen-deciduous forests had shifted southward and were located throughout the Gulf coastal plain. Concomitantly, these forests became separated from those in the Appalachians and central Mexico, and some tropical taxa apparently became extinct in the Southeast (Graham, 1964; Wolfe, 1985, 1986). Only a few species of tropical families of trees (e.g., *Dirca palustris*, Thymelaeaceae; *Diospyros virginiana*, Ebenaceae; *Asimina triloba*, Annonaceae) are still present in warm temperate southeastern forests. In contrast, a large number of tropical species of mosses (Schornherst, 1943) and ferns (Lakela and Long, 1976) are still present, especially in Florida hammocks.

The origin of Florida's hammocks is a subject of varying opinions. While data from Monk (1967) are consistent with Braun's (1950) hypothesis that coastal plain forests are derived from mixed mesophytic forests in the Appalachians, Axelrod (1975) suggests that mixed species forests of Florida and the mixed mesophytic Appalachian forests are both derived from mixed evergreen-deciduous forests present in the early Cenozoic era. Cooling trends during the latter part of the Cenozoic are hypothesized to have resulted in differential loss of species, especially evergreen taxa, from Appalachian and coastal plain forests. At the same time, mixed species hardwood forests have become restricted to watercourses as a result of more xeric conditions. Thus, coastal plain forests in the Southeast became fragmented during the Cenozoic (Alexrod, 1975). Mixed species hardwood forests may closely resemble ancestral forests, since they have retained the mixed evergreen-deciduous character.

A more detailed history of southern mixed hardwood forests is available from the last full glacial-interglacial cycle of the Pleistocene. Quaternary palynological records that include portions of the Altonian stadial of the early Wisconsinan glaciation (80,000–30,000 YBP), the Farmdalian interstadial of the middle Wisconsinan glaciation (30,000–24,000 YBP), the Woodfordian stadial of the late Wisconsinan glaciation (24,000–10,000 YBP), and the present Holocene interglacial (<10,000 YBP), as well as climatic studies (Kutzbach and Wright, 1985), indicate that the interior of peninsular Florida was not a refuge for tropical or warm temperate species during the Wisconsinan glaciation (Watts, 1980). Records from Lake Annie, located near Highlands Hammock State Park in Highlands County (no. 12, fig. 7.1), indicate that xeric rosemary scrub, oak/pine scrub, and savannas with grasses and forbs have been predominant at the southern end of the Lake Wales Ridge from 44,300 to 13,000 YBP (Watts, 1975, 1980). Before 8000 YBP, most sinkhole lakes in south Florida were dry (Watts and Stuiver, 1980). Water tables lowered by as much as 20 m (Kutzbach and Wright, 1985) would have resulted in very xeric conditions along the central ridge during the glacial periods. Similarly, low areas of south Florida also were more xeric than at the present time (Beriault et al., 1981). During the late Quaternary period, however, hammocks could have been present on exposed surfaces of the Florida platform; palynological samples from one core taken off the Atlantic coast included hickory pollen (Field et al., 1979).

Conditions in peninsular and southern Florida became more mesic at the end of the Pleistocene (Duever et al., 1986). Pines, probably *Pinus clausa*, were present in oak scrub and savannas around Lake Annie from 13,000 to 5000 YBP (Watts, 1980). Over the past 5000 years, there have been further changes in vegetation at Lake Annie, coincident with an increase in the elevation of the water table (Scholl et al., 1969; Milliman and Emery, 1968); this suggests more mesic conditions in southern Florida (Watts, 1971). Moreover, palynological data from Little Salt Springs in Charlotte County (no. 14, fig. 7.1) indicate that temperate hammock species (e.g., *Quercus, Ilex, Nyssa, Myrica*) have been present in the immediate vicinity of the spring for the past 8500 years (Clausen et al., 1979; J. G. Brown, 1981).

Table 7.1. Dominant species in exemplary Florida hammocks

Marianna Lowlands[a] Map reference: 1	Apalachicola Bluffs[b] 2	Woodyard Hammock[c] 3	Titi Hammock[c] 3	San Felasco[d] 4	Goldhead Branch[e] 5	Pineola Grotto[f] 7
Overstory						
Xeric						
Quercus virginiana	*Quercus virginiana* *Q. stellata* *Q. hemisphaerica* *Carya pallida* *C. glabra*		*Pinus glabra* *P. echinata* *Quercus alba* *Q. hemisphaerica* *Carya glabra*	*Quercus falcata* *Carya tomentosa*	*Quercus virginiana* *Q. hemisphaerica*	*Quercus virginiana*
Mesic						
Magnolia grandiflora *Fagus grandifolia* *Pinus glabra* *Quercus nigra* *Liquidambar styraciflua* *Carya* spp.	*Magnolia grandiflora* *Fagus grandifolia*	*Magnolia grandiflora* *Fagus grandifolia* *Pinus glabra* *Liquidambar styraciflua* *Carya glabra* *C. cordiformis* *Quercus michauxii* *Q. nigra* *Nyssa sylvatica*	*Magnolia grandiflora* *Fagus grandifolia* *Pinus glabra*	*Magnolia grandiflora* *Quercus hemisphaerica* *Carya glabra* *C. tomentosa* *Persea borbonia* *Liquidambar styraciflua*	*Magnolia grandiflora* *Carya* spp. *Liquidambar styraciflua*	*Quercus michauxii* *Q. shumardii* *Ulmus floridana* *Tilia americana* *Celtis laevigata* *Liquidambar styraciflua*
Hydric						
None given	*Magnolia virginiana* *Pinus taeda* *Nyssa sylvatica*		*Liriodendron tulipifera* *Magnolia virginiana* *Nyssa sylvatica* *Pinus taeda* *Liquidambar styraciflua*	*Quercus virginiana* *Q. hemisphaerica* *Q. nigra* *Liquidambar styraciflua* *Carya glabra* *Pinus glabra* *P. taeda*	*Magnolia virginiana* *Pinus taeda*	
Understory						
Xeric						
None given	*Vaccinium arboreum*		*Cornus florida* *Ostrya virginiana*	*Cornus florida* *Chionanthus virginicus* *Prunus angustifolia*	*Osmanthus americana* *Lyonia ferruginia* *Quercus virginiana* *Q. hemisphaerica* *Carya glabra*	
Mesic						
None given	*Ostrya virginiana* *Cornus florida* *Osmanthus americana* *Ilex opaca*	*Ostrya virginiana* *Cornus florida* *Ilex opaca* *Carpinus caroliniana* *Symplocos tinctoria*	*Ilex opaca* *Symplocos tinctoria*	*Ostrya virginiana* *Cornus florida* *Aralia spinosa* *Osmanthus americana* *Ilex opaca* *Symplocos tinctoria*	*Quercus hemisphaerica* *Q. virginiana* *Cornus florida* *Magnolia grandiflora*	*Sabal palmetto*
Hydric						
None given	*Illicium floridanum* *Ilex coriacea*		*Carpinus caroliniana*	*Acer rubrum* *Cornus foemina* *Fraxinus caroliniana* *Carpinus caroliniana*	*Persea palustris* *Ilex cassine* *Agarista populifolia* *Quercus hemisphaerica* *Magnolia virginiana*	

Welaka Reserve[g] Map reference: 8	Anastasia Island[h] 9	St. Mark's[i] 10	Highlands Hammock[j] 12	Alafia River[k] 13	Myakka River; Northport[l]:14	Highlander Hammock[m] 15
Overstory						
Xeric						
Quercus virginiana	*Quercus virginiana*			*Quercus virginiana*		
Q. incana	*Sabal palmetto*			*Q. nigra*		
Q. hemisphaerica	*Quercus hemisphaerica*			*Q. hemisphaerica*		
Sabal palmetto	*Magnolia grandiflora*			*Carya glabra*		
Pinus palustris	*Carya glabra*			*Liquidambar styraciflua*		
P. taeda				*Sabal palmetto*		
Mesic						
Magnolia grandiflora			*Quercus virginiana*	*Quercus nigra*		*Quercus virginiana*
Q. hemisphaerica			*Sabal palmetto*	*Sabal palmetto*		*Celtis laevigata*
Q. nigra			*Carya glabra*	*Quercus virginiana*		*Prunus serotina*
Q. virginiana			*Celtis laevigata*	*Q. hemisphaerica*		*Carya glabra*
Persea borbonia			*Quercus hemisphaerica*	*Liquidambar styraciflua*		*Sabal palmetto*
Liquidambar styraciflua			*Liquidambar styraciflua*			
Carya glabra						
Hydric						
Quercus nigra		*Sabal palmetto*		*Liquidambar styraciflua*	*Quercus virginiana*	
Liquidambar styraciflua		*Pinus taeda*		*Quercus hemisphaerica*	*Sabal palmetto*	
Sabal palmetto		*Quercus virginiana*		*Q. nigra*	*Quercus hemisphaerica*	
Pinus elliottii		*Q. hemisphaerica*		*Magnolia virginiana*	*Pinus elliottii*	
		Liquidambar styraciflua		*Ulmus americana*		
Understory						
Xeric						
	Persea borbonia			*Juniperus silicola*		
	Ilex vomitoria			*Cornus florida*		
	I. opaca			*Prunus serotina*		
	Osmanthus americanus			*Serenoa repens*		
	Serenoa repens					
Mesic						
Ilex opaca			*Acer rubrum*	*Carpinus caroliniana*		*Acer rubrum*
Osmanthus americana			*Serenoa repens*	*Acer rubrum*		*Prunus caroliniana*
				Myrica cerifera		*Citrus aurantium*
						Psychotria nervosa
						Ardisia escallonoides
Hydric						
Ilex coriacea		*Ilex vomitoria*		*Acer rubrum*	*Serenoa repens*	
Myrica cerifera		*Fraxinus pauciflora*		*Gordonia lasianthus*	*Morus rubra*	
		Myrica cerifera		*Carpinus caroliniana*	*Persea borbonia*	
		Acer rubrum		*Fraxinus caroliniana*	*Myrica cerifera*	
		Persea palustris			*Psychotria nervosa*	
					Styrax americana	
					Viburnum obovatum	
					Citrus sp.	

Sources: a. Mitchell (1963) and Stalter and Dial (1986).
b. Clewell (1986) and M. Schwartz (unpublished data).
c. Platt (1985) and Platt and Hermann (1986).
d. Monk (1960) and Skeate (1987).
e. White and Judd (1985).
f. Lakela (1964).
g. Laessle (1942).
h. Laessle and Monk (1961).
i. Thompson (1980).
j. Stalter et al. (1981).
k. Clewell et al. (1982).
l. Miller et al. (1983) and J. M. Huffman (unpublished data).
m. Genelle and Fleming (1978).

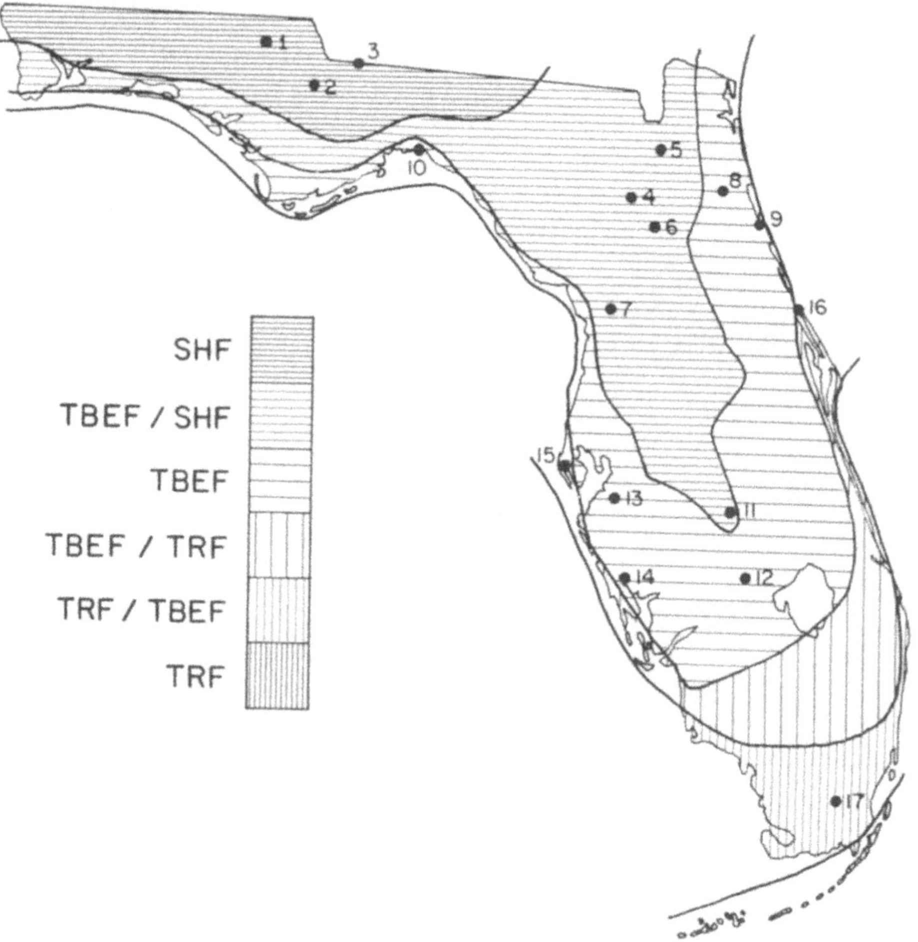

Fig. 7.1. Hammock vegetation zones of Florida, modified after Greller, 1980. Vegetation codes: SHF = Southern Hardwood Forest; TBEF = Temperate Broad-Leaved Evergreen Forest; TRF = Tropical Rain Forest. Sites: 1, Florida Caverns State Park (Jackson County); 2, Apalachicola River Bluffs (Liberty, Gadsden counties); 3, Woodyard and Titi hammocks (Leon County, Fla.; Thomas County, Ga.); 4, San Felasco Hammock (Alachua County); 5, Goldhead Branch State Park (Clay County); 6, Mud Lake, Ocala National Forest (Marion and Lake counties); 7, Pineola Grotto (Citrus County); 8, Welaka Reserve (Putnam County); 9, Anastasia Island State Park (Flagler County); 10, St. Marks Wildlife Refuge (Wakulla County); 11, Tiger Creek Preserve (Polk County); 12, Highlands Hammock State Park (Highlands County); 13, Alafia River hammocks (Hillsborough County); 14, Little Salt Spring, Northport, Myakka River State Park (Charlotte and Sarasota counties); 15, Highlander Hammock (Pinellas County); 16, Turtle Mound (Volusia County); 17, Everglades National Park (Dade County).

It has been hypothesized that tree species currently present in subtropical hammocks have invaded southern Florida since the end of the last full glacial (Harper, 1927; Davis, 1943; Long, 1974; Lakela and Long, 1976; Delcourt and Delcourt, 1985). Cores from the Everglades (no. 17, fig. 7.1) indicate the return of sea level to its current position by 5000 YBP and subsequent establishment of the coastal vegetation including tropical species that are currently found in subtropical hammocks (Riegel, 1965; Spackman, et al., 1966). There are no earlier palynological data from the southern tip of Florida. If tropical species occurred only in restricted locations, such as along the coast during glacial times of lowered sea levels (Field et al., 1979), it is unlikely that they would be represented in pollen records from the interior of the Florida peninsula—that is, those of xeric sites with longer palynological records.

Farther north on the coastal plain, the floristic composition of forests appears to have changed little since the last full glacial (Delcourt and Delcourt, 1987). Although boreal species were displaced south of their present distributions during the Wisconsinan glaciation, they did not reach Florida. The Tunica Hills of West Feliciana Parish, Louisiana, is the southernmost site from which there is clear evidence of boreal species. There, white spruce (*Picea glauca*) occurred with cool-temperate deciduous trees as late as about 13,000 YBP (P. A. Delcourt and H. R. Delcourt, 1977).

For more than 20,000 years, hardwoods—most notably oaks and hickories—have alternated with southern pines as the dominant species in pollen cores taken from northern Florida (Lake Sheelar in Goldhead Branch State Park, Clay County [no. 5, fig. 7.1] [Watts and Stuiver, 1980] and Mud Lake in the Ocala National Forest, Marion County [no. 6, fig. 7.1] [Watts, 1969]), southern Georgia (Lake Louise [Watts, 1971]), and southern Alabama (Goshen Springs [Delcourt, 1980]), as well as from sites in central Texas (Graham, 1964; Larson et al., 1972; Bryant, 1977; Bryant and Holloway, 1985). Delcourt (1980) presents two possible interpretations of these shifts. First, sand/clayhill vegetation may have been present, but dominance shifted between scrub oaks (*Quercus laevis, Q. incana, Q. geminata, Q. virginiana, Q. marilandica*) and pines (*Pinus palustris*). Alternatively, there may have been shifts in forest types, with high hammocks dominated by *Quercus falcata, Q. stellata, Carya glabra*, and *P. echinata* alternating with sand/ clayhill vegetation. If the latter scenario is correct, sand/clayhill vegetation may have been more restricted to southern latitudes—along the Gulf coast—during periods of increased abundance of high hammocks in the Southeast (Delcourt, 1980).

Species typical of midslope and low hammocks appear to have been present throughout the southern coastal plain during the period for which palynological data are available. *Fagus grandifolia* was present at Mud Lake before the late Wisconsinan glaciation and thus occurred farther south than at present (Watts, 1969, 1971; Ward, 1967). Likewise, hammock species have been present at Goshen Pond in southern Alabama for the past 35,000 years (Delcourt, 1980). Goshen Pond is notable for an increase in pollen of *Magnolia grandiflora* over the past 5000 years, which may reflect an increase in the areal abundance of midslope hammocks (see also Quarterman, 1981).

Late Quaternary shifts in the climate of the southeastern United States—increase in precipitation, warming, and a rise in sea level—have been proposed by Delcourt (1985) and Delcourt and Delcourt (1985, 1987) to be responsible for shifts in paleohydrology and forest vegetation. Delcourt (1985) hypothesized that increases in sediment accumulation rates within lake basins of the Gulf coastal plain and Florida peninsula between 8000 and 6000 YBP reflect increases in the overland flow of surface water and transport of sediments. Coniferous forests are more likely to reflect these increases in sediment accumulation (Wright, 1981). The observed increase in the abundance of coniferous forests dominated by *Pinus palustris* (Delcourt, 1980) during the period from 8000 to 6000 YBP (Watts, 1980) could be a result of an increased fire frequency associated with more frequent summer thunderstorms (Platt et al., 1988a). Concomitantly, increased summer rainfall would have enabled species of mesic hammocks to increase in abundance in areas protected from fire.

Relict Forests

Mixed species hardwood forests of northern Florida (e.g., Marianna Lowlands, Apalachicola Bluffs/Ravines, and Tallahassee Red Hills regions [nos. 1–3, fig. 7.1]) appear unusual among southern hardwood forests (Harper, 1948a,b, 1949). Not only do these forests contain among the largest numbers of tree species per unit area within the temperate forests of the eastern United States (Marks and Harcombe, 1975; Platt, 1985), but also the Apalachicola Bluffs are the only hammocks containing endemic species of trees. In addition, a number of northern species of understory trees, shrubs, herbs, and mosses in these forests have populations disjunct from the Appalachian Mountains (Harper, 1914a; Small, 1933, 1938; Kurz, 1927, 1933, 1938b; Schornherst, 1943; Thorne, 1949, 1954; Knight, 1986). A similar pattern occurs for some animals (Neill, 1957). While closely related floristically to Appalachian forests (Long, 1974), hardwood forests in northern Florida may be ecologically more similar to Mexican temperate cloud forests in that both are mixed evergreen-deciduous and are present in warm temperate, but seasonal, climates (Greller and Rachele, 1983).

Hardwood forests in northern Florida probably originated during the Miocene, when portions of northern Florida initially emerged above sea level. Taxa that are now endemic or disjunct in distribution probably migrated southward at this time (cf. James, 1961; Deevey, 1949). Thus, the presence of disjuncts and endemics in northern Florida hammocks likely predated the Pleistocene (cf. Garren, 1943; Kurz, 1927, 1933, 1938a; Small, 1938; Braun, 1950; Mitchell, 1963). It has been suggested that the current restriction of certain species to ravines and other cool, moist habitats in the coastal plain reflects changes in climate that resulted in warmer and drier habitats in areas in which these species were once present (Schornherst, 1943; Thorne, 1949; Neill, 1957).

The species richness of these north Florida forests may have increased during the Pleistocene, when temperate species may have migrated southward. Florida hammocks north of the Cody scarp—the break between the clay-rich Miocene soils along the northern tier of counties and the Pleistocene sands along the coast—remained above sea level during the Pleistocene (Neill, 1957). Some northern Florida disjuncts may have reexpanded their ranges into the mixed mesophytic forests of the Appalachian Mountains during interglacial times of warmth, especially via the Apalachicola River system, which has its headwaters in the Appalachians (Thorne, 1949; James, 1961; Mitchell, 1963; Knight, 1986; see also H. R. Delcourt and P. A. Delcourt, 1977).

Northern Florida hardwood forests may represent true relict forests, as the southeastern coastal plain was characterized by a relatively constant climate during glacial and interglacial periods (Delcourt and Delcourt, 1984). Although decreased precipitation resulted from the slight cooling of the Atlantic Ocean and the Gulf of Mexico that occurred during the last full glacial (sea surface temperatures decreased by 1–2°C), the general climate of the warm temperate Southeast from 29°30' to 33°N) appears not to have changed dramatically over the past 20,000 years (Delcourt and Delcourt, 1984, 1987). We note, however, that it is difficult to distinguish between a relict forest and forest species with a long historical record. Many hardwood species have a long record of presence in north Florida, but adequate evidence does not exist to document a continual presence of the same forest types since the Miocene.

Current Distribution and Abundance

Records of travelers (mainly in the Panhandle) before 1800 provide fascinating but nonquantitative descriptions of Florida forests (e.g., Cabeza de Vaca, Garcilaso de la Vega, William and John Bartram, Andre Michaux, Thomas Nuttall; see Small, 1921a,b; Harper, 1948a; Tebo, 1985). The first quantitative estimates of percentages of land in hardwood forests were provided by Williams (1827, 1837) as he traveled through the Panhandle between Tallahassee and Pensacola. Approximately 8 percent of the land was estimated to contain midslope and low hammocks; another 10 percent was estimated to contain high hammocks that included both pines and hardwoods (see table 7.1). Original public land surveys provide another quantitative measure of plant community abundance. Land surveys in the Panhandle of Florida, conducted between 1822 and 1835, indicate that less than 5 percent of the land contained midslope and low hammocks; high hammocks comprised an additional 5 percent of the land (Schwartz, 1990). Hammocks similar to those described in early accounts and land surveys have also been described more recently in various locations in the southeastern United States (e.g., H. R. Delcourt and P. A. Delcourt, 1974, 1977; Blaisdell et al., 1974; Harper, 1943; Monk, 1965; Marks and Harcombe, 1981; Platt, 1985; Clewell, 1986; White, 1987).

Harper (1914a) provides extensive quantitative surveys of the abundance of different tree species in phytogeographic regions of northern Florida. His description of the distribution and abundance of hammocks in the early 1900s is similar to that of Williams. The only region with greater than 20 percent hammock hardwoods was the small area of the river bottoms, ravines, and bluffs along the Apalachicola River. In central and southern Florida, Harper (1921, 1927) described hammocks as a minor component of the landscape and restricted to low areas or along margins of watercourses. Small (1933) also described hammocks as covering only a small proportion of southern Florida.

More recent quantitative studies indicate that the proportion of forested land in hammocks has changed little over the past 200 years. In the middle of the twentieth century, hammocks composed 16 to 18 percent of the total forested land area in Florida north of Charlotte, Glades, and Martin counties, and 6 percent of the land area in the rest of the peninsula (McCormack, 1949a, b, 1950a, b). Descriptions of the regional distribution and abundance of hammocks are available for the Panhandle (Clewell, 1977, 1986) and for north-central (Monk, 1965, 1968; Dunn, 1982; Ansley, 1952) and northeastern (Laessle, 1942, 1958b) Florida. These studies indicate that hammocks occur primarily as narrow bands of forest vegetation along the edges of watercourses or around the margins of lakes and sinkholes. These forests are characterized by a wide variety of soil types and moisture conditions, although most (80–90 percent of the forested land area in hammocks north of, and 100 percent south of, Charlotte, Glades, and Martin counties) are midslope-low hammocks (McCormack, 1949a, b, 1950a, b). Statewide distribution patterns of hammocks (Davis, 1967) indicate a fragmented but ubiquitous distribution throughout the state.

Biogeography of Temperate Mixed Species Hardwood Forests

The Transition from Warm Temperate to Tropical Hammocks

Merriam (1898) and Livingston and Shreve (1921) divided the Southeast into three life zones: northernmost austroriparian, middle lower austral, and southern tropical zones. Subsequent studies also have tended to recognize warm temperate and tropical floras in Florida (e.g., Schimper, 1903; Harshberger, 1914; Rubel, 1930; Braun, 1950; Polunin, 1960; Küchler, 1967; Davis, 1967; Daubenmire, 1978). The most recent study (Greller, 1980) identified three climatic zones in Florida (fig. 7.1). Tropical and temperature forests were distinguished by the proportion of tropical taxa present. Based on proportions of evergreen trees in overstory strata, Greller (1980) further divided the temperate zone of Florida into southern mixed species hardwood forests (<30 percent overstory species evergreen) along the northern tier of counties from Escambia to Madison and temperate broad-leaved evergreen forests (>50 percent overstory species evergreen) spanning most of the peninsula. Broad transition areas were designated between the three zones.

A marked decrease in number of species occurs along many peninsulas; this has been termed the *peninsula effect* (Simpson, 1964). The diversity of birds (Simpson, 1964; Wamer, 1978; Cook, 1969), reptiles, and amphibians (Means and Simberloff, 1987) decreases from the base to the tip of the Florida peninsula. However, there is no overall decrease in the numbers of species of trees and shrubs towards the tip of the Florida peninsula (Schwartz, 1988). Ranges of temperate species do terminate mainly in northern and central Florida, but ranges of tropical species extend into these regions of the state. As a result, there are sharp gradients in the distribution of both groups along the peninsula, and these gradients result in more rapid changes in species composition along the Florida peninsula than in regions of similar area in other parts of the United States (Schwartz, 1988).

The shift from temperate to tropical taxa along the peninsula does not occur as a broad intermixing of these two groups. Instead, temperate species tend to occur farther south in the center of the state than they do along the coasts, while tropical species tend to occur farther north along the coasts than in the center (fig. 7.2). Thus, species richness decreases in hammocks along the central ridge, with fewer temperate species occurring at lower latitudes and very few tropical species found inland. In contrast, species rich-

Fig. 7.2. Composite range termini maps for trees and shrubs of Florida as described by Little, 1978 and modified after Schwartz, 1988: (*A*) the southern extent of the range of temperate woody species; (*B*) the northern extent of the range of tropical woody species.

ness increases southward along the coast because woody coastal vegetation is dominated by tropical species.

The rapid changes in species composition with respect to latitude in Florida reflect in part a shift in dominance between deciduous and evergreen species of trees in hammocks. Harper's estimates of the proportions of hammock floras that were evergreen (Harper, 1914a, 1921, 1927) ranged from 40 percent to 60 percent in the Panhandle, 60 to 80 percent in central Florida (see also Monk, 1965, 1968; Daubenmire, 1978), and almost 100 percent in south Florida. The shift from deciduous to evergreen vegetation in southern Florida is reflected in both an increased proportion of temperate species that are evergreen and an increased abundance of tropical species, nearly all of which are evergreen. This pattern appears to be associated with climatic differences (Livingston and Shreve, 1921; Polunin, 1960; Laessle and Monk, 1961; Monk, 1965, 1966a). The importance of cold temperature in determining the evergreen or deciduous nature of forests has been suggested by Axelrod (1966, 1975), Axelrod and Bailey (1969), and Schlesinger and Chabot (1977). The transition between temperate and tropical hammocks is congruent with the 5.5°C (41.9°F) mean winter minimum isotherm (Greller, 1980).

In addition to changes in species composition, changes in forest structure also occur along the peninsula. Panhandle hammocks have a multilayered overstory 20–30 m or more above ground, a discrete understory, and sparse gound cover (Platt, 1985; Platt and Hermann, 1986). In contrast, peninsular hammocks have a somewhat lower and less layered overstory that grades into the understory and abundant ground cover (Clewell et al., 1982). The increased abundance of vegetation in understory and shrub layers, as well as the presence of epiphytes, presumably reflects increased light penetration of the overstory in southern hammocks. As a result, the diversity of these groups, especially epiphytes, increases southward along the peninsula (Small, 1904, 1920a,b, 1923b, 1924b, 1938; Luer, 1972, Lakela and Long, 1976). Wamer (1978) suggests that structural changes in the vegetation along the length of the peninsula are responsible for a lower diversity of birds in southern Florida forests.

Exemplary Mixed Species Hardwood Forests

In general, the mixed species hardwood forests of northern Florida resemble other lowland hardwood forests that occur throughout the coastal plain of the southeastern United States (Quarterman and Keever, 1962; Delcourt and Delcourt, 1974; Marks and Harcombe, 1975, 1981; White, 1987). Nonetheless, the three most widely studied northern Florida hammock regions—the Marianna Lowlands, Apalachicola River Bluffs, and Tallahassee Red Hills—are each characterized by distinctive floras (Schornherst, 1943; Neill, 1957;

Mitchell, 1963; Harper, 1948a,b, 1949; Thorne, 1949, 1954). Overstory vegetation tends to be rather similar in all three regions (Platt, 1985; Clewell, 1986), but each area contains different species of understory trees and herbs, especially endemic or disjunct species. These three regions almost certainly are not sufficiently isolated from one another to prevent interchange of species. Postglacial rates of spread of trees in eastern North America indicate that even a minimal period of 5000 years is likely to be ample time for invasion of nearby areas (Davis, 1981; Webb, 1981; Bennett, 1985). We suggest that local site characteristics maintain differences among hammocks in these regions of northern Florida.

The first region, the Marianna Lowlands (Harper, 1914a; Kurz, 1927, 1938b), is Eocene-Recent in age and may have been the initial area of the state to appear and remain above sea level (Moore, 1955; Mitchell, 1963). This area—part of the Dougherty River Valley Lowlands (Hendry and Yon, 1958)—is characterized by a mixture of clay-rich soils and calcareous slopes with limestone outcrops and a rolling topography within the basin formed by the Chipola, Chattahoochee, and Choctawahatchee rivers (Moore, 1955; Reves, 1961). The flora of Florida State Caverns Park in Jackson County (no. 1, fig. 7.1) has been most often studied. Stalter and Dial (1986) have characterized hammocks (table 7.1), and Mitchell (1963) has listed endemics, disjunct species, and numerous herbaceous plants at the southern extremity of their ranges (see also Knight, 1986). Calciphilic ferns and mosses, both tropical and temperate species, as well as an endemic moss (*Plagiothecium mariannae*) are also present in Marianna Lowlands hammocks (Schornherst, 1943).

Hammocks of the second region, the Apalachicola River Bluffs, are notable for a large number of locally endemic plants and animals, as well as many species at the southern terminus of their ranges; these hammocks are found in one of the most interesting geological formations in Florida. The Apalachicola-Flint-Chattahoochee river system has originated in the Appalachian Mountains since the early Cenozoic (Puri and Vernon, 1964; Stringfield, 1966). Although the river system has shifted course during that time (Moore, 1955; Hendry and Yon, 1958), upper stretches of the Apalachicola watershed have been above sea level since the Miocene. Along the eastern shore of the Apalachicola River in Gadsden and Liberty counties, about 65 km from the Gulf, there are steep bluffs and ravines, both above the Cody scarp on clay-rich Miocene soils and below on Pleistocene sands (no. 2., fig. 7.1). Below the scarp, water flows along the upper surface of a limestone layer and then seeps out of the ground onto the surface, producing springs and runs. These have cut channels into the substrate, lowering water levels and causing the springs gradually to shift away from the mouth of the stream. Lateral sapping of the water table has resulted in steep sides produced by headward undercutting (Sharp, 1938). Sheet erosion has also occurred along such slopes, especially following removal of litter and vegetation by fires. Thus one of Florida's unique hammock habitats, the steephead, has been formed (Means, 1975).

Steepheads are restricted to habitats south of the Cody scarp dividing Miocene and Plio-Pleistocene sediments, but deep ravine forests, similar to steephead forests, are found north of the scarp along the Apalachicola River to the Georgia border. Steepheads are present along several tributaries—Big and Little Sweetwater creeks, Beaverdam Creek, Kelly Branch—in Liberty County but are rare east of the Ochlockonee River (e.g., Goldhead Branch State Park [White and Judd, 1985] no. 5, fig. 7.1 and table 7.1). Steepheads are more common farther west in the Panhandle, especially in Okaloosa, Walton, and Santa Rosa counties (Wolfe et al., 1988).

Clewell (1986) has described the rapid transition from sandhill to high hammocks dominated by overstory oaks and hickories along continually eroding steep upper slopes of Apalachicola ravines (table 7.1). Along lower slopes, where sand from upslope habitats accumulates until the stream channel cuts into the base or slipping occurs, there are midslope hammocks containing *Magnolia grandiflora*, *Fagus grandifolia*, and large numbers of understory species, especially on north-facing slopes. These forests contain endemic species—such as *Torreya taxifolia*, which is on the verge of extinction (see Godfrey and Kurz, 1962; Stalter and Dial, 1984a), and *Taxus floridana*—as well as species such as *Rhododendron austrinum* and *Magnolia ashei* that are restricted to the southeastern United States. Along unstable and continually changing stream banks, midslope hammocks grade into mixed species hydric evergreen swamp forests with a flora reminiscent of bayheads.

Oddly, some rare understory trees and shrubs, which are often thought to be sensitive to disturbance, occur on the highly unstable substrate of steepheads and ravines (Chapman, 1885; Nash, 1895; Harper, 1911b, 1914a; Kurz, 1927, 1933, 1938a,b; Stalter and Dial, 1984a; Redmond, 1984). We suggest that these species may be restricted in distribution, not because they occur in some stable relict forest but rather because they have adapted to the regime of localized geomorphic disturbance that characterizes these hardwood forests. The patterns of distribution and growth form of *Taxus floridana*, for example, suggest a species adapted to chronic disturbance. Genetic individuals (genets) of this species move downslope as a result of shifting sand: stems fall over, then root adventitiously and produce new upright stems (Redmond, 1984). Thus, while genets of this species may be long-lived, they are likely to shift location along slopes. Not surprisingly, the largest genets occur on lower slopes of the steephead forests (Redmond, 1984).

Although the Apalachicola River bluff and ravine forests have been chronically disturbed, evidence from historical records suggests that the degree of disturbance may have increased in recent years. After Florida was acquired by the United States in 1819, the state was surveyed in square mile blocks by the U.S. General Land Office (see Bourdo, 1956). Forest vegetation (c. 1825) within a 400 km^2 area (four townships) along the Apalachicola River has been reconstructed from these surveys by H. R. Delcourt and P. A. Delcourt (1977); their generalized maps show mixed species hardwood forests located along ravine slopes of tributary creeks. These data indicate that the presettlement abundances of *M. grandiflora* and *F. grandifolia* may have been greater than at present.

Clewell (1986) indicated that the present distribution of species in Apalachicola ravine forests differs from that reported by H. R. Delcourt and P. A. Delcourt (1977); in particular, *M. grandiflora* and *F. grandifolia* are less abundant and more restricted to lower slopes than they were in the early 1800s. H. R. Delcourt and P. A. Delcourt (1977) noted that distances to witness trees were no different for beech and magnolia than for other species; they found no statistical evidence for inherent biases that would have resulted in overestimation of the abundances of these species. We note that the ravine slopes of the Apalachicola River Bluffs are currently extremely unstable; about one out of every four steepheads along Little Sweetwater and Beaverdam creeks shows signs of pronounced slipping or slumping. It is possible that site conditions have changed since the early 1800s. Clearcutting of adjacent upslope sand/clayhill longleaf pine forests might have accelerated rates of groundwater seepage, thus increasing the frequency of slumping and ultimately changing the flora of steephead slopes.

The third region, the Tallahassee Red Hills, is the most thoroughly studied of the north Florida hammock areas (Kurz, 1944; Blaisdell, 1966; Blaisdell et al., 1974; Platt, 1985; Platt and Hermann, 1986). This area, characterized by fine clay soils and consisting of dissected hills and drainages derived from alluvial sediments, has remained above sea level since the Miocene (Cooke, 1945; Hendry and Yon, 1958; Puri, 1953; Puri and Vernon, 1964; Stringfield, 1966). Hardwood forests are more extensive in this area than anywhere else in Florida. Vegetation of old-growth hammocks predating European settlement has been described quantitatively; approximately 25–35 species of trees are likely to occur in areas of about one hectare in size (Platt, 1985). Red Hills hammocks are the southernmost extension of the range of important temperate species such as *F. grandifolia* and *Quercus alba*, with the exception of a few isolated sites farther south (Ward, 1967). Herbaceous plants tend to be less abundant in these closed canopy, mixed evergreen-deciduous forests than in more northern deciduous forests; there are, for example, very few species typical of the spring herbaceous flora of northern forests.

The character of Tallahassee Red Hills hammocks may be affected by topography. Woodyard Hammock (no. 3, fig. 7.1, and fig. 7.3), one of the most thoroughly studied forests in the southeastern United States, is located along a flat lake margin in Leon County (Blaisdell et al., 1974; Clewell,

Fig. 7.3. Woodyard Hammock, an exemplary old-growth forest, Tall Timbers Research Station, Leon County. Photo by R. Myers.

1986; Hirsh, 1981; Hirsh and Platt, 1981; Platt, 1985; Platt and Hermann, 1986). This forest has a multilayered overstory dominated by a number of species and a well-developed understory containing as many species as the overstory (table 7.1). In other forests located along steeper topographic gradients, both overstory and understory vegetation tend to be separated into distinct associations (Platt, 1985). High, midslope, and low hammock associations characterized by distinct overstory and understory species of trees occur along a 20 m topographic gradient in Titi Hammock, which is located along slopes of a stream bank in Thomas County, Georgia, just north of the Georgia-Florida state line (no. 3, fig. 7.1, and table 7.1).

In the Tallahassee Red Hills region, Clewell (1986) found that more than 50 percent of the early 1800s survey lines were dominated by hardwoods, primarily oaks and hickories. He attributed the abundance of these species to an abundance of high hammocks in this region of the state before settlement and to residual effects of extensive Apalachee Indian agriculture before and during the period of Spanish exploration and settlement (Spellman, 1948). Furthermore, Stoddard (1931, 1962) estimated that 75 to 90 percent of the Tallahassee Red Hills was cleared before the Civil War. Most of this area was not farmed after the war (Brubaker, 1956), and forests of hardwoods or mixed hardwoods and pines have regrown. As a result, hardwood forests in the Tallahassee Red Hills region have increased in abundance since the Civil War.

Exemplary Temperate Broad-Leaved Evergreen Forests

The central Florida hammock belt (Harper, 1914a, 1915, 1921), which runs along the central ridge of the peninsula, contains numerous hammocks (Monk, 1960; Ansley, 1952; Easterday, 1982; Laessle, 1942; Mohlenbrock, 1976; White and Judd, 1985). Like the Panhandle, this region contains high, midslope, and low hammocks. Unlike those of the Panhandle, however, these central ridge hammocks are located south of the range limit of two important southern mixed hardwood forests species: beech (*Fagus grandifolia*) and white oak (*Quercus alba*). One of the more extensively studied north-central Florida hardwood forests is San Felasco Hammock in Alachua County (no. 4, fig. 7.1, and table 7.1). Vegetation in San Felasco Hammock spans the range from high to low hammocks (Dunn, 1982) and includes a diversity of overstory and understory species (Noss, 1988). As many as 20 tree species are present per hectare (Noss, 1988). Other studies of hammock floras in the upland north-central region of Florida (e.g., Cross Creek, Newnan's Lake, and Alachua Sink hammocks in Alachua County; Goldhead Branch Hammock in Clay County [no. 5, fig. 7.1]; and Ocala National Forest [no. 6, fig. 7.1] in Marion County [see Ansley, 1952; Easterday, 1982; White and Judd, 1985; Mohlenbrock, 1976]) indicate floras similar to those in San Felasco Hammock.

To the east and west of the central ridge in northern peninsular Florida are topographcally lower areas containing scattered hammocks (Monk, 1965). The Gulf hammock region along the Big Bend area of north-central Florida (Harper, 1914a, 1921) is a relatively low-lying area containing hammock islands (Swindell, 1949; Ansley, 1952; Pearson, 1954) on dolomite soils. Midslope sites from this region, exemplified by Pineola Grotto in Citrus County (no. 7, fig. 7.1), contained mixed evergreen and deciduous vegetation somewhat similar to that of San Felasco and Woodyard hammocks (table 7.1). Monk (1965) found that hammocks in the Big Bend region, however, contained fewer total species of trees and a larger proportion of deciduous species than hammocks in the central highlands of the peninsula. Understory species in hammocks of this region are similar to those in San Felasco Hammock, but *Sabal palmetto* is more prominent (Greller, 1980). We note, however, that *S. palmetto* is present in San Felasco Hammock as scattered trees and appears to be increasing in abundance in many north-central Florida hammocks.

In contrast to the depauperate flora of trees in the Gulf hammock region, the ferns are diverse, especially along outcrops in lime sinks (Harper, 1916; St. John, 1936; St. John and St. John, 1935). Sinks create moist microhabitats that are cooler in the summer because of the shade afforded by the depressions but warmer in the winter as a result of constant water flow. Almost all species are terrestrial and most are of tropical origin; one endemic species (*Asplenium curtissii*) is present in these fern grottoes (Small, 1920a,b,c; Lakela, 1964).

Hammocks east of the central uplands in northern Florida are characterized by fewer species but a greater proportion of evergreen trees (Monk, 1965). Laessle (1942) described xeric, mesic, and hydric hammocks on the Welaka Reserve in Putnam County (no. 8, fig. 7.1). He noted that sandhill forbs and grasses occur in open areas of high hammocks, the canopy is not closed, and there are abundant shrubs. The overstory of midslope hammocks (table 7.1) is more closed than in the high hammocks, and ground cover is more sparse. Low hammocks on the Welaka Reserve occur as narrow strips between midslope hammocks and swamps along the St. Johns River. These forests are not flooded for extensive periods of time, but many have a water table close to the soil surface.

Hammocks located right along the Atlantic and Gulf coasts, as well as at the southern end of the central Florida ridge, are south of the ranges of most temperate overstory trees (fig. 7.4). As a result, these hammocks tend to be similar and are dominated by evergreen species. Highlands Hammock in Highlands County (no. 12, fig. 7.1) (Stalter et al., 1981), the banks of Tiger Creek in Polk County (no. 11, fig. 7.1) (Small, 1921b), and slopes of tributary creeks of the Alafia River in Hillsborough County (no. 13, fig. 7.1) (Clewell et al., 1982) contain forests dominated by *Q. virginiana* and *S. palmetto*. Only a few other temperate species are present in these forests (table 7.1). Likewise, the flora of hammocks at Little Salt Spring, Northport, and Myakka River State Park in Charlotte and Sarasota counties (no. 14, fig. 7.1) is dominated by temperate overstory (*Q. virginiana*, *S. palmetto*, *Q. hemisphaerica*, *Persea borbonia*) and understory (*Serenoa repens*, *Ilex* sp.) species (J. G. Brown, 1981; Miller et al., 1983; J. M. Huffman, unpublished data). More, but still evergreen, species are dominant in coastal hammocks that occur along narrow zones of the Gulf coast in the Panhandle and the Atlantic coast of northeastern Florida. Low coastal hammocks in the St. Marks Wildlife Refuge, Wakulla and Jefferson counties (no. 10, fig. 7.1) are dominated by evergreen oaks, palms, and loblolly pine (*Pinus taeda*) (table 7.1). Similar species predominate in coastal dunes hammocks of Anastasia Island State Park in Flagler County (no. 9, fig. 7.1). The ground cover in most temperate broad-leaved evergreen forests consists primarily of evergreen shrubs; only a few herbaceous species are present. While epiphytic species are dominated by Spanish moss (*Tillandsia usneoides*) along the Atlantic and Gulf coasts, a greater diveristy of epiphytes—including ferns, bromeliads, and orchids—is present in south Florida hammocks. Low, temperate broad-leaved evergreen hammocks, especially in south Florida, do contain numerous ferns in the ground cover. The abundance of epiphytes and ferns may reflect a more open and lower overstory, as well as a milder climate (Greller, 1980; Stalter et al., 1981).

Ranges of tropical tree species extend up both Atlantic and Gulf coasts (fig. 7.2). Coastal hammocks in the transition zone between temperate broad-leaved evergreen forest and tropical rain forest tend to be limited mixtures, however, of temperate and tropical species. Along both coasts, tropical hammocks with 60–70 percent or more tropical species often are considered distinct from low, hydric hammocks dominated by *Q. virginiana* and *S. palmetto* in the overstory (Austin et al., 1977; Herwitz, 1977; Richardson, 1977). In general, more mixing of temperate and tropical species occurs in the understory trees and shrubs and ground cover than in overstory trees. For example, the overstory of Highlander Hammock in Pinellas County (no. 15, fig. 7.1) (Genelle and Fleming, 1978) consists exclusively of temperate species, resembling that of hammocks at the southern end of the central ridge. The understory, however, has a mixture of temperate and tropical species (table 7.1), and tropical ferns (*Thelypteris*, *Nephrolepis*, *Dryopteris*) dominate the ground cover. Similar patterns occur farther south in Myakka River State Park and Northport (Miller et al., 1983; J. M. Huffman, unpublished data, table 7.1), as well as in the Big Cypress National Preserve (Duever et al., 1986).

Coastal hammocks dominated by tropical species occur in increasing abundance southward through Florida. The northernmost sites for many tropical species of trees are in hammocks on old shell middens that predate European settlement of Florida (Harper, 1921; Small, 1921a; Norman, 1976). These sites tend to be dominated by tropical overstory species, although some temperate species may also be present. For example, the forest on Turtle Mound in Volusia County (no. 16, fig. 7.1) is dominated by evergreen tropical taxa, but temperate species such as *Celtis laevigata* and *P. borbonia* also are present (Small, 1923a; Norman, 1976). Such middens often are tropical islands surrounded by low, temperate hammocks dominated by *Q. virginiana* and *S. palmetto*.

Local Distribution of Mixed Species Hardwood Forests

Abiotic variables appear to be overwhelmingly important in determining the location of hardwood forests along the usually subtle topographic gradients that characterize the Florida landscape. Fire and drought have been hypothesized to limit upslope invasion of hardwoods (Harper, 1943; Monk, 1965; Marks and Harcombe, 1981; Blaisdell et al., 1974; Komarek, 1983; Platt, 1985), while seepage and flooding have been hypothesized to limit downslope invasion of these same species (Wharton et al., 1977; Penfound and Hathaway, 1938; Penfound, 1952; Putnam et al., 1960). Effects of these variables also are predicted to depend on soil type (Monk, 1960; Marks and Harcombe, 1981) and slope (Penfound, 1952; Clewell, 1977, 1986).

The Role of Fire

Fire influences vegetation in many different types of habitats (see reviews in White, 1979; Heinselman, 1973; Christensen, 1981; Mueller-Dombois, 1981; Sousa, 1984). Traditionally, fire has been considered a rare, catastrophic disturbance in most deciduous forests of eastern North America (Ahlgren, 1974; Bormann and Likens, 1979a; Braun, 1950; Oliver, 1981). Its role in Florida forests has been debated for more than a century (see Long, 1899). Many studies of Florida forests also have assumed that fire acts destructively (e.g., Bessey, 1911; Small, 1924b; Laessle, 1958b; Monk, 1960, 1965; Quarterman and Keever, 1962; Veno, 1976; H. R. Delcourt and P. A. Delcourt, 1977). Harper (1914a, 1962) has reviewed the controversy, which has continued into the 1980s (Komarek, 1974; Clewell, 1986; see also Quarterman, 1981).

Boundaries often exist between habitats differing in flammability; fire regimes may determine the location of these boundaries (Abrams, 1986; Anderson and Brown, 1983; Buell and Cantlon, 1950; Graham, 1941; Grimm, 1983; Myers, 1985). Streng and Harcombe (1982) used a model for flammability developed by Rothermel (1972) to predict that differences in fuel between bluestem savannas and adjacent pine-oak woodlands in the coastal plain of eastern Texas would result in savannas being more likely to burn during the growing season (especially under conditions of high humidity) than pine-oak woodlands. They further suggested that such community-specific differences in flammability may be self-perpetuating (Mutch, 1970). Unlike grasses, dead leaves of shrubs and trees are likely to burn only when dry and at low humidity (Stoddard, 1962; Neel, 1967; Komarek, 1974). Streng and Harcombe (1982) predict that if intervals between fires become long enough that hardwoods suppress grasses, a two-stage change in flammability will occur. First, addition of hardwood leaves to litter results in retention of moisture, decreasing the likelihood of fires during the growing season. Second, accumulation of litter compacts fuel beds and further lowers the likelihood of fire since gas exchange during combustion is reduced. Thus a long interval without fire could cause the boundary between these two habitats to shift. Frequent fires could presumably cause a shift in the other direction.

One likely consequence of fire frequency patterns predicted by the Streng-Harcombe model is that while fires might become less likely with a shift from grass to hardwood dominance, the intensity of any fire occurring during drought conditions would increase because of increased fuel loads (Heinselman, 1973, 1981; Franklin and Hemstrom, 1981). Cover and biomass of the shrub stratum increase in the intervals between fires (Oosting, 1944; Wenger, 1956; Brender and Nelson, 1954; Boerner, 1981, 1982). Increased fire intensity might be especially likely following windstorms, such as hurricanes or tornadoes (see Glitzenstein and Harcombe, 1988) when there would be a large amount of fallen wood. A single high-intensity fire, perhaps during a drought, could alter the species composition and direction of vegetation change (Hough and Forbes, 1943; Henry and Swan, 1974; see also Holling, 1973, 1981). For example, if a high intensity fire were to occur in low areas that are seasonally flooded, hardwood forests might be replaced by pinelands, marshes, or canebrakes (Small, 1904; Beaver and Oosting, 1939; Putnam, 1951; Penfound, 1952; Hughes, 1957, 1966).

High intensity fires can occur in live oak–cabbage palm hammocks of southern and coastal Florida. Under dry conditions, fires burning into hammocks from surrounding pinelands may ignite saw palmetto and ferns in the ground cover, producing a fire hot enough to ignite cabbage palms in the understory or even the overstory. Fire-sensitive species, such as *Quercus hemisphaerica* and tropical hammock species, may be killed, while less fire-sensitive species such as *Q. virginiana* may resprout (Laessle and Monk, 1961; Duever et al., 1986). *Sabal palmetto* is highly resistant to fire; its vertical growth form and bud protected by a sheath of green leaves make this species relatively invulnerable even to hot fires. This species produces flammable litter that would facilitate fires, at least under xeric conditions. Intense fires could result in cabbage palms becoming the major overstory tree in low hammocks (Miller et al., 1983). Furthermore, regeneration by pines in open areas following hot fires could even change hammocks into pine-palm forests. Observations by Small (1904) also indicate that high intensity fires that destroy live oak–cabbage palm hammocks may open the habitat to invasion by flatwoods species. It appears possible that low, temperate broad-leaved evergreen forests dominated by live oaks and cabbage palms are related to flatwoods in the same way that scrub forests are related to sandhill pinelands (Myers, 1985). Infrequent crown fires may favor oak-palm hammocks, while frequent ground cover fires may favor flatwoods (but see Vince et al., 1989).

In contrast to the temperate broad-leaved evergreen forests, high intensity running or crown fires have almost never been recorded in mixed species hardwood forests (Barden and Woods, 1974). Direct observations indicate that north Florida hammock fires creep and burn only litter (Blaisdell et al., 1974). In addition, large areas are not likely to be burned (Barden and Woods, 1974) unless highly flammable species are present. Moreover, virtually all fires recorded in hardwood forests originate in surrounding habitats. Lightning strikes, the most significant natural origin of fire (Komarek, 1964, 1968; Taylor, 1974; Vogl, 1973b), do occur in hardwood forests (Baker, 1974; Barden and Woods, 1974) but are unlikely to initiate fires after trees have leafed out (which occurs in late February–early March in Florida, before the onset of the lightning season; see Komarek, 1964).

Frequent low-intensity fires that originate in longleaf pine forests (Platt et al., 1988a, 1990) may burn downslope into hardwood forests and create high hammock zones between sand/clay hills and midslope hammocks. It has been hypothesized that fires prevent establishment and growth of hardwoods in sandhill habitats (Nash, 1895; Schwarz, 1907; Harper, 1962; see also Monk, 1960; Veno, 1976; Myers, 1985; Rebertus, 1988; Rebertus et al., 1989). While this is likely for species with thin bark—especially at small sizes (see Hodgkins, 1958; Harmon, 1984)—once established, some hardwoods appear to be capable of resprouting and growing rapidly after at least some kinds of low-intensity fires (Buell and Cantlon, 1950; Monk, 1960; Abrahamson, 1984a,b; Chapman, 1942; Hodgkins, 1958; Boyle, 1973; De Selm et al., 1974; Thor and Nichols, 1974; Komarek, 1974; Auclair, 1975; McGee, 1980; Huntley and McGee, 1981). Thus, recurrent low-intensity fires may not result in the same changes in vegetation as occur following high-intensity fires or in the absence of fire (e.g., Maissurow, 1941; Lorimer, 1977; Delcourt et al., 1983).

The presettlement high hammock zone between upslope sand/clayhills and midslope hammocks likely contained a mixture of species from both habitats. The degree of intermixing depends on slope and frequency of fire. Oaks (*Q. alba*, *Q. falcata*, *Q. stellata*, *Q. hemisphaerica*, *Q. incana*) and hickories (*Carya pallida*, *C. glabra*, *C. tomentosa*) are characteristic of this zone. Some of these hardwoods, as well as shortleaf pine (*Pinus echinata*), may have occurred almost entirely within the transition zone (Pessin, 1933; Chapman, 1942; Harper, 1943; Clewell, 1986). High hammock zones were noted by travelers in the Tallahassee Red Hills region as early as the 1800s (Young, 1818; Vignoles, 1823). Open pine barrens were noted to contain large pines but few other species of trees. High hammocks contained pines, oaks, and hickories, as well as a dense growth of coppicing hardwoods along interfaces with pinelands. Similar pine-oak-hickory forests, in which low-intensity fires occur every one to two decades, also occur in other parts of the country (Ahlgren, 1974; Lyon and Stickney, 1976; Little and Moore, 1949; Buell and Cantlon, 1950; Boerner, 1981, 1982).

The only experimental data regarding effects of differences in fire frequency on the composition of hardwood forests come from a long-term study begun in 1959 by H. L. Stoddard at Tall Timbers Research Station (Leon County) in the Tallahassee Red Hills region. Replicated 0.2 ha plots were located in second growth pine (*P. taeda*, *P. echinata*) forests with a ground cover of herbaceous vegetation (Tall Timbers, 1962). Plots removed from annual winter burning have been reburned in March at prescribed intervals. In 1982, species composition, relative abundance, and physiognomy were measured within each of two plots burned at intervals of every one, two, three, seven, and twenty years, and unburned since 1959, to determine if differences in fire frequency affected forest composition and structure. In each plot thirty points were selected randomly from a 1 × 1 m grid (eliminating a 5 m perimeter). The highest point at which each plant intersected a pole marked at 2 m intervals was recorded. All heights above 8 m were included in a single stratum. In addition, all species of trees present in each

Table 7.2 Comparison between annually burned plots and plots not burned since 1959

	Annual burns		Unburned	
Plot	1A	1B	UC	UB
Percent cover	10	3	61	57
Number of woody species sampled	4	3	10	12
Total number of woody species	7	8	14	17
H′ (species)	0.51	0.48	0.68	0.82
H′ (strata)	0.14	0.00	0.68	0.65

plot were recorded. The Shannon-Weiner species/diversity index, H′, was calculated for species within 2 m strata in plots.

We assessed development of hardwood forests in the absence of fire by comparing unburned plots with annually burned plots, which constituted a "reference" fire regime of frequent, low-intensity winter ground cover fires (table 7.2). Hardwoods present in the latter plots were unable to reach a developmental stage invulnerable to fire and thus were root sprouts confined to the lowest stratum. In the absence of fire, three major changes occurred in the woody vegetation: the cover of woody plants increased by an order of magnitude; diversity increased in all strata; and species composition changed. Of the twelve species in annually burned plots, only six were also found in unburned plots. The twelve additional species in unburned plots were primarily those dispersed by birds—such as *Nyssa sylvatica* and *Cornus florida*—and included evergreen hardwoods (*Magnolia grandiflora, Ilex opaca*).

The hardwood forest formed on a site may depend on immigration and growth capabilities of species in the vicinity. Initial colonization most likely will involve species with good dispersal capability but also may be somewhat stochastic (Whelan, 1986). In the Tall Timbers study, both unburned plots differed from the forests that would have been expected if trees had colonized at random (table 7.3). Two species, *Liquidambar styraciflua* and *Q. nigra*, were more abundant than expected on the basis of chance colonization. Abundance and distribution of species differed, however, between plots and among strata within plots. Furthermore, once cover of woody species increased to a point that forest-dwelling birds were likely to use trees as perches, bird-dispersed hammock species invaded rapidly. Differences in arrival times—which result from unequal dispersal capability—coupled with unequal growth rates of invading species, can explain patterns of forest development following fire exclusion that have traditionally been attributed to differential shade tolerance (i.e., secondary succession [Laessle, 1942; Quarterman and Keever, 1962; Beckwith, 1967]).

Effects of differences in fire frequency on woody plant communities were assessed by comparing plots burned every two, three, seven, and twenty

Table 7.3. Replicated goodness of fit test on the distribution of individuals among species and among strata on unburned plots

Species			Strata		
Test	df	G	Test	df	G
Pooled	9	21.5[a]	Pooled	4	6.18
Heterogeneity	9	130.6[a]	Heterogeneity	4	14.42[a]
Total	18	151.7[a]	Total	8	20.60[a]
Plot			Plot		
UC	9	23.3[a]	UC	4	7.70
UB	9	128.4[a]	UB	4	12.92[a]

Note: Only species that occur on both plots are included.
a. Null hypothesis of random variation rejected at the 0.05 level.

Table 7.4. Friedman rank sums (s) for two-way layouts contrasting different burning frequencies with unburned plots

Fire frequency	(years)	2	3	7	20	Unburned	S	P
Percent cover	A	34	28	37	41	61	5.6	0.25
	B	28	52	32	51	57		
H′ (species)	A	0.81	0.75	0.75	0.75	0.81	1.2	0.93
	B	0.71	0.81	0.90	0.62	0.68		
H′ (strata)	A	0.31	0.56	0.47	0.34	0.65	7.6	0.04
	B	0.11	0.35	0.44	0.34	0.67		

years with unburned plots. Friedman rank sum analyses for two-way layouts were used (Hollander and Wolfe, 1973). Fire frequency affected strata diversity but did not affect numbers of species or species diversity (table 7.4). Varying fire frequency had only subtle effects on initial formation of a hardwood forest, suggesting that the rate, but not the actual process, of transition from second-growth pine to hardwood forest would be influenced by periodic, low intensity fire (see also McGee, 1980).

This study indicates that when fires periodically occur between growing seasons, assemblages of species—many of which resprout and grow rapidly—may become dominant in transition areas between pine forests and midslope hammocks. Species abundant in the Tall Timbers fire plots include *Q. nigra*, *Q. hemisphaerica*, *Q. virginiana*, *Q. falcata*, *Q. alba*, *L. styraciflua*, *C. glabra*, *C. pallida*, *C. tomentosa*, *Prunus serotina*, *Pinus taeda*, and *Pinus echinata*, some of which were not recorded in transition zones between pine and hardwood forests at the turn of the century. Harper (1943) suggested that fires occurring every decade in Alabama clayhills would result in pine-oak hardwood forests containing *Pinus palustris*, *P. echinata*, *Q. falcata*, *Q. alba*, and *C. glabra*. These forests did not include *P. taeda*, *Q. nigra*, or *L. styraciflua*, species that currently are often dominant in upland clayhill pine-oak forests throughout much of the southeastern coastal plain. Such species, which occur as dominants in some bottomland floodplain forests (Jones et al., 1981; Stalter, 1971; Wharton et al., 1982), first appeared in species lists for upland hardwood forests after the pyrogenic longleaf pine had been removed by logging and fire regimes had been shifted to winter burns (Chapman, 1942; Clewell, 1986; see also Delcourt et al., 1983). Data from studies of effects of fire on species with differences in bark thickness (Hodgkins, 1958; Harmon, 1984) and of effects of differences in the season of burn on the extent to which hardwoods are killed (Chaiken, 1952; Ferguson, 1957, 1961; Harrington and Stephenson, 1955; Lindenmuth and Byram, 1948; Lotti, 1956; Woods, 1955) also indicate that bottomland species like *Q. nigra* and *L. styraciflua* may have been excluded from upslope forests by periodic summer fires. The presence of *P. palustris* needles also would have increased the intensity of periodic groundcover fires (Williamson and Black, 1981; Platt et al., 1990) and thus the likelihood that fire-sensitive species would be excluded from high hammocks.

The northern Florida hardwood forests currently developing in transition zones between sand/clayhill pine forests and mesic hammocks appear to be a result of fire suppression and current fire management practices. Data from the Tall Timbers fire plots further suggest that these forests will be invaded by species less tolerant of fire if only a few years occur between recurrent fires; even the most sensitive species of hardwoods resprouted following low-intensity winter fires 7–20 years after the study began. Blaisdell et al. (1974) noted that low-intensity fires creeping through Titi Hammock did not kill large trees of *M. grandiflora* and *Fagus grandifolia.* Such species are likely to increase in importance over time under low-intensity winter fire regimes as well as following fire exclusion. Thus, altered fire regimes have probably induced changes in composition of high hammocks present at the time of settlement, as well as initiated the ongoing formation of hammocks in upland sand/clayhill habitats.

The Effects of Moisture

In the coastal plain, soils along upper slopes typically are entisols and ultisols, well-drained sandy soils of washed quartz and overlying variable amounts of clay (e.g., Dunn, 1982). Marks and Harcombe (1981) suggest that because moisture levels may be limiting, especially on sandy sites (see also Wells, 1928; Heyward, 1939a), there may be restrictions on the extension of mixed species hardwood forests upslope even in the absence of fire. There are, however, numerous empirical observations in a number of habitats and some quantitative data (Veno, 1976; Platt, 1985; Myers and White, 1987) indicating that midslope or even bottomland hardwood species are capable of invading upland sand/clayhill habitats when fires are suppressed. In the absence of fire, at least some type of hardwood vegetation appears likely to develop even on xeric sites. Hardwood hammocks are present on certain types of xeric sites protected from fire, such as xeric sandhill bluffs along the Apalachicola River (MacGowan, 1935, 1937; Kurz, 1938a; Clewell, 1977, 1986), and on isolated clayhills in northern Florida (data in Florida Natural Areas Inventory).

Several characteristics of fluctuations in water levels appear to affect the distribution of woody species along lower slopes, where the water table is close to the surface (Ware and Penfound, 1949; Buell and Wistendahl, 1955; Wistendahl, 1958; Weaver, 1960; Monk, 1966b; Dabel and Day, 1977; Franz and Bazzaz, 1977; Day and Dabel, 1978; Day, 1985). Water depth affects tree survival in several ways (Penfound, 1952; Broadfoot and Williston, 1973). The frequency, duration, and severity of flooding/drought affect germination (Putnam, 1951; Hosner, 1957), survival (Streng et al., 1989), and growth and reproduction (Hosner, 1958, 1959; Lindsey et al., 1961; Dickson et al., 1965; Broadfoot, 1973; Broadfoot and Williston, 1973). Periodic aeration of sites may be necessary for germination and establishment (Shunk, 1939; Penfound, 1952; Nixon et al., 1977).

The influence of flooding on zonation of vegetation along lower slopes where low hammocks grade into bottomland forests has been best described for rivers in the southeastern United States. Different forest associations along river floodplains are related to differences in tolerance of flooding (Hosner, 1960; Hook et al., 1972; Broadfoot, 1973; Whitlow and Harris, 1979; Wharton et al., 1982) and thus occur in areas with different drainage patterns (Penfound, 1952; Shelford, 1954; Putnam et al., 1960; Hosner and Minkler, 1963; Conner and Day, 1976; Wharton et al., 1977; Leitman, 1978). Along the Apalachicola River, floodplain distribution of tree species is variable (Harper, 1911b, 1914a; Kurz, 1938a; Hubbell et al., 1956; Clewell, 1977; Leitman, 1978; Elder and Cairns, 1982; Leitman et al., 1982). Low hammock species (*Liquidambar styraciflua*, *Quercus nigra*, *Pinus taeda*, *Carpinus caroliniana*) are mixed with floodplain species (*Celtis laevigata*, *Carya aquatica*, *Quercus laurifolia*, *Q. lyrata*, *Fraxinus pennsylvanica*, *Ilex decidua*) in areas infrequently and briefly flooded (Leitman, 1978; Leitman et al., 1982). Because these same low hammock species also are adventive in more xeric upper slope habitats, they appear not to be strongly influenced by soil moisture.

Composition and Dynamics of Hardwood Forests

Coastal plain hardwood forests most often have been compared to mixed mesophytic forests of the Appalachians (Braun, 1950; Quarterman and Keever, 1962; Monk, 1965, 1967; Marks and Harcombe, 1975; Platt, 1985). As a result of different measurements, these comparisons have led to different conclusions regarding relative diversity of tree species in these forests.

Monk (1967) indicated lower diversity of trees in north-central peninsular Florida hammocks than in Appalachian cove forests. Schwartz (1988) has shown, however, that the diversity in hammocks along the central ridge of Florida decreases. Furthermore, hammocks along the northern tier of Panhandle counties in Florida—the southern mixed species forest region of Greller (1980)—contain as many overstory species of trees as Appalachian cove forests, or even slightly more. These hammocks also contain many more species of smaller-statured understory trees and shrubs than do the Appalachian forests (Marks and Harcombe, 1975; Platt, 1985). Postulated reasons for large numbers of species of trees, especially in northern Florida hammocks, have centered on vertical (physiognomic) structure, habitat differences (topography), as well as *in situ* dynamics involving limited resources (nutrients and light) or succession and disturbance.

Structure

Smith (1973) has documented increased layering of vegetation in tropical compared to temperate forests. This layering results in part from increased solar radiation and hence more light penetrating the overstory at lower latitudes (Harcombe and Marks, 1977). This is also true of Florida's hammocks, where increased insolation leads to increased layering of vegetation compared to temperate forests. There are both more trees in the overstory layer and numerous small-statured understory and shrub species (Marks and Harcombe, 1975; Platt, 1985).

The increased number of smaller-statured species in southern hardwood forests appears to reflect the ability of these species to colonize localized gaps resulting from canopy damage or windthrows of overstory trees. In Woodyard Hammock, small trees (2–10 cm diameter at breast height, or dbh) of all dominant understory species are positively associated with gaps (Platt and Hermann, 1986). Furthermore, recruitment of understory species into the understory stratum also occurs almost exclusively in gaps. Densities of understory trees increase in recent gaps but decline beneath overstory trees (W. J. Platt, unpublished data). Within gaps, rapidly growing, short-lived deciduous fugitive species (*Carpinus caroliniana*, *Ostrya virginiana* and *Cornus florida*) tend to be replaced in the understory stratum by slower-growing but longer-lived evergreen species (*Ilex opaca* and *Symplocos tinctoria*) (W. J. Platt, unpublished data). Increased numbers of smaller-statured species in north Florida hammocks thus appear to result partly from sequential replacement within gaps of smaller-statured species with different life histories.

Understory species, as a whole, dominate gaps in Woodyard Hammock for a period of several decades after formation. These species probably suppress growth of overstory species into the understory stratum (Platt and Hermann, 1986; W. J. Platt, unpublished data). Harcombe and Marks

(1977) also have demonstrated a negative association between abundances of overstory and understory species, suggesting that understory species can suppress overstory species and vice versa (see also Ehrenfeld, 1980).

It appears to be primarily in north Florida hammocks that understory trees are present as a guild of species forming a discrete but transient understory stratum in gaps. The reason for this may well be the presence of beech (*Fagus grandifolia*), a species noted for shade tolerance (Hough and Forbes, 1943; Horn, 1971; Woods, 1979, 1984; Runkle, 1981, 1982; Glitzenstein et al., 1986). Small beech trees may be recruited at the same time as more rapidly growing overstory trees, but they grow slowly and hence enter the understory stratum beneath overstory trees (Glitzenstein et al., 1986; Platt and Hermann, 1986). Maps of the crowns of trees in Woodyard Hammock (Platt and Hermann, 1986) also indicate that beech trees frequently have large crowns that are partially beneath crowns of other trees. Multiple layers of leaves (especially those including both the evergreen southern magnolia and beech) cast dense shade; almost no small trees of either overstory or understory species occur beneath such a multilayered overstory (Kurz, 1944; Glitzenstein et al., 1986; Platt and Hermann, 1986). Hence, in hardwood forests of northern Florida, where beech is abundant, understory species may be restricted to gaps.

In central and southern Florida, south of the range of beech, there is no multilayered overstory stratum. There commonly is, however, a well-developed shrub–small tree stratum that includes understory and overstory species, as well as shrubs that do not commonly reach overstory height (Wamer, 1978; Clewell et al., 1982). Thus, smaller-statured species that tend to occur primarily in gaps in north Florida hammocks also occur beneath overstory trees in peninsular hammocks. The increased continuity of small tree and shrub strata in peninsular Florida hammocks may well result from the absence of beech and, hence, a multilayered, continuous overstory.

Restricted Distributions along Topographic Gradients

Distributions and abundances of hammock species are generally recognized to depend on an often subtle topographic gradient (Bessey, 1911; Quarterman and Keever, 1962; Monk, 1965; Clewell et al., 1982; Clewell, 1986). Whether associations of species can be discerned depends on the slope. In Woodyard Hammock, located along a flat lake margin, there are few spatial patterns to the distribution of dominant species attributable to elevation within a 4.5 ha mapped plot in which the greatest topographic differences are 2.5 meters (Platt and Hermann, 1986; W. J. Platt, unpublished data). In contrast, in Titi Hammock, located along a steep creek bank, segregation analysis of trees in a 5 ha mapped plot indicated distinct associations (Platt, 1985).

The importance of interspecific interactions in determining the occurrence of species in different areas within Woodyard and Titi hammocks was assessed by comparing observed species occurrences in quadrats to those expected if species were randomly and independently distributed within quadrats composing the plot. Each plot was divided into a grid of 25 × 25 m quadrats. For each plot, species area curves based on observed distributions of species were generated by selecting quadrats in random order and obtaining the cumulative number of species as the number of quadrats increased. This process was repeated 10 times to obtain mean observed cumulative numbers of species with increasing area. Mean observed distributions of species-area curves were compared to expected species-area curves generated by 100 Monte Carlo simulations in which the same numbers of species (in the same relative abundances) were independently distributed among quadrats. Confidence intervals that contained 90 percent of the cumulative number of species expected within areas of different size were constructed.

Species-area curves (fig. 7.4) indicate that species of trees are broadly intermixed in both forests despite the differences in slope. The number of species increases rapidly with increasing area in both forests. One-third to one-half the species are likely to occur in a single 25 × 25 m area, and more than 80 percent are likely to occur in a hectare. In addition, the species-area curves differ only minutely from ones expected if species were indepen-

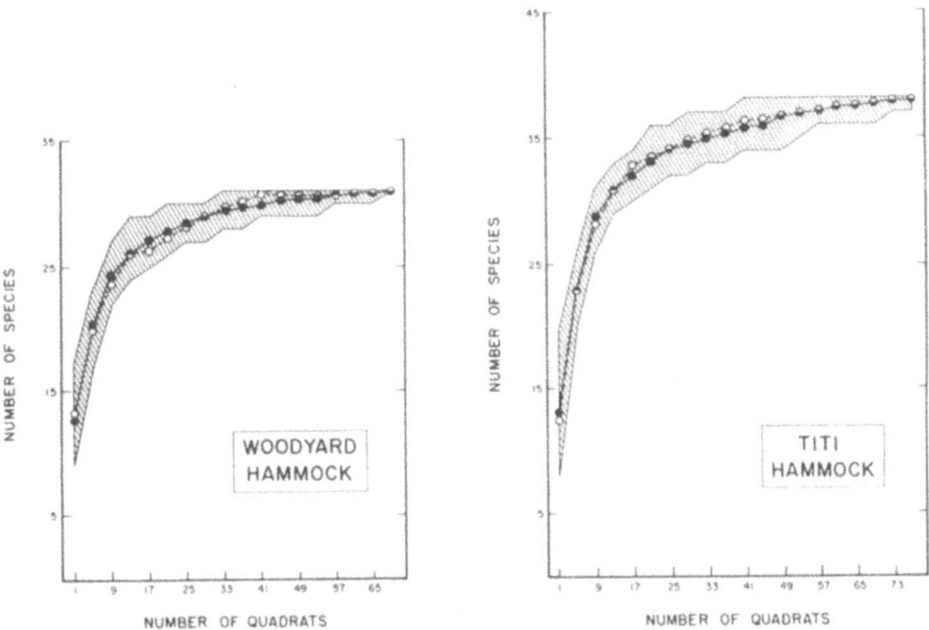

Fig. 7.4. Species-area curves for a flat lake margin forest (Woodyard Hammock) and steep-banked creek slope forest (Titi Hammock). Quadrat sizes are 625 m^2. *Open circles*: observed species area curve. *Closed circles*: species area curves predicted based upon random distribution of species within plots. *Shaded areas* represent 95% confidence intervals for the expected species area curves.

dently and randomly distributed among quadrats composing plots. Although patterns in the distribution of populations result in distinct associations based on segregation analysis when there is a steep topographic gradient (Platt, 1985), such associations contain some trees of a number of species not typical of that association.

Abiotic conditions are more extreme along the ends of topographic gradients in hammocks (Monk, 1965, 1967; Marks and Harcombe, 1981). Although species diversity may be higher in transition zones between habitats, effects of fire and xeric conditions along upper slopes and of flooding along lower slopes may tend to result in fewer species of trees at the extremes of the topographic gradient (but see Streng et al., 1989). Marks and Harcombe (1981) have quantitatively described the distribution of tree species along topographic gradients in eastern Texas. Stand-to-stand variation in species composition was interpreted—based on a reciprocal averaging ordination—as being most strongly related to soil moisture. Numbers of overstory and understory species increased from xeric upland to mesic slope forests, then declined somewhat in more hydric bottomland forests (see also Monk, 1965).

While patterns in the distribution of species along the topographic gradient in hammocks have most commonly been attributed to soil moisture (Harper, 1914a; Quarterman and Keever, 1962; Wells, 1928, 1942; Monk, 1960, 1965; H. R. Delcourt and P. A. Delcourt, 1977), fire frequency varies along slopes in a manner similar to soil moisture. Fires burning into hammocks become slow creeping ground fires, but even these may kill aboveground stems (especially of small juveniles) as well as open up space by removing leaf litter. Increased moisture of downslope soils also may influence the frequency and type of fire. Regardless of the relative importance of fire and moisture, subtle changes in these abiotic variables along the upper ends of topographic gradients appear to exert a major influence on species distributions and thus, to some extent, the diversity of species in hammocks. Similarly subtle changes, especially in moisture (expressed both as flooding and as drought), appear important along the lower ends of topographic gradients (Streng et al., 1989).

Nutrient Availability

Mixed species hardwood forests have long been recognized to occur on soils that contain more organic matter and cations than adjacent sandhills (Harper, 1914a; Monk, 1960). Within hardwood forests, soils vary considerably in organic matter, exchangeable cations, and pH (DeVall, 1943; Monk, 1965, 1966a; Marks and Harcombe, 1981). Moisture and cation exchange are influenced by soil texture, especially layers of clay (hardpans) in subsurface soil layers. An excellent description of local variation in soil types and the correlation with different vegetation types is given by Dunn (1982) for San Felasco Hammock in Alachua County.

Harper (1914a, 1921, 1927) and Small (1923b) hypothesized that nutrient availability influences the proportion of evergreen species in hammocks. Monk (1965, 1966a), using stepwise regression analysis to determine how much of the variation in evergreenness of stands could be explained by various soil properties, found that there tended to be more evergreen trees on hardwood forest sites low in calcium, potassium, and phosphorus. Greller (1980 and personal communication) suggests, however, that the distribution of *Quercus virginiana*, the most abundant evergreen hardwood in Florida, is more closely associated with climatic conditions (the 5.5° C [42°F] mean January minimum) than with low soil nutrients.

Monk hypothesized that the greater occurrence of evergreen species on xeric, infertile sites may be related to more gradual return of nutrients to soil by evergreen species or to the establishment of a more closed mineral cycle through leaching of nutrients from leaves and/or leaf fall that occurs year-round. Data from a study of mineral nutrient cycling in a forty-five-year-old hardwood stand in north-central Florida (Ewel et al., 1975) suggest continual leaching of phosphorus and calcium from leaves and perhaps higher concentrations in stem flow. This stand, however, was dominated by two deciduous (*Q. nigra* and *Carya glabra*) and an evergreen (*Q. hemisphaerica*) overstory species that are associated with gaps in hardwood forests (Platt and Hermann, 1986; Platt, 1985) and also typically invade abandoned agricultural land. Continual leaching could, therefore, be a characteristic not just of evergreen species but also of inefficient utilization of nutrients by rapidly growing gap or pioneer species.

More and different species, especially shrubs and herbs, occur on soils high in calcium and phosphate (Monk, 1965, 1967; Marks and Harcombe, 1975, 1981). It has been hypothesized that nutrient use efficiency varies inversely with soil nutrient availability (Vitousek, 1982, 1984). In fact, a number of deciduous understory (*Cornus florida, Hamamelis virginiana, Acer rubrum*) and overstory (*Q. alba, Fagus grandifolia*) species appear to become less efficient in use of calcium and phosphorus as soil fertility increases (Kost and Boerner, 1985; Boerner, 1984, 1985). The importance of nutrients in limiting growth of hardwood trees also depends on soil moisture and availability (Boerner, 1984, 1985). On mesic sites with calcareous material in subsurface soil layers, therefore, increased calcium and higher pH may occur near the soil surface as a result of leaching (Ewel et al., 1975) or leaf fall (turnover of leaves occurs within six to twelve months [Elder and Cairns, 1982; Lugo et al., 1978]). Increased nutrient availability near the soil surface may result in presence of species (especially small-statured trees and shrubs capable of utilizing such nutrients) that otherwise might be excluded. Such increased nutrient availability in forests on calcareous soils thus could partly account for large numbers of smaller-statured species in northern Florida hammocks.

Succession and Disturbance

Comparisons of the diversity of hammocks and adjacent pinelands in the southeastern coastal plain have shown that the former have more species of trees (Quarterman and Keever, 1962; Monk, 1965, 1967, 1968; Marks and Harcombe, 1981). Several hypotheses have been proposed to explain this phenomenon. Laessle (1942), Quarterman and Keever (1962), and Monk (1967, 1968) interpreted the increased diversity of hammocks to be a result of succession in which harsh environmental conditions characterizing open pinelands were ameliorated by pioneer species, thus enabling more specialized species to invade and partition the habitat in the absence of any subsequent fires (Whittaker, 1953; Drury and Nisbet, 1973; but see also Connell and Slatyer, 1977). Much of the literature dealing with the dynamics of mixed species forests has attempted to delineate replacement processes and to discern patterns produced by succession (e.g., Gano, 1917; Kurz, 1944; Ewel et al., 1975; Hubbell et al., 1956; Laessle, 1942, 1958b; Monk, 1965, 1967, 1968; Blaisdell et al., 1974; H. R. Delcourt and P. A. Delcourt, 1974, 1977). These studies have emphasized replacement of pines by oaks and hickories (Laessle, 1942; Quarterman and Keever, 1962; Monk, 1965, 1967) and of oaks and hickories by magnolias and beeches (H. R. Delcourt and P. A. Delcourt, 1974, 1977; Blaisdell et al., 1974; Glitzenstein et al., 1986). There is no general agreement, however, regarding the nature of putative climax forests (Harper, 1911a; Quarterman and Keever, 1962; Monk, 1965; Blaisdell et al., 1974; H. R. Delcourt and P. A. Delcourt, 1977; Glitzenstein et al., 1986).

The role of succession in mixed species hardwood forests has been questioned. Analysis of coastal plain hardwood forests in Texas has indicated no patterns related to succession (Harcombe and Marks, 1977, 1978; Marks and Harcombe, 1981). Studies of populations of trees in mapped plots (Platt, 1984, 1985; Glitzenstein et al., 1986; Platt and Hermann, 1986; W. J. Platt, unpublished data) and of long-term population trends (Glitzenstein et al., 1986) also do not indicate replacement of overstory species as being of major importance in determining the species composition of hammocks. Instead, these studies implicate a very complex disturbance regime involving frequent disruptions of variable intensity (also see Streng et al., 1989). Such a regime would maintain hammocks in nonequilibrium states frequently opened to invasion (see also Lorimer, 1980; Barden, 1980, 1981; Hubbell and Foster, 1983, 1986).

Studies of disturbance of hammocks have produced hypotheses regarding both the nature of forest dynamics in coastal plain hammocks and the basic population biology of the species that are different from the hypotheses produced by studies of succession. The disturbance-based studies have indicated a few patterns to replacement in the absence of disturbance. For example, because it is more tolerant of shade, beech tends to enter the understory and overstory beneath other trees (Glitzenstein et al., 1986). Likewise, shade tolerance appears to play a role in capture of localized gaps by oaks and hickories (Platt and Hermann, 1986). Nonetheless, such replacement processes are only a small part of forest dynamics in coastal plain hammocks. Disturbances open overstory layers of hammocks to different degrees and at different frequencies. Several studies (e.g. Harcombe and Marks, 1978; Platt, 1985; Platt and Hermann, 1986; Glitzenstein et al., 1986) suggest that dominant species (core species of Quarterman and Keever, 1962) in mixed species hardwood forests coexist as nonequilibrium populations responding independently to patterns of overstory disturbance (Platt and Hermann, 1986). Relative abundances of species in forests are predicted to depend on the disturbance regime and responses to disturbance, within the context of background environmental conditions such as moisture and soil nutrient levels.

While advance recruits of most dominant species are present as juveniles scattered across the forest floor of Woodyard and Titi hammocks, most of these species do not enter the overstory in localized treefalls or beneath overstory trees. This pattern suggests that larger-scale disturbances, such as fires and hurricanes (see Simpson and Lawrence, 1971), may have a major influence on overstory composition (also see Lorimer, 1989). Several dominant overstory species (*Magnolia grandiflora*, *Nyssa sylvatica*, *Liquidambar styraciflua*) are clonal; the presence of basal or root sprouts enhances the likelihood of recovery from damage. Genetic individuals of these species, because they can recapture space following large-scale disruptions, may be long-lived (Platt, 1984 and unpublished data). New individuals appear to be recruited rarely into populations of these species. Another dominant overstory species present in these hammocks, spruce pine (*Pinus glabra*), is much shorter-lived but grows more rapidly (Hirsh and Platt, 1981). Spruce pine has advance recruits in localized light gaps; these recruits, capable of rapid growth at high light intensities, capture space following large-scale disruptions. Thus species indigenous to hammocks and dependent on large-scale disturbance exhibit a wide range of life histories (see also Veblen et al., 1979, 1980; Poulson and Platt, 1989). Similar patterns characterize other mixed evergreen-deciduous forests elsewhere in the world (e.g., Japan [Naka, 1982], Southeast Asia [Whitmore, 1975], and Chile [Veblen, 1985]).

Disruption of hammocks by hurricanes or fires appears unlikely to be catastrophic in nature (cf. Canham and Loucks, 1984). Damage is likely to vary locally in magnitude, producing open patches of variable size and intensity of disruption. For example, in 1985, Woodyard Hammock bore the impact of Hurricane Kate: 21 new gaps were formed, and the sizes of many of the 38 extant gaps in a mapped area of 4.5 hectares increased. Sizes of gaps after the hurricane ranged from 50 to 4800 m^2 (W. J. Platt, unpubl. data). In addition, some areas of forests may be affected repeatedly by disturbance, while other areas may escape extensive damage for many years. Thus species with potentially long life spans as a result of clonal growth and escape from damage persist in the same forest with short-lived, damage-prone, nonclonal species (cf. Stearns and Crandall, 1981). While relative abundances of species may vary over space and time as a function of idiosyncratic effects of specific large-scale disturbances, species may persist even over long periods of time (see also Lorimer, 1980).

The complex disturbance regime may act as a filter, determining which species persist as indigenous components of the forest flora. While the forest is frequently opened to invasion from outside, an invading species either must respond rapidly to conditions produced by disturbances or must be capable of surviving repeated disturbance if it is to persist (cf. Connell, 1989). Shade-tolerant species with advance recruits or species capable of recovery are likely to have an edge over shade-intolerant species whose seeds germinate after large-scale disturbances such as hurricanes, unless the growth rates of the latter are rapid (Canham and Marks, 1985; Canham, 1989; see also Whitmore, 1975, 1989). Species adapted to wind disturbance, however, may not be as resistant to fires, since advance recruits or clonal sprouts may be killed by even low-intensity creeping fires. Hence, the flora of hammocks may change with the type of widespread disruption that is most likely to occur (see also Brokaw and Scheiner, 1989).

Frequent disturbance, which repeatedly opens areas of forests to invasion, is probably the reason that interactions among species seem to have so little effect on the distribution of species in hammocks. The stochastic nature of immigration makes it unlikely that species can be competitively excluded from the forest or that species will necessarily differ in habitat requirements, such as regeneration niches (Grubb, 1977). Species that resprout or have advance recruits may have an edge on growth into the overstory after certain types of disturbances; they are not likely to dominate completely because they are unlikely to capture all space or survive all types of disturbance better than species without such characteristics. Hence, trees of species typically found in other habitats in the vicinity of hammocks (especially those in upslope pinelands or downslope bottomland forest) may colonize areas opened by disturbance, increasing the numbers of species found in these forests. Populations of such species may even persist for several generations once present in hammocks. Frequent and variable disturbance regimes, coupled with restrictions on the distribution of species over the ranges of environmental conditions occurring in hammocks, thus appear to be a major reason behind the presence of large numbers of species within small areas of hammocks. This hypothesis, supported by data on the population dynamics and life histories of tree species, indicates that these are not "stable, climax forests" of the Southeast, but instead are frequently disrupted, nonequilibrium, nonsuccessional forests. Although these forests are open to invasion, they nonetheless have a number of persistent, core species (Quarterman and Keever, 1962) adapted to different and recurrent characteristics of disturbance regimes; the continual presence of such species provides some notion of community consistency and predictability over time.

Coda

In this review, we have explored the nature of mixed species hardwood forests, as indicated by studies of the geological and recent history, biogeographical differences among different parts of the state, abiotic and biotic variables that affect the distribution and abundance of hammocks, and internal forest dynamics. Results of these studies emphasize a common theme: Mixed species hardwood forests have changed continually. While these assemblages have a long history, over the past 100 million years they have undergone changes in geographic location as well as in abundance and distribution within localized areas. The composition and structure of these forests change markedly, not only with latitude but also over subtle differences in topography. In addition, the composition and abundances of species, as well as the structure and dynamics of these forests, are affected by complex disturbance regimes that vary at different scales over space and time. Most recently, anthropogenic disturbance has been added to natural disturbance, still further modifying disturbance regimes. Hence, combinations of species and forest communities not present in presettlement Florida are currently being formed. Relationships between historically and anthropogenically derived forests have not been studied in detail, but available data suggest that these forests are essentially new variations of mixed species hardwood forests.

We conclude that the vegetation of hardwood forests is kaleidoscopic, changing over a number of different temporal and spatial scales. The environmental variables most important in determining the characteristics of a hardwood forest appear to be abiotic in nature but are complex and continually change locally over space and time. As a result, hammocks should not be viewed as stable, equilibrium "climax" forests produced by intricate biotic interactions among component species. A more accurate paradigm appears to be one in which these forests are considered as continually changing in character in response to a continually changing and variable environment. Hence, these are nonequilibrium forests responding dynamically to local environmental conditions.

8

South Florida Rockland

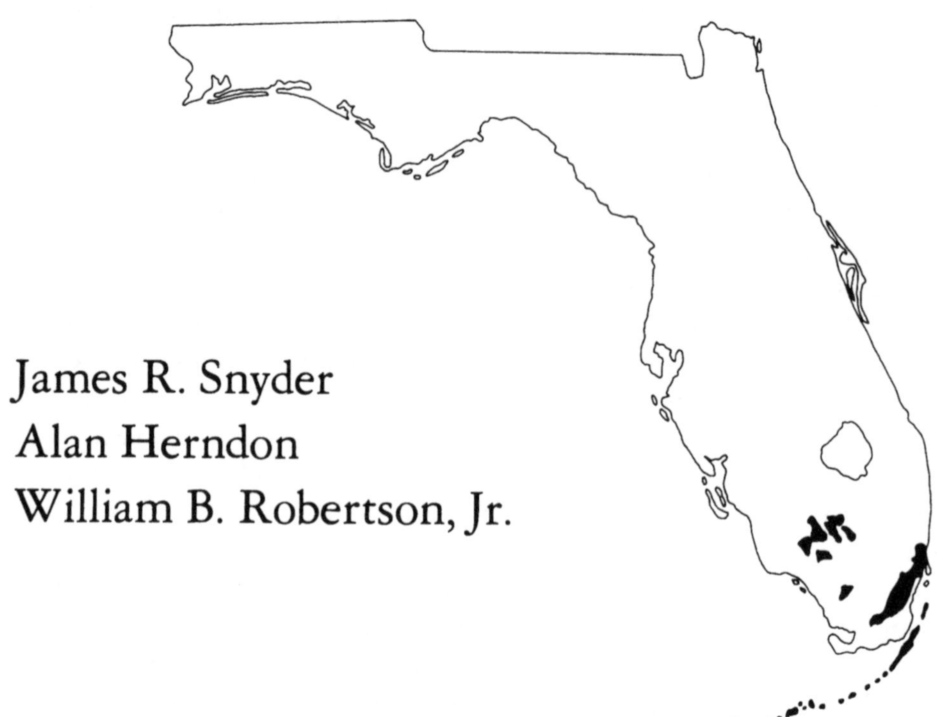

James R. Snyder
Alan Herndon
William B. Robertson, Jr.

With the exception of a few coastal ridges and beaches, the upland areas of extreme southern Florida are associated with outcroppings of limestone. Pinelands and tropical hardwood hammocks cover virtually all of these outcrops and are the rockland ecosystems considered in this chapter. Hammocks are evergreen, broad-leaved forests composed predominantly of trees common to the Bahamas and Greater Antilles. They are well endowed with tropical epiphytes such as orchids, bromeliads, and ferns. In the continental United States, most of these species are found only in south Florida. The fire-maintained pine forests have a diverse understory with a mixture of tropical and temperate shrubs, palms, and herbs. Many of the taxa are endemic to the ecosystem (table 8.1). In contrast to the flora, the fauna is derived primarily from temperate species, although several taxa are considered to be endemic (table 8.2).

The area covered by the rockland ecosystems was never large, and it has been rapidly shrinking because of the pressure of economic development. Land required by the burgeoning population of greater Miami and the Florida Keys has been obtained largely by clearing pineland and hammock,

Table 8.1. Vascular plants endemic to southern Florida and found in rockland ecosystems

Scientific name	Common name[a]	Listing status[a]	
		Federal	State
Herbs			
Argythamnia blodgettii	Blodgett's wild mercury	UR2	—
Aster concolor var. *simulatus*	—	—	—
Borreria terminalis	—	—	—
Cassia keyensis	Big Pine partridge pea	UR1	E
Chamaesyce conferta	—	—	—
Chamaesyce deltoidea subsp. *deltoidea* var. *adhaerens*	wedge spurge	E	—
Chamaesyce deltoidea subsp. *deltoidea* var. *deltoidea*	wedge spurge	E	—
Chamaesyce deltoidea subsp. *serpyllum*	wild thyme spurge	URI	—
Chamaesyce garberi	Garber's spurge	T	—
Chamaesyce pinetorum	—	—	—
Chamaesyce porteriana var. *keyensis*	Keys hairy-podded spurge	UR1	—
Chamaesyce porteriana var. *porteriana*	Porter's hairy-podded spurge	UR1	—
Chamaesyce porteriana var. *scoparia*	Porter's broom spurge	UR1	—
Digitaria pauciflora	Florida crabgrass	UR2	—
Dyschoriste oblongifolia var. *angusta*	—	—	—
Encyclia cochleata var. *triandra**	shell orchid	—	—
Evolvulus sericeus var. *averyi*	—	—	—
Galactia pinetorum	narrow-leaf milkpea	UR2	—
Galactia smallii	Small's milkpea	E	—
Hedyotis nigricans var. *floridana*	—	—	—
Hyptis alata var. *stenophylla*	—	—	—
Indigofera keyensis	—	—	—
Jacquemontia curtissii	pineland clustervine	UR2	E
Kuhnia eupatorioides var. *floridana*	—	—	—
Lantana depressa	—	—	—
Linum arenicola	sand flax	UR2	E
Linum carteri var. *carteri*	Carter's small-flowered flax	UR1	—
Melanthera parvifolia	small-leaved cat tongue	UR2	—
*Peperomia floridana**	Everglades peperomia	UR2	E

(*continued*)

Table 8.1. (continued)

Scientific name	Common name[a]	Listing status[a]	
		Federal	State
Phyllanthus pentaphyllus var. *floridanus*	Florida five-petaled leaf flower	UR2	—
Poinsettia pinetorum	—	—	—
Polygala smallii	tiny milkwort	E	E
Ruellia caroliniensis var. *succulenta*	—	—	—
Schizachyrium rhizomatum	Florida autumn grass	UR4	—
Stillingia sylvatica subsp. *tenuis*	slender queen's delight	UR2	—
Tragia saxicola	Florida Keys noseburn	UR2	—
Tripsacum floridanum	Florida grama grass	UR1	—
Trees and shrubs			
Amorpha crenulata	crenulate lead plant	E	E
Cereus robinii var. *deeringii**	Key tree cactus	E	E
Colubrina cubensis var. *floridana**	—	—	—
Forestiera segregata var. *pinetorum*	pine wood privet	UR1	—
Myrcianthes fragrans var. *simpsonii**	Simpson's stopper	UR2	—

Source: Modified from Avery and Loope (1980). Elements of the *Croton glandulosus* complex have been described as endemic taxa, but the taxonomy remains confused. *Salvia blodgettii* was originally described from specimens found in hammocks of Key West, but no recent collections have been seen.

Note: All are native to pinelands except those marked with an asterisk, which are native to hammocks.

a. Based on Wood (1986). Codes for federal and state listing status:

E = endangered.
T = threatened.
UR1 = under review for federal listing, and substantial evidence of biological vulnerability or threat exists.
UR2 = under review for federal listing, but substantial evidence of biological vulnerability or threat is lacking.
UR4 = under review for federal listing, but no longer being considered because current taxonomic understanding indicates species is an invalid taxon.

threatening or endangering the existence of a large number of species (especially endemics) in these ecosystems (tables 8.1 and 8.2).

The tropical tip of Florida has long fascinated biologists from more temperate regions. More than any other individual, John K. Small of the New York Botanical Garden made the vegetation of south Florida known. From 1902 to 1938 he published more than 100 articles and books on south Florida botany, including several floras (Loope, 1980a). Long before the recent population explosion, he decried the loss of south Florida's natural habitats (Small, 1929). The popular writings of Simpson (1920, 1923, 1932) pre-

Table 8.2. Vertebrates endemic to southern Florida and chiefly found in rockland ecosystems

Scientific name	Common name	Listing status[a] Federal	State
Mammals			
Eumops glaucinus floridanus	Florida mastiff bat	UR2	—
Neotoma floridana smallii	Key Largo wood rat	E	E
Nycticeius humeralis subtropicalis	evening bat	—	—
Odocoileus virginianus clavium	Key deer	E	T
Oryzomys argentatus	silver rice rat	UR1	E
Peromyscus gossypinus allapaticola	Key Largo cotton mouse	E	E
Procyon lotor auspicatus	Key Vaca raccoon	UR2	T
Procyon lotor incautus	Key West raccoon	UR2	—
Procyon lotor inexperatus	Upper Keys raccoon	—	—
Sigmodon hispidus exsputus	Lower Keys cotton rat	—	—
Reptiles			
Diadophis punctatus acricus	Big Pine Key ringneck snake	UR2	T
Elaphe obsoleta deckerti	Keys rat snake	—	—
Eumeces egregius egregius	Florida Keys mole skink	UR2	SSC
Kinosternon bauri bauri	Key mud turtle	UR2	E
Tantilla oolitica	Miami black-headed snake	UR2	T

Source: Derived from Stevenson (1976), Layne (1978), and McDiarmid (1978).

a. Based on Wood (1986). Codes for federal and state listing status:
E = endangered.
SSC = species of special concern.
T = threatened.
UR1 = under review for federal listing, and substantial evidence of biological vulnerability or threat exists.
UR2 = under review for federal listing, but substantial evidence of biological vulnerability or threat is lacking.

sented an early naturalist's observations of south Florida. Harshberger (1914), Harper (1927), and Davis (1943) provided general accounts of the ecosystems of southern Florida, including rockland hammocks and pinelands. More detailed descriptions of rocklands include those by Robertson (1955) and Craighead (1971). Duever (1984) briefly summarized the plant communities of the south Florida rockland ecosystems. Nomenclature for plant species mentioned in this discussion generally follows Avery and Loope (1983) and Long and Lakela (1971).

Physical Environment

Surface Geology

South Florida rocklands are outcrops of primarily mid-Pleistocene marine limestone representing three distinct geological formations: the Miami, Key

Largo, and Tamiami limestones (Hoffmeister, 1974). The rocklands also occur in three distinct geographical regions, which are only partially correlated with the geological formations (fig. 8.1).

The largest outcrop is the Miami rock ridge, composed of Miami limestone, which occupies a broad area from Miami to Homestead and narrows westward through the Long Pine Key area of Everglades National Park. At the northern end of this outcrop, in the Silver Bluff area of Miami near the shore of Biscayne Bay, the ridge reaches elevations in excess of 7 m above sea level. Elevations decrease rapidly westward and more gradually southward. The highest points of the Miami rock ridge in the Homestead area are about 4 m above sea level. The westward extension of the rock ridge shows a further decrease in elevation, the surface of Long Pine Key being less than 2 m above sea level. At its southwestern extremity in the vicinity

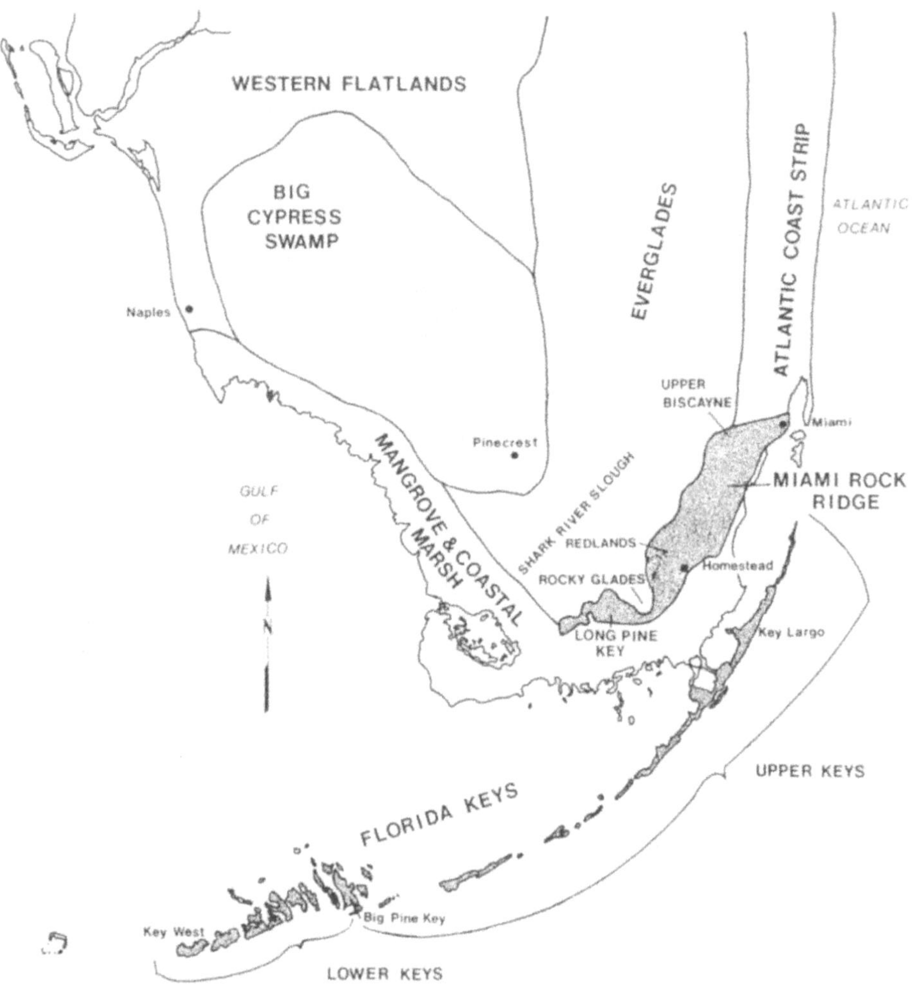

Fig. 8.1. Generalized map of south Florida with major areas of limestone outcropping shown by shading. Outcropping is less extensive in the Big Cypress region than in the Miami rock ridge or the Florida Keys.

of Mahogany Hammock in Everglades National Park, the outcrop is largely mantled by marl soil with only occasional patches of exposed limestone.

The Florida Keys are composed almost entirely of rock outcrops representing two different formations. The upper Keys (Soldier Key to Big Pine Key) represent outcrops of the Key Largo limestone, and the lower Keys (Big Pine Key to Key West) represent outcrops of the Miami limestone. The two formations meet at the southeastern corner of Big Pine Key, where a small peninsula of the Key Largo limestone is found. Most of the Keys are low (elevations 1 to 2 m above sea level), but small areas 4 to 5 m above sea level occur on Key West and Lignumvitae Key.

The third region of outcropping is the southeastern third of the Big Cypress Swamp. This region is also where the Miami limestone thins to a feather edge and disappears, baring the older Tamiami limestone. The outcrops are most extensively exposed around Pinecrest near their southern end, but they extend for many kilometers to the north.

The surficial rocks of the Miami rock ridge and lower Florida Keys are the oolitic facies of the Miami limestone, a rock composed of small spherical or ovoid pellets of calcium carbonate originally precipitated in a shallow marine environment (Hoffmeister et al., 1967; Hoffmeister, 1974). These ooids became cemented together when sea level fell, exposing the unconsolidated mass to air. The Miami oolite was deposited during the Pleistocene, around 130,000 YBP (Perkins, 1977). Only a shallow layer of this rock near the surface is fully hardened. A few feet below the surface the ooids are so weakly cemented that the rock can be easily cut and shaped with hand tools. Early settlers took advantage of the softness of this rock. Blocks quarried below the surface were shaped as desired and left to harden with exposure to air.

The Tamiami limestone, which underlies Big Cypress Swamp, is much more fossiliferous than the Miami limestone and has generally been considered to be older (Hoffmeister, 1974). However, Perkins (1977) suggests that the latest levels of the formation were contemporaneous with the early layers of the Miami limestone. Like the Miami limestone, the Tamiami limestone hardens only on exposure to air.

The Key Largo limestone, which underlies the upper Florida Keys, is formed from consolidated reef corals and associated rubble (fig. 8.2) and is considered to be contemporaneous with the Miami oolite. This limestone covers a small area in comparison with the other two formations and was apparently formed by a patch reef–sand shoal complex during a period of high sea level, between 200,000 and 130,000 YBP (Perkins, 1977).

Although Hoffmeister (1974) suggested that the limestones in southern Florida were most recently exposed about 5000 YBP, numerous lines of evidence suggest that the actual date is much earlier. The most direct evidence is the recent discovery of archaeological remains within the rockland region that date from 8000 YBP or earlier. Indirect evidence consists of a recent

Fig. 8.2. Exposed Key Largo limestone in a tropical hammock on upper Key Largo. Note fossilized brain coral.

sea level curve that shows an increase in sea level over the last 14,000 years, with the Miami oolite and Key Largo limestone exposed throughout this episode of rising sea level (Robbin, 1984). Finally, several endemic plant species are closely associated with the rocklands of southern Florida (table 8.1). These seem to be mostly calciphiles, and many have no apparent adaptations for long-distance dispersal. Their presence suggests a long period of evolution on rocky substrate in southern Florida.

Solution features dominate the appearance of the rock surface in southern Florida. The most conspicuous of these features are solution holes (fig. 8.3), steep-sided pits of varying sizes formed by the dissolution of rock below the surface followed by collapse of the top. They are usually most abundant within hammocks. Shallower depressions in the rock surface are probably formed by the same process. Pinnacle rock, one of the most spectacular erosional features, appears to represent pillars left between subterranean flow channels. The collapse of the rock shell over the channels gives rise to the steep-sided, linear walls characteristic of pinnacle rock. A feature seen most often in the Long Pine Key area is karren erosion, locally known as "dogtooth" limestone. This surface rock has intricate sculpturing with numerous small holes and sharp edges. It is generally assumed that this feature developed after the induration of the rock surface and the establishment of vegetation.

Soils

Soils of pinelands and hammocks in south Florida differ greatly from the predominantly deep, acid, sandy soils elsewhere in the state. Pine soils, in fact, are most notable for their paucity, as is particularly apparent where fire has removed litter and understory vegetation; hammock soils are largely or-

Fig. 8.3. Solution hole in Miami limestone in Long Pine Key pineland, Everglades National Park. Pole is 1 m long.

ganic matter. Soil surveys are available for Dade and Collier counties (Soil Conservation Service, 1954, 1958), but Monroe County soils have never been mapped. These surveys predate the advent of current soil taxonomy, so that the nomenclature is archaic, though mapping units such as "Rockdale" and "Rockland" are quite descriptive.

In the pinelands of Long Pine Key the "soil" surface is almost entirely limestone, varying in character from a solid surface interrupted by solution holes to an uneven surface covered by loose rock rubble. The actual rooting medium in the channels and fissures in the rock includes 30–50 percent organic matter and is circumneutral in reaction. Occasional shallow depressions in the rock surface contain fine, reddish-brown, sandy loam. These residual soils are slightly acid (pH 6 to 6.5) and have less than 10 percent organic matter (Snyder, 1986). North and west of Homestead such soils are more common and are responsible for the name "Redlands" given to the area. In some of the lowest pinelands and surrounding wetlands, alkaline marl soils have been deposited over the limestone. In the northerly parts of the Miami rock ridge and in the eastern Big Cypress pinelands, deposits of sand that date from higher sea stands mantle the limestone to depths of several centimeters. Because of the pervasive underlying limestone, these sandy soils are at most only slightly acid. The soils of the lower Keys pinelands are scanty, much like those of Long Pine Key. All the pineland soils have good internal drainage and remain saturated only when flooded by high water tables.

In hammocks the rooting medium is an uneven layer of highly organic soil overlying the rock. The thickness of the layer ranges from nothing, where the limestone outcrops, to several centimeters over the general rock surface, to 0.5 m or more where soil has accumulated in solution holes. Olmsted et al. (1980) found mean soil depths ranging form 8 to 15 cm in five rockland hammocks. The organic content of these soils is so high that they burn readily when dry. The depth of the organic soil layer in a given hammock represents a balance between the processes of litter deposition and decomposition and the periodic destruction of soil by fire. Alexander (1953) reported a soil pH of 6.7 for a hammock on Key Largo, again indicating the influence of the underlying calcareous rock.

Climate

Rainfall is unevenly distributed over the rocklands of southern Florida. The northern portions of the Miami rock ridge receive the greatest rainfall, with an average 1525 to 1650 mm of rain per year. This amount decreases gradually to the south and west. The Pinecrest and southern Miami rock ridge regions have 1400 to 1525 mm of rain in an average year; the upper Keys have 1015 to 1145 mm; and the lower Keys have the lowest rainfall, 890 to 1015 mm per year (MacVicar and Lin, 1984).

Rainfall also varies temporally, with a dry season from October through May and a wet season from June through September, when about 75 percent of the yearly rainfall occurs. Onset of the rainy season may occur from the latter part of May through July; those years in which the start of the rainy season is delayed past the end of June are generally considered drought years. Within the rainy season, rainfall tends to be unevenly distributed. The first and last months generally have the greatest precipitation, while July and August are relatively dry.

Average temperature is uniform across the entire rockland area, with July averages ranging from 27°C (81°F) in the vicinity of Pinecrest to 29°C (84°F) in the Florida Keys. A similarly small difference is found during winter; the average January temperatures range from 18°C to 21°C (64 to 70°F) (Thomas, 1974). Of much greater significance than these minor variations in average temperatures is the susceptibility of the various regions to freezing weather during winter. In the Miami rock ridge and Pinecrest areas, a freeze is possible any year, but most winters pass without freezing temperatures. Freezing weather is rare in the Florida Keys, but even these rare freezes may have long-lasting effects by killing cold-sensitive species that could otherwise become established on the Keys.

Hurricanes strike south Florida about every three years (Gentry, 1974).

The high winds, heavy rains, and storm surge can all have significant effects on these ecosystems, though specific areas are affected only sporadically.

Vegetation

Tropical Hammock

Rockland tropical hammocks occupy elevated, rarely inundated, and relatively fire-free sites in all three of the major rockland areas: the Miami rock ridge, the eastern Big Cypress Swamp, and the Florida Keys. Typically, tropical hammocks on the mainland and in the lower Florida Keys are relatively small "islands," or patches, of broad-leaved forest surrounded by other vegetation types. The discrete nature of these stands encouraged the naming of individual hammocks, often by early settlers or landowners. Collectors of tree snails developed an elaborate nomenclature to designate individual hammocks in more remote areas such as Big Cypress Swamp and Long Pine Key (Pilsbry, 1946; Craighead, 1974). On the upper Florida Keys, tropical hammock once occupied virtually the entire upland area.

Craighead (1974) estimated that there were originally more than 500 hammocks ranging in size from 0.1 ha to over 40 ha scattered within the pine forests that dominated the Miami rock ridge. Hammocks are generally on the highest ground, but not necessarily higher than adjacent pinelands (Olmsted et al., 1983). The relative coverage of pineland and hammock on upland sites is obviously controlled to a considerable extent by fire (discussed later in this chapter), but Craighead (1974) also suggested that the limestone underlying hammocks differs from most of the surface rock. Hammocks often border seasonally flooded prairies, or glades, that transect the ridge. Robertson (1955) pointed out that hammocks are generally found on the leeward side of these glades, which may act as firebreaks. Along Biscayne Bay, hammocks come into contact with mangrove and buttonwood forests on their seaward edges.

Hammocks of the Big Cypress Swamp region are rarely associated with pine forests. Generally these hammocks are located on plateaus or mesas of outcropping rock slightly higher than surrounding graminoid marsh or open cypress forest (fig. 8.4). At least in the southern hammocks near Pinecrest, these rock platforms are apparently remnants of Miami limestone overlying the Tamiami limestone, and they are often surrounded by moats created by solution of the limestone (Duever et al., 1986).

Tropical hammock covers the well-drained areas of the upper Florida Keys not normally exposed to flooding by salt water, and the transition from hammock to salt-tolerant mangrove communities tends to be abrupt. Most tropical hammocks of the lower Keys are closely associated with pineland, but only on Big Pine Key is the area of pineland much greater than

Fig. 8.4. Tropical hammock in eastern Big Cypress Swamp bordered by open cypress (*Taxodium ascendens*) wetland.

that of hammock. On the lower Keys broader transition areas are found between the hammock and the mangrove fringes or occasional freshwater wetlands.

Woody Vegetation

Tropical hardwood hammocks are closed, broad-leaved forests that contain a large number of evergreen and semievergreen tropical tree species. More than 150 species of trees and shrubs are native to the rockland hammocks of Dade, Monroe, and Collier counties (see Appendix), and less than a fourth of these are found north of Florida. The vast majority of the species are at or near their northern range limits in south Florida and are more widespread in the West Indies and elsewhere in the Neotropics (Little, 1978).

A number of tree species are found throughout the range of the rockland hammocks, but few are common or dominant in all regions. Gumbo limbo (*Bursera simaruba*) and pigeon plum (*Coccoloba diversifolia*) are canopy species likely to be found in hammocks from Big Cypress to the lower Florida Keys. White stopper (*Eugenia axillaris*) is a small tree found in nearly every tropical hardwood hammock. Numerous other species are common over most of the range but are rare or absent in either the Big Cypress or the lower Keys hammocks. The distribution of woody species in the various rockland hammock areas is shown in the Appendix.

The structure and composition of tropical rockland hammocks are variable and are influenced by several factors, including regional gradients of rainfall and minimum temperature, disturbances such as fire and hurricanes, local gradients of saline influence (especially in the Keys), surrounding vegetation types, and, to some extent, the elevation and character of the limestone substrate. It should be pointed out that probably no present hammock stands are entirely unaltered by human disturbance through cutting of trees, burning, or drainage.

Tropical hammocks have been most studied on the Miami rock ridge (e.g., Phillips, 1940; Alexander, 1958a, 1967b; Robertson, 1955; Craighead, 1974; Olmsted et al., 1980, 1983). Here a reasonably mature hammock has a closed canopy at 18 m or less, with a few emergents extending above, and a subcanopy of small trees. The closed nature of the canopy creates a forest interior with low light levels and moderated moisture and temperature conditions. Relatively few shrubs, lianas, and herbs are found in intact hammock interiors, but they are common in disturbed areas. Because hammocks are usually surrounded by more open vegetation, such as pineland or prairie, the ecotonal margins are often densely vegetated and nearly impenetrable. These dense margins and the tangled growth in disturbed areas have led numerous authors to comment on the jungle-like appearance of tropical hammocks.

Common canopy species in Miami rock ridge hammocks include pigeon plum, wild tamarind (*Lysiloma latisiliqua*), gumbo limbo, live oak (*Quercus virginiana*), mastic (*Mastichodendron foetidissimum*), willow bustic (*Bumelia salicifolia*), and strangler fig (*Ficus aurea*). The strangler fig generally begins its existence as an epiphyte on another tree and sends down roots that eventually "strangle" the host. Cabbage palms (*Sabal palmetto*) are frequently found in hammocks and are often hosts for strangler figs (fig. 8.5).

The understory of small trees and shrubs includes additional species such as lancewood (*Nectandra coriacea*), inkwood (*Exothea paniculata*), white stopper, marlberry (*Ardisia escallonioides*), red mulberry (*Morus rubra*), satinleaf (*Chrysophyllum oliviforme*), myrsine (*Myrsine guianensis*), West Indies cherry (*Prunus myrtifolia*), *Tetrazygia bicolor*, wild coffee (*Psychotria nervosa, P. sulzneri*), crabwood (*Ateramnus lucidus*), black ironwood (*Krugiodendron ferreum*), and rough velvetseed (*Guettarda scabra*), among many others.

Woody vines and sprawlers are common, particularly in disturbed hammocks and in hammock margins. The devil's claw (*Pisonia aculeata*) is armed with wicked curved spines and can have a basal diameter of 15 cm and reach 30 m in length (Bessey, 1911). Other woody vines include muscadine (*Vitis rotundifolia*), Virginia creeper (*Parthenocissus quinquefolia*), and poison ivy (*Toxicodendron radicans*). Snowberry (*Chiococca alba*) is a common sprawling shrub.

Many of the hardwoods found in the rock ridge (and lower Keys) hammocks are found in adjacent pinelands (see Appendix). Regardless of their stature in the hammocks, they are generally maintained as shrubs by frequent fires in the pinelands.

Royal Palm Hammock (also referred to as Paradise Key), at the eastern end of Long Pine Key, is one of the best known hammocks in south Florida (Safford, 1919; Small, 1916, 1918). It was part of Royal Palm State Park before being incorporated into Everglades National Park. Although no one hammock can be representative of all rock ridge hammocks, portions of

Fig. 8.5. Strangler fig (*Ficus aurea*) on cabbage palm (*Sabal palmetto*), Snead Island, Manatee County. Photo by Allan Horton.

Royal Palm Hammock provide an example of a reasonably mature tropical forest. The royal palm (*Roystonea elata*) is native to hammocks and major swamp forests (e.g., Fakahatchee Strand) of the extreme southern mainland. Robertson (1955) found 45 percent of the canopy trees in Royal Palm Hammock to be live oak, with poisonwood, gumbo limbo, willow bustic, myrtle-of-the-river (*Calyptranthes zuzygium*), and strangler fig making up most of the remainder. Occasional royal palms were emergents. Olmsted et al. (1980) found 183 stems greater than 2 m tall in three 100 m^2 plots in the most mature part of the hammock. Live oaks and willow bustics were the tallest at 14 to 16 m; poisonwood, myrtle-of-the-river, and lancewood had stems up to 12 m tall. Most of the stems were 4 to 7 m tall and belonged to myrtle-of-the-river, lancewood, and inkwood. Live oak dominated in terms of basal area, although a strangler fig was one of the larger trees. Forty-four species of trees and shrubs were found in the entire hammock (ignoring ecotonal or solution-hole species), only seven of which were temperate species.

Three additional Long Pine Key hammocks were studied by Olmsted et al. (1980). Wright and Deer hammocks had live oaks as their tallest trees (up to 14 m). In Deer Hammock crabwood and pigeon plum were the most numerous, while in Wright Hammock rough velvetseed and lancewood had the highest numbers. Osteen Hammock was dominated by wild tamarinds reaching 13 m in height. Gumbo limbo and poisonwood also contributed some of the larger trees. The most numerous trees in Osteen Hammock were marlberry, pigeon plum, and lancewood.

Some quantitative information is available for Castellow Hammock (Phillips, 1940; Alexander, 1967b), which lies farther north on the Miami rock ridge and is now a Dade County park. Alexander's data showed the dominance of basal area by wild tamarind, with gumbo limbo and pigeon plum each contributing about half as much. Pigeon plum had the highest density of stems, but lancewood and paradise tree (*Simarouba glauca*) were also numerous.

Canopy species in hammocks near Miami include those found elsewhere, but the trees probably reach larger sizes than those of the Long Pine Key area. Bessey (1911) estimated that mastics reached more than 20 m with diameters of 60 to 100 cm. Alexander (1958a) counted stems in plots in several Miami area hammocks. Pigeon plum, marlberry, lancewood, and white stopper had the highest frequencies and densities. Bitterbush (*Picramnia pentandra*), a rare species in Florida, was found in one-fourth of the quadrats. The presence of Jamaica dogwood (*Piscidia piscipula*) and blackbead (*Pithecellobium guadalupense*) in these hammocks indicates their coastal location. Only five of the thirty woody species recorded have primarily temperate distributions.

The hammocks of the Pinecrest region of eastern Big Cypress (fig. 8.6) closely resemble those of the Miami rock ridge in species composition (Alexander, 1958b; Gunderson and Loope, 1982b). Dominant canopy trees include wild tamarind, gumbo limbo, live oak, laurel oak (*Quercus laurifolia*), willow bustic, and mastic. Laurel oak is the only additional temperate species that assumes much importance in these hammocks. Twinberry stopper (*Myrcianthes fragrans*) is a common understory species; others include pigeon plum, myrsine, marlberry, and lancewood. Species common in the Miami rock ridge but missing from Big Cypress include rough velvetseed and tetrazygia. Scrubby borders of live oak, wax myrtle (*Myrica cerifera*), and cabbage palm, which are probably fire-induced, frequently surround Big Cypress hammocks.

A Pinecrest hammock (called Pinecrest #40 by tree snail collectors) studied by Olmsted et al. (1980) had basal area dominated by wild tamarind, mastic, and gumbo limbo. The tallest trees were tamarinds that reached

Fig. 8.6. Interior of tropical hammock near Pinecrest, Big Cypress National Preserve. Photo by Holly Tuck.

17 m; gumbo limbo and willow bustic were slightly shorter. Pigeon plum and lancewood accounted for about half the stems in the sampled area. Of the thirty-three woody species in the hammock, twenty-seven were tropical.

North of the Pinecrest region the number of tropical species decreases, and the dominance of oaks increases (Gunderson and Loope, 1982c; Duever et al., 1986). The understory retains a more tropical character because it is protected from cold temperatures by the canopy. Thus, myrsine, wild coffee, and white stopper are present in most Big Cypress hardwood hammocks regardless of canopy composition.

The hammocks of the Florida Keys are similar floristically to those of the mainland, although temperate species are less common—for example, live oak is rare, and sugarberry (*Celtis laevigata*) and red mulberry are absent—and additional tropical species are present. Canopy trees in hammocks of the Keys tend to be smaller than in mainland hammocks. This characteristic becomes more pronounced toward the southwestern extreme of the archipelago, apparently because of decreasing rainfall.

Weiner (1979) described many hammock remnants of the Keys. Upper Keys hammocks typically have a canopy 9 to 12 m tall with gumbo limbo, pigeon plum, poisonwood, mahogany (*Swietenia mahagoni*), black ironwood, wild tamarind, willow bustic, Jamaica dogwood, mastic, and strangler fig as common trees (fig. 8.7). The subcanopy contains, in addition to smaller individuals of canopy species, white stopper, Spanish stopper (*Eugenia foetida*), crabwood, torchwood (*Amyris elemifera*), wild coffee, marlberry, milkbark (*Drypetes diversifolia*), both velvetseeds (*Guettarda elliptica* and *G. scabra*), cinnamon-bark (*Canella winterana*), strongbarks (*Bourreria ovata* and *B. succulenta*), soapberry (*Sapindus saponaria*), and tallowwood (*Ximenia americana*). In intact hammocks the understory is open and easy to walk through. Where rock elevations approach sea level, there is a transition to mangrove vegetation. Here the hammock contains large buttonwood (*Conocarpus erectus*) and blolly (*Guapira discolor*), and several other species are more common than in the more elevated portions of the hammock: blackbead, cat's claw (*Pithecellobium unguis-cati*), Spanish stopper, saffron plum (*Bumelia celastrina*), darling plum (*Reynosia septentrionalis*), limber caper (*Capparis flexuosa*), and Jamaica caper (*C. cynophallophora*). Cacti such as dildo cactus (*Cereus pentagonus*), prickly pear cactus (*Opuntia stricta*), and prickly apple cactus (*Cereus gracilis*) are also commonly found in these transition zones.

Soldierwood (*Colubrina elliptica*) and lignum vitae (*Guaiacum sanctum*) are trees presently limited to the upper Keys, although lignum vitae was once known from Key West (Little, 1976). A few species are found only on the upper Keys and the coastal hammocks of the Miami rock ridge, including bitterbush and red stopper.

Fig. 8.7. Recent road cut through an upper Keys tropical hammock on Upper Matecumbe Key. The large, dark-barked trees in the left foreground are gumbo limbo (*Bursera simaruba*).

In the lower Keys and much of the upper Keys south of lower Matecumbe Key, the dominant vegetation is a stunted, xeric form of tropical hammock known as "low hammock" (Weiner, 1979; not *sensu* Alexander, 1955) or "Keys hammock thicket" (Duever, 1984). Here the canopy height is only 6 to 7.5 m, with occasional emergents, and the trees have smaller diameters and grow closer together. The tallest trees include poisonwood, buttonwood, blolly, and Key thatch palm (*Thrinax morrisii*). Other common tree species include Spanish stopper, wild dilly (*Manilkara bahamensis*), Jamaica dogwood, and white stopper. Mastic and mahogany are absent from the lower Keys, and wild tamarind is less common there.

In the gradual transition to the halophytic vegetation on the seaward side of these low hammocks, the vegetation becomes scrubbier and a number of species become more prominent: black torch (*Erithalis fruticosa*), saffron plum, sea grape (*Coccoloba uvifera*), blackbead, indigo berry (*Randia aculeata*), tallowwood, darling plum, joewood (*Jacquinia keyensis*), dildo cactus, and prickly pear cactus. Because of the prevalence of thorn-bearing species, this transitional type of hammock is often called thorn scrub.

Several trees are native to the United States only in the lower Keys, including cupania (*Cupania glabra*), pisonia (*Pisonia rotundata*), pitch apple (*Clusia rosea*), and false boxwood (*Gyminda latifolia*) (Little, 1976). In spite of the rarity of many of the rockland tropical hammock tree species in the United States, none has federal protection as endangered species except the Key tree cactus (*Cereus robinii*), which has varieties native to both the upper and lower Keys (U.S. Fish and Wildlife Service, 1986; Little, 1976).

Herbs

The tropical hardwood hammocks of southern Florida are notably deficient in terrestrial herbaceous species. Few shade-tolerant herbs have found their way into the community from either the north or the south, leaving the floor of a mature hammock essentially barren beneath areas with a dense tree canopy.

Two grasses, *Panicum dichotomum* and *Oplismenus setarius*, are commonly found in hammocks, usually near margins or canopy gaps. *Paspalum caespitosum* is infrequently found in the same habitats. *Lasiacis divaricata*, a viny grass, is common in the drier hammocks. Several terrestrial ferns are found commonly in hammocks, including Boston fern (*Nephrolepis exaltata*), sword fern (*N. biserrata*), and *Thelypteris kunthii.* In sites with sufficient light and moisture the two *Nephrolepis* species can form dense stands on the hammock floor.

The most speciose group of terrestrial herbs within the hammocks, though far less common in number of individual plants than the species mentioned, is the orchids. These are mainly spiranthoid species that are widespread in the West Indies. Several of the terrestrial orchids are known from only a single locality, and many of the species are found only sporadically. The species that seem most widespread at present are *Eulophia alta* (not restricted to hammocks and apparently never producing inflorescences in hammock habitats), *Spiranthes costaricensis, S. cranichoides, S. lanceolata,* and *Centrogenium setaceum.* A recent introduction to the flora, *Oeceoclades maculata* (originally from Brazil), has found the essentially vacant terrestrial niche suitable for growth and is now more widespread and abundant than any native orchid.

The bare rock walls of solution holes—a specialized habitat within hammocks—hosts several conspicuous ferns. These include maidenhair fern (*Adiantum tenerum*), halberd ferns (*Tectaria heracleifolia* and *T. lobata*), and shield ferns (*Thelypteris reptans* and *T. sclerophylla*). The species adapted to this habitat are more akin to epiphytic than terrestrial species, but the epipetric and epiphytic niches differ in significant respects. The epipetric species receive somewhat more protection from desiccation than the epiphytic species, and the root environment of the epipetric species in southern Florida is basic while that of the epiphytic species is acidic.

Compared to the terrestrial herbs, herbaceous epiphytes are abundant and conspicuous in hammocks (fig. 8.8). The three major groups of epiphytes are ferns, bromeliads, and orchids (Small, 1931; Craighead, 1963; Benzing, 1980; Luer, 1972). Among the ferns, the most widespread and con-

Fig. 8.8. Interior of a Miami rock ridge hammock with three bromeliad species visible: *Guzmania monostachya, Tillandsia valenzuelana*, and *T. setacea*. The large tree in the background is a live oak (*Quercus virginiana*).

spicuous epiphytes are strap fern (*Campyloneuron phyllitidis*), resurrection fern (*Polypodium polypodioides*), golden polypody (*Phlebodium aureum*), and shoestring fern (*Vittaria lineata*). Bromeliads are represented by several species of *Tillandsia*, most of which are found exclusively in the canopy (e.g., *T. fasciculata, T. balbisiana,* and *T. flexuosa*). *Tillandsia valenzuelana* and *T. setacea,* in contrast, are normally found below the canopy. *Guzmania monostachya* (fig. 8.8) and *Catopsis berteroniana* are found in relatively few hammocks. Spanish moss (*Tillandsia usneoides*) and ball moss (*T. recurvata*) are less common than might be expected, considering their abundance in the rest of Florida. They are found in scattered locations and are not abundant where found. Several epiphytic orchids are widespread in hammocks. *Encyclia cochleata, E. tampensis, Epidendrum nocturnum,* and *Polystachya concreta* are found in most hammocks on the mainland. Other species are more restricted in distribution. *Oncidium luridum* and *Encyclia boothiana,* for instance, are found only in coastal hammocks. The conspicuous cowhorn orchid (*Cyrtopodium punctatum*) was once common but has suffered from heavy collecting pressure (Craighead, 1963).

Less commonly seen epiphytes include a few species of *Peperomia,* with populations in the Miami rock ridge treated as an endemic species (*P. floridana*) by some authors (e.g., Small, 1933; Long and Lakela, 1971). An epiphytic cactus (*Rhipsalis baccifera*) was also found in rock ridge hammocks, although no wild plants are now known (Ward, 1978). Mistletoes, semiparasitic shrubby plants that live in tree crowns, are represented by red mistletoe (*Phoradendron rubrum*), which parasitizes mahogany (Ward, 1978). The common mistletoe of northern Florida (*P. serotinum*) is not known to occur in rockland hammocks.

The factors that determine the distribution of herbaceous species in the hammocks are light and water availability. None of the herbaceous species in southern Florida can tolerate the deep shade in the interior of a dense hammock. Terrestrial herbaceous species and subcanopy epiphytes are concentrated in areas near canopy gaps or the hammock margins. Therefore, neighboring hammocks can have drastically different herbaceous floras, depending on the number of gaps present in the canopy. The importance of natural disturbances that produce canopy gaps, particularly hurricanes and fires, in maintaining the diversity of the herbaceous flora has not been adequately studied.

The influence of the second factor—reduced water availability—is most apparent in the lower diversity and abundance of epiphytes in the Florida Keys. Desiccation of mainland hammocks resulting from drainage along the coast has affected the herbaceous flora, though only a handful of cases can be documented. For example, from the reports of Small (1931) and Phillips (1940) we know that the filmy ferns *Trichomanes krausii* and *T. punctatum* were common in the rockland hammocks during the first decades of this century. Their ranges have greatly contracted in the intervening years, and now the species are known from only two sites.

Other Rockland Hammock Areas

Although the Miami rock ridge, Florida Keys, and Big Cypress Swamp account for most tropical hammocks on limestone, a few other areas of outcropping limestone have tropical hammock vegetation.

Between the Miami rock ridge and the Shark River Slough at the southern end of the Everglades lies an area of shallow soils over Miami limestone. The area is mostly seasonally flooded prairie and is known as "rocky glades" or "East Everglades" (fig. 8.1). Scattered in this area are thousands of small hammocks on slightly elevated platforms of rock (Loope and Urban, 1980). The hammocks are dominated by poisonwood, gumbo limbo, willow bustic, strangler fig, and pigeon plum. Important smaller trees include myrsine, white stopper, wild coffee, and marlberry. The hammocks also contain a number of bayhead species characteristic of seasonally inundated conditions: red bay (*Persea borbonia*), wax myrtle, dahoon (*Ilex cassine*), sweet bay (*Magnolia virginiana*), and cocoplum (*Chrysobalanus icaco*). These species dominate the hammock margins where solution holes break up the elevated platform. Both live oak and wild tamarind are less common than in rock ridge hammocks. Several other tropical and temperate species of rock ridge hammocks are infrequent or missing, so that woody species diversity is generally less than twenty species per hammock. Epiphyte numbers and species diversity are also low. Bracken fern (*Pteridium aquilinum* var. *caudatum*) often dominates severely burned hammocks.

The southern Everglades marshes contain teardrop-shaped tree islands with their long axes oriented in the direction of water flow. Near the blunt upstream end of many of these islands is a small area of tropical hammock (Craighead, 1971; Loveless, 1959b). As far as is known these hammocks occur on rock platforms (presumably Miami limestone) 30 cm or more above the surrounding wetlands. Around the tropical hammock is a zone of bayhead species growing in peat that makes up most of the tree island (Olmsted and Loope, 1984). The species diversity of these hammocks is even less than that of the "rocky glades" hammocks. Panther Mound, one of the larger hammocks in Shark River Slough, has a canopy dominated by sugarberry, cabbage palm, gumbo limbo, and strangler fig. Craighead (1971) attributed the common occurrence of species such as fishpoison vine (*Dalbergia* spp.), sugarberry, persimmon (*Diospyros virginiana*), red mulberry, and cabbage palm to earlier Indian habitation.

North of Miami along the Atlantic coastal ridge are other areas of outcropping limestone that support tropical hammock vegetation. Austin et al. (1977) and Richardson (1977) described hammocks on Anastasia and Ft.

Thompson limestones in eastern Palm Beach County. These hammocks are similar to Miami rock ridge hammocks but have somewhat lower numbers of tropical species.

Related Tropical Hammock Types

Tropical hammocks can apparently develop anywhere in Florida that has a sufficiently elevated calcareous substrate within the climatic tolerance of the tropical flora. On the southern tip of the mainland, coastal hammocks are found on ridges of marl or calcareous sand (Robertson, 1955; Craighead, 1971; Olmsted et al., 1981). These hammocks are more like those of the Florida Keys than the Miami rock ridge, both in physiognomy and floristics.

Shell mounds, or Indian middens, are anthropogenic elevations that support tropical hammock vegetation along southern coastal areas. The species composition is influenced by the coastal location and the introduction of useful plants by people (Craighead, 1971). Many midden sites in the interior of Big Cypress Swamp, while often dominated by temperate oaks, have at least a subcanopy composed largely of tropical species.

The greatest extension of the range of tropical hammocks, however, occurs along both coasts where sands contain a substantial quantity of shell fragments (Alexander, 1958a; Austin and Weise, 1972; Austin et al., 1977). The diversity of tropical species in these coastal hammocks declines rapidly to the north as the cold tolerance of individual species is exceeded; few tropical hardwoods reach as far north as Cape Canaveral (Little, 1978).

Floristically the south Florida tropical hammocks closely resemble the coastal hardwood forests of the Bahamas and Greater Antilles (Robertson, 1955). For example, in a dry forest in southern Puerto Rico about half the trees are species found in south Florida hammocks (Murphy and Lugo, 1986). In physiognomy, however, the West Indian forests of similar species composition differ considerably from the south Florida hammocks. Typically they are scrubbier in appearance, more deciduous, and with fewer herbs and lianas, probably due to drier conditions (Robertson, 1955).

Pineland

Rockland pine forests in southern Florida occur in locally elevated areas of the limestone bedrock bordered primarily by wet prairies and, to a small extent, by mangroves. These peaks in elevation may be several meters higher than the surrounding lowlands or as little as a few centimeters higher, leading to great variation in the hydroperiod experienced by pinelands at different sites. Pinelands a meter or more above the surrounding glades flood only during extreme weather events, and flooding seldom persists for more than a few days. Lower pinelands flood regularly during the wet season and may remain flooded for several months. Pinelands near the coast, especially in the Florida Keys, are subject to flooding by ocean waters during severe hurricanes.

Pinelands were probably present on the upper Florida Keys during historical time (Alexander, 1953). However, the available evidence consists only of scattered pine trees (stumps and dead trunks, none living) and a few associated pineland plants (live oak, saw palmetto, *Crossopetalum ilicifolium*, and rough velvetseed) within hammock vegetation. We do not know whether an extensive pineland community ever existed in this region.

The Miami rock ridge pinelands encompass a diversity of habitats. The northern Biscayne region has the least exposed rock and best-drained soil; flooding is rare and local. In the Redlands (or southern Biscayne) region, exposed rock is the predominant surface and the soils are still well drained, but flooding is more frequent. In the Long Pine Key region exposed rock makes up 70 percent or more of the surface, and erosional features like sinkholes are more common than in the other areas; the soil is commonly saturated, or the surface is flooded, for extended periods during the rainy season.

Much of the original Miami rock ridge pineland was in close proximity to wet prairies, either the "transverse glades" and the eastern rim of the Everglades in the northern Biscayne and Redlands regions, or the "finger glades" and surrounding wet prairies of the Long Pine Key region (fig. 8.9). In addition, the northern Biscayne pineland had a substantial border with the mangroves fringing Biscayne Bay.

In the lower Keys, fairly extensive pinelands occur on Big Pine (fig. 8.10), Little Pine, No Name, Cudjoe, and Sugarloaf keys; smaller stands occur on other keys. More than 50 percent of the ground surface is exposed rock. The low rainfall of this area compared to the mainland imposes more xeric conditions on the pinelands, but they may be flooded by salt water for brief periods (one to three days) when hurricanes pass over the islands.

The pinelands of eastern Big Cypress are on slightly elevated bedrock and are subject to frequent flooding. A thin layer of sandy soil is present, but, unlike the sandy soil of the northern Biscayne pineland, the soil in Big Cypress is usually wet for several months of the year. Many of the pinelands in Big Cypress lack areas of outcropping bedrock and could just as well be treated as the southernmost extension of the pine flatwoods. Because of their geographic position and edaphic conditions, the eastern Big Cypress pinelands are best considered as a connecting link between the pine flatwoods of the southeastern coastal plain and the rocky pinelands of southern Florida.

Canopy

The single canopy species in the rocky pinelands is the south Florida variety of slash pine (*Pinus elliottii* var. *densa*). Slash pine is closely related to

Fig. 8.9. Rockland pine forest in Long Pine Key, Everglades National Park, with seasonally flooded marl prairie (finger glade) in the foreground.

Fig. 8.10. Lower Keys pineland on Big Pine Key, National Key Deer Refuge, with Key thatch palm (*Thrinax morrisii*) in the foreground.

longleaf pine (*P. palustris*) and Caribbean pine (*P. caribaea*). For the first half of this century, south Florida slash pine was treated as an element of Caribbean pine (Small, 1933; Lückhoff, 1964) either separated from or united with typical slash pine from northern Florida. Little and Dorman (1954b) reviewed the problem and proposed a varietal name *Pinus elliottii* var. *densa* for south Florida slash pine, indicating a closer relationship between northern and southern Florida populations than between southern Florida and Caribbean populations.

Quantitative data on stand characteristics of the pine canopy are available only for Long Pine Key—the most recently logged (about 1935 to 1947) and least elevated region of the Miami rock ridge and also that with the poorest soil development. In one of the more vigorous pine stands in Long Pine Key, trees form a canopy below 24 m, with a median diameter at breast height (dbh) of about 20 cm and few trees greater than 30 cm dbh. Stand density is about 500 trees per hectare, and total basal area is 17 m^2 /ha. Elsewhere in Long Pine Key, pines may form a canopy well below 20 m with median dbh about 13 cm (Snyder, 1986). Typically, the less vigorous stands have a higher density due to a large number of small trees.

Subcanopy

Subcanopy development is rare in most of the rocky pinelands; only occasional hardwoods growing on sites protected from fire reach tree size. Wild tamarind and live oak are the species that most often reach tree size in the Miami rock ridge pinelands. There are a few exceptions to the scarcity of subcanopy trees. In some of the lower Florida Keys pinelands, there is a well-developed subcanopy of silver palm and Key thatch palm (fig. 8.10). In rocky pinelands that have not burned for many years, the hardwood shrubs grow to form a subcanopy, as is the case in some of the lower Keys pinelands (e.g., Cudjoe Key). In many of the pineland remnants on the Miami rock ridge, the past several decades of fire suppression have allowed the development of a subcanopy.

Shrub Layer

Pinelands do not provide as much buffering against extreme environmental conditions as do hammocks. The relatively open canopy provides little protection against freezes, and the near absence of soil exacerbates the effects of drought. As a result, many tropical plants have much more restricted ranges in pinelands than in hammocks. The distribution of woody species in rocky pinelands is given in the Appendix.

The shrub stratum of the rocky pinelands of southern Florida includes more than ninety taxa (Appendix; see also Olmsted et al., 1983). Most of these taxa derive from the tropical flora of the West Indies. Only about seven species representing the flatwoods flora occur. The diversity of the pine shrub stratum is significantly affected by the presence of other plant communities. Gumbo limbo, inkwood, and wild tamarind, for instance, are normally found in pinelands only near hardwood hammocks. Pinelands bordering on glades generally have a depauperate shrub stratum, although some shrub species, such as *Acacia pinetorum* and *Solanum donianum*, are found mainly near these interfaces. A number of wetland species also enter the pineland shrub stratum at these margins, although some species—including pond cypress (*Taxodium ascendens*), pond apple (*Annona glabra*), buttonbush (*Cephalanthus occidentalis*), willow (*Salix caroliniana*), and elderberry (*Sambucus canadensis*)—are restricted to deep solution holes.

About fifteen species occur in all three pineland areas in southern Florida, including willow bustic, coco plum, strangler fig, shortleaf fig, wax myrtle, myrsine, red bay, indigo berry, southern sumac, cabbage palm, and saw palmetto. Temperate and tropical species are both well represented in this group. Most are relatively conspicuous in all pineland areas in southern Florida, but a few are rare or have restricted distributions in some regions.

Species often found in the understory of Big Cypress and Miami rock ridge pinelands but not in the lower Florida Keys are buckthorn (*Bumelia reclinata*), beauty berry (*Callicarpa americana*), varnish leaf (*Dodonaea viscosa*), dahoon, and live oak. With the exception of varnish leaf, these species are adapted to more temperate climates.

Species found in the understory of Miami rock ridge and lower Florida Keys pinelands but not in Big Cypress pinelands include *Bourreria cassinifolia*, locust berry (*Byrsonima lucida*), silver palm, pineland croton (*Croton linearis*), rough velvetseed, wild sage (*Lantana involucrata*), and long-stalked stopper (*Psidium longipes*). All of these are tropical forms and, except for the widely distributed but rare *Bourreria cassinifolia*, all are common in the pineland shrub stratum on the lower Florida Keys and Long Pine Key. Their abundance rapidly decreases northward along the Miami rock ridge.

Pinelands of the lower Florida Keys are distinguished by a number of tropical shrubs not found in pine forests elsewhere in southern Florida. Several of these tropical species are not known from the mainland of Florida: *Caesalpinia pauciflora*, *Catesbaea parviflora*, pisonia, and *Strumpfia maritima*. A few other species are known from hammocks, but not pineland areas, on the mainland. Marked differences exist in the composition and density of shrub understory vegetation from site to site in the lower Keys pineland. In many parts of Big Pine Key the shrub stand is low and sparse, and the forest floor is scantily covered with grasses or consists of smooth, bare limestone under the pine and thatch palm/silver palm layers. In contrast, the main pine area of Cudjoe Key has an almost continuous hardwood understory 6 m or more high. Here also the forest floor is covered with a deep mat of pine straw and dead grasses. The pineland shrub stratum of Little Pine Key and No Name Key is similar, but somewhat less dense.

The Long Pine Key pinelands of the Miami rock ridge are similar to the lower Keys pinelands in the number of tropical shrubs. Notably, a number of West Indian species found in the Long Pine Key pinelands are not found in the pine forests of the lower Keys, for example, alvaradoa (*Alvaradoa amorphoides*), Cuba colubrina (*Colubrina cubensis*), varnish leaf, *Eupatorium villosum*, tawnyberry holly (*Ilex krugiana*), and tetrazygia. The relatively xeric nature of the lower Keys pinelands seems to be at least partially responsible for the failure of these species to grow there. Many shrubs that are abundant and generally distributed in the Long Pine Key region are markedly restricted to moister sites in the pine forests of the lower Keys. Examples include satinleaf, white stopper, shortleaf fig, both velvetseeds, and myrsine.

Shrub diversity in the Redlands pineland is slightly lower than on Long Pine Key. The most evident difference between these two regions is the decrease in abundance of the tropical hardwoods. Tropical hardwoods are prominent in the pineland understory in the Redlands only near hammocks, and hammocks are widely separated in the Redlands compared to Long Pine Key.

With the appearance of relatively continuous sandy soils in the northern Biscayne pinelands, a number of flatwoods species such as staggerbush (*Lyonia fruticosa*), dwarf live oak (*Quercus minima*), running oak (*Q. pumila*), and shiny blueberry (*Vaccinium myrsinites*) become common. Tropical hardwoods become even less abundant and more restricted in their distribution. In general, the tropical species are restricted to and dominate rocky outcrops in this region.

Herb Layer

Spots within the rocky pinelands that are not densely covered by shrubs support a diverse herbaceous flora. More than 250 indigenous herbaceous species have been recorded in this ecosystem (many are listed in Loope et al., 1979). Nearly half of these species are largely limited to the rocky pineland community. Examples of herbaceous species restricted to rockland pine forests and commonly found in Miami rock ridge pinelands include *Angadenia sagrae, Melanthera parvifolia, Jacquemontia curtissii* (fig. 8.11), *Crossopetalum ilicifolium, Acalypha chamaedrifolia, Cassia deeringiana, Crotalaria pumila, Andropogon cabanisii*, and *Anemia adiantifolia.* Coontie (*Zamia pumila*), a cycad common in pinelands, grows in tropical hardwood hammocks as well. *Dyschoriste oblongifolia* var. *angusta* and *Phyllanthus pentaphyllus* are common in pinelands and also in the driest of the peripheral glades.

The herbaceous flora contains a mixture of tropical and temperate species with a high percentage of endemic taxa. A great majority of the herbaceous species represent southern populations of temperate species, but

Fig. 8.11. Pineland cluster vine (*Jacquemontia curtissii*), an herb endemic to south Florida rockland pine forests.

about 15 percent represent the northernmost populations of tropical species. More than thirty taxa are endemic to southern Florida (table 8.1).

Temperate species are most common in the Big Cypress and northern Biscayne pinelands where a layer of sand covers much, but not all, of the rock surface. Examples of herbs found only in association with a deep sand layer in northern Biscayne pinelands are *Asclepias verticillata*, *Liatris chapmanii*, *Opuntia compressa*, *Bulbostylis* sp., *Aristida patula*, *Euphorbia polyphylla*, *Tragia linearifolia*, *Aeschynomene viscidula*, and *Polygala smallii*. With the exception of the last species named, these are temperate forms that reach their southern limit in Dade County. *Polygala smallii* is endemic to the Miami rock ridge pinelands but is closely related to a temperate species, *P. nana* (Ward, 1979). In the wetter Big Cypress pinelands, species common in the sandy areas include *Pluchea rosea*, *Aletris lutea*, and *Helenium pinnatifidum*.

Tropical species are most common in the Redlands, Long Pine Key, and lower Florida Keys pinelands, but are distributed throughout the area. In the northern Biscayne and Big Cypress pinelands, the tropical species tend to be limited to areas of rock outcropping.

The herbaceous flora of the lower Florida Keys pinelands is impoverished in comparison with the mainland flora, having fewer than 150 recorded species. The common temperate herbs of the mainland pinelands are found in the lower Keys along with a very few tropical species not found on the mainland (*Cassia keyensis*, *Evolvulus grisebachii*, *Linum arenicola*, and *Spiranthes torta*). The failure of many temperate species to reach the lower Florida Keys accounts for the lower herbaceous diversity.

One striking feature of the indigenous herbaceous flora is the overwhelming predominance of perennial species. Only two species, *Agalinis purpurea* and *Sabatia stellaris*, are annuals, and *Polygala smallii* is a biennial (Ward, 1979). Although a few of these perennials seem to have a brief life span (e.g., *Ocimum micranthum* and *Satureja rigida*), others apparently live for many years.

Relationship to Other Pineland Types

In northern Dade County, rocky pinelands grade into the neighboring sandhill-scrub complex. A mosaic of these ecosystems is found near the northern limit of the rocklands, with species typical of sandhill scrub in pockets of deep sand and species characteristic of rocklands in areas of rock outcrop. Sandhill-scrub species can be found throughout the northern Biscayne region of the Miami rock ridge pineland, but their numbers diminish rapidly from north to south.

Rocky pinelands in the Pinecrest region of Big Cypress show a similar relationship with the wet flatwoods common to the northwest. A mosaic develops with flatwoods species in areas of deep sandy soil and rockland species associated with outcrops of limestone.

The distinctiveness of the rockland flora is due to its association with outcrops of limestone bedrock. The flora of peninsular Florida is dominated by species adapted to deep, acidic soils. Many of these species are not able to invade the shallow, basic soils of the southern Florida rocklands, leaving an empty habitat for invasion by West Indian calciphiles.

There is a strong resemblance between the rocky pinelands of southern Florida (especially the lower Keys pinelands) and the pinelands of the Bahamas (March, 1949; Lückhoff, 1964). These pinelands share the distinction, unusual for this type of vegetation, of occupying a calcareous substrate. Many of the tropical species found in the understory of the rocky pinelands in Florida are also found in the understory of the Bahaman pine forests (Robertson, 1955; Correll and Correll, 1982), though the canopy pine in the Bahamas is Caribbean pine (*P. caribaea* var. *bahamensis*).

Fire Ecology

Fire is required for the maintenance of rockland pine forest and controls, at least in part, the relative dominance of upland habitats by pineland and hammock. Wade et al. (1980) and Robertson (1955) reviewed fire effects in south Florida pinelands and hammocks. Fires in rockland pine forests are surface fires that consume only litter and some understory vegetation (fig. 8.12). The pine canopy is usually too open to support a crown fire. On the mainland, fires often start in surrounding graminoid wetlands and sweep into the pinelands. Fires usually go out when they reach hammock margins, whether entering from pineland or some other community. However, soil fires can occur in hammocks, especially during severe droughts.

Rockland pine forests burn readily because fuel conditions are favorable. Pine needles accumulate on or near the ground and decompose slowly. The grassy herb layer contributes a small amount of fuel and also keeps pine needles from matting on the ground, as does the rough rock surface. The open canopy of the pine forest allows for the rapid drying of fuels, so that fires are possible within a day after rain. In contrast, hammocks have hardwood leaf litter lying directly on moist organic soil and little herbaceous fuel. The shaded, humid microclimate of hammocks is not conducive to fire spread. A fire with flame lengths greater than 1 m burning through pine land can reach a hammock margin and die out within seconds.

Fig. 8.12. Recently burned rockland pine forest, Long Pine Key, Everglades National Park.

Pineland plants show obvious adaptation to fire. South Florida slash pine has long needles that shield vulnerable apical buds and a thick, insulating bark that protects the living inner bark and cambium; it shares these characters with the typical variety of slash pine and with longleaf pine (Byram, 1948; Hare, 1965). Most prescribed fires, and presumably natural fires as well, kill few, if any, large trees. Fires often "prune" lower branches and may even scorch all the needles, but the trees generally recover. The seedlings have thicker stems and are more fire-resistant than typical slash pine seedlings (Ketcham and Bethune, 1963), though there is still high seedling mortality from fires. Pine seedling establishment is improved when fires occur soon before seed release (Klukas, 1973; Snyder, 1986).

The aboveground portion of hardwood shrubs is usually killed by fires, but all species can resprout from below ground within a few months (Robertson, 1953; Hofstetter, 1974). Robertson (1953) found 0–10 percent mortality in nine hardwood species after a December fire. A few species, such as sumac, are prolific root sprouters; most species resprout from near the base of the stem. Because individual stems often send up multiple sprouts, a fire can actually result in a temporary increase in the number of hardwood stems. Topkilling by fires typically eliminates fruiting for one to two years after burning. There is no massive mortality of shrubs followed by regeneration from seed, as in some chaparral species (Keeley and Keeley, 1981). However, seedlings of varnish leaf and sumac have been observed in the first year after a fire and must be derived from a soil seed bank.

Shrub layer palms experience little mortality as well. Generally all the expanded leaves are killed by fires, but the apical buds are unaffected and new leaf and flower stalk production continues unabated. Palms with developed trunks are susceptible to fire damage but, because of their internal anatomy, die only if repeated fires burn through the trunk and cause the tree to fall over.

The pineland herbs respond to fire with rapid regrowth and increased flowering (Robertson, 1953, 1962). Many species flower very infrequently except in recently burned pineland. This group includes grasses (e.g., *Tripsacum floridanum*, *Imperata brasiliensis*, and *Andropogon cabanisii*) and forbs with showy inflorescences (e.g., *Liatris tenuifolia* var. *laevigata* [Herndon, 1987b], *Stenandrium dulce*, and *Ipomoea microdactyla*). *Hypoxis* flowers more profusely in recently burned pineland than in long-unburned habitat (Herndon, 1987a). The amount of flowering of some species depends heavily on the time of year of burning. For example, the endemic *Schizachyrium rhizomatum* flowers much more profusely after spring burning than after fall or winter burning (Snyder and Ward, 1987).

Pineland fires do not result in significant changes in species composition because almost all species are perennials that survive and recover in place. However, the relative importance in terms of cover or biomass shifts initially from hardwoods to herbs because herbs respond more quickly. As the post-fire period lengthens, the development of larger hardwoods and the accumulation of litter shift the balance back in favor of hardwoods (Snyder, 1986).

Within two or three decades of fire exclusion, Miami rock ridge pine lands become tropical hammocks with a relict overstory of pine (Robertson, 1953; Alexander, 1967b; Loope and Dunevitz, 1981a). The hardwood shrubs develop into a closed canopy, a more humid microclimate is created, a thick organic detritus layer accumulates, and the characteristic herbaceous flora of the pineland disappears. This is the basic sequence proposed for the development of hammock islands in pineland (Safford, 1919; Simpson, 1920). The rate of succession from pineland to hardwood forest on rockland is more rapid than it is in most flatwoods sites. It is likely that this process is slower in areas of the rock ridge where hammocks are less frequent. Alexander and Dickson (1972) estimated that in the lower Keys it may take fifty years for hardwoods to overgrow pineland completely, presumably because of water-limited productivity.

Under drought conditions, fires can enter hammocks. If the flames pass through quickly, consuming only the loose litter on the forest floor, relatively little damage results. Greater disturbance is caused by slow combustion of the organic soil, which can proceed for weeks (Craighead, 1974; Robertson, 1955). Depending on the moisture content, either all or only the upper portions of the organic mat overlying the rock may be consumed. Olmsted and Loope (1984) point out that hammocks usually burn in a mosaic fashion, with some portions less affected by the fire than others. The trees may be completely killed, but often they resprout or coppice from below-ground parts. Live oak is the most fire-resistant of the common hardwoods. After a severe fire a number of "fireweed" species dominate the site for a few years. Florida trema (*Trema micrantha*), bracken fern, *Baccharis* spp., potato tree (*Solanum erianthum*), and the exotic papaya (*Carica papaya*) are common in burned mainland hammocks. Woody vines such as poison ivy, Virginia creeper, and pepper vine (*Ampelopsis arborea*) often form dense tangles.

A number of hammock tree species appear to be shade-intolerant and therefore require disturbances such as fire to open up the forest canopy for regeneration. Species such as live oak, wild tamarind, gumbo limbo, willow bustic, and mahogany are in this group (Olmsted et al., 1980). On the upper Florida Keys, where mahogany is common, hurricanes were probably the common natural disturbance (Craighead and Gilbert, 1962); however, human-caused fires have been frequent during historical times.

A fundamental question concerning the fire ecology of south Florida pinelands involves the fire regime before settlement by Europeans: how frequently and at what time of year did pinelands burn before the fire pattern was affected by drainage, artificial barriers such as roads and canals, and accidental or intentional ignition by humans? Reconstructing the fire history of south Florida from physical evidence such as fire scars has not been possible (Taylor, 1980). An alternative approach is to infer the answer from observations of present-day fire patterns and fire effects.

The upper limit of natural fire frequency can be inferred from the time it takes the endemic herbaceous plants to be shaded out by the development of a closed hardwood layer; the lower limit, from the time it takes for sufficient fuel to accumulate. In the Miami rock ridge these limits are approximately ten to fifteen years and two to three years. Such extremes in fire frequency would result in differences in forest structure and dynamics. Frequent fires would produce open, savanna-like stands with relatively little hardwood growth and a heavy herbaceous layer. Pine regeneration would occur in small patches where one or a few canopy trees died. In contrast, a long fire interval would result in greater litter accumulation, a heavier hardwood understory, and less herbaceous growth. The high fuel loads would result in more intense fires that would kill canopy trees in patches hectares in size. The presettlement fire frequency was probably somewhere between these two extremes and undoubtedly varied considerably during the history of these pinelands.

The time of year at which these fires occurred also would have affected forest structure and dynamics. It is known that the season of burning influences the flowering of herbaceous species and the establishment of pine seedlings. Elsewhere in the Southeast, the mortality and regrowth of hardwood understories have been shown to depend on season of burning (e.g., Lewis and Harshbarger, 1976), but studies in rockland pine forests have been ambiguous on this point (Snyder, 1986). Lightning, the only nonanthropogenic source of fire ignition, is common in south Florida (Taylor, 1980). Lightning strikes and lightning-caused fires occur mainly during the rainy season (May through October), but larger fires tend to occur in the earlier part of the season before water levels are highest and in years when the onset of the summer rains is delayed (fig. 8.13a).

On the other hand, human-caused wildfires are most common in November through May, with the greatest area burned when conditions are usually driest (April and May) (fig. 8.13b; Taylor and Rochefort, 1981). Prescribed burning in the pinelands of Everglades National Park until 1980 was mainly done in the cooler months of October to April under mild burning conditions (Taylor, 1981); since that time it has been done mostly during the rainy season.

It is difficult, perhaps impossible, to know with any degree of certainty what the presettlement fire regime in south Florida was. The fact that Indians have lived in the area for thousands of years introduces the greatest level of uncertainty because they may have burned at times other than the lightning season. One as yet unexplored avenue to address the question of season of burning would be to examine the responses of the numerous endemic taxa found in these pinelands (table 8.1) to different fire regimes. It

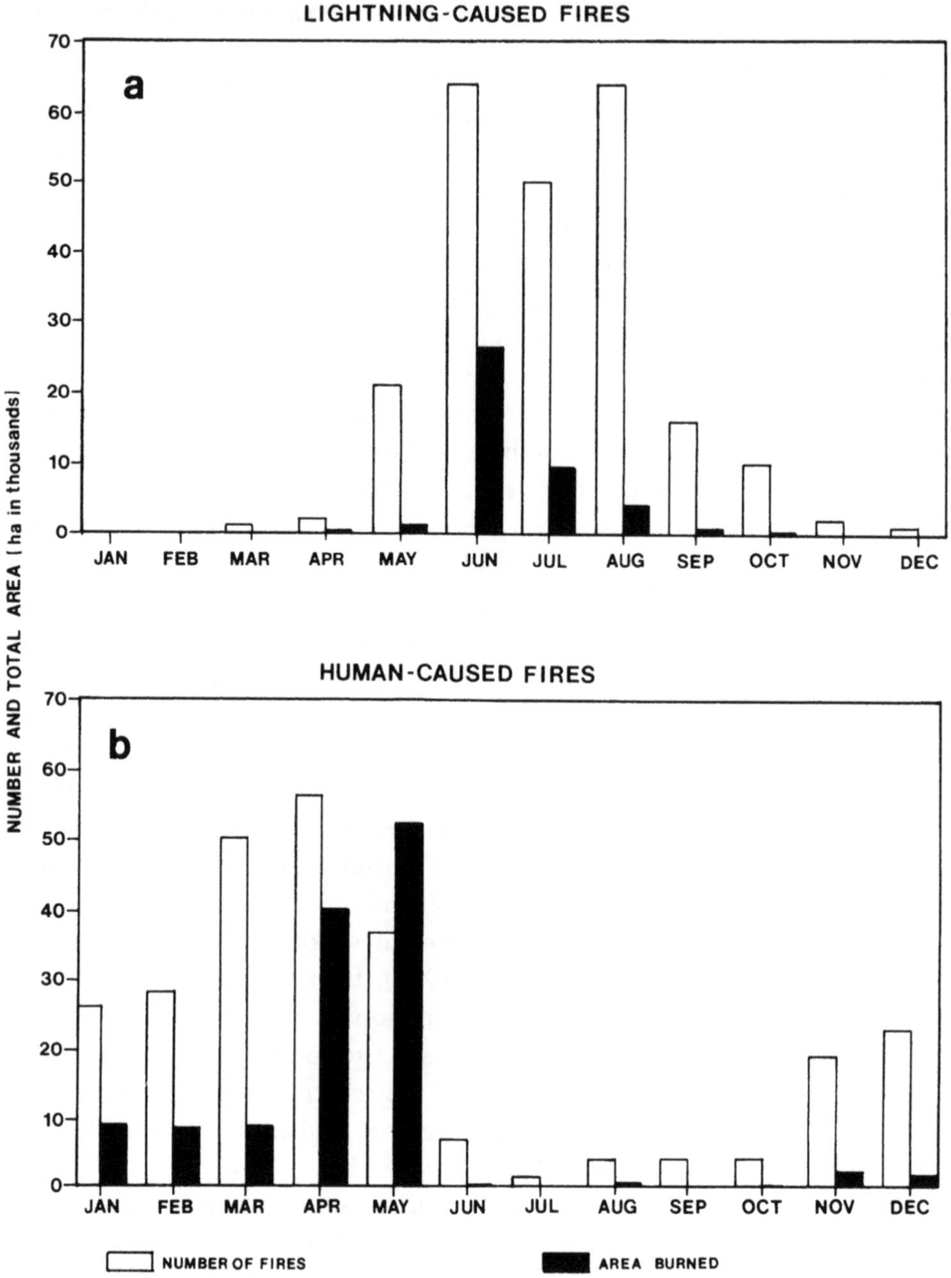

Fig. 8.13. Monthly distribution of (*a*) lightning fires and (*b*) human-caused fires (excluding prescribed fires) in Everglades National Park recorded from 1948 to 1981. The data are derived from Taylor (1981) and Doren and Rochefort (1984) and include fires in all habitats.

is not unreasonable to expect that there would be a favorable population response—increased flowering, fruiting, and establishment—of endemic taxa to the fire regime in which they evolved.

Phenology

Conditions favorable to year-round plant growth and the mixture of temperate and tropical species in the rockland communities of southern Florida introduce much variety into vegetative and reproductive phenology in the region. There are species in flower and fruit throughout the year.

South Florida slash pine is a true evergreen, with needles living for more than a year. Leaf abscission, or needlefall, occurs year-round with a minimum from January to March (Herndon and Taylor, 1985; Snyder, 1986). The trees also grow in diameter and height throughout the year, though diameter increase is slight during December and January (Langdon, 1963). The timing of height growth varies considerably from year to year, with over half the extension occurring from March through May.

Some of the temperate hardwoods, such as sumac, willow, and persimmon, are obligately deciduous. Willows, however, lose their leaves by October but flower and leaf out in December and January, so they are green during most of the winter. None of the tropical hardwoods is strictly deciduous, but several species—including wild tamarind, Jamaica dogwood, poisonwood, pond apple, and gumbo limbo—gradually lose a large percentage of their leaves during the winter, the percentage depending on the severity of the dry season. These trees begin to flower and produce new leaves about April, flowering on leafless or nearly leafless shoots. The temperate live oak follows the same pattern but flowers a month or two earlier. In yet another variation, mahogany maintains a relatively dense canopy throughout the winter season but then loses virtually all foliage just before flowering near the end of the dry season.

Only a few of the hardwood species in the rocklands have short, well-defined flowering periods. Data contained in Tomlinson (1980) indicate flowering periods of two months or less for willow, live oak, persimmon, sugarberry, pond apple, mahogany, West Indies cherry, and Jamaica dogwood. South Florida slash pine could also be added to the list. Several species, including scarletbush (*Hamelia patens*), satinleaf, Florida trema, black ironwood, blolly, red mangrove, buttonwood, and lancewood, can be found in flower for more than six months of the year (Loope, 1980b; Tomlinson, 1980). Other hardwoods have flowering periods between these extremes, with most flowering during the late spring and summer months (April to August).

The herbaceous species of the rocklands exhibit a similar diversity of flowering patterns. A few—such as *Cladium jamaicense*, *Muhlenbergia filipes*, *Teucrium canadense*, and most orchid species—have short, well-defined blooming periods. Most of the herbs—including *Borreria terminalis*, *Crotalaria pumila*, *Chamaesyce pinetorum*, *Croton linearis*, *Dichromena floridensis*, *Hedyotis nigricans*, *Phyllanthus pentaphyllus*, *Physalis viscosa*, and *Samolus ebracteatus*—flower and fruit for more than six months (Loope, 1980b; Gunderson et al., 1983). A relatively small number have blooming periods of intermediate duration.

Fire influences reproductive phenology in the pinelands, besides stimulating flowering in many species. Fire can shift blooming periods slightly for some species, though it is noticeable only for species with short blooming periods. A summer fire, for instance, can change the flowering period of *Liatris gracilis* from September and October to December and January. The most pronounced effect of fire, however, is to stimulate and synchronize the reproductive activity of herbaceous species. For several months following burning, all individuals of a given species flower simultaneously. In unburned pineland, many of these same individuals would not flower at all, and those that did would only occasionally flower at the same time as nearby conspecifics.

Fauna

The native fauna of the rockland ecosystems has been largely determined by two characteristics of southern Florida geomorphology. First, the rock lands are at the distal end of a peninsula 600 km long connected to southeastern North America. Second, though much of the rockland vegetation has a decidedly West Indian character, no land connection with the West Indies has ever existed. The Florida peninsula has been available throughout its existence to overland colonization by animals from the North American mainland subject only to the constraints imposed by climate and habitat and by distance down a long, relatively narrow corridor. Conversely, potential West Indian colonists of upland ecosystems in southern Florida have been effectively limited to animals able to fly and to those small enough and resistant enough to survive transport across an ocean barrier by wind or on floating debris.

Thus, in sharp contrast to the predominantly West Indian flora, the vertebrate fauna of southern Florida rocklands is derived almost completely from southeastern temperate North America (Robertson, 1955; Duellman and Schwartz, 1958; Robertson and Kushlan, 1984; Layne, 1984). Except for a few West Indian land birds of the Florida Keys and southeastern mainland, virtually all of the common and conspicuous native vertebrates of the rockland hammocks and pinelands are widely distributed in the southeastern United States coastal plain and beyond. Examples include the southern toad (*Bufo terrestris*), green treefrog (*Hyla cinerea*), black racer (*Coluber constrictor*), rough green snake (*Opheodrys aestivus*), green anole (*Anolis caroliniensis*), red-bellied woodpecker (*Melanerpes carolinus*), Carolina wren (*Thryothorus ludovicianus*), pine warbler (*Dendroica pinus*), northern cardinal (*Cardinalis cardinalis*), opossum (*Didelphis virginiana*), hispid cotton rat (*Sigmodon hispidus*), raccoon (*Procyon lotor*), and white-tailed deer (*Odocoileus virginianus*) (fig. 8.14).

The West Indian element in the indigenous rockland vertebrate fauna is apparently negligible except for birds, but the record is clouded by considerable uncertainty as to whether certain species are native or introduced by humans. Duellman and Schwartz (1958) suggested that the greenhouse frog (*Eleutherodactylus planirostris*), Cuban treefrog (*Hyla septentrionalis*), reef gecko (*Sphaerodactylus notatus*), and brown anole (*Anolis sagrei*) may have reached south Florida from Cuba or the Bahamas by natural means. Wilson and Porras (1983) included all of these species, except the reef gecko, as members of the introduced herpetofauna; however, they considered the bark anole (*Anolis distichus*), a Bahaman lizard established in and near Miami

Fig. 8.14. Key deer (*Odocoileus virginianus clavium*), noted for their small stature, in Big Pine Key pineland. The large-leafed shrub in the foreground is sea grape (*Coccoloba uvifera*). Photo by J. C. Oberhew. Courtesy U.S. Fish and Wildlife Service.

coastal hammocks, to be a probable native. The reef gecko, with its extensive distribution in tropical hammocks of the Florida Keys and southern mainland, seems to be the most likely self-introduced West Indian species of the rocklands, but it also has been thought by some to have been introduced by people (e.g., Schmidt, 1953).

Among the mammals, the extant West Indian fauna of terrestrial species is limited, but the region supports a diversity of bats, two species of which have reached southern Florida. The Jamaican fruit bat (*Artibeus jamaicensis*) is known from several records in the Florida Keys, but there seems to be no evidence that an established population exists there (Layne, 1984). Since 1936, several colonies of the Florida mastiff bat (*Eumops glaucinus floridanus*) have been found in older buildings (those with chimneys and attics) in Miami. The Florida population has been described as a distinct subspecies said to be the same as a Pleistocene fossil bat from Florida (Koopman, 1971; Layne, 1978, 1984). Although the known occurrences are in areas formerly occupied by rockland vegetation, almost no information is available concerning the species' role, if any, in unaltered ecosystems.

Compared to the equivocal record in other groups of terrestrial vertebrates, the nine undoubtedly native West Indian land birds constitute a robust representation. Two additional land birds, the zenaida dove (*Zenaida aurita*) and the Key West quail-dove (*Geotrygon chrysia*), are said to have inhabited the Florida Keys in the 1800s, but, if correctly reported as breeding species, these populations were extirpated at an early date (Kale, 1978). The West Indian birds that have established breeding populations exhibit several common characteristics that probably contributed to their ability to colonize southern Florida. Most are widely distributed in the Bahamas and Greater Antilles, where they are among the most common and characteristic species of coastal habitats. Many inhabit mangrove forests as well as upland communities, and the extensive mangrove areas of southern Florida doubtless facilitated their establishment. Finally, several species appear to have colonized southern Florida fairly recently, and there is reason to believe that additional colonization may occur.

In the rockland ecosystems, the West Indian land birds are limited to the Florida Keys and southeastern coastal areas and are absent from the rock lands of the Big Cypress Swamp. The mangrove cuckoo (*Coccyzus minor*) and black-whiskered vireo (*Vireo altiloquus*) are widespread in tropical hammocks of the Florida Keys, and, more sparingly, in those of the Miami rock ridge; both are closely limited to coastal mangroves in their more northerly range in Florida (Kale, 1978). The white-crowned pigeon (*Columba leucocephala*) nests on isolated mangrove islets in Florida Bay and the Florida Keys but feeds primarily on the fleshy fruits of tropical hardwoods (e.g., fig and poisonwood) in the rockland hammocks and pinelands of the Florida Keys and southern mainland (Kale, 1978). The gray kingbird (*Tyrannus dominicensis*) is ubiquitous in open habitats of the Florida Keys and southeastern coast. The smooth-billed ani (*Crotophaga ani*) is widely distributed in brushy secondary vegetation of southeastern Florida rocklands but is presently much less numerous than it was before the severe freezes of the late 1970s. Both the gray kingbird and the smooth-billed ani, very typical West Indian birds, have extensive ranges in Florida beyond the rockland area, especially along coasts.

The remaining four West Indian species appear to be recent colonists. The Cuban yellow warbler (*Dendroica petechia gundlachi*), first found nesting in 1941 (Greene, 1942), is largely limited to mangrove islands of Florida Bay but has a broader ecological amplitude in its West Indian range (Kale, 1978). Recent colonization by other West Indian birds may have depended upon the alteration of rockland ecosystems by humans. Thus, the Antillean nighthawk (*Chordeiles gundlachii*), first found in the lower Florida Keys in the 1940s (Greene, 1943), often nests where rocklands are being cleared for development (Kale, 1978); the Greater Antillean subspecies of the mourning dove (*Zenaida m. macroura*) (Aldrich and Duvall, 1958) mainly inhabits yards and plantings in residential developments; and the West Indian cave swallow (*Hirundo f. fulva*), discovered in 1987 (P. W. Smith et al., 1988), has been found nesting only under highway bridges. Because of the evident recent invasions and the growing list of West Indian land birds known to reach southern Florida as vagrants (now about twenty species), colonization by additional species seems likely (Robertson and Kushlan, 1984).

Invertebrates have not been well studied in the rocklands, but the few relatively well-known groups show diverse biogeographic patterns. The resident ants of the rocklands are overwhelmingly derived from the fauna of the southeastern United States (M. Deyrup, personal communication), while the resident butterflies and skippers are largely West Indian (Lenczewski, 1980). Twenty-seven of the sixty native land snails have tropical affinities (Hulbricht, 1985). Notable invertebrates include the endemic (and endangered) Schaus swallowtail (*Heraclides aristodemus ponceanus*, fig. 8.15), whose larvae feed exclusively on torchwood foliage in upper Keys hammocks (Loftus and Kushlan, 1984). The Florida tree snail (*Liguus fasciatus*, fig. 8.16), is native to hammocks of southern Florida and Cuba, where it feeds on the algae and fungi growing on tree bark (Franz, 1982; Pilsbry, 1946). It was sought after by collectors because of the wide variety of color forms that have evolved, but the state now requires a special permit to collect this species.

Although the vertebrate fauna of rockland ecosystems is mostly of northern derivation, only a considerably diminished selection of the fauna of northern Florida and the adjacent Southeast reached the southern end of the long peninsula and the Florida Keys. The "peninsula effect" of reduced species diversity is seen in all vertebrate groups (Duellman and Schwartz, 1958; Dalrymple, 1988; Simpson, 1964; Layne, 1984; Robertson and Kushlan, 1984); numerous historical and ecological arguments have been advanced to

Fig. 8.15. Schaus swallowtail (*Heraclides aristodemus ponceanus*), an endangered species known only from upper Keys hammocks. Photo by George Krizek. Courtesy U.S. Fish and Wildlife Service.

Fig. 8.16. Florida tree snail (*Liguus fasciatus*) on wild tamarind (*Lysiloma latisiliqua*).

account for it. The isolation and relatively limited extent of the rockland ecosystems doubtless had an important role in limiting both original access by upland species and recolonizing after local extirpation. The extent of reduction of species diversity varies among the vertebrate groups. In the case of breeding land birds, for example, seventy species inhabit northern Florida while only forty are found in the southern peninsular area that includes the rocklands and, despite the addition of West Indian species, only twenty breed in the lower Florida Keys (Robertson and Kushlan, 1984).

The reduced species diversity of land birds in rockland ecosystems contributes to the substantially lower total population density found in rockland pine forests and tropical hammocks, compared with similar habitats farther north in Florida (Robertson and Kushlan, 1984). Habitat disturbance by humans may partially account for lower breeding-bird population density in some of the areas studied, but similarly reduced density has also been found in remote, virgin stands of rockland pine forest in the Big Cypress Swamp (Patterson et al., 1980). Reduced species diversity and low total population give a depauperate, oddly constituted appearance to the avifauna of some rockland areas. Thus, the pine forests of the lower Florida Keys have none of the breeding birds characteristic of southeastern coastal plain pine flatwoods, and the interiors of extensive tropical hammocks on the southern mainland are often without breeding birds, except where the black-whiskered vireo occurs or where canopy gaps provide habitat for forest-edge species (Robertson, 1955).

The endemic vertebrates of rockland ecosystems (table 8.2) are mainly relict populations of North American species stranded in the Florida Keys. Most are distinct at the subspecies level, and the survival of most is more or less imminently threatened by massive habitat destruction. Endemic mammals in the rocklands of the Florida Keys (Layne, 1978, 1984) include four rodents, three subspecies of raccoon, and the well-known Key deer (*Odocoileus virginianus clavium*) (fig. 8.14). The Key deer is the smallest subspecies of white-tailed deer in the United States and is restricted to Big Pine Key and several surrounding keys. The decimation of the population to as few as twenty-five individuals in the 1950s prompted the establishment of the National Key Deer Refuge (Dickson, 1955; Hardin et al., 1984). Recently the population has been estimated at 250 to 300 deer (U.S. Fish and Wildlife Service, 1985). In mainland areas, the mangrove fox squirrel (*Sciurus niger avicennia*), Florida panther (*Felis concolor coryi*), and Florida black bear (*Ursus americanus floridanus*) are all considered endangered or threatened (Layne, 1978). All occur in rockland ecosystems but also have extensive geographic and ecologic ranges outside the rocklands. There are threatened endemic subspecies of turtles, lizards, and snakes in the Florida Keys (table 8.2). The Miami black-headed snake (*Tantilla oolitica*), an endemic species, has been found at a few localities in Key Largo and the Miami rock ridge (McDiarmid, 1978). The southern Florida rockland ecosystems have no endemic birds, but a remnant population of one endangered bird species, the red-cockaded woodpecker (*Picoides borealis*), persists in old-growth pine forests of the Big Cypress region (Patterson and Robertson, 1981).

It has been noted that the southern Florida ranges of a number of pine forest birds of northern derivation have contracted within the period of historical record in patterns not wholly attributable to habitat disturbance (Robertson, 1955; Robertson and Kushlan, 1984). The species concerned are the American kestrel (*Falco sparverius*), red-cockaded woodpecker, hairy woodpecker (*Picoides villosus*), brown-headed nuthatch (*Sitta pusilla*), eastern bluebird (*Sialia sialis*), and summer tanager (*Piranga rubra*). All are known to have nested in the Miami rock ridge pinelands (as recently as the 1960s, in the case of the eastern bluebird, hairy woodpecker, and red-cockaded woodpecker), and all, possibly excepting the hairy woodpecker, have since disappeared from the area as breeding species. Populations of five of the six species persist in the pine forests of Big Cypress National Preserve, but the hairy woodpecker and summer tanager are rare there, and no breeding American kestrels have been located in extensive surveys of areas of old-growth pine forest (Patterson et al., 1980). The absence of all typical pine forest birds in the lower Florida Keys pinelands (where no extensive lumbering has occurred), the disappearance of species from the Long Pine Key section of the Miami rock ridge well after lumbering ended, and the availability of fairly extensive uncut forest in some areas (Olmsted et al., 1983) suggest causative factors other than (or added to) habitat disruption. The range contractions might represent the effects of long-term changes in climate upon small populations at their range extremes.

A last point to be made about the vertebrate fauna of southern Florida rocklands is that the drama of range change by native species is being thoroughly eclipsed by introductions of exotic species. By rough tally, the introduced species that may have established self-maintaining populations in south Florida include seven mammals (Layne, 1984), about thirty birds (Owre, 1973; American Ornithologists' Union, 1983; W. B. Robertson, Jr., personal observation), four amphibians, and about twenty-five reptiles (Wilson and Porras, 1983). The predominant groups are lizards, with around eighteen species (seven or more species of West Indian *Anolis*), parrots, parakeets, and other psittacids, with as many as fifteen species known to have nested in the wild. Most populations apparently were founded by animals that escaped or were released from the stream of imports through Miami. The majority are species of neotropical origin, but also included are numerous representatives of the Old World tropics. Most populations are still closely limited to urban/suburban areas of the southeast coast, where landscape plantings provide many forms with habitats similar to those of their native areas (Owre, 1973). A striking, perhaps ominous, characteristic of the introduced vertebrate fauna is its rapid increase in recent decades. For example, Wilson and Porras (1983) point out that the species diversity of the known introduced hereptofauna tripled from 1958 (Duellman and Schwartz, 1958) to the early 1980s. This growth is likely to have continued, and a similar rate of increase probably applies for bird species.

It is still unknown to what extent introduced vertebrates may become established in natural rockland areas and what impact they may have on the native vertebrate fauna. However, some exotics have spread widely into agricultural and disturbed natural habitats fringing the suburban area. It has been suggested that spread of the Cuban treefrog may have depressed populations of native *Hyla* species and that the brown anole may have similarly affected populations of the green anole, but Wilson and Porras (1983) point out that documentation is scanty in these and other suggested cases. The principal instances of introduced species that are widely established in natural rockland areas are found among mammals (Layne, 1984). Mexican red-bellied squirrels (*Sciurus aureogaster*) are relatively common in tropical hammocks on Elliott Key and nearby islands in Biscayne National Park; races of the black rat (*Rattus rattus*) are widely distributed in some natural communities; and the nine-banded armadillo (*Dasypus novemcinctus*) and feral hog (*Sus scrofa*) are common in the Big Cypress Swamp. It remains to be seen what potential for invasion into natural areas exists among more recently introduced vertebrates.

Land Use History and Conservation

The earliest settlers in southern Florida were concentrated on the Florida Keys. Key West was the largest city in the region from the time of its settlement in the 1820s through the early years of the twentieth century. The hammocks on the Keys were exploited extensively during this period. The valuable timbers, especially mahogany, were logged out first. Many of the early settlers used slash-and-burn agriculture around homesteads within the hammocks. The most intensive exploitation of the hammocks during this period, however, was for firewood and charcoal. As Key West grew, its need for fuel grew correspondingly, and this fuel was supplied by hammock trees (Small, 1917).

Early settlers on the mainland followed practices similar to those of their counterparts on the Keys. Hammocks were cleared for farming and the pinelands and glades were used as range for livestock. Large solution holes within the pinelands ("banana holes") were often planted by homesteaders (Harshberger, 1914). Limited logging of the pinelands took place until the Florida East Coast Railroad reached Miami in 1896. Industrial logging quickly followed, and the pinelands were clear-cut over the next fifty years. Only a few marginal pine stands escaped this logging.

The earliest industry in the Miami region was the preparation of flour from the "root" (stem and rootstock) of coontie (Burkhardt, 1952; Gearhart, 1952). This industry, which lasted from 1840 through 1925, certainly reduced the abundance of coontie in the Miami area but probably had little other effect on the rockland ecosystem.

Several entrepreneurs recognized the potential for growing new crops in the tropical climate of southern Florida. Sisal (*Agave sisalana*) was introduced by Dr. Henry Perrine to the Florida Keys to establish a new source of fiber for cordage. Coconut palms and pineapple were widely planted. Commercial plantings of tropical tree crops were developed around the turn of the century (Dorn, 1956). The most important of these crops were grapefruit, limes, mangoes, and avocadoes. The groves were generally established on the well-drained rocklands, primarily cleared pinelands.

Row-crop farming was initially concentrated in the glades rather than the rocklands due to the lack of workable soil in pinelands. After 1950, however, farm machinery—in particular, the "rock plow" (fig. 8.17)—was developed that allowed farmers to modify the rock/soil surface of the pineland, making agricultural operations feasible. Large-scale clearing of pinelands for row crops followed.

The low water-holding capacity and lack of nutrients in plowed pineland "soils" are countered by liberal irrigation and chemical fertilization. On abandonment, the physical and chemical alterations of the soil (Orth and Conover, 1975) result in successional vegetation that bears little resemblance to the native pineland and is often dominated by the exotic *Schinus terebinthifolius* (Loope and Dunevitz, 1981b).

Residential development has also increasingly encroached upon the rocklands from the beginning of the century. Outside of Long Pine Key in Everglades National Park, the combined effect of clearing for agriculture and residential development has left perhaps 2 percent of the original Miami rock ridge pinelands intact, and only three individual blocks of these remnant pinelands are larger than 50 ha. Hardwood hammocks were also cleared for agricultural and residential development, though only the latter irrevocably destroyed the vegetation. Brickell Hammock, the largest tropical hardwood hammock on the Miami rock ridge, occupied an area in the present-day center of Miami (Young, 1951). It was largely cleared early in this century as the city grew. Other hammocks visited by Small during his early explorations were likewise destroyed (Small, 1916).

Most of the remaining hammocks on the Miami rock ridge are not in

Fig. 8.17. A rock plow preparing an agricultural field southwest of Homestead. The field was formerly pineland; in the background is a tropical hammock.

danger of being cleared for development at this time. In addition to the hammocks of the Long Pine Key area, which are protected by the National Park Service, many important hammocks on the Miami rock ridge (Snapper Creek, Matheson, Castellow, Fuchs, Addison) are owned by Dade County. Most of the remaining hammocks have been proposed for purchase by the State of Florida's Conservation and Recreation Lands (CARL) program. Overall, despite the loss of such large and important forests as Brickell Hammock, more than half of the tropical hardwood hammocks found in Dade County at the beginning of settlement are still extant.

In contrast to the situation on the mainland, most hardwood hammocks on the Keys are privately owned and are not protected against clearing. Demand for the commercial and residential development on the Keys is such that all privately held land is almost certain to be cleared eventually. A few large tracts are protected by the federal government, particularly in Biscayne National Park in the upper Keys and the National Key Deer Refuge in the lower Keys. Two major land acquisition programs that are under way on Key Largo—the Crocodile Lakes National Wildlife Refuge of the U.S. Fish and Wildlife Service and the North Key Largo Hammock Preserve of the Florida Department of Natural Resources—will add substantially to the total area of protected rocklands in the Keys.

Exotic plants present a major threat to hammocks throughout the rock lands. Several trees widely planted as ornamentals in southern Florida, including *Schinus terebinthifolius*, *Bischofia javanica*, and *Schefflera actinophylla*, invade hammocks and displace native species. *Colubrina asiatica*, a woody vine, smothers hammocks in coastal areas. Several herbaceous invaders, however, are likely to be more troublesome. The worst are the vine *Syngonium* and the ground-covering *Sansevieria*. Active management will be necessary to control these exotic species.

On the mainland, pineland areas have been much more devastated than have the hardwood hammocks. Aside from Long Pine Key in Everglades National Park, the only large areas of pineland on the Miami rock ridge are Navy Wells Pineland Preserve (owned primarily by Dade County), those around the old Richmond Air Field (owned by several different government agencies), and those in the Deering Estate at Cutler (owned by Dade County). The largest of the remaining pineland remnants on the rock ridge have been proposed for purchase by the CARL program.

Unfortunately, passive protection is not sufficient to preserve the pineland system. Pinelands must be burned regularly, and both the small size of the remaining pinelands and the presence of residential and commercial development on the borders of the preserves greatly restrict burning programs. *Schinus* is the worst invader of infrequently burned pinelands (Loope and Dunevitz, 1981a). In addition, some of the other weeds likely to disrupt the pinelands (e.g., *Neyraudia reynaudiana*, *Pennisetum purpureum*, and *Albizzia lebbeck* in the Miami rock ridge) cannot be controlled by burning and must be removed by hand on a regular basis.

Pinelands in the lower Keys are in much better condition because there has been less development in that region. Still the pinelands are slowly being cleared for homes and fragmented by the roads connecting the homes. The lower Keys pinelands will be lost as viable habitats if this pattern continues.

Of the three rockland areas in southern Florida, the Big Cypress region is the least disturbed by civilization. The entire region lies within the boundaries of Big Cypress National Preserve and is protected against commercial development. The Big Cypress region has also been less affected by hydrologic modifications of the upstream watershed than has the Miami rock ridge region. The major threat to this section of the rocklands is invasion by exotic plants, including *Melaleuca quinquenervia.*

Despite the limited area covered by the rocklands and sustained development pressure, only a few species have been lost. Among the plants, *Tephrosia angustissima* is presumed extinct; it was described as endemic to the rocky pinelands by Small (1933), but no plants of this species have been found for several decades. Several epiphytes, including *Rhipsalis baccifera, Brassia caudata,* and *Macradenia lutescens,* have been extirpated from south Florida, primarily due to overcollecting. Among the animals, several color forms of the tree snail *Liguus* have been lost in the wild. Most of these were lost to urban development, but in one case the form was lost to a hurricane (A. Jones, personal communication).

Several other species are in a precarious position and could easily be lost in the near future. The endemic plants *Polygala smallii* and *Amorpha crenulata,* for instance, are known from only a few populations each. Preservation of representative areas of the rockland communities in a viable state will be a major challenge. There is some urgency in acquiring representative sites in advance of development, but, in the long term, increased active management will be just as necessary to ensure the continued existence of these unique ecosystems.

Appendix. Distribution of woody plant species native to rockland hammocks (H) and pinelands (P) of southern Florida

Scientific Name	Common Name	Florida Keys		Miami Rock Ridge				Big Cypress
		UK	LK	—	LP	RL	NB	
Trees and Shrubs								
Acacia farnesiana	sweet acacia	—	P	—	—	—	P	—
Acacia pinetorum	pineland acacia	—	P	H	P	—	—	—
Acer rubrum var. *tridens*[a,b]	red maple	—	—	—	—	—	—	H
Alvaradoa amorphoides	alvaradoa	—	—	H	P	P	—	—
Amorpha crenulata	crenulate lead plant	—	—	—	—	—	P	—
Amyris elemifera	torchwood	H	—	H	—	—	—	H
Annona glabra[b]	pond apple	H	P	H	P	P	P	H
Ardisia escallonioides	marlberry	H	P	H	P	P	—	H
Asimina reticulata[a]	pawpaw	—	—	—	—	—	—	P
Ateramnus lucidus	crabwood	H	—	H	—	—	—	—
Avicennia germinans[b]	black mangrove	H	H	—	—	—	—	—
Baccharis angustifolia[a]	false willow	—	P	H	—	—	—	—
Baccharis glomeruliflora[a]	groundsel tree	—	H	H	P	P	P	H
Baccharis halimifolia[a]	groundsel tree	H	H,P	H	P	P	P	P
Befaria racemosa[a]	tarflower	—	—	—	—	—	—	P
Bourreria cassinifolia	smooth strongbark	—	P	—	P	P	P	—
Bourreria ovata	strongbark	H	H	—	—	—	—	—
Bourreria succulenta	rough strongbark	H	—	—	—	—	—	—
Bumelia celastrina var. *angustifolia*	saffron plum	H	H,P	—	P	—	—	—
Bumelia reclinata	buckthorn	—	—	H	P	P	P	H,P
Bumelia salicifolia	willow bustic	H	H,P	H	P	P	P	H,P
Bursera simaruba	gumbo limbo	H	H,P	H	P	P	—	H
Byrsonima lucida	locust berry	H	H,P	H	P	P	P	—
Caesalpinia pauciflora	—	—	P	—	—	—	—	—
Callicarpa americana[a]	beauty berry	H	—	H	P	P	P	H,P
Calyptranthes pallens	pale lidflower	H	—	H	—	—	—	H
Calyptranthes zuzygium	myrtle-of-the-river	H	—	H	—	—	—	—
Canella winterana	cinnamon-bark	H	—	—	—	—	—	—
Capparis cynophallophora	Jamaica caper	H	—	—	—	—	—	—
Capparis flexuosa	limber caper	H	H	—	—	—	—	—
Casasia clusiifolia	seven-year apple	H	—	—	—	—	—	—
Cassia chapmanii	Bahama senna	—	H,P	H	P	P	P	P
Cassia ligustrina	—	H	—	H	—	—	—	—
Catesbaea parviflora	—	—	P	—	—	—	—	—
Celtis laevigata[a]	sugarberry	—	—	H	—	—	—	H
Cephalanthus occidentalis[a,b]	buttonbush	—	—	H	P	P	—	H
Chrysobalanus icaco	coco plum	H	P	H	P	P	P	H,P
Chrysophyllum oliviforme	satinleaf	H	H,P	H	P	—	—	H
Citharexylum fruticosum	fiddlewood	H	—	H	P	P	—	H
Clusia rosea	pitch apple	—	H	—	—	—	—	—
Coccoloba diversifolia	pigeon plum	H	H,P	H	P	—	—	H
Coccoloba uvifera	sea grape	H	H,P	—	—	—	—	—
Colubrina arborescens	coffee colubrina	—	—	H	P	—	—	H
Colubrina cubensis	Cuba colubrina	—	—	H	P	—	—	—
Colubrina elliptica	soldierwood	H	—	—	—	—	—	—
Conocarpus erecta	buttonwood	H	H,P	H	P	P	—	—
Cordia globosa	—	H	—	—	—	—	—	H
Cordia sebestena	Geiger tree	H	H	—	—	—	—	—
Cornus foemina[a,b]	stiff cornel	—	—	—	—	—	—	H
Crossopetalum rhacoma	rhacoma	H	H,P	H	P	P	—	—
Croton linearis	pineland croton	—	P	—	P	P	P	—
Cupania glabra	cupania	—	H	—	—	—	—	—
Diospyros virginiana[a]	persimmon	—	—	H	P	—	—	H,P
Dodonaea viscosa	varnish leaf	H	—	H	P	P	P	P
Drypetes diversifolia	milkbark	H	H,P	—	—	—	—	—
Drypetes lateriflora	Guiana plum	H	—	H	—	—	—	H
Erithalis fruticosa	black torch	H	H,P	—	—	—	—	—
Erythrina herbacea[a]	coral bean	—	—	H	—	—	—	H
Eugenia axillaris	white stopper	H	H,P	H	P	P	—	H,P
Eugenia confusa	redberry stopper	H	—	H	—	—	—	H
Eugenia foetida	Spanish stopper	H	H,P	H	—	—	—	—
Eugenia rhombea	red stopper	H	—	—	—	—	—	—
Eupatorium villosum	—	—	—	H	P	P	—	—
Exostema caribaeum	princewood	H	H	—	—	—	—	—
Exothea paniculata	inkwood	H	H	H	P	P	—	H
Ficus aurea	strangler fig	H	H,P	H	P	P	P	H,P
Ficus citrifolia	shortleaf fig	H	H,P	H	P	P	P	H,P

(*continued*)

Scientific Name	Common Name	Florida Keys		Miami Rock Ridge				Big Cypress
		UK	LK	—	LP	RL	NB	
Forestiera segregata var. *pinetorum*	pineland olive	—	P	H	P	P	—	—
Guaiacum sanctum	lignum vitae	H	—	—	—	—	—	—
Guapira discolor	blolly	H	H,P	H	P	P	—	—
Guettarda elliptica	velvetseed	H	H,P	H	P	P	—	—
Guettarda scabra	rough velvetseed	H	H,P	H	P	P	P	—
Gyminda latifolia	false boxwood	—	H	—	—	—	—	—
Hamelia patens	scarletbush	H	H	H	—	—	—	H
Hippomane mancinella	manchineel	—	H,P	—	—	—	—	—
Hypelate trifoliata	white ironwood	H	P	H	P	—	—	—
Ilex cassine[a]	dahoon	—	—	H	P	P	P	H,P
Ilex glabra[a]	gallberry	—	—	—	—	—	—	P
Ilex krugiana	tawnyberry holly	—	—	H	P	P	—	—
Jacquinia keyensis	joewood	H	H,P	H	P	—	—	—
Krugiodendron ferreum	black ironwood	H	H	H	—	—	—	H
Laguncularia racemosa[b]	white mangrove	H	H,P	—	—	—	—	—
Lantana involucrata	wild sage	H	H,P	H	P	P	P	—
Lyonia fruticosa[a]	staggerbush	—	—	—	—	—	P	P
Lysiloma latisiliqua	wild tamarind	H	—	H	P	P	—	H
Magnolia virginiana[a,b]	sweet bay	—	—	H	P	—	—	H
Manilkara bahamensis	wild dilly	H	H,P	—	—	—	—	—
Mastichodendron foetidissimum	mastic	H	—	H	—	—	—	H
Maytenus phyllanthoides	gutta-percha mayten	H	—	—	—	—	—	—
Metopium toxiferum	poisonwood	H	H,P	H	P	P	P	H,P
Morus rubra[a]	red mulberry	—	—	H	—	—	—	H
Myrcianthes fragrans	twinberry stopper	H	—	H	P	P	—	H
Myrica cerifera[a]	wax myrtle	—	H,P	H	P	P	P	H,P
Myrsine guianensis	myrsine	H	H,P	H	P	P	P	H,P
Nectandra coriacea	lancewood	H	—	H	—	—	—	H
Persea borbonia[a]	red bay	H	P	H	P	P	P	H,P
Pinus elliottii var. *densa*	S. Fla. slash pine	—	H,P	H	P	P	P	P
Piscidia piscipula	Jamaica dogwood	H	H,P	H	—	—	—	—
Pisonia rotundata	pisonia	—	H,P	—	—	—	—	—
Pithecellobium guadalupense	blackhead	—	P	—	—	—	—	—
Pithecellobium unguis-cati	cat's claw	H	H	H	—	—	—	—
Prunus myrtifolia	West Indies cherry	—	—	H	—	—	—	—
Psidium longipes	long-stalked stopper	—	H,P	H	P	P	P	—
Psychotria ligustrifolia	Bahama wild coffee	H	—	—	—	—	—	—
Psychotria nervosa	wild coffee	H	H,P	H	P	P	—	H
Psychotria sulzneri	wild coffee	—	—	H	—	—	—	H
Quercus laurifolia[a]	laurel oak	—	—	—	—	—	—	H
Quercus minima[a]	dwarf live oak	—	—	—	—	—	P	P
Quercus pumila[a]	running oak	—	—	H	—	—	P	P
Quercus virginiana[a]	live oak	H	—	H	P	P	P	H,P
Quercus virginiana var. *geminata*[a]	sand live oak	—	—	—	—	—	P	P
Randia aculeata	indigo berry	H	H,P	H	P	P	P	H,P
Reynosia septentrionalis	darling plum	H	H,P	—	—	—	—	—
Rhizophora mangle[b]	red mangrove	H	H,P	—	—	—	—	—
Rhus copallina[a]	sumac	—	P	H	P	P	P	H,P
Salix caroliniana[a,b]	willow	—	—	H	P	P	P	H,P
Sambucus canadensis[a,b]	elderberry	—	—	H	—	—	P	H
Sapindus saponaria	soapberry	H	—	H	—	—	—	—
Savia bahamensis	maiden bush	—	H	—	—	—	—	—
Schaefferia frutescens	Florida boxwood	H	—	—	—	—	—	—
Schoepfia chrysophylloides	gray twig	H	—	H	—	—	—	H
Simarouba glauca	paradise tree	H	H	H	—	—	—	H
Solanum bahamense	Bahama nightshade	H	—	—	—	—	—	—
Solanum donianum[b]	—	—	H,P	H	P	—	—	—
Solanum erianthum	potato-tree	H	H,P	H	—	—	—	H
Sophora tomentosa	necklace pod	—	P	—	—	—	—	—
Strumpfia maritima	—	—	P	—	—	—	—	—
Swietenia mahagoni	mahogany	H	—	H	—	—	—	—
Taxodium ascendens[a,b]	pond cypress	—	—	H	—	—	—	P
Tetrazygia bicolor	tetrazygia	—	—	H	P	P	P	—
Trema lamarckiana	West Indies trema	H	—	—	—	—	P	—
Trema micrantha	Florida trema	—	H,P	H	P	P	P	H,P
Vaccinium myrsinites[a]	shiny blueberry	—	—	—	—	—	P	P
Vallesia glabra	pearl berry	H	—	—	—	—	—	—
Viburnum obovatum[a,b]	black haw	—	—	—	—	—	—	H
Ximenia americana	tallowwood	H	H	H	—	—	P	H
Zanthoxylum fagara	wild lime	H	—	H	—	—	—	H

(*continued*)

Appendix (continued)

Scientific Name	Common Name	Florida Keys UK	Florida Keys LK	Miami Rock Ridge —	Miami Rock Ridge LP	Miami Rock Ridge RL	Miami Rock Ridge NB	Big Cypress
Vines and Scandent Shrubs								
Ampelopsis arborea[a]	pepper vine	—	—	H	—	—	—	H
Berchemia scandens[a,b]	rattan vine	—	—	—	—	—	—	H
Caesalpinia bonduc	yellow nicker	—	H	—	—	—	—	—
Caesalpinia crista	gray nicker	H	—	—	—	—	—	—
Chiococca alba	snowberry	H	H	H	—	—	—	H
Cissus sicyoides	possum grape	—	—	H	—	—	—	H
Dalbergia brownei	—	H	—	—	—	—	—	—
Dalbergia ecastophyllum	fishpoison vine	H	—	H	—	—	—	—
Gouania lupuloides	chew stick	H	—	—	—	—	—	H
Hippocratea volubilis	doctor vine	H	—	H	—	—	—	—
Parthenocissus quinquefolia[a]	Virginia creeper	H	H	H	—	—	—	H
Pisonia aculeata	devil's claw	H	H	H	—	—	—	H
Smilax spp.[a]	greenbrier	H	H,P	H	P	P	P	H,P
Tournefortia hirsutissima	—	—	—	H	—	—	—	H
Tournefortia volubilis	soldier vine	H	H	—	—	—	—	H
Toxicodendron radicans	poison ivy	H	H,P	H	P	P	P	H,P
Vitis spp.[a]	grape	H	—	H	—	—	—	H
Vitis rotundifolia[a]	muscadine	H	H	H	P	—	—	H,P
Palms								
Coccothrinax argentata	silver palm	H	H,P	H	P	P	P	—
Pseudophoenix sargentii	buccaneer palm	H	—	—	—	—	—	—
Roystonea elata	royal palm	—	—	H	—	—	—	—
Sabal palmetto[a]	cabbage palm	H	H,P	H	P	P	P	H,P
Serenoa repens[a]	saw palmetto	H	H,P	H	P	P	P	H,P
Thrinax morrisii	Key thatch palm	H	H,P	—	—	—	—	—
Thrinax radiata	Florida thatch palm	H	H,P	—	—	—	—	—

Sources: Distributions are based on Alexander (1958a, 1967b), Dickson (1955), Gunderson and Loope (1982b), Hilsenbeck (1976), McGuire and Brown (1974), Olmsted et al. (1980, 1983), Phillips (1940), Robertson (1955), Weiner (1979), and observations of the authors.

Note: UK = Upper Keys; LK = Lower Keys; LP = Long Pine Key; RL = Redlands; NB = Northern Biscayne.

a. Species with distributions mainly north of south Florida.

b. Species of solution holes or ecotones; more characteristic of other habitats.

Part III

Freshwater Wetlands and Aquatic Ecosystems

9
Swamps

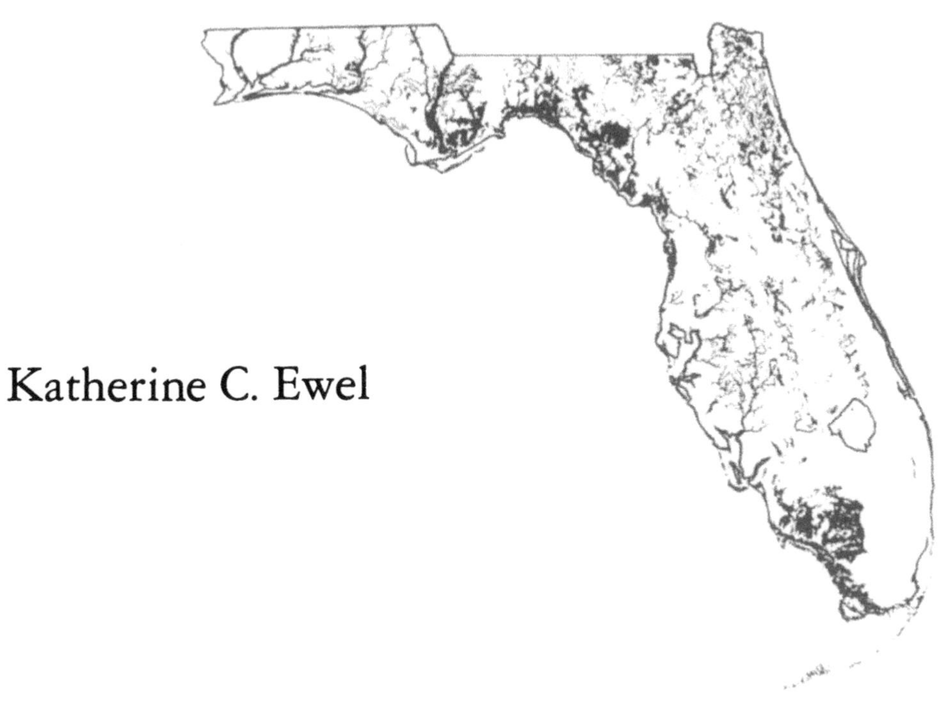

Katherine C. Ewel

Wetlands—marshes and swamps together—are a major component of the Florida landscape. More than half of the state was originally covered by wetlands (Shaw and Fredine, 1956). Even today, after more than half of them have been lost, these ecosystems exemplify the degree to which seemingly distinct communities can be interconnected and interdependent.

Although forested wetlands, or swamps, have been reduced in area and number by drainage and filling, they still comprise 10 percent of Florida's land area (Wharton et al., 1982). These swamps are widely distributed throughout the state (fig. 9.1), fringing rivers and lakes, following drainages that grow from seepage basins into meandering sloughs, and occupying small, shallow ponds. Heads, galls, domes, bogs, sogs, bays, strands, and hammocks are only a few of the types of swamps that can be identified, indicating the diversity of both the ecosystems themselves and the challenges and opportunities they presented to the earliest settlers.

In spite of reduction in both their names and numbers over the years, most of Florida's swamps are as much a mystery now as when they were first described. Considerable research has been conducted in some swamps,

Fig. 9.1. Distribution of swamps in Florida, with locations of swamps and regions mentioned in chapter 9. By M. T. Brown in Odum, 1984.

including the Apalachicola River floodplain forest in the Florida Panhandle, the Oklawaha River floodplain forest in central Florida, and cypress swamps throughout the state. But many other kinds of swamps, such as bayheads, shrub bogs, cedar swamps, and even the swamps lining spring runs, are poorly understood.

Just as poorly understood are the relationships among adjacent swamps and between swamps and uplands. Florida's flat topography and high water tables often allow water and nutrient flows to weave adjacent ecosystems into a closely integrated landscape. Large areas, such as Tate's Hell in the Panhandle, the Osceola National Forest in northeast Florida, San Pedro Bay near Perry, Gulf Hammock near Cedar Keys, the Green Swamp in central Florida, and the Big Cypress Swamp in south Florida, are characteristic landscapes in which uplands, hydric hammocks, poorly drained pine flatwoods, bay swamps, shrub bogs, and cypress swamps intermingle, producing a complex, distinctive landscape.

Important Environmental Variables

At least four major environmental variables are necessary to explain the range of structural and functional diversity within and among Florida swamps (table 9.1). Differences in (1) hydroperiod (the length of time that soils are saturated during a year), (2) fire frequency, and (3) organic matter accumulation have all been used effectively to explain the coexistence of different kinds of wetlands in the Southeast (e.g., Sharitz and Gibbons, 1982; Duever et al., 1984b). In addition, (4) source of water is, in Florida, closely correlated with water quality, which has a major impact on nutrient cycling and hence productivity of a swamp (e.g., S. Brown, 1981).

The presence of saturated soils or standing water for at least part of the year is the dominant environmental control over the ecological characteristics of a swamp. Hydroperiod affects soil aeration and the ability of plants to survive and reproduce. When flooding persists, oxygen in the soil is gradually depleted, imposing increasingly stressful conditions on roots. Only a handful of species can tolerate the lack of oxygen and high concentrations of soluble iron and manganese, and sometimes even hydrogen sulfide, that develop in the root zone under such conditions. The adaptations of these tolerant species are not well understood. They appear to be both morphological, such as the development of aerenchymous tissue that allows air to be transported to the roots, and metabolic, such as the accumulation of malate rather than ethanol during anaerobic respiration (Hook, 1984). Wetlands are inhabited by a small number of flood-tolerant species; therefore, swamps with longer hydroperiods, requiring greater physiological tolerance and morphological plasticity to cope with the reducing conditions that develop, should have fewer species and be less productive than those with shorter hydroperiods.

Fire is common in many wetlands throughout the world, especially still-water swamps with peat-lined basins and fluctuating water levels. Swamps burn primarily during dry seasons, when fire is sustained by dry litter and peat, and may continue to burn slowly for weeks. Fire is probably important in reducing organic matter accumulation and preventing subsequent succession from wetlands into mesic ecosystems—a transition that is commonly believed to occur but is probably rare anywhere in the world. Fire also affects the diversity of plants in a swamp. Many species are incapable of surviving fire (e.g., Ewel and Mitsch, 1978), but other species, such as pond pine (*Pinus serotina*), black titi (*Cliftonia monophylla*), and titi (*Cyrilla racemiflora*) depend on fire for regeneration. The mix of cypress swamps, gum ponds, bay swamps, and shrub bogs that composes the Okefenokee

Table 9.1. Proposed ranges of important environmental characteristics of major types of Florida swamps

Type of swamp	Average hydroperiod[a]	Approximate fire frequency[b]	Organic matter accumulation[c]	Main water source
River swamps				
Whitewater floodplain forest	Short	Low	Low	River
Blackwater floodplain forest	Short	Low	Low	River
Spring run swamp	Short	Low	Low	Deep groundwater
Stillwater swamps				
Bay swamp	Long	Low	High	Shallow groundwater
Cypress pond	Moderate	Moderate	High	Shallow groundwater
Cypress savanna	Moderate	High	Low	Rain
Cypress strand	Moderate	Moderate	High	Shallow groundwater
Gum pond	Long	Low	High	Shallow groundwater
Hydric hammock	Short	Low	Low	Deep groundwater
Lake fringe swamp	Moderate	Low	High	Lake
Melaleuca swamp	Moderate	High	Low	Shallow groundwater
Mixed hardwood swamp	Moderate	Low	High	Shallow groundwater
Shrub bog	Long	Moderate-high	High	Shallow groundwater

a. Short = <6 mo; moderate = 6–9 mo; long = >9 mo. b. Low = 1/century; moderate = 5/century; high = 1/decade.
c. Low = <1 m; high = >1 m.

Swamp in Georgia and northeastern Florida demonstrates the ability of different fire frequencies and intensities not only to shape swamps but also to create a mosaic of lakes, marshes, and swamps within a single basin (Hamilton, 1984).

A swamp's source of water affects its nutrient supply, hydroperiod, and flow rate. Swamps fed solely by rainfall are nutrient-limited and exhibit water level fluctuations as wet and dry seasons alternate. Groundwater supply may lengthen the hydroperiod, but substantial differences in pH and nutrient concentrations between shallow and deep groundwater create different communities, depending on the origin of the water. Short hydroperiods, flowing water, and high dissolved oxygen levels characterize river swamps, making organic matter removal rates rapid and fire uncommon.

Differences in organic matter accumulation result from differences in hydroperiod, fire frequency, and water source. Litter decomposition is slow in swamps with long hydroperiods, especially if pH and dissolved oxygen levels are low. This is a function of both the physical-chemical environment of the swamp and the plant community that it supports. Acid, stillwater swamps are generally nutrient-limited, and many plants have thick, hard leaves with low nutrient concentrations (Larsen, 1982), so neither live nor dead leaves are consumed rapidly. Organic matter therefore builds up, slowing only when the amount of litter decomposing becomes equal to litter production, or when fire burns away the accumulation. This accumulation increases water retention (and therefore hydroperiod), decreases pH if *Sphagnum* mosses are present, and may decrease nutrient availability as well (Clymo, 1983; Dierberg and Brezonik, 1984c).

These environmental variables affect swamps throughout the world, but the unique combination in Florida of high fire frequency, low topography, high surficial groundwater tables, and seepage from deep groundwater aquifers has produced a collage of wetlands that is unmatched in diversity. In this chapter, differences in the four chief environmental variables are used to distinguish thirteen kinds of swamps that fit into two major categories (table 9.1). Few of the ranges listed for these variables are based on data collected in rigorous studies. Instead, they represent a set of hypotheses that constitutes a framework for understanding the differences among swamps as they are now perceived, as well as for identifying needs for further research.

A hierarchical classification system based on hydrologic, geomorphologic, chemical, and biological characteristics of a wetland has been devised by the National Wetlands Inventory, a unit of the U.S. Fish and Wildlife Service (Cowardin et al., 1979). This system was intended to assist wetland inventory and analysis by transcending regional differences and terminologies. Classes, subclasses, and modifiers for the thirteen types of swamps discussed in this chapter are proposed in the Appendix to facilitate comparison with swamps outside Florida.

Vegetation

The diversity of vegetation in Florida swamps reflects the variety of types of swamps, the range in temperatures throughout the state, and the origins of the plant species themselves. Approximately 100 species of woody vines, shrubs, and trees are commonly found in one or more types of Florida swamps (table 9.2). Several of these species, such as guava (*Psidium guajava*) and wild coffee (*Psychotria* spp.), are found only in subtropical south Florida, but most are derived from north temperate regions. This unusual mix of north temperate to subtropical plants in a warm temperate to subtropical climate helps to explain the floristic uniqueness of Florida swamps among North American wetlands.

River swamps (fig. 9.2), which are Florida's most diverse and productive swamps, are similar floristically to north temperate swamps, perhaps because they are most common in north Florida. In other types of swamps, however, the range of climates and mixture of biogeographic influences have produced several anomalies that make it difficult to extrapolate information about floristic patterns of other swamps in North America, or indeed in the world, to Florida. For instance, many Florida stillwater, peat-lined swamps, like temperate and high latitude bogs around the world, are dominated by conifers, and evergreen vegetation with leathery, waxy leaves is common. However, the main conifer in Florida swamps, cypress (*Taxodium*), is deciduous. Also, palms, which are not found in North American swamps outside the southeastern coastal plain, are common in some Florida swamps, especially on limestone outcrops. They are not found, however, on significant peat accumulations, as is characteristic of tropical palm swamps.

Nor are the taxonomic relationships of swamp trees straightforward. Many genera, such as cypress, black gum (*Nyssa*), red maple (*Acer*), and oak (*Quercus*) contain species/variety pairs that are similar. Whereas one member may be characteristic of one kind of swamp, another is characteristic of either another type of swamp (e.g., cypress) or an upland ecosystem (e.g., black gum).

Conifers

Cypress

Cypress is the most common wetland tree in Florida and is usually the dominant species in swamps with fluctuating water levels. It is a deciduous conifer, losing its needles by the end of November and flushing again in March. Cypress seeds cannot germinate when soils are flooded, and—although seedlings grow best in saturated but unflooded soils (Dickson and Broyer, 1972)—they grow too slowly to survive competition with faster growing hardwoods. Nor do they survive extended submergence (Demaree, 1932), making successful regeneration of a cypress swamp virtually depend-

Table 9.2. Common woody plants in Florida swamps

Scientific name	Common name	Type of swamp[a]									
		BS	CS	CV	GP	HH	LF	ME	MS	RS	SB
Conifers											
Chamaecyparis thyoides	Atlantic white cedar									X	X
Juniperus silicicola	southern red cedar					X					
Pinus elliottii	slash pine	X	X	X				X			X
P. glabra	spruce pine									X	
P. palustris	longleaf pine	X	X								
P. serotina	pond pine	X									X
P. taeda	loblolly pine					X				X	X
Taxodium distichum	cypress	X	X	X	X		X	X	X	X	X
Palms											
Rhapidophyllum hystrix	needle palm					X				X	
Roystonea elata	Floridian royal palm								X		
Sabal minor	bluestem; dwarf palmetto					X				X	
S. palmetto	cabbage palm	X	X			X			X	X	
Hardwoods											
Acer rubrum	southern red maple	X	X			X			X	X	X
Alnus serrulata	hazel alder									X	
Annona glabra	pond apple	X	X						X		
Betula nigra	river birch									X	
Carpinus caroliniana	American hornbeam	X				X				X	
Carya aquatica	water hickory									X	
C. glabra	pignut hickory									X	
Celtis laevigata	hackberry					X				X	
Cornus foemina	stiff cornel					X					
Diospyros virginiana	persimmon					X				X	
Fraxinus caroliniana	water ash		X			X	X		X	X	
F. pennsylvanica	green ash, red ash									X	
F. profunda	pumpkin ash									X	
Gleditsia aquatica	water locust									X	
Gordonia lasianthus	loblolly bay	X	X			X				X	X
Liquidambar styraciflua	sweet gum	X	X			X				X	
Magnolia grandiflora	southern magnolia									X	
M. virginiana	sweet bay	X	X			X			X	X	X
Melaleuca quinquenervia	melaleuca, punk tree		X					X			
Nyssa aquatica	water tupelo									X	
N. ogeche	Ogeechee lime									X	
N. sylvatica	black gum	X	X		X		X			X	X
Persea palustris	swamp bay	X	X			X			X		
Planera aquatica	planer tree									X	
Platanus occidentalis	American sycamore					X				X	
Populus deltoides	cottonwood										X
P. heterophylla	swamp cottonwood										X
Psidium guajava	guava		X								
Quercus laurifolia	swamp laurel oak	X	X			X			X	X	
Q. lyrata	overcup oak									X	

(*continued*)

Table 9.2. (continued)

Scientific name	Common name	Type of swamp[a]									
		BS	CS	CV	GP	HH	LF	ME	MS	RS	SB
Q. michauxii	basket oak					X				X	
Q. nigra	water oak	X				X				X	
Q. shumardii	shumard oak, spanish oak					X					
Q. virginiana	live oak	X				X				X	
Salix caroliniana	coastal plain willow		X							X	X
S. nigra	black willow									X	
Ulmus americana	American elm					X				X	
Shrubs											
Aronia arbutifolia	red chokeberry									X	
Cephalanthus occidentalis	buttonbush		X							X	X
Chrysobalanus icaco	coco plum	X	X	X							
Clethra alnifolia	sweet pepperbush	X	X		X					X	X
Cliftonia monophylla	black titi		X							X	X
Crataegus aestivalis	may haw					X					
C. marshallii	parsley haw					X				X	
Cyrilla racemiflora	titi	X	X		X					X	X
Ilex cassine	dahoon holly	X	X			X			X	X	X
I. coriacea	large gallberry					X					X
I. decidua	possum haw					X				X	
I. glabra	gallberry		X								
I. myrtifolia	myrtle-leaf holly										X
I. vomitoria	yaupon									X	
Itea virginica	Virginia willow	X	X		X	X				X	X
Leucothoe axillaris	dog-hobble									X	X
L. racemosa	fetterbush		X								
Lyonia ferruginea	rusty lyonia										X
L. lucida	fetterbush	X	X		X					X	X
Myrica cerifera	wax myrtle	X	X			X				X	
M. heterophylla	northern bayberry		X			X					
Myrsine floridana	myrsine								X		
M. guianensis	myrsine		X								
Psychotria sulzneri	wild coffee		X								
P. undata	wild coffee		X			X					
Rhododendron viscosum	swamp honeysuckle	X								X	
Rubus argutus	blackberry		X							X	
R. betulifolius	blackberry	X								X	
Sambucus canadensis	elderberry				X	X				X	
Schinus terebinthifolius	Brazilian pepper		X								
Sebastiana fruticosa	sebastian bush									X	
Vaccinium arboreum	sparkleberry		X								
V. corymbosum	highbush blueberry	X									
Viburnum nudum	swamp haw									X	
V. obovatum	small viburnum, black haw									X	

(*continued*)

Table 9.2. (continued)

Scientific name	Common name	Type of swamp[a]									
		BS	CS	CV	GP	HH	LF	ME	MS	RS	SB
Vines											
Ampelopsis arborea	pepper vine		X							X	
Aster carolinianus	climbing aster									X	
Ficus aurea	strangler fig		X						X		
F. citrifolia	wild banyan tree		X								
Gelsemium sempervirens	yellow jessamine	X									
Smilax bona-nox	catbrier	X									
S. glauca	wild sarsaparilla	X									
S. laurifolia	bamboo-vine, catbrier	X	X			X				X	
S. walteri	coral greenbrier									X	
Toxicodendron radicans	poison ivy	X				X				X	
Vitis aestivalis	summer grape	X	X								
V. rotundifolia	muscadine grape	X								X	
V. shuttleworthii	calusa grape		X								

Sources: Argus (1986); Best et al. (1981); Brown et al. (1984b); Carter et al. (1973); Clewell (1971); Clewell et al. (1982); Duever et al. (1982); Duever et al. (1984b, 1986); Elder and Cairns (1982); Ewel (1984); Florida Game and Freshwater Fish Commission (1976); Godfrey (1988); Laessle (1942); Leitman et al. (1982); Marois and Ewel (1983); McJunkin (1977); Monk (1965, 1966b); Monk and Brown (1965); Myers (1984); Pearson (1954); Richardson et al. (1983); Snedaker and Lugo (1972); J. Stout (unpublished data); S. Vince (personal communication); Wade et al. (1980); C. Wharton (personal communication); Wharton et al. (1977); White (1983). Long and Lakela (1971), Godfrey and Wooten (1981), Wunderlin (1982), and Clewell (1985) were consulted for nomenclature.

a. BS = bay swamp; CS = cypress pond and strand; CV = cypress savanna; GP = gum pond; HH = hydric hammock; LF = lake fringe swamp; ME = melaleuca swamp; MS = mixed hardwood swamp; RS = river swamp; SB = shrub bog.

Fig. 9.2. Winter view of Apalachicola River floodplain forest. Photo by R. Myers.

ent on regular water level fluctuation. When mature, however, cypress is the most flood-tolerant of all tree species in Florida (e.g., Harms et al., 1980).

Like many wetland trees, cypress may have buttresses of various sizes and shapes. In addition, their root systems often develop unusual but characteristic "knees," which are narrow, contorted outgrowths that can occur when a lateral root bends downward (fig. 9.3). Knees may help support the tree, but their relatively high respiration rates when oxygen levels are low (Brown et al., 1984a) indicate that they may assist the trees in coping with low oxygen levels in the root zone. The heights of knees and buttresses appear to be related to depth of flooding, but this relationship has not been verified.

Cypress trees may be identified as bald cypress or pond cypress, recognized by some (e.g., Wunderlin, 1982; Clewell, 1985; Godfrey, 1988) as separate species (*T. distichum* and *T. ascendens*, respectively) and by others (e.g., Little, 1979; Elias, 1980) as separate varieties (*T. distichum* var. *distichum* and *T. distichum* var. *nutans*). Bald cypress is characteristic of flowing-water swamps, whereas pond cypress is commonly found in still-water swamps. Although seedlings of the two species may be readily distinguishable when germinated under the same conditions (Gunderson, 1977; Neufeld, 1983), and mature trees often have distinct foliage and bark, gradients in these characteristics from one site to another prevent unequivocal identification of many individuals in the field (e.g., Duever et al., 1984b).

Fire frequency may be a major environmental factor favoring eventual speciation of bald cypress and pond cypress, though there is no direct evidence for this supposition. Cypress ponds burn occasionally, but fire appears to be rare in most river swamps. The thicker, shaggier bark on pond cypress may provide more protection to the cambium (e.g., Ewel and Mitsch, 1978), though both trees can produce adventitious branches after burning, which help them to recover. Bald cypress is less resistant to fire than the most common southern pines, but more resistant than many hardwoods (Hare,

Fig. 9.3. A cypress tree's root system, exposed by erosion.

1965). There has been no comparative study of fire resistance of the two varieties of cypress.

Pond cypress is more likely than bald cypress to grow on nutrient-limited sites. Like many species under such circumstances, it transfers nutrients from leaves to twigs before abscission, conserving nutrients for use the following spring (Dierberg et al., 1986). A stunted form of pond cypress, called dwarf cypress, hat-rack cypress, or scrub cypress (fig. 9.4), is common in south Florida cypress savannas as well as in other nutrient-poor areas on clay soils, such as Tate's Hell in the Panhandle. Trees that are hundreds of years old may be no more than 2 m tall or 10 cm in diameter, and larger individuals, such as those in the Apalachicola National Forest, may have lived for more than a millennium.

Pines

Although pines are commonest on dry sites, several species occur on poorly drained soils and in swamps. Many pines are known to transport oxygen to their roots (e.g., Philipson and Coutts, 1980) and may form hypertrophied lenticels (pores in the stems), presumably to assist in this process (Kozlowski, 1984).

Slash pine (*Pinus elliottii*) is common but never dominant in Florida swamps. Two recognized varieties that differ in range, taproot length, needle size, and wood density (summarized by Duever et al., 1986) are found at the northern and southern ends of the state. *P. elliottii* var. *elliottii*, in north

Fig. 9.4. "Dwarf" or "hat rack" cypress in Big Cypress National Preserve. Photo by J. N. Layne.

Florida, may originally have been restricted by fire to bay swamps and to shrub and herb bogs (Hebb and Clewell, 1976; Wharton et al., 1977). Measurement of unusually low bulk density and water-filled volume in green tap and sinker roots in slash pine roots indicates that oxygen entering through stem lenticels is available for respiration of roots as much as one or two meters below the water table (Fisher and Stone, 1990). Slash pine is now planted widely throughout north Florida in commercial plantations. *P. elliottii* var. *densa*, in south Florida, ranges from well-drained, sandy soils to cypress swamps.

Other pines are also common in some north Florida swamps. Pond pine (*P. serotina*) is found in bay swamps and in shrub bogs that burn every fifteen to twenty years (Edmisten, 1965). Its cones are serotinous, requiring fire to open, and, like cypress, pond pine will produce branches from epicormic buds after a fire. Loblolly pine (*P. taeda*) is common in hydric hammocks, and both loblolly pine and longleaf pine (*P. palustris*) are also found occasionally on hummocks in other swamps.

Cedars

Atlantic white cedar swamps (dominated by *Chamaecyparis thyoides*) are found throughout the Atlantic coastal plain. In Florida, however, Atlantic white cedar is common on perennially moist soils where neither flooding nor fire is frequent (Clewell and Ward, 1987). In Apalachicola National Forest, it occasionally dominates shallow peat swamps. It is neither shade- nor fire-tolerant, but it is a rapid colonizer, perhaps replacing bay trees—such as sweet bay (*Magnolia virginiana*) and loblolly bay (*Gordonia lasianthus*)—after a fire but relinquishing dominance to bays in the absence of fire (Wells, 1942). In Ocala National Forest, Atlantic white cedar also occurs along spring runs and creeks where little peat accumulates and pH is close to neutral (Ward, 1963b; Collins et al., 1964).

Southern red cedar (*Juniperus silicicola*) is more common than Atlantic white cedar in Florida, though it has never fully recovered from large-scale harvesting, concentrated in Gulf Hammock, for the pencil industry that dominated the Cedar Key economy in the late nineteenth century. This tree is salt-tolerant and is frequently found in coastal hydric hammocks near the boundary between brackish and freshwater wetlands (Wharton et al., 1977), as well as in hammocks along the upper St. Johns River.

Palms

Palms are common in tropical and subtropical environments, but only a few species can tolerate subfreezing temperatures. They are particularly common in wet habitats, often growing aerial roots that can obtain oxygen easily. Palms are common but not dominant in Florida swamps. Needle palm

(*Rhapidophyllum hystrix*) extends north into bordering states, and cabbage palm (*Sabal palmetto*) is found along the coast into North Carolina.

Palms are generally fire-resistant (Tomlinson, 1979). Cabbage palm is considered to be an indicator of fire (Laessle, 1942), and its fire-charred trunks serve as relatively long-lived markers (Clewell and Ward, 1987).

Hardwoods

Black Gum, Water Tupelo

Nyssa is one of the most flood-tolerant hardwoods in Florida swamps. Its seeds float readily and are also bird-dispersed; like cypress, *Nyssa* requires periodic drought for germination. The most common species is *N. sylvatica*, which—again like cypress—comprises two varieties, *N. sylvatica* var. *sylvatica* (black gum) and *N. sylvatica* var. *biflora* (swamp black gum), which is considered by many (e.g., Clewell, 1985) to be a distinct species (*N. biflora*). The former grows primarily on upland sites and occasionally on floodplains, whereas the latter is commonly found with pond cypress in stillwater swamps. Water tupelo (*N. aquatica*) is common in river swamps, with bald cypress.

As with many bottomland hardwoods, both lenticels and new roots commonly develop on the stems of *Nyssa* seedlings when they are submerged, and adventitious "water roots" often develop when the stems are continuously flooded with moving water (Hook et al., 1970). The flood tolerance of a black gum tree is related to the age of its first exposure to flooding; the tree apparently depends on internal oxygen transport through its root system to ameliorate low oxygen levels in the soil immediately surrounding the roots (Keeley, 1979).

Oaks

Several evergreen oaks are common in hydric hammocks and the upper zones of floodplains. Overcup oak (*Quercus lyrata*) and swamp laurel oak (*Q. laurifolia*) are the most flood-tolerant (Teskey and Hinckley, 1977), dominating areas that are generally inundated for less than half the growing season (Wharton et al., 1982); they are common only in north Florida. Because birds and mammals feed extensively on mast produced by oaks and associated hardwoods, floodplain forests and hydric hammocks are among the most important wetlands per unit area for supporting vertebrate wildlife species (Wharton et al., 1981; Vince et al., 1989).

Willows

Two species of willows are common in Florida: coastal plain willow (*Salix caroliniana*) in northeast and peninsular Florida and black willow (*S. nigra*) in north-central and northwestern Florida; they are closely related and hybridize where they overlap (Argus, 1986). Willows often form large thickets and grow best on unshaded, well-oxygenated, flowing water sites. They appear as early successional species in the Everglades around tree islands, on rock outcrops, and in abandoned farmlands, as well as on severely burned sites where cypress swamps eventually reestablish (Schomer and Drew, 1982; Duever et al., 1984b; Argus, 1986). A third species (*S. floridana*) is endemic to Florida and Georgia and is found primarily along spring runs.

Other Hardwoods

Melaleuca quinquenervia was introduced from Australia within the last 100 years. It is an evergreen hardwood that is highly flood-tolerant and fire-resistant and therefore capable of rapidly recolonizing burned wetlands (Myers, 1984).

Sweet bay, loblolly bay, and swamp bay (*Persea palustris*) are common in acid stillwater swamps throughout the Southeast, but little is known about the autecology of these evergreen hardwoods. Loblolly bay sprouts readily after a fire and appears to colonize best after severe site disturbance (Gresham and Lipscomb, 1985).

Other Plants

Shrubs

Shrub bogs are frequently dominated by titi and black titi, which are common in other acid Florida swamps as well. Both species sprout readily from their roots after a fire (Thomas, 1961).

Shrubs in the heath family (Ericaceae) are common in acid swamps around the world. These plants have several characteristics often associated with low transpiration rates and nutrient-poor sites: evergreen, thick leathery leaves, often with a waxy cuticle on the surface and a mat of wind-blocking hairs beneath, and stomates in pits or grooves (Larsen, 1982). They depend on a characteristic suite of mycorrhizal fungi to obtain sufficient nutrients from the infertile soils on which they grow. *Lyonia* is especially common in Florida swamps, sprouting readily after either cutting or burning and often becoming abundant or even dominant in shrub bogs (Judd, 1981). The stomates of fetterbush (*L. lucida*) close at midday, decreasing the rate of transpiration (Schlesinger and Chabot, 1977).

Vines

As many as twenty-three species of woody and herbaceous vines may be found in Florida swamps (Clewell et al., 1982). They are densest in bay swamps and shrub bogs and are also common in cypress swamps. Bamboo-vine (*Smilax laurifolia*) is the most ubiquitous species, although poison ivy (*Toxicodendron radicans*) is also common. Strangler figs (*Ficus aurea*) in south Florida swamps often grow into the canopy.

Fig. 9.5 Epiphytic bromeliads on pond cypress, Big Cypress National Preserve. Photo by H. Tuck.

Epiphytes

Epiphytes are not listed in table 9.2 but are common in Florida, and both species richness and biomass of these plants increase dramatically from north to south. Certain swamp trees, such as cypress, some oaks, and mangroves, are most likely to bear epiphytes. High densities of both bromeliads and orchids are found in the open canopies of dwarf cypress and pond cypress swamps (fig. 9.5) as well as in heavily shaded canopies in south Florida mixed hardwood swamps, where they are protected from occasional cold spells (Benzing, 1980).

Mycorrhizae and special nutrient-absorbing organs on the leaves of epiphytes assist in scavenging the nutrients that are available primarily in rainfall and stem flow (Benzing and Renfrow, 1971). Nutrients appear to be more readily obtained from cypress than from upland pines (Schlesinger and Marks, 1977).

Many of the epiphytes in south Florida swamps are not found elsewhere in the United States. Because of rapid habitat alteration as well as uncontrolled collection for many years, many of them, as well as subtropical species of palms and ferns, are now considered to be rare or endangered. The list of endangered plants in the Big Cypress Swamp, particularly in the Fakahatchee Strand, continues to grow as the area becomes more and more accessible to the public (Ward, 1979; Duever et al., 1986).

Insectivorous Plants

Insectivorous plants are another notable feature of many Florida swamps. Four genera are common: bladderworts (*Utricularia*) just beneath the surface of the water in cypress ponds and other stillwater swamps, and sundews (*Drosera*), butterworts (*Pinguicula*), and pitcher plants (*Sarracenia* spp.) in shallow sites in and around acid swamps (fig. 9.6).

All four genera are common in the Panhandle in seepage zones interposed between pine flatwoods and swamps or streams. These "herb bogs" (fig. 9.7) may be acidic, with sand or *Sphagnum* substrates, and may sometimes be large enough to contain open water. Pond pines often fringe these areas, but frequent fires prevent woody plants from dominating (Folkerts, 1982).

Hydrology, Fire, and Diversity

Hydrology

The increasingly severe reducing conditions imposed by progressively longer hydroperiods suggest an inverse relationship between number of plant species and hydroperiod (fig. 9.8). However, variations in water depth, water residence time, and water quality allow swamps with similar hydroperiods to differ in such critical factors as fire and depth of organic matter accumulation, which in turn may affect the number of species. Consequently, swamps with similar hydroperiods may vary considerably in species richness.

Two major categories of swamps may be distinguished by water regimes (source of water, hydroperiod, and flow rate). River swamps are dominated by surface flow early in the growing season and have both a short hydroperiod and a perceptible flow rate for at least part of each year. Stillwater swamps, which have longer hydroperiods and virtually no perceptible flow, are fed primarily by rainfall and groundwater. This category includes a large number of distinctive types, including some in which soils are saturated for several months but standing water is seldom present.

Not all swamps can be easily classified, and individual swamps may be influenced by different water sources at different times of the year. For instance, cypress strands are listed as stillwater swamps, although sometimes there is slow flow in them. Coastal river swamps may be affected by lunar tides that damp normal seasonal fluctuations, as well as by wind tides and spring tides that accentuate them.

River Swamps

River swamps constitute approximately one-third of Florida's swampland (Wharton et al., 1982) and are found primarily in north Florida (fig. 9.9). Swamps may occupy the floodplains of whitewater (alluvial) rivers (rivers that carry colloidal clays and suspended matter in their floodwaters), blackwater rivers (rivers that carry primarily dissolved organic matter), and spring runs, but there are no data to suggest major differences among them in plant species richness. In all three, hydroperiods are short except in depressions in the floodplain where deposits of clay and organic matter retain water.

Fig. 9.6. Trumpet pitcher plants (*Sarracenia flava*) growing along the edge of a shrub bog, Apalachicola National Forest. Photo by R. Myers.

Fig. 9.7. Herb bog or seepage meadow between pine flatwoods and cypress/titi swamp. Photo by R. Myers.

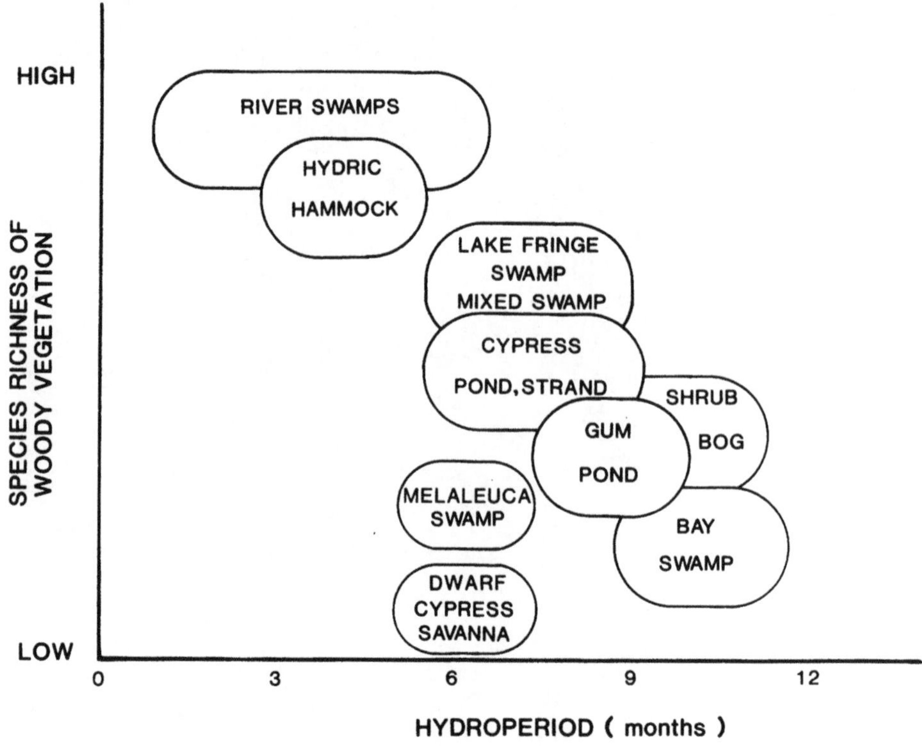

Fig. 9.8. Proposed relationships between species richness of woody vegetation in swamps and hydroperiod.

Four distinct zones can be distinguished in bottomland forests in the Southeast on the basis of soil moisture and hydrology, from streamside levees through low-lying backwaters to upper zones that are only occasionally flooded (Huffman and Forsythe, 1981). Reduced topography and abrupt changes in soil type in Florida river swamps may blur, compress, or obliterate individual zones, though the same range of conditions exists. Because of this ecological diversity, river swamps appear to be the most diverse of Florida swamps.

Whitewater Floodplain Forests. The Apalachicola is the only major whitewater river in Florida. It has the third largest discharge among all the rivers on the Atlantic and Gulf coastal plain. Its floodplain forest covers 450 km^2 and has more than forty species of trees (fig. 9.2).

Five forest types have been distinguished in the Apalachicola River floodplain forest on the basis of relief, hydrology, and species diversity (Leitman et al., 1982). In three of these, tree diversity is high. Type A, characterized by sweet gum (*Liquidambar styraciflua*), hackberry (*Celtis laevigata*), and water oak (*Quercus nigra*), occurs on levees and high ridges, where soils are only occasionally saturated by flooding. Water hickory (*Carya aquatica*), green ash (*Fraxinus pennsylvanica*), overcup oak, and swamp laurel oak are dominant in Type B, which is found on high flats and low

Fig. 9.9. Locations of major river swamps in Florida. After Wharton et al., 1982.

ridges where flooding is more common. Water tupelo, the most common tree in terms of both basal area and density, dominates Type C along with Ogeechee lime (*Nyssa ogeche*) and bald cypress. This forest type occurs in low areas where ridges or hummocks provide some drainage.

The two less diverse types are located in low, flat, poorly drained areas where soils are predominantly clay and saturation is almost continuous. They are both dominated by water tupelo; black gum is a codominant in Type D, which is found only in the lower reaches of the river, and bald cypress is a codominant in Type E, which occurs in low areas throughout the river's length.

Blackwater Floodplain Forests. The sandy soils underlying flatwoods in watersheds of blackwater rivers contribute few nutrients to the runoff that supplies the rivers. Flooding is closely related to local rain events, and water levels rise and fall rapidly. Floodplains on blackwater rivers may be underlain by impermeable soil layers extending into them from the surrounding landscape, so that horizontal groundwater flow may contribute as much as runoff to base flow in the river, and also to standing water in the floodplain (Clewell et al., 1982; Wharton et al., 1982).

Floodplains of blackwater rivers are seldom as diverse as whitewater river floodplains, and the zones occupied by different forest types are narrower or absent, except for gum/cypress communities, which may be extensive (C. Wharton, personal communication). One species, such as cypress or American elm, may dominate in certain areas, perhaps because of local differences in hydroperiod or flow rate. Few blackwater river swamps have been studied; one major exception is the Oklawaha River swamp, parts of which were inundated by the construction of Rodman Dam.

Spring Run Swamps. Flooding is less dramatic in river swamps along spring runs, and hydroperiods may be short. Because spring runs are fed from the limestone aquifer, flood events are damped and chemical characteristics differ from those of silt-laden whitewater rivers and dark, acidic, blackwater rivers.

Many spring runs discharge directly into larger rivers. During rainy seasons, water spilling over berms and backing up into the spring runs may obscure the subtle differences between a river swamp and a spring run swamp.

Stillwater Swamps

In other Florida swamps, groundwater seepage and rainfall dominate the water budget; the source of groundwater has a substantial impact on the characteristics of a swamp. Hydric hammocks, which are similar floristically to the upper zones of river swamps, often form where deep groundwater seeps slowly from limestone outcrops, as in north-central Florida along the Gulf coast, from Tide Swamp through Gulf Hammock (Vince et al., 1989). Most stillwater swamps, however, are supplied by shallow, acid groundwater.

Plant species richness is lower in acid groundwater swamps than in river swamps (e.g., Monk, 1968). Most have saturated soils, and sometimes standing water, for more than six months in a year. Single species may dominate large areas in swamps with long hydroperiods, but vegetation along the edges of stillwater swamps, where the soil is better aerated, is often denser and more diverse than in the deeper centers. Less flood-tolerant species may also germinate and grow on pockets of organic matter on stumps, hummocks, and other sites that are elevated above normal water level.

Cypress Swamps. Cypress ponds, the most common and widespread of Florida's stillwater swamps, occur where depressions expose the shallow water table (fig. 9.10). In north Florida, they are scattered throughout a matrix of poorly drained pine flatwoods and plantations. The impermeable clay layers that underlie this landscape are found beneath ponds as well (fig. 9.11). It is not clear if the slumping that often characterizes these layers under cypress ponds occurred before colonization by cypress communities, or if it resulted from percolation of increasingly acid water from accumulating organic matter (Odum, 1984; Spangler, 1984).

Cypress ponds in south Florida (fig. 9.12) occupy depressions in the mineral soil underlain by marl and limestone bedrock (Duever et al., 1986). Decomposition is slow, and, as in north Florida ponds, peat accumulates in the depressions.

Water level in a cypress pond normally fluctuates dramatically once or twice during the year, exposing the peat floor for a few weeks to several

Fig. 9.10. A cypress strand and several cypress ponds in the Upper St. Johns River basin.

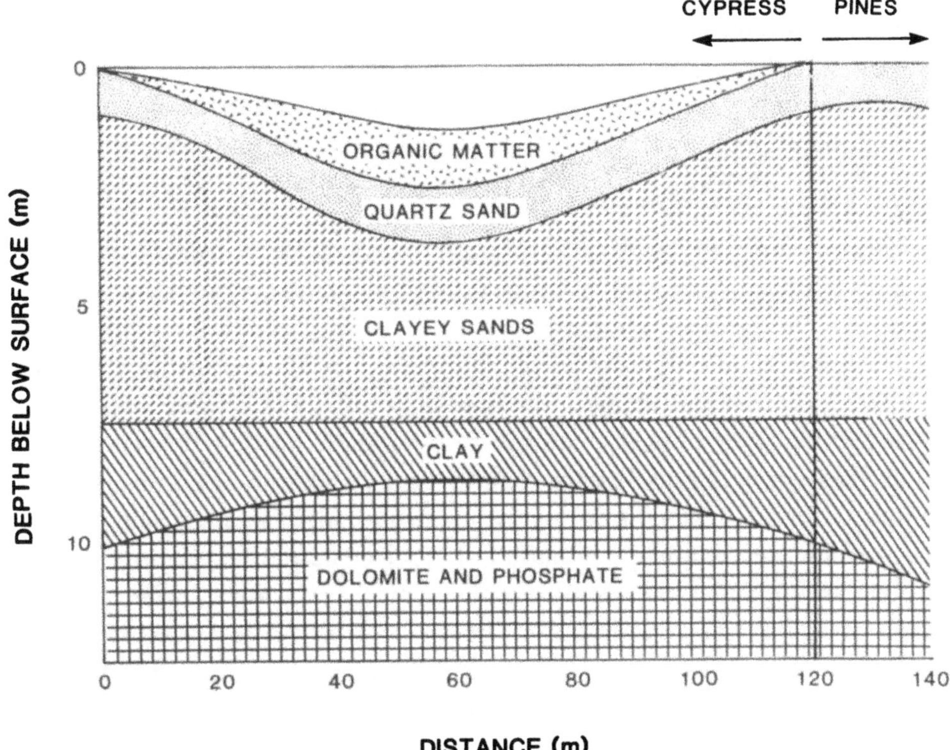

Fig. 9.11. Generalized soil profile beneath a north Florida cypress pond.

Fig. 9.12. Characteristic dome-shaped stand of pond cypress, Big Cypress National Preserve. Photo by R. Myers.

months at a time. When water is present, dissolved oxygen is low. Litter decomposition rates are slow, and organic acids accumulate in the water column, where they impart a reddish-brown stain to the water, decreasing the amount of light available to phytoplankton and hence reducing gross primary productivity and oxygen production. There is little wind at the water surface; it is blocked by the swamp trees themselves, eliminating another source of oxygenation.

The xeromorphic leaves of pond cypress and the thick, leathery leaves of at least one common shrub, fetterbush (*Lyonia lucida*), have low transpiration rates (Schlesinger and Chabot, 1977; S. Brown, 1981). Evapotranspiration rates from stillwater cypress ponds are only 75 percent of estimated transpiration losses from pine flatwoods (Ewel, 1985). Similar patterns in leaf morphology are found in northern bogs, where nutrient conservation is more likely to be a causal factor than low evapotranspiration rates (Larsen, 1982). Occasional drought during summer, normally Florida's rainy season, often results in complete defoliation of cypress. Low transpiration rates in cypress swamps may therefore be a major mechanism for alleviating water stress during normal dry seasons (S. Brown, 1981). Where melaleuca has invaded drained cypress swamps in south Florida, as in the Six-Mile Cypress Swamp in Lee County, increased transpiration during the dry season may affect shallow groundwater levels.

Cypress strands are common throughout Florida, forming where there is sufficient water and flow to generate a depression channel, but the gradient is low, and actual flow is seldom observed (fig. 9.10). The transition between cypress ponds and cypress strands is gradual, and some ponds become strands for several weeks when connected during unusually high rainfall. This is a common occurrence in the Green Swamp in central Florida, for instance. The term *cypress head* is believed to refer to the cypress pond at the head of such a strand (J. H. Davis, personal communication).

In south Florida, mixed hardwoods regenerate readily in strands that are protected from fire, displacing cypress from dominance. Shallow lakes with fluctuating water levels are ringed by cypress trees, grading into mixed hardwoods around the landward edge. These swamps are often dominated by bald cypress and appear to be more productive than cypress ponds. At the other end of the spectrum are dwarf cypress savannas, widespread throughout the Everglades and the Big Cypress in south Florida. In these swamps, rainfall is the most significant source of water, and vegetation density and diversity are low.

Bay Swamps and Shrub Bogs. The soil layers beneath bay swamps and shrub bogs appear to be similar to those beneath cypress ponds (Wharton et al., 1977). These swamps occupy peat-filled depressions (perhaps with shallower water and deeper peat than cypress ponds), occasionally underlain by deep sands (as in the "titi sogs" in San Pedro Bay, Jarvis and Beers, 1965) and impermeable clays. An organic hardpan has been found beneath at least one shrub bog (Coultas et al., 1979). These swamps are characterized by dense, low vegetation (fig. 9.13) and are believed to be fed by groundwater draining from higher terrain (Wharton et al., 1977). Unlike cypress ponds, they are drained by small blackwater streams, perhaps because of restricted downward flow as well as slow evapotranspiration.

In the Panhandle, shrub bogs and pine flatwoods are often separated by herb bogs, or savannas, which are dominated by a variety of grasses and forbs but characterized by insectivorous plants, especially pitcher plants. The shallow layer of organic matter in these bogs is generally underlain by acid soils, either sandy or organic, and usually by a shallow or deep clay layer. These are fire-dependent ecosystems that normally burn every three to eight years; unburned herb bogs eventually become shrub bogs (Wharton et al., 1977; Coultas et al., 1979; Folkerts, 1982).

Gum Ponds. Gum ponds, found primarily from the Panhandle northward along the coastal plain, also occupy depressions. They are believed to be underlain by clay lenses, resulting in longer hydroperiods, less extreme water level fluctuations, and lower fire frequency than in cypress ponds (Clewell, 1971; Wharton et al., 1977).

Fire

Differences among swamps due to fire frequency can be measured best in decades or even centuries, so they are difficult to quantify. However, a few

Fig. 9.13. Profile of a titi/slash pine shrub bog in Tate's Hell, Franklin County. Photo by J. Ewel.

long-term records and observations permit a general framework to be constructed (fig. 9.14). Fire is rarest in the driest swamps where rapid decomposition and occasional floods prevent organic matter from accumulating. No swamps appear to be entirely free from burning, however (fig. 9.15). In certain river swamps, such as the Oklawaha, the occurrence of cabbage palm suggests occasional fire. Generally, however, charred trees in floodplains can be attributed to isolated lightning strikes or to human activity, such as hunters burning hollow trees to smoke out raccoons (C. Wharton, personal communication). Among groundwater swamps, bay swamps seldom burn; shrub bogs that include black titi, titi, pond pine, and other species such as fetterbush and greenbriar burn fairly frequently; and shrub bogs dominated by black titi burn only occasionally (Wharton et al., 1977).

The waxy cuticles on understory vegetation, including many species in the family Ericaceae, are particularly flammable, increasing the fuel content of cypress swamps and shrub bogs in which this type of vegetation is common. Where forest management has decreased fire frequency in pine plantations in the Panhandle, shrub bogs have expanded into the plantations, accompanied by wetter soil conditions (Coultas et al., 1979). Lower transpiration rates from the invading vegetation may facilitate this process.

Cypress ponds may burn several times each century in north Florida. Pond cypress trees survive fire more readily than hardwoods in these swamps (Ewel and Mitsch, 1978). As in shrub bogs, shrub species diversity is relatively high in cypress swamps that have burned frequently; evergreen species are more common in areas that burn less frequently (Schlesinger, 1978b).

Fires are more frequent in south Florida than in north Florida. From 1970 through 1977, four fires per year in swamps in the Big Cypress National Preserve were reported, with an average of 499 ha (nearly 2 square miles) burned per fire (Duever et al., 1986). Fire frequency in the dwarf cy-

Fig. 9.14. Proposed relationships between fire frequency and hydroperiod in swamps.

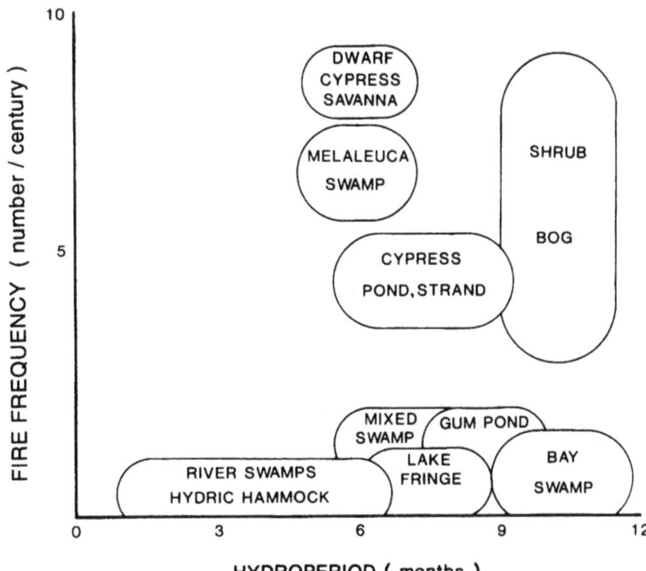

Fig. 9.15. A burned swamp in Baker County, Florida. Loss of peat around the bases of trees may leave surviving trees precariously tilted. Photo taken in 1931 by L. T. Miland. From Florida State Archives.

press savannas in south Florida is probably limited primarily by the slow rate of peat accumulation (Wade et al., 1980).

The nature of fires in swamps in both south and north Florida has changed dramatically within the last century. Severe burning after logging or drainage may destroy both seeds and roots in the soil, favoring replacement in south Florida by willows and subsequently succession to mixed hardwoods (fig. 9.16). On many sites, however, melaleuca rapidly invades cypress swamps that have been drained and severely burned. These new eco-

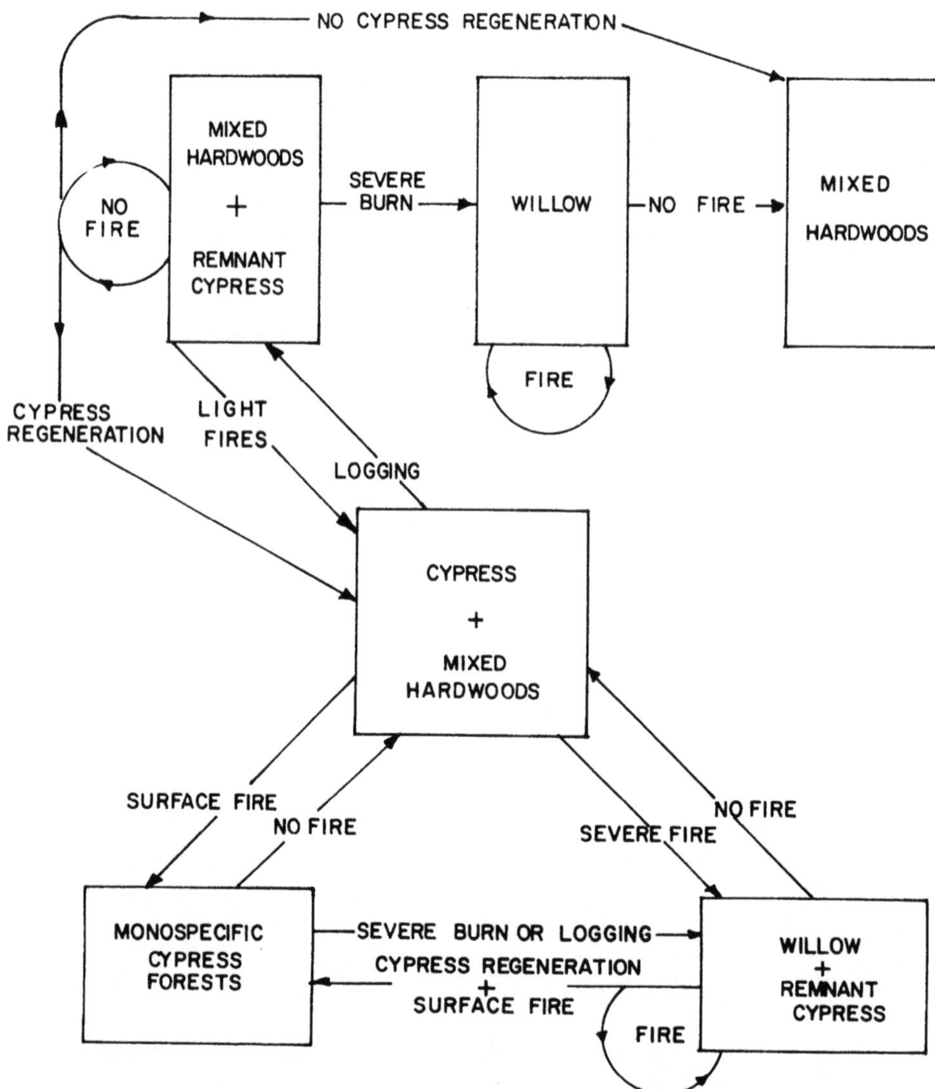

Fig. 9.16 Generalized succession scheme for south Florida swamps (Gunderson, 1984).

systems are still poorly understood, but greater water loss via transpiration from the evergreen vegetation may mean a slightly shorter hydroperiod and lower dry season water levels than in the original cypress pond.

In north Florida, drainage and protection from fire increase dominance of slash pine, bays, and black gum in cypress swamps (Marois and Ewel, 1983). But the combination of frequent extensive fires in the Okefenokee Swamp (approximately every twenty-five years, Izlar, 1984) and logging is probably responsible for shifting dominance from cypress to mixed hardwoods or bay swamps (Hamilton, 1984). No exotic species has become well enough established in a north Florida swamp to dominate its flora.

Productivity and Nutrients

Studies in both natural and enriched swamps throughout eastern North America indicate that nutrient availability and productivity are closely correlated (fig. 9.17). Florida swamps obtain nutrients primarily from rainfall, shallow and deep groundwater, and surface flow from rivers. Each of these sources differs from the others in nutrient content and delivery rate. Because groundwater inflow and outflow are especially difficult to measure, however, complete water budgets—and therefore nutrient budgets—of Florida swamps do not exist. Nevertheless, some generalizations can be made relating nutrient inflows to productivity.

Nutrient Storages and Indices of Availability

One index of nutrient availability in a swamp is pH, which is an inverse measure of acidity. Acid peatlands around the world have low levels of available nutrients. Inflows are low, primarily from rainfall, and the domi-

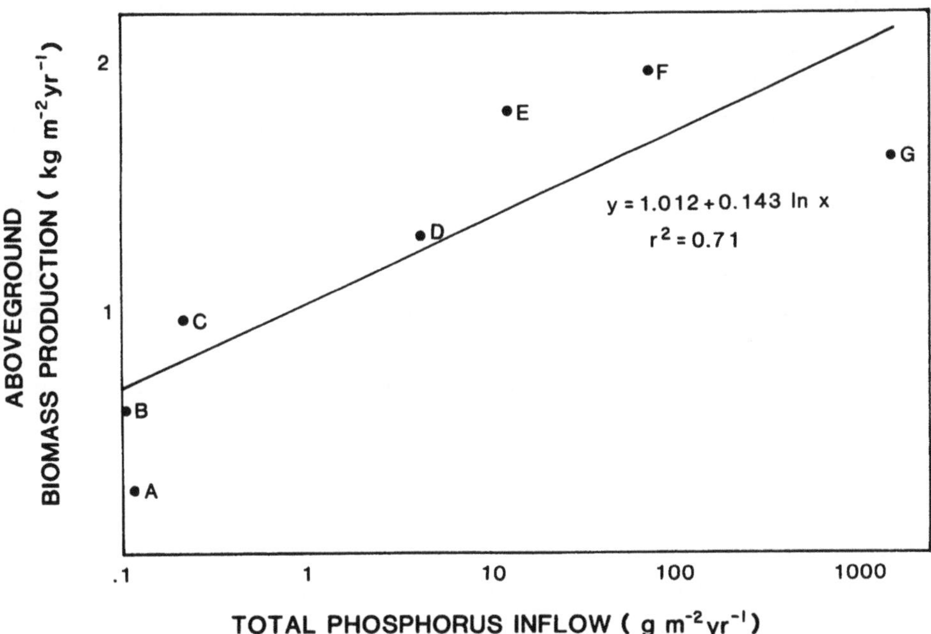

Fig. 9.17. Relationship between total phosphorus inflow and above-ground biomass production in cypress swamps. After S. Brown, 1981. *A* = dwarf cypress savanna, south Florida (S. Brown, 1981); *B* = Okefenokee Swamp, south Georgia (Schlesinger, 1978a); *C* = cypress dome, north Florida (S. Brown, 1981); *D* = sewage-enriched cypress strand, north Florida (Nessel and Bayley, 1984); *E* = sewage-enriched cypress dome, north Florida (S. Brown, 1981); *F* = cypress/tupelo forest, Illinois (Mitsch et al., 1979); *G* = blackwater river forest, north Florida (S. Brown, 1981).

nance of hydrogen ions on exchange sites in the soil reduces nutrient retention. Substantial quantities of nutrients may exist in the dead organic matter itself, but slow decomposition rates keep them unavailable to the plant community for years. Even when mineralization does occur, inorganic phosphorus may form compounds with iron and aluminum that are not available for plant uptake, and inorganic nitrogen in the form of nitrate may be lost to the atmosphere via denitrification. Although nitrogen-fixing organisms may be present, either free-living in the litter or associated with plants such as water fern (*Azolla caroliniana*) and wax myrtle (*Myrica cerifera*), they do not add appreciably to the overall nitrogen budget of a swamp (e.g., Dierberg and Brezonik, 1981, 1984b).

Water level fluctuation may mitigate nutrient limitation, allowing more rapid decomposition and nutrient mineralization (but with increased denitrification) when low water levels permit oxidation. This effect may be insignificant, however, in acid, peat-based swamps. Cypress litter decomposed just as slowly over one year in the temporarily inundated edge of a cypress dome as in the middle, which was flooded nearly the entire year (Deghi et al., 1980). Low nutrient levels in the litter may have been responsible.

Specific conductance, which is often used as an index of fertility of lakes or streams, is a measure of dissolved mineral concentration in water. It is directly correlated with pH, though interpretation is difficult for water with high concentrations of dissolved organic matter.

Substantial differences in pH and specific conductance exist among the major sources of water for Florida swamps (table 9.3). These data suggest that swamps fed by deep groundwater are most productive and swamps depending on rainfall are least productive. Other aspects of the water regime must also be taken into account, however; flow, hydroperiod, and degree of water level fluctuation are clearly important factors in determining the productivity of a swamp.

Productivity

Most studies of productivity in Florida swamps have been conducted in cypress swamps and river swamps. These swamps span a wide range in both gross primary productivity (GPP), the rate at which carbon is fixed and becomes part of the plant, and net primary productivity (NPP), the difference between gross primary productivity and plant respiration (table 9.4). Both GPP and NPP are high in swamps with flowing water. They are intermediate in cypress strands, which are supplied by sufficient surface and groundwater flow to generate faster turnover than in the other stillwater swamps. GPP and NPP are low in swamps supplied primarily by rainfall and with little nutrient-storing capability in the soil. The fact that wastewater enrichment of cypress swamps increases both GPP (S. Brown, 1981) and NPP (fig. 9.17) (Deghi et al., 1980; Nessel et al., 1982), in spite of in-

Table 9.3. Variability of pH and specific conductance of major sources of water for Florida swamps

Water source	Location	pH	Specific conductance (μmho/cm)	Source
Rainfall	All Florida	4.3–4.7		1
	North Florida	4.63	19	2
Shallow groundwater	Panhandle	5.3–7.5	35–46	3
	North Florida	5.4 (0.7)	90 (67)	2
	South Florida	6.8–8.2	364–708	4
Deep groundwater	North Florida	7.21 (0.32)	432 (98)	5
	South Florida	7.4–8.0	1160–5900	4
Blackwater river	Oklawaha River	7.6 (0.3)	375 (28)	6
	Satilla-Suwannee (Ga.)	4.9	40–59	7
	Ocklockonee (Ga.)	7.0	49–327	7
Whitewater river	Apalachicola	5.7–7.8	57–127	3

Sources: (1) Swihart et al. (1984); (2) Dierberg and Brezonik (1984c); (3) Mattraw and Elder (1984); (4) summarized in Duever et al. (1986); (5) Dierberg and Brezonik (1984a); (6) Lugo and Brown (1984); (7) summarized in Wharton and Brinson (1979).

Note: Numbers in parentheses are standard deviations. Numbers without ranges or standard deviations are annual averages.

creased hydroperiod and the near-absence of dissolved oxygen, indicates that nutrient inflow is the critical component (S. Brown, 1981).

These data suggest that productivity increases as groundwater and surface flow become more important elements in a water budget (fig. 9.18). Hydric hammocks and spring run swamps should have high productivity rates because both are fed by deep groundwater with a neutral pH and a high concentration of inorganic ions; spring run swamps have a moderate to fast delivery rate when flooded. In neither swamp type are soils continually saturated. Productivity in river swamps is also high; whitewater river swamps may be more productive than blackwater swamps because of higher sediment loads with associated inorganic forms of nutrients in the floodwaters. Similarly, lake fringe swamps, which experience periodic drawdowns and are influenced by surface runoff as well as by the stream flow and groundwater flow that supply the lakes, also appear to be very productive. South Florida mixed swamp forests are similar hydrologically to cypress strands; data from two stands in the cypress strand at Corkscrew Swamp suggest that productivity decreases as hardwoods assume dominance (Duever et al., 1984a).

Where shallow groundwater is the primary source of water and nutrients for a swamp, the rate of groundwater flow probably determines productivity. Cypress strands, even with virtually imperceptible surface water flow rates, appear to be more productive than cypress ponds (table 9.4). Quality of shallow groundwater may account for higher productivity in cypress

Table 9.4. Above-ground productivity measurements in Florida swamps

Swamp	Gross primary productivity ($g\ C\ m^{-2}\ day^{-1}$)	Net Primary Productivity ($tonnes\ dry\ weight\ ha^{-1}\ yr^{-1}$) Litter fall	Stem growth	Total	Source
River swamps					
North Florida blackwater	13.73	5.97	10.86	16.83	1
river swamps			3.36		2
		5.78			3
North Florida whitewater					
river swamps		7.95			4
Stillwater swamps					
South Florida dwarf					
cypress savanna	1.82–2.41	2.24	0.44	2.68	1, 5
North and central	6.97	3.87–4.88	5.41	9.28–10.29	1, 6, 7
Florida cypress domes			1.54–3.72		1, 2
		3.35–4.26	4.33–4.77	8.12–8.59	1
South Florida cypress	6.74	5.97	7.72	13.69	8
strands		7.12–7.26	1.84–8.16	8.96–15.42	9

Sources: (1) S. Brown (1981); (2) Mitsch and Ewel (1979); (3) Richardson et al. (1983); (4) Elder and Cairns (1982); (5) Flohrschutz (1978); (6) Deghi et al. (1980); (7) Dierberg and Ewel (1984); (8) Burns (1984); (9) Duever et al. (1984a).

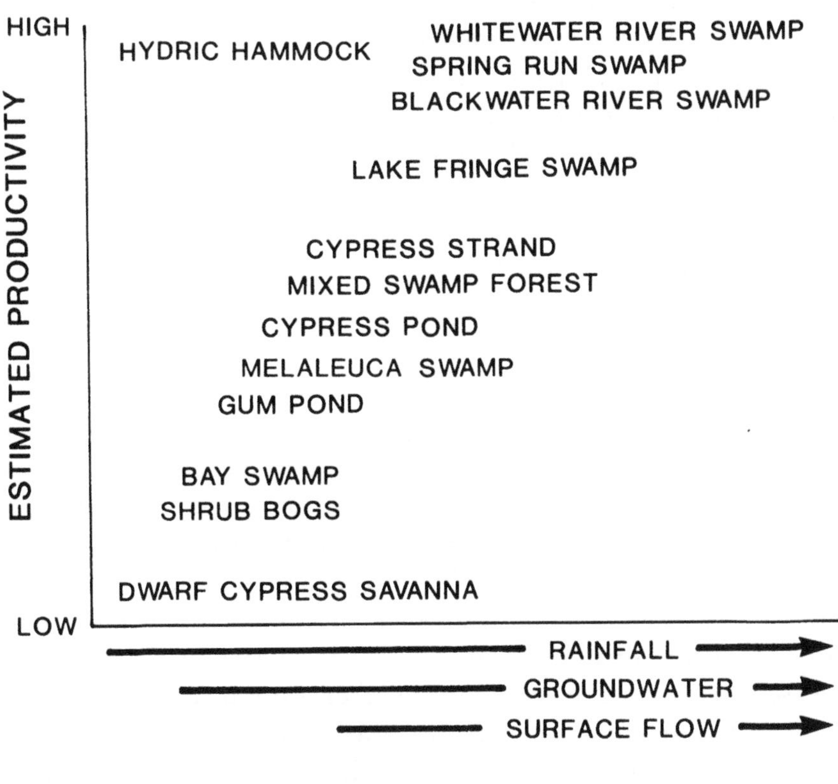

Fig. 9.18. Proposed productivity rankings of Florida swamps and importance of different water sources. Swamps at the left are believed to be influenced most by rainwater, swamps at the center by groundwater, and swamps at the right by surface flow, including both river and lake water. Actual productivity rates for some swamps are listed in table 9.4.

ponds in south Florida than in north Florida (table 9.3). Cypress ponds, with slightly shorter hydroperiods and damped water level fluctuations, may be slightly more productive than gum ponds.

Bay swamps have been considered more productive than cypress ponds by virtue of their higher mineral content (Monk, 1966b; Wharton et al., 1977). However, productivity is more likely to be related to uptake, which is not necessarily a function of content in the soil. Longer hydroperiod, less water level fluctuation, and less apparent surface water inflow suggest instead that bay swamps are less productive than either cypress swamps or gum ponds.

Bay swamps are also considered to be climax communities, developing from cypress domes in the absence of fire (Monk, 1966b; Clewell, 1971). It is not clear how common this successional sere was when natural fire frequencies prevailed. If evapotranspiration rates from bay trees are lower than from cypress trees, lengthening hydroperiods may accompany (or cause) the development of a bay swamp community.

Shrub bogs are probably the least productive of the stillwater swamps that are common in north Florida. South Florida cypress savannas, fed primarily by precipitation, are likely the least productive of all Florida swamps. Fire, which infrequently but periodically destroys the peat substrate in the shallow limestone depressions and the meager nutrient storage associated with it, clearly shapes this ecosystem.

Animals and Swamps

Wetlands interact with terrestrial and aquatic ecosystems primarily via the flow of water and its associated nutrients and suspended solids—runoff draining from uplands into wetlands and floodwaters moving between rivers and floodplains. Animals also can contribute to this integration of ecosystems within a landscape by moving propagules and nutrients from one ecosystem into another. Swamps provide food, cover, nesting sites, and hibernating places for a variety of animals, but most spend only part of their lives in swamps, moving to uplands or to other water bodies as water levels rise and fall. Movement of animals from one ecosystem to another may be particularly important when it represents the only significant flow of nutrients and energy in that direction, such as from wetland to upland.

Invertebrates

Benthic invertebrates, including leeches and worms, immature and mature insects, mites and spiders, crustaceans, and molluscs, are often the base of swamp food chains. The diversity of this group of organisms is strongly related to water quality. In low oxygen, stillwater swamps such as cypress ponds and shrub bogs, immature chironomids (a family of flies in the order Diptera) dominate the benthic fauna (Haack, 1984; Brightman, 1984). Spatial variation in swamps with gradients in water quality parameters, such as pH and dissolved oxygen, leads to patchy distributions in invertebrate populations. In shrub bogs, for instance, sites with sphagnum moss and very low pH have relatively sparse invertebrate populations and are dominated by crustaceans that are generalist feeders (Haack, 1984). More diverse assemblages of invertebrates, including immature forms of hemipterans (bugs), coleopterans (beetles), and odonates (dragonflies and damselflies), all characteristic of north temperate acid water bodies and wetlands, occur in open sites with flowing water.

Topographic heterogeneity in river swamps generates what is probably the greatest diversity and productivity of benthic invertebrates among Florida swamps (e.g., Wharton et al., 1981). Snails, clams, and crayfish are particularly abundant in river swamps. Snails and clams are especially common along spring runs. Invertebrate production in the floodplain can be orders of magnitude greater than in the river channel, providing a major resource not only for terrestrial predators but also for fish during high water (Wharton et al., 1977).

Invertebrates, especially insects and other arthropods, are common on the water surface and in the canopy as well as in the substrate. High diversities have been recorded in cypress ponds and in a dwarf cypress savanna (Flohrschutz, 1978; Harris and Vickers, 1984; McMahan and Davis, 1984), but no studies have been reported for other swamps. In cypress ponds, dipterans and spiders are the most prominent groups in the vegetation above the water; the community on the water surface is more diverse, with dipterans, hemipterans, and collembolans dominating. Among the dipterans in cypress ponds are at least eighteen species of mosquitoes (Davis, 1984).

Many canopy insects graze on live foliage. Most of the vegetation in stillwater swamps does not appear to be palatable, although some of the deciduous species, such as sweet pepperbush (*Clethra alnifolia*), are regularly defoliated by herbivores, primarily insects, within weeks of leafing out in the spring (Schlesinger and Chabot, 1977). Casual observation suggests that much more leaf material is eaten in river swamps than in stillwater swamps, but these canopy insect communities have not yet been described.

Fish

Swamps adjacent to rivers and lakes are more likely than isolated swamps to have large and diverse fish populations, including many species that use them during only part of their life cycle (e.g., Wharton et al., 1981). Anadromous fish entering from the Gulf of Mexico or the Atlantic Ocean to seek spawning sites may be common in the larger rivers. Because water quality and food availability may be substantially different in floodplains than in the main water bodies, however, populations may still become isolated. At least two species of fish found in floodplain backwaters—the cypress minnow (*Hybognathus hayi*) and the cypress darter (*Etheostoma proeliare*)—are described as rare and endangered in Florida, although they occur in contiguous drainages farther west in the United States (Gilbert, 1978).

Periodic drawdowns in most isolated stillwater swamps preclude the development of a diverse or important fish fauna. Large swamps often have deep pools or seasonal inflows that permit fish populations to survive year-round. For instance, during the dry season in areas such as the Big Cypress Swamp, fish concentrate in small, deep holes (e.g., Carlson and Duever, 1977), and fish population densities are as high as, and sometimes higher than, in habitats with more permanent water (summarized in Duever et al., 1986).

Amphibians and Reptiles

Pronounced wet-dry cycles make many stillwater swamps ideal year-round habitat for amphibians, and frogs dominate the fauna in north Florida cypress swamps in summer (Harris and Vickers, 1984). Amphibians may be common, if not abundant, in bay swamps, but ground-dwelling reptiles, including turtles, are rare.

In river swamps, such as the Oklawaha, where flood events are shorter and flow rates stronger than in the stillwater swamps, amphibians and reptiles are not common, and arboreal species outnumber ground-dwelling species (Florida Game and Freshwater Fish Commission, 1976). Nevertheless, a variety of these herpetofauna, such as alligators (*Alligator mississippiensis*), amphiumas (*Amphiuma means*), and the less common glossy crayfish snake (*Regina rigida*) and striped crayfish snake (*R. alleni*), may be found (often feeding on crayfish) (Wharton et al., 1981). In general, tree-climbing snakes and burrowing sirens (*Siren* spp.) and amphiumas occur in the zones closer to the river, whereas salamanders may be closer to the uplands.

South Florida cypress swamps, with a relatively sparse understory to provide cover, do not have large populations of either amphibians or reptiles. Mixed swamp forests, on the other hand, with their deep, more permanent pools, are heavily used by turtles and snakes. Both types of swamps commonly have alligators (Duever et al., 1986), which are also frequently found in lake fringe swamps in north Florida.

Many common amphibians and reptiles depend on swamps for reproduction and are also found in other aquatic and terrestrial ecosystems. Others, such as the marbled salamander (*Ambystoma opacum*), four-toed salamander (*Hemidactylium scutatum*), dwarf siren (*Pseudobranchus striatus*), bird-voiced tree frog (*Hyla avivoca*), mud snake (*Farancia abacura*), and rainbow snake (*F. erytrogramma*), are seldom found outside swamps (C. Wharton, personal communication).

Isolated swamps may harbor populations of rare and endangered species. The Pine Barrens tree frog (*Hyla andersoni*) is found where north Florida herb bogs and shrub bogs provide habitat for both larvae and adults, respectively (Means and Moler, 1979), and the carpenter frog (*Rana virgatipes*) is found in bayheads and cypress ponds in north Florida (McDiarmid, 1978). Among Florida swamps, nine species of amphibians and reptiles are reported as rare or endangered in hardwood swamps, five in cypress swamps, and one in scrub cypress.

Birds and Mammals

Swamps differ considerably in their importance to birds and mammals (table 9.5), which are more mobile than the lower vertebrates and tend to use a wider variety of habitats during a lifetime. The presence of water in all swamps is important for drinking and for the protection it affords to

Table 9.5. Relative contributions (based on subjective observations) of Florida swamps to bird and mammal habitat

Swamps	Canopy insect production	Production of edible fruits and seeds	Cavity density	Density of vegetation	Presence of water
Bay swamp	Low	Low	Low	High	High
Cypress pond	Low	Low	High	Low	High
Cypress strand	Low	Low	High	Low	High
Dwarf cypress	Low	Low	Low	Low	High
Gum pond	Low	High	Low	Low	High
Hydric hammock	High	High	High	Low	Low
Lake fringe	Low	Low	High	Low	High
Melaleuca swamp	Low	High	Low	Low	High
Mixed swamp	High	Low	High	Low	High
River swamp	High	High	High	Low	Low
Shrub bog	Low	Low	Low	High	High

canopy-nesting species. Hardwood swamps provide several additional key habitat components: mast is an important food item; edible foliage supports insect populations, another major food source; tree cavities, both at the base and in the canopy, provide nest sites; broad-leaved evergreen trees and shrubs provide cover in the winter; and dense vegetation of any kind provides refuge, especially to large mammals (Harris and Mulholland, 1983). The edges of floodplain forests, with mast-producing bottomland hardwoods and proximity to other species in the adjoining mesic forests, therefore support perhaps the greatest density and diversity of wildlife in Florida. Bay swamps and shrub bogs provide cover, which is increasingly important to the shrinking populations of large mammals. Conversely, dwarf cypress savannas are important for their lack of cover, providing perching sites for predatory birds—both raptors and water birds—that search for small organisms in an open environment.

Birds are more abundant in swamps than in uplands in Florida during migration and in the summer (Harris and Mulholland, 1983). They dominate the winter vertebrate fauna in north Florida cypress swamps; yellow-rumped warblers (*Dendroica coronata*) and pine warblers (*D. pinus*) are particularly common (Harris and Vickers, 1984). More than fourteen species of birds are common in south Florida swamps but do not breed there (Duever et al., 1986). The greatest diversity and biomass probably occur in river swamps. Not only is insect production likely to be greater there, but a higher percentage of plants produces fruit and seeds from spring to fall in hardwood swamps than in cypress swamps (Ewel and Atmosoedirdjo, 1987).

Water birds are especially conspicuous in and around Florida swamps and are often year-round residents. Limpkins (*Aramus guarauna*), which feed primarily on snails, are characteristic of both cypress swamps and river swamps. White ibis (*Eudocimus albus*) and glossy ibis (*Plegadis falcinellus*) use crayfish extensively (Wharton et al., 1981). Cypress swamps commonly contain rookeries of wood storks (*Mycteria americana*) and of at least nine species of herons and their allies; hardwood swamps and willow thickets, often bordering cypress swamps, are also common nesting sites (Nesbitt et al., 1982; Duever et al., 1986). Among the waterfowl, only wood ducks (*Aix sponsa*) are common in Florida swamps, and south Florida mixed swamp forests are considered critical habitat for them (Duever et al., 1986).

Wild turkeys (*Meleagris gallopavo*), which also often feed on crayfish, and at least three species of woodpeckers often nest in cypress or hardwood swamps. Mississippi kites (*Ictinia mississippiensis*) and swallow-tailed kites (*Elanoides forficatus*) breed only in swamps (Wharton et al., 1981). Swainson's warblers (*Limnothlypis swainsonii*) and prothonotary warblers (*Protonotaria citrea*) are characteristic of southern swamps.

Several mammals are most commonly found in swamps, such as the southeastern shrew (*Sorex longirostris*) and the cotton mouse (*Peromyscus gossypinus*). Some small mammals, such as golden mice (*Ochrotomys nuttalli*), nest in trees to escape floodwaters. River otters (*Lutra canadensis*) and mink (*Mustela vison*) feed heavily on crayfish in river swamps (Wharton et al., 1981). The beaver (*Castor canadensis*), which was trapped out of Florida by the middle of the twentieth century, has returned to north Florida, where it is most common in floodplains of small streams (Evers, 1976).

Many mammals are common in swamps but are not necessarily confined to them. Raccoons (*Procyon lotor*), for instance, are common in bay swamps in central Florida (Florida Game and Fresh Water Fish Commission, 1976). They eat crayfish in river swamps and range widely in the uplands as well. Large, uncommon mammals, such as the black bear (*Ursus americanus*) and the Florida panther (*Felis concolor*), are now concentrated in swamps because of widespread destruction of upland habitat. Bears in north Florida feed heavily on berries in the summer, including many swamp species such as blueberry and sparkleberry (*Vaccinium* spp.), gallberry (*Ilex glabra*), and needle palm (Maehr and Brady, 1984). They often use bay swamps as refuge.

Rare and endangered birds and mammals are more likely to be found in cypress swamps and mixed hardwood swamps than in other kinds of swamps. Of the sixty-eight birds listed as rare and endangered in all of Florida's ecosystems, twelve are found in cypress swamps and hardwood swamps (Kale, 1978). In the Big Cypress region, six of the nineteen birds listed as rare, endangered, or threatened use these swamps for breeding and feeding (Duever et al., 1986). These include the wood stork, short-tailed hawk (*Buteo brachyurus*), southern bald eagle (*Haliaeetus leucocephalus*), and osprey (*Pandion haliaetus*). A fifth species, roseate spoonbill (*Ajaja ajaja*), uses dwarf cypress savannas. The demise of the sixth species, the ivory-billed woodpecker (*Campephilus principalis*), now considered to be extinct in

North America, has been associated with widespread logging of bottomland hardwoods.

All four of the terrestrial mammals considered to be rare, endangered, or threatened in south Florida and known to occur in the Big Cypress commonly use cypress swamps and mixed swamps (Duever et al., 1986). These include the Florida panther, mangrove fox squirrel (*Sciurus niger*), black bear, and mink.

Because swamps are used by many species of mammals with large territories, and in particular by endangered species as refugia, the spatial arrangement of the remaining wilderness area in Florida must be carefully examined when formulating land acquisition policies. Linking large wilderness areas with corridors of natural vegetation is attractive: for example, joining the Okefenokee Swamp and the Osceola National Forest by protecting the Pinhook Swamp or connecting the Okefenokee Swamp with coastal marshes and swamps along the Gulf coast by preserving the Suwannee River floodplain (Noss and Harris, 1986). This strategy may be the only way remaining to provide sufficient contiguous habitat for the survival of many vertebrate species.

Swamps in a Changing Landscape

Throughout Florida's history, swamps have been drained, impounded, polluted, logged, and excavated. Although some of these activities have yielded short-term profits, most have led to long-term economic losses, many of them indirectly. Much can be learned about how an ecosystem functions from its response to alteration, and close examination of these practices is useful in formulating future management guidelines for both conservation and wise use of these ecosystems (see Brandt and Ewel, 1989).

Changes in Hydroperiod

Alteration of hydroperiod affects swamp communities rapidly and often profoundly. Drainage, which is particularly common in Florida, allows species with low flood tolerance to become established. Significant decreases in GPP, NPP, and biomass were recorded in a drained portion of the Fakahatchee Strand in south Florida (Burns, 1984). In north Florida, cypress swamp drainage led to poor cypress regeneration, increased density of shrubs and hardwoods, increased fire potential, and a dramatic shift from aquatic and wading animals to arboreal species (Marois and Ewel, 1983; Harris and Vickers, 1984).

Lengthening a hydroperiod affects a swamp more if its hydroperiod is normally short than if it is already accustomed to long periods of flooding. Hardwood trees in river swamps, for instance, may show signs of stress due to increased flooding in less than a year (e.g., Broadfoot and Williston, 1973; Richardson et al., 1983). Cypress trees are the most tolerant of Florida trees to long hydroperiods, though even they will die if floodwaters are too deep (Harms et al., 1980).

Changes in Water Quality

Changes in swamp water quality are usually caused by wastewater discharge, which increases hydroperiod as well. Cypress swamps are attractive as wastewater disposal sites because their plant communities can tolerate long hydroperiods and low dissolved oxygen levels (Ewel and Odum, 1984). Water drains from these swamps through the peat, sands, and clays underneath; nutrients are retained in the substrate and vegetation; and eutrophication is restricted to the swamp itself. Wastewater disposal has been sustained in some swamps for more than forty-five years, increasing tree growth rates throughout the entire duration (Nessel et al., 1982). However, severe reducing conditions can develop and kill even cypress trees if large quantities of poorly treated wastewater are discharged into a swamp (Lemlich and Ewel, 1984).

Silviculture

Timber production is a major land use activity in Florida swamps, which make up more than 25 percent of commercial forest land (Dippon, 1983). Virtually every swamp in the state was logged between the late 1800s and 1950, the most valuable products coming from centuries-old bald cypress trees with large volumes of durable, attractive heartwood (marketed as tidewater red cypress) (fig. 9.19). The second-growth cypress now being harvested from Florida swamps (fig. 9.20) is marketed as yellow cypress; it has little heartwood and no unusually rot-resistant properties. Until recently it was used primarily for specialty items such as ladders and crab traps. Development of chippers that can process entire trees, including the stringy bark, has recently made mulch a major product.

When access roads were built into large swamps, topography and drainage patterns were often drastically changed. A large cypress strand that drains into Lake Panasoffkee in central Florida regenerated ash, maple, gum, and bay after logging (Wharton et al., 1977), and probably few of the large strands and river swamps bear much resemblance to the original stands. Long-term effects of changes in community composition on evapotranspiration rates, wildlife populations, and downstream water quality have not been determined.

Stillwater swamps are less vulnerable to logging because hydroperiod is less likely to be affected. Virtually all the cypress ponds in north Florida have been logged, but many appear to have retained their essential charac-

Fig. 9.19. Cutting old-growth bald cypress along the Suwannee River. Photo taken for the journal *American Lumberman* and used as an advertisement for the Putnam Lumber Company. Appeared in the June 15, 1929, issue of *The Southern Lumber Journal.*

teristics after regeneration (Parendes, 1983; Terwilliger and Ewel, 1986; Ewel et al., 1989).

The best silvicultural management practices currently promoted for Florida swamps emphasize protection of rivers and lakes by prohibiting logging within a buffer zone (Riekerk, 1983). Even if site degradation within the

Fig. 9.20. Skidder removing trees in a central Florida cypress swamp.

swamps can be prevented and regeneration of characteristic tree species can be assured, the long-term effects on wildlife populations of maintaining young, even-aged stands may be detrimental. The disappearance from Florida swamps of both the ivory-billed woodpecker and the Carolina parakeet (*Conuropsis caroliniensis*) has been attributed to logging during the early part of this century, primarily to removal of large trees, decrease in availability of cavities, and decrease in overall structural heterogeneity (Harris and Mulholland, 1983; Harris and Vickers, 1984).

Substrate Removal

Removal of peat from a stillwater swamp—for example, for use as an energy source—is tantamount to destruction of the swamp; the low nutrient status and low productivity rates that characterize most of these wetlands indicate that centuries are required for replacement. Even more devastating is the removal of the geologic substrate beneath. Much of the phosphate mined in Florida is taken from beneath poorly drained pine flatwoods, cypress swamps, and bay swamps in both north and south Florida. Until recently, most of the mined areas were reclaimed as uplands—for example, as pastures. Considerably more effort is being devoted to restoring the original ecosystems, but swamp restoration has yet to be demonstrated.

When swamps are managed, indirect effects on other ecosystems should be considered just as carefully as direct impacts on the swamp itself. One of the major reasons for protecting and restoring swamps is their importance to downstream water bodies. Changes in stream water quality (though not necessarily from peat or phosphate mining) have led to drastic changes in downstream estuaries—in benthic macroinvertebrate distribution, phytoplankton production, and dominance and abundance of fish both in Florida (Livingston, 1984b) and North Carolina (Richardson, 1983). This illustrates the close dependence between ecosystems that are connected by the flow of water.

Even stillwater swamps can significantly affect water relations in a region because of their low evapotranspiration rates and their buffering effect on runoff during summer storms. A simulation model demonstrated that drainage of 80 percent of the swamps in the Green Swamp region in central Florida and replacement by plant communities that have greater evapotranspiration losses during the winter and less flood retention capability would result in 45 percent less water entering the surface aquifer and becoming available to the region (Brown, 1984). Incorporating into Brown's model the lower summer evapotranspiration rates that are being reported for cypress swamps would increase the estimated loss even more.

Outlook for Swamps

Although Florida has lost more than half of its wetlands during its short history, some large, important swamps have been saved and studied. In the mid-1900s, the National Audubon Society purchased Corkscrew Swamp in southwest Florida and later established its Ecosystem Research Unit there. When the proposed Cross-Florida Barge Canal threatened the diverse, productive river forest that bordered the Oklawaha River, the Florida Defenders of the Environment was organized to define and protect the swamp's values. Although much of this swamp was destroyed in the formation of Lake Ocklawaha, studies on the remaining portion have provided basic information on the structure and function of river swamps (Harms et al., 1980; Lugo and Brown, 1984).

Big Cypress Swamp in southwest Florida and Green Swamp in central Florida were named areas of critical state concern in 1973 and 1974, respectively—landmark dates in the state's growing awareness of the importance of its vanishing natural resource base. Big Cypress subsequently became a national preserve, representing a milestone in cooperation among private, state, and federal interests. The Conservation and Recreation Lands Trust Fund, established in 1979, assisted in purchase of environmentally endangered lands, including swamps. The passage of the Warren S. Henderson Wetlands Protection Act in 1984 demonstrated the willingness of the state government to limit further exploitation and development. Actions taken by the state's water management districts to protect major wetlands, particularly floodplains, are further evidence of the growing recognition of the values of these swamps and Florida's interest in preserving them.

Undisturbed swamps provide a number of benefits to society without appreciable cost. Wildlife production is high in areas with mixtures of upland and wetland ecosystems, such as San Pedro Bay and Green Swamp. Floodplain forests serve as flood control areas without dams or other water level manipulations. Stillwater swamps can serve as nutrient retention areas in wastewater treatment systems and water retention areas in stormwater management systems. They may also serve as water conservation areas, perhaps allowing more water to percolate into aquifers or into estuaries than if drained and replaced by communities with higher evapotranspiration rates. Although no direct profit is gained by recognizing these services, expensive installations for flood control or water purification may be necessary if the natural functions of swamps are destroyed.

The importance of the four key ecological characteristics of different kinds of swamps (hydroperiod, fire, organic matter, and water quality) can be identified and incorporated into management plans. More difficult to define, but just as important both economically and ecologically, are relationships among swamps and other ecosystems. Low topography, high water tables, and abundant animal populations mean that wetlands are closely linked with both uplands and aquatic ecosystems, thus demanding that they be managed as part of a landscape rather than as individual ecosystems.

Appendix. Classification of 13 Florida swamps according to the National Wetlands Inventory system

Class	Subclass	Swamp	Dominant	Modifers		
				Water	pH	Soil
Scrub-shrub Wetland	Narrow-leaved Deciduous	Cypress savanna	*Taxodium*	Seasonally flooded	Acid-circumneutral	Organic
	Broad-leaved Evergreen	Shrub bog	*Cliftonia, Cyrilla*	Semi-permanently flooded	Acid	Organic
Forested Wetland	Narrow-leaved Deciduous	Cypress pond	*Taxodium*	Seasonally flooded	Acid-circumneutral	Organic
		Cypress strand	*Taxodium*	Seasonally flooded	Acid-circumneutral	Organic
		Lake fringe swamp		Seasonally flooded	Acid-circumneutral	Organic
	Broad-leaved Deciduous	Whitewater floodplain forest		Temporarily flooded	Circumneutral-alkaline	Mineral
		Blackwater floodplain forest		Temporarily flooded	Acid-circumneutral-alkaline	Mineral
		Spring run swamp		Temporarily flooded	Circumneutral-alkaline	Mineral
		Hydric hammock		Temporarily flooded	Circumneutral-alkaline	Mineral
		Mixed hardwood swamp		Seasonally flooded	Circumneutral-alkaline	Organic
		Gum swamp	*Nyssa*	Seasonally flooded	Acid-circumneutral	Organic
	Broad-leaved Evergreen	Bay swamp	*Gordonia, Magnolia, Persea*	Semi-permanently flooded	Acid	Organic
		Melaleuca swamp	*Melaleuca*	Seasonally flooded	Circumneutral	Mineral

Source: Cowardin et al. (1979).
Note: All swamps are included in the Palustrine System. Where no dominant is listed, any of several species may dominate, as described in the text.

10
Freshwater Marshes

James A. Kushlan

Wetland ecosystems dominate much of the Florida landscape, and marshes make up about one-third of those wetlands (Hefner, 1986). The largest of these marshlands, the Everglades, is a well-known symbol of natural Florida. Yet the history of Florida has been punctuated by campaigns to reclaim the wetlands; between the mid-1950s and mid-1970s alone, 24 percent of Florida's remaining marshes were drained (Hefner, 1986). Many more, including the Everglades, were severely altered by both drainage and unnatural flooding.

Marshes are wetlands dominated by herbaceous plants rooted in and generally emergent from shallow water that stands at or above the ground surface for much of the year. In general, less than one-third of the cover of a marsh consists of trees and shrubs. Marsh ecosystems include bogs, fens, mires, prairies, wet prairies, savannas, wet savannas, reed swamps, and swamps. The term *swamp*, however, is more appropriately restricted to forested or wooded wetlands. Marshes are classified as palustrine emergent wetlands by Cowardin et al. (1979). The Florida Natural Areas Inventory (1988) lists nine marsh types in Florida: basin marsh, bog, depression marsh, floodplain marsh, marl prairie, seepage slope, slough, swale, and wet prairie. In this chapter, marshes are classified either according to their general physiognomy, such as floodplain marsh, swale marsh, basin or depression marsh, and wet prairie, and by their characteristic plants, such as saw grass marsh and flag marsh.

Florida's marshes are characterized by their subtropical location, fluctuating water levels, recurring fires, and hard water. Owing to differences in climate and geology, the distribution and character of marshes vary across the state; yet notable similarities in appearance, constituent species, and controlling factors can be discerned among them.

Distribution

Marshes are not uniformly distributed throughout the state (fig. 10.1d). The greatest expanse is the Everglades of southern Florida (fig. 10.2). Several other relatively large marshes are associated with river floodplains, notably along the Kissimmee and St. Johns rivers. Smaller marshes are scattered throughout the peninsula, but the Panhandle has few marshes.

Topography is the principal factor controlling the distribution of marshes over the Florida peninsula (White, 1970) (fig. 10.1a). Land form and elevation affect marsh development primarily by determining the depth to the water table and the fate of runoff from local rainfall. Because the northern Panhandle and central core of the peninsula are elevated and well drained, they lack expanses of marshland. The remainder of the peninsula has a greater area of marshland because it is low, flat, and poorly drained. In southern Florida, water runs off slowly and is impounded by topographic rises and coastal ridges of limestone and sand. It is behind one of these coastal ridges that the enormous swale marsh of the Everglades is found. Elsewhere, marshes occur anywhere local topography and impermeable soils prevent rapid runoff or infiltration—either near rivers and lakes or in small basins and other depressions.

A relatively large surplus of annual rainfall over annual potential evaporation in Florida further contributes to the existence of marshland. This effect is particularly pronounced along Florida's southeast coast (figs. 10.1b, 10.1c), where it contributed to the development of the Everglades marshes, those in the vicinity of Lake Okeechobee, and those in the St. Johns River basin.

Thus the distribution of marshes in Florida (fig. 10.1d) may be explained through a combination of local and regional topography, rainfall, evaporation, and geology. Because these factors vary from one physiographic region to the next, it is possible to categorize the state's marshlands into five major groups. From higher to lower elevation, these are highland marshes, flatwoods marshes, the Kissimmee marsh complex, the St. Johns marshes, and the Everglades (fig. 10.2).

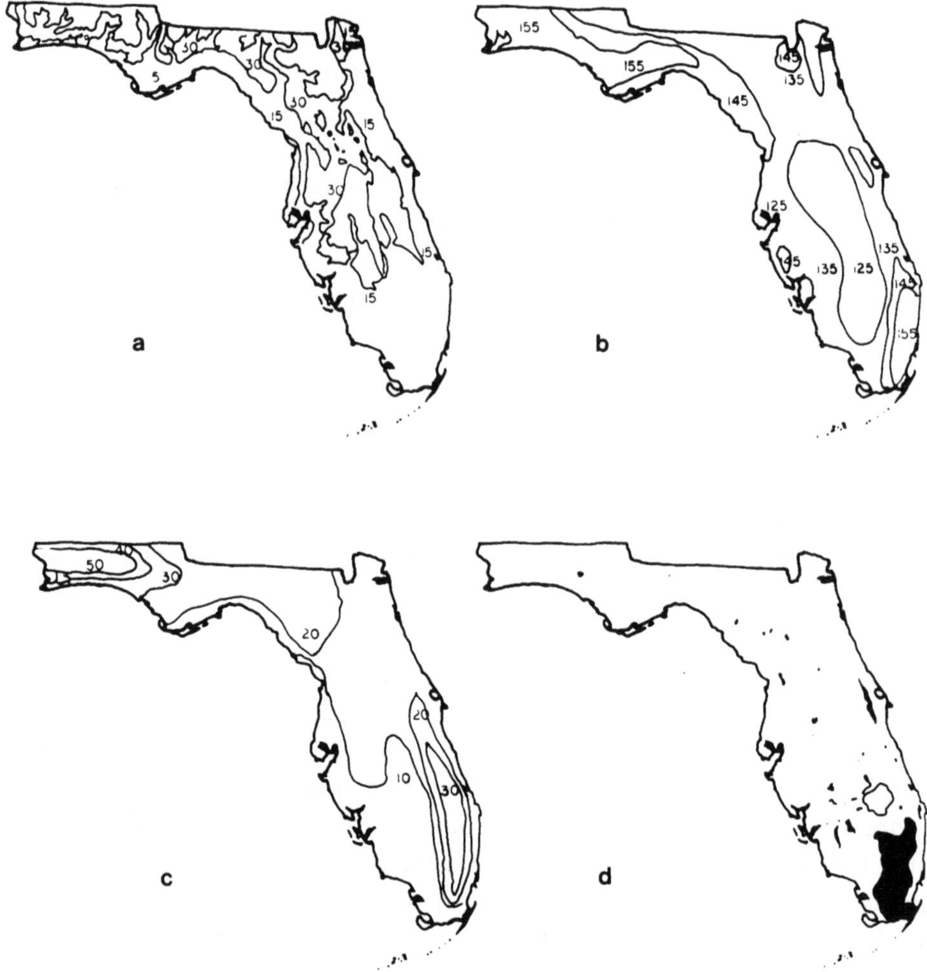

Fig. 10.1 The location of Florida's freshwater marshes and the environmental features that affect them: (*a*) topography in 15 m increments; (*b*) annual rainfall (cm); (*c*) difference between annual rainfall and potential evaporation (cm); (*d*) present distribution of marshes. Redrawn from Fernald and Patton, 1984.

Highland Marshes

The uneven topography of the central ridge produces an array of marshes occupying different types of depressions: former lake basins, shallow peat-filled valleys between existing lakes, and depressions landward of swamps that ring some lakes. Many of these marshes exist because of the shifting balance between two processes: the compaction of surficial sediments that retards loss of surface water and the periodic development of solution features that drain surface water into the aquifer (Pirkle, 1956; Pirkle and Brooks, 1959). Marshes and lakes in this region are unstable because subsurface drainage patterns change frequently as solution features appear or previous drainageways become plugged. A single site may alternately be lake, marsh, and dry land within a relatively short time span.

Fig. 10.2. Former distribution of major marshland areas in Florida and names of larger examples. Not shown are areas that include numerous small flatwoods marshes, wet savannas, and wet prairies scattered throughout much of the state.

Paynes Prairie, a large highland marsh located near Gainesville, is a famous example of this phenomenon (fig. 10.3). The character of Paynes Prairie has varied substantially during recorded history in response to changes in inflows, drainage, and fluctuations of the Floridan Aquifer. When William Bartram visited the area in 1774, the basin consisted of a dry grassland known as the Alachua Savannah (Bartram, 1791). In the early 1870s, Alachua Sink—the prairie's major drainageway—became plugged, and the basin became a lake deep enough for steamboat operations. The lake level began falling in 1891, and a marsh formed within two years.

Other large highland marshes are the Peace Creek marshes near Lake Wales; the Lake Apopka marsh near Zellwood; the Clermont marsh between Lake Minneola and Lake Minehaha; Emeralda and Fruitland Park marshes near Lake Griffin; Eustis Meadows near Eustis; Florahome, Fowler's, Hawthorne, and Levy's prairies in Putnam County; Jumper Creek marsh in Sumter County; Lake Panasoffkee marsh and Black Sink Prairie in Marion County; and the marshes of Orange Lake in Alachua County. Numerous small marshes dotted the Oklawaha River valley before it was impounded in the 1960s.

Fig. 10.3. The Alachua Savannah of William Bartram's day is now known as Paynes Prairie. It is an example of a large, highlands-type marsh created by the coalescence of solution holes. Photo by R. Myers.

Flatwoods Marshes

Flatwoods marshes, also known as flatwoods or seasonal ponds, occur throughout Florida's extensive pine flatwoods but are most common between the central highlands and the Atlantic and Gulf coasts (fig. 10.4). These marshes occur within slight depressions in an otherwise flat landscape. Although shallow (less than a meter deep) and small (usually only ten to a few hundred meters across), they reach a density of seventy per square kilometer in Sarasota County (Winchester et al., 1985). In places they make up a large portion of the area covered by flatwoods (Laessle, 1942; Abrahamson et al., 1984). The best-studied area where these marshes occur is the Ringling-MacArthur Reserve in Sarasota County (Winchester et al., 1985; Winchester, 1986). Preserved as a water recharge area, it encompasses 13,400 ha of flatwoods and associated flatwoods marsh habitat.

The St. Johns Marshes

The St. Johns marshes once encompassed the upper reaches of the St. Johns River floodplain (St. Johns River Water Management District, 1977). Before alteration by humans, all but the northernmost 100 km of the 480 km river basin was an extensive freshwater system of swamps, marshes, and lakes. The river originated in the 120,000-ha Blue Cypress Lake marsh, and other marshes occurred along the flat river floodplain, which falls less than 1.5 m over the entire upper St. Johns River basin (Lowe et al., 1984).

The Kissimmee Marsh Complex

The Kissimmee marsh complex includes the drainage basin of the Kissimmee River, Lake Istokpoga–Indian Prairie, and Fisheating Creek. The marshes along the Kissimmee River floodplain historically occupied 5000 km^2. Prior to its channelization in the 1960s, the river followed a 160-km

Fig. 10.4. Flatwoods marshes of the Ringling-MacArthur Reserve in eastern Sarasota County. Photo by Allan Horton.

meandering course from its headwaters at Orlando to its terminus in Lake Okeechobee. Undulating topography within the Kissimmee Valley created numerous isolated swale marshes, which blended into drier grasslands known as the Kissimmee Prairie.

One of the largest marshes in the Kissimmee complex was the 12,000 ha Istokpoga or Indian Prairie, which originated at Lake Istokpoga and then drained southward to Lake Okeechobee. It was once covered by shallow marsh, embedded with numerous deeper marshes. Similar marshes dot the swamp forests within the Fisheating Creek basin, located southwest of the Kissimmee River valley. The Ordway-Whittell Prairie Preserve and Avon Park Bombing Range also contain portions of the Kissimmee marsh complex (Tanner et al., 1982).

The Everglades

The Everglades marsh, the largest in Florida, originally encompassed over 10,000 km^2 in an elongated basin spanning 100 km and sloping a mere 3 cm/km (fig. 10.5). The basin, a bedrock depression known as the Everglades trough, is juxtaposed between the Atlantic coastal ridge, the Immokalee rise, and Big Cypress Swamp. Formerly, the marsh covered the entire central portion of southern Florida, from Lake Okeechobee southwestward to Florida Bay.

Some other marshes in southern Florida were hydrologically linked to

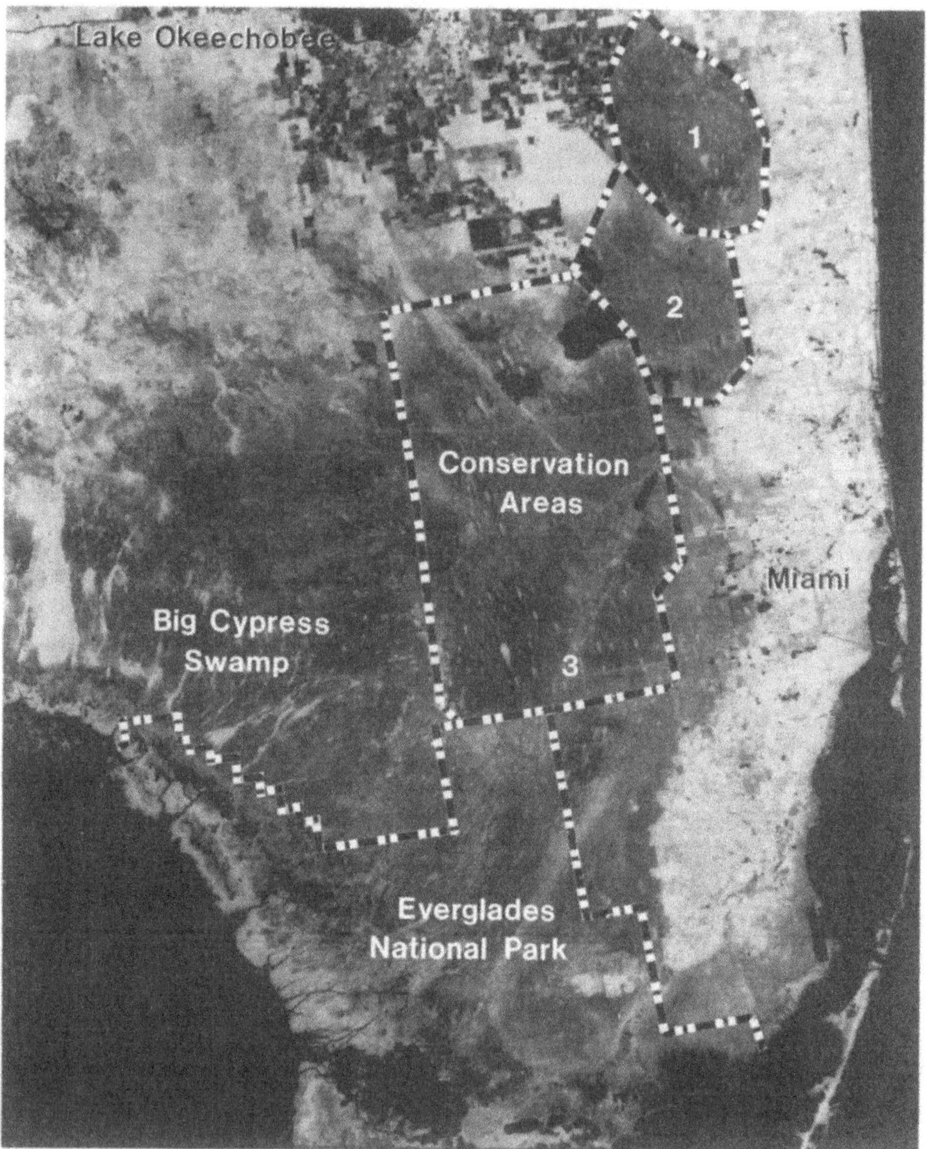

Fig. 10.5. Aerial image of southern Florida showing interior marshes of the Everglades as they exist today. Conservation Area 1 encompasses the Arthur R. Marshall Loxahatchee National Wildlife Refuge. The agricultural lands in the upper part of the Everglades basin are "muck farms," primarily sugarcane, commercial sod, and vegetable crops.

the Everglades or to Lake Okeechobee (Davis, 1943; Parker et al., 1955). For example, the Allapattah marsh, the Loxahatchee marsh and Hungryland Slough, and the Hillsborough Lakes marsh, together covering 81,000 ha, all drained into the northern Everglades. On the other hand, the southeast saline Everglades, or East Glades (Egler, 1952), and Taylor Slough drain south or southeast and are, for the most part, hydrologically independent of Everglades flow except during periods of high water. Big Cypress Swamp, situated topographically higher than the Everglades basin, contains a mosaic of various marshes and cypress swamps (Duever et al., 1986). Much of its waters historically flowed into the Everglades basin.

Physical Environment

Geology

Most of Florida is underlain by permeable sand or limestone, neither of which is particularly conducive to the formation of marshes. Where marshes do occur, one of three geological conditions is present: surficial deposits are impermeable, the water table emerges through the permeable substrate, or the marsh is hydrologically connected to a river.

Marshes perched above impermeable surficial deposits include many of the highlands and flatwoods marshes. Paynes Prairie, for example, is situated over a 2-m layer of sandy clay, which was deposited in the basin by ancient surface water flow. Many flatwoods marshes, particularly the deep, peat-filled ones, are underlain by an impermeable clay layer. Some low-lying flatwoods marshes, on the other hand, lack the clay deposit (Winchester, 1986), demonstrating the second condition: where water tables are high or overflow occurs, marshes do not require an impermeable basement deposit. The third condition holds in floodplain marshes, where the peat substrate clearly maintains both subsurface and surface connections with the river basin water table.

The southern Everglades fits into the second category: peat directly overlies permeable limestone, but the water table emerges through the limestone. In the northern Everglades, as in some other marshes, the determining factor has not been conclusively identified. A layer of marl underlies the peat, but it is uncertain whether it is responsible for the marsh's existence (Gleason et al., 1984).

Soils

The occurrence and character of the three principal soil materials of Florida marshes—peat, marl, and sand—are influenced by hydroperiod, height of flooding, and depth to the water table during the dry season.

Peat tends to accumulate in deep water marshes exhibiting long hydroperiods (over nine months in southern Florida; Duever et al., 1978) and limited recession of surface water during the dry season. The lengthy flooding maintains the anaerobic conditions conducive to peat formation and prevents oxidation because the peat typically remains somewhat damp throughout the year, even during seasonal dry periods. Completely dry peat, on the other hand, undergoes oxidation, consolidation, and compaction, which cause reduced porosity and irreversible loss of part of its water-holding capacity (Stephens and Johnson, 1951; Parker et al., 1955; Bay, 1966; Stephens, 1984).

The capacity of peat soils to retain water in the dry season is crucial to marsh development. Not only does peat hold water longer into the dry season than do other soils, but it also absorbs and retains scarce dry season rainfall (Parker et al., 1955). Such water retention maintains the high soil moisture necessary for the survival of marsh plants. Even in severe droughts, water typically is held within the root zone of the plants. Some marshes may lack surface water for many months during infrequent droughts, with no effect on soil or plant associations. However, deep, long-term drying of the soil causes changes in plant composition, productivity, and subsequent rates of peat accumulation.

Peat varies in color, structure, and acidity, depending on the source of plant material and the hydroperiod (Davis, 1946). It can range from red to brown to nearly black, from fibrous to spongy, and from neutral to acidic. Peats can be classified by their major plant components (Cohen and Spackman, 1984). For example, there are distinctive peats derived from saw grass and from water lilies.

Peat accumulation reached depths of 4 m at the south end of Lake Okeechobee. This mass of peat blocked water flow, thereby defining the lake. South of Lake Okeechobee, peat thickness ranges from 1.5 m in the upper reaches of the Everglades to 0.75 m in the lower end, and the peat layer smooths out the topographic irregularities of the basin.

In marshes with moderate hydroperiods and seasonal drying sufficient to oxidize organic matter, a marl substrate may develop. Most marl derives from precipitation of carbonates by the metabolic activities of encrusting algae, which form a "periphyton" mat on the surfaces of submerged sediments and plant stems. Occasionally, a substantial water level decline results in marl subsidence (Winchester, 1986).

A sand substrate is maintained on sites with short hydroperiods and extensive drying of the soil in the dry season. Frequent or extensive oxidation and fires preclude the accumulation of either peat or marl.

Hydrology

The marked seasonality of Florida's rainfall and evaporation plays an important role in the functioning of marsh ecosystems by creating a seasonal fluctuation in surface water (fig. 10.6). This seasonal fluctuation is most

Fig. 10.6. Mean annual fluctuation of rainfall, evaporation, and water depth in the Everglades.

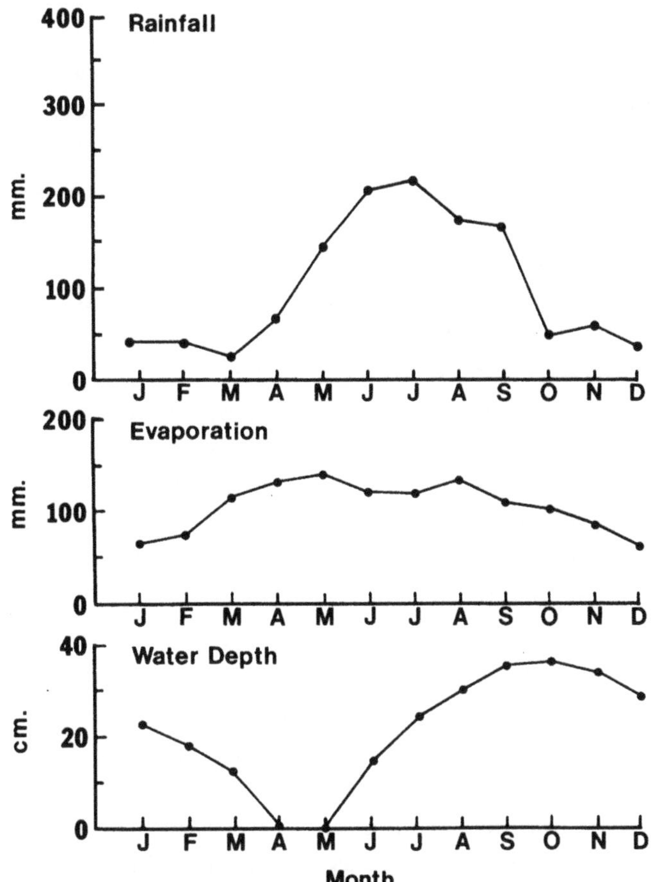

pronounced in southern Florida because it experiences less winter rainfall than occurs farther north. Water levels rise during the summer rainy season, gradually decline during the winter, and annually reach drought conditions as evapotranspiration increases in the spring. In most years, standing water is absent from southern Florida marshes at the height of the dry season, a condition that may last from a couple of weeks to several months. In northern Florida, water levels remain high through the winter and early spring because of higher winter rainfall.

Most marshes flood during each rainy season, but some may flood only in very wet years. Annual variation in rainfall may cause substantial differences in the depth and extent of flooding in various years at a single marsh site.

The timing and extent of water level fluctuations determine flooding depth, drying depth, drying rate, and hydroperiod (Duever et al., 1975; Pesnell and Brown, 1977). Various marsh plants, plant assemblages, and animals require specific ranges of these variables. In general, marshes in Florida have hydroperiods of seven to twelve months, water depths of less than 50 cm, and drying depths of less than 30 cm.

Those marshes of the highlands and flatwoods that are perched above the water table depend on local rainfall, sporadic surface runoff, and seepage from adjacent uplands for their water. In flatwoods marshes of the coastal lowlands, however, water source and water level fluctuation are linked to the water table (Winchester, 1986). These marshes tend to dry almost completely during periods of low rainfall, but the central peat zones usually retain water, and the marshes reflood rapidly as the water table rises during the wet season.

Some of the Kissimmee and St. Johns marshes are hydrologically connected to water flows in their river systems, whereas others are more isolated. Along the Kissimmee River, lower lying, river-edge marshes receive overflow water, but others are isolated in swales and obtain water from rainfall, localized runoff, and the seasonal rise in the water table. Historically, water level fluctuations averaged 1 m but may have been as great as 3.7 m during floods (Perrin et al., 1982). During the wet season the entire floodplain became inundated, while during the dry season only deeper sloughs, ponds, and the river channel retained surface water. Similar conditions prevailed in the St. Johns basin, where water accumulated in the marshes of the headwaters before flowing slowly over 20 km of marshland to Lake Helen Blazes, where the river channel itself begins.

Historically, the Everglades originated at Lake Okeechobee, which in turn received its inflow from the extensive catchment that included the entire Kissimmee basin. Outflow from the lake into the Everglades occurred intermittently in high water periods (Parker et al., 1955) but did not markedly affect the hydrology of the marsh farther south. Surface water conditions in the Everglades resulted primarily from *in situ* rainfall and extremely slow runoff from marshes immediately up-gradient (Leach et al., 1972).

Fire

Fire plays a crucial role in the ecology of Florida's marshes by limiting the invasion of woody vegetation, affecting the composition of the herbaceous community, and retarding, or occasionally reversing, peat accumulation (Alexander, 1971; Vogl, 1973a; Hofstetter, 1975; Van Arman and Goodrick, 1979; Wade et al., 1980). A sharp demarcation of plant associations in Florida marshes often indicates the boundary of a previous burn. Fires also burn dead but undecayed plant material, thereby releasing nutrients.

Fires have always been frequent occurrences in Florida's marshes. In the Everglades and elsewhere, charcoal embedded in the peat attests to a history of repeated fires (Parker, 1984). In fact, Everglades peat owes its black color to charcoal from ancient fires (Smith, 1968).

Summer, when lightning is most frequent, is the natural fire season. Thus, natural fires generally occur when soil moisture levels are high and plants are growing. Because organic soils fail to ignite when moisture content is above 65 percent (Wade et al., 1980), wet season fires are typically confined to the above-water vegetation and seldom consume the soil. All of Florida's marsh plant associations carry fire to varying degrees. In sparse stands, fire can be carried by the burning alga mat that forms on the top of the soil. Except during severe droughts, deeper water marshes serve as natural firebreaks.

Fire periodicity in most deep water marshes is about three to five years, whereas shallow water marshes burn on one- to three-year cycles, provided plant growth is sufficient to carry a fire (Wade et al., 1980).

Nutrients

The water in most Florida marshes is highly buffered because it is in contact with limestone, marl, or calcareous sand. In most cases, pH is circumneutral to slightly basic, but in some flatwoods ponds, where the groundwater is acidic, pH may be lower. Dissolved solids (especially carbonates and bicarbonates) and conductivity are generally high (Gonyea and Hunt, 1970; Flora and Rosendahl, 1982b). Oxygen concentrations are usually low (Kushlan, 1979c; Kushlan and Hunt, 1979; Perrin et al., 1982), yet decomposition can be rapid (Reeder and Davis, 1983).

Nutrients in flatwoods, highlands, and Everglades marshes are derived primarily from rainfall rather than from upland runoff or bedrock, so levels are typically low (Waller, 1975; Waller and Earle, 1975; Flora and Rosendahl, 1982a). Even given the influence of anthropogenic discharges, 78 percent of the nitrogen and 90 percent of the phosphorus entering the northern Everglades are from rainfall; 74 percent and 96 percent, respectively, of the incoming nitrogen and phosphorus are retained within the marsh (Waller, 1975). Inorganic nitrogen concentrations in Everglades waters are less than 0.1 mg/l. Phosphorus levels (Boyd and Hess, 1970) are especially low and limiting, being on the order of 0.003 to 0.005 mg/l in the water. Peat soils are typically deficient in minor elements (particularly copper, manganese, zinc, and boron), high in organic nitrogen, and low in phosphorus and potash (Forsee, 1940; Bryan, 1958). In contrast, floodplain marshes gain additional nutrients from river overflow.

Hurricanes

Hurricanes have little long-term influence on inland freshwater marshes in Florida (Craighead and Gilbert, 1962). Water depths may increase during storms, but basin overflow and runoff limit excessive levels. For example, hurricane-enhanced water levels in the Everglades in 1947, before the institution of control measures, did not exceed 0.3 m above normal high water. Freshwater marshes along the coast, on the other hand, can be adversely affected by the intrusion of saline water, especially in areas where runoff has been artificially blocked (Alexander, 1967a).

Marsh Plants

Flora

Although much of the flora of Florida is tropical (Long, 1974), many of the plants in Florida marshes (table 10.1) are from highly cosmopolitan taxa (Long and Lakela, 1971). The dominant marsh species are primarily temperate.

Although most Florida marshes are dominated by only a few species, the entire flora of a marsh may be large. For example, several Kissimmee marshes contained more than 100 species of forbs, grasses, and sedges (Tanner et al., 1982). Deep water marshes in southern Florida have more than 110 species (Long, 1984). In shallower wet-prairie sites, the species number increases to about 175 (Long, 1984). In the Paynes Prairie complex, 326 species of herbaceous and woody hydrophytes were found in a mosaic of deep water marshes, shallow wet prairies, and pasture (Easterday, 1982; Patton and Judd, 1986).

Table 10.1. Dominant plant species in marsh associations of Florida

	Marsh association[a]					
Species	WL	SB	CT	FL	SG	WP
Nymphaea odorata (white water lily)	x					
Orontium aquaticum (neverwet)	x					
Nelumbo lutea (yellow lotus)	x					
Najas guadalupensis (naiad)	x	x				
Utricularia spp. (bladderwort)	x	x		x		
Potamogeton spp. (pondweed)		x				
Typha spp. (cattail)			x			
Pontederia lanceolata (pickerelweed)				x		
Sagittaria latifolia (arrowhead)				x		
Eleocharis spp. (spikerush)				x		
Panicum hemitomon (maidencane)				x		x
Thalia geniculata (fire flag)				x		
Scirpus spp. (bulrush)			x			
Rynchospora tracyi (Tracy's beakrush)				x		x
Cladium jamaicensis (saw grass)					x	x
Muhlenbergia fillipes (muhly)						x
Spartina bakeri (cordgrass)						x
Dichromena colorata (white-topped sedge)						x
Hypericum fasciculatum (St. John's-wort)						x

a. WL = water lily marsh; SB = submersed marsh; CT = cattail marsh; FL = flag marsh; SG = saw grass marsh; WP = wet prairie.

Major Associations

Throughout Florida, freshwater marshes support a similar set of plant associations (table 10.1). Each association occurs under a particular range of environmental conditions defined by the hydrologic regime, fire frequency, and soils (table 10.2). Of these factors, hydroperiod (the percentage of time a marsh is flooded) and timing of drying are the most important.

The abilities of various species to become established and persist under specific environmental conditions determine the composition of the plant community at a specific site. The establishment phase is critical, as most species cannot germinate under water. Thus, the timing and length of the dry season relative to the types of seeds available in the substrate determine which species gain a foothold. Once established, individuals may persist under conditions that might otherwise be unsuitable for germination. Their subsequent spread is primarily vegetative.

Plant associations vary markedly along hydrological gradients, but species tolerances to inundation overlap broadly. For example, in the marshes of the upper St. Johns River, both maidencane and saw grass grow where the hydroperiod exceeds 290 days (Lowe, 1983). Other flood tolerances include white water lily, 90–100 percent inundation; naiad, 95–100 percent; arrowhead, 85–95 percent; pickerelweed, 70–95 percent; spikerush, 70–90 percent; and white-topped sedge, 10–65 percent. The importance of water level fluctuation and hydroperiod are apparent from the changes in plant distribution that have been brought about by water level stabilization (Ager and Kerce, 1970, 1974; McPherson, 1973b; Goodrick and Milleson, 1974).

Six major categories of freshwater marsh are recognized in Florida:

Table 10.2. Important environmental characteristics of marsh associations in Florida

Marsh association	Hydroperiod[a]	Fire frequency[b]	Organic matter accumulation[c]
Water lily	Long	Low	High
Submersed	Long	Low	High
Cattail	Moderate	Moderate	High
Flag	Moderate	Moderate	Moderate to high
Saw grass	Moderate	Moderate	Moderate to high
Wet prairie	Short	High	Low

a. Short = < 6 months flooding; moderate = 6 to 9 months; long = > 9 months.

b. Low = < once per decade; moderate = about once per decade; high = > once per decade.

c. Low = a few centimeters to nonexistent; moderate = usually < 1 meter deep; high = usually > 1 meter deep.

water lily marsh, submersed marsh, cattail marsh, flag marsh, saw grass marsh, and wet prairie. Each is characterized by a distinct assemblage of dominant plant species (table 10.1).

Water Lily Marsh

Water lily marsh is dominated by floating-leaf plants including white water lily, neverwet, and yellow lotus (fig. 10.7). These marshes generally occur in the deepest water, where emergent plants cannot thrive. They are usually rooted in poorly decomposed plant material, which seldom dries out completely.

Submersed Marsh

Submersed marsh occurs in deep water where emergent plants are thinly distributed. The more important species are naiad, pondweed, and bladderwort. In the Everglades, water hyssop (*Bacopa caroliniana* and *B. monnieri*), primrose willow (*Ludwigia repens*), spikerush (*Eleocharis elongata*), *Chara*, and string lily (*Crinum americanum*) are also characteristic.

Cattail Marsh

Cattail marsh is found in relatively deep, nutrient-rich water, usually on deep soils (fig. 10.8). It is not generally dominant over large areas but forms

Fig. 10.7. Water lily marsh along the shore of Lake Jackson, Leon County. Dominants are water lotus, white water lily, and maidencane. Photo by R. Myers.

Fig. 10.8. Cattail marsh at the transition between freshwater saw grass marsh and salt marsh, Collier County. The abundance of cattail may be the result of freshwater damming by U.S. 41 (Tamiami Trail). Photo by R. Myers.

nearly monospecific stands in some places, particularly those that are disturbed.

Flag Marsh

Flag marshes are named after pickerelweed, fire flag, arrowhead, and other species with flag-like leaves. These are diverse associations and may be dominated not only by flag species but also by maidencane, spikerush, beakrush, or bulrush. Flag marshes occur where the wet season water depth is between 0.3 and 1 m and the hydroperiod extends more than 200 days per year. They require seasonal drying; under prolonged inundation plants uproot and die.

Pickerelweed- and maidencane-dominated marshes are the most widespread types of flag marsh (fig. 10.9). Of these two, pickerelweed is more dependent on continually wet conditions. Beakrush and maidencane, at the other extreme, cannot tolerate long-term flooding. Both types disappear from marshes in which the seasonal drawdown has been eliminated, as occurred in parts of the northern Everglades in the 1970s. Spikerush can tolerate both flooding and drying, and thus is less affected by changes in hydrological conditions.

Fig. 10.9. Maidencane marsh flanking Myakka River in Myakka River State Park, Sarasota County. Photo by Allan Horton.

Saw Grass Marsh

Saw grass marsh is widespread in Florida and is the predominant association in the Everglades, where it once covered over 800,000 ha; it still accounts for 70 percent of the remaining Everglades landscape (Loveless, 1959a; Stephens, 1984) (fig. 10.10). The nearly total dominance of this species over such a large area is one of the distinguishing features of the Everglades.

Saw grass marsh is impressive. The plants may exceed 3 m in height and form an impenetrable mass. Two categories of saw grass marsh are recognizable: dense and sparse. The dense type occurs on higher ground and is underlain by deep organic soils. Although it appears monospecific, dense saw grass marsh includes other tall emergents such as cattail, ferns, and small shrubs. The transition between dense saw grass and adjacent marsh communities is often sharply defined, probably owing to fire effects. Where flooding conditions increase, flag marsh or water lily marsh replaces saw grass marsh. Under prolonged dry conditions, woody vegetation becomes more prevalent. Where nutrients are elevated, cattail tends to invade and may eventually displace saw grass.

Sparse saw grass, which usually occurs at lower elevations than the dense saw grass, occupies similar sites to those of flag marsh and thus may include spikerush, arrowhead, and maidencane. The substrate under sparse saw grass marsh is shallow peat or marl.

Periphyton is a typical component of these sparse stands of saw grass and of similar marshland environments with alkaline water (fig. 10.11). It consists of an algal mat composed mostly of filamentous blue-green algae (Swift, 1981), but its composition varies with ionic and nutrient concentrations and with hydroperiod (Van Meter-Kasanof, 1973; Swift, 1981).

Periphyton becomes attached to submerged surfaces, such as sediment and plant stems, and its development is enhanced in sparse communities because light penetrates into the water. In deeper-water marshes, it often

Fig. 10.10. Saw grass marsh with elongated tree islands that lie parallel to the direction of water flow, Shark Valley, Everglades National Park. Photo by J. Snyder.

Fig. 10.11. Sparse saw grass marsh with periphyton, Shark Valley, Everglades National Park. Photo by R. Myers.

attaches to the floating purple bladderwort (*Utricularia purpurea*) and thereby covers much of the water surface.

Wet Prairie

Wet prairies are the least frequently flooded of any Florida marsh type. Their short hydroperiods (50–150 days per year) preclude peat development. In southern Florida, the substrate is a periphyton-derived marl, but the acid substrates of shallow flatwoods marshes and wet savannas of the Florida Panhandle also support wet prairie vegetation. Species composition varies greatly depending on hydroperiod, soils, and site history. Because of their short hydroperiods, wet prairies are the most species-rich of Florida's marshes and include a variety of grasses, sedges, and flowering forbs (fig. 10.12). Dominants include maidencane, cordgrass, beakrush, or muhly. Saw grass may be present, but it is sparsely distributed and of shorter stature than in saw grass–dominated marshes.

Wet prairie species have considerable tolerance to both flooding and drying. Many shallowly rooted species typical of the wet prairies associated with coastal flatwoods (like St. John's-wort) are killed by drying but reseed readily. As a result, their zone of dominance migrates up- and downslope in response to changing water conditions (B. H. Winchester, personal communication). Higher wet prairies may, under some conditions, be invaded by saw palmetto (*Serenoa repens*).

Geographic Differences among Plant Associations

Although the six major marsh plant associations occur throughout the state, their extent differs within and among Florida's major marsh systems (table 10.3).

Large highland marshes, such as Paynes Prairie, typically include a mosaic of saw grass marshes; water lily marshes; and arrowhead, beakrush, and maidencane flag marshes (White, 1975; Easterday, 1982; Patton and Judd, 1986). Water lily marshes of Paynes Prairie are dominated by white water lily, banana water lily (*Nymphaea mexicana*), fanwort (*Cabomba caroliniana*), bladderwort (*Utricularia foliosa*), naiad, and water pennywort (*Hydrocotyle ranunculoides*). Floating mats of water hyacinth (*Eichhornia crassipes*), pickerelweed, and pennywort also develop in stabilized deep water, particularly in the canals, but also in waters having high nutrient content (Morris, 1974) (fig. 10.13). Saw grass and pickerelweed marshes occupy the middle ground, while maidencane marshes, intermixed with southern cut-

Fig. 10.12. Shallow flatwoods marsh supporting wet prairie vegetation, Lake Kissimmee State Park, Polk County. Photo by R. Myers.

grass (*Leersia hexandra*) and rush (*Juncus acuminatus*, *J. effusus*), dominate higher ground.

Flatwoods marshes typically consist of concentric rings of marsh associations defined by hydroperiod and water depth. Maximum depth usually occurs in the center; thus water lily marshes or flag marshes occupy this zone. Arrowhead flag marshes are most common, but in some cases the central zone is open water, creating what is known as a flatwoods pond. In a number of places, pickerelweed, maidencane, redroot (*Lachnanthes caroliniana*), cordgrass, or saw grass predominates. The abundance of pickerelweed relative to arrowhead frequently depends on the severity of the drought period. Arrowhead, because of its greater drought tolerance, is the usual dominant. Over time, peat accumulation may elevate the central portion of the marsh above peripheral plant zones.

The intermediate zones of flatwoods marshes are generally dominated by Tracy's beakrush or maidencane marsh. Maidencane marshes on sandy substrates typically have a *Sphagnum* moss mat. In many of the coastal flatwoods, however, there is a dense mat of periphyton (B. H. Winchester, personal communication).

The upper zone, which completely dries out each year, supports wet prairie associations. Species composition is particularly variable from one place to the next. It may be dominated by St. Johns wort, blue maidencane

Table 10.3. Predominant plant associations in the marsh systems of Florida

Marsh	Predominant marsh association
Highlands marshes	Water lily marsh
	Arrowhead flag marsh
	Beakrush flag marsh
	Maidencane flag marsh
	Dense saw grass marsh
Flatwoods marshes	Beakrush marsh
	Maidencane marsh
	Wet prairie
The St. Johns marshes	Dense saw grass marsh
	Maidencane flag marsh
	Pickerelweed flag marsh
The Kissimmee marshes	Pickerelweed flag marsh
	Maidencane flag marsh
	Beakrush marsh
The Everglades	Dense saw grass marsh
	Sparse saw grass marsh
	Spikerush flag marsh
	Beakrush flag marsh
	White water lily marsh
	Wet prairie

Fig. 10.13. Water hyacinth, a troublesome exotic, clogs drainageway of Rainey Slough, Glades County. Photo by M. McMillian.

(*Amphicarpum muhlenbergianum*), cutthroat grass (*Panicum abscissum*), or yellow-eyed grass (*Xyris* spp.). The St. John's-wort marsh is particularly characteristic of southeast peninsular flatwoods in Sarasota County (Winchester et al., 1985).

Flatwoods marshes often abruptly terminate in a border of saw palmetto, buttonbush (*Cephalanthus occidentalis*), willow (*Salix caroliniana*), pop ash (*Fraxinus caroliniana*), gallberry (*Ilex glabra*), fetterbush (*Lyonia lucida*), slash pine (*Pinus elliottii*), or dry prairie.

At one time the marshes of the upper St. Johns basin were similar to the Everglades (Sincock, 1959; Lowe, 1983, 1986). White water lily marsh predominated in deeper areas, but saw grass marshes covered extensive areas. Maidencane marshes have expanded at the expense of saw grass marshes following deep-burning fires. They now cover 37 percent of the headwater wetlands (Lowe, 1983). Pickerelweed flag marshes are common in places, while flag marshes of water hemp (*Amaranthus australis*), moonflower (*Ipomoea alba*), dog fennel (*Eupatorium capillifolium*), arrow arum (*Peltandra virginica*), string lily, and redroot also occur.

The marsh associations of the Kissimmee basin are particularly complex (Goodrick and Milleson, 1974; Milleson et al., 1980; Perrin et al., 1982; Pierce et al., 1982). The most widespread are pickerelweed flag marshes (Tanner et al., 1982). Associated species include arrowhead, maidencane, torpedo grass (*Panicum repens*), smartweed (*Polygonum* spp.), primrose, pennywort, horsehair sedge (*Eleocharis equisetoides*), Tracy's beakrush, southern cutgrass, and several woody plants, such as swamp hibiscus (*Hibiscus grandiflorus*) and buttonbush.

Maidencane flag marshes dominate large areas where sandy substrates occur. Maidencane makes up 50 percent to 60 percent of the biomass in some of these marshes (Van Arman and Goodrick, 1979). Associated with it are pickerelweed, arrowhead, pennywort, beakrush (*Rhynchospora inundata*), and smartweed. Beakrush flag marshes replace maidencane marshes as higher ground is approached. Both associations contain much the same complement of species, differing only in their relative abundances.

Saw grass marshes occur in a few locations in the Kissimmee basin, primarily as patches within maidencane and beakrush marshes. Maidenhair sedge (*Eleocharis vivipara*), blue maidencane, and shrubs such as buttonbush and hibiscus are associates.

Some sites support marsh associations not distinguished by any consistent dominants but rather by a mixture of torpedo grass, maidencane, broomsedges (*Andropogon* spp.), water grass (*Hydrochloa caroliniensis*), southern cutgrass, and false maidencane (*Sacciolepis striata*).

The Everglades are predominantly saw grass and flag marshes. As elsewhere, inundation patterns determine species distribution. Deeply flooded areas support water lily marshes, whereas in slightly shallower zones, beakrush marsh and spikerush marsh predominate (Loveless, 1959b; Goodrick, 1984). Redroot and yellow-eyed grasses are common in the Loxahatchee Wildlife Refuge but are rarely found farther south. Flag marshes often support periphyton mats that cover floating bladderwort. Saw grass marshes, of course, are the characteristic association of the Everglades. Sparse saw grass occurs throughout the southern part, especially along the periphery, while dense saw grass covers much of the core. In some places, standing stocks exceed 28,000 kg/ha (Hofstetter, 1976). A common pattern in the Everglades is strand and slough physiography—saw grass marshes alternating with flag or water lily marshes (fig. 10.10).

In the Everglades, wet prairies are primarily oriented laterally to the main drainage (Gleason and Spackman, 1974). Interspersed among vast expanses of these wet prairies are deeper-water marshes and unflooded rises. The most prominent species in Everglades wet prairies are muhly, foxtail grass (*Setaria corrugata*), black rush (*Schoenus nigricans*), plume grass (*Erianthus giganteus*), love grass (*Eragrostis* spp.), and white-topped sedge.

Adaptations of Marsh Plants

As mentioned, marshes are characterized by three key environmental factors: rainfall, evaporation, and water level. The timing and extent of water level fluctuations influence the colonization and survival of marsh plants by creating extremes either of submergence and waterlogged substrates or of drought conditions conducive to fire. Additional adaptive challenges are presented by such factors as periodic freezes and water chemistry.

Flooding

Living in a flooded environment requires special adaptations. Inundation results in saturated substrates and, if prolonged, an anaerobic environment. To counteract anaerobiosis and the attendant presence of toxic chemicals, some marsh plants possess internal air channels that facilitate oxygenation of their roots. Oxygen leaks from these channels, forming an aerobic microlayer around the roots.

Most marsh plants can neither germinate nor survive as seedlings under water (Teskey and Hinckley, 1977; Pesnell and Brown, 1977; van der Valk, 1981); thus, most propagate vegetatively. Even dominants such as saw grass seldom sprout from seed (Alexander, 1971). Germination and establishment are rare events, and many marsh species rely on seed stored in persistent seed banks in the marsh substrate. The seeds germinate when the marsh is dry. Interestingly, few of the long-lived dominants in marshes form large, persistent seed banks.

Besides being the period for germination, the dry season serves to release the bulk of nutrients tied up in the vegetation and detritus. As water levels recede, leaves and stems fall over, die, and decay. The nutrient release, coupled with aerobic soil conditions, initiates a burst of aerial vegetative growth. Upon reflooding, decaying plant material becomes available to the marsh food chains. Thus seasonal drying is essential to maintaining energy and nutrient flows.

Excessive drying of the marsh substrate during drought also limits plant growth. Root systems of most marsh plants are shallow, mostly within the upper 15 cm of soil, and few roots extend below 50 cm (Duever et al., 1986).

Because of their relatively short hydroperiods, flatwoods marshes experience marked seasonal variation. One outcome is seasonal dominance by different species. For example, in maidencane flag marshes, maidencane and floating heart (*Nymphoides aquatica*) are dominant in spring, but beakrush and bald rush (*Psilocarya nitens*) become more apparent as the dry season progresses (Winchester et al., 1985). Similarly, flowering phenology is related to seasonal hydrology (Abrahamson et al., 1984). The species of shorter stature bloom in early spring before water levels rise, whereas the taller emergent species flower in summer and fall.

Fire

Plants in Florida marshes are also adapted to recurring fires. Most marsh plants—including long hydroperiod species, such as saw grass, pickerelweed, arrowhead, and maindencane—regrow quickly following fire, their growth enhanced by the release of bound-up nutrients and reduced competition for space (Loveless, 1959b; Forthman, 1973; Goodrick and Milleson, 1974; Wade et al., 1980). Fire is at least partly responsible for the mosaic of marsh associations and for the sharp demarcations between them (Craighead, 1971; Lowe, 1986). Fire's impact depends on how fast and how deeply the organic soil burns and how slowly the water rises after the fire.

Saw grass is particularly suited for surviving fire (Wade et al., 1980). Its growing bud is buried in the soil and surrounded by overlapping leaves that insulate it from fire. Saw grass leaves are highly flammable and can support fire even when standing water is present. Saw grass responds quickly after a fire, reaching a height of as much as 20 to 40 cm in two weeks (Forthman, 1973). The rapid regrowth permits saw grass to outpace rising water levels. If complete submergence occurs, however, the resprouting stem is killed. If large areas are affected in this way, saw grass may be eliminated from the site. Saw grass declines when there is extended flooding coupled with a lack of fire; this decline is reversed by drying and burning.

Flag marsh species also respond rapidly after fire. Significant regrowth of maidencane occurs within one month after fire (Loveless, 1959b; Vogl, 1973a), and within six months little evidence of fire remains (Van Arman and Goodrick, 1979). Fire influences the competitive relationship between saw grass and maidencane; the latter frequently invades marshes after fires severe enough to kill saw grass. Saw grass, however, eventually reinvades (Lowe, 1983, 1986).

Fires limit peat build-up and prevent invasion of trees and shrubs into marshes (Craighead, 1971). In the absence of fire, invasion by wax myrtle (*Myrica cerifera*), willow, buttonbush, and nonnative woody species such as Brazilian pepper (*Schinus terebinthifolius*), Australian pine (*Casuarina* spp.), and melaleuca (*Melaleuca quinquenervia*) occurs rapidly if seed sources are nearby and water levels are conducive to establishment (fig. 10.14). The spread of melaleuca, an Australian native, is also enhanced by fires, which open serotinous seed capsules (see Myers, 1983, 1984, and Ewel, 1986, for assessments of melaleuca's invasibility in south Florida marshes).

Nutrients

Most plant species in Florida marshes have low nutrient requirements and tend to accumulate available nutrients (Steward and Ornes, 1975). The ability of saw grass to sequester nutrients beyond its immediate needs may account for its competitive advantage over other species in nutrient-poor Florida marshes. Although marsh systems have considerable assimilative capability (Sloey et al., 1978), this capacity may not be unlimited. Increased nutrient loading in streams entering many marshes may have affected species composition. For example, high nutrient loads have been responsible for an increase in cattail along canals and perhaps elsewhere.

Fig. 10.14. Melaleuca, an aggressive exotic pest plant from Australia, scattered in a wet prairie/dwarf cypress landscape, Big Cypress National Preserve. Melaleuca is a serious threat to the marshes and wet prairies of southern Florida. Frost limits its northerly advance. Photo by R. Myers.

Periphyton growth is limited by low nutrient concentrations in the marsh and altered by changing nutrient loads. Periphytic blue-green algae can fix nitrogen and may be important sources of this nutrient in Florida marshes.

Temperature

Seasonal variation in temperature has important effects on Florida marshes, though the presence of surface water during the coldest months of the year tends to offset the effect of drastic temperature changes to some extent. Frost, however, determines the northward spread of tropical species. A notable example is pond apple (*Annona glabra*), which finds its northern limit on the marshy fringes of islands in Lake Istokpoga.

Above-ground stems of water lilies, maidencane, pickerelweed, and other more northerly ranging species die back in winter and resprout from roots or tubers in spring (Milleson, 1976). Saw grass, on the other hand, is one of the most cold-tolerant of Florida's marsh species (Steward, 1974). Cold-death of leaves is limited, and above-ground biomass shows no seasonality.

Plant growth in Florida's more northerly marshes, such as Paynes Prairie, varies markedly with season (White, 1975). Standing crop is greatest in July and August. In late fall and winter, above-ground portions of many plants (including pickerelweed, arrowhead, cattail, water lily, spadderdock, and maidencane) die, creating great rafts of recumbent leaves in late winter.

Succession

The extant wetland communities in Florida have existed in their present form for only a few thousand years (Long, 1984), and there is clear evidence for large-scale primary succession within this period. Some highland marshes represent late successional stages in the filling of solution basins by endogenous peat and allochthonous sediment. Marl and older peats underlying surficial peat layers indicate that Lake Okeechobee and the Everglades basin have filled by successional processes. In some cases, shallow marshes can be completely replaced by woody thickets within five to ten years. In the Everglades, peat derived from tree islands overlies peat derived from marsh vegetation, demonstrating that tree islands have developed on former deepwater marsh sites (Stone, 1978). In many places, it is clear that present-day emergent marshes have succeeded from deeper water associations.

Relatively frequent fires coupled with fluctuating water levels maintain the integrity of Florida marshes. For example, Winchester (1986) found no major change in the zonal configurations of flatwoods marshes over forty years. The importance of fire frequency and water level in arresting succession is demonstrated by the rapid change that occurs when these factors are altered. Succession occurs quickly when water levels are raised or stabilized or when lowered (McPherson, 1973b; Alexander and Crook, 1984; Pierce et al., 1982; Lowe, 1983; Lowe et al., 1984). The vegetation history of Paynes Prairie demonstrates that successional processes are reversible, given changes in the hydrology and fire regime.

Marsh Animals

Fauna

Aquatic animal populations are among the great glories of Florida's marshes and are in fact the stated reason Congress established Everglades National Park. Although abundant, this animal life, with the exception of birds, is not diverse. The aquatic invertebrates, fishes, reptiles, amphibians, and mammals are derived from temperate North America, and their diversity decreases southward down the peninsula. In contrast, the bird fauna is enhanced by species derived from both North America and tropical sources, especially waterbirds (Robertson and Kushlan, 1984).

Invertebrates

Small invertebrates serve as important components of marsh food chains. Amphipods are extremely abundant where they are secure from predation, especially within periphyton, naiad, bladderwort, or water grass. Dragonflies and mayflies are diverse and abundant in marshes throughout Florida. Fly larvae are also common and locally abundant. These include the infamous mosquitoes and gnats as well as the larger deerflies and horseflies. Many species of water bugs and water beetles are widely distributed. When fish numbers decrease after dry periods, ostracods may become abundant. Leeches are not common in Florida marshes but do occur locally, especially on turtles and alligators.

Macroinvertebrates figure importantly in food chains. Among the most conspicuous in many marshes are prawns, crayfish (*Procambarus alleni* in the south and *P. fallax* in the north), and snails such as the apple snail (*Pomacea paludosus*) (Kushlan, 1975; Kushlan and Kushlan, 1979). Prawns abound in submersed marshes where they are sheltered by aquatic plants such as naiad and water grass (Kushlan and Kushlan, 1980b).

Fishes

The fish fauna of Florida marshes is depauperate, especially toward the southern end of the peninsula. Nearly all fish species are derived from temperate North America, with the exception of a few species in the Everglades (e.g., *Rivulus* spp.) that have affinities with the West Indies (Loftus and Kushlan, 1987). In some places, particularly the lower Everglades, the fish fauna is augmented by marine and estuarine species that are able to penetrate inland because of the chemically hard water (Odum, 1953).

Most of the fish found in Florida marshes are small, minnow-sized species, typically the livebearing mosquitofish (*Gambusia affinis*) and least killifish (*Heterandria formosa*), along with the cyprinodonts: flagfish (*Jordanella floridae*), golden topminnow (*Fundulus chrysotus*), seminole killifish (*F. seminolis*), and bluefin killifish (*Lucania goodei*). Also abundant are small sunfishes, such as pygmy sunfish (*Elassoma spp.*), bluespotted sunfish (*Enneacanthus gloriosus*), and dollar sunfish (*Lepomis marginatus*). Smaller individuals of larger species, such as warmouth (*L. gulosus*) and redear sunfish (*L. microlophus*), may be found in fluctuating marshes.

Dominance of small fishes arises from differential mortality during drying periods, when the smaller species are at an advantage (Kushlan, 1974a). Thus the size and relative abundances of species vary seasonally. One study found that small fishes—especially mosquitofish and least killifish—as well as prawns and crayfish, increased rapidly during the first six months following reflooding of a previously drained marsh (Milleson, 1976). In floodplain marshes, alternating water levels produce an explosive expansion of fish production as water levels rise (Perrin et al., 1982).

If water levels become stabilized, larger fish survive and assume dominance (Kushlan, 1980). These larger species, such as Florida gar (*Lepisosteus platyrhincus*), bullhead catfish (*Ictalurus natalis* and *I. nebulosus*), bowfin (*Amia calva*) and pirate perch (*Aphredoderus sayanus*), occur in deep marshes, ponds, and rivers and lakes adjacent to marshes. At one time, the St. Johns River supported a large freshwater fishery that was probably based on marsh productivity (Cox et al., 1976). Decreases in river fish populations followed by decline of the fisheries occurred in both the St. Johns and Kissimmee rivers after they were channelized (Perrin et al., 1982).

The fishes of the Everglades are the most studied in Florida (Kushlan and Lodge, 1974; Dineen, 1984; Kushlan, 1976a, 1980; Loftus and Kushlan, 1987). The fish community is dominated by mosquitofish, which can compose 60 percent of a sample, followed by other livebearers and killifishes, such as golden topminnow, bluefin killifish, and seminole killifish. Under typical fluctuating conditions, sunfishes are rare and small, except near canals and ponds.

Fishes of the Kissimmee marshes are also numerically dominated by mosquitofish, but Florida gar accounts for the greatest biomass (Perrin et al., 1982). Other common components are the least killifish, bluefin killifish, sailfin molly (*Poecilia latipinna*), bluegill (*Lepomis macrochirus*), flagfish, and redear sunfish. Game species, including crappie (*Pomoxis nigromaculatus*), largemouth bass (*Micropterus salmoides*), and channel catfish (*Ictalurus punctatus*), are common in the river but not in the marsh.

Nonnative fish species have spread via canals throughout the state (Courtenay and Robins, 1973). By the mid-1970s the exotic walking catfish (*Clarias batrachus*) was present throughout the southern Florida canal system and had invaded the Kissimmee marshes (Courtenay, 1978; Perrin et al., 1982). As of the mid-1980s, nonnative species had not become a problem in the fish communities of undisturbed parts of the Everglades, though a substantial threat exists, especially from the blue tilapia (*Tilapia niloticus*) (Kushlan, 1986b).

Amphibians and Reptiles

Amphibians characteristic of deeper Florida marshes include the leopard frog (*Rana sphenocephala*), pig frog (*Rana grylio*), bullfrog (*Rana catesbeiana*), green tree frog (*Hyla cinerea*), fire-bellied newt (*Notophthalamus viridescens*), and dwarf newt (*Pseudobranchus striatus*). Water snakes, abundant in some Florida marshes, include the green water snake (*Nerodia cyclopion*), swamp snake (*Seminatrix pygaea*), cottonmouth (*Agkistrodon piscivorus*), and mud snake (*Farancia abacura*). Turtles of the deeper marshes include the mud turtle (*Kinosternon bauri* and *K. subrubrum*), musk turtle (*Sternotherus odoratus*), Florida cooter (*Chrysemys floridana*) in the north, and the red-bellied turtle (*C. nelsoni*) in the south.

Shallower marshes and wet prairies support more species of amphibians and reptiles. These include the little grass frog (*Limnaoedus ocularis*), narrow-mouthed toad (*Gastrophryne carolinensis*), leopard frog, pygmy rattlesnake (*Sistrurus miliarius*), and chicken turtle (*Deirochelys reticularia*).

The American alligator (*Alligator mississippiensis*) (fig. 10.15) assumes a dominant ecological position in many of Florida's marshes because of the "gator holes" it creates and maintains. These ponds supply dry season habitat for other aquatic organisms (Kushlan, 1974b) and serve as staging areas for recolonization of the marshlands when floodwaters return. Alligator populations throughout the state were depressed by hunting, and for a period during the 1960s the species was threatened with extinction. With protection, populations have rebounded to the point where, in some places, alligators are becoming a nuisance. Management of these large reptiles, including the reinstitution of hunting, is a matter of concern in wildlife conservation (Hines and Woodward, 1980; Jacobsen and Kushlan, 1986).

Mammals

Mammals are not as abundant in Florida marshes as they are elsewhere in North America. The Florida water rat (*Neofiber alleni*) is found throughout the state, replacing the larger muskrat (*Ondatra zibethica*), which is a dominant influence in many North American marshes. The white-tailed deer (*Odocoileus virginianus*) inhabits shallow marshes throughout Florida and is surprisingly well adapted to wetland conditions. Deer in the Everglades are distinguished from populations elsewhere by their small size and aquatic habits (Loveless, 1959a). It has recently been found that the endangered

Fig. 10.15. Alligator in an artificial "gator hole" at the mouth of a culvert, Shark Valley Loop Road, Everglades National Park. Photo by R. Myers.

Florida panther (*Felis concolor coryi*) uses marshland extensively (C. Belden, personal communication).

Birds

Waterbirds that are particularly dependent on freshwater marsh habitat include the least bittern (*Ixobrychus exilis*), American bittern (*Botaurus lentiginosus*), green-backed heron (*Butorides striatus*), white ibis (*Eudocimus albus*), glossy ibis (*Plegadis falcinellus*), limpkin (*Aramus guarauna*), rails (such as the king rail, *Rallus elegans*), marsh wren (*Cistothorus palustris*), common yellowthroat (*Geothlypis trichas*), red-winged blackbird (*Agelaius phoeniceus*), and boat-tailed grackle (*Quiscalus major*). A few species characteristic of Florida marshes are now considered to be rare or endangered. The original distribution of the snail kite (*Rostrahamus sociabilis*) was coincident with that of Florida's marshes (fig. 10.16; cf. fig. 10.1d) (Sykes, 1979, 1983a,b, 1984; Kushlan and Bass, 1983b). Its historic habitat included the Everglades, the marshes surrounding Lake Okeechobee and Lake Istokpoga, those along the Kissimmee and St. Johns rivers, and numerous smaller marshes. At present, the kite population is in most years limited to stabilized, deeply flooded marshes of the Everglades Conservation Areas (fig. 10.5). The Cape Sable seaside sparrow (*Ammodramus maritimus mirabilis*) occurs in muhly-dominated wet prairies bordering the southern Everglades (Kushlan and Bass, 1983a). Resident and wintering sandhill cranes (*Grus canadensis*) (fig. 10.17) are found primarily in the marshes of north and central Florida but range into the southern marshes in limited numbers (Williams and Phillips, 1972; Walkinshaw, 1976; Kushlan, 1982).

Wading birds, including the endangered wood stork (*Mycteria americana*) and a variety of herons, egrets, and ibis, depend on freshwater marshes, particularly those of southern Florida (Kushlan, 1973, 1976b, 1978; Kushlan and White, 1977). Resident species often nest in swamp forest vegetation and forage in nearby marshes. Mixed species colonies, usually dominated by white ibis, have exceeded 35,000 birds. Other birds that nest over much of the eastern United States use Florida's freshwater marshes in winter, when they number in the tens of thousands. For example, more than 14,000 birds were counted in the eastern Everglades each year during the mid-1970s.

The number and variety of nesting waterfowl are limited in Florida marshes. Wintering waterfowl are also not abundant (relative to sites farther north), as most of them frequent estuarine areas (Chamberlain, 1960; Goodwin, 1979; Kushlan et al., 1982; Perrin et al., 1982; Johnson and Montalbano, 1984). Mottled ducks (*Anas fulvigula*) are among the most common, and fulvous whistling duck (*Dendrocygna bicolor*) populations are increasing in the state's interior marshes. Canvasback ducks (*Aythya valsineria*) were once common winter residents of the marshes that existed

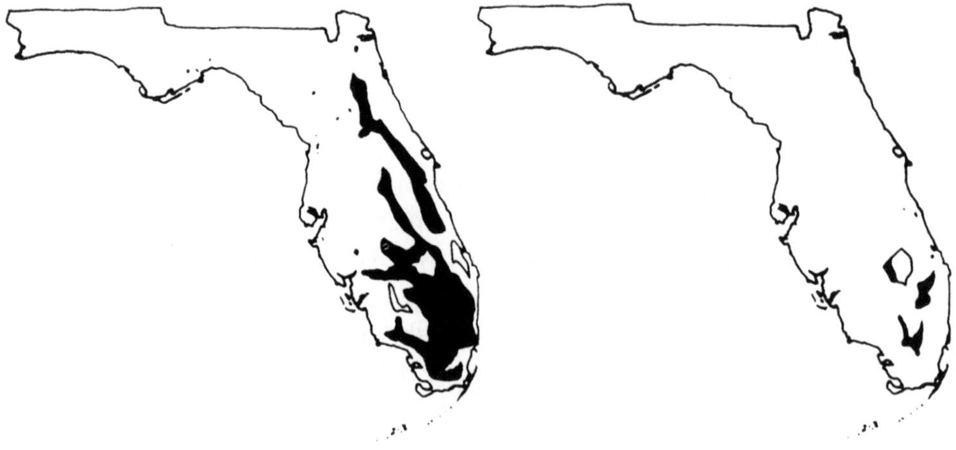

Fig. 10.16. Historic (*left*) and present (*right*) ranges of the snail kite in Florida. After Sykes, 1984.

Fig. 10.17. Nesting sandhill crane. Photo by J. N. Layne.

along the Kissimmee River, and the river floodplain was historically a major waterfowl corridor (Belrose, 1976). The most common duck overwintering in freshwater marsh habitats is the ring-necked (*Aythya collaris*). It is found throughout the state, especially in the peripheral marshes of Lake Okeechobee, along the St. Johns River, and in the deep water areas of the Everglades. Coots (*Fulica americana*) still winter in large numbers throughout Florida's fresh waters.

The diversity of other bird groups is limited by seasonal high waters.

Nesting species in the Everglades include the red-winged blackbird, common yellowthroat, boat-tailed grackle, cardinal (*Cardinalis cardinalis*), Carolina wren, king rail, purple gallinule, and red-shouldered hawk (*Buteo lineatus*); their density averages about 96 birds per km^2 (Kushlan and Kushlan, 1978). In winter, bird density increases to about 380 individuals per km^2 and includes such migrants as the eastern phoebe (*Sayornis phoebe*), belted kingfisher (*Ceryle alcyon*), palm warbler (*Dendroica palmarum*), yellow-rumped warbler (*Dendroica coronata*), and marsh wren (Kushlan and Kushlan, 1977).

Adaptations of Marsh Animals

Like the plants, animals living in marshes possess specific adaptations for surviving periodic fires and seasonal fluctuations in water levels, dissolved oxygen, and temperature (Kushlan, 1990a). An example of a bird adapted to Florida's fluctuating marshes is the snail kite (Sykes, 1983b; Kushlan, 1975; Kushlan and Bass, 1983b; Beissinger and Takekawa, 1983). These birds are nomadic, concentrating in marshes where water levels have been relatively high because their primary food, the apple snail (*Pomacea paludosus*), requires prolonged flooding. In drought, the birds are forced to use the small, widely scattered patches of marsh that remain. Historically the kites roamed throughout the state to find such patches of suitable marshes. As the density and abundance of these patches have declined through drainage, so have the kite populations.

The Cape Sable seaside sparrow requires not only specific water levels but also a predictable fire regime (Werner and Woolfenden, 1983). Marshes that burn on a five- to seven-year cycle provide optimum habitat; sparrow populations decline rapidly with longer fire-free periods.

Alligators are closely attuned to hydrological fluctuations and position their nest sites relative to water depths (Kushlan and Jacobsen, 1990).

Mammals also have specific adaptations to fluctuating water levels. Water rats move between higher and lower marshes as water levels fluctuate, and they burrow when water levels fall below the ground (Tilmant, 1975). To forage, deer wade or even swim through water that can be shoulder-deep.

The accommodations that marsh-dwelling animals make in response to hydrological fluctuations in southern Florida (Kahl, 1964; Kolipinski and Higer, 1969; Kushlan, 1974a,b, 1975, 1976a, 1977, 1979b, 1986d, 1990b; Kushlan et al., 1975; Kushlan and Kushlan, 1979, 1980b) appear to be generally applicable throughout the state (Collopy and Jelks, 1986; Perrin et al., 1982). The basic pattern consists of the annual cycle of water level fluctuation, which Dineen et al. (1974) called the "rejuvenation process." The pattern can best be illustrated by considering the annual cycle faced by marsh fishes and their major predators, the wading birds. During high water in the summer and fall, fish populations increase in number and in total biomass. When water levels recede in the late winter, standing surface water becomes shallow, higher elevations dry out, and fishes and other mobile aquatic organisms become increasingly concentrated in depressions. Densities in these pools can exceed hundreds of individuals per square meter of water surface. Alligator ponds provide one of the principal sources of dry-season pools. Another set of refugia is supplied by crayfish burrows.

A consequence of falling water levels is a decrease in dissolved oxygen. Aquatic organisms can survive in pools as long as densities are low enough that total community metabolism does not exhaust available oxygen. Predation by birds on fishes has the beneficial effect of increasing the probability that the remaining fish will survive through the dry season.

Dry-season refugia are also crucial to the survival of wading birds (Kahl, 1964; Kushlan, 1976c, 1977, 1979b, 1986d; Kushlan et al., 1975). Both wintering and nesting birds use the concentrated food resource, and continued low water level determines the nesting success of some species. The white ibis, for example, chooses its nesting colony sites near marsh areas where drying conditions are appropriate. Wood storks depend on specific falling water conditions over a prolonged four-month nesting season; the faster the marsh dries, the earlier they nest. If water levels rise, nesting success declines. This pattern is consistent in several herons (Frohring and Kushlan, unpubl.).

As the wet season commences, water levels rise. Invertebrates, which spend the dry season as eggs or cysts, hatch soon after reflooding. Mobile aquatic organisms recolonize the marsh, either from refugial ponds or from rivers. In flatwoods and highland marshes, recolonization depends on the degree of isolation. Fishes appear to be more abundant in flatwoods marshes that have a wet-season connection to deep-water habitats than in hydrologically isolated marshes (B. H. Winchester, personal communication).

Ecosystem Function

Standing crop of the vegetation in Florida marshes is quite variable. Saw grass can achieve 2800 g/m^2, while flag marshes may reach 688 g/m^2 (Hofstetter, 1976; Bayley et al., 1985). Periphyton standing crop can achieve 350 g/m^2 (Brock, 1970).

The productivity of Florida's marshes has not been thoroughly studied, but data suggest that natural rates of accumulation are relatively low. Net production is on the order of 320 g m^2 yr for a flag marsh and 150 g m^2 yr in a wet prairie (Duever et al., 1986). These values compare poorly with productivity of 700 to 2800 g m^2 yr in a marsh in the northern prairies (de la Cruz, 1978).

The relatively low productivity may be a function of the low nutrient levels of most Florida marshes. However, the primary factor influencing the productivity of Florida's marshes is the seasonal fluctuation of water level. Bayley et al. (1985) found that nutrient enrichment of a flag marsh did not increase production over that achieved by the drying and flooding cycle alone. The loss of biomass through dry-season death and decay stimulates production during the following wet period. Periodic drying and reflooding also mobilize nutrients bound in plant material and in the soil.

Human Influences and Management

Highland Marshes

Most small highland marshes have been drained for farming or used in conjunction with adjacent dry prairies for cattle grazing (Camp, 1932). Some, such as Florahome and Black Sink prairies, have been mined for peat (Davis, 1946).

Among the larger remaining highland marshes, few are afforded any permanent protection. At Paynes Prairie, which is a Florida State Preserve, the principal management goal is "to restore, as nearly as possible, the conditions that existed on and around the basin during Bartram's visit" (i.e., 1774) (Florida Department of Natural Resources, 1981). Management involves imitating natural processes with manipulations, including regulating water inflow and outflow, conducting controlled burns, controlling exotic plants, and grazing.

Because water depth and its fluctuations have determined the character of Paynes Prairie throughout its history, water entering and draining from the prairie is regulated by structural means to simulate water cycles that would have occurred naturally. Control of incoming nutrients is a problem that needs attention (Dugger, 1976). Managing as a historic landscape does ignore the fact that marsh systems such as Paynes Prairie are highly dynamic. An alternate management strategy has been proposed to manipulate water levels to reset successional patterns every thirty to fifty years (White, 1975). The objective of such a plan would be to perpetuate a natural successional cycle rather than to mimic perpetually the conditions that prevailed at a particular time in the past.

Flatwoods Marshes

Many flatwoods marshes have been drained, either by general lowering of the groundwater or by ditching. Most are used for cattle grazing, and the composition of plant associations is often the result of the grazing and burning (Laessle, 1942). St. John's-wort and maidencane become scarce in areas of heavy cattle use and may be replaced by smartweed and prairie grasses.

Rooting by hogs also adversely affects these marshes (Winchester et al., 1985). The recognition that complexes of flatwoods marshes serve as groundwater recharge areas has led to their use as well fields, but wells can draw down water levels, with attendant changes in plant associations (Rochow, 1985).

Management of flatwoods marshes involves protection from development followed by active management to counteract the effects of groundwater lowering. Additionally, these marshes require prescribed fire. It is likely that with proper management flatwoods marshes can be used judiciously as groundwater recharge areas and well fields while being maintained in a relatively natural state (Winchester, 1986).

The St. Johns Marshes

Alteration of the St. Johns floodplain began with the construction of a road and levee between 1910 and 1914, which cut off Blue Cypress Lake and the St. Johns River from their headwater marshes. Reclamation for agriculture and channelization of the river followed (Goolsby and McPherson, 1978). More than 70 percent of the basin is now used for cattle production, and the marshes and swamps feeding the river have been reduced by 65 percent (Lowe, 1983).

The results of these changes have been segmentation of the continuous floodplain, isolation of remnant marsh patches, loss of floodplain water storage capacity, rapid movement of water between previously unconnected basins, decrease in water storage, increase in flood stages in the river, and reduced dry-season river flow (Tai and Rao, 1982; Lowe, 1983). The remaining marsh is confined to a few reservoirs and lake edges.

These changes—particularly those that affect the frequency of inundation—caused the replacement of saw grass marshes by cordgrass and woody species, which increased in coverage by 89 percent between 1943 and 1980–81 (Cox et al., 1976; Lowe et al., 1984). Waterfowl and wading bird populations have decreased markedly in recent decades (Sincock, 1959; Florida Game and Fresh Water Fish Commission, 1981; Lowe et al., 1984). From 1948–58 to 1972–80, wintering waterfowl decreased 75 percent. Numbers of wading birds, which nested in nine colony sites in the late 1970s, are similarly much reduced. In 1930, for example, 15,000 white ibis were reported to have nested in the marshes of Lake Washington, but nowhere near that number of birds nests there today. Likewise, snail kites bred in considerable numbers in the early part of the century (Howell, 1932), but today they are rare.

After several decades of planning and implementing ill-advised flood control projects, the management plan of the St. Johns River basin now emphasizes the preservation and restoration of plant and animal resources and takes into account the importance of the hydrologic gradient and associated fire regimes. Primary management emphasis is placed on the river and its lakes because of their roles in water supply and flood control. However, the historic importance of the surrounding marshes in maintaining the quality of the deeper water habitats is now recognized (Brooks and Lowe, 1984). Plans call for a semistructural approach to flood control and water management to be implemented through purchase and restoration of the marshes and the development of water conservation areas (St. Johns River Water Management District, 1977, 1979; Brooks and Lowe, 1984).

A semistructural approach, which involves small structural modifications, may be the best management strategy for nearly all Florida marshes. This approach allows natural hydrologic regimes to be reestablished, corrects reversible changes, and maintains the managers' ability to manipulate the system if required.

Several other aspects of this plan merit special notice by the managers of Florida's marshes. One is its acknowledgement that acquisition of additional marshland is necessary. Another is the recognition that changes in the floodplain are mostly irreversible (Brooks and Lowe, 1984). Computer simulations indicate that drained marshes can never be restored to their primitive condition because elevations have been lowered by soil subsidence and oxidation. A third aspect is the realization that existing wetlands must be actively managed by structural means. Restoration of marsh function will require manipulation of the fluctuations and depths required by the plant communities and other aquatic organisms (Lowe, 1983; Brooks and Lowe, 1984).

The Kissimmee Marshes

Like the St. Johns basin, the Kissimmee floodplain has been drastically altered by drainage and flood control projects (Dineen et al., 1984). A plan to manage the river was authorized by Congress in 1948. It involved using lakes as reservoirs, connecting them by canals, and channelizing the river to carry floodwaters south into Lake Okeechobee. The resulting channel, which is half the length of the original river, is flanked by discontinuous spoil piles. Flow is regulated by six control structures that drop water in 2 m decrements. Water levels behind these structures were stabilized; the downstream portion of each pool is constantly inundated by up to a meter of water while the upstream portion remains relatively dewatered.

Hydrologic modifications and dewatering in the Kissimmee basin have resulted in the overall loss of marshes and alteration of those that remain (Goodrick and Milleson, 1974; Heaney and Huber, 1975; Pruitt and Gatewood, 1976). Grazing also has had an impact; improved pasture covers more than 30 percent of the original floodplain (Frederico et al., 1978). Milleson et al. (1980) found that more than 42 percent of the land in one area had been developed and that only 24 percent remained as marsh vegetation. The complexity of the present plant associations—such as floating tussocks, mixed grass marshes, and nearly floating pickerelweed marsh—is the result of stabilized high water levels (Milleson et al., 1980). Hydrologic modifications have also increased the rate of eutrophication of Lake Okeechobee and caused reductions in waterfowl populations (U.S. Fish and Wildlife Service, 1958; Perrin et al., 1982). Animals using the Kissimmee marshes and other parts of the basin have been greatly affected by the changes (Perrin et al., 1982). Fish populations in both the marsh and the river have been reduced by hydrologic stabilization. Waterfowl food, and therefore waterfowl populations, have also been reduced.

For decades, the appropriate management of the Kissimmee basin has been a matter of intense debate. It has centered on the recognized need to abate the environmentally adverse effects of channelizing the Kissimmee River (Marshall et al., 1972; Dineen et al., 1974). The largest remaining marshes are near the lake and in the southern flooded portions of each impoundment. As in the case of the St. Johns River, marsh acquisition is an important first step, and several sites in the Kissimmee basin have been proposed for preservation.

Management of the remnant marshes of the Kissimmee basin requires restoration of a fluctuating water regime. It is clear from the studies of Perrin et al. (1982) that restoration would enhance fish and wildlife habitat, improve water quality, increase water storage capacity, and restore aspects of the riverine-wetland ecosystem. It is generally believed that backfilling the canal is an important overall first step. The efficacy of the second step—semistructural management of isolated marshes—has been shown by Perrin et al. (1982), and the possibility of dechannelization is being studied in a demonstration project (Palmer, 1986). Other aspects of the state's management strategy are to purchase additional floodplain, expand management to abate nonpoint pollution, and develop a model of dechannelization effects.

It is clear, however, that complete restoration of the Kissimmee Marsh is not possible, given existing flood control requirements. As in the St. Johns marshes, the best alternative is to reestablish as much marsh and river flow as possible and otherwise impede the downgradient flow of water by structural controls. Restoration of functioning marshes both adjacent to and isolated from the river would require additional structural control.

The Everglades

The Everglades have been much altered by flood control and water management (Blake, 1980; Kushlan, 1986a,c, 1990b). Despite early attempts at drainage, the vastness of the Everglades prevented the near total loss of marsh habitat experienced in the St. Johns and Kissimmee valleys. Nevertheless, cross-Everglades canals were operable by 1921, and a levee around

Lake Okeechobee was completed in 1924. Drainage was most effective along the periphery, particularly along the east coast.

Most of the loss of marshland in the Everglades resulted from drainage for farming, the largest loss occurring immediately south of Lake Okeechobee (Jones, 1948). Additional land was "reclaimed" east of the Everglades, a loss consisting primarily of wet prairie and sparse saw grass marshes (Birnhak and Crowder, 1974; Hull and Meyer, 1973). Drainage of the Loxahatchee Slough began in 1913 and led to the near total reclamation of that marsh. Overall, 65 percent of the original Everglades has been irretrievably drained; in completely drained places, dewatered peat has subsided at a rate of about 3 cm per year (Stephens, 1984; Stephens and Johnson, 1951).

The central core of the Everglades proved exceptionally difficult to drain and was unsuited for agricultural development. The lack of control of seasonal and catastrophic high water, however, led to the establishment of a flood control district in 1949; this in turn led to the enclosure of the remaining Everglades and its isolation from reclaimed lands to the north and east.

Superimposed on the dramatic loss of peripheral marsh habitat were the effects of water impoundment within the leveed core of the Everglades for flood control and water storage. These impoundments are known as "conservation areas." The former Hillsborough Lakes marsh is enclosed in Conservation Area 1, the Loxahatchee National Wildlife Refuge (see fig. 10.5). South of the conservation areas lies Everglades National Park and the undeveloped wet prairie to its east, known as the East Everglades. The compartmentalization of the Everglades system preserved the marsh character of the landscape, but it also markedly altered water flow and flood cycles.

Flood control and water regulation have had profound effects on the marsh plant communities (McPherson, 1973b; Alexander and Crook, 1984). From 1940 to 1970, swamp trees and shrubs nearly disappeared from the flooded southern end of Conservation Area 3, and saw grass marsh was displaced by water lily marsh. Conversely, marsh associations have been replaced by drier communities in the dewatered northern end. In Conservation Area 2, prolonged flooding caused loss of swamp islands and flag marsh and changed the depositional characteristics of the peat (Worth, 1983).

Bird populations responded dramatically to the changes. The wood stork and other species of wading birds have decreased in numbers as a direct result of hydrologic alterations (Kushlan et al., 1975; Kushlan and Frohring, 1986; Kushlan, 1990b). These same alterations have had a beneficial effect on the snail kite (Sykes, 1983a, 1984). In addition, excessive water discharges from the conservation areas into the national park have increased the flooding of alligator nests (Kushlan and Jacobsen, 1990).

Water management practices have also changed the chemistry of Everglades water. In Conservation Area 2, for example, 57 percent of the surface water in the interior marsh is derived from canal inflows that have been mineralized by contact with the limestone bedrock (Millar, 1981). The ionic composition of water flowing into the southern Everglades has been similarly affected by canal deliveries. Chloride concentration has increased from 10 to 70 mg/L since 1959 (Klein et al., 1975; Flora and Rosendahl, 1982b).

Management of the Everglades, like the management of the Kissimmee marshes, has been the source of considerable debate. As in the Kissimmee marshes, appropriate management of the Everglades must take into account the irreversible loss of marsh habitat, the requirements of individual species, and the valid needs of the many human users of Everglades resources (Kushlan, 1979a, 1983, 1986a,c, 1990b). It must involve restoration of meteorologically based patterns of water level fluctuations in the natural-area zone, most notably Everglades National Park. However, flood control and human water supply needs must continue to be met by retaining water in the conservation areas, conserving water in the dry season, and releasing excess in the wet season. Thus, ironically, restoration may require additional structural and semistructural controls of water movement and active management of all component areas just as in the St. Johns and Kissimmee.

Conclusion

Given their distinctive plant and animal populations, Florida's marshes are clearly worth conserving for their own sake and for their scientific value. In addition, they maintain the overall quality of human life in the state. Environmental services performed by marshes include recreation, flood control, water storage and supply, production of fish and wildlife, provision of habitat for nonharvestable species including endangered and rare animals, some agriculture, water quality maintenance, and wastewater renovation. Concerning the last, state legislation—the Warren S. Henderson Wetland Protection Act of 1984 (FS 403.918)—mandates permit issuance, consideration of cumulative impacts, and establishment of regulatory criteria for using wetlands for wastewater disposal.

The principal cause of ecological degradation of Florida's marshes has been dewatering, a dominant force in the political and social history of the state. Loss of marsh has continued in recent decades, mostly due to agricultural conversion (Hefner, 1986). The initial objective of marshland conservation in the state is the purchase and reflooding of drained marshes. Considerable progress has been made in reclaiming Florida wetlands, especially after phosphate mining (Clewell, 1981; Shuey and Swanson, 1979; Erwin and Best, 1985).

Although the loss of marsh area is the most obvious component of the degradation of Florida wetlands, a second factor is more subtle but no less important: the loss of wetland function in those marshes that remain

(Kushlan, 1990b). Given the dependence of plants and animals on specific inundations, it should be clear that modifications of the hydrologic cycle alter the distribution and abundance of various species and, therefore, the character of the wetland ecosystem. Such changes have been repeatedly documented in Florida marshes. The natural history and population status of the snail kite and the wood stork in Florida reflect the history of drainage and functional alterations of the state's marshes.

The similarities in the ecology of Florida marshes and the demonstrated effects of changes in the plant and animal populations dependent on them hold promise for their effective management. Several generalizations emerge from a consideration of the history and character of Florida marshes.

1. Most of the loss of Florida marshes was due to drainage, and only a small but important part of this loss is reversible.

2. Loss of the natural fluctuation of water levels in the remaining marshes has caused drastic changes in the functioning of these ecosystems.

3. Marshes are useful for flood control and water supply management, and these services can be supplied conveniently to nearby developed areas.

4. Storage of water in wetlands has led to their alteration because the area available for storage now is so much less than when the entire natural marsh area was intact. There is more water to be stored on less land; thus water levels may be higher and dry seasons shorter. As a result, remnant marshes can have higher than natural water levels in the dry season.

5. Because of the above factors, structural control and continued managed manipulation of water levels is not only inevitable but desirable. Semi-structural solutions emphasizing natural fluctuations, restoration of sheet flow, and reduction of canal flow except when absolutely required for health and safety would yield substantial returns.

6. The diverse demands placed on marshes, ranging from flood control to wildlife conservation, can be coordinated through management techniques that simulate the natural fluctuation of water levels but are constrained by criteria based on biological and hydrologic goals.

7. To the extent that these needs cannot be coordinated, management goals must be chosen for a particular patch of marsh; different patches may be zoned for different purposes. It may be that only in a large natural zone would the appropriate management goal be to restore a naturally functioning marsh ecosystem.

8. Because of history, conflicting demands, and management limitations, some of the natural functioning of Florida's marshes can never be recovered.

9. Only active management will assure the future of the remnants of Florida's once great marshlands.

11
Lakes

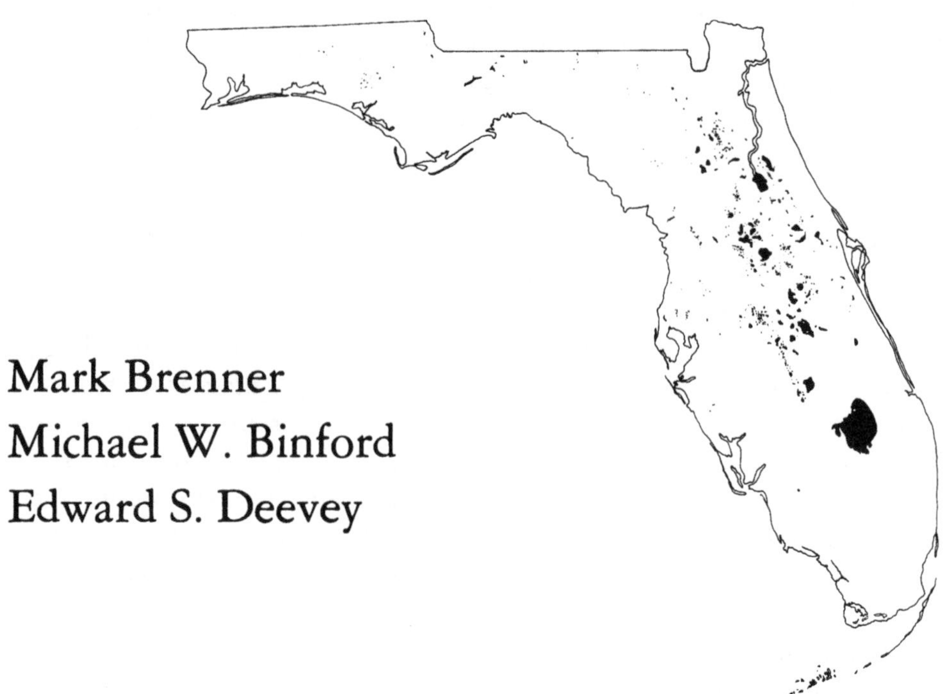

Mark Brenner
Michael W. Binford
Edward S. Deevey

Florida's climate and numerous tourist attractions draw thousands of visitors, while the population of residents increases at a high annual rate. For naturalists, the beaches, springs, and subtropical flora are the major attractions. Except for those who fish for bass and bream, or who sail or ski on the inland waters, few visitors or residents appreciate the number and diversity of Florida's lakes. Tourists who travel in the coastal areas may miss the lakes altogether. An airplane trip, however—even a short trip from Orlando to Gainesville—will give the traveler a view of an extraordinary, watery world.

Florida contains about 7800 lakes with surface area greater than 0.4 ha. Covering at least 9270 km^2—about 6 percent of the landscape—they are collectively about half the size of Lake Ontario, the smallest of the Great Lakes. Lake Okeechobee alone covers about one-fifth of the total area (Canfield and Hoyer, 1988).

Florida has a few large lakes and thousands of small ones (fig. 11.1). Five natural lakes in the state have surface areas greater than 100 km^2. They include Lake Okeechobee (1770 km^2), Lake George (190 km^2), Lake Kissimmee (140 km^2), Lake Apopka (125 km^2), and Lake Istokpoga (112 km^2). Most of

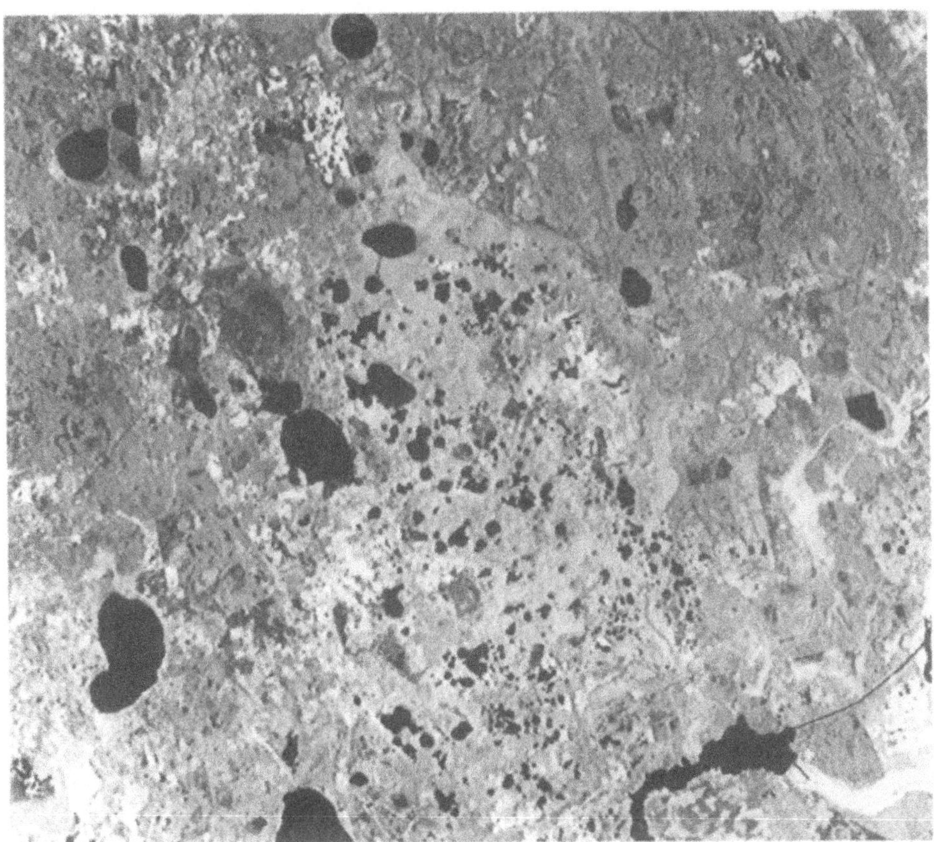

Fig. 11.1. Northern section of the peninsular Florida lake district. From photo 018-039, 17 March 1976, 7, CN 30-18/W082-27, NN 30-18/W082-23, NASA ERTS E-2420-15180-701,T2 S D E 011-1.0, C000-044.

the lakes are much smaller. Surface area is reported for 625 lakes in the Florida Lakes Data Base (FLADAB), and about half are smaller than 60 ha. As fig. 11.2 suggests, the lakes are distributed unevenly in the state. No county is wholly without them, though a total of only seven lakes is reported for the tri-county area (Union, Baker, Nassau) in the northeast part of the state (Edmiston and Myers, 1983). More than half of all the lakes occur in the fourteen counties that make up the central sandy ridge system, where the Mio-Pliocene mantle is thickest. In Lake County alone, 1345 lakes and wetlands cover 32 percent of the area (Knochenmus and Hughes, 1976), making the county's waterfront ecotone at least 4800 km long.

Most Florida lakes are quite shallow (Kenner, 1964). About three-fourths of the lakes listed in FLADAB have maximum depths less than 5 m. Most of the large lakes are very shallow. For instance, Lake Okeechobee has a maximum depth less than 5 m (Canfield and Hoyer, 1988), and Lake Apopka has a maximum depth of only about 3.5 m (Kenner, 1964). Few lakes are deeper than 25 m, and they are small. Deep Lake (Collier County) is more than 29 m deep (Gonyea and Hunt, 1969).

Fig. 11.2. Florida lake distribution.

No other southern state contains a lake district like Florida's; the nearest counterparts are in Canada and the formerly glaciated northern states from Minnesota to Maine. With about 125 cm of annual rainfall, Florida shares the humid climate of those regions. There are other similarities, apart from the sheer abundance of lakes, but the main difference is in the proportion of unevaporated rainwater that runs off to sea—about 50 percent in the north, almost zero in Florida. The similarities include the landscape and vegetation, for Florida's sandhills are ecologically rather like glacial outwash plains. The seepage lakes that fill kettles in outwash—Walden Pond is the most famous—are similar to sinkhole lakes in mantled karst. Whereas kettled outwash is relatively rare in the north, most Florida lakes are seepage lakes. Some estimates suggest that as many as 70 percent of Florida lakes lack overland outflows (Palmer, 1984). For these lakes at least, and probably for most of the others, much or most of the inflow and all of the unevaporated outflow is groundwater.

Dominance of subterranean over surface drainage, which is characteristic of karst terrain, imposes a very special stamp on Florida's limnology. One ecological consequence is to obscure the complex interaction between water, the "universal solvent," and land, the source of all the water-soluble substances that compose, nourish, or damage aquatic organisms. Naturalists find Florida lakes to be diverse habitats because of the range of sizes, of shoreline convolutions, and of concentrations of certain chemicals. For limnologists, who are especially interested in ecosystem dynamics, the processes of system metabolism vary between lakes in proportion to the rates of inflow and outflow of chemicals, not to their concentrations; and rates of inflow and outflow are very difficult to measure in Florida lakes. Limnologists sometimes try to get an idea of rates of inflow and outflow by noting the proportion of watershed area to lake area. In Florida, unfortunately, this measure cannot be obtained from a topographic map, because the ecologically relevant watershed is underground.

Nevertheless, the chemicals exported to lakes have their sources in the rocks, soils, airsheds, and vegetation of adjacent uplands. As both the amounts and the rates of export can be radically altered by human activities, changing land use requires close attention from limnologists. In Florida, the exports that have drawn most attention are the waterborne nutrients, chiefly phosphorus and nitrogen, that cause cultural eutrophication. Limnologists have classified certain watersheds with respect to their inferred influence on nutrient supply. This methodology describes amounts of nutrients supposedly supplied under certain kinds of land use (Baker et al., 1981). The approach fails to consider inputs to lakes from the air, like oxides of sulfur, and gives no idea of rates of soil erosion from recently deforested watersheds.

Human populations are increasing at exceptionally high rates throughout Florida. People rely on the availability of high-quality water for home use, recreation, agriculture, and industry. Activities that degrade water quality usually begin with forest clearance; heavy siltation of lakes is a common consequence. Among other more or less deleterious activities are mining; construction and road building; channelization or damming of surface drainage; pumping of groundwater; discharge of pollutants and excess nutrients from homes, farms, and industry; introduction of exotic plants and animals; and spread of airborne plant and animal pathogens. Acid rain is particularly insidious, because most Florida lake waters are poorly buffered.

This chapter presents an overview of limnological information on Florida lakes, drawn largely from FLADAB, a compilation of data produced by county, state, and federal agencies and by university scientists. The data set is maintained at the Water Resources Research Center at the University of Florida in Gainesville. Some information is available for 788 lakes, about 10 percent of the total. Analyses and summaries of some problems are presented by Canfield (1981), Baker et al. (1981), Huber et al. (1982), in the National Eutrophication Survey (EPA, 1978), and in three volumes produced by the U.S. Environmental Protection Agency's National Acid Precipitation Assessment Program (Linthurst et al., 1986; Overton et al., 1986; Kanciruk et al., 1986). The acid deposition data set has not yet been melded with FLADAB. Statistics of location, size, and drainage type are given in the "Gazetteers" (Florida Board of Conservation, 1969; Shafer et al., 1986). Bathymetric maps of a few lakes were published by Kenner (1964). The Water Resources Atlas of Florida (Fernald and Patton, 1984) is a mine of information compiled for the general reader.

Lake Origins

Lakes can be formed in limestone terrain by dissolution of the bedrock. The process is effected by downward percolation of acidic waters under pressure. Rainwater is naturally acidic from carbonic acid and can gain acidity from acid soils. The air pollutants nitrate and sulfate contribute additional acidity as nitric and sulfuric acids. Acidic groundwater can form large caverns in limestone. On uplift or drying of the country, the roofs of caverns may collapse, forming sinkholes. Sinkholes are the most distinctive landforms of classical karst districts (Jennings, 1985). But Florida's karst is not classical, and the traditional view of sinkhole formation in Florida (Stubbs, 1940; Pirkle and Brooks, 1959) has been modified.

In Florida the Eocene Ocala limestone is buried, in places to depths of hundreds of feet, under a mantle of Miocene, Pliocene, and Pleistocene deposits. This overburden is dominantly sandy, with beds of clay, phosphatic mudstone, and peat. Dissolution of the deep Ocala limestone creates fissures into which the unconsolidated material of the mantle can fall or be forced by hydraulic pressure (Arrington and Lindquist, 1987). In much of Florida, sinkhole formation is expressed on the land surface by collapse of the loose overburden, and in some areas sinks form at a rate of several per km^2 per year (Upchurch and Littlefield, 1987).

Away from the sandhills, where limestone is near the surface and is demonstrably cavernous, solution has undoubtedly played a role in enlarging, if not in forming, lake basins. Lake Tsala Apopka (Citrus County), though apparently a drowned river system (Hutchinson, 1957), is believed to have been enlarged by solution (Shannon and Brezonik, 1972a). Lake Okeechobee, an uplifted sea-floor depression (Edmiston and Myers, 1983), may also have been enlarged. Little Salt Spring and Warm Mineral Spring (Sarasota County) have limestone caverns well below lake level (Clausen et al., 1979). The steep walls of Deep Lake (Collier County), cited as a perfect doline by Hutchinson (1957), are of limestone, but the composition of the floor is unknown. Doline (circular) form is not proof of origin by solution, however; some of the finest dolines—Kingsley Lake (Clay County) and Santa Rosa Lake (Putnam County)—are in the sandhills.

Fluvial, or riverine, processes have produced only a few of Florida's lakes.

Cut-off oxbows and other riverine backwaters are found in the valleys of the St. Johns, Peace, Kissimmee, and other rivers. Nine lakes, including four of Florida's largest, are reservoirs. Hundreds of smaller lakes have been created in borrow-pits and strip-mined areas. Semipermanent ponds and roadside ditches are common throughout the state, but these have received little attention from limnologists (Dickinson, 1948).

Age of Florida Lakes

Surprising as it is that any lakes persist in Florida's unstable terrain, some sinkholes have held water continuously for the past 8000 years (Watts, 1969, 1971). Two deep lakes in Highlands County, Lake Annie (fig. 11.3) and Lake Tulane, are older than 30,000 years. They held water through the late Wisconsin glacial age (Watts, 1975; Watts and Hansen, 1988). That is even more surprising, for when much water was frozen in glaciers the world's sea level was lower than today's by more than 100 m. Local water tables, graded to lower sea level, should also have been lower. Not only should shallow lakes have gone dry, but also semidesert conditions should have prevailed, particularly in the central sandy ridges. Semidesert vegetation is in fact shown by pollen in the lake mud of late Wisconsin time. However, as all the pollen evidence comes from sandhill lakes, one cannot say whether it indicates a drier climate, a lower local water table, or both.

Fig. 11.3. Lake Annie, a small, deep sinkhole lake in Highlands County. Photo by Paige Martin.

Another deep lake, Lake Sheelar (Clay County), deposited silty sediments from 23,860 to 18,500 years ago and organic sediments from 14,600 years ago to the present (Watts and Stuiver, 1980). The 4000-year disconformity records the lowered water table. Lake Sheelar began to refill when sea level began to rise, but refilling of shallower lakes was delayed until 8000 or 6000 years ago, when about half the rise had been completed. By 3000 or 2000 years ago, when the sea stood nearly at its present level, pollen of bald cypress became more abundant in lake sediments. It seems that cypress spread through most of Florida's interior wetlands not because the climate was moister or cooler but because wetlands had come to occupy more numerous and larger sinkholes.

Hydrology and Lake Levels

In Florida's mantled karst, a subtropical climate with variable rainfall interacts with the regional geology to make both hydrology and limnology decidedly unusual. The rainfall varies both seasonally and annually, because much of it comes with thunderstorms in summer and with hurricanes in late summer or autumn. Lake evaporation, though about equal to rainfall on the average (Deevey, 1988), is not curtailed by freezing and is much more constant from year to year. As one result, dry years are frequent and can be very dry; the chance of a rainfall deficiency 30 percent greater than normal is about one in ten. Moreover, in Florida's flat, porous terrain the usual fate of any unevaporated water is not to run off but to sink downward.

These circumstances affect lake levels so that "normal" years do not exist: what is normal is extreme variability, the condition limnologists call *astatic*. Some lakes clearly fluctuate more than others. Deevey's (1988) analysis of data from the northern part of the lake district shows that Kingsley Lake (Clay County) is one of the least variable. The lake surface rose and fell by no more than a meter over three decades (1954–1984). The lake is said to be stabilized by its outlet (Palmer, 1984). Pebble Lake, only a few kilometers away, is at the other extreme. It has fallen by 93 cm in one month and risen by 79 cm in another month; over forty years it has changed by 9.6 m.

Monthly and annual lake level fluctuations are related to net rainfall (regional precipitation minus lake evaporation), but the relation is not strong. In a statistical study of sixteen Florida lakes, Deevey (1988) concluded that lake levels respond to wet and dry months with little or no lag period. Net precipitation accounts for 34 percent to 62 percent of the variance in lake levels; that means that the fraction *not* accounted for is 38 percent to 66 percent.

Hydrographs from lakes as far apart as 280 km show that water levels often fluctuate in sympathy with each other (Deevey, 1988). The strongest of the statewide variations, the low-level periods of the mid-1950s and early 1980s, occurred in years that were not much drier than average. These were periods of exceptionally low artesian pressure in the deep limestone aquifer. In ten lakes with adequate records, lake levels are highly correlated with water levels in artesian wells (Deevey, 1988). In four of the ten lakes, statistical analysis showed that net rainfall did not contribute to regulation of lake level (Deevey, 1988). For Lake Weir (Marion County), the combined effects of weather and artesian pressure account for all but 23 percent of the variance of lake level.

If artesian pressure raises and lowers lake levels, hydrologists might assume that water from the deep limestone aquifer mixes upward into lake waters. But chemical evidence contradicts the assumption; these lakes have soft waters and contain no trace of any carbonate-rich source. It appears that artesian pressure is exerted indirectly, through many meters of confining beds, shatter zones, surficial or water table aquifers, and the sediments that hold up the lakes.

In north-temperate regions, where hydrologic throughflow is both rapid and measurable, at least at lake outlets, limnologists construct rough water budgets as a first step toward nutrient budgets. Nutrient concentrations are measured in incoming, standing, and outflowing surface waters and are then multiplied by their respective volumes. The budget of sources and sinks is then said to be "based on a hydrologic model." As a trickle of groundwater can bring in a lot of nutrients (Belanger et al., 1985), seepage inflow is often measured in seepage meters, which are buckets with stopcocks, inverted over the lake bottom. Seepage outflow, however, is thought to be unmeasurable. In defense of northern limnologists' assumption that it is not worth measuring, note that groundwater outflow will always seem negligible when the sum of surface outflows plus evaporation exceeds the sum of all known inflows. Seepage lakes have no outlets, and all unevaporated water must exit to groundwater, but few seepage lakes in north-temperate regions are "problem lakes," and most limnologists ignore them.

In Florida, where many lakes lack surface outflow, total water inputs normally exceed measured outputs. When seepage inflow is measured, as in Lakes Conway and Apopka in Orange County (Fellows and Brezonik, 1980, 1981), seepage outflow can be estimated from the remaining imbalance in the water budget (table 11.1). In these cases, it proved to be substantial—11.7 percent of the total outflow, or nearly half the nonevaporative outflow in both lakes.

For Lake Kerr (Marion County), a seepage lake, Hughes (1974) used lake-stage data to estimate outseepage, or downward leakage, in months when lake level fell by an amount greater than the net precipitation deficiency for that month. After confirming Hughes's estimate of 0.1 foot per month, we applied his method to measure leakage from twenty lakes (Deevey, 1988) and found eighteen of them to leak downward at rates between

Table 11.1. Water budgets for Lakes Conway and Apopka for water-year 1976 (October 1975–September 1976)

	Lake Conway		Lake Apopka	
	10^6 m^3	Percent	10^6 m^3	Percent
Sources				
Precipitation	8.87	69.5	131.7	61.9
Springs	—	—	21.7	10.2
Surface inflow	n.s.	—	1.2	0.6
Muck farm pumpage	—	—	54.0	25.4
Seepage (nearshore)	2.24	17.5	4.2	2.0
Storm water runoff	1.66	13.0	—	—
Total	12.77	100.0	212.8	100.1
Sinks				
Evaporation	9.41	73.7	163.8	75.0
Surface outflow	1.87	14.6	29.2	13.4
Other[a]	1.49	11.7	25.5	11.7
Total	12.77	100.0	218.5	100.0
Change in storage	—	—	−5.7	—

Source: From Fellows and Brezonik (1980, Table I). Used with permission of the American Water Resources Association.

a. Calculated by difference.

about 30 cm and about 50 cm per year. Higher values (90 cm and 141 cm) were observed in two notoriously astatic lakes (Brooklyn and Pebble lakes, Clay County). Although fifteen of the twenty lakes are reported to have some surface outflow, we found no consistent difference in leakage between drainage and seepage lakes.

Lakes that leak 51 cm of water per year also lose about 125 cm by evaporation. If there are no other losses, and if the mean depth (volume ÷ area) is 5 m, water resides in the lake for 2.8 years. A few centimeters of loss by surface outflow, as in Lake Weir (Brezonik and Messer, 1977) will shorten that time by a few percent. The mean residence time for the twenty lakes in our data set was 2.67 ± 1.33 years. In the northern states, lakes of comparable volume have residence times of about three to six months—that is, they are flushed five to ten times more rapidly than Florida lakes. Long residence times give more time for nutrients and pollutants to exert their effects. Here, then, is one reason why Florida's sandhill lakes are vulnerable to eutrophication by a few septic tanks and to acidification by tiny inputs of airborne acids.

Stratification and Thermics

During winter, Florida lakes maintain uniform water temperatures well above freezing. Mean monthly temperatures, even in the coldest months, are typically above 10°C (50°F) (Dye et al., 1980, Beaver et al., 1981). In spring and summer, lakes become thermally stratified because warm water, which is lighter than cold water, is forced downward by wind with increasing difficulty. (The reason is that higher temperatures greatly increase the density difference per degree difference in temperature.) A stratified lake is divided into a warm upper stratum, the *epilimnion*, and a colder, lower stratum, the *hypolimnion*.

Many Florida lakes are too shallow to develop stable summer stratification. Others, of moderate depth, are so large that wind disrupts incipient stratification. Of fifty-five lakes and ponds studied in north-central Florida, only thirteen showed stable summer stratification (Shannon and Brezonik, 1972a). In deep lakes such as Lake Mize in Alachua County (maximum depth 25.3 m), the period of stratification may last from March to November, with late summer surface temperatures 20°C (36°F) warmer than bottom temperatures (Harkness and Pierce, 1940; Nordlie, 1972).

In stratified lakes, biotic production is largely confined to the warm, well-lighted epilimnion, also called the *euphotic* or *trophogenic zone*. Respiratory or consumptive processes (mainly microbial decomposition of organic matter) dominate in the colder, darker hypolimnion, also called the *anoxic*, *dysphotic*, or *tropholytic zone*. Dissolved oxygen, distributed throughout the water column during an earlier period of complete mixing, is rapidly exhausted in the hypolimnion, while respiratory gases (CO_2, CH_4, NH_3, N_2O, H_2, and H_2S) accumulate. Except for CO_2, which is also respired by animals and plants, these gases are produced anaerobically, and their production is inhibited by free oxygen. It is rare, therefore, for the full intensity of all these consumption processes to be displayed in deep water of any lake, though it is often displayed in bottom mud. Although fish kills occasionally result from anoxia (Reid, 1964), the only Florida lake known to attain permanent anoxia in deep water is Johnson Pond in Gainesville (Whitmore, et al., 1988). Few others are likely to do so, for the highly productive lakes are shallow and weakly stratified, with at least a little oxygen at all depths (McDiffett, 1980, 1981). Lake Mize, though deep and thermally well stratified for nine months each year, is very unproductive (Brezonik and Harper, 1969; Keirn and Brezonik, 1971).

The presence of dense aquatic vegetation alters physico-chemical properties of lake waters in several ways. Dense mats of water hyacinth (*Eichhornia crassipes*) can cover the water surface, modifying heat transfer and reducing gas exchange from the atmosphere. Temperatures below the mat are often moderated, and decomposition can result in low oxygen concentrations (0.2 to 0.3 mg/L) in the water (Reddy, 1981; Mitsch, 1976; Ultsch, 1973). Heavy growths of submerged plants such as *Potamogeton* or *Hydrilla* reduce wind-driven turbulence, thereby promoting stable thermal stratification.

Some of the heat stored in a lake is exchanged with the atmosphere when air and water are at different temperatures, so lakes affect the microclimates of their surroundings. Effects are most important in winter, as citrus groves are protected from cold damage (Bill et al., 1979). Thus, management schemes that propose to increase or decrease lake volumes may have unwanted consequences for lakeside crops.

Annual heat budgets express heat gain or loss between seasons. When calculated for subtropical or tropical lakes, they are minimal estimates of annual heat storage, as they ignore temperature fluctuations due to nocturnal cooling and diurnal heating. The largest heat budgets 30 to 40 $\times 10^3$ cal/cm of lake surface, occur in large, deep northern lakes like New York's Finger Lakes, much of whose large volume is annually warmed from about 0°C to about 25°C (32°F to 77°F). No such annual budgets are expected in the shallow lakes of subtropical Florida, but a shallow lake with a winter temperature of 10°C (50°F) nevertheless stores a good deal of heat.

Lake Mize, with a maximum depth of 25.3 m, is one of the deepest lakes in Florida. Using data from Harkness and Pierce (1940), Nordlie (1972) calculated that the lake gained and lost 6003 cal/cm in 1940. In 1964 and 1965, Nordlie found values of 4391 and 3767 cal/cm. L. E. Battoe (personal communication) reported 8425 and 8519 cal/cm for Lake Annie (Highlands County), another deep lake.

Light Transmission

Public perception of a lake's quality is frequently based on water clarity, which is easily measured by the Secchi disk. In Florida, acceptably clear waters have Secchi depths greater than 2 m. Lower values indicate plankton blooms, turbidity from silt or organic detritus, and/or dissolved humic stain. The Secchi depth, or lake transparency, is the depth of penetration of roughly 10 percent of visible surface light. Transparency is used as a proxy for algal biomass in the water column and thus (despite serious reservations) for the system's productivity. Algal biomass is independently measured by the chlorophyll *a* concentration, which proves to be inversely and hyperbolically related to Secchi depth (Carlson, 1977; Canfield and Hodgson, 1983; Brezonik 1978).

Optical properties of lake water are measured and expressed in terms of color, which is governed primarily by colored organic compounds in solution. Living phytoplankton and pondweeds liberate some colored compounds, but most color is humic stain, derived from decayed vegetation in peat and organic soil. The color of filtered lake water is matched against that of a colored platinum compound and measured in units of milligrams of platinum per liter. Dissolved color data are available for 558 lakes in the FLADAB; they show that more than 60 percent of the lakes have less than 40 mg/L. About 10 percent of the lakes have more than 100 mg/L, or enough dissolved color that even in the absence of algal cells and inorganic turbidity, Secchi disk transparency is restricted to less than 3 m. At the upper end of the scale are the highly stained waters of darkwater or blackwater lakes.

Dissolved organic matter can also be measured independently. Values of 10 to 100 mg/L in South Florida waters (Gonyea and Hunt, 1969), combined with the highly skewed distribution of water color in the FLADAB data set, suggest that the tea-colored or blackwater lakes contain opaque material that is not algal. This material can inhibit photosynthesis, and in high concentrations (corresponding to more than 50 mg/L) is probably inversely related to algal biomass and productivity. Nevertheless, chlorophyll *a* and color are both inversely related to Secchi depth in many lakes. The combined statistical relationship was evaluated in 205 lakes by Canfield and Hodgson (1983). It preserves the usefulness of the Secchi disk for survey purposes but conceals much that ecologists need to know about plankton and system productivity. One component of the system, the zooplankton, is negatively correlated with color in nine lakes and may be restricted by food limitation in blackwater lakes (Bienert, 1982).

Carbonates, Alkalinity, and Acid Rain

The Florida peninsula is underlain by marine limestone, giving rise to the popular misconception that Florida lake waters are hard (that is, having high concentrations of $CaCO_3$) and have high pH. In fact, many, perhaps most, Florida lakes are soft-water, acid systems with low alkalinity. They are thus poorly buffered against acid deposition. Canfield (1983b) assessed their sensitivity to acid rain, by examining pH, alkalinity, and other variables across major geologic and physiographic regions. The data indicate a general increase in pH and alkalinity from northwest to southeast across the state and from inland highlands (the sandhills) to lowlands.

Both in northwestern Florida (Canfield et al., 1983b) and on the highland ridges, the lakes are hydrologically isolated from contact with carbonate-rich soils or bedrock. The northwest-to-southeast gradient coincides with a geologic shift from the North Gulf Sedimentary Province, consisting of sandy, noncarbonate sediments, to the Florida Peninsula Sedimentary Province (Fenneman, 1938), containing carbonates, phosphates, and sulfates. Lakes in the center of the state show a broad range of pH and alkalinity, reflecting the diverse geology and physiography. Proximity of a lake to the underground source of its solutes is related to the height of the *piezometric surface* (the hydrostatic pressure boundary), which in turn is measured by the water level in artesian wells. In the sandy highlands, small sinkhole lakes abound on the ridges and lie above the piezometric surface. Larger, shallow lakes and wetland systems occupy the valley floors and are below the piezometric surface.

Total alkalinity expresses the acid-neutralizing capacity of lake water; and as pH can vary diurnally with the photosynthetic activity of plankton, alkalinity is the appropriate measure of susceptibility to acid deposition. Below concentrations of 10 mg/L (as $CaCO_3$), lakes are considered sensitive, while basins in the range of 10 to 20 mg/L are moderately sensitive. Canfield found that 98 of the 165 lakes in his study, or 59 percent, contained less than 20 mg/L. The proportion is nearly identical (58 percent) for the 601 lakes in the larger FLADAB set. (This data set does not yet include results of the national acidity survey conducted by the Environmental Protection Agency.) If these studies are representative, some 4600 Florida lakes may be susceptible to acidification.

While acidification is clearly a problem in the northeastern United States and Canada (Schindler, 1988) and in Europe, attention has turned to Florida only recently. Over the northern portion of the state, the annual mean pH of rainfall is below 4.7, with summer averages generally 0.2 to 0.3 units below winter values. Although hydrogen ion concentrations in rainfall are not notably high, the total amount that reaches land and water surfaces can be substantial (300 to 500 equivalents per hectare where yearly rainfall is high (Brezonik et al., 1980). By this measure about as much acidity falls in Florida as in the heavily affected northeastern states. There is evidence that the pH of rainfall and the alkalinity of acid-sensitive lakes both declined between the late 1950s and the late 1970s. On the other hand, some lakes that lie in residentially or agriculturally developed watersheds show increases in alkalinity and pH, perhaps as a result of pumping and discharge of carbonate-rich water from the deep aquifer.

The biological effects of lake acidification in Florida are poorly understood. They are difficult to assess because many other limnological variables—such as solubility of phosphorus, aluminum, and other metals—are correlated with pH and alkalinity. Studies show decreased abundance of submerged plants (Garren, 1982) and phytoplankton (Schulze, 1980) with increasing acidity, but nutrient availability may be the limiting factor. For the most part, zooplankton abundance, numbers of benthic invertebrates, and fish diversity appear little affected down to pH 4.5 (Schulze, 1980; Crisman and Bienert, 1983). Abundance and biomass of ciliated Protozoa decline with increasing acidity (Beaver and Crisman, 1981). Keller (1984) found that lake pH influences diversity of fishes, but lake surface area was also a determinant of diversity. Growth rate and condition of bass and other fish species have been investigated in acid-clear, acid-colored, and circumneutral lakes by Canfield et al. (1985). Some damage was found at pH levels below 3.7, but other results are difficult to interpret, owing to confounding by factors other than acidity.

If biological damage from acidification is more difficult to demonstrate in Florida than elsewhere, one reason may be that Florida waters have been acidic throughout their history, and natural selection has favored acid tolerance. The history of acidity, determined in several affected regions by study of diatom assemblages in lake sediments (Charles and Norton, 1986; Smol et al., 1986), has just begun to be studied in Florida (Whitmore, 1989). Several investigators (Canfield, 1983b; Crisman and Bienert, 1983) have noted that certain factors that increase susceptibility of northern lakes to damage are absent in Florida. One such factor is the strong springtime flush of hydrogen ions that results from melting snow. Another may be the paucity (or previous removal by leaching) of aluminum and industrial toxic metals in the sandy soils of Florida watersheds.

Conductivity and Ionic Composition

The concentration of dissolved ions in lake waters can be expressed in several ways. In careful studies, the concentration of each ion is reported in g/L or eq/L (the latter value an expression of dissociated ionic charge). Sometimes filtered lake water is evaporated and the residue reported as total dissolved solids (TDS) per volume of water. More commonly, specific conductance (conductivity) is measured. An inexpensive meter measures the inverse of the electrical resistance of a sample (in Siemens/cm). Conductivity is systematically related to TDS or the sum of ions, usually by a line of uniform slope for all the natural waters of a geologically homogeneous district (which Florida is not).

The principal components of salinity in inland waters are the cations calcium (Ca^{2+}), magnesium (Mg^{2+}), sodium (Na^{+}), and potassium (K^{+}) and the anions carbonate (CO_3^{2-}), bicarbonate (HCO_3^{-}), sulfate (SO_4^{2-}), and chloride (Cl^{-}). Most inland waters are dominantly calcium bicarbonate waters, and many of Florida's waters are typical. High sodium and chloride imply marine influence, either from maritime air or from buried salt deposits, but high sulfate, though also marine (or, more recently, industrial) commonly results from gypsum interbedded in marine carbonate rocks.

As might be expected in a region where the hydrologic input to lakes is dominated by direct precipitation and flow over or through sands, there is a large population of very dilute or soft-water lakes. A substantial number of lakes, though harder, are nevertheless fresh and not brackish. More than half of the 609 lakes listed in the FLADAB have conductivities less than 150 Siemens/cm. Statistics of ionic composition, given in table 11.2, are a little surprising. Calcium bicarbonate waters probably dominate in the sandhills, but the average lake of this data set has the sodium, chloride, and sulfate proportions characteristic of sea water. Canfield (1981, 1984) noticed the general increase of these ions from northwest to southeast across the state, but it appears that coastal lakes with distinctively marine compositions were

Table 11.2. Important ions in Florida lakes

Ion	Number of lakes	Average	S.D.	Median	Q25	Q75
Calcium	187	16.98	17.76	12.00	4.05	24.00
Magnesium	187	5.08	7.25	3.55	1.80	6.28
Sodium	241	21.44	71.71	7.80	4.85	13.68
Potassium	241	2.53	3.79	1.45	0.50	2.86
Bicarbonate	385	44.90	54.74	19.00	5.00	69.25
Sulfate	250	19.07	28.28	10.52	5.40	22.09
Chloride	267	39.72	133.88	15.33	8.83	24.50
Silica	179	1.46	2.07	0.67	0.21	1.74
Iron	189	0.19	0.21	0.13	0.04	0.25

Note: Data are from the Florida Lakes Data Base. Entries were calculated using the median value of the variable for each lake. All units are in mg/L. S.D. is the standard deviation of the concentrations. Q25 and Q75 are the concentration values of the ion at the 25 percent and 75 percent quartiles, which is a measure of variability about the median. For example, 25 percent of the lakes have calcium concentrations below 4.05 and 25 percent above 24.00 mg/L.

underrepresented in his sample of 165 lakes. We therefore infer that the source of ions in most of the harder lakes is not marine carbonate rocks, or soils derived from them, but maritime air.

Trophic State and Nutrients

Trophic state, in the original and accepted sense of the term, refers to the nutritional status of a lake. *Eutrophic* lakes are "well nourished" and *oligotrophic* lakes are "poorly nourished." Analyzed for nitrogen and phosporus, the principal waterborne nutrients, eutrophic lakes have high concentrations, oligotrophic lakes have low concentrations, and mesotrophic lakes are intermediate.

Concentrations of phytoplankton, routinely measured by chlorophyll *a* concentration, normally range from high to low on the same continuum. Other, statistically weaker correlatives of nutrient status include Secchi depth, total dissolved solids, dissolved inorganic and organic carbon, pigments specific to blue-green algae, and the ratio of calcium and magnesium to sodium and potassium ions. In a few studies the "primary productivity," the rate of carbon assimilation or oxygen production in an isolated water sample, proves to be positively correlated with chlorophyll *a* concentration (Shannon and Brezonik, 1972a,b). However, the methodology is inapplicable to macrophytes and beset with other difficulties. Rates of production may perhaps be inferred from concentrations but should not be confused with them. Therefore, most limnologists describe trophic states empirically, hoping eventually to deduce the mechanisms by which they have been attained. Unfortunately, in addressing the interested public, the temptation to consider oligotrophic lakes as "unproductive systems" is frequently too strong to be resisted.

The trophic status of Florida lakes is frequently described by use of a numerical scale called a trophic state index (TSI). Shannon and Brezonik (1972b) developed an index that incorporates seven indicators: primary productivity, chlorophyll *a*, total phosphorus, total organic nitrogen, Secchi depth, conductivity, and the ratio of monovalent (sodium and potassium) to divalent (calcium and magnesium) cations. It has been superseded (Huber et al., 1982) by a modification of the "Carlson index" (Carlson, 1977). Developed originally for north-temperate lakes, it incorporates Secchi depth and chlorophyll *a* and total phosphorus concentrations.

Carlson's assumption that nitrogen can be disregarded—drawn from the widely admired work of Vollenweider (1968) and Dillon and Rigler (1974)—is untenable in Florida. Many of the state's lakes receive excess phosphorus either from the air (Hendry and Brezonik, 1980) or from phosphate mines and thus have abnormally low nitrogen-to-phosphorus ratios (Baker et al., 1981). In such cases trophic states are plainly nitrogen-limited (Kratzer and Brezonik, 1981). This point is particularly clear from Canfield's study (1983a). In current use (Huber et al., 1982) the trophic state index incorporates nitrogen concentration when the N:P ratio is below 10, values above 20 being indications of "normal" phosphorus limitation. In our own work (Flannery et al., 1982; Whitmore, 1985; Deevey et al., 1986; Binford and Brenner, 1986; Binford et al., 1987; Brenner and Binford, 1988) we avoid Secchi depth as an ambiguous measure and use trophic state indices derived singly from chlorophyll *a*, phosphorus, or nitrogen concentrations.

Nutrient data available for more than 500 lakes in the FLADAB show that the lakes run the gamut from ultra-oligotrophic in the sandhills to hypereutrophic near sewage plants, muck farms, and phosphate deposits. While it might be assumed that most subtropical lakes in karst terrain are eutrophic, such a gross generalization does not hold in Florida. More than half the lakes reported in the FLADAB contain less than 1 mg/L total nitrogen. About one-third of the lakes contain less than 20 μg/L total phosphorus and on this criterion alone would be considered oligotrophic to mesotrophic. Both geologic and cultural factors clearly play a role in regulating lacustrine nutrient content, and a large limnological and engineering literature summarizes the impact of various riparian land uses on lake trophic state. The issue is addressed in general by Chapra and Reckhow (1983) and summarized for Florida by Baker et al. (1981) and Huber et al. (1982). These studies try to evaluate "nonpoint source" exports of phosphorus and nitrogen from variously urbanized or agriculturally developed drainage basins. The objective is to develop models that will allow prediction of lacustrine trophic state changes given proposed land use shifts.

When chlorophyll *a* concentration is used to evaluate the trophic state of

Florida lakes, it corroborates the finding that the majority of lakes fall in the oligotrophic to mesotrophic range. For 305 lakes in the FLADAB, more than 70 percent had less chlorophyll *a* than 20 mg/m^3. Despite the fact that low concentrations of chlorophyll *a* suggest low concentrations of algae in the water column, low system productivity should not be inferred. In Florida's prevailing shallow lakes, a large fraction of the nutrient pool may be used by larger plants (macrophytes), which are not considered when measuring the chlorophyll *a* content of open waters (Canfield et al., 1983a).

Plants

Plants form the foundation of the lacustrine trophic pyramid. Aquatic plants occupy several habitats and include the algae of the phytoplankton as well as larger forms growing on the lake bottom and on other plants. Macrophytes—macroalgae, mosses, ferns, and flowering plants—are particularly important in Florida's numerous shallow lakes. The relative contribution of each life form, either to total biomass or to productivity, depends on physical factors such as morphometry and the nature of the substratum, on chemical factors such as nutrients and ions, and on biological factors such as competition and predation.

Species composition of phytoplankton communities varies with trophic state. Eutrophic Newnan's Lake and Biven's Arm, both in Alachua County, were dominated by the cyanophyte (blue-green) genera *Anacystis* and *Anabaena*, and by chlorophytes (green algae) such as *Ankistrodesmus, Pediastrum*, and *Scenedesmus* (Nordlie, 1976). *Aphanizomenon*, another blue-green alga, was the commonest genus in Newnan's Lake, but was absent from the other two lakes in Nordlie's study. Lake Mize, also in Alachua County, is a nutrient-poor, acidic, colored lake; the phytoplankton was composed largely of the diatom *Asterionella*, two chrysophyte (yellow-brown) genera (*Dinobryon* and *Synura*), and two pyrrhophyte (dinoflagellate) species of the genus *Peridinium*. *Peridinium* demonstrates a preference for low pH, oligotrophic systems and can form algae-rich layers in deep water of clear lakes (Battoe, 1985).

Total cell density of phytoplankton increased with trophic state in Orange County's Lakes Beauclair (hypereutrophic), Corner (mesotrophic), and Bay (oligotrophic). There was also a shift in community structure along the trophic gradient (Elmore et al., 1984). Lake Beauclair was dominated by blue-green algae (52 percent), with greens representing 38 percent. In Corner Lake the relative abundances were reversed, with greens accounting for 59 percent and blue-greens for 35 percent. In Bay Lake greens were also dominant (54 percent) but were followed in importance by cryptophytes (31 percent).

Brezonik et al. (1984) found that green algae dominated in acid lakes while blue-greens were more important at higher pH. However, as phosphorus concentrations were low in the acidic systems, the algae may be controlled by nutrient limitation.

Mud Lake, in the Ocala National Forest, is a shallow, alkaline lake with moderate color. *Spirogyra* is the dominant green alga, followed by a species of *Sirogonium*. Eighteen species and varieties of diatoms were recorded, though in small numbers (Bradley and Beard, 1969). The sediments are composed largely of midge fecal pellets containing blue-green algae (Iovino and Bradley, 1969), and benthic primary productivity is apparently important in this lake.

Whitmore (1989) examined diatom remains from surficial sediments of thirty Florida lakes representing a trophic gradient. Skeletons of benthic, epiphytic, and planktonic forms are quantitatively preserved in lake mud, and the samples contained a total of 287 taxa. Relative abundances of species varied as a function of trophic state and permitted construction of a diatom index of trophic status, to be compared with the diatom index of acidity in sedimentary histories (Binford et al., 1987).

Laboratory studies have provided supplemental evidence that nutrient limitation controls algal cell densities and species composition. Water samples from soft-water Lake Jackson, near Tallahassee, were enriched with nitrogen, phosphorus, or silica (Glooschenko and Alvis, 1973). Nitrogen or phosphorus added singly or in combination resulted in higher numbers and changes in community composition, suggesting that these nutrients limit primary production and may control algal species succession in the lake. Addition of silica stimulated diatom growth, implying that the scarcity and low diversity of diatoms in Lake Jackson are attributable to silica deficiency.

Aquatic macrophytes play an important role in the structure and function of Florida's lakes, where long growing seasons, high insolation, and shallow depths are conducive to prolific growth. They compete with microalgae for dissolved nutrients and affect physical, chemical, and biological conditions in lakes. Macrophytes represent an important component of total biomass and primary productivity (Canfield et al., 1983a). For example, phytoplankton accounted for 44 percent of gross primary production in Little Lake Conway, the balance being attributed to macrophytes and their associated epiphytes (Fontaine and Ewel, 1981). Macrophytes also play a significant role in nutrient cycling, by taking up materials from the sediments and releasing them to the water column (Ewel and Fontaine, 1983).

Aquatic macrophytes are represented by numerous species in Florida, many of which are not native (Tarver et al., 1979). The introduction of exotics and their subsequent proliferation have caused major changes in many lakes, rendering some nearly useless for recreation. In 1983, 332 Florida lakes, representing 418,770 ha, were surveyed. Weeds occupied 117,894 ha, or 28 percent coverage of the surfaces of these lakes. Twenty-nine of the

154 species found in the survey (which included flowing waters as well as lakes) were exotic, and these accounted for 32 percent of the total weed coverage for all water bodies (Schardt, 1983).

Among the most problematic of the nuisance species are the free-floating water hyacinth (*Eichhornia crassipes*) and the rooted, submerged hydrilla (*Hydrilla verticillata*). Water hyacinth may have been introduced into the United States in 1884 at the Cotton Centennial Exposition in New Orleans. The plant can double its biomass in two weeks in nutrient-rich waters (Mitsch, 1976). This Brazilian exotic spread quickly and by 1983 was found in 287 of 332 surveyed Florida lakes. It was ranked the fourth most abundant aquatic plant in Florida with respect to coverage (Schardt, 1983). The plant clogs waterways and can change chemical conditions in the underlying water (Ultsch, 1973). Recent efforts to control hyacinths with herbicides have been relatively successful.

Hydrilla, introduced by the aquarium trade in the early 1960s, remains the most troublesome weed in Florida waters. Though found in only 36 percent of the 332 lakes surveyed in 1983, hydrilla was second only to cattails (*Typha*) with respect to areal coverage (Schardt, 1983). Hydrilla demonstrates several growth characteristics that may enable it to outcompete other weed species. Experiments show that green light stimulates rapid stem elongation. Green wavelengths penetrate deep into lake water and initiate rapid stem growth toward the surface. Red wavelengths penetrate poorly, but when absorbed by plants at or near the surface they trigger extensive branching (Van et al., 1977). The thick mat that forms has a high ratio of stems and leaves to roots, and it propagates rapidly by budding. Furthermore, the surface mat severely attenuates light, thereby shading other plant species below. In open water, light energy was reduced some 29 percent in the upper 0.3 m of the water column, but in hydrilla beds a 95 percent reduction was measured over the same vertical distance (Haller and Sutton, 1975).

The case history of Lake Apopka, at the head of the Oklawaha drainage, demonstrates the severity of the weed problem. During the 1940s the lake was dominated by pondweed, *Potamogeton illinoiensis*, which grew throughout the basin at depths above 2.4 m, together with the codominant eelgrass, *Vallisneria americana* (Chesnut and Barman, 1974). Plankton blooms commenced in 1947 as a consequence of sewage discharge, disposal of citrus wastes, and muck farming in the basin. In 1959, hyacinths were encountered around the lake shores and in some isolated mats, and increasing eutrophication had reduced the abundance of game fish by the mid-1950s (Clugston, 1963). Studies in 1971 and 1972 indicated that hyacinths had greatly expanded their coverage and that submerged, attached macrophytes had been eliminated. Former dominants, *Potamogeton* and *Vallisneria*, were not found.

Aquatic weed infestations not only limit navigability but also affect biological characteristics of lakes. Watkins et al. (1983) studied zooplankton and benthic invertebrate communities of vegetated and nonvegetated areas of Orange Lake (Alachua County). The greatest numbers of invertebrate species were found in vegetated regions, and hydrilla supported higher numbers of invertebrates than did other macrophytes. Watkins et al. hypothesized that hydrilla's dissected leaves provide abundant surface area where animals can hide, thereby escaping predation.

Weed-infested Florida lakes are likely to support many kinds of zooplankton, as many types avoid open water and live only in weed beds (Shireman and Martin, 1978; Watkins et al., 1983; Schmitz and Osborne, 1984; Flannery, 1984; Richard et al., 1985). Zooplankton in lakes heavily infested with hydrilla is dominated by cladocerans and calanoid copepods, while rotifers are relatively scarce (Shireman and Martin, 1978; Flannery, 1984).

Aquatic weed beds support large numbers of many fish species (Barnett and Schneider, 1974), but weed infestations often have negative impact on sport fish in particular (Colle and Shireman, 1980; Shireman and Maceina, 1981). Killing of floating and submerged macrophytes with herbicides is often effective, but the nutrients in the dead plants are returned to the lake by decomposition. Biological control—of hydrilla in particular—has proved effective in several lakes after experimental introduction of the Asiatic grass carp (*Ctenopharyngodon idella*). Introduction of any exotic species requires careful management, and close attention is being given to the limnological effects of reduction of a major nuisance by this method (Canfield et al., 1983c, 1984; Leslie et al., 1983; Richard et al., 1984, 1985; Van Dyke et al., 1984).

Zooplankton

Invertebrate animals are separated by habitat into two communities, the zooplankton and the benthos. Zooplankters are the floating or weakly swimming animals of the water column, while benthic invertebrates inhabit the lake bottom. Some types divide their time between habitats, living mainly in surficial sediments but migrating at times into the waters above. Larvae of the nonbiting midge *Chaoborus* migrate daily and often dominate the zooplankton at night. Other zooplankters (chydorid cladocerans and amphipods) avoid open water, living only among weed beds near shore. Invertebrates occupy several trophic levels, feeding on planktonic algae, organic detritus, bacteria, or other invertebrates. Larvae of freshwater mussels (Unionidae) are obligate parasites on gills of fishes and appear in the plankton for a few minutes before attachment.

Surveys in many states demonstrate that zooplankton communities change in biomass and composition as a function of trophic state. As a rule, diversity—of crustaceans in particular—is higher in oligotrophic systems, while smaller forms such as rotifers and protozoans dominate at higher trophic states.

In a study of thirty-nine Florida lakes, total zooplankton biomass was positively correlated with trophic state, and the microzooplankton (ciliates, rotifers, and copepod nauplii) was largely responsible for the relationship (Bays and Crisman, 1983). Among the eutrophic systems, microzooplankton composed 50 percent to 90 percent of the biomass. For eight north-central lakes, total zooplankton numbers were highly correlated with the inverse of Secchi depth (Blancher, 1984). Average annual concentrations ranged from 23 to 381 animals per liter. Abundance under unit area of lake surface ranged from $1 \times 10^5/m^2$ in systems of low productivity to $8.2 \times 10^5/m^2$ in eutrophic lakes. Copepods made up the highest percentage of annual biomass in all the lakes, but while cladocerans or copepods were more important numerically in oligotrophic and mesotrophic systems, rotifers clearly dominated in eutrophic lakes, with 78 percent or more of annual mean numbers of animals.

Similar results were obtained in three Orange County lakes (Bay, Corner, and Beauclair) by Elmore et al. (1984). In a spring and summer survey of 165 lakes, mean numerical zooplankton abundance was quite variable, ranging from 7.3 to $1500/L^1$, and there was a significant positive correlation (r = 0.66) with chlorophyll *a* concentration (Canfield and Watkins, 1984).

Ciliated protozoans were collected monthly over an annual cycle in twenty Florida lakes (Beaver and Crisman, 1982). Abundance and biomass were highly correlated with trophic state, and larger animals were replaced by smaller individuals in more productive systems. Ciliates are effective bacterial grazers (Crisman et al., 1981), and the exclusion of smaller ciliates from oligotrophic systems may be related to low bacterial densities (Crisman et al., 1984). The larger types that dominate in these systems are probably capable of ingesting minute planktonic algae. Five kinds of supposedly autotrophic algae have been shown to ingest particles of the size of bacteria and picoplankton (Porter, 1986), so grazing of algae by ciliates would not be surprising.

Zooplankton communities have been examined in lakes of varying pH (Brezonik et al., 1984), but because pH and chlorophyll *a* covary, it is difficult to separate acidity from food limitation. Zooplankton abundance and diversity may be controlled by either factor, by both, or by neither. Alone or in combination, factors known to influence zooplankton include predation and competition (Bays and Crisman, 1983; Blancher, 1984; Elmore, 1983; Elmore et al., 1983; Foran, 1986a,b); water chemistry (Crisman, 1980; Brezonik et al., 1984); food availability (Beaver and Crisman, 1981, 1982; Canfield and Watkins, 1984; Elmore et al., 1984; Brezonik et al., 1984); temperature (Blancher, 1984; Foran, 1986a,b); life history patterns and behavior (Billets and Osborne, 1985), and structure of habitat, which is affected by aquatic macrophytes (Fry and Osborne, 1980; Richard et al., 1985; Schmitz and Osborne, 1984; Shireman and Martin, 1978; Watkins et al., 1983). Seasonal and diurnal factors also influence the kinds and numbers of animals collected (Wyngaard et al., 1982; Shireman and Martin, 1978; Reid and Blake, 1970; Schmitz and Osborne, 1984).

Benthos

The benthic or bottom-dwelling community contains animals of most of the invertebrate phyla, but the conspicuous animals encountered by naturalists and anglers are mainly molluscs, crustaceans, and larval or adult insects. Limnologists regularly encounter a fourth group, the oligochaete worms of muddy bottoms. Fishes encounter animals of all four groups. While juvenile and other small fishes may feed on zooplankton, and larger fishes on smaller fishes, the common Florida fishes of intermediate size subsist mainly on amphipod and isopod crustaceans and immature insects. In general, the abundance and composition of the benthic community depend heavily on the nature of the substratum, which is most diverse and richest in food and shelter in weed beds (Osborne et al., 1976). Offshore, or in depths too great for macrophytes to grow, the benthos of soft mud bottoms is restricted to oligochaete worms and midge larvae, which tolerate low oxygen concentrations and gain a supply of food—organic mud—that is also their refuge from predation.

Assemblages of benthic invertebrates in eutrophic Lake Thonotosassa form three distinct groups according to depth (Cowell and Vodopich, 1981). Forty-two species were found at shallow stations, twenty-four at mid-depth, and twenty-two at deep stations. Mean annual densities were 2255, 9809, and 12,255 animals per square meter, respectively. The whole-lake, depth-weighted annual mean value was $7424/m^2$. Oligochaetes dominated the fauna, representing 56.1 percent of the mean annual figure and were followed by chironomid midges (37.1 percent) and *Chaoborus* (5.7 percent).

Oligochaetes and chironomids also dominated the benthos of hydrilla-infested Little Lake Barton, near Orlando (Scott and Osborne, 1981). Chironomids made up 60 percent of the assemblage. Mean monthly abundance of all animals ranged from $176/m^2$ (September) to $9195/m^2$ (February), with a mean annual figure of $1717/m^2$. Taxonomic diversity was also greatest in winter. The low summer figures for both abundance and diversity were attributed to insect emergence and low oxygen concentrations.

Organic deposits in Mud Lake are composed largely of fecal pellets of several chironomid species: *Chironomus* sp., *Procladius bellus, P. culiciformis*, and *Tanytarsus* sp. (Iovino and Bradley, 1969). Samples were collected on four dates through the year, yielding mean benthic densities of 120 to 580 animals per m^2. Such densities are low as compared to temperate lakes, or even to other Florida lakes, and are attributed to fish predation, which probably occurs throughout this shallow lake.

Fuller and Cowell (1985) tested responses of benthic invertebrates to disturbance of the habitat. The surface mud of Lake Thonotosassa was raked flat, simulating the nests of the exotic cichlid fish *Sarotherodon* (= *Tilapia*) *aurea*. Nests occupy about 11.5 percent of the littoral (near shore) zone. Experiments were conducted in spring, summer, and winter to correspond to nesting periods. The artificial disturbances removed 91.6 percent of the benthos. Community recovery proceeded more quickly in spring and summer than in winter. The chironomid *Polypedilum halterale* rapidly colonized in spring and summer, whereas another chironomid (*Glyptotendipes paripes*) and the amphipod *Hyalella azteca* were the principal winter colonizers.

Fish

Game fish—species attracted to lures—are at or near the top of the trophic pyramid in lakes. Florida's lakes support about forty species of native fishes; table 11.3 lists them by family. Sport fishing is an important recreational activity in the state, and much research has been concerned with sport fish populations. Florida lake fisheries were reviewed in detail by Williams et al. (1985). The most important species are members of the centrarchid family: largemouth bass (*Micropterus salmoides*), bluegill (*Lepomis macrochirus*), and black crappie or speckled perch (*Pomoxis nigromaculatus*) and other sunfish. Several ictalurid catfishes are important to commercial and recrea-

Table 11.3. Native fish species common to Florida lakes

Scientific name	Common name
Family Lepisosteidae	gars
1. *Lepisosteus platyrhinchus*	Florida gar
Family Amiidae	bowfins
2. *Amia calva*	bowfin
Family Cyprinidae	carps and minnows
3. *Notemigonus crysoleucas*	golden shiner
4. *Notropis maculatus*	taillight shiner
*5. *Notropis emiliae peninsularis*	Florida pugnose minnow
*6. *Notropis petersoni*	coastal shiner
Family Catostomidae	suckers
7. *Erimyzon sucetta*	Lake chubsucker

(*continued*)

Table 11.3 (continued)

Scientific name	Common name
Family Ictaluridae	freshwater catfishes
8. *Ictalurus catus*	white catfish
9. *Ictalurus natalis*	yellow bullhead
10. *Ictalurus nebulosus*	brown bullhead
11. *Ictalurus punctatus*	channel catfish
12. *Noturus gyrinus*	tadpole madtom
Family Cyprinodontidae	killifishes
13. *Fundulus chrysotus*	golden topminnow
14. *Fundulus lineolatus*	lined topminnow
15. *Fundulus seminolis*	Seminole killifish
16. *Jordanella floridae*	flagfish
17. *Lucania goodei*	bluefin killifish
Family Poeciliidae	livebearers
18. *Gambusia holbrooki*	Eastern mosquitofish
19. *Heterandria formosa*	least killifish
Family Atherinidae	silversides
20. *Labidesthes sicculus*	brook silverside
Family Centrarchidae	sunfishes
21. *Lepomis gulosus*	warmouth
22. *Lepomis macrochirus mystacalis*	southern bluegill
23. *Lepomis marginatus*	dollar sunfish
24. *Lepomis microlophus*	redear sunfish
25. *Lepomis punctatus*	spotted sunfish
26. *Micropterus salmoides floridanus*	Florida largemouth bass
27. *Pomoxis nigromaculatus*	black crappie
*28. *Elassoma evergladei*	Everglades pygmy sunfish
*29. *Elassoma okefenokee*	Okefenokee pygmy sunfish
*30. *Enneacanthus gloriosus*	bluespotted sunfish
*31. *Enneacanthus obesus*	banded sunfish
Family Esocidae	pikes
32. *Esox niger*	chain pickerel
*33. *Esox americanus: americanus* × *vermiculatus*	redfin pickerel
Family Percidae	
34. *Etheostoma fusiforme barratti*	scalyhead darter
Family Clupeidae	
35. *Dorosoma cepedianum*	gizzard shad
36. *Dorosoma petenense*	threadfin shad
Family Aphredoderidae	pirate perches
*37. *Aphredoderus sayanus*	pirate perch

Note: List from C. R. Gilbert and G. Burgess (personal communication). The listed species are those found throughout much of the state. Species designated with an asterisk are restricted in distribution or are more typical of habitats peripheral to the lake proper (e.g., weedy sloughs). Species limited to lakes of the St. Johns River drainage were excluded.

tional fishing. Two members of the pike family (Esocidae), the chain pickerel (*Esox niger*) and redfin pickerel (*Esox americanus*), are also taken by anglers.

SCUBA divers evaluated the fish populations of Lake Annie, a small, oligotrophic acid lake in Highlands County (Werner et al., 1978). Eighteen of nineteen species known from the lake were recorded. The assemblage was dominated by seven species of centrarchids. Bluegill and bass accounted for 81 percent of the fish biomass in the lake. Compared to a typical small lake in the northern states with about the same number of species (Lawrence Lake, Michigan, for example), presence of poeciliids (livebearers) and absence of esocids are noteworthy; and while minnows (cyprinids) are the dominant small fishes in north-temperate systems, killifish (cyprinodontids) and poeciliids are the prevalent small forms in Florida. Yellow perch (*Perca flavescens*), walleye (*Stizostedion vitreum*), cisco (Coregonidae), and all the trout and salmon (Salmonidae), so prevalent in cooler waters, have no ecological equivalents in Florida.

Of thirty-seven species collected from Orange Lake, Alachua County, two families (twelve species of centrarchids and six species of cyprinodontids) contain nearly half the species (Reid, 1950). Seine hauls over a thirteen-month period in Lake Panasoffkee (Sumter County) yielded 3×10^5 pounds of fish, of which one-third were game fish (Moody, 1957). The gizzard shad, *Dorosoma cepedianum*, was an important component of the nongame assemblage; gizzard shads, members of the herring family, subsist on zooplankton when adult. Of the game species captured by seining, 78 percent were bream (sunfishes, Centrarchidae), 15 percent were bass, and 7 percent were crappie. Creel censuses involving 18,000 game fish yielded similar proportions.

Cultural eutrophication of Florida lakes has prompted studies of fish community responses to changing trophic state. Among three lake types—oligotrophic, mesoeutrophic, and hypereutrophic—Kautz (1980) found no statistically significant differences in sport fish and forage fish density or biomass. Biomass of commercial species (catfish and eel) was significantly greater in hypereutrophic lakes, as were biomass and density of rough fish (shad, gar, bowfin) and the exotic cichlid, *Tilapia aurea*. Species diversity was higher in mesoeutrophic lakes than in other categories.

Florida has the largest number of exotic fish species in the forty-eight contiguous states. Warm surface water in the southern part of the state has encouraged the establishment of tropical fishes. Exotic fishes are widespread in rivers and canals, especially in southern Florida, but have not yet become widely distributed in lakes. As of 1983 (table 11.4), twenty-one alien species had established breeding populations (Courtenay et al., 1984). An additional thirty-one exotic species are known but not established. Deliberate introductions have occurred for several reasons, including food production (common

Table 11.4. Exotic fishes established in Florida fresh waters

Scientific name	Common name
Group A	
Family Cichlidae	cichlids
1. *Astronotus ocellatus*	Oscar
2. *Cichlasoma bimaculatum*	black acara
3. *Cichlasoma citrinellum*	Midas cichlid
4. *Cichlasoma meeki*	firemouth
5. *Cichlasoma octofasciatum*	Jack Dempsey
6. *Tilapia aurea*	blue tilapia
7. *Tilapia mariae*	spotted tilapia
8. *Tilapia melanotheron*	blackchin tilapia
9. *Tilapia mossambica*	Mozambique tilapia
10. *Hemichromis bimaculatus*	jewelfish
Family Clariidae	air-breathing catfishes
11. *Clarias batrachus*	walking catfish
Group B	
Family Poeciliidae	livebearers
12. *Belonesox belizanus*	pike killifish
13. *Xiphophorus helleri*	green swordtail
14. *Xiphophorus maculatus*	southern platyfish
15. *Xiphophorus variatus*	variable platyfish
Family Loricariidae	suckermouth catfishes
16. *Hypostomus* sp.	suckermouth catfish
Family Anabantidae	gouramies
17. *Trichopsis vittata*	croaking gourami
Group C	
Family Cyprinidae	carps and minnows
18. *Cyprinus carpio*	common carp
Group D	
Family Loricariidae	suckermouth catfishes
19. *Pterygoplichthys multiradiatus*	
Family Cichlidae	cichlids
20. *Geophagus surinamensis*	redstriped eartheater
Family Poeciliidae	livebearers
21. *Poecilia reticulata*	guppy

Note: Data from Courtenay et al. (1984). Group A includes species with expanding populations, group B species with localized distributions, group C species with apparently broad and stable distributional limits, and group D species for which there is insufficient information to determine population status.

carp, *Cyprinus carpio*) and weed control (grass carp, *Ctenopharyngodon idella*). Disposal of unwanted aquarium fishes accounts for some, and escape from fish farms accounts for others, such as several species of *Tilapia* and *Cichlasoma* (cichlids), catfishes, livebearers, and others.

Several exotic species compete with and soon replace native fishes. The cichlids, originating in Africa and Central and South America, fill niches occupied by native centrarchids. The Asiatic walking catfish (*Clarias batrachus*) threatens to displace native bullheads and is difficult to eradicate because it disperses readily over land. The pike killifish (*Belonesox belizanus*) attains greater lengths at maturity than native livebearers (poeciliids), and is a voracious feeder on other fish (Turner and Snelson, 1984).

Prospects

Florida's thousands of lakes, with their many thousand miles of waterfront, are extremely valuable natural resources. Their waters, bottoms, shorelines, and drainage basins are the habitat of a remarkably diverse flora and fauna. To an extent that is unusual among the lake districts of the world, the lakes are set *into* as well as *on* the landscape and are profoundly influenced by subsurface drainage. One result, little understood as yet, is that downward percolation through the bottoms of Florida lakes contributes to recharge, and potentially to contamination, of deep aquifers.

Inland waters are used for bathing, boating, skiing, fishing, and irrigation, as well as for drinking. The very existence of a lake moderates the climate of its surroundings, with incalculable consequences for human health as well as for agriculture. Although no dollar value can be placed on all the benefits of lakeside living, waterfront property sells at a premium and increases the tax base for county governments.

Florida lakes display a wide range of natural variation of limnological properties. Many have exceptionally soft, clear waters, which are naturally acidic and deficient in phosphorus and nitrogen. These properties make them vulnerable to even modest additions of waterborne and airborne nutrients, acids, and toxins. Case studies—for example in Lake Apopka—demonstrate that human activities have many kinds of impact, mostly deleterious, on water quality. Limnological changes indicate ecological changes in watershed ecosystems as wholes; but while some obvious changes affect water clarity, birdlife, color of plankton, or abundance of nuisance pondweeds, many changes result from overuse or chemical alteration of groundwater and are concealed from public view.

Human populations in Florida will continue to grow, and watershed ecosystems will inevitably be subjected to further development. Environmental problems are receiving increasing public attention, and water quality issues—eutrophication, acidification, groundwater contamination, and others—arouse increasing concern. Groups involved in research on and protection of water resources include the state water management districts, state departments of natural resources and environmental regulation, the Florida Game and Fresh Water Fish Commission, the U.S. Geological Survey, the U.S. Environmental Protection Agency, and university scientists from numerous departments. Data gathered by these agencies have greatly increased our knowledge of Florida's warm-temperate and subtropical lakes, but many important problems remain unstudied. Successful policies designed to protect the state's aquatic resources will depend on agreed-on management objectives and a firm understanding of ecological processes in lakes and their watersheds (fig. 11.4).

Fig. 11.4. Lake Istokpoga, Florida's fifth-largest lake, covers 11 km^2 in Highlands County. Photo by J. N. Layne.

12
Rivers and Springs

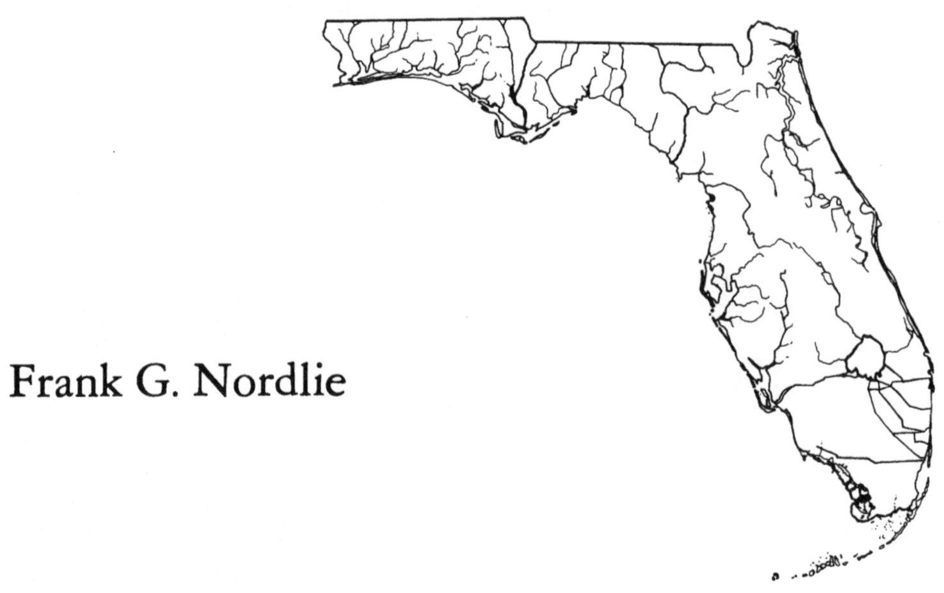

Frank G. Nordlie

Florida, with its unique geographical location, morphometry, and climate, has developed a multitude of rivers—more than 1700 counting those of all sizes, most of the larger ones discharging directly into the sea. The area that is now the southeastern United States was repeatedly inundated to various extents by marine waters as the earth's climate changed through geological time, layering these areas with limestones (calcium and magnesium carbonates) produced as marine sediments. As the water retreated, the limestones were subsequently covered to varying depths by clays and sands. An extensive aquifer system (the Floridan Aquifer) developed in the upper strata of these limestones, producing more than 300 artesian springs within what is now the state of Florida. Artesian springs combine with surface drainage to produce the extensive discharge systems of northern and central Florida.

The climate and geology of Florida, and of the southeastern region in general, have been discussed in earlier chapters of this book and are also discussed by Bass and Cox (1985) in their consideration of Florida rivers and fishery resources. Only a few especially pertinent points will be reviewed here to help the reader focus on processes that have shaped and continue to influence Florida's flowing water ecosystems.

Topography and Stratigraphy

Peninsular Florida is the highest part of the Floridan plateau, most of which lies submerged under waters of the Gulf of Mexico and, to a much lesser extent, the Atlantic Ocean. The maximum elevation in Florida is roughly 106 m above sea level, in Walton County in northwest Florida, and the maximum elevation in the peninsula is 95 m, at Sugarloaf Mountain, Lake County, in the central Highlands area (Fernald, 1981). While the modest elevations of the Florida peninsula do not produce fast-flowing streams, several of those discharging into the Gulf along the Florida Panhandle have their origins at higher elevations inland above the fall line in Alabama or Georgia. The longest river completely within the political boundaries of Florida is the St. Johns River, which originates in Kissimmee Prairie, west of Malabar, and flows northward for a distance of 512 km to its point of discharge into the Atlantic Ocean 34 km northeast of Jacksonville (Pierce, 1947).

Surficial deposits over the Florida peninsula (and the southeastern United States in general) are relatively diverse, though largely shaped by marine processes; they are distributed over underlying limestone formations that are frequently rich in phosphates and other substances, including sodium chloride, derived from ocean waters. It is in these limestones that the artesian Floridan Aquifer formed (Rosenau et al., 1977). This aquifer extends from southern South Carolina across the lower half of Georgia and the southeastern corner of Alabama and underlies all of Florida. Areas of recharge develop where surface waters percolate through permeable regions in overlying sediments into breaks in the limestones. Acidity of surface waters produced by the solution of carbon dioxide (carbonic acid) and of organic acids from plant materials further erodes these limestones by converting the $CaCO_3$ to soluble Ca^{2+} and HCO_3^-, thus creating cavities and chambers. The confinement of water within such cavities by overlying sediments (the confining bed) results in the establishment of a "pressure head" within the aquifer and forces water to the surface anywhere downslope that the confining bed is broached, producing artesian springs. Water table springs, or seeps, result from the reemergence at the surface of water that has percolated through only the most surficial sediments and moved downslope over the surface of impermeable sediments, principally clays.

Florida's physiography has been evaluated over the years by geologists who have subdivided or combined regions in various ways. Perhaps the earliest comprehensive approach was to divide the state into five physiographic divisions: Coastal Lowlands, Central Highlands, Tallahassee Hills, Marianna

Lowlands, and Western Highlands (Stubbs, 1940; Cooke, 1945). The Coastal Lowlands extend around the coastal periphery of the state where elevations are generally below 30 m. The Central Highlands area, also known as "The Ridge," runs southward down the peninsula from the Georgia boundary to just below Lake Istokpoga in Highlands County, where the elevation drops abruptly to the Coastal Lowlands. The Tallahassee Hills lie to the west of the Central Highlands and extend westward to the Apalachicola River. The Marianna Lowlands in Holmes, Jackson, and Washington counties extend westward from the Apalachicola River to the eastern edge of the Western Highlands. The Western Highlands extend farther westward in the Panhandle to the Perdido River (Cooke, 1945; Stubbs, 1940).

These five physiographic divisions were combined into three major regions by Puri and Vernon (1964). The Northern Region, consisting of the Western Highlands, Marianna Lowlands, and Tallahassee Hills, includes much high ground at elevations above the piezometric surface (the height to which water will rise in a tightly cased pipe driven into limestone of the Floridan Aquifer). This area is well drained with existing lakes generally "perched" above the Floridan Aquifer. Most of the largest springs in Florida are found along river valleys in this region. The second region, the Central Highlands, is a region of extremes, with longitudinally oriented ridges, upland plains, and valleys. Here the piezometric surfaces are below the levels of the higher ground and above those of lower areas, resulting in the presence of standing waters in depressions and the development of springs in lowlands. The third region, Coastal Lowlands, includes areas of low elevation along the coasts and the flat areas from Lake Okeechobee southward, much of which is occupied by the Everglades. The land surfaces of the Coastal Lowlands are almost entirely below the piezometric surface, resulting in a flow to the surface of artesian water wherever there is a break in the overlying strata.

Surface Runoff

The availability of water for surface runoff in any region is roughly a function of the difference between the annual rainfall and evapotranspiration in that area. This relationship is altered by a number of factors; perhaps the most important, over much of Florida, is the extent to which rainfall percolating to the artesian aquifer is discharged through spring flow at a distance from the recharge point. The difference between annual rainfall and potential evapotranspiration of Florida varies considerably. It is greatest in the Panhandle, followed by the southeastern portion of the peninsula, where there is a net recharge of the aquifer. In southwestern Florida (Charlotte, Glades, Lee, and Hendry counties) the potential difference is a negative one with evaporation exceeding annual rainfall (Visher and Hughes, 1975). There is greater variation in annual rainfall over Florida (112–163 cm) than in evaporation (117–137 cm), so the variations in runoff are more influenced by rainfall than by evapotranspiration (Visher and Hughes, 1975). Seasonal variations in stream flow patterns show greatest discharge during winter and spring months in the Panhandle and as far east as the Suwannee River drainage, and in summer and fall months in the St. Johns River drainage and southward through the peninsula (Kenner, 1975). The marked climatic differences from north to south in Florida make comparisons of various riverine ecosystems more interesting but also more difficult.

Rivers

Florida's Major Waterways

The major river systems of Florida are most numerous in the northern and western regions of the state—in the Panhandle and along the Gulf coast of the peninsula (fig. 12.1 and accompanying information in table 12.1). There is great variation among Florida's major river systems in areal extents of drainage basins; average rates of flow; lengths of the rivers, along with portion of the distance traversed in Florida before discharge; and average gradient along the stream course (table 12.2). The Apalachicola River has the largest drainage basin (51,800 km^2), the greatest average discharge (702.4 m^3/s), and the greatest total length (805 km), but only a small fraction of the total system is within Florida. This drainage system includes three states. The Apalachicola River itself is located exclusively in Florida but is formed by the confluence of two large rivers, the Flint and Chattahoochee, draining southward from Alabama and Georgia. The area of confluence was impounded by the construction of the Jim Woodruff Dam, creating the large, shallow Lake Seminole, now effectively the headwaters of the Apalachicola. Another large river, the Chipola, also discharges into the Apalachicola well downstream from Lake Seminole. The Suwannee River has the second largest drainage basin (26,641 km^2), the second largest mean flow (304.7 m^3/s), and the second longest stretch of river within Florida. The St. Johns has the third largest drainage basin (22,792 km^2).

Of the twenty-three major rivers that discharge directly into the sea, twenty-one are located on the Gulf coast; only the St. Johns and St. Marys rivers drain into the Atlantic. Five of the six major canals listed—Miami, North New River, Hillsboro, West Palm Beach, and St. Lucie—discharge directly into the Atlantic, whereas the Tamiami Canal discharges much water southward through the Everglades before it joins the Miami Canal, which discharges into Biscayne Bay on the Atlantic coast.

The general patterns of stream flow are southward in the Panhandle, westward along the Gulf coast, southward in the central region of the peninsula, eastward in the lower eastern portion of the peninsula and northward (St. Johns River) or eastward in the upper eastern area of the peninsula. The only major system that does not discharge directly on a coast is the

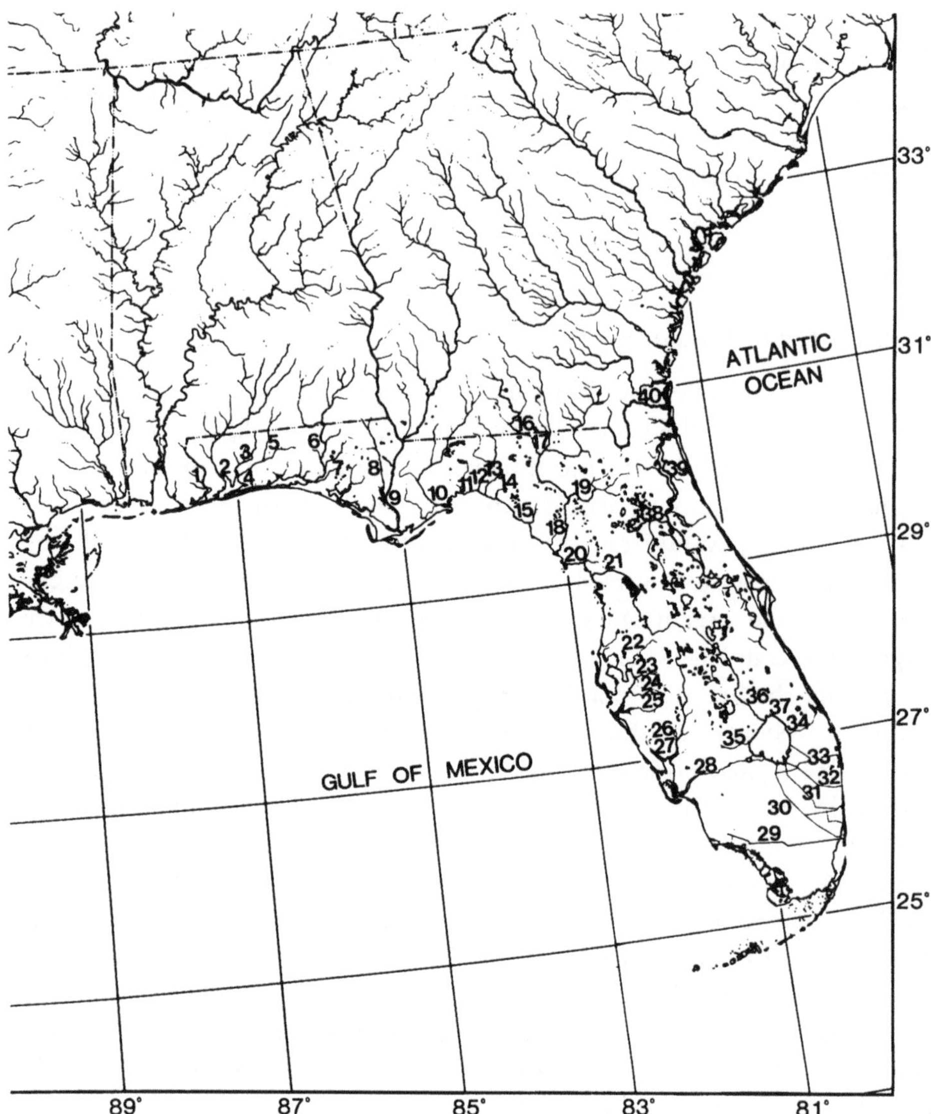

Fig. 12.1. Florida's major waterways, including their headwaters. Numbers correspond to those of rivers listed in table 12.1.

Table 12.1. Principal waterways of Florida

Waterway	Location of headwaters
Gulf	
1. Perdido River	Alabama
2. Escambia River	Alabama (the Conecuh River a major tributary)

(*continued*)

Table 12.1 (continued)

Waterway	Location of headwaters
3. Blackwater River	Florida and Alabama
4. Yellow River	Florida and Alabama
5. Shoal[a]	Florida and Alabama
6. Choctawhatchee River	Alabama
7. Holmes Creek[a]	Alabama
8. Chipola River[a,d]	Mostly Florida
9. Apalachicola River	Alabama and Georgia (the Flint and Chattahoochee rivers major tributaries)
10. Ochlockonee River	Georgia
11. St. Marks River[d]	Florida
12. Aucilla River	Mostly Florida
13. Econfina River	Florida
14. Fenholloway River	Florida
15. Steinhatchee River	Florida
16. Withlacoochee (North) River[a,e]	Georgia
17. Alapaha River[a,e]	Georgia
18. Suwannee River[d]	Several sources including Okeefenokee Swamp and nos. 16 and 17 above—Georgia
19. Santa Fe River[a,d]	Florida
20. Waccasassa River	Florida
21. Withlacoochee (South) River[d]	Florida
22. Hillsborough River	Florida
23. Alafia River	Florida
24. Little Manatee River	Florida
25. Manatee River	Florida
26. Myakka River	Florida
27. Peace River	Florida
28. Caloosahatchee River[c]	Florida
Atlantic	
29. Tamiami Canal[b]	Florida
30. Miami Canal[b]	Florida
31. North New River Canal[b]	Florida
32. Hillsboro Canal	Florida
33. West Palm Beach Canal[b]	Florida
34. St. Lucie Canal[b]	Florida
35. Fisheating Creek[a]	
36. Kissimmee River[a]	Florida
37. Taylor Creek[a]	
38. Oklawaha River[a]	Florida
39. St. Johns River[d]	Florida
40. St. Marys River[d]	Okeefenokee Swamp, Georgia

Note: River numbers indicate their locations on map (fig. 12.1).

a. Tributary streams—do not discharge directly into a marine water.

b. Canals.

c. A canal in area adjacent to Lake Okeechobee.

d. Receive flow from one or more first magnitude springs.

e. Tributaries of the Suwannee located almost totally in Georgia.

Kissimmee River, a tributary of Lake Okeechobee. It flows southward through the Osceola Plain (Puri and Vernon, 1964; White, 1970) on its path to the lake. The St. Johns River, which originates to the east of the Kissimmee Valley, flows northward in the Eastern Valley (Puri and Vernon, 1964; White, 1970). The various canals listed are all involved in water level regulation in the south Florida area, the Tamiami canal with the Everglades and the others with Lake Okeechobee. The unaltered pathways of discharge from Lake Okeechobee were generally southward, following the surface elevation gradients, with discharge primarily to Florida Bay and the Gulf of Mexico (Tebeau, 1974; Parker, 1984).

There are dramatic differences among waterways in chemical features, including total phosphorus, total nitrogen, hardness, and specific conduc-

Table 12.2. Physical features of selected Florida rivers

River	Total length (km)	Florida length (km)	Gradient (m/km)	Drainage (km^2)	Average flow (m^3/s)
Apalachicola	805	161	0.40	51,800	702.4
Aucilla	111	98	0.55	2279	15.7
Blackwater	94	79	0.64	2227	30.0
Caloosahatchee	121	121	0.04		40.8
Chipola	201	136	0.17	3124	42.8
Choctawhatchee	280	201	0.27	12,033	204.8
Escambia	148	87	0.72	10,878	185.1
Fenholloway	55	55	0.49	855	3.7
Fisheating Creek	85	85	0.27	1129	7.3
Hillsborough	88	88	0.27	1787	16.8
Kissimmee	172	172	0.07	7550	62.0
Little Manatee	63	63	0.64	386	4.8
Myakka	87	87	0.34	1399	7.1
Ochlockonee	257	180	0.47	5957	45.7
Oklawaha	121	121	0.13	5517	45.2
Peace	169	169	0.19	5957	32.7
Perdido	105	93	0.80	2396	21.8
St. Johns[a]	512	512	0.02	22,792	156.2
St. Marys	193	161	0.17	3885	19.3
Santa Fe	113	113	0.36	3730	46.0
Shoal	53	53	0.63	1292	31.4
Steinhatchee	46	46	0.40	1528	9.3
Suwannee	394	333	0.09	26,641	304.7
Waccasassa	62	62	0.38	1373	9.4
Wakulla	16	16	0.00	spring	11.0
Withlacoochee (N)	185	45	0.44	6035	47.6
Withlacoochee (S)	253	253	0.17	5180	32.0
Yellow	148	98	0.57	3626	65.0

Source: Bass (1983).

a. The average flow given for the St. Johns River is the average *net* flow, corrected for tidal flow. The maximum *net* flow for the St. Johns given by Anderson and Goolsby (1973) is 2463.6 m^3/s.

tance (table 12.3). Thus, it is not surprising that the diversity of sources and of geological formations drained by both surface flow and artesian spring flow produces such great variations in chemical features. Total phosphorus concentrations (means) range from a low of 0.08 mg/kg (Yellow River) to a very high 8.26 mg/kg (Peace River); total nitrogen concentrations from

Table 12.3. Chemical features of selected Florida streams

River	Total phosphorus (mg/kg)	Total nitrogen (mg/kg)	Hardness (mg/kg)	Specific conductance (μS/cm)
Perdido	0.10	1.8	3.6	22.0
	(0.00–0.15)	(0.44–3.2)	(3–5)	(20–25)
Escambia	0.13	2.5	22.9	78.7
	(0.03–0.28)	(1.5–3.5)	(13–40)	(40–130)
Blackwater			6.6	25.1
			(0–20)	(12–29)
Yellow	0.08	2.1	20.7	54.3
	(0.00–0.15)	(1.0–4.1)	(9–33)	(20–75)
Choctawhatchee	0.10	2.6	37.9	98.3
	(0.06–0.15)	(1.5–4.5)	(15–65)	(45–150)
Apalachicola	0.14	3.3	34.3	93.8
	(0.00–0.25)	(1.1–5.6)	(19–55)	(60–132)
Chipola	0.09	5.4	93.0	207.1
	(0.00–0.15)	(3.2–8.6)	(58–110)	(168–225)
Ochlockonee	0.64	6.0	25.8	120.8
	(0.18–1.00)	(4.0–8.5)	(13–53)	(75–217)
Aucilla	0.17	3.1	55.2	115.7
	(0.00–0.28)	(1.8–4.4)	(15–170)	(33–338)
Suwannee	0.93	4.7	95.2	207.9
	(0.34–4.00)	(3.4–5.7)	(21–160)	(64–330)
St. Marys	0.21	3.1	20.0	66.2
	(0.09–0.6)	(1.0–5.0)	(6–40)	(40–104)
St. Johns	0.21	5.4	178.0	869.5
	(0.12–0.27)	(1.4–8.5)	(170–200)	(645–1150)
Withlacoochee	0.12	3.7	125.4	264.3
	(0.06–0.18)	(2.4–5.9)	(69–150)	(159–308)
Hillsborough	2.3	10.5	138.8	286.6
	(0.66–8.1)	(5.5–26)	(45–180)	(100–465)
Kissimmee	0.26	5.6	44.8	142.1
	(0.15–0.51)	(4.9–6.4)	(40–61)	(121–205)
Peace	8.26	11.1	117.6	316.0
	(3.6–13.2)	(7.7–16)	(53–150)	(142–445)
Myakka	0.65	5.5	89.0	224.5
	(0.09–1.38)	(3.5–6.7)	(31–130)	(90–300)
Caloosahatchee	0.40	10.5	178.3	563.0
	(0.18–1.14)	(6.9–19)	(140–230)	(445–665)

Source: Bass (1983).

Note: Mean values are given with ranges below each in parentheses. All data are for the 1980 water-year.

1.8 mg/kg (Perdido River) to 11.1 mg/kg (Peace River); hardness from 3.6 mg/kg (Perdido River) to 178 mg/kg (St. Johns and Caloosahatchee); and specific conductances from 22.0 μS/cm (Perdido River) to 869.5 μS/cm (St. Johns River). While the hardness and conductance values may be influenced by tide waters, the general pattern is of an increase in plant nutrients and dissolved inorganic materials from the Florida Panhandle to the peninsula, with highest concentrations in south and east Florida.

Classification of Florida's Streams and Rivers

Rivers have not escaped the inevitable efforts to categorize and classify ecosystems. Most of these have utilized combinations of physical, chemical, and biological features. The utility of such categorization of a river depends on the extent of natural variation that exists between the headwaters and tailwaters of the system and is confounded by cultural alterations such as dam construction and channelization along the river course.

Variations in velocity of flow, substratum, temperature, dissolved oxygen concentration, and water hardness determine the suitability of a particular stream for various organisms (Beck, 1965). All of these characteristics have been considered in developing stream classifications. Among these factors temperature would seem to vary least, and since some of the rivers are wholly or partially fed by artesian springs, their temperatures fluctuate even less than do those of streams fed exclusively or primarily by surface waters. Thus, some springs harbor species incapable of surviving in rivers subject to wide variations in temperature.

Several systems have been developed and used for categorizing Florida rivers (Rogers, 1933; Carr, 1940; Berner, 1941, 1950; Hobbs, 1942; Herring, 1951; Beck, 1965). A new system of river classification has been used by the Florida Natural Areas Inventory. This scheme includes four categories of riverine systems: seepage streams, alluvial streams, blackwater streams, and spring-run streams. However, this new system suffers from the same disadvantages that other systems do and seems to offer no additional advantages.

The most widely used system of river classification is that of Beck (1965), who divided Florida's flowing waters into five categories: sand-bottomed, calcareous, swamp-and-bog, larger rivers, and canals. Brief descriptions of each of these categories will be given.

Thirty-three of Florida's major waterways were classified using Beck's system and information from his paper (Beck, 1965), along with information from Bass (1983) and personal observations (table 12.4). The largest group, consisting of twelve of these thirty-three waterways, was classified as sand-bottomed streams, with the second largest group of eight classified as canals. Only seven of the group were classified as calcareous streams and two as swamp-and-bog streams. The remaining four are the larger rivers.

Table 12.4. Classification of Florida's major waterways

Category / Waterway
Sand-bottomed streams
Perdido River
Blackwater River
Yellow River
Shoal River
Ochlockonee River
Econfina River
Withlacoochee River (North)
Waccasassa River (sand-bottomed/calcareous)
Withlacoochee River (South)
Hillsborough River
Myakka River
Oklawaha River[a]
Calcareous streams
Holmes Creek (calcareous/sand-bottomed)
Chipola River
St. Marks River
Aucilla River (calcareous/sand-bottomed)
Alapaha River
Suwannee River
Santa Fe River
Swamp-and-bog streams
Steinhatchee River
St. Marys River
Large rivers
Escambia River
Choctawhatchee River
Apalachicola River
St. Johns River
Canals
Caloosahatchee River
Tamiami Canal
Miami Canal
North New River Canal
Hillsboro Canal
West Palm Beach Canal
St. Lucie Canal
Kissimmee River

Source: following Beck (1965).

a. A portion of the lower Oklawaha River channel near its point of discharge to the St. Johns River was impounded by the construction of the Rodman Dam to become a part of the now de-authorized Cross-Florida Barge Canal. This impoundment is called Lake Oklawaha or the Rodman Reservoir.

Sand-Bottomed Streams

Sand-bottomed streams are the most widely distributed and abundant type in Florida. They are prominent in the Central Highlands (fig. 12.2), Coastal Lowlands, Marianna Lowlands, and Western Highlands. Currents in these streams are moderate to swift, and the typical faunal elements are various species of immature insects, such as mayflies, caddisflies, and blackflies, that are adapted to swift waters (and are used as indicator species of such habitats).

Chemically such streams are circumneutral to slightly acid (pH 5.7–7.4) with low to moderate buffering capacities, hardnesses from 5 to 120 mg/kg, and moderately high color. Streambeds are frequently of shifting sands. Plant growth is variable in density and variety. Rivers of the Panhandle and upper Gulf coast are typical examples.

Calcareous Streams

Calcareous streams are predominantly of spring origin. Their waters are relatively cool and clear (some have slight turbidities due to suspended carbonates and/or clay), frequently with dense growths of submerged plants.

Fig. 12.2. Tiger Creek is a sand-bottomed stream fed by seepage from the Central Highlands, Polk County. Photo by J. N. Layne.

They are widely distributed in the Central Highlands, Coastal Lowlands, Marianna Lowlands, and southern portion of the Tallahassee Hills. Velocities range from low to high. Their benthic faunas are characterized by high densities of molluscs, especially snails of the genera *Elimia* (*Goniobasis*), *Campeloma*, *Viviparus*, and *Pomacea*.

Waters of the calcareous streams are alkaline (pH 7.0–8.2) and well buffered, with hardnesses in the range of 25–300 mg/kg (ignoring saline springs).

The Larger Rivers

The category of larger rivers is one of convenience. There are only four examples in Florida, three of which are interstate: the Escambia, the Apalachicola, and the Choctawhatchee. The fourth, the St. Johns, is entirely within the state. All of these rivers carry significant loads of silt and clay and are always turbid. The Choctawhatchee is regarded as the "muddiest" of Florida rivers (Bass and Cox, 1985).

The four rivers classified as larger rivers represent distinctive river systems, the Apalachicola (fig. 12.3) being the largest and perhaps best known scientifically (Livingston and Joyce, 1977). The St. Johns River is unique even among Florida waterways in that the lower portion is really an exten-

Fig. 12.3. Florida's largest river, the Apalachicola. Photo by R. Myers.

sive estuary that receives drainage from a chain of lakes in the upper basin. The flora, and especially the fauna, of such river systems are mixtures of freshwater and marine organisms. One can see, for example, blue crabs and mullet in the river channel and in adjacent springs well into the headwaters of the St. Johns system.

Swamp-and-Bog Streams

Swamp-and-bog streams are very acidic, highly colored, sluggish streams most common in the Coastal Lowlands, with a few occurring in the Central Highlands. They originate in swamps, sphagnum bogs, and marshes. An increase in gradient, and thus in velocity, would convert them to sand-bottomed streams (fig. 12.4).

Such streams are very acidic (pH ranges from 3.8 to 6.5) and poorly buffered and have hardnesses well below 40 mg/kg. Their invertebrate faunas are generally depauperate, with *Physa pumilia* the only mollusc present in these systems. However, some support surprisingly large fish faunas.

Canals

Artificial waterways range widely in morphometry and show the characteristics of the waters to which they are connected. Most canals harbor plants and animals more typical of standing than of running waters.

Fig. 12.4. Fisheating Creek originates in the marshes and swamps of Highlands and Glades counties and empties into Lake Okeechobee. Photo by Lovett Williams. Courtesy of the Florida Game & Fresh Water Fish Commission.

Summary of Classification

It is difficult to give a single classification to many streams because there may be several sources of inflow to the river along its course from headwater to point of discharge. A number of rivers originate from artesian springs and become brown, acidic waters due to swamp discharge and surface runoff below the headwaters (for example, the Aucilla River, fig. 12.5), or they may originate as acidic brownwater streams and receive spring input in their midreaches (for example, the Suwannee and Waccasassa rivers). Many rivers have been culturally modified in one way or another. Dams have been constructed on some of these rivers (Apalachicola and Oklawaha are two excellent examples), producing lakes in portions of the drainage basin and altering physical, chemical, and biotic features of the system. Extensive channelization has also altered the characteristics of several rivers (Apalachicola, Caloosahatchee, Kissimmee, and Oklawaha). While many Florida rivers have been affected in some way by pollutants, several have been significantly altered by such cultural influences. Perhaps the Fenholloway River is the prime example of such degradation, now classified as a water fit only for industrial use. The Escambia, Peace, and St. Johns rivers have been sites of massive fish kills produced by pollutants—largely industrial wastes in the Escambia, phosphatic slimes in the Peace, and plant nutrients that produced overenrichment and subsequent oxygen depletion in the St. Johns.

Fig. 12.5. One of many "sinks" that characterize the lower Aucilla River. Photo by R. Myers.

Major Biotic Components of Florida Streams

Few comprehensive studies have been carried out on Florida's stream ecosystems, and few of these have been published in the scientific literature. Much effort has been expended recently assessing impacts of various types of potential or actual environmental alterations on river systems, but the vast bulk of this information is hidden in agency reports that have only limited distribution.

Most of the earlier biological investigations of rivers dealt with individual taxonomic groups, especially the insect and other arthropod faunas, but in recent years the emphasis has been on fishes. Other animal groups such as molluscs have also been studied, and new interest has recently been given to aquatic plants, largely because of problems created by several exotic species. Most of the studies highlighted here have value beyond simply identifying the presence of members of a particular taxonomic group. Various conclusions regarding biogeographical or ecological relationships were also expressed by the authors of several of these studies. Unfortunately, the only extensive evaluations to date of primary production in Florida's flowing waters are those of Odum (1956, 1957a,b) in springs and spring runs. These will be discussed in the section on springs.

Vegetation

Several intensive efforts have been made to determine the principal species of higher aquatic vegetation in various Florida waters, especially to keep track of the distributions of the nuisance forms. There are at least 130 aquatic macrophytes in Florida—likely significantly more because the taxonomy at the specific level is unknown or in question in several cases—that are known from rivers or adjacent marsh areas (Schardt, 1984).

Nuisance species of aquatic vegetation that often become locally abundant enough to create "problems" in running waters of Florida include floating water hyacinth (*Eichhornia crassipes*), alligator-weed (*Alternanthera philoxeroides*), coontail (*Ceratophyllum demersum*), variable leaf milfoil (*Myriophyllum heterophyllum*), Brazilian elodea (*Egeria densa*), and hydrilla (*Hydrilla verticillata*). Control of these species, plus a few others, costs the taxpayers vast amounts each year. Most aquatic weed control is accomplished with herbicides, though physical removal and biological control, especially through the use of such fishes as grass carp, are also used in Florida.

Many Florida waters would be totally unusable for recreation, transportation, or other purposes if weed control were not practiced regularly. What makes most of these nuisance species troublesome is a high intrinsic growth potential under prevailing environmental conditions and an absence of natural controlling agents. For example, modest growth of hydrilla or water hyacinth provides excellent cover for fishes. However, the dense beds produced by uncontrolled growth of hydrilla may undergo regular nighttime oxygen depletion, and the areas under dense water hyacinth beds may be continuously devoid of dissolved oxygen. Water hyacinths are among the most productive of all kinds of plants, capable of doubling their biomass several times over in a single season.

Plankton

Small, swift-flowing streams develop little in the way of a plankton while large, slow-flowing rivers support extensive plankton populations, especially wide areas of rivers such as Lake George in the St. Johns River. Pierce (1947) conducted a study of the seasonality of chemical conditions and of plankton at two stations in the St. Johns River near Welaka and one station at the mouth of the Oklawaha River (a tributary of the St. Johns River); he compared these conditions with those in an adjacent lake. Dominant zooplankters were found to be cladocerans of the genera *Bosmina*, *Daphnia*, and *Diaphanosoma*; copepods of the genera *Cyclops* and *Diaptomus*; and rotifers of the genera *Brachionus*, *Filinia*, *Keratella*, and *Pedalia*. The dominant phytoplankters included blue-greens of the genera *Anabaena*, *Microcystis*, and *Raphidiopsis*; diatoms of the genera *Asterionella*, *Coscinodiscus*, and *Melosira*; the dinoflagellate genus *Ceratium*; and greens of the genera *Clos-*

terium, Desmodium, Docidium, Euastrum, Micrasterias, and *Staurastrum.* These are all typical forms in freshwater plankton of lakes in this region. The estuarine nature of the lower St. Johns was demonstrated in a study of phytoplankton of the lower 42 km of the river by DeMort and Bowman (1985). Unlike Pierce's upstream stations, this part of the river was brackish, and marine diatoms dominated the phytoplankton.

Molluscs

The riverine mollusc fauna of Florida consists of at least sixty species of clams (Heard, 1979) and eighty-three species of snails (Thompson, 1984). All of the clams known from the state are found in flowing waters, and some are also found in standing waters. The same appears true for snails. Florida's largest river system, the Apalachicola (taken as a whole), has a snail fauna consisting of twenty species, five of which are endemic to the system, and a clam fauna of forty species, three of which are endemic to the system (Heard, 1977).

Clench and Turner (1956) compared the numbers of species of molluscs found in several rivers in west Florida with those of the "Orange Island," or central Florida area, and areas to the south and east. The general trend in species richness among molluscs was a reduction in numbers of species from west to east, with the most reduced faunas in the lower peninsula. One can ask, as Kushlan and Lodge (1974) did with respect to a similar distribution pattern in the fishes, whether it is a lack of suitable habitat in the lower peninsula or a lack of avenues of invasion that has limited the mollusc fauna in that area.

Snails of the genus *Elimia* (*Goniobasis*) are abundant and widely distributed in hard-water rivers of Florida. Chambers (1980) conducted a study of the morphology and genetics of populations of these snails from river systems throughout Florida. He concluded that while there is much morphological diversification from stream to stream, morphological differences among populations (or even among forms that had been described as separate species) were not well correlated with the extent of reproductive isolation.

The freshwater mussel fauna of North America is declining, according to Heard (1979), and all forms are threatened by various kinds of water pollution and other habitat alterations such as stream channelization. Seventeen species of molluscs endemic to a single drainage system in Florida consequently face possible extinction from environmental alterations in those systems (Heard, 1979).

The introduction and rapid dispersal in recent years of the Asiatic clam *Corbicula manilensis* (also referred to as *fluminalis, fluminea,* or *leana*), accompanying declines in the abundances of native species throughout central North America, has raised serious questions about the impact of this exotic on native species (Britton and Fuller, 1979; Gottfried and Osborne, 1982). Populations of the Asiatic clam were found to range in abundance from 4 to 1210/mg^2 in the Wekiva River (Gottfried and Osborne, 1982), indicating the ability of this species to dominate appropriate habitats.

Aquatic Insects

Few insects are aquatic as adults. Immature stages of many species, representing a diversity of insect orders, develop in aquatic environments, but they are by no means all restricted to flowing waters. The groups that have been studied on a relatively wide geographical scale and on an ecological basis in Florida include craneflies (Order Diptera, Family Tipulidae, studied by Rogers, 1933); dragonflies and damselflies (Order Odonata, studied by Byers, 1930; Johnson and Westfall, 1970); mayflies (Order Ephemeroptera, studied by Berner, 1941, 1950, 1977); aquatic and semiaquatic bugs (Order Hemiptera, studied by Herring, 1951); aquatic beetles (Order Coleoptera, studied by Young, 1954); chironomids (Order Diptera, Family Chironomidae, studied by Beck and Beck, 1959, 1966, 1969); and stoneflies (Order Plecoptera, studied by Stark and Gaufin, 1979). Perhaps mayflies best typify flowing waters, for immatures of all species develop in aquatic habitats, and the greatest diversity and likely the most extreme adaptations to environmental conditions are seen among the forms developing in running waters (the rheophiles). The diversity of adaptations in this group is such that the forms present in a particular habitat can be used as indicators of the extreme environmental conditions of that situation. The presence of various types of indicator species has been used extensively in the development of systems of stream classification for the assessment of cultural influences on these waters.

Crayfishes

Crayfishes, which are conspicuous inhabitants in the clear spring runs of the state, are generally abundant in both flowing and standing waters of Florida. These large crustaceans are important elements of aquatic food chains and are favorite items in the diet of Florida's foremost freshwater sport fish, the largemouth black bass.

Flatwoods streams of the Panhandle and northern Florida support the greatest numbers of crayfishes among Florida's flowing waters (Hobbs, 1942). Even semipermanent sluggish, blackwater, acid streams can support sizeable populations where survival is possible in deep pools or through burrowing in areas that remain moist during times when there is little or no flow in these streams. Hobbs (1942) suggested that large silt-laden rivers, such as the Apalachicola and Choctawhatchee, were least suitable for crayfish, while their smaller tributaries might have more abundant and diverse crayfish faunas.

Some of the smaller rivers that are at least partially spring-fed, such as the Sante Fe, support abundant crayfish populations but of only a few species. The largest of Florida's crayfishes, *Procambarus spiculifer*—a form restricted to flowing waters with relatively high oxygen concentrations—is found in the more alkaline portions of streams such as the Santa Fe (Hobbs, 1942).

The large, sluggish rivers of the western part of the peninsula have an abundance and diversity of crayfishes but of forms more typical of standing waters than of flowing waters.

Included among the crayfishes known from Florida are at least thirteen species adapted to life in underground waters (spelean or troglobitic forms), according to Hobbs and Franz (1986). One of these species, *Procambarus acherontis*, was found by Hobbs (1942) to live in a sulfur spring (Palm Spring in Seminole County near Orlando).

Fishes of Florida Rivers

Biogeography. Fishes are the best-known animal group in Florida waters. The fauna is a highly interesting one, especially because of the involvement of marine forms. There are 126 native fishes in fresh waters of the Florida region, of which 72 are considered to be freshwater species but only 50 are primary division species—fishes that are strictly limited to fresh waters (Gilbert, 1986).

An especially interesting zoogeographic phenomenon in Florida waters is the replacement of cyprinids, catostomids, and percids (minnows, suckers, and perches) by centrarchids, ictalurids, and cyprinodontids (sunfishes and basses, catfishes, and killifishes) along with an abundance of many species of euryhaline marine species (Gilbert, 1987).

The large Apalachicola River system, which flows through three states and includes the Flint, Chattahoochee, and Chipola rivers, has a fish fauna including 116 species, 83 of which are strictly freshwater forms and three of which—the bluestripe shiner, the bandfin shiner, and the grayfin redhorse—are endemic to that system (Yerger, 1977).

More species of freshwater fishes are found in streams of west Florida than elsewhere in the state, followed closely by the Kissimmee and St. Marys rivers, with fewer species of freshwater fishes in other streams of the peninsula. The same general pattern of distribution holds for molluscs, as has been pointed out. The trend extends all the way to the drainages of South Carolina (Swift et al., 1986). Repeated inundations of the Florida peninsula by sea water during the Pleistocene obviously eliminated its freshwater fauna, which was reestablished by dispersal from the mainland as the sea level receded. Three suggested reasons for the present distribution pattern (Swift et al., 1977) are distance from the large Mississippian fauna to the west; the fact that the more eastern streams do not originate (or have few tributaries) above the fall line; and the fact that many of the fishes involved are tied to stream habitats and do not disperse readily through standing waters.

Euryhaline Fishes. Euryhaline fishes—species that tolerate wide ranges of salinity—are abundant in Florida streams that have unimpeded connections with marine waters. An example of the impact of marine and brackish-water fishes on the riverine fish fauna is provided by data for the St. Johns River given by Tagatz (1967). He lists 170 species, of which 115 are either brackish-water or marine forms. Some of these species enter the lower end of the estuary only on high tides or during periods of little freshwater discharge, but many are true euryhaline species, capable of extending well up into the river system. This situation is roughly similar to the situation in south Florida streams, where only 29 percent of the native fish fauna consists of strictly freshwater fishes (Kushlan and Lodge, 1974).

The composition and abundance of the fish fauna of rivers is known to vary seasonally, as was shown by Swift et al. (1977) in the Ochlockonee River. Florida sport anglers are well aware of the presence of tarpon in rivers in summer and anticipate the arrival in the lower reaches of rivers of spotted sea trout (*Cynoscion nebulosus*) and the red drum or redfish (*Sciaenops ocellatus*), when water temperatures begin to drop in the autumn.

Snorkelers and SCUBA divers, who frequent springs and spring runs, become familiar with such euryhaline fishes as the hogchoker (*Trinectes maculatus*), found in fresh waters only in immature stages; Gulf pipefish (*Syngnathus scovelli*), which has breeding populations in some of the spring-fed river systems such as the Ichetucknee and Santa Fe; striped mullet (*Mugil cephalus*), a species that seems ubiquitous in Florida fresh waters with marine connections; and Atlantic needlefish (*Strongylura marina*). Even bull sharks (*Carcharhinus leucas*) have been seen far inland in some Florida river systems.

The most extensive analysis of the presence of marine fishes in Florida's freshwater streams was that of Odum (1953), which showed that these invasions were correlated with the quantity of salt (chloride) being introduced into a stream by spring discharge.

Exotic Fishes. The fish fauna of Florida, especially that of canals and ditches in south Florida, has been significantly enriched by accidental and intentional additions of exotic species. (I have ignored range extensions produced by accidental or intentional introductions of native species.) Twenty-one species of exotic fishes are reported to be established in Florida (see table 11.4). An additional thirty-one exotic species have been collected in Florida but are not thought to have established reproducing populations

(Courtenay et al., 1984). Most of these aliens were brought into the state as aquarium fish and likely escaped from holding ponds or were released by aquarists who had tired of their pets. The list includes the common carp—a species introduced into North America many years ago and now present throughout the lower forty-eight states, in many of which it is a serious problem species. A close relative, the grass carp (*Ctenopharyngodon idella*), introduced into Florida waters as an agent of aquatic weed control, apparently has not established reproducing populations in this area.

Because most exotic species were introduced from tropical areas, their northward migrations are probably restricted by low winter temperatures. There is little documentation of problems created by these species in areas where they have become established, but walking catfish created psychological problems for south Florida residents when these fish were first seen wandering across fields and roads. Fortunately, reports of establishment of such potentially dangerous forms as the piranhas have proved false (Shafland, 1979).

Introductions of exotic fishes will likely continue as various species are introduced on an experimental basis as sport fishes or for aquatic weed control. Also, since the aquarium fish industry is a large one in Florida, additional accidental introductions will undoubtedly continue. Pond culture of food fishes is now a developing industry and is certain to involve some fast-growing exotic species. It seems inevitable that some of these fishes also will be added to the exotic fish fauna of the state.

Rare and Endangered Florida Riverine Fishes. Several Florida fishes are presently rare or may become rare because of existing or expected circumstances. Four classes of rarity were established by Gilbert (1978).

Endangered species are species whose habitat is so reduced that their continued existence is unlikely unless special steps are taken to alter existing circumstances. Gilbert's (1978) list included the Okaloosa darter (*Etheostoma okaloosae*) and the shortnose sturgeon (*Acipenser brevirostrum*).

Threatened species are those thought likely to become endangered in the future if present population trends continue and include the Atlantic sturgeon (*Acipenser oxyrhynchus*), river redhorse (*Moxostoma carinatum*), grayfin redhorse (*Moxostoma* undescribed species), cypress minnow (*Hybognathus hayi*), speckled chub (*Hybopsis aestivalis*), bluestripe shiner (*Notropis callitaenia*), blackmouth shiner (*Notropis* undescribed species), saltmarsh topminnow (*Fundulus jenkinsi*), crystal darter (*Ammocrypta asprella*), harlequin darter (*Etheostoma histrio*), tesselated darter (*E. olmstedi*), goldstripe darter (*E. parvipinne*), cypress darter (*E. proeliare*), saddleback darter (*Percina ouachitae*), and shoal bass (*Micropterus* undescribed species).

Rare species are those showing restricted ranges or habitats and include the sea lamprey (*Petromyzon marinus*, which certainly would not be mourned by Great Lakes area residents if it were exterminated in that region), bannerfin shiner (*Notropis leedsi*), bandfin shiner (*N. zonistius*), snail bullhead (*Ictalurus brunneus*), spotted bullhead (*I. serracanthus*), Eastern mudminnow (*Umbra pygmaea*), opossum pipefish (*Oostethus brachyurus*), mountain mullet (*Agonostomus monticola*), mud sunfish (*Acantharchus pomotis*), Suwannee bass (*Micropterus notius*), and river goby (*Awaous tajasica*).

Species of special concern are groups that may be exploited to the point of becoming endangered or may pose potential threats of damage to other vulnerable species. Gilbert's list included the dusky shiner (*Notropis cummingsae*) and the bluenose shiner (*N. welaka*).

The Florida Game and Fresh Water Fish Commission (Wood, 1986) recognizes the Okaloosa darter, blackmouth shiner, and shortnose sturgeon as endangered riverine species. Its list of threatened species, however, includes only the crystal darter. Species of special concern are the Atlantic sturgeon, bluestripe shiner, tessellated darter, harlequin darter, shoal bass, and Suwannee bass. It has not designated a "rare" category.

The extent to which cultural impacts and unanticipated vagaries of nature affect Florida's flowing water ecosystems will determine which of these species go extinct and which other species, not presently of concern, will be added to these lists.

The Manatee Problem

The West Indian manatee (*Trichechus manatus*), a native mammal in southern Florida waters, is an endangered species. A major conflict exists between manatees and motor boaters in the several rivers on the Gulf and Atlantic coasts of Florida that these mammals enter during the colder months of the year (Odell and Reynolds, 1979; Tiedemann, 1983; Irvine and Scott, 1984). Manatees must come to the surface to breathe and are frequently hit by motor boat propellers as they do so. Efforts have been made to restrict boating activities, or at least to enforce speed limits, in areas where manatees are known to congregate. Manatees have also been injured or killed by water control devices in south Florida (Odell and Reynolds, 1979). Another problem occurs when manatees are attracted in autumn to warm waters discharged by electric power generating plants. Power plant effluent streams may be located considerably farther north than the rivers and springs that were originally inhabited by manatees. No problem exists as long as a plant continues to discharge warm water, but if it is shut down in the colder part of the year, the results may prove devastating to the manatees (Odell and Reynolds, 1979; Tiedemann, 1983; Shane, 1984). These aquatic mammals are undergoing intensive study because of both the precarious nature of their existence and their potential in the control of such noxious weed species as hydrilla and water hyacinth (Campbell and Irvine, 1977; Reynolds, 1981; Lomolino and Ewel, 1984).

Subterranean Rivers

Subterranean rivers and pools are relatively common in the Floridan Aquifer, where in some areas large caverns are present and overlying strata have remained intact. One such situation that has received considerable public attention is the Santa Fe River, which disappears into a sinkhole in O'Leno State Park northeast of the city of High Springs (Skirvin, 1962). The river reemerges east of the city of High Springs, roughly 3 km southwest of where it entered the ground.

The underground portion of the Santa Fe River system serves as a barrier to movement of at least some species of fishes (Hellier, 1967). Hellier discovered that of the sixty species of fishes found in the Santa Fe River system, roughly a dozen were known only from the waters downstream from the underground portion and another dozen only from the waters upstream of the subterranean channel. Those restricted to the lower portion of the system were mainly euryhaline forms.

No species of animal adapted to life in underground water is known from this system, though a number of such forms, especially of crayfishes (Hobbs, 1942), are known from Florida. There are no true troglobitic fishes (forms adapted to an underground existence and found nowhere but in such habitats) in Florida (Gilbert, 1987), though the redeye chub (*Notropis harperi*), a species closely associated with springs (Hubbs, 1956; Marshall, 1947), frequently enters the aquifer, as does the yellow bullhead (*Ictalurus natalis*) (Relyea and Sutton, 1973). The distribution of these species in isolated sinkholes reflects this subterranean route of travel. There are also reports of mosquito fish (*Gambusia affinis*) from caves (Marshall, 1947) and of American eels (*Anguilla rostrata*) (Pylka and Warren, 1958) in one cave. A troglobitic salamander (*Haideotriton wallacei*) has also been found in an underground stream near Marianna in Jackson County (Pylka and Warren, 1958).

Springs

Florida has a large number of springs for its size, with more than 300 known in the state. Most of these springs are artesian, and twenty-seven of these springs are of first magnitude, with an average discharge of at least 2.83 m^3/s (100 ft^3/s) (table 12.5)—roughly one-third of all first magnitude springs in the United States. The total daily discharge from all of Florida's springs is approximately 30,284,000 m^3 (8×10^9 gal), nearly 80 percent of it discharged by the twenty-seven first magnitude springs (Rosenau et al., 1977).

Artesian springs are by no means a homogeneous group, differing significantly in physical and chemical features. The chemical contents of springs depend on the origin of the water, residence time in the ground, and local

Table 12.5. The 27 first magnitude springs and spring groups of Florida

Spring	Discharge Average (m^3/s)	Discharge Range (m^3/s)	Average water temper-ature(°C)	Average dissolved solids (mg/kg)
Alachua County				
Hornsby Spring	4.62	2.15–7.08	22.5	230
Bay County				
Gainer Springs	4.50	3.71–5.24	22.0	60
Citrus County				
Chassahowitzka Springs	3.94	0.91–5.58	23.5	740
Crystal River Springs	25.94		25.0	144
Homosassa Springs	4.96	3.54–7.28	23.0	1800
Columbia County				
Ichetucknee Springs	10.22	5.82–16.37	22.5	170
Hamilton County				
Alapaha Rise	17.22	14.38–19.79	19.0	130
Holton Spring	8.16	1.95–13.65	—	—
Hernando County				
Weeki Wachee Springs	4.98	2.86–7.79	23.5	150
Jackson County				
Blue Springs	5.38	1.59–8.13	21.0	116
Jefferson County				
Wacissa Springs Group	11.02	7.93–17.13	20.5	150
Lafayette County				
Troy Spring	4.70	4.19–5.80	22.0	171
Lake County				
Alexander Springs	3.40	2.10–4.59	23.5	512
Leon County				
Natural Bridge Spring	3.00	2.24–3.74	20.0	138
St. Marks Spring	14.70	8.78–26.90	20.5	154
Levy County				
Fannin Springs	2.92	1.81–3.94	22.0	194
Manatee Spring	5.13	3.11–6.74	22.0	215
Madison County				
Blue Spring	3.26	2.12–4.11	21.0	146
Marion County				
Rainbow Springs	21.61	13.79–34.83	23.0	93
Silver Glen Springs	3.17	2.55–3.65	23.0	1200
Silver Springs	23.22	15.26–36.53	23.0	245
Suwannee County				
Falmouth Spring	4.47	1.70–6.23	21.0	190
Volusia County				
Blue Spring	4.59	1.78–6.06	23.0	826
Wakulla County				
Kini Spring	4.98	—	20.0	110
River Sink Spring	4.64	2.89–6.09	20.0	110
Wakulla Springs	11.04	0.71–54.09	21.0	153
Spring Creek Springs	56.72		19.5	2400

Source: after Rosenau et al. (1977).

variations in the sediments through which the water travels from point of entry to point of discharge. Such chemical features as calcium, magnesium, sodium, bicarbonate, chloride, and sulfate ions, and specific conductance, color, pH, and temperature vary appreciably among springs.

Classification of Florida Springs

Florida springs were divided into six categories by Whitford (1956):

1. *Soft, freshwater*: Examples include some of the water table springs or seeps.
2. *Hard, freshwater*. Examples include Silver Springs, Weeki Wachee, Ichetucknee, and Crystal.
3. *Oligohaline* (chlorides typically up to 600 mg/kg). Examples include Homosassa (chlorides 640–1100 mg/kg), Silver Glen (chlorides 520–610 mg/kg), and Chassahowitzka Springs (chlorides 53–320 mg/kg).
4. *Mesohaline* (chlorides up to 9000 mg/kg). An example is Salt Springs, Marion County (chlorides 1900–2800 mg/kg).
5. *Sulfide*. Examples include Hampton and Beecher springs. Beecher Springs is a hard, freshwater spring, anoxic and high in sulfates and sulfides.
6. *Salt, sulfide*. An example is Warm Mineral Springs (chlorides 9200–9600 mg/kg, most saline of Florida springs). The water temperature here is 30°C (86°F), warmer than any other Florida spring. Water discharging from the boil is anoxic and high in sulfides and sulfates (1700 mg/kg). There are no aquatic flowering plants in the pool or run, but sparse beds of *Chara honemani* are present in shallows of the pool.

To provide a representative sample of physical and chemical variation, data were summarized for the group of springs involved in the various studies to be considered in the remainder of this chapter (table 12.6).

There are wide variations, among the springs discussed here, in calcium, magnesium, sodium, bicarbonate, chloride, sulfate, hardness, and specific conductance, but pH, color, and temperature are less variable. There are some exceptions even in these, however, as the waters of Hampton Spring are moderately colored and those of Warm Mineral Springs are appreciably warmer than any of the others.

The Silver Springs Ecosystem

Perhaps the best known of Florida springs is Silver Springs in Marion County. Certainly it is the most studied, has served as the site for numerous motion pictures and television shows, and is a major tourist attraction. Silver Springs is large even among Florida's first magnitude springs, with

Table 12.6. Physical and chemical conditions of selected Florida springs

Spring	Calcium (mg/kg)	Magnesium (mg/kg)	Sodium (mg/kg)	Bicarbonate (mg/kg)	Chloride (mg/kg)	Sulfate (mg/kg)	Hardness (as mg/kg $CaCO_3$)	pH	Specific conductance (μS/cm at 25°C)	Color (platinum-cobalt units)	Temperature (°C)
Beecher (Putnam Co.)	33.0	8.3	41.0	110	74.0	11.0	120.0	7.9	446	10	23.5
Blue (Gilchrist Co.)	54.0	5.0	2.9	180	6.2	7.9	160.0	7.4	340	5	22.5
Blue (Volusia Co.)	52–76	20–51	128–419	128–150	245–780	37–110	212–399	7.5–7.8	1060–2840	0–5	23.0
Chassahowitzka (Citrus Co.)	46–55	11–29	29–180	160–180	53–320	13–56	160–260	7.5–8.2	470–1370	8–10	22.2–26.0
Crystal (Citrus Co.)	41.0	14.0	110.0	130	180.0	29.0	160.0		555	5	23.0
Green Cove (Clay Co.)	28.0	15–16	2.4–4.6	96–100	5.7–6.1	49–55	130–140	7.3–8.0	289–290	0–5	25.0
Hampton (Taylor Co.)	150–190	70–85	6.5–7.0	270–290	5–10	430–560	660–820	6.9–7.6	1120–1320	25–30	21.1–22.8
Homosassa (Citrus Co.)	48–65	48–86	340–600	130–140	640–1100	84–150	320–480	6.9–8.2	2370–3740	0–10	23.5
Ichetucknee (Columbia Co.)	52–58	6.0–6.6	3.1–3.4	170–200	3.6–4.4	6.9–8.4	150–170	7.6–7.7	290–329	0–1	21.0–22.2
Rainbow (Marion Co.)	20–21	3.1–5.1	1.4–2.9	64–78	3.0–3.5	4.3–16	63–73	7.8–7.9	121–145	0–2	22.5
Salt (Hernando Co.)	56–64	43–68	260–540	150–160	490–1900	73–140	15–440	7.3–7.6	1800–6430	2–5	24.0–25.0
Salt (Marion Co.)	220–440	140–170	1400–1500	84–87	1900–2800	540–610	1000–1300	7.1–8.1	6500–9330	0	24.0
Silver (Marion Co.)	68–73	9.2–9.6	4.0–9.8	200–220	7.7–8.0	34–44	210–220	7.8–8.1	401–420	0–4	23.5
Silver Glen (Marion Co.)	74–87	38–46	290–330	84–85	520–610	190–200	340–410	7.4–7.8	2220–2480	0	22.8–23.0
Warm Mineral (Sarasota Co.)	500–770	470–630	4900–5200	160–170	9200–9600	1600–1700	3700–3900	7.0–7.3	26,000–27,000	5–6	29.5–30.0
Weeki Wachee (Hernando Co.)	44–50	5.0–7.8	3.0–4.0	160–170	4.0–8.0	6.4–9.6	140–150	7.7–8.0	262–284	1–5	21.5–24.0

Source: Rosenau et al. (1977).

an average discharge of 23.22 m^3/s (Rosenau et al., 1977). It is a clear, hardwater spring of alkaline pH, with low to modest sodium, chloride, and sulfate concentrations. The numerous boils of the Silver Springs complex give rise to the Silver Springs River, a tributary of the Oklawaha, which in turn discharges into the St. Johns River.

Primary Production and Respiration

The structure and energy flow of the Silver Springs ecosystem were described in great detail by Odum (1956, 1957a,b) and are reviewed here principally from his studies.

Net primary production in Silver Springs amounted to 6390 g m^{-2} yr^{-1} of organic matter (roughly 3195 g C m^{-2} $year^{-1}$, assuming that carbon content is 50 percent of average organic material). Most of this production comes from a single species of plant, *Sagittaria lorata*, and the algae growing on its leaves. Primary production in the spring run showed an efficiency of solar energy utilization of 5.3 percent, while the efficiency dropped to 1.1 percent in headwater areas where there was little or no current. The bulk of net primary production was utilized within the system, with only 12 percent being exported downstream.

The primary producer level of the ecosystem appeared structurally simple, largely *Sagittaria*, but the diversity of epiphytic algae allowed for the establishment of a species-rich herbivore fauna. Perhaps the most spectacular consumers in this crystal-clear spring system are the forty species of fish (Hubbs and Allen, 1943). Fishes of a wide array of species and sizes belonging to three (perhaps four) trophic levels are present but may be aggregated into schools of only a single or a few species in certain areas of the system.

Marine fishes such as mullets (*Mugil cephalus* and *M. curema*) and Atlantic needlefish (*Strongylura marina*) were found to occur in the river and springs. The mullets, along with several species of freshwater catfishes, were principal consumers at the time of Odum's studies. Both mullet and catfishes were found to be rare in Silver Springs in a recent reanalysis of structure and function of the spring system by Knight (1980). These fishes are now prevented from ascending the Oklawaha to Silver Springs by the Rodman Dam, the mullet coming from the Atlantic and the catfish from the St. Johns River. However, blue shad (*Dorosoma cepedianum*) appears to have increased in importance since the time of Odum's studies, replacing the mullets and catfish as dominant consumers (Knight, 1980).

The general area of Silver Springs has been undergoing alteration at least since 1929, as it has developed as a tourist attraction. The main spring was originally surrounded by a marsh that provided spawning area for some of the fish species, but this area was filled in as development proceeded, reducing the abundance of fish in the spring system (Hubbs and Allen, 1943). Also, the giant freshwater shrimp (*Macrobrachium jamaicense*) was common in the spring until 1936, when it disappeared (Hubbs and Allen, 1943).

Comparisons of Primary Production among Florida Springs

Odum (1957a) compared rates of primary production in several Florida springs under roughly comparable environmental conditions (table 12.7). Primary production values varied from a low of 0.26 g C m^{-2} day^{-1} in the anoxic waters of Beecher to a high of 23.93 g C m^{-2} day^{-1} in Homosassa Springs. While the low value is not truly low in comparison with nutrient-poor waters or the world's deserts, the high value is extremely high compared to natural or managed ecosystems listed by Whittaker (1975).

Environmental conditions—including the extent of shading by surrounding trees; depth of water where measurements were made; types of vegetation; levels of nitrate-nitrogen and phosphate-phosphorus; N/P ratio; and carbon dioxide and oxygen concentrations—all varied among springs. The springs studied were aerobic, with the exception of Beecher Springs. Odum (1957b) suggested that the principal controller of primary production in these spring systems was the quantity of light reaching the photosynthetic areas of a community.

Recreational Use of Springs—The Ichetucknee Springs Group

Many of the larger springs and spring runs are used extensively for recreation (fig. 12.6), particularly fishing, SCUBA diving, snorkling, tubing, and swimming. Most of the springs that have been developed or are being developed for recreational use—whether for water sports alone or combined with picnicking, camping, and hiking—are in private ownership. A notable exception is the Ichetucknee Springs system.

The Ichetucknee Springs system in Columbia County is a favorite recreational spring run in north Florida, which has remained relatively undeveloped because it was acquired by the state and designated a state park. Ichetucknee is another first magnitude spring with a mean discharge of 10.22 m^3/s (range 6.82–16.37 m^3/s; Rosenau et al., 1977). The spring run from its origin at the main spring to its point of discharge into the Santa Fe River is approximately 8.85 km long. The Ichetucknee River is produced by the discharge of a group of springs, nine of which are large enough to have individual names. The two largest and best known of the springs in the system are Ichetucknee (or Head) Spring, with an average discharge of 1.3 m^3/s, and Blue Hole (or Jug) Spring, with an average discharge of 2.4 m^3/s. The Ichetucknee system may be the surface manifestation of a much longer underground stream system (Stubbs, 1940).

The system is of hard water with moderately high calcium concentration, of alkaline pH, and low in sodium and chloride concentrations (table 12.6). The water is virtually without coloring matter or turbidity.

Table 12.7. Rates of gross primary production (GPP) in Florida springs

Spring community	GPP[a] g C m^{-2} day^{-1}
Beecher (an anoxic spring)	0.26
Blue (Alachua County)	1.95
Blue (Alachua County)—*Utricularia*	0.75
Blue (Volusia County)[b]	2.03
Weeki Wachee[b]	4.01
Green Cove	5.81
Silver[b] (mean of three July–August 1954–55 values)	6.75
Manatee[b]	7.28
Rainbow[b]	8.96
Chassahowitzka[b] (side run)	10.01
Homosassa[b]	23.93

Source: Odum (1957a).

a. Values were converted from g O_2 m^{-2} day^{-1} to g C m^{-2} day^{-1} by using the mass relationships from $CO_2 + H_2O \rightleftharpoons (CH_2O)_n + O_2$ where 12 g C = 32 g O_2.

b. First magnitude springs.

Fig. 12.6. Juniper Springs Run in Ocala National Forest is a favorite of canoeists. Photo courtesy of USDA Forest Service.

A great deal of basic biological work has been carried out there in recent years, evaluating the actual and potential impact of human use (principally tubing and SCUBA diving) on the system. More than 5000 people per day used the spring and river on a few occasions in 1979, with an annual tally of more than 300,000 people before daily quotas and use restrictions were established by the Florida Department of Natural Resources (Dutoit, 1979).

Heavy use by swimmers, tubers, and SCUBA divers devastated rooted vegetation in certain areas of the river channel as well as in the spring holes and in adjacent marshes.

Twelve species of aquatic plants are common in this system (table 12.8). Fishes—especially mullet, chubsuckers, and some of the sunfishes—are the most obvious animals of the spring and run, while crayfishes and snails of the genus *Elimia* (*Goniobasis*) are extremely abundant benthic forms, the latter found in densities of up to 17,000/m^2. Other larger but less abundant animals seen by swimmers, tubers, and canoeists include alligators, turtles of several species, brown water snakes, an occasional otter, and, in recent years, beaver (Dutoit, 1979).

I anticipate that the pressures accompanying the continued economic and population growth in Florida will result in demands for greater and more diverse use of such semiwild areas and will generate the need for the acquisition and development of more such areas either by private enterprise or as state parks. Certainly only with carefully controlled development and use can the existing ecosystems survive under such circumstances.

The Oligohaline Spring Fish Bowl—Homosassa Springs

Another well-known tourist attraction along the Florida Gulf coast is Homosassa Springs, famous for its "Fish Bowl," where large numbers of individuals of a number of freshwater and marine fishes congregate. It is a somewhat smaller spring, with a discharge only 20 percent that of Silver Springs and about 50 percent that of Ichetucknee Springs. The Homosassa River extends roughly 14.5 km between the headspring and its point of discharge to the Gulf of Mexico. It is an alkaline, hard water, oligohaline spring with a relatively high chloride concentration (table 12.6). Its famous fish fauna consists of thirty-five species, including eighteen marine species

Table 12.8. Common macrophytes of the Ichetucknee Springs group and Spring Run

Ceratophyllum demersum	coontail
Chara sp.	muskgrass
Cicuta maculata	water-hemlock
Fontinalis sp.	water-moss
Ludwigia repens	red ludwigia
Myriophyllum heterophyllum	variable-leaf milfoil
Najas guadalupensis	southern naiad
Nasturtium officinale	watercress
Pistia stratiotes	water-lettuce
Sagittaria kurziana	eelgrass
Vallisneria americana	tape grass
Zizania aquatica	wild rice (extensive marshes)

Source: Dutoit (1979).

and three euryhaline, salt marsh species (Herald and Strickland, 1949). Thus, twenty-one of the thirty-five species known from the Homosassa Spring and River have marine affinities. Among the marine invaders are such eye-catching forms as the stingray (*Dasyatis sabina*), tarpon (*Tarpon atlanticus*), gaff-topsail catfish (*Galeichthys felis*), snook (*Centropomus undecimalis*), mangrove snapper (*Lutjanus griseus*), redfish (*Sciaenops ocellatus*), seatrout (*Cynoscion nebulosus*), and jack (*Caranx hippos*).

Sloan (1956) made an effort to determine qualitatively and quantitatively the environmental bases of distributions of insect larvae in Homosassa Springs and Homosassa River and also in Weeki Wachee Springs, a spring of similar size but of lower salinity. Maximum numbers of immature insect species were taken some distance downstream from the springhead in both systems, beyond which point diversities again decreased. While he arrived at no definite conclusions, Sloan pointed out as possible causal factors that dissolved O_2 was lowest at the springheads, and chloride concentrations were highest downstream, because of tidal influences. Sloan's results may be generally applicable to similar spring runs influenced by tides.

Algal Communities of Florida Springs

The great interest in Florida spring communities generated by Odum in the mid-1950s attracted others to work in conjunction with him but frequently on separate topics or using different approaches. One such spin-off was Whitford's (1956) study of algal communities of Florida springs. He proposed four algal communities: a *Cocconeis/Stigeoclonium* community of hard, freshwater springs; a *Cladophora/Cocconeis/Enteromorpha* community of oligohaline springs; an *Enteromorpha/Lyngbya/Licmophora* community of mesohaline springs; and a *Phormidium/Lyngbya* community of sulfide springs.

Attached (epiphytic) algae were by far the most abundant forms present in all types of springs. Such attached algae were found principally on three common higher plants: *Najas guadalupensis, Sagittaria lorata,* and *Vallisneria neotropicalis*. *Najas* was typically found near the boil or spring vent and in deeper portions of pools, but it was not found in shaded areas. Epiphytes were most abundant on *Sagittaria* and less abundant on *Vallisneria*. Few algae were found on aquatic mosses. Muskgrass (*Chara*), a large multicellular alga, was abundant in several springs and supported growths of epiphytes, including diatoms. Many diatoms and small blue-green algae were epiphytic on the filaments of another alga, *Plectonema wollei*, which formed large and abundant mats in the freshwater springs. Two algal species of the genus *Enteromorpha* and the pondweed (*Potamogeton pectinatus*) formed important attachment surfaces for epiphytes in the oligohaline and mesohaline springs.

Former Springs, Pseudosprings, and Submarine Springs

A number of Florida springs have been known to go dry or to vary greatly in rate of discharge, depending on variations in local recharge and ground-water pumping. Several water table springs in south Florida have stopped flowing due to heavy pumping from the water table. Kissingen Spring in the Peace River system of Polk County shows intermittent flow determined by adjacent pumping activity (Rosenau et al., 1977).

Some of the "springs" in south Florida are in reality artesian wells or pseudosprings. These include, for example, Hot Springs in Charlotte County, which discharges water with a temperature of 35.6°C (96.8°F) and a chloride concentration of 19,200 mg/kg; Pennekamp Spring on Key Largo in Monroe County, with a temperature of 27°C (80.6°F) and a chloride concentration of 2440 mg/kg; and Mineral Springs in the Everglades of Dade County with a temperature of 24.5°C (76.1°F) and a chloride concentration of 1300 mg/kg.

Artesian springs are not confined to the present land areas of Florida—submarine springs are known from both coasts (Brooks, 1961). The best known of these offshore springs is located roughly 4 km east of Crescent Beach in St. Johns County. The discharge from this spring, which originates in the Floridan Aquifer, was estimated to be in the range of 0.3–8.5 m^3/s, with a chloride content of 7680 mg/kg or 38 percent that of the coastal sea water of the region. The chloride concentration increases to 19,800 mg/kg (98.5 percent of local sea water) by the time water reaches the surface of the "boil" (Brooks, 1961). No living creatures were seen by Brooks in his explorations of the bottom of the crater from which the discharge emanated, though marine invertebrates characteristic of the adjacent benthic areas were found on the upper slopes of the crater.

Prospects

Management policies involving riverine systems incorporate complex considerations regarding usages of the water itself, the river channel, the adjacent floodplain, and the drainage basin. Obviously what happens at any particular point along a river course potentially alters the system from that point on downstream, including the system into which the river discharges, whether a lake or an estuary—and in the latter case, far beyond the estuary into the marine realm. It is especially difficult to develop integrated management plans for rivers in the Florida Panhandle and the Suwannee because these rivers or their tributaries originate in other states. Even where a drainage system lies entirely within the state boundaries it would be rare indeed to find all parties concerned about the management of a river system in accord regarding its use. An excellent example of such disagreements regarding best use of a river system is the long conflict over the development of the Cross-Florida Barge Canal, whose construction involved altering a stretch of the Oklawaha River by channelization and impounding an area through construction of the Rodman Dam. While efforts by environmentalists ultimately convinced political leaders to vote to deauthorize completion of the canal, the decision was made that existing structures, including the Rodman Dam, should remain in place. The conflict continues as to whether the dam should be removed.

Another such conflict involves the Kissimmee River, originally a meandering river, which was turned into a canal (C38) to hasten the removal of floodwaters from its large watershed. The restoration of the river was mandated by the Florida legislature more than a decade ago, but disagreements as to how and whether this should be accomplished continue, and restoration has not been undertaken.

A third example involves the Apalachicola River, which originates in Alabama and Georgia. Significant efforts have been made to "improve" the system (including portions of the Flint and Chattahoochee rivers), especially to produce a commercial navigation channel. Modifications have involved constuction of the Jim Woodruff Dam and a considerable amount of excavating to widen and deepen the river channel. Additional proposals are pending for further development including dam construction and channel development. In this situation, citizens and political bodies in three states operate directly and also indirectly through their federal politicians in the continuing discussion of proposed developments in the system.

In the examples cited, opponents and proponents of the developments have expended significant amounts of time and money in building cases for their particular viewpoints. A Florida environmentalist group, Florida Defenders of the Environment, has been involved in all three conflicts mentioned. It sponsored a symposium on the Apalachicola River development and published the proceedings (Livingston and Joyce, 1977), in which a wide array of concerns was analyzed: considerations of water quality in the river and its influences on the estuary into which it discharges; the river biota; the floodplain and its direct and indirect effects on water quality and river and estuarine productivity; and the watershed, including its biota and various types of interactions among these and the river system. Other important aspects of the symposium involved legal and economic considerations of the various alternatives presented. Economic projections that included evaluations of the values of wildlife and of recreational activities as well as of other economic features were carried out by traditional as well as by energy-based calculations; these revealed that the greatest economic benefits would be realized by minimizing further alterations of natural conditions of the riverine system, including its floodplain and watershed. Certainly the case presented in this book provides a model for the kinds of information that should be obtained and considered in making river management decisions.

Water is certainly a major limiting factor in the economic growth of Florida, which has one of the most rapidly increasing populations among all the states. It can only become more important as time goes on. As a result, more and more diverse demands—agricultural, domestic, and industrial—will be placed on water resources. There is great need for expanded water supplies for domestic and industrial purposes in the rapidly growing coastal cities where local pumping of groundwater has brought salt water into the aquifer. Their needs are leading to the development of well fields in rural areas remote from the cities to be supplied. In recent years questions have been posed regarding the taking of water from rivers and springs far from the places of need. Obviously the answers will be unacceptable to some, no matter what the outcome. If such exploitation is allowed, residents of the presently water-rich but more sparsely populated areas may see their water supplies dwindle and their own supply costs increase. Certainly the transport of surface waters to distant areas will alter their existing recreational uses. Great political and economic pressures will be exerted by residents of the coastal urban and industrialized regions of the peninsula to ensure that they continue to have adequate water supplies to meet present demands as well as for future expansions.

The vast bulk of water being used in agricultural, industrial, and domestic activities—and likely being significantly altered by usage—is returned to surface waters. Flowing waters are the preferred receiving waters in such managed disposal. Alteration of these waters is an inevitable result, with the implications not fully predictable from present knowledge.

Development of land within the watershed of a river, and especially of its floodplain, whether for agriculture, housing, or industrial plants, affects the adjacent river as well as systems to which the river may be tributary. Such influences were largely neglected in the past and are as yet too little considered in decisions concerning land use. Water supply problems and nutrient enrichment in the upper St. Johns River system provide dramatic evidence of this.

Certainly the recreational and aesthetic values of our flowing waters must be factored into cost/benefit analyses when decisions are made with respect to water use. Perpetuation of native flora and fauna, spring and river systems, and the environmental heritage in general must head at least some of the lists of priorities in planning for the continued development of Florida. A population growing as rapidly as Florida's has vast needs for outdoor recreation. The value of flowing water systems in providing a portion of these recreational possibilities is vast, with the economic returns of such usage, when evaluated in monetary units, frequently far greater than those possible from alternative agricultural, domestic, or industrial ones. A discouraging, yet likely, eventuality is that with continued population growth surface water resources will be inadequate to provide for all the diverse demands for their use. Limited regulations have already been imposed on recreational uses of the Ichetucknee Spring system, as well as on several other waters. It is likely that uses considered in such resource apportionments will ultimately include industrial and domestic ones as well as various types of recreation.

Present laws regarding water and watershed usage and management plans and strategies will need to be reviewed and scaled up to meet the greater and more diverse demands. It is abundantly clear that integrated plans must be made for development within Florida, with all types of water resources being given a prominent place in this plan. Accompanying enforceable regulatory statutes must be developed.

Detailed, integrated, long-term studies of Florida's flowing water systems—rivers and springs—are only now being made. Legislators and policy makers in local, state, and federal agencies should make the implementation of such programs top priority items, to furnish the kinds of information necessary for intelligent planning for the benefit of all portions of society and the environment. It does seem evident that much new interest is being focused on Florida's running water systems. Various local, state, and federal agencies are sponsoring extensive studies, while other investigations are being carried out privately to meet various permit requirements. Examples of the work now being carried out by state agencies are the river-monitoring program of the Game and Fresh Water Fish Commission and the studies of rivers being undertaken by the staffs of the several water management districts. However, such information needs to be made more readily available than is now the case.

Another encouraging sign has been the establishment of state and federal programs through which several agencies identify various waters to be set aside or protected in some way, to preserve existing ecosystems. In some cases the usage of a system or an area of a system may be limited to particular recreational activities. The agencies involved have been able to propose guidelines to appropriate legislative bodies as to the types and extents of use that may be allowed and the kinds and extents of alterations that are acceptable in such waters. The Outstanding Florida Waters program, the Florida Scenic and Wild Rivers program, and the National Wild and Scenic Rivers Act are all involved in this. A list of waters of all types included in Florida programs up to 1984 is found in Fernald and Patton (1984). More recent listings are found in Florida Department of Environmental Regulation publications of water quality standards. It is hoped that these programs will be perpetuated and further expanded to help protect Florida's river and spring ecosystems.

Part IV

Coastal Ecosystems

13
Dunes and Maritime Forests

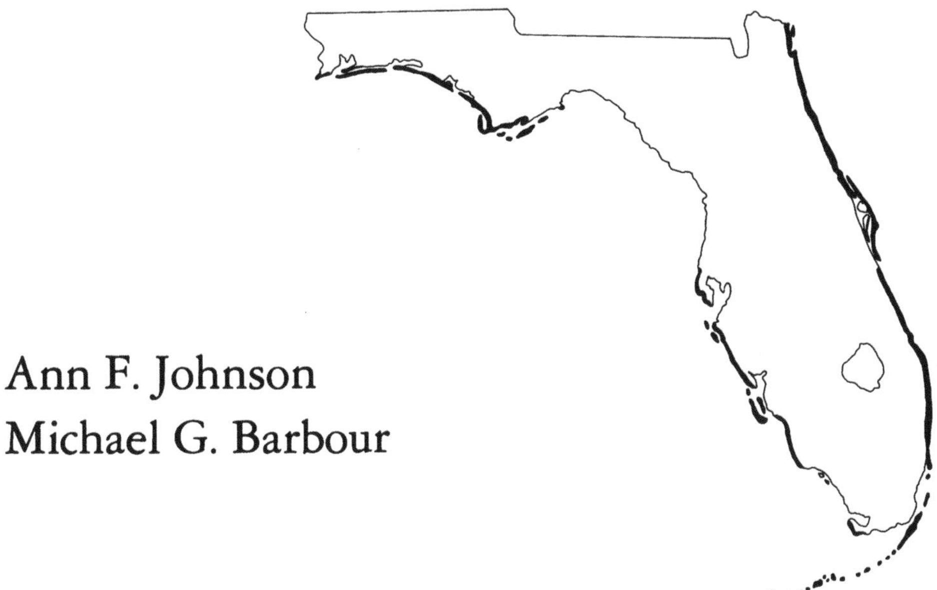

Ann F. Johnson
Michael G. Barbour

Florida's 1900-km coastline (exclusive of the Keys) is easily the longest in the coterminous United States. Of those 1900 km, 1200 km are sandy, mostly in the form of offshore barrier islands (fig. 13.1). The major non-sandy portions are the mangrove-bordered southern tip and the Big Bend of the Gulf coast, where the peninsula curves around to join the Panhandle. Both of these are areas of low or zero wave energy (Tanner, 1960a), where extremely gradual offshore slopes prevent large waves from breaking near shore; this, combined with a lack of sandy sediment (Hine and Belknap, 1986), permits marshes or mangrove swamps to develop on open, unbarred coastlines (fig. 13.2).

Physical Setting

Source of Sand

Florida's beaches are composed primarily of quartz sand in the north and of quartz plus calcium carbonate sand (shell fragments and oolite grains) in the south. The ultimate source of quartz is the granitic Appalachians.

Fig. 13.1. Sandy coastline in Florida.

Fig. 13.2. Zero wave energy coast along Florida's Big Bend. Photo by R. Myers.

Quartz sand was brought to the coastal plain and continental shelf by rivers draining the Piedmont, including the Apalachicola and Ochlockonee rivers in the Florida Panhandle and the Santee, Savannah, and Altamaha rivers in Georgia and South Carolina. Little sediment is supplied to the coast by rivers whose drainage area encompasses only the coastal plain, which includes all those in peninsular Florida (Giles and Pilkey, 1965). As sea level rose and fell across the continental shelf during the Pleistocene, these quartz sands were reworked by waves to form beaches and barrier islands fringing the coast (Swift, 1975). The sand that forms the present barriers on both the Atlantic and Gulf coasts of Florida appears to have come from reworked offshore deposits rather than from the present rivers, which are depositing their sandy sediment in bays and estuaries instead of on the open coast (Otvos, 1981; Pilkey and Field, 1972).

Longshore drift moves sand south along the Atlantic coast of Florida. The percentage by volume of calcium carbonate sand increases from less than 10 percent north of Jacksonville (fig. 13.3a) to more than 40 percent at Miami (Martens, 1931; Giles and Pilkey, 1965; Duane and Meisburger, 1969). No quartz sand is deposited south of Cape Florida (fig. 13.3b).

Beaches in the Florida Keys, Cape Sable, and the Ten Thousand Islands are mostly calcium carbonate sand. Quartz sand beaches resume on the peninsular Gulf coast near Cape Romano (Tanner et al., 1963) and continue north to Anclote Keys (fig. 13.3c). Like the sands of the southern barriers on the Atlantic coast, the sands of these peninsular Gulf barriers contain a high percentage of shell. South of Indian Rocks Beach (fig. 13.3c) longshore drift moves sand both north and south on this coast, with south weakly predominating. North of Indian Rocks Beach drift is predominantly northward.

Barriers fringing the Panhandle coast are 99 percent quartz sand (Drehle, 1973), again originally deposited by rivers draining the Piedmont (Kwon, 1969; van Andel and Poole, 1960). West of Cape San Blas (fig. 13.3d) longshore drift is mainly westward; east of Cape San Blas, drift moves sand both east and west.

Barrier Formation

Barrier islands are linear islands of sand that parallel many gently sloping coastlines around the world. They are thought to have been formed in three ways (Schwartz, 1971): by the growth of spits from headlands and their subsequent breaching by inlets; by the emergence of underwater shoals; and by the drowning and isolation of mainland dunelines as sea level rose. Once formed, barrier islands may migrate landward, as many on the Atlantic coast have done in historical times, leaving marsh peats exposed on the ocean shore (Field and Duane, 1976).

Otvos (1981), not finding lagoon peats seaward of barriers on the Florida Panhandle, hypothesizes that these islands formed in place through shoal emergence and longshore drift. Crooked Island and several others along this coast have emerged from shoals in historical times (Shepard and Wanless, 1971). Evans et al. (1985) concluded that Pinellas County barriers on the peninsular Gulf coast had migrated to their present position, since lagoon sediments are found seaward of them. Whether the barriers on the Atlantic coast of Florida migrated to their present position or were formed in place is not known.

Barriers on both the Panhandle and peninsular Gulf coasts occur on "highs" in the underlying Pleistocene surface, which consists of limestone rock in the peninsula and unconsolidated mud and sand in the Panhandle. Tanner (1960b) hypothesized that the Atlantic barriers are also perched on a rise in the underlying coquina rock or Anastasia formation—itself thought to be a Pleistocene beach and nearshore deposit that lithified in places to form beachrock (Cooke, 1939). This process is presently occurring at more

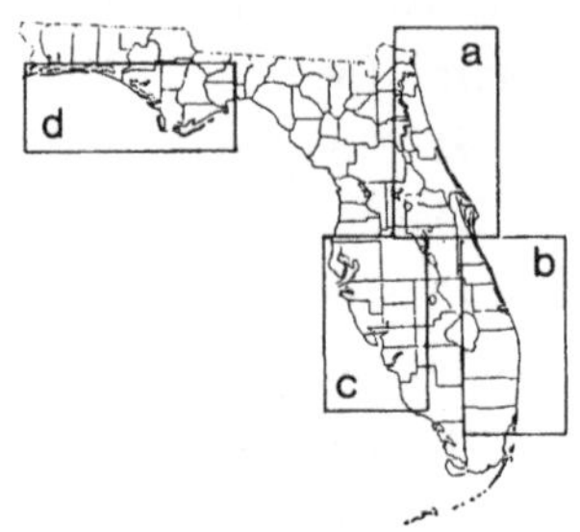

Fig. 13.3 a–d. Maps of coastal regions of Florida with portions of natural vegetation shown in black. *A*, northeast; *B*, southeast; *C*, southwest; *D*, Panhandle. Abbreviations used: *SP*, state park; *SRA*, state recreation area; *NM*, national monument; *NWR*, national wildlife refuge; *NS*, national seashore; *SPR*, state preserve; *AFB*, Air Force base; *I*, island; *K*, key.

southerly locations such as the Dry Tortugas (Ginsberg, 1953). The Anastasia formation (fig. 13.4) is found from St. Augustine to Boca Raton, where it grades into the oolitic Miami limestone; it also outcrops on the west coast of the peninsula (Puri and Vernon, 1964).

The two northernmost Atlantic barriers in Florida, Amelia and Little Talbot islands (fig. 13.3a), are the southernmost of the sea islands, a chain of barriers extending from South Carolina to Florida (White, 1970). These islands are short and broad, in contrast to the long narrow shape of most Atlantic barriers, and their Recent sands are often welded onto older Pleistocene barriers (Hoyt and Hails, 1967), as Little Talbot is to Big Talbot Island. Hayes (1979) attributed their short "drumstick" shape to the higher tidal range (relative to wave energy) found along this coastal sector. The mean tidal range is 2+ m, compared to ranges of less than 1 m for most of the Florida coast. Greater tidal ranges generate stronger tidal currents that can maintain the inlets open against the tendency of longshore drift to occlude them. The underwater ebb tidal deltas deposited by these currents seaward of the inlets deflect longshore drift, leading to the deposition of a sequence of beach ridges at the tips of the islands—hence their "drumstick" shape.

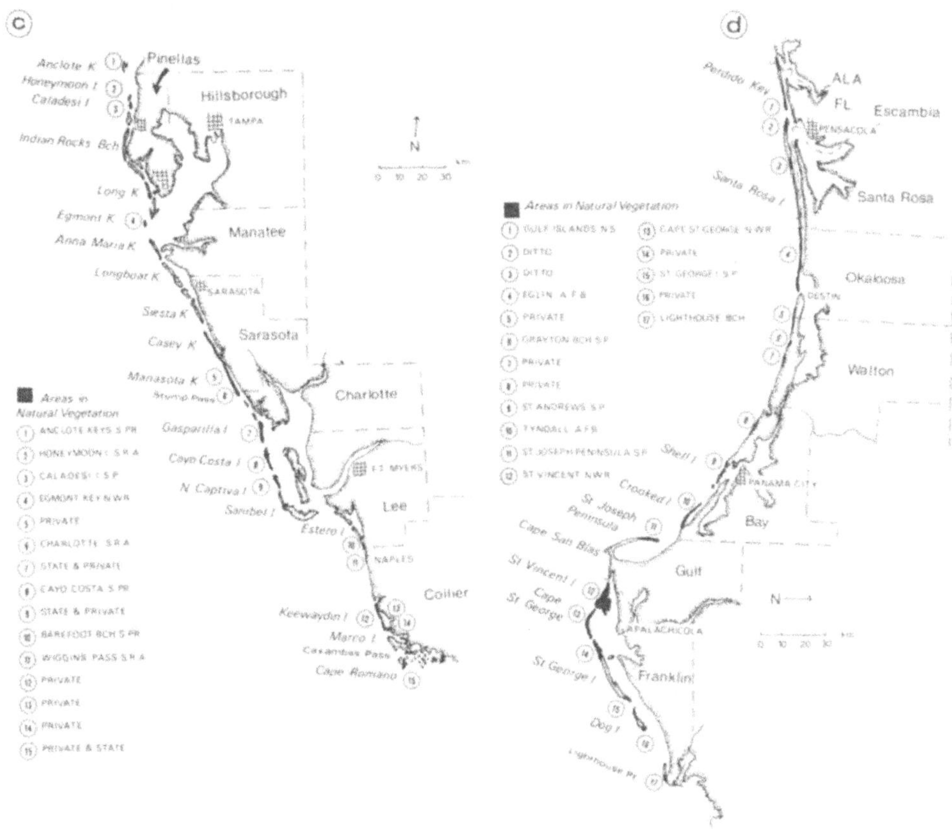

Fig. 13.4. Exposure of coquina rock (Anastasia formation) in Martin County. Photo by Allan Horton.

Beach Ridges

Sandy capes and the broader barrier islands of Florida are composed of sets of parallel ridges with intervening swales, as an aerial photo of St. Vincent Island in the Panhandle clearly shows (fig. 13.5). The ridges are old berms left inland as the island built seaward or parallel to the coast (Stapor, 1975). The wave-deposited berms may or may not be topped by wind-deposited dunes. Each set of parallel ridges represents one episode of progradation, one set having been truncated by erosion before the next set—with a different orientation—was laid down. Carbon-14 dating of beach ridge sets on the islands of St. Vincent (Stapor, 1975), Dog (Stapor, 1975), Sanibel (Missimer, 1973), and Cayo Costa (Stapor and Matthews, 1980) dates the oldest ridge sets at 2000 to 4000 YBP. Thus the Gulf barrier islands appear to have been at their present position since the slowing of the rate of sea level rise at about 3500 YBP (Scholl et al., 1969). Tide gauge data show that the average rate of sea level rise in Florida over the last fifty years (1–2 mm/yr; Evans and Hine, 1983) is greater than the average for the last several thousand years (0.4 mm/yr; Scholl et al., 1969). In the last century most of the

Florida coast has been undergoing net erosion (Pilkey et al., 1984; Doyle et al., 1984). Sea level rise alone, however, does not account for this erosion. Local sediment supply to the coast and coastal slope interacts with the rate of sea level rise to determine whether a given shoreline will advance, retreat, or remain in position (Curry, 1964; Nummedal, 1983).

Dynamics

Barrier islands are dynamic habitats. Their topographic and vegetation profiles result from the interaction of plant growth habits and physical processes, principally wind-driven sand movement and salt spray deposition and wave-driven erosion, accretion, and overwash (Barbour et al., 1975). Zonation of species from the coast inland has been related to tolerance to salt spray (Oosting, 1945; Boyce, 1954; Stalter, 1976) and to sand burial (Olson, 1958; van der Valk, 1974; Tyndall, 1985). However, several authors have pointed out that if a seedling cannot survive normal sand burial conditions obtaining in a zone, its tolerance or intolerance to salt spray may be irrelevant. On a larger scale, Godfrey (1977) studied the recovery of barrier systems from storm overwash and was able to link the topographic differences between barriers in Massachusetts and North Carolina to differences in plant responses to storms in the two areas. To take one example, the Carolina variety of the principal high marsh grass (*Spartina patens* var. *monogyna*) grows up through a layer of sand deposited over it by large

Fig. 13.5. Aerial photograph of St. Vincent Island, Franklin County, Florida, taken in 1984. National High Altitude Photography, U.S. Geological Survey.

storm waves (which frequently attack this part of the coast), thus quickly stabilizing the overwash deposit and preventing the sand behind the beach from being piled into dunes; the barrier profile remains low and flat. The northern variety (*S. patens* var. *patens*) is killed by such sand deposition, leaving the sand surface free to be piled into dunes and resulting in the higher, more irregular profile of the northern barriers.

To our knowledge, no studies in Florida have looked at mechanisms or rates of reestablishment of vegetation zones after storms or of their initial establishment on newly formed portions of barriers, though individual species' reactions to erosion and progradation have been studied (Platt, 1987; Iverson, 1984). Nonetheless, it may be useful to note some general correlations between barrier vegetation profiles and the different physical conditions obtaining along Florida's coasts.

Wind

Dunes are built as stems of dune grasses increase the surface roughness, causing wind to slow and to drop sand grains being moved across the beach (Bagnold, 1941). It follows that only winds blowing onshore—across the loose sand of the beach—will cause dune formation, at least where the barrier is covered by vegetation. Offshore winds will merely move sand alongshore or into the water. The threshold wind speed needed to move sand grains of medium diameter (0.25 mm) along a beach is about 6 m/sec (Mitsudera et al., 1965). Generally coastlines that face the prevailing wind direction have higher foredunes and are more apt to have blowouts—i.e., moving sand invading the backdune zone—than are those that do not. Because most of peninsular Florida lies in the path of the prevailing easterlies, foredunes on the Atlantic coast are generally higher (3–6 m; Pilkey et al., 1984) than those on the southwest coast (1–2 m; Doyle et al., 1984). The south-facing Panhandle coast receives generally light southerly winds in summer and is protected from the stronger northwest winds of winter. The fine to medium diameter (0.25 mm) quartz sands of this coast can be moved by lighter winds than the coarser shelly sands of the southern peninsular coasts, and foredunes are 4–6 m high.

Extraordinary waves of a hurricane may destroy the foredune, while its winds may start the loose sand in permanent motion in sectors of coast historically well stabilized by vegetation. Grayton Beach State Park in the Panhandle was hit by Hurricane Eloise in 1975 and Hurricane Frederick in 1979 (Doyle et al., 1984), and a large wave of loose sand is now invading its woody backdune vegetation. Once started, such a migrating slipface may continue until it engulfs the whole barrier, if conditions are too dry or too unstable for vegetation to colonize its crest. Shackleford Bank on the North Carolina coast, shown on old maps as completely forested, was hit by a hurricane in 1899 that started a sheet of sand slowly burying the forest (Johnson, 1900). By 1969 only the northwestern bayside, making up 4 percent of the island's area, still had a fringe of the original forest left unburied (Au, 1974).

Like sand, salt spray is carried only by winds blowing onshore across open water. Salt droplets kill the terminal buds, producing the "pruned" canopies of woody species seen along the coast (Boyce, 1954). Low, upwardly slanting canopies of dwarf live oak or sea grape are common on the east coast (fig. 13.6). Their absence on southwest Florida shores (fig. 13.7) can probably best be explained by the relative infrequency of onshore winds along this coast. In the Panhandle the light southerly onshore winds of summer produce a more compact growth form in the rosemary shrubs growing in the transitional zone than is seen in those growing in the more inland and protected scrubs of the stabilized dunes.

Waves

Waves are continually adding new parts to barrier islands and eroding the old, either through continuous processes such as longshore drift, or by single events, such as winter storms and hurricanes. Over the last several decades most of the Florida coast has been eroding landward at an average rate of 0.3–0.6 m/yr (Doyle et al., 1984; Pilkey et al., 1984). Accretion has been parallel to the coast or at the downdrift ends of barrier islands or capes, rather than seaward. This accretion is usually accompanied by losses on the updrift ends. Major changes occur during storms, including opening and closing of inlets, overwash of narrow parts of barriers, and formation of new barriers from submarine shoals. A few prominent examples will illustrate these processes.

Along the Panhandle coast accretion occurs on the western ends of islands in the direction of longshore drift. Perdido Key (fig. 13.3d) grew westward 6.4 km in 108 years (Price, 1975), and Santa Rosa Island grew westward 0.8 km in the 67 years before 1935 (Doyle et al., 1984). The western shore of Cape San Blas has been retreating landward at the rate of 11

Fig. 13.6. View south at Canaveral National Seashore on the Atlantic coast north of Cape Canaveral in 1986. Note spray-pruned scrub and hammock canopies and height of foredune relative to person.

Fig. 13.7. View south at Caladesi Island on the Gulf coast north of Tampa in 1986. Note low foredune and absence of spray-pruned canopies.

m/yr, one of the highest erosion rates in Florida (Tanner, 1975). St. George and Dog islands, east of Cape San Blas, have been eroding at their centers and building at both ends. St. George Island extended eastward 1.6 km from 1855 to 1935 (Doyle et al., 1984).

Panhandle barriers have been repeatedly struck by hurricanes in the past decade; at present there is hardly a stretch on the entire coast that is not in the process of recovery. As much as 90 percent of Perdido Key and Santa Rosa Island was awash during Hurricane Frederick in 1979; much of their vegetative cover was destroyed (Doyle et al., 1984). The stretch of nonbarrier coast from Destin to Panama City was damaged by Hurricane Eloise in 1975, with serious effects on Grayton Beach State Park, as described earlier. On Franklin County barriers, hurricanes Elena and Kate in 1985 cut back or destroyed the foredunes from St. Joseph Peninsula to Dog Island and overwashed narrow portions of Dog and St. George islands (Clark, 1986a).

Islands that have emerged from submarine shoals along this coast include Crooked Island, which appeared on maps after 1779, and a lunate sandspit east of Shell Island, which emerged in 1950–51 (Shepard and Wanless, 1971). Potential new barriers may be represented by sand shoals extending 16 km east of Dog Island (Shepard and Wanless, 1971).

On Florida's Atlantic coast all inlets are jettied. Major changes in these narrow barriers are confined largely to accretion on the updrift (or northern) side of the jetties and erosion on their downdrift (or southern) side. Since construction of the long jetties at the mouth of the St. Johns River, the outer set of beachfront lots at Jacksonville has been lost to erosion (Pilkey et al., 1984). Landward erosion at the north end of Jupiter Island, Martin County, has totaled 500 m since the north jetty was constructed on St. Lucie inlet in 1930—ocean waves now break on mangrove roots at some points along this coast (Pilkey et al., 1984). In Dade County the jetties at Government Cut have starved beaches on Virginia Key of sand, causing 90 m of landward erosion in this century (Pilkey et al., 1984).

Storms on the Atlantic coast generally erode the foredune without overwashing or breaching the barriers to form new inlets as they do on the Gulf coast. Winter storms, or nor'easters, have in recent decades caused as much or more erosion on the Atlantic coast of Florida as have hurricanes (Pilkey et al., 1984). The granddaddy of all nor'easters was the 1962 Ash Wednesday storm, which accelerated coastal erosion in Florida from Nassau to Palm Beach counties. Winter storms in 1973, 1981, and 1983 also produced coastal erosion in northern counties. Hurricanes Dora in 1964 and David in 1979 affected northern counties, but no major hurricane has struck the southern counties for the past twenty years.

Barriers along the southwest coast are lower than those along the east coast. Some are broadened at their tips by sets of beach ridges and are separated from the mainland by substantial bays, such as Tampa Bay, Sarasota Bay, Charlotte Harbor, and Estero Bay (fig. 13.3c). These larger bodies of water have a greater tidal flux than do the linear east coast lagoons, causing sand to be stored in underwater tidal deltas on either side of inlets. Occasionally these shoals emerge above water, forming new barrier islands. Lover's Key in Lee County was formed in this way in the 1950s (Doyle et al., 1984).

South of Indian Rocks Beach, Pinellas County, drift is generally southward. On Anna Maria and Longboat keys, Banks (1975) found that recent erosion rates of 0.5 to 3 m/yr are greater than those prevailing during the previous sixty years. Beaches on the south sides of passes have receded. North Captiva Island (south of Captiva Pass), Captiva Island (south of Redfish Pass), and Morgan Island (south of Caxambas Pass) have all receded about 0.3 km landward from the late 1800s to the mid-1900s (Doyle et al., 1984). Several peninsular Gulf barriers have inner barrier islands parallel to the outer barrier near inlets (e.g., Stump Pass between Manasota Key and Knight Island in Charlotte County). Inner barriers are formed when the updrift barrier overlaps the downdrift barrier, forming a long, narrow tidal channel parallel to the coast. When a storm opens a new direct inlet through these overlapped islands, part of the downdrift barrier becomes an inner barrier adjacent to a new inlet. A recent example is Keewaydin Island in Collier County, which has extended southward 2.4 km since 1952 to overlap completely Little Marco Island, cutting it off from the Gulf and forming the long, narrow Little Marco Pass (Harvey et al., 1984). Inlets along this coast constantly open, close, and migrate southward. The only inlets that can maintain their positions are those that open to bays with sufficient tidal prism to generate a current capable of counteracting the occluding tendency of longshore drift (Evans and Hine, 1983).

Although beaches on the Gulf may experience winter erosion, this coast is largely protected from the severe nor'easters that strike the Atlantic side; tropical storms or hurricanes cause most of the dramatic changes. During Hurricane Donna in 1960 water overtopped all the barriers in Lee and Collier counties (Doyle et al., 1984). In this one storm the southern end of Manasota Key was extended southward 0.6 km, cutting off Peterson Island from the Gulf. Even fourteen years later this new land had only 50 percent cover of such pioneer species as sea oats (*Uniola paniculata*), beach elder (*Iva imbricata*), and beach berry (*Scaevola plumieri*; Reynolds, 1976). Tanner (1961) estimates that Hurricane Donna did the work of about 100 years of ordinary processes on this low wave energy coast.

Besides wave energy and land elevation, tidal range influences the amount of damage that can be done by a storm. Coasts with greater tidal ranges are more buffered against storm surges than are those with low tidal ranges, except when the storm strikes at high tide. Mean tidal range decreases southward along the Atlantic coast from 2.1 m at the Georgia border to 0.6 m in Palm Beach County. Tidal range is 0.8 m along the Gulf coast, except in the extreme south (Cape Romano and Cape Sable) where it is 0.9 to 1.2 m (Fernald, 1981). In short, because of its lower elevations and lower wave energy regime, the west coast of the peninsula is more subject to major changes during storms than is the east coast. Thus it is a more dynamic and unstable coast even though historically it has had a lower frequency of hurricane strikes than the Atlantic side.

Plant Reactions

The reaction of plants to these physical conditions produces the zonation and topographic profiles observed. The responses of several species have been studied in Florida.

Plants on the upper beach must be able to recolonize after winter storm erosion. The annual beach peanut (*Okenia hypogaea*) has pedicels that turn down as the fruit ripens, burying the fruit in the sand (Ward, 1979). Iverson (1984) found that winter storm waves may excavate the fruit, which is then deposited with the drift at the upper limit of storm wave penetration, where it germinates the following spring. If storm waves do not excavate it, the fruit may germinate in place, producing a plant in the same site the following year. Seedlings do not survive unless the seeds have been buried to a depth of at least 5 cm (G. B. Iverson, personal communication). In Mexico, *Okenia* is also confined to coasts with regular winter storms called *nortes* (Moreno-Casasola, 1985). Another set of upper beach annuals, the sea rockets (*Cakile*), also produce fruits that can either hold the same site if no storms intervene or colonize new ones if they do. Sea rockets have a two-stage fruit: the bottom half remains attached to (and buried with) the dead parent plant, while the buoyant top half is detachable and can be carried by waves to new sites.

Upper beach species on prograding beaches are faced with the problem of keeping up with their moving habitat. Platt (1987) considered this problem in two colonial railroad vines (*Ipomoea pes-caprae* and *I. stolonifera*) on the east end of St. George Island (fig. 13.3d), which was prograding at the rate of 2–10 m/yr. He found that both species germinate on the upper beach and produce their longest stolons at right angles to the coast—

ensuring they will have ramets both on the newest foredune if the coast is prograding and on the old foredune if the upper beach is eroding.

Foredunes are usually built by grasses whose upward growth keeps pace with sand burial and whose lateral growth helps build a continuous dune ridge. Growth and tillering in sea oats, the major dune builder in Florida, is stimulated by sand burial (Wagner, 1964). Two other grasses on the dunes, bitter panicum (*Panicum amarum*) and beach cordgrass (*Spartina patens*), may have similar reactions (Oertel and Lassen, 1976). The growth of other species colonizing the foredune built by these grasses must also be able to keep pace with burial. Many have relatively large seeds that produce seedlings able to reach the surface from depths of 5–10 cm (van der Valk, 1974).

Species growing in the lee of the foredune are subjected to lesser amounts of sand burial and salt spray, depending on the height and orientation of the foredune. These factors still seem to be of sufficient intensity to prevent inland plant communities, such as are found on stabilized backdunes, from becoming established in this zone. Another possible factor is lack of sufficient time between storms for inland plant communities to become established. Comparative research that takes account both of past storm history and present environmental factors is needed to interpret the variability in the vegetation found in the transitional zone. Our observations suggest, for example, that the saw palmetto (*Serenoa repens*), so prominent on the lee slope of Atlantic coast dunes, may be sensitive to salt spray. Where the protecting sea oats foredune is low, as at Cape Canaveral, grassland replaces the saw palmetto scrub behind the foredune. Farther south, at J. D. MacArthur and Boynton Beach parks in Palm Beach County, the low sea oats plateau is backed by an upward-slanting canopy of dwarfed sea grape (*Coccoloba uvifera*), rather than by palmetto scrub.

The question of whether the grasslands found in the transitional zone at Cape Canaveral, Cape Sable, Cape Romano, Cayo Costa Island, and Sanibel Island will maintain themselves or will succeed in time to coastal scrub has yet to be answered.

Vegetation

Although the familiar postcard pictures of waving sea oats might give visitors the impression that Florida's barrier islands have a fairly uniform vegetation, a short walk inland from the foredune would quickly dispel that notion. On northeasternmost Amelia Island walkers would find themselves in the deep shade of spreading live oaks and magnolias; at Palm Beach in a shorter but more diverse forest of smooth-barked tropical sea grapes, stoppers, and gumbo limbos; on Cayo Costa Island, opposite Fort Myers on the west coast, in a shadeless cabbage palm savanna; on St. Vincent Island in the Panhandle, in either a waist-high scrub of oaks and rosemary on the ridges or a tall slash pine flatwoods in the swales, both strongly reminiscent of the interior peninsula. Sea oats would be uniformly present, to be sure, but as one moves inland, away from the stresses of storm waves, sand burial, and salt spray, climate and substrate play an increasing role in differentiating the vegetation.

The Florida coast can be divided into five regions, the beaches within each region having roughly similar vegetation: the northeast coast from the Georgia border to Cape Canaveral; the southeast coast from Cape Canaveral to Cape Florida; the south coast comprising the "shell hash" and calcium carbonate sand beaches of Cape Sable, the Ten Thousand Islands, and the Florida Keys; the southwest coast from Cape Romano to Anclote Keys north of Tampa; and the Panhandle from the mouth of the Ochlockonee River west to the Alabama border (fig. 13.8). (This regional subdivision is based on a species × site table available on request from Ann Johnson.)

It is widely recognized that coastal vegetation occurs in zones parallel to the coast (Doing, 1981); accordingly, we have organized our discussion of the vegetation in each sector under three headings: beach and foredune

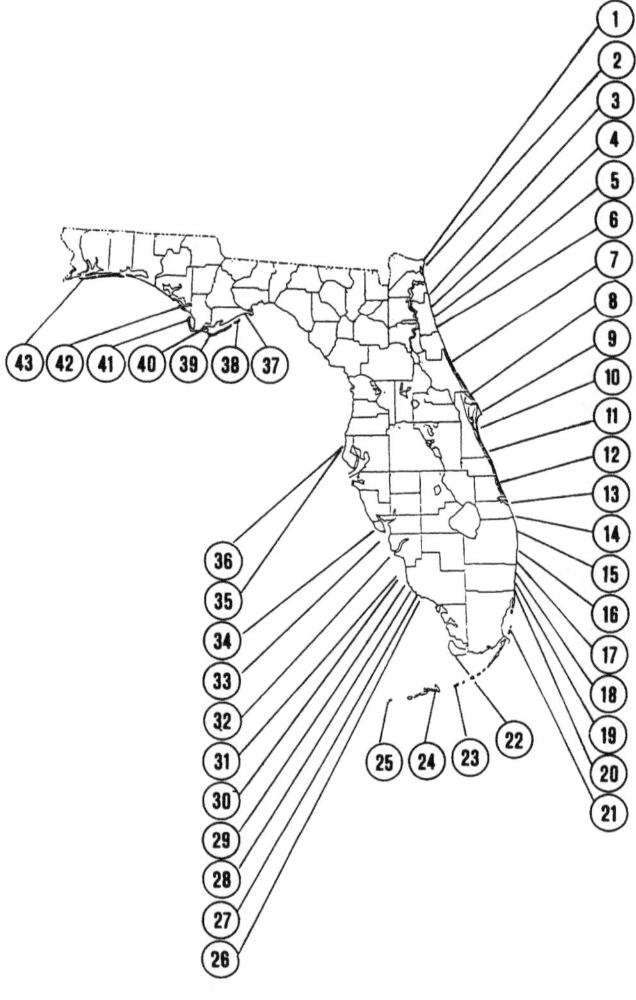

Fig. 13.8. Locations and sources for vegetative and floristic descriptions on which is based the subdivision of Florida coast into five regions. *First author* refers to field notes taken in 1985–86.

1. Fort Clinch State Park (first author; Carlton, 1977).
2. Little Talbot Island State Park (first author; Stalter and Dial, 1984b).
3. Ponte Vedra (Kurz, 1942).
4. Vilano Beach (Kurz, 1942).
5. St. Augustine to Flagler Beach (Laessle and Monk, 1961).
6. Crescent Beach (Kurz, 1942).
7. Daytona Beach (Kurz, 1942).

8. Canaveral National Seashore (Carlton, 1977; Kirkman, 1979).
9. Cape Canaveral (first author; Kurz, 1942; Stout, 1979; Sweet, 1976).
10. Brevard County coast (Poppleton et al., 1977).
11. Sebastian Inlet (first author; Carlton, 1977).
12. Ft. Pierce Inlet (unplant list by Jane Brooks, Florida Division of Recreation and Parks, Hobe Sound).
13. St. Lucie Inlet (unpublished plant list by R. Roberts and D. Austin, Florida Division of Recreation and Parks, Hobe Sound).
14. Blowing Rocks Preserve, Jupiter Island (Kurz, 1942; unpublished plant list by R. Roberts, 1983, Florida Division of Recreation and Parks, Hobe Sound).
15. John D. MacArthur State Park (unpublished plant list, Florida Division of Recreation and Parks, Hobe Sound; Duever et al., 1981).
16. Boynton Beach (Austin and Weise, 1972).
17. Boca Raton Inlet (Austin and Coleman-Marois, 1977).
18. Pompano Beach (Alexander, 1958a).
19. Hugh Taylor Birch State Park (Buckley and Hendrickson, 1983).
20. John U. Lloyd State Recreation Area (unpublished plant list by A. Buckley and T. Hendrickson, 1985, Florida Division of Recreation and Parks, Ft. Lauderdale).
21. Elliot Key, Biscayne National Monument (first author; Carlton, 1977).
22. Cape Sable, Everglades National Park (first author; Robertson, 1955).
23. Long Key State Recreation Area (first author).
24. Southeast Beach, Big Pine Key (first author; W. B. Robertson, personal communication, 1987, Everglades National Park).
25. Sand Keys (Davis, 1942; Millspaugh, 1907; Stoddart and Fosberg, 1981; G. Avery, unpublished ms., 1978, Everglades National Park).
26. Cape Romano (first author).
27. Marco Island (first author; Small, 1923).
28. Little Marco Island (first author).
29. Wiggins Pass State Recreational Area (first author; Carlton, 1977).
30. Barefoot Beach State Preserve, Bonita Beach (unpublished plant list, 1982, Florida Division of Recreation and Parks, Estero).
31. Sanibel Island (Cooley, 1955).
32. North Captiva Island (Morrill and Harvey, 1980).
33. Cayo Costa Island State Preserve (Herwitz, 1977).
34. Stump Pass (Reynolds, 1976).
35. Caladesi Island State Park (unpublished plant list, Florida Division of Recreation and Parks, Clermont).
36. Honeymoon Island State Recreation Area (unpublished plant list, Florida Division of Recreation and Parks, Clermont).
37. Cochran's Beach (Kurz, 1942).
38. Dog Island (Anderson Alexander, 1985).
39. Cape St. George (first author).
40. St. Vincent Island (first author).
41. St. Joseph Peninsula State Park (first author; Carlton, 1977).
42. Beacon Hill (Kurz, 1942).
43. Fort Pickens State Park (Carlton, 1977).

zone, transitional zone, and stable dune zone. The *upper beach and foredune zone* is the most easily recognized, being clearly controlled by physical processes. The upper beach is continuously recolonized by plants, since waves of storms or high tides disturb it every year or two. Beyond the limit of yearly wave action, windblown sand can accumulate around plants as they grow upward to form the foredune. Since a supply of loose sand from the beach is always present, sand burial is a constant factor on the foredune, its rate dependent on the force and direction of the winds and the mobility of the sand grains.

The remaining two zones we define in terms of the characteristics of the plant communities within them rather than in terms of physical processes, though these are assumed to control them. The *transitional zone* begins in the shelter of the foredune and continues inland until a recognized inland plant community—such as hammock, palm savanna, scrub, or flatwoods—is reached. Presumably the same coastal stresses that operate in the upper beach and foredune zone operate at lower frequency or intensity in the transitional zone and prevent its being colonized by ordinary inland plant communities. Vegetation in this zone is often patchy and variable from site to site within the same coastal sector (fig. 13.9).

Fig. 13.9. Zones of coastal vegetation in the process of becoming reestablished after storm erosion at St. Joseph Peninsula State Park in the Florida Panhandle. *Foreground*, sea oat dune; *middle ground*, Gulf bluestem (*Schizachyrium maritimum*); *background*, scrub oak (*Quercus geminata*).

In Florida the term *strand* has been used both to denote what we are calling the transitional zone (Austin and Coleman-Marois, 1977) and to denote both the foredune and the transitional zone (Herwitz, 1977). In ordinary speech, strand usually refers either to the unvegetated beach or to the entire sand deposit bordering the coast. To avoid confusion we have chosen to use a more neutral term for this discussion.

To illustrate zonation and community composition we have used a series of nine profiles of vegetation and topography representing all sectors of the coast (figs. 13.10–12 and 13.14–20). Five of these are original, and four were taken from the literature. All have been redrawn to the same scale to facilitate comparisons. Except where noted, nomenclature follows Wunderlin (1982), Clewell (1985), and Long and Lakela (1971).

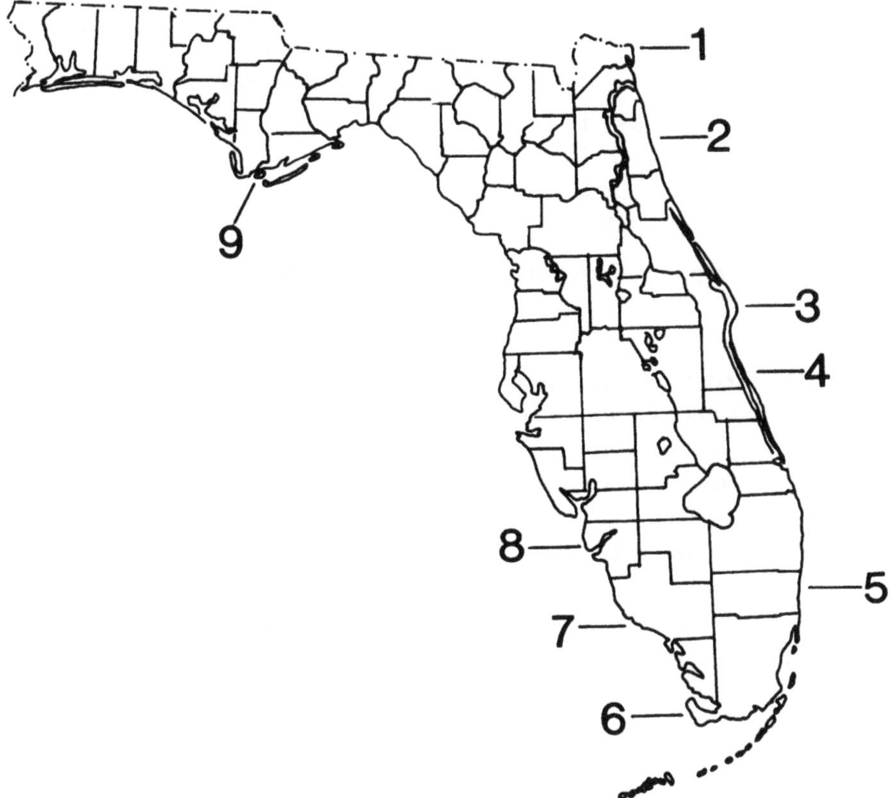

Fig. 13.10 Location of topographic and vegetation profiles across beaches in Florida (shown in figs. 13.11, 13.12, 13.14–20).

Northeast Coast

The northeast coast from the Georgia border to Cape Canaveral can be further subdivided into a northern "sea island" portion from the border to Jacksonville and a southern portion from Jacksonville to the Cape.

Vegetation, as well as topography, link Amelia and Little Talbot islands more closely to the Georgia Sea Islands than to Florida barriers to the south.

① AMELIA ISLAND (Fort Clinch State Park) 30° 45′N

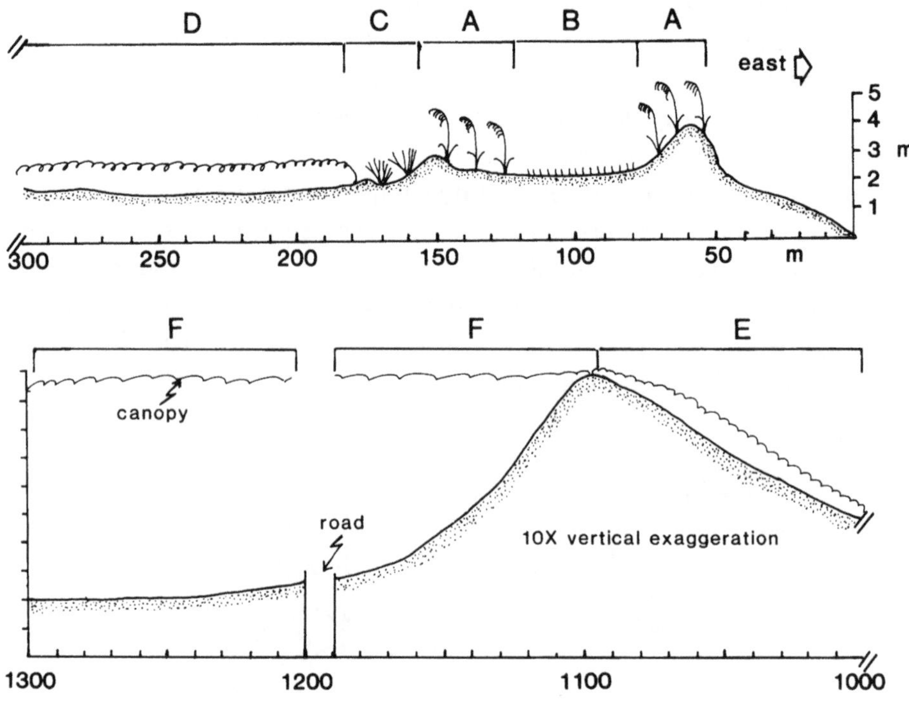

Fig. 13.11. Topographic and vegetation profile across Amelia Island, Nassau County, Florida.

(*A*) Sea oats foredune: *Uniola paniculata, Ipomoea stolonifera, Hydrocotyle bonariensis, Panicum amarum* (inland: *Cladonia leporina, Opuntia pusilla*).

(*B*) Herbaceous flat: *Hydrocotyle bonariensis, Smilax auriculata, Phyla nodiflora, Oenothera humifusa, Heterotheca subaxillaris, Cirsium horridulum, Myrica cerifera, Opuntia stricta, Distichlis spicata,* plus low grasses and forbs.

(*C*) Muhlenbergia grassland: *Muhlenbergia capillaris, Eupatorium capillaceum, Spartina patens.*

(*D*) Wax myrtle scrub: *Myrica cerifera, Baccharis halimifolia, Ilex vomitoria, Sabal palmetto, Juniperus silicicola.*

(*E*) Oak scrub: *Quercus myrtifolia, Juniperus silicicola, Sabal palmetto, Bumelia tenax, Persea borbonia, Magnolia grandiflora.*

(*F*) Oak forest: (*a*) canopy: *Quercus virginiana, Quercus hemisphaerica, Magnolia grandiflora, Prunus serotina, Juniperus silicicola, Celtis laevigata, Sabal palmetto;* (*b*) understory trees and shrubs: *Ilex vomitoria, Persea borbonia, Serenoa repens, Juniperus silicicola, Ilex opaca, Osmanthus americana, Bumelia tenax, Zanthoxylum clava-herculis, Vaccinium arboreum, Callicarpa americana;* (*c*) vines: *Smilax auriculata, Vitis munsoniana, Toxicodendron radicans;* (*d*) herbs: *Salvia lyrata, Verbesina virginica.*

29° 55'N

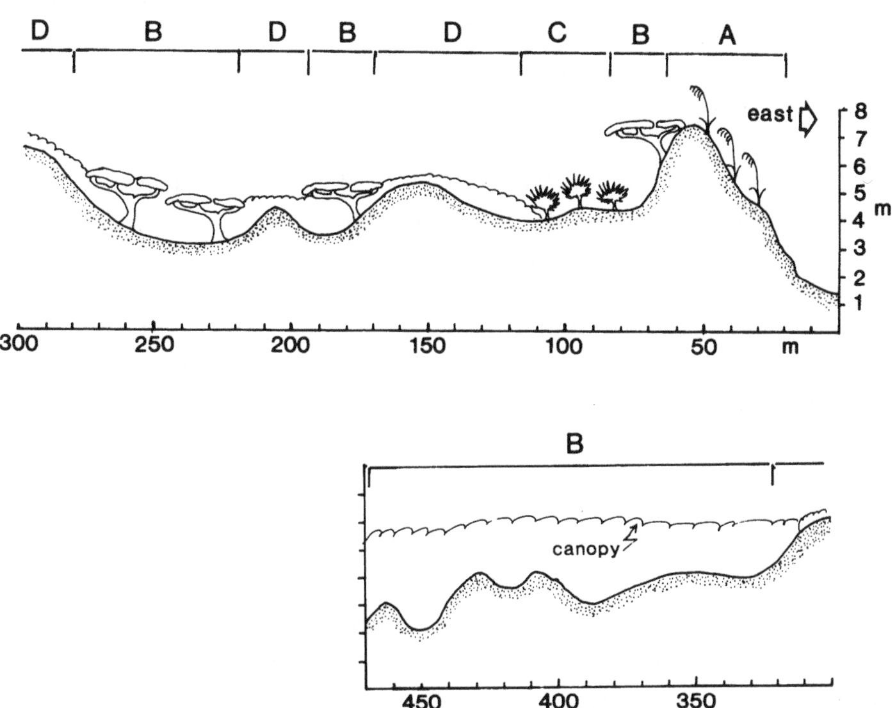

Fig. 13.12. Topographic and vegetation profile across Vilano Beach, St. Johns County, Florida. After Kurz, 1942.

(*A*) Sea oats foredune: *Uniola paniculata, Cakile edentula* ssp. *harperi, Ipomoea pes-caprae, Croton punctatus, Yucca aloifolia, Oenothera humifusa, Salsola kali, Sporobolus virginicus, Chamaesyce bombensis, Helianthus debilis, Cirsium horridulum.*

(*B*) Oak forest: (*a*) canopy: *Quercus hemisphaerica, Persea borbonia, Quercus virginiana, Magnolia grandiflora;* (*b*) understory: *Lyonia ferruginea, Ilex vomitoria, Myrica cerifera, Vaccinium arboreum, Smilax auriculata.*

(*C*) Saw palmetto scrub: *Serenoa repens, Bumelia tenax, Ilex vomitoria, Myrica cerifera, Vaccinium arboreum.*

(*D*) Oak scrub: *Quercus virginiana, Quercus myrtifolia,* plus same species as in saw palmetto scrub above.

Missing from Amelia and Little Talbot are two endemic Florida species characteristic of the lee foredune slope of the more southern barriers: beach verbena (*Glandularia maritima*) and beach sunflower (*Helianthus debilis*). Present on the two northern islands and not southward is the tuna cactus (*Opuntia pusilla*), which is found northward to the Carolinas and on the barriers of the Panhandle.

Upper Beach and Foredunes

Species consistently found seaward of the foredune throughout this sector are the sea rocket (*Cakile edentula* ssp. *harperi*) and beach elder (*Iva imbricata*), which are both succulents (figs. 13.11 and 13.12). Also frequently found on the upper beach are the halophytes, salt grass (*Distichlis spicata*) and beach orach (*Atriplex pentandra*). Usually the first to invade the upper beach after storm erosion is the white-flowered beach morning glory or railroad vine (*Ipomoea stolonifera*), whose stolons extend seaward from a rooted ramet on the face of the foredune. The foredune itself is built by the upward growth of grasses, primarily sea oats (*Uniola paniculata*) but also including beach cordgrass (*Spartina patens*) and bitter panicum (*Panicum amarum*). Other wide-ranging herbs characteristic of the foredune zone are silver-leaf croton (*Croton punctatus*), sand cherry (*Physalis walteri*; Sullivan, 1985), evening primrose (*Oenothera humifusa*), and the prostrate beach spurge (*Chamaesyce bombensis*).

Transitional Zone or Backdunes

The transitional vegetation of the two northern islands contrasts sharply with that found to the south. The immediate backdune zone on the two northern islands is usually a broad flat area occupied by a mixture of low-growing grasses and forbs, such as beach pennywort (*Hydrocotyle bonariensis*), capeweed (*Phyla nodiflora*), and *Dicanthelium* spp. Slightly lower areas are dominated by tall bunches of purple muhly grass (*Muhlenbergia capillaris*) or by beach cordgrass (*Spartina patens*). In lower areas farther inland scattered wax myrtle shrubs may coalesce into a solid stand interspersed with silverling (*Baccharis halimifolia*), southern red cedar (*Juniperus silicicola*), and cabbage palm (*Sabal palmetto*). Farther inland the drier parts of the flat may be covered by scattered mounds of intermingled vines (*Smilax auriculata, Toxicodendron radicans, Ampelopsis arborea, Vitis munsoniana*, and *Parthenocissus quinquefolia*), either growing on the sand itself or clambering over shrubs. Still farther inland is a zone of scattered shrubs and trees; these same species compose the forest that develops behind the protection of taller dunes, whose exposed seaward faces are covered by spray-pruned oak scrub.

All of these plant communities have been described by others on barriers to the north, from Georgia to the Carolinas (Hillestad et al., 1975; Stalter, 1974; Brown, 1959). Godfrey and Godfrey (1976) described similar grassy flats behind foredunes on Cape Lookout, North Carolina, which they found to be old washover fans where waves had breached the sea oats foredune, carrying sand inland. The duneline had subsequently re-formed, leaving a broad flat area behind it. Au (1974) mapped a "Myrica-Juniper" flat in a low area on Shackleford Bank, North Carolina, and also mentioned vines colonizing the dunes behind the grassy interdunal zone. On Waiters Island,

South Carolina, Rayner and Batson (1976) described a "shrub-vine" zone (*Myrica, Baccharis*, and *Toxicodendron*), which they considered successional to closed, woody vegetation.

The transitional zone vegetation of the barriers south of Amelia and Little Talbot Islands is primarily woody. The low-growing saw palmetto (*Serenoa repens*) favors the protected lee slopes and flats behind the steeply eroded foredunes. It forms dense stands 1.5 m tall intermingled with shrubs of the same height, above which the crowns of dwarfed cabbage palms occasionally protrude. Austin and Coleman-Marois (1977) refer to the zone occupied by saw palmetto scrub as "strand." This palmetto zone has been described as far north as Vilano Beach, St. Johns County (Kurz, 1942), and as far south as Boca Raton in southern Palm Beach County (Austin and Coleman-Marois, 1977). Long stretches of it are still found north of Ormond Beach, St. Johns County, and at Canaveral National Seashore, Volusia County.

The palmetto scrub gives way farther inland to spray-pruned oak scrub and the scrub to forest. Actually, almost all of the forest trees are already present in dwarfed form in the coastal scrub—live oak (*Quercus virginiana*), red bay (*Persea borbonia*), magnolia (*Magnolia grandiflora*), wild olive (*Osmanthus americana*), and cabbage palm (*Sabal palmetto*). As the land slopes down toward the lagoon, the dwarfed trees of the scrub may grow to tree height while the canopy level remains the same or slopes up gently. Some members of the coastal scrub community remain as understory shrubs in the forest: yaupon (*Ilex vomitoria*), wax myrtle (*Myrica cerifera*), and buckthorn (*Bumelia tenax*). Others, such as myrtle oak (*Quercus myrtifolia*), are primarily found in the unshaded coastal scrub.

Although both are oak-dominated shrub communities, *coastal scrub* as used here is not synonymous with *Florida scrub*, also referred to simply as *scrub* (see chapter 6). Coastal scrub occurs behind foredunes on Atlantic barriers; Florida scrub occurs on acid sands of mainland dunes and in the interior of Panhandle barriers. The low growth form of at least some of the component species of coastal scrub is probably due to salt spray injury to the terminal buds; the low growth form of Florida scrub species is generally controlled by other factors, such as nutrient supply or fire frequency. The same or closely related oak species are found in both communities: myrtle oak (*Quercus myrtifolia*), Chapman's oak (*Q. chapmanii*, rare in coastal scrub), and live oak (*Q. virginiana*). Populations of live oak may have diverged in the two communities to form a distinct species, sand live oak (*Q. geminata*), in the Florida scrub, while remaining merely a shrubby ecotype of *Q. virginiana* in the coastal scrub, but there is no taxonomic consensus about this possibility. The shrub form of live oak on the coast was described as a separate variety (*Q. virginiana* var. *maritima*). This variety was later synonymized with *Q. geminata* (Small, 1933), itself originally described as a variety of *Q. virginiana*. Field and experimental work is needed to clarify the taxonomic status of these segregates of live oak, about which there is no consensus (Clewell, 1985; Fernald, 1950; Godfrey, 1988; Radford et al., 1968; Small, 1933; Wunderlin, 1982). Coastal and Florida scrub communities differ in their principal associated species as well, with rosemary (*Ceratiola ericoides*) and sand pine (*Pinus clausa*) characterizing the Florida scrubs, and yaupon holly (*Ilex vomitoria*) and cabbage palm (*Sabal palmetto*) the coastal scrubs.

Stable Dunes

Live oak forests occur on stable portions of barrier islands from Nags Head, North Carolina, to north of Daytona Beach, Florida, and their species composition has been well documented (Bourdeau and Oosting, 1959; Brown, 1959; Burk, 1962; Coker, 1905; Hillestad et al., 1975; Johnson, 1900; Johnson et al., 1974; Laessle and Monk, 1961; Rayner and Batson, 1976; Stalter and Dial, 1984b; Wells, 1939).

Live oak (*Quercus virginiana*) dominates throughout. This large tree with a spreading canopy reaches 9–18 m in height with trunks 0.6–1.2 m in diameter. Its crowns are often planed to a uniform level by salt winds off the ocean (fig. 13.13). Evergreen canopy species accompanying the live oak throughout its range are laurel oak (*Q. hemisphaerica*), whose cover increases in more protected sites, and red bay (*Persea borbonia*), which is often the principal understory tree. Two other characteristic evergreens,

Fig. 13.13. Salt- and wind-sculpted oak forest, near Matanzas Inlet, Flagler County. Photo by A. E. Laessle.

cabbage palm and magnolia (*Magnolia grandiflora*), range only as far north as Smith Island, North Carolina; a third, the southern red cedar (*Juniperus silicicola*), is replaced in North Carolina by its northern relative or vicariad, *Juniperus virginiana* (Barry, 1980). Deciduous species contribute little canopy cover, but several are consistently present throughout: mulberry (*Morus rubra*), pignut hickory (*Carya glabra*), and hackberry (*Celtis laevigata*).

From Florida to North Carolina the percentage canopy cover contributed by deciduous species increases as one moves inland or northward along the coast. Deciduous trees, such as water oak (*Quercus nigra*), southern red oak (*Q. falcata*), willow oak (*Q. phellos*), and sweet gum (*Liquidambar styraciflua*) in the overstory, and ironwood (*Carpinus caroliniana*) and flowering dogwood (*Cornus florida*) in the understory, are all consistently mentioned in descriptions of forests on North Carolina's outer barriers. They are rarely encountered on the outer barriers of South Carolina, though frequent on the inner barrier islands and mainland peninsulas of that state (Rayner and Batson, 1976). In northeastern Florida, Laessle and Monk (1961, Table 1) likewise found that a set of deciduous trees (*Quercus nigra, Liquidambar styraciflua, Nyssa biflora*) distinguished mature inland oak hammocks from those on the coast.

Loblolly pine (*Pinus taeda*) and longleaf pine (*P. palustris*) are also found on the barriers, either in pure stands or mixed with hardwoods. Bozeman (in Hillestad et al., 1975) and Bratton (1985) provide historical evidence from the Georgia Sea Islands that the pines are successional following fire, clearing, or timbering of the original hardwood hammock, as has similarly been suggested for the mainland by Quarterman and Keever (1962). Indeed the prevalence of pines may be a good index of human disturbance on Atlantic barrier islands. Naturally caused fire, which could also produce pine forest, probably has a lower incidence on barrier islands (considering the water barriers to its spread) than on the mainland.

Southeast Coast

From Cape Canaveral southward the tropical West Indian element in the coastal vegetation becomes increasingly prominent.

Upper Beach and Foredune

At Cape Canaveral and continuing southward, the warm temperate beach species mingle with tropical species to form a rich beach flora (fig. 13.14). The pantropical halophytes, sea purslane (*Sesuvium portulacastrum*) and beach dropseed (*Sporobolus virginicus*), join Mexican beach peanut (*Okenia hypogaea*) and a West Indian sedge (*Remirea maritima*) on the upper beach. After storm erosion two stoloniferous species, the larger pink-flowered railroad vine (*Ipomoea pes-caprae*) and seashore paspalum (*Paspalum distichum*), may recolonize the upper beach from the foredune. On the foredunes themselves several spray-tolerant tropical shrubs appear among the grasses: sea lavender (*Argusia [=Tournefortia] gnaphalodes*), beach berry (*Scaevola plumieri*), and bay cedar (*Suriana maritima*).

Transitional Zone

Cape Canaveral (fig. 13.14) is one of the few broad, low barriers on the east coast, and its backdune zone is unique in that it is dominated by grasses: purple muhly grass (*Muhlenbergia capillaris*), beardgrasses (*Andropogon virginicus* and *A. glomeratus*), and a sedge (*Fimbristylis caroliniana*). Whether this grassland is successional to shrubs is an open question. Cape Sable on the south coast and Cape Romano on the southwest also have grasslands behind the sea oats foredune, and aerial photographs suggest that Cape Florida once did also, before it was covered by dredge spoil in the 1950s (Pilkey et al., 1984).

On the remainder of the narrow barriers along the southeast coast, woody species dominate the transitional zone. At Canaveral National Seashore tropical shrubs first begin to mingle with temperate species in the palmetto and coastal scrub vegetation. The West Indian nakedwood (*Myrcianthes fragrans*), also known as twinberry or Simpson's stopper, is prominent on the coast only in this temperate-tropical transition zone, extending between Canaveral National Seashore and Fort Pierce Inlet (fig. 13.15). South of Fort Pierce Inlet the shrub form of live oak drops out, and tropical shrubs predominate. In exposed areas an upward-slanting scrub of dwarfed sea grape (*Coccoloba uvifera*) replaces saw palmetto behind the sea oats dune. At the border between the sea oats and sea grape is often a "prickly zone" of spiny species: Spanish bayonet (*Yucca aloifolia*), agave (*Agave decipiens*), and prickly pear (*Opuntia stricta*).

Stable Dune Vegetation

Some of the tropical shrubs in the transitional zone become canopy trees as the land slopes down to the lagoon—sea grape, cabbage palm, and Spanish stopper (*Eugenia foetida*). Some, such as nakedwood (*Myrcianthes fragrans*) and white indigoberry (*Randia aculeata*), remain as understory shrubs. Some are found primarily in the open scrub—blackbead (*Pithecellobium keyensis*), lantana (*Lantana involucrata*), and coin vine (*Dalbergia ecastophyllum*). Many trees in the tropical forest canopy are not found in the preceding shrub zone—e.g., poisonwood (*Metopium toxiferum*), mastic (*Mastichodendron foetidissimum*), strangler fig (*Ficus aurea*), lancewood (*Nectandra coriacea*), pigeon plum (*Coccoloba diversifolia*), and many others.

South of Daytona Beach the forest canopy gradually changes from one dominated by temperate species to one dominated by tropical species. In pinpointing where the change occurs, one has to take into account both topography and substrate (fig. 13.16). Low, wet sites support temperate cabbage palm–live oak forests throughout southern Florida, a vegetation type termed "low hammock" by Richardson (1977). Aboriginal shell middens support tropical species well to the north of their range on sand (Norman, 1976; Small, 1923). Many tropical species reach their northern limits at Cape Canaveral, but dominate the canopy in this area only on shell mounds. On sandy substrates temperate oaks still form the canopy, though tropical species may be found in the understory. The northernmost (extant) tropical forest growing on sand is found at J. D. MacArthur State Park in northern Palm Beach County (fig. 13.3b). Here both oak-dominated "low" hammock and tropical hammock occur on sandy substrate (Duever et al., 1981). The few natural hammocks remaining on the highly urbanized barriers south of here are all tropical (Alexander, 1958a; Austin and Coleman-Marois, 1977; Richardson, 1977). Obviously the transition from temperate to tropical canopy occurred somewhere between Cape Canaveral and northern Palm Beach County. Hammocks at Sebastian Inlet (fig. 13.8) and Fort Pierce Inlet have a mixture of temperate and tropical trees in the canopy; farther south at St. Lucie inlet in Martin County, fragmentary tropical hammock exists, but most of the site is now covered by a dense stand of Australian pine.

Southern Coast

The carbonate sand beaches of the Keys and the mangrove islands at the southern tip of Florida are mostly small, scattered cove beaches, with a few exceptions—notably Cape Sable, which forms a shelly coastline 14 km long. Its beaches are low, with a narrow sea oats foredune backed by a broad grassy zone that is gradually invaded by the shrubs and trees that form a forest farther inland (fig. 13.17). The vegetation of shell hash beaches is not well enough known to say with certainty whether it differs from that found on the southernmost quartz sand beaches at Cape Romano and (formerly) at Cape Florida. The endemic spurge *Chamaesyce garberi* appears to be confined to shell hash or calcium carbonate sand beaches; it is found on the Sand Keys and Florida Keys and at Cape Sable. Saw palmetto is rare and sea grape less frequently encountered than on quartz sand beaches. Jamaica dogwood (*Piscidia piscipula*) and blackbead (*Pithecellobium keyensis*) are more common in this region than to the north. West Indian bluestem (*Schizachyrium semiberbe*) is prominent in the transitional zone.

In its tropical sector Florida lacks an exposed limestone coast and two communities associated with this habitat in the Bahamas, Cuba, and Yucatan. One is a rocky foreshore community consisting of prostrate shrubs and mat-forming succulents (*Rachicallis americana, Strumpfia maritima, Conocarpus erectus* forma *procumbens, Sesuvium portulacastrum*, and *Blutaparon vermiculare*; Samek, 1973). The second community is a dense, spray-shorn coastal thicket with endemic species in the woody genera (*Bumelia, Citharexylum, Coccoloba, Randia,* and *Pithecellobium*; Espejel, 1986; Moreno-Casasola, 1985; Samek, 1973).

Southwest Coast

Dune vegetation on the southwest coast is also dominated by tropical species but differs from the southeast coast in two respects: it is not as diverse, and grasslands and palm savannas replace dwarfed trees and shrubs in the transitional zone.

Upper Beach and Foredunes

Upper beach and foredune vegetation on the west coast is practically identical to that of the east coast south of Cape Canaveral. The western beach sunflower (*Helianthus debilis* ssp. *vestitus*) replaces *H. d.* ssp. *debilis* (Ward, 1978), but it is much less prominent on the Gulf dunes than is its counterpart on the Atlantic. The sand cherry on the Atlantic coast (*Physalis walteri*) may hybridize on the Gulf coast with *P. angustifolia*, whose range centers in the Florida Panhandle (Sullivan, 1985). Two West Indian species present on eastern foredunes are missing on the west: a sedge (*Remirea maritima*) and sea lavender (*Argusia gnaphalodes*).

Transitional Zone

In the backdunes is a diverse assemblage of coastal shrubs characteristic of the West Indies, including nickerbean (*Caesalpinia bonduc*), sea grape (*Coccoloba uvifera*), bay cedar (*Suriana maritima*), and coin vine (*Dalbergia ecastophyllum*) (fig. 13.18). Farther inland, other shrubs and small trees join these: cats claw (*Pithecellobium unguis-cati*), Florida privet (*Forestiera segregata*), buckthorn (*Bumelia celastrina*), lantana (*Lantana involucrata*), white indigoberry (*Randia aculeata*), and joewood (*Jacquinia keyensis*). These shrubs may occur as a solid band or as scattered clumps interspersed with grasses (*Muhlenbergia capillaris, Aristida patula, Chloris petraea, Schizachyrium semiberbe*) and forbs (*Ambrosia hispida, Croton glandulosus* var. *floridanus, Alternanthera ramosissima, Flaveria floridana*). Cover usually is highest just behind the sea oats foredune, diminishing inland until the stable dune zone is reached. The spray-planed scrub and forest canopies seen on the east coast (fig. 13.6) are absent on the west coast (fig. 13.7), probably because the prevailing easterlies blow offshore.

Stable Dunes

Cabbage palm dominates stable dunes, either in a palm savanna with purple muhly grass or grama grass (*Bouteloua hirsuta*) in the low broad sectors or in a forest with tropical understory on the higher ridges (fig. 13.19;

Cooley, 1955; Herwitz, 1977; Morrill and Harvey, 1980). Shell mounds or shelly storm ridges may support a tropical hammock of gumbo limbo, strangler fig, mastic, stoppers, and sea grapes, reminiscent of the east coast. These Gulf coast hammocks, however, are less diverse, lacking several tree species prominent in the east coast hammocks: torchwood (*Amyris elemifera*), butterbough (*Exothea paniculata*), ironwood (*Krugiodendron ferreum*), poisonwood (*Metopium toxiferum*), lancewood (*Nectandra coriacea*), silver palm (*Coccothrinax argentata*), and paradise tree (*Simarouba glauca*). At scattered sites the palm forests may develop a spiny understory of agaves (*Agave decipiens, A. sisalana*), yucca (*Y. aloifolia*), and cacti (*Cereus pentagonus, C. gracilis, Opuntia stricta*), which Harper (1927) refers to as "cactus thickets" and notes as peculiar to the west coast.

At the latitude of Caladesi Island near Tampa (ca. 28° N), frost regularly damages sea grapes and mangroves. Tropical species are no longer found in the canopy, which is instead dominated by live oak and cabbage palm—a situation analogous to that seen at Cape Canaveral on the east coast.

Panhandle Coast

The flora of the Panhandle coast is similar to that of the northeast sector, but the vegetation differs in that scrub and flatwoods, rather than oak hammock, are found on the stable dunes and the transitional zone is dominated by a grass/forb community composed of species endemic to the northern Gulf coast from Mississippi to Florida.

Upper Beach and Foredune

The beach and foredune vegetation in the Panhandle is identical to that found in northeast Florida, except that the Atlantic sea rocket (*Cakile edentula* ssp. *harperi*) is replaced by a Gulf species (*C. constricta*; Rodman, 1974).

Transitional Zone

The climate of Apalachicola on the Panhandle is nearly identical to that of Jacksonville on the northeast coast, but the transitional and stable dune vegetation of barriers off the two coasts are very different. Although occasionally a spray-shorn scrub of live oak, yaupon, saw palmetto, and dwarfed cabbage palm comes in behind the foredunes in the Panhandle, as at Cape St. George, the most commonly encountered vegetation in the transitional backdune zone is patches of the rhizomatous Gulf bluestem (*Schizachyrium maritimum*) interspersed with scattered shrubs of woody goldenrod (*Chrysoma pauciflosculosa*) and rosemary (*Ceratiola ericoides*). Vegetation cover is usually less than 50 percent.

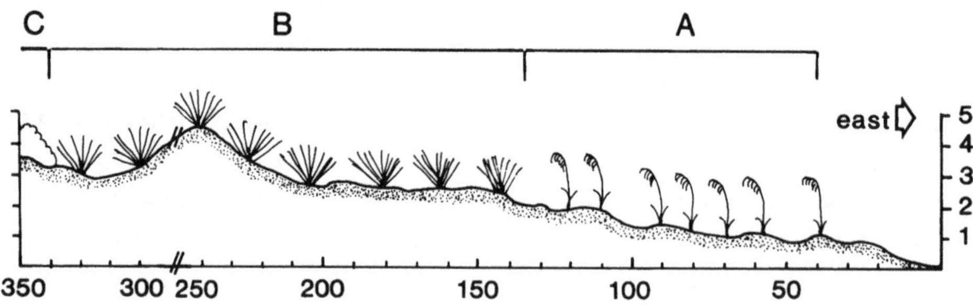

Fig. 13.14. Topographic and vegetation profile across Cape Canaveral, Brevard County. After Kurz, 1942.

(*A*) Sea oats foredune: *Uniola paniculata, Atriplex pentandra, Sesuvium portulacastrum, Scaevola plumieri, Iva imbricata, Ipomoea pes-caprae.*

(*B*) Muhlenbergia grassland: *Muhlenbergia capillaris, Andropogon virginicus, Uniola paniculata, Andropogon glomeratus, Serenoa repens, Dodonea viscosa, Myrica cerifera, Bumelia tenax, Coccoloba uvifera.*

(*C*) Oak forest: canopy: *Persea borbonia, Quercus virginiana, Zanthoxylum clava-herculis, Bumelia tenax, Quercus myrtifolia.*

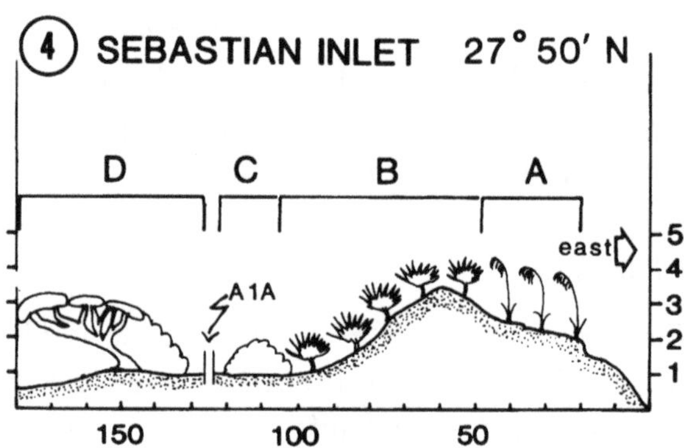

Fig. 13.15. Topographic and vegetation profile at Sebastian Inlet, Brevard County.

(*A*) Sea oats foredune: *Iva imbricata, Canavalia maritima, Helianthus debilis, Chamaesyce mesembryanthemifolia, Cnidoscolus stimulosus.*

(*B*) Saw palmetto scrub: *Serenoa repens, Coccoloba uvifera, Echites umbellata, Randia aculeata, Alternanthera ramosissima, Erythrina herbacea, Heterotheca subaxillaris, Andropogon glomeratus, Opuntia stricta.*

(*C*) Oak scrub: *Quercus virginiana, Sabal palmetto, Lantana camara, Schinus terebinthifolius, Osmanthus americana, Bumelia tenax, Chrysobalanus icaco, Ximenia americana.*

(*D*) Oak forest: (*a*) canopy: *Quercus virginiana, Sabal palmetto, Persea borbonia, Eugenia foetida, Bursera simarouba, Coccoloba diversifolia, Eugenia axillaris, Exothea paniculata;* (*b*) understory: *Chiococca alba, Ardisia escallonioides, Myrcianthes fragrans, Psychotria nervosa, Myrica cerifera, Callicarpa americana, Rhus copallina, Rivina humilis, Bumelia tenax, Randia aculeata.*

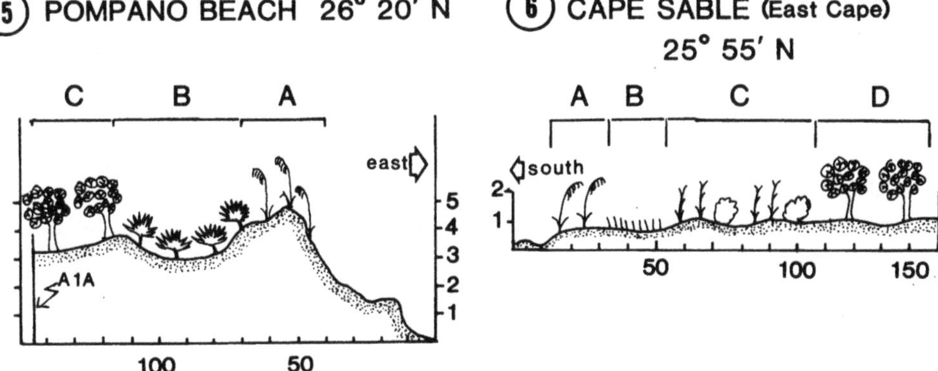

Fig. 13.16. Topographic and vegetation profile at Pompano Beach, Broward County. After Alexander, 1958a.

(*A*) Sea oats foredune: *Uniola paniculata, Sesuvium portulacastrum, Distichlis spicata, Ipomoea pes-caprae, Helianthus debilis.*

(*B*) Sea grape scrub: *Coccoloba uvifera, Serenoa repens, Sabal palmetto, Dalbergia ecastophyllum.*

(*C*) Tropical forest: (*a*) canopy: *Eugenia foetida, Sabal palmetto, Ardisia escallonioides, Bursera simaruba, Eugenia axillaris, Metopium toxiferum, Coccoloba uvifera, Coccothrinax argentata, Mastichodendron foetidissimum, Zanthoxylum fagara, Amyris elemifera, Krugiodendron ferreum, Nectandra coriacea, Casuarina equisetifolia, Pithecellobium keyensis, Simarouba glauca, Guapira discolor;* (*b*) understory: *Psychotria nervosa, Chrysobalanus icaco, Rivina humilis.*

Fig. 13.17. Topographic and vegetation profiles at Cape Sable, Dade County.

(*A*) Sea oats foredune: *Uniola paniculata, Sporobolus virginicus, Panicum amarum, Sesuvium portulacastrum, Bidens pilosa, Alternanthera ramosissima, Commelina erecta, Suriana maritima.*

(*B*) Grassland: *Eustachys petraea, Andropogon glomeratus, Schizachyrium semiberbe, Ipomoea, pes-caprae, Chamaesyce garberi, Cirsium horridulum, Waltheria indica, Croton glandulosus* var. *floridanus, Spartina patens.*

(*C*) Grass-shrub savanna: *Schizachyrium semiberbe, Muhlenbergia capillaris, Pithecellobium keyensis, Lantana involucrata, Piscidia piscipula, Forestiera segregata, Agave sisalana, Caesalpinia bonduc, Bumelia celastrina.*

(*D*) Tropical forest: (*a*) canopy: *Pithecellobium keyensis, Eugenia foetida, Piscidia piscipula, Zanthoxylum fagara, Bursera simaruba, Coccoloba uvifera, Mastichodendron foetidissimum, Ficus aurea;* (*b*) understory: *Cereus pentagonus, Agave sisalana.*

a) south end

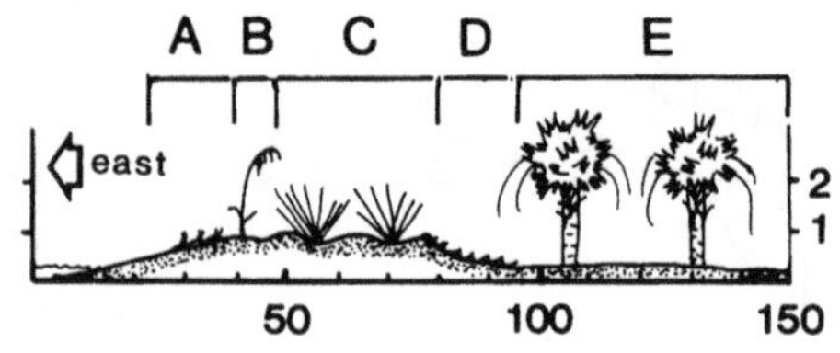

b) north end

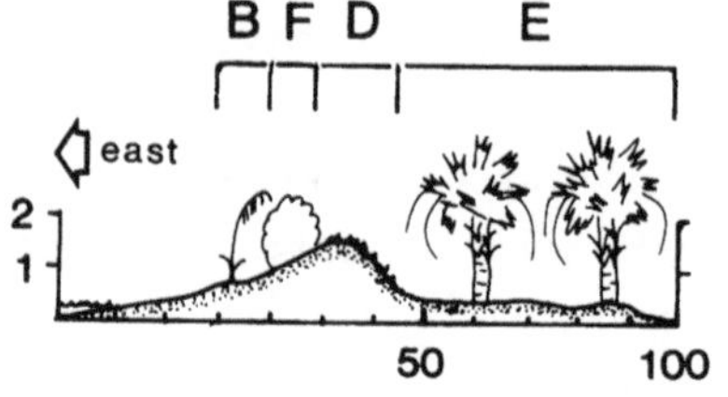

Fig. 13.18. Topographic and vegetation profile at Cape Romano, Collier County.

(*A*) Upper beach: *Paspalum distichum, Ipomoea pes-caprae, Iva imbricata, Sporobolus virginicus.*

(*B*) Sea oats foredune: *Uniola paniculata, Eustachys petraea, Scaevola plumieri, Dalbergia ecastophyllum, Sophora tomentosa.*

(*C*) Muhlenbergia grassland: *Muhlenbergia capillaris, Urechites lutea, Opuntia stricta, Cirsium horridulum, Trichostema suffrutescens,* plus scattered shrubs of *Coccoloba uvifera, Randia aculeata.*

(*D*) Zone of sparse cover: *Andropogon glomeratus, Schizachyrium semiberbe, Randia aculeata, Opuntia stricta, Waltheria indica, Stachytarpheta jamaicensis, Capraria biflora, Urechites lutea, Lantana involucrata.*

(*E*) Palm forest: (*a*) canopy: *Sabal palmetto, Bursera simaruba, Coccoloba uvifera, Piscidia piscipula, Conocarpus erecta;* (*b*) understory: *Eugenia foetida, Bumelia celastrina, Zanthoxylum fagara, Cereus pentagonus, Hymenocallis latifolia, Parthenocissus quinquefolia, Galium hispidulum, Ipomoea indica, Verbesina virginica.*

Stable Dune

Instead of live oak hammock, the ridges and swales of Panhandle backdunes are covered on the ridges by low scrub of oak (*Quercus myrtifolia, Q. geminata*) and rosemary (*Ceratiola ericoides*) and in the intervening swales by slash pine (*Pinus elliottii*) flatwoods (fig. 13.20). Sands of the Panhandle barriers contain less than 1 percent shell, compared to the 5–10 percent shell in the sands of northeastern barriers (Martens, 1931). The scrub and flatwoods strongly resemble the vegetation found on the leached, white "sugar sands" of the interior peninsula. Panhandle scrubs are distinguished from those on the peninsula by two characteristic northern Gulf coast subshrubs: a shrubby mint (*Conradina canescens*) and woody goldenrod (*Chry-*

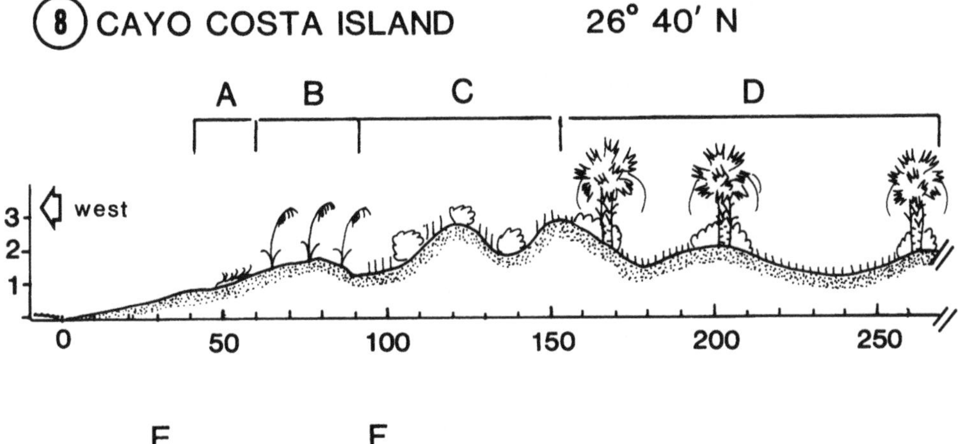

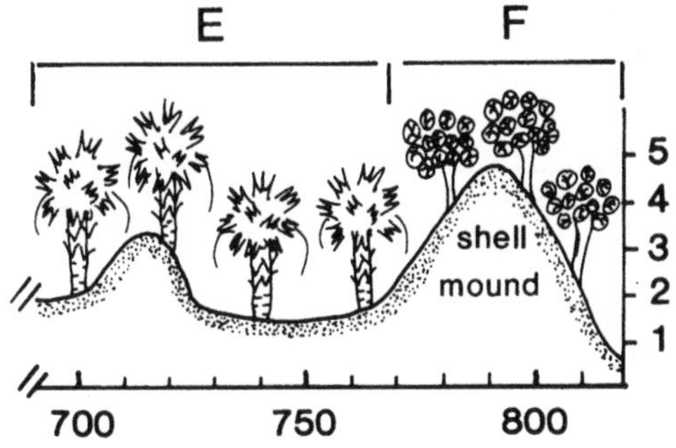

Fig. 13.19. Topographic and vegetation profile across Cayo Costa Island, Lee County. After Herwitz, 1977.

(*A*) Upper beach: *Cakile lanceolata, Sesuvium portulacastrum, Paspalum distichum, Ipomoea pes-caprae, Sporobolus virginicus.*

(*B*) Sea oats foredune: *Uniola paniculata, Iva imbricata, Chamaesyce mesembryanthemifolia, Croton punctatus, Scaevola plumieri.*

(*C*) Grass-shrub savanna: *Muhlenbergia capillaris, Eustachys petraea, Yucca aloifolia, Scaevola plumieri, Zanthoxylum clava-herculis, Ernodea littoralis, Jacquinia keyensis, Sophora tomentosa, Ipomoea pes-caprae, Trichostema dichotomum, Physalis angustifolia, Bidens pilosa, Poinsettia cyathophora, Chrysobalanus icaco, Bumelia celastrina, Alternanthera ramosissima, Coccoloba uvifera.*

(*D*) Palm savanna: (*a*) palm-shrub islands on ridges: *Sabal palmetto, Toxicodendron radicans, Smilax auriculata, Rapanea punctata, Myrica cerifera, Quercus virginiana;* (*b*) Bouteloua grassland in swales: *Bouteloua hirsuta, Muhlenbergia capillaris, Opuntia stricta, Cnidoscolus stimulosus, Licania michauxii, Dodonea viscosa.*

(*E*) Palm forest: (*a*) canopy: *Sabal palmetto, Quercus virginiana, Persea borbonia, Eugenia axillaris;* (*b*) understory: *Serenoa repens, Myrica cerifera, Psychotria nervosa, Ximenia americana, Ardisia escallonioides, Callicarpa americana, Forestiera segregata, Rivina humilis, Vitis munsoniana.*

(*F*) Tropical forest: (*a*) canopy: *Bursera simaruba, Coccoloba uvifera, Eugenia axillaris, Eugenia foetida, Ficus aurea, Mastichodendron foetidissimum, Sabal palmetto, Capparis cyanophallophora;* (*b*) understory: *Ardisia escallonioides, Chiococca alba, Petiveria alliacea, Psychotria nervosa, Rivina humilis, Ipomoea acuminata, Zanthoxylum fagara, Toxicodendron radicans, Vitis aetivalis.*

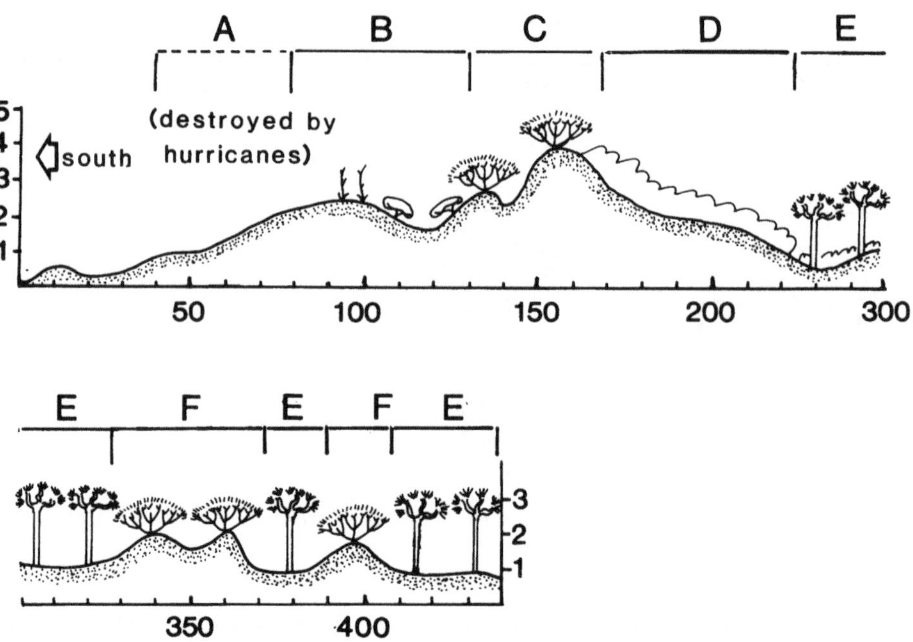

Fig. 13.20. Topographic and vegetation profile across St. Vincent Island, Franklin County.

(*A*) Sea oats foredune (destroyed by hurricanes Elena and Kate, 1985).

(*B*) Woody goldenrod zone: *Chrysoma pauciflosculosa, Schizachyrium maritimum, Uniola paniculata, Dicanthelium* sp., *Opuntia pusilla, Cladonia leporina, Oenothera humifusa, Physalis angustifolia, Helianthemum arenicola, Cnidoscolus stimulosus.*

(*C*) Rosemary zone: *Ceratiola ericoides,* plus the species in the preceding zone.

(*D*) Tall oak scrub: *Quercus myrtifolia, Quercus geminata, Serenoa repens, Myrica cerifera, Conradina canescens, Ceratiola ericoides.*

(*E*) Flatwoods: (*a*) canopy: *Pinus elliotii, Sabal palmetto;* (*b*) understory: *Ilex glabra, Myrica cerifera, Serenoa repens, Lyonia lucida.*

(*F*) Rosemary scrub: *Ceratiola ericoides, Quercus geminata, Quercus myrtifolia, Conradina canescens, Chrysoma pauciflosculosa, Serenoa repens, Smilax auriculata, Cladonia evansii, Cladonia leporina, Lyonia ferruginea, Vaccinium arboreum.*

soma pauciflosculosa). Oak-palm forests, so characteristic of the northeast Florida barriers, are found on Panhandle barriers only on special substrates, such as shell middens, shelly ridges built by storms on the lagoon side of barrier islands, and some mainland sands (Kurz, 1942). Apparently a certain amount of nutrient enrichment of the regional quartz sand by shells, clay, or humus buildup is necessary to support live oak hammocks.

Ranges of Coastal Plant Species

Along Florida shores the warm temperate flora of the southeastern U.S. coastal plain meets, and to some extent mingles with, the tropical flora of the West Indies. The areas of transition lie in the vicinity of Cape Canaveral on the east coast and Tampa Bay on the west. The incidence of hard freezes is undoubtedly a major factor limiting the northward spread of tropical species. Most tropical trees have a U-shaped distribution in Florida, the sides of the U extending up the coasts (fig. 13.21). Their northern limit roughly coincides with the 12°C (53.6°F) isotherm for average minimum daily temperature in January (Tomlinson, 1980).

Many tropical species are even more narrowly confined to the coast than this isotherm would indicate, not by temperature but by their apparent preference for calcareous substrates (Kurz, 1942). Only Recent coastal sand deposits in Florida (i.e., the barrier islands) have much shell admixed; whatever shell was once in the Pleistocene sands of the mainland has long since been leached away (White, 1970). On leached acid sands, temperate scrub vegetation is found well into the tropical zone along the coast: as far south as Marco Island on the Gulf coast and (formerly) to within a few miles of Miami on the east coast (Small, 1924a). On calcareous substrates, tropical trees may dominate the canopy up to their northern climatic limits. On shell mounds a few tropical herbs and shrubs (*Rivina humilis, Mentzelia floridana*, and *Bumelia celastrina*) extend even beyond the usual northern climatic limits to the Cedar Keys on the west coast (Garber, 1877) and to the mouth of the St. Johns River on the east (Curtiss, 1879). Small (1927) suggested that shell mounds store heat and thus are not only chemically but also climatically distinct from surrounding substrates, but a year's record of soil temperature data taken on Turtle Mound and adjacent sands by Norman (1976) failed to substantiate Small's claim. Norman found that, while the shells were slightly warmer during the day, they were also colder at night than the adjacent sands. It may be that, within broad climatic limits, tropical species are the better competitors on well-drained calcareous substrates and temperate species on acid ones. Each set of species dominates on the type of substrate that is extensive along coastlines within its center of origin.

The northward extension of tropical trees along the coast in Florida has a parallel in the northward extension of live oak (*Quercus virginiana*) and other temperate broad-leaved evergreen trees (*Q. laurifolia, Sabal palmetto, Magnolia grandiflora, Persea borbonia*) along the coast to the Carolinas (Little, 1971). Greller (1980) found that the northern limit of temperate

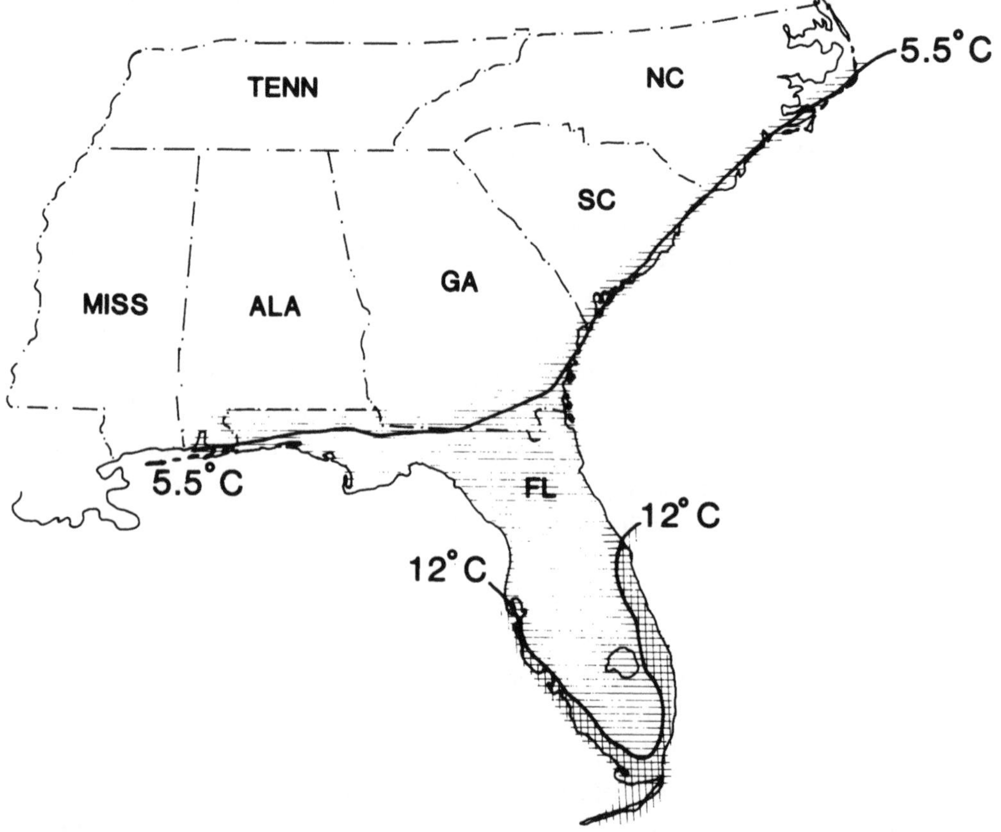

Fig. 13.21. Range limits of live oak (*Quercus virginiana*) (*horizontal lines*) and tropical trees (*vertical lines*) in Florida in relation to the 5.5°C and 12°C isotherms for average daily minimum temperatures in January (Greller, 1980; Tomlinson, 1980).

broad-leaved evergreen forest in Florida coincided with the 5.5°C (41.9°F) isotherm for the average minimum daily temperature of the coldest month. When extended to North Carolina this isotherm also roughly coincides with the coastal distribution of live oak (fig. 13.21). Wells (1939) suggested that the live oak forests along the Carolina coasts were a "salt spray climax," replacing the deciduous forests of the Carolina mainland because of superior tolerance to salt spray. It appears probable from the climatic data, however, that live oak forests are the climatic climax on the Carolina coast; special tolerance to coastal conditions need not be invoked to account for their presence there. Greller (1980) considers temperate broad-leaved evergreen forests to be the zonal vegetation in central Florida, gradually replacing deciduous species over a broad transition zone as one moves south of the 5.5°C isotherm. The question of climax forest composition in this region is obscured by the prevalence of azonal soils, citrus groves, and (putatively seral) pines.

Unlike trees on stable dunes, many herbaceous species on the beach and foredune range across the warm temperate/subtropical boundary at Cape Canaveral and Tampa Bay, including such pantropical species as railroad vine (*Ipomoea pes-caprae*), beach morning glory (*Ipomoea stolonifera*), sea purslane (*Sesuvium portulacastrum*), and beach dropseed (*Sporobolus virginicus*), as well as the temperate dune-building grasses, sea oats (*Uniola paniculata*), bitter panicum (*Panicum amarum*), and beach cordgrass (*Spartina patens*). Beach and foredune species tend to have wider ranges than species in the other two zones—37 percent of the former range throughout Florida, as opposed to only 16 percent of the latter.

Several wide-ranging halophytes on the beaches and upper salt marshes in Florida become more and more confined to salt marshes in the northern parts of their ranges: *Atriplex pentandra* (= *hastata*), *Distichlis spicata, Spartina patens, Suaeda linearis*, and the shrub *Baccharis halimifolia*. In addition, there are three pairs of closely related (or doubtfully distinct) species in which one of the species has a more northern range in salt marshes while the other has a more southern range on both beaches and marshes. These are *Sesuvium maritimum/S. portulacastrum, Paspalum distichum/P. vaginatum*, and *Fimbristylis castanea/F. spadicea*.

Halophytism is not a requirement for plants on beaches and dunes as is sometimes assumed (Duncan, 1974). The water table beneath is fresh, at least in temperate climates, and it has been shown that saltwater around the roots injures several prominent foredune species, including sea oats (Seneca, 1972), beach grass (*Ammophila breviligulata*; Seneca, 1972) and red sand verbena (*Abronia maritima*; Johnson, 1985). Nonetheless, the north/south pattern in halophyte distribution suggests that *periodic* salinization of the water table in warmer regions may favor the establishment of halophytes, if not on the dunes themselves, at least on the lower-lying beaches and swales between them.

The transitional zone vegetation is the most physiognomically variable and species-rich of the three zones. It also harbors most of the coastal endemics. Unlike the foredunes, which are dominated by sea oats in all sectors of the coast, the transitional zone is dominated by different species in each sector. Wax myrtle (*Myrica cerifera*) is prominent on Amelia and Little Talbot islands in the northeast; saw palmetto (*Serenoa repens*) in the central Atlantic sector; sea grape (*Coccoloba uvifera*) in the southeast; and woody goldenrod (*Chrysoma pauciflosculosa*), Gulf bluestem (*Schizachyrium maritimum*), and rosemary (*Ceratiola ericoides*) in the Panhandle. Purple muhly grass (*Muhlenbergia capillaris*), on the other hand, may dominate grassy flats behind the foredunes in all sectors.

Vicarious Species

North Carolina/Virginia represents the northern limit of many of the warm-temperate coastal species that reach Florida, including several that are replaced there by northern vicariants: *Myrica cerifera* by *M. pensylvanica;*

Juniperus silicicola by *J. virginiana; Cakile edentula* ssp. *harperi* by *C. e.* ssp. *edentula*. In southern Florida *C. e. harperi* gives way to the West Indian *C. lanceolata*. In the Panhandle this species is replaced by *C. constricta*, which ranges west to the Mississippi barriers (Rodman, 1974). Like *Cakile*, two other genera have related taxa on the east and west coasts of Florida: the beach sunflower, *Helianthus debilis* ssp. *debilis* on the east coast, *H. d.* ssp. *vestitus* on the west, and *H. d.* ssp. *tardiflorus* in the Panhandle (Ward, 1978); and the sand cherry, *Physalis walteri* on the east coast and *P. angustifolia* on the Panhandle coasts, with hybrids in southwest Florida (Sullivan, 1985).

Coastal Endemics

At latest count twenty-two species are endemic to the coast of Florida. Seven others range only slightly beyond the state's boundaries: two to the Bahamas and five to the barrier islands of Mississippi (table 13.1). Changes in this list should be expected, particularly for the southern coast, where taxonomic relations with the West Indies are incompletely understood. For ex-

Table 13.1. Plant species endemic to the Florida coast

East coast
Glandularia maritima[a] (Small) Small
Frequent on dunes, Flagler County to Dade County
Helianthus debilis Nutt.
Common on dunes, St. Johns County to Florida Keys
Jacquemontia reclinata House
Local on dunes, Palm Beach County to Dade County
South coast
Chamaesyce cumulicola Small
Rare on dunes, Martin County to Lee County
C. garberi[a] (Engelm. ex Chap.) Small
Frequent on beaches and pinelands, Monroe and Dade counties
C. porteriana Small var. *keyensis*[a] (Small) Burch
Dunes and pinelands, Long Key to Cudjoe Key
Cereus gracilis Mill. var. *simpsonii* (Small) L. Bens.
Rare in hammocks, Ten Thousand Islands to Cape Canaveral
Croton glandulosus L. var. *floridanus* (Ferg.) R. W. Long
Common on dunes, Monroe County to Collier County
Indigofera keyensis Small
On strands, Key Largo to Key Vaca
Lantana depressa[a] Small var. *floridanus* (Moldenke) R. Sanders
Coastal dunes, Volusia County to Dade County
Lantana depressa[a] Small var. *sanibelensis* R. Sanders
Coastal dunes, Levy County to Collier County
Lechea lakelae[a] Wilbur
Dunes and scrub, Collier and Broward counties

(*continued*)

Opuntia eburnispina Small
Sand ridges, Cape Romano to Ten Thousand Islands
West coast
Cereus gracilis Mill. var. *aboriginum* (Small) L. Bens.
Rare in hammocks, Tampa to Ten Thousand Islands
Eragrostis tracyi Hitchc.
Common on dunes and shell mounds, Pinellas County to Lee County
Eriochloa michauxii (Poin.) Hitchc. var. *simpsonii* Hitchc.
Rare on dunes and brackish areas, Sarasota County to Dade County
Flaveria floridana[a] J. R. Johnston
Frequent on dunes, Pinellas County to Collier County
Helianthus debilis Nutt. ssp. *vestitus* (Wats.) Heiser
Rare on backdunes, Pinellas County to Charlotte County
South Florida and the Bahamas
Coccothrinax argentata[a] (Jacq.) Bailey
Dunes and hammocks, Miami to Florida Keys
Mentzelia floridana Nutt.
Common on dunes, Brevard County to Lee County
Panhandle and Alabama Coast
Chrysopsis godfreyi Semple
Dunes and scrub, Franklin County to Baldwin County, Alabama
Chrysopsis gossypina (Michx.) Ell. ssp. *cruiseana* (Dress.) Semple
Dunes, Walton County to Escambia County
Helianthus debilis Nutt. ssp. *tardiflorus*[a] Heiser
Rare on backdunes, Franklin County to Sarasota County
Liatris provincialis[a] Godfrey
Local on dunes and sandhills, Bay County to Wakulla County
Lupinus westianus[a] Small
Local on dunes and sandhills, Okaloosa County to Franklin County
Polygonella macrophylla[a] Small
Coastal dunes and scrub, Franklin County to Baldwin County, Alabama
Florida Panhandle to Mississippi
Chrysoma pauciflosculosa[a] (Michx.) Greene
Dominant on dunes and sandhills, inland to North Carolina
Conradina canescens[a] (T&G) Gray
Dominant in dunes and scrub, Escambia County to Wakulla County
Helianthemum arenicola[a] Chapm.
Occasional on backdunes to Franklin County
Paronychia erecta (Chapm.) Shinners
Common on backdunes to Wakulla County
Schizachyrium maritimum (Chapm.) Nash
Dominant on beaches, dunes, and swales, to Franklin County
East and west coasts and westward
Cakile constricta Rodman
Locally common on upper beach, south to Dade and Pinellas counties and west to Mississippi
Phyllanthus abnormis Baillon var. *abnormis*
Rare in openings on backdunes, peninsular Florida coasts excluding the Keys, and inland in Texas

a. Species also found inland.

ample, Long and Lakela (1971) err in listing *Coccothrinax argentata* as West Indian—it is endemic to Florida and the Bahamas (Bailey, 1939). *Coccothrinax argentea*, on the other hand, is West Indian. Long and Lakela list *Ageratum littorale* as endemic to Florida, when it is found in the Cayman Islands (Sauer, 1982), Belize (Stoddart, 1969), and Yucatan (Espejel, 1986). *Hymenocallis latifolia* is likewise listed as endemic, when it has been reported from the Bahamas (Correll and Correll, 1982) and Cuba (Sealy, 1954).

Although the southern coast has the most endemic taxa (nine), only five of these are at the species level. Two of the latter (*Jacquemontia reclinata* and *Coccothrinax argentata*) have become rare following the intensive development of the southeast coast. Characteristic peninsular endemics include the beach sunflower (*Helianthus debilis*) and beach verbena (*Glandularia maritima*) on the east coast, poor man's patch (*Mentzelia floridana*) on the south, and Florida yellowtop (*Flaveria floridana*) on the west.

The vegetation of the Panhandle coast is the most distinctive in terms of coastal endemics. Besides several narrowly local endemics, it has five species that are endemic to the entire stretch of barriers from the Florida Panhandle west to Mississippi (table 13.1). These five species make up a fair proportion of the vegetative cover on the transitional backdunes of this northern Gulf region. Part of the explanation for such a high degree of endemism may be that this region forms a natural unit (Barbour et al., 1987): its beaches share a common climate and substrate and are physically isolated from other barrier islands by low wave energy coasts—on the west by marshy shore in Louisiana and eastern Texas, on the east by marshes in the Big Bend region of Florida.

Disjunct Species

Four coastal species skip the Panhandle, having a disjunct distribution between the western Gulf of Mexico and the Atlantic. Dune bluestem (*Schizachyrium littorale*; DeSelm, 1975), not to be confused with the endemic Gulf bluestem (*Schizachyrium maritimum*), occurs on coastal dunes from Texas (Dahl et al., 1975) to Vera Cruz, Mexico (Sauer, 1967), and from North Carolina (Au, 1974) to northern Florida. A white-flowered evening primrose (*Oenothera drummondii*) ranges from Texas to Vera Cruz (Sauer, 1967) and is also found at Isle of Palms, South Carolina (Stalter, 1974). It was collected at Cape Canaveral by Small (1923a) but has not been found there recently (Poppleton et al., 1977). Beach peanut (*Okenia hypogaea*) ranges from Vera Cruz to Yucatan, Mexico, and from St. Lucie to Dade counties in Florida (Iverson, 1984). A fourth disjunct, *Phyllanthus abnormis*, occurs on both the Atlantic and peninsular Gulf coasts of Florida (but not on the Panhandle coast) and inland in Texas as a separate variety.

The disjunct distributions of *Oenothera* and *Okenia* may be the result of human introduction from Mexico to Florida, since Mexico is clearly the center of their range and they are both pioneer beach species whose seeds are apt to be carried in ballast. This explanation seems less likely for the disjunct ranges of dune bluestem (*S. littorale*) and *Phyllanthus*. Webster (1970) speculates that the absence of *Phyllanthus* from the Panhandle (a gap in distribution also found in several animal groups) may be due to a cold event in the Pleistocene that caused extinction in this region.

Colonizing Abilities of Beach Species: The Sand Keys

The Sand Keys consist of three groups of small sand and mangrove islands west of Key West: the "near islands," an unnamed group of about fourteen islands 8 km to 16 km west of Key West; the Marquesas, a ring of seven islands about 30 km west; and the Dry Tortugas, a group of seven islands 105–115 km west. All but two of these islands are less than 2 km long, ranging in area from a few tenths of a hectare to 20 ha and in elevation from 0.6 to 2.5 m. The Marquesas and near islands have large mangrove borders; the Tortugas are mostly carbonate sand. These three groups of islands and their floras have been repeatedly surveyed: in 1904 (Millspaugh, 1907); in 1915 (Bowman, 1918); in 1937 (Davis, 1942); and in 1962 and 1977 (Stoddart and Fosberg, 1981). MacArthur and Wilson (1963) used the Dry Tortugas as an example in presenting their theory of island biogeography. However, Stoddart and Fosberg (1981) found that some of the early maps were inaccurate and that several of the islands changed in area radically from one sampling period to the next. In fact, some disappeared altogether and others appeared. They are also skeptical of the completeness of the collecting done in the early surveys.

If not of general interest to island theory, the surveys are of interest for what they tell us about the colonizing abilities of beach species and the differences between island and mainland vegetation, since the islands are essentially isolated beaches. All the principal foredune species on mainland beaches have reached the islands, as have a subset of the transitional and stable dune species. There follows a listing of species in descending order of their presence on seventeen islands, according to surveys by Millspaugh (1907) and Davis (1942).

Suriana maritima	15 of 17
Chamaesyce mesembryanthemifolia	14
Sesuvium portulacastrum	14
Uniola paniculata	14
Cyperus planifolius	11
Borrichia arborescens	10
Cenchrus tribuloides	10
Iva imbricata	10

Melanthera aspera	9
Argusia gnaphalodes	9
Hymenocallis latifolia	8
Pithecellobium keyensis	7
Andropogon glomeratus	6
Atriplex pentandra	5
Paspalum distichum	5
Sporobolus virginicus	4
Alternanthera ramosissima	3

The first four species are all dispersed by ocean currents; the fruits of most of the remainder are dispersed by birds (Linhart, 1980). All of these species are also frequently found on similar sand keys off the coasts of Yucatan (Bonet and Rzedowski, 1962) and Belize (Linhart, 1980; Stoddart, 1969).

Although most of the foredune colonizers reach the Sand Keys, only a subset of the transitional species do, including *Andropogon glomeratus, Eustachys petraea, Cyperus planifolius, Lantana involucrata*, and *Melanthera* cf. *aspera*. Others, equally or more abundant in this zone on the mainland, are absent on the islands—e.g., *Forestiera segregata, Muhlenbergia capillaris, Piscidia piscipula*, and *Schizachyrium semiberbe*.

A peculiarity of island vegetation is the formation of monospecific stands of bay cedar (*Suriana maritima*) and also occasionally of sea lavender (*Argusia gnaphalodes*) in the interior. On mainland coasts these shrubs seldom occur in pure stands, but rather are scattered among sea oats or backdune grasses, while the more inland zones are occupied by a diversity of woody species. In the absence of these woody species, bay cedar appears to take over the more inland portions of the islands. Many forest species, typified by *Pithecellobium keyensis*, reach the near islands and the Marquesas but not the Dry Tortugas, and it is here that bay cedar scrubs are well developed. Similar bay cedar scrubs are also known from the sand keys off Yucatan and Belize.

Animals Dependent on Beaches

Sea Turtles

Sea turtles are marine reptiles that spend most of their lives at sea but depend on beaches for nesting sites. Of the seven sea turtle species, five have worldwide distributions in tropical and subtropical seas, including the waters off the Florida coast: green (*Chelonia mydas*), hawksbill (*Eretmochelys imbricata*), loggerhead (*Caretta caretta*), olive ridley (*Lepidochelys olivacea*), and leatherback (*Dermochelys coriacea*). Two others are of more restricted distribution: the flatback (*Chelonia depressa*), a relative of the green restricted to Australia, and Kemp's ridley (*Lepidochelys kempi*), found in the Gulf of Mexico and occasionally on the east coast of the United States.

Florida's beaches (as well as those of Georgia and South Carolina) are the most important nesting sites of the loggerhead in its New World range (fig. 13.22). Important sites in other parts of its range are Natal, South Africa, the island of Misirah in the Red Sea, and the northeast coast of Australia (Bustard, 1972). The green and leatherback sea turtles also nest in Florida but not in significant numbers. Their principal New World nesting beaches are in Costa Rica and French Guiana, respectively. The green may once have been more numerous in Florida, but overfishing—this species is used in making turtle soup—has drastically reduced its numbers throughout its West Indian range (Carr, 1984). Turtle fishing and importation continued in the United States until 1975, when the United States as a signatory to the CITES treaty (Convention on International Trade in Endangered Species of Wild Flora and Fauna) listed all sea turtles as endangered and banned trade in their products.

Loggerhead turtles can easily be distinguished from greens by their relatively larger heads (they crush shellfish and crabs for food, while the greens are vegetarians) and the presence of five (rather than four) plates along the sides of their back shell or carapace. It is harder to distinguish loggerheads from ridleys; the main indicator is the absence of pores along the sides of their undershell (plastron). Loggerheads and greens nest from May through August, while leatherbacks nest earlier, typically beginning in February. Sea turtles come ashore at night to lay about 120 eggs per female in an excavated pit that is then re-covered. About 70 to 80 percent of the eggs in a nest hatch, and the young hatchlings then head toward the sea. Tagging projects have shown that adult females nest several times in one season and then skip two or three years before nesting again (Hopkins and Richardson, 1984). Tagging has also shown that females return repeatedly to the same beaches to nest, and it is widely assumed that these are their natal beaches—however, no tag has yet been designed that will last from baby turtle to breeding adult stage. The total population of nesting females along the east coast of the United States is estimated to be about 14,000 (Hopkins and Richardson, 1984). This figure is in the same range as that found for green turtles at their major nesting site at Tortugero, Costa Rica (23,000), and for leatherbacks in French Guiana (15,000; Hopkins and Richardson, 1984).

Major threats to the species in Florida are destruction of suitable beach habitat above high tide by the building of seawalls; predation of eggs by raccoons (by one count, 70 percent of the nests on uninhabited beaches of Cape Sable are thus lost); and lights, which disorient the hatchlings and cause them to head toward the lights (and often toward the coastal highway) instead of toward the sea (Carr, 1984). Nesting is much more concentrated on some parts of the Florida coast than on others (fig. 13.22). Highest nest

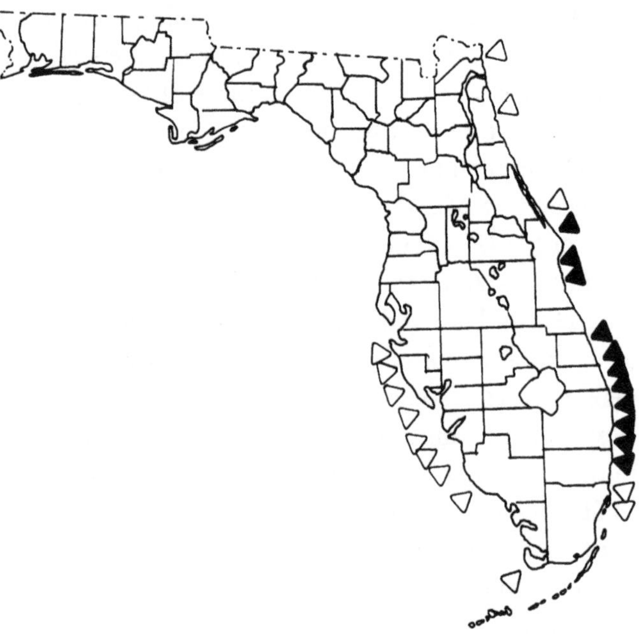

Fig. 13.22. Nesting sites of loggerhead turtles (*Caretta caretta*) in Florida (Hopkins and Richardson, 1984). *Filled triangles* = nest densities greater than 50 per km of beach; *empty triangles* = less than 50 per km of beach.

densities are found in southern Brevard County from Cape Canaveral to Sebastian Inlet (Hopkins and Richardson, 1984), which, with the exception of the Cape itself, is one of the most rapidly developing sectors of the Florida coast. However, even along the highly developed coasts of Palm Beach and Broward counties, surprisingly high nest densities are still encountered. In Broward County about 60 percent of these nests must be dug up and the eggs either reburied in more suitable sites or hatched artificially and released in order for them to survive threats from human activities (Fletemeyer, 1985). Whether such labor-intensive programs can be continued permanently remains to be seen.

Birds

Florida beaches are important as nesting sites for several species of shore birds and as wintering grounds for many others.

Thirteen species nest on Florida beaches, generally between April and August (Sprunt, 1954). All nest on the ground, the nest consisting of a scrape in the sand. The species differ in the degree of vegetative cover preferred. Five prefer bare sand beaches with no vegetation whatsoever: least (*Sterna antillarum*), royal (*S. maxima*), and sandwich (*S. sandvicensis*) terns; black skimmer (*Rynchops niger*); and snowy plover (*Charadrius alexandrinus*). Three species prefer nest sites covered with sparse grass or herbs: American oystercatcher (*Haematopus palliatus*), Wilson's plover (*Charadrius wilsonia*), and willet (*Catoptrophorus semipalmatus*). Three prefer denser grass or bushes that shield the nests from the sight of each other: laughing gull (*Larus atricilla*), gull-billed tern (*Sterna nilotica*), and Caspian tern (*S. caspia*). The two remaining nesting species, sooty (*Sterna fuscata*) and noddy (*Anous stolidus*) terns, are mainly tropical in range, found in Florida only at the Dry Tortugas during the nesting season.

Nesting shore bird populations in Florida, like those of sea turtles, have declined due to loss of beach habitat to real estate development. On the remaining natural beaches, human visitors disrupt nesting birds more than they do turtles, since birds stay at the nest for a longer time. The Tampa Bay and Charlotte Harbor areas, in particular, once supported large numbers of nesting black skimmers, snowy plovers, American oystercatchers, and royal and sandwich terns, all of whose nesting sites are presently concentrated along the less populated Panhandle and northeast Florida coasts (Sprunt, 1954; Schreiber and Schreiber, 1978). The snowy plover, which in Florida nests only on the Gulf coast, has been placed on the state's endangered species list. Its population began to decline in the 1970s and today is estimated at fewer than 100 breeding pairs for the state (Kale, 1978)

Some species have proved adaptable to new nesting sites. Since the 1950s least terns have been reported nesting on rooftops; this "habitat" accounts for over half the young fledged in northeast Florida (Schreiber and Schreiber, 1978). Many other species have adopted as nest sites the dredge spoil islands created by maintenance of inlets and the inland waterway. Most laughing gulls in Florida nest on dredge spoil, where they form colonies of up to 20,000 birds (Schreiber and Schreiber, 1978). Caspian terns appear recently to have extended their breeding range to Florida on spoil, having first been reported nesting in 1962 on a spoil island in Pinellas County and more recently on spoil in Brevard County (Schreiber and Schreiber, 1978).

Christmas bird counts show the largest concentrations of wintering shore birds to be in the Tampa Bay region, followed by Everglades National Park (Below, 1985). The most abundant winter residents are sanderling (*Calidris alba*), western sandpiper (*C. mauri*), dunlin (*C. alpina*), short-billed dowitcher (*Limnodromus griseus*), red knot (*Calidris canutus*), black-bellied plover (*Pluvialis squatarola*), and willet (*Catoptrophorus semipalmatus*). Florida (along with Texas) is also the main wintering ground of the piping plover (*Charadrius melodus*), listed by the state as a "species of special concern" (Kale, 1978).

Rodents

In vagile groups such as plants, birds, and larger mammals, barrier island populations are not distinct from those on the mainland, but in the more sedentary populations of small rodents differentiation of barrier island populations has occurred at the subspecific level. Barrier island subspecies are found in the old field mouse, cotton mouse, cotton rat, and rice rat.

Five subspecies of old field mouse (*Peromyscus polionotus*) occur on Panhandle barriers and three on the barriers of the Atlantic coast. The Panhandle subspecies are all isolated by inlets: *P. p. ammobates* west of Perdido Inlet, *P. p. trisyllepsis* on Perdido Key, *P. p. leucocephalus* on Santa Rosa Island, *P. p. allophrys* between Destin and Panama City on the mainland, and *P. p. peninsularis* on St. Joseph peninsula and adjacent mainland beaches (Bowen, 1968). Oddly, the four eastern Panhandle barriers (St. Vincent, St. George, Dog, and St. James) have no beach mice on them.

On the east coast, *P. p. phasma* occurs on barriers from the St. Johns River to Anastasia Island, *P. p. decoloratus* from Matanzas to Mosquito (= Ponce) inlets, and *P. p. niveiventris* from Cape Canaveral (Stout, 1979) to Sebastian Inlet and recently at Hillsboro Inlet (Hall, 1981). All beach mice on both the Panhandle and Atlantic coasts are paler than their inland counterparts and are found primarily in open sand habitats of sea oats foredunes and scrub (Blair, 1951; Bowen, 1968). They feed on the fruits of sea oats, Gulf bluestem (*Schizachyrium maritimum*), and various herbs (Blair, 1951). In scrub, they probably take acorns of scrub oaks (*Quercus virginiana, Q. geminata, Q. chapmanii*, and *Q. myrtifolia*) and fruits of rosemary (*Ceratiola ericoides*), as do the inland subspecies (Johnson, 1982).

A subspecies of cotton mouse (*Peromyscus gossypinus anastasae*) was collected from mesic hammocks on Anastasia Island in 1901 (Pournelle and Barrington, 1953), but it has not been collected there since, though a population is still extant on Cumberland Island, Georgia. Likewise, trapping data indicate that the Chadwick Beach cotton mouse (*P. gossypinus restricta*), described by Howell (1939) from Manasota Key in Sarasota County, is probably extinct (Repenning and Humphrey, 1986).

The cotton rat (*Sigmodon hispidus*), which lives on the fringes of salt and freshwater marshes, has two subspecies on barrier islands: *S. h. insulicola* from Captiva, Sanibel, and Pine islands on the Gulf coast and *S. h. littoralis* on the northeast coast from Sebastian Inlet to Cape Canaveral (Hall, 1981).

The rice rat (*Oryzomys palustris*), which inhabits wetter parts of marshes than the cotton rat, occurs on most of the larger barrier islands. It has one described barrier subspecies—*O. p. sanibeli* from Sanibel Island—and another (*O. p. planirostris*; Hall, 1981) from an isolated piece of the mainland, Pine Island.

Of the twelve barrier subspecies mentioned, six are listed by the state as in trouble (Layne, 1978): *Peromyscus polionotus decoloratus*, listed as "endangered" (i.e., extinction imminent); *P. p. allophrys* and *P. p. trisyllepsis* as "threatened"; and *P. gossypinus anastasae* and *Sigmodon hispidus insulicola* as "status unknown." Trapping data from Alabama (Holliman, 1983) suggest that *P. p. trisyllepsis* was on the verge of extinction in the aftermath of Hurricane Frederick in 1979, during which Perdido Key was flooded to a depth of 2.4 m. Holliman attributes its decline to the destruction of the foredune habitat by wave overwash and to the loss to development of areas of higher ground that would have served as refuges for the mice during the storm. House cats are also major predators of beach mice on developed portions of the islands (Bowen, 1968). Trapping data from the east coast (Humphrey et al., 1987) reveal *Peromyscus gossypinus anastasae* to be probably extinct in Florida and populations of *P. polionotus niveiventris* and *P. p. phasma* to be much constricted by development of their habitat.

Alteration of the Coast

Real Estate Development

Experience with the effects of storms on coastal structures has led to wider acknowledgment among planners of the concept that the foredune is part of the dynamic beach-shoreface system (Psuty, 1983). Sand stored in the foredune is moved offshore by storm waves and restored to the beach with the return of normal wave conditions. Winds move the sand back to the line of plant growth, and a new dune is built up. When structures built on the foredune and the beachfront are "hardened" with seawalls, this store of sand is removed from the system and storm waves may permanently scour the beach.

Development of Florida's beachfront has been most intense near large cities (fig. 13.23 a and b). Jacksonville, Palm Beach, Fort Lauderdale, Miami, and Clearwater–St. Petersburg all have strips of high-rise buildings along their shores and have had much the same history (Pilkey et al., 1984; Doyle et al., 1984). After high-rises were constructed on the foredune, a storm cut back the beach in front of the buildings, and a seawall was built to protect the property. The waves of the next storm, deflected against the seawall, eroded away the beach; sand was then dredged from offshore to replace it. The cycle was continued with each storm.

"Beach nourishment" is an expensive process. Miami Beach recently replaced eleven miles of eroded beach with coral sand dredged from offshore, at a cost of about $6 million per mile. Miami's new beach is still in place (fig. 13.23b), but Delray, Hobe Sound, Cocoa Beach, and other east coast communities have repeatedly lost their newly restored beaches to erosion, often within five years. Taxpayers may subsidize private beachfront construction at three points in this sequence of events: to insure the buildings under the Federal Flood Insurance Act, to construct the seawall to protect the buildings, and finally to replace the beach once the seawall has caused its destruction. Recent federal and state legislation has sought to limit public subsidies to some extent by declaring certain high-risk barrier beach areas ineligible for federal flood insurance (or any other federal assistance), and by enforcing a set-back line to prevent construction on the foredune. Neither piece of legislation affects structures already in existance.

In contrast to the peninsula, the lightly developed Panhandle coast, though repeatedly battered by hurricanes in the last decade, still has its

Fig. 13.23. (*a*) Miami Beach in 1920. Photo by Roland Harper. (*b*) Miami Beach in 1980, showing the new artificial beach. Photo courtesy of U.S. Army Corps of Engineers, Jacksonville.

beaches intact. Indeed, differences in recent storm history (as well as differences in population density) may be a contributing factor in the contrasting degrees of development on the peninsular and Panhandle coasts.

Hurricanes

Weather summaries between 1885 and 1971 show that Florida coasts were affected by eighty-four hurricanes, an average of about one a year (Funk, 1980). When the eleven major Florida hurricanes of this century are numbered chronologically (fig. 13.24), the lower numbers (1–6) are clustered in south Florida and the higher numbers in the Panhandle and Mississippi. Memorable dates in south Florida are mostly in the first half of this century (Gentry, 1974): 1921 (Tampa), 1926 (Miami), 1928 (Lake Okeechobee overflowed, drowning more than 2000 people), 1935 (Key West), and 1960 (Donna destroyed the Everglades mangrove forests). Memorable dates in the Panhandle occurred in the second half of the century: 1969 (Camille, Biloxi, Mississippi), 1972 (Agnes, Grayton Beach), 1975 (Eloise, Panama City), 1979 (Frederick, Pensacola), and 1985 (Elena and Kate, Apalachicola).

The south Florida coast has been developed to the point where even a

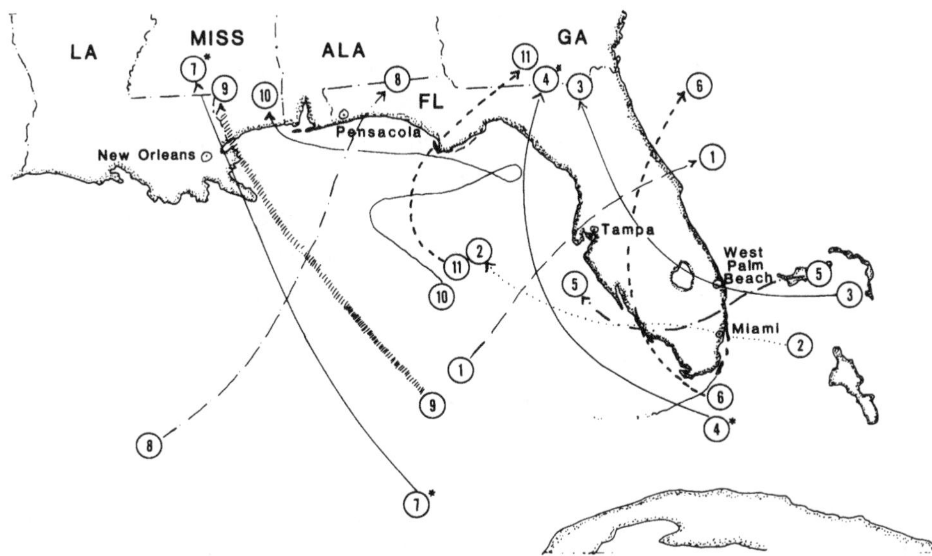

Fig. 13.24. Paths of major hurricanes affecting Florida in the twentieth century. Asterisk denotes a Class Five hurricane (winds 248+/km/h; storm surge 5.5+/m). (*1*) October 1921, (*2*) September 1926, (*3*) September 1928, (*4*) September 1935—Labor Day storm, (*5*) September 1947, (*6*) September 1960—Donna, (7) August 1969—Camille, (8) June 1972—Agnes, (*9*) September 1979—Frederick, (*10*) September 1985—Elena, (*11*) November 1985—Kate. To improve legibility the paths of two major hurricanes are not mapped: Betsy, which struck Key Largo in 1965, and Eloise, which struck Panama City in 1975 (Case, 1985; Doyle et al., 1984; Funk, 1980; Pilkey et al., 1984).

minor storm or distant hurricane can have a large economic effect. Hurricane Elena in 1985 did more structural damage in Pinellas County than in any Panhandle county, even though it passed 80 km closer to the Panhandle coast and produced storm tides there that were twice as high (Balsillie, 1985). The effects of Hurricane Elena in Pinellas County were compounded that same year by Hurricane Juan, which made landfall in New Orleans and was never closer than 756 km to the coast of Florida (Clark, 1986b).

Exotic plants

Exotics are most prominent in the vegetation of the tropical portions of Florida. There are two categories of naturalized exotics on south Florida beaches—those that blend into the native plant communities and those that take over coastal habitats to the exclusion of native vegetation. There are many species in the first category, including eleven prominent ones: Spanish bayonet (*Yucca aloifolia*), introduced from Mexico for fiber; cultivated coconut (*Cocos nucifera*); guava (*Psidium guajava*); papaya (*Carica papaya*); *Agave decipiens; Catharanthus roseus; Colubrina asiatica; Dactyloctenium aegypticum; Manilkara zapota; Sapindus saponaria*; and *Sarcostemma clausa.*

Three exotics tend to take over habitats they invade. Sisal (*Agave sisalana*) is locally dominant in forest understories at Cape Sable and in the Ten Thousand Islands. The ubiquitous Brazilian pepper (*Schinus terebinthifolius*) is found in many inland habitats and, on the coast, occurs at mangrove borders and on the fringes of tropical forests. Australia pine (*Casuarina equisetifolia*) has spread primarily on beaches. Of all the exotics listed, Australian pine poses by far the greatest threat to native beach vegetation.

Three species of Australian pine were introduced into Florida from their native western Pacific region around the turn of the century, most probably by the U.S. Department of Agriculture experiment station in Homestead. From this source they were widely planted as windbreaks around houses and along roads. The three species of Australian "pines" are flowering plants; their "needles" are composed of the fused edges of the whorled leaves with only the leaf tips free. This cylinder of fused leaves is in turn fused to the stem. The number of leaf tips and the bark help to distinguish the species: *C. equisetifolia* (= *C. litorea*) has six to eight leaf tips and nonfurrowed bark and is the primary beach invader; *C. glauca* has ten to fourteen leaf tips and furrowed bark and prefers mangrove fringes; *C. cunninghamiana* has seven to ten leaf tips and furrowed bark and is found in freshwater sites (Woodall and Geary, 1985).

Casuarina equisetifolia has the same range limits as other tropical species in south Florida and is most likely distributed by seeds that are washed up and deposited on beaches as drift (fig. 13.25). It tends to invade newly exposed sand, such as newly accreted beaches (e.g., Keewaydin Island in Collier County), beaches where dredge spoil has been dumped (e.g., Cape Flor-

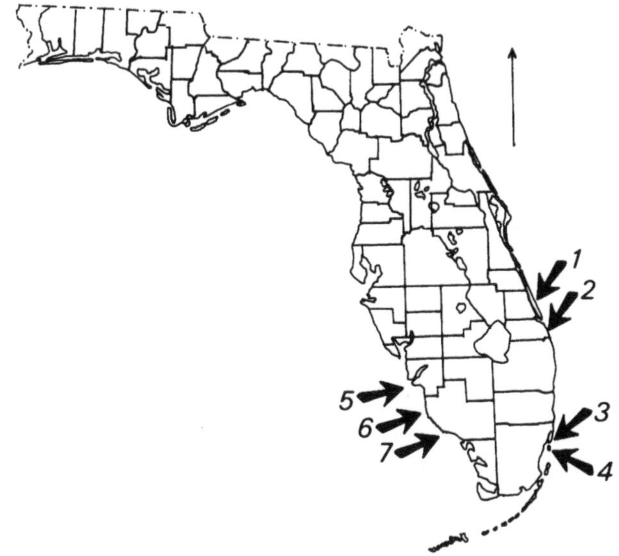

Fig. 13.25. Coastal areas in Florida that have dense stands of *Casuarina equisetifolia.*

ida State Recreation Area in Dade County), or beaches where storm overwash has destroyed the existing vegetation (e.g., Cape Sable in Everglades National Park after Hurricanes Donna in 1960 and Betsy in 1965). Once having gained a foothold on disturbed areas, it may continue to invade native grassland behind the foredune, since it is more resistant to salt spray (and can thus grow taller closer to the water) than any of the native woody species. The primary native species it displaces are sea grape (*Coccoloba uvifera*), several coastal shrubs (*Chrysobalanus, Sophora, Ernodea, Suriana, Argusia, Pithecellobium, Caesalpinia*), and coastal grasses (*Muhlenbergia, Schizachyrium*, etc.) found in the transitional zone.

The dense shade and thick litter layer (10+ cm) of monospecific stands of Australian pine prevent germination and growth of native species that otherwise would provide food for birds and mice. When erosion brings stands of "pine" close to the waterline, its dense root mat inhibits sea turtles and American crocodiles from digging their nests (Klukas, 1969). For these reasons Everglades National Park began an eradication program when Australian pine began to spread on the beaches after the 1960 and 1965 hurricanes. Eradication was accomplished by cutting down or girdling trees and applying herbicide to the cuts to prevent resprouting, and pulling by hand saplings up to 1.5 m tall (Klukas, 1969). Park beaches have since been maintained "pine free" by periodic uprooting of seedlings, and cover of native vegetation is now complete.

In areas where stands of Australian pines are old and well established, removal followed by planting of native species may be necessary to regenerate native plant communities. In 1986, The Nature Conservancy, a private conservation organization, pioneered such an effort at its Blowing Rocks Preserve in Martin County. A pine-removal project on Sanibel Island, however, was recently vetoed by voters who wanted the trees to remain because of the shade they provide. Perhaps a compromise will have to be reached on recreational beaches that would allow some pines to be left standing near the beach for shade while the dense stands behind them are removed. The public could be educated to pull up the seedlings as they appear.

Percentage of the Coast in Natural Vegetation

Development of the approximately 200,000 ha of barrier islands along the Florida coast has proceeded rapidly. By 1975 nearly 20 percent of Florida's barriers had been developed, compared to 11 percent of the remaining 500,000 ha of barrier islands from Texas to Maine in the same period (Lins, 1980).

The percentage of coast in natural vegetation (fig. 13.26) is highest in the Panhandle and northeastern Florida and tends to diminish southward, especially on the east coast. Manatee, Dade, and Broward counties all have little natural shoreline remaining. In terms of absolute length of coast, Palm Beach County is the most developed, with construction on 61 of its 75 km. Pinellas County is a close second, with 56 out of 78 km developed. Pinellas, Palm Beach, Broward, and Dade are the most densely populated counties in Florida, with more than 3 million residents among them, according to the 1980 census (Fernald, 1981). Several less populated counties, however, have developed more than 40 percent of their coastlines; these include Bay, Collier, and Nassau counties.

Perhaps the best preserves are the largest. Existing large preserves include Santa Rosa Island, Crooked Island, St. Vincent Island, and Cape St. George on the Panhandle coast; Little Talbot Island and the Cape Canaveral–Merritt Island complex on the Atlantic coast; Cape Sable on the southern "shell hash" coast; and Cayo Costa and Caladesi islands on the Gulf coast.

Even preserved portions of the coastline may still be adversely affected by certain management practices. Raking drift off the beach on local recreational beaches is a practice that removes seeds and nutrients from the upper beach habitat, thus interfering with healing of the foredunes after storms (Oertel and Lassen, 1976). Bulldozing a new foredune after storms have destroyed the original, instead of letting dune grasses build one up naturally, may lead to sand being blown inland, if the crest is too dry or too unstable for dune grasses to gain a foothold. Dumping dredge spoil on natural beaches not only alters their topography but, in south Florida, creates sites for the invasion of Australian pine. Burning dune scrub at intervals shorter than fifteen to twenty years prevents the dominant rosemary shrubs (*Ceratiola ericoides*) from reaching reproductive maturity (Johnson, 1982).

The five sectors of Florida's coast differ markedly in the degree to which representative natural coastline is preserved. The Panhandle coast, with three state parks, part of a national seashore, two national wildlife refuges,

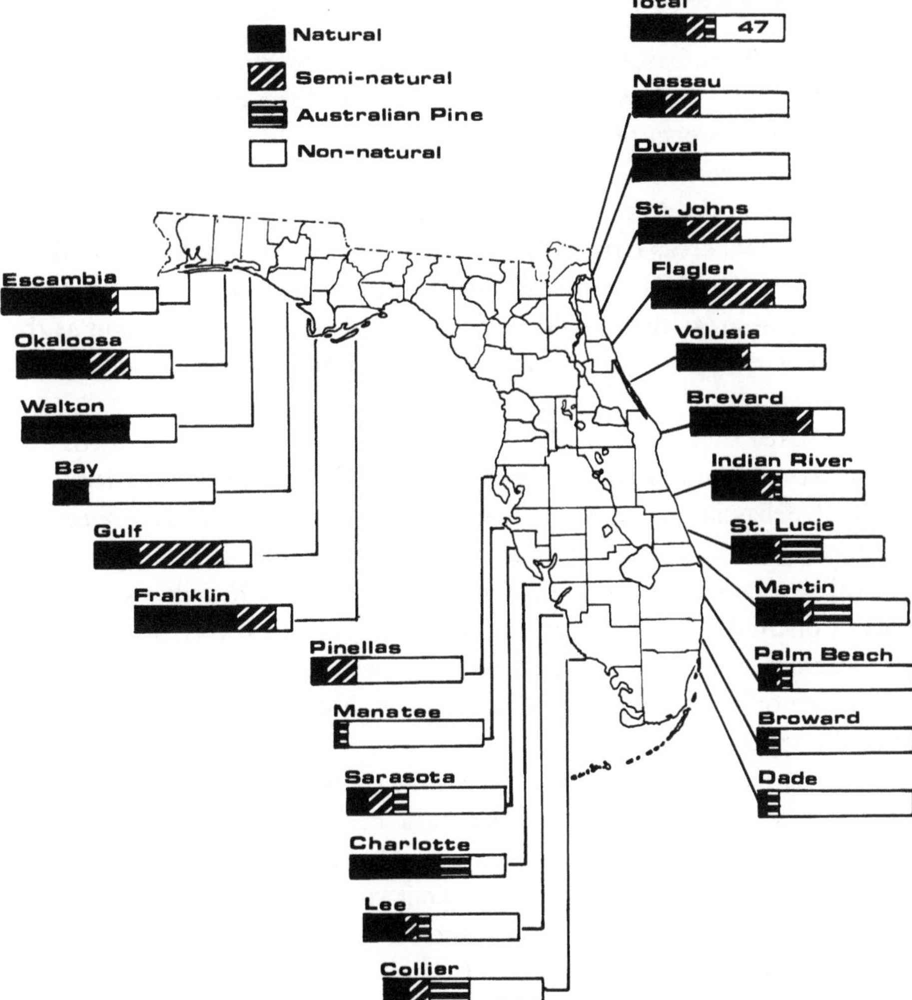

Fig. 13.26. Percent of sandy coastline (measured in tenths of a mile) in natural vegetation by county. The eastern, southwestern, and Panhandle coast east of Panama City were examined in detail via aerial photographs, field reports of other investigators, or personal visits. Western Panhandle coast was determined from latest available U.S. Geological Survey 7.5-minute topographic maps. Coastline was considered natural if sufficient transitional zone and stable dune vegetation were present to allow reconstruction of the vegetation profile across the barrier island; seminatural if part of these zones remained; nonnatural if only beach and foredune or mangrove communities remained; and Australian Pine if *Casuarina equisetifolia* had displaced native communities to the extent that they could not be reconstructed from the native elements remaining.

and two Air Force bases, has a relatively high proportion of its coastline in public ownership and would be an excellent site for a comparative study of the processes of storm recovery .

On the northeast coast, the "sea island" barriers are well represented in preserves, as is the Cape Canaveral complex, but the narrow barriers between these two areas have only short stretches in state parks. Natural portions of these barriers are found north of St. Augustine and north of Ormond Beach—areas that would be good candidates for preservation as they constitute a type of barrier coast whose dynamics are now poorly understood.

From Cape Canaveral south to Cape Florida no large pieces of coastline are protected. Natural coast in private ownership extends for a few miles north of Sebastian Inlet State Recreation Area—an area of interest for preservation both because it is a transition point between temperate and tropical vegetation and because it is one of the most heavily used nesting beaches of the loggerhead turtle (*Caretta caretta*) on the Atlantic coast. It is probable that in Broward and Dade counties there is no natural coastline left outside of what is already in parks, a condition that Palm Beach County is rapidly approaching.

The relatively inaccessible shell hash beaches of Cape Sable and part of the Ten Thousand Islands, on which basic descriptive work remains to be done, are protected as a part of Everglades National Park.

The largest protected areas of the Gulf coast are Caladesi Island in the north and Cayo Costa Island in the center. Two smaller islands near Tampa, Anclote Keys and Egmont Key, are also preserved in their natural state. No large areas are preserved on the southern Gulf coast, which is developing at a rapid rate. The broadest and most ecologically diverse barrier on the southwestern Gulf coast, Marco Island (Small, 1923a), has already been largely lost to development. However, several privately owned islands in this region are still undeveloped, including the rapidly elongating outer barrier, Keewaydin; several inner barriers with well-developed stable dune vegetation (Little Marco, Cannon, Sea Oat, and Horrs islands); and the southernmost quartz sand beach on this coast, Cape Romano. Three considerations would tend to place these barrier islands at the top of the list for preservation on the Florida coast. (1) They are the last large representative portions of natural quartz sand coast in this tropical Gulf sector. (Keewaydin, though covered with Australian pine, probably has enough natural vegetation left to act as a seed source to revegetate the island without artificial planting, once the pines are removed.) (2) They are part of a coast that is currently undergoing rapid development, which could easily become as complete as that seen in Manatee or Dade counties. (3) The islands are low, with an extremely dynamic history of erosion and accretion, which makes them risky as building sites, but desirable as natural laboratories for studying coastal processes.

14
Salt Marshes

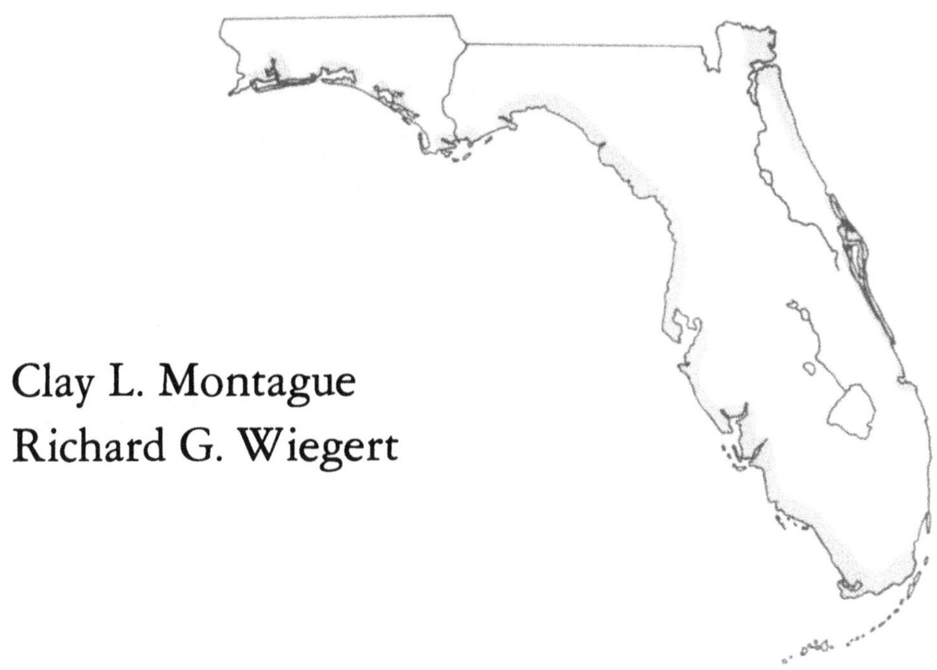

Clay L. Montague
Richard G. Wiegert

The salt marshes of Florida (fig. 14.1) are coastal ecosystems with communities of nonwoody, salt-tolerant plants occupying intertidal zones that are at least occasionally inundated with salt water. They exist at the interface of land and marine waters, wherever wave energy is sufficiently low to allow their development and where mangrove trees are not dense enough to shade out the characteristic vegetation. Within these constraints, the areal extent of salt marshes is determined in large part by the size of the intertidal zone. Regions of low relief and high tidal range are likely to have extensive salt marshes (fig. 14.2).

The rate of net primary production (photosynthetic production minus plant respiration) in salt marshes is among the highest in any of the world's ecosystems. This production results in some features of marshes that are valued by humans—such as sediment stabilization, storm protection, beauty, and wildlife—and gives rise to terrestrial and marine food webs involving many fascinating animals, some of commercial and recreational value. Estimates of the total area of salt marsh in Florida vary considerably. McNulty et al. (1972) estimated 214,000 ha of nonmangrove "emergent tidal marshes" along the Gulf coast of Florida. Eleuterius (1976), combining this

Fig. 14.1. Florida salt marshes: (*a*) *Juncus roemerianus*–dominated salt marsh of the Big Bend area (near St. Marks); (*b*) *Spartina alterniflora*–dominated salt marsh near Crescent Beach.

estimate with his own observations of the Atlantic coast of Florida, calculated a total of 304,000 ha of marshes. A recent National Wetlands Inventory estimate, which used 1982 preliminary data, is much lower: 155,000 ha of tidal salt and brackish water emergent marshes (U.S. Fish and Wildlife Service, 1984). This figure is in closer agreement with the earlier Coastal Coordinating Council (1973) estimate of 189,000 ha of tidal marshes in Florida (Provost, 1973b; Lewis et al., 1985). The estimate by McNulty et al. (1972) may be too high because it included numerous small areas of high ground and mangroves. A figure of 170,000 ha is probably a more accurate estimate.

Salt marshes exhibit characteristics of both terrestrial and marine ecosystems. Indeed, the food web that arises from grazing the dominant vegetation consists of species (mostly insects, spiders and passerine birds) that generally do not tolerate submersion in saline water for any appreciable length of time (Wiegert et al., 1981). A distinct watershed and network of drainage creeks is often present (fig. 14.3). Salt marsh sediments, under the influence of colonizing plants and animals, begin to develop layered soil horizons, similar to those of terrestrial soils. The rooted plants form what may be described as "periodically flooded grassland, with an herbivorous fauna of

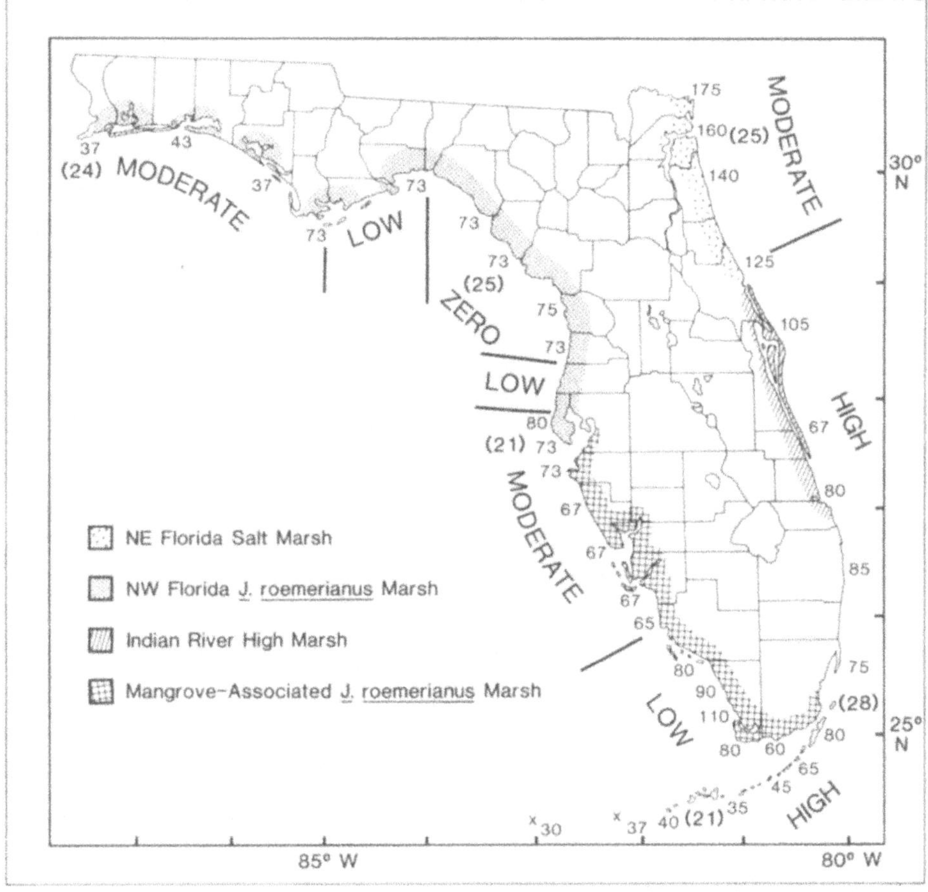

Fig. 14.2. Occurrence of salt marshes in Florida and physical features of the coast: tidal range in cm (*small numbers*), relative wave energy (*block letters*), and relative sea level rise in cm per century (*numbers in parentheses*). Adapted from Tanner (1960) and Provost (1973a).

terrestrial arthropods supporting a typical predator-parasitoid food web" (Wiegert and Freeman, 1989).

At times of flooding, however, the marsh surface becomes an extension of the continuum of coastal marine benthic sediments. Intertidal marsh sediments, despite their similar appearance to terrestrial soils, are largely anaerobic and are microbiologically similar to marine benthic sediments. Benthic marine microalgae and organic detritus fuel a food chain of intertidal marine animals (Subrahmanyam et al., 1976; Daiber, 1982). Furthermore, the tidal water abounds with marine organisms that move in and out of the marsh, using it for food and cover.

Often, marine and terrestrial attributes mingle: a shoot of black needlerush (*Juncus roemerianus*) may support both a grazing grasshopper (*Orchelimum concinnum*) and a snail (*Littorina irrorata*) that feeds on organisms attached to plants (called *aufwuchs*). Below mean low water, the sea is

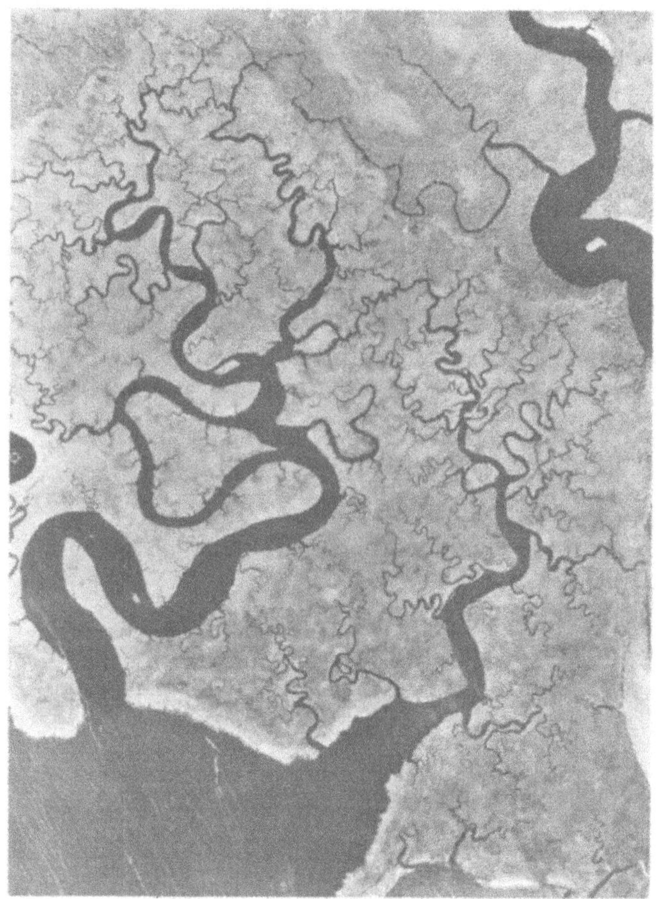

Fig. 14.3. Aerial view of the network of tidal creeks in a salt marsh near the mouth of the Suwannee River.

the dominant physical influence. Above mean high water, terrestrial features predominate. Because of low tidal amplitude and frequency, most of the marsh surface area in Florida is above mean high water (Provost, 1973a, 1976).

Salt Marsh Plants and Plant Zonation

Vascular Plants

The principal species of salt marsh plants in Florida are *Juncus roemerianus* and *Spartina alterniflora*, which generally occur in monotypic stands (Kurz and Wagner, 1957). The most seaward nonwoody salt marsh plant in Florida is smooth cordgrass (*Spartina alterniflora*), though in many Florida marshes this plant occurs only in narrow bands, often less than 10 m wide, near the water's edge. In the high salt marsh above mean high water, many species of plants can be found in addition to black needlerush. A list of salt marsh plants common to Florida is given in table 14.1. Many of the high marsh plants are succulents or are otherwise adapted to soils of high salinity. Water in such soils can be as difficult for plants to extract as it is in

Table 14.1. Common salt marsh plants of Florida

Species	Common name	Notes[a]
Plants of the upper edge of the high marsh		
Baccharis halmifolia	Saltbush	Sol.
Iva frutescens	Marsh elder	Sol.
Lycium carolinianum	Christmas berry	Sol.
Solidago sempervirens	Seaside goldenrod	Sol.
Sueda linearis	Sea blite	Suc.
Plants generally found above mean high water (high marsh)		
Acrostichum aureum	Leather fern	E
Aster tenuifolius	Salt marsh aster	
Batis maritima	Saltwort	E, Suc.
Borrichia arborescens	Sea oxeye	E (S. Fla.)
B. frutescens	Sea oxeye	E
Distichlis spicata	Salt grass	E
Monanthochloe littoralis	Key grass	(S. Fla.)
Paspalum vaginatum	Salt jointgrass	E
Salicornia bigelovii	Annual glasswort	Suc.
S. virginica	Perennial glasswort	E, Suc.
Sesuvium portulacastrum	Sea purslane	Suc.
Spartina bakerii	Clumped cordgrass	E (Merr. Is.)
S. patens	Saltmeadow cordgrass	E
Sporobolus virginicus	Coastal dropseed	E
Sueda maritima	Sea blite	Suc.
Plants found from high to low marsh		
Juncus roemerianus	Black needlerush	E
Limonium carolinianum	Sea lavender	Sol.
Spartina alterniflora	Smooth cordgrass	E
Mangroves that often occur sparsely in generally nonwoody salt marsh		
Avicennia germinans	Black mangrove	
Conocarpus erecta	Button mangrove	(S. Fla.)
Laguncularia racemosa	White mangrove	(S. Fla.)
Rhizophora mangle	Red mangrove	(S. Fla.)

Sources: Carlton (1975, 1977), Leenhouts and Baker (1982).

a. E = can form extensive colonies; Suc. = a succulent plant; Sol. = usually found as solitary plants; (S. Fla.) = found primarily in south Florida salt marshes; (Merr. Is.) = found as a salt marsh plant on Merritt Island.

some deserts. Vegetation will often be some combination of glasswort (*Salicornia* spp.), saltwort (*Batis maritima*), salt grass (*Distichlis spicata*), sea purslane (*Sesuvium portulacastrum*), sea lavender (*Limonium carolinianum*), and several other species (Kurz and Wagner, 1957; Carlton, 1975, 1977). Saltmeadow cordgrass (*Spartina patens*), which is prevalent in high marshes along the northern Atlantic coast (Nixon, 1982), is found only in small fringing patches shoreward of smooth cordgrass or needlerush communities (Kurz and Wagner, 1957; Carlton, 1977).

If the slope is gradual near the landward limit of salt marshes, a bare "salt pan" may develop and persist for years or decades. In salt pans, interstitial salinity is too great for any vascular plants to survive. Salt pans are perhaps caused by evaporation of the thin film of seawater that only rarely reaches areas of high elevation and low relief. Although they occur in all of the salt marsh types around Florida, they are perhaps most extensive inland of the mangroves and mangrove-associated *J. roemerianus* marshes of the southwest coast of Florida.

Flood frequency and soil salinity are two principal determinants of the types and productivity of salt marsh vegetation (Eleuterius, 1976, 1984; Eleuterius and Eleuterius, 1979; Stout, 1984). Although both *S. alterniflora* and *J. roemerianus* grow best in fresh water and tolerate a wide range of salinities (Smart and Barko, 1978, 1980; Eleuterius, 1984), the former is apparently limited to areas that receive sufficient flooding. In a comparison of *S. alterniflora* marshes and nearby *J. roemerianus* marshes in Mississippi, Eleuterius and Eleuterius (1979) determined that the latter were flooded only 0.8 percent to 5 percent of the time, whereas the former are flooded 35 percent to 87 percent of the time. *J. roemerianus* does not require low soil salinity. Stunted *J. roemerianus* has been found in salinities of up to 360 parts per thousand (ppt), though individuals from another population did not grow in the laboratory in water above 30 ppt (Eleuterius, 1984). While *S. alterniflora* apparently tolerates greater flooding, *J. roemerianus* perhaps tolerates greater fluctuation in soil salinity (Stout, 1984). The prevalence of *J. roemerianus* in Florida indicates the prevalence of high marsh.

Salt Marsh Algae

Several hundred species of benthic microalgae and phytoplankton occur in salt marshes and creeks, as well as a few species of large, multicellular seaweeds. The more common benthic microalgae are also found as aufwuchs on the dead stems of *Spartina alterniflora.* Although salt marsh algae are generally ten times less productive than salt marsh vascular plants, microalgae may be ten times more nutritious for consumers of algae and detritus, such as fiddler crabs and snails, because they are assimilated live, rather than after a period of decomposition (Peterson, 1981; Montague et al., 1987a,b).

Salt marsh algae have been censused in detail in Georgia (Williams, 1962; Pomeroy et al., 1981) and Mississippi (Sullivan, 1978; Sage and Sullivan, 1978; Stout, 1984). The similarity of the algae in these two studies strengthens the idea that one edaphic algal community is common to both Gulf and Atlantic salt marshes (Stout, 1984). The results of these studies should also be applicable to north Florida.

Diatoms form 75 percent to 93 percent of the benthic microalgal biomass (Williams, 1962). Most of the rest consists of blue-green algae. Although several hundred species of diatoms have been found, 90 percent of the cells are in only four genera: *Navicula, Nitzschia, Gyrosigma,* and *Cylindrotheca* (Williams, 1962). Likewise, twenty-five species of blue-green algae were reported in a Mississippi salt marsh, but only a few were dominant, including the filamentous blue-greens *Anabaena oscillarioides, Microcoleus lyngbyaceous,* and *Schizothrix calciola* (Sage and Sullivan, 1978; Pomeroy et al., 1981).

Salt marsh seaweeds include the red alga *Caloglossa leprieurii*, found attached to stems of *S. alterniflora* in some marshes. The green algae *Ulva, Enteromorpha*, and *Cladophora* and the yellow-green alga *Vaucheria* occur on low marsh sediments, especially in the cooler months (Kurz and Wagner, 1957; Pomeroy et al., 1981).

Phytoplankton are a principal food of the numerous zooplankton and filter-feeding bivalves (oysters, clams, and mussels) that live in salt marshes and tidal creeks. Like the edaphic microalgae, most phytoplankton are diatoms. The species composition overlaps somewhat with the benthic microalgae because tidal currents suspend cells from the marsh surface. At slack tide, suspended cells settle onto the marsh surface. Several species of green flagellates and dinoflagellates are also part of the phytoplankton associated with salt marshes. Dinoflagellates periodically grow to noticeable "blooms" in tidal creeks (Odum, 1968).

Availability of light and nutrients—such as inorganic nitrogen and phosphorus—limits algal production in salt marshes (Darley et al., 1981). Turbid coastal waters and shade from the stems of marsh plants reduce production of benthic microalgae. The number of cells is greatest on the exposed creek banks, where the marsh surface is not shaded by plant stems. Phytoplankton production is often light-limited in turbid waters (Ragotzkie, 1959; Thomas, 1966; Sellner and Zingmark, 1976; Pomeroy et al., 1981). In the clearer water adjacent to some of Florida's salt marshes, nutrients alone may limit phytoplankton production.

Differences among Florida Salt Marshes

The types of plants as well as the extent of salt marshes vary considerably around the state owing to a combination of a large latitudinal change and geographic differences in tidal range, local relief, and wave energy (fig. 14.2). Carlton (1977) described many relatively dissimilar plant communities in Florida salt marshes, but differences (fig. 14.4) are especially distinctive among four parts of the state: northeast Florida, northwest Florida, the Indian River Lagoon, and south Florida. These areas differ primarily with respect to annual average temperature and frequency and amplitude of tides.

North of both Tampa on the west coast and Merritt Island on the east coast nonwoody vegetation dominates the intertidal zone. Isolated mangrove trees occur as far north as St. Augustine and throughout the northwest coast of Florida (the Panhandle), but the freezes of 1983 and 1984 have temporarily reduced the pockets of mangrove ecosystems that occurred as far north as Cedar Key on the Gulf coast and Crescent Beach on the Atlantic coast.

Northeast Florida salt marshes, from the Georgia border south to Marineland, are similar in vegetation, hydrology, and climate to the well-studied marshes of Georgia (Wiegert, 1979; Pomeroy and Wiegert, 1981). This type of marsh, however, accounts for only about 20 percent of the total area of nonwoody salt marsh in Florida. These salt marshes contain large expanses of smooth cordgrass (*Spartina alterniflora*) and are flooded and drained twice daily by the highest tides in the state. *Spartina alterniflora* in these marshes has a distinctly taller growth near the edges of tidal creeks (fig. 14.4a). Closer to land, shorter *S. alterniflora* gives way to typical high marsh plants. Similar marshes near Sapelo Island, Georgia, are described in Teal (1962), Teal and Teal (1969), and Pomeroy and Wiegert (1981).

Half of the salt marsh area in Florida occurs from Tampa Bay north and west to the Alabama border. The greatest development of salt marshes in northwest Florida is in the Big Bend area, from Aripeka (Pasco-Hernando county line) to Apalachicola Bay. In this region, tidal range is higher than in the western Panhandle and relief and wave energy are low (fig. 14.2). Salt marshes here are irregularly flooded by a combination of lunar and wind-blown tides and a seasonal rise in sea level. Similar marshes occur in Alabama, Mississippi, and Louisiana. The ecology of these irregularly flooded salt marshes has recently been described by Stout (1984).

About 60 percent of northwest Florida salt marshes are covered with monospecific stands of black needlerush (*Juncus roemerianus*) (Kurz and Wagner, 1957; Subrahmanyam and Drake, 1975; Eleuterius, 1976; Rey, 1981; Kruczynski, 1982). These expansive stands often grow nearly to the water's edge. Like the *S. alterniflora* of northeast Florida salt marshes, these plants often have a distinctly taller form nearer open water and a shorter form nearer land (Jackson, 1952; Kruczynski et al., 1978; Kruczynski, 1982). A variety of high marsh plants occurs landward of these stands (fig. 14.4b).

Smooth cordgrass (*S. alterniflora*) is not as prevalent as it is in northeast Florida salt marshes. A narrow fringe of *S. alterniflora* may occur at the edges of creeks. Monospecific stands of *S. alterniflora* sometimes occur in pockets and islands at the lowest elevations of emergent vegetation (Turner and Gosselink, 1975; Rey, 1981). Cordgrass fringe is often separated from the needlerush by a berm or levee (fig. 14.4b), which may be occupied by various high marsh plants, shrubs (wax myrtle), and trees (live oak). This berm reduces the hydrological connection between much of the marsh surface and the adjacent coastal marine waters.

About 10 percent of the nonwoody salt marshes of Florida occur along the Indian River Lagoon (Volusia to Martin counties). Like the salt marshes of northwest Florida, these are almost wholly above mean high water and are naturally inundated only by windblown tides and a seasonal rise in sea level. A berm occurs here, too, approximately at the level of mean high water (Provost, 1973a). Unlike northwest Florida marshes, nearly all of the Indian River high marsh has been diked and semipermanently flooded to control the hordes of salt marsh mosquitoes that once bred there (Bidling-

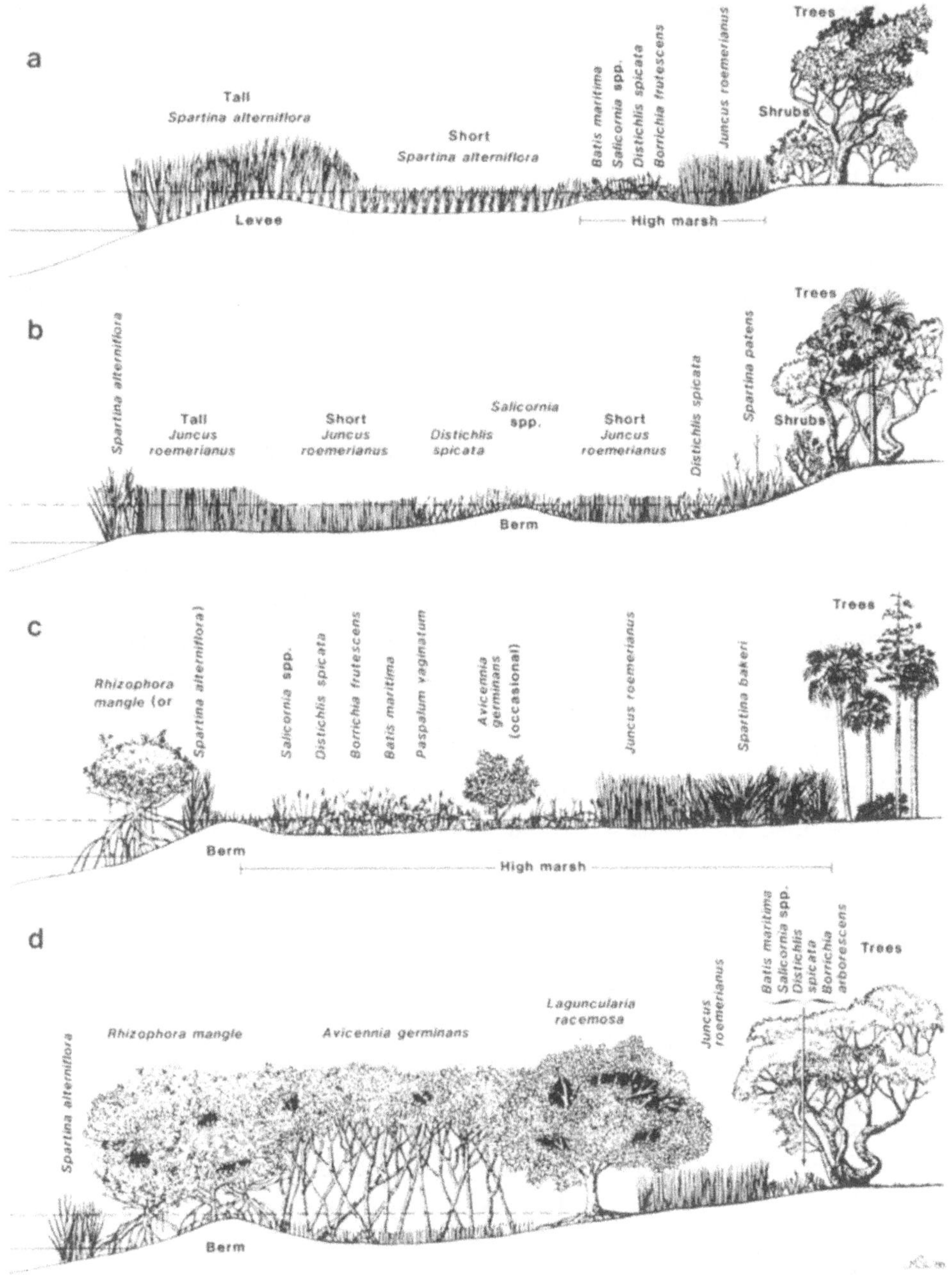

Fig. 14.4. Profiles of Florida salt marshes. *Dashed line* indicates approximate level of mean high water; *solid line* is estimate of mean low water (illustration by Marjorie LaRoe Summers). (*a*) Typical northeast Florida *Spartina alterniflora* marsh (see also Teal, 1962; de la Cruz, 1981). (*b*) Typical northwest Florida salt marsh (see also Kurz and Wagner, 1957; Kruczynski, 1982; Woods et al., 1982). (*c*) Typical Indian River high marsh (see also Provost, 1973a; with data from Leenhouts and Baker, 1982). (*d*) Typical south Florida mangrove-associated *Juncus roemerianus* marsh (see also Davis, 1940; Lewis et al., 1985).

mayer and McCoy, 1978; Bidlingmayer, 1982; Montague et al., 1984, 1985, 1987a,b). Photographs of many of these marshes before impoundment show only small patches of black needlerush (*J. roemerianus*) (Montague et al., 1984). As illustrated in figure 14.4c, natural marshes consisted of monotypic and mixed stands of a variety of high marsh plants together with black mangroves, the latter especially in marshes to the south and east. On Merritt Island, Baker's cordgrass (*Spartina bakeri*, a grass also found on sand dikes and in lowland pastures) is found just landward of the more typical high marsh plants (Leenhouts and Baker, 1982). Because of low relief, this grass was occasionally inundated by high wind-driven tides, especially during the fall and winter rise in sea level, so it is included here as part of the salt marsh.

The northern part of Indian River (Volusia and Brevard counties) has a minute daily lunar tidal component, so the intertidal zone below mean high water is narrow (Provost, 1973a, 1976). In a few places, a narrow (10 m) band of smooth cordgrass (*S. alterniflora*) occurs in this zone. Nearer to Sebastian Inlet—100 km south—tidal range increases, but mangroves, rather than nonwoody vegetation (e.g., *S. alterniflora*), occupy the more extensive lower intertidal zone (Provost, 1973a, 1976).

Where mangroves are best developed in south Florida, nonwoody vegetation is confined to the seaward and landward intertidal fringes. A narrow strip of smooth cordgrass (*S. alterniflora*) occurs seaward of some red mangrove forests. In the landward fringe, seldom inundated by salt water, narrow strips to extensive zones of black needlerush (*J. roemerianus*) and high marsh plant communities often occur (fig. 14.4d). These salt marshes account for perhaps 20 percent of those in Florida. They are most extensive in Dade County south of Homestead and less extensive at the inland fringe of mangroves along the southwest coast north to Tampa Bay (Eleuterius, 1976; Odum et al., 1982; Durako et al., 1985; Lewis et al., 1985). Little is known of these salt marshes other than their general appearance (Davis, 1940; Schomer and Drew, 1982). Farther landward, they may give way to barren salt pans, or they may border vast expanses of saw grass (*Cladium jamaicense*), one of the most prevalent grasses in the Everglades. In brackish, wet areas, extensive stands of leather fern (*Acrostichum aureum*) may also occur in southwest Florida.

Plant Zonation

Among the most easily observed characteristics of salt marshes are their vast expanses of vegetation separated into distinctive zones, each dominated by a different species. The zonation generally corresponds to subtle changes in elevation, which result in changes in the depth, duration, and frequency of inundation by saline water to which coastal marsh plants are especially sensitive. Vegetation often changes abruptly, which may reflect abrupt changes in environmental conditions or intense plant competition.

The abrupt change from monospecific stands of smooth cordgrass (*S. alterniflora*) to similarly monospecific stands of black needlerush (*J. roemerianus*) is a conspicuous feature of many north Florida salt marshes (fig. 14.5). This phenomenon has not been completely explained. Elevation often does not change abruptly at the interface, nor does the interface occur at a consistent elevation (Eleuterius and Eleuterius, 1979). Soil conditions (perhaps partly created by the different community types themselves) and direct biotic interactions, such as competition, may account for this phenomenon (Eleuterius and Eleuterius, 1979; Stout, 1984). Such an abrupt change in vegetation, however, does not always occur between these two species. Stout (1984) reported more frequent intermingling of *S. alterniflora* and *J. roemerianus* along steeper elevation gradients. The reason for this is unknown.

In some Florida high marshes, distinct zonation also occurs, but in others high marsh plants intermingle. In salt marshes of Merritt Island, for example, monotypic zones of *Distichlis spicata, Paspalum vaginatum, Batis maritima,* and *Salicornia* spp. occur with little overlap. In other areas of Merritt Island, these same four plants intermingle. Reasons for this difference are also unknown.

Fig. 14.5. Abrupt change from *Spartina alterniflora* to *Juncus roemerianus* in a salt marsh near Crescent Beach.

Salt Marsh Development and Production

Plant Succession and Salt Marsh Development

The zonation of salt marsh vegetation has provoked considerable discussion of the contributions of autogenous succession and of relatively static environmental gradients in producing such a zonation (Davis, 1940; Kurz and Wagner, 1957; Odum et al., 1982). In the view of autogenous succession, plant communities of the lowest elevations are pioneers. These plants trap and hold sediments (Meade, 1982), thereby increasing the elevation until, supposedly, it is no longer as suitable for the initial plants as it is for the next community, the high marsh plants. Presumably, this process continues on until dry land is developed. This land-building view was championed by Davis (1940) from his work in south Florida mangroves. Conversely, in the static gradient view, the slope of the intertidal area is established by local physical and geological processes of the coast (wind and water motion). Marsh plants simply occupy the elevations to which they are best adapted. Since sea level has continually risen over the past several thousand years, these zones should be moving inland rather than outward as in the land-building scenario.

This controversy was tested by Kurz and Wagner (1957) in northwest Florida salt marshes. They reasoned that if land building was occurring in the marsh, then marshes should be underlain by marine sediments, perhaps with evidence of sea grasses. On the other hand, if rising sea level was the primary determinant of changes in plant communities, then cores of sediment from the marsh should reveal peat deposits of those communities characteristic of higher elevations. They found peat deposits from terrestrial communities that existed when sea level was lower. This finding required a modification of the notion of coastal marshes as significant land builders and added evidence to static gradients as the primary cause of zonation. The supply rate of sediment, however, is central to these issues of land building and zonation.

Most Florida marshes exist in waters with little inorganic sediment load (Meade and Parker, 1985). This is reflected in the high sand content of soils in *Spartina alterniflora* marshes of northwest Florida (70 percent to 90 percent), compared to those of Georgia and northeast Florida (<20 percent to 70 percent) (Kurz and Wagner, 1957; Edwards and Frey, 1977). Even in the marshes of Georgia—where inorganic sediment load is great and where sedimentation occurs in excess of that explained by a rise in sea level (Meade, 1982)—the layer of fine sediments over the parent Pleistocene sands thins and then disappears in the high marsh. The exposed sand surface at higher marsh elevations indicates that even this high marsh vegetational zonation is not created by the building of land by low marsh vegetation.

If a sufficient supply of sediment is available, however, the sediment-trapping characteristics of marsh plants can lead to the seaward expansion of salt marsh boundaries (Frey and Basan, 1985). Furthermore, during major storm tides, resuspended subtidal sediments can be trapped by marsh vegetation to create locally higher elevations upon the recession of the storm tides (Hoffmeister, 1974).

On a more rapid time scale, and where mangroves occur, *S. alterniflora* may commonly appear first in a newly forming marsh, to be displaced later by mangroves in what is apparently a successional replacement. *Spartina alterniflora* is said to be the first species to colonize new intertidal zones and to trap additional sediments and mangrove seeds, which eventually eliminate the grass by shading (Davis, 1940; Lewis, 1982a). In areas where mangroves are subject to periodic freezes, *S. alterniflora* is the first plant to return. At Seahorse Key in Levy County, seedlings of black mangrove (*Avicennia germinans*) have grown rapidly since the freeze of 1984. By 1986 they were well above the height of the grass and were in full flower in July 1987.

Vascular Plant Production

Although net primary production in salt marshes is relatively high, it is also variable (Marinucci, 1982; Montague et al., 1987a). Production has been estimated in only a few Florida salt marshes. Estimates of net production of above-ground plant material (stems and leaves) in Florida range from 130 to 2500 grams of dry mass per square meter per year (g m^{-2} yr^{-1}), depending in part on location.

Estimates of net above-ground production in a northwest Florida salt marsh (St. Marks National Wildlife Refuge) range from 250 to 950 g m^{-2} yr^{-1} for *Juncus roemerianus* and from 130 to 700 g m^{-2} yr^{-1} for *S. alterniflora* (Kruczynski et al., 1978). For both plants, production was highest at lower elevations. These estimates are similar to others taken near Crystal Bay, 135 km to the south (Young, 1974; Montague et al., 1981b; Knight and Coggins, 1982).

Unimpounded marshes on Merritt Island are often densely vegetated with plants typical of Indian River high marshes. High marshes in the southeastern United States are usually not so densely vegetated, and production is low (Kruczynski et al., 1978). On Merritt Island, however, Chynoweth (1975) measured above-ground net productions of 2000 and 2500 g m^{-2} yr^{-1} at two sites in a restored, formerly impounded salt marsh. One site was dominated by *Spartina bakeri, Distichlis spicata,* and *Sesuvium portulacastrum*; the other was dominated by *S. portulacastrum* and *D. spicata* alone. It is not clear why these marshes are so productive. They have a long growing season and perhaps lower soil salinity than many other high marshes.

Plant production in northeast Florida salt marshes is probably similar to that in Georgia marshes or perhaps slightly higher owing to the almost year-round growing season (Kurz and Wagner, 1957; Carlton, 1977). Aboveground production in salt marshes near Sapelo Island, Georgia, is around 1300 to 1400 g m^{-2} yr^{-1} for *S. alterniflora* and 2200 g m^{-2} yr^{-1} for *J. roemerianus* marshes (Pomeroy et al., 1981). Aerial production of the taller form in Georgia is around 3700 g m^{-2} yr^{-1} (Pomeroy et al., 1981). Greater production near tidal creeks has been attributed to the work of the tides (Schelske and Odum, 1961; Odum, 1980; Odum et al., 1983). Mechanisms for such an effect may include improved access to nutrients and better removal of accumulations of growth-reducing substances in the soil, such as sulfides and salt. Reduction in height of both *J. roemerianus* and *S. alterniflora* has been correlated with a decrease in flood frequency and an increase in soil salinity (Nestler, 1977; Eleuterius and Caldwell, 1981).

Within the soil, the major constraints on plant growth arise from the generally stagnant and anaerobic nature of the interstitial water. The organic content of salt marsh soils ranges from 3 percent to 40 percent (Kurz and Wagner, 1957; Stout, 1984). Anaerobic decomposition of this organic matter through sulfate reduction often produces large amounts of hydrogen sulfide, which stresses marsh plants. Evapotranspiration increases salinity—another potential stress to plants. Stagnant circulation restricts the removal of these stressful agents and the replenishment of essential nutrients, such as inorganic nitrogen and iron. On the creek banks and levees, a greater hydraulic head is established at low tide by the depth of the low water combined with the height of the levee. This head pressure causes more interstitial movement of water. The pore spaces in the sediment thus emptied at low tide are refilled on the subsequent high tide. This pattern is not sufficient for complete reoxygenation, but it does reduce the sulfide accumulation, a result readily inferred from the weaker odor of cores taken from the creek banks and levees compared to cores taken in the interior portions of the marsh. In various studies, growth of short *S. alterniflora* has been experimentally increased by adding nitrogen, fresh water, oxygen, and fiddler crab burrows (Linthurst, 1980; Chalmers, 1982; Montague, 1982). *Juncus roemerianus* may be affected similarly. Direct experimental evidence of the effect of interstitial water movement in regulating *S. alterniflora* biomass and production was provided by Wiegert et al. (1982).

Only about 10 percent of the vascular plant production is consumed alive by herbivores, mostly insects (Pfeiffer and Wiegert 1981). Most of the plant dies, falls to the marsh surface, and decomposes. The fates and functions of salt marsh detritus have been thoroughly reviewed by Montague et al. (1987a). Some of this detritus may leave the marsh during storms or floods, but most decomposes in place (see also Hackney and de la Cruz, 1979; Harriss et al., 1980). The relatively high elevation of Florida salt marshes, together with the berm often present at mean high water, impede the hydrological connection with coastal waters, probably reducing both the amount of detritus that reaches the estuary from the marsh and the amount of detritus imported into the marsh from elsewhere in the estuary (from sea grasses, for example) (Montague et al., 1987a). Within the salt marsh, however, detritus, benthic and planktonic microalgae, and live vascular plants form the base of a food web consisting of a variety of productive resident animals and vertebrate visitors.

Salt Marsh Animals

Introduction to Salt Marsh Animals

Because of the high net primary production and the high density of plant stems, salt marshes contain abundant food and cover for a variety of resident and transient animals (fig. 14.6). To utilize salt marshes, however, animals must either tolerate or avoid the rigorous conditions created by the alternating terrestrial and aquatic environments. Those few species that have adapted to these difficult conditions are often abundant; thus, animal production is high in salt marshes, but diversity is low.

The large, irregular, and often sudden fluctuations in salinity and water level, with accompanying variations in dissolved oxygen and temperature, create a physiologically stressful environment, especially at the sediment surface. Few species have the necessary physiological and behavioral adaptations for thriving within this varying environment. Permanent residents of such environments must be, simultaneously, able to withstand extremes in

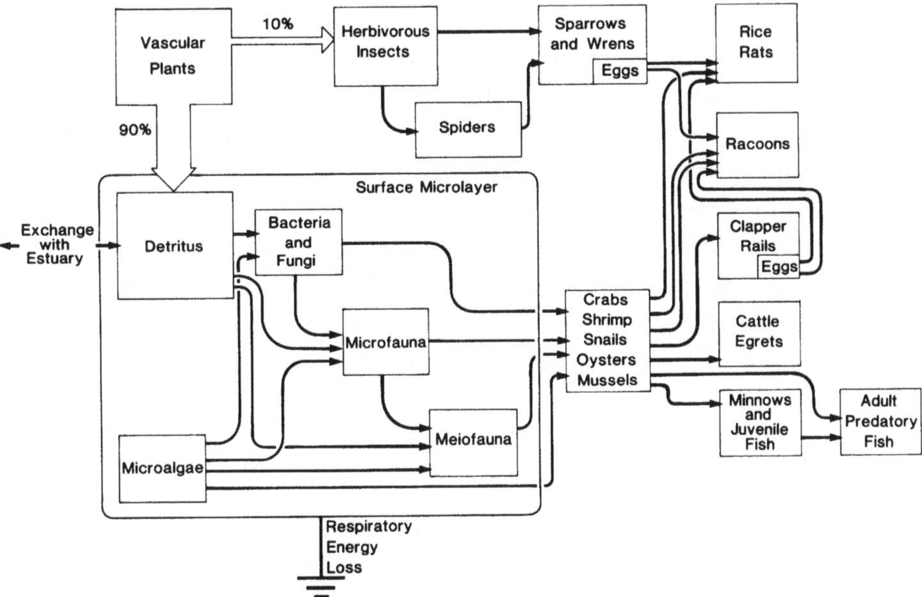

Fig. 14.6. Salt marsh food web: a grazing food chain is depicted across the top, a detritus-algae food chain along the bottom.

temperature (*eurythermal*) and in the concentrations of salts (*euryhaline*) and dissolved oxygen.

Transient vertebrates tend to use the fringes of the marsh. The high marsh fringe adjacent to coastal fields and forests is most heavily used by terrestrially based visitors, such as raccoons and marsh rabbits. The raccoon (*Procyon lotor*) is the most common mammal visitor. Raccoon scat filled with fiddler and squareback crab parts can be found on nearly any trip to the marsh. Other visitors to the higher elevations of the salt marsh include minks (*Mustela vison*), marsh rabbits (*Sylvilagus palustris*), cotton rats (*Sigmodon hispidus*), and cotton mice (*Peromyscus gossypinus*) (Johnson et al., 1974; Woods et al., 1982; Stout, 1984). For estuarine organisms, marsh creeks are the main corridors of access. Salt marsh creeks and the associated marsh edges are used by a variety of transient vertebrates of commercial, recreational, and environmental significance. These include adult fish, wading birds, and a few marine mammals, such as the bottlenose dolphin (*Tursiops truncatus*). The food and cover available in these creeks are used by a variety of juvenile estuarine fish and shellfish found in other coastal habitats as adults. For this reason, salt marshes are said to be nursery grounds for fish and shellfish of commercial and recreational importance (Durako et al., 1985).

The few resident species that are well adapted to the salt marsh environment are widely distributed among the salt marshes of Florida and the southeastern United States. The species compositions and numbers of animals are remarkably similar from site to site. Faunal differences undoubtedly occur among the various Florida salt marshes, but most are subtle, often at the level of subspecies or species. Greater variation occurs among the scarcer organisms.

Accounts of salt marsh fauna from other areas are, therefore, generally applicable to Florida. The guide by Heard (1982a) and the community profile by Stout (1984) are especially relevant to the *Juncus*-dominated salt marshes of northwest Florida. The discussion by Montague et al. (1981a) for Georgia salt marshes is relevant to the marshes of northeast Florida. Extensive discussions of the fauna of tidal marshes in general can be found in the books and monographs by Daiber (1977, 1982). Other accounts for various parts of the Gulf and Atlantic coasts include those of Davis and Gray (1966), Teal and Teal (1969), Davis (1978), Nixon (1982), and Gosselink (1984).

Effects of Salt Marsh Animals

Feeding is an important direct influence of animals on the distributions and abundances of their foods. Because assimilation of food leads to animal production, the importance of animals in ecosystems is often assumed to relate to their feeding and production. The behavior and by-products of animals, however, can have significant effects that are not apparent in measures of secondary (animal) production. Animals may inadvertently kill some organisms and stimulate growth of others during their daily activities. Such effects produce a degree of interdependency among biota that may considerably exceed that indicated by the food web alone. Sometimes these influences feed back to the animals that produce them in the form of enhanced food production.

Fiddler crabs, for example, excavate hundreds of burrows per m^2, from small ones (a few millimeters in diameter and depth) to large (10 to 20 mm in diameter and 25 to 80 cm in depth). The deeper burrows pass through the root zone of marsh plants. In a Georgia salt marsh, experimentally added burrows stimulated growth of *Spartina alterniflora*. Judging from these results and the quantity of deep burrows present in the salt marsh, an estimated 20 percent of the production of this plant was attributed to the presence of fiddler crab burrows (Montague, 1982). Detritus from this plant is consumed by fiddler crabs, and added detritus stimulates crab population growth; therefore, burrowing may result in a greater supply of a limiting resource (Montague, 1980a,b, 1982; Genoni, 1985, 1987).

Animal Habitats and Diversity

More species occur in salt marsh habitats where some of the stressful fluctuations can be avoided. Four major habitats can be identified within salt marshes: an aerial habitat amongst the leaves and stems of salt marsh plants; the intertidal sediment-water interface beneath the stems and leaves; salt marsh creeks and associated marsh edges; and salt marsh tidepools. These habitats differ significantly in environmental rigor and species composition, though some overlap of fauna occurs. The environment in the aerial portions of marsh plants, for example, is terrestrial-like much of the time and inundated only during extremely high tides. Considerably more species are found in this habitat than in the other three. For example, more than 500 species of insects occur in the aerial community in Florida salt marshes (McCoy, 1977).

Not all of this variety can be attributed to stable conditions; rapid growth is also a factor. Many salt marsh insects are common as adults for only a short time, but they grow rapidly when favorable conditions occur and leave behind environmentally resistant eggs as conditions change. Only about 10 percent of the terrestrial arthropod species found in a St. Marks salt marsh were listed as abundant at least one month of the year (McCoy and Rey, 1981, 1987; Rey and McCoy, 1982, 1983, 1986). The diversity of insects and spiders is low compared to most terrestrial arthropod communities. The vegetative cover of salt marshes, however, is often a monotypic stand. Diversity of terrestrial arthropods in salt marshes is high relative to that of arthropods in monospecific agricultural crops (Pfeiffer and Wiegert, 1981).

In contrast, beneath the stems and leaves, the number of species of resident macrofauna in the intertidal sediment-water interface is lower by an order of magnitude. Heard (1982a) lists eighty-eight species of noninsect macroinvertebrates found in salt marshes of the northeastern Gulf of Mexico (excluding oligochaete worms). In St. Marks *Juncus roemerianus* marshes, Subrahmanyam et al. (1976) found forty-eight species; in three South Carolina *S. alterniflora* marshes, Fox and Ruppert (1985) found thirty-one to forty-nine species per marsh. As with the insects of the aerial habitat, few (perhaps 20 percent) macroinvertebrate species of the intertidal sediment-water interface are abundant (Subrahmanyam et al., 1976; Fox and Ruppert, 1985). All have special adaptations for living in alternating aquatic and terrestrial conditions. The success of the abundant fiddler crab, for example, can be attributed in large part to its burrow. Burrows, which are excavated to just below the water table, provide water at low tide. Although fiddler crabs are most active when the tide is out, physiologically they are aquatic organisms, so they must carry respiratory water with them in their gill chambers. Water must frequently be replenished because it is also used for evaporative cooling and for feeding (particle sorting before ingestion). In addition, burrows provide protection from predators and from temperature extremes (Montague, 1980a,b).

Few species of fish, reptiles, birds, or mammals (five or six) can be considered residents of salt marshes. Larger, longer-lived organisms are not as able to avoid environmental fluctuation. However, a variety of transient vertebrates visit the salt marsh. In four years of annual breeding bird surveys, for example, a total of forty-four species of bird visitors were seen foraging or resting in 15 to 30 ha of Cedar Key salt marsh and adjacent creeks; twenty-eight occurred in all four surveys (Post, 1981b; McDonald, 1982, 1983, 1984).

When conditions are suitable, vagile estuarine and terrestrial organisms use the abundant food and cover of salt marshes. They avoid some of the rigors of environmental variation by leaving when conditions become unbearable. As conditions vary over time, sequential replacement of transients occurs (Zale et al., 1987). Over several years, many species of transient juvenile and adult fauna may visit the creeks and edges of a salt marsh.

The Aerial Habitat and Grazing Food Chain

Among the stems and leaves of salt marsh plants is a terrestrial-like grazing food web based on the consumption of the juices and tissues of the living plants (top of fig. 14.6). Nearly all the abundant salt marsh insects are herbivores. Tissue-eating tettigoniid grasshoppers (*Orchelimum concinnum* and *Conocephalus* spp.) and juice-feeding planthoppers (*Prokelesia marginata*) are the most abundant (Parsons and de la Cruz, 1980; Pfeiffer and Wiegert, 1981; Rey and McCoy, 1982). The herbivore community supports a predatory food web that includes eight abundant species of spiders, a large variety of parasitic wasps, and the predatory beetle *Collops* sp. (Pfeiffer and Wiegert, 1981; McCoy and Rey, 1981, 1987; Rey and McCoy, 1982, 1983, 1986).

Even though only about 10 percent of the net primary production of salt marsh vascular plants is consumed by herbivores, net primary production in salt marshes is so large that the per-unit-area secondary production in this food chain—81 kcal m^{-2} yr^{-1}—is one of the greatest recorded for any grassland (Wiegert and Evans, 1967).

The stems and leaves of salt marsh plants are also visited by aufwuchs-feeding snails: the salt marsh periwinkle (*Littorina irrorata*) and the pulmonate "coffee bean" snail (*Melampus* spp.). These snails also feed on the detritus and microalgae of the sediment surface. Marsh crabs (*Sesarma* spp.), which also commonly feed at the sediment surface, occasionally visit the aerial habitat to eat the leaves of *S. alterniflora* (Jackewicz, 1973; Pfeiffer and Wiegert, 1981; Heard, 1982a).

A number of birds forage on the aerial invertebrate community, including cattle egrets (*Bubulcus ibis*), migratory insectivores (swallows), and two salt marsh residents: the marsh wren (*Cistothorus palustris*) and the seaside sparrow (*Ammodramus maritimus*) (Howell, 1932; Kale, 1964; Post et al., 1983). On average, slightly more than one long-billed marsh wren occurs per hectare in both Georgia and Cedar Key salt marshes (Kale, 1965; McDonald, 1986). They feed mostly on the smaller types of insects and spiders. In Kale's (1964) study, planthoppers made up 23 percent of the volume of stomach contents. Other foods included ants and wasps (15 percent), small dictynid and linyphiid spiders (12 percent), and a variety of other insects, small crustaceans, and molluscs. Larger foods taken but fed to nestlings include the tettigoniid grasshopper (*Orchelimum fidicinium*), wolf spiders (Lycosidae), and large moth larvae (Kale, 1964). Foods of the Gulf coast subspecies are probably similar, though no study similar to Kale's has been published either for this species or for adult seaside sparrows.

Nestling seaside sparrows are fed a diet similar to that of nestling long-billed marsh wrens. Tettigoniid grasshoppers (e.g., *Orchelimum*) made up 44 percent of the volume of nestling foods; spiders (especially wolf spiders) contributed 32 percent, and moths 13 percent (Post et al., 1983).

The stems and leaves of salt marsh plants are also nesting sites for resident salt marsh birds. Nests are built high enough to avoid all but the highest tides. Long-billed marsh wrens nest high in the tall vegetation near marsh creeks; clapper rails (*Rallus longirostris*) nest in medium-height vegetation; and seaside sparrows nest in the high marsh areas in *Juncus*, *Distichlis*, *Salicornia*, and *Spartina patens* (Howell, 1932; Kale, 1965, 1978; Post, 1981a; Post et al., 1983; McDonald, 1986). Although easily detected from the ground, nests built in the taller vegetation are somewhat camouflaged from the air, which discourages egg predation by fish crows (*Corvus ossifragus*) (Meanley, 1985). During a study at Cedar Key, more than 50 percent of seaside sparrow nests were destroyed by fish crows (Post, 1981a). Most of these nests were in the less dense vegetation (*Salicornia* and *Distichlis*).

Egg predators are the top carnivores of the aerial, grazing food chain. In addition to fish crows, rice rats (*Oryzomys palustris*) and raccoons (*Procyon lotor*) are also significant egg predators (Kale, 1965; Sharp, 1967; Post, 1981a; Meanley, 1985; McDonald, 1986). The rice rat nests in medium and tall *S. alterniflora* and *J. roemerianus* in the vicinity of nests built by long-billed marsh wrens and seaside sparrows. The breeding season for rice rats (March through July) overlaps with that of the birds (Kale, 1965; Sharp, 1967; Post, 1981a). Rice rats construct their own nests but will also occupy nests of both species of birds after they have consumed the birds' eggs. In four years of study of long-billed marsh wrens in a Georgia salt marsh, an average of almost 50 percent of all eggs or young were lost to predators (Kale, 1965). Most of this predation (an average of 57 percent) was attributed to rice rats, and much of the rest was attributed to raccoons. Post (1981a) reported that 26 percent of the nests of seaside sparrows in a Cedar Key salt marsh were preyed upon by rice rats, mainly in nests built in *J. roemerianus*, where predation by fish crows was lower. In this marsh, rice rat density was 7 to 10 per ha. The population of seaside sparrows renests frequently and is apparently stable at a density of about 2.5 males per ha (McDonald, 1986).

Fly and rice borer moth larvae are also among the foods of the rice rat (Sharp, 1967; Post, 1981a). Sharp (1967) speculated that to obtain the rice borer larvae, the rat must chew into the stalks of *S. alterniflora*, where the rice borer resides and consumes the plant. He did not speculate further about the survival of the plant relieved of its rice borers by such a method!

The Sediment-Water Interface and Detritus-Algae Food Chain

Beneath the stems and leaves that harbor the aerial community lives a community of macrofauna that forage on the sediment surface and filter floodwaters (fig. 14.7). The common resident macroinvertebrates include polychaetes (e.g., *Neanthes succinea* and *Scoloplos fragilis*); gastropod molluscs (e.g., *Littorina irrorata, Melampus bidentatus, M. coffeus*, and *Cerithidea* spp.); bivalve molluscs (e.g., *Geukensia demissa, Polymesoda caroliniana, Cyrenoidea floridana*, and *Crassostrea virginica*); and crustaceans (e.g., *Uca* spp., *Cyathura polita*, tanaid mysids, and gammarid amphipods). Distributions of these organisms change somewhat from the lower to the upper marsh.

These macroinvertebrates become food for a variety of predators, including some salt marsh residents (such as xanthid mud crabs, killifish, and diamondback terrapins) and foraging visitors, such as blue crabs and red drum (at high tide) and raccoons and cattle egrets (at low tide). The most conspicuous of these is undoubtedly the clapper rail or marsh hen (*Rallus longirostris*), whose repeated clack can be heard every few minutes at most times of year. Clapper rails feed primarily on the abundant crabs and snails of the marsh and, less frequently, on salt marsh grasshoppers and annelid worms (Heard, 1982b; Meanley, 1985). Density of this bird in a Cedar Key marsh is about 1 bird per 2 ha (McDonald, 1986).

The food web of the sediment-water interface is based both on microalgae (sediment algae and phytoplankton) and on a community of microbes and meiofauna associated with decomposing plant detritus, dissolved organic matter, and particles of organic floc—a sediment-based, microalgae-detritus food chain (bottom of fig. 14.6). The top few millimeters of sediment (the surface microlayer) contain most of the microalgae, detritus, bacteria, microfauna, and meiofauna. Numbers greatly diminish below this layer as the oxidation state declines (Fenchel, 1969; Bell, 1979, 1980).

Marsh-dwelling animals can be subdivided into those that can forage at low as well as high tide, such as fiddler crabs and marsh snails, and those that forage only when submerged, such as marsh clams and mussels. This distinction is important because of the variation among Florida salt marshes in the frequency and duration of flooding. Where marshes are less frequently inundated, as in most *J. roemerianus* marshes, less of the available food can be consumed by filter feeding marsh dwellers and aquatic estuarine visitors.

Filter feeders, such as ribbed mussels (*Geukensia demissa*), consume suspended particles available in floodwaters and transfer unwanted particles to the marsh surface (Montague et al., 1981a). Suspended particles both enter with floodwaters and are resuspended from local sediments. Deposit feed-

Fig. 14.7. The sediment-water interface in a salt marsh near Crescent Beach. Concealed in this photo are ribbed mussels, periwinkle snails, and a mud fiddler crab.

ers, such as fiddler crabs (*Uca* spp.), feed on microalgae, microbes associated with decomposing vascular plant detritus, and meiofauna, all in the surface microlayer (Montague, 1980a,b; Bell, 1980; Hoffman et al., 1984; Genoni, 1985). Because 90 percent of the plant production eventually becomes detritus, sediment-based organisms would at first appear to live in a food-rich environment, but this is apparently not true. Fiddler crab recruitment and production increased following experimental additions of *S. alterniflora* detritus in a marsh near Crescent Beach, Florida (Genoni, 1985, 1987).

Secondary production of the resident macrofaunal community of the sediment-water interface is approximately 70 kcal m^{-2} yr^{-1} (Teal, 1962), and literally hundreds of snails and crabs occur per square meter of marsh (Montague et al., 1981a). Although this is a high rate of secondary production, it is remarkably similar to the production of the aerial herbivore community, which consumes only 10 percent of the net aerial vascular plant production. Why secondary production of these resident animals is not much higher probably relates to four factors: a relative lack of nutrition in vascular plant detritus; a relatively low production of the more nutritious benthic microalgae in the shade of the vascular plants; loss of energy by the respiration of microbes and meiofauna associated with decomposing detritus; and greater energy allocation by species of the resident sediment community to physiological control and less to production because of the rigorous environment (see also Montague et al., 1987a).

The Surface Microlayer

Salt marsh vascular plants constantly grow and shed leaves throughout most of the year in Florida. In north Florida, additional detritus is added in the months following frost, as dead stems break and fall to the marsh surface. Even before the dead leaves and stems fall, fungi and bacteria attach and begin the process of decomposition. Most of the detritus is decomposed at the aerobic-anaerobic interface in the top few millimeters of sediment.

The organic matter decomposing in the sediment creates a high demand for oxygen. Just a few millimeters into the fine, water-saturated salt marsh sediment, dissolved oxygen is used faster than it can be replaced by diffusion from the air, so the sediment becomes anaerobic. Complex organics in detritus must slowly decompose by fermentation, which results in simple organic compounds, such as organic acids. These simple compounds can be metabolized by sulfur bacteria, which can use sulfate (the third most common ion in seawater) in place of oxygen for their metabolism. The resulting sulfate reduction produces the characteristic sulfide smell found in the black subsurface sediment of salt marshes.

Much of the microalgae, bacteria, and fungi of the surface microlayer is consumed by protozoans (mainly ciliates and foraminiferans) and by tiny metazoans, such as nematodes, harpacticoid copepods, annelids, turbellarians, rotifers, and larval stages of larger invertebrates (Fenchel, 1969; Bell, 1979). These microfauna and meiofauna consume the same foods as many larger deposit feeders and filter feeders. The smaller fauna themselves become food for many large fauna, but not before they have used much of the energy available lower on the food chain (bottom of fig. 14.6). In their metabolic wastes, however, are nutrients for the regrowth of plants and bacteria.

Microfauna and meiofauna are the least well known sizes of salt marsh animals. Only a few studies of microfauna exist anywhere (e.g., Fenchel, 1969; Phleger, 1970). Meiofaunal studies from salt marshes in Alabama (Harp, 1980, cited in Stout, 1984), Georgia (Teal and Wieser, 1966), and South Carolina (Coull and Bell, 1979; Bell, 1979, 1980) may be generally applicable to Florida. Densities in these studies ranged from 10^5 to 10^7 microfauna and meiofauna per m^2. Microfauna include both foraminiferans and ciliated protozoans. Densities of foraminiferans are low in high marsh. Ciliates are much more common in sandier, submerged sediments. Nematodes, harpacticoid copepods, and small annelid worms (oligochaetes and polychaetes) are the most common meiofauna (table 14.2).

Larger animals can have a considerable impact on the microbial community of the surface microlayer. The feeding activities of fiddler crabs, for example, mix almost all the surface at every low tide. Fiddler crabs also regenerate nitrogen on the surface (Montague, 1980a,b). The net result of these activities can be enhanced microalgal production and microbial community respiration in the surface microlayer (and thus more food for fiddler crabs).

The Importance of Salt Marsh Creeks and Pools

The principal salt marsh habitats for fish are tidal creeks and pools (fig. 14.8). Some commercially important species (table 14.3) spend all or a great portion of their lives in marsh creeks and estuaries (Seaman, 1985). These include mullet, spot, blue crabs (*Callinectes sapidus*), oysters (*Crassostrea virginica*), and penaeid shrimp (*Penaeus* spp.).

More than 90 percent of the numbers and biomass of fish collected in salt marsh creeks and pools, however, are minnows: killifishes (Cyprinodontidae, e.g., *Fundulus* spp. and *Cyprinodon variegatus*), livebearers (Poeciliidae, e.g., *Gambusia* spp. and *Poecilia latipinna*), and silversides (Atherinidae, e.g., *Menidia* spp.). Spot (*Leiostomus xanthurus*) is the major nonminnow exception; both juveniles and adults of this species are abundant in northern Florida tidal creeks. Mullet (*Mugil* spp.) and pinfish (*Lagodon rhomboides*) are also abundant (Kilby, 1955; Harrington and Harrington, 1961, 1982; Subrahmanyam and Drake, 1975; Subrahmanyam and Coultas, 1980; Schooley, 1980; Gilmore, 1984).

Larval and juvenile fish and shellfish seasonally remain in estuaries—

including the creeks of fringing marshes—to feed and find refuge from predation. Juvenile white shrimp (*Penaeus setiferus*), for example, enter estuarine marsh creeks and remain until they are about 5 cm long, when they move to the estuary and, later, offshore to spawn (Anderson, 1970). In fact, many commercially and recreationally important species that utilize the estuary as nursery grounds spawn offshore (fig. 14.9). Soon after spawning, the larvae appear in the estuary. The mechanisms of larval recruitment to estuaries, unfortunately, have not yet been determined.

The abundant minnows and juvenile spot, mullet, and pinfish provide forage for less common but more recreationally valuable predatory fish, wading birds, and the occasional dolphin that ventures there to feed. Salt marsh creeks and ditches contain tarpon (*Megalops atlanticus*), snook (*Centropomus undecimalis*), and several drums and croakers (Sciaenidae), including red drum (*Sciaenops ocellatus*), seatrout (*Cynoscion* spp.), and kingfish (*Menticirrhus* spp.). Sharks and rays are also common visitors in tidal creeks, as are needlefishes (Belonidae, e.g., *Strongylura* spp.). Snowy and great egrets (*Egretta thula* and *Casmerodius albus*) and great blue, tricolor, and green-backed herons (*Ardea herodias, Egretta tricolor*, and *Butorides striatus*) are common sights near the edges of the marsh along tidal creeks (Post, 1981b; McDonald, 1982, 1983, 1984).

Despite the presence of many predators, it is undoubtedly the marsh creek edges that account for the presence of juvenile stages of commercially and recreationally important fish and shellfish (Zale et al., 1987; Montague et al., 1985; Browder et al., 1985). Indeed this is where most "salt marsh" fish collections have been made (e.g., Subrahmanyam and Drake, 1975). These benefit from the simultaneous food and cover provided by the great production of grasses and microalgae in the salt marsh. The edge of the marsh creek (fig. 14.8) provides the cover of shallow water and creekside vegetation. Foods include not only the organisms of the intertidal and sub-

Table 14.2. Meiofauna community composition in an Alabama salt marsh

Dominant plant	Meofaunal group	Proportion of total number of individuals (%)
Juncus roemerianus		
	Nematodes	55
	Harpacticoid Copepods	26
	Oligochaete Worms	10
	Polychaete Worms	3
Spartina alterniflora		
	Nematodes	70
	Harpacticoid Copepods	25
	Oligochaete Worms	2

Source: Stout (1984).

Fig. 14.8. The salt marsh creek and associated edge habitat (illustration by Edgar Rivera).

Table 14.3. Average annual landings of top 10 fishery organisms (by weight) on Florida Gulf and Atlantic coasts (1982–1984)

Gulf coast			Atlantic coast		
Organism type	Weight (1000 lbs)	Value (1000 $)	Organism type	Weight (1000 lbs)	Value (1000 $)
Shrimps	24,274	47,057	Calico Scallop	19,795	14,783
Mullets	19,970	4675	Menhaden	8291	285
Groupers	10,118	12,099	Shrimps	7340	12,848
Blue crabs	10,107	2714	Blue Crabs	5558	1595
Oyster meats	5202	5215	Span. Mackerel	4208	1260
Other crabs[a]	4705	7327	King Mackerel	3341	3212
Spiny lobster	4612	11,562	Swordfish	2783	7493
Red snapper	3017	5997	Mullets	2071	436
Other snapper	2479	3193	Bluefish	1671	341
Seatrouts	1922	1642	Tilefish	1608	1512
Total Florida landings	112,560	112,787		68,139	54,138

Sources: National Marine Fisheries Service (1983, 1984, 1985).
a. Other crabs are mostly stone crabs.

tidal sediments but also a zooplankton community based on phytoplankton and the microbes associated with suspended detrital particles and dissolved organic matter.

Zooplankton in tidal creeks are an important food for larval and postlarval fish. Minnows, arrow worms (chaetognaths), and barnacles are also voracious predators of zooplankton. Zooplankton species in salt marsh creeks and in the water that floods salt marshes are similar in composition

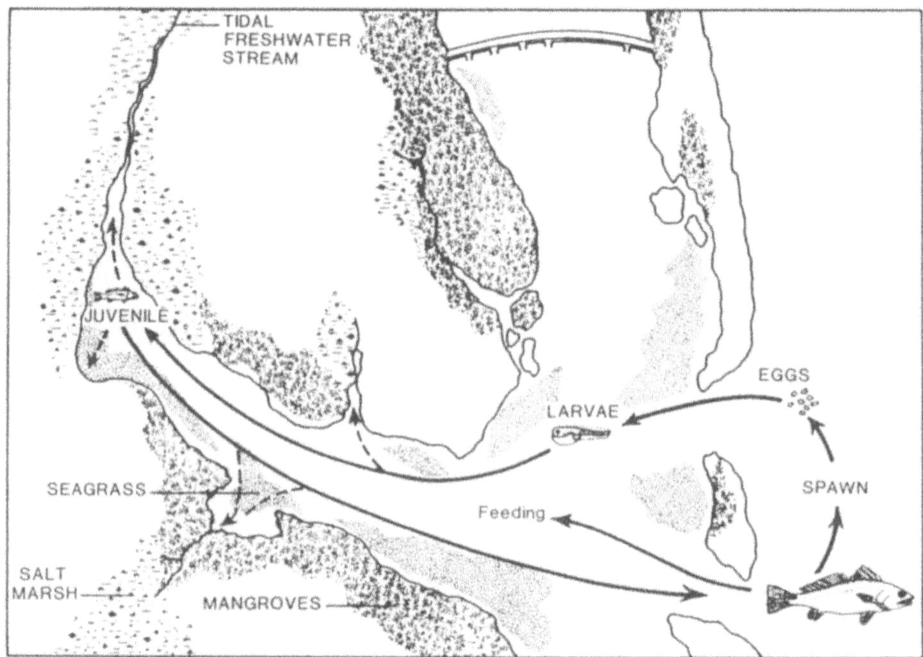

Fig. 14.9. Life cycle of the red drum. Many estuarine fish and shellfish have similar life cycles, including spotted seatrout, pink shrimp, and blue crabs. Reproduced from Lewis et al, 1985.

and abundance to those of nearby open estuarine water (Rey et al., 1984, 1987; Odum et al., 1982). In many Florida estuaries, the *holoplankton* (organisms that are planktonic their entire life) consist of about 10^5 individuals per m^3, together weighing around 40 mg, and distributed among perhaps twenty species, including copepods, ostracods, and the predatory chaetognaths. Invariably, however, one ubiquitous species dominates: the calanoid copepod *Acartia tonsa* (Livingston, 1984a; Turner and Hopkins, 1985; Odum et al., 1982; Youngbluth, 1976; Rey et al., 1984; Jacobs, 1968). About half the number (perhaps 15 percent of the biomass) are larvae. Planktonic larvae include not only those of holoplankton, but also *meroplankton*, larvae of animals found elsewhere as adults, such as crabs, barnacles, polychaetes, snails, and fish (Stout, 1984; Rey et al., 1984; Turner and Hopkins, 1985).

Ironically, the creek edge is simultaneously a good place for juvenile fish to avoid being eaten and a good place for adult fish to find a meal consisting in part of juvenile fish (Montague et al., 1985). The risk to each individual forage fish is presumably reduced, however, by the simultaneous presence of food and cover. Hence, salt marsh creeks not only provide nursery grounds for commercially important species but also facilitate the flow of energy to highly valued predatory organisms, such as snook, red drum, herons, and ibises.

Although the main fish habitat is the creek and associated marsh edge, fish and shellfish venture from tidal creeks partway into the marsh when water covers it. Some creek residents and transient visitors will move far into the marsh to feed. During high tides, the red drum may enter the marsh to feed. Its tail sometimes thrashes the surface of the water as it extracts fiddler crabs from burrows. Minnows (killifish and livebearers) and grass shrimp (*Palaemonetes* spp.) also move onto the marsh surface and back to the creeks with the flood and ebb of tidal water. These vagile organisms are lifetime residents of marsh creeks and tidal pools. They are probably very important links between the production of plants and animals within the salt marsh and the growth and survival of predatory juvenile and adult fishes in adjacent creeks (Montague et al., 1985; Zale et al., 1987).

When the water recedes, small fish may remain in water-filled depressions and larger pools in the marsh. Many may be eaten by wading birds or may die of exposure to heat, drought, or low dissolved oxygen. Minnows that can tolerate extreme conditions are usually the only living fish found on the marsh at low tide. More species can be found in deeper ponds; however, far fewer species are collected in interior pools than in creeks. Subrahmanyam and Coultas (1980) reported fifty-five species from creeks and only nineteen from pools in St. Marks salt marshes. Near Cedar Key and Bayport, Kilby (1955) reported twenty to thirty species from pools at the marsh creek edge but only half this number from pools in the interior of marshes. In a study of the effects of a completely closed Indian River salt marsh impoundment, Harrington and Harrington (1982) found eleven of only sixteen species present before impoundment. On revisiting this impoundment after tidal fluctuation was restored, Gilmore (1984) reported forty species, twenty-eight of which were transients. This large increase in transient species after reopening the impoundment was attributed to utilization of the creek-like perimeter ditch habitat that had not been an original feature of the marsh.

Gunter (1967) stated that more than 97 percent of the total commercial catch by states bordering the Gulf of Mexico was dependent in some way on estuaries. To what extent this conclusion extends to the tidal marshes bordering estuaries is an open question. Most species of coastal fish are not commonly collected in salt marshes or their creeks. For example, Snelson (1983) reported 141 species in waters adjacent to Merritt Island, but Schooley (1980) collected only 44 of these in nearshore sea grass beds and only 14 in adjacent salt marsh impoundments. Marshes with a greater density of creeks and longer duration of flooding are undoubtedly much more important as nursery areas for estuarine fish and shellfish and foraging grounds for predatory fish and wading birds.

Salt marshes are among several types of intertidal and shallow water habitats that are both nursery and feeding grounds for estuarine animals. Others include shallow mudflats, sea grasses, mangroves, and even perhaps lines of flotsam at converging water masses and well-developed fouling communities on bulkhead walls. It is probably the diversity of all these habitats that ensures the continued production of a variety of seafoods, wading birds, and game fish along the coast of Florida.

Animals of Special Interest

The vast openness of the salt marsh allows observation of a multitude of visiting birds. Even from a distance, masses of cattle egrets can be seen on most mornings foraging in the high marsh. Wood storks (*Mycteria americana*), roseate spoonbills (*Ajaia ajaja*), and a variety of herons and egrets (family Ardeidae) are often seen feeding, roosting, or flying over Florida salt marshes. Willets (*Catoptrophorus semipalmatus*) both feed and nest in salt marshes as well as along beaches (Howell, 1932). Many salt marsh residents and transients are not easily seen. Most are cryptically colored; some are rare and potentially endangered. Two Florida subspecies of seaside sparrow are believed extinct. Other vertebrates are simply well hidden, however, and may be unexpectedly common.

Mammals

Although the rice rat (*Oryzomys palustris*) is the most common mammal that both feeds and nests in salt marshes, other, perhaps unexpected, mammal residents have been found. A relict population of meadow vole (*Microtus pennsylvanicus*) from a Cedar Key salt marsh has been described as a new subspecies (*M. p. dukecampbelli*; Woods et al., 1982). This unusual meadow vole lives wholly within a band of *Distichlis* marsh that exists seaward of a *Juncus* marsh. Also, roundtailed muskrats (*Neofiber alleni*) are reported from high marshes on Merritt Island (Ehrhart, 1984).

Unusual visitors are also found. The West Indian manatee (*Trichechus manatus*) is a wide-ranging, occasional visitor to salt marsh tidal creeks, where it grazes *Spartina alterniflora* from the creek banks (Hardisky, 1979; T. O'Shea, personal communication, U.S. Fish and Wildlife Service, Sirenia Laboratory, Gainesville, Florida).

Conspicuously absent, however, are coypu (*Myocastor coypus*, also called nutria), which are often found in Gulf and Atlantic salt marshes in other states. Although present in Florida, coypu has been reported only from freshwater marshes (C. A. Woods, personal communication, Florida Museum of Natural History, Gainesville). Why it has not been found in Florida salt marshes is unknown.

Reptiles and Amphibians

Neill (1958) reported ten species of reptiles and amphibians to be common on Merritt Island salt and brackish marshes—including several species each of frogs, toads, turtles, and snakes, as well as the American alligator (*Alligator mississippiensis*). Merritt Island is perhaps unique in its harboring of salt-tolerant reptiles and amphibians (Neill, 1958), or at least it was before impoundment of salt marshes for mosquito control. More recently, however, salt-tolerant southern leopard frogs (*Rana sphenocephala*) have been collected from Merritt Island marshes as well as from marshes on the Gulf coast of Florida (Christman, 1974).

Most reptiles, however, are not exclusive residents of salt marshes. Only the diamondback terrapin (*Malaclemys terrapin*) and certain subspecies of the water snake (*Nerodia fasciata*) have this distinction. Both of these species have been of special concern in Florida salt marshes.

Diamondback Terrapin (*Malaclemys terrapin*). Diamondback terrapins roam or bask in the marsh by day and apparently bury themselves completely in the mud at night (Carr, 1952; Ernst and Barbour, 1972). On Merritt Island, mating occurs from March through April, and nesting occurs from April through July (Seigel, 1980a,b). Females lay four to twelve pinkish-white eggs in shallow nests dug into the sand above the high water mark. Nests on Merritt Island are found exclusively on impoundment dikes despite the presence of natural sand dunes nearby (Seigel, 1980b). Raccoons are common nest predators (Carr, 1952; Ernst and Barbour, 1972), and adult terrapins on Merritt Island may be taken frequently by raccoons on impoundment dikes (Seigel, 1980c). The terrapins feed on small crabs and snails (Carr, 1952; Ernst and Barbour, 1972) or occasionally on roots and shoots of marsh vegetation (Neill, 1958).

Although the diamondback terrapin is now relatively common in salt marshes, it was nearly exterminated in many places by collectors who sold them for the high price they commanded as a popular food during the first part of this century (Ernst and Barbour, 1972). Even the less highly regarded subspecies in Florida (*M. t. centrata* and *M. t. tequesta* on the Atlantic coast and *M. t. macrospilota* along the Gulf coast) were collected for shipment to market (Carr, 1952). After this practice subsided in the 1940s, the terrapin recovered. Recent density estimates for two Merritt Island populations (*M. t. tequesta*) were high—324 and 441 per ha (Seigel, 1984).

Salt Marsh Snake (*Nerodia fasciata*). Salt marsh snakes are secretive, mostly nocturnal, and rarely seen. In more than four years of intensive study of seaside sparrows in Cedar Key marshes, McDonald (1986) reported sighting the Gulf salt marsh snake (*N. f. clarki*) only three times. Few people have ever collected the endangered Atlantic salt marsh snake (*N. f. taeniata*), which is reported only from Volusia, Brevard, and Indian River counties (Neill, 1958; Kochman and Christman, 1978) and may now be found only in Volusia County (Hebrard and Lee, 1981; Kochman and Christman, n.d.). Salt marsh snakes are livebearers and feed on small fishes that venture into dense marsh vegetation on the incoming tides. Although generally nocturnal, the Atlantic salt marsh snake is reported to feed in daylight when water floods the marsh (Neill, 1958). This occurs perhaps because lunar tides are nearly imperceptible in the northern part of the

Indian River and Mosquito lagoons, so flooding is infrequent and irregular. Hence, feeding opportunities may be taken whenever possible.

Salt marsh snakes are salt-tolerant subspecies (or perhaps species; see Lawson, 1987) of the globally distributed natricine subfamily of water snakes (Dunson, 1980; Hebrard and Lee, 1981). Florida has three subspecies of salt marsh snake, all of which form hybrids with the freshwater banded water snake (*N. f. pictiventris*) (Dunson, 1979). Concern has been expressed that impoundment for mosquito control will enhance the opportunity for the Atlantic salt marsh snake (listed as endangered by the State of Florida) to interbreed with the banded water snake and hence lose its genetic identity. Impounded water is generally less saline than ambient Indian River Lagoon water, but in 80 percent of the impoundments, salinity stays above 5 ppt (Montague et al., 1987a). The banded water snake is intolerant of full-strength seawater (Dunson, 1980), but tests in lower salinities have not been reported. A survey of Merritt Island in 1978 showed no Atlantic salt marsh snakes but showed instead a healthy population of mangrove snakes (Hebrard and Lee, 1981). The Atlantic salt marsh snake may simply be a longitudinally striped variant of the mangrove snake; the distributional range and scale pattern of both these snakes overlap (Dunson, 1979). Nevertheless, a healthy population of striped Atlantic salt marsh snakes still exists in Volusia County. It may be a genetically distinct, relict population of salt marsh snakes (Kochman and Christman, n.d.).

Birds

The three exclusively resident salt marsh birds (clapper rails, long-billed marsh wrens, and seaside sparrows) are not easily seen or easily distinguished from migratory relatives. They are cryptically colored and generally well hidden, but all have distinctive sounds and call or sing regularly, especially during the April-to-June breeding season in Florida (Howell, 1932; Kale, 1965; Meanley, 1985; McDonald, 1986). The status of one of these species, the seaside sparrow, has been of special concern in Florida salt marshes.

Seaside Sparrow (*Ammodramus maritimus*). Despite the apparently stable population of seaside sparrows at Cedar Key (McDonald, 1986), a decline in these birds has occurred statewide (Kale, 1983). In the last fifteen years, considerable attention has been brought to the decline of the now extinct dusky seaside sparrow (*A. m. nigrescens*). Dusky seaside sparrows (fig. 14.10) occurred in a small area on north Merritt Island and in other marshes along 40 km of coastline, including some nearby inland areas of the St. Johns River marsh (Howell, 1932). These seaside sparrows were reported as abundant in 1925 by Howell (1932) but were reduced to seventy pairs on north Merritt Island by 1963, thirty pairs in 1969, two in 1973, and none after 1977 except for one single bird reported in 1980 (Leenhouts and

Fig. 14.10. One of the last dusky seaside sparrows. ©1988 by the Walt Disney Company.

Baker, 1982). Some captive birds kept at Disney World never successfully mated. Eventually, only males remained, and attempts to breed these with other subspecies (Webber and Post, 1983) resulted in only a few living offspring. The last captive dusky died in mid-June 1987. The offspring consist of one 75 percent dusky male and four females, ranging from 25 percent to 87.5 percent dusky (C. Cook, personal communication, Disney World). A breeding program continues at Disney World to try to restore related seaside sparrows to nature.

Why these birds did not survive in the wild is a matter of speculation; it could relate to loss of habitat by permanent flooding of high marsh for mosquito control on Merritt Island. Impoundment construction began in the area inhabited by dusky seaside sparrows in 1961 and was completed in 1962 (Leenhouts and Baker, 1982; Montague et al., 1985). Unfortunately, little information is available about this bird's status before 1961 (Leenhouts and Baker, 1982). DDT was extensively and frequently sprayed in the area for mosquito control between the late 1940s and the completion of the impoundments. It is possible that much of the food of this insectivore was eliminated by DDT spraying and that DDT accumulated in its tissues (see also Trost, 1968; Kale, 1983). It is also possible that the bird was in decline before the onset of DDT spraying, perhaps due to natural changes in habitat.

Efforts to restore seaside sparrow habitat began in 1972, and habitat was considered successfully restored in 1980 (Leenhouts and Baker, 1982). Dusky seaside sparrows did not return in this habitat, however, perhaps because too few birds remained at the beginning of the effort.

The range of the Smyrna seaside sparrow (*A. m. pelonota*) ends just north of Merritt Island. No Smyrna seaside sparrows were found in intensive searching of their habitat in either 1975 or 1976 (Kale, 1983). It is not known why this seaside sparrow has disappeared. This bird was in decline before DDT spraying, and mosquito control impoundments were not built throughout its range. Invasion of the lower reaches of its habitat by mangroves (before the freeze of 1983) has been offered as a possible explanation, but suitable habitat remained in the northern part of its former range (Kale, 1983).

Human Uses of Salt Marshes

History and Present Status

Before the 1940s, most salt marshes were neither highly valued nor greatly altered in Florida, though they were recognized as breeding sites for nearly indescribable hordes of salt marsh mosquitoes (*Aedes taeniorhynchus*). At that time, Florida's population was much lower, and much of the coastline that harbored expanses of salt marsh was not heavily developed. Development still lags near the marshes of northwest Florida, north of Tampa to St. Marks, and modern development around the salt marshes of the Everglades National Park will not occur in the foreseeable future.

Nevertheless, various salt marshes have been used or destroyed for a variety of reasons, and many such sites are still in use today. Salt marshes were used as dumping grounds for domestic and industrial solid wastes and as discharge sites for liquid industrial wastes near cities, such as Jacksonville and Tampa. A large mound of phosphogypsum (a by-product of phosphate ore processing) has continuously accumulated for forty years on the Archie Creek salt marsh in East Tampa. It is a dominant feature of the landscape along U.S. Highway 41. Many small towns and large cities discharged domestic sewage in or near salt marshes, and some have only recently taken steps to eliminate this practice (e.g., Jacksonville Beach). Marshes have been used as convenient sites for disposal of dredged material at various points along shipping channels and the Intracoastal Waterway. Such a site is easily seen from U.S. Highway A1A along the Matanzas River between Crescent Beach and Marineland. As Florida became more heavily populated, additional salt marshes near population centers were bulkheaded and filled for the construction of business and housing developments and shipping ports. Tampa Bay, for example, lost perhaps 40 percent of its tidal marshes between 1948 and 1978 (Estevez and Mosura, 1985).

The most extensive human impact on Florida's salt marshes, however, has been associated with mosquito control practices, which continue to be in great demand in Florida. Some of the highest densities of mosquitoes ever recorded in the continental United States occurred in Florida before mosquito control (Provost, 1949). Mosquito landings of 500 per minute on a single person were recorded by the Brevard County Mosquito Control District (Leenhouts, 1983). To prevent mosquito bites, residents of Merritt Island are said to have stuffed their clothes with crumpled newspaper

(W. P. Leenhouts, personal communication). Marshes were ditched during the 1930s as part of a Works Projects Administration (WPA) effort to control mosquitoes in coastal zones all along the east coast of the United States. This simplistic, parallel-grid ditching at sea level did not have much effect on marsh water level or vegetation in Florida marshes, nor was it effective at mosquito control (Provost, 1977), although it did put unemployed people to work.

Following the development of DDT in the 1940s, salt marshes near population centers were heavily sprayed for mosquito control. By the mid-1950s, the effectiveness of this method had declined with the appearance of DDT-resistant strains of mosquitoes. Negative side effects on fish and wildlife had also become apparent. Extensive spraying of DDT was subsequently discontinued in favor of the more effective and nontoxic method of removing the source of mosquitoes by impounding water in salt marshes (fig. 14.11). Holding water on breeding sites in the marshes above mean high water during the breeding season (May to October) effectively breaks the life cycle of salt marsh mosquitoes (*Aedes taeniorhynchus* and *A. sollicitans*) and sandflies (*Culicoides* spp.). Females will not lay eggs on standing water. Other nuisance mosquitoes do not develop well in standing brackish or salty waters, so the nuisance is effectively controlled at the source (Clements and Rogers, 1964).

Increasing tourism and the construction of rocket-launching facilities created a surge in demand for mosquito control in the 1960s along the Indian River. Plans were made to impound all mosquito-breeding marshes there. Because of the low tidal range, nearly all of the marshlands (about 32,000 ha) were above mean high water, so they were considered potential breeding sites for mosquitoes (Provost, 1973a,b, 1976). Extensive impounding began in 1954 and peaked in 1961, but it declined by 1972 as tidal marshes began to be considered more valuable for a variety of marsh functions (Provost, 1976). A total of 14,090 ha of marshes had been impounded, with 74 percent of the impounded area in Brevard County alone (Montague et al., n.d.). All but 5 percent of Brevard County's salt marshes had been impounded by 1972.

Semipermanent flooding after impoundment killed many salt marsh plants. In some cases, the original vegetation has been replaced by freshwater emergent plants, such as cattail (*Typha* spp.), or submerged vegetation, such as the green alga (*Chara* sp.) or widgeongrass (*Ruppia maritima*). Pre-impoundment vegetation can be restored in many places, however, simply by reopening impounded marsh. Vegetative changes during impoundment and following reopening of an impoundment on Merritt Island are described by Leenhouts and Baker (1982; see also Provost, 1959; Clements and Rogers, 1964; Chynoweth, 1975; Montague et al., 1984, 1987a; Leenhouts, 1985). During the development of these impoundments, much was written about serendipitous benefits of impoundment to waterfowl, wading birds, and other wildlife (e.g., Provost, 1959, 1969a,b). Currently, about 84 percent of the impoundments in Brevard County are secondarily managed as much as possible for waterfowl and other wildlife by personnel of the Merritt Island National Wildlife Rufuge (Leenhouts, 1983). Mosquito control impoundments at the Ding Darling National Wildlife Refuge on Sanibel Island and the Hobe Sound National Wildlife Refuge are also managed for wildlife. Salt marsh impoundments at the St. Marks National Wildlife Refuge were constructed primarily for wildlife management.

Continued environmental concerns—especially relating to the demise of the dusky seaside sparrow and fear of negative effects on estuarine fish and shellfish production—have recently led to the reopening or complete restoration of some formerly impounded marshes. Reopening of impoundments has occurred also because private landowners have requested it and because some water control structures have not been maintained. The evidence for the environmental concerns raised in connection with salt marsh impoundments has been reviewed in several publications (Montague et al., 1985, 1987a,b, n.d.; Zale et al., 1987; Percival et al., 1987). In 1986, 12,505 ha of mosquito control impoundments were still managed or flooded along the Indian River (Montague et al., 1987a).

Future Trends

The demand for mosquito control will surely increase as Florida's population continues to expand, but so too will the concerns about the effects of mosquito control activities on other aspects of human existence in Florida.

Fig. 14.11. Mosquito control impoundments on Merritt Island.

Mosquito control districts in Florida have always been responsive to human environmental needs, and these districts—together with the Florida Medical Entomology Laboratory and the National Wildlife Refuges—have continuously advanced the knowledge of how to control mosquitoes effectively while minimizing toxic chemical releases, reducing mangrove death due to overflooding, and reducing damage to fish, shellfish, and other species of special concern. In addition, techniques of impoundment management have been developed within the constraints of mosquito control for the benefit of some species of vertebrates, including waterfowl, sport fish, reptiles and amphibians, and several species of special concern, including alligators, woodstorks, eagles, and roundtail muskrats.

Therefore, salt marsh impoundments carry known environmental benefits and suspected environmental risks. Managers of salt marsh continue to argue about the values and fate of salt marsh impoundments. Currently, marsh regulation in Florida is restrictive for any type of alteration. Ironically, it may even be difficult to obtain a permit to develop new mosquito management techniques that could replace impoundments. These techniques, called open-marsh water management, allow the return of natural hydrological regimes to most of the marsh (Ferrigno and Jobbins, 1968; Ferrigno et al., 1969, 1975; Whigham et al., 1982; Meredith et al., 1985). However, they require the ditching of breeding "hotspots" in marshes and a commitment to several years of management trials.

Although ditching the marsh is apparently the major objection to open-marsh water management, the impact of these ditches may be much less than flooding huge expanses of high marsh. Furthermore, the ditches may allow greater utilization of marsh production by estuarine fish and shellfish. Trials on Merritt Island National Wildlife Refuge allowed restoration of natural marsh vegetation, but so far the effectiveness of mosquito control has been somewhat less than desired (Leenhouts, 1985; J. Salmela, personal communication, Brevard County Mosquito Control District, retired). Additional trials will be necessary to improve mosquito control with this method. Current regulatory practices, however, may prevent or retard the development of this alternative. Fear of setting precedents that could allow other practices, such as filling, that irreversibly eliminate salt marshes may be the reason. If so, perhaps a specific exception for alterations that lead to partial restoration or enhancement of natural marsh values will be considered.

Rising sea level may eventually eliminate significant areas of marsh in Florida. Concern about this has recently arisen because of the possibility of a global acceleration in the rate of rise caused by the greenhouse effect from burning fossil fuels (Mehta et al., 1987). Relative sea level is presently rising in Florida between 20 and 40 cm per century (Tanner, 1960a; Wanless, 1989). Much of Florida's two northern coasts is bound by sandhills that are part of ancient shorelines (MacNeil, 1950). Although the current rate of rise may be slow enough to allow salt marshes to advance inland with the sea, the change in elevation near these sandhills would decrease the width of the intertidal zone. Unless tidal range also increases sufficiently, suitable area for salt marsh development will be decreased (Mehta et al., 1987). If the rate accelerates, habitat may change too rapidly for many specialized salt marsh animals, such as seaside sparrows, to adapt.

Values of marshes have been variously described, hypothesized, studied, modified, and refuted in both scientific and legal case studies; however, the public has a great desire to maintain natural wetland areas (Smardon, 1983). The remaining vast areas of salt marsh surprise and delight travelers along some of Florida's more developed coasts. They provide the impression of wilderness, where wading birds are easily spotted and wild seafoods may still thrive. Even people who will never visit any wilderness areas may want to feel assured that some still exist in Florida. Vast expanses of salt marsh still remain along much of Florida's coast, and future development of salt marshes is restricted for now. Florida's population, however, continues to grow, mostly by immigration, at the staggering rate of 1000 people per day (Bureau of Economic and Business Research, 1987, 1988). Pressure to develop all types of Florida ecosystems, including salt marshes, will undoubtedly increase and will only be retarded in proportion to the collective desire of both the current and the immigrating public to preserve these areas for many reasons, scientifically supportable or not (for example, religious and aesthetic).

15
Mangroves

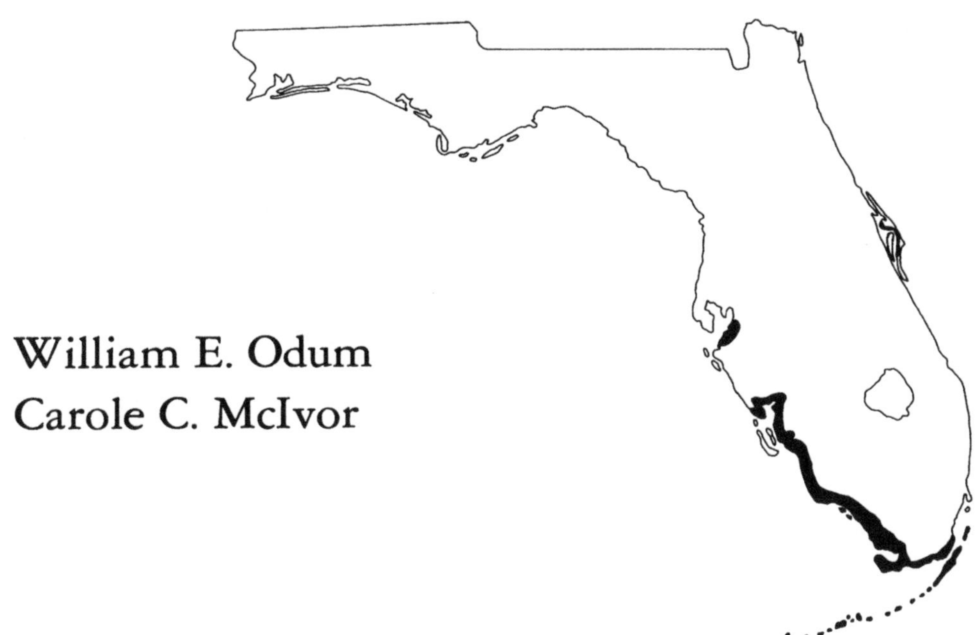

William E. Odum
Carole C. McIvor

The word *mangrove* has been closely intertwined with much of the written history of the Florida peninsula. Spanish explorers were fascinated by these strange, often contorted trees that extended into the shallow edges of the sea. Early settlers and naturalists noted the diversity of fishes, birds, and other wildlife living in close association with stands of mangroves. Until the middle of the twentieth century, however, mangrove forests were given little protection from alteration and development, with the result that thousands of acres were destroyed and replaced with filled and developed land. Since the late 1960s, planners, developers, managers, environmentalists, and scientists have heatedly debated the importance of mangrove ecosystems to society and have often resorted to legislative and legal battles to decide between preservation or alteration for commercial development (fig. 15.1).

Mangrove Species in Florida

Mangrove Terminology

The word *mangrove* comes from a combination of the Portuguese word for tree (*mangue*) and the English word for a stand of trees (*grove*) (Dawes,

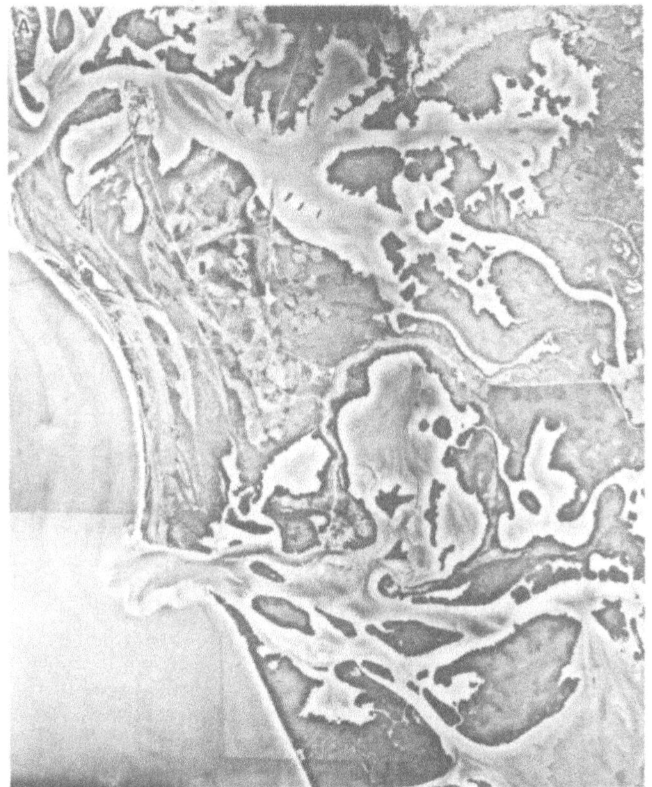

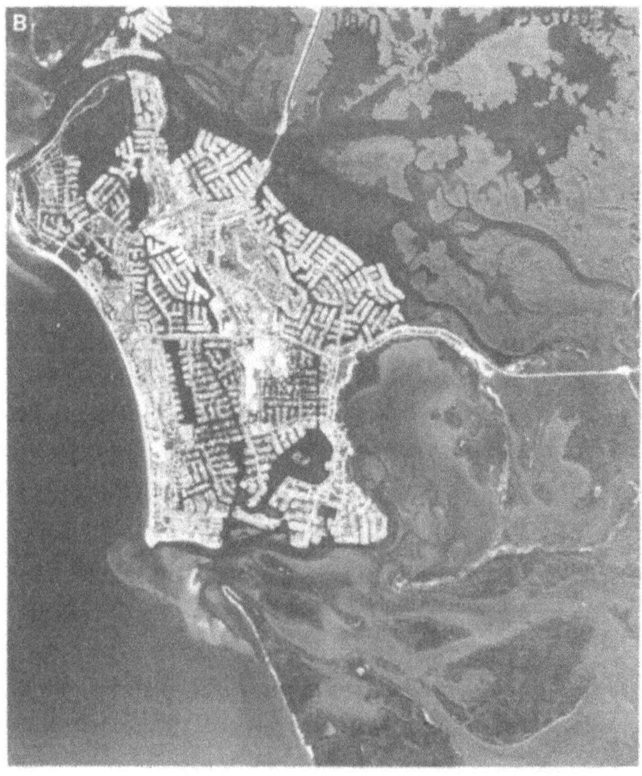

Fig. 15.1. Aerial photographs of Marco Island in (*a*) 1952 before development and (*b*) 1974, after extensive development and destruction of more than 800 hectares of mangrove forests. From Patterson, 1986.

1981). The word is used in two different ways. First, it is employed as a general catch-all term for species of trees or shrubs (dicots and monocots) that may not be closely related but do have certain common characteristics. Tomlinson (1986) defines the characteristics of true mangrove species as (1) *morphological specialization* that adapts them to their environment, such as aerial roots and vivipary; (2) some physiological mechanism for *salt exclusion* and often the ability to excrete salt; (3) complete *fidelity* to the mangrove environment so that they do not extend into terrestrial communities; and (4) *taxonomic isolation* from terrestrial relatives at least at the generic level and often at the subfamily or family level. He further differentiates between species that are "major elements" or "minor elements," based on whether they have a major role in the structure of mangrove communities and have the ability to form pure stands.

Worldwide, Tomlinson (1986) considers thirty-four species in nine genera and five families to be "major elements" and a further twenty species in eleven genera and eleven families as "minor elements." He also lists a host of other plant species found in mangrove forests that he considers to be "associated species."

The second usage of the word *mangrove* includes the entire plant community. Synonymous terms include *tidal forest*, *tidal swamp forest*, *mangrove community*, *mangrove ecosystem*, *mangal* (Macnae, 1968), and *mangrove swamp*.

In this book we will follow the most common, current usage. *Mangrove* here refers to the individual species of trees as defined by Tomlinson (1986). *Mangrove community*, *mangrove ecosystem*, or *mangrove forest* are used to refer to the entire assemblage of "mangroves."

Mangrove Species

According to Tomlinson's (1986) criteria, three species of true mangroves are "major elements" in Florida mangrove forests: the red mangrove (*Rhizophora mangle* L.), the black mangrove (*Avicennia germinans* L.), and the white mangrove (*Laguncularia racemosa* L.). A fourth species, the buttonwood (*Conocarpus erecta* L.), is classified only as a "mangrove associate" since it does not have any degree of root modification for saturated, saline soils or viviparity of propagules. Because it constitutes an important upland fringe of many Florida mangrove ecosystems (Tomlinson, 1980), buttonwood will be discussed occasionally in this chapter.

The following mangrove descriptions come largely from Carlton (1975) and Savage (1972). These publications, along with Dawes (1981) and Tomlinson (1986), contain further taxonomic information, photographs, and detailed descriptions of leaves, flowers, and propagules.

The black mangrove (*Avicennia germinans*) is a member of the family Avicenniaceae. It is most easily recognized by the system of shallow "cable" roots that radiate out from the tree and have short, vertical aerating branches (*pneumatophores*) that extend from 2 cm to 20 cm or more above the soil (fig. 15.2). These finger-like projections often form an extensive carpet under the tree. Black mangroves may reach a height of 20 m and have narrowly elliptic or oblong leaves that are often encrusted with salt. Propagules are lima-bean-shaped and several centimeters long. The tree flowers in spring and early summer.

The red mangrove (*Rhizophora mangle*) is in the family Rhizophoraceae. Its most distinctive characteristic is the complex network of "prop roots" that arise from the trunk and branches and shallowly penetrate the soil below the tree (fig. 15.3). Although usually shorter, it may reach 25 m in height and has leaves that are shiny, deep green above and paler below. The pencil-shaped propagules can be as long as 25–30 cm after germination. Although flowering can occur throughout the year, in Florida it happens predominantly in spring and summer.

The white mangrove (*Laguncularia racemosa*) is in the family Combretaceae. It is a tree or shrub that reaches 15 m or more in height and has broad,

Fig. 15.2. Black mangrove (*Avicennia germinans*) with pneumatophores, Snead Island, Manatee County. Photo by Allan Horton.

Fig. 15.3. Red mangrove prop roots. Photo by R. Myers.

flattened oval leaves up to 7 cm long. The propagules are small (approximately 1 cm). Flowering occurs in spring and early summer.

The buttonwood (*Conocarpus erecta*) is also in the family Combretaceae and grows as a shrub or tree to heights of 12–14 m. It has oval leaves 4–9 cm long that are wedge-shaped at the base. There is no true propagule; the fruit is a persistent woody aggregate.

Abiotic Constraints on Mangroves

The distribution of mangroves and the extent of ecosystem development appear to be limited by five principal factors (Odum et al., 1982): climate, salt water, water fluctuation, runoff of terrestrial nutrients, and substrate and wave energy.

Mangroves are essentially tropical tree species that usually do not occur in regions where the annual average temperature is much below 19°C (66°F) (Waisel, 1972). Temperature fluctuations greater than 10°C (18°F) over short periods of time and below freezing for more than a few hours are detrimental. Lugo and Patterson-Zucca (1977) have found that low-temperature stress leads to decreased structural complexity (decreased tree height, leaf area index, and leaf size and increased tree density). The black mangrove exists on portions of the northern coast of the Gulf of Mexico by maintaining a semipermanent shrub form through regeneration from the roots after severe freeze damage (Sherrod and McMillan, 1985).

Another important aspect of climate in relation to mangrove forest development involves the periodicity and intensity of hurricanes. In regions such as Puerto Rico, the Bahamas, Cuba, and south Florida, which have frequent, severe hurricanes, mangrove forests tend to be periodically damaged or destroyed before they reach their maximum height and development. In other regions, such as parts of Central America and northern South America where hurricanes are largely absent, the forests tend to have much larger trees if other factors—such as nutrient supply and suitable substrate—are favorable.

Mangroves are facultative halophytes; in other words, salt water is not required for good growth (Bowman, 1917; Egler, 1948). For example, Sternberg and Swart (1987) analyzed the stable isotope ratios of oxygen and hydrogen from the stem water of mangroves growing at various locations in south Florida. They determined that mangroves were able to utilize either fresh water or salt water depending upon availability.

While Florida mangroves can grow quite well in fresh water (Teas, 1979), mangrove ecosystems do not develop in strictly freshwater environments, apparently because of ecological competition from freshwater vascular plant species (Simberloff, 1983; Tomlinson, 1986). Therefore, salt water plays a key role in mangrove ecosystem development by excluding potential competing species (Kuenzler, 1974).

Water fluctuations—both tidal and due to freshwater runoff—are important to mangrove forest development. For example, tidal action carries mangrove propagules into the upper portion of the estuary. Water fluctuations transport nutrients and relatively clean water to the mangroves while flushing out accumulations of hydrogen sulfide and salts from sediment pore waters. Lugo and Snedaker (1974) have pointed out that mangrove forests reach their greatest extent in height and biomass where they can intercept significant quantities of nutrients, such as phosphorus and nitrogen, from terrestrial runoff.

Because of these factors, termed *tidal* or *fluctuating water subsidies* by E. P. Odum (1971), mangrove ecosystems often reach their greatest areal extent in low-lying regions with relatively large tidal ranges. Other types of water fluctuation, such as the seasonal runoff of fresh water along the edge of the Everglades, can provide similar subsidies. The combination of significant tidal amplitude, heavy rainfall, and terrestrial runoff, and lack of hurricanes, as occurs on the west coast of Panama, can result in expansive forests with remarkably large trees.

Two other important interrelated factors affecting mangroves are the type of substrate and the amount of wave energy. Mangroves flourish in depositional environments with low wave energy. High wave energy prevents establishment of propagules, destroys the relatively shallow root system, and prevents the accumulation of fine anaerobic sediment. Anaerobic conditions further limit potential competing vascular plants (Mitsch and Gosselink, 1986), and mangroves are adapted for life in anaerobic sediments. Still, they must pay a metabolic cost that results in lowered net primary production (Miller, 1972).

As in salt marshes, salt water, fluctuating water levels, and waterlogged anaerobic sediments appear to combine synergistically to exclude most competing vascular plants from the mangrove environment. Even aggressive, introduced species, such as *Melaleuca quinquenervia*, cannot invade mangrove forests in south Florida with much success (Myers, 1983).

Morphological Adaptations

Unlike most vascular plants, mangroves have managed to adapt to a harsh environment characterized by unstable, anaerobic sediments, fluctuating water levels, and waters with high concentrations of salt. They have accomplished this through evolutionary adaptations of their root systems, morphological and physiological mechanisms for maintaining salt balance, and reproductive dispersal strategies. Individual species and genera have evolved different solutions to the same problems.

Root Systems

Mangroves have adapted to life in highly anaerobic soils by developing shallow root systems and lacking a deep taproot (see Gill and Tomlinson [1971, 1977] and Tomlinson [1986] for reviews of anatomical features of mangrove roots). Some species, such as the red mangrove, have developed *prop roots* from the lower part of the stem and *drop roots* from branches and upper parts of the stem that extend only a few centimeters into the soil. The above-ground portion of these roots contains many small pores (*lenticels*) that allow oxygen to diffuse into the plant and down to the underground roots by means of air space tissues in the cortex called *aerenchyma* (Scholander et al., 1955). The lenticels are highly hydrophobic and prevent water penetration into the aerenchyma during high tide (Waisel, 1972).

A different strategy has been evolved by certain other species, such as the black mangrove. They have a system of cable roots, a few centimeters deep, which radiate outward for many meters from the stem base. Extending upward from the cable roots there may be erect aerial roots called pneumatophores. These contain lenticels and arenchyma for gas exchange and may extend as high as 20 to 30 cm above the soil—occasionally almost 1 m when the depth of flooding is great (A. E. Lugo, personal communication). Apparently because of the dense network of pneumatophores, the black mangrove has a greater ability to oxidize the reduced substrate surrounding its roots than does the red mangrove (Thibodeau and Nickerson, 1986).

The drop, prop, and cable roots produce anchoring and feeding types of associated roots (Dawes, 1981). The feeding roots are small, horizontal fibrous roots with plentiful root hairs; they occur at a shallow depth and function in absorption. The anchoring roots have a thick protective cork layer and may extend, though rarely, as deep as 1 m into the substrate (Zieman, 1972).

Other mangrove species have combinations and variations of these root systems. For example, the white mangrove usually does not have either prop roots or cable roots but uses lenticels in the lower trunk to satisfy the respiratory demand of the root system. "Peg roots" and pneumatophores are often present in poorly flushed or strongly reduced sediments (Jenik, 1967).

Unfortunately, the root structure that allows mangroves to thrive in anaerobic soils is also one of its most vulnerable points (Odum and Johannes, 1975). As will be discussed, the lenticels in the exposed portions of any of the aerial root systems are susceptible to clogging by fine suspended sediments (e.g., processed bauxite ore) and crude oil, attack by root borers, and prolonged flooding from artificial dikes or causeways. Extended stress on the aerial roots can kill the entire tree.

Maintenance of Salt Balance

Mangroves use a variety of mechanisms to offset fluctuations and extremes of water and soil salinity. Scholander et al. (1962) identified two major groups of species that used different methods of internal ion regulation: the salt exclusion species and the salt excretion species.

The salt exclusion species, including the red mangrove, separate fresh water from sea water at the root surface by means of a nonmetabolic ultrafiltration system (Scholander, 1968). This is a "reverse osmosis" process powered by high negative pressure in the xylem resulting from transpiration at the leaf surface. Sulfide is also excluded at mangrove root surfaces, sometimes leading to elevated pore water sulfide concentrations in poorly flushed sediments (Carlson and Yarbro, 1987).

Salt-excreting species, including the black and white mangroves and the buttonwood, use salt glands on the leaf surface to excrete excess salt (Fahn, 1979). This is probably an active transport process with a requirement for biochemical energy input (Atkinson et al., 1967). As a group, the salt excreters have sap salt concentrations approximately ten times higher than the salt excluders.

Most species of mangroves probably use a combination of salt exclusion and excretion (Albert, 1975). For example, most salt excreters, including the black and white mangroves, are capable of limited salt exclusion at the root surface. Additionally, all mangroves have a variety of xerophytic adaptations that further aid osmoregulation, including thickened, succulent leaves (Teas, 1979), a thick leaf cuticle, and sunken stomates confined to the lower leaf surface (Dawes, 1981). Finally, mangroves appear to have complex biochemical mechanisms of salt tolerance, including changes in stomatal responses (Ball and Farquhar, 1984), enzyme activation, protein synthesis, and other ways to alter osmotic relationships and ionic potentials across membranes (reviewed in Flowers et al., 1977).

In Florida, the red mangrove appears to be limited by soil salinities above 60 to 65 ppt (Cintrón et al., 1978). On the other hand, white and black mangroves may grow at salinities greater than 80 to 90 ppt (Macnae, 1968; Cintrón et al., 1978). Mangrove-free or bare sand flats in the center of mangrove ecosystems have been described by many authors (e.g., Davis, 1940; Fosberg, 1961). These features have been called *salinas, salterns, salt flats,* and *salt barrens.* They are usually found above mean high water and are only irregularly flushed with sea water. Evidently, they result from a combination of low seasonal rainfall, high ambient temperatures, high evaporation rates, and occasional inundation by sea water, creating high soil salinities, lowered buffering capacity, lowered pH, and mangrove death (Teas, 1979). Once established, salinas tend to persist unless tidal or rainfall flushing becomes reestablished.

Reproductive Dispersal Strategies

Mangroves have solved the problem of successful reproduction in the marine environment with two special adaptations (reviewed in Rabinowitz, 1978a): vivipary and dispersal of propagules by means of water (fig. 15.4). *Vivipary* means that the embryo initiates germination and begins development while still on the tree. This continuous development without intermediate resting stages makes the word *seed* inappropriate for mangroves; the term *propagule* is used instead. In general, mangrove species in the higher part of the intertidal zone (e.g., the white and black mangrove) have small propagules, and those in the lower part (e.g., the red mangrove) have large propagules. As will be discussed, this difference may have implications for intertidal mangrove species distribution and zonation.

Propagules of all three true mangrove species in Florida float and remain viable for extended periods of time. There is an obligate dispersal time (i.e., period during dispersal for germination to be completed). Rabinowitz (1978a) estimated the obligate dispersal period at approximately eight days for the white, fourteen days for the black, and forty days for the red mangrove. She further estimated the time for root establishment at five, seven, and fifteen days for white, black, and red mangroves, respectively. Her estimate for longevity of the propagule is 35 days for white and 110 days for black mangroves. Davis (1940) found viable red mangrove propagules that had been floating for more than twelve months.

This combination of viviparity and long-lived floating propagules allows mangroves to disperse over wide areas and to establish seedlings rapidly once an appropriate substrate and wave energy regime are encountered.

Fig. 15.4. Red mangrove seedling. Photo by Allan Horton.

Geographical Distribution

Statewide

Although not well documented, it is likely that short-term climatic fluctuations, on the order of decades and centuries, have caused the northern limits for the red and white mangroves to vary in Florida. For example, in 1962 and particularly during the late 1970s and early 1980s, a series of short-term intrusions of severe cold weather down the Florida peninsula resulted in widespread but uneven mortality of all mangrove species as far south as Naples on the Gulf coast and West Palm Beach on the Atlantic coast. Black mangroves, because of their ability to resprout from their root system, will continue to persist even on the northern edge of their range, where they occur in a more shrub-like form. Fully developed stands of red and white mangroves, however, probably tend to retreat farther south during these periods of more frequent incursions of severe cold.

Because of the fluctuating nature of the northern limits of mangrove species, it is difficult to give exact delineations of their ranges in Florida (fig. 15.5). Both the red and white mangrove have been reported as far north as Cedar Key on the west coast (Rehm, 1976) and north of the Ponce

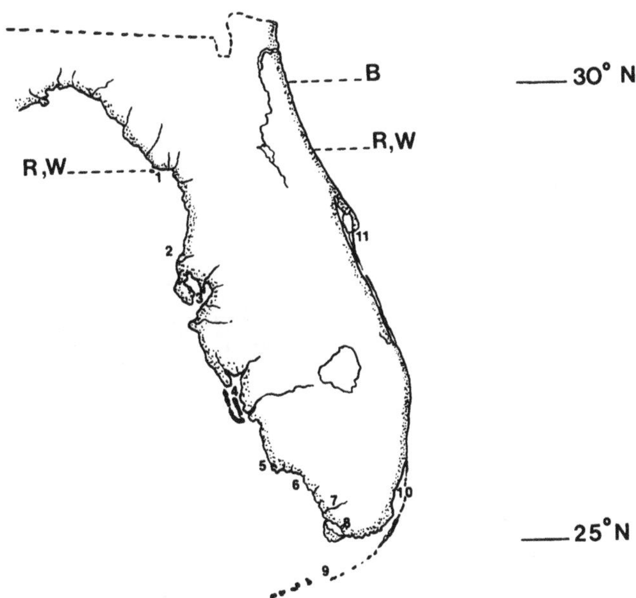

Fig. 15.5. Map of Florida showing distribution of mangrove species. From Odum et al., 1982.

de Leon Inlet on the east coast (Teas, 1977); both of these locations lie at approximately 29° 10' N latitude. Significant stands lie south of Cape Canaveral on the east coast and Tarpon Springs on the west coast. The black mangrove has been reported as far north as 30° N latitude on the east coast (Savage, 1972) and as scattered shrubs along the north coast of the Gulf of Mexico.

Areal Extent of Mangroves in Florida

Estimates of mangrove area vary due to difficulties interpreting aerial photography and limited "ground truth" observations. The National Wetlands Inventory in 1982 (from Lewis et al., 1985) estimated Florida mangrove area as 272,873 ha. Coastal Coordinating Council (1974) estimated a total of 189,725 ha of mangroves in the state. The expected margin of error was ± 15 percent. They further estimated that 90 percent of the mangrove area in Florida is located in the four southern counties of Lee (14,275 ha), Collier (29,126 ha), Monroe (94,810 ha), and Dade (32,931 ha).

Community Structure and Dynamics

Intertidal Distribution, Zonation, and Succession

In general, red and black mangroves are distributed relative to the intertidal zone as shown in figure 15.6. In this idealized scenario first hypothesized by Davis (1940), the red mangrove dominates the middle and lower portions of the intertidal and the upper subtidal zone, while the black mangrove predominates in the upper part of the intertidal zone and into the irregularly

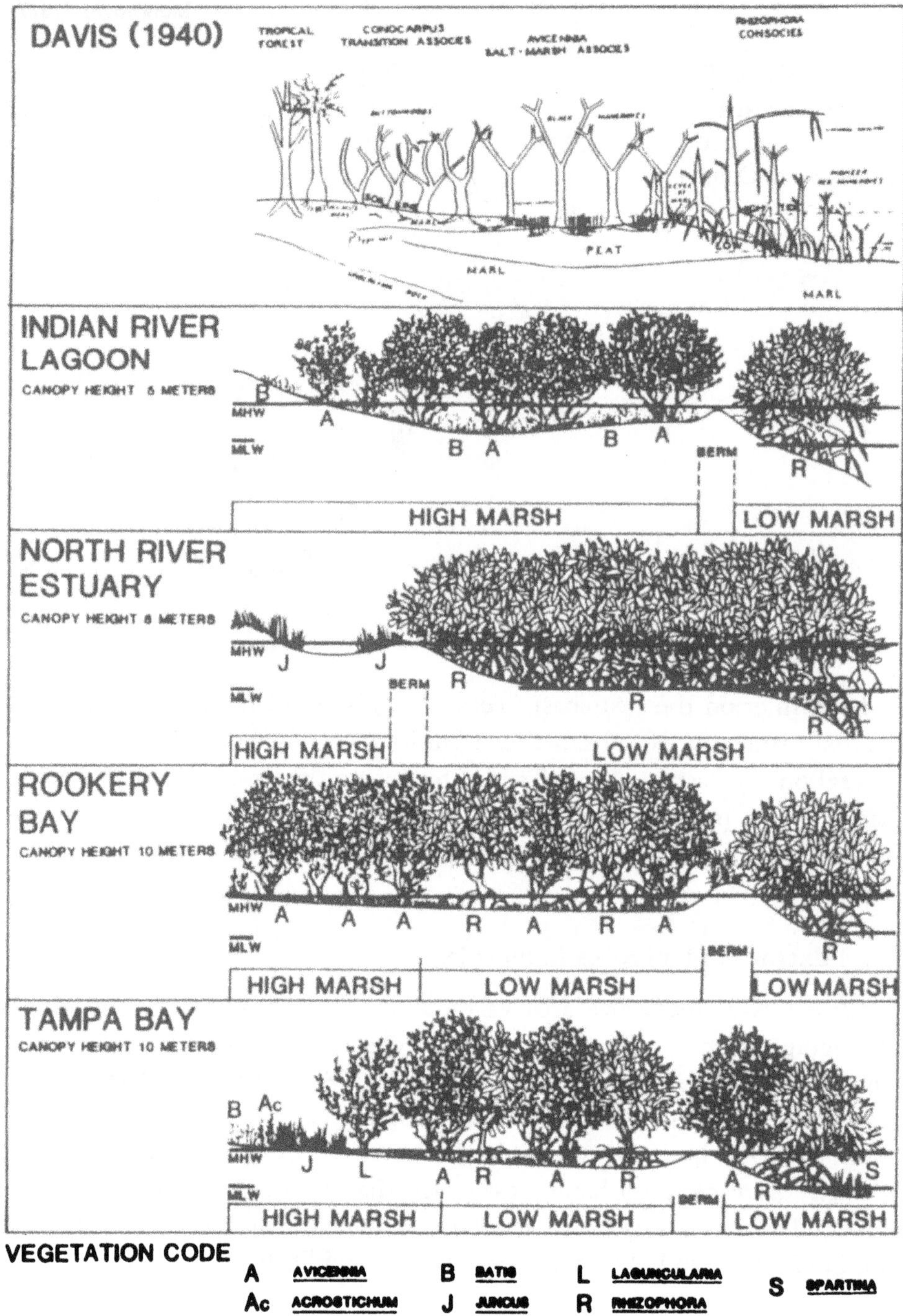

Fig. 15.6. Intertidal distribution of Florida mangroves. *Top diagram* depicts zonation as hypothesized by Davis (1940). *Lower diagrams* show variations at four specific sites (from Lewis et al., 1985). Note that the term *marsh* is incorrect; this should be low and high *swamp*.

flooded higher elevations. This distribution is similar to that in temperate marshes of smooth cordgrass (*Spartina alterniflora*) in the low marsh and salt marsh hay (*Spartina patens*) in the high marsh. The white mangrove typically is found in patches, often ones that have been created by lightning, storm, or human disturbance; it occurs throughout the intertidal zone, but predominantly in the irregularly flooded higher portions of the swamp (Ball, 1980). Buttonwood usually occurs at higher elevations than white mangrove, in areas of sand/strand vegetation (such as sea grape and sabal palm) (Tomlinson, 1986).

There are many variations and exceptions to this generalized description of the distribution of the mangrove species in Florida (fig. 15.6). Factors such as climate, differences in substrate type and wave energy, local variations in the subsidence rate of the land, and the effects of rising sea level can alter the classical pattern of Florida mangrove distribution. Moreover, the seasonal change in sea level (i.e., tendency for sea level to be higher in the fall than in the spring), which is typical in many areas of Florida (Provost, 1974), makes intertidal distribution even more complex. As a result, it is not uncommon at a specific location to find black mangrove as the outer fringe in the intertidal zone and red mangrove at higher elevations than black. In southeast Asia and parts of the Pacific, species of *Avicennia* may occur as the seaward fringe and species of *Rhizophora*, complete with prop roots, may dominate the higher elevations of the swamp.

Davis (1940), one of the first in Florida to describe the classical pattern of mangrove zonation, further suggested that mangrove zonation patterns were equivalent to seral stages of succession. In this interpretation, the red mangrove zone was the "pioneer stage," more landward zones dominated by black and white mangroves and buttonwood were regarded as more mature stages, and the adjacent tropical forest was the climatic climax. The entire mangrove ecosystem was hypothesized to be moving seaward through a process of sediment accumulation and colonization. This argument was based upon both zonation, as observed in the field, and sediment cores that showed red mangrove peat underlying black mangrove peat, which in turn occurred under terrestrial plant communities.

Subsequently, the pioneering work and hypotheses of Davis (1940) have been modified in the following ways. Egler (1952) and Thom (1967, 1975) argued that mangrove zonation was a response to external physical forces rather than a temporal sequence induced by the plants themselves. Spackman et al. (1966) emphasized the role of sea level change in determining changes in mangrove zonation, through both sea level rise and land subsidence. Lewis and Dunstan (1975) found that black and white mangroves are often the earliest colonizers of dredge spoil islands in central Florida. Cohen and Spackman (1984) suggested that the peat identification work of Davis (1940) may have been too simplistic in ignoring the complexities of peat formation. In particular, they question the existence of pure, identifiable black mangrove peat.

Rabinowitz (1975) provided a new perspective on the mangrove zonation debate. Using reciprocal planting experiments in Panamanian swamps with species of *Rhizophora, Laguncularia, Avicennia,* and *Pelliciera,* she demonstrated that each species could grow vigorously within any of the mangrove zones. This meant that physical and chemical factors, such as soil salinity, along with frequency and depth of inundation were not solely responsible for excluding species from that zone. Although her views were not widely accepted, she revived the hypothesis of tidal sorting of propagules based upon propagule size (Watson, 1928) as an important mechanism affecting zonation (Rabinowitz, 1978b).

T. J. Smith and coworkers (Smith, 1987b,c; Smith et al., 1989) have hypothesized that seed predators may influence intertidal distribution of mangroves. In Australia, Smith (1987b) found that heavy predation from grapsid crabs appears to limit the distribution of *Avicennia marina* to the upper and lower portions of the intertidal zone and to exclude this species from the midintertidal where seed predation is the highest. In south Florida, Smith et al. (1989) found heavy seed predation by the crab *Sesarma curacoaense*, along with the snails *Littorina angulifera* and *Melampus coffeus*, on the propagules of black mangrove but not on those of red mangrove.

Based on research of mangrove secondary succession patterns adjacent to Biscayne Bay, Ball (1980) made a compelling case for the importance of interspecific competition in zonation. She found that white mangrove grew best in intertidal areas but rarely occurred there in mature mangrove stands. Instead, white mangrove dominates higher, drier locations above mean high water where the red mangrove does not appear to have a competitive advantage. Central to Ball's argument is the differential influence of physical factors on the competitive abilities of the different mangrove species. In support of this hypothesis, Smith (1987a) has demonstrated the importance of light and intertidal position in mangrove seedling survival and growth.

Thibodeau and Nickerson (1986) added an interesting new twist to the understanding of mangrove zonation. Previously, Carlson et al. (1983) and Nickerson and Thibodeau (1985) had reported that the red mangrove tends to occur in areas with lower sulfide concentrations in substrate pore water and less severely reduced conditions than the black mangrove. Thibodeau and Nickerson (1986) demonstrated that the black mangrove has a much greater ability to oxidize anaerobic substrates in the vicinity of its roots than does the red mangrove. They suggest that the black mangrove has a competitive advantage in areas where strongly reducing substrates with high sulfide concentrations are present. According to their hypothesis, red mangrove occurs in areas that are well flushed by the tides, do not have strongly reduced peat deposits, and are flooded too deeply for the pneumatophores of black mangrove to function properly.

In summary, zonation of mangrove species does not appear to be controlled solely by physical and chemical factors but rather by the interplay of these factors with interspecific competition and, possibly, seed predation. Lugo (1980) has suggested that established mangrove ecosystems are steady-state cyclical or catastrophic climax (Odum, 1971) systems. This means that succession proceeds in response to periodic external perturbations rather than in the classicial biological fashion. External perturbations might include incursions of freezing temperatures, hurricanes, periodic droughts causing unusually high soil salinities (Cintrón et al., 1978) or sulfide concentrations (Carlson et al., 1983), or fire spreading into mangrove forests from terrestrial sources and lightning strikes. Such fires can produce a mosaic of regenerating patches (Taylor, 1980, 1981) within a mature stand.

Land Building

Davis (1940) introduced the concept of mangrove forests actively extending seaward through a process of sediment accumulation around the root systems, elevation of the soil surface, and seaward colonization. Although replaced by subsequent hypotheses, the idea of mangroves as "land builders" or "walking trees" has persisted, particularly in the popular press.

Both Egler (1952) and Spackman et al. (1966), along with Wanless (1974), Carlton (1974), and Thom (1967, 1975, 1982), have suggested and demonstrated that mangroves react passively rather than actively to strong physical processes. Geomorphological, sedimentary, and hydrological processes, and particularly changes in relative sea level (Thom, 1975), appear to be the dominant forces in determining whether mangrove shorelines recede or grow. The role of mangroves is to stabilize sediments deposited by physical processes, so mangroves should be regarded as "land stabilizers" rather than "land builders" (fig. 15.7).

Community Types—A Hydrologic Continuum

Mangrove forests in Florida vary tremendously in their structural appearance. For example, mature red and black mangrove trees along the Shark River are 20 m tall and extremely dense. In contrast, the dwarf scrub forests that grow on marl prairies in southeast Florida have scattered trees rarely exceeding 1.5 m in height, even though many of the trees are more than fifty years old.

Lugo and Snedaker (1974) proposed a classification system consisting of six types of mangrove communities arranged along a continuum of hydrologic flushing. While generally based on physiognomic differences under different environmental conditions, this system could also be related to functional attributes, such as primary production and movement of nutrients. More recently, Lugo and Snedaker's (1974) system has been simplified to

Fig. 15.7. Red mangroves and oysters stabilizing sediments. Photo by R. Myers.

three major mangrove community types (Cintrón et al., 1985; Lugo et al., 1989).

Riverine forests occur along tidal rivers and creeks and receive the greatest amount of tidal flushing and freshwater runoff of nutrients from terrestrial ecosystems. The trees may exceed 20 m in height, have high rates of primary production, and export considerable quantities of dissolved and particulate carbon. Zonation of mangrove species may be very complex.

Fringing forests usually form a relatively thin fringe along waterways and embayments; mangrove islands occurring in bays and along the Florida Keys are included in this category. Typically, fringing forests are flushed by tidal waters but do not receive as much runoff of terrestrial nutrients as riverine forests. Zonation is often as described by Davis (1940). Primary production and carbon export are typically lower than in riverine forests and trees rarely exceed 10 m.

Basin forests occur inland from the fringing and riverine forests. They may take a variety of forms, including forests in depressions channeling terrestrial runoff, hammock forests on slightly raised platforms, and dwarf scrub forests on marl substrates. Tidal flushing of these forests can be infrequent but fairly predictable, with those nearest the coast receiving regular flooding and those farthest inland flooded only by storm tides or precipitation runoff. Export of carbon appears to be largely dissolved (Lugo et al., 1980; Twilley, 1985); primary production and nutrient movements vary considerably between the different types of basin forests.

While the simpler categorization of Florida mangrove forests into three physiognomic types has shortcomings and pitfalls, it does provide a convenient basis for comparing various ecosystem functions. The following sections will discuss functions such as primary production, litter fall, and movement of elements using the riverine-fringing-basin hydrologic continuum.

Forest Structure, Primary Production, and Peat Formation

Biomass Partitioning

Little is known about relative biomass distribution in mangrove trees, partly because of the difficulty in retrieving and weighing fine root material. This problem is confounded by the apparent high variation among different types of mangrove communities (e.g., basin/scrub forests versus riverine forests) and forests of different ages.

In one of the few studies of mangrove biomass partitioning, Lugo et al. (1976) reported values for a fringing forest in south Florida (values are in dry grams per square meter plus or minus one standard error): 710 ± 22 g/m^2 of leaves, 12.8 ± 15.3 g/m^2 of propagules, 7043 ± 7 g/m^2 of wood, 4695 ± 711 g/m^2 of prop roots, and 1565 ± 234 g/m^2 of detritus on the forest floor. Golley et al. (1962) studied a smaller-stature Puerto Rican red mangrove fringing forest and found 778 g/m^2 of leaves, 4070 g/m^2 of branches and trunk, and 1437 g/m^2 of prop roots. In addition, they estimated root biomass (excluding fine roots) as 4997 g/m^2. Inclusion of these fine living roots would probably mean that below-ground biomass exceeded above-ground biomass.

At present, there are not enough data to draw many conclusions concerning biomass distribution in mangrove forests, except that it must be highly variable from one site to the next. One preliminary observation is that red mangrove leaf biomass appears to be fairly constant (700–800 g/m^2) in most forest types except scrub forests (Odum and Heald, 1975b). This may be related to self-shading of leaves lower in the canopy of mature forests.

Vertical Structure

Golley et al. (1962) have shown that red mangrove canopies are extremely efficient interceptors of light. They found that 95 percent of available light was intercepted within the first four meters below the top of the canopy. Not surprisingly, 90 percent of the leaf biomass was found in the upper four meters of the canopy.

The leaf area index (LAI) of mangrove forests appears to be relatively low, with values ranging from 1 to 5 m^2/m^2 (Pool et al., 1977; Odum et al., 1982). The model developed by Miller (1972) suggests an optimum LAI of 2.5 for red mangrove canopy photosynthesis in south Florida. This amount compares to typical values for most tropical forests of 10–20 m^2/m^2 (Golley et al., 1975). Presumably, the low values in mangrove forests result from a combination of factors including limitation of leaf area by physiological stresses placed on wetland plants, efficient light interception at the top of the canopy, and the usual lack of an understory (Odum et al., 1982). Janzen (1985) and Lugo (1986) discuss some of the hypotheses explaining why a highly developed understory has not evolved in most mangrove forests (shading, salt stress, etc.). Corlett (1986) notes that in certain situations there may be a modest understory present, particularly on the landward side of the forest.

Primary Production

Productivity estimates for mangroves come from four methods: harvest of trees of known age, changes in tree diameter, litter fall, and gas exchange. Estimates of mangrove productivity vary widely and are affected by a host of factors, including nutrient availability, degree of salt stress, and amount of tidal flushing (Clough and Attiwill, 1982). The literature dealing with primary production of Florida mangroves can be summarized as follows.

Although there is some controversy concerning this point (Tomlinson, 1986), mangroves generally appear to have low transpiration rates (Waisel, 1972). Lugo et al. (1975) reported transpiration rates of 2500 g H_2O m^{-2} day^{-1} for a fringing red mangrove forest and 1482 g H_2O m^{-2} day^{-1} for a basin black mangrove forest. These values are approximately one-third to one-half the value found in temperate broad-leaved forests but comparable to those of tropical rain forests (Odum and Jordan, 1970). Low transpiration rates of mangroves are probably linked to the energetic costs of maintaining sap pressures of −35 to −60 atmospheres (Scholander et al., 1965).

Litter fall (leaves, twigs, bark, fruit, and flowers) of Florida mangroves averages 2 to 3 dry g m^{-2} day^{-1} in most well-developed stands of mangroves (Odum et al., 1982).

Gross primary production ranges from about 3 to 24 g C m^{-2} day^{-1} and net primary production from 1 to 12 g C m^{-2} day^{-1} (Miller, 1972; Carter et al., 1973; Lugo and Snedaker, 1974; Hicks and Burns, 1975; Lugo et al., 1976; Teas, 1979). This amount of production places mangrove ecosystems among the most productive in the world.

In general, red mangroves are the highest net producers, black mangroves are intermediate, and white mangroves are the lowest (Lugo et al., 1975). This generalization assumes that the plants occur within the zone for which they are best adapted and are not existing in an area with extreme limiting factors.

Black mangroves tend to have higher respiration rates than red mangroves and, therefore, lower net productivity (conclusion from the data of Miller, 1972; Carter et al., 1973; Lugo and Snedaker, 1974; Hicks and Burns, 1975). These higher rates probably result from the greater salinity stress under which black mangroves normally exist.

Carter et al. (1973) and Lugo et al. (1976) have proposed that an inverted U-shaped relationship exists between mangrove net production and position along a hydrologic gradient. At the upland, freshwater end of the gradient, mangroves are limited by competition with freshwater macrophytes, even though nutrient inputs from the terrestrial environment may be high. At the seaward end of the gradient, salinity stress limits net primary production in spite of high gross primary production. The highest net production was hypothesized to occur in the middle, where moderate nutrient levels and tidal flushing enhance productivity and salinity is high enough to reduce competition but not to become a severe stress. This remains only a general hypothesis, since many other local factors can influence net production.

As mentioned earlier, Thibodeau and Nickerson (1986) have hypothesized that black mangroves are better at oxygenating highly reduced substrates than are red mangroves. Not only might this explain the prevalence of black mangrove in areas of highly reduced substrates, but it may also explain apparent lowered net production in older stands of red mangrove growing on peat with strong reducing conditions.

Peat Formation

As previously emphasized, mangroves can grow on a wide variety of substrates, ranging from fine mud to sand and peat. Where mangroves persist for some time in low wave energy, depositional environments, they may modify the underlying substrate through peat formation. Peat deposits in Florida have been described by Davis (1940, 1943, 1946), Egler (1952), Craighead (1964), Cohen and Spackman (1984), and others.

Red mangrove produces the most easily recognized peat. Recent deposits are spongy, fibrous, and composed largely of fine rootlets (0.2–3.0 mm in diameter). Other components include larger pieces of roots, bits of wood and leaves, and inorganic materials, such as pyrite, carbonate minerals, and quartz. Older deposits become less differentiated though still somewhat fibrous. The pore water within mangrove peat is often acidic (Zieman, 1972, measured a pH range of 4.9–6.8), though presence of carbonate materials can raise the pH above 7.0. In addition, mangrove peat pore water is almost always anaerobic; Lee (1969) recorded Eh values of −100 to −400 mv.

When drained, dried, and aerated, mangrove soils and peats usually undergo a dramatic increase in acidity (pH 3.5–5.0 in pore water when reflooded) due to oxidation of reduced sulfur compounds. This fact greatly complicates their conversion to agricultural land (Macnae, 1968).

Movements of Nutrients and Carbon

Nutrient Flux

Many mangrove ecosystems, like many tidal wetlands (Mitsch and Gosselink, 1986), probably tend to act as *sinks* (net accumulators) for a variety of elements, including nitrogen, phosphorus, trace elements, and heavy metals. These are intercepted and sequestered from the water flowing through mangrove stands by the concerted actions of mangrove prop roots, prop root algae, the associated sediments, fallen mangrove litter, the fine root system of the mangrove trees, and a variety of invertebrates (such as oysters), as well as microorganisms attached to all of these surfaces. Although turnover times for these elements probably vary widely among different types of mangrove ecosystems, elements may be stored in wood, sediments, and peat for many years.

Although mangrove ecosystems tend to accumulate nutrients, they also have a continual loss through export of gaseous, dissolved, and particulate forms from processes such as denitrification and flushing by heavy rains and tidal action. Theoretically, unless imports of nutrients exceed exports, both nutrient storage and primary production will be low (Lugo et al., 1976). This is presumably the case with scrub basin forests, which apparently have limited nutrient inputs (though other biogeochemical factors may be involved, such as pH-related nutrient unavailability). Lugo et al. (1976) further hypothesize, based on a simulation model, that if inputs of nutrients to mangrove ecosystems are reduced, nutrient storage levels within the system will be reduced, as will primary production.

Carter et al. (1973) and Snedaker and Lugo (1973) have hypothesized that major nutrient inputs for mangroves come from upland, terrestrial sources. Not surprisingly, many of the most productive and luxuriant mangrove forests in Florida occur in riverine locations or adjacent to significant upland drainage. A variety of authors (summarized in Twilley et al., 1986) have further suggested that mangrove ecosystems with greater tidal activity and water turnover generally are more productive than mangroves in stagnant areas, presumably because of the greater input of nutrients. Finally, localized sources of nutrients, such as bird rookeries, can result in greater nutrient storage and higher mangrove productivity (Onuf et al., 1977).

To summarize, the net flux of nutrients in a mangrove ecosystem depends on position relative to terrestrial nutrient sources and localized sources such as rookeries and on the amount of tidal flushing. Factors internal to the ecosystem, however, may also play an important role, among them nitrogen fixation and nutrient-recycling mechanisms.

Nitrogen fixation apparently occurs in Florida mangrove stands at a rate comparable to other shallow tropical waters (Gotto and Taylor, 1976; Zuberer and Silver, 1978; Gotto et al., 1981). Because the process appears to be limited by the availability of labile carbon compounds, the highest rates have been measured in association with decaying mangrove leaves. Zuberer and Silver (1978) have speculated that the nitrogen fixation rates observed in Florida mangrove swamps may be sufficient to supply a significant portion of the mangrove's growth requirements. If this is the case, it might explain why moderately productive mangrove stands occur in waters that are severely depleted in nitrogen.

It has been suspected that mangrove ecosystems with low nutrient inputs might have more efficient internal recycling mechanisms than ecosystems with large nutrient inputs. Twilley et al. (1986) compared nitrogen recycling among riverine, fringing, and basin forests. Inland basin forests, which have the lowest inputs of nitrogen, had relatively low recycling efficiency in litter fall but made up for it with a higher internal recycling of nitrogen in litter on the forest floor, due in part to longer litter residence time on the forest floor and nitrogen immobilization during litter decomposition and peat deposition.

Our understanding of nutrient fluxes and mangrove ecosystems remains incomplete. While external nutrient sources clearly affect nutrient storage (and primary productivity) within mangrove ecosystems, internal mechanisms may partially offset the limiting effects of low nutrient inputs.

Carbon Flux

Litter Fall

Litter fall is one of the major inputs of organic carbon to consumers in mangrove ecosystems (Odum, 1970). We define *litter* as including leaves, wood (twigs and small branches), leaf scales, propagules, bracts, flowers, and insect frass that fall from the tree. Inputs of larger pieces of wood such as large branches, prop roots, and trunks have not been adequately estimated in Florida mangrove swamps. Depending on the site, litter fall can be partitioned roughly into 68–86 percent leaves, 3–15 percent twigs, and 8–21 percent miscellaneous (Pool et al., 1975). Litter fall in Florida mangrove swamps is continuous throughout the year, with minor peaks before the beginning of the summer wet season and after periods of stress (Heald, 1969; Pool et al., 1975; Twilley et al., 1986).

The first estimate of litter fall in Florida mangrove swamps was made by E. J. Heald and W. E. Odum (Heald, 1969; Odum, 1970; Odum and Heald, 1975b). They estimated that litter fall in a fringing swamp averaged 2.4 dry g m^{-2} day^{-1} (or 876 g m^{-2} yr^{-1} or 8.8 metric tons ha^{-1} yr^{-1}). Subsequent estimates have been similar but with considerable variation depending on site characteristics. Twilley et al. (1986) reviewed most of the available literature and found these averages (in metric tons ha^{-1} yr^{-1}): scrub basin forests = 1.86 ± 0.55, basin forests = 6.61 ± 0.70, fringing forests = 9.00 ± 0.72, and riverine forests = 12.98 ± 1.01. As a rule, black mangroves have rates of litter fall about one-half (1.0–1.5 g m^{-2} day^{-1}) those of red mangroves (2.0–3.0 g/m^2/day) (Lugo et al., 1980). In Australia, Bunt (1982) found a negative relationship between litter fall and topographic height above mean sea level; highest rates were in the intertidal zone.

Decomposition

Decomposition rates of mangrove leaves in Florida have been reported by a number of investigators (Heald, 1969; Odum, 1970; Odum and Heald,

1975b; Pool et al., 1975; Lugo and Snedaker, 1975; Twilley, 1982; Twilley et al., 1986). In general, black mangrove leaves decompose more rapidly than red mangrove leaves (Heald et al., 1979; Lugo et al., 1980; Twilley et al., 1986). Pool et al. (1975) and Flores-Verdugo et al. (1987) have found that mangrove litter decomposes and is exported most rapidly from frequently flooded riverine and fringing forests. Systems, such as basin forests, that are not as well flushed by the tides have slower rates of decomposition and lower export rates.

Heald (1969) and Odum (1970) showed that decomposition of red mangrove leaves proceeds most rapidly under marine conditions, somewhat more slowly in fresh water, and very slowly on dry substrates. They also found relative increases in nitrogen, protein, and caloric content as mangrove leaves progressively decayed. Fell and Master (1973), Fell et al. (1980), Fell and Newell (1980), and Fell (1980) have provided extensive information on decomposition, the role of fungi in decomposition, and nitrogen changes and nitrogen immobilization during decomposition.

Other Carbon Sources

Additional significant sources of net primary production in Florida mangrove ecosystems are prop root algae, algae on the mud surface, phytoplankton in the water column, and associated vascular plants. Rehm (1974) has described the characteristic association of algae on Florida mangrove prop roots. Of seventy-four species of marine algae recorded as prop root epiphytes between Tampa and Key Largo, thirty-eight were Rhodophyta; twenty-nine, Chlorophyta; four, Phaenophyta; and three, Cyanophyta. Lugo et al. (1975) found a prop root community's net primary production rate in a well-lighted area to be 1.1 g C m^{-2} day^{-1}, a level comparable to leaf fall. Production of this magnitude occurs only on the edge of the forest and is much lower in the dark center of the swamp.

The mud adjacent to mangroves is often heavily populated with green and blue-green algae (Marathe, 1965) and many species of benthic diatoms and dinoflagellates (Wood, 1965). Production of benthic algae may be appreciable and important to secondary production (Cooksey et al., 1975).

Phytoplankton production from tidal creeks and other waters within Florida mangrove swamps is poorly studied. Wood (1965) found that the net plankton is usually dominated by diatoms (including benthic forms if turbulence is high), though blooms of dinoflagellates may be important at times. Studies of nannoplankton and total phytoplankton productivity are needed.

Many vascular plants are associated with mangrove swamps, but their relative importance in terms of productivity is both variable and poorly understood. All of the Florida sea grasses are present in adjacent submerged bottoms (see Zieman [1982] and Zieman et al. [1984] for reviews of possible energy linkages with mangrove systems). Within the mangrove swamps there may be marsh areas (Carter et al., 1973; Olmsted et al., 1981). In addition, a variety of other vascular plants occur in a spotty fashion on the landward edge of the swamp (reviewed in Carter et al., 1973).

While definitive data are lacking, we hypothesize that the productivity of sea grasses and phytoplankton is probably highly significant in many Florida mangrove ecosystems. Productivity of prop root and mud algae is probably less significant but still important. The other associated vascular plants are probably of little importance except in areas where the area of marsh plants is appreciable.

Carbon Export

Estimation of the movement of dissolved and particulate carbon from tidal wetlands into nearby bodies of water has proven to be an extremely difficult undertaking (see reviews in Odum et al. [1979] and Nixon [1980]). In spite of these difficulties, a number of carbon import/export studies have been conducted in mangrove ecosystems, and the results appear reasonably consistent. Unfortunately, dissolved organic carbon fluxes were not estimated in most of these studies.

In this discussion, *export* refers to the movement of mangrove carbon from immediately under the tree into nearby tidal creeks, rivers, and embayments. Not unexpectedly, Florida basin forests—which are the most isolated from tidal flooding—have the lowest estimated carbon export rates, ranging from 0.15 to 0.18 g m^{-2} day^{-1} of organic matter (Twilley et al., 1986). Fringing forests have been estimated to export between 0.5 and 0.7 g m^{-2} day^{-1} (Pool et al., 1975; Odum and Heald, 1975b; Lugo and Snedaker, 1975). Estimates from riverine forests range from 1.2 to 2.7 g m^{-2} day^{-1} (Boto and Bunt, 1981; Flores-Verdugo et al., 1987). The high estimate of 2.7 g m^{-2} day^{-1} comes from a Mexican coastal lagoon with an ephemeral inlet and a strong seasonal pulse of freshwater scouring and flooding during the rainy season; this figure represents 90 percent of the estimated annual litter fall (Flores-Verdugo et al., 1987).

It seems certain that large mangrove ecosystems typically export quantities of organic carbon into contiguous bodies of water and even many miles offshore. Because most studies have omitted dissolved organic fluxes (Twilley, 1985, is an exception), bedload transport of particulate material, and fluxes during storm events, most of the quoted rates are probably significant underestimates.

Secondary Production

While there is general agreement that mangrove ecosystems export appreciable quantities of organic carbon, at least over short distances, there remains much uncertainty concerning the importance of this material in secondary production of invertebrates, fishes, birds, and so forth. Odum (1970) and Odum and Heald (1972, 1975a) hypothesized that mangrove carbon (leaf, propagule, and wood tissues) may contribute to detritus-based food webs in adjacent coastal waters. They also emphasized the importance of other sources of carbon, such as sea grass, phytoplankton, and benthic microalgae, and pointed out that, like most coastal food webs, those in mangrove ecosystems are probably fueled by a variety of carbon sources. In later publications (Odum et al., 1979, 1982), emphasis was placed on the ratio of mangrove area to open water area (fig. 15.8). In regions that have large expanses of mangroves and relatively little surface water (such as the Shark River valley of southwest Florida), mangrove detritus could be the most important source of organic carbon. In areas with expanses of open water and a fringe of mangrove forests, such as around south Biscayne Bay, algae, sea grasses, and phytoplankton should be the dominant carbon source. While these hypotheses have existed for more than fifteen years, good data concerning secondary production and energy flow in mangrove ecosystems are limited.

Thayer et al. (1987) have quantitatively documented the habitat value of the red mangrove prop root environment for a variety of fishes and invertebrates. Their data and the data of Robertson and Duke (1987) suggest that the prop root habitat may be equally or more important to juveniles than are sea grass beds, on a comparable area basis. Other information detailing the habitat value of mangrove ecosystems to fishery organisms has been reviewed by Lewis et al. (1985) (see fig. 15.9 for an example).

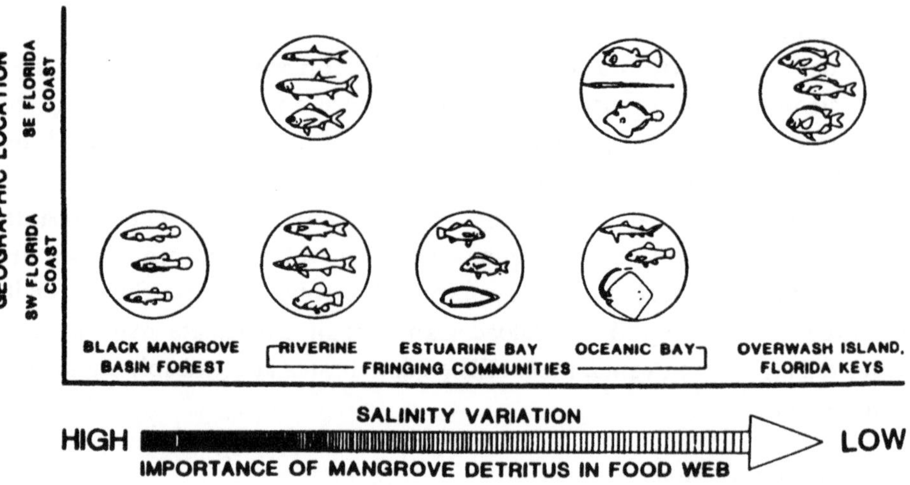

Fig. 15.8. Gradient of mangrove-associated fish communities, showing the theoretical importance of mangrove detritus in food webs. The axis of salinity variation/detritus importance is positively correlated with terrestrial freshwater runoff. Modified from Odum et al., 1982, by Lewis et al., 1985.

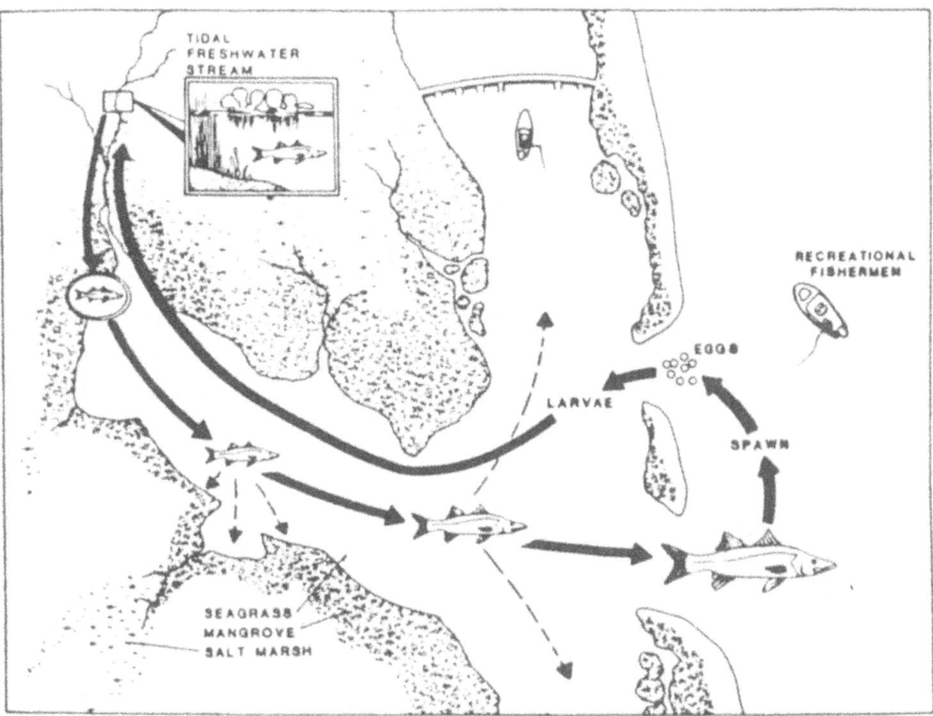

Fig. 15.9. Summary of the life history and habitat relationships of the snook (*Centropomus undecimalis*), which uses mangrove habitat as a juvenile. From Lewis et al., 1985.

Recently, stable isotope ratios have been used to trace the fate of organic carbon in mangrove ecosystems. Rodelli et al. (1984) found that several commercially important species of bivalves, shrimp, crabs, and fishes in a Malaysian mangrove swamp appeared to obtain most of their carbon from mangrove trees. Zieman et al. (1984) and J. C. Zieman (personal communication) found that the stable carbon signal for the pink shrimp (*Penaeus duorarum*) in the upper portions of Rookery Bay, Florida, was close to values for mangrove carbon. The same organism sampled from the grass beds of the lower Florida Keys had carbon signatures close to those for sea grass carbon.

Benner et al. (1986) have shown that dissolved organic matter from red mangrove leaves is readily utilized by the microbial community. They found an overall efficiency of conversion of mangrove leachate into microbial biomass of 64–94 percent. Camilleri and Ribi (1986) have demonstrated that dissolved organic carbon (DOC) originating from mangrove leaves forms flakes of particulate matter that are subsequently consumed by crustaceans, such as copepods, shrimp, amphipods, and crabs. The data from both of these papers support the hypothesis discussed by Odum (1970), Odum and Heald (1975a), Lugo et al. (1980), and Snedaker (1989) that dissolved organic matter from mangroves might be a significant carbon source for higher consumers.

On a different note, Alongi (1987) presents evidence that hydrolyzable tannins leached from mangrove leaves may have a negative influence on meiobenthos in mangrove forest sediments. This finding suggests that mangrove forest-derived DOC may play a complex, multiple role—as inhibitor and food source—in benthic communities.

Currently, details concerning the link between mangrove primary production and secondary production in surrounding waters remains largely hypothetical and little tested. Future research using multiple stable isotopes (carbon, nitrogen, sulfur) as tracers should greatly increase knowledge in this area.

Associated Fauna

Mangrove forests and associated waters provide valuable habitat for a wide range of invertebrates, fishes, amphibians, reptiles, birds, and mammals in Florida. Odum et al. (1982) reviewed the scattered literature dealing with mangrove habitat utilization and found numbers of species reported from Florida mangrove ecosystems: 220 species of fishes; 24 species of reptiles and amphibians, including turtles, snakes (fig. 15.10), lizards, and frogs; 18 species of mammals, including the raccoon (*Procyon lotor*), mink (*Mustela*

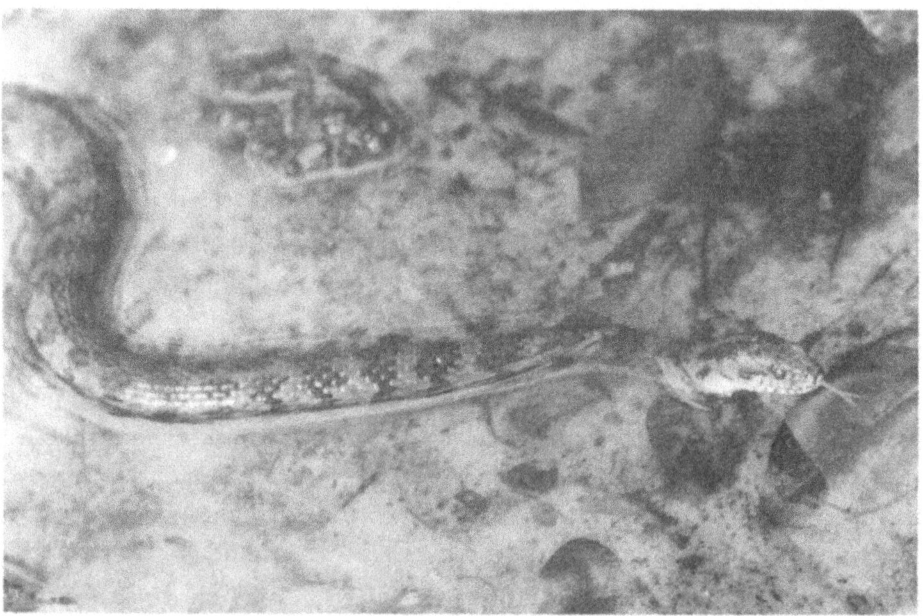

Fig. 15.10. Mangrove water snake (*Nerodia fasciata compressicauda*), Snead Island mangroves, Manatee County. Photo by Allan Horton.

vison), river otter (*Lutra canadensis*), black bear (*Ursus americanus*), and striped skunk (*Mephitis mephitis*); and 181 bird species (guilds include 18 wading birds, 25 probing shore birds, 29 floating and diving water birds [fig. 15.11], 14 aerially searching birds, 20 birds of prey, and 71 arboreal birds). Complete lists of invertebrates that utilize mangrove swamps are not available, but limited descriptions are given by Kaplan (1988) and Odum et al. (1982).

Human Use and Impact

Values

Mangrove ecosystems provide a variety of services that are of value to human society. They are able to stabilize intertidal sediments in depositional environments but not where strong erosional forces exist (Egler, 1952; Gill, 1970; Thom, 1975; Savage, 1972). This function lets them provide shoreline protection and be used to stabilize dredge spoil in suitable locations (Lewis and Dunstan, 1975). Although not well documented, it appears that thick

Fig. 15.11. Brown pelican (*Pelicanus occidentalis*) rookery, Ten Thousand Islands, Collier County. Photo by Lovett Williams. Courtesy of Florida Game and Fresh Water Fish Commission.

stands of fringing mangroves offer some protection on their landward edge from hurricane-generated waves (Fosberg, 1971).

Currently, there is a controversy in Florida concerning the ability of fringing mangroves to intercept nutrient runoff from upland areas. The operational hypothesis suggests that nutrient concentrations in shallow groundwater (less than 1.0 m) may be reduced significantly while passing through stands of mangroves. Processes responsible for this reduction could include nutrient uptake by the mangroves, adsorption onto mangrove swamp sediments, and possibly denitrification, if a suitable aerobic/anaerobic transition zone exists in the sediments. At this point, suitable evidence to test the hypothesis is lacking, though the implications for regulatory agencies and other types of management activities are considerable.

As mentioned earlier, mangrove ecosystems provide valuable habitat for a wide range of animals. Included are seven species and four subspecies listed by the U.S. Fish and Wildlife Service as endangered (E), threatened (T), or of concern (C): American crocodile (*Crocodylus acutus*, E), hawksbill sea turtle (*Eretmochelys imbricata*, E), Atlantic ridley sea turtle (*Lepidochelys kempi*, E), Florida manatee (*Trichechus manatus*, E), bald eagle (*Haliaeetus leucocephalus*, E), American peregrine (*Falco peregrinus*, T), brown pelican (*Pelicanus occidentalis*, C), Key deer (*Odocoileus virginianus clavium*, E), Florida panther (*Felis concolor coryi*, E), Atlantic salt marsh snake (*Nerodia fasciata taeniata*, T), and eastern indigo snake (*Drymarchon corais couperi*, T).

Mangroves can also be important nursery areas for sport and commercial fishes and invertebrates, such as the spiny lobster (*Panulirus argus*), pink shrimp (*Penaeus duorarum*), mullet (*Mugil cephalus*), tarpon (*Megalops atlanticus*), snook (*Centropomus undecimalis*), and mangrove snapper (*Lutjanus apodus*) (Heald and Odum, 1970; Lewis et al., 1985). Finally, many wading birds nest and roost in mangroves, such as the wood stork (*Mycteria americana*), white ibis (*Eudocimus albus*), roseate spoonbill (*Ajaia ajaja*), cormorant (*Phalacrocorax* spp.), pelicans (*Pelicanus* spp.), egrets, and herons.

The critical value of mangrove systems as nursery habitats for fishes and invertebrates is well established (see review by Lewis et al., 1985). Both sport and commercial fisheries decline when mangrove ecosystems are destroyed.

One of the greatest values of mangrove swamps in Florida is their aesthetic appeal. Although not everyone views mangrove swamps as beautiful, the fact remains that in heavily settled urban areas, such as Dade County and around Tampa Bay, mangrove-dominated areas are virtually the only near-pristine habitat remaining. Moreover, the huge mangrove belt along the seaward edge of the Everglades forms part of the most significant wilderness in this area of the United States. Because of their unaltered status and because they offer refuge to organisms as diverse as white ibis and tarpon, the value to humans of mangrove ecosystems in an increasingly urbanized landscape grows greater every year.

Effects of Pollution

Two factors render mangroves susceptible to certain types of pollutants. First, because they are growing under metabolically stressful conditions, any factor that further stresses the tree may be potentially fatal. Second, their modified root systems with lenticels and pneumatophores are especially vulnerable to clogging (Odum and Johannes, 1975).

Petroleum and its by-products pose a particularly serious threat to mangroves. Crude oil kills mangroves by coating and clogging pneumatophores; severe metabolic alterations occur when petroleum is absorbed by lipophylic substances on mangrove surfaces (Baker, 1971). Both Lewis (1980) and de la Cruz (1982) present reviews of the effects of oil spills in mangrove ecosystems.

As was discovered in South Vietnam, many species of mangroves are highly susceptible to herbicides. At least 100,000 ha of mangroves were defoliated and killed by the U.S. military (Walsh et al., 1973). In Florida, Teas and Kelly (1975) reported that black mangroves are somewhat resistant to most herbicides but that red mangroves are extremely sensitive. They hypothesized that this vulnerability is related to the small reserves of leaf buds in the red mangrove.

Although mangroves are not negatively affected by highly eutrophic waters, they can be killed by heavy suspended loads of fine, flocculent material. These can come from untreated sugarcane wastes, pulp mill effluent, and ground bauxite and other ore wastes (Odum and Johannes, 1975).

Other Destructive Alterations

In Florida it is likely that more mangroves have been killed by diking, impounding, and permanent flooding of the aerial root system than by any other activity except, perhaps, outright destruction through dredge and fill. Any activity that covers the root systems with water or mud for a long period will kill the trees by preventing oxygen transport to the deeper roots (Odum and Johannes, 1975; Patterson-Zucca, 1978; Lugo, 1981). Restriction of tidal circulation with causeways and undersized culverts can also damage stands of mangroves, particularly if salinities are lowered sufficiently to allow freshwater vegetation to flourish.

Mitigation Techniques

In situations where mangroves do not exist or have been destroyed, they can be replanted or replaced in suitable alternate areas through mitigation procedures. This was done in Florida as early as 1917 to protect the right-of-way of the overseas railway in the Florida Keys (Teas, 1977). Lewis (1982b) provides a useful review of the extensive literature on planting and mitigation techniques for mangroves.

In comparison to the red mangrove, the black mangrove is easier to transplant as a seedling. In addition, it establishes its pneumatophore system rapidly, has an underground root system that is better adapted to holding sediments, is more cold-hardy, and can better tolerate "artificial" substrates such as dredge spoil (Teas, 1977). Transplants do best when planted in the intertidal zone where wave energy is not too great (Teas, 1977). Mitigation practices are widespread in Florida, and several private firms specialize in transplanting mangroves.

Effect of Rising Sea Level

Over the past few centuries, the relative sea level appears to have been rising at a rate of 10–15 cm a century along the east coast of North America (Aubrey and Emery, 1983). Most scientists feel that this rate will probably accelerate significantly in the near future, as a result of either global warming (and ice cap melting) or groundwater withdrawal. Recent estimates have been as great as a meter or more a century (Hoffman, 1984).

At this point, any discussion of the effect of accelerated sea level rise on mangrove ecosystems in Florida remains speculative. It is likely that mangroves can keep pace with relatively high rates of sea level rise if sedimentation rates are high. Since sedimentation rates are highly variable in different locations in Florida, some areas will probably keep pace with sea level rise and some will become inundated. In the latter case, if the shore gradient is low—as occurs along the lower southwest coast of Florida—mangrove swamps will simply "roll over" in an inland direction. The result will be steady or even increased mangrove area. In other locations, where a steeper terrestrial gradient exists or there is no low-lying land for inland expansion, mangrove area will shrink. It is possible, given different scenarios of sea level rise, to simulate anticipated changes in areas of mangrove and other intertidal wetlands. An initial modeling attempt (Armentano et al., 1986) suggests that moderate rates of sea level rise along the lower southwest coast of Florida would result in an increase in mangrove area.

Status and Prognosis

As discussed earlier, there are approximately 190,000 ha of mangroves remaining in Florida (Coastal Coordinating Council, 1974), and about 90 percent of this area lies in the four southern counties of Lee, Collier, Monroe, and Dade (fig. 15.12). Lindall and Saloman (1977) estimated that the loss of coastal wetlands in Florida to dredge and fill activities has been 9522 ha, but this figure includes intertidal marshes in addition to mangrove swamps.

Fig. 15.12. Extensive mangrove ecosystem, Ten Thousand Islands, Collier County. Photo by Allan Horton.

Birnhak and Crowder (1974) estimated a loss of approximately 4453 ha of mangroves between 1943 and 1970 in the three southern counties of Collier, Monroe, and Dade.

At first glance, these statistics seem to indicate only a modest loss of mangrove ecosystem area in Florida. Unfortunately, the pattern of loss has not been even across the state. High percentages of mangrove area have been lost in Tampa Bay, near Sarasota, around Marco Island, in the Florida Keys, and along the lower east coast of Florida. For example, Lewis et al. (1979) estimate a 44 percent loss of the intertidal vegetation in the Tampa Bay estuary over the past 100 years. In a detailed study using historical aerial photography, ground truth, and the ERDAS GIS system, Patterson (1986) estimated that 1083 ha of the mangrove area around Marco Island were permanently altered between 1952 and 1984 (fig. 15.1).

Future trends are difficult to predict. The pressures for development in Florida are intense and are continually fueled by increasing population growth. It seems likely that developmental pressure will increase at the greatest rate in areas that have already lost the largest percentage of mangrove shoreline, such as Tampa Bay. It remains to be seen whether the citizens of the state have the resolve to continue to preserve and protect mangrove ecosystems by means of strong legislative and regulatory procedures. From a scientific point of view, continued stringent preservation seems to be in the best interest of society.

16

Inshore Marine Habitats

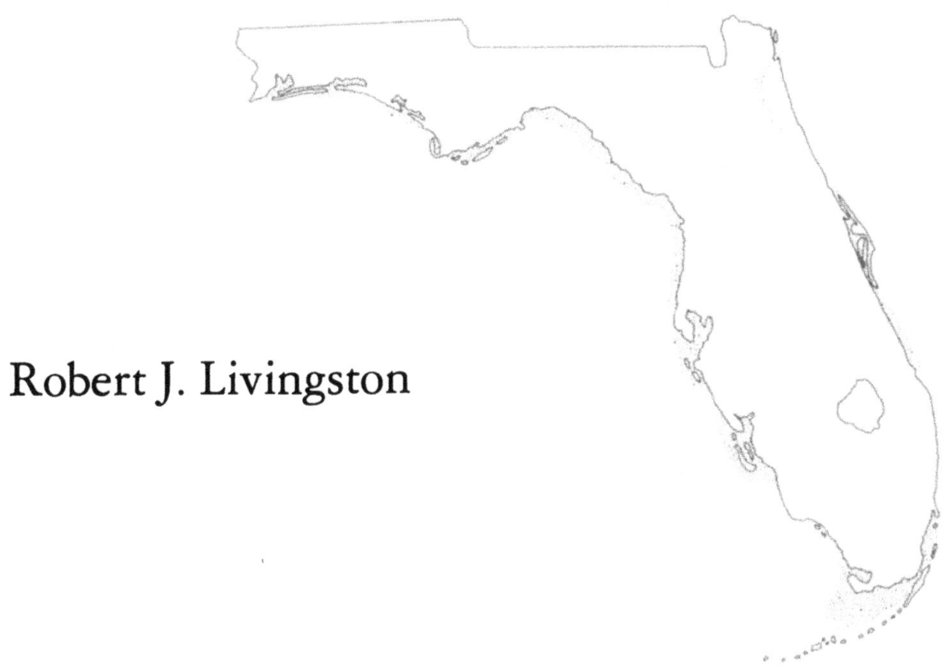

Robert J. Livingston

Florida's inshore marine systems are characterized by diversity of habitats—sea grass beds, tidal flats and marshes, soft sediments, hard substrates, shellfish beds, and a series of transition zones including those affected by people. When compared to other such habitats in the northern hemisphere, Florida's coastal systems are unique because their combination of climatological and physiographic features occurs nowhere else. Florida's shallow marine habitat is far more than a transition area between land and sea. The entire inshore marine habitat could be called an *estuary*, if the term is broadly defined as any area where sea water is diluted by land runoff. Early definitions of estuaries as semi-enclosed bodies of water with free connections to the open sea and measurable dilution from land drainage (Pritchard, 1967) are too restrictive when Florida's inshore waters are considered, because they are based on narrow physical conditions rather than key ecological characteristics. Biological characteristics of this diverse habitat include high productivity, high dominance, and low species diversity. Unique species, from the spiny lobster to the manatee, occupy Florida's coastal systems. Such areas are essential to most of Florida's extensive recreational and commercial fisheries. Many species, both freshwater and marine, spend at least part of their life histories in the nearshore marine environment. Penaeid shrimp (*Penaeus* spp.), blue crabs (*Callinectes sapidus*), oysters (*Crassostrea virginica*), and spotted seatrout (*Cynoscion nebulosus*) are just a few of the important species that occupy this region. Overall, the habitats that make up this particular zone represent a diverse and important part of an ecological continuum that extends from freshwater areas to the deep sea along the Atlantic and Gulf coasts.

Environmental Characteristics

Physiography and Geomorphology

Florida is a massive platform of sedimentary rock that has been deposited in a warm shallow sea over the past 200 million to 300 million years (Fernald, 1981). The alluvial Panhandle rivers originate in Georgia and Alabama; the nonalluvial rivers to the east and south flow through areas of low relief. The submarine portion of the platform is broad along the west coast and relatively narrow along the east coast. The primary topographic relief on land (exceeding 60 m) is in the northwest section of the state. Peninsular Florida is generally flat; most coastal areas and the Everglades region have elevations of less than 2 m.

The shoreline of Florida is the longest of any state in the conterminous United States (13,676 km), with more than 1.2 million ha of open estuarine area and tidal marshes along the Gulf coast. About 30 percent of the land area of Florida is wetlands (marshes, swamps, cypress forests) (Seaman, 1985). Details of the geographic distribution of coastal habitats in Florida are available elsewhere in this volume; the geographic distribution of Florida's inshore marine systems is given in figure 16.1. Individual embayments and estuaries vary considerably in size, physiographic structure, productivity, freshwater input, and human impact. The east coast, from the St. Johns estuary in Jacksonville to Biscayne Bay near Miami, is a high-energy shoreline bounded by areas characterized as lagoons behind barrier islands (Seaman, 1985). South of Biscayne Bay are coral reefs, inshore lagoons, and the Florida Bay system. Shoreline vegetation in north and central east coast areas is dominated by marshes, whereas the southeastern peninsula is forested mainly by mangroves. In contrast to the high wave energy east coast systems that are usually characterized by high salinities, the west coast inshore marine systems are dominated by low-energy conditions and distinct salinity gradients caused by land runoff. Many such systems are located behind barrier islands, which form lagoons in southwest and northwest Florida. Mangrove vegetation in the south grades into *Juncus-Spartina* marshes to the north. The midsection, stretching from the Anclote Keys to the Ochlockonee River drainage in the Panhandle, is characterized by a series of marshes and small river drainages. The northwest coast systems are dominated by

Fig. 16.1 Inshore marine systems of Florida.

freshwater flows from springs, creeks, and rivers of varying sizes; higher wave energy systems prevail in this region. There are also major river-fed estuaries (the Pensacola Bay system, Choctawhatchee Bay system, Apalachicola Bay system) clustered behind barrier islands.

Climate

Florida extends from a south-temperate to a subtropical climate. Mean annual temperature in north Florida ranges between 18 and 20.5°C (64–69°F), whereas south Florida annual means approximate 23–25°C (73–77°F). Maximum differences between north and south are noted during winter. Mean annual rainfall in the state ranges from 120 cm to 150 cm; seasonal peaks usually occur during the summer. Annual precipitation is highest in the northwestern and extreme southeastern portions of Florida. Drought periods around the state usually occur in the spring (April–May) and fall (October–November), at which times the influence of low-pressure systems is minimal (Fernald and Patten, 1984). Although most areas in Florida have a distinct summer peak of precipitation, north Florida also has a secondary winter maximum. These climatological conditions physically control the major habitat features of Florida's inshore marine areas.

Freshwater Resources and Watershed Delineations

Rain-derived water in Florida takes various paths. More than 26 percent of such water enters the Atlantic Ocean and the Gulf of Mexico by means of groundwater discharge to rivers by springs. Most of the remaining rain-derived water returns to the atmosphere by evapotranspiration. Much of the subsurface flow for northern Florida originates in Alabama and Georgia (Fernald and Patten, 1984). In peninsular Florida, groundwater originates in the Central Upland limestones of the Floridan Aquifer, where recharge occurs at or near the ground surface. Florida is underlain by this aquifer and has more available groundwater than any other state. Because much of Florida is low lying, the water table is often at depths of less than 1 m. It is exposed in some streams, lakes, swamps, and other wetlands and has seasonal fluctuations in coastal areas of up to 1 m. In general, groundwater moves toward areas of low pressure along streams and coastlines. Some groundwater also discharges as springs within a few kilometers of the coast. Topographic relief, though low in Florida, does influence surface drainage into the sea. Such drainage is regional; major watersheds include portions of Georgia, Alabama, and Florida.

Most of Florida's rivers discharge to bays around the state or are tributaries to rivers that have such discharge. The average annual state runoff approximates 35.6 cm, though local average values vary considerably. According to Fernald and Patton (1984), river systems in the northern part of the state, because of greater topographic relief, increased infiltration and percolation, and reduced evapotranspiration, generally have higher stream flows than do rivers farther south. Streams in the north have peak flows in late winter and early spring, whereas southern rivers tend to have the highest flows in late summer and early fall. Such differences have a considerable effect on the rate of flow and the timing of salinity cycles in coastal regions.

In Florida, inshore marine systems are strongly influenced by offshore energy conditions as well as overland runoff. Wave height and wave energy density are highest along the east coast from Daytona Beach to the Florida Keys. Substrate conditions are strongly influenced by such factors. North of Biscayne Bay, quartz (SiO_2) sand is predominant, whereas south of this system, the substrate is composed primarily of shell and coral ($CaCO_3$) fragments (Fernald, 1981). Florida Bay is a low wave energy system, while the region from Cape Romano to Tampa Bay is of moderate wave energy. The Big Bend area from Tarpon Springs to Apalachicola Bay is another low wave energy system. In such areas, substrates are dominated by fine particles, such as silts and clays. Regions west of Apalachicola Bay are characterized by moderate wave energy and predominantly sandy beaches. When the influence of the major watersheds on the coastal systems is analyzed, it is important to consider the energy conditions and physiographic features.

Major Drainage Systems

The unique geological conditions of the Florida peninsula, together with abundant rainfall, define the ecological characteristics of the major drainage systems of the state. The inshore marine habitats make up only one portion of what is actually a continuous distribution of freshwater runoff from the upper basins to the sea.

The St. Johns drainage system includes a fluvial drainage of 7400 km^2 and an estuarine drainage of 1680 km^2. The entire estuarine zone totals 670 km^2, with an average depth of 4.3 m (U.S. Department of Commerce, 1985). The St. Johns River is about 435 km long and is one of the few rivers in the United States that flows northward. The St. Johns and its principal tributary, the Oklawaha, are meandering, relatively sluggish rivers that contribute a broad seasonal range of freshwater flows to the estuary (Anderson and Goolsby, 1973). Average daily flows approximate 220 m^3/s. Major portions of the Oklawaha–St. Johns system have been severely altered by agriculture and industrial activities in the basin. Currently, the St. Johns estuary is polluted by a variety of sources, both point and nonpoint. Farther south, along Florida's east coast, the Indian River system includes a drainage area of 3280 km^2 with a total estuarine zone of 740 km^2. This flow is entirely behind a barrier island system and averages 40 m^3/s. To the south of the Indian River system, a series of canals and rivers, with a combined average daily flow of 91 m^3/s, forms the drainage to the Biscayne Bay system. The drainage area for this watershed approximates 480 km^2. The natural drainage characteristics of this area have been severely altered by urbanization and industrialization.

Before the human depredations of this century, the Kissimmee/Okeechobee/Everglades system represented the most biologically distinctive wetlands in the northern hemisphere. Located largely in a karst terrain of limestone, covered by a moderate to thick overburden of sand and a water table at or near the ground surface, this area was characterized by a complex of drainage systems considered to be important to the inshore marine systems around the southern extremity of Florida. The relatively low terrain of this vast system was dominated by a series of freshwater marshes and swamps, with mangrove swamps along the coast. Recently, natural drainage characteristics have been substantially altered by human activities, such as agriculture. Florida Bay, a shallow marine system between the mainland and the Keys, is still influenced by Everglades drainage, though the history of this influence is unclear because of a lack of scientific data. A low rock ridge that extends from north of Miami to the Homestead area deflects water toward the southwest in the Shark River Slough and Taylor Slough. Shark Slough contributes primarily to Whitewater Bay and the Gulf coast, whereas Taylor Slough drains into Florida Bay. During high water periods, Shark Slough may merge into northern Taylor Slough, thus contributing fresh water to Florida Bay. The Ten Thousand Islands drainage area, including a series of interconnected passes, tidal creeks, mangrove forests, and islands, is fed by sheet flow from the Everglades and a series of tributaries draining the Everglades system. This entire drainage area approximates 10,880 km^2 with an estuarine zone of 368 km^2. Average daily flow rates for the region are about 51 m^3/s.

North of the Ten Thousand Islands, the estuarine zone is fronted by a series of barrier islands that extend in a broken string up to the Anclote drainage. Major estuaries in this region include Estero Bay, Caloosahatchee Bay, Charlotte Harbor, Sarasota Bay, and the Tampa Bay system. The Caloosahatchee drainage approximates 3680 km^2, with an average daily freshwater flow of 54 m^3/s. According to Seaman (1985), the Caloosahatchee River flow is controlled by artificial structures. Charlotte Harbor has a drainage area of more than 1295 km^2 and is primarily affected by drainage from the Peace River. Daily average freshwater inflows are 136 and 68 m^3/s, respectively. Sarasota Bay has freshwater input in the eastern section and remains relatively high in salinity as a result of restricted freshwater flow and numerous passes in the barrier island system. Tampa Bay, with a drainage system of nearly 6735 km^2, is associated with a series of rivers (Hillsborough, Palm, Alafia, Little Manatee, Manatee); open Gulf water mixes with such freshwater inflows to form estuarine salinity gradients. The Tampa Bay system has been severely disturbed by municipal and industrial activities.

The region from the Anclote Keys north to the Ochlockonee River drainage can be viewed as one massive estuary. This open estuarine system is supplied by freshwater from the Anclote, Pithlachascotee, Weeki Wachee, Homosassa, Chassahowitzka, Crystal, Withlacoochee, Waccasassa, Suwannee, Steinhatchee, Spring Warrior, Fenholloway, Econfina, Aucilla, St. Marks, and Ochlockonee rivers. This combined drainage system of springs and streams contributes approximately 1 billion gallons of fresh water per day to Apalachee Bay in the northeast Gulf of Mexico. This massive drainage is associated with relatively intact wetlands. The associated estuarine area, still undisturbed by human activities, is one of the least polluted coastal regions of the continental United States.

The Apalachicola River has a drainage area of 60,780 km^2 (Apalachicola/Flint/Chattahoochee system) with an estuarine drainage area of nearly 7772 km^2. The average daily flow rate of 824 m^3/s is the highest in Florida. Like the basins of other northwest Florida streams, the Apalachicola drainage lies in part outside the state; 88 percent of its basin is in Georgia and Alabama (Livingston, 1984a). Nearly 80 percent of the Apalachicola stream flow originates in these two states. Variations in flow are based largely on rainfall, evapotranspiration of the wetlands vegetation, and the resultant runoff (including groundwater discharge). The barrier islands, together with high river flow and generally shallow water depths, strongly influence the estuarine conditions within the highly productive Apalachicola Bay system (East Bay, Apalachicola Bay, St. Vincent Sound, St. George Sound, Alligator Harbor). The Apalachicola River estuary represents one of the last major alluvial systems to remain undammed with relatively unbroken wetlands.

Other northwest Florida rivers (Econfina, Choctawhatchee, Blackwater, and Escambia) are associated with a series of inshore estuaries in northwest Florida, including St. Andrews Bay (2930 km^2 drainage area), Choctawhatchee Bay (13,900 km^2 drainage area), and the Escambia Bay system (18,100 km^2 drainage area; Escambia Bay, Blackwater Bay, East Bay, Pensacola Bay). The Choctawhatchee Bay and Escambia Bay systems are connected by the Santa Rosa Sound. Spring and groundwater contributions are high in various rivers in this area.

Tides

Lunar tides in Florida vary considerably in range and periodicity. Along most of the east coast, semidiurnal tides predominate (two almost equal high tides and two nearly equal low tides each day). Around the southern tip and north along the west coast to the Apalachicola estuary, mixed tides prevail (two unequal high and unequal low tides each day). Across the northwest Panhandle coast, diurnal tides occur (one high and one low tide each day). Tidal ranges vary from 0.6 to 2.4 m along the east coast (increasing northward); those along the Gulf coast average 0.6–1.0 m. Wind-generated (storm) tides are generally higher along the Gulf coast than along the rest of Florida's coastline. The relatively small tidal ranges along the Gulf coast can be strongly affected by wind and other meteorological factors.

Wind and Storms

During winter, winds come predominantly from the northeast along the Panhandle and Gulf coasts and from the northwest along the east coast. In spring and summer, air flows come mainly from the southeast along the peninsula and the southwest along the Panhandle coast. In the fall, predominant flows are from the northeast along both coasts. Thunderstorm frequency is highest in central and southern Florida. Florida has more hurricanes than any other state; peak activity extends from June through November, and the risk is highest in south and northwest Florida. Florida also has frequent tornadoes. Such storms may have long-lasting effects on inshore marine systems.

Principal Abiotic Features

The shallow inshore marine habitats of Florida are physically stressed systems. Water temperature is an important limiting factor in these inshore areas where wind-mixing of the water column leads to rapid air-water equilibration (Livingston, 1984a). In north Florida, seasonal variation is considerable, with temperatures ranging from 5°C to 33°C (41–91°F) over a twelve-month period. Water temperatures can be a primary limiting factor in northern inshore areas on both coasts, where temperatures can go as low as 2–3°C (36–37°F) during particularly cold winters. There is some evidence that peak summer temperatures may also stress inshore organisms in north Florida estuaries. Low water temperature becomes a less important factor along the south Florida coasts, though high temperature in inshore areas can be a factor in limiting the distribution of some organisms in this area (Zieman, 1970).

Salinity can also be a major limiting feature, as a determinant of osmoregulatory functions of aquatic organisms. Spatial and temporal variation of salinity can be extreme in inshore marine systems, depending on proximity to shore and the specific characteristics of the drainage basin. Extreme variation (both short- and long-term) is found in areas around major rivers (Livingston, 1984a). Salinity can also be affected by depth, basin configuration, wind speed and direction, and water currents. In addition to absolute values, the rate of change in salinity in a given situation may affect the distribution of organisms. In many inshore areas, organisms are euryhaline (adapted to a wide range of salinity) and must be able to withstand rapid changes of salinity over varying time periods. Changes may occur seasonally or from year to year (Livingston, 1984a). Such salinity patterns affect productivity, population distribution, community composition, predator-prey interactions, and food web structure in the inshore marine habitat. In many ways, salinity is a master ecological variable that controls important aspects of community structure and food web organization in coastal systems.

Dissolved oxygen is another important limiting factor in inshore marine systems. Low dissolved oxygen in such areas can be due to various factors, both natural and anthropogenous (Simon, 1974). High nutrient/organic loading, outbreaks of red tide, and low water exchange rates (stagnation), combined with natural cycles of seasonal temperature changes, can produce broad changes in the available dissolved oxygen. Maximum levels usually occur during winter months or periods of high wind. Cultural (human-made) *eutrophication* (nutrient excess leading to overproduction of microalgae and associated trophic imbalance) is common in various estuaries near human population centers (Livingston, 1987; Simon, 1974). This condition is characterized by exaggerated fluctuations of dissolved oxygen from supersaturation to hypoxia and anoxia.

Other water quality features can also be limiting to inshore marine organisms (Livingston et al., 1974). Water color and turbidity influence productivity and food web structure (Livingston, 1982a,b, 1984b). A broad range of natural variation of these factors tends to limit and alter both the quantity and quality of primary productivity in estuarine and coastal systems. Natural levels vary with the type of freshwater runoff and the physiography of the receiving area. The alluvial rivers of northwest Florida generally have high levels of turbidity and color, while levels farther south tend to be lower.

Sediment type—in terms of particle size distribution, percent organics, and interstitial water quality—is also an important habitat feature of inshore marine systems. Usually, inshore sediments are mixtures of sand, silt, clay, and shell fragments, produced by complicated physical and biological processes that ultimately have considerable influence on the biological organization of the individual estuarine and coastal systems.

Complex geological, physiographic, and watershed conditions contribute to certain unique features of the estuaries along the Florida coast. That is not to say that most inshore marine areas do not have common features. Many such systems are highly productive as a result of nutrient fluxes and the translation of wind and tidal energy into highly nutritious microbial production, which forms the basis of the important detrital food webs in coastal systems (Livingston, 1984a). Salinity variations limit the influx of stenohaline offshore predators, thus providing a sanctuary from predation for euryhaline types adapted to the highly variable inshore marine habitat. The combination of emergent vegetation (marshes and swamps), submergent vegetation (sea grass beds), and phytoplankton productivity in nearshore areas provides the autochthonous basis for coastal food webs. More than 90 percent of the species that provide the basis of sport and commercial fisheries use such inshore habitats for at least part of their life histories. Florida's marine commercial fishery ranks sixth in the United States, with dockside landings valued at $168 million (Seaman, 1985). The sport fisheries are even more valuable, involving just over 3.4 million people. The specific and common attributes that make inshore marine systems highly productive and economically important are the same factors that limit these habitats to relatively few highly salt-tolerant populations. In addition, each coastal system has its own attributes that lead to interesting deviations from the basic model.

Ecosystem Processes

In a functional sense, inshore marine systems encompass a biological continuum from upland, freshwater portions of individual drainage basins to the deep sea. Inshore marine systems represent a combination of habitats with complex physical, chemical, and biological interactions. Livingston (1984a,b) has established some basic models for such systems (figs. 16.2 and 16.3).

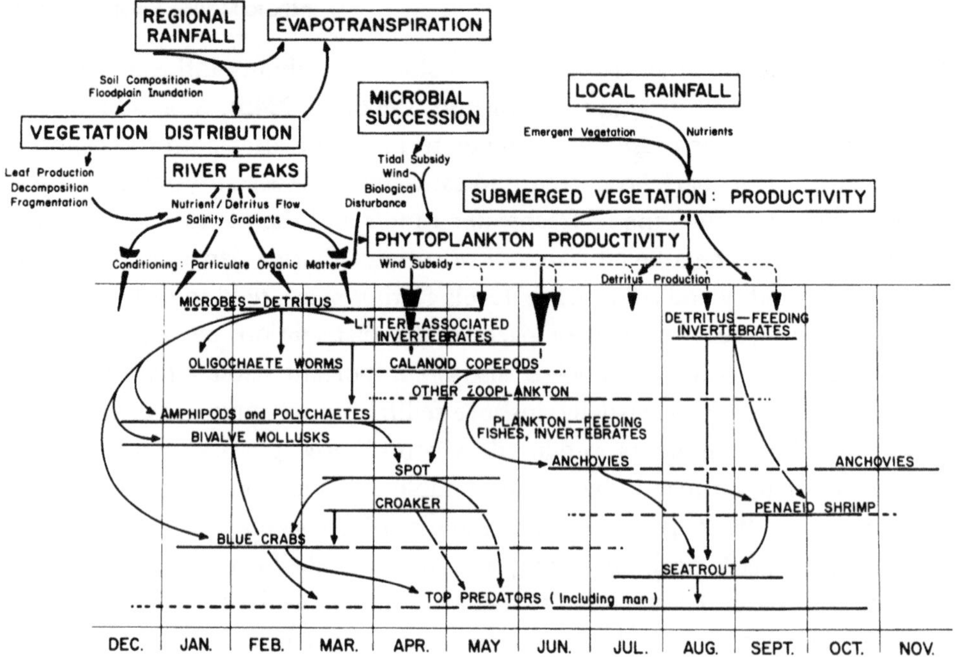

Fig. 16.2. Model of the Apalachicola river-bay system. This model is derived from a series of studies that have been summarized by Livingston, 1984a, 1985.

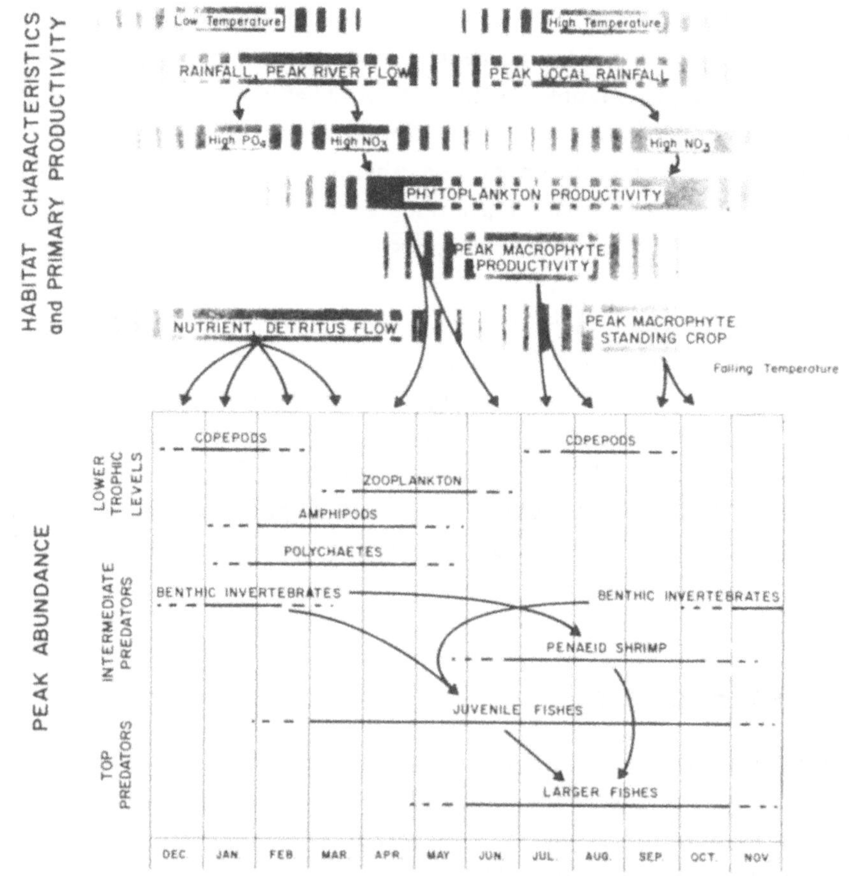

Fig. 16.3. Model of the Apalachee Bay inshore sea grass systems. This model is derived from a series of studies summarized by Livingston, 1984b.

High nutrient levels, multiple sources of primary and secondary production, shallow depths, organically rich sediments, energy inputs from wind, tidal currents, and freshwater inflow all combine to establish unique sets of conditions that still have certain universal characteristics. For instance, low/variable salinity is often a controlling ecological factor that determines the community characteristics of an inshore area. Different combinations of controlling factors, together with specific patterns of inshore-offshore migration of marine forms and offshore movements of euryhaline species, contribute to the often area-specific characteristics of the particular inshore marine system.

The acknowledged uniqueness of different estuarine and coastal systems overlies a series of common attributes that are often a function of the physical conditions of such areas. The basic characteristics of a system are determined by physiographic conditions (depth, area, access to freshwater runoff, and open ocean conditions) and freshwater input (i.e., dilution of seawater) with accompanying input of dissolved nutrients (inorganic and organic) and particulate organic matter. Seasonal cycles of temperature and rainfall, particularly in south-temperate north Florida, add a dimension of recurrent, time-related changes. The particular combination of habitat features and temporal biological responses to such conditions determines the basic ecological attributes of each system.

One of the important characteristics of many inshore coastal areas is high productivity. The multiple sources of nutrients, together with more or less continuous disturbance by wind and tidal currents, form an ideal situation for microbial production in sediments and on the surface of particulate organic matter (Livingston, 1984a). Microbial biomass is the highest living particulate component in coastal systems and forms the basis for the nitrogen- and phosphorus-enriched detrital food webs that predominate in estuarine areas. Inputs from freshwater and saltwater wetlands (*allochthonous* and *autochthonous*), *in situ* phytoplankton productivity, and submerged aquatic vegetation all contribute to the rich coastal soup. In addition to organisms that spend their entire life cycles in such systems—such as shellfish and spotted seatrout—there are many marine species that migrate in- or offshore during their larval and juvenile stages. Often, such species spawn offshore. Many commercially important species, such as oysters, penaeid shrimp, blue crabs, and various finfishes, are euryhaline, capable of living in rapidly changing conditions of salinity and other habitat variables. These species utilize the abundant food resources of coastal systems while remaining relatively free from predation by the stenohaline (salinity-restricted) marine forms offshore and the inshore freshwater predators. Thus, the inshore marine habitat often serves as a physically stressed but highly productive sanctuary for developing stages of offshore forms, many of which are used directly and indirectly by humans. Gradients of physical variables, together with forms of food availability and utilization, provide the basic components for the highly complex food webs of the inshore marine systems.

The rapidly changing physical conditions and intermittent cycling of organic production are important determinants of the form of the trophic organization in coastal areas. However, the final form of such biological systems is determined by complex processes, such as predator-prey interactions and competition. The importance of these processes is determined in part by physical gradients of salinity (Livingston, 1984a). Inshore areas of low but highly variable salinity are dominated by opportunistic species accustomed to natural disturbance. Community interactions in such habitats are controlled less by biological processes, such as predation and competition, than by physical factors, such as salinity changes. High productivity, high dominance, and low species richness prevail under such conditions. Along the increasing salinity gradient, biological features become more important as determinants of community structure. With increasing salinity, population distribution becomes more even, with a corresponding decrease in relative dominance and an increase in species richness and diversity. Seasonal changes in predation pressure as well as recruitment characteristics of species with high abundance and biomass may modify this general rule. At any time, the community structure may be the result of various combinations of such variables. The coexisting estuarine assemblages may reach different levels of equilibrium depending on the exact temporal sequence of such interacting factors. This model would explain the unique characteristics of individual coastal systems while also accounting for the features that are common to most such systems.

As examples of these generalizations, models have been generated for two intensively studied areas along the northeastern Gulf coast of Florida, the Apalachicola estuary (fig. 16.2) and Apalachee Bay (fig. 16.3). The Apalachicola Bay system is dominated by freshwater input from the Apalachicola River, which determines important habitat factors (low, variable salinity and high color and turbidity), productivity features (high levels of allochthonous detritus and nutrients and enhanced phytoplankton production), and the development of associated, commercially important species. These species include oysters, penaeid shrimp, blue crabs, and young finfishes, such as anchovies and sciaenids (spot, croaker). Submerged aquatic vegetation is restricted to areas less than 1 m deep. Much of the bay bottom is composed of unvegetated mud and oyster bars. High phytoplankton productivity and imported organic matter from the river (fig. 16.4) contribute to microbial activities, which form the basis of the detritivorous food webs (fig. 16.5). Wind and tidal disturbance of the shallow system enhance such secondary productivity, which is then utilized by a seasonal succession of euryhaline dominants. The result is one of Florida's most productive inshore systems in terms of seafood such as oysters, shrimp, and finfishes.

Apalachee Bay, on the other hand, receives less surface freshwater runoff

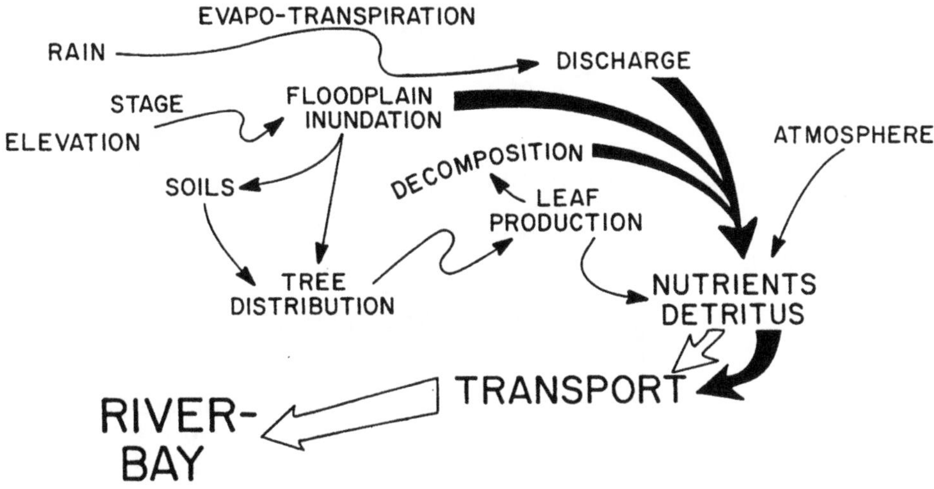

Fig. 16.4. Model of the movement of nutrients and organic matter from alluvial wetlands into associated river-estuary systems. After Livingston, 1984a.

(Livingston, 1984b). These clear, nutrient-poor waters are dominated by turtle grass beds. In this situation, where conditions favor the development of sea grass beds, phytoplankton is a secondary source of organic matter (fig. 16.3). Salinity is generally higher here; species richness and diversity are high, and dominance relatively low. Species such as pink shrimp, spotted seatrout, and various offshore finfishes (many of which are important to the sport fisheries in the region) constitute the food webs based on sea grass. In this case, the sea grasses provide both the major habitat and the most important source of organic matter for the system. Even though similar basic components are important to the Apalachicola and Apalachee Bay systems, the peculiar combination of physical/chemical variables leads to distinctive habitat conditions and productivity cycles, which in turn form the basis for very different species assemblages and food web organizations.

Primary Inshore Habitats and Biotas

Sea Grass Beds

Sea grass beds represent one of the most productive and important habitats in the nearshore marine systems of Florida. Such areas are also quite vulnerable to the impact of human population increases.

There is a considerable and growing scientific literature concerning submerged aquatic vegetation (Livingston, 1982a,b, 1984b; Durako et al., 1987). Sea grasses modify sedimentation rates and current patterns while mediating predator-prey relationships and defining the community structure of such systems (Stoner, 1980). In addition to being extremely productive, sea grass beds are used by a wide range of species as feeding grounds, nurseries,

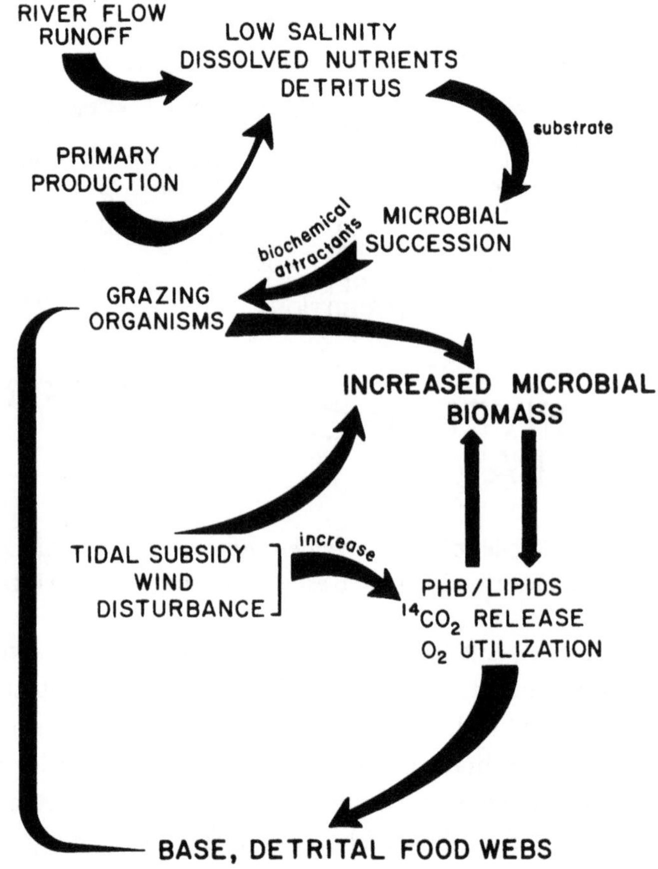

Fig. 16.5. Model of microbial interactions and secondary production that contributes significantly to coastal detrital food webs. After Livingston, 1984a.

and refuges from predation, providing food for various organisms both directly (herbivory) and indirectly (as the base of detrital food webs). The sea grasses act as substrates for epiphytic algae, which are an important component of the sea grass food webs.

The physical habitat of the sea grass bed provides a refuge from predation for different species. As a result, the sea grasses are an important factor in predator-prey interactions, giving differential advantages to species that are able to take advantage of the refuge factor (Livingston, 1985). In this way, the overall community structure is defined in part by the sea grass habitat per se. Sea grass beds are thus essential for the propagation and growth of many commercially important species.

Turtle grass (*Thalassia testudinum*) is temperature-limited and does not occur along the northeast Florida coast. The northward limit of *Syringodium filiforme* and *Halophila engelmannii* is the Indian River west of Cape Canaveral. Shoal grass (*Halodule wrightii*) and widgeongrass (*Ruppia maritima*) appear in various inlets along the Florida east coast. Farther south, from Biscayne Bay to the Dry Tortugas, turtle grass forms extensive beds. Along the western Gulf coast, in the region from Tarpon Springs to Cape Romano, sea grasses are found primarily inside of barrier islands, though there is little such development in the Ten Thousand Islands area. The most diverse associations of sea grasses and marine algae in the Gulf of Mexico are found off the southwest coast of Florida. Two of the most extensive sea grass beds in continental North America occur along the southwest and north Florida Gulf coasts. Coverage in Florida Bay approximates 5000 km^2, while the beds lining the north Florida Gulf coast (Apalachee Bay) cover 3000 km^2. The northern beds form an almost continuous band, from 10 to 35 km wide, at depths from 1 to 5 m. Scattered beds occur along inshore areas of the northwest Florida (Panhandle) coast.

Oyster Bars

Oysters (primarily *Crassostrea virginica*) are found along inshore coastal habitats on both coasts of Florida. Predominant habitats include estuaries (especially near mouths of rivers) in areas less than 10 m deep with firm substrates such as mud/shell bottom (fig. 16.6). This filter-feeding, sedentary invertebrate depends on unicellular algae, suspended particulate organic matter, and, possibly, dissolved organic substances for sustenance and growth. Spawning occurs in estuarine areas primarily during late spring, summer, and early fall; planktonic larvae require a firm substrate for further development. Adult oysters are concentrated mainly in inshore areas along the Gulf coast. In the Apalachicola estuary, factors such as salinity and food availability are influenced by the Apalachicola River (Livingston et al., 1974). Nowhere else in Florida are such ecological conditions available, where comparatively pollution-free freshwater runoff provides prime habitat and sustenance for shellfish concentrations. According to Whitfield and Beaumarriage (1977), approximately 40 percent of the Apalachicola estuary is suitable for the growth of oysters (fig. 16.7). During the fall of 1985, Hurricane Elena destroyed more than 90 percent of the most valuable oyster

Fig. 16.6. The mouth of the Apalachicola River as it enters the oyster-rich estuary that contributes more than 90 percent of Florida's commercial oyster crop.

Fig. 16.7. Apalachicola oyster tongers in action.

bars in the Apalachicola estuary. Two and a half months later, Hurricane Kate caused further damage. By the late spring of 1987, oyster production in the bay exceeded that just before the hurricanes of 1985. Although the storms caused considerable economic problems in the region, the oysters—worth $6 million to $10 million per year—made a substantial recovery as a result of a spectacular spatfall just weeks after Hurricane Elena. This example illustrates the resilience of estuarine species, such as oysters, in the face of natural disturbances, which are common along the Florida Gulf coast.

Oysters provide food and habitat for a variety of estuarine species, including various boring sponges, gastropod molluscs (*Thais haemastoma, Melongena corona*), polychaete worms, and decapod crustaceans (*Menippe mercenaria*). Low and varying salinity limits predation on oysters by organisms such as *Menippe* and *Thais*. Oysters over 5 cm long are relatively rare in areas of high salinity, in large part because of predation by offshore species. In addition, the incidence of certain diseases of oysters may be related to high salinities and chronic stress due to pollution. Thus, freshwater runoff not only provides food for oysters but allows relief from predation and disease.

Soft-Bottom (Unvegetated) Areas

Soft-bottom sediments, composed primarily of sand, sand-gravel, and shell, make up a dominant benthic habitat along both coasts of Florida. In extreme south Florida, mud-sand and combinations of coral rock ($CaCO_3$) bottom types prevail; the $CaCO_3$ sediments of southeast Florida are composed primarily of codacean algal plates. Considerable portions of offshore southwest Gulf substrates are composed of hard bottoms, scattered coral heads, and rocky outcrops.

The fauna in such areas is dominated by *microorganisms* (< 52 μm), *meiobenthic organisms* (between 62 and 250 μm), and *macrobenthos* (> 250 μm). Considerable scientific information exists concerning the complex relationships of these organisms, including those animals living at or near the sediment-water interface (*epibenthic organisms*) and those living within the substrate (*infauna*). Spatial gradients of salinity, productivity, water quality, and sediment type affect the community composition of such associations (Santos and Simon, 1980). Predation and competition, along with seasonal changes of recruitment, can also affect the infaunal assemblages. The fauna is dominated by polychaete worms, crustaceans, molluscs, and insect larvae. Some cosmopolitan dominants include polychaete worms (*Mediomastus ambiseta, Streblospio benedicti, Paraprionospio pinnata*), tubificid worms, tanaids, and amphipods. Many of these species are eurythermal and euryhaline, with specific distributions dependent on life history factors such as recruitment and feeding habits. These organisms are primarily detritivores, selective and nonselective deposit feeders, filter feeders, and predators. The benthos is an important food web component (Sheridan, 1979), which determines to a considerable degree the community that lives in the overlying water column (motile macroinvertebrates and fishes).

Dominant Epibenthic Populations

Distributions of important inshore marine species in Florida have been outlined in the Gulf of Mexico data atlas (U.S. Department of Commerce, 1985). Florida's east and west coasts are ecologically different. The west (Gulf) coast has a broad, shallow shelf in a low-energy system lined with mangrove and *Juncus-Spartina* marshes. Barrier island systems form a string of inshore estuaries with salinity gradients based on freshwater flows of surface and groundwater. The east (Atlantic) coast has a high-energy system with a relatively narrow shelf that grades into a series of beaches. There are fewer estuarine systems. Small tidal amplitudes along with low wave energy marshes and swamps predominate along the west coast. These features determine the composition of the inshore marine assemblages, along with specific natural history attributes of the dominant populations.

Invertebrates

Different species of penaeid shrimp occupy a range of habitats along Florida's coasts. Brown shrimp (*Penaeus aztecus*) prefer mud or sandy mud substrates along both coasts; nurseries are found primarily in the Panhandle estuaries. A major summer fishery for this species extends along the Atlantic coast of Georgia to just below the St. Johns drainage area. The pink shrimp (*Penaeus duorarum*), found along both coasts, is commercially important primarily from St. Joseph Bay in the Panhandle to Florida Bay. Juveniles use the shallow sea grass beds along the west coast as nurseries. Adults favor higher salinities and substrates of shell sand, sand, and coral. White shrimp

(*Penaeus setiferus*) are located only in estuaries and offshore areas along the northwest and northeast coasts. This species prefers inshore (brackish water) areas with mud or clay substrates. Primary commercial catches of white shrimp are taken off the northeast Florida coast during fall and winter.

The stone crab (*Menippe mercenaria*), another important commercial species, is taken mainly along the southwest Gulf coast from the Florida Keys and Florida Bay to Tampa Bay. Stone crabs are also numerous in Apalachee Bay. Juveniles are located in estuaries with shells, rock, or sea grass substrates, but maturing crabs move to deeper water, where they burrow in soft substrates or live in sea grass areas. The blue crab (*Callinectes sapidus*), located along both coasts, is harvested primarily along the northern Gulf coast and the east coast of Florida. Tagging studies (Oesterling and Evink, 1977) indicate that mature females migrate northward along the Gulf coast to spawn in the general region of Apalachicola Bay (fig. 16.8). The migrating female blue crab swims up to hundreds of kilometers to spawn in the northeast Gulf region. Blue crabs prefer muddy and sandy bottoms in shallow estuarine areas and are often associated with submerged aquatic vegetation.

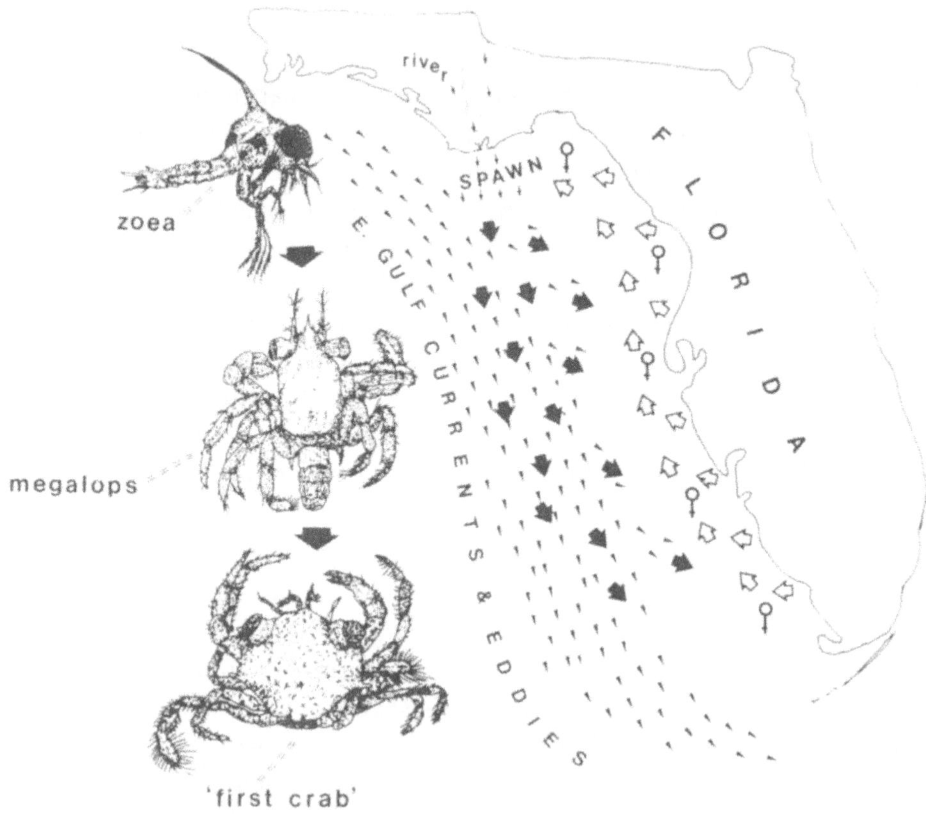

Fig. 16.8. Schematic representation of life history stages of the blue crab (*Callinectes sapidus*) along Florida's Gulf coast. After Livingston, 1984a.

Most commercially important epibenthic invertebrates are located primarily along the Gulf coast. Wetlands, freshwater runoff (and estuarine conditions), and sea grass beds are associated with these species at some stage of their development, despite distinctive species-specific life history patterns. Such conditions, together with the shallow coastal embayments, provide the habitat and productivity that support the major sport and commercial fisheries along Florida's Gulf coast.

Another group of commercially important invertebrate species is found primarily along the Atlantic coast of Florida. This group includes the calico scallop (*Aequipecten gibbus*), which is caught in offshore regions of east Florida characterized by gravel substrate at depths from 20 to 60 m. The rock shrimp (*Sicyonia brevirostris*) forms concentrated aggregates on hard sand and shell substrates at depths between 25 and 65 m off the northeast coast of Florida and is the basis of a small commercial fishery in this region. Farther offshore in this general region, the royal red shrimp (*Pleoticus robustus*) concentrates above various substrates. These shrimp are usually found at depths of 180 to 600 m. No major commercial fishery exists for this species.

The inshore clam (*Mercenaria*) fishery in the Indian River system has recently become economically important. The spiny lobster (*Panulirus argus*) used to be commercially important along the mid-Florida east coast from south of Biscayne Bay to the Florida Keys and Florida Bay. Adult spiny lobster occur near reefs and rubble areas from the shore to depths of 80 m; postlarvae and juveniles use shallow inshore coastal areas as nurseries. However, this species, together with the queen conch (*Strombus gigas*), has been severely damaged by overfishing in south Florida. In 1922, 300,000 lbs of spiny lobster were harvested by twenty-four fishermen in twelve boats (i.e., 12,500 lb per fisherman). By 1984, 6,062,637 lbs of lobster were harvested by 2372 fishermen (i.e., 256 lbs per fisherman).

Fishes

The family Sciaenidae is a group of fishes that is particularly important to the commercial and sport fisheries of Florida. The sand seatrout (*Cynoscion arenarius*) is fished commercially along Florida's Gulf coast; favorite habitats include sandy and muddy areas in coastal and shelf waters. The spotted seatrout (*C. nebulosus*) is fished on both coasts but is a commercially important species along the state's west coast. This species is found in shallow coastal areas associated with salt marshes, sand flats, and sea grass beds. The spot (*Leiostomus xanthurus*) is an important commercial species on both coasts. The croaker (*Micropogonias undulatus*) forms the basis of a commercial fishery along the northern Gulf coast. The black drum (*Pogonias cromis*) is commercially important in bay areas along both coasts, whereas the red drum (*Sciaenops ocellatus*) is a grass bed species that is of commercial and sport fishing importance along Florida's west coast. In many instances, the general ecological features of Florida's Gulf coast are important for the sciaenid fishes.

Another group of fishes forms the basis of vast commercial and sport fisheries primarily in southern portions of both the east and west coasts of Florida. It includes the bonefish (*Albula vulpes*), tarpon (*Megalops atlanticus*), snook (*Centropomus undecimalis*), Florida pompano (*Trachinotus carolinus*), mutton snapper (*Lutjanus analis*), gray snapper (*L. griseus*), lane snapper (*L. synagris*), and yellowtail snapper (*Ocyurus chrysurus*). Two migratory species are commercially important and support sport fisheries on both coasts: king mackerel (*Scomberomerus cavalla*) and Spanish mackerel (*S. maculatus*). The striped mullet (*Mugil cephalus*) forms the basis of important fisheries on both coasts. Another group of species is important commercially primarily along the Gulf coasts: Gulf menhaden (*Brevoortia patronus*), Atlantic thread herring (*Opisthonema oglinum*), and Spanish sardine (*Sardinella aurita*).

The overwhelming majority of the fishes listed here spend at least some time in the inshore marine habitats of Florida's Gulf and Atlantic coasts. It has been postulated that overfishing and habitat deterioration have had harmful effects on species such as red drum. Such suppositions are controversial because there are few good scientific data concerning the species. When compared with the enormous value of the commercial and sport fisheries of Florida, the amount of money spent by Florida officials and federal environmental agencies for basic and applied research on such species is minuscule. Because of the absence of such information and the state's burgeoning growth, various fisheries are poorly managed and consequently are in severe trouble. The Apalachicola oyster industry is a good example of such a fishery, where overfishing and the illegal taking of oysters have not been controlled. Consequently, the oyster industry remains in constant turmoil, with considerable economic problems in the Apalachicola region. Other troubled fisheries include queen conch, lobster, red drum (redfish), snook, and mackerel (king and Spanish). In most instances, state officials have chosen political rather than scientific methods of resource management along Florida's coasts. Consequently, habitat deterioration (fig. 16.9) and overfishing have accelerated to a point where entire fisheries are in jeopardy.

Human Impact

Population Growth in Florida

At the beginning of this century, the population of Florida was approximately 500,000. By 1980, it approached 10 million, with population centers primarily along both coasts on urban strips from Palm Beach to Miami and

Fig. 16.9. Dredging in the salt marshes along Florida's northern Gulf coast.

from Sarasota to Tarpon Springs. In 1987, Florida became the fourth most populous state in the country. Between 1970 and 1980, coastal counties in Florida had the greatest percent population increases in the United States (44 percent). Populous metropolitan areas include Miami, Tampa–St. Petersburg, Fort Lauderdale–Hollywood, Jacksonville, Orlando, West Palm Beach, and Pensacola. Estimates for the year 2000 range as high as 15 million. It is projected that, by that time, the east coast will feature a continuous urban area between Jacksonville and Miami. The southwest coast will have been urbanized between Crystal River and Naples, with a cross-state corridor of urbanization between Tampa and Daytona Beach (Fernald, 1981).

Economic Activities

The leading forms of economic activity in Florida include agriculture, forestry, mineral production, sport and commercial fisheries, manufacturing, construction, and tourism. Farmland is located primarily in the central and south-central counties. Manufacturing activities, power plants, and municipal wastewater treatment plants are located mainly along the southeast coast and in the Tampa–St. Petersburg area, Jacksonville, and Pensacola. Most pulp mills are in the northern part of the state, fifteen located between Jacksonville and Pensacola. Hazardous waste sites and landfills tend to be concentrated around population centers, as are industrial wastewater discharges and stormwater runoff. Such areas are high in oxygen-demanding substances, nutrient concentrations, and fecal coliform bacteria. Agricultural activities and human alterations in the hydrological relationships of upland drainage systems have had a major impact on the Kissimmee-Okeechobee-Everglades system, which borders the highly productive Florida Bay and various estuaries along the southwest Gulf coast.

An enumeration of the overall impact of such activities on the coastal systems of Florida is beyond the scope of this chapter. Appreciable losses of wetlands have resulted from a variety of agricultural activities (fig. 16.10). It has been estimated that less than half the wetlands that existed in Florida at the time of early European settlement are still present. Urban development has altered the basic processes in various river basins, with attendant effects on the associated estuarine and coastal systems. The relentless destruction of the Florida Everglades by agricultural interests, sanctioned by public agencies, represents one of the most important habitat losses in the United States in recent times. The loss of fresh water to Florida Bay as a result of such changes is currently a primary concern because there are indications that the fisheries of this region may be in trouble. Problems due to upland restrictions of freshwater flow, the loss of wetlands, and the proliferation of toxic substances are currently recognized in various inland marine systems around Florida. Areas such as the St. Johns estuary, Indian River, Biscayne Bay, Tampa Bay, Choctawhatchee Bay, and Escambia Bay have suffered major losses of habitat as a result of industrialization, agricultural activities, physical changes in the drainage basins, and stormwater runoff. It is clear that Florida's coastal zone is under pressure as a result of the lack of proper management of its explosive population increase.

Submerged Aquatic Vegetation as an Indicator

Submerged aquatic vegetation (SAV) is a sensitive indicator of water quality and pollution in shallow coastal areas. According to recent reviews (Livingston, 1987; Zieman, 1982), sea grass beds are vulnerable to various forms of anthropogenous stress. Thermal effluents, toxic agents, dredging, industrial discharges, cultural eutrophication, oil spills, commercial fishing, and changes in light transmission due to turbidity and color, have been associated with reductions in SAV. Such effects have been documented in other regions, such as the Chesapeake Bay system (Orth and Moore, 1984), where unprecedented declines of SAV have been caused by combinations of natural fluctuations and human activities. Thus, because of its sensitivity to certain types of human activity, SAV can be viewed as a "canary" of coastal habitats and can be used as a sensitive index of the impact of human activities.

During the rapid population increase over the past thirty to forty years, SAV has declined in inshore marine areas around Florida. Urbanization and industrialization have been accompanied by extensive losses of SAV in the Pensacola Bay system, where recent surveys have found little sea grass cover in areas where SAV was once well developed. This deterioration was asso-

Fig. 16.10. Agricultural dikes and drainage ditches in the Apalachicola wetlands, which simultaneously cut off natural flooding and concentrate toxic substances, nutrients, and pathogenic organisms that are eventually pumped back into the natural drainage system.

ciated with sewage and industrial discharges, dredging and filling, cultural eutrophication, and alterations in upland watersheds. Such changes led to severe losses in the fisheries of the region.

Extensive losses of SAV in Choctawhatchee Bay since 1949 have been postulated, though the cause is unknown. Recent studies indicate a 20 percent loss of SAV in this bay system over the past thirty years. Less populated areas along the northwest Florida coast (St. Joseph Bay and the Apalachicola estuary) appear to have experienced no substantial losses of SAV in recent times. The massive sea grass beds of Apalachee Bay remain largely intact, though pulp mill effluents discharged into the Fenholloway River have caused severe local damage to portions of these grass beds (Zimmerman and Livingston, 1976a,b, 1979); such changes have been associated with losses of benthic productivity, lowered species richness at various levels of biological organization, and altered food web interactions (Livingston, 1975, 1982a,b, 1984a,b; Heck, 1976; Hooks et al., 1976). Farther south along the Gulf coast, the once productive sea grass beds of the Tampa Bay system have been lost to a variety of human activities (Simon, 1974). Lewis and Phillips (1980) found that sea grass cover in Tampa Bay, Hillsborough Bay, and Old Tampa Bay had decreased from 6140 ha in 1876 to 1250 ha in 1980. In Boca Ciega Bay, hydraulic dredging and filling accounted for the loss of 1400 ha of bay bottom (1131 metric tons of turtle grass) (Taylor and Saloman, 1968). Deterioration of water quality in Hillsborough Bay and Old Tampa Bay eliminated several species of algae and replaced them with "obnoxious species" of *Gracilaria, Ulva*, and *Enteromorpha* (Simon, 1974). Overall, more than 80 percent of the SAV noted in 1948 had been lost by 1980. Recent analyses of Charlotte Harbor (K. Haddad, personal communication) indicate a decline of 29 percent of the sea grass beds (11,740 ha) from 1943 and to 1984, although no causative factors have been identified. These estimates of sea grass losses in Charlotte Harbor have been challenged by some workers in the region (T. Fraser, personal communication).

The sea grass habitat is extensive but deteriorating in Florida Bay and is of considerable importance for numerous species (Tabb et al., 1962). Recent losses of 10–20 percent of SAV in Florida Bay have baffled scientists. Zieman (1982) indicated that changes in salinity and turbidity due to altered freshwater input to eastern Florida Bay have changed sea grass distribution by giving turtle grass a competitive advantage over shoal grass. Some deterioration of SAV in northern Biscayne Bay has been observed (McNulty, 1961). In southern portions of the bay, heated power plant effluents destroyed 120 ha of SAV (Zieman, 1970). Farther north along the east coast, urbanization in the Vero Beach area has been associated with losses of SAV (R. Virnstein, personal communication). Loss of 25 percent of the sea grass beds around Fort Pierce Inlet from 1951 to 1984 has been noted (K. Haddad, personal communication). In the Sebastian Inlet region, a 38 percent decline of SAV (494 ha) has been noted over the same period (K. Haddad, personal communication).

Overall, recent population growth, together with attendant forms of human impact, has been associated with substantial losses of sea grass beds in inshore marine areas. Coastal engineering projects—including beach nourishment, the construction of seawalls, bridges, and other coastal structures, and massive dredging and filling activities—have had a major adverse impact on SAV distribution. Long-term monitoring of sea grass beds is lacking, and effective planning in the face of multiple and varied assaults on marine habitats is almost nonexistent. These problems are due in part to lack of attention to an ecosystem approach in present-day methods of scientific research and management. Consequently, the future outlook for nearshore habitats around Florida in the face of projected population growth is not optimistic.

Summary

The inshore marine habitats of Florida represent a diverse, highly productive series of biological systems. Areas such as the Everglades and Florida Bay are unique in the northern hemisphere. The mangrove forests of south Florida, together with the wetlands systems of Florida's northern river estuaries, represent important habitats in terms of biological activity and diversity. Numerous species of economic importance are closely associated with specific basin features, climatological conditions, and water quality characteristics of Florida's inshore systems. The combination of wetlands, submerged aquatic vegetation, and phytoplankton productivity provides the conditions for proliferation and development of various life stages of migratory marine species that utilize such areas as nurseries and sanctuaries from predation. Recent rapid population increases along Florida's coasts—associated with urbanization, industrialization, and agricultural activities—have already taken a severe toll of the natural resources in such areas, as exemplified by the losses of emergent vegetation and submerged aquatic vegetation around the state in the past thirty to fifty years. The general lack of scientific data of sufficient scale and quality to evaluate insidious long-term anthropogenous changes in freshwater flows to marine systems and water quality of the coastal habitats has contributed to an atmosphere of confusion and indecision on the part of those responsible for environmental policy. Until now the trend has been to allow widespread environmental destruction by agricultural, industrial, and development interests and then, if there is adverse public response, to implement expensive mitigation procedures. Because inexpensive yet effective planning and management procedures have been neglected *before* the resource problems appear, serious environmental problems have occurred that often defy immediate solution. Physical alteration of watersheds, the release of agricultural and industrial wastes, and the lack of control of stormwater runoff from municipal developments remain the chief threats to the inshore marine systems of Florida. The development of progressive management programs is needed *now* if Florida's marine inshore systems are to remain viable.

17
Coral Reefs

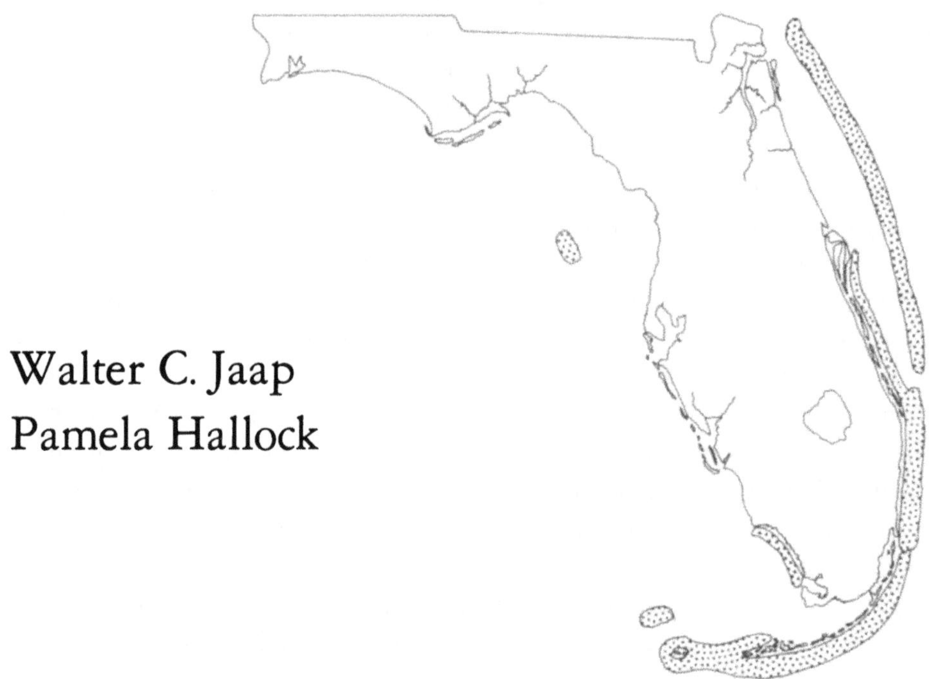

Walter C. Jaap
Pamela Hallock

Coral reefs are well known for their beauty and complex diversity of life. Reef communities in the oceans are in some ways similar to forest communities on land: in both cases, the dominant organisms provide other members of the community with food and shelter. Shelter, however, is the primary contribution of coral reefs, for food is less abundant there than in many other marine communities. The massive and intricate frameworks constructed by reef-building organisms provide an almost infinite array of habitats for other plants and animals, leading to greater biologic activity and diversity than in most marine environments.

Florida is richly endowed with reefs, both modern and ancient. Modern reefs include intertidal worm reefs, tropical shallow-water coral reefs, and deep-water coral banks. These reefs contribute to the economy of Florida through fisheries and tourism. Reefs serve as living breakwaters, dissipating storm and hurricane wave energies before they reach the coast. Moreover, the very existence of much of Florida is the result of limestone deposition. Without the ancient reefs that have occupied the Florida peninsula intermittently over the past 150 million years, most of the state would lie several kilometers below sea level.

Nontropical Reef Types and Associated Communities

Although tropical, shallow-water coral reefs are most familiar to the public, other types of reef communities in Florida deserve mention, as do communities closely associated with reefs: live-bottom, sea grass, mangrove, and sedimentary communities. The last two types are covered elsewhere in this book.

Live-Bottom Communities

Live-bottom biotas are among the most widely distributed marine communities in Florida waters. They are found virtually anywhere, from subtidal areas to the continental shelf edge. The main criterion is solid substratum upon which members of this epibiotic community attach. Attached biotas occupy everything from reef limestones to rocky outcrops on the sea floor to artificial reefs, seawalls, buoys, bridge pilings, and boat bottoms. Flora and fauna naturally vary throughout this range of depths and substrata, but algae, sponges, octocorals, hardy stony corals, and bryozoans are often visually dominant (fig. 17.1). In general, shallow-water ($<$ 6 m) live-bottom biotas

Fig. 17.1. Live-bottom community off Tarpon Springs in the eastern Gulf of Mexico, about 15 m deep. Large white object on left is a sponge attached to the edge of a low relief limestone outcropping.

throughout Florida show temperate, Carolinian affinities, with tropical West Indian affinities becoming increasingly important to the south (Collard and D'Asaro, 1973). West Florida shelf communities in deeper water (> 18 m), which is buffered from seasonally low temperatures, are dominated by tropical species (Lyons and Camp, 1982).

Although live-bottom communities do not construct reefs, they often contribute to the three-dimensionality of the environment by destructive processes. Where limestones outcrop on the seafloor, rock-boring organisms, such as clionid sponges and *Lithophaga* clams, undermine rock ledges. Such *bioerosion* produces caverns that are used as refuges by fish and invertebrates. By pitting and undercutting, bioerosion also increases the surface area and diversity of attachment sites for sessile organisms. Large basket sponges, octocorals, stony corals, and algae also contribute to the three-dimensionality of the habitat, providing living substrata for attached organisms.

On the west Florida shelf, at depths of 12 to 30 m, numerous limestone outcrops jut upwards 0.5 m to 2 m, often forming table-like structures above surrounding sediments. Ledges are covered with abundant plant and animal life. Stony corals are common on these outcrops, though they seldom construct significant three-dimensional structures. Cavernous vertical faces provide refuges for crabs, lobsters, and fish. Octocorals dominate upper surfaces. Brittlestars often seek shelter in the branches of flexible octocorals and feed on plankton or suspended particles in the water. Limestone outcrops provide oases of vertical relief in the vast expanses of sands that cover most of the west Florida shelf. Snapper (*Lutjanus* spp.), grouper (*Epinephelus* spp.), and sea bass (*Centropristis* spp.) are frequently found in these habitats (Smith, 1976).

The Florida Middle Ground northwest of Tampa Bay (fig. 17.2) is the best developed live-bottom habitat on the west Florida shelf. At shelf depths of about 40 m, outcropping limestone has relief of up to 18 m. This limestone is thought to be fossil remains of a Pleistocene interglacial coral reef system (Brooks, 1962). The high relief provides extreme spatial heterogeneity, which in turn provides excellent habitat for attached biota and fish populations, including economically important demersal fish species (Smith and Ogren, 1974). Other sources of information on the Florida Middle Ground include Austin and Jones (1974), Cheney and Dyer (1974), Smith and Ogren (1974), Lyons (1976), Grimm and Hopkins (1977), Hopkins et al. (1977), Shaw and Hopkins (1977), and Vittor and Johnson (1977).

Live-bottom communities off the east coast are similar to those in the Gulf of Mexico. They are more frequent south of Cape Canaveral, particularly upon knolls, ridges, and rocky outcrops (Moe, 1963; Jones et al., 1986). Seaward of Jupiter Island, extensive limestone outcrops occur in depths of 5 to 15 m. Large boulders provide complex refuges. Attached organisms in-

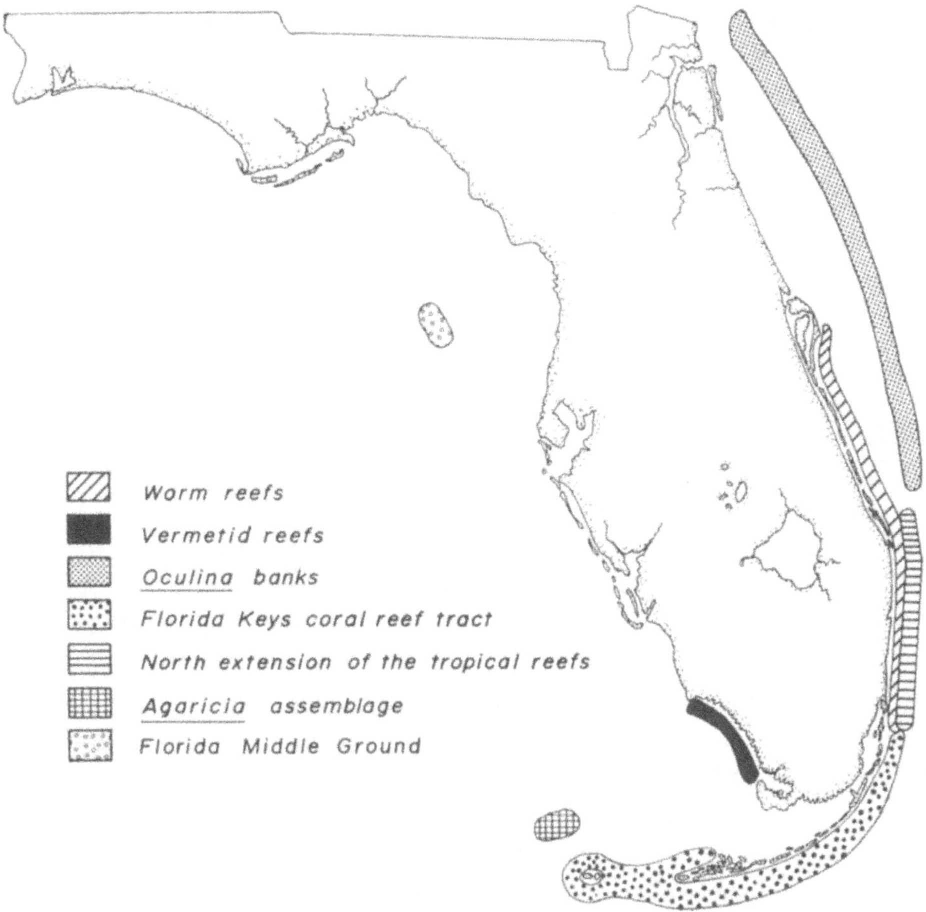

Fig. 17.2. Distribution of Florida reef assemblages. Map units describe extent of potential habitat distribution; actual occurrences are often disjunct (patchy).

clude sponges, algae, octocorals, and stony corals (*Oculina* spp.). Caves within the rocks harbor fish and lobster.

Sea Grass Communities

One of the most productive communities on earth, the sea grass community is found in estuaries, lagoons, and shallow open shelves off the coast of Florida. These vast meadows are habitat for large populations of invertebrates and fishes and provide the richest nursery and feeding ground in Florida's coastal waters. Most of the following information was summarized from Zieman's (1982) community profile of the sea grasses of south Florida.

Sea grasses are the only flowering plants that live their entire lives completely and obligately in seawater. Forty-five species are known worldwide; six of those occur in Florida, and only three are of major importance. Turtle grass (*Thalassia testudinum*) is the best known, with its large, ribbon-like leaves that are 4–12 mm wide and 10–35 cm long. Two to five leaves per shoot grow from stout rhizomes that may be found as deep as 25 cm in the sediment. Turtle grass is the major species in the extensive meadows of south and west Florida. Manatee grass (*Syringodium filiforme*) is commonly found in mixed sea grass beds or in small, dense monospecific patches. Its leaves are string-like: round in cross-section, about 1 mm in diameter, and up to 50 cm long. The rhizomes are less robust than those of turtle grass and seldom penetrate as deep into the sediment. The blades of shoal grass (*Halodule wrightii*) are like thin ribbons, typically 1–3 mm wide and 10–20 cm long, with two or three points. Shoal grass is an early colonizer of disturbed areas.

Of the 10,000 km^2 of sea grasses in the Gulf of Mexico, more than 85 percent occur in Florida waters (Iverson and Bittaker, 1986). Sea grass beds totaling more than 5500 km^2 are found in the warm, shallow waters of Florida Bay and adjacent to the Florida coral reef tract; they cover 80 percent of the sea bottom between Cape Sable, north Biscayne Bay, and the Dry Tortugas. Sea grass cover declines sharply north of this area on both coasts. The shifting sand beaches of the high wave energy Atlantic coast restrict sea grasses to protected bays and inlets. On the Gulf coast, high turbidity and low salinity inhibit sea grass development off the Everglades. Along the southwest coast of Florida, sea grasses are found primarily in bays and estuaries. Extensive meadows of sea grass blanket the broad shallow shelf of the northeastern Gulf in the Big Bend region, from Tarpon Springs to St. Marks.

Sea grasses require sediment of sufficient depth to allow roots to anchor the plants. A variety of sediments, from fine muds to coarse sands, support their growth. Shoal grass can colonize thin sediments (Fonesca et al., 1981); turtle grass requires at least 7 cm of sediment depth to colonize (Scoffin, 1970) and about 50 cm to achieve lush growth (Zieman, 1972). Once sea grasses are established, they greatly influence local sedimentation. Deposition of fine inorganic and organic particles is facilitated by the baffling effect of the sea grass blades, the entrapment of waterborne particles in epiphytic growth on the sea grass, the production of particles within the grass beds, and the binding and stabilizing of the substrate by the root and rhizome systems.

Like terrestrial grasslands, sea grass meadows support a diverse assemblage of other organisms. Macroalgae live among the sea grasses, and both may have epiphytes attached to them. Epibenthic organisms find shelter as well as food within the meadow. Infaunal organisms live hidden within sediments stabilized by the sea grass roots and rhizomes. Grazers and predators move through the community harvesting these resources.

Several types of calcareous green algae are important contributors to the subtropical sea grass community in south Florida. They include *Halimeda, Penicillus, Rhipocephalus,* and *Udotea.* Besides being producers of organic matter, these algae secrete calcium carbonate skeletons, which, upon death of the algae, are incorporated into the sediments.

Sea grass and associated benthic macroalgae provide substrate for epiphytic organisms; Humm (1964) found 113 species of algae epiphytic on turtle grass in south Florida, including the coralline reds, *Fosliella* and *Melobesia*, that encrust grass blades. On tropical sea grasses, heavy overgrowth by epiphytes occurs only after the leaves have been colonized by these encrusters (Zieman, 1982). The coralline algae also contribute calcium carbonate to the sediments. Foraminifera (Hallock et al., 1986) and micromolluscs (Zieman, 1982) are commonly found living on the epiphytic algae; shells of these tiny animals also contribute to the sediments, as do the skeletal remains of serpulid worms and bryozoans that live attached to the sea grass blades.

The invertebrate fauna is exceedingly rich in sea grass communities of south Florida. Larger epibenthic organisms include the queen conch (*Strombus gigas*) and other gastropods, the West Indian sea star (*Oreaster reticulata*), sea urchins, sea cucumbers, pink shrimp (*Penaeus duorarum*), and spiny lobster (*Panulirus argus*). A few corals (e.g., *Manicina areolata* and *Porites furcata*) and sponges can be found. Infauna include a variety of clams and annelid worms. A multitude of small crustaceans lives on or in the epiphytes and sediments.

Sea grass meadows are inhabited or visited by a diverse and abundant fish fauna. Resident fishes are typically small, cryptic, and of little commercial value. Seasonal residents spend their juvenile, subadult, or spawning season feeding in the grass beds. Commercially and recreationally important drums (Sciaenidae), sea bass (Serranidae), porgies (Sparidae), grunts (Pomadasyidae), snappers (Lutjanidae), and mojarras (Gerridae) use sea grass meadows as nursery grounds. Coral reefs near sea grass beds shelter animals like snappers and lobster that feed in the meadows at night.

Some higher vertebrates can also be found in sea grass meadows. Turtle grass was named for its appeal to green sea turtles (*Chelonia mydas*). Manatee (*Trichechus manatus*), bottlenose dolphin (*Tursiops truncatus*), and a variety of wading and diving birds also use sea grass beds as feeding grounds (Zieman, 1982).

Sea grasses have potential for extremely high primary productivity; values of 0.9 to 16 g C m^{-2} day^{-1} have been reported in south Florida (Zieman, 1982). That production is available to other organisms by direct grazing and as detritus and dissolved organic carbon. Traditionally, detrital food webs within grass beds have been considered the primary pathway. Greenway (1976), however, found that nearly 50 percent of the turtle grass production in Kingston Harbor, Jamaica, was directly grazed by urchins, 42 percent was deposited on the bottom, and the rest was exported from the system. Ogden (1980) questioned the general applicability of Greenway's study because urchin densities were unusually high. Urchins, conchs, fishes, green sea turtles, and manatees are all important grazers on sea grasses and their epiphytes (Zieman, 1982). Sea grass detritus, with its microflora, and epiphytes are important food sources for the variety of epibenthic organisms as well as seasonal or nocturnal visitors. Furthermore, dissolved organic carbon from sea grasses provides a source of food for microorganisms (Zieman, 1982).

Sea grasses are extremely efficient at capturing and utilizing nutrients, a major factor in their ability to maintain high productivity in relatively low nutrient environments (Zieman, 1982). They are apparently capable of absorbing nutrients through either their leaves or their roots. *Zostera*, a sea grass common in somewhat higher latitudes, can take up ammonia and phosphate from the sediments and transport the nutrients to the leaves, where they can be pumped into the surrounding water (McRoy and Barsdate, 1970). If turtle grass has the same capability, it should be of tremendous benefit to epiphytic algae on the sea grass blades, particularly in the nutrient-poor waters associated with coral reefs. Sediment depth may play an imporant role in nutrient dynamics in the sea grass bed, for deeper sediments allow more extensive development of roots and rhizomes. Furthermore, extensive root systems may be needed to sustain growth in sediments that contain few nutrients (Zieman, 1982). Burkholder et al. (1959) found that the ratio of leaf to root and rhizome diminished as sediments became coarser in turtle grass beds in Puerto Rico. Sources of nitrogen include the water column, regeneration in the sediments, and nitrogen fixation by bacteria associated with the leaves, roots, and rhizomes. Capone and Taylor (1980) estimated that most nitrogen comes from recycling in the sediments, though up to 50 percent can come from nitrogen fixation within the root and rhizome system.

The value of estuarine regions to commercial and recreational fisheries is difficult to overemphasize. About 90 percent of the total Gulf of Mexico and south Atlantic commercial fishery landings is estuarine-dependent (Lindall and Saloman, 1977). The pink shrimp fishery, economically the most important in Florida, is centered on the Tortugas shrimping grounds. The nursery grounds for this species are the vast mangrove and sea grass meadows of south Florida.

Recognition of the economic value of sea grass beds as nursery areas for commercial and recreational species has sparked concern for the preservation of sea grass habitats. Dredge-and-fill activities have probably been the principal agent of destruction of sea grass habitat in south Florida (Zieman, 1982). Such operations typically dredge one area to fill another, destroying habitat in both areas. Furthermore, because turtle grass requires high light intensity for photosynthesis (Zieman and Wetzel, 1980), turbidity caused by dredging affects nearby habitats. Phytoplankton blooms stimulated by nutrient enrichment of estuarine waters by urban sewage and phosphate mining discharges have reduced sea grass beds in Hillsborough Bay to small, sparse patches (Zieman, 1982). Damage or destruction of sea grass resources in other bays, such as Tampa Bay and Boca Ciega Bay, further demonstrates how susceptible this community is to human influence.

Worm Reefs

Off the east coast of central Florida, aggregations of the tropical marine worm *Phragmatopoma lapidosa* construct low reefs of tubes consisting of sand grains cemented together by protein (fig. 17.3). The reefs expand as worm larvae settle on existing tube masses. Reef growth is controlled by waves bringing planktonic food and sand to the worms. These reefs harbor a diverse community of live-bottom plants and animals (Van Montfrans, 1981). Besides supporting recreational fisheries for lobster and fish, worm reefs provide a nursery for numerous coastal fish species.

Worm reefs are found from Cape Canaveral to Key Biscayne (fig. 17.2) and are best developed off St. Lucie and Martin counties. They occur intertidally to about 10 m depth. Hurricanes, winter storms, burial during beach renourishment (Nelson and Main, 1985), pollution (Mulhern, 1976), and physical destruction by persons trampling on the delicate structures during low tide threaten these reefs. Other literature on worm reefs includes Multer and Milleman (1967), Gram (1968), Kirtley (1974), Mauro (1975), and Gore et al. (1978).

Vermetid Reefs

Another unusual reef form, built by a worm-like gastropod mollusc, *Petaloconchus*, is found intertidally seaward of the outer islands in Ten Thousand Islands (Dall and Harris, 1892) (fig. 17.2). These reefs, which are now inactive, grew on shallow offshore bars, often providing nuclei for the accretion of islands. Although living *Petaloconchus* may be found in the area, they are no longer building reefs (Shier, 1969).

An estuarine live-bottom biota, which includes juvenile and adult stone crabs (*Menippe mercenaria*), inhabits the remaining reef masses. The reef masses probably provide temporary refuge to a variety of fish species during high tide. Other references on vermetid reefs include Heald (1970), Brooks (1973), and Laborel (1977).

Oculina Banks

Coral banks that occur offshore from Jacksonville to St. Lucie Inlet at depths of 50 to 100 m (fig. 17.2) are another of Florida's little-known reef types. These banks are constructed by the ivory tree coral (*Oculina varicosa*). Individuals may grow to 1.5 m in height. In some places, corals coalesce to form dense thickets covering hectares of seafloor (Reed, 1980), while in other areas they produce isolated ridges and mounds. *Oculina* banks often grow on pinnacles and ridges on the underlying oolitic and algal limestones that par-

Fig. 17.3. *Phragmatopoma* worm reef in the intertidal zone, north side of St. Lucie Inlet.

allel the coast at the continental shelf margin (Macintyre and Milliman, 1970). Inshore, isolated colonies of *O. varicosa* occur in depths as shallow as 3 m.

Oculina banks function as refuge, feeding and breeding grounds, and nurseries for many other species (Reed et al., 1982; Reed and Mikkelsen, 1987). A single coral colony may support hundreds of animals, including crabs, shrimps, bivalve and gastropod molluscs, worms, anemones, solitary corals, and small fish. Large fish commonly observed feeding or seeking refuge in the *Oculina* habitat include black sea bass (*Centropristis striata*), gag grouper (*Mycteroperca microlepis*), snowy grouper (*Epinephelus niveatus*), red grouper (*E. morio*), and warsaw grouper (*E. nigritus*).

Because light levels are extremely low on these banks, the food source for this benthic community is primary production by phytoplankton in overlying waters. Periodic upwelling of cold, nutrient-rich waters over the banks undoubtedly contributes to that phytoplankton productivity. Zooplankton and organic particulate detritus are the major direct food sources for the bank inhabitants. Among the fifty species of decapod crustaceans that Reed et al. (1982) found associated with *O. varicosa* in depths ranging from 6 m to 80 m, most were omnivorous detritivores. A few species were obligate commensals, feeding upon coral mucus.

Like other kinds of coral communities, *Oculina* banks are relatively fragile because the principal architects grow so slowly. Reed (1981) found *O. varicosa* growth rates averaging 1.6 cm/yr at 80 m; thus, growth to 1.5 m requires nearly a century. Because growth rates are correlated with temperature, current velocity, and light, environmental events that may influence *Oculina* banks include bottom currents, upwelling of cold-water masses, and red tides. And because *Oculina* is a fragile, branching coral, it is prone to damage by fishing gear; trawl nets, dredges, bottom long lines, and traps, as well as anchors, can scar or crush coral branches. Oil and gas development in this region should avoid placing drilling and production platforms on *Oculina* banks.

Deep Coral Banks

Deep-water coral banks occur on the continental slope margins of Florida at depths of 400–800 m (distribution of deep coral banks is *not* shown in figure 17.2 because knowledge of their extent is incomplete). *Lophelia prolifera* and *Enallopsammia profunda* are the primary framework builders (Cairns and Stanley, 1983), with minor contributions by *Madrepora carolina* and *Solenosmilia variabilis* (Cairns, 1979). *Enallopsammia profunda* dominates the banks, while *L. prolifera* is typically limited to upper portions (Stetson et al., 1962). These fragile, branching corals create structures, sediment accumulations, and habitat similar to *Oculina* banks.

Coral growth is relatively slow, 5–7 mm/yr (Wilson, 1979). Several environmental characteristics seem necessary for these banks to develop, including hard substrata, vigorous currents, and temperatures ranging from 5° to 10°C (41° to 50°F) (Cairns and Stanley, 1983). Habitat depths indicate dependence upon planktonic and detrital food sources. Because these reefs are so inaccessible, little else is known of their ecology.

Large, commercially exploited deep-sea crabs (*Geryon quinquedens* and *G. fenneri*) are found associated with coral banks in the Gulf of Mexico and off southeast Florida (Neumann and Ball, 1970). Corals provide both food and shelter for fish (Squires, 1964). Isopods and other crustaceans are also associated with these banks. Other publications that deal with Florida's deep-coral banks include Teichert (1958), Moore and Bullis (1960), and Neumann et al. (1977).

Artificial Reefs

Artificial reefs are structures or materials accidentally or purposefully placed in the sea. Shipwrecks, engineering structures, bridge pilings, piers, wrecked aircraft, pipelines, and navigation aids are examples of artificial hard-substrate habitats. They occur throughout the coastal and offshore waters of Florida.

Larger structures in place for many years develop diverse communities. Bridge pilings in the Florida Keys often support a biota similar to nearshore patch reefs and live-bottom communities. The submerged structures are heavily colonized by algae, sponges, corals, tunicates, and bryozoans. Mobile fauna include spiny lobsters, stone crabs, and reef fish. Strong tidal currents through the channels bring planktonic larvae that settle on the pilings and provide a continuous supply of food and oxygenated water to the piling community.

In offshore areas, sunken ships attract biota common to local live-bottom or bank reef habitats. The *Benwood* wreck off Key Largo and the *Black-*

thorn off Pinellas County are representative of offshore artificial reefs. These ships provide substrata for algae and sessile animals, thereby providing food as well as shelter for numerous demersal and pelagic fish species. Time required for an artificial reef to become an effective fishery resource depends upon location, current patterns, local bottom type, and other variables. Typically, the biologic community must develop over several years before larger invertebrate and fish species take up residence in an artificial reef. Literature relevant to artificial reefs includes Randall (1963), Unger and Bolster (1966), Colunga and Stone (1974), Aska (1978, 1981), Southwest Regional Research Institute (1981), and the *Bulletin of Marine Science* (1985).

Tropical Coral Reefs

The Florida Keys shallow water, tropical, coral reef ecosystem (fig. 17.2) is unique on the continental shelf of North America. These reefs are similar to Caribbean-Bahamas tropical reefs in species composition and physiographic characteristics. Bank reefs are the major reefal structures in the Florida Keys. Most occur at the continental margin seaward of the larger islands of the Florida Keys. The area between the bank reefs and the islands supports sea grass meadows and patch reefs. Patch reefs are smaller, roughly circular features that occur in waters less than 10 m deep.

Coral reefs are interdependent with other marine and terrestrial communities that make up the coastal ecosystem. Energy, chemical constituents, and mobile species move between the reefs and other communities, including mangrove, sea grass, sediment, and hard ground.

Coral reefs are vital to Florida's economy. Commercial and recreational fishing focuses on numerous species that inhabit reefs during all or parts of their life cycles. Nonconsumptive uses, such as boating, SCUBA diving, snorkeling, and educational and natural history activities, are major producers of revenue. If lodging, meals, transportation, equipment rental, and boat charters are included, a coral reef such as Molasses Reef generates $400 million annually (Mattson and DeFoor, 1985).

Ecologic studies of Florida Keys coral reefs began during the late nineteenth century (Agassiz, 1883; Mayer, 1914; Vaughan, 1915, 1918; Longley and Hildebrand, 1941). More recently, research on western Atlantic coral reef ecosystems has focused on the Caribbean basin: Jamaica, St. Croix–U.S. Virgin Islands, Barbados, the Netherlands Antilles, Belize, and the San Blas Islands of Panama, where field stations provide laboratories and logistic infrastructure to support reef research. After the Carnegie Laboratory on Loggerhead Key, Dry Tortugas, burned in 1937, laboratory facilities in the Florida Keys were lacking until the recent opening of a facility on Long Key.

Thus, understanding of Florida corals and reefs is based heavily upon research findings from other Caribbean–western Atlantic areas.

Tropical coral reefs are characterized by high species diversity (Loya, 1972; Connell, 1978; Huston, 1985); rapid recycling of nitrogen and phosphorus (Pilson and Betzer, 1973; Webb et al., 1975; Muscatine, 1980; Johannes et al., 1983); high gross primary productivity and low net primary productivity (Lewis, 1977; Atkinson and Grigg, 1984; Gladfelter, 1985; Kinsey, 1985); highly transparent water (Wells, 1957; Yonge, 1963; Wethey and Porter, 1976); many species with specialized food requirements, narrow niches, and complex life cycles (Ebbs, 1966; Colin, 1976; Kissling and Taylor, 1977); symbiotic relationships (Limbaugh, 1961; Goreau and Hartman, 1966; Meyer et al., 1983); and primary productivity by microscopic symbiotic algae (zooxanthellae) within the reef-dwelling Cnidaria (Goreau and Goreau, 1960; Chalker, 1983; Porter et al., 1984).

Because this chapter can highlight only certain aspects of the Florida Keys coral reefs, readers are encouraged to seek details from the cited literature and from the following brief bibliography. Geological background is presented by Hoffmeister (1974). Synoptic overviews of south Florida coral reefs are found in Jaap (1984) and Voss (1988). General guides to western Atlantic coral reefs include Colin (1978) and Kaplan (1982). The four volumes of *Biology and Geology of Coral Reefs* (Jones and Endean, 1973–1977) cover a wide spectrum of reef science, as do the proceedings of the International Coral Reef Symposia (Mukudan and Pillai, 1972; Cameron et al., 1974; Taylor, 1977; Gomez et al., 1981; Delesalle et al., 1985); and the quarterly journal *Coral Reefs*. A compendium on a portion of the barrier reef off Belize, Central America, provides intensive documentation of a small area of this reef (Rützler and Macintyre, 1982). Marine invertebrates frequenting Florida reefs are identified in Zeiller (1974) and Voss (1976). Field guides to coral reef fish are provided by Chaplin and Scott (1972), Greenberg (1977), and Stokes and Stokes (1980). A diver's guide to the Florida Keys by Halas et al. (1984) contributes practical information on reef diving sites.

Environmental Setting

Geography

The Florida reef tract is the only shallow-water, tropical coral reef ecosystem on the continental shelf of North America. Representatives of the tropical reef biota occur as far north as Jupiter Island near Stuart (27°N lat.) and become increasingly important southward to Miami (Cape Florida). Fossil reef structures off Miami and Palm Beach support corals, octocorals, and sponges of the same species found in Keys reefs. However, corals are not presently building reefs in this region (Lighty, 1977). Development of extensive three-dimensional reef structures is restricted to south and west of

Cape Florida, offshore of the Florida Keys archipelago (fig. 17.4). This chain of islands, which extends from Soldier Key to Dry Tortugas, exhibits a diverse array of hard grounds, patch reefs, and bank reefs from 25 m to 13 km offshore (Jaap, 1984). Coral reefs also extend into the Gulf of Mexico from Key West and Smith Shoal to the Content Keys.

The Florida Keys archipelago arcs to the southwest. West and north of the Keys lie a series of shallow embayments (e.g., Biscayne Bay and Florida Bay) and the continental shelf off southwest Florida. East and south of the Keys are the Straits of Florida and the Florida Current. The latter, a subsystem of the Gulf Stream, is crucial to Florida's coral reefs. Moderate winter temperatures and warm, clear, relatively nutrient-poor waters permit the slow-growing, reef-building corals to compete successfully with faster growing live-bottom biotas.

Coral reef distribution patterns reflect the extent of water exchange between the continental shelf and the Atlantic. Heavy rainfall, drought, summer doldrums, and winter cold fronts influence temperature, salinity, nutrient supply, and turbidity in the shallow bays and sounds, producing water quality generally unfavorable to reef development. Large islands act as barriers to off-shelf transport from Florida Bay and Biscayne Bay; thus Key Largo and Elliott Key have extensive offshore reefs. The middle Keys, which are smaller and separated by numerous wide channels communicating with Florida Bay, have limited reef development. The island mass from Big Pine Key to Key West also provides a barrier to water transport, allowing extensive reef development off this area.

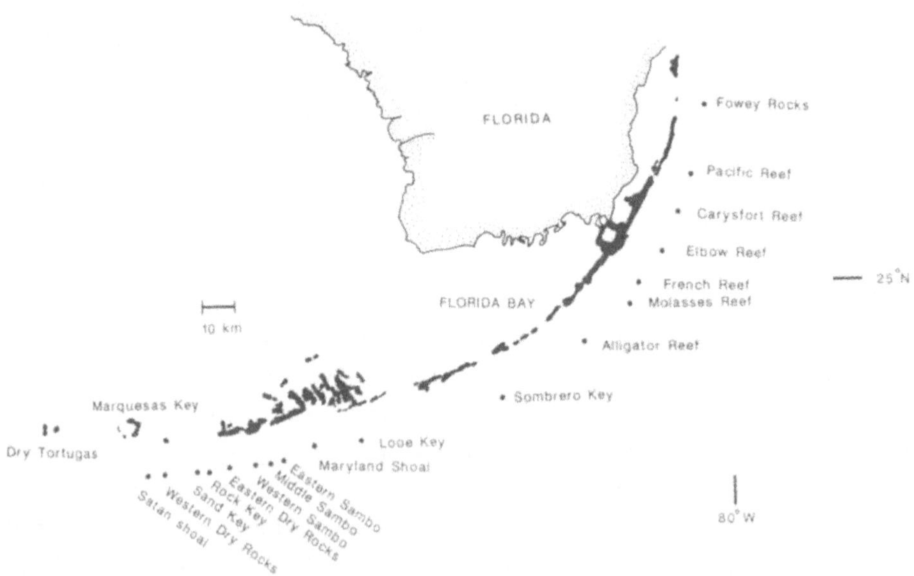

Fig. 17.4. Major bank reefs of the Florida Keys.

Geology

The Florida-Bahamas region is part of an extensive carbonate platform that once extended into the Gulf coast region. The Florida platform is a massive southward-thickening wedge of limestones that is at least 6000 m thick beneath Cay Sal Bank (Antoine et al., 1974). These limestones have been accumulating for approximately 150 million years. About 15 million YBP, middle and high latitude climates began to cool, sea level began to drop, and coral reefs retreated to lower latitudes. Over the past million years (during the Ice Ages), with each continental glacial advance, sea level dropped further and coral reef communities withdrew from Florida. During interglacial episodes, sea level rose, waters warmed, and corals returned.

Key Largo limestone, which is the fossil coralline reef rock found in the upper Keys, provides evidence of coral reef development during the last major interglacial period before the present. This formation extends from Miami Beach to the Dry Tortugas and seaward into the Straits of Florida. It varies in thickness from 23 m to 61 m or more and principally represents low wave energy patch reef conditions (Hoffmeister and Multer, 1968; Hoffmeister, 1974).

The last glacial advance ended about 18,000 YBP, and sea level began to rise. Coring in reefs from Miami Beach to the Dry Tortugas indicates that modern reef growth began 5000 to 7000 YBP (Shinn et al., 1977; Shinn, 1980). Reefs developed on topographic highs, including Pleistocene reef limestones, mangrove peat deposits, and lithified sand dunes (Shinn et al., 1977). Rates of sea level rise controlled early reef development.

Coral reefs are three-dimensional limestone frameworks produced principally by the skeletons of coral and coralline algae. Upward growth of a reef occurs because these organisms secrete calcium carbonate as they grow. Lime sands and muds, produced by breakdown of shells and skeletons of invertebrates and calcareous algae, also contribute to the reef mass by collecting in spaces within the reef framework. They are cemented into the reef by encrusting coralline algae and by high magnesium calcite cements produced by geochemical processes. Lime sands and muds also accumulate in backreef environments.

At the same time as growth processes build reefs, destructive forces erode and undermine the structures. Physical agents of destruction include waves, especially those generated by storms and hurricanes. Biological processes are no less important: fungi, sponges, marine worms, molluscs, and other organisms actively bore and erode reef framework (Ebbs, 1966; Hein and Risk, 1975; Hudson, 1977) at rates ranging from 0.05 mm to 4 mm/yr (Hutchings, 1986). Hein and Risk (1975) estimated that rates of bioerosion on some inner patch reefs of the Florida reef tract are equal to rates of carbonate production. Bioerosion also weakens the framework, making it more susceptible to wave damage (Jaap, 1984).

While some boring organisms chemically dissolve limestone, other bioerosion is mechanical; that is, reef framework is reduced to sediments and rubble. Thus, although bioerosion reduces the rate of upward growth of the reef framework itself, at least some of the sediments produced by bioerosion contribute to the accretion of the overall reef tract. Over the past 5000–7000 years, upward growth of Florida's reefs has occurred at rates of 0.65 to 4.85 m/1000 yr (table 17.1). The most rapid accretion rate reported for the Caribbean area is 15 m/1000 yr at an *Acropora palmata*-dominated reef of St. Croix, U.S. Virgin Islands (Adey, 1977).

Climate

The climate of southeast Florida is characterized as subtropical marine in Miami and tropical maritime in Key West. Monthly mean air temperatures range from 20° to 22°C (68° to 72°F) in winter to 28° to 29°C (82° to 84°F) in summer, with minima of 14°C (57°F) reported for Miami and maxima of nearly 32°C (90°F) reported for both Miami and Key West. Annual precipitation averages 152 cm in Miami and 101 cm in Key West; most rain falls between May and October. Winter winds are typically from the north or northeast from October through January, with monthly mean velocities of 15 km/hr in Miami and nearly 20 km/hr in Key West. Through the remainder of the year, southeast winds of 13–20 km/hr prevail, with lightest winds during summer.

The Florida Keys have the highest probability of hurricane impact of any coastal area of Florida (Florida Department of Natural Resources, 1974). Although hurricane season runs from June 1 to November 30, twelve of thirteen major hurricanes that struck the Keys between 1894 and the late 1960s struck between August and October (Sugg et al., 1970).

Table 17.1. South Florida coral reef age, accretion, and growth rates

Reef	Base age (YBP) with confidence limits	Accretion (m)	Growth rate (m/1000 yr)
Long Key	5630 (120)	5.0	0.65
Carysfort	5250 (85)	7.3	0.86–4.85
Grecian Rocks	5950 (100)	9.5	6–8
Bahia Honda	7160 (85)	4.6–8.2	1.14
Looe Key	6580 (90)	7.3	1.12
Bird Key	6017 (90)	13.7	1.36–4.85
Hillsboro[a]	8900 (95)	10.0	—

Sources: Lighty (1977), Shinn et al. (1977), and Shinn (1980).

a. Hillsboro Reef is a fossil Holocene reef off Broward County that appears to have died about 6000 YBP.

Oceanography

An extensive data base of seawater temperatures was established during the late nineteenth and early twentieth centuries from daily measurements taken by lighthouse keepers in the Keys and at Fort Jefferson, Dry Tortugas. These data, as well as more recent data from Biscayne National Park (Jaap, 1984), show winter mean temperatures of about 22°C (72°F) and summer means of 28–30°C (82–86°F). In some years, abnormally cold polar air masses have cooled coastal waters, causing fish and coral kills, particularly off Loggerhead Key, Dry Tortugas, and Plantation Key (Jaap, 1984).

As noted earlier, the Florida Current is responsible for the mild winter temperatures that permit reef development in the Florida Keys. The current flows about 150 cm/s, carrying two water masses in its surface layer (Wennekens, 1959). The eastern core is composed of Caribbean water that flows into the Gulf of Mexico through the Straits of Yucatan. The western portion, which encounters the Florida reef tract, is composed of water from the Gulf of Mexico.

Tidal range is less than a meter throughout the Florida Keys. The Atlantic coast from Miami to Key West experiences semidiurnal tides. Areas influenced by the Gulf of Mexico have semidiurnal to diurnal tides. The major effect of tides on reef communities occurs when extremes in weather coincide with spring low tides when shallow reef flats are near-emergent. During summer, if winds are calm, the water temperature over the reef flat can exceed 32°C (90°F) and induce zooxanthellae expulsion (Jaap, 1979, 1985). During winter, cold air masses can cool waters on the reef flat. Because the chilled water is denser than ambient water, it sinks to the bottom and flows downslope, stressing both reef flat and reef slope organisms (Hudson et al., 1976).

Normal marine salinities (34–37 percent) occur throughout the reef tract (Jaap, 1984). Heavy rainfall can reduce salinities temporarily in the enclosed bays.

Over the reef tract, dissolved oxygen in the water column ranges diurnally from 90 percent to 125 percent oxygen saturation, with daily maxima occurring between 2 P.M. and 4 P.M. (Jones, 1963). Oxygen availability in the water column is probably not a limiting factor for corals under most circumstances (Jones, 1963). However, bacterial blooms in coral mucus can produce oxygen stress at the coral surface if corals are stimulated to secrete more mucus than they can shed (Mitchell and Chet, 1975). Suspended sediments (Dodge et al., 1974), pollutants, and even excess food supply (Mitchell and Chet, 1975) all stimulate mucus secretion. Wave action normally carries away excess mucus, but during summer periods of calm winds and waves, mucus buildup accompanied by warm temperatures that spur bacterial growth could produce stressful conditions, particularly at night. Surface sediments generally are oxygenated on open shelves, in passes, and reef margins (Jaap, 1984) but can be organic-rich and suboxic in the sea grasses, mangroves, and enclosed bays and sounds (Lynts, 1966).

Clear waters are crucial to reef-building corals because their zooxanthellae require sunlight. The clearer the water, the deeper corals can live (Hallock and Schlager, 1986). Water transparency over Florida reefs can vary considerably, from nearly opaque following storms to exceptional clarity during prolonged calm (Jaap, 1984). Plankton, suspended organic matter, and sediments all diminish water transparency. Zooxanthellate corals require a minimum of about 4 percent of surface radiation for reef development (Kanwisher and Wainwright, 1967) and about 0.15 percent for survival (Reed, 1985). Data on water transparency in the Florida Keys area, summarized by Jaap (1984), indicate reef growth in the Keys can normally occur to about 30 m and zooxanthellate corals can survive to about 40–45 m maximum.

Reef Biology and Ecology

Coral Biology

Reef corals are found in two classes of the Phylum Cnidaria (Coelenterata): Hydrozoa and Anthozoa. In the Florida Keys, *Millepora* (fire coral) is the only hydrozoan coral on shallow reefs (<30 m); *Stylaster* and *Distichopora* occur in deep reef habitats. The anthozoans include octocorals (Octocorallia), zoanthids (Zoantharia), stony corals (Scleractinia), false corals (Corallimorpharia), and anemones (Actinaria). Reef corals are colonial, often containing thousands of individual members or polyps (fig. 17.5).

Milleporina. The fire coral, whose name comes from the burning sensation inflicted by nematocysts (microscopic stinging organs), secretes a limestone skeleton with microscopic pores in which the individuals (zooids) live. Patterns of larger central pores surrounded by smaller pores can be distinguished with a microscope. Within a colony, the larger pores house the gastrozooids, which, by possessing a mouth and the ability to secrete digestive enzymes, are morphologically adapted to digest food. Dactylozooids bearing nematocysts dwell in the smaller pores; they defend the colony and capture food, providing the colony with nutrients and some energy. The porous limestone skeleton is covered with tissues containing dense concentrations of zooxanthellae that provide most of the carbon used by the colony. The golden-yellow color of the fire coral comes from these microscopic algae.

Two species of fire coral are found on Florida reefs. The bladed fire coral (*Millepora complanata*) is a keel-shaped species restricted to shallow windward reef tops. Mergner (1977) found that this species is restricted to turbulent and highly illuminated reef habitats. Crenulated fire coral (*M. alcicornis*) is a branching species found in a much wider range of reef habitats.

The life cycle of hydrozoan corals involves asexual colonial generations, which produce microscopic planktonic medusae by budding. The medusa is

Fig. 17.5. Photograph of rose coral (*Manicina areolata*) with tentacles extended.

the sexual stage, producing gametes that are released into the water. Following fertilization, a planktonic larva develops and then settles to the bottom and produces a new fire coral colony. Although growth data for *Millepora* are nonexistent, we estimate from personal observation that fire corals extend upward at about 10 cm/yr.

Octocorallia. The octocorals, which include the sea whips, sea plumes, sea fans, gorgonians, and soft corals, are a conspicuous and diverse faunal element on most Florida Keys reefs (table 17.2). Their common characteristic is that their polyps bear eight tentacles. Octocorals vary in form from irregular mats to large sea fans; polyps are distributed along the branches, fan surfaces, or mats. Organic skeletons are commonly reinforced by calcareous spicules, which are secreted by the polyps. Taxonomy of octocorals is based upon the microscopic morphology of the spicules (Bayer, 1961).

Life histories of most octocoral species are poorly known. One species, *Plexaura homomalla*, has been intensively studied in the Cayman Islands (Kinzie, 1974). Colonies of this dioecious species become sexually mature at 25–35 mm in height. Male individuals release sperm into the water, and fertilization occurs within the female polyps. Larvae spend a brief time in the plankton before settling on appropriate substrata and starting new colonies. Growth rates vary from 10 to 40 mm/yr.

Octocorals are extremely abundant in some reef habitats, occurring in densities up to 50 colonies/m^2 (Opresko, 1973). Many octocoral species inhabit shallow patch reef and bank reef habitats in areas with substantial turbulence and high light intensities. Highest rates of mortality occur during larval and juvenile life stages. Mortality is also high among adult colonies dislodged by storms. Invertebrate predators include the snails *Cyphoma gibbosum* and *Coralliophila caribaea* and the worm *Hermodice carunculata.*

Scleractinia. The Scleractinia, or stony corals, include common reef-building species. Taxonomy is based on external skeletal morphology and

Table 17.2. Florida Keys octocoral fauna (<30 m)

Briarium asbestinum	*Plexaurella dichotoma*
Iciligorgia schrammi	*P. nutans*
Erythropodium caribaeorum	*P. grisea*
Plexaura homomalla	*P. fusifera*
P. flexuosa	*Muricea muricata*
Pseudoplexaura porosa	*M. atlantica*
P. flagellosa	*M. laxa*
P. wagenaari	*M. elongata*
P. crucis	*Lophogorgia hebes*
Eunicea palmeri	*Pseudopterogorgia bipinnata*
E. pinta	*P. kallos*
E. mammosa	*P. rigida*
E. succinea	*P. acerosa*
E. fusca	*P. americana*
E. laciniata	*P. elisabethae*
E. tourneforti	*P. navia*
E. asperula	*Gorgonia ventalina*
E. clavigera	*Pterogorgia citrina*
E. knighti	*P. anceps*
E. calyculata	*P. guadalupensis*
Muriceopsis flavida	*Nicella schmitti*

Sources: Bayer (1961); Opresko (1973); Wheaton, Florida Department of Natural Resources (in preparation).

calyx characteristics (Vaughan and Wells, 1943; Wells, 1956; Zlatarski and Estalella, 1982). The Scleractinia are thought to have evolved from the anemones (Wells, 1956) by developing the ability to secrete limestone skeletons.

Although sixty-three coral taxa (species and subspecies or forma), living at depths of <1 m to 45 m, have been recognized in the Florida Keys (table 17.3), information on their life cycles comes largely from other Caribbean areas or from work completed before 1920 at Dry Tortugas. Stony coral generation times vary greatly, ranging from a few years in small finger corals to hundreds of years in massive star and brain corals. Sexual maturity appears to depend upon both size and age of a colony. Large, sexually mature colonies, if broken into small fragments, cease gamete production until they grow to a minimum size (Kojis and Quinn, 1984; Szmant-Froelich, 1985).

Individuals of *Montastraea annularis* (fig. 17.6) must be at least 40–50 mm in diameter, representing at least four years' growth or about 350 polyps, before they are sexually mature (Szmant-Froelich, 1985). Polyps bear gametes of both sexes, but female gametes mature before male gametes. On Puerto Rican reefs, gametes begin to develop in mid-May, and spawning occurs in September (Szmant-Froelich, 1984). Gonad development is nearly synchronous within colonies; individual polyps produce twelve gonads that each contain six to fourteen eggs. Both eggs and sperm are released into the water column where fertilization takes place.

Table 17.3. Florida Keys Scleractinia (<45 m)

Order Scleractinia
Suborder Astrocoeniina Vaughan and Wells
  Family Astrocoeniidae Koby
    Stephanocoenia michelinii (Milne Edwards and Haime)
  Family Pocilloporidae Gray
    Madracis decactis (Lyman)
    M. formosa Wells
    M. mirabilis (*sensu* Wells)
  Family Acroporidae Verrill
    Acropora palmata (Lamarck)
    A. cervicornis (Lamarck)
    A. prolifera (Lamarck)
Suborder Fungiina (Verrill)
  Family Agariciidae Gray
    Agaricia agaricites (Linné)
    A. agaricites danai Milne Edwards and Haime
    A. agaricites carinata Wells
    A. agaricites purpurea (LeSueur)
    A. lamarcki Milne Edwards and Haime
    A. undata (Ellis and Solander)
    A. fragilis (Dana)
    Leptoseris cucullata (Ellis and Solander)
  Family Siderastreidae Vaughan and Wells
    Siderastrea radians (Pallas)
    S. siderea (Ellis and Solander)
  Family Poritidae Gray
    Porites astreoides (Lamarck)
    P. porites (Pallas)
    P. porites divaricata LeSueur
    P. porites furcata Lamarck
    P. porites clavaria Lamarck
    P. branneri Rathbun
Suborder Faviina Vaughan and Wells
  Family Faviidae Gregory
    Favia fragum (Esper)
    F. gravida (Verrill)
    Diploria labyrinthiformis (Linné)
    D. clivosa (Ellis and Solander)
    D. strigosa (Dana)
    Manicina areolata (Linné)
    M. areolata mayori Wells
    Colpophyllia natans (Houttyn)
    C. amaranthus (Müller)
    C. breviseralis Milne Edwards and Haime
    Cladocora arbuscula (LeSueur)
    Montastraea annularis (Linné)
    M. annularis (Ellis and Solander)
    Solenastrea hyades (Dana)
    S. bournoni Milne Edwards and Haime

(*continued*)

Table 17.3. (continued)

Family Rhizangiidae d'Orbigny
Astrangia astreiformis (Milne Edwards and Haime)
A. solitaria (LeSueur)
Phyllangia americana Milne Edwards and Haime
Family Oculinidae Gray
Oculina diffusa Lamarck
O. varicosa LeSueur
O. robusta Pourtalès
Family Meandrinidae Gray
Meandrina meandrites (Linné)
M. meandrites brasiliensis (Milne Edwards and Haime)
Dichocoenia stellaris Milne Edwards and Haime
D. stokesii Milne Edwards and Haime
Dendrogyra cylindrus Ehrenberg
Family Mussidae Ortman
Mussa angulosa (Pallas)
Scolymia lacera (Pallas)
S. cubensis (Milne Edwards and Haime)
Isophyllia sinuosa (Ellis and Solander)
I. multiflora Verrill
Isophyllastraea rigida (Dana)
Mycetophyllia lamarckiana Milne Edwards and Haime
M. danaana Milne Edwards and Haime
M. ferox Wells
M. aliciae Wells
Suborder Caryophylliina Vaughan and Wells
Family Caryophylliidae Gray
Eusmillia fastigiata (Pallas)
Paracyathus pulchellus (Phillippi)
Suborder Dendrophylliina Vaughan and Wells
Family Dendrophylliidae Gray
Balanophyllia floridana Pourtalès

Among other stony coral species, internal fertilization, external fertilization, broadcasting of gametes, and larval brooding all have been reported (Fadlallah, 1983). After fertilization and embryonic development, free-living planula larvae are formed, which can be either planktonic or benthic. After periods that vary from species to species and also with environmental conditions, the larvae settle and metamorphose into juvenile corals. A larva attaches itself to the substratum by secreting a basal plate, the initial skeletal structure. Walls and axial structures are secreted next (Wells, 1956). Growth involves a harmonious integrated increase in coral tissue, zooxanthellae, and skeleton (Barnes, 1973). When the larva is fully transformed into a polyp, growth proceeds with the budding of daughter polyps by asexual division.

Growth rates of Florida's reef-building corals have not been studied extensively. X-ray photographs of *Montastraea annularis* reveal annual growth

Fig. 17.6. A colony of star coral (*Montastraea annularis*) approximately 2 m high.

rings, which can be used to determine growth and environmental conditions (Hudson et al., 1976; Hudson, 1981). Growth rate in this species is relatively slow; the extension rate is <11 mm/yr (table 17.4). In contrast, the growth rate of *Acropora cervicornis* is rapid (> 100 mm/yr).

Nutrients and Reef Productivity

Inorganic nutrients are essential for plant growth. Seawater concentrations of some nutrients—such as sulphate, magnesium, and potassium—are high, whereas other essential nutrients, like fixed nitrogen, phosphorus, and iron, are present only in minute amounts. Subtropical sea surface waters typically contain less than 0.3 μM inorganic phosphorus and less than 1 μM inorganic fixed nitrogen (Crossland, 1983). Nutrient levels in surface waters of the Florida reef tract can vary from barely detectable to in excess of 1 μM inorganic phosphorus and 3 μM inorganic fixed nitrogen (R. Skinner and W. Jaap, unpubl. data).

There is a disagreement over which nutrient, fixed nitrogen or phosphate, limits coral growth (Gladfelter, 1985), though the abundance of nitrogen-fixing bacteria in reef systems (Johannes et al., 1972; Pilson and Betzer, 1973) supports the argument for phosphate (e.g., Littler and Littler, 1984). The lowest nitrogen values are often accompanied by relatively high phosphate levels and vice versa.

Coral reefs provide a fascinating paradox: healthy, well-developed reefs

Table 17.4. Growth rates of Florida reef Scleractinia

Species	Growth rate[a] (mm $year^{-1}$)	Location	Source
Acropora cervicornis	40	Dry Tortugas	Vaughan (1915)
	109	Key Largo Dry Rocks	Shinn (1966)
	115	Eastern Sambo	Jaap (1974)
A. palmata	105	Eastern Sambo	Jaap (1974)
Agaricia agaricites	4	Dry Tortugas	Vaughan (1916)
Porites porites	18	Dry Tortugas	Vaughan (1916)
	15	Lower Keys	Landon (1975)
P. astreoides	10	Dry Tortugas	Vaughan (1916)
Siderastrea radians	2	Dry Tortugas	Vaughan (1916)
S. siderea	4	Dry Tortugas	Vaughan (1916)
	3	Lower Keys	Landon (1975)
Favia fragum	4	Dry Tortugas	Vaughan (1916)
Diploria labyrinthiformis	4	Key Largo	Ghiold and Enos (1982)
D. clivosa	6	Dry Tortugas	Vaughan (1916)
Manicina strigosa	7	Dry Tortugas	Vaughan (1916)
	5	Carysfort	Shinn (1976)
M. areolata	8	Dry Tortugas	Vaughan (1916)
M. areolata mayori	6	Dry Tortugas	Vaughan (1916)
Montastraea cavernosa	5	Dry Tortugas	Vaughan (1916)
M. annularis	9	Key West	Agassiz (1890)
	6	Dry Tortugas	Vaughan (1916)
	11	Carysfort	Hoffmeister and Multer (1964)
	8	Lower Keys	Landon (1975)
	8	Carysfort	Shinn (1976)
	9	Key Largo	Hudson (1981)
Oculina diffusa	14	Dry Tortugas	Vaughan (1916)
Dichocoenia stokesii	5	Dry Tortugas	Vaughan (1916)
Eusmilia fastigiata	6	Dry Tortugas	Vaughan (1916)

a. Values, averaged and rounded to nearest mm, are for increase in height and/or outward extension.

are found in the most nutrient-deficient waters in the world. Hallock and Schlager (1986) summarized why reefs are best developed in such conditions. If nutrients are readily available in the water column, plankton growth stimulated by nutrients will diminish water transparency. The more nutrient-deficient the water, the clearer it is and the deeper corals can live. Besides diminishing water clarity, increased plankton abundances favor larval survival, recruitment and growth of coral predators, competitors, and bioeroders (Hallock and Schlager, 1986). Abundant nutrients also stimulate benthic algal growth. Overgrowth by benthic algae is harmful to living corals (e.g., Smith et al., 1981) and inhibits coral recruitment (Birkeland, 1977, 1987).

Understanding that coral reefs are adapted to nutrient-deficient conditions helps explain why reefs are so dependent upon associated ecosystems, particularly mangrove and sea grass communities. Nutrients and sediments shed from terrestrial environments are intercepted by mangrove and sea grass communities before they reach the reef margin. With their more plentiful supplies of nutrients, these communities also provide nursery areas for juveniles and foraging areas for adult animals that inhabit the reef.

This interdependence of various community elements is exemplified by the life cycle of the spiny lobster (*Panulirus argus*). Mature spiny lobsters live, breed, and spawn on coral reefs. The planktonic larvae live for several months in the oceanic water column. Juveniles settle near shore in algae associated with sea grass communities (Marx and Herrnkind, 1985). Larger juveniles live in live-bottom habitats or mangroves before moving offshore to patch reefs and finally to reef margins as mature adults (Lyons et al., 1981). Adult lobsters also use different ecosystem components on a diurnal cycle, seeking refuge in reef dens during the day and moving into sea grass beds and sedimentary environments to forage for small molluscs, crustaceans, and other prey at night.

Because reefs are highly adapted to nutrient deficiency, nutrient pollution can be a serious threat (Weiss and Goddard, 1977; Smith et al., 1981). Florida reefs that are already near their temperature limits may be particularly vulnerable. Cold fronts and hurricanes periodically decimate Florida reefs. As long as nutrient levels remain favorable for reef development, the communities can recover over several years or decades. However, if nutrient pollution diminishes water quality, recovery of reefs after physical disturbances is retarded or prevented.

Trophic Relationships and Community Structure

The visible biological richness of a coral reef is remarkable. Literally thousands of species are known from the Florida reef tract (table 17.5), even though groups such as bacteria, sponges, and crustaceans have not been studied intensively. Complexity is further enhanced by transitory animals, such as birds and turtles, that feed, breed, or seek temporary shelter on coral reefs. Floating algae, with associated organisms, are also transitory constituents.

The function of corals in the reef ecosystem is similar to that of trees in a forest. Each is not only the major primary producer in its ecosystem but also the principal source of spatial complexity. Coral reefs are often compared to tropical rainforests in the way space and resources are stratified: canopy, understory, and substory.

Corals, together with some octocorals and larger sponges, form the canopy. Although these are animals, they function as primary producers in the reef system via their zooxanthellae. However, since many corals are highly specialized predators (Yonge, 1930), they also capture plankton from the

Table 17.5. Numbers of species that live in association with Florida Keys reefs

Taxonomic category	No. of species[a]	Source
Algae	60	Eiseman (1981)
Sponges	120	Schmahl (1984)
Octocorals (soft corals)	42	Jaap (1984)
Stony corals	63	Table 17.4
Crustaceans	500	Camp (1)
Polychaetes (marine worms)	450	Perkins (1)
Molluscs	1200	Lyons (1)
Echinoderms	75	Miller (2)
Fish	450	Tilmant (1984)
Birds	40	Robertson (3)

a. Values represent the taxa known or estimated from reef habitats in depths <1 m to 30 m. Unpublished sources are the best estimates of specialists based on their expertise. Unpublished sources are affiliated with

(1) Florida Marine Research Institute, Florida Department of Natural Resources, 100 8th Ave. SE, St. Petersburg, FL 33701;

(2) Harbor Branch Oceanographic Institution, 5600 Old Dixie Highway, Ft. Pierce, FL 33450;

(3) Research Center, Everglades National Park, P.O. Box 279, Homestead, FL 33030.

water column. Some species ingest bacteria from seawater (DiSalvo, 1971); some can feed on dissolved organics in seawater (Stephens, 1962); and some may utilize organic matter in detritus (Goreau and Goreau, 1960). Many species even digest the tissues of other coral species using mesenterial filaments (Lang, 1971, 1973). Despite the variety of sources, direct feeding often supplies less than 10 percent of the corals' energy needs (Muscatine and Porter, 1977). In such cases, most energy comes from photosynthesis by zooxanthellae (Kanwisher and Wainwright, 1967; Lewis, 1977; Gladfelter, 1983; Chalker et al., 1984). The zooxanthellae, in turn, obtain nutrients from metabolic waste products of the coral host as well as from seawater or detritus.

Algal symbiosis allows the coral to function as a "free link" in the food chain; the coral-symbiont system, by recycling nutrients, can potentially produce nearly as much biomass as originally captured by the coral (Hallock, 1981). Even though inorganic nutrients and food are scarce in the environment, the coral has a variety of ways to acquire those scarce resources; once acquired, the nutrients are retained within the system, where they are used by the zooxanthellae to photosynthesize more organic matter. Thus, the coral-symbiont system concentrates scarce and dispersed nutrients from a variety of sources and uses them for maintenance, growth, and reproduction.

Nutrient recycling also helps explain why gross primary productivity on coral reefs can exceed that of areas where nutrients are abundant (Sournia, 1977). Gross primary productivity seems to be controlled principally by light availability and by rates of nutrient recycling within the community (Smith et al., 1981). In the clear waters over a healthy reef, light is readily available, recycling rates are high, and so is gross primary productivity. Yet net (i.e., harvestable) primary productivity is low because most of the organic matter produced is quickly metabolized, freeing nutrients to be reused in photosynthesis.

Photosynthesis by zooxanthellae also promotes production of skeletal limestones that make up the reef framework (Kawaguti and Sakumoto, 1948; Goreau, 1959). Zooxanthellae provide coral with the energy needed to calcify. They also may prevent phosphate poisoning of calcification by removing phosphatic wastes and any phosphates in the microenvironment; phosphate inhibits precipitation of aragonite crystals, the skeletal building blocks of corals (Simkiss, 1964).

Photosynthesis uses carbon dioxide from the water and from respiration, thereby raising the pH of the system and enhancing aragonite precipitation (Borowitzka and Larkum, 1976). During calcification (fig. 17.7), calcium ions, which are abundant in seawater, combine with bicarbonate ions, which are also readily available in the environment. Goreau (1961) postulated that the reaction proceeds in steps. Calcium bicarbonate is formed first:

$$Ca^{2+} + 2HCO_3^- \longrightarrow Ca(HCO_3)_2 \quad (1)$$

then calcium carbonate and carbonic acid are produced:

$$Ca(HCO_3)_2 \longrightarrow CaCO_3 + H_2CO_3. \quad (2)$$

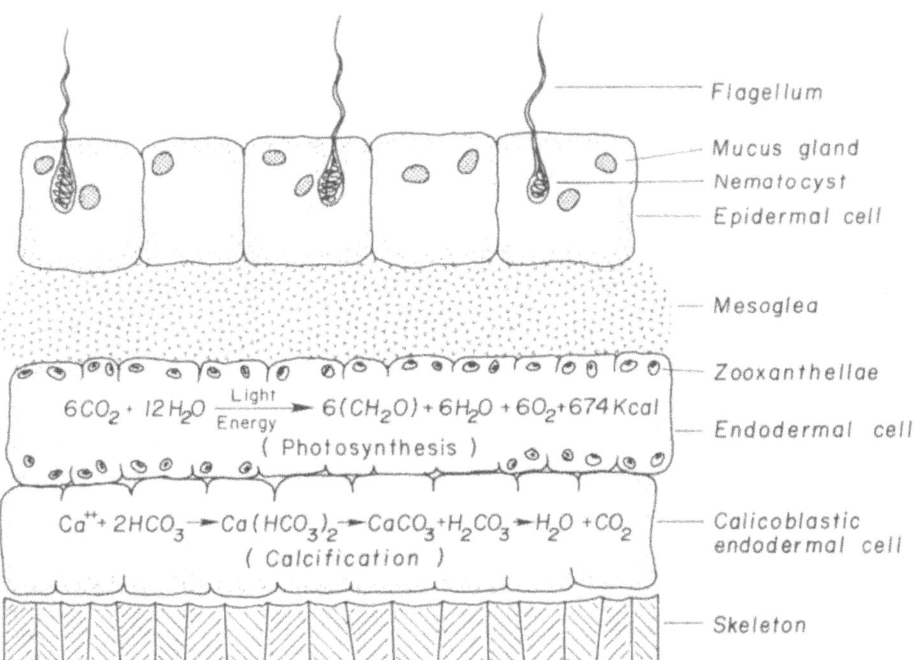

Fig. 17.7. Coral tissues, skeleton, and physiological processes.

But carbonic acid cannot coexist with calcium carbonate, so the carbonic acid must be ionized:

$$H_2CO_3 \longrightarrow H^+ + HCO_3^- \quad (3)$$

or converted to water and carbon dioxide:

$$H_2CO_3 \longrightarrow H_2O + CO_2. \quad (4)$$

Reactions (3) and (4) are catalyzed by the enzyme carbonic anhydrase, which is concentrated in the calicoblastic epithelium, the coral tissue layer in which calcium metabolism is most active (Isa and Yamazato, 1984). Calcium carbonate is apparently stored, then actively transported in a system of microvesicles to the deposition site (Johnston, 1980), where it is deposited as aragonite crystals (Barnes, 1973; Gladfelter, 1982; Oliver et al., 1983). Chalker (1983), Gladfelter (1985), and Kinsey (1985) review this subject.

Branching corals, as well as the reef framework, provide shelter for fish that feed upon the plankton in the overlying water column. These fish might be compared to the small birds and bats that dwell in the forest canopy and venture out to feed on insects. The coral canopy provides shelter from larger predators, such as sharks and barracuda, that prowl the reef margins. The reef also provides shelter for organisms, such as lobsters, that hunt in the sea grass behind the reef. There is mutual benefit to the reef and the organisms that seek refuge in the reef. The fish and crustaceans that seek refuge in the reef (fig. 17.8) transfer nutrients and organic matter, by means of their excreta, from the water column or sea grass flat to the reef (Faulkner and Chesher, 1979; Meyer et al., 1983). Faulkner and Chesher (1979) observed coral ingesting fecal pellets of fish. Thus, nutrients are available to corals and to algae living in the understory but do not promote phytoplankton growth in the overlying water column—growth that would reduce light reaching the benthos.

Understory biota includes photosynthetic organisms, such as algae and many kinds of sponges, ascidians, and foraminifera that harbor algal symbionts, all contributing to the productivity of the reef while benefiting from the nutrients brought in by mobile organisms. These and other epibenthic organisms, such as polychaetes and bryozoans, live upon the dead portions of the coral surface.

Substory biota, also known as cryptofauna, live within the coral framework. Boring organisms—including fungi, certain algae, polychaete and sipunculid worms, *Lithophaga* clams, and sponges (Bromley, 1978; Risk and MacGeachy, 1978)—excavate the limestone structure, providing habitat for themselves and ultimately producing a labyrinth of tunnels and caves. Smaller caves are occupied by small crustaceans, molluscs, and worms. Larger, deeper excavations, often found at the reef base, provide shelter for fish, crabs, and lobsters. The excavations also provide surfaces on and

Fig. 17.8. Schools of goat fish (*Mulloidichthys martinicus*) sheltered among broad branches of elkhorn coral (*Acropora palmata*).

within the reef for sessile organisms, such as bryozoans, ascidians, and serpulid worms.

Diversity

Biogeographic and environmental factors together determine how many species will be found on a particular reef. Biogeographic factors determine what species are regionally available. Thus, a healthy Florida reef will not have a coral fauna as diverse as a comparable western Pacific reef, simply because West Indian reef biotas have declined in diversity more during the past 15 million years than have Indo–west Pacific biotas (Frost, 1977). Because Florida's reefs are located near the northern limit of West Indian biotas, their diversities are further diminished relative to comparable central Caribbean reefs, such as those of the Cayman Islands. The actual number of plant and animal species on a particular reef is primarily controlled by local environmental factors, such as water transparency, spatial heterogeneity, depth, age of the reef, frequency and magnitude of physical disturbance (environmental predictability), and organismal life histories (Grassle, 1973).

To date, no one has completed an intensive investigation of floral and faunal diversity of a single Florida reef. Voss (1983) reported 62 algal species, 3 sea grasses, 55 sponges, 73 cnidarians, 22 worms, 67 molluscs, 37 crustaceans, 7 tunicates, and 224 fish species from the Key Largo area, including sedimentary, sea grass, live-bottom, and coral reef habitats. Those numbers represent only a small fraction of the species that actually live there.

Water transparency controls the depth ranges of photosynthesizing organisms. On well-developed reefs worldwide, coral and algal species diversity increases from the reef crest to maxima at depths of 20–30 m (Huston, 1985). Because light penetrates only about half as deeply on Florida's reefs as on many other Caribbean reefs, maximum diversity on Florida's reefs would be expected at about 8–15m.

Spatial heterogeneity is an obvious factor controlling reef diversity. If more kinds of microhabitats are available, more kinds of species can be supported. Depth, water transparency, and age of the reef influence spatial heterogeneity. Coral species show depth zonation: branching species thrive in relatively shallow water where at least 60 percent of surface light is available; star and brain corals flourish down to 20 percent of surface light (Huston, 1985); and plate corals thrive down to about 4 percent (Kanwisher and Wainwright, 1967) and can occur at depths with as little as 0.15 percent of surface light (Reed, 1985). On a Florida Keys reef, the depths to which those light levels are available are approximately 5 m, 15 m, 30 m, and in excess of 43 m, respectively (calculated from values reported in Jaap, 1984). On a mature reef, three-dimensional spatial heterogeneity is well developed in the massive head coral zone, possibly declining somewhat upward into the branching coral zone, and declining substantially with increasing depth as massive head corals give way to low-lying plate corals. Topography of the original substratum upon which the reef grew can also influence spatial heterogeneity.

Environmental predictability influences how close a reef's diversity can approach its maximum potential. Overall, diversity on a reef recently devastated by a hurricane, cold front, or other major disturbance will be lower than on one that has developed for decades with only minor disturbances. Florida's reefs are particularly vulnerable to cold fronts (Jaap, 1984), compared to reefs at lower latitudes.

Environmental predictability is also a major factor creating depth-related diversity gradients. Though spatial heterogeneity on a shallow reef margin may be comparable to that of the deeper head coral zone, lack of environmental predictability limits diversity on the shallow margin. Ultraviolet radiation, thermal extremes, desiccation during extremely low spring tides, high wave energy, and abrasion by sediments carried by storm waves all act to reduce diversity. Connell's (1978) intermediate magnitude and frequency disturbance model, when applied to Florida's reefs, indicates that disturbance occurs at such magnitude and frequency as to prevent development of highly diverse reef communities at depths < 2 m.

Biological Interactions

Complex biological interactions are particularly characteristic of coral reef communities. Grazing and predation can be readily observed in any euphotic community. But on coral reefs disease, competition, chemical "warfare," bioerosion, and symbioses are also common.

Pathogens may injure or kill corals (Mitchell and Chet, 1975; Ducklow and Mitchell, 1979; Antonius, 1974, 1981a,b) and other reef-associated organisms. The most common coral disease reported is the "black band" disease originally described by Antonius (1974). A series of papers redescribed the black band pathogen (*Phormidium corallyticum*: Cyanobacterium: Oscillatoriaceae) and discussed its distribution, ecology, infective mechanism, and growth (Rützler and Santavy, 1983; Rützler et al., 1983; Taylor, 1983). The cyanobacterium attaches to a coral—usually a massive species such as *Montastraea annularis*—following tissue damage. The pathogen then proliferates, feeding on the coral tissues. Other coral pathogens include bacteria (Peters et al., 1983; Peters, 1984) and fungi (Ramos, 1983; Jaap, 1985). An epidemic of unknown cause decimated black sea urchin (*Diadema antillarum*) populations throughout the Caribbean and the Florida Keys during 1983–84 (Bak et al., 1984; Lessios et al., 1984a,b).

Competitive interactions include overgrowth of understory species by species with rapid growth rates, such as the stony coral (*Acropora cervicornis*). Rapidly growing species deny light and water movement, with associated nutritional resources, to the understory corals (Shinn, 1976). Fire coral (*Millepora*) is successful in colonizing living octocoral branches (Whale, 1980), and some bryozoa can overgrow other sessile reef organisms (Buss, 1980). Scleractinian corals expand and defend territory by extracoelentric digestion of adjacent coral tissues through use of mesenterial filaments (Lang, 1971, 1973). Other coral species defend themselves from such attack with specialized sweeper tentacles (den Hartog, 1977; Richardson et al., 1979; Wellington, 1980; Bak et al., 1982; Chornesky and Williams, 1983). Allelopathy (chemical defense and offense) is another mechanism employed by some organisms to prevent overgrowth and gain living space (Cameron, 1974; Glynn, 1980; Bak et al., 1981; Tursch, 1982; Sullivan et al., 1983). Octocorals are perhaps most notorious for the toxic chemicals they produce and excrete.

Damselfish (*Pomacentrus planifrons*) destroy coral tissue and farm algae on the dead coral, defending their territory with bravado (Kaufman, 1977; Brawley and Adey, 1981). The black sea urchin crops algae from the reef, as well as from adjacent areas (Sammarco et al., 1974; Bak and Van Eys, 1975;

Ogden and Lobel, 1978). The urchin provides settlement habitat for coral larvae by rasping off algae and exposing clean limestone substrate (Sammarco, 1980).

Sponges interact in the coral reef in both beneficial and destructive ways. Many sponge species bore into coral skeletons, structurally weakening them (Goreau and Hartman, 1963; Neumann, 1966; Hein and Risk, 1975; Rützler, 1975; Hudson, 1977). Other sponges bind coral skeletons to the reef substrate (Wulff and Buss, 1979; Wulff, 1984), and some sponges protect the coral undersurface from attacks by boring organisms (Goreau and Hartman, 1966). Under low light conditions, sponges are successful competitors for space (Bryan, 1973; Vicente, 1978; Jackson and Winston, 1982).

Numerous organisms live in close association with coral, gaining shelter and food, often devouring mucus that is prevalent on the coral tissue surface. Several copepod species with worm-like body forms live within coral polyps (Patton, 1976). The crab *Domecia acanthophora* and certain pyrogomatid barnacles induce the coral skeleton to grow around them, forming a den or pit that shelters the symbiont (Patton, 1967). The crab has specialized legs that permit it to feed from its den on mucus and suspended matter in the water column.

Predation is another biological interaction that influences coral community structure. The marine worm *Hermodice carunculata* feeds on numerous coral species, including staghorn coral (Marsden, 1960, 1962; Glynn, 1962; Ebbs, 1966; Antonius, 1974; Lizama and Blanquet, 1975). Gastropod molluscs known to feed on corals include *Coralliophila abbreviata, Calliostoma javanicum*, and *Cyphoma gibbosum* (Glynn, 1964, 1973; Robertson, 1970; Ott and Lewis, 1972). Fish that feed on corals include parrotfish (Scaridae), spadefish (Ephippidae), damselfish (Pomacentridae), and butterfly fish (Chaetodontidae) (Glynn, 1973).

Major Reef Types

Bank Reefs

Bank reefs occur 7.4 to 13 km seaward of the Florida Keys, paralleling the coast and continental shelf margin. Major bank reefs are shown in figure 17.4. As noted previously, most occur off Key Largo and from Big Pine Key to Key West where major islands protect the reefs from the detrimental influence of Florida Bay waters.

A reef flat (figs. 17.9, 17.10) is located on the inshore side of the reef. This relatively barren area is characterized by coral rubble encrusted by coralline algae and mustard hill coral (*Porites astreoides*). Waves, intensive solar radiation, and often tidal exposure severely limit the reef flat community. Shoreward, the reef flat grades into a mosaic of sedimentary or sea grass habitats.

Spur and groove formations are a prominent characteristic of bank reefs (figs. 17.9, 17.10). *Spurs* are elongate reefal limestone formations covered with living corals. *Grooves* are valleys containing carbonate sand and rubble that separate the spurs. Spur tops are less than 1 m deep at shoreward ends and as deep as 10 m at seaward margins; spurs may extend a linear distance of several hundred meters. Grooves may be less than 1–4 m deep. Most spur and groove formations extend laterally 1–2 km along reefs within the 1–10 m depth contours. Spur formations are usually aligned perpendicular to the coast and continental shelf margin. In particular, they face into the predominant wind-sea direction. The groove system allows sediments to pass through the reef with minimal damage to attached biota. Grooves also channel water through the reef, delivering oxygen and plankton while removing metabolic wastes.

Spurs are constructional features in Florida reefs (Shinn, 1963; Shinn et al., 1981). The major spur builder is elkhorn coral (*Acropora palmata*); excavations and cores reveal fossil *A. palmata*, in growth position, aligned linearly. Other corals, algae, and limestone debris fill spaces between *A. palmata* colonies. Under optimum environmental conditions, this species can monopolize large areas (Glynn, 1973; Adey, 1977). Spur construction occurs in several stages. The initial stage includes recruitment, exploitation, and

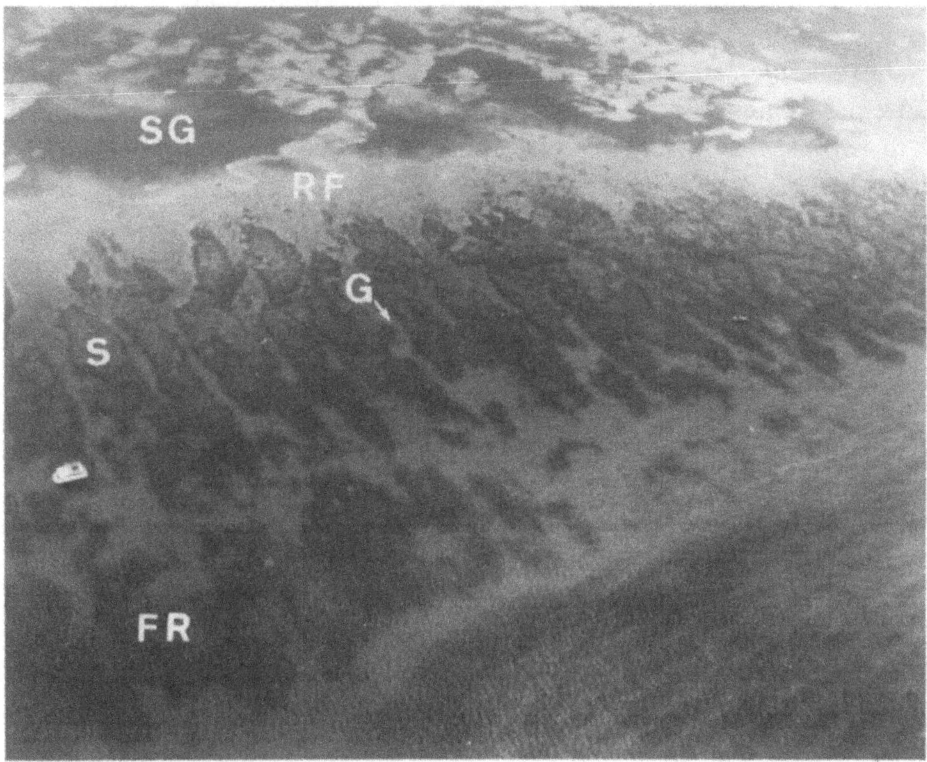

Fig. 17.9. Aerial photograph of Looe Key Reef, photographed from seaward toward land. *G*, groove; *S*, spur; *SG*, sea grass; *RF*, reef flat rubble zone; *FR*, forereef area in depths of 9–10 m.

monopolization of shallow (< 5 m) reef habitat by *A. palmata*. Not only does this species have one of the highest growth rates of any stony coral, but it also recruits vegetatively from broken fragments that fuse to the substratum and develop new colonies. Rubble and debris broken from *A. palmata* and cemented into a solid platform by encrusting coralline algae provide substrata for further coral recruitment. As the population grows upward to low tide level and increases in density, localized reduction in water circulation limits planktonic food supply and may also influence oxygen and carbon dioxide exchange and sediment removal. Overcrowding can increase incidence of disease (Gladfelter, 1982; Peters et al., 1983). When coral growth reaches low tide level, corals die back from environmental stress. Dead corals are encrusted with coralline algae, producing a pavement upon which other organisms can live. Meanwhile, the *A. palmata* population continues to colonize seaward, building upon the skeletons of deeper dwelling corals that grew upward into the *A. palmata* zone or upon debris from its own population.

Communities occupying and constructing spurs are zoned by depth; the major controlling parameters are wave energy and water transparency. A guild of specialized coral and zoanthid species occupies the shallow (< 2 m) spur habitats. This guild is dominated by *Palythoa caribaeorum* (golden sea mat) and *Millepora complanata* (bladed fire coral); other members include *Zoanthus sociatus* (green sea mat) and *Ricordea florida* (false coral) (Wheaton and Jaap, 1988). These species are adapted to the environmental extremes of intense solar radiation and high wave energy. Between 2 m and 5 m depths, *Acropora palmata* dominates, especially in terms of surface area. *Agaricia agaricites* is abundant on vertical surfaces (spur sides). Diversity increases and specific dominance diminishes with increasing depth. Below 6 m, large haystack colonies of *Montastraea annularis* (Fig. 17.6) are major contributors to coral cover in the buttress zone (fig. 17.10).

Some reefs show little or no development seaward of the spur and groove zone, whereas others have a well-developed forereef that slopes to 30–40 m (fig. 17.10). Local conditions and reef age may influence forereef development. Where forereefs are developed, they may be characterized by low relief spur and groove complexes running seaward downslope. Although relief is generally low, corals are often abundant and diverse. Octocorals and sponges are also common.

The deepest portions of Florida bank reefs are in 37–40 m depths (Jaap, 1981) and occur as isolated outcrops surrounded by sediments. Species that seem more abundant in this habitat include *Madracis decactis, Agaricia fragilis, A. lamarcki* (fig. 17.11), *Leptoseris cucullata, Meandrina meandrites* forma *brasiliensis, Mycetophyllia lamarckiana*, and *M. aliciae*.

Stony corals have been surveyed on several bank reefs in the Florida Keys (Jaap, 1984). With the exception of shallow spur and groove habitats,

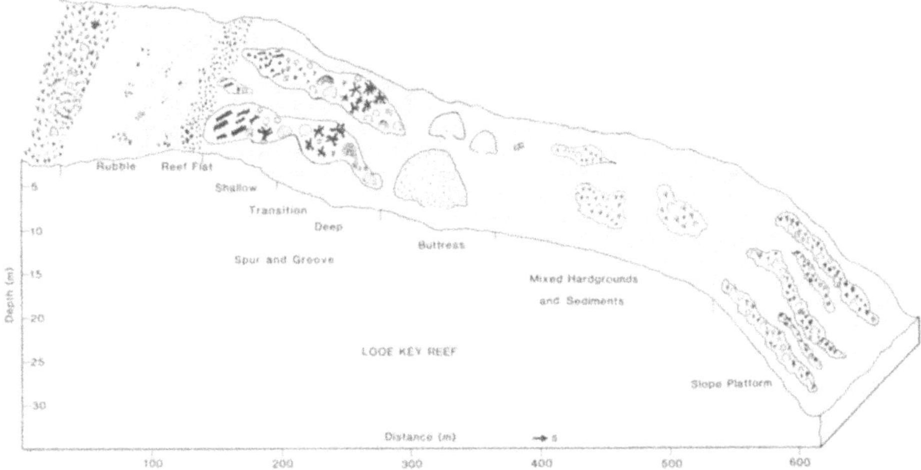

Fig. 17.10. Cross-sectional diagram of Looe Key Reef showing reef zonation.

Fig. 17.11. Lettuce coral (*Agaricia lamarcki*) in about 40 m depth at French Reef, Key Largo National Marine Sanctuary.

there is considerable variability among species associations from similar habitats (fig. 17.12). Intrareef similarity is usually greater than interreef similarity.

Temporal dynamics of bank reef habitats are demonstrated in figure 17.13. Intermediate depth habitats show high degrees of similarity between years and over a five-year period. The Carysfort forereef experienced more change during the study than the spur and groove habitats. In these cases, change was often the result of coral spatial rearrangement rather than mortality and recruitment.

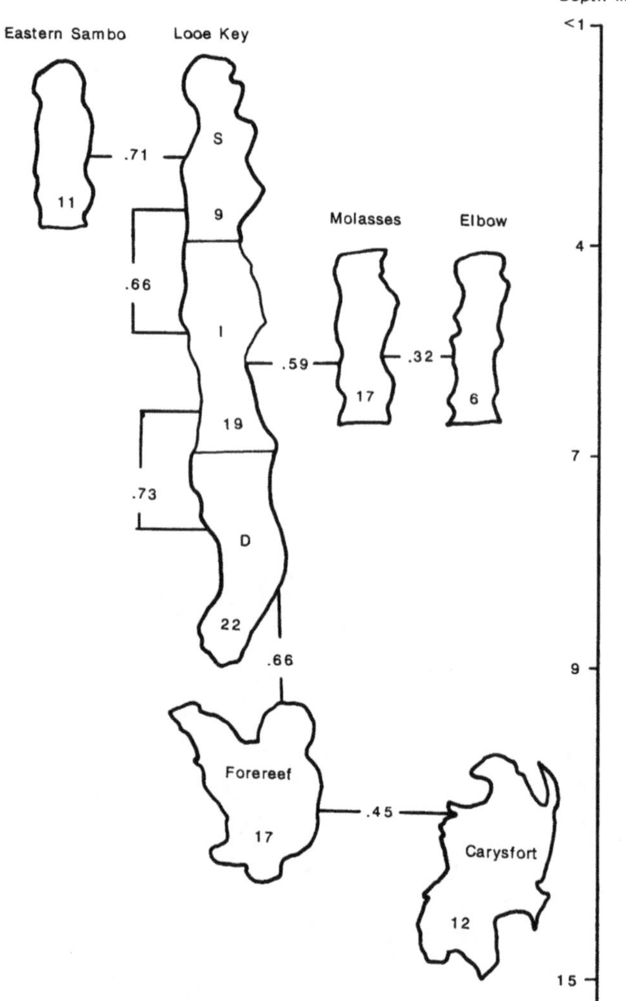

Fig. 17.12. Stony coral spatial similarity of bank reef zones. Data were collected with a quadrat (1 m²); all stony corals within the quadrat perimeter were censused. Classification analysis was employed to analyze similarity. *S*-shallow; *I*-intermediate; *D*-deep. Numbers within reefs are number of species censused during sampling.

Patch Reefs

Patch reefs are found throughout most of the Florida reef tract (Jones, 1977; Marszalek et al., 1977; Davis, 1979, 1982). They are the principal reef form between northern Elliott Key and north Key Largo (fig. 17.4), where approximately 5000 patch reefs are found (Marszalek et al., 1977). Most patch reefs are situated seaward of Hawk Channel and inshore of the outer reef line; exceptions occur between Plantation Key and Newfound Harbor Keys, where patch reefs occur close to the coast. Patch reefs, which typically occur in water depths of about 2–9 m, are usually roughly circular in outline and range from 30 m to 700 m in diameter.

Patch reefs provide topographic relief and biotic diversity in sea grass and sedimentary habitats. The region directly adjacent to the reef is usually barren because reef-dwelling herbivores venture from the reef to graze algae and sea grass (Randall et al., 1964; Randall, 1965; Sammarco et al., 1974). Local environmental conditions, physical characteristics, and reef age deter-

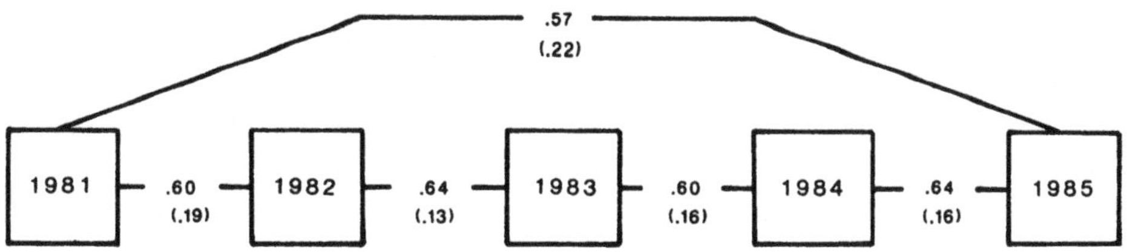

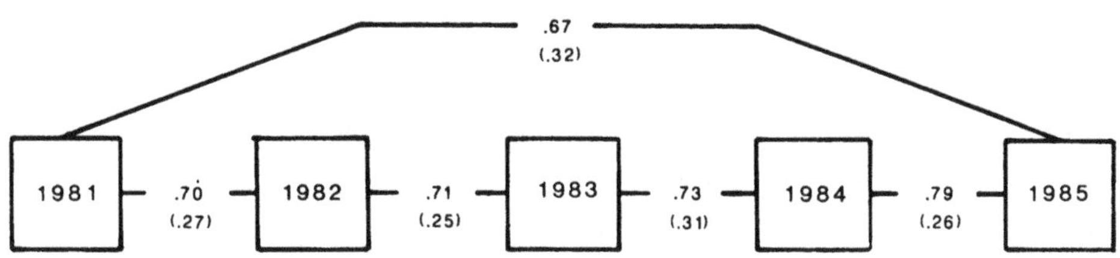

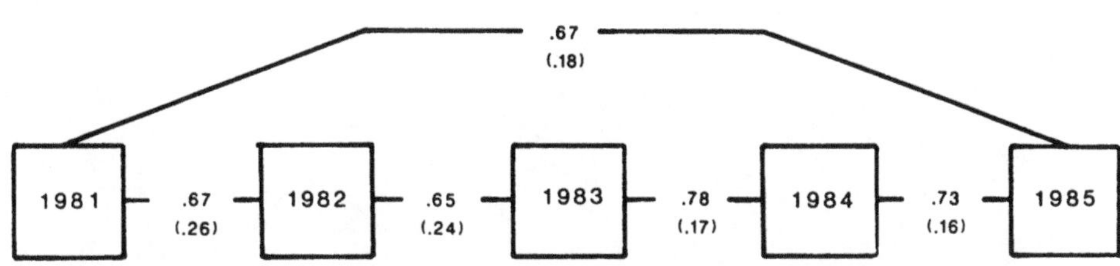

Fig. 17.13. Temporal similarity of three bank reef stations in Key Largo National Marine Sanctuary; refer to figure 17.4 for locations of the reefs. Similarity values are the mean and (standard deviation); *N*-number of quadrats (1 m^2) sampled each year; *S*-standard deviation.

mine physiography. Smith and Tyler (1975) and Jones (1977) proposed a model that considers the patch reef a superorganism with distinctive life stages. In the initial stage, the pioneer corals settle on available hard substrata, such as rocky outcrops and conch shells. These pioneers—*Siderastrea radians, Porites porites, Favia fragum, Cladocora arbuscula*, and *Manicina areolata*—are short-lived, though their skeletal remains provide a foundation upon which the primary framework-building species can settle. Following the establishment of these framework builders—which include *Siderastrea siderea, Diploria strigosa, D. labyrinthiformis, Copophyllia natans*, and *Montastraea annularis*—other corals, sponges, algae, and bryozoans begin to settle and occupy the newly created habitats. As the framework corals grow upward, they add to the heterogeneity of the environment, thereby creating additional niches for other plants and animals. The creation of caverns and tunnels by merging of the coral canopy and bioerosion provides habitat for shade-dwelling organisms and shelter for fish and larger mobile invertebrates.

As the reef approaches sea level, growth is limited to lateral expansion. The upper central portions of older patch reefs are often hard grounds occupied by dense populations of octocorals (fig. 17.14). The reef margins are dominated by stony corals. This pattern can be seen in the coral community of Dome Reef patch reef in Biscayne National Park (Jaap, 1984). The major difference between the interior and the periphery is exemplified by the abundance and cover of star coral (*Montastraea annularis*). At the reef periphery, star coral was the most abundant stony coral, accounting for 17 percent of all coral colonies and 87 percent of stony coral cover. In the reef interior, octocorals were the dominant element, while star coral accounted for 7 percent of all individuals and 55 percent of stony coral cover.

Classification analysis showed a 79 percent similarity level between interior and periphery transects at Dome Reef in 1979. An evaluation of tem-

Fig. 17.14. Dense octocoral populations on a reef in Biscayne National Park, approximately 4 m deep.

poral stability between 1977 and 1981, again using classification analysis of these elements with identical sampling methods (fig. 17.15), showed that change occurred at a level of 30–40 percent each year. Changes were caused by mortality, spatial rearrangement of substratum and its attached benthos by storm activity, and recruitment, mostly by fragmentation (Jaap, 1983).

Dry Tortugas Reefs

Dry Tortugas is composed of islands, shoals, and reefs located about 117 km west of Key West (fig. 17.4). Massive thickets of staghorn coral (*Acropora cervicornis*; fig. 17.16) occur west and north of Loggerhead Key. Early work in the region (Agassiz, 1883) documented wide distribution of staghorn corals at Dry Tortugas. Mayer (1902) reported that an environmental perturbation referred to as "black water" nearly eliminated staghorn corals at Dry Tortugas in 1878. Because staghorn corals are shown in Agassiz's 1883 map, they must have partially recovered in the intervening period. Vaughan (1911) reported that staghorn corals were recovering west of Loggerhead Key.

Cold fronts have dramatically reduced staghorn populations at least twice this century. Populations were reduced by roughly 95 percent during the winter of 1962–63 and again in 1976–77 when cold fronts lowered temperatures to 14°C (57.2°F). Mayer (1914) reported the lower thermal tolerance

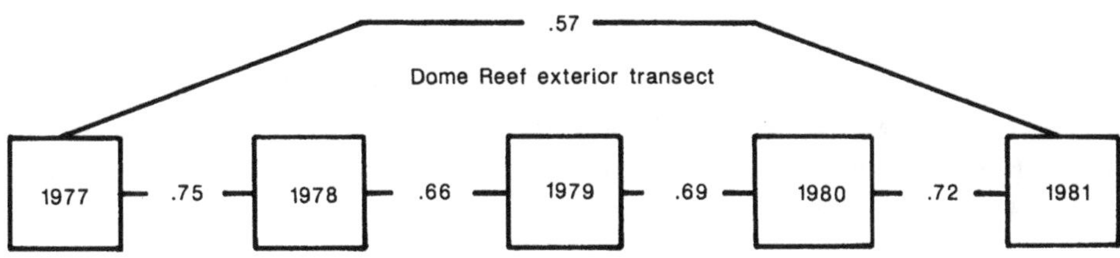

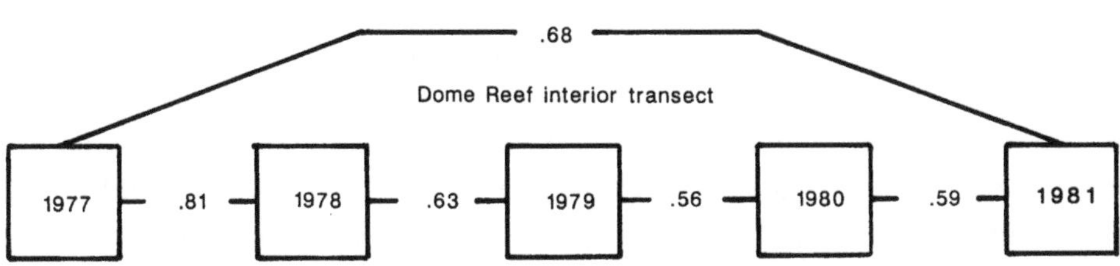

Fig. 17.15. Temporal similarity of peripheral and interior transects at Dome Reef, Biscayne National Park. Species abundance data were classified using Czekanowski's quantitative coefficient; values of 1 document complete similarity and values of 0 complete dissimilarity.

Fig. 17.16. Staghorn coral (*Acropora cervicornis*) thicket west of Loggerhead Key, Dry Tortugas, 2–3 m deep.

of *A. cervicornis* to be 13.5–15°C (56.3–59°F). Staghorn coral proliferates during favorable periods by rapid growth and by fragmentation, which propagates new colonies. Populations recovered to form massive thickets of at least 0.5 m relief by 1981. Those thickets were more than 1 m high in 1984.

In a remote area northwest of Dry Tortugas (fig. 17.4) in depths of 64 m to 76 m, a zone of highly irregular relief supports an unusual biological assemblage visually dominated by frondose green algae (*Anadyomene menziesii*) and large plates of lettuce coral (*Agaricia* spp.). This assemblage was discovered during petroleum environmental impact surveys in 1982 (D. Gettleson, personal communication, Continental Shelf Associates) and may be similar to those found on vertical escarpment habitats of the Bahamas and central Caribbean basin (Ginsburg and James, 1973; Goreau and Land, 1974; Lang, 1974; Reed, 1985). Dredge samples contained five species of octocorals, seventeen stony corals, twelve molluscs, eleven crustaceans, eight bryozoans, two brachiopods, seventeen echinoderms, twenty-seven bony fishes, and numerous species of sponges (D. Gettleson, personal communication).

Human Factors

History of Human Exploitation

Calusa Indians were the early inhabitants of southern Florida. Aboriginal artifacts 2000 years old have been found on Plantation Key, and settlements are also known from Upper and Lower Matecumbe keys. Their society was based on a marine-oriented, subsistence economy; fish, lobster, shellfish, and sea turtles were harvested from coastal waters (Windhorn and Langley, 1974).

The Spanish arrived in Florida in 1513 but did not establish permanent settlements in the Keys. However, many Spanish ships wrecked on reefs and shoals between 1520 and 1763. Nineteen vessels of various sizes were lost between Long Key and Key Largo during one hurricane in 1733. The Spanish established temporary camps in the Keys during salvage operations.

In 1818, the United States purchased Florida from Spain for $5 million. John Simonton settled Key West in 1822, and, in that same year, Commodore David Porter based a flotilla there to combat Caribbean pirates. Because navigation along the Florida Keys reef tract was treacherous, many ships were lost on the poorly charted reefs. Key West residents conducted a thriving industry salvaging cargo and wood from wrecked vessels; during the mid-1800s, the salvage industry was worth approximately $1.5 million annually.

The salvage industry waned as the U.S. Lighthouse Service posted lightships and built lighthouses on major reefs in the Florida Keys between 1825 and 1886. Lighthouses were costly; Carysfort lighthouse, constructed between 1848 and 1852, cost $100,000.

Maritime commerce was the only communication between the Keys and the outside world. Communities developed around coastal, deep water anchorages. The economy was also linked to marine resources. In 1897, the sponge fishery employed 1400 people and was worth $284,640 (Smith, 1897). Harvest of fish, lobster, manatee, sea turtles, crabs, and sponges provided both food and products for export. Fish were transported live to Havana. Exploitation of resources in some cases threatened species survival. The Caribbean monk seal is now extinct, and manatees and sea turtles are endangered or threatened.

In 1912, the Flagler railroad was completed to Key West, effectively linking the Keys to peninsular Florida. The railroad enhanced transport of seafood to northern markets and stimulated tourism to the Keys. The deadly 1935 hurricane destroyed the railroad, but a highway eventually replaced it, opening previously unsettled areas to urbanization.

The principal reef-related fishery in the Keys is for spiny lobster (*Panulirus argus*). Before 1930, lobstering was primarily a subsistence fishery for local markets. In 1908, the lobster catch was worth $3600. Most were used for fish bait (Crawford and DeSmidt, 1922). In 1922, the lobster fishing fleet consisted of twelve boats and twenty-four men. Today the fleet exceeds 600 boats, and the value of the catch is more than $15 million (FDNR, 1984).

The commercial fishing industry also harvests grouper, snapper, and yellowtail from coral reef habitats. Today's fishing fleet is equipped with modern vessels, electronic navigation equipment, hydraulic winches to recover traps and nets, and freezing plants to preserve the harvest. Exploitation of commercial species is intense; catch per unit effort indicates that some fisheries are in danger.

Recreational fishing is important to the Florida Keys economy. Much of the activity is focused on demersal reef fish (grouper, yellowtail, hogfish, and snapper). Divers also harvest lobster and finfish. These activities are staged from privately owned or chartered vessels. Although economic data on recreational fishing are limited, when the entire spectrum of activities associated with recreation is considered—purchase and charter of vessels, equipment sales and service, bait and lure sales, food and lodging for fishermen, and so forth—the recreational fishery probably exceeds the commercial fishery in its contribution to the Florida Keys economy.

Reef Management

A variety of government agencies is responsible for specific areas of reef management. This fragmentation of responsibility contributes to inefficiency and limits the ability to solve problems. The state boundary is three nautical miles seaward of the coast on the Atlantic (ocean) side and nine nautical miles on the Gulf (bay) side, except around islands and bays where there are special considerations. The area between the state boundary and the 200-mile national conservation boundary is under federal jurisdiction. Thus, most patch reefs in the upper Keys are under state jurisdiction, while bank reefs are under federal administration. In the lower Keys off Key West, the islet of Sand Key extends state jurisdiction to the outer bank reefs from Maryland Shoal to Satan Shoal. The complexity of boundaries makes enforcement difficult.

The State of Florida and the federal government have statutes protecting stony corals and the sea fan *Gorgonia* from harvest, sale, or damage on the seafloor. Permits from the Florida Department of Natural Resources (state waters) or the National Marine Fisheries Service (federal zone) are required for all coral collections. Parks, sanctuaries, and national monuments receive special management. Florida marine refuges with reef resources include Biscayne National Park (708 km^2), John Pennekamp Coral Reef State Park (217 km^2), Key Largo National Marine Sanctuary (259 km^2), Looe Key National Marine Sanctuary (111 km^2), and Fort Jefferson National Monument (190 km^2). Responsibilities for fisheries and environmental management of Florida's coral reefs are divided among twelve different state and federal agencies. Fragmentation of responsibility makes it difficult for a management agency to react quickly to information on destructive human activities.

Issues currently faced by management include limiting SCUBA diving and snorkling on popular reefs, such as Molasses Reef. Options include sinking larger ships offshore of the reefs to create alternative recreational dive sites, closing some reefs to the general public to allow recovery, limiting numbers of divers that may visit a reef over certain periods, and directing visitors to less popular reefs.

An anchor buoy system was developed and installed on many reefs in the Key Largo and Looe Key National Marine Sanctuaries to mitigate anchor damage by small boats to coral reefs (Halas, 1985). Expansion of the system to other reefs will further relieve the chronic problem of anchors that break and scar coral.

As noted, many vessels have run aground on Florida reefs. Such impacts not only damage or destroy the vessels but also damage reef, sea grass, and mangrove habitats. Coral reef communities require at least several decades to recover from major natural disturbances; recovery following human impacts is less predictable if habitat has been permanently altered (Pearson, 1981). Large vessels, such as the freighter *Wellwood* that ran aground in August 1984, devastate extensive areas of the reef. Even small boats can drive antifouling paint or fiberglass into coral surfaces, cut deep gashes into coral heads, shatter stands of elkhorn coral, or split large head corals that are hundreds of years old. In addition to overt physical damage, impacts seem to make corals more susceptible to disease. The great number of boats operating in the waters of the Keys results in numerous groundings every year, many of which could be avoided. Most are caused by navigational errors or poor knowledge of local water hazards. Shallow patch reefs, such as Mosquito Bank off Key Largo, are particularly prone to damage by pleasure boats; boaters seeking shortcuts to offshore reefs commonly run aground on the patch reefs.

Fishing activities that cause reef damage include deployment and recovery of lobster and fish traps. When deployed on a reef, the traps can crush and scar corals and other biota. During recovery, traps may be pulled across the reef until they clear the bottom, often abrading or dislodging algae, corals, sponges, and octocorals.

Terrestrial vegetation and mangroves are crucial to the survival of sea grass and coral reef communities because they act as filters and absorb runoff, which carries sediments, organic debris, and nutrients, before it reaches the sea grass beds and reefs. Coastal urbanization threatens sea grass and reef habitats by removing these natural filters. At the same time, urban activities such as landscaping, dredging, and domestic waste disposal increase the need for the filters (LaPointe and O'Connell, 1988). Turbidity caused by sediments and plankton blooms reduces the depths to which sea grass and coral reefs can live. Eutrophication also stimulates benthic algal growth, which can prevent larval corals from recruiting, and increases microbial use of oxygen, reducing its availability in the environment. To the north, beach renourishment to counter erosion on the barrier islands of Dade, Broward, and Palm Beach counties has damaged reefs. Increased sedimentation rates, burial, and physical damage by dredge cables and anchors have all occurred there (Courtenay et al., 1974; Jaap, 1984; Goldberg et al., 1985).

Why Preserve Florida's Reefs?

Economic incentives for effective reef management are compelling and involve the sustained vitality of the commercial and recreational fishing and diving industries. These industries contribute not only to Florida's economy but also to the quality of life for residents and visitors.

A long-term incentive is the protection of low elevation human settlements, especially in the Florida Keys. The importance of Florida's shallow water reefs as offshore breakwaters is taken for granted. Sea level is rising several centimeters per decade; healthy coral reefs can build at that rate and thus continue to function as a self-tending breakwater. However, pollution not only will kill most corals but also will stimulate bioerosion of the reef framework, compounding the problem of rising sea level.

Finally, society has an ethical responsibility to conserve unique natural resources for future generations. Rational management seeks to maintain the organic evolutionary process responsible for the diversity of life found in the biosphere (Bradbury and Reichelt, 1981).

Part V

Conclusion

18

Problems, Prospects, and Strategies for Conservation

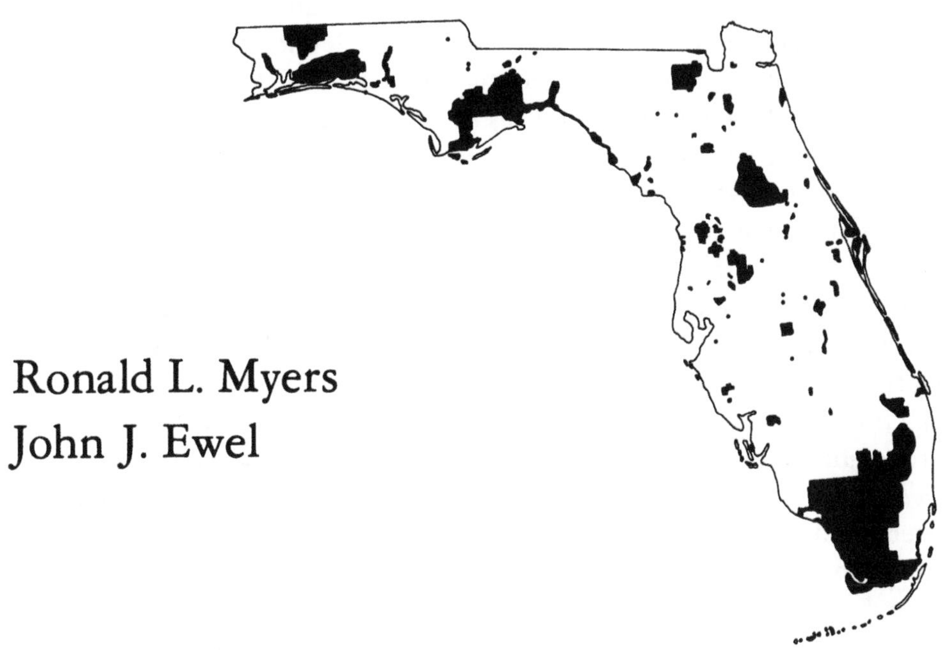

Ronald L. Myers
John J. Ewel

> Where do you go when all the fair places have been ruined? Where do you go from Florida?
>
> Raymond F. Dasmann, *No Further Retreat*

Florida's burgeoning human population is frequently identified as its primary environmental problem. Yet its population growth, coupled with the accompanying economic prosperity, has made possible much that is good for conservation, too. Most immigrants are attracted to Florida because of the quality of its environment: mild winters, lush forests, sunshine, clean air, and ready access to lakes, rivers, and seas. Floridians not only are interested in environmental quality but also are willing to invest in conservation, as demonstrated by the success of countless bond issues as well as private sector conservation activities.

In 1971, Raymond F. Dasmann wrote *No Further Retreat*, an overview of what had been lost in Florida and an outline of a strategy to save what remained. The inevitable was conceded: development would continue as

Map: *black areas* are managed areas with significant natural habitat.

Florida's population increased. The book is an odd mixture of lament, indignation, and optimism. Dasmann pointed out that much had been lost, particularly during the first seven decades of this century. Unbridled subdivision of the Florida landscape was rampant. But much had been saved, too, however precariously. He concluded that "the opportunity to win exists in Florida. The consequences of failure are unacceptable."

Two milestones have been passed since Dasmann wrote those words: Florida's population has doubled, and conservation and environmental concerns in the state have come of age. Growth and development continue, but further colossal environmental boondoggles, such as the Cross-Florida Barge Canal, are unlikely. Nor will the likes of a Gulf America Corporation again be able to do to wetlands what was done to those of southwest Florida. Today's efforts to save the last vestiges of natural Florida may involve fighting over crumbs, but also under discussion is restoration—actually undoing some of the monumental mistakes of the past.

It may be possible to put the meanders back into the Kissimmee River (fig. 18.1) and to rid the Oklawaha River of Rodman Pool and see it flowing free again. Companies now restore phosphate strip-mined lands and oil well pads; in addition, the raw materials extracted are taxed to purchase environmentally significant lands elsewhere (fig. 18.2). The Florida panther (*Felis concolor coryi*) is approaching oblivion (fig. 18.3), but Floridians are determined not to let it go. There is talk of re-introduction and recovery. The State of Florida is acquiring lands and considering corridors to connect them. For the panther itself the effort may be futile, but the cat has become the icon of conservation in Florida. Lands acquired for it will also capture less charismatic species and their habitats; corridors it might use may be used by others. In addition, Florida residents have decided to support the cause of all nongame wildlife in the state by assessing a fee when new arrivals register their automobiles.

Florida residents and visitors may soon see an Apalachicola River that is no longer dredged and national forests where maintaining natural communities takes precedence over producing timber. With nearly 2 million visitors a year, Ocala National Forest alone rivals many national parks in use by visitors. Its wildland and recreation values are superseding those of more traditional forest uses. It may even be possible to gain control over at least one of Florida's troublesome naturalized aliens: the Australian cajeput (*Melaleuca quinquenervia*). A movement is building in Florida; long a mecca for the naturalist, the state is now an exciting place for the conservation-minded.

Conservation Status of Florida Ecosystems

Two themes recur in this book: today each ecosystem is a mere fraction of what it was at the beginning of this century, and nature can no longer maintain the examples that are protected without biological management.

Fig. 18.1. Relict channel fragments of the Kissimmee River straddle the excavated banks of the artificial drainage canal linking Lake Kissimmee to Lake Okeechobee near State Road 70 in Okeechobee County. Photo by Allan Horton.

Fig. 18.2. Phosphate strip mining operation in Polk County.

Fig. 18.3. Florida panther. Photo by J. N. Layne.

Reviews of the conservation status of Florida's natural ecosystems are mixed. The virgin forests are long gone. Old-growth forests are rare, but some examples remain: *bald cypress* at Corkscrew Swamp Sanctuary and possibly inaccessible portions of Bradwell Bay in the Apalachicola National Forest, Big Gum Swamp in the Osceola National Forest, and the interior sloughs of Tosohatchee State Reserve; *slash pine stands* in the pine/cabbage palm flatwoods of Tosohatchee; *south Florida slash pine sandhills and flatwoods* at Archbold Biological Station; *subtropical pine rockland* on Big Pine Key; *bottomland hardwood forest* of Woodyard Hammock at Tall Timbers Research Station; a 65 ha pocket of *upland hardwood forest* in San Felasco State Preserve; and some inaccessible *tropical hammocks* in the Everglades.

There are surely other examples, but they are unlikely to be pristine woods. Old-growth longleaf pine forests, which might have covered more than half of the state, are gone. The flatwoods complex of communities still is extensive, but in places its character has been altered beyond recognition. The pine/grass/pitcher plant savannas (fig. 18.4) of the Panhandle lowlands once stretched from at least the Ochlockonee River westward to the Florida Parishes of Louisiana (at one time part of Florida) and served as a

Fig. 18.4. Lowland savanna with intact ground cover community, Bay County north of Panama City in 1936. The original photo caption read, "Cut-over, denuded, burned wastelands. Note lack of seedlings or seed trees." Photo by H. E. Whitehead. From Florida State Archives.

vast matrix for seepage areas, bogs, titi-lined drainages, and cypress sloughs and bays fringed with slash pine forests. In a matter of a few decades, they have been reduced to ecotonal status between titi swamps and pine plantations. Tate's Hell in Franklin County was once savanna-like; today it is a mosaic of titi thickets and slash pine plantations. Remnant savannas occur in Apalachicola National Forest and the unprotected Garçon Point near Pensacola. The pond apple (*Annona glabra*) sloughs that once fringed Lake Okeechobee are gone. Hints of what these may have been like can be found in the interior of the Big Cypress National Preserve. We will be lucky to save a small fraction of the ancient scrubs on the Lake Wales Ridge. The list could go on.

Florida does have some reasonably well protected wetlands. In south Florida, extensive tracts are maintained in freshwater marshes and mangrove swamps—the marshes in Everglades National Park, Big Cypress National Preserve, the conservation areas of the South Florida Water Management District, Loxahatchee National Wildlife Refuge, and the mangrove swamps in Everglades National Park and Rookery Bay National Estuarine Research Reserve. In north Florida, salt marshes and estuaries are protected in a nearly unbroken crescent that extends along the Gulf coast from Chassahowitzka National Wildlife Refuge northward through Waccasassa Bay State Preserve, Cedar Keys and Lower Suwannee River national wildlife refuges, The Nature Conservancy's Big Bend purchase (Big Bend, Aucilla, and Jena wildlife management areas) to St. Marks National Wildlife Refuge.

The only upland associations that appear to be secure are second-growth broad-leaved forests and young even-aged pine stands. Considered artifacts of recent human land use, these are of little interest to conservationists today but will become increasingly important in the future as green spaces, corridors, and refuges for migratory song birds and species yet to reach threatened or endangered status. Most other upland ecosystems occur as altered or degraded expanses, as isolated fragments on the verge of development, as beachfront property sprouting "for sale" signs, or as hydric hardwood hammocks slated for conversion to pine plantations.

It is difficult to identify which natural ecosystems are most vulnerable—all are in danger. Wetlands are afforded the most legislated protection, but all ecosystem groups—wetland, upland, aquatic, and marine—are threatened: coral reefs and inshore marine habitats face offshore oil drilling and increased turbidity; lakes, streams, and estuaries receive contaminated runoff and seepage; wetlands that do not fall within the legislative definition are subject to drainage and filling; scrubs face development because they afford few other uses and are high and dry; the pineland ground cover suffers from intensive site preparation; flatwoods and dry prairies in the lower peninsula are being converted to citrus groves; and all pyric communities are changing because fires no longer sweep across an uninterrupted landscape, while liability and air quality concerns are restricting the use of prescribed fires.

On the positive side, significant lands are being purchased by the State of Florida for conservation and recreational purposes. In 1972, the Florida Legislature established the Environmentally Endangered Lands (EEL) Program to acquire lands containing relatively unaltered ecosystems or providing critical habitat for endangered species. Acquisitions comprised 149,952 ha, including Paynes Prairie, San Felasco Hammock, Rock Springs Run, and Cape St. George. In 1979, the EEL Program was folded into the broader Conservation and Recreation Lands (CARL) Program. Both programs have been funded from an excise tax on the severance of minerals, primarily phosphate, and from a percentage of a documentary excise tax. Under the CARL program, an additional 49,724 ha have been purchased, and fifty-nine projects totaling 211,617 ha are being evaluated.

Freshwater aquatic ecosystems are finally receiving attention. In response to the degradation of the water quality and scenic values of its rivers, Florida in 1981 expanded the documentary stamp tax fee to create a Save Our Rivers Program. It has allowed the state's water management districts to acquire riparian lands deemed necessary to maintain water quality. Lakes have received similar attention. Few of Florida's 7800 lakes lack shoreline development. Two of the largest, Lake Okeechobee and Lake Apopka, once prime bass fishing lakes, have been so severely polluted that special efforts are under way to restore them. In 1987, Florida established the Surface Water Improvement and Management Program (SWIM) to promote lake restoration.

Parks, preserves, and management areas protect exemplary remnants of most of Florida's natural ecosystems. In fact, surprisingly large amounts of Florida—nearly 20 percent of the state—are within administrative units that at least allow for *potential* ecosystem protection and restoration (table 18.1). Probably fewer than half of these, however, are managed solely as natural areas.

Protection of representative examples of each of Florida's ecosystems does not ensure sufficient habitat for all of their characteristic species. Wide-ranging species like the Florida panther and the black bear are victims not only of habitat loss but also of limits imposed by habitat size. They have little future in Florida unless large blocks of their habitats are set aside.

Many species with special habitat requirements are also becoming victims of habitat loss. Beaches remain, but sea turtles rarely find them suitable for nesting. Two federally endangered plants, Harper's beauty (*Harperocallis flava*) and Bartram's ixia (*Sphenostigma coelestinum*), prefer natural seeps but are now found primarily in roadside ditches. The *Sarracenia* species (pitcher plants) may soon be joining them there. Most isolated scrub islands are too small to maintain scrub jays, which have stringent requirements for territory size.

Table 18.1. Managed areas in Florida possessing significant natural habitats

Agency/organization	No. units	Area (hectares)
Federal		
National Park Service		
National parks, monuments, preserves, and seashores	10	1,003,958
(Wilderness areas)	(1)	(524,899)
U.S. Forest Service		
National forests	3	444,569
(Wilderness areas)	(7)	(29,704)
(Research natural areas)	(2)	(341)
U.S. Air Force		
Military reservations	2	230,449
U.S. Fish and Wildlife Service		
National wildlife refuges	26	210,502
(Wilderness areas)	(11)	(20,750)
National Oceanic and Atmospheric Administration		
Estuarine reserves and marine sanctuaries (upland only)	4	329
State		
Florida Game and Fresh Water Fish Commission		
Wildlife management areas	34	285,490
Wildlife and environmental areas (state-owned only)	7	19,940

(*continued*)

Table 18.1. (continued)

Agency/organization	No. units	Area (hectares)
Water management districts		
St. Johns River	37	71,589
Southwest Florida	40	56,820
South Florida	10	44,634
Northwest Florida	3	35,913
Suwannee River	23	6,577
Florida Division of Recreation and Parks		
State preserves	8	48,889
State parks	37	45,268
State reserves	9	30,857
State recreation areas	47	16,983
State botanical sites	3	581
Historic sites	8	435
State gardens	4	180
Archaeological sites	5	118
Geologic sites	1	26
Florida Division of Forestry		
State forests	5	132,522
State universities	3	1,740
County		
Parks, reserves, and nature centers	>70	5,821
Private		
The Nature Conservancy	33	8,475
National Audubon Society	6	6,867
Other	36	8,290
	TOTAL	2,487,372

Note: Where administrative jurisdiction overlaps, the unit is included under the lead agency. Not included are 70,755 ha of submerged lands associated with some units or 40 aquatic preserves totaling 1,420,541 ha. One hectare = 2.47 acres.

Anticipated Changes

We envision four major threats to conservation and ecosystem management in Florida in the years ahead: land conversion, fire exclusion, exotic species, and water use demands.

Land Conversion

At one time, the conversion of natural ecosystems to farms and tree plantations was the major agent of landscape change in Florida. In the future, housing developments, suburban sprawl, city growth, and new roads are likely to be the greatest threats to natural communities. One important difference between these two types of conversion is that deforestation for farming or forestry is reversible, whereas concrete and asphalt are essentially permanent. Once urbanized, a forest is gone for good.

Furthermore, most construction occurs on uplands. Unlike legislatively protected wetlands, uplands are afforded little protection. An effective conservation strategy for Florida requires the identification and protection of significant areas of uplands as well as wetlands.

The waste associated with much upland development is appalling. Take, for example, 1500 acres of farm or forest, divide it into 300 lots, dig 300 wells, plant one septic tank on each plot, and add a home for three people. You will have accommodated just one day's worth of immigrants to Florida. This five-acre-ization of Florida consumes vast areas while supporting low population densities, a luxury that Floridians will not be able to afford for long if the quality of the environment is to be protected.

Fire

The expansion of housing developments and highways does not bode well for the continued use of the most important tool available to any land manager in Florida: fire (fig. 18.5). Smoke and fire are simply not compatible with suburban residents and travelers. Resource managers must prepare now for the days when burning regulations will become increasingly restrictive. The wisdom of conserving small tracts should be reconsidered, given the difficulty of conducting prescribed burns in these sites. It is also important to investigate less desirable management alternatives to fire, such as mowing, grazing, herbicides, and water level manipulation.

Fig. 18.5. Prescribed burning for ecosystem maintenance and restoration at Lower Wekiva River State Reserve, Seminole County. This reserve is located just north of the rapidly growing Orlando metropolitan area.

Exotics

Naturalized alien species present a special threat to the ecosystems of south Florida. Many plants and animals have been intentionally introduced over the years, while others have found their way to south Florida as unnoticed hitchhikers. The southern third of the peninsula is island-like, surrounded on three sides by water and on one side by frost. Like other islands, it appears to have an impoverished native biota, making it vulnerable to invasions of new species. Furthermore, modifications of south Florida's landscape by drainage, diking, burning outside the natural fire season, urbanization, and rock plowing have created vacant habitats ripe for colonization; some nonnative species have been exceptionally successful at moving into such areas.

There is some argument as to whether exotic species actively displace natives or whether they primarily colonize disturbed habitats that are not optimum sites for native species. Whichever is the case, habitat permanently occupied by aliens is unavailable to natives. Exotic species usurp resources that might be used by the native flora and fauna, resulting in a tradeoff that biologists and conservationists find objectionable. Exotic trees also change the aspect of the landscape. The afforestation of the treeless Everglades marshes by Australian cajeputs is not a welcome sight. Furthermore, many of south Florida's exotic plants are serviced by an exotic fauna. The seeds of peppertrees (*Schinus terebinthifolius*) from Brazil are dispersed by the red-whiskered bulbul (*Pycnonotus jocosus*) from India (Owre, 1973), though dispersal by Florida's resident mockingbirds (*Mimus polyglottos*) and wintering robins (*Turdus migratorius*) and waxwings (*Bombycilla cedrorum*) is infinitely more important at this time. Introduced parrots (*Aratinga* spp., *Amazona* spp.) probably would not thrive in southeast Florida without exotic fruiting trees, especially the figs. The wasp that pollinates the most widely planted exotic fig (*Ficus benjamina*) in Florida has recently found its way to Miami (D. McKey, Univ. of Miami, personal communication).

Potentially pestiferous species are seldom recognized as serious threats until their foothold is firm. For example, few people are aware that cogon grass (*Imperata cylindrica*), a pantropical grass whose spread is facilitated by fire, is moving southward down the Florida peninsula and invading disturbed pineland. The tenacity with which this species has held on to formerly forested areas in the Philippines and elsewhere should cause concern in Florida. Some exotics, like the brown anole (*Anolis sagrei*), seem destined to occur in all urban and suburban parts of Florida. The armadillo (*Dasypus novemcinctus*) occupies virtually all of Florida by now.

Anyone who has gazed over a canal filled with walking catfish and two-spot cichlids to watch parrots and parakeets cavorting in an overgrown fencerow of Australian pines, cajeputs, and peppertrees knows that exotics are in south Florida to stay. Exotic species invasions can be slowed, and perhaps even prevented, by maintaining vigorous, healthy communities of native species (Ewel, 1986). Where exotic species already dominate, however, resource managers must be prepared to face new challenges: crown fires racing through dense stands of cajeput, displacement of sparse species from intercommunity transition zones (fig. 18.6), and subtle impacts of new vegetation on hydrology, to mention only a few.

Substrate modification, such as rock plowing, diking, strip-mining, and bedding, has created soils and topographic features heretofore unknown to Florida. These human-created soils, or *anthrosols*, are likely to support new ecosystems in which exotic species play dominant roles. The Hole-in-the-Doughnut in Everglades National Park exemplifies this situation. Despite efforts by the National Park Service to restore native vegetation to this rock plowed land, a peppertree/wax myrtle/saltbush ecosystem persists there.

Water

Finally, there is the perennial issue of the use and limits of Florida's surface waters and groundwater. Development in Florida has been accomplished at the cost of immense damage to its water supplies: saltwater intrusion, contamination with agricultural pesticides and toxic wastes, and nutrient enrichment from fertilizers and sewage. Few Floridians realize that most of Florida's population draws from the same underground "river," the Floridan Aquifer, and its interconnected "tributaries." As with any watershed, impacts

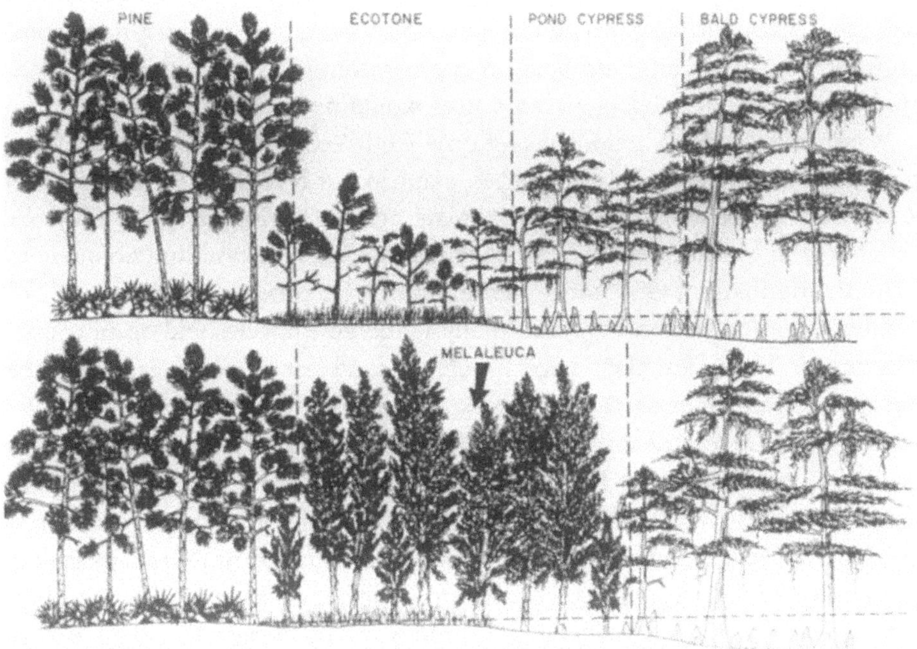

Fig. 18.6. *Melaleuca quinquenervia*, the Australian cajeput, readily invades the transition between flatwoods and pond cypress swamps. From Myers, 1984.

at the upper reaches affect quality and quantity downstream. On the bright side, in the past twenty years Florida has made tremendous progress in protecting its water and associated wetlands. The water storage and purification services that wetlands provide are no longer questioned. The role of uplands as recharge areas may be receiving the attention it deserves.

Conservation Issues and Strategies for the Future

Tomorrow's conservation issues will center on the four anticipated changes already discussed. Coping with the problems associated with land conversion, fire exclusion, the spread of alien species, and water quality degradation requires ecosystem-level strategies.

Retention of Interconnectedness

Land conversion leads to landscape fragmentation followed by piecemeal conservation efforts. One inevitable consequence is the loss of the interconnections among ecosystems. The water quality of the freshwater ponds of the Middle Keys, for example, depends on the surrounding pine and hardwood forests; the Key deer that inhabit those forests rely on the ponds for water. The oyster beds of Apalachicola Bay are dependent on the waters percolating through upland substrates located considerable distances upriver.

Land-water links are relatively obvious. Other connections are equally important, yet more subtle. Many communities that depend on occasional fires for their continued existence ignite only when more fire-prone communities that surround them burn. A cypress dome or pitcher plant bog isolated from pine flatwoods-generated fires would not survive for long.

When conservation actions target only well-recognized community types, some species inevitably suffer. Species, alas, do not recognize the community boundaries delineated by conservationists and ecologists. Rather, they are distributed in a continuum across the landscape, each responding uniquely to various combinations of environmental and biotic conditions. As a result of community-oriented conservation, many vulnerable species end up in transition zones. These are the "edges," left to fend for themselves while the manager concentrates on the hammock, the spring, the scrub, or the seep.

One solution to the problems of interconnected ecosystems and edge-dwelling species is to save larger units than would at first seem necessary. In general, to conserve a system, one must protect the next largest system of which it is a part. Thus, to save a species, save its community; to save a community, save a portion of the landscape mosaic of which it is a part. Unfortunately, for many species and communities in Florida, it is too late to engage in "ocean liner" conservation; the lifeboats are all that are left.

In comparison with other eastern states, however, Florida has done remarkably well with respect to protection of large landscape units. On a recent map of the conterminous forty-eight states illustrating areas more than 8 km from a road, one of the largest shaded areas is in the Everglades and Big Cypress Swamp of south Florida. Yet little is being done to capitalize on other opportunities. Pine flatwoods—consisting of a matrix of pine forests, pine savannas, seeps, bogs, meadows, swamps, and ponds—still occupy large areas of Florida (thanks to their economic value) and harbor species of concern to conservationists, but there is no effort under way to conserve a large unit of this landscape mosaic. In the south-central peninsula lie the flatwood landscapes of the Cecil M. Webb and J. W. Corbett wildlife management areas and the Ringling-MacArthur Reserve of Sarasota County, but no extensive flatwood landscapes are protected in the northern peninsula or the Panhandle, though opportunities still exist.

Another solution involves linking reserves through strips or corridors of natural communities (Harris, 1984). Corridors are appropriate under two circumstances. First, they are useful when they can expand the habitat available to a wide-ranging animal. A black bear or a panther, for example, might be accommodated in two reserves linked by a corridor through which the animal could commute from one habitat to the other, even though either reserve alone would be too small to maintain the animal. Second, corridors that facilitate gene flow among members of a population that might otherwise be genetically isolated are a useful conservation investment. The key to the utility of corridors is that something must move along them. If not, a corridor becomes nothing more than a long, slender, hard-to-manage reserve, and conservation investments might better be made elsewhere.

Maintenance of Community Heterogeneity

Once an area is protected, its managers are faced with a number of management dilemmas. Triage decisions are sometimes necessary, particularly on small preserves. For example, scrub jays do not inhabit scrubs containing dense stands of mature sand pine. Should scrubs be managed for the jays at the expense of the pine? Is it preferable to strive for open stands of longleaf pine that would benefit the red-cockaded woodpecker, at the expense of the Sherman fox squirrel, which prefers pine/oak woodlands? Species and communities become trendy. Experts point out that the upland longleaf pine forests have been reduced to 3 percent of their former distribution, not recognizing or acknowledging that associated oak woods have had a similar fate. Thus, current management prescriptions target only the former.

There is a tendency to look for a single management prescription for each community type, but rigid adherence to these is ill-founded and often leads to landscape homogenization and loss of diversity. All flatwoods, for example, should not look alike. Historic landscapes are useful models for management only if community dynamics are also appreciated. Many examples of each community need to be protected if the natural variability among sites is to be preserved. Frequently, the focus is on the flashy, the rare, and the unusual as targets of protection and management, while the hordes of species in the "lower" classes of organisms—arthropods, fungi, lichens, and slime molds that not only contribute to biological diversity but also perform important ecosystem functions—are ignored.

Ecosystem-Level Conservation

Preservation of rare species and communities is a noble conservation goal, but it has two unfortunate drawbacks: it promotes a piecemeal approach to preservation, and it frequently results in species or communities being ignored until they become endangered. The Herculean efforts made to protect these rarities sometimes involve the purchase of either exorbitantly expensive and unmanageable remnants or sites where the species' natural habitat no longer exists. Impossible to burn, subject to exotic species invasions, and isolated from associated systems, they are likely transitory and of little global significance.

Although decline toward endangerment and extinction is progressive, the imperiled species and communities of tomorrow are seldom identified beforehand. In the long run, large units of the natural landscape probably capture more biological diversity than do small units containing species or communities that are currently sparse. The biological importance of Lake Wales Ridge scrub and the Dade County pine rocklands was recognized decades ago. Fortunately, a significant portion of the latter was included in Everglades National Park. In the case of scrub, the opportunity for an intact natural landscape no longer exists, and the future of the few protected pieces is uncertain. Although small conservation units do serve the important function of preserving biological curiosities for education and scientific study, an ecosystem-level approach contributes to achieving our primary goal: *sustaining the biosphere.*

References

Abrahamson, W.G. (1980). Demography and vegetative reproduction. *In* "Demography and Evolution of Plant Populations" (O.T. Solbrig, ed.), pp. 89–106. Blackwell, Oxford.

Abrahamson, W.G. (1984a). Post-fire recovery of Florida Lake Wales Ridge vegetation. *Am. J. Bot.* 71, 9–21.

Abrahamson, W.G. (1984b). Species responses to fire on the Florida Lake Wales Ridge. *Am. J. Bot.* 71, 35–42.

Abrahamson, W.G., Johnson, A.F., Layne, J.N., and Peroni, P.A. (1984). Vegetation of the Archbold Biological Station, Florida: an example of the southern Lake Wales Ridge. *Fla. Sci.* 47, 209–250.

Abrams, M.D. (1986). Historical development of gallery forests in northeast Kansas. *Vegetatio* 65, 29–37.

Adey, W. (1977). Shallow water Holocene bioherms of the Caribbean Sea and West Indies. *Proc. Int. Coral Reef Symp., 3d, Miami, Fla.* 2, xxi–xxiv.

Agassiz, A. (1883). The Tortugas and Florida reefs. *Mem. Am. Acad. Arts Sci.* 11, 107–134.

Agassiz, A. (1890). On the rate of growth of corals. *Bull. Mus. Comp. Zool.* 20, 61–64.

Ager, L.A., and Kerce, K.E. (1970). Vegetation changes associated with water level stabilization in Lake Okeechobee, Florida. *Proc. Annu. Conf. S.E. Assoc. Game Fish Comm.* 24, 338–351.

Ager, L.A., and Kerce, K.E. (1974). "Lake Okeechobee Investigations and Development Completion Report for Aquatic Plant Communities–Associated Fauna Investigation," Mimeo Rep., Fla. Game Fresh Water Fish Comm., Tallahassee.

Ahlgren, C.E. (1974). Effects of fires on temperate forests: north central United States. *In* "Fire and Ecosystems" (C.E. Ahlgren and T.T. Kozlowski, eds.), pp. 195–223. Academic Press, New York.

Albert, R. (1975). Salt regulation in halophytes. *Oecologia* 21, 57–71.

Aldrich, J.W., and Duvall, A.J. (1958). Distribution and migration of races of the mourning dove. *Condor* 60, 108–128.

Alexander, T.R. (1953). Plant succession of Key Largo, Florida, involving *Pinus caribaea* and *Quercus virginiana*. *Q.J. Fla. Acad. Sci.* 16, 133–138.

Alexander, T.R. (1955). Observations on the ecology of low hammocks of southern Florida. *Q.J. Fla. Acad. Sci.* 18, 21–27.

Alexander, T.R. (1958a). Ecology of the Pompano Beach hammock. *Q.J. Fla. Acad. Sci.* 21, 299–304.

Alexander, T.R. (1958b). High hammock vegetation of the southern Florida mainland. *Q.J. Fla. Acad. Sci.* 21, 293–298.

Alexander, T.R. (1967a). Effect of hurricane Betsy on the southeastern Everglades. *Q.J. Fla. Acad. Sci.* 30, 10–24.

Alexander, T.R. (1967b). A tropical hammock in the Miami (Florida) limestone: a twenty-five year study. *Ecology* 48, 863–867.

Alexander, T.R. (1971). Sawgrass biology related to the future of the Everglades ecosystem. *Proc. Soil Sci. Soc. Fla.* 31, 72–74.

Alexander, T.R., and Crook, A.G. (1984). Recent vegetational changes in south Florida. *In* "Environments of South Florida: Present and Past II" (P.J. Gleason, ed.), pp. 199–210. Miami Geol. Soc., Coral Gables, Florida.

Alexander, T.R., and Dickson, J.D., III (1972). Vegetational changes in the National Key Deer Refuge II. *Q.J. Fla. Acad. Sci.* 35, 85–96.

Allen, L.H., Jr., Knisel, W.G., Jr., and Yates, P. (1982). Evapotranspiration, rainfall, and water yield in south Florida research watersheds. *Proc. Soil Crop Sci. Soc. Fla.* 41, 127–139.

Allen, R.M. (1956). Relation of saw-palmetto to longleaf pine reproduction on a dry site. *Ecology* 37, 195–196.

Alongi, D.M. (1987). The influence of mangrove-derived tannins on intertidal meiobenthos in tropical estuaries. *Oecologia* 71, 537–540.

American Ornithologists' Union (1983). "Checklist of North American Birds," 6th Ed. Am. Ornithol. Union, Allen Press, Lawrence, Kansas.

Anderson, L.C., and Alexander, L.L. (1985). The vegetation of Dog Island, Florida. *Fla. Sci.* 48, 232–251.

Anderson, R.C., and Brown, L.E. (1983). Comparative effects of fire on trees in a midwestern savannah and an adjacent forest. *Bull. Torrey Bot. Club* 110, 87–90.

Anderson, W.W. (1970). Contribution to the life histories of several penaeid shrimps (Penaeidae) along the south Atlantic coast of the United States. *U.S. Fish Wildl. Serv. Spec. Sci. Rep.* No. 605.

Anderson, W., and Goolsby, D.A. (1973). Flow and chemical characteristics of the St. Johns River at Jacksonville, Florida. *Fla. Bur. Geol. Inf. Circ.* No. 82.

Ansley, C.C. (1952). An ecological comparison of the mesic hardwoods of central Florida. M.S. Thesis. Univ. of Florida, Gainesville.

Antoine, J.W., Brant, W.R., and Pyle, T.E. (1974). Structural framework of the west Florida continental shelf and recommendations for further research. *In* "Procedures in Marine Environment Implications of Offshore Drilling, Eastern Gulf of Mexico" (R.E. Smith, ed.), pp. 295–300. Inst. Oceanogr., State Univ. Syst., Florida, St. Petersburg.

Antonius, A. (1974). New observations on coral destruction in reefs. *Assoc. Isl. Mar. Lab. Caribb., 10th Meet., Mayagüez, P.R., 1973* Abstr.

Antonius, A. (1981a). The "band" diseases in coral reefs. *Proc. Int. Coral Reef Symp., 4th, Manila* 2, 7–14.

Antonius, A. (1981b). Coral pathology: a review. *Proc. Int. Coral Reef Symp., 4th, Manila* 2, 3–6.

Argus, G.W. (1986). The genus *Salix* (Salicaceae) in the southeastern United States. *Syst. Bot.* 9.

Armentano, T.V., Park, R.A., and Cloonan, C.L. (1986). "The Effect of Future Sea Level Rise on U.S. Coastal Wetland Areas." Final rep. to USEPA from Holcomb Res. Inst., Butler Univ., Indianapolis, Indiana.

Arnade, C.W. (1965). Cattle raising in Spanish Florida: 1513–1763. *St. Augustine Hist. Soc. Publ.* No. 21.

Arrington, D.V., and Lindquist, R.C. (1987). Thickly mantled karst of the Interlachen, Florida area. *In* "Karst Hydrogeology: Engineering and Environmental Applications" (B.F. Beck and W.L. Wilson, eds.), pp. 31–39. Balkema, Boston, Massachusetts.

Art, H.W., and Marks, P.L. (1971). A summary table of biomass and net annual primary production in forest ecosystems of the world. *In* "Forest Biomass Studies" (H.E. Young, ed.), pp. 3–32. Univ. Maine Life Sci. Agric. Exp. Stn., Orono. Reprinted *in* "Patterns of Primary Production in the Biosphere" (H.F. Lieth, ed.), pp. 177–192. Dowden, Hutchinson, & Ross, Stroudsburg, Pennsylvania.

Aska, D., ed. (1978). Artificial reefs in Florida. *Fla. Sea Grant Rep.* No. 24. Gainesville, Florida.

Aska, D., ed. (1981). Proceedings of artificial reef conference. *Fla. Sea Grant Rep.* No. 41. Gainesville, Florida.

Atkinson, M.J., and Grigg, R.W. (1984). Model of a coral reef ecosystem. II. Gross and net benthic primary production at French Frigate Shoals, Hawaii. *Coral Reefs* 3, 13–22.

Atkinson, M.R., Findlay, G.P., Hope, A.B., Pitman, M.G., Saddler, H.D.W., and West, H.R. (1967). Salt regulation in the mangroves *Rhizophora mangle* Lam. and *Aerialitis annulata* R. *Aust. J. Biol. Sci.* 20, 589–599.

Au, S.-F. (1974). Vegetation and ecological processes on Shackleford Bank, North Carolina. *Natl. Park Serv. Sci. Monogr. Ser.* No. 6.

Aubrey, D.G., and Emery, K.O. (1983). Eigenanalysis of recent U.S. sea levels. *Shelf Res.* 2, 21–33.

Auclair, A.N. (1975). Sprouting response in *Prunus serotina* Ehrh.: multivariate analysis of site, forest structure and growth rate relationships. *Am. Midl. Nat.* 94, 72–87.

Auffenberg, W.A. (1963). "Present Problems about the Past." *Biol. Sci. Curric. Study Pam.* No. 6. Heath, Boston, Massachusetts.

Austin, D.F. (1976). Vegetation of southeastern Florida, USA. Part 1. Pine Jog. *Fla. Sci.* 39, 230–235.

Austin, D.F., and Coleman-Marois, K. (1977). Vegetation of southeastern Florida. II. Boca Raton hammock site. *Fla. Sci.* 40, 331–338.

Austin, D.F., and Weise, J.G. (1972). Annotated checklist of the Boynton Beach hammock. *Q.J. Fla. Acad. Sci.* 35, 145–154.

Austin, D.F., Coleman-Marois, K., and Richardson, D.R. (1977). Vegetation of southeastern Florida II–V. *Fla. Sci.* 40, 331–361.

Austin, H., and Jones, J.I. (1974). Seasonal variation of physical parameters on the

Florida middle ground in relation to zooplankton biomass on the west Florida shelf. *Q.J. Fla. Acad. Sci.* 37, 16–32.

Avery, G.N., and Loope, L.L. (1980). Endemic taxa in the flora of south Florida. *Everglades Natl. Park South Fla. Res. Cent. Rep.* No. T-558.

Avery, G.N., and Loope, L.L. (1983). Plants of Everglades National Park: a preliminary checklist of vascular plants. *Everglades Natl. Park South Fla. Res. Cent. Rep.* No. T-574.

Axelrod, D.I. (1958). Evolution of the Madro-Tertiary geoflora. *Bot. Rev.* 24, 432–509.

Axelrod, D.I. (1966). Origin of deciduous and evergreen habits in temperate forests. *Evolution* 20, 1–15.

Axelrod, D.I. (1975). Evolution and biogeography of Madrean-Tethyan sclerophyll vegetation. *Ann. Mo. Bot. Gard.* 62, 280–334.

Axelrod, D.I., and Bailey, H.P. (1969). Paleotemperature analysis of Tertiary floras. *Palaeogeogr. Palaeoclimatol. Palaeoecol.* 6, 163–195.

Bagnold, R.A. (1941). "The Physics of Blown Sand and Desert Dunes." Methuen, London.

Bailey, L.H. (1939). *Coccothrinax* in the southern Greater Antilles. *Gentes Herbarum* 4, 247–259.

Bak, R.P.M., and Van Eys, G. (1975). Predation of the sea urchin *Diadema antillarum* Phillippi on living coral. *Oecologia* 20, 111–115.

Bak, R.P.M., Sybesma, J., and VanDuyl, F.C. (1981). The ecology of the compound ascidian *Trididemnum solidum*. II. Abundance, growth and survival. *Mar. Ecol. Prog. Ser.* 6, 43–52.

Bak, R.P.M., Termaat, R.M., and Dekker, R. (1982). Complexity of coral interaction: influence of time, location of interaction, and epifauna. *Mar. Biol. (Berlin)* 69, 215–222.

Bak, R.P.M., Carpay, M.J.E., and de Ruyter van Steveninck, E.D. (1984). Densities of the sea urchin *Diadema antillarum* before and after mass mortalities on the coral reefs of Curaçao. *Mar. Ecol. Prog. Ser.* 17, 105–108.

Baker, J.M. (1971). The effects of oil on plant physiology. *In* "Ecological Effects of Oil Pollution" (E.B. Cowell, ed.), pp. 88–98. Appl. Sci. Pub., London.

Baker, L.A., Brezonik, P.L., and Kratzer, C.R. (1981). Nutrient loading–trophic state relationships in Florida lakes. *Univ. Fla. Water Resour. Res. Cent. Publ.* No. 56.

Baker, W.W. (1974). Longevity of lightning-struck trees and notes on wildlife use. *Proc. Tall Timbers Fire Ecol. Conf.* 13, 497–504.

Ball, M.C. (1980). Patterns of secondary succession in a mangrove forest in south Florida. *Oecologia* 44, 226–235.

Ball, M.C., and Farquhar, G.D. (1984). Photosynthetic and stomatal responses of the grey mangrove, *Avicennia marina*, to transient salinity conditions. *Plant Physiol.* 74, 7–11.

Ball, M.J., III, Hunter, D.H., and Swindel, B.F. (1979). Understory development in north Florida bedded slash pine plantations. *Univ. Fla. Intensive Manage. Pract. Assess. Cent. (IMPAC) Rep.* No. 4(6).

Balmer, W.E., and Mobley, H.E. (1983). Damaged stands: appraisal of damages, recovery potential and management decisions. *In* "The Managed Slash Pine Ecosystem," Proc. Symp. (E.L. Stone, ed.), pp. 288–303. Sch. For. Resour. Conserv., Univ. of Florida, Gainesville.

Balsillie, J.H. (1985). Post-Storm Report: Hurricane Elena of 29 August to 2 September 1985. *Fla. Dep. Nat. Resour. Beaches Shores Post-Storm Rep.* No. 85-2.

Banks, R.S. (1975). Beach erosion along the lower west coast of peninsular Florida. *Trans. Gulf Coast Assoc. Geol. Soc.* 25, 391–392.

Barbour, M.G., DeJong, T.M., and Pavlik, B.M. (1975). Marine beach and dune plant communities. *In* "Physiological Ecology of North American Plant Communities" (B.F. Chabot and H.A. Mooney, eds.), pp. 296–322. Chapman & Hall, New York.

Barbour, M.G., Rejmanek, M., Johnson, A.F., and Pavlik, B.M. (1987). Beach vegetation and plant distribution patterns along the northern Gulf of Mexico. *Phytocoenologia* 15, 201–233.

Barden, L.S. (1980). Tree replacement in a cove hardwood forest of the southern Appalachians. *Oikos* 35, 16–19.

Barden, L.S. (1981). Forest development in canopy gaps of a diverse hardwood forest of the southern Appalachian mountains. *Oikos* 37, 205–209.

Barden, L.S., and Woods, F.W. (1974). Characteristics of lightning fires in southern Appalachian forests. *Proc. Tall Timbers Fire Ecol. Conf.* 13, 345–361.

Barnard, E.L., Blakeslee, G.M., English, J.T., Oak, S.W., and Anderson, R.L. (1985). Pathogenic fungi associated with sand pine root disease in Florida. *Plant Dis.* 69, 196–199.

Barnes, D.J. (1973). Growth in colonial scleractinians. *Bull. Mar. Sci.* 23, 280–298.

Barnett, B.S., and Schneider, R.W. (1974). Fish populations in dense submersed plant communities. *Hyacinth Control J.* 12, 12–14.

Barry, J.M. (1980). "Natural Vegetation of South Carolina." Univ. of South Carolina Press, Columbia.

Bartram, J. (1766). "Diary of a Journey through the Carolinas, Georgia, and Florida" (F. Harper, ed. and annot.), *Trans. Am. Philos. Soc.,* Vol. 33, Part 1. Am. Philos. Soc., Philadelphia, Pennsylvania, 1942.

Bartram, W. (1791). "The Travels of William Bartram" (M. Van Doren, ed.). Dover, New York, 1955.

Bass, D.G., Jr. (1983). "Rivers of Florida and Their Fishes." Completion Rep. for Invest. Proj., Dingell–Johnson Proj. F-36, North Fla. Streams Res. Study III. Florida Game Fresh Water Fish Comm. 1980–1983. Tallahassee.

Bass, D.G., Jr., and Cox, D.T. (1985). River habitat and fishery resources of Florida. *In* "Florida Aquatic Habitat and Fishery Resources" (W. Seaman, Jr., ed.), pp. 121–187. Florida Chap., Am. Fish. Soc., Kissimmee.

Bastos, T.X., and Smith, W.H. (1979). Influence of pine forest removal on flatwood soil temperature and moisture conditions. *Univ. Fla. Intensive Manage. Pract. Assess. Cent. (IMPAC) Rep.* No. 4(3).

Battoe, L.E. (1985). Changes in vertical phytoplankton distribution in response to natural disturbances in a temperate and a subtropical lake. *J. Freshwater Ecol.* 3, 167–174.

Bay, R.R. (1966). Factors influencing soil-moisture relationships in undrained bogs. *Int. Symp. For. Hydrol.* (W.E. Soper and H.W. Hull, eds.), pp. 335–343. Pergamon, New York.

Bayer, F. (1961). "The Shallow-Water Octocorallia of the West Indian Region." Nijhoff, The Hague.

Bayley, S.E., Zoltek, J., Jr., Hermann, A.J., Dolan, T.J., and Tortora, L. (1985). Experimental manipulation of nutrients and water in a freshwater marsh: effects on biomass, decomposition, and nutrient accumulation. *Limnol. Oceanogr.* 30, 500–512.

Bays, J.S., and Crisman, T.L. (1983). Zooplankton and trophic state relationships in Florida lakes. *Can. J. Fish. Aquat. Sci.* 40, 1813–1819.

Beaver, G.F., and Oosting, H.J. (1939). Pocomoke Swamp: a study of a cypress swamp on the eastern shore of Maryland. *Bull. Torrey Bot. Club* 66, 367–389.

Beaver, J.R., and Crisman, T.L. (1981). Acid precipitation and the response of ciliated protozoans in Florida lakes. *Int. Ver. Theor. Angew. Limnol.* 21, 353–358.

Beaver, J.R., and Crisman, T.L. (1982). The trophic response of ciliated protozoans in freshwater lakes. *Limnol. Oceanogr.* 27, 246–253.

Beaver, J.R., Crisman, T.L., and Bays, J.S. (1981). Thermal regimes of Florida lakes. *Hydrobiologia* 83, 267–273.

Beck, B.F., and Sinclair, W.C. (1986). "Sinkholes in Florida: An Introduction." Rep. 85–86–4. Sinkhole Res. Ins., Coll. Eng., Univ. Central Florida in coop. with U.S. Geol. Surv., Orlando.

Beck, E.C., and Beck, W.M., Jr. (1959). A checklist of the Chironomidae (Insecta) of Florida (Diptera: Chironomidae). *Bull. Fla. State Mus. Biol. Sci.* 4, 85–96.

Beck, E.C., and Beck, W.M., Jr. (1969). Chironomidae (Diptera) of Florida. III. The Harnischia complex (Chironominae). *Bull. Fla. State Mus. Biol. Sci.* 13, 277–313.

Beck, W.M., Jr. (1965). The streams of Florida. *Bull. Fla. State Mus. Biol. Sci.* 10, 91–126.

Beck, W.M., Jr., and Beck, E.C. (1966). Chironomidae (Diptera) of Florida. II. Pentaneurini (Tanypodinae). *Bull. Fla. State Mus. Biol. Sci.* 10, 305–379.

Beckwith, S.L. (1967). Chinsegut Hill–McCarty Woods, Hernando County, Florida. *Q.J. Fla. Acad. Sci.* 30, 250–268.

Bein, F.L. (1971). Geographic shifts of Florida citrus. M.S. Thesis, Univ. of Florida, Gainesville.

Beissinger, S.R., and Takekawa, J.E. (1983). Habitat use by and dispersal of snail kites in Florida during drought conditions. *Fla. Field Nat.* 11, 89–106.

Belanger, T.V., Mikutel, D.F., and Churchill, P.A. (1985). Groundwater seepage nutrient loading in a Florida lake. *Water Res. 19,* 773–781.

Bell, S.S. (1979). Short and long-term variation in a high marsh meiofauna community. *Estuarine Coastal Mar. Sci.* 9, 331–350.

Bell, S.S. (1980). Meiofauna-macrofauna interaction in a high salt marsh habitat. *Ecol. Monogr.* 50, 487–505.

Below, T.H. (1985). Shorebirds in south-west Florida. *Natl. Audubon Soc., Naples, Fla., Wader Study Group Bull.* No. 44.

Belrose, F.C. (1976). "Ducks, Geese and Swans of North America." Stackpole Books, Harrisburg, Pennsylvania.

Bengtson, G.W., and Smart, G.C., Jr. (1981). Slash pine growth and response to fertilizer after application of pesticides to the planting site. *For. Sci.* 27, 487–502.

Benner, R., Peele, E.R., and Hodson, R.E. (1986). Microbial utilization of dissolved organic matter from leaves of the red mangrove, *Rhizophora mangle,* in the fresh creek estuary, Bahamas. *Estuarine Coastal Shelf Sci.* 23, 607–619.

Bennett, K.D. (1985). The spread of *Fagus grandifolia* across eastern North America during the last 18,000 years. *J. Biogeogr.* 12, 147–164.

Benzing, D.H. (1980). "The Biology of the Bromeliads." Mad River Press, Eureka, California.

Benzing, D.H., and Renfrow, A. (1971). The biology of the atmospheric bromeliad *Tillandsia circinata* Schlecht. I. The nutrient status of populations in south Florida. *Am. J. Bot.* 58, 867–873.

Beriault, J., Carr, R., Stipp, J., Johnson, R., and Meeder, J. (1981). The archeological salvage of the Bay West Site. *Fla. Anthropol.* 34, 39–58.

Berner, L. (1941). The mayflies of Florida (Ephemeroptera). Ph.D. Thesis, Univ. of Florida, Gainesville.

Berner, L. (1950). "The Mayflies of Florida." *Bio. Sci. Ser.,* Univ. of Florida Press, Gainesville.

Berner, L. (1977). Distributional patterns of southeastern mayflies (Ephemeroptera). *Bull. Fla. State Mus. Biol. Sci.* 22, 1–55.

Berry, E.W. (1916). The physical conditions and age indicated by the flora of the Alum Bluff Formation. *Geol. Surv. Prof. Pap. (U.S.)* No. 98, 41–53.

Bessey, E.A. (1911). The hammocks and everglades of southern Florida. *Plant World* 14, 268–276.

Best, G.R., Schwartz, L.N., Sonnenburg, L., Kidd, S., and McCreary, J.J. (1981). Low-energy wastewater recycling through wetland ecosystems: Apalachicola Study—experimental use of a freshwater shrub swamp. *Univ. Fla. Cent. Wetlands Tech. Rep.* No. 39.

Bethune, J.E. (1960). Distribution of slash pine as related to certain climatic factors. *For. Sci.* 6, 11–17.

Bethune, J.E. (1966). Performance of two slash pine varieties planted in south Florida. *U.S. For. Serv. Res. Pap.* No. SE-24.

Bidlingmayer, W.L. (1982). Surveying salt marsh mosquito control impoundments of central Florida. *J. Fla. Anti-Mosq. Assoc.* 53, 4–7.

Bidlingmayer, W.L., and McCoy, E.D. (1978). "An Inventory of the Salt Marsh Mosquito Control Impoundments in Florida." Florida Med. Entomol. Lab., Vero Beach.

Bienert, R.W., Jr. (1982). The plankton communities of selected colored lakes in north-central Florida. M.S. Thesis, Univ. of Florida, Gainesville.

Bill, R.G., Jr., Bartholic, J.F., Sutherland, R.A., Georg, J.G., and Chen, E. (1979). The moderating effect of Lake Apopka on downwind temperatures. *Univ. Fla., Inst. Food Agric. Sci. Tech. Bull.* No. 808.

Billets, B.D., and Osborne, J.A. (1985). Zooplankton abundance and diversity in Spring Lake, Florida. *Fla. Sci.* 48, 129–139.

Binford, M.W., and Brenner, M. (1986). Dilution of ^{210}Pb by organic sedimentation in lakes of different trophic states, and application to studies of sediment-water interactions. *Limnol. Oceanogr.* 31, 584–595.

Binford, M.W., Brenner, M., Whitmore, T.J., Higuera-Gundy, A., Deevey, E.S., and Leyden, B. (1987). Ecosystems, paleoecology and human disturbance in subtropical and tropical America. *Q. Sci. Rev.* 6, 115–128.

Birkeland, C. (1977). The importance of rate of biomass accumulation in early successional stages of benthic communities to the survival of coral recruits. *Proc. Int. Coral Reef Symp., 3d, Miami, Fla.* 1, 16–21.

Birkeland, C. (1987). Nutrient availability as a major determinant of differences among coastal hard-substratum communities in different regions of the tropics. *In* "Differences between Atlantic and Pacific Tropical Marine Coastal Ecosystems: Community Structure, Ecological Processes, and Productivity" (C. Birkeland, ed.), pp. 45–90. UNESCO Reports in Marine Science, Paris.

Birnhak, B.I., and Crowder, J.P. (1974). "An Evaluation of the Extent of Vegetative Habitat Alteration in South Florida, 1943–1970." *Ecol. Rep.* No. DI-SFEP-74-22 of South Fla. Environ. Proj., Bur. Sport Fish. Wildl., U.S. Dep. Inter., Atlanta, Georgia.

Blair, W.F. (1951). Population structure, social behavior, and environmental relations in a natural population of the beach mouse (*Peromyscus polionotus leucocephalus*). *Univ. Mich. Contrib. Lab. Vertebr. Biol.* No. 48, 1–46.

Blaisdell, R.S. (1966). The role of *Magnolia grandiflora* and *Fagus grandifolia* in forest processes in northwestern Florida. M.S. Thesis, Florida State Univ., Tallahassee.

Blaisdell, R.S., Wooten, J., and Godfrey, R.K. (1974). The role of magnolia and beech in forest processes in the Tallahassee, Florida, Thomasville, Georgia area. *Proc. Tall Timbers Fire Ecol. Conf.* 13, 363–397.

Blake, N.M. (1980). "Land into Water—Water into Land: A History of Water Management in Florida." Univ. Presses of Florida, Tallahassee.

Blancher, E.C. (1984). Zooplankton–trophic state relationships in some north and central Florida lakes. *Hydrobiologia* 109, 251–263.

Bloom, A.L. (1983). Sea level and coastal morphology of the United States through the Late Wisconsin glacial maximum. *In* "Late Quaternary Environments of the United States" (H.E. Wright, Jr., ed.), Vol. 1, pp. 215–229. Univ. of Minnesota Press, Minneapolis.

Bloom, S. (1981). Similarity indices in community studies: potential pitfalls. *Mar. Ecol. Prog. Ser.* 5, 125–128.

Bloom, S., Santos, S., and Field, J. (1977). A package of computer programs for benthic community analysis. *Bull. Mar. Sci.* 27, 577–580.

Boerner, R.E.J. (1981). Forest structure dynamics following wildfire and prescribed burning in the New Jersey Pine Barrens. *Am. Midl. Nat.* 105, 321–333.

Boerner, R.E.J. (1982). Fire and nutrient cycling in temperate ecosystem. *BioScience* 32, 187–192.

Boerner, R.E.J. (1984). Foliar nutrient dynamics and nutrient use efficiency of four deciduous tree species in relation to site fertility. *J. Appl. Ecol.* 21, 1029–1040.

Boerner, R.E.J. (1985). Foliar nutrient dynamics, growth, and nutrient use efficiency of *Hamamelis virginiana* in three forest microsites. *Can. J. Bot.* 63, 1476–1481.

Bonet, F., and Rzedowski, J. (1962). La vegetación de las islas del Arrecife Alacranes, Yucatán (México). *Ann. Esc. Nac. Cienc. Biol.* 11, 15–50.

Bormann, F.H., and Likens, G.E. (1979a). Catastrophic disturbance and the steady state in northern hardwood forests. *Am. Sci.* 67, 660–669.

Bormann, F.H., and Likens, G.E. (1979b). "Pattern and Process in a Forested Ecosystem." Springer-Verlag, New York.

Borowitzka, M.A., and Larkum, A.W.D. (1976). Calcification in the green alga *Halimeda.* II. The exchange of Ca^{2+} and the occurrence of age gradients in calcification and photosynthesis. *J. Exp. Bot.* 27, 879–893.

Boto, K.G., and Bunt, J.S. (1981). Tidal export of particulate organic matter from a northern Australian mangrove system. *Estuarine Coastal Shelf Sci.* 13, 247–257.

Bourdeau, P.F., and Oosting, H.J. (1959). The maritime live oak forest in North Carolina. *Ecology* 40, 148–152.

Bourdo, E.A., Jr. (1956). A review of the general land office survey and of its use in quantitative studies of former forests. *Ecology* 37, 754–768.

Bowen, W.W. (1968). Variation and evolution of Gulf coast populations of beach mice (*Peromyscus polionotus*). *Bull. Fla. State Mus. Biol. Sci.* 12, 1–91.

Bowman, H.H.M. (1917). Ecology and physiology of red mangroves. *Proc. Am. Philos. Soc.* 56, 589–672.

Bowman, H.H.M. (1918). Botanical ecology of the Dry Tortugas. *Carnegie Inst. Wash. Publ.* No. 252.

Boyce, S.G. (1954). The salt spray community. *Ecol. Monogr.* 24, 29–67.

Boyd, C.E., and Hess, L.W. (1970). Factors influencing shoot production and mineral nutrient levels in *Typha latifolia*. *Ecology* 51, 296–300.

Boyle, J.R. (1973). Forest soil chemical changes following fire. *Comm. Soil Sci. Plant Anal.* 4, 369–374.

Bradbury, R., and Reichelt, R. (1981). The reef and man: rationalizing management through ecological theory. *Proc. Int. Coral Reef Symp., 4th, Manila* 1, 219–223.

Bradley, J.T. (1972). "The Climate of Florida," *Climatography of the United States* No. 60-8. Natl. Ocean. Atmos. Adm., Silver Spring, Maryland.

Bradley, W.H., and Beard, M.E. (1969). Mud Lake, Florida: its algae and alkaline brown water. *Limnol. Oceanogr.* 14, 889–897.

Brandt, K., and Ewel, K.C. (1989). Ecology and management of cypress swamp: a review. *Univ. Fla. Ext. Bull.* 252. Gainesville.

Bratton, S.P. (1985). The vegetation history of Fort Frederica, St. Simons Island, GA. *Castanea* 50, 133–145.

Braun, E.L. (1950). "Deciduous Forests of Eastern North America." Blakiston, Philadelphia, Pennsylvania.

Brawley, S.H., and Adey, W.H. (1981). The effect of micrograzers on algal community structure in a coral reef microcosm. *Mar. Biol. (Berlin)* 61, 167–177.

Breininger, D.R. (1981). Habitat preferences of the Florida scrub jay (*Aphelocoma coerulescens coerulescens*) on Merritt Island National Wildlife Refuge, Florida. M.S. Thesis, Florida Inst. of Technol., Melbourne.

Breininger, D.R., Schmalzer, P.A., Rydene, D.A., and Hinkle, C.R. (1988). "Burrow and Habitat Relationships of the Gopher Tortoise in Coastal Scrub and Slash Pine Flatwoods on Merritt Island, Florida." Final rep., Project No. GFC 84–016. Florida Game Fresh Water Fish Comm., Nongame Wildl. Prog., Tallahassee.

Brender, E.V., and Nelson, T.C. (1954). Behavior and control of understory hardwoods after clearcutting a Piedmont stand. *U.S. For. Serv. Res. Note* No. SE-44.

Brenner, M., and Binford, M.W. (1988). Relationships between concentrations of sedimentary variables and trophic state in Florida lakes. *Can. J. Fish. Aquat. Sci.* 45, 294–300.

Brezonik, P.L. (1978). Effect of organic color and turbidity on Secchi disk transparency. *J. Fish. Res. Board. Can.* 35, 1410–1416.

Brezonik, P.L., and Harper, C.L. (1969). Nitrogen fixation in some anoxic lacustrine environments. *Science* 164, 1277–1279.

Brezonik, P.L., and Messer, J.J. (1977). Analysis of trophic conditions and eutrophication factors in Lake Weir, Florida. *In* "North American Project—A Study of Water Bodies" (L. Seyb and K. Randolph, eds.), EPA-600/3-77-086, pp. 1–24. Environ. Res. Lab., U.S. Environ. Prot. Agency, Corvallis, Oregon.

Brezonik, P.L., Edgerton, E.S., and Hendry, C.D. (1980). Acid precipitation and sulfate deposition in Florida. *Science* 208, 1027–1029.

Brezonik, P.L., Crisman, T.L., and Schulze, R.L. (1984). Planktonic communities in Florida softwater lakes of varying pH. *Can. J. Fish. Aquat. Sci.* 41, 46–56.

Brightman, R.S. (1984). Benthic macroinvertebrate response to secondarily treated wastewater in north-central Florida cypress domes. *In* "Cypress Swamps" (K.C. Ewel and H.T. Odum, eds.), pp. 186–196. Univ. Presses of Florida, Gainesville.

Britton, J.C., and Fuller, S.L.H. (1979). "The Freshwater Bivalve Mollusca (Unionidae, Sphaeriidae, Corbiculidae) of the Savannah River Plant, South Carolina." Savannah River Ecol. Lab., Natl. Environ. Res. Park Program, U.S. Dep. Energy, Aiken, South Carolina.

Broadfoot, W.M. (1973). Raised water tables affect southern hardwood growth. *U.S. For. Serv. Res. Note* No. SO-168.

Broadfoot, W.M., and Williston, H.L. (1973). Flooding effects on southern forests. *J. For.* 71, 584–587.

Brock, T.D. (1970). Photosynthesis by algal epiphytes of *Utricularia* in Everglades National Park. *Bull. Mar. Sci.* 20, 952–956.

Broerman, F.S. (1978). Cultural practices in industrial forest management. *Proc. Fifth North Amer. For. Biology Workshop, Gainesville*, 150–166.

Brokaw, N.V.L., and Scheiner, S.M. (1989). Species composition in gaps and structure of a tropical forest. *Ecology* 70, 538–541.

Bromley, R.G. (1978). Bioerosion of Bermuda reefs. *Palaeogeogr., Palaeoclimatol., Palaeoecol.* 23, 169–197.

Brooks, H.K. (1961). The submarine spring off Crescent Beach, Florida. *Q. J. Fla. Acad. Sci.* 24, 122–134.

Brooks, H.K. (1962). Observations on the Florida Middle Ground. *Geol. Soc. Am. Spec. Publ.* 68, 65–66. (Abstr.)

Brooks, H.K. (1973). Geological oceanography. *In* "A Summary of Knowledge of the Eastern Gulf of Mexico," pp. IIE-1–IIE-49. Inst. Oceanogr., State Univ. Syst. of Florida, St. Petersburg.

Brooks, H.K. (1982). "Guide to the Physiographic Divisions of Florida." Fla. Coop. Ext. Serv., Inst. Food Agric. Sci., Univ. of Florida, Gainesville.

Brooks, J.E., and Lowe, E.F. (1984). "U.S. EPA Clean Lakes Program, Phase I, Diagnostic-Feasibility Study of the Upper St. Johns River Chain of Lakes, Volume II—Feasibility Study." St. Johns River Water Manage. Dist. Tech. Publ. SJ 84-15. Palatka, Florida.

Browder, J.A., Bartley, H.A., and Davis, K.S. (1985). A probabilistic model of the relationship between marshland-water interface and marsh disintegration. *Ecol. Modell.* 29, 245–260.

Brown, C.A. (1959). Vegetation of the outer banks of North Carolina. *La. State Univ. Coastal Stud. Ser.* No. 4.

Brown, J.G. (1981). Palynologic and petrographic analyses of bayhead hammock and marsh peats at Little Salt Spring archeological site (85018), Florida. M.S. Thesis, Univ. of South Carolina, Columbia.

Brown, M.J., and Thompson, M.T. (1988). Forest statistics for Florida, 1987. USDA For. Serv., S.E. For. Exp. Station SE-101.

Brown, S. (1981). A comparison of the structure, primary productivity, and transpiration of cypress ecosystems in Florida. *Ecol. Monogr.* 51, 403–427.

Brown, S. (1984). The role of wetlands in the Green Swamp. *In* "Cypress Swamps" (K.C. Ewel and H.T. Odum, eds.), pp. 405–415. Univ. Presses of Florida, Gainesville.

Brown, S.L., Cowles, S.W., and Odum, H.T. (1984a). Metabolism and transpiration of cypress domes in north-central Florida. *In* "Cypress Swamps" (K.C. Ewel and H.T. Odum, eds.), pp. 145–163. Univ. Presses of Florida, Gainesville.

Brown, S.L., Flohrschutz, E.W., and Odum, H.T. (1984b). Structure, productivity, and phosphorus cycling of the scrub cypress ecosystem. *In* "Cypress Swamps" (K.C. Ewel and H.T. Odum, eds.), pp. 304–317. Univ. Presses of Florida, Gainesville.

Brubaker, H.F. (1956). Land classification, ownership, and use in Leon County, Florida. Ph.D. Thesis, Univ. of Michigan, Ann Arbor.

Bryan, O.C. (1958). The soils of Florida and their crop adaptation. *Fla. Dep. Agric. Bull.* No. 42.

Bryan, P.G. (1973). Growth rate, toxicity and distribution of the encrusting sponge, *Terpios* sp. (Hadromerida: Subertides) in Guam, Mariana Islands. *Micronesica* 9, 237–242.

Bryant, V.M., Jr. (1977). A 16,000 year pollen record of vegetational change in central Texas. *Palynology* 1, 143–156.

Bryant, V.M., Jr., and Holloway, R.G. (1985). A late-Quaternary paleoenvironmental record of Texas: an overview of the pollen evidence. *In* "Pollen Records of Late-Quaternary North American Sediments" (V.M. Bryant and R.G. Holloway, eds.), pp. 39–70. Am. Assoc. Stratigr. Palynol. Found.

Buckley, A., and Hendrickson, T.O. (1983). "Vascular Plants of Hugh Taylor Birch State Recreation Area." Florida Dep. Nat. Resour., Tallahassee.

Buckley, A., and Hendrickson, T.O. (1988). The distribution of *Cladonia perforata* Evans on the southern Lake Wales Ridge in Highlands County, Florida. *The Bryologist* 9, 354–356.

Buckner, J.L. (1983). Wildlife concerns in the managed slash pine ecosystem. *In* "The Managed Slash Pine Ecosystem," Proc. Symp. (E.L. Stone, ed.), pp. 369–374. Sch. For. Resour. Conserv., Univ. of Florida, Gainesville.

Buell, M.F., and Cantlon, J.E. (1950). A study of two communities of the New Jersey pine barrens and a comparison of methods. *Ecology* 31, 567–586.

Buell, M.F., and Wistendahl, W.A. (1955). Flood plain forests of the Raritan River. *Bull. Torrey Bot. Club* 82, 463–472.

Bulletin of Marine Science (1985). "Third International Artificial Reef Conference Proceedings." *Bull. Mar. Sci.* 37, 1–402.

Bunt, J.S. (1982). Studies of mangrove litter fall in tropical Australia. *In* "Mangrove Ecosystems in Australia" (B.F. Clough, ed.), pp. 223–237. Australian Natl. Univ. Press, Canberra.

Buol, S.W., Hole, F.D., and McCracken, R.J. (1980). "Soil Genesis and Classification," 2nd Ed. Iowa State Univ. Press, Ames.

Bureau of Economic and Business Research (1987). "Florida Estimates of Population: April 1, 1986." Coll. Bus. Adm., Univ. of Florida, Gainesville.

Bureau of Economic and Business Research (1988). "Florida Estimates of Population: April 1, 1987." Coll. Bus. Adm., Univ. of Florida, Gainesville.

Burk, J.C. (1962). The North Carolina outer banks: a floristic interpretation. *J. Elisha Mitchell Sci. Soc.* 78, 21–28.

Burkhardt, H.J. (1952). Starch making: a pioneer Florida industry. *Tequesta* 12, 47–53.

Burkholder, P.R., Burkholder, L.M., and Rivero, J.A. (1959). Some chemical constituents of turtle grass, *Thallasia testudinum*. *Bull. Torrey Bot. Club* 85, 88–93.

Burns, L.A. (1984). Productivity and water relations in the Fakahatchee Strand of south Florida. *In* "Cypress Swamps" (K.C. Ewel and H.T. Odum, eds.), pp. 318–333. Univ. Presses of Florida, Gainesville.

Burns, R.M. (1973). Sand pine: distinguishing characteristics and distribution. *Proc. Sand Pine Symp.*, pp. 13–27. *U.S. For. Serv. Gen. Tech. Rep.* No. SE-2.

Burton, G.W., and Hughes, R.H. (1961). Effects of burning and 2,4,5-T on gallberry and saw palmetto. *J. For.* 59, 497–500.

Buss, L. (1980). Bryozoan overgrowth interactions: the interdependence of competition for space and food. *Nature (London)* 281, 475–477.

Bustard, R. (1972). "Sea Turtles." Taplinger, New York.

Byers, C.F. (1930). A contribution to the knowledge of Florida Odonata. *Univ. Fla. Publ. Biol. Sci. Ser.* 1, 1–327.

Byers, H.R., and Rodebush, H.R. (1948). Causes of thunderstorms of the Florida peninsula. *J. Meteorol.* 5, 275–280.

Byram, G.M. (1948). Vegetation temperature and fire damage in the southern pines. *U.S. For. Serv. Fire Control Notes* 9, 34–46.

Cairns, S. (1979). The deep water Scleractinia of the Caribbean Sea and adjacent waters. *Uitqaven Natuurwet. Stud. Suriname Ned. Antillen* 96, 1–341.

Cairns, S., and Stanley, G. (1983). Ahermatypic coral banks: living and fossil counterparts. *Proc. Int. Coral Reef Symp., 4th, Manila* 1, 611–618.

Caldwell, R.E., and Johnson, R.W. (1982). "General Soil Map—Florida." U.S. Dep. Agric., Soil Conserv. Serv. in coop. with Univ. of Florida, Soil Sci. Dep., Inst. Food Agric. Sci. Agric. Exp. Stn., Gainesville.

Cameron, A. (1974). Toxicity phenomena in coral reef waters. *Proc. Int. Coral Reef Symp., 2nd, Brisbane* 1, 513–518.

Cameron, A., Campbell, B., Cribb, A., Endean, R., Jell, J., Jones, O., Mather, P., and Talbot, F., eds. (1974). *Proc. Int. Coral Reef Symp., 2nd.* 2 vols. Courier-Mail Print. Serv., Bowen Hills, Queensland, Australia.

Camilleri, J.C., and Ribi, G. (1986). Leaching of dissolved organic carbon (DOC) from dead leaves, formation of flakes from DOC, and feeding on flakes by crustaceans in mangroves. *Mar. Biol. (Berlin)* 91, 337–344.

Camp, P.D. (1932). A study of range cattle management in Alachua County, Florida. *Fla. Agric. Exp. Stn. Bull.* No. 248.

Campbell, H.W., and Christman, S.P. (1982). The herpetological components of Florida sandhill and sand pine scrub associations. *U.S. Fish Wildl. Serv. Wildland Res. Rep.* No. 13, pp. 163–171.

Campbell, H.W., and Irvine, A.B. (1977). Feeding ecology of the West Indian manatee (*Trichechus manatus* Linnaeus). *Aquaculture* 12, 249–251.

Campbell, R.S. (1957). Grazing in southern pine forests. *Proc. Annu. For. Symp., 6th,* pp. 13–20. Sch. of For., Louisiana State Univ., Baton Rouge.

Canfield, D.E., Jr. (1981). "Chemical and Trophic State Characteristics of Florida Lakes in Relation to Regional Geology." Final rep. to Fla. Coop. Fish Wildl. Unit, Univ. of Florida, Gainesville.

Canfield, D.E., Jr. (1983a). Prediction of chlorophyll *a* concentrations in Florida lakes: the importance of phosphorus and nitrogen. *Water Resour. Bull.* 19, 255–262.

Canfield, D.E., Jr. (1983b). Sensitivity of Florida lakes to acidic precipitation. *Water Resour. Res.* 19, 833–839.

Canfield, D.E., Jr. (1984). A survey of sodium and chloride concentrations in Florida lakes. *Fla. Sci.* 47, 44–54.

Canfield, D.E., Jr., and Hodgson, L.M. (1983). Prediction of Secchi disc depths in Florida lakes: impact of algal biomass and organic color. *Hydrobiologia* 99, 51–60.

Canfield, D.E., Jr., and Hoyer, M.V. (1988). The eutrophication of Lake Okeechobee. *Lake and Reservoir Management* 4, 91–99.

Canfield, D.E., Jr., and Watkins, C.E., II (1984). Relationships between zooplankton abundance and chlorophyll *a* concentrations in Florida lakes. *J. Freshwater Ecol.* 2, 335–344.

Canfield, D.E., Jr., Langeland, K.A., Maceina, M.J., Haller, W.T., Shireman, J.V., and Jones, J.R. (1983a). Trophic state classification of lakes with aquatic macrophytes. *Can. J. Fish Aquat. Sci.* 40, 1713–1718.

Canfield, D.E., Jr., Maceina, M.J., Hodgson, L.M., and Langeland, K.A. (1983b). Limnological features of some northwestern Florida lakes. *J. Freshwater Ecol.* 2, 67–79.

Canfield, D.E., Jr., Maceina, M.J., and Shireman, J.V. (1983c). Effects of *Hydrilla* and grass carp on water quality in a Florida lake. *Water Resour. Bull.* 19, 773–778.

Canfield, D.E., Jr., Shireman, J.V., Colle, D.E., Haller, W.T., Watkins, C.E., II, and Maceina, M.J. (1984). Prediction of chlorophyll *a* concentrations in Florida lakes: importance of aquatic macrophytes. *Can. J. Fish Aquat. Sci.* 41, 497–501.

Canfield, D.E., Jr., Maceina, M.J., Nordlie, F.G., and Shireman, J.V. (1985). Plasma osmotic and electrolyte concentrations of largemouth bass from some acidic Florida lakes. *Trans. Am. Fish. Soc.* 114, 423–429.

Canham, C.D. (1989). Different responses to gaps among shade-tolerant tree species. *Ecology* 70, 548–550.

Canham, C.D., and Loucks, O.L. (1984). Catastrophic windthrow in the presettlement forests of Wisconsin. *Ecology* 65, 803–809.

Canham, C.D., and Marks, P.L. (1985). The response of woody plants to disturbance: patterns of establishment and growth. *In* "The Ecology of Natural Disturbance and Patch Dynamics" (S.T.A. Pickett and P.S. White, eds.), pp. 197–216. Academic Press, New York.

Capone, D.G., and Taylor, B.F. (1980). Microbial nitrogen cycling in a seagrass community. In "Estuarine Perspectives" (V.S. Kennedy, ed.), pp. 153–162. Academic Press, New York.

Carlisle, V.W. (1953). Some important soil series of Florida planted to slash pine. M.S. Thesis, Univ. of Florida, Gainesville.

Carlisle, V.W., Caldwell, R.E., Sodek, F., III, Hammond, L.C., Calhoun, F.G., Granger, M.A., and Breland, H.L. (1978). "Characterization Data for Selected Florida Soils." *Soil Sci. Res. Rep.* No. 78-1. Soil Charact. Lab., Inst. Food Agric. Sci., Univ. of Florida, in coop. with U.S. Dep. Agric. Soil Conserv. Serv., Gainesville.

Carlisle, V.W., Hallmark, C.T., Sodek, F., III, Caldwell, R.E., Hammond, L.C., and Berkheiser, V.E. (1981). "Characterization Data for Selected Florida Soils." *Soil Sci. Res. Rep.* No. 81-1, Soil Charact. Lab., Inst. Food Agric. Sci., Univ. of Florida, in coop. with U.S. Dep. Agric. Soil Conserv. Serv., Gainesville.

Carlson, J.E., and Duever, M.J. (1977). Seasonal fish population fluctuations in south Florida swamp. *Proc. Annu. Conf. Southeast Assoc. Fish Wildl. Agencies* 31, 603–611.

Carlson, P.R., and Yarbro, L.A. (1987). Physical and biological control of mangrove pore water chemistry. *In* "The Ecology and Management of Wetlands" (D.D. Hook et al., eds.), pp. 112–132. Croom Helm, London.

Carlson, P.R., Yarbro, L.A., Zimmermann, C.F., and Montgomery, J.R. (1983). Pore water chemistry of an overwash mangrove island. *Fla. Sci.* 46, 239–249.

Carlson, R.E. (1977). A trophic state index for lakes. *Limnol. Oceanogr.* 22, 361–369.

Carlton, J.M. (1974). Land-building and stabilization by mangroves. *Environ. Conserv.* 1, 285–294.

Carlton, J.M. (1975). A guide to common Florida salt marsh and mangrove vegetation. *Fla. Mar. Res. Publ.* No. 6.

Carlton, J.M. (1977). A survey of selected coastal vegetation communities of Florida. *Fla. Mar. Res. Publ.* No. 30.

Carr, A. (1940). A contribution to the herpetology of Florida. *Univ. Fla. Publ. Biol. Sci. Ser.* 3, 1–118.

Carr, A. (1952). "Handbook of Turtles." Comstock, Ithaca, New York.

Carr, A. (1984). "So Excellent a Fishe." Scribner's, New York.

Carter, L.J. (1974). "The Florida Experience: Land and Water Policy in a Growth State." Johns Hopkins Univ. Press, Baltimore, Maryland.

Carter, M.R., Burns, L.A., Cavinder, T.R., Dugger, K.R., Fore, P.L., Hicks, D.B., Revells, H.L., and Schmidt, T.W. (1973). "Ecosystems Analysis of the Big Cypress Swamp and Estuaries." U.S. Environ. Prot. Agency Reg. IV., Atlanta, Georgia.

Case, R.A. (1985). "Atlantic Hurricane Season of 1985." Natl. Hurricane Cent., NWS, Natl. Oceanogr. Atmos. Admin., Miami, Florida.

Cattelino, P.J., Noble, I.R., Slatyer, R.O., and Kessell, S.R. (1979). Predicting the multiple pathways of plant succession. *Environ. Manage.* 3, 41–50.

Chaiken, L.E. (1952). Annual summer fires kill hardwood root stocks. *U.S. For. Serv. Res. Note* No. SO-19.

Chalker, B.E. (1983). Calcification by corals and other animals on the reef. *In* "Perspectives on Coral Reefs" (D.J. Barnes, ed.). *Aust. Inst. Mar. Sci. Contrib.* 200, 29–45.

Chalker, B.E., Cox, T., and Dunlap, W.C. (1984). Seasonal changes in primary production and photoadaptation by the reef building coral *Acropora granulosa* on the Great Barrier Reef. *In* "Marine Plankton and Productivity" (O. Holm-Hansen, L. Bolis, and R. Giles, eds.), pp. 73–87. Springer-Verlag, Berlin.

Chalmers, A.G. (1982). Soil dynamics and the productivity of *Spartina alterniflora*. *In* "Estuarine Comparisons" (V.S. Kennedy, ed.), pp. 231–242. Academic Press, New York.

Chamberlain, E.B. (1960). Florida waterfowl populations, habitats, and management. *Fla. Game Fresh Water Fish Comm. Tech. Bull.* No. 7.

Chambers, S.M. (1980). Genetic divergence between populations of *Goniobasis* (Pleuroceridae) occupying different drainage systems. *Malacologia* 20, 63–81.

Chaplin, C., and Scott, P. (1972). "Fish Watchers' Guide to Western Atlantic Coral Reefs." Livingston, Wynnewood, Pennsylvania.

Chapman, A.W. (1885). *Torreya taxifolia* Arnott.: a reminiscence. *Bot. Gaz.* 10, 251–254.

Chapman, H.H. (1909). A method of studying growth and yield of longleaf pine applied in Tyler Co., Texas. *Proc. Soc. Am. For.* 4, 207–220.

Chapman, H.H. (1932a). Is the longleaf type a climax? *Ecology* 13, 328–334.

Chapman, H.H. (1932b). Some further relations of fire to longleaf pine. *J. For.* 30, 602–604.

Chapman, H.H. (1942). Management of loblolly pine in the pine-hardwood region in Arkansas and in Louisiana west of the Mississippi River. *Yale Univ. Sch. For. Bull.* No. 49.

Chapman, H.H. (1950a). Lightning in the longleaf. *Am. For.* 56, 10–11, 34.

Chapman, H.H. (1950b). Longleaf yellow pine owes its existence to fire. *Coastal Cattleman* 16, 10–13.

Chapra, S.C., and Reckhow, K.H. (1983). "Engineering Approaches to Lake Management. Vol. 1: Data Analysis and Empirical Modelling." Butterworth, Boston, Massachusetts.

Charles, D.F., and Norton, S.A. (1986). Paleolimnological evidence for trends in atmospheric deposition of acids and metals. *In* "Acid Deposition: Long-term Trends" (Committee on Monitoring and Assessment of Trends in Acid Deposition, J.H. Gibson, chm.), pp. 335–431. National Academy Press, Washington, D.C.

Chen, C.S. (1965). The regional lithostratigraphic analysis of Paleocene and Eocene rocks of Florida. *Fla. Geol. Surv. Geol. Bull.* 45, 1–105.

Chen, E., and Gerber, J.F. (1985). Minimum temperature cycles in Florida. *Proc. Fla. State Hortic. Soc.* 98, 42–46.

Chen, E., and Gerber, J.F. (1986). Effects of 1980's freezes on citrus crops in Florida. *In* "Conference on Human Consequences of 1985's Climate," prepr. vol., pp. 196–199. Am. Meteorol. Soc. Asheville, North Carolina.

Chen, E., and Martsolf, J.D. (1982). "The Development of Nocturnal GOES Infrared Data as a Source of Climate Information." Natl. Clim. Program Off., Natl. Ocean. Atmos. Adm., U.S. Dep. Commer., Washington, D.C.

Chen, E., Allen, L.H., Jr., Bartholic, J.F., and Gerber, J.F. (1982). Delineation of cold-prone areas using nighttime SMS/GOES thermal data: effects of soils and water. *J. Appl. Meteorol.* 21, 1528–1537.

Chen, E., Allen, L.H., Jr., Bartholic, J.F., and Gerber, J.F. (1983). Comparison of winter-nocturnal geostationary satellite infrared-surface temperature with shelter-height temperature in Florida. *Remote Sens. Environ.* 13, 313–327.

Cheney, D., and Dyer, J., III (1974). Deep-water benthic algae of the Florida middle ground. *Mar. Biol. (Berlin)* 27, 185–190.

Chesnut, T.L., and Barman, E.H., Jr. (1974). Aquatic vascular plants of Lake Apopka, Florida. *Fla. Sci.* 37, 60–64.

Chornesky, E., and Williams, S. (1983). Distribution of sweeper tentacles on *Montastraea cavernosa*. *In* "The Ecology of Deep and Shallow Coral Reefs" (M. Reaka, ed.), *Symp. Underwater Res.,* Vol. 1, pp. 61–67. Natl. Ocean. Atmos. Adm., Rockville, Maryland.

Christensen, N.L. (1981). Fire regimes in southeastern ecosystems. *In* "Fire Regimes and Ecosystem Properties" (H.A. Mooney, T.M. Bonnickson, N.L. Christensen, J.E. Lotan, and W.A. Reiners, eds.). *U.S. Dep. Agric. For. Serv. Gen. Tech. Rep.* No. WO-26, pp. 112–136.

Christensen, N.L. (1988). Vegetation of the southeastern coastal plain. *In* "North American Terrestrial Vegetation" (M.G. Barbour and W.D. Billings, eds.), 317–363. Cambridge Univ. Press, New York.

Christman, S.P. (1974). Geographic variation for salt water tolerance in the frog *Rana sphenocephala*. *Copeia* No. 3, pp. 773–778.

Christman, S.P. (1988). "Endemism and Florida's Interior Sand Pine Scrub." Final Proj. Rep. GFC-84-101, Florida Game Fresh Water Fish Comm., Tallahassee.

Chynoweth, L.A. (1975). "Net Primary Production of *Spartina* and Species Diversity of Associated Macroinvertebrates of a Semi-Impounded Salt Marsh." *Tech. Rep.* No. 1, Grant No. NGR 10-019-009. Natl. Aeronaut. Space Adm., Kennedy Space Cent., Florida.

Cintrón, G., Lugo, A.E., Pool, D.J., and Morris, G. (1978). Mangroves of arid environments in Puerto Rico and adjacent islands. *Biotropica* 10, 110–121.

Cintrón, G., Lugo, A.E., and Martinez, R. (1985). Structural and functional properties of mangrove forests. *In* "The Botany and Natural History of Panama" (W.G. Darcy and M.D. Correa, eds.), *Monogr. Syst. Bot.,* Vol. 10, pp. 53–66. Missouri Bot. Gard., St. Louis.

Clark, R. (1986a). Hurricane Kate, November 15–23, 1985. *Fla. Dep. Nat. Resour., Beaches Shores Post-Storm Rep.* No. 86-1.

Clark, R. (1986b). The impact of hurricane Elena and tropical storm Juan on coastal construction in Florida. *Fla. Dep. Nat. Resour., Beaches Shores Post-Storm Rep.* No. 85-3.

Clausen, C.J., Cohen, A.D., Emiliani, C., Holman, J.A., and Stipp, J.J. (1979). Little

Salt Spring, Florida: a unique underwater site. *Science* 203, 609–614.
Clements, B.W., Jr., and Rogers, A.J. (1964). Studies of impounding for the control of salt marsh mosquitos in Florida, 1958–1963. *Mosq. News* 24, 265–276.
Clench, W.J., and Turner, R.D. (1956). Freshwater mollusks of Alabama, Georgia and Florida from the Escambia to the Suwannee River. *Bull. Fla. State Mus. Biol. Sci.* 1, 97–239.
Clewell, A.F. (1971). "The Vegetation of the Apalachicola National Forest: an Ecological Perspective." Final Rep. to U.S. For. Serv., Atlanta, Georgia.
Clewell, A.F. (1977). Geobotany of the Apalachicola River region. *Fla. Mar. Res. Publ.* No. 26, pp. 6–15.
Clewell, A.F. (1981). Vegetational restoration techniques on reclaimed phosphate strip mines in Florida. *Wetlands* 1, 158–170.
Clewell, A.F. (1985). "Guide to the Vascular Plants of the Florida Panhandle." Univ. Presses of Florida, Gainesville.
Clewell, A.F. (1986). "Natural Setting and Vegetation of the Florida Panhandle." COESAM/PDEI-86/001, Contract No. DACW01-77-C-0104. U.S. Army Corps Eng., Mobile, Alabama.
Clewell, A.F. (1989). Natural history of wiregrass (*Aristida stricta* Michx. Gramineae). *Natural Areas J.* 9, 223–233.
Clewell, A.F., and Ward, D.B. (1987). White cedar in Florida and along the northern Gulf coast. *In* "Atlantic White Cedar Wetlands" (A.D. Lederman, ed.), pp. 69–82. Westview Press, Boulder, Colorado.
Clewell, A.F., Goolsby, J.A., and Shuey, A.G. (1982). Riverine systems of the South Prong Alafia River System, Florida. *Wetlands* 2, 21–72.
Clough, B.F., and Attiwill, P.M. (1982). Primary productivity of mangroves. *In* "Mangrove Ecosystems in Australia" (B.F. Clough, ed.), pp. 213–222. Australian Natl. Univ. Press, Canberra.
Clugston, J.P. (1963). Lake Apopka, Florida, a changing lake and its vegetation. *Q. J. Fla. Acad. Sci.* 26, 168–174.
Clymo, R.S. (1983). Peat. *In* "Mires: Swamp, Bog, Fen and Moor." Ecosystems of the World 4A (A.J.P. Gore, ed.), pp. 159–224. Elsevier, New York.
Coastal Coordinating Council, State of Florida (1973). "Statistical Inventory of Key Biophysical Elements in Florida's Coastal Zone." Coastal Coord. Counc., Tallahassee.
Coastal Coordinating Council, State of Florida (1974). "Florida Coastal Zone Management Atlas." Coastal Coord. Counc., Tallahassee.
Cohen, A.D., and Spackman, W. (1984). The petrology of peats from the Everglades and coastal swamps of southern Florida. *In* "Environments of South Florida: Present and Past II" (P.J. Gleason, ed.), pp. 352–374. Miami Geol. Soc., Coral Gables, Florida.
Coker, W.C. (1905). Observations on the flora of the Isle of Palms, Charleston, South Carolina. *Torreya* 5, 135–14.
Colin, P.L. (1976). Filter feeding and predation on the eggs of *Thalassoma* sp. by the scombrid fish *Rastrelliger kanagurta. Copeia,* pp. 596–597.
Colin, P.L. (1978). "Caribbean Reef Invertebrates and Plants." T.F.H. Publ., Neptune City, New Jersey.
Collard, S., and D'Asaro, C. (1973). Benthic invertebrates of the eastern Gulf of Mexico. *In* "A Summary of Knowledge of the Eastern Gulf of Mexico" (J. Jones, R. Ring, M. Rinkle, and R. Smith, eds.), pp. IIIG-1–IIIG-27. Inst. Oceanogr., State Univ. Syst. of Florida, St. Petersburg.
Colle, D.E., and Shireman, J.V. (1980). Coefficients of condition for largemouth

bass, bluegill, and redear sunfish in *Hydrilla*-infested lakes. *Trans. Am. Fish. Soc.* 109, 521–531.

Collins, E.A., Monk, C.D., and Spielman, R.H. (1964). White-cedar stands in northern Florida. *Q. J. Fla. Acad. Sci.* 27, 107–110.

Collins, M.E. (1985). Key to soil orders in Florida. *Soil Sci. Fact Sheet* SL-43. Fla. Coop. Ext. Serv., Inst. Food Agric. Sci., Univ. of Florida, Gainesville.

Collins, M.E., and Carlisle, V.W. (1984). New horizon designations and definitions. *Soil Sci. Fact Sheet* SL-41. Fla. Coop. Ext. Serv., Inst. Food Agric. Sci., Univ. of Florida, Gainesville.

Collins, M.E., Schellentrager, G.W., Doolittle, J.A., and Shih, S.F. (1986). Using ground-penetrating radar to study changes in soil map unit composition in selected Histosols. *Soil Sci. Soc. Am. J.* 50, 408–412.

Collopy, M.W., and Jelks, H.L. (1986). "The Distribution of Foraging Wading Birds in Relation to the Physical and Biological Characteristics of Freshwater Wetlands in Southwest Florida." Rep. to CH2M Hill, Inc. and Cty. of Sarasota.

Colunga, L., and Stone, R., eds. (1974). *Proc. Int. Conf. Artif. Reefs.* Tex. A&M Univ. Sea Grant. Publ. 74-103.

Connell, J.H. (1978). Diversity in tropical rain forests and coral reefs. *Science* 199, 1302–1310.

Connell, J.H. (1989). Some processes affecting the species composition in forest gaps. *Ecology* 70, 560–562.

Connell, J.H., and Slatyer, R.O. (1977). Mechanisms of succession in natural communities and their role in community stability and organization. *Am. Nat.* 111, 1119–1144.

Conner, W.H., and Day, J.W., Jr. (1976). Productivity and composition of a bald cypress-water tupelo site and a bottomland hardwood site in a Louisiana swamp. *Am. J. Bot.* 63, 1354–1364.

Cook, R.E. (1969). Variation in species density in North American birds. *Syst. Zool.* 18, 63–84.

Cooke, C.W. (1939). Scenery of Florida interpreted by a geologist. *Fla. Geol. Surv. Bull.* No. 17.

Cooke, C.W. (1945). Geology of Florida. *Fla. Geol. Surv. Bull.* No. 29.

Cooksey, K.E., Cooksey, B., Evans, P.M., and Hildebrand, E.L. (1975). Benthic diatoms as contributors to the carbon cycle in a mangrove community. *Eur. Symp. on Marine Biology,* 10th, Ostend, Belg. 2, pp. 165–178.

Cooley, G.R. (1955). The vegetation of Sanibel Island, Lee County, Florida. *Rhodora* 57, 269–289.

Coombs, M.C. (1978). Reevaluation of early Miocene North American *Moropus* (Perissodactyla, Chalicotheriidae, Schizotheriinae). *Bull. Carnegie Mus. Nat. Hist.* 4, 1–62.

Cooper, R.W., Schopmeyer, C.L., and McGregor, W.H.D. (1959). Sand pine regeneration on the Ocala National Forest. *U.S. For. Serv. Prod. Res. Rep.* No. 30, Washington, D.C.

Corlett, R.T. (1986). The mangrove understory: some additional observations. *J. Trop. Ecol.* 2, 93–94.

Correll, D.S., and Correll, H.B. (1982). "Flora of the Bahama Archipelago." Lubrecht & Cramer, Forestburgh, New York.

Coull, B.C., and Bell, S.S. (1979). Perspectives of meiofaunal ecology. *In* "Ecological Processes in Coastal and Marine Systems" (R.J. Livingston, ed.), pp. 189–216. Plenum, New York.

Coultas, C.L., Clewell, A.F., and Taylor, E.M., Jr. (1979). An aberrant toposequence of soils through a titi swamp. *Am. J. Soil Sci.* 43, 377–383.

Courtenay, W.R., Jr. (1978). Additional range expansion in Florida of the introduced walking catfish. *Environ. Conserv.* 5, 273–275.

Courtenay, W.R., Jr., and Robins, C.R. (1973). Exotic aquatic organisms in Florida with emphasis on fishes: a review and recommendations. *Trans. Am. Fish. Soc.* 102, 1–12.

Courtenay, W.R., Jr., Herrema, D.J., Thompson, M.J., Azzinaro, W. P., and van Montfrans, J. (1974). Ecological monitoring of beach erosion control projects, Broward County, Florida, and adjacent areas. *U.S. Army Corps Eng. Tech. Memo.* No. 42. Coastal Eng. Res. Cent., Fort Belvoir, Virginia.

Courtenay, W.R., Jr., Hensley, D.A., Taylor, J.N., and McCann, J.A. (1984). Distribution of exotic fishes in the continental United States. *In* "Distribution, Biology, and Management of Exotic Fishes" (W.R. Courtenay, Jr. and J.R. Stauffer, Jr., eds.), pp. 41–77. Johns Hopkins Univ. Press, Baltimore, Maryland.

Cowardin, L.M., Carter, V., Golet, F.C., and LaRoe, E.T. (1979). "Classification of Wetlands and Deepwater Habitats of the United States." *U.S. Fish Wildl. Serv. Off. Biol. Serv. [Tech. Rep],* FWS/OBS 79-31.

Cowell, B.C., and Vodopich, D.S. (1981). Distribution and seasonal abundance of benthic macroinvertebrates in a subtropical Florida lake. *Hydrobiologia* 78, 97–105.

Cox, D.T., Vosatka, E.D., and Rawlings, K.E. (1976). "D-J F-25 Stream Investigations Completion Report, Upper St. Johns River." Florida Game Fresh Water Fish Comm., Tallahassee.

Cox, J. (1987). The breeding bird survey in Florida: 1969–1983. *Fla. Field Nat.* 15, 29–56.

Cox, J., Inkley, D., and Kautz, R. (1987). Ecology and habitat protection needs of gopher tortoise (*Gopherus polyphemus*) populations on lands slated for large-scale development in Florida. *Nongame Wildl. Program Tech. Rep.* No. 4. Florida Game Fresh Water Fish Comm., Tallahassee.

Cox, J.A. (1981). Distribution, habitat, and social organization of the Florida scrub jay, with a discussion of the evolution of cooperative breeding in New World jays. Ph.D. Thesis, Univ. of Florida, Gainesville.

Craighead, F.C. (1963). "Orchids and Other Air Plants of the Everglades National Park." Univ. of Miami Press, Coral Gables, Florida.

Craighead, F.C. (1964). Land, mangroves and hurricanes. *Fairchild Trop. Gard. Bull.* 19, 5–32.

Craighead, F.C. (1971). "The Trees of South Florida. Vol. 1. The Natural Environments and Their Succession." Univ. of Miami Press, Coral Gables, Florida.

Craighead, F.C. (1974). Hammocks of south Florida. *In* "Environments of South Florida: Present and Past" (P.J. Gleason, ed.), Mem. No. 2, pp. 53–60. Miami Geol. Soc., Miami, Florida.

Craighead, F.C., and Gilbert, V.C. (1962). The effects of Hurricane Donna on the vegetation of southern Florida. *Q. J. Fla. Acad. Sci.* 25, 1–28.

Crawford, D., and DeSmidt, W. (1922). The spiny lobster *Panulirus argus* of southern Florida, its natural history and utilization. *Bull. Bur. Fish. (U.S.)* 38, 281–310.

Crisman, T.L. (1980). Chydorid cladoceran assemblages from subtropical Florida. *In* "Evolution and Ecology of Zooplankton Communities" (W.C. Kerfoot, ed.), pp. 657–668. Univ. Press of New England, Hanover, New Hampshire.

Crisman, T.L., and Bienert, R.W., Jr. (1983). Perspectives on biotic responses to acidification in Florida lakes. *In* "Acid Deposition Causes and Effects: A State

Assessment Model" (A.E.S. Green and W.H. Smith, eds.), pp. 307–315. Gov. Inst., Rockville, Maryland.

Crisman, T.L., Beaver, J.R., and Bays, J.S. (1981). Examination of the relative impact of microzooplankton and macrozooplankton on bacteria in Florida lakes. *Verh. Int. Ver. Theor. Angew. Limnol.* 21, 359–362.

Crisman, T.L., Scheuerman, P., Bienert, R.W., Jr., Beaver, J.R., and Bays, J.S. (1984). A preliminary characterization of bacterioplankton seasonality in subtropical Florida lakes. *Verh. Int. Ver. Theor. Angew. Limnol.* 22, 620–626.

Critchfield, H.J. (1966). "General Climatology." Prentice-Hall, Englewood Cliffs, New Jersey.

Croker, T.C. (1968). Longleaf pine: an annotated bibliography 1946–1967. *U.S. For. Serv. South. For. Exp. Stn.* SO-35, New Orleans, Louisiana.

Croker, T.C. (1987). Longleaf pine: a history of man and a forest. *U.S. For. Serv. South. Reg. For. Rep.* No. R8-FR 7, Atlanta, Georgia.

Cronin, T.M. (1982). Rapid sea level and climate change: evidence from continental and island margins. *Quat. Sci. Rev.* 1, 177–214.

Crossland, C.J. (1983). Dissolved nutrients in coral reef waters. *In* "Perspectives on Coral Reefs" (D.J. Barnes, ed.). *Aust. Inst. Mar. Sci. Contrib.* 200, 56–68.

Curry, J.R. (1964). Transgressions and regressions. *In* "Papers in Marine Geology" (R.L. Miller, ed.), pp. 175–203. Macmillan, New York.

Curtiss, A.H. (1879). A visit to the shell islands of Florida. *Bot. Gaz.* 2, 117–119, 132–137, 154–158.

Dabel, C.V., and Day, F.P., Jr. (1977). Structural comparisons of four plant communities in the Great Dismal Swamp, Virginia. *Bull. Torrey Bot. Club* 104, 352–360.

Dahl, B.E., Fall, B.A., Lohse, A., and Appan, S.G. (1975). "Construction and Stabilization of Coastal Foredunes with Vegetation: Padre Island, Texas." U.S. Army Corps Eng., Coastal Eng. Res. Cent., Fort Belvoir, Virginia.

Daiber, F.C. (1977). Salt-marsh animals: distribution related to tidal flooding, salinity, and vegetation. *In* "Ecosystems of the World. I: Wet Coastal Ecosystems" (V.J. Chapman, ed.), pp. 79–108. Elsevier, Amsterdam.

Daiber, F.C. (1982). "Animals of the Tidal Marsh." Van Nostrand-Reinhold, New York.

Dall, W.H., and Harris, G.D. (1892). Correlation papers: Neogene. *U.S. Geol. Surv. Bull.* No. 84.

Dallmayer, R.D. (1987). $^{40}Ar/^{39}Ar$ age of detrital muscovite within Lower Ordovician sandstone in the coastal plain basement of Florida: implications for west African terrane linkages. *Geology* 15, 998–1001.

Dalrymple, G.H. (1988). The herpetofauna of Long Pine Key, Everglades National Park in relation to vegetation and hydrology. *In* "Management of Amphibians, Reptiles, and Small Mammals in North America," pp. 72–86. USDA Forest Service General Technical Report RM—166. R.C. Szaro, K.E. Severson, and D.R. Patton, tech. coordinators.

Daniels, J.J. (1855). "The United States Survey of Florida Township 30 South, Range 29 East." Florida Dep. Nat. Resour., Tallahassee.

Darley, W.M., Montague, C.L., Plumley, F.G., Sage, W.W., and Psalidas, A.T. (1981). Factors limiting edaphic algal biomass and productivity in a Georgia salt marsh. *J. Phycol.* 17, 122–128.

Dasmann, R.F. (1971). "No Further Retreat: The Fight to Save Florida." Macmillan, New York.

Daubenmire, R. (1978). "Plant Geography with Special Reference to North America." Academic Press, New York.

Davis, F.T. (1910). "The Cold Waves of the Florida Peninsula." A.B. Caldwell, Tallahassee, Florida.

Davis, F.T. (1937). Early orange culture and the epochal cold of 1835. *Fla. Hist. Q.* 15, 232–241.

Davis, G.E. (1979). "Outer Continental Shelf Resource Management Map Coral Distribution Fort Jefferson National Monument, the Dry Tortugas." U.S. Natl. Park Serv. and Bur. Land Manage., New Orleans, Louisiana.

Davis, G.E. (1982). A century of natural change in coral distribution at the Dry Tortugas: a comparison of reef maps from 1881 and 1976. *Bull. Mar. Sci.* 32, 608–623.

Davis, G.R. (1963). The influence of Santa Fe Lake on nearby minimum air temperatures. *Weather Forecasting Mimeo* No. 63-17. Fed.-State Frost Warning Serv., Natl. Weather Serv., Lakeland, Florida.

Davis, H. (1984). Mosquito populations and arbovirus activity in cypress domes. *In* "Cypress Swamps" (K.C. Ewel and H.T. Odum, eds.), pp. 210–215. Univ. Presses of Florida, Gainesville.

Davis, J.H., Jr. (1940). The ecology and geologic role of mangroves in Florida. *Pap. Tortugas Lab.* 32, 304–412. *Carnegie Inst., Wash. Publ.* No. 517.

Davis, J.H., Jr. (1942). The ecology of the vegetation and topography of the sand keys of Florida. *Pap. Tortugas Lab.* 33 (prepri. from *Carnegie Inst. of Wash. Publ.* No. 524, pp. 113–195).

Davis, J.H., Jr. (1943). The natural features of southern Florida, especially the vegetation and the Everglades. *Fla. Geol. Surv. Bull.* No. 25.

Davis, J.H., Jr. (1946). The peat deposits of Florida: their occurrence, development, and uses. *Fla. Geol. Surv. Bull.* No. 30.

Davis, J.H., Jr. (1967). "General Map of the Natural Vegetation of Florida." Circ. S-178, Inst. Food Agric. Sci., Agric. Exp. Stn., Univ. of Florida, Gainesville.

Davis, J.M., and Sakamoto, C.M. (1976). An atlas and tables of thunderstorm and hail day probabilities in the southeastern United States. *Ala. Agric. Exp. Stn. Bull.* No. 477.

Davis, L.V. (1978). Class Insecta. *In* "An Annotated Checklist of the Biota of the Coastal Zone of South Carolina" (R.G. Zingmark, ed.), pp. 186–220. Univ. of South Carolina Press, Columbia.

Davis, L.V., and Gray, I.E. (1966). Zonal and seasonal distribution of insects in North Carolina salt marshes. *Ecol. Monogr.* 36, 275–295.

Davis, M.B. (1981). Quaternary history and the stability of forest communities. *In* "Forest Succession: Concepts and Application" (D.C. West, H.H. Shugart, and D.B. Botkin, eds.), pp. 132–153. Springer-Verlag, New York.

Davison, K.L., and Bratton, S.P. (1986). The vegetation history of Canaveral National Seashore. *CPSU Tech. Rep.* No. 22. Natl. Park Serv. Coop. Unit, Athens, Georgia.

Dawes, C.J. (1981). "Marine Botany." Wiley, New York.

Day, F.P., Jr. (1985). Tree growth rates in the periodically flooded Great Dismal Swamp. *Castanea* 50, 89–95.

Day, F.P., Jr., and Dabel, C.V. (1978). Phytomass budgets for the Dismal Swamp ecosystem. *Va. J. Sci.* 29, 220–224.

DeBrahm, S.G. (1773). "DeBrahm's Report of the General Survey in the Southern District of North America" (L. DeVorsey, ed.). Univ. of South Carolina Press, Columbia, 1971.

Deevey, E.S., Jr. (1949). Biogeography of the Pleistocene, Part I. Europe and America. *Bull. Geol. Soc. Am.* 60, 1315–1416.

Deevey, E.S. (1988). Estimation of downward leakage from Florida lakes. *Limnol. Oceanogr.* 3, 1308–1320.

Deevey, E.S., Binford, M.W., Brenner, M., and Whitmore, T.J. (1986). Sedimentary records of accelerated nutrient loading in Florida lakes. *Hydrobiologia* 143, 49–53.

Deghi, G.S., Ewel, K.C., and Mitsch, W.J. (1980). Effects of sewage effluent application on litter fall and litter decomposition in cypress swamps. *J. Appl. Ecol.* 17, 397–408.

de la Cruz, A.A. (1978). Primary production processes: summary and recommendations. *In* "Freshwater Wetlands, Ecological Processes and Management Potential" (R.E. Good, D.F. Whigham, and R.L. Simpson, eds.), pp. 79–86. Academic Press, New York.

de la Cruz, A.A. (1981). Differences between south Atlantic and Gulf coast marshes. *In* "Proceedings, U.S. Fish and Wildlife Service Workshop on Coastal Ecosystems of the Southeastern United States" (R.C. Carey, P.S. Markovits, and J.B. Kirkwood, eds.). *U.S. Fish Wildl. Serv. Off. Biol. Serv., [Tech Rep.]* FWS/OBS 80-59, pp. 10–20.

de la Cruz, A.A. (1982). The impact of crude oil and oil-related activities on coastal wetlands—a review. *Proc. Int. Wetlands Conf., Delhi.*

Delaney, K.R., R.P. Wunderlin, and B.F. Hansen (1989). Rediscovery of *Ziziphus celata* (Rhamnaceae). *Sida* 13, 325–330.

Delcourt, H.R., and Delcourt, P.A. (1974). Primeval magnolia-holly-beech climax in Louisiana. *Ecology* 55, 638–644.

Delcourt, H.R., and Delcourt, P.A. (1977). Presettlement magnolia-beech climax of the Gulf coastal plain: quantitative evidence from the Apalachicola River bluffs, north-central Florida. *Ecology* 58, 1085–1093.

Delcourt, H.R., and Delcourt, P.A. (1985). Quaternary palynology and vegetational history of the southeastern United States. *In* "Pollen Records of Late-Quaternary North American Sediments" (V.M. Bryant, Jr. and R.G. Holloway, eds.), pp. 1–37. Am. Assoc. Stratigr. Palnyol. Found.

Delcourt, H.R., Delcourt, P.A., and Webb, T., III (1982). Dynamic plant ecology: the spectrum of vegetational change in space and time. *Quat. Sci. Rev.* 1, 153–175.

Delcourt, H.R., Delcourt, P.A., and Spiker, E.C. (1983). A 12,000 year record of forest history from Cahaba Pond, St. Clair County, Alabama. *Ecology* 64, 874–887.

Delcourt, P.A. (1980). Goshen Springs: Late-Quaternary vegetation record for southern Alabama. *Ecology* 61, 371–386.

Delcourt, P.A. (1985). The influence of Late-Quaternary climatic and vegetational change on paleohydrology in unglaciated eastern North America. *Ecol. Mediterr.* 11, 17–26.

Delcourt, P.A., and Delcourt, H.R. (1977). The Tunica Hills, Louisiana–Mississippi: late glacial locality for spruce and deciduous forest species. *Quat. Res.* 7, 218–237.

Delcourt, P.A., and Delcourt, H.R. (1983). Late-Quaternary vegetational dynamics and community stability reconsidered. *Quat. Res.* 19, 265–271.

Delcourt, P.A., and Delcourt, H.R. (1984). Late-Quaternary paleoclimatic and biotic responses in eastern North America and the western North Atlantic Ocean. *Pa-*

laeogeogr. Palaeoclimatol. Palaeoecol. 48, 263–284.

Delcourt, P.A., and Delcourt, H.R. (1987). "Long-Term Forest Dynamics of the Temperate Zone: a Case Study of Late-Quaternary Forest History in Eastern North America." *Ecol. Stud. Ser.* No. 63. Springer-Verlag, New York.

Delesalle, B., Galzin, R., and Salvat, B., eds. (1985). *Proc. Int. Coral Reef Congr., 5th, Tahiti.* 6 vols. Antenne Mus. EPHE, Moorea, French Polynesia.

Demaree, D. (1932). Submerging experiments with *Taxodium. Ecology* 13, 258–262.

DeMort, C., and Bowman, R.D. (1985). Seasonal cycles of phytoplankton populations and total chlorophyll of the lower St. Johns River estuary, Florida. *Fla. Sci.* 48, 96–107.

Den Hartog, J. (1977). The marginal tentacles of *Rhodactis sanctithomae* (Corallimorpharia) and the sweeper tentacles of *Montastraea cavernosa* (Scleractinia): their cnidom and possible function. *Proc. Int. Coral Reef Symp., 3rd, Miami, Fla.* 2, 463–469.

DeSelm, H.R. (1975). Keys and descriptions to "*Andropogon*" (Gramineae) of the southeasten United States. Unpubl. ms.

Deselm, H.R., Clebsch, E.E.C., Nichols, G.M., and Thor, E. (1974). Response of herbs, shrubs and tree sprouts in prescribed-burn hardwoods in Tennessee. *Proc. Tall Timbers Fire Ecol. Conf.* 13, 331–334.

DeVall, W.B. (1943). The correlation of soil pH with distribution of woody plants in the Gainesville area. *Q. J. Fla. Acad. Sci.* 6, 9–24.

Deyrup, M.A. (1989). Arthropods endemic to Florida Scrub. *Fla. Scientist* 52, 254–271.

Diamond, J.M., and Gilpin, M.E. (1983). Biogeographic umbilici and the origin of the Philippine avifauna. *Oikos* 41, 307–321.

Dickinson, J.C., Jr. (1948). An ecological reconnaissance of the biota of some ponds and ditches in northern Florida. *Q. J. Fla. Acad. Sci.* 11, 1–28.

Dickson, J.D., III (1955). An ecological study of the Key deer. *Fla. Game Fresh Water Fish Comm. Tech. Bull.* No. 3.

Dickson, R.E., and Broyer, T.C. (1972). Effects of aeration, water supply, and nitrogen source on growth and development of tupelo gum and bald cypress. *Ecology* 53, 626–634.

Dickson, R.E., Hosner, J.F., and Hosley, N.W. (1965). The effects of four water regimes upon the growth of four bottomland tree species. *For. Sci.* 11, 299–305.

Dierberg, F.E., and Brezonik, P.L. (1981). Nitrogen fixation (acetylene reduction) associated with decaying leaves of pond cypress (*Taxodium distichum* var. *nutans*) in a natural and a sewage-enriched cypress dome. *Appl. Envir. Microbiol.* 41, 1413–1418.

Dierberg, F.E., and Brezonik, P.L. (1984a). The effect of wastewater on the surface water and groundwater quality of cypress domes. *In* "Cypress Swamps" (K.C. Ewel and H.T. Odum, eds.), pp. 83–101. Univ. Presses of Florida, Gainesville.

Dierberg, F.E., and Brezonik, P.L. (1984b). Nitrogen and phosphorus mass balances in a cypress dome receiving wastewater. *In* "Cypress Swamps" (K.C. Ewel and H.T. Odum, eds.), pp. 112–118. Univ. Presses of Florida, Gainesville.

Dierberg, F.E., and Brezonik, P.L. (1984c). Water chemistry of a Florida cypress dome. *In* "Cypress Swamps" (K.C. Ewel and H.T. Odum, eds.), pp. 34–50. Univ. Presses of Florida, Gainesville.

Dierberg, F.E., and Ewel, K.C. (1984). The effects of wastewater on decomposition and organic matter accumulation in cypress domes. *In* "Cypress Swamps" (K.C. Ewel and H.T. Odum, eds.), pp. 164–170. Univ. Presses of Florida, Gainesville.

Dierberg, F.E., Straub, P.A., and Hendry, C.D. (1986). Leaf-to-twig transfer conserves nitrogen and phosphorus in nutrient poor and enriched cypress swamps. *For. Sci.* 32, 900–913.

Dilcher, D.L. (1973). A paleoclimatic interpretation of the Eocene floras of southeastern North Atlantic. *In* "Vegetation and Vegetational History of Northern Latin America" (A. Graham, ed.), pp. 39–59. Elsevier, New York.

Dillon, P.J., and Rigler, F.H. (1974). A test of a simple nutrient budget model predicting the phosphorus concentration in lake water. *J. Fish. Res. Board Can.* 31, 1771–1778.

Dineen, J.W. (1984). The fishes of the Everglades. *In* "Environments of South Florida: Present and Past" (P.J. Gleason, ed.), Mem. No. 2., Miami Geol. Soc., Miami, Florida.

Dineen, J.W., Goodrick, R.L., Hallett, D.W., and Milleson, J.F. (1974). "The Kissimmee River Revisited." In-Depth Rep. No. 2, Cent. and South Fla. Water Manage. Dist.

Dippon, D. (1983). Florida's wetland hardwood resource. *In* "Appraisal of Florida's Wetland Hardwood Resource" (D.M. Flinchum, G.B. Doolittle, and K.R. Munson, eds.), pp. 1–11. Sch. For. Resour. Conserv., Univ. of Florida, Gainesville.

DiSalvo, L. (1971). Ingestion and assimilation of bacteria by two scleractinian coral species. *In* "Experimental Coelenterate Biology" (H. Lenhoff, L. Muscatine, and L. Davis, eds.), pp. 129–136. Univ. of Hawaii Press, Honolulu.

Dodge, R.E., Aller, R.C., and Thomson, J. (1974). Coral growth related to resuspension of bottom sediments. *Nature (London)* 247, 574–577.

Doing, H. (1981). Coastal fore-dune zonation and succession in various parts of the world. *In* "Ecology of Coastal Vegetation" (W.G. Beeftink, J. Rozema, and A.H.L. Huiskies, eds.), pp. 65–77. Junk, The Hague.

Domning, D.P., Morgan, G.S., and Ray, C.E. (1982). North American Eocene sea cows (Mammalia: Sirenia). *Smithson. Contrib. Paleobiol.* 52, 1–69.

Doren, R.F., and Rochefort, R.M. (1984). Summary of fires in Everglades National Park and Big Cypress National Preserve, 1981. *Everglades Natl. Park South Fla. Res. Cent. Rep.* No. SFRC-84/01.

Doren, R.F., Richardson, D.R., and Roberts, R.E. (1987). Prescribed burning of the sand pine scrub community: Yamato Scrub, a test case. *Fla. Sci.* 50, 184–192.

Dorn, H.W. (1956). Mango growing around early Miami. *Tequesta* 16, 37–53.

Doyle, L.J., Sharma, D.C., Hine, A.C., Pilkey, O.H., Jr., Neal, W.J., Pilkey, O.H., Sr., Martin, D., and Belknap, D.F. (1984). "Living with the West Florida Shore." Duke Univ. Press, Durham, North Carolina.

Drehle, W.F. (1973). Anomalous beach ridges of Sangamon Age. *Trans. Gulf Coast Assoc. Geol. Soc.* 23, 333–340.

Drury, W.H., and Nisbet, I.C.T. (1973). Succession. *J. Arnold Arbor.* 54, 331–368.

Duane, D.B., and Meisburger, E.P. (1969). Geomorphology and sediments of the nearshore continental shelf Miami to Palm Beach, Florida. *U.S. Army Corps Eng. Tech. Mem.* No. 29. Coastal Eng. Res. Cent. Fort Belvoir, Virginia.

Ducklow, H.W., and Mitchell, R. (1979). Observations on naturally and artificially diseased tropical corals: a scanning electron microscope study. *Microbial Ecol.* 5, 215–223.

Duellman, W.E., and Schwartz, A. (1958). Amphibians and reptiles of southern Florida. *Bull. Fla. St. Mus. (Biol. Sci.)* 3, 181–324.

Duever, L.C. (1984). Natural communities of Florida's rocklands. *Palmetto* 4, 8–11.

Duever, L.C. (1984–1985). Natural communities of Florida's flatwoods. *Palmetto* 4, 6.

Duever, L.C., Iverson, G.B., Lund, P.F., Duever, M.J., Pozel, P.P., Burch, J.N., and

Meeder, J.F. (1981). "Resource Inventory and Analysis of the J.D. MacArthur Beach State Recreation Area." Unpubl. rep. for The Nature Conservancy, Winter Park, Florida.

Duever, L.C., Meeder, J.F., and Duever, M.J. (1982). "Ecological Portion, Florida Peninsula Natural Region Theme Study." Final Rep. to Natl. Park Serv., Natl. Audubon Soc., Ecosyst. Res. Unit, Naples, Florida.

Duever, M.J., Carlson, J.E., and Riopelle, L.A. (1975). Ecosystem analysis at Corkscrew Swamp. *In* "Cypress Wetlands for Water Management, Recycling, and Conservation," pp. 627–725. 2nd Annu. Rep. to Natl. Sci. Found. and Rockefeller Found., Cent. Wetlands, Univ. of Florida, Gainesville.

Duever, M.J., Carlson, J.E., Riopelle, L.A., and Duever, L.C. (1978). Ecosystem analysis at Corkscrew Swamp. *In* "Cypress Wetlands for Water Management, Recycling, and Conservation," pp. 534–570. 4th Annu. Rep. to Natl. Sci. Found. and Rockefeller Found., Cent. Wetlands, Univ. of Florida, Gainesville.

Duever, M.J., Carlson, J.E., and Riopelle, L.A. (1984a). Corkscrew Swamp: a virgin cypress strand. *In* "Cypress Swamps" (K.C. Ewel and H.T. Odum, eds.), pp. 334–348. Univ. Presses of Florida, Gainesville.

Duever, M.J., Meeder, J.F., and Duever, L.C. (1984b). Ecosystems of the Big Cypress Swamp. *In* "Cypress Swamps" (K.C. Ewel and H.T. Odum, eds.), pp. 294–303. Univ. Presses of Florida, Gainesville.

Duever, M.J., Carlson, J.E., Meeder, J.F., Duever, L.C., Gunderson, L.H., Riopelle, L.A., Alexander, T.R., Myers, R.L., and Spangler, D.P. (1986). "The Big Cypress National Preserve." Res. Rep. No. 8, Natl. Audubon Soc., New York.

Dugger, K.R. (1976). A management model for Paynes Prairie. M.S. Thesis, Univ. of Florida, Gainesville.

Duncan, D.V., and Terry, T.A. (1983). Water management. *In* "The Managed Slash Pine Ecosystem" (E.L. Stone, ed.), Proc. Symp., pp. 91–111. Sch. For. Resour. Conserv., Univ. of Florida, Gainesville.

Duncan, W.H. (1974). Vascular halophytes of the Atlantic and Gulf coasts of North America north of Mexico. *In* "Ecology of Halophytes" (R.J. Reinhold and W.H. Queen, eds.), pp. 23–50. Academic Press, New York.

Dunn, W.J. (1982). Plant communities and vascular flora of San Felasco Hammock, Alachua County, Florida. M.S. Thesis, Univ. of Florida, Gainesville.

Dunson, W.A. (1979). Occurrence of partially striped forms of the mangrove snake *Nerodia fasciata compressicauda* Kennicott and comments on the status of *N. f. taeniata* Cope. *Fla. Sci.* 42, 102–112.

Dunson, W.A. (1980). The relation of sodium and water balance to survival in sea water of estuarine and freshwater races of the snakes *Nerodia fasciata, N. sipedon* and *N. valida. Copeia,* pp. 268–280.

Durako, M.J., Browder, J.A., Kruczynski, W.L., Subrahmanyam, C.B., and Turner, R.E. (1985). Salt marsh habitat and fishery resources of Florida. *In* "Florida Aquatic Habitat and Fishery Resources" (W. Seaman, Jr., ed.), pp. 189–280. Florida Chap. Am. Fish. Soc., Kissimmee.

Durako, M.J., Phillips, R.C., and Lewis, R.R., III (1987). Proceedings of the symposium on subtropical-tropical seagrasses of the southeastern United States. *Fla. Mar. Res. Publ.* No. 42.

Dutoit, C.H. (1979). The carrying capacity of the Ichetucknee Springs and River. M.S. Thesis, Univ. of Florida, Gainesville.

Duvall, V.L., and Linnartz, N.E. (1967). Influence of grazing and fire on vegetation and soils of longleaf pine-blue stem range. *J. Range Manage.* 20, 241–246.

Dye, C.W., Jones, D.A., Ross, L.T., and Gernert, J.L. (1980). Diel variations of selected physico-chemical parameters in Lake Kissimmee, FL. *Hydrobiologia* 71, 51–60.

Easterday, J.C. (1982). A flora of Paynes Prairie Basin and Alachua Sink Hammock. M.S. Thesis, Univ. of Florida, Gainesville.

Ebbs, N.K., Jr. (1966). The coral inhabiting polychaetes of the northern Florida reef tract, Part I. *Bull. Mar. Sci.* 16, 455–485.

Edmisten, J.E. (1963). The ecology of the Florida pine flatwoods. Ph.D. Thesis, Univ. of Florida, Gainesville.

Edmisten, J.E. (1965). Some ecological aspects of pond pine. *Bull. Ga. Acad. Sci.* 23, 39–44.

Edmiston, H.L., and Myers, V.B. (1983). "Florida Lakes: A Description of Lakes, Their Processes, and Means of Protection." Florida Department of Environmental Regulation. Wilderness Graphics, Tallahassee.

Edwards, J.M., and Frey, R.W. (1977). Substrate characteristics within a Holocene salt marsh, Sapelo Island, Georgia. *Senckenbergiana Marit.* 9, 215–259.

Egler, F.E. (1948). The dispersal and establishment of the red mangrove, *Rhizophora,* in Florida. *Caribb. For.* 9, 299–310.

Egler, F.E. (1952). Southeast saline Everglades vegetation, Florida and its management. *Vegetatio* 3, 213–265.

Ehrenfeld, J.G. (1980). Understory response to canopy gaps of varying size in a mature oak forest. *Bull. Torrey Bot. Club* 107, 29–41.

Ehrhart, L.M. (1984). Some avian predators of the round-tailed muskrat. *Fla. Field Nat.* 12, 98–99.

Eiseman, N. (1981). Algae. *In:* "Key Largo Coral Reef National Marine Sanctuary Deep-Water Resource Survey" (S. Jameson, ed.), Tech. Rep. CZ/SP1, pp. 31–35, 141–144. NOAA, Washington, D.C.

Elder, J.F., and Cairns, D.J. (1982). Production and decomposition of forest litter fall on the Apalachicola River flood plain, Florida. *U.S. Geol. Surv. Water-Supply Pap.* No. 2196-B.

Eleuterius, L.N. (1976). The distribution of *Juncus roemerianus* in the salt marshes of North America. *Chesapeake Sci.* 17, 289–292.

Eleuterius, L.N. (1984). Autecology of the black needlerush *Juncus roemerianus*. *Gulf Res. Rep.* 7, 339–350.

Eleuterius, L.N., and Caldwell, J.D. (1981). Growth kinetics and longevity of the salt marsh rush, *Juncus roemerianus*. *Gulf Res. Rep.* 7, 27–34.

Eleuterius, L.N., and Eleuterius, C.K. (1979). Tide levels and salt marsh zonation. *Bull. Mar. Sci.* 29, 394–400.

Elias, T.S. (1980). "The Complete Trees of North America." Van Nostrand Reinhold, New York.

Elmore, J.L. (1983). Factors influencing *Diaptomus* distributions: an experimental study in subtropical Florida. *Limnol. Oceanogr.* 28, 522–532.

Elmore, J.L., Vodopich, D.S., and Hoover, J.J. (1983). Selective predation by bluegill sunfish (*Lepomis macrochirus*) on three species of *Diaptomus* (Copepoda) from subtropical Florida. *J. Freshwater Ecol.* 2, 183–192.

Elmore, J.L., Cowell, B.C., and Vodopich, D.S. (1984). Biological communities of three subtropical Florida lakes of different trophic character. *Arch. Hydrobiol.* 100, 455–478.

Engstrom, T., Crawford, R.L., and Baker, W.W. (1984). Breeding bird populations in relation to changing forest structure following fire exclusion: a 15-year study. *Wilson Bull.* 96, 437–450.

EPA (U.S. Environmental Protection Agency) (1978). "A Compendium of Lake and

Reservoir Data Collected by the National Eutrophication Survey in Eastern, North-Central, and Southeastern United States." Working Pap. No. 475, Environ. Res. Lab., Corvallis, Oregon.

Ernst, C.H., and Barbour, R.W. (1972). "Turtles of the United States." Univ. Press of Kentucky, Lexington.

Erwin, K.L., and Best, G.R. (1985). Marsh development in a central Florida phosphate surface-mined reclaimed wetland. *Wetlands* 5, 155–166.

Espejel, I. (1986). Studies on coastal sand dune vegetation of the Yucatan Peninsula. Ph.D. Thesis, Inst. Ecol. Bot., Univ. of Uppsala.

Estevez, E.D., and Mosura, E.L. (1985). Emergent vegetation. *Proc. Tampa Bay Area Sci. Inf. Symp., 1982* (S.F. Treat, J.L. Simon, R.R. Lewis III, and R.L. Whitman, Jr., eds.), pp. 248–278. Bellwether Press, Tampa, Florida.

Evans, A.W. (1952). The *Cladoniae* of Florida. *Trans. Conn. Acad. Arts Sci.* 38, 249–336.

Evans, M.W., and Hine, A.C. (1983). Basic control of barrier island evolution. *In* "The Crisis of Our Beaches." Environ. Stud. Publ. No. 35, pp. 21–40. New Coll., Sarasota, Florida.

Evans, M.W., Hine, A.C., Belknap, D.B., and Davis, R.A. (1985). Bedrock control on barrier island development—west central Florida coast. *Mar. Geol.* 63, 263–283.

Evers, J.H. (1976). Florida beaver: distribution and modification of their environment. M.S. Thesis, Univ. of Florida, Gainesville.

Ewel, J.J. (1986). Invasibility: lessons from south Florida. *In* "Ecology of Biological Invasions of North America and Hawaii" (H.A. Mooney and J.A. Drake, eds.), Ecol. Stud. Vol. 58. Springer-Verlag, New York.

Ewel, K.C. (1984). Effects of fire and wastewater on understory vegetation in cypress domes. *In* "Cypress Swamps" (K.C. Ewel and H.T. Odum, eds.), pp. 119–126. Univ. Presses of Florida, Gainesville.

Ewel, K.C. (1985). Effects of harvesting cypress swamps on water quality and quantity. *Univ. Fla. Water Resour. Res. Cent. Publ.* No. 87.

Ewel, K.C., and Atmosoedirdjo, S. (1987). Flower and fruit production in three north Florida ecosystems. *Fla. Sci.* 50, 216–222.

Ewel, K.C., and Fontaine, T.D., III (1983). Structure and function of a warm monomictic lake. *Ecol. Modell.* 19, 139–161.

Ewel, K.C., and Golkin, K.R. (1982). Predicting long-term changes in managed forests. *Fla. Agric. Exp. Stn. J. Ser.* No. 3959, pp. 85–90.

Ewel, K.C., and Mitsch, W.J. (1978). The effects of fire on species composition in cypress dome ecosystems. *Fla. Sci.* 41, 25–31.

Ewel, K.C., and Odum, H.T., eds. (1984). "Cypress Swamps." Univ. Presses of Florida, Gainesville.

Ewel, K.C., Davis, H.J., and Smith, J.E. (1989). Recovery of Florida cypress swamps from clearcutting. *South. J. Appl. For.* 13, 123–126.

Ewel, K.C., Gamble, J.F., and Lugo, A.E. (1975). Aspects of mineral-nutrient cycling in a southern mixed-hardwood forest in north central Florida. *In* "Mineral Cycling in Southeastern Ecosystems" (F.G. Howell, J.B. Gentry, and M.H. Smith, eds.), *ERDA Symp. Ser.* (CONF-740513), pp. 700–714.

Fadlallah, Y.H. (1983). Sexual reproduction, development and larval biology in scleractinian corals. A review. *Coral Reefs* 2, 129–150.

Fahn, A. (1979). "Secretory Tissues in Plants." Academic Press, London.

Faulkner, D., and Chesher, R. (1979). "Living Corals." Clarkson N. Potter, New York.

Fell, J.W. (1980). The association and potential role of fungi in mangrove detrital systems. *Bot. Mar.* 23, 257–263.

Fell, J.W., and Master, I.M. (1973). Fungi associated with the degradation of mangrove (*R. mangle*) leaves in south Florida. *In* "Estuarine Microbial Ecology" (H.L. Stevenson and R.R. Colwell, eds.), pp. 455–466. Univ. of South Carolina Press, Columbia.

Fell, J.W., and Newell, S.Y. (1980). Role of fungi in carbon flow and nitrogen immobilization in coastal marine plant litter systems. *In* "The Fungal Community: Its Organization and Role in the Ecosystem" (D.T. Wicklow and G.C. Carroll, eds.). Dekker, New York.

Fell, J.W., Master, I.M., and Newell, S.Y. (1980). Laboratory model of the potential role of fungi (*Phytophthora* spp.) in the decomposition of red mangrove (*Rhizophora mangle*) leaf litter. *In* "Marine Benthic Dynamics" (K.R. Tenore and B.C. Coull, eds.). Univ. of South Carolina Press, Columbia.

Fellows, C.R., and Brezonik, P.L. (1980). Seepage flow into Florida lakes. *Water Resour. Bull.* 16, 635–641.

Fellows, C.R., and Brezonik, P.L. (1981). Fertilizer flux into two Florida lakes via seepage. *J. Environ. Qual.* 10, 174–177.

Fenchel, T. (1969). The ecology of marine microbenthos. IV. Structure and function of the benthic ecosystem, its chemical and physical factors and the microfauna communities with special reference to the ciliated protozoa. *Ophelia* 6, 1–182.

Fenneman, N.M. (1938). "Physiography of Eastern United States." McGraw-Hill, New York.

Ferguson, E.R. (1957). Stem-kill and sprouting following prescribed fires in a pine-hardwood stand in Texas. *J. For.* 55, 426–429.

Ferguson, E.R. (1961). Effects of prescribed fires on understory stems in pine-hardwood stands in Texas. *J. For.* 59, 356–359.

Fernald, E.A., ed. (1981). "Atlas of Florida." Florida State Univ. Found., Tallahassee.

Fernald, E.A., and Patton, D.J., eds. (1984). "Water Resources Atlas of Florida." Inst. Sci. Public Aff., Florida State Univ., Tallahassee.

Fernald, M.L. (1950). "Gray's Manual of Botany." Van Nostrand-Reinhold, New York.

Fernald, R.T. (1989). Coastal xeric scrub communities of the Treasure Coast region, Florida: a summary of their distribution and ecology, with guidelines for their preservation and management. *Nongame Wildl. Prog. Tech. Rep.* No. 6. Tallahassee.

Ferrigno, F., and Jobbins, D.M. (1968). Open marsh water management. *Proc. Annu. Meet. N.J. Mosq. Exterm. Assoc.* 55, 104–115.

Ferrigno, F., MacNamara, L.G., and Jobbins, D.M. (1969). Ecological approach for improved management of coastal meadowlands. *Proc. Annu. Meet. N.J. Mosq. Exterm. Assoc.* 56, 188–202.

Ferrigno, F., Slavin, P., and Jobbins, D.M. (1975). Saltmarsh water management for mosquito control. *Proc. Annu. Meet. N.J. Mosq. Exterm. Assoc.* 62, 30–38.

Field, J., Clarke, J., and Warwick, M. (1982). A practical strategy for analyzing multispecies distribution patterns. *Mar. Ecol. Prog. Ser.* 8, 37–52.

Field, M.E., and Duane, D.B. (1976). Post-Pleistocene history of the United States inner continental shelf: significance to the origin of barrier islands. *Bull. Geol. Soc. Am.* 84, 691–702.

Field, M.E., Meisburger, E.P., Stanley, E.A., and Williams, S.J. (1979). Upper Quaternary peat deposits on the Atlantic inner shelf of the United States. *Bull. Geol. Soc. Am.* 90, 618–628.

Fisher, H.M., and Stone, E.L. (1990). Air-conducting porosity in slash pine roots from saturated soils. *For. Sci.* 36, 18–33.

Fisher, R.F. (1982). Impact of intensive silviculture on soil and water quality in a coastal lowland. *In* "Tropical Agricultural Hydrology" (R. Lal and E.W. Russell, eds.), pp. 299–301. Wiley, New York.

Flannery, M.S. (1984). Seasonal variations in water chemistry and zooplankton communities in four macrophyte infested central Florida lakes. M.S. Thesis, Univ. of Florida, Gainesville.

Flannery, M.S., Snodgrass, R.D., and Whitmore, T.J. (1982). Deepwater sediments and trophic conditions in Florida lakes. *Hydrobiologia* 92, 597–602.

Fletemeyer, J.R. (1985). "1985 Sea Turtle Monitoring Project Report." Environ. Qual. Control Board Broward Cty., Ft. Lauderdale, Florida.

Flohrschutz, E.W. (1978). Dwarf cypress in the Big Cypress Swamp of southwestern Florida. M.S. Thesis, Univ. of Florida, Gainesville.

Flora, M.D., and Rosendahl, P.C. (1982a). The impact of atmospheric deposition on the water quality of Everglades National Park. *Int. Symp. Hydrometeorol.* pp. 55–61.

Flora, M.D., and Rosendahl, P.C. (1982b). The response of specific conductance to environmental conditions in the Everglades National Park, Florida. *Water Air Soil Pollut.* 17, 51–59.

Flores-Verdugo, F.J., Day, J.W., and Briseno-Duenas, R. (1987). Structure, litter fall, decomposition, and detritus dynamics of mangroves in a Mexican coastal lagoon with an ephemeral inlet. *Mar. Ecol. Prog. Ser.* 35, 83–90.

Florida Board of Conservation, Division of Water Resources (1969). "Florida Lakes, Part III, Gazetteer." Tallahassee.

Florida Department of Natural Resources (1974). "Florida Keys Coastal Zone Management Study." Tallahassee.

Florida Department of Natural Resources (1981). "Resources Management Plan for the Paynes Prairie State Preserve, Basin and Rim." Paynes Prairie State Preserve, Dist. III, Fla. State Parks.

Florida Game and Fresh Water Fish Commission (1976). "Cross Florida Barge Canal Restudy Report. Wildlife Study," Vol. 1. Dep. Army, Jacksonville Dist., Corps Eng.

Florida Game and Fresh Water Fish Commission (1981). "An Evaluation of the Waterfowl Potential on Lands of the St. Johns Water Management District lying between SR 60 and US 192." Rep., Florida Game Fresh Water Fish Comm., Tallahassee.

Florida Game and Fresh Water Fish Commission (1986). Florida Wildlife Code, title 39. Tallahassee.

Florida Natural Areas Inventory (FNAI) (1988). "Natural Community Classification and Element Abstracts." Tallahassee.

Flowers, T.J., Troke, P.F., and Yeo, A.R. (1977). The mechanism of salt tolerance in halophytes. *Annu. Rev. Plant Physiol.* 28, 89–121.

Folkerts, G.W. (1982). The Gulf Coast pitcher plant bogs. *Am. Sci.* 70, 260–267.

Fonesca, M.S., Kenworthy, W.J., and Thayer, G.W. (1981). "Transplanting of the Seagrasses *Zostera marina* and *Halodule wrightii* for the Stabilization of Subtidal Dredged Material." Annu. Rep. Natl. Mar. Fish. Serv., Beaufort Lab. to U.S. Army Corps Eng.

Fontaine, T.D., III, and Ewel, K.C. (1981). Metabolism of a Florida lake ecosystem. *Limnol. Oceanogr.* 26, 754–763.

Foran, J.A. (1986a). A comparison of the life history features of a temperate and a subtropical *Daphnia* species. *Oikos* 46, 185–193.

Foran, J.A. (1986b). The relationship between temperature, competition and the potential for colonization of a subtropical pond by *Daphnia magna*. *Hydrobiologia* 134, 103–112.

Forest Industries Council (1980). "Forest Productivity Report." Natl. For. Prod. Assoc., Washington, D.C.

Forsee, W.T., Jr. (1940). Recent plant responses to some of the microelements on Everglades peat. *Proc. Soil Sci. Soc. Fla.* 2, 53–58.

Forthman, C.A. (1973). The effects of prescribed burning on sawgrass *Cladium jamaicense* (Crantz) in south Florida. M.S. Thesis, Univ. of Miami, Coral Gables, Florida.

Fosberg, F.R. (1961). Vegetation-free zones of dry mangrove coasts. *U.S. Geol. Surv. Prof. Pap.* No. 365, 216–218.

Fosberg, F.R. (1971). Mangroves versus tidal waves. *Biol. Conserv.* 4, 38–39.

Fox, R.S., and Ruppert, E.E. (1985). "Shallow-Water Marine Benthic Macroinvertebrates of South Carolina." Univ. of South Carolina Press, Columbia.

Frailey, D. (1978). An early Miocene (Arikareean) fauna from north-central Florida (SB-1A local fauna). *Occas. Pap. Mus. Nat. Hist. Univ. Kans.* 75, 1–20.

Frailey, D. (1979). The large mammals of the Buda local fauna (Arikareean: Alachua County, Florida). *Bull. Fla. St. Mus.* 24, 123–173.

Frailey, D. (1980). The beginning of the age of mammals in Florida. *Plaster Jacket* 33, 1–13. Florida State Mus., Gainesville.

Frank, N.L., Moore, P.L., and Fisher, G.E. (1967). Summer shower distribution over the Florida peninsula as deduced from digitized radar data. *J. Appl. Meteorol.* 6, 309–316.

Franklin, J.F., and Hemstrom, M.A. (1981). Aspects of succession in the coniferous forests of the Pacific Northwest. *In* "Forest Succession: Concepts and Application" (D.C. West, H.H. Shugart, and D.B. Botkin, eds.), pp. 221–229. Springer-Verlag, New York.

Franz, E.H., and Bazzaz, F.A. (1977). Simulation of vegetation response to modified hydrologic regimes: a probabilistic model based on niche differentiation in a floodplain forest. *Ecology* 58, 176–183.

Franz, R., ed. (1982). "Rare and Endangered Biota of Florida, Vol. 6: Invertebrates." Univ. Presses of Florida, Gainesville.

Frederico, A.C., Milleson, J.F., Millar, P.S., and Rosin, P. (1978). Environmental studies in the Chandler Slough watershed. *South Fla. Water Manage. Dist. Tech. Publ.* No. 78-2.

Frey, R.W., and Basan, P.B. (1985). Coastal salt marshes. *In* "Coastal Sedimentary Environments" (R.A. Davis, Jr., ed.), pp. 225–301. Springer-Verlag, New York.

Frost, C.C., and Musselman, L.J. (1987). History and vegetation of the Blackwater Ecological Preserve. *Castanea* 52, 16–46.

Frost, C.C., Walker, J., and Peet, R.K. (1986). Fire-dependent savannas and prairies of the southeast: original extent, preservation status and management problems. *In* "Wilderness and Natural Areas in the Eastern United States: A Management Challenge" (D.L. Kulhavy and R.H. Conner, eds.). Cent. Appl. Stud., Stephen F. Austin State Univ., Nacogdoches, Texas.

Frost, S.H. (1977). Cenozoic reef systems of Caribbean—prospects for paleoecologic synthesis. *In* "Reefs and Related Carbonates—Ecology and Sedimentology" (S.H. Frost, M.P. Weiss, and J.B. Saunders, eds.), *Stud. Geol.* (Tulsa, Okla.) No. 4, pp. 93–110.

Fry, D.L., and Osborne, J.A. (1980). Zooplankton abundance and diversity in central

Florida grass carp ponds. *Hydrobiologia* 68, 145–155.

Fuller, A., and Cowell, B.C. (1985). Seasonal variation in benthic invertebrate recolonization of small-scale disturbances in a subtropical Florida lake. *Hydrobiologia* 124, 211–221.

Funk, B. (1980). Hurricane! *Natl. Geogr.* 157, 346–367.

Gaines, E.M. (1950). Scrub oak as a nurse crop for longleaf pine on deep sandy soils. *Proc. Ala. Acad. Sci.* 22, 107–108.

Gallatin, M.H., and Henderson, J.R. (1943). Progress report on the soil survey of the Everglades. *Soil Sci. Soc. Fla. Proc.* V-A, 95–104.

Gano, L. (1917). A study in physiographic ecology in northern Florida. *Bot. Gaz.* 63, 337–372.

Garber, A.P. (1877). The April flora of Cedar Keys, FL. *Bot. Gaz.* 2, 112–114.

Garren, K.H. (1943). Effects of fire on vegetation of the southeastern United States. *Bot. Rev.* 9, 617–654.

Garren, R.A. (1982). Macrophyte species composition-trophic state relationships in fourteen north and north-central Florida lakes. M.S. Thesis, Univ. of Florida, Gainesville.

Gearhart, E.G., Jr. (1952). South Florida's first industry. *Tequesta* 12, 55–57.

Geiger, R. (1980). "The Climate Near the Ground." Harvard Univ. Press, Cambridge, Massachusetts.

Genelle, P., and Fleming, G. (1978). The vascular flora of "The Hammock," Dunedin, Florida. *Castanea* 43, 29–54.

Genoni, G.P. (1985). Food limitation in salt marsh fiddler crabs *Uca rapax* (Smith) (Decapoda: Ocypodidae). *J. Exp. Mar. Biol. Ecol.* 87, 97–110.

Genoni, G.P. (1987). Farming of cordgrass, *Spartina alterniflora* Loisel., by fiddler crabs, *Uca rapax* (Smith) (Decapoda: Ocypodidae). Ph.D. Thesis, Univ. of Florida, Gainesville.

Gentry, R.C. (1974). Hurricanes in south Florida. *In* "Environments of South Florida: Present and Past" (P.J. Gleason, ed.), Mem. No. 2, pp. 73–81. Miami Geol. Soc., Miami, Florida.

Georg, J.G. (1974). Note on Florida inversions. *Lakeland Agric. Res. Educ. Cent. Rep.* No. WEA-3.

Georg, J.G. (1977). Lake Apopka area wind study. Unpubl. data.

Ghiold, J., and Enos, P. (1982). Carbonate production of the coral *Diploria labyrinthiformis* in south Florida patch reefs. *Mar. Geol.* 45, 281–296.

Gholz, H.L., and Fisher, R.F. (1982). Organic matter production and distribution in slash pine plantation ecosystems. *Ecology* 63, 1827–1839.

Gholz, H.L., and Fisher, R.F. (1984). The limits to productivity: fertilization and nutrient cycling in coastal plain slash pine forests. *In* "Forest Soils and Treatment Impacts" (E.L. Stone, ed.). *Proc. North Am. For. Soils Conf., 6th, Univ. Tenn., Knoxville,* pp. 105–120.

Gholz, H.L., Fisher, R.F., and Pritchett, W.L. (1985a). Nutrient dynamics in slash pine plantation ecosystems. *Ecology* 66, 647–659.

Gholz, H.L., Perry, C.S., Cropper, W.P., Jr., and Hendry, L.C. (1985b). Litterfall, decomposition, and nitrogen and phosphorus dynamics in a chronosequence of slash pine (Pinus elliottii) plantations. *For. Sci.* 31, 463–478.

Gilbert, C.R., ed. (1978). "Rare and Endangered Biota of Florida. Vol. 4. Fishes." Univ. Presses of Florida, Gainesville.

Gilbert, C.R. (1987). Zoogeography of the freshwater fish fauna of southern Georgia and peninsular Florida. *Brimleyana* 13, 25–54.

Giles, R.T., and Pilkey, O.H., Sr. (1965). Atlantic beach and dune sediments of the southern United States. *J. Sediment. Petrol.* 35, 900–910.

Gill, A.M. (1970). The mangrove fringe on the eastern Pacific. *Fairchild Trop. Gard. Bull.* 25, 7–11.

Gill, A.M., and Tomlinson, P.B. (1971). Studies on the growth of red mangrove (*Rhizophora mangle* L.). II. Growth and differentiation of aerial roots. *Biotropica* 3, 63–77.

Gill, A.M., and Tomlinson, P.B. (1977). Studies on the growth of red mangrove (*Rhizophora mangle* L.). IV. The adult root system. *Biotropica* 9, 145–155.

Gilmore, R.G. (1984). Fishes and macrocrustacean population dynamics in a tidally influenced impounded sub-tropical marsh. *In* "Impoundment Management. Final Report: CM-47 and CM-73" (D.B. Carlson, R.G. Gilmore, and J. Rey, eds.), Sect. 2. Unpubl. rep. to Florida Dep. Environ. Regul., Coastal Zone Manage. Dep., Tallahassee.

Ginsburg, R.N. (1953). Beach rock in south Florida. *J. Sediment. Petrol.* 23, 85–92.

Ginsburg, R.N., and James, N.P. (1973). British Honduras by submarine. *Geotimes* 18, 23–24.

Givens, K.T., Layne, J.N., Abrahamson, W.G., and White-Schuler, S.C. (1984). Structural changes and successional relationships of five Florida Lake Wales Ridge plant communities. *Bull. Torrey Bot. Club* 63, 8–18.

Gladfelter, E. (1982). Skeletal development in *Acropora cervicornis.* I. Patterns of calcium carbonate accretion in the axial corallite. *Coral Reefs* 1, 45–51.

Gladfelter, E. (1983). The role of Scleractinian corals in the trophodynamics of the reef ecosystem. *In* "Coral Reefs, Seagrass Beds, and Mangroves: Their Interaction in the Coastal Zones of the Caribbean" (J. Ogden and E. Gladfelter, eds.), *UNESCO Rep. Mar. Sci.* 23, 35–50. Montevideo, Uruguay.

Gladfelter, E. (1985). Metabolism, calcification and carbon production. II. Organism-level studies. *Proc. Int. Coral Reef Congr. 5th, Tahiti* 4, 527–539.

Gleason, P.J., and Spackman, W., Jr. (1974). Calcareous periphyton and water chemistry in the Everglades. *In* "Environments of South Florida: Present and Past" (P.J. Gleason, ed.), Mem. No. 2, pp. 287–341. Miami Geol. Soc., Miami, Florida.

Gleason, P.J., Cohen, A.D., Stone, P., Smith, W.G., Brooks, H.K., Goodrick, R., and Spackman, W., Jr. (1984). The environmental significance of holocene sediments from the Everglades and saline tidal plain. *In* "Environments of South Florida: Present and Past II" (P.J. Gleason, ed.), pp. 297–351. Miami Geol. Soc., Coral Gables, Florida.

Glitzenstein, J.S., and Harcombe, P.A. (1988). Effects of the December 1983 tornado on forest vegetation of the Big Thicket, SE Texas, USA. *For. Ecol. Manage.* 25, 269–290.

Glitzenstein, J.S., Harcombe, P.A., and Streng, D.R. (1986). Disturbance history, succession, and the maintenance of species diversity in an east Texas forest. *Ecol. Monogr.* 56, 243–258.

Glooschenko, W.A., and Alvis, C. (1973). Changes in species composition of phytoplankton due to enrichment by N, P, and Si of water from a north Florida lake. *Hydrobiologia* 42, 285–294.

Glynn, P.W. (1962). *Hermodice carunculata* and *Mithraculus sculptus,* two hermatypic coral predators. *Assoc. Isl. Mar. Lab. Caribb. Meet., 4th.* Abstr.

Glynn, P.W. (1964). Common marine invertebrate animals of the shallow waters of Puerto Rico. *In* "Historia Natural de Puerto Rico," pp. 12–20. Univ. of Puerto Rico, Mayagüez.

Glynn, P.W. (1973). Aspects of the ecology of coral reefs in the western Atlantic region. *In* "Biology and Geology of Coral Reefs" (O.A. Jones and R. Endean, eds.), Vol. 2, pp. 271–324. Academic Press, New York.

Glynn, P.W. (1980). Defense by symbiotic crustacea of host corals elicited by chemical cues from predator. *Oecologia* 47, 287–290.

Godfrey, P.J. (1977). Climate, plant response, and development of dunes on barrier beaches along the United States east coast. *Int. J. Biometeorol.* 21, 203–215.

Godfrey, P.J., and Godfrey, M.M. (1976). "Barrier Island Ecology of Cape Lookout National Seashore and Vicinity, North Carolina." Natl. Park Serv. Sci. Monogr. Ser. No. 9. U.S. Gov. Print. Off., Washington, D.C.

Godfrey, R.K. (1988). "Trees, Shrubs, and Woody Vines of Northern Florida and Adjacent Georgia and Alabama." University of Georgia Press, Athens.

Godfrey, R.K., and Kurz, H. (1962). The Florida Torreya destined for extinction. *Science* 136, 900–902.

Godfrey, R.K., and Wooten, J.W. (1981). "Aquatic and Wetland Plants of Southeastern United States. Dicotyledons." Univ. of Georgia Press, Athens.

Goldberg, W., McLaughlin, P.L., and Fisher, L. (1985). Long term effects of beach restoration in a coralline environment: impact on macrobenthic and infaunal communities. *Proc. Int. Coral Reef Congr., 5th, Tahiti* 2, 150. (Abstr.)

Golkin, K.R., and Ewel, K.C. (1984). A computer simulation of the carbon, phosphorus, and hydrologic cycles of a pine flatwoods ecosystem. *Ecol. Modell.* 24, 113–136.

Golley, F.B., Odum, H.T., and Wilson, R.F. (1962). The structure and metabolism of a Puerto Rican red mangrove forest in May. *Ecology* 43, 1–19.

Golley, F.B., McGinnis, J.T., Clements, R.G., Child, G.I., and Duever, M.J. (1975). "Mineral Cycling in a Tropical Marsh Forest Ecosystem." Univ. of Georgia Press, Athens.

Gomez, E., Birkeland, C., Buddemeier, R., Johannes, R., Marsh, J., Jr., and Tsuda, R., eds. (1981). *Proc. Int. Coral Reef Symp., 4th.* 2 vols. Paragon Print Corp., Quezon City, Philippines.

Gonyea, W.J., and Hunt, B.P. (1970). Organic matter in fresh waters of southern Florida. *Q. J. Fla. Acad. Sci.* 32, 171–184.

Goodrick, R.L. (1984). The wet prairies of the northern Everglades. *In* "Environments of South Florida: Present and Past II" (P.J. Gleason, ed.), pp. 185–190. Miami Geol. Soc., Coral Gables, Florida.

Goodrick, R.L., and Milleson, J.F. (1974). Studies of floodplain vegetation and water level fluctuation in the Kissimmee River Valley. *Cent. South. Fla. Flood Control Dist. Tech. Publ.* No. 74-2.

Goodwin, T.M. (1979). Waterfowl management practices employed in Florida and their effectiveness on native and migratory waterfowl populations. *Fla. Sci.* 42, 123–129.

Goolsby, D.A., and McPherson, B.F. (1978). Limnology of Taylor Creek impoundment with reference to other water bodies in upper St. Johns River basin, Florida. *U.S. Geol. Surv. Water Resour. Invest.* No. 78–91.

Gore, R., Scotto, L., and Becker, L. (1978). Community composition, stability, and trophic partitioning in decapod crustaceans inhabiting some subtropical sabellarid worm reefs. *Bull. Mar. Sci.* 28, 221–248.

Goreau, T.F. (1959). The ecology of Jamaican coral reefs. I. Species composition and zonation. *Ecology* 40, 67–90.

Goreau, T.F. (1961). The structure of Jamaican reef communities: geological aspects. *N.Y. Acad. Sci.* 109, 127–167.

Goreau, T.F., and Goreau, N. (1960). The uptake and distribution of labelled carbon in reef building corals with and without zooxanthellae. *Science* 131, 668–669.

Goreau, T.F., and Hartman, W.D. (1963). Boring sponges as controlling factors in the formation and maintenance of coral reefs. *Am. Assoc. Adv. Sci. Publ.* 75, 25–54.

Goreau, T.F., and Hartman, W.D. (1966). Sponge: effect on the form of reef corals. *Science* 151, 343–344.

Goreau, T.F., and Land, L. (1974). Forereef morphology and depositional processes, north Jamaica. *In* "Reefs in Time and Space" (L. Laporte, ed.). *Spec. Publ. Soc. Econ. Paleontol. Mineral.* No. 18, pp. 77–89.

Gosselink, J.G. (1984). "The Ecology of Delta Marshes of Coastal Louisiana: a Community Profile." *U.S. Fish Wildl. Serv. Off. Biol. Serv. [Tech. Rep.] FWS/OBS* 84-09.

Gottfried, P.K., and Osborne, J.A. (1982). Distribution, abundance and size of *Corbicula manilensis* (Phillippi) in a spring-fed central Florida stream. *Fla. Sci.* 45, 178–188.

Gotto, J.W., and Taylor, B.F. (1976). N_2 fixation associated with decaying leaves of the red mangrove, *Rhizophora mangle*. *Appl. Environ. Microbiol.* 31, 781–783.

Gotto, J.W., Tabita, F.R., and Baalen, C.V. (1981). Nitrogen fixation in intertidal environments of the Texas gulf coast. *Estuarine Coastal Shelf Sci.* 12, 231–235.

Graham, A. (1964). Origin and evolution of the biota of southeastern North America: evidence from the fossil plant record. *Evolution* 18, 571–585.

Graham, S.A. (1941). Climax forests of the upper peninsula of Michigan. *Ecology* 22, 355–362.

Gram, R. (1968). A Florida Sabellarid reef and its effect on sedimentary distribution. *J. Sediment. Petrol.* 38, 863–886.

Grassle, J. (1973). Variety in coral reef communities. *In* "Biology and Geology of Coral Reefs" (O. Jones and R. Endean, eds.), Vol. 2, pp. 247–270. Academic Press, New York.

Greenberg, I. (1977). "Guide to the Corals and Fishes of Florida, the Bahamas and the Caribbean." Seahawk Press, Miami, Florida.

Greene, E.R. (1942). Golden warbler nesting in Lower Florida Keys. *Auk* 59, 114.

Greene, E.R. (1943). Cuban nighthawk nesting in Lower Florida Keys. *Auk* 60, 105.

Greene, S.W. (1931). The forest that fire made. *Am. For.* 37, 583–584.

Greenway, M. (1976). The grazing of *Thalassia testudinum* in Kingston Harbor, Jamaica. *Aquat. Bot.* 2, 117–126.

Grelen, H.E. (1962). Plant succession on cleared sandhills in northwest Florida. *Am. Midl. Nat.* 67, 36–44.

Grelen, H.E. (1983). May burning favors survival and early height growth of longleaf pine seedlings. *South. J. Appl. For.* 7, 16–20.

Greller, A.M. (1980). Correlation of some climate statistics with distribution of broadleaved forest zones in Florida, USA. *Bull. Torrey Bot. Club* 107, 189–219.

Greller, A.M., and Rachele, L.D. (1983). Climatic limits of exotic genera in the Legler palyroflora, Miocene, New Jersey, USA. *Rev. Paleobot. Palynol.* 40, 149–163.

Gresham, C.A., and Lipscomb, D.J. (1985). Selected ecological characteristics of *Gordonia lasianthus* in coastal South Carolina. *Bull. Torrey Bot. Club* 112, 53–58.

Griffin, G.M., Wieland, C.C., Hood, L.Q., Good, R.W., III, Sawyer, R.K., and McNeill, D.F. (1982). "Assessment of the Peat Resources of Florida, with a Detailed Survey of the Northern Everglades." Dep. Geol., Univ. of Florida for U.S.

Dep. Energy under Grant DE-FG18-81FCO5114. State of Florida, Governor's Energy Off., Tallahassee.

Grimm, D., and Hopkins, T. (1977). Preliminary characterization of the octocorallian and scleractinian diversity at the Florida middle ground. *Proc. Int. Coral Reef Symp., 3rd, Miami, Fla.* 1, 135–141.

Grimm, E.C. (1983). Chronology and dynamics of vegetation change in the prairie-woodland region of southern Minnesota, USA. *New Phytol.* 93, 311–350.

Grubb, P.J. (1977). The maintenance of species-richness in plant communities: the importance of the regeneration niche. *Biol. Rev.* 52, 107–145.

Guerin, D.N. (1988). Oak dome establishment and maintenance in a longleaf pine community in Ocala National Forest, Florida. M.S. Thesis, Univ. of Florida, Gainesville.

Gunderson, L.H. (1977). Regeneration of cypress, *Taxodium distichum* and *Taxodium ascendens,* within logged and burned cypress strands at Corkscrew Swamp Sanctuary, Florida. M.S. Thesis, Univ. of Florida, Gainesville.

Gunderson, L.H. (1984). Regeneration of cypress in logged and burned strands at Corkscrew Swamp Sanctuary, Florida. *In* "Cypress Swamps" (K.C. Ewel and H.T. Odum, eds.), pp. 349–357. Univ. Presses of Florida, Gainesville.

Gunderson, L.H., and Loope, L.L. (1982a). An inventory of the plant communities of the Levee 28 Tieback area, Big Cypress National Preserve. *Everglades Natl. Park South Fla. Res. Cent. Rep.* No. T-664.

Gunderson, L.H., and Loope, L.L. (1982b). A survey and inventory of the plant communities in the Pinecrest area, Big Cypress National Preserve. *Everglades Natl. Park South Fla. Res. Cent. Rep.* No. T-655.

Gunderson, L.H., and Loope, L.L. (1982c). A survey and inventory of the plant communities in the Raccoon Point area, Big Cypress National Preserve. *Everglades Natl. Park South Fla. Res. Cent. Rep.* No. T-665.

Gunderson, L.H., and Loope, L.L. (1982d). A survey of the plant communities within the Deep Lake Strand area, Big Cypress National Preserve. *Everglades Natl. Park South Fla. Res. Cent. Rep.* No. T-666.

Gunderson, L.H., Loope, L.L., and Maynard, W.R. (1982). An inventory of the plant communities of the Turner River area, Big Cypress National Preserve, Florida. *Everglades Natl. Park South Fla. Res. Cent. Rep.* No. T-648.

Gunderson, L.H., Taylor, D., and Craig, J. (1983). Fire effects on flowering and fruiting patterns of understory plants in pinelands of Everglades National Park. *Everglades Natl. Park South Fla. Res. Cent. Rep.* No. SFRC-83/04.

Gunderson, L.H., Loope, L.L., and Irish, G. (1986). Vegetation cover types of Shark River Slough, Everglades National Park, derived from Landsat Thematic Mapper data. *Everglades Natl. Park South Fla. Res. Cent. Rep.* No. SRFC-86/03.

Gunter, G. (1967). Some relationships of estuaries to the fisheries of the Gulf of Mexico. In "Estuaries" (G.H. Lauff, ed.). *Am. Assoc. Adv. Sci. Publ.* No. 83, pp. 621–638.

Gunter, H. (1921). *Fla. Geol. Surv. Rep.* 13, 207–209.

Haack, S.K. (1984). Aquatic macroinvertebrate community structure in a forested wetland: interrelationships with environmental parameters. M.S. Thesis, Univ. of Florida, Gainesville.

Hackney, C.T., and de la Cruz, A.A. (1979). Patterns of suspended particle transport in a Mississippi tidal marsh system. *Gulf Res. Rep.* 6, 217–224.

Haines, L.W., and Gooding, J. (1983). Slash pine versus other species. *In* "The Managed Slash Pine Ecosystem" (E.L. Stone, ed.), Proc. Symp., pp. 112–130. Sch. For. Resour. Conserv., Univ. of Florida, Gainesville.

Halas, J. (1985). A unique mooring system for reef management in the Key Largo National Marine Sanctuary. *Proc. Int. Coral Reef Congr., 5th, Tahiti* 4, 237–242.

Halas, J., Halas, J., and Kincaid, D. (1984). "Diving and Snorkeling Guide to the Florida Keys." Pisces Books, New York.

Hall, B. (1829). "Travels in North America, in the Years 1827 and 1828." Cadell & Co., Edinburgh.

Hall, E.R. (1981). "The Mammals of North America," Vol. II. Wiley, New York.

Haller, W.T., and Sutton, D.L. (1975). Community structure and competition between *Hydrilla* and *Vallisneria. Hyacinth Control J.* 13, 48–50.

Hallock, P. (1981). Algal symbiosis: a mathematical analysis. *Mar. Biol. (Berlin)* 62, 249–255.

Hallock, P., and Schlager, W. (1986). Nutrient excess and the demise of coral reefs and carbonate platforms. *Palaios* 1, 389–398.

Hallock, P., Cottey, T.L., Forward, L.B., and Halas, J. (1986). Population biology and sediment production of *Archaias angulatus* (Foraminiferida) in Largo Sound, Florida. *J. Foraminiferal Res.* 16, 1–8.

Hamilton, D.B. (1984). Plant succession and the influence of disturbance in Okefenokee Swamp. In "The Okefenokee Swamp" (A.D. Cohen, D.J. Casagrande, M.J. Andrejko, and G.R. Best, eds.), pp. 86–106. Wetland Surv., Los Alamos, New Mexico.

Haq, B.U., Hardenbol, J., and Vail, P.R. (1987). Chronology of fluctuating sea levels since the Triassic. *Science* 238, 1156–1167.

Harcombe, P.A., and Marks, P.L. (1977). Understory structure of a mesic forest in southeast Texas. *Ecology* 58, 1144–1151.

Harcombe, P.A., and Marks, P.L. (1978). Tree diameter distributions and replacement processes in southeast Texas forests. *For. Sci.* 24, 153–166.

Hardin, J.W., Klimstra, W.D., and Silvy, N.J. (1984). Florida Keys. *In* "White-tailed Deer: Ecology and Management" (L.K. Halls, ed.), pp. 381–390. Stackpole Books, Harrisburg, Pennsylvania.

Hardisky, M. (1979). Marsh habitat development: a feasible alternative to dredged material disposal. *Ga. Coastline* 1, 5–6.

Hare, R.C. (1965). Contribution of bark to fire resistance of southern trees. *J. For.* 63, 248–251.

Harkness, W.J.K., and Pierce, E.L. (1940). The limnology of Lake Mize, Florida. *Q. J. Fla. Acad. Sci.* 5, 96–116.

Harmon, M.E. (1984). Survival of trees after low-intensity surface fires in Great Smoky Mountains National Park. *Ecology* 65, 796–802.

Harms, W.R., Schreuder, H.T., Hook, D.D., Brown, C.L., and Shropshire, F.W. (1980). The effects of flooding on the swamp forest in Lake Ocklawaha, Florida. *Ecology* 61, 1412–1421.

Harper, R.M. (1905). "Hammock," "Hommock," or "Hummock?" *Science* 22, 400–402.

Harper, R.M. (1911a). The relation of climax vegetation to islands and peninsulas. *Bull. Torrey Bot. Club* 38, 515–525.

Harper, R.M. (1911b). The river-bank vegetation of the lower Apalachicola, and a new principle illustrated thereby. *Torreya* 11, 225–234.

Harper, R.M. (1914a). Geography and vegetation of northern Florida. *Fla. Geol. Surv., 6th Annu. Rep.* pp. 163–451.

Harper, R.M. (1914b). A superficial study of the pine-barren vegetation of Mississippi. *Bull. Torrey Bot. Club* 41, 551–567.

Harper, R.M. (1915). Vegetation types. *In* "Natural Resources of an Area in Central Florida" (E.H. Sellards, R.M. Harper, E.N. Mooney, W.J. Latimer, H. Gunter, and E. Gunter, eds.), pp. 135–188. *Fla. Geol. Surv.,* 7th Annu. Rep.

Harper, R.M. (1916). Fern grottoes of Citrus County, Florida. *Am. Fern J.* 6, 68–81.

Harper, R.M. (1921). Geography of central Florida. *Fla. Geol. Surv., 13th Annu. Rep.* pp. 71–307.

Harper, R.M. (1927). Natural resources of southern Florida. *Fla. Geol. Surv., 18th Annu. Rep.* pp. 27–206.

Harper, R.M. (1943). Forests of Alabama. *Ala. Geol. Surv. Monogr.* 10, 1–230.

Harper, R.M. (1948a). A preliminary list of the endemic flowering plants of Florida. Part I. Introduction and history of exploration. *Q. J. Fla. Acad. Sci.* 11, 25–35.

Harper, R.M. (1948b). A preliminary list of the endemic flowering plants of Florida. Part II. List of species. *Q. J. Fla. Acad. Sci.* 11, 39–57.

Harper, R.M. (1949). A preliminary list of the endemic flowering plants of Florida. Part III. Notes and summary. *Q. J. Fla. Acad. Sci.* 12, 1–19.

Harper, R.M. (1962). Historical notes on the relation of fires to forests. *Proc. Tall Timbers Fire Ecol. Conf.* 1, 11–29.

Harrington, R.W., and Harrington, E.S. (1961). Food selection among fishes invading a high subtropical salt marsh: from onset of flooding through the progress of a mosquito brood. *Ecology* 42, 646–666.

Harrington, R.W., and Harrington, E.S. (1982). Effects on fishes and their forage organisms of impounding a Florida salt marsh to prevent breeding by salt marsh mosquitoes. *Bull. Mar. Sci.* 32, 523–531.

Harrington, T.A., and Stephenson, G.K. (1955). Repeat burns reduce small stems in Texas Big Thicket. *J. For.* 53, 847.

Harris, D.L. (1982). "The Prediction of Hurricane Storm Surges." SGR-4, Florida Sea Grant Coll., Gainesville.

Harris, L.D. (1984). "The Fragmented Forest: Island Biogeography Theory and the Preservation of Biotic Diversity." Univ. of Chicago Press, Chicago, Illinois.

Harris, L.D., and Mulholland, R. (1983). Southeastern bottomland ecosystems as wildlife habitat. *In* "Appraisal of Florida's Wetland Hardwood Resource" (D.M. Flinchum, G.B. Doolittle, and K.R. Munson, eds.), pp. 63–73. Sch. For. Resour. Conserv., Univ. of Florida, Gainesville.

Harris, L.D., and Vickers, C.R. (1984). Some faunal community characteristics of cypress ponds and the changes induced by perturbations. *In* "Cypress Swamps" (K.C. Ewel and H.T. Odum, eds.), pp. 171–185. Univ. Presses of Florida, Gainesville.

Harriss, R.C., Ribelin, B.W., and Dreyer, C. (1980). Sources and variability of suspended particulates and organic carbon in a salt marsh estuary. *In* "Estuarine and Wetland Processes" (P. Hamilton and K.B. MacDonald, eds.), pp. 371–384. Plenum, New York.

Harshberger, J.W. (1914). The vegetation of south Florida. *Trans Wagner Free Inst. Sci. Philos.* 3, 51–189.

Hartnett, D.C. (1987). Effect of fire on clonal growth and dynamics of *Pityopsis graminifolia* (Asteraceae). *Am. J. Bot.* 74, 1737–1745.

Hartnett, D.C., and Richardson, D. (1989). Reproduction, population dynamics and responses to fire in the perennial herb *Bonamia grandiflora* (Convolvulaceae). *Am. J. Bot.* 76, 361–369.

Harvey, J.W., Benedict, M.A., Gore, R.A., and Curran, M.E. (1984). Natural resources of Collier County, Florida. Part II. Coastal barrier resources. *Collier Cty. Nat. Resour. Manage. Dep. Tech. Rep.* No. 84-2. Naples, Florida.

Hayes, M.O. (1979). Barrier island morphology as a function of tidal and wave regime. *In* "Barrier Islands from the Gulf of St. Lawrence to the Gulf of Mexico" (S.P. Leatherman, ed.). Academic Press, New York.

Heald, E.J. (1969). The production of organic detritus in a south Florida estuary. Ph.D. Thesis, Univ. of Miami, Coral Gables, Florida.

Heald, E.J. (1970). The Everglades estuary: an example of seriously reduced inflow of freshwater. *Trans. Am. Fish. Soc.* 99, 847–848.

Heald, E.J., and Odum, W.E. (1970). The contribution of mangrove swamps to Florida fisheries. *Proc. Gulf Caribb. Fish. Inst.* 22, 130–135.

Heald, E.J., Roessler, M.A., and Beardsley, G.L. (1979). Litter production in a southwest Florida black mangrove community. *Proc. Fla. Anti-Mosq. Assoc. Meet., 50th* pp. 24–33.

Healey, H.G. (1975). Terraces and shorelines of Florida. *Bur. of Geol. Map Ser.* No. 71. U.S. Geol. Serv. in coop. with Fla. Dep. Environ. Regul., Bur. Water Resour. Manage., Tallahassee. Tallahassee, Florida.

Heaney, J.P., and Huber, W.C. (1975). "Environmental Resources Management Studies in the Kissimmee River Basin." Rep. ENV-05-75-1. Univ. of Florida, Gainesville.

Heard, R.W. (1982a). "Guide to Common Tidal Marsh Invertebrates of the Northeastern Gulf of Mexico." Mississippi-Alabama Sea Grant Consortium, MASGP-79-004, Univ. of South Alabama, Mobile.

Heard, R.W. (1982b). Observations on the food and food habits of clapper rails (*Rallus longirostris* Boddaert) from tidal marshes along the east and gulf coasts of the United States. *Gulf Res. Rep.* 7, 125–135.

Heard, W.H. (1977). Freshwater mollusca of the Apalachicola drainage. *Proc. Conf. Apalachicola Drain. Syst., Gainesville, Fla. 1976* (R.J. Livingston and E.A. Joyce, Jr., eds.). *Fla. Mar. Res. Publ.* No. 26., pp. 20–21. Florida Dep. Nat. Resour., Tallahassee.

Heard, W.H. (1979). "Identification Manual of the Freshwater Clams of Florida." Tech. Ser., Vol. 4, No. 2, Florida Dep. Environ. Regul., Tallahassee.

Heath, R.C., and Conover, C.S. (1981). Hydrologic almanac of Florida. *U.S. Geol. Surv. Open-File Rep.* No. 81-1107. Tallahassee, Florida.

Hebb, E.A. (1957). Regeneration in the sandhills. *J. For.* 55, 210–212.

Hebb, E.A. (1971). Site preparation decreases game food plants in Florida sandhills. *J. Wildl. Manage.* 35, 155–162.

Hebb, E.A., and Burns, R.M. (1973). Methods and goals in preparing sand pine sites. *Proc. Sand Pine Symp., U.S. For. Serv. Gen. Tech. Rep.* No. SE-2, pp. 82–92.

Hebb, E.A., and Clewell, A.F. (1976). A remnant stand of old-growth slash pine in the Florida panhandle. *Bull. Torrey Bot. Club* 103, 1–9.

Hebrard, J.J., and Lee, R.C. (1981). A large collection of brackish water snakes from the central Atlantic coast of Florida. *Copeia,* pp. 886–889.

Heck, K.L., Jr. (1976). Community structure and the effects of pollution in seagrass meadows and adjacent habitats. *Mar. Biol.* (*Berlin*) 35, 345–357.

Hefner, J.M. (1986). Wetlands of Florida, 1950s to 1970s. *In* "Managing Cumulative Impacts in Florida Wetlands" (E.D. Estevez, J. Miller, J. Morris, and R. Hamman, eds.), pp. 23–31. Omnipress, Madison, Wisconsin.

Hein, F.J., and Risk, M.J. (1975). Bioerosion of coral heads: inner patch reefs, Florida reef tract. *Bull. Mar. Sci.* 25, 133–138.

Heinselman, M.L. (1973). Fire in the virgin forests of the Boundary Waters Canoe Area, Minnesota. *Quat. Res.* 3, 329–382.

Heinselman, M.L. (1981). Fire intensity and frequency as factors in the distribution and structure of northern ecosystems. *In* "Fire Regimes and Ecosystem Properties" (H.A. Mooney, T.M. Bonnickson, N.L. Christensen, J.E. Lotan, and W.A. Reiners, eds.). *U.S. For. Serv. Gen. Tech. Rep.* No. WO-26, pp. 7–57.

Hellier, T.R., Jr. (1967). The fishes of the Santa Fe River system. *Bull. Fla. State Mus. Biol. Sci.* 2, 1–44.

Hendry, C.D., and Brezonik, P.L. (1980). Chemistry of precipitation at Gainesville, Florida. *Environ. Sci. Technol.* 14, 843–849

Hendry, C.W., and Yon, J.W. (1958). Geology in and around Jim Woodruff Reservoir. *Fla. Geol. Surv. Rep.* 16, 1–52.

Henry, J.D., and Swan, J.M.A. (1974). Reconstructing forest history from live and dead plant material—an approach to the study of forest succession in southwest New Hampshire. *Ecology* 55, 772–783.

Herald, E.S., and Strickland, R.R. (1949). An annotated list of the fishes of Homosassa Springs, FL. *Q. J. Fla. Acad. Sci.* 11, 99–109.

Herndon, A. (1987a). Ecology and systematics of *Hypoxis wrightii* and *H. sessilis* in southern Florida. M.S. Thesis, Florida Int. Univ., Miami.

Herndon, A. (1987b). Variation in resource allocation and reproductive effort within a single population of *Liatris laevigata* Nuttall (Asteraceae). *Am. Midl. Nat.* 118, 406–413.

Herndon, A., and Taylor, D. (1985). Litterfall in pinelands of Everglades National Park. *Everglades Natl. Park South Fla. Res. Cent. Rep.* No. SFRC-85/01.

Herring, J.L. (1951). The aquatic and semi-aquatic Hemiptera of northern Florida. Part 4: Classification of habitat and keys to the species. *Fla. Entomol.* 34, 146–161.

Herwitz, S. (1977). "The Natural History of Cayo-Costa Island." Environ. Stud. Program Publ. No. 14., New Coll., Sarasota, Florida.

Heyward, F. (1937). The effects of frequent fires on profile development on longleaf pine forest soils. *J. For.* 35, 23–27.

Heyward, F. (1939a). The relation of fire to stand composition of longleaf pine forests. *Ecology* 20, 287–304.

Heyward, F. (1939b). Some moisture relationships of soils from burned and unburned longleaf-pine forests. *Soil Sci.* 47, 313–325.

Hicks, D.B., and Burns, L.A. (1975). Mangrove metabolic response to alterations of natural freshwater drainage to southwestern Florida estuaries. *Proc. Int. Symp. Biol. Manage. Mangroves* (G. Walsh, S. Snedaker, and H. Teas, eds.), pp. 238–255. Univ. of Florida, Gainesville.

Hillestad, H.O., Bozeman, J.R., Johnson, A.S., Berisford, C.W., and Richardson, J.I. (1975). "The Ecology of Cumberland Island National Seashore, Camden County, Ga." *Tech. Rep. Ser.* No. 75-5, Georgia Mar. Sci. Cent., Skidaway Island.

Hilmon, J.B., and Lewis, C.E. (1962). Effect of burning on south Florida range. *U.S. For. Serv. Southeast. For. Exp. Stn. Res. Pap.* No. 146.

Hilsenbeck, C.E. (1976). A comparison of forest sampling methods in hammock vegetation. M.S. Thesis, Univ. of Miami, Coral Gables, Florida.

Hine, A.C., and Belknap, D.F. (1986). Recent geological history and modern sedimentary processes of the Pasco, Hernando, and Citrus County coastline: west-central Florida. *Florida Sea Grant Rep.* No. 79. Florida Sea Grant Coll., Gainesville.

Hines, T.C., and Woodward, A.R. (1980). Nuisance alligator control in Florida. *Wildl. Soc. Bull.* 8, 234–241.

Hirsh, D.W. (1981). Physiognomy and spatial patterns of a beech-magnolia hammock in north-central Florida. M.S. Thesis, Florida State Univ., Tallahassee.

Hirsh, D.W., and Platt, W.J. (1981). Dynamics of regeneration within a spruce pine (*Pinus glabra*) population in a beech-magnolia forest in north-central Florida. *Bull. Ecol. Soc. Am.* 62, 71–72.

Hobbs, H.H., Jr. (1942). The crayfishes of Florida. *Univ. Fla. Publ. Biol. Sci. Ser.* 11, 1–179.

Hobbs, H.H., Jr., and Franz, R. (1986). New troglobitic crayfish with comments on its relationship to epigean and other hypogean crayfishes of Florida. *J. Crustacean. Biol.* 6(3), 509–519.

Hodgkins, E.J. (1958). Effects of fire on undergrowth vegetation in upland southern pine forests. *Ecology* 39, 36–46.

Hoffman, J.A., Katz, J., and Bertness, M.D. (1984). Fiddler crab deposit feeding and meiofaunal abundance in salt marsh habitats. *J. Exp. Mar. Biol. Ecol.* 82, 161–174.

Hoffman, J.S. (1984). Estimates of future sea level rise. *In* "Greenhouse Effect and Sea Level Rise" (M.C. Barth and J.G. Titus, eds.). Van Nostrand-Reinhold, New York.

Hoffmeister, J.E. (1974). "Land from the Sea, The Geologic Story of South Florida." Univ. of Miami Press, Coral Gables, Florida.

Hoffmeister, J.E., and Multer, H.G. (1964). Growth rate estimates of a Pleistocene coral reef of Florida. *Geol. Soc. Am. Bull.* 75, 353–358.

Hoffmeister, J.E., and Multer, H.G. (1968). Geology and origin of the Florida Keys. *Geol. Soc. Am. Bull.* 79, 1487–1502.

Hoffmeister, J.E., Stockman, K.W., and Multer, H.G. (1967). Miami limestone and its recent Bahamian counterpart. *Geol. Soc. Am. Bull.* 78, 175–190.

Hofstetter, R.H. (1974). The effect of fire on the pineland and sawgrass communities of southern Florida. *In* "Environments of South Florida: Present and Past" (P.J. Gleason, ed.), Mem. No. 2, pp. 201–212. Miami Geol. Soc., Miami, Florida.

Hofstetter, R.H. (1975). Effects of fire in the ecosystem. Part II, Appendix K. *In* "South Florida Environmental Project." Univ. of Miami, Coral Gables, Florida.

Hofstetter, R.H. (1976). Current status of vegetation and possible indications of vegetational trends in the Everglades. *Everglades Natl. Park Rep.* No. 18-492.

Hollander, M., and Wolfe, D.A. (1973). "Nonparametric Statistical Methods." Wiley, New York.

Holliman, D.C. (1983). Status and habitat of Alabama Gulf coast beach mice, *Peromyscus polionotus ammobates* and *P. p. trisyllepsis*. *Northeast Gulf Sci.* 6, 121–129.

Holling, C.S. (1973). Resilience and stability of ecological systems. *Annu. Rev. Ecol. Syst.* 4, 1–23.

Holling, C.S. (1981). Forest insects, forest fires, and resilience. *In* "Fire Regimes and Ecosystem Properties" (H.A. Mooney, T.M. Bonnickson, N.L. Christensen, J.E. Lotan, and W.A. Reiners, eds.), *U.S. For. Ser. Gen. Tech. Rep.* WO-26, pp. 445–464.

Hollis, C.A., Fisher, R.F., and Pritchett, W.L. (1978). Effects of some silvicultural practices on soil-site properties in the lower coastal plains. *In* "Forest Soils and Land Use" (C.T. Youngberg, ed.), Proc. 5th North Am. For. Soil Conf., pp. 585–606. Colorado State Univ., Fort Collins.

Hook, D.D. (1984). Adaptations to flooding with fresh water. *In* "Flooding and Plant Growth" (T.T. Kozlowski, ed.), pp. 265–294. Academic Press, New York.

Hook, D.D., Brown, C.L., and Kormanik, P.P. (1970). Lenticel and water root development of swamp tupelo under various flooding conditions. *Bot. Gaz.* 131, 217–224.

Hook, D.D., Brown, C.L., and Wetmore, R.H. (1972). Aeration in trees. *Bot. Gaz.* 133, 443–454.

Hooks, T.A., Heck, K.L., Jr., and Livingston, R.J. (1976). An inshore marine invertebrate community: structure and habitat associations in the northeastern Gulf of Mexico. *Bull. Mar. Sci.* 26, 99–109.

Hopkins, S.R., and Richardson, J.J., eds. (1984). "Recovery Plan for Marine Turtles." Mar. Turtle Recovery Team, Natl. Mar. Fish. Serv., U.S. Dep. Agric., Washington, D.C.

Hopkins, T., Blizzard, D., Brawley, S., Earle, S., Grimm, D., Gilbert, D., Johnson, P., Livingston, E., Lutz, C., Shaw, J., and Shaw, B. (1977). Preliminary characterization of the biotic components of composite strip transects on the Florida Middle Ground, northeastern Gulf of Mexico. *Proc. Int. Coral Reef Symp., 3rd, Miami, Fla.* 1, 31–37.

Horn, H.S. (1971). "The Adaptive Geometry of Trees." Princeton Univ. Press, Princeton, New Jersey.

Hosner, J.F. (1957). Effects of water upon the seed germination of bottomland trees. *For. Sci.* 3, 67–70.

Hosner, J.F. (1958). The effects of complete inundation upon seedlings of six bottomland tree species. *Ecology* 39, 371–373.

Hosner, J.F. (1959). Survival, root, and shoot growth of six bottomland tree species following flooding. *J. For.* 57, 927–928.

Hosner, J.F. (1960). Relative tolerance to complete inundation of fourteen bottomland tree species. *For. Sci.* 6, 246–251.

Hosner, J.F., and Minkler, L.S. (1963). Bottomland hardwood forests of southern Illinois—regeneration and succession. *Ecology* 44, 29–41.

Hough, A.F., and Forbes, R.D. (1943). The ecology and silvics of forests in the high plateaus of Pennsylvania. *Ecol. Monogr.* 13, 299–320.

Hovis, J.A., and Labisky, R.F. (1985). Vegetative associations of red-cockaded woodpecker colonies in Florida. *Wildl. Soc. Bull.* 13, 307–314.

Howell, A.H. (1932). "Florida Bird Life." Florida Dep. Game Fresh Water Fish, Tallahassee.

Howell, A.H. (1939). Descriptions of five new mammals from Florida. *J. Mammol.* 20, 363–365.

Hoyt, J.H. (1969). Late Cenozoic structural movements, northern Florida. *Trans. Gulf Coast Assoc. Geol. Soc.* 19, 1–9.

Hoyt, J.H., and Hails, J.R. (1967). Pleistocene shoreline sediments in coastal Georgia: deposition and modification. *Science* 115, 1541–1543.

Hubbell, S.P., and Foster, R.B. (1983). Diversity of canopy trees in a neotropical forest and implications for conservation. *In* "Tropical Rain Forest: Ecology and Management" (S.L. Sutton, T.C. Whitmore, and A.C. Chadwick, eds.), Br. Ecol. Soc. Spec. Publ. No. 2, pp. 25–41. Blackwell, Oxford.

Hubbell, S.P., and Foster, R.B. (1986). Commonness and rarity in a neotropical forest: implications for tropical tree conservation. *In* "Conservation Biology" (M.E. Soule, ed.). Sinauer, Sunderland, Massachusetts.

Hubbell, T.H., Laessle, A.M., and Dickinson, J.C., Jr. (1956). The Flint–Chattahoochee–Apalachicola region and its environments. *Bull. Fla. State Mus. Biol. Sci.* 1, 1–63.

Hubbs, C.L. (1956). Preliminary analysis of the American cyprinid fishes, seven new, referred to the genus *Hybopsis,* subgenus *Erimystax. Univ. Mich. Mus. Zool. Occas. Pap.* 578, 1–8.

Hubbs, C.L., and Allen, E.R. (1943). Fishes of Silver Springs, Florida. *Proc. Fla. Acad. Sci.* 6, 110–130.

Huber, W.C., Brezonik, P.L., Heaney, J.P., Dickinson, R.E., Preston, S.D., Dwornik, D.S., and DeMaio, M.A. (1982). "A Classification of Florida Lakes." Final Rep. ENV-05-82-1 to Florida Dep. Environ. Regul., Tallahassee.

Huck, R.B. (1987). Plant communities along an edaphic continuum in a central Florida watershed. *Fla. Sci.* 50, 111–128.

Huck, R.B., Judd, W.S., Whitten, W.M., Skean, J.D., Wunderlin, R.P., and Delaney, C.R. (1989). A new *Dicerandra* (Labiatae) from the Lake Wales Ridge of Florida. *Syst. Bot.* (in press).

Hudson, J.H. (1977). Long-term bioerosion rates on a Florida reef: a new method. *Proc. Int. Coral Reef Symp., 3rd, Miami, Fla.* 2, 491–497.

Hudson, J.H. (1981). Response of *Montastraea annularis:* a record of environmental change in Key Largo Coral Reef Marine Sanctuary, Florida. *Bull. Mar. Sci.* 31, 444–459.

Hudson, J.H., Shinn, E., Halley, R., and Lidz, B. (1976). Sclerochronology: a tool for interpreting past environments. *Geology* 4, 361–364.

Huffman, R.T., and Forsythe, S.W. (1981). Bottomland hardwood forest communities and their relation to anaerobic soil conditions. *In* "Wetlands of Bottomland Hardwood Forests" (J.R. Clark and J. Benforado, eds.), pp. 187–196. Elsevier, New York.

Hughes, G.H. (1974). Water balance of Lake Kerr—a deductive study of a landlocked lake in north-central Florida. *U.S. Geol. Surv. & Fla. Dep. Nat. Resour. Rep. Invest.* 73, 1–49. Tallahassee, Florida.

Hughes, R.H. (1957). Response of cane to burning in the North Carolina coastal plain. *N.C. Agric. Exp. Stn. Bull.* 402, 3–24.

Hughes, R.H. (1966). Fire ecology of canebrakes. *Proc. Tall Timbers Fire Ecol. Conf.* 5, 149–158.

Hulbert, R.C., Jr. (1982). Population dynamics of the three-toed horse *Neohipparion* from the late Miocene of Florida. *Paleobiology* 8, 159–167.

Hulbert, R.C., Jr. (1987). A new *Cormohipparion* (Mammalia, Equidae) from the Pliocene (latest Hemphillian and Blancan) of Florida. *J. Vert. Paleont.* 7, 451–468.

Hulbricht, L. (1985). The distribution of the native land mollusks of the eastern United States. *Fieldiana: Zool., New Ser.* 24.

Hull, J.E., and Meyer, F.W. (1973). Salinity studies in East Glades agricultural area southeastern Dade County, Florida. *Fla. Bur. Geol. Rep. Invest.* No. 66.

Humm, H.J. (1964). Epiphytes of the seagrass, *Thalassia testudinum,* in Florida. *Bull. Mar. Sci. Gulf Caribb.* 14, 306–341.

Humphrey, S.R., Kern, W.H., Jr., and Ludlow, M.W. (1987). Status survey of seven Florida mammals. *Coop. Fish Wildl. Res. Unit Tech. Rep.* No. 25. Sch. For. Resour. Conserv., Inst. Food Agric. Sci., Univ. of Florida, Gainesville.

Huntley, J.C., and McGee, C.E. (1981). Timber and wildlife implications of fire in young upland hardwoods. *U.S. For. Serv. South. For. Exp. Stn. Gen. Tech. Rep.* SO-34, 56–66.

Husted, J.E. (1972). Shaler's line and the Suwannee Strait, Florida and Georgia. *Am. Assoc. Pet. Geol. Bull.* 56, 1557–60.

Huston, M. (1985). Patterns of species diversity on coral reefs. *Annu. Rev. Ecol. Syst.* 16, 149–177.

Hutchings, P.A. (1986). Biological destruction of coral reefs—a review. *Coral Reefs* 4, 239–252.

Hutchinson, G.E. (1957). "A Treatise on Limnology. Vol. 1: Geography, Physics, and Chemistry." Wiley, New York.

Iovino, A.J., and Bradley, W.H. (1969). The role of larval Chironomidae in the production of lacustrine copropel in Mud Lake, Marion County, Florida. *Limnol. Oceanogr.* 14, 898–905.

Irvine, A.B., and Scott, M.D. (1984). Development and use of marking techniques to study manatees in Florida. *Fla. Sci.* 47, 12–26.

Isa, Y., and Yamazato, K. (1984). The distribution of carbonic anhydrase in a staghorn coral, *Acropora hebes* (Dana). *Galaxea* 3, 25–36.

Iverson, G.B. (1984). Ecological adaptation of beach peanut (*Okenia hypogaea*) on Florida subtropical east coast beaches. *Fla. Sci.* 47, 45. (Abstr.)

Iverson, R.L., and Bittaker, H.F. (1986). Seagrass distribution and abundance in the eastern Gulf of Mexico coastal waters. *Estuarine Coastal Shelf Sci.* 22, 577–602.

Izlar, R.L. (1984). Some comments on fire and climate in the Okefenokee marsh-swamp complex. In "The Okefenokee Swamp" (A.D. Cohen, D.J. Casagrande, M.J. Andrejko, and G.R. Best, eds.), pp. 70–85. Wetland Surv., Los Alamos, New Mexico.

Jaap, W.C. (1974). Scleractinian growth rate studies. *Proc. Fla. Keys Coral Reef Workshop,* p. 17. Fla. Dep. Nat. Resour., Tallahassee. (Abstr.)

Jaap, W.C. (1979). Observations on zooxanthellae expulsion at Middle Sambo Reef, Florida Keys, USA. *Bull. Mar. Sci.* 29, 414–422.

Jaap, W.C. (1981). Stony corals (Milleporina and Scleractinia). *In* "Key Largo Coral Reef National Marine Sanctuary Deep Water Resource Survey" (S. Jameson, ed.), *Tech. Rep.* CZ/SP1, pp. 7–13. NOAA, Washington, D.C.

Jaap, W.C. (1983). Population dynamics of stony corals in Biscayne National Park patch reefs, Florida, USA. *Coll. Annu. Int. Soc. Reef Stud.* p. 19. (Abstr.)

Jaap, W.C. (1984). "The Ecology of the South Florida Coral Reefs: a Community Profile." *U.S. Fish Wildl. Serv. Off. Biol. Serv. [Tech. Rep.]* FWS/OBS 82–108.

Jaap, W.C. (1985). An epidemic zooxanthellae expulsion during 1983 in the lower Florida Keys coral reefs: hyperthermic etiology. *Proc. Int. Coral Reef Cong., 5th, Tahiti* 6, 143–148.

Jackewicz, J.R. (1973). Energy utilization in the marsh crab, *Sesarma reticulatum* (Say). M.S. Thesis, Univ. of Delaware, Newark.

Jackson, C.R. (1952). Some topographic and edaphic factors affecting plant distribution in a tidal marsh. *Q. J. Fla. Acad. Sci.* 15, 137–146.

Jackson, D.A. (n.d.). Late Oligocene vertebrate fauna from Hillsborough County, Florida. Unpubl. ms.

Jackson, D.R., and Milstrey, E.R. (1988). The fauna of gopher tortoise burrows. *Proc. Gopher Tortoise Relocation Symp.* (J.E. Diemer, D.R. Jackson, J.L. Landers, J.N. Layne, and D.A. Wood, eds.). Nongame Wildl. Program Tech. Rep., Florida Game Fresh Water Fish Comm., Tallahassee.

Jackson, J. (1854–1855). "The United States Survey of Florida Township 31 South, Range 28–29 East." Florida Dep. Nat. Resour., Tallahassee.

Jackson, J.A., Lennartz, M.R., and Hooper, R.G. (1979). Tree age and cavity initiation by red-cockaded woodpeckers. *J. For.* 77, 102–103.

Jackson, J.B.C., and Winston, J.E. (1982). Ecology of cryptic coral reef communities. I. Distribution and abundance of major groups of encrusting organisms. *J. Exp. Mar. Biol.* 57, 135–147.

Jacobs, J. (1968). Animal behavior and water movement as co-determinants of plankton distribution in a tidal system. *Sarsia* 34, 355–370.

Jacobsen, T., and Kushlan, J.A. (1986). Alligators in natural areas: choosing conservation policies consistent with local objectives. *Biol. Conserv.* 36, 181–196.

James, C.W. (1961). Endemism in Florida. *Brittonia* 13, 225–244.

Janzen, D.H. (1985). Mangroves: where's the understory? *J. Trop. Ecol.* 1, 89–92.

Jarvis, W.T., and Beers, W.L. (1965). Reclamation of a wasteland in central Gulf coastal Florida. *J. For.* 63, 3–7.

Jenik, J. (1967). Root adaptations in west African trees. *J. Linn. Soc. London Bot.* 60, 126–140.

Jennings, J.N. (1985). "Karst Geomorphology." Blackwell, Oxford.

Johannes, R.E., and the Project Symbios Team (1972). The metabolism of some coral reef communities. *BioScience* 22, 541–543.

Johannes, R.E., Wiebe, W.J., and Crossland, C.J. (1983). Three patterns of nutrient flux in a coral reef community. *Mar. Ecol. Prog. Ser.* 12, 105–111.

Johnson, A.F. (1982). Some demographic characteristics of the Florida rosemary *Ceratiola ericoides* Michx. *Am. Midl. Nat.* 108, 170–174.

Johnson, A.F. (1985). Ecologia de *Abronia maritima,* especie pionera de las dunas del oeste de México. *Biotica* 10, 19–34.

Johnson, A.F., and Abrahamson, W.G. (1982). *Quercus inopina:* a species to be recognized from south-central Florida. *Bull. Torrey Bot. Club* 109, 392–395.

Johnson, A.S., Hillestad, H.O., Shanholzer, S.F., and Shanholzer, G.F. (1974). "An Ecological Survey of the Coastal Region of Georgia." Natl. Park Serv. Sci. Monogr. Ser. No. 3. U.S. Gov. Print. Off., Washington, D.C.

Johnson, C., and Westfall, M.J., Jr. (1970). Diagnostic keys and notes on the damselflies (Zygoptera) of Florida. *Bull. Fla. State Mus. Biol. Sci.* 15, 45–89.

Johnson, D.S. (1900). Notes on the flora of the banks and sounds at Beaufort, N.C. *Bot. Gaz.* 30, 405–410.

Johnson, F.A., and Montalbano, F., III (1984). Selection of plant communities by wintering waterfowl on Lake Okeechobee, Florida. *J. Wildl. Manage.* 48, 174–178.

Johnson, W.O. (1963). The big freeze of December 1962. *Weather Forecasting Mimeo* No. 63-1. Fed.-State Frost Warning Serv., Natl. Weather Serv., Lakeland, Florida.

Johnson, W.O. (1970). Minimum temperatures in the agricultural areas of peninsular Florida, summary of seasons 1937–1967. *Univ. Fla. Inst. Food Agric. Sci. Publ.* No. 9.

Johnston, I.S. (1980). The ultrastructure of skeletogenesis in hermatypic corals. *Int. Rev. Cytol.* 67, 171–214.

Jones, A.C., Berkeley, S.A., Bohnsack, J.A., Bortone, S.A., Camp, D.K., Darcy, G.H., Davis, J.C., Haddad, K.D., Hedgepeth, M.Y., Irby, E.W., Jr., Jaap, W.C., Kennedy, F.S., Jr., Lyons, W.G., Nakamura, E.L., Perkins, T.H., Reed, J.K., Steidinger, K.A., Tilmant, J.T., and Williams, R.O. (1986). Oceanic habitat and fishery resources of Florida. *In* "Florida Aquatic Habitat and Fishery Resources" (W. Seaman, Jr., ed.), pp. 437–542. Florida Chap. Am. Fish. Soc., Kissimmee.

Jones, J.A. (1963). Ecological studies of the southeastern Florida patch reefs. I: Diurnal and seasonal changes in the environment. *Bull. Mar. Sci. Gulf Caribb.* 13, 282–307.

Jones, J.A. (1977). Morphology and development of southeast Florida patch reefs. *Proc. Int. Coral Reef Symp., 3rd, Miami, Fla.* 2, 231–235.

Jones, J.I., Ring, R.E., Rinkel, M.O., and Smith, R.E. (eds.) (1973). A summary of knowledge of the Eastern Gulf of Mexico. State Univ. Syst. Fla. Inst. Oceanog. pp. I-1–Vii-74.

Jones, J.W., Allen, L.H., Shih, S.F., Rogers, J.S., Hammond, L.C., Smajstrala, A.G., and Martsolf, J.D. (1984). Estimated and measured evapotranspiration for Florida climate, crops, and soils. *Univ. Fla. Inst. Food Agric. Sci. Agric. Exp. Stn. Tech. Bull.* No. 840.

Jones, L.A. (1948). Soils, geology, and water control in the Everglades region. *Univ. Fla. Agric. Exp. Stn. Bull.* No. 442.

Jones, O., and Endean, R., eds. (1973–1977). "Biology and Geology of Coral Reefs," 4 vols. Academic Press, New York.

Jones, S.M., Van Lear, D.H., and Cox, S.K. (1981). Composition and density-diameter pattern of an old-growth forest stand of the Boiling Springs Natural Area, South Carolina. *Bull. Torrey Bot. Club* 108, 347–353.

Jordan, C.L. (1984). Florida's weather and climate: implications for water. *In* "Water Resources Atlas of Florida" (E.A. Fernald and D.J. Patton, eds.), pp. 18–35. Inst. of Sci. Pub. Aff., Florida State Univ., Tallahassee.

Judd, W.S. (1981). A monograph of *Lyonia* (Ericaceae). *J. Arnold Arbor.* 62, 63–128.

Judd, W.S., and Hall, D.W. (1984). A new species of *Ziziphus* (Rhamnaceae) from Florida. *Rhodora* 86, 381–387.

Kahl, M.P., Jr. (1964). Food ecology of the work stork (*Mycteria americana*) in Florida. *Ecol. Monogr.* 34, 97–117.

Kale, H.W., II (1964). Food of the long-billed marsh wren, *Telmotodytes palustris griseus,* in the salt marshes of Sapelo Island, Georgia. *Oriole* 29, 47–61.

Kale, H.W., II (1965). Ecology and bioenergetics of the long-billed marsh wren *Telmotodytes palustris griseus* (Brewster), in Georgia salt marshes. *Nuttall Ornithol. Club Publ.* No. 5.

Kale, H.W., II, ed. (1978). "Rare and Endangered Biota of Florida. Vol. 2: Birds." Univ. Presses of Florida, Gainesville.

Kale, H.W., II (1983). Distribution, habitat, and status of breeding seaside sparrows in Florida. In "The Seaside Sparrow, Its Biology and Management, Proc. Symp. Raleigh, N.C., 1981" (T.L. Quay, J.B. Funderburg, Jr., D.S. Lee, E.F. Potter, and C.S. Robbins, eds.), Occas. Pap. N.C. Biol. Surv. 1983–1985, pp. 41–48. North Carolina State Mus. Nat. Hist., Raleigh.

Kale, H.W., II (1987). Who is your neighbor? *Fla. Nat.* 60, 14.

Kalisz, P.J. (1982). The longleaf pine islands of the Ocala National Forest: a soil study. Ph.D. Thesis, Univ. of Florida, Gainesville.

Kalisz, P.J., and Stone, E.L. (1984a). The longleaf pine islands of the Ocala National Forest, Florida: a soil study. *Ecology* 65, 1743–1754.

Kalisz, P.J., and Stone, E.L. (1984b). Soil mixing by scarab beetles and pocket gophers in north-central Florida. *Soil Sci.* 48, 169–172.

Kalisz, P.J., Dorian A.W., and Stone, E.L. (1986). Prehistoric land-use and the distribution of longleaf pine on the Ocala National Forest, Florida: an interdisciplinary synthesis. *Fla. Anthropol.* 39, 183–193.

Kanciruk, P., Eilers, J.M., McCord, R.A., Landers, D.H., Brakke, D.F., and Linthurst, R.A. (1986). "Characteristics of Lakes in the Eastern United States. Vol. 3. Data Compendium of Site Characteristics and Chemical Variables." EPA/600/4-86/007c, U.S. Environ. Prot. Agency, Washington, D.C.

Kanwisher, J.W., and Wainwright, S.A. (1967). Oxygen balance in some reef corals. *Biol. Bull.* (*Woods Hole, Mass.*) 133, 378–390.

Kaplan, E.H. (1982). "A Field Guide to Coral Reefs of the Caribbean and Florida." Peterson Field Guide Ser. 27, Houghton, Boston, Massachusetts.

Kaplan, E.H. (1988). Mangrove communities of Florida and the Carribean. *In* "A Field Guide to Southeastern and Carribean Seashores," pp. 173–197. Houghton, Boston, Massachusetts.

Kaufman, L. (1977). The three spot damsel fish: effects on benthic biota of Caribbean coral reefs. *Proc. Int. Coral Reef Symp., 3rd, Miami, Fla.* 1, 559–564.

Kautz, R.S. (1980). Effects of eutrophication on the fish communities of Florida lakes. *Proc. Annu. Conf. Southeast Assoc. Fish Wildl. Agencies* 34, 67–80.

Kawaguti, S., and Sakumoto, S. (1948). The effect of light on the calcium deposition of corals. *Bull. Oceanogr. Inst. Taiwan* 4, 65–70.

Keeley, J.E. (1979). Population differentiation along a flood frequency gradient: physiological adaptations to flooding in *Nyssa sylvatica*. *Ecol. Monogr.* 49, 89–108.

Keeley, J.E., and Keeley, S.C. (1981). Post-fire regeneration of southern California chaparral. *Am. J. Bot.* 68, 524–530.

Keirn, M.A., and Brezonik, P.L. (1971). Nitrogen fixation by bacteria in Lake Mize, Florida, and in some lacustrine sediments. *Limnol. Oceanogr.* 16, 720–731.

Keller, A.E. (1984). Fish communities in Florida lakes: relationship to physicochemical parameters. M.S. Thesis, Univ. of Florida, Gainesville.

Kenner, W.E. (1964). Maps showing depths of selected lakes in Florida. *Fla. Geol. Surv. Inf. Circ.* No. 40. Tallahassee, Florida.

Kenner, W.E. (1975). "Seasonal Variation of Streamflow in Florida," Map Ser. No. 31 (updated). Bur. Geol., Florida Dep. Nat. Resour., Tallahassee.

Ketcham, D.E., and Bethune, J.E. (1963). Fire resistance of the south Florida slash pine. *J. For.* 61, 529–530.

Kilby, J.D. (1955). The fishes of two gulf coastal marsh areas of Florida. *Tulane Stud. Zool.* 2, 175–247.

Kinsey, D.W. (1985). Metabolism, calcification and carbon production. I. System level studies. *Proc. Int. Coral Reef Congr., 5th, Tahiti* 4, 505–526.

Kinzie, R.A. (1974). *Plexaura homomalla:* the biology and ecology of a harvestable marine resource. *Stud. Trop. Oceanogr.* 12, 22–38.

Kirkman, K.L. (1979). "Vegetation of a Selected Portion of Canaveral National Seashore." Unpubl. Rep. for U.S. Natl. Park Serv. Southeast Reg. Off., Atlanta, Georgia.

Kirtley, D. (1974). Geological significance of polychaetous annelid family Sabellariidae. Ph.D. Thesis, Florida State Univ., Tallahassee.

Kissling, D., and Taylor, G. (1977). Habitat factors for reef-dwelling ophiuroids in the Florida Keys. *Proc. Int. Coral Reef Symp., 3rd, Miami, Fla.* 1, 225–231.

Klein, H., Armbruster, J.T., McPherson, B.F., and Freiberger, H.J. (1975). Water and the south Florida environment. *U.S. Geol. Surv. Water Resour. Invest.* No. 24-75.

Klukas, R.W. (1969). "The Australian Pine Problem in Everglades National Park. Part 1. The Problem and Some Possible Solutions." Unpubl. Rep. for South Fla. Res. Cent., Everglades Natl. Park, Homestead, Florida.

Klukas, R.W. (1973). Control burn activities in Everglades National Park. *Proc. Tall Timbers Fire Ecol. Conf.* 12, 397–425.

Knight, G.R. (1986). A floristic study of Three Rivers state recreation area and Apalachee game management area, Jackson County, Florida. M.S. Thesis, Florida State Univ., Tallahassee.

Knight, R.L. (1980). Energy basis of control in aquatic ecosystems. Ph.D. Thesis,

Univ. of Florida, Gainesville.

Knight, R.L., and Coggins, W.F. (1982). "Record of Estuarine and Salt Marsh Metabolism at Crystal River, Florida, 1977–1981." Final Summ. Rep. to Fla. Power Corp., Contract No. QEA-000045, Syst. Ecol. Energy Anal. Group, Dep. Environ. Eng. Sci., Univ. of Florida, Gainesville.

Knochenmus, D.D., and Hughes, G.H. (1976). Hydrology of Lake County, Florida. *U.S. Geol. Surv. Water Res. Invest.* No. 76-72.

Kochman, H.I., and Christman, S.P. (1978). Atlantic salt marsh snake. *In* "Rare and Endangered Biota of Florida. Vol. 3: Amphibians and Reptiles" (R.W. McDiarmid, ed.), pp. 27–28. Univ. Presses of Florida, Gainesville.

Kochman, H.I., and Christman, S.P. (n.d.). Atlantic salt marsh snake. *In* "Rare and Endangered Biota of Florida," 2d ed., vol. 3, "Amphibians and Reptiles" (P.E. Moler, ed.). Univ. Presses of Florida, Gainesville. In press.

Kojis, B., and Quinn, N. (1984). Puberty in corals: an examination of Connell's hypotheses. *Adv. Reef Sci., Abstr. Pap. Jt. Meet. Atl. Reef Comm. Int. Soc. Reef Stud.,* p. 62. Univ. of Miami, Coral Gables, Florida.

Kolipinski, M.C., and Higer, A.L. (1969). Some aspects of the effects of the quantity and quality of water on biological communities in Everglades National Park. *U.S. Geol. Surv. Open-File Rep.* No. FL-69007.

Komarek, E.V., Sr. (1964). The natural history of lightning. *Proc. Tall Timbers Fire Ecol. Conf.* 3, 139–183.

Komarek, E.V., Sr. (1965). Fire ecology—grasslands and man. *Proc. Tall Timbers Fire Ecol. Conf.* 4, 169–197.

Komarek, E.V., Sr. (1968). Lightning and lightning fires as ecological forces. *Proc. Tall Timbers Fire Ecol. Conf.* 8, 169–197.

Komarek, E.V., Sr. (1974). Effects of fire on temperate forests and related ecosystems: southeastern United States. *In* "Fire and Ecosystems" (C.E. Ahlgren and T.T. Kozlowski, eds.), pp. 251–277. Academic Press, New York.

Komarek, E.V., Sr. (1983). Fire as an anthropogenic factor in vegetation ecology. *In* "Man's Impact on Vegetation" (W. Holzner, M.J.A. Werger, and I. Ikusima, eds.), pp. 77–82. Junk, The Hague.

Koopman, K.F. (1971). The systematic and historical status of the Florida *Eumops* (Chiroptera, Molossidae). *Am. Mus. Novit.* No. 2478, pp. 1–6.

Kost, J.A., and Boerner, R.E.J. (1985). Foliar nutrient dynamics and nutrient use efficiency in *Cornus florida. Oecologia* 66, 602–606.

Kozlowski, T.T. (1984). Responses of woody plants to flooding. *In* "Flooding and Plant Growth" (T.T. Kozlowski, ed.), pp. 129–163. Academic Press, New York.

Kral, R. (1983). Endangered species, perennial plants of moist pine flatwood savannas, northwest Florida. *U.S. For. Serv. Tech. Publ.* No. R8-TP.

Kratzer, C.R., and Brezonik, P.L. (1981). A Carlson-type trophic state index for nitrogen in Florida lakes. *Water Resour. Bull.* 17, 713–715.

Kruczynski, W.L. (1982). Salt marshes of the northeastern Gulf of Mexico. *In* "Creation and Restoration of Coastal Plant Communities" (R.R. Lewis III, ed.), pp. 71–87. CRC Press, Boca Raton, Florida.

Kruczynski, W.L., Subrahmanyam, C.B., and Drake, S.H. (1978). Studies on the plant community of a north Florida salt marsh. Part I. Primary production. *Bull. Mar. Sci.* 28, 316–334.

Küchler, A.W. (1964). Potential natural vegetation of the conterminous United States. *Am. Geogr. Soc. Spec. Publ.* No. 36.

Küchler, A.W. (1967). "Potential Natural Vegetation," Map, Rev. Ed. (1965), Sheet No. 90, U.S. Geol. Surv., Washington, D.C.

Kuenzler, E.J. (1974). Mangrove swamp systems. *In* "Coastal Ecological Systems" (H.T. Odum, B.J. Copeland, and E.A. McMahon, eds.), Vol. 1, pp. 346–371. Conservation Found., Washington, D.C.

Kurz, H. (1927). A new and remarkable habitat for the endemic Florida yew. *Torreya* 27, 90–92.

Kurz, H. (1933). Northern disjuncts in northern Florida. *Annu. Rep. Fla. State Geol. Surv. (1930–1932)* 23/24, 50–53.

Kurz, H. (1938a). A physiographic study of the tree associations of the Apalachicola River. *Q. J. Fla. Acad. Sci.* 3, 78–90.

Kurz, H. (1938b). *Torreya* west of the Apalachicola River. *Q. J. Fla. Acad. Sci.* 3, 66–77.

Kurz, H. (1942). Florida dunes and scrub, vegetation and geology. *Fla. Geol. Surv. Bull.* 23, 1–154.

Kurz, H. (1944). Secondary forest succession in the Tallahassee Red Hills. *Proc. Fla. Acad. Sci.* 7, 59–100.

Kurz, H., and Godfrey, R.K. (1962). "Trees of Northern Florida." Univ. of Florida Press, Gainesville.

Kurz, H., and Wagner, K. (1957). "Tidal Marshes of the Gulf and Atlantic Coasts of Northern Florida and Charleston, South Carolina." Florida State Univ. Study No. 24. Florida State Univ., Tallahassee.

Kushlan, J.A. (1973). White ibis nesting in the Florida Everglades. *Wilson Bull.* 58, 230–231.

Kushlan, J.A. (1974a). Effects of a natural fish kill on the water quality, plankton, and fish population of a pond in the Big Cypress Swamp, Florida. *Trans. Am. Fish. Soc.* 103, 235–243.

Kushlan, J.A. (1974b). Observations on the role of the American alligator (*Alligator mississippiensis*) in the southern Florida wetlands. *Copeia,* pp. 993–996.

Kushlan, J.A. (1975). Population changes of the apple snail (*Pomacea paludosa*) in the southern Everglades. *Nautilus* 89, 21–23.

Kushlan, J.A. (1976a). Environmental stability and fish community diversity. *Ecology* 57, 821–825.

Kushlan, J.A. (1976b). Site selection for nesting colonies by the American white ibis *Eudocimus albus* in Florida. *Ibis* 118, 590–593.

Kushlan, J.A. (1976c). Wading bird predation in a seasonally fluctuating pond. *Auk* 88, 464–476.

Kushlan, J.A. (1977). Population energetics of the white ibis. *Auk* 94, 114–122.

Kushlan, J.A. (1978). Wading bird use of the East Everglades. *Fla. Field Nat.* 6, 46–47.

Kushlan, J.A. (1979a). Design and management of continental wildlife reserves: lessons from the Everglades. *Biol. Conserv.* 15, 281–290.

Kushlan, J.A. (1979b). Foraging ecology and prey selection in the white ibis. *Condor* 81, 376–389.

Kushlan, J.A. (1979c). Temperature and oxygen in an Everglades alligator pond. *Hydrobiologia* 67, 267–271.

Kushlan, J.A. (1980). Population fluctuations of Everglades fishes. *Copeia,* pp. 870–874.

Kushlan, J.A. (1982). The sandhill crane in the Everglades. *Fla. Field Nat.* 10, 72–74.

Kushlan, J.A. (1983). Special species and ecosystem preserves: colonial waterbirds in U.S. national parks. *Environ. Manage.* 7, 201–207.

Kushlan, J.A. (1986a). The Everglades: management of cumulative ecosystem degradation. *In* "Managing Cumulative Impacts in Florida Wetlands" (E.D. Estevez, J. Miller, J. Morris, and R. Hamman, eds.), pp. 61–82. Omnipress, Madison, Wisconsin.

Kushlan, J.A. (1986b). Exotic fishes in the Everglades, a reconsideration of proven impact. *Environ. Conserv.* 13, 67–69.

Kushlan, J.A. (1986c). External threats and internal management: the hydrologic regulation of the Everglades. *Environ. Manage.* 11, 109–119.

Kushlan, J.A. (1986d). Responses of wading birds to seasonally fluctuating water levels: strategies and their limits. *Colonial Waterbirds* 9, 155–162.

Kushlan, J.A. (1990a). Avian use of fluctuating wetlands. *In* "Wetlands and Wildlife" (R. Sharitz and W. Gibbons, eds.). DOE Tech. Publ. Ser.

Kushlan, J.A. (1990b). Wetlands and wildlife: the Everglades perspective. *In* "Wetlands and Wildlife" (R. Sharitz and W. Gibbons, eds.). DOE Tech. Publ. Ser.

Kushlan, J.A., and Bass, O.L., Jr. (1983a). Habitat use and the distribution of the Cape Sable sparrow. *In* "The Seaside Sparrow, Its Biology and Management, Proc. Symp. Raleigh, N.C., 1981" (T.L. Quay, J.B. Funderburg, Jr., D.S. Lee, E.F. Potter, and C.S. Robbins, eds.), Occas. Pap. N.C. Biol. Surv. 1983–1985, pp. 139–146. North Carolina State Mus. Nat. Hist., Raleigh.

Kushlan, J.A., and Bass, O.L., Jr., (1983b). Snail kite in the southern Everglades. *Fla. Field Nat.* 11, 108–111.

Kushlan, J.A., and Frohring, P.C. (1986). The history of the wood stork in southern Florida. *Wilson Bull.* 98, 368–386.

Kushlan, J.A., and Hunt, B.P. (1979). Limnology of an alligator pond in south Florida. *Fla. Sci.* 42, 65–84.

Kushlan, J.A., and Jacobsen, T. (1990). Environmental variability and the reproductive success of Everglades alligators. *J. Herp.* In press.

Kushlan, J.A., and Kushlan, M.S. (1977). Winter bird census: Everglades marsh. *Am. Birds* 30, 1006–1067.

Kushlan, J.A., and Kushlan, M.S. (1978). Breeding bird census: Everglades marsh. *Am. Birds* 31, 83.

Kushlan, J.A., and Kushlan, M.S. (1979). Observations on crayfish in the Everglades. *Crustaceana, Suppl.* 5, 116–120.

Kushlan, J.A., and Kushlan, M.S. (1980a). Everglades alligator nests: nesting sites for marsh reptiles. *Copeia,* pp. 930–932.

Kushlan, J.A., and Kushlan, M.S. (1980b). Population fluctuations of the prawn, *Palaemonetes paludosus,* in the Everglades. *Am. Midl. Nat.* 103, 401–403.

Kushlan, J.A., and Lodge, T.E. (1974). Ecological and distributional notes on the freshwater fish of southern Florida. *Fla. Sci.* 37, 110–128.

Kushlan, J.A., and White, D.A. (1977). Nesting wading bird populations in southern Florida. *Fla. Sci.* 40, 65–72.

Kushlan, J.A., Ogden, J.C., and Higer, A.L. (1975). Relation of water level and fish availability to wood stork reproduction in southern Everglades, Florida. *U.S. Geol. Surv. Open-File Rep.* No. 75-434. Tallahassee, Florida.

Kushlan, J.A., Bass, O.L., Jr., and McEwan, L.C. (1982). Wintering waterfowl in the Everglades estuaries. *Am. Birds* 36, 815–819.

Kutzbach, J.E., and Wright, H.E., Jr., (1985). Simulation of the climate of 18,000 years BP: results for the North American/North Atlantic/European sector and comparison with the geological record of North America. *Quat. Sci. Rev.* 4, 147–187.

Kwon, H.J. (1969). "Barrier Islands of the Northern Gulf of Mexico Coast: Sediment Source and Development." Louisiana State Univ. Coastal Stud. Ser. No. 25.

Louisiana State Univ. Press, Baton Rouge.
Laborel, J. (1977). Are reef-building vermetids disappearing in the south Atlantic? *Proc. Int. Coral Reef Symp., 3rd, Miami, Fla.* 1, 233–237.
Laessle, A.M. (1942). "The Plant Communities of the Welaka Area with Special Reference to Correlation between Soils and Vegetational Succession." *Biol. Sci. Ser.* 4. Univ. of Florida Pub., Gainesville.
Laessle, A.M. (1958a). The origin and successional relationships of sandhill vegetation and sand-pine scrub. *Ecol. Monogr.* 28, 361–387.
Laessle, A.M. (1958b). A report on succession studies of selected plant communities on the Univ. of Florida Conservation Reserve, Welaka, Florida. *Q. J. Fla. Acad. Sci.* 21, 101–112.
Laessle, A.M. (1968). Relationships of sand pine scrub to former shore lines. *Q. J. Fla. Acad. Sci.* 30, 269–286.
Laessle, A.M., and Monk, C.D. (1961). Some live oak forests of northeastern Florida. *Q. J. Fla. Acad. Sci.* 24, 39–55.
Lakela, O. (1964). Fewer Florida rarities: changing flora of Pineola Grotto, Citrus County. *Sida* 1, 299–305.
Lakela, O., and Long, R.W. (1976). "Ferns of Florida: an Illustrated Manual and Identification Guide." Banyan Books, Miami, Florida.
Landers, J.L., and Speake, D.W. (1974). Management needs of sandhill reptiles in southern Georgia. *In* "Effects of Intensive Forestry on Succession and Wildlife in Florida Sandhills" (R.W. Umber and L.D. Harris, eds.), pp. 686–693. Proc. Southeast Game Fish Comm. Conf.
Landon, S. (1975). Environmental controls on growth rates in hermatypic corals from the lower Florida Keys. M.S. Thesis, State Univ. of New York, Binghamton.
Lang, J. (1971). Interspecific aggression by Scleractinian coral. 1. The rediscovery of *Scolymia cubensis* (Milne Edwards and Haime). *Bull. Mar. Sci.* 21, 952–959.
Lang, J. (1973). Interspecific aggression by Scleractinian coral. 2. Why the race is not to the swift. *Bull. Mar. Sci.* 23, 260–279.
Lang, J. (1974). Biological zonation at the base of a reef. *Am. Sci.* 62(3), 272–281.
Langdon, O.G. (1963). Growth patterns of *Pinus elliottii* var. *densa*. *Ecology* 44, 825–827.
LaPointe, B.E., and O'Connell, J. (1988). The effects of on-site sewage disposal systems on nutrient relations of groundwaters and nearshore waters of the Florida Keys. Tech. Rep., Monroe Cty. Planning Dep., Key West, Florida.
Larsen, J.A. (1982). "Ecology of the Northern Lowland Bogs and Conifer Forests." Academic Press, New York.
Larson, D.A., Brant, V.M., and Patty, T.S. (1972). Pollen analysis of a central Texas bog. *Am. Midl. Nat.* 88, 358–367.
Lawson, R. (1987). Molecular studies of thamnophiine snakes: I. The physiology of the genus *Nerodia*. *J. Herpetol.* 21, 140–157.
Layne, J.N. (1974). Ecology of small mammals in a flatwoods habitat in north-central Florida, with emphasis on the cotton rat (*Sigmodon hispidus*). *Am. Mus. Novit.* No. 2544, 48 pp.
Layne, J.N., ed. (1978). "Rare and Endangered Biota of Florida. Vol. 1: Mammals." Univ. Presses of Florida, Gainesville.
Layne, J.N. (1984). The land mammals of South Florida. *In* "Environments of South Florida: Past and Present II" (P.J. Gleason, ed.), pp. 269–296. Miami Geol. Soc., Coral Gables, Florida.
Layne, J.N., Stallcup, J.A., Woolfenden, G.E., McCauley, M.N., and Worley, D.J.

(1977). "Fish and Wildlife Inventory of the Seven-County Region included in the Central Florida Phosphate Industry Areawide Environmental Impact Study." U.S. N.T.I.S. *PB Rep:* PB-287 456, 3 vols.

Leach, S.D., Klein, H., and Hampton, E.R. (1972). Hydrologic effects of water control and management of southeastern Florida. *Fla. Bur. Geol. Rep. Invest.* No. 60.

Lee, C.C. (1969). The decomposition of organic matter in some shallow water, calcareous sediments of Little Black Water Sound, Florida Bay. Ph.D. Thesis, Univ. of Miami, Coral Gables, Florida.

Leenhouts, W.P. (1983). "Marsh and Water Management Plan, Merritt Island National Wildlife Refuge." U.S. Fish Wildl. Serv., Merritt Isl. Natl. Wildlife Refuge, Titusville, Florida.

Leenhouts, W.P. (1985). Soil and vegetation dynamics in a rotary ditched mosquito control impoundment on the Merritt Island National Wildlife Refuge. *Proc. Annu. Conf. Wetlands Restoration Creat., 12th* (F.J. Webb, ed.), pp. 181–192. Hillsborough Community Coll., Tampa, Florida.

Leenhouts, W.P., and Baker, J.L. (1982). Vegetation dynamics in dusky seaside sparrow habitat on Merritt Island National Wildlife Refuge. *Wildl. Soc. Bull.* 10, 127–132.

Leitman, H.M. (1978). Correlation of Apalachicola River floodplain tree communities with water levels, elevation, and soils. M.S. Thesis, Florida State Univ., Tallahassee.

Leitman, H.M., Sohm, J.E., and Franklin, M.A. (1982). Wetland hydrology and tree distribution of the Apalachicola River Flood Plain, Florida. *U.S. Geol. Surv. Water-Supply Pap.* No. 2196-A.

Lemlich, S.K., and Ewel, K.C. (1984). Effects of wastewater disposal on growth rates of cypress trees. *J. Environ. Qual.* 13, 602–604.

Lemon, P.C. (1949). Successional responses of herbs in the longleaf-slash pine forests after fire. *Ecology* 30, 135–145.

Lenczewski, B. (1980). Butterflies of Everglades National Park. *Everglades Natl. Park, South Fla. Res. Cent. Rep.* No. T-588.

Leslie, A.J., Jr., Nall, L.E., and Van Dyke, J.M. (1983). Effects of vegetation control by grass carp on selected water quality variables in four Florida lakes. *Trans. Am. Fish. Soc.* 112, 777–787.

Lessios, H., Cubit, J., Robertson, D., Shulman, M., Parker, M., Garrity, S., and Levings, S. (1984a). Mass mortality of *Diadema antillarum* on the Caribbean coast of Panama. *Coral Reefs* 4, 173–182.

Lessios, H., Robertson, D., and Cubit, J. (1984b). Spread of *Diadema* mass mortality through the Caribbean. *Science* 226, 335–337.

Lewis, C.E. (1972). Chopping and webbing control saw-palmetto in south Florida. *U.S. For. Serv. Res. Note* No. SE-177.

Lewis, C.E., and Harshbarger, T.J. (1976). Shrub and herbaceous vegetation after 20 years of prescribed burning in the South Carolina coastal plain. *J. Wildl. Manage.* 29, 13–18.

Lewis, C.E., and Hart, R.H. (1972). Some herbage responses to fire on pine wiregrass range. *J. Range Manage.* 25, 209–213.

Lewis, C.E., Swindel, B.F., Conde, L.F., and Smith, J.E. (1984). Forage yields improved by site preparation in pine flatwoods of north Florida, USA. *South. J. Appl. For.* 25, 181–185.

Lewis, J.B. (1977). Processes of organic production on coral reefs. *Biol. Rev.* 52, 305–347.

Lewis, R.R., III (1980). Impact of oil spills on mangrove forests. *Int. Symp. Biol. Manage. Mangroves Trop. Shallow Water Communities, 2nd, Port Moresby, Madang, Papau, New Guinea*, p. 36.

Lewis, R.R., III (1982a). Low marshes, peninsular Florida. *In* "Creation and Restoration of Coastal Plant Communities" (R.R. Lewis III, ed.), pp. 147–152. CRC Press, Boca Raton, Florida.

Lewis, R.R., III (1982b). Mangrove forests. *In* "Creation and Restoration of Coastal Plant Communities" (R.R. Lewis III, ed.), pp. 153–171. CRC Press, Boca Raton, Florida.

Lewis, R.R., III, and Dunstan, F.M. (1975). Use of spoil islands in re-established mangrove communities in Tampa Bay, Florida. *Proc. Int. Symp. Biol. Manage. Mangroves* (G.E. Walsh, S. Snedaker, and H. Teas, eds.), pp. 766–775. Univ. of Florida, Gainesville.

Lewis, R.R., and Phillips, R.C. (1980). "Seagrass Mapping Project, Hillsborough County, Florida." Tampa Port Authority, Tampa.

Lewis, R.R., III, Lewis, C.S., Fehring, W.K., and Rodgers, J.A. (1979). Coastal habitat mitigation in Tampa Bay, Florida. *Proc. Mitigation Symp.*, Gen. Tech. Rep. RM-65, pp. 136–140. U.S. Dep. Agric., Fort Collins, Colorado.

Lewis, R.R., III, Gilmore, R.G., Jr., Crewz, D.W., and Odum, W.E. (1985). Mangrove habitat and fishery resources of Florida. *In* "Florida Aquatic Habitat and Fishery Resources" (W. Seaman, Jr., ed.), pp. 281–336. Florida Chap. Am. Fish. Soc., Kissimmee.

Lighty, R.G. (1977). Relict shelf-edge Holocene coral reef: southeast coast of Florida. *Proc. Int. Coral Reef Symp., 3rd, Miami, Fla.* 2, 215–222.

Limbaugh, C. (1961). Cleaning symbiosis. *Sci. Am.* 205, 42–49.

Lindall, W.M., Jr., and Saloman, C.H. (1977). Alteration and destruction of estuaries affecting fisheries resources of the Gulf of Mexico. *Mar. Fish. Rev.* 39, Pap. No. 1262.

Lindenmuth, A.W., and Byram, G.M. (1948). Headfires are cooler near the ground than backfires. *Fire Control Notes* 9, 8–9.

Lindsey, A.A., Petty, R.O., Sterling, D.K., and Van Asdall, W. (1961). Vegetation and environment along the Wabash and Tippecanoe Rivers. *Ecol. Monogr.* 31, 105–156.

Linhart, Y.B. (1980). Local biogeography of plants on a Caribbean atoll. *J. Biogeogr.* 7, 159–171.

Lins, H.F., Jr. (1980). Patterns and trends of land use and land cover on Atlantic and Gulf coast barrier islands. *U.S. Geol. Surv. Prof. Pap.* No. 1156.

Linthurst, R.A. (1980). An evaluation of aeration, nitrogen, pH and salinity as factors affecting *Spartina alterniflora* growth: a summary. *In* "Estuarine Perspectives" (V.S. Kennedy, ed.), pp. 235–247. Academic Press, New York.

Linthurst, R.A., Landers, D.H., Eilers, J.M., Brakke, D.F., Overton, W.S., Meier, E.P., and Crowe, R.E. (1986). "Characteristics of Lakes in the Eastern United States. Vol. 1: Population Descriptions and Physico-chemical Relationships." EPA/600/4-86/007a, U.S. Environ. Prot. Agency, Washington, D.C.

Little, E.L., Jr. (1971). "Atlas of United States Trees. Vol. 1: Conifers and Important Hardwoods." *U.S. For. Serv. Misc. Publ.* No. 1146. U.S. Govt. Print. Off., Washington, D.C.

Little, E.L., Jr. (1976). Rare tropical trees of south Florida. *U.S. For. Serv. Conserv. Res. Rep.* No. 20.

Little, E.L., Jr. (1978). "Atlas of United States Trees. Vol. 5: Florida." *U.S. For. Serv. Misc. Publ.* No. 1361. U.S. Government Print. Off., Washington, D.C.

Little, E.L., Jr. (1979). "Checklist of United States Trees (Native and Naturalized)." *U.S. Dep. Agric. Handb.* No. 541.

Little, E.L., Jr., and Dorman, K.W. (1954a). Slash pine (*Pinus elliottii*), including south Florida slash pine: nomenclature and description. *U.S. For. Serv. Southeast. For. Exp. Stn. Pap.* No. 36.

Little, E. L., Jr., and Dorman, K.W. (1954b). Slash pine (*Pinus elliottii*), its nomenclature and varieties. *J. For.* 50, 918–923.

Little, S., and Moore, E.B. (1949). The ecological role of prescribed burns in the pine-oak forests of southern New Jersey. *Ecology* 30, 223–233.

Littler, M.M., and Littler, D.S. (1984). Models of tropical reef biogenesis: the contribution of algae. *Prog. Phycol. Res.* 3, 323–364.

Livingston, B.E., and Shreve, F. (1921). The distribution of vegetation in the United States, as related to climatic conditions. *Carnegie Inst. Wash. Publ.* No. 284.

Livingston, R.J. (1975). Impact of kraft pulp-mill effluents on estuarine and coastal fishes in Apalachee Bay, Florida, USA. *Mar. Biol.* (*Berlin*) 32, 19–48.

Livingston, R.J. (1982a). Long-term variability in coastal systems: background noise and environmental stress. *In* "Ecological Stress and the New York Bight: Science and Management" (G. Mayer, ed.), pp. 605–620. U.S. Dep. Commer., Washington, D.C.

Livingston, R.J. (1982b). Trophic organization of fishes in a coastal seagrass system. *Mar. Ecol. Prog. Ser.* 7, 1–12.

Livingston, R.J. (1984a). "The Ecology of the Apalachicola Bay System: an Estuarine Profile." *U.S. Fish and Wildl. Serv. Off. Biol. Serv. [Tech. Rep.] FWS/OBS* 82-05.

Livingston, R.J. (1984b). Trophic responses of fishes to habitat variability in coastal seagrass systems. *Ecology* 65, 1258–1275.

Livingston, R.J. (1985). Application of scientific research to resource management: case history, the Apalachicola Bay system. *Proc. Int. Symp. Util. Coastal Ecosyst.: Plann., Pollut., Prod.* (N.L. Chao and W. Kirby-Smith, eds.), Vol. 1, pp. 103–125.

Livingston, R.J. (1987). Historic trends of human impacts on seagrass meadows in Florida. *Proc. Symp. Subtrop.-Trop. Seagrasses Southeast. U.S.* (M.J. Durako, R.C. Phillips, and R.R. Lewis III, eds.), Fla. Mar. Res. Publ. No. 92, pp. 139–156. Florida Dep. Nat. Resour., Tallahassee.

Livingston, R.J., and Joyce, E.A., Jr., eds. (1977). *Proc. Conf. Apalachicola Drain. Syst., Gainesville, Fla., 1976.* Fla. Mar. Res. Publ. No. 26, Florida Dep. Nat. Resour., Tallahassee.

Livingston, R.J., Iverson, R.L., Estabrook, R.H., Keys, V.E., and Taylor, J., Jr. (1974). Major features of the Apalachicola Bay system: Physiography, biota, and resource management. *Fla. Sci.* 37, 245–271.

Lizama, J., and Blanquet, R. (1975). Predation on sea anemones by the amphinomid polychaete *Hermodice carunculata. Bull. Mar. Sci.* 25, 442–443.

Lockwood, J.G. (1979). "Causes of Climate." Wiley, New York.

Loftus, W.F., and Kushlan, J.A. (1984). Population fluctuations of the Schaus swallowtail (Lepidoptera: Papilionidae) on the islands of Biscayne Bay, Florida, with comments on the Bahaman swallowtail. Fla. Entomol. 67, 277–28.

Loftus, W.F., and Kushlan, J.A. (1987). The fresh water fishes of southern Florida. *Bull. Fla. State Mus.* 31, 147–344.

Lomolino, M.V., and Ewel, K.C. (1984). Digestive efficiencies of the West Indian manatee (*Trichechus manatus*). *Fla. Sci.* 47, 176–179.

Long, E.C. (1899). Forest fires in the southern pines. *For. Leaves* 2, 94.

Long, R.W. (1974). The vegetation of southern Florida. *Fla. Sci.* 37, 33–45.

Long, R.W. (1984). Origin of the vascular flora of Florida. *In* "Environments of South Florida: Present and Past II" (P.J. Gleason, ed.), pp. 118–126. Miami Geol. Soc., Coral Gables, Florida.

Long, R.W., and Lakela, O. (1971). "A Flora of Tropical Florida." Univ. of Miami Press, Coral Gables, Florida.

Longley, W.H., and Hildebrand, S.F. (1941). Systematic catalogue of the fishes of Tortugas, Florida, with observations on color, habits and local distribution. *Pap. Tortugas Lab.* 34, 1–331.

Loope, L.L. (1980a). A bibliography of south Florida botany. *Everglades Natl. Park South Fla. Res. Cent. Rep.* No. T-600.

Loope, L.L. (1980b). Phenology of flowering and fruiting in plant communities of Everglades National Park and Biscayne National Monument, Florida. *Everglades Natl. Park South Fla. Res. Cent. Rep.* T-593.

Loope, L.L., and Dunevitz, V.L. (1981a). Impact of fire exclusion and invasion of *Schinus terebinthifolius* on limestone rockland pine forests of southeastern Florida. *Everglades Natl. Park South Fla. Res. Cent. Rep.* No. T-645.

Loope, L.L., and Dunevitz, V.L. (1981b). Investigations of early plant succession on abandoned farmland in Everglades National Park. *Everglades Natl. Park South Fla. Res. Cent. Rep.* No. T-644.

Loope, L.L., and Urban, N.H. (1980). A survey of fire history and impacts in tropical hardwood hammocks in the East Everglades and adjacent portions of Everglades National Park. *Everglades Natl. Park South Fla. Res. Cent. Rep.* No. T-592.

Loope, L.L., Black, D.W., Black, S., and Avery, G.N. (1979). Distribution and abundance of flora in limestone rockland pine forests of southeastern Florida. *Everglades Natl. Park South Fla. Res. Cent. Rep.* No. T-547.

Lorimer, C.G. (1977). The presettlement forest and natural disturbance cycle of northeastern Maine. *Ecology* 58, 139–148.

Lorimer, C.G. (1980). Age structure and disturbance history of a southern Appalachian virgin forest. *Ecology* 61, 1169–1184.

Lorimer, C.G. (1989). Relative effects of small and large disturbances on temperate hardwood forest structure. *Ecology* 70, 565–567.

Lotti, T. (1956). Eliminating understory hardwoods with summer prescribed fires in coastal plain loblolly pine stands. *J. For.* 54, 191–192.

Loughridge, R.H. (1884). Report on the cotton production of the state of Georgia. *Annu. U.S. Census, 10th,* 6, 259–450.

Loveless, C.M. (1959a). The Everglades deer herd life history and management. *Fla. Game Fresh Water Fish Comm. Tech. Bull.* No. 6.

Loveless, C.M. (1959b). A study of the vegetation in the Florida Everglades. *Ecology* 40, 1–9.

Lowe, E.F. (1983). Distribution and structure of floodplain plant communities in the upper basin of the St. Johns River, Florida. *St. Johns River Water Manage. Dist. Tech. Publ.* SJ 83-8.

Lowe, E.F. (1986). The relationship between hydrology and vegetational pattern within the floodplain marsh of a subtropical Florida lake. *Fla. Sci.* 49, 213–233.

Lowe, E.F., Brooks, J.E., Fall, C.J., Gerry, L.R., and Hall, G.B. (1984). U.S. EPA clean lakes program, phase I, diagnostic-feasibility study of the upper St. Johns River chain of lakes. Vol. 1. Diagnostic study. *St. Johns River Water Manage. Dist. Tech. Rep.* SJ 84-15.

Loya, J. (1972). Community structure and species diversity of hermatypic corals at

Eilat, Red Sea. *Mar. Biol. (Berlin)* 13, 100–123.

Lückhoff, H.A. (1964). The natural distribution, growth and botanical variation of *Pinus caribaea* and its cultivation in South Africa. *Ann. Univ. van Stellenbosch* 39, 1–160.

Luer, C.A. (1972). "The Native Orchids of Florida." New York Bot. Gard., New York.

Lugo, A.E. (1980). Mangrove ecosystems: successional or steady state? *Biotropica* 12, 65–73.

Lugo, A.E. (1981). Mangrove issue debates in courtrooms. *Proc. U.S. Fish Wildl. Serv. Workshop Coastal Ecosyst. Southeast. U.S.* (R.C. Carey, P.S. Markovits, and J.B. Kirkwood, eds.), *U.S. Fish Wildl. Serv. Off. Biol. Serv. [Tech. Rep.] FWS/OBS* 80-59, pp. 48–60.

Lugo, A.E. (1986). Mangrove understory: an expensive luxury. *J. Trop. Ecol.* 2, 287–288.

Lugo, A.E., and Brown, S.L. (1984). The Oklawaha River forested wetlands and their response to chronic flooding. *In* "Cypress Swamps" (K.C. Ewel and H.T. Odum, eds.), pp. 365–373. Univ. Presses of Florida, Gainesville.

Lugo, A.E., and Patterson-Zucca, C. (1977). The impact of low temperature stress on mangrove structure and growth. *J. Trop. Ecol.* 18, 149–161.

Lugo, A.E., and Snedaker, S.C. (1974). The ecology of mangroves. *Annu. Rev. Ecol. Syst.* 5, 39–64.

Lugo, A.E., and Snedaker, S.C. (1975). Properties of a mangrove forest in southern Florida. *Proc. Int. Symp. Biol. Manage. Mangroves* (G. Walsh, S. Snedaker, and H. Teas, eds.), pp. 170–211. Univ. of Florida, Gainesville.

Lugo, A.E., Evink, G., Brinson, M.M., Broce, A., and Snedaker. S.C. (1975). Diurnal rates of photosynthesis, respiration, an transpiration in mangrove forests in south Florida. *In* "Tropical Ecological Systems" (F. Golley and G. Medina, eds.), pp. 335–350. Springer-Verlag, New York.

Lugo, A.E., Sell, M., and Snedaker, S.C. (1976). Mangrove ecosystem analysis. *In* "Systems Analysis and Simulation in Ecology" (B.C. Patten, ed.), pp. 113–145. Academic Press, New York.

Lugo, A.E., Gamble, J.F., and Ewel, K.C. (1978). Organic matter budget in a mixed-hardwood forest in north-central Florida. *In* "Environmental Chemistry and Cycling Processes" (D.C. Adriano and I.L. Brisbin, eds.). *DOE Symp. Ser.* No. 45 (CONF-760429), pp. 790–800.

Lugo, A.E., Twilley, R.R., and Patterson-Zucca, C. (1980). "The Role of Black Mangrove Forests in the Productivity of Coastal Ecosystems in South Florida." Rep. to EPA Corvallis Environ. Res. Lab., Corvallis, Oregon.

Lugo, A.E., Brinson, M.M., and Brown, S. (1989). "Forested Wetlands." Ecosyst. World Ser. Elsevier, Amsterdam. In press.

Lynts, G.W. (1966). Relationship of sediment-size distribution to ecologic factors in Buttonwood Sound, Florida. *J. Sediment. Petrol.* 36, 66–74.

Lyon, L.J., and Stickney, P.F. (1976). Early vegetational succession following large northern Rocky Mountain wildfires. *Proc. Tall Timbers Fire Ecol. Conf.* 14., 355–376.

Lyons, W. (1976). Distribution of *Cerithium litteratum* (Born) (Gastropoda: Cerithiidae) off western Florida. *Veliger* 18, 375– 377.

Lyons, W.G., and Camp, D.K. (1982). Zones of faunal similarity within the Hourglass Study Area. *Proc. Annu. Gulf Mex. Inf. Transfer Meet., 3rd,* pp. 44–46. U.S. Dep. Interior/Mineral Manage. Serv., Washington, D.C.

Lyons, W.G., Barber D., Foster, S., Kennedy, F., and Milano, G. (1981). The spiny lobster, *Panulirus argus,* in the middle and upper Florida Keys: population structure, seasonal dynamics, and reproduction. *Fla. Mar. Res. Publ.* No. 38.

MacArthur, R.H., and Wilson, E.O. (1963). An equilibrium theory of insular biogeography. *Evolution* 17, 373–387.

McCaleb, J.E., and Hodges, E.M. (1960). Climatological records at range cattle experiment station, 1942–1958. *Range Cattle Exp. Stn. Circ.* No. S-124, Ona, Florida.

McCormack, J.F. (1949a). Forest resources of central Florida, 1949. *U.S. For. Serv. Southeast. For. Exp. Stn. Surv. Release* No. 31.

McCormack, J.F. (1949b). Forest resources of northeast Florida, 1949. *U.S. For. Serv. Southeast. For. Exp. Stn. Surv. Release* No. 30.

McCormack, J.F. (1950a). Forest resources of northwest Florida, 1949. *U.S. For. Serv. Southeast. For. Exp. Stn. Surv. Release* No. 32.

McCormack, J.F. (1950b). Forest resources of south Florida, 1949. *U.S. For. Serv. Southeast. For. Exp. Stn. Surv. Release* No. 33.

McCoy, E.D. (1977). The diversity of terrestrial arthropods in northwest Florida salt marshes. Ph.D. Thesis, Florida State Univ., Tallahassee.

McCoy, E.D., and Rey, J.R. (1981). Terrestrial arthropods of northwest Florida salt marshes: Coleoptera. *Fla. Entomol.* 64, 405–411.

McCoy, E.D., and Rey, J.R. (1987). Terrestrial arthropods of northwest Florida salt marshes: Hymenoptera (Insecta). *Fla. Entomol.* 70, 90–97.

McCulley, R.D. (1950). Management of natural slash pine stands in the flatwoods of south Georgia and north Florida. *U.S. Dep. Agric. Circ.* No. 845.

McCune, B. (1988). Ecological diversity in North American pines. *Am. J. Bot.* 75, 353–368.

McDiarmid, R.W., ed. (1978). "Rare and Endangered Biota of Florida. Vol. 3: Amphibians and Reptiles." Univ. Presses of Florida, Gainesville.

McDiffett, W.F. (1980). Limnological characteristics of several lakes on the Lake Wales Ridge, south-central Florida. *Hydrobiologia* 71, 137–145.

McDiffett, W.F. (1981). Limnological characteristics of eutrophic Lake Istokpoga, Florida. *Fla. Sci.* 44, 172–181.

McDonald, M.V. (1982). Gulf coast salt marsh. *In* "Forty-fifth Breeding Bird Census" (W.T. Van Velzen and A.C. Van Velzen, eds.), *Am. Birds* 36, 100.

McDonald, M.V. (1983). Gulf coast salt marsh. *In* "Forty-sixth Breeding Bird Census" (W.T. Van Velzen and A.C. Van Velzen, eds.), *Am. Birds* 37, 100.

McDonald, M.V. (1984). Gulf coast salt marsh. *In* "Forty-seventh Breeding Bird Census" (W.T. Van Velzen and A.C. Van Velzen, eds.), *Am. Birds* 38, 119.

McDonald, M.V. (1986). The ecology and vocalizations of Scott's Seaside Sparrows (*Ammodramus maritimus peninsulae*). Ph.D. Thesis, Univ. of Florida, Gainesville.

McDowell, L.L., Stephens, J.C., and Stewart, E.H. (1969). Radiocarbon chronology of the Florida Everglades peat. *Soil Sci. Soc. Am. Proc.* 33, 743–745.

McGee, C.E. (1980). The effect of fire on species dominance in young upland hardwood stands. *U.S. For. Serv. State Public For. S.E. Area Tech. Publ.* SA-TP-12, pp. 97–104.

MacGowan, W.L. (1935). Growth-ring studies of certain forest trees of north Florida. M.S. Thesis, Florida State Coll. for Women, Tallahassee.

MacGowan, W.L. (1937). Growth-ring studies of trees of northern Florida. *Q. J. Fla. Acad. Sci.* 1, 57–65.

McGuire, R.J., and Brown, L.N. (1974). A phytosociological analysis of two subtropical hammocks on Elliot Key, Dade Co., Florida. *J. Elisha Mitchell Sci. Soc.* 90, 125–131.

Macintyre, I.G., and Milliman, J.D. (1970). Physiographic features on the outer shelf and upper slope, Atlantic continental margin, southeastern United States. *Geol. Soc. Am. Bull.* 81, 2577–2598.

McJunkin, D.M. (1977). Aspects of cypress domes in southeastern Florida. M.S. Thesis, Florida Atlantic Univ., Boca Raton, Florida.

McKey D.B. (1988). Naturalization of exotic *Ficus* species (Moraceae) in south Florida, Proc. Symp. Exotic Pest Plants. USDI National Park Service, Miami.

McMahan, E.A., and Davis, L.R., Jr. (1984). Density and diversity of microarthropods in manipulated and undisturbed cypress domes. *In* "Cypress Swamps" (K.C. Ewel and H.T. Odum, eds.), pp. 197–209. Univ. Presses of Florida, Gainesville.

McMinn, J.W., and McNab, W.H. (1971). Early growth and development of slash pine under drought and flooding. *U.S. For. Serv. Res. Pap.* No. SE-89.

Macnae, W. (1968). A general account of the fauna and flora of mangrove swamps and forests in the Indo-West-Pacific region. *Adv. Mar. Biol.* 6, 73–270.

MacNeil, F.S. (1950). Pleistocene shorelines in Florida and Georgia. *Geol. Surv. Prof. Pap. (U.S.)* No. 221-F.

McNulty, J.K. (1961). Ecological effects of sewage pollution in Biscayne Bay, Florida: sediments and distribution of benthic and fouling organisms. *Bull. Mar. Sci. Gulf Caribb.* 11, 394–447.

McNulty, J.K., Lindall, W.N., and Sykes, J.E. (1972). Cooperative Gulf of Mexico estuarine inventory and study, Florida: Phase I, area description. *NOAA Tech. Rep. Natl. Mar. Fish. Serv. Circ.* No. 368, Washington, D.C.

McPhee, J. (1966). "Oranges." Farrar, Straus, Giroux, New York.

McPherson, B.F. (1973a). "Vegetation Map of Southern Parts of Subareas A and C, Big Cypress Swamp, Florida." Hydrol. Invest. Atlas HA-492, U.S. Geol. Surv., Washington, D.C.

McPherson, B.F. (1973b). Vegetation in relation to water depth in Conservation Area 3, Florida. *U.S. Geol. Surv. Open-File Rep.* No. FL-73025. Tallahassee, Florida.

McReynolds, R.D. (1983). Gum naval stores production from slash pine. *In* "The Managed Slash Pine Ecosystem" (E.L. Stone, ed.), Proc. Symp., pp. 375–384. Sch. For. Resour. Conserv., Univ. of Florida, Gainesville.

McRoy, C.P., and Barsdate, R.J. (1970). Phosphate absorption in eel grass. *Limnol. Oceanogr.* 15, 14–20.

MacVicar, T.K. (1981). Frequency analysis of rainfall maximums for central and south Florida. *South Fla. Water Manage. Dist. Tech. Publ.* No. 81-3.

MacVicar, T.K., and Lin, S.S.T. (1984). Historical rainfall activity in central and southern Florida: average, return period estimates and selected extremes. *In* "Environments of South Florida: Present and Past II" (P.J. Gleason, ed.), pp. 477–509. Miami Geol. Soc., Coral Gables, Florida.

Maehr, D.S., and Brady, J.R. (1984). Food habits of Florida black bears. *J. Wildl. Manage.* 48, 230–235.

Maissurow, D.K. (1941). The role of fire in the perpetuation of virgin forests of northern Wisconsin. *J. For.* 39, 201–207.

Marathe, K.V. (1965). A study of the subterranean algae flora of some mangrove swamps. *J. Indian Soc. Soil Sci.* 13, 81–84.

March, E.W. (1949). The pine forests of the Bahamas. *Emp. For. Rev.* 28, 33–37.

Marinucci, A.C. (1982). Trophic importance of *Spartina alterniflora* production and decomposition to the marsh-estuarine ecosystem. *Biol. Conserv.* 22, 35–58.

Marion, W.R., and O'Meara, T.E. (1982). Wildlife dynamics in managed flatwoods of north Florida. *Annu. Symp. Proc. Impacts Intensive For. Manage. Pract., 14th,* pp. 63–67. Sch. For. Resour. Conserv., Univ. of Florida, Gainesville.

Marks, P.L., and Harcombe, P.A. (1975). Community diversity of coastal plain forests in southern east Texas. *Ecology* 56, 1004–1008.

Marks, P.L., and Harcombe, P.A. (1981). Forest vegetation of the Big Thicket, southeast Texas. *Ecol. Monogr.* 51, 287–305.

Marois, K.C., and Ewel, K.C. (1983). Natural and management-related variation in cypress domes. *For. Sci.* 29, 627–640.

Marsden, J.R. (1960). Polychaetous annelids from the shallow waters around Barbados and other islands of the West Indies, with notes on larval forms. *Can. J. Zool.* 38, 989–1020.

Marsden, J.R. (1962). A coral-eating polychaete. *Nature (London)* 193, 598.

Marshall, A.R., Hartwell, J.H., Anthony, D.S., Betz, J.V., Lugo, A.E., Veri, A.R., and Wilson, S.U. (1972). "The Kissimmee-Okeechobee Basin." Rep. to Florida Cabinet, Tallahassee.

Marshall, N. (1947). The spring run and cave inhabitats of *Erimystax harperi* (Fowler). *Ecology* 28, 68–75.

Marszalek, D., Babashoff, G., Noel, M., and Worley, P. (1977). Reef distribution in south Florida. *Proc. Int. Coral Reef Symp., 3rd, Miami, Fla.* 2, 223–230.

Martens, J.H.C. (1931). "Beaches of Florida." Florida Geol. Surv. Annu. Rep. 21st and 22nd, pp. 67–119, Tallahassee.

Marx, J.M., and Herrnkind, W.F. (1985). Macroalgae (Rhodophyta: *Laurencia* spp.) as habitat for young juvenile lobsters, *Panulirus argus. Bull. Mar. Sci.* 36, 423–431.

Mattraw, H.C., Jr., and Elder, J.F. (1984). Nutrient and detritus transport in the Apalachicola River, Florida. *U.S. Geol. Surv. Water-Supply Pap.* No. 2196-C.

Mattson, J., and DeFoor, J. (1985). Natural resource damages: restitution as a mechanism to slow destruction of Florida's natural resources. *J. Land Use Environ. Law* 1, 295–319.

Mauro, N.A. (1975). The premetamorphic development rate of *Phragmatopoma lapidosa* Kinberg, 1867, compared with that in temperate sabellariids (Polychaete: Sabellariidae). *Bull. Mar. Sci.* 25, 387–392.

Mayer, A. (1902). The Tortugas as a station for research in biology. *Science* 17, 190–192.

Mayer, A.G. (1914). The effects of temperature upon tropical marine animals. *Pap. Tortugas Lab. Carnegie Inst. Wash.* 6, 1–14.

Meade, R.H. (1982). Sources, sinks, and storage of river sediment in the Atlantic drainage of the United States. *J. Geol.* 90, 235–252.

Meade, R.H., and Parker, R.S. (1985). Sediment in rivers of the United States. *In* "National Water Summary 1984: Hydrologic Events, Selected Water-Quality Trends, and Ground-Water Resources." *U.S. Geol. Surv. Water-Supply Pap.* No. 2275, pp. 49–60.

Meanley, B. (1985). "The Marsh Hen: a Natural History of the Clapper Rail of the Atlantic Coast Salt Marsh." Tidewater Publ., Centerville, Maryland.

Means, D.B. (1975). Competitive exclusion along a habitat gradient between two species of salamaders (*Desmognathus*) in western Florida. *J. Biogeogr.* 2, 253–263.

Means, D.B., and Campbell, H.W. (1982). Effects of prescribed burning on amphibians and reptiles. *In* "Prescribed Fire and Wildlife in Southern Forests" (G.W. Wood, ed.), pp. 89–97. Belle W. Baruch For. Sci. Inst. Clemson Univ., Georgetown, South Carolina.

Means, D.B., and Grow, G. (1985). The endangered longleaf pine community. *ENFO* 85, 1–12.

Means, D.B., and Moler, P.E. (1979). The pine barrens treefrog: fire, seepage bogs, and management implications. *Proc. Rare Endangered Wildl. Symp.* (R.R. Odom and L. Landers, eds.), Tech. Bull. WL4, pp. 77–83. Georgia Dep. Nat. Resour. Game Fish Div., Atlanta.

Means, D.B., and Simberloff, D. (1987). The peninsula effect: habitat-correlated species decline in Florida's herpetofauna. *J. Biogeogr.* 14, 551–568.

Mehta, A.J., Dean, R.G., Dally, W.R., and Montague, C.L. (1987). "Some Considerations on Coastal Processes Relevant to Sea Level Rise." Final Rep. to Oak Ridge Natl. Lab., Coastal Oceanogr. Eng. Dep., Univ. of Florida, UFL/COEL-87/012.

Meredith, W.H., Saveikis, D.E., and Stachecki, C.J. (1985). Guidelines for "open marsh water management" in Delaware's salt marshes—objectives, system designs, and installation procedures. *Wetlands* 5, 119–133.

Mergner, H. (1977). Hydroids as indicator species for ecological parameters in Caribbean and Red Sea coral reefs. *Proc. Int. Coral Reef Symp., 3rd, Miami, Fla.* 2, 119–126.

Merriam, C.H. (1898). "Life zones and crop zones of the United States." *Bull. USDA Div. Biol. Surv.* No. 10.

Meyer, J.L., Schulte, E.T., and Helfman, G.S. (1983). Fish schools: an asset to corals. *Science* 220, 1047–1049.

Meylan, P.A. (1982). The squamate reptiles of the Inglis IA fauna (Irvingtonian: Citrus County, Florida). *Bull. Fla. State Mus.* 27, 1–85.

Meylan, P.A. (1984). A history of fossil Amphibians and Reptiles in Florida. *Plaster Jacket* 44, 5–29.

Milanich, J.T., and Fairbanks, C.H. (1980). "Florida Archeology." Academic Press, New York.

Millar, P.S. (1981). "Water Quality Analysis in the Water Conservation Areas 1978 and 1979." South Florida Water Manage. Dist. Rep.

Miller, J., Huffman, J., and Morris, J. (1983). "The Changing Landscape of Northport, Florida, as Related to Wildlife Habitat and Burning." Environ. Stud. Program Rep., New Coll. of Univ. of South Florida, Sarasota.

Miller, P.C. (1972). Bioclimate, leaf temperature, and primary production in red mangrove canopies in south Florida. *Ecology* 53, 22–45.

Miller, R. (1950). Ecological comparisons of plant communities of the xeric pine type on sand ridges in central Florida. M.S. Thesis, Univ. of Florida, Gainesville.

Milleson, J.F. (1976). Environmental responses to marshland reflooding in the Kissimmee River Basin. *South Fla. Water Manage. Dist. Tech. Publ.* No. 76-3.

Milleson, J.F., Goodrick, R.L., and Van Arman, J.A. (1980). Plant communities of the Kissimmee River Valley. *South Fla. Water Manage. Dist. Tech. Rep.* No. 80-7.

Milliman, J.D., and Emery, K.O. (1968). Sea levels during the past 35,000 years. *Science* 162, 1121–1123.

Millspaugh, C.F. (1907). "Flora of the Sand Keys of Florida." Publ. No. 118, Bot. Ser. Vol. II, No. 5. Field Columbian Mus., Chicago, Illinois.

Mincey, E.F., Yates, H.E., and Butson, K.D. (1967). "South Florida weather summary. Weather Forecasting Mimeo WEA 68-1." Fed.-State Agric. Weather Serv., Lakeland, Florida.

Minno, M. (1987). "The pollination biology and ecology of Curtiss' milkweed (*Asclepias curtissii*)." Proj. No. GFC-86-027, Florida Game Fresh Water Fish Comm., Tallahassee.

Mirov, N.T. (1967). "The Genus *Pinus*." Ronald Press, New York.

Missimer, T.M. (1973). Growth rates of beach ridges on Sanibel Island, Florida. *Trans. Gulf Coast Assoc. Geol. Soc.* 23, 383–393.

Mitchell, R.S. (1963). Phytogeography and floristic survey of a relic area in the Marianna Lowlands, Florida. *Am. Midl. Nat.* 69, 328–366.

Mitchell, R., and Chet, I. (1975). Bacterial attack of corals in polluted seawater. *Microb. Ecol.* 2, 227–233.

Mitsch, W.J. (1976). Ecosystem modeling of water hyacinth management in Lake Alice, Florida. *Ecol. Modell.* 2, 69–89.

Mitsch, W.J., and Ewel, K.C. (1979). Comparative biomass and growth of cypress in Florida wetlands. *Am. Midl. Nat.* 101, 417–426.

Mitsch, W.J., and Gosselink, J.G. (1986). "Wetlands." Van Nostrand-Reinhold, New York.

Mitsch, W.J., Dorge, C.L., and Wiemhoff, J.R. (1979). Ecosystem dynamics and a phosphorus budget of an alluvial cypress swamp in southern Illinois. *Ecology* 60, 1116–1124.

Mitsudera, M.S., Nemoto, S., and Numata, N. (1965). Ecological studies on the coastal pine forest. III. Investigation on environmental factors checking growth. *J. Coll. Arts Sci. Chiba Univ.* 4, 277–288.

Moe, M.A., Jr. (1963). A survey of offshore fishing in Florida. *Fla. State Board Conserv. Mar. Lab. Prof. Pap. Ser.* No. 4, pp. 1–117.

Mogil, H.M., Stern, A., and Hagan, R. (1984). The great freeze of '83: analyzing the causes and the effects. *Weatherwise,* pp. 304–308.

Mohlenbrock, R.H. (1976). Woody plants of the Ocala National Forest, Florida. *Castanea* 41, 309–319.

Monk, C.D. (1960). A preliminary study on the relationships between the vegetation of a mesic hammock community and a sandhill community. *Q. J. Fla. Acad. Sci.* 23, 1–12.

Monk, C.D. (1965). Southern mixed hardwood forests of north central Florida. *Ecol. Monogr.* 35, 335–354.

Monk, C.D. (1966a). An ecological significance of evergreenness. *Ecology* 47, 504–505.

Monk, C.D. (1966b). An ecological study of hardwood swamps in north-central Florida. *Ecology* 47, 649–654.

Monk, C.D. (1967). Tree species diversity in the eastern deciduous forest with particular reference to north-central Florida. *Am. Nat.* 101, 173–187.

Monk, C.D. (1968). Successional and environmental relationships of the forest vegetation of north-central Florida. *Am. Midl. Nat.* 79, 441–457.

Monk, C.D., and Brown, T.W. (1965). Ecological consideration of cypress heads in north-central Florida. *Am. Midl. Nat.* 74, 126–140.

Montague, C.L. (1980a). A natural history of temperate western Atlantic fiddler crabs (genus *Uca*) with reference to their impact on the salt marsh. *Contrib. Mar. Sci. 23,* 25–55.

Montague, C.L. (1980b). The net influence of the mud fiddler crab, *Uca pugnax,* on carbon flow through a Georgia salt marsh: the importance of work by macroorganisms to the metabolism of ecosystems. Ph.D. Thesis, Univ. of Georgia, Athens.

Montague, C.L. (1982). The influence of fiddler crab burrows and burrowing on metabolic processes in salt marsh sediments. *In* "Estuarine Comparisons" (V.S. Kennedy, ed.), pp. 283–301. Academic Press, New York.

Montague, C.L., Bunker, S.M., Haines, E.B., Pace, M.L., and Wetzel, R.L. (1981a). Aquatic macroconsumers. *In* "The Ecology of a Salt Marsh" (L.R. Pomeroy and R.G. Wiegert, eds.), pp. 69–85. Springer-Verlag, New York.

Montague, C.L., Caldwell, J.W., and Knight, R.L. (1981b). "Record of Metabolism of Estuarine Ecosystems at Crystal River, Florida, 1977–1980." Final Rep. to Fla. Power Corp., Contract No. QEA-000045. Syst. Ecol. Energy Anal. Group, Univ. of Florida, Gainesville.

Montague, C.L., Zale, A.V., and Percival, H.F. (1984). Photographic analysis of natural and impounded salt marsh in the vicinity of Merritt Island, Florida. *Fla. Coop. Fish Wildl. Res. Unit Univ. Fla. Tech. Rep.* No. 11.

Montague, C.L., Zale, A.V., and Percival, H.F. (1985). Final report: a conceptual model of salt marsh management of Merritt Island National Wildlife Refuge, Florida. *Fla. Coop. Fish Wildl. Res. Unit Univ. Fla. Tech. Rep.* No. 17.

Montague, C.L., Zale, A.V., and Percival, H.F. (1987a). Ecological effects of coastal marsh impoundments: a review. *Environ. Manage.* 11, 743–756.

Montague, C.L., Zale, A.V., and Percival, H.F. (1987b). The nature of export from fringing marshes, with reference to the production of estuarine animals and the effect of impoundments. *In* "Waterfowl and Wetlands Symposium: Proc. Symp. Waterfowl and Wetlands Management in the Coastal Zone of the Atlantic Flyway" (W.R. Whitman and W.H. Meredith, eds.), pp. 437–450. Del. Coastal Manage. Program, Delaware Dep. Nat. Resour. Environ. Control, Dover.

Montague, C.L., Zale, A.V., and Percival, H.F. (n.d.). "The Ecology and Management of Impounded Coastal Wetlands of the Southeastern United States: Literature Synthesis and Management Options." Draft ms. submitted to U.S. Fish Wildl. Serv., Off. Biol. Serv., Fort Collins, Colorado.

Moody, H.L. (1957). A fisheries study of Lake Panasoffkee, Florida. *Q. J. Fla. Acad. Sci.* 20, 21–88.

Moore, B.J. (1968). The macrolichen flora of Florida. *Bryologist* 71, 161.

Moore, D., and Bullis, H., Jr. (1960). A deep-water coral reef in the Gulf of Mexico. *Bull. Mar. Sci. Gulf Caribb.*, 10, 125–128.

Moore, W.E. (1955). Geology of Jackson County, Florida. *Fla. State Geol. Surv. Geol. Bull.* No. 37.

Moore, W.H., and Swindel, B.F. (1981). Effects of site preparation on dry prairie vegetation in south Florida. *South. J. Appl. For.* 5, 89–92.

Moore, W.H., and Terry, W.S. (1980). Effects of clearcut harvest followed by site preparation on a north Florida flatwoods site. *Univ. Fla. Intensive Manage. Pract. Assess. Cent. (IMPAC) Rep.* No. 5(1).

Moore, W.H., Swindel, B.F., and Terry, W.S. (1982). Vegetation responses to prescribed fire in a north Florida flatwoods forest. *J. Range Manage.* 35, 386–389.

Moreno-Casasola, P. (1985). Ecological studies on sand dune vegetation along the Mexican Gulf coast. Ph.D. Thesis, Inst. Ecol. Bot., Uppsala Univ.

Morgan, G.S., and Pratt, A.E. (1988). An early Miocene (late Hemingfordian) vertebrate fauna from Brooks Sink, Bradford Co., Florida. *In* "Southeastern Geological Society Annual Field Trip Guidebook," pp. 53–69.

Morgan, G.S., and Ridgeway, B. (1987). Late Pliocene (late Blancan) vertebrates from the St. Petersburg Times Site, Pinellas County, Florida, with a brief review of Florida Blancan Faunas. *Fla. Papers in Paleontology*, vol. 1, pp. 1–22.

Morrill, S., and Harvey, J. (1980). "An Environmental Assessment of North Captiva Island, Lee County, Florida." Environ. Stud. Program Publ. No. 23. New Coll., Sarasota, Florida.

Morris, L.A. (1981). Redistribution and mobilization of nutrients as a result of harvest and site preparation of a pine flatwoods forest. Ph.D. Thesis, Univ. of Florida, Gainesville.

Morris, T.L. (1974). Water hyacinth *Eichornia crassipes* (Mart.) Solms: its ability to invade aquatic ecosystems of Paynes Prairie Preserve. M.S. Thesis, Univ. of Florida, Gainesville.

Mueller-Dombois, D. (1981). Fire in tropical ecosystems. *In* "Fire Regimes and Ecosystems Properties" (H.A. Mooney, T.M. Bonnickson, N.L. Christensen, J.E. Lotan, and W.A. Reiners, eds.), *U.S. For. Serv. Gen. Tech. Rep.* No. WO-26, pp. 137–176.

Mukudan, C., and Pillai, C., eds. (1972). *Symp. Corals Coral Reefs.* Cochin Mar. Biol. Assoc., Cochin, India.

Mulhern, E. (1976). A toxicity study of three refined fuel oils and a reference toxicant with respect to the sabellarid worm *Phragmatopoma lapidosa.* M.S. Thesis, Florida Inst. Technol., Melbourne.

Multer, H., and Milleman, J. (1967). Geologic aspects of sabellarid reefs, south eastern Florida. *Bull. Mar. Sci.* 17, 257–267.

Mulvania, M. (1931). Ecological survey of the Florida scrub. *Ecology* 12, 528–540.

Munn, R.E. (1966). "Descriptive Micrometeorology," Vol. 37, No. 6. Academic Press, New York.

Murphy, P.G., and Lugo, A.E. (1986). Structure and biomass of a subtropical dry forest in Puerto Rico. *Biotropica* 18, 89–96.

Muscatine, L. (1980). Productivity of zooxanthellae. *In* "Primary Productivity in the Sea" (P. Falkowski, ed.), pp. 381–402. Plenum, New York.

Muscatine, L., and Porter, J.W. (1977). Reef corals: mutualistic symbiosis adapted to nutrient-poor environments. *BioScience* 27, 454–460.

Mutch, R.W. (1970). Wildland fires and ecosystems—a hypothesis. *Ecology* 51, 1046–1051.

Myers, R.L. (1983). Site susceptibility to invasion by the exotic tree *Melaleuca quinquenervia* in southern Florida. *J. Appl. Ecol.* 20, 645–658.

Myers, R.L. (1984). Ecological compression of *Taxodium distichum* var. *nutans* by *Melaleuca quinquenervia* in southern Florida. *In* "Cypress Swamps" (K.C. Ewel and H.T. Odum, eds.), pp. 358–364. Univ. Presses of Florida, Gainesville.

Myers, R.L. (1985). Fire and the dynamic relationship between Florida sandhill and sand pine scrub vegetation. *Bull. Torrey Bot. Club* 112, 241–252.

Myers, R.L. (1986). Florida's freezes: an analog of short-duration nuclear winter events in the tropics. *Fla. Sci.* 49, 104–115.

Myers, R.L. (1989). Condominiums, trailer parks, and high-intensity fires: the future of sand pine scrub preserves in Florida. 17th Tall Timbers Fire Ecology Conference, Tallahassee.

Myers, R.L., and White, D.L. (1987). Landscape history and changes in sandhill vegetation in north-central and south-central Florida. *Bull. Torrey Bot. Club* 114, 21–32.

Myers, R.L., Boettcher, S.E., and Tuck, H.A. (1987). Seeding response of sand pine (*Pinus clausa*) following fire. *ASB Bull.* 34, 68–69.

Mytinger, L. (1979). A successional survey of the fire climax communities of Myakka River State Park. Senior Thesis, New Coll. of Univ. of South Florida, Sarasota, Florida.

Naka, K. (1982). Community dynamics of evergreen broadleaf forests in southwestern Japan. I. Wind damaged trees and canopy gaps in an evergreen oak forest. *Bot. Mag.* (Tokyo) 95, 385–399.

Namias, J. (1978). The enigma of drought—a challenge for terrestrial and extra terrestrial research. *In* "Solar-Terrestrial Influences on Weather and Climate" (B.M. McCormac and T.A. Seliga, eds.), pp. 41–43. Reidel, Boston, Massachusetts.

Nash, G.V. (1895). Notes on some Florida plants. *Bull. Torrey Bot. Club* 22, 141–161.

National Marine Fisheries Service (1983). "End-of-year Report: Annual Landings by Distance Caught from Shore—Southeast Region for CY82 (Preliminary)." Natl. Mar. Fish. Serv., Southeast Fish. Cent., Miami, Florida.

National Marine Fisheries Service (1984). "End-of-year Report: Annual Landings by Distance Caught from Shore—Southeast Region for CY83 (Preliminary)." Natl. Mar. Fish. Serv., Southeast Fish. Cent., Miami, Florida.

National Marine Fisheries Service (1985). "End-of-year Report: Annual Landings by Distance Caught from Shore—Southeast Region for CY84 (Preliminary)." Natl. Mar. Fish. Serv., Southeast Fish. Cent., Miami, Florida.

Neel, L. (1967). Head fires in southeastern pines. *Proc. Tall Timbers Fire Ecol. Conf.* 4, 231–240.

Neill, W.T. (1957). Historical biogeography of present-day Florida. *Bull. Fla. State Mus.* 2, 175–221.

Neill, W.T. (1958). The occurrence of amphibians and reptiles in saltwater areas, and a bibliography. *Bull. Mar. Sci. Gulf Caribb.* 8, 1–97.

Nelson, W., and Main, M. (1985). Criteria for beach nourishment: biological guidelines for sabellariid worm reef. *Fla. Sea Grant Tech. Pap.* No. 33.

Nesbitt, S.A., Ogden, J.C., Kale, H.W., II, Patty, B.W., and Rowse, L.A. (1982). "Florida Atlas of Breeding Sites for Herons and Their Allies: 1976–78." *U.S. Dep. Fish Wildl. Serv. Off. Biol. Serv. [Tech. Rep.] FWS/OBS* 81-49.

Nessel, J.K., and Bayley, S.E. (1984). Distribution and dynamics of organic matter and phosphorus in a sewage-enriched cypress swamp. *In* "Cypress Swamps" (K.C. Ewel and H.T. Odum, eds.), pp. 262–278. Univ. Presses of Florida, Gainesville.

Nessel, J.K., Ewel, K.C., and Burnett, M.S. (1982). Wastewater enrichment increases mature pond cypress growth rates. *For. Sci.* 28, 400–403.

Nestler, J. (1977). Interstitial salinity as a cause of ecospheric variation in *Spartina alterniflora. Estuarine Coastal Mar. Sci.* 5, 707–714.

Neufeld, H.S. (1983). Effects of light on growth, morphology, and photosynthesis in bald cypress (*Taxodium distichum* (L.) Rich) and pondcypress (*T. ascendens* Brongn.) seedlings. *Bull. Torrey Bot. Club* 110, 43–54.

Neumann, A.C. (1966). Observations on coastal erosion in Bermuda and measurements of the boring rate of the sponge, *Cliona lampa. Limnol. Oceanogr.* 11, 92–108.

Neumann, A.C., and Ball, M. (1970). Submersible observations in the Straits of Florida: geology and bottom currents. *Geol. Soc. Am. Bull.* 81, 2861–2874.

Neumann, A.C., Kofoed, J., and Keller, G. (1977). Lithoherms in the Straits of Florida. *Geology* 5, 4–10.

Neumann, C.J., Cry, G.W., Caso, E.L., and Jarvinen, B.R. (1985). "Tropical Cyclones of the North Atlantic Ocean, 1871–1980, with Storm Track Maps Updated through 1984." Natl. Clim. Data Cent., Asheville, North Carolina.

Nickerson, N.H., and Thibodeau, F.R. (1985). Association between pore water sulfide concentrations and the distribution of mangroves. *Biogeochemistry* 1, 183–192.

Nieuwolt, S. (1977). "Tropical Climatology." Wiley, New York.

Nixon, E.S., Trotty, W.F., Bates, B.L., and Wilkinson, D.L. (1977). Analysis of stump vegetation in an east Texas pond. *Tex. J. Sci.* 28, 366–367.

Nixon, S.W. (1980). Between coastal marshes and coastal waters—a review of twenty years of speculation and research on the role of salt marshes in estuarine productivity and water chemistry. *In* "Estuarine and Wetland Processes" (P. Hamilton and K.B. MacDonald, eds.), pp. 437–525. Plenum, New York.

Nixon, S.W. (1982). "The Ecology of New England High Salt Marshes: a Community Profile." *U.S. Fish Wildl. Serv. Off. Biol. Serv. [Tech. Rep.] FWS/OBS* 81-55.

NOAA (National Oceanographic and Atmospheric Administration) (1930–1985). "Climatological Data Florida." Natl. Clim. Data Cent., Asheville, North Carolina.

Nordlie, F.G. (1972). Thermal stratification and annual heat budget of a Florida sinkhole lake. *Hydrobiologia* 40, 183–200.

Nordlie, F.G. (1976). Plankton communities of three central Florida lakes. *Hydrobiologia* 48, 65–78.

Norman, E.M. (1976). An analysis of the vegetation at Turtle Mound. *Fla. Sci.* 39, 19–31.

Noss, R.F. (1988). The longleaf pine landscape of the southeast: almost gone and almost forgotten. *Endangered Species Update* 5, 1–8.

Noss, R.F., and Harris, L.D. (1986). Nodes, networks, and MUMs: preserving diversity at all scales. *Environ. Manage.* 10, 299–309.

Nummedal, D. (1983). Barrier Islands. *In* "CRC Handbook of Coastal Processes and Erosion" (P.D. Komar, ed.), pp. 77–121. CRC Press, Boca Raton, Florida.

Ober, L.D. (1954). Plant communities of the flatwood forests in Austin Cary Memorial Forest. M.S. Thesis, Univ. of Florida, Gainesville.

Odell, D.K., and Reynolds, J.E. (1979). Observations on manatee mortality in south Florida. *J. Wildl. Manage.* 43, 572–577.

Odum, E.P. (1971). "Fundamentals of Ecology." Saunders, Philadelphia, Pennsylvania.

Odum, E.P. (1980). The status of three ecosystem-level hypotheses regarding salt marsh estuaries: tidal subsidy, outwelling, and detritus-based food chains. In "Estuarine Perspectives" (V.S. Kennedy, ed.), pp. 485–495. Academic Press, New York.

Odum, E.P., Birch, J.B., and Cooley, J.L. (1983). Comparison of giant cutgrass productivity in tidal and impounded marshes with special reference to tidal subsidy and waste assimilation. *Estuaries* 6, 88–94.

Odum, H.T. (1953). Factors controlling marine invasion into Florida fresh waters. *Bull. Mar. Sci. Gulf Caribb.* 3, 134–156.

Odum, H.T. (1956). Primary production in flowing waters. *Limnol. Oceanogr.* 1, 102–117.

Odum, H.T. (1957a). Primary production measurements in eleven Florida springs and a marine turtle grass community. *Limnol. Oceanogr.* 2, 85–97.

Odum, H.T. (1957b). Trophic structure and productivity of Silver Springs, Florida. *Ecol. Monogr.* 27, 55–112.

Odum, H.T. (1984). Summary: cypress swamps and their regional role. *In* "Cypress Swamps" (K.C. Ewel and H.T. Odum, eds.), pp. 416–443. Univ. Presses of Florida, Gainesville.

Odum, H.T., and Jordan, C.F. (1970). Metabolism and evapotranspiration of the lower forest in a giant plastic cylinder. *In* "A Tropical Rain Forest" (H.T. Odum and R.F. Pidgeon, eds.), pp. I-165–I-189. Div. Tech. Inf., USAEC, Oak Ridge, Tennessee.

Odum, W.E. (1968). Mullet grazing on a dinoflagellate bloom. *Chesapeake Sci.* 9, 202–204.

Odum, W.E. (1970). Pathways of energy flow in a south Florida estuary. Ph.D. Thesis, Univ. of Miami, Coral Gables, Florida.

Odum, W.E., and Heald, E.J. (1972). Trophic analyses of an estuarine mangrove community. *Bull. Mar. Sci.* 22, 671–738.

Odum, W.E., and Heald, E.J. (1975a). The detritus-based food web of an estuarine mangrove community. In "Estuarine Research," pp. 265–286. Academic Press, New York.

Odum, W.E., and Heald, E.J. (1975b). Mangrove forests and aquatic productivity. *In* "An Introduction to Land-Water Interactions," Chapt. 5. Ecol. Study Ser. Springer-Verlag, New York.

Odum, W.E., and Johannes, R.E. (1975). The response of mangroves to man-induced environmental stress. *In* "Tropical Marine Pollution" (E.J.F. Wood and R.E. Johannes, eds.), pp. 52–62. Oceanogr. Ser. Elsevier, Amsterdam.

Odum, W.E., Fisher, J.S., and Pickral, J. (1979). Factors controlling the flux of particulate organic carbon from estuarine wetlands. *In* "Ecological Processes in Coastal and Marine Systems" (R.J. Livingston, ed.), pp. 69–80. Plenum, New York.

Odum, W.E., McIvor, C.C., and Smith, T.J., III (1982). "The Ecology of the Mangroves of South Florida: a Community Profile." *U.S. Fish Wildl. Serv. Off. Biol. Serv., [Tech. Rep.] FWS/OBS* 81-24.

Oertel, G.F., and Lassen, M. (1976). Developmental sequences in Georgia coastal dunes and distribution of dune plants. *Bull. Ga. Acad. Sci.* 34, 35–48.

Oesterling, M.E., and Evink, G.L. (1977). Relationship between Florida's blue crab population and Apalachicola Bay. *Proc. Conf. Apalachicola Drain. Syst.* (R.J. Livingston and E.A. Joyce, eds.), Publ. No. 26, pp. 101–121. Florida Dep. Nat. Resour. Mar. Res. Lab., Tallahassee.

Ogden, J.C. (1980). Faunal relationships in Caribbean seagrass beds. *In* "Handbook of Seagrass Biology" (R.C. Phillips and C.P. McRoy, eds.). Garland STPM Press, New York.

Ogden, J., and Lobel, P. (1978). The role of herbivorous fishes and urchins in coral reef communities. *Environ. Biol. Fishes* 3, 49–63.

Oliver, C.D. (1978). Subsurface geological formation and site variation in the upper sand hills of South Carolina. *J. For.* 76, 352–354.

Oliver, C.D. (1981). Forest development in North America following major disturbances. *For. Ecol. Manage.* 3, 153–168.

Oliver, J., Chalker, B., and Dunlap, W. (1983). Bathymetric adaptations of reef-building corals at Davis Reef, Great Barrier Reef, Australia. I. Long-term growth responses of *Acropora formosa* (Dana, 1846). *J. Exp. Mar. Biol. Ecol.* 73, 11–35.

Olmsted, I.C., and Loope, L.L. (1984). Plant communities of Everglades National Park. *In* "Environments of South Florida: Present and Past II" (P.J. Gleason, ed.), pp. 167–184. Miami Geol. Soc., Coral Gables, Florida.

Olmsted, I.C., Loope, L.L., and Hilsenbeck, C.E. (1980). Tropical hardwood hammocks of the interior of Everglades National Park and Big Cypress National Preserve. *Everglades Natl. Park South Fla. Res. Cent. Rep.* No. T-604.

Olmsted, I.C., Loope, L.L., and Russell, R.P. (1981). Vegetation of the southern coastal region of Everglades National Park between Flamingo and Joe Bay. *Everglades Natl. Park South Fla. Res. Cent. Rep.* No. T-620.

Olmsted, I.C., Robertson, W.B., Jr., Johnson, J., and Bass, O.L., Jr. (1983). The vegetation of Long Pine Key, Everglades National Park. *Everglades Natl. Park South Fla. Res. Cent. Rep.* No. SFRC-83/05.

Olson, J.S. (1958). Lake Michigan dune development. 1. Wind velocity profiles. 2. Plants as agents and tools in geomophology. *J. Geol.* 66, 254–263; 345–351.

Onuf, C.P., Teal, J.M., and Valiela, I. (1977). Interactions of nutrients, plant growth, and herbivory in a mangrove ecosystem. *Ecology* 58, 514–526.

Oosting, H.J. (1944). The comparative effect of surface and crown fire on the composition of a loblolly pine community. *Ecology* 25, 61–69.

Oosting, H.J. (1945). Tolerance to salt spray of plants of coastal dunes. *Ecology* 26, 85–89.

Opdyke, N.D., Spangler, D.P., Smith, D.L., Jones, D.S., and Lindquist, R.C. (1984). Origin of the epeirogenic uplift of Pliocene-Pleistocene beach ridges in Florida and development of the Florida karst. *Geology* 12, 226–228.

Opdyke, N.D., Jones, D.S., MacFadden, B.J., Smith, D.L., Mueller, P.A., and Shuster, R.D. (1987). Florida as an exotic terrane: paleomagnetic and geochronologic investigation of lower Paleozoic rocks from the subsurface of Florida. *Geology* 15, 900–903.

Opresko, D. (1973). Abundance and distribution of shallow-water gorgonians in the area of Miami, Florida. *Bull. Mar. Sci.* 23, 535–558.

Orth, P.G., and Conover, R.A. (1975). Changes in nutrients resulting from farming the Hole-in-the-Doughnut, Everglades National Park. *Proc. Fla. State Hortic. Soc.* 88, 221–225.

Orth, R.J., and Moore, K.A. (1984). Distribution and abundance of submerged aquatic vegetation in Chesapeake Bay: an historical perspective. *Estuaries* 7, 531–540.

Osborne, J.A., Wanielista, M.P., and Yousef, Y.A. (1976). Benthic fauna species diversity in six central Florida lakes in summer. *Hydrobiologia* 48, 125–129.

Ott, B., and Lewis, J. (1972). The importance of the gastropod *Coralliophila abbreviata* (Lamarck) and the polychaete *Hermodice carunculata* (Pallas) as coral reef predators. *Can. J. Zool.* 50, 1651–1656.

Otvos, E.G. (1981). Barrier island formation through nearshore aggradation—stratigraphic and field evidence. *Mar. Geol.* 43, 195–243.

Outcalt, K.W. (1983). A comparison of sand pine varieties in central Florida. *South. J. Appl. For.* 7, 58–59.

Overton, W.S., Kanciruk, P., Hook, L.A., Eilers, J.M., Landers, D.H., Brakke, D.F., Blick, D.J., Jr., Linthurst, R.A., DeHaan, M.D., and Omernik, J.M. (1986). "Characteristics of Lakes in the Eastern United States. Vol. 2: Lakes Sampled and Descriptive Statistics for Physical and Chemical Variables." EPA/600/4-86/007b, U.S. Environ. Prot. Agency, Washington, D.C.

Owre, O.T. (1973). A consideration of the exotic avifauna of southeastern Florida. *Wilson Bull.* 85, 491–500.

Palmer, C.E., and Nguyen, H. (1986). "Long Term Rainfall Deficits in Central Florida: Implications for Water Management." Water Resour. Dep., Imperial Polk

Cty., Bartow, Florida.

Palmer, M.G. (1986). Restoration of the Kissimmee River. *Fla. Defenders Environ. Bull.* No. 17.

Palmer, S.L. (1984). Surface water. *In* "Water Resources Atlas of Florida" (E.A. Fernald and D.J. Patton, eds.), pp. 54–67. Florida State Univ., Tallahassee, Florida.

Parendes, L.A. (1983). An ecological comparison of three sizes of cypress swamps with management implications. M.S. Thesis, Univ. of Florida, Gainesville.

Parker, G.G. (1951). Geologic and hydrologic factors in the perennial yield of the Biscayne Aquifer. *Am. Water Works Assoc. J.* 43, 810–843.

Parker, G.G. (1974). Hydrology of the pre-drainage system of the Everglades in southern Florida. *In* "Environments of South Florida: Present and Past II" (P.J. Gleason, ed.), pp. 28–37. Miami Geol. Soc., Coral Gables, Florida.

Parker, G.G., Ferguson, G.E., Love, S.K., et al. (1955). Water resources of southeastern Florida. *U.S. Geol. Surv. Water-Supply Pap.* No. 1255.

Parrish, F.K., and Rykiel, E.J., Jr. (1979). Okefenokee swamp origin: review and reconsideration. *J. Elisha Mitchell Soc.* 95, 17–31.

Parrott, R.T. (1967). A study of wiregrass (*Aristida stricta* Michx.) with particular reference to fire. M.S. Thesis, Duke Univ., Durham, North Carolina.

Parsons, K.A., and de la Cruz, A.A. (1980). Energy flow and grazing behavior of concephaline grasshoppers in a *Juncus roemerianus* marsh. *Ecology* 61, 1045–1050.

Patterson, G.A., and Robertson, W.B., Jr. (1981). Distribution and habitat of the red-cockaded woodpecker in Big Cypress National Preserve. *Everglades Natl. Park South Fla. Res. Cent. Rep.* No. T-613.

Patterson, G.A., Robertson, W.B., Jr. and Minsky, D.E. (1980). Slash pine–cypress mosaic. *Am. Birds* 34, 61–62.

Patterson, S.G. (1986). Mangrove community boundary interpretation and detection of areal changes in Marco Island, Florida: application of digital image processing and remote sensing techniques. *U.S. Fish Wildl. Serv. Biol. Rep.* No. 86(10).

Patterson-Zucca, C. (1978). The effects of road construction on a mangrove ecosystem. M.S. Thesis, Univ. of Puerto Rico, Rio Piedras.

Patton, J.E., and Judd, W.S. (1986). Vascular flora of Paynes Prairie Basin and Alachua Sink Hammock, Alachua County, FL. *Castanea* 51, 88–110.

Patton, T.H. (1969). An Oligocene land vertebrate fauna from Florida. *J. Paleontol.* 43, 544–546.

Patton, W.K. (1967). Studies on *Domecia acanthophora,* a commensal crab from Puerto Rico, with particular reference to modifications of the coral host and feeding habits. *Biol. Bull. (Woods Hole, Mass.)* 132, 56–67.

Patton, W.K. (1976). Animal associates of living reef corals. *In* "Biology and Geology of Coral Reefs," Vol. 3 (O.A. Jones and R. Endean, eds.), pp. 1–36. Academic Press, New York.

Pearson, P.G. (1954). Mammals of Gulf Hammock, Levy Co., Florida. *Am. Midl. Nat.* 51, 468–485.

Pearson, R. (1981). Recovery and recolonization of coral reefs. *Mar. Ecol. Prog. Ser.* 4, 105–122.

Penfound, W.T. (1952). Southern swamps and marshes. *Bot. Rev.* 18, 413–446.

Penfound, W.T., and Hathaway, E.S. (1938). Plant communities in the marshlands of southeastern Louisiana. *Ecol. Monogr.* 8, 1–56.

Penfound, W.T., and Watkins, A.G. (1937). Phytosociological studies in the pinelands of southeastern Louisiana. *Am. Midl. Nat.* 18, 661–682.

Percival, H.F., Montague, C.L., and Zale, A.V. (1987). A summary of positive and negative aspects of coastal wetland impoundments as habitat for waterfowl. *In* "Waterfowl and Wetlands Symposium: Proc. Symp. Waterfowl and Wetlands Management in the Coastal Zone of the Atlantic Flyway" (W.R. Whitman and W.H. Meredith, eds.), pp. 223–230. Del. Coastal Manage. Program, Delaware Dep. Nat. Resour. Environ. Control, Dover.

Perkins, C.J. (1974). Silvicultural practice impacts on wildlife. *Timber-Wildlife Manage. Symp.* (J.P. Slusher and T.M. Hinckley, eds.). *Mo. Acad. Sci. Occas. Pap.* No. 3, pp. 43–48.

Perkins, P.D. (1977). Depositional framework of Pleistocene rocks in South Florida. Part II. *Geol. Soc. Am. Mem.* No. 147.

Peroni, P.A., and Abrahamson, W.G. (1985). Post-settlement vegetation loss on the southern Lake Wales Ridge, Florida. *Palmetto* 5, 6–7.

Peroni, P.A., and Abrahamson, W.G. (1986). Succession in Florida sandridge vegetation: a retrospective study. *Fla. Sci.* 49, 176–191.

Perrin, L.S., Allen, M.J., Rowse, L.A., Montalbano, F., III, Foote, K.J., and Olinde, M.W. (1982). "A Report on Fish and Wildlife Studies in the Kissimmee River Basin and Recommendations for Restoration." Florida Game Fresh Water Fish Comm., Okeechobee.

Perry, C.S. (1983). Needle litterfall, decomposition, and nitrogen immobilization in an age sequence of slash pine plantations in north Florida. M.S. Thesis, Univ. of Florida, Gainesville.

Pesnell, G.L., and Brown, R.T., III (1977). The major plant communities of Lake Okeechobee, Florida, and their associated inundation characteristics as determined by gradient analysis. *South Fla. Water Manage. Dist. Tech. Publ.* No. 77-1.

Pessin, L.J. (1933). Forest associations in the uplands of the lower gulf coastal plain (longleaf pine belt). *Ecology* 14, 1–14.

Peters, E. (1984). A survey of cellular reactions to environmental stress and disease in Caribbean scleractinian corals. *Helgol. Wiss. Meeresunters* 37, 113–137.

Peters, E., Oprandy, J., and Yevich, P. (1983). Possible causal agent of "white band disease" in Caribbean acroporid corals. *J. Invertebr. Pathol.* 41, 394–396.

Peterson, C.H. (1981). The ecological role of mud flats in estuarine systems. *Proc. U.S. Fish Wildl. Serv. Workshop Coastal Ecosyst. Southeast. U.S.* (R.C. Carey, P.S. Markovits, and J.B. Kirkwood, eds.), pp. 184–192. *U.S. Fish Wildl. Serv. Off. Biol. Serv. [Tech. Rep.] FWS/OBS* 80-59.

Pfeiffer, W.J., and Wiegert, R.G. (1981). Grazers on *Spartina* and their predators. *In* "The Ecology of a Salt Marsh" (L.R. Pomeroy and R.G. Wiegert, eds.), pp. 87–112. Springer-Verlag, New York.

Philipson, J.J., and Coutts, M.P. (1980). The tolerance of tree roots to waterlogging. III. Oxygen transport in lodgepole pine and sitka spruce roots of primary structure. *New Phytol.* 80, 341– 349.

Phillips, W.S. (1940). A tropical hammock on the Miami (Florida) limestone. *Ecology* 21, 166–175.

Phleger, F.B. (1970). Foraminiferal populations and marine marsh processes. *Limnol. Oceanogr.* 15, 522–534.

Pielke, R.A. (1974). A three-dimensional numerical model of the sea breezes over south Florida. *Mon. Weather Rev.* 102, 115–139.

Pielou, E. (1975). "Ecological Diversity." Wiley (Interscience), New York.

Pierce, E.L. (1947). An annual cycle of the plankton and chemistry of four aquatic habitats in northern Florida. *Univ. Fla. Stud. Biol. Sci. Ser. IV,* pp. 1–67.

Pierce, G.J., Amerson, A.B., and Becker, L.R., Jr. (1982). "Pre-1960 Floodplain Vegetation of the Lower Kissimmee River Valley, Florida." Rep. to U.S. Army Corps Eng., Jacksonville, Florida.

Pilkey, O.H., and Field, M.E. (1972). Onshore transportation of continental shelf sediment: Atlantic southeastern United States. *In* "Shelf Sediment Transport: Process and Pattern" (D.J.P. Swift, D.B. Duane, and O.H. Pilkey, eds.). Dowden, Hutchinson, Ross, Stroudsburg, Pennsylvania.

Pilkey, O.H., Jr., Sharma, D.C., Wanless, H.R., Doyle, L.J., Pilkey, O.H., Sr., Neal, W.J., and Gruver, B.L. (1984). "Living with the East Florida Shore." Duke Univ. Press, Durham, North Carolina.

Pilsbry, H.A. (1946). "Land Mollusca of North America (North of Mexico)." Vol. II, Part I. Acad. Nat. Sci. Philadelphia, Monogr. No. 3. Philadelphia, Pennsylvania.

Pilson, M.E.Q., and Betzer, S.B. (1973). Phosphorus flux across a coral reef. *Ecology* 54, 581–588.

Pirkle, E.C., Jr. (1956). Notes on physiographic features of Alachua County, Florida. *Q. J. Fla. Acad. Sci.* 19, 168–182.

Pirkle, E.C., Jr., and Brooks, H.K. (1959). Origin and hydrology of Orange Lake, Santa Fe Lake, and Levys Prairie lakes of north-central peninsular Florida. *J. Geol.* 67, 302–317.

Pirkle, E.C., Pirkle, W.A., and Yoho, W.H. (1977). The highland heavy-mineral sand deposit on trail ridge in northern peninsular Florida. *Bur. Geol. Div. Resour. Manage. Fla. Dep. Nat. Resour. Rep. Invest.* No. 84.

Platt, W.J. (1984). Composition and demography of a sweetgum (*Liquidambar styraciflua*) population in an old-growth magnolia-beech forest. *Bull. Ecol. Soc. Am.* 65, 149.

Platt, W.J. (1985). "The Composition and Dynamics of the Mixed-Species Hardwood Forest in Titi Hammock Preserve, Thomas County, Georgia." Rep. for The Nature Conservancy.

Platt, W.J. (1987). Adaptation to accreting coastal dunes: the myth of the immobile plant. Unpubl. ms.

Platt, W.J., and Hermann, S.M. (1986). Relationships between dispersal syndrome and characteristics of populations of trees in a mixed-species forest. *In* "Frugivores and Seed Dispersal" (A. Estrada, T.H. Fleming, C. Vasques-Yanes, and R. Dirzo, eds.), pp. 309–321. Junk, The Hague.

Platt, W.J., and Platt, M.M. (1990). Life history of a beach morning glory (*Ipomoea stolonifera*: Convolvulaceae) along accreting shorelines of a barrier island. *Oecologia* (in press).

Platt, W.J., Evans, G.W., and Rathbun, S.L. (1988a). The population dynamics of a long-lived conifer (*Pinus palustris*). *Am. Nat.* 131, 491–525.

Platt, W.J., Evans, G.W., and Davis, M.M. (1988b). Effects of fire season on flowering of forbs and shrubs in longleaf pine forests. *Oecologia* 76, 353–363.

Platt, W.J., Glitzenstein, J.S., and Streng, D.R. (1990). Evaluating pyrogenicity and its effects on longleaf pine savannas. *Proc. Tall Timbers Fire Ecol. Conf.* (in press).

Pojeta, J., Jr., Kriz, J., and Berdan, J.M. (1976). Silurian-Devonian pelecypods and Palaeozoic stratigraphy of sub-surface rocks in Florida and Georgia and related Silurian pelecypods from Bolivia and Turkey. *U.S. Geol. Surv. Prof. Pap.* No. 879, pp. 1–39.

Polunin, N. (1960). "Introduction to Plant Geography." McGraw-Hill, New York.

Pomeroy, L.R., and Wiegert, R.G., eds. (1981). "The Ecology of a Salt Marsh." Springer-Verlag, New York.

Pomeroy, L.R., Darley, W.M., Dunn, E.L., Gallagher, J.L., Haines, E.B., and Whitney, D.M. (1981). Primary production. *In* "The Ecology of a Salt Marsh" (L.R. Pomeroy and R.G. Wiegert, eds.), pp. 39–67. Springer-Verlag, New York.

Pool, D.J., Lugo, A.E., and Snedaker, S.C. (1975). Litter production in mangrove forests of southern Florida and Puerto Rico. *Proc. Int. Symp. Biol. Manage. Mangroves* (G. Walsh, S. Snedaker, and H. Teas, eds.), pp. 213–237. Univ. of Florida, Gainesville.

Pool, D.J., Snedaker, S.C., and Lugo, A.E. (1977). Structure of mangrove forests in Florida, Puerto Rico, Mexico, and Central America. *Biotropica* 9, 195–212.

Poppleton, J.E., Shuey, A.G., and Sweet, H.C. (1977). Vegetation of central Florida's east coast: a checklist of vascular plants. *Fla. Sci.* 40, 362–389.

Porter, J., Muscatine, L., Dubinski, Z., and Falkowski, P. (1984). Primary production and photoadaptation in light- and shade-adapted colonies of the symbiotic coral, *Stylophora pistillata. Proc. Soc. London Ser. B* 222, 161–180.

Porter, K.G. (1986). Particle feeding by pigmented phytoflagellates from five phyla: evidence for the ubiquity of algal myxotrophy in freshwater microbial food webs. *Int. Congr. Ecol., 4th, Syracuse, N.Y.* Program abstr.

Post, W. (1981a). The influence of rice rats *Oryzomys palustris* on the habitat use of the seaside sparrow *Ammospiza maritima. Behav. Ecol. Sociobiol.* 9, 35–40.

Post, W. (1981b). Salt marsh. *In* "Forty-fourth Breeding Bird Census" (W.T. Van Valen, ed.). *Am. Birds* 35, 99, 104.

Post, W., Greenlaw, J.S., Merriam, T.L., and Wood, L.A. (1983). Comparative ecology of northern and southern populations of the seaside sparrow. *In* "The Seaside Sparrow, Its Biology and Management, Proc. Symp. Raleigh, N.C., 1981" (T.L. Quay, J.B. Funderburg, Jr., D.S. Lee, E.F. Potter, and C.S. Robbins, eds.), pp. 123–136. Occas. Pap. N.C. Biol. Surv. 1983–1985, North Carolina State Mus. Nat. Hist., Raleigh.

Poulson, T.L., and Platt, W.J. (1989). Gap light regimes influence canopy tree diversity. *Ecology* 70, 553–555.

Pournelle, G.H., and Barrington, B.A. (1953). Notes on the mammals of Anastasia Island, St. Johns County, Florida. *J. Mammal.* 34, 133–135.

Pratt, A.E. (1990). Taphonomy of the large vertebrate fauna from the Thomas Farm locality (Miocene, Hemingfordian), Gilchrist County, Florida. *Bull. Fla. Mus. Ntl. Hist., Biol. Sci.* 35, 35–130.

Price, D.J. (1975). The apparent growth of Gulf Beach, extreme western Florida. *Trans. Gulf Coast Assoc. Geol. Soc.* 25, 369–371.

Pritchard, D.W. (1967). What is an estuary: physical viewpoint. *In* "Estuaries" (G.H. Lauff, ed.), pp. 3–5. Am. Assoc. Adv. Sci., Washington, D.C.

Pritchett, W.L. (1968). Progress in the development of techniques and standards for soil and foliar diagnosis of phosphorus deficiency in slash pine. *In* "Forest Fertilization—Theory and Practice," pp. 81–87. Proc. Symp. For. Fertilization, Tennessee Valley Authority.

Pritchett, W.L. (1981). Site preparation in the coastal flatwoods. *Univ. of Fla. Intensive Manage. Pract. Assess. Cent. (IMPAC) Rep.* No. 6(7).

Pritchett, W.L., and Comerford, N.B. (1982). Long-term response to phosphorus fertilization on selected southeastern coastal plain soils. *Soil Sci. Soc. Am. J.* 46, 640–644.

Pritchett, W.L., and Comerford, N.B. (1983). Nutrition and fertilization of slash pine. *In* "The Managed Slash Pine Ecosystem" (E.L. Stone, ed.), Proc. Symp., pp. 69–90. Sch. For. Resour. Conserv., Univ. of Florida, Gainesville.

Pritchett, W.L., and Morris, L.A. (1982). Implications of intensive forest management for long-term productivity of *Pinus elliottii* flatwoods. *Proc. Annu. Symp. Impacts Intensive For. Manage. Pract., 14th,* pp. 27–34. Sch. For. Resour. Conserv., Univ. of Florida, Gainesville.

Pritchett, W.L., and Smith, W.H. (1974). Management of wet savanna forest soils for pine production. *Fla. Agric. Exp. Stn. Tech. Bull.* No. 762.

Pritchett, W.L., and Smith, W.H. (1975). Forest fertilization in the U.S. southeast. *In* "Forest Soils and Forest Land Management" (B. Bernier and C.H. Winget, eds.), pp. 467–476. Laval Univ. Press, Quebec.

Pritchett, W.L., and Wells, C.G. (1978). Harvesting and site preparation increase nutrient mobilization. *Proc. Symp. Maintaining Prod. Prepared Sites* (T. Tippen, ed.), pp. 98–110. Mississippi State Univ., State College.

Provost, M.W. (1949). Mosquito control and mosquito problems in Florida. *Proc. Annu. Meet. Calif. Mosq. Control Assoc., 17th,* pp. 32–35.

Provost, M.W. (1959). Impounding salt marshes for mosquito control—and its effects on bird life. *Fla. Nat.* 32, 163–169.

Provost, M.W. (1969a). Ecological control of salt marsh mosquitoes with side benefits to birds. *Proc. Tall Timbers Conf. Ecol. Anim. Control Habitat Manage.* 1, 193–206.

Provost, M.W. (1969b). Man, mosquito, and birds. *Fla. Nat.* 42, 63–67.

Provost, M.W. (1973a). Mean high water mark and use of tidelands in Florida. *Fla. Sci.* 36, 50–66.

Provost, M.W. (1973b). Salt marsh management in Florida. *Proc. Tall Timbers Conf. Ecol. Anim. Control Habitat Manage.* 5, 5–17.

Provost, M.W. (1976). Tidal datum planes circumscribing salt marshes. *Bull. Mar. Sci.* 26, 558–563.

Provost, M.W. (1977). Source reduction in salt-marsh mosquito control: past and future. *Mosq. News* 37, 689–698.

Pruitt, B.C., and Gatewood, S.E. (1976). "Kissimmee River Floodplain Vegetation and Cattle Capacity Before and After Canalization." Div. State Plann., Florida Dep. Adm., Tallahassee.

Psuty, N.P. (1983). Options and alternatives. *In* "Crisis of Our Beaches," *Environ. Sci. Publ.* No. 35, pp. 123–132. New Coll., Sarasota, Florida.

Puri, H.S. (1953). Contribution to the study of the Miocene of the Florida panhandle. *Fla. Geol. Surv. Geol. Bull.* No. 36.

Puri, H.S., and Vernon, R.O. (1964). Summary of the geology of Florida and a guidebook to the classic exposures. *Fla. Geol. Surv. Spec. Publ.* No. 5 (revised).

Putnam, J.A. (1951). Management of bottomland hardwoods. *U.S. For. Serv. South. For. Exp. Stn. Occas. Pap.* No. 116.

Putnam, J.A., Gurnival, G.M., and McKnight, J.S. (1960). Management and inventory of southern hardwoods. *U.S. For. Serv. Agric. Handb.* No. 181.

Pylka, V.M., and Warren, R.D. (1958). A population of *Haideotriton* in Florida. *Copeia,* pp. 334–336.

Pyne, S.J. (1982). "Fire in America: A Cultural History of Wildland and Rural Fire." Princeton Univ. Press, Princeton, New Jersey.

Quarterman, E. (1981). A fresh look at climax forests of the Coastal Plain. *ASB Bull.* 28, 143–148.

Quarterman, E., and Keever, C. (1962). Southern mixed hardwood forest: climax in the southeastern coastal plain, U.S.A. Ecol. Monogr. 32, 167–185.

Quiroz, R.S. (1984). Season climate summary of the 1983–84 winter—a season of strong blocking and severe cold in North America. *Mon. Weather Rev.* 112, 426–433.

Rabinowitz, D. (1975). Planting experiments in mangrove swamps of Panama. *Proc. Int. Symp. Biol. Manage. Mangroves* (G. Walsh, S. Snedaker, and H. Teas, eds.), pp. 385–393. Univ. of Florida, Gainesville.

Rabinowitz, D. (1978a). Dispersal properties of mangrove propagules. *Biotropica* 10, 47–57.

Rabinowitz, D. (1978b). Early growth of mangrove seedlings in Panama, and an hypothesis concerning the relationship of dispersal and zonation. *J. Biogeogr.* 5, 113–133.

Radford, A.E., Ahles, H.E., and Bell, C.R. (1968). "Manual of the Vascular Flora of the Carolinas." Univ. of North Carolina Press, Chapel Hill.

Ragotzkie, R.A. (1959). Plankton productivity in estuarine waters of Georgia. *Inst. Mar. Sci. Univ. Tex.* 6, 146–158.

Ramos, H. (1983). Lower marine fungus associated with the black line disease in star coral *Montastraea annularis*. *Biol. Bull.* 165, 429–435.

Randall, J.E. (1963). An analysis of the fish populations of artificial and natural reefs in the Virgin Islands. *Caribb. J. Sci.* 3, 1–16.

Randall, J.E. (1965). Grazing effect of sea grasses by herbivorous reef fishes in the West Indies. *Ecology* 46, 255–260.

Randall, J.E., Schroeder, R.E., and Stark, W.A., II (1964). Notes on the biology of the echinoid *Diadema antillarum*. *Caribb. J. Sci.* 4, 421–433.

Randazzo, A.F., and Saroop, H.C. (1976). Sedimentology and paleoecology of middle and upper Eocene carbonate shoreline sequences, Crystal River, Florida, USA. *Sediment. Geol.* 15, 259– 291.

Randolph, A.M. (1849). "United States Survey of Florida Township 12 South, Range 26 East." Florida Dep. Nat. Resour., Tallahassee.

Rawlings, M.K. (1933). "South Moon Under." Scribner's, New York.

Rayner, D.A., and Batson, W.T. (1976). Maritime closed dunes vegetation in South Carolina. *Castanea* 41, 58–70.

Rebertus, A.J. (1988). The effects of fire on forest community composition, structure, and pattern in Florida sandhills. Ph.D. Thesis, Louisana State University, Baton Rouge.

Rebertus, A.J., Williamson, G.B., and Moser, E.B. (1989). Longleaf pine pyrogenicity and turkey oak mortality in Florida xeric sandhills. *Ecology* 70, 60–70.

Reddy, K.R. (1981). Diel variations of certain physico-chemical parameters of water in selected aquatic systems. *Hydrobiologia* 85, 201–207.

Redmond, A.M. (1984). Population ecology of *Taxus floridana,* a passively cloning, dioecious tree. M.S. Thesis, Florida State Univ., Tallahassee.

Reed, J.K. (1980). Contribution and structure of deep water *Oculina varicosa* coral reefs off central eastern Florida USA. *Bull. Mar. Sci.* 30, 667–677.

Reed, J.K. (1981). In situ growth rates of the scleractinian coral *Oculina varicosa* occurring with zooxanthellae on 6-m reefs and without on 80-m banks. *Proc. Int. Coral Reef Symp., 4th, Manila* 2, 201–206.

Reed, J.K. (1985). Deepest distribution of Atlantic hermatypic corals. *Proc. Int. Coral Reef Cong., 5th, Tahiti* 6, 249–254.

Reed, J.K., and Mikkelsen, P.M. (1987). The molluscan community associated with the scleractinian coral *Oculina varicosa*. *Bull. Mar. Sci.* 40, 99–131.

Reed, J.K., Gore, R., Scotto, L., and Wilson, K. (1982). Community composition, structure, areal, and trophic relationships of decapods associated with shallow- and deep-water *Oculina varicosa* coral reefs. *Bull. Mar. Sci.* 32, 761–786.

Reeder, P.B., and Davis, S.M. (1983). Decomposition, nutrient uptake and microbial colonization of sawgrass and cattail leaves in Water Conservation Area 2A.

South Fla. Water Manage. Dist. Tech. Publ. No. 83-4.

Rehm, A.E. (1974). A study of the marine algae epiphytic on the prop roots of *Rhizophora mangle* L. from Tampa to Key Largo, Florida. Ph.D. Thesis, Univ. of South Florida, Tampa.

Rehm, A.E. (1976). The effects of the wood-boring isopod, *Sphaeroma terebrans,* on the mangrove communities of Florida. *Environ. Conserv.* 3, 47–57.

Reid, G.K., Jr. (1950). The fishes of Orange Lake, Florida. *Q. J. Fla. Acad. Sci.* 12, 173–183.

Reid, G.K., Jr. (1964). Oxygen depletion in a Florida lake. *Q. J. Fla. Acad. Sci.* 27, 120–126.

Reid, G.K., Jr., and Blake, N.J. (1970). Diurnal zooplankton ecology in a phosphate pit lake. *Q. J. Fla. Acad. Sci.* 32, 275–284.

Relyea, K.G., and Sutton, B. (1973). Cave dwelling yellow bullheads in Florida. *Fla. Sci.* 36, 31–34.

Repenning, R.W., and Humphrey, S.R. (1986). The Chadwick Beach cotton mouse (Rodentia: *Peromyscus gossypinus restrictus*) may be extinct. *Fla. Sci.* 49, 259–262.

Repenning, R.W., and Labisky, R.F. (1985). Effects of even-age timber management on bird communities of the longleaf pine forest in northern Florida. *J. Wildl. Manage.* 49, 1088–1098.

Reves, W.D. (1961). The limestone resources of Washington, Holmes, and Jackson Counties, Florida. *Fla. State Geol. Surv. Bull.* 42, 1–121.

Rey, J.R. (1981). Ecological biogeography of arthropods on *Spartina* islands in northwest Florida. *Ecol. Monogr.* 5, 237–265.

Rey, J.R., and McCoy, E.D. (1982). Terrestrial arthropods of northwest Florida salt marshes: Hemiptera and Homoptera (Insecta). *Fla. Entomol.* 65, 241–248.

Rey, J.R., and McCoy, E.D. (1983). Terrestrial arthropods of northwest Florida salt marshes: Araneae and Pseudoscorpiones (Arachnida). *Fla. Entomol.* 66, 497–503.

Rey, J.R., and McCoy, E.D. (1986). Terrestrial arthropods of northwest Florida salt marshes: Diptera (Insecta). *Fla. Entomol.* 69, 197–205.

Rey, J.R., Kain, T.R., Crossman, R.A., Vose, F.E., and Perez, F. (1984). Zooplankton and marsh vegetation in a recently re-opened mosquito control impoundment. *In* "Impoundment Management," Final Rep. CM-47 and CM-73 (D.B. Carlson, R.G. Gilmore, and J. Rey, eds.), Sect 3. Unpubl Rep. to Florida Dep. Environ. Regul., Coastal Zone Manage. Dep., Tallahassee.

Rey, J.R., Crossman, R.A., Kain, T.R., Vose, F.E., and Peterson, M.S. (1987). Sampling zooplankton in shallow marsh and estuarine habitats: gear description and field tests. *Estuaries* 10, 61–67.

Reynolds, J.E., III (1981). Behavior patterns in the West Indian manatee, with emphasis on feeding and diving. *Fla. Sci.* 44, 233–242.

Reynolds, W. (1976). "Botanical, geological and sociological factors affecting the management of barrier islands adjacent to Stump Pass." Unpubl. Rep. Environ. Stud. Program, New Coll., Sarasota, Florida.

Rich, T.H.V., and Patton, T.H. (1975). First record of a fossil hedgehog from Florida (Erinaceidae, Mammalia). *J. Mammal.* 56, 692–696.

Richard, D.I., Small, J.W., Jr., and Osborne, J.A. (1984). Phytoplankton responses to reduction and elimination of submerged vegetation by herbicides and grass carp in four Florida lakes. *Aquat. Bot.* 20, 307–319.

Richard, D.I., Small, J.W., Jr., and Osborne, J.A. (1985). Response of zooplankton to the reduction and elimination of submerged vegetation by grass carp and herbicide in four Florida lakes. *Hydrobiologia* 123, 97–108.

Richards, H.G., and Palmer, K.V.W. (1953). Eocene mollusks from Citrus and Levy Counties, Florida. *Fla. Geol. Surv. Geol. Bull.* 35, 1–95.

Richardson, C., Dustan, P., and Lang, J. (1979). Maintenance of living space by sweeper tentacles of *Montastraea cavernosa,* a Caribbean reef coral. *Mar. Biol. (Berlin)* 55, 181–186.

Richardson, C.J. (1983). Pocosins: vanishing wastelands or valuable wetlands? *Bio-Science* 33, 626–633.

Richardson, D.R. (1977). Vegetation of the Atlantic coastal ridge of Palm Beach County, FL. *Fla. Sci.* 40, 281–330.

Richardson, D.R. (1985). Allelopathic effects of species in sandpine scrub in Florida. Ph.D. Thesis, Univ. of South Florida, Tampa.

Richardson, J., Straub, P.A., Ewel, K.C., and Odum, H.T. (1983). Sulfate-enriched water effects on a floodplain forest in Florida. *Environ. Manage.* 7, 321–326.

Richmond, E.A. (1962). The fauna and flora of Horn Island, Mississippi. *Gulf Res. Rep.* 1, 59–106.

Riebsame, W.E., and Woodley, W.L. (1974). Radar inference of Lake Okeechobee rainfall for use in environmental studies. *Weatherwise* 27, 206–211.

Riegel, W.L. (1965). Palynology of environments of peat formation in southwestern Florida. Ph.D. Thesis, Pennsylvania State Univ., Philadelphia.

Riehl, H. (1954). "Tropical Meteorology." McGraw-Hill, New York.

Riekerk, H. (1983). Forested wetlands, environmental rules and silvicultural practices. In "Appraisal of Florida's Wetland Hardwood Resource" (D.M. Flinchum, G.B. Doolittle, and K.R. Munson, eds.), pp. 74–92. Sch. For. Resour. Conserv., Univ. of Florida, Gainesville.

Riekerk, H., Swindel, B.F., and Replogle, J.A. (1980). Initial hydrologic effects of forestry practices in Florida flatwoods watersheds. *Univ. Fla. Intensive Manage. Pract. Assess. Cent. (IMPAC) Rep.* No. 4(4).

Riggs, S.R. (1984). Paleoceanographic model of neogene phosphorite deposition, U.S. Atlantic continental margin. *Science* 223, 123–131.

Risk, M.J., and MacGeachy, J.K. (1978). Aspects of bioerosion of modern Caribbean reefs. *Rev. Biol. Trop.* 26, Suppl. 1, 85–105.

Robbin, D.M. (1984). A new Holocene sea level curve for the Upper Florida Keys and Florida reef tract. *In* "Environments of South Florida: Past and Present II" (P.J. Gleason, ed.), pp. 437–458. Miami Geol. Soc., Coral Gables, Florida.

Robbins, L.E., and Myers, R.L. (1990). Seasonal effects of prescribed burning in Florida: a review. *Tall Timbers Res. Sta. Misc. Publ.* No. 8.

Robertson, A.I., and Duke, N.C. (1987). Mangroves as nursery sites: comparisons of the abundance and species composition of fish and crustaceans in mangroves and other nearshore habitats in tropical Australia. *Mar. Biol. (Berlin)* 96, 193–205.

Robertson, J.S. (1976). Latest Pliocene mammals from Haile XV A, Alachua County, Florida. *Bull. Fla. State Mus.* 20, 111–186.

Robertson, R. (1970). Review of the predators and parasites of stony corals, with special reference to symbiotic prosobranch gastropods. *Pac. Sci.* 24, 43–54.

Robertson, W.B., Jr. (1953). "A Survey of the Effects of Fire in Everglades National Park." Natl. Park Serv., Homestead, Florida.

Robertson, W.B., Jr. (1955). An analysis of the breeding-bird populations of tropical Florida in relation to the vegetation. Ph.D. Thesis, Univ. of Illinois, Urbana.

Robertson, W.B., Jr. (1962). Fire and vegetation in the Everglades. *Proc. Tall Timbers Fire Ecol. Conf.* 1, 67–80.

Robertson, W.B., Jr., and Kushlan, J.A. (1984). The southern Florida avifauna. *In*

"Environments of South Florida: Present and Past II" (P.J. Gleason, ed.), pp. 219–257. Miami Geol. Soc., Coral Gables, Florida.

Robinson, A.F. (1981). *Dicerandra immaculata.* Status rev. for U.S. Fish Wildl. Serv., Jacksonville, Florida.

Rochow, T.F. (1985). Hydrologic and vegetational changes resulting from underground pumping at the Cypress Creek wellfield, Pasco County, FL. *Fla. Sci.* 48, 65–80.

Rodelli, M.R., Gearing, J.N., Gearing, P.J., Marshall, N., and Sasekumar, A. (1984). Stable isotope ratio as a tracer of mangrove carbon in Malaysian ecosystems. *Oecologia* 61, 326–333.

Rodman, J.E. (1974). Systematics and evolution of the genus *Cakile* (Cruciferae). *Contrib. Gray Herb. Harv. Univ.* No. 205.

Rogers, J.S. (1933). The ecological distribution of the crane-flies of northern Florida. *Ecol. Monogr.* 3, 1–74.

Rogers, J.S., Allen, L.H., Jr., and Calvert, D.V. (1983). Evapotranspiration from a humid-region developing citrus grove with grass cover. *Trans. Am. Soc. Agric. Eng.*, 26, 1778–1783.

Romans, B. (1775). "A Concise Natural History of East and West Florida." Reprinted, Pelican Publ. Co., New Orleans, Louisiana, 1961.

Romeo, J.T., and Weidenhamer, J. (1986). "Allelopathic Properties of *Polygonella myriophylla* and *Cladonia leporina.*" Unpubl. proposal submitted to Fla. Nongame Wildl. Program, Univ. of South Florida, Tampa.

Rosenau, J.C., and Faulkner, G.L. (1975). "An Index to Springs of Florida." Bur. Geol. Map Ser. No. 63 (revised). U.S. Geol. Surv. in coop. with Bur. Geol., Dep. Nat. Resour., Tallahassee.

Rosenau, J.C., Faulkner, G.L., Hendry, C.W., Jr., and Hull, R.W. (1977). "Springs of Florida." Bur. Geol. Bull. No. 31 (revised). U.S. Geol. Surv. in coop. with Bur. Geol., Dep. Environ. Regul. Bur. Water Resour. Manage., Florida. Dep. Nat. Resour., Tallahassee.

Rothermel, R.C. (1972). A mathematical model for predicting fire spread in wildland fuels. *U.S. For. Serv. Res. Pap.* No. INT-16.

Rowse, L.A. (1980). Avian community composition of a north Florida flatwoods. M.S. Thesis, Univ. of Florida, Gainesville.

Rubel, E. (1930). "Pflanzengesellschaften der Erde." Huber, Berlin.

Runkle, J.R. (1981). Gap regeneration in some old-growth forests of the eastern United States. *Ecology* 62, 1041–1051.

Runkle, J.R. (1982). Patterns of disturbance in some old-growth mesic forests of eastern North America. *Ecology* 63, 1533–1546.

Rützler, K. (1975). The role of burrowing sponges in bioerosion. *Oecologia* 19, 203–216.

Rützler, K., and Macintyre, I.G., eds. (1982). The Atlantic Barrier Reef ecosystem at Carrie Bow Cay, Belize. I. Structure and communities. *Smithson. Contrib. Mar. Sci.* 12.

Rützler, K., and Santavy, D. (1983). The black band disease of Atlantic reef corals. I. Description of the Cyanophyte pathogen. *Mar. Ecol.* 4, 301–319.

Rützler, K., Santavy, D., and Antonius, A. (1983). The black band disease in Atlantic reef corals. III. Distribution, ecology, and development. *Mar. Ecol.* 4, 329–358.

Safford, W.E. (1919). "Natural History of Paradise Key and the Nearby Everglades of Florida." Smithson. Rep. for 1917, pp. 377–434. Smithson. Inst., Washington, D.C.

Sage, W.W., and Sullivan, M.J. (1978). Distribution of bluegreen algae in a Mississippi gulf coast salt marsh. *J. Phycol.* 14, 333–337.

St. John, E.P. (1936). Rare ferns of central Florida. *Am. Fern J.* 16, 41–50.

St. John, E.P., and St. John, R.P. (1935). Fern study in central Florida. *Am. Fern J.* 25, 33–44.

St. Johns River Water Management District (1977). "Water Resource Management Plan," Phase 1. St. Johns River Water Manage. Dist., Palatka, Florida.

St. Johns River Water Management District (1979), "Upper St. Johns River Basin Surface Water Management Plan," Vol. 2. St. Johns River Water Manage. Dist., Palatka, Florida.

Samek, V. (1973). Vegetación litoral de la costa norte de la Provincia de la Habana. *Acad. Cienc. Cuba Dep. Ecol. For., Ser. For.* No. 18.

Sammarco, P.W. (1980). *Diadema* and its relationship to coral spat mortality: grazing, competition, and biological disturbance. *J. Exp. Mar. Biol. Ecol.* 45, 245–272.

Sammarco, P.W., Levinton, J., and Ogden, J. (1974). Grazing and control of coral reef community structure by *Diadema antillarum* Phillippi (Echinodermata: Echinoidea): a preliminary study. *J. Mar. Res.* 32, 47–53.

Sanders, M.L. (1980). The great freeze of 1894–95 in Pinellas County. *Tampa Bay Hist.* 2, 5–14.

Sanders, R.W. (1987). Identity of *Lantana depressa* and *L. ovatifolia* (Verbenaceae) of Florida and the Bahamas. *Syst. Bot.* 12, 44–60.

Santos, S.L., and Simon, J.L. (1980). Marine soft-bottom community establishment following annual defaunation: larval or adult recruitment. *Mar. Ecol. Prog. Ser.* 2, 235–241.

Sargent, C.S. (1884). "Report on the Forests of North America." USDI Census Off., Washington, D.C.

Saucier, J.R., and Dorman, K.W. (1969). Intraspecific variation in growth and wood characteristics of two slash pine varieties grown in south Florida. *Proc. South. For. Tree Improv. Conf., 10th,* pp. 49–57.

Sauer, J. (1967). Geographic reconnaissance of seashore vegetation along the Mexican Gulf coasts. *La. State Univ. Coastal Stud. Ser.* No. 21.

Sauer, J. (1982). "Cayman Islands Seashore Vegetation." Univ. of Calif. Publ. Geogr. Vol. 25. Univ. of California Press, Berkeley.

Savage, T. (1972). Florida mangroves as shoreline stabilizers. *Fla. Dep. Nat. Resour. Prof. Pap.* No. 19.

Schardt, J.D. (1983). "1983 Aquatic Flora of Florida Survey Report." Bur. Aquat. Plant Res. Control, Florida Dep. Nat. Resour., Tallahassee.

Schardt, J.D. (1984). "1984 Florida Aquatic Plant Survey." Bur. Aquat. Plant Res. Control, Florida Dep. Nat. Resour., Tallahassee.

Schelske, C.L., and Odum, E.P. (1961). Mechanisms maintaining high productivity in Georgia estuaries. *Proc. Gulf Caribb. Fish. Inst.* 14, 75–80.

Schimper, A.F.W. (1903). "Plant Geography Upon a Physiological Basis." Clarendon Press, Oxford.

Schindler, D.W. (1988). Effects of acid rain on fresh water ecosystems. *Science* 239, 149–157.

Schlesinger, W.H. (1978a). Community structure, dynamics and nutrient cycling in the Okefenokee cypress swamp–forest. *Ecol. Monogr.* 48, 48–65.

Schlesinger, W.H. (1978b). On the relative dominance of shrubs in Okefenokee Swamp. *Am. Nat.* 112, 949–954.

Schlesinger, W.H., and Chabot, B.F. (1977). The use of water and minerals by evergreen and deciduous shrubs in the Okefenokee Swamp. *Bot. Gaz.* 138, 490–497.

Schlesinger, W.H., and Marks, P.L. (1977). Mineral cycling and the niche of Spanish moss, *Tillandsia usneoides* L. *Am. J. Bot.* 64, 1254–1262.

Schmahl, G.P. (1984). Sponges. *In* "The Ecology of the South Florida Coral Reefs: a Community Profile," pp. 37–40. *U.S. Fish Wildl. Serv. Off. Biol. Serv. [Tech. Rep.]* FWS/OBS 82–08.

Schmalzer, P.A., and Hinkle, C.R. (1987). "Effects of Fire on Composition, Biomass, and Nutrients in Oak Scrub Vegetation on John F. Kennedy Space Center, Florida." *NASA Tech. Memo.* NASA TM-X-100305.

Schmidt, K.P. (1953). "A Check List of North American Amphibians and Reptiles," 6th Ed. Am. Soc. Ichthyol. Herpetol. Univ. of Chicago Press, Chicago, Illinois.

Schmitz, D.C., and Osborne, J.A. (1984). Zooplankton densities in a *Hydrilla* infested lake. *Hydrobiologia* 111, 127–132.

Scholander, P.F. (1968). How mangroves desalinate seawater. *Physiol. Plant.* 21, 258–268.

Scholander, P.F., van Dam, L., and Scholander, S.I. (1955). Gas exchange in the roots of mangroves. *Am. J. Bot.* 42, 92–98.

Scholander, P.F., Hammel, H.T., Hemmingsen, E., and Cary, W. (1962). Salt balance in mangroves. *Plant Physiol.* 37, 722–729.

Scholander, P.F., Hammel, H.T., Bradstreet, E.D., and Hemmingsen, E.A. (1965). Sap pressure in vascular plants. *Science* 148, 339–346.

Scholl, D.W., Craighead, F.C., and Stuiver, M. (1969). Florida submergence curve revised: its relation to coastal sedimentation rates. *Science* 163, 562–564.

Schomer, N.S., and Drew, R.D. (1982). "An Ecological Characterization of the Lower Everglades, Florida Bay, and the Florida Keys." *U.S. Fish Wildl. Serv. Off. Biol. Serv. [Tech. Rep.]* FWS/OBS 82/58.1.

Schooley, J.K. (1980). The structure and function of warm temperate estuarine fish communities. Ph.D. Thesis, Univ. of Florida, Gainesville.

Schornherst, R.O. (1943). Phytogeographic studies of the mosses of northern Florida. *Am. Midl. Nat.* 29, 509–532.

Schreiber, R.W., and Schreiber, E.A. (1978). "Colonial Bird Use and Plant Succession on Dredged Material Islands in Florida. Vol. 1: Sea and Wading Bird Colonies." *Dredged Mater. Res. Program Tech. Rep.* No. D-78-14, U.S. Army Eng. Waterways Exp. Stn., Vicksburg, Mississippi.

Schultz, R.P. (1972). Root development of intensively cultivated slash pine. *Soil Sci. Soc. Am. Proc.* 36, 158–162.

Schultz, R.P. (1973). Site treatment and planting methods alter root development of slash pine. *U.S. For. Serv. Res. Pap.* No. SE-109.

Schultz, R.P. (1976). Environmental change after site preparation and slash pine planting on a flatwood site. *U.S. For. Serv. Res. Pap.* No. SE-156.

Schultz, R.P., and Wilhite, L.P. (1975). Changes in a flatwoods site following intensive site preparation. *For. Sci.* 20, 230–237.

Schulze, R.L. (1980). The biotic response to acid precipitation in Florida lakes. M.S. Thesis, Univ. of Florida, Gainesville.

Schwartz, M.L. (1971). Multiple causality of barrier islands. *J. Geol.* 79, 91–94.

Schwartz, M.W. (1988). Species diversity patterns in woody flora on three North American peninsulas. *J. Biogeogr.* 15, 759–774.

Schwartz, M.W. (1990). Conserving forest diversity in panhandle Florida: a multiscale approach. Ph.D Thesis, Florida State University, Tallahassee.

Schwarz, G.F. (1907). "The Longleaf Pine in Virgin Forest. A Silvical Study." Wiley, New York.

Scoffin, T.P. (1970). The trapping and binding of subtidal carbonate sediments by marine vegetation in Bimini Lagoon, Bahamas. *J. Sediment. Petrol.* 40, 249–273.

Scott, S.L., and Osborne, J.A. (1981). Benthic macroinvertebrates of a *Hydrilla* infested central Florida lake. *J. Freshwater Ecol.* 1, 41–49.

Scott, T.M. (1988). The lithostratigraphy of the Hawthorn Group (Miocene) of Florida. *Fla. Geol. Surv. Bull.* 59, 1–148.

Sealy, J.R. (1954). Review of the genus *Hymenocallis*. *Kew Bull.* 9, 201–214.

Seaman, W., Jr., ed. (1985). "Florida Aquatic Habitat and Fishery Resources." Florida Chap. Am. Fish. Soc., Kissimmee.

Seamon, P.A., Myers, R.L., Robbins, L.E., and Seamon, G.S. (1989). Wiregrass reproduction and community restoration. *Natural Areas J.* 9, 264–265.

Seigel, R.A. (1980a). Courtship and mating behavior of the diamondback terrapin *Malaclemys terrapin tequesta*. *J. Herpetol.* 14, 420–421.

Seigel, R.A. (1980b). Nesting habits of diamondback terrapins (*Malaclemys terrapin*) on the Atlantic coast of Florida. *Trans. Kans. Acad. Sci.* 83, 239–246.

Seigel, R.A. (1980c). Predation by raccoons on diamondback terrapins, *Malaclemys terrapin tequesta*. *J. Herpetol.* 14, 87–89.

Seigel, R.A. (1984). Parameters of two populations of diamondback terrapins (*Malaclemys terrapin*) on the Atlantic coast of Florida. *In* "Vertebrate Ecology and Systematics—A Tribute to Henry S. Fitch" (R.A. Seigel, L.E. Hunt, J.L. Knight, L. Malaret, and N.L. Zuschlag, eds.), *Mus. Nat. Hist. Spec. Publ.* No. 10, pp. 77–87. Univ. of Kansas, Lawrence.

Sellner, K.G., and Zingmark, R.G. (1976). Interpretations of the 14C method of measuring the total annual production of phytoplankton in a South Carolina estuary. *Bot. Mar.* 19, 119–125.

Seneca, E.D. (1972). Seedling response to salinity in four coastal dune grasses from the outer banks of North Carolina. *Ecology* 50, 465–471.

Shafer, M.D., Dickinson, R.E., Heaney, J.P., and Huber, W.C. (1986). Gazetteer of Florida Lakes. *Florida Water Resour. Res. Cent. Publ.*, No. 96. Univ. of Florida, Gainesville.

Shafland, P.L. (1979). Non-native fish introductions with special reference to Florida. *Fisheries* 4, 18–24.

Shane, S.H. (1984). Manatee use of power plant effluents in Brevard County, Florida. *Fla. Sci.* 47, 180–187.

Shannon, C., and Weaver, W. (1948). "The Mathematical Theory of Communication." Univ. of Illinois Press, Urbana.

Shannon, E.E., and Brezonik, P.L. (1972a). Limnological characteristics of north and central Florida lakes. *Limnol. Oceanogr.* 17, 97–110.

Shannon, E.E., and Brezonik, P.L. (1972b). Relationships between lake trophic state and nitrogen and phosphorus loading rates. *Environ. Sci. Technol.* 6, 719–725.

Sharitz, R.R., and Gibbons, J.W. (1982). "The Ecology of Southeastern Shrub Bogs (Pocosins) and Carolina bays: A Community Profile." *U.S. Fish Wildl. Serv. Off. Biol. Serv. [Tech. Rep.]* FWS/OBS 82-04.

Sharp, H.F. Jr. (1967). Food ecology of the rice rat, *Oryzomys palustris* (Harlan), in a Georgia salt marsh. *J. Mammal.* 48, 557–563.

Sharp, H.S. (1938). Steepheads and spring sapping in Florida—Holt and Niceville quadrangles, Florida. *J. Geomorphol.* 1, 247–248.

Shaw, J., and Hopkins, T. (1977). The distribution of the family Haplocarcinidae (Decapoda, Brachyura) on the Florida Middle Ground with a description of *Pseudocryptochirus hypostegus* n. sp. *Proc. Int. Coral Reef Symp., 3rd, Miami,*

Fla. 1, 177–184.

Shaw, S.P., and Fredine, C.G. (1956). Wetlands of the United States, their extent and their value for waterfowl and other wildlife. *U.S. Fish and Wildl. Serv. Circ.* No. 39.

Sheffield, R.M., Knight, H.A., and McClure, J.P. (1983). The slash pine resource. *In* "The Managed Slash Pine Ecosystem" (E.L. Stone, ed.), Proc. Symp., pp. 4–23. Sch. For. Resour. Conserv., Univ. of Florida, Gainesville.

Shelford, V.E. (1954). Some lower Mississippi Valley flood plain biotic communities: their age and elevation. *Ecology* 35, 126–142.

Shepard, F.P., and Wanless, H.R. (1971). "Our Changing Coastlines." McGraw-Hill, New York.

Sheridan, P.F. (1979). Trophic research utilization by three species of sciaenid fishes in a northwest Florida estuary. *Northeast Gulf Sci.* 3, 1–15.

Sherrod, C.L., and McMillan, C. (1985). The distributional history and ecology of mangrove vegetation along the northern Gulf of Mexico coastal region. *Contrib. Mar. Sci.* 28, 129–140.

Shier, D. (1969). Vermetid reefs and coastal development in the Ten Thousand Islands, Southwest Florida. *Geol. Soc. Am. Bull.* 80, 485–508.

Shih, S.F., and Chen, E. (1984). On the use of GOES thermal data to study effects of land use on diurnal temperature fluctuation. *J. Clim. Appl. Meteorol.* 23, 426–433.

Shinn, E.A. (1963). Spur and groove formation on the Florida Reef tract. *J. Sediment. Petrol.* 33, 291–303.

Shinn, E.A. (1966). Coral growth-rate: an environmental indicator. *J. Paleontol.* 40, 233–240.

Shinn, E.A. (1976). Coral reef recovery in Florida and the Persian Gulf. *Environ. Geol.* 1, 241–254.

Shinn, E.A. (1980). Geologic history of Grecian Rocks, Key Largo Coral Reef Marine Sanctuary. *Bull. Mar. Sci.* 30, 646–656.

Shinn, E.A., Hudson, J.H., Halley, R.B., and Lidz, B. (1977). Topographic control and accumulation rate of some Holocene coral reefs: South Florida and Dry Tortugas. *Proc. Int. Coral Reef Symp., 3rd, Miami, Fla.* 1, 1–7.

Shinn, E.A., Hudson, J.H., Robin, D.M., and Lidz, B. (1981). Spur and grooves revisited: construction versus erosion. *Proc. Int. Coral Reef Symp., 4th, Manila* 1, 475–484.

Shireman, J.V., and Maceina, M.J. (1981). The utilization of grass carp, *Ctenopharyngodon idella* Val., for hydrilla control in Lake Baldwin, Florida. *J. Fish Biol.* 19, 629–636.

Shireman, J.V., and Martin, R.G. (1978). Seasonal and diurnal zooplankton investigations of a south-central Florida lake. *Fla. Sci.* 41, 193–201.

Shuey, A.J., and Swanson, L.J., Jr. (1979). Creation of freshwater marshes in west central Florida. *Proc. Annu. Conf. Restoration Creat. Wetlands* 6, 57–76.

Shunk, I.V. (1939). Oxygen requirements for germination of seeds of *Nyssa aquatica,* tupelo gum. *Science* 90, 253–261.

Simberloff, D.S. (1983). Mangroves. *In* "Costa Rican Natural History" (D.H. Janzen, ed.), pp. 273–276. Univ. of Chicago Press, Chicago, Illinois.

Simkiss, K. (1964). Phosphates as crystal poisons of calcification. *Biol. Rev.* 39, 487–505.

Simmons, W.H. (1822). "Notices of East Florida." A.E. Miller, Charleston, South Carolina.

Simon, D.M. (1986). Fire effects in coastal habitats of east-central Florida. *Natl.*

Park Serv. Coop. Unit, Athens, Ga., CPSU Tech. Rep. No. 27.

Simon, J.L. (1974). Tampa Bay estuarine system—a synopsis. *Fla. Sci.* 37, 217–244.

Simpson, C.T. (1920). "In Lower Florida Wilds." Putnam, New York.

Simpson, C.T. (1923). "Out of Doors in Florida." E.B. Douglas, Miami, Florida.

Simpson, C.T. (1932). "Florida Wildlife: Observations on the Flora and Fauna of the State and the Influence of Climate and Environment on Their Development." Macmillan, New York.

Simpson, G.G. (1964). Species densities of North American mammals. *Syst. Zool.* 12, 57–73.

Simpson, R.H., and Lawrence, M.B. (1971). Atlantic hurricane frequencies along the U.S. coastline. *Natl. Ocean. Atmos. Adm. Tech. Memo* No. NWS ST-58.

Simpson, R.H., and Riehl, H. (1981). "The Hurricane and its Impact." Louisiana State Univ. Press, Baton Rouge.

Sinclair, W.C., and Stewart, J.W. (1985). "Sinkhole Type, Development, and Distribution in Florida." *Bur. Geol. Map Ser.* No. 110, U.S. Geol. Surv. in coop. with Dep. Environ. Regul., Bur. Water Resour. Manage., Florida Dep. Nat. Resour., Tallahassee.

Sincock, J.L. (1959). "Waterfowl Ecology in the St. Johns River Valley as Related to the Proposed Conservation Areas and Changes in the Hydrology from Lake Harney to Fort Pierce, Florida." Florida Game Fresh Water Fish Comm., Tallahassee.

Skeate, S.T. (1987). Interactions between birds and fruits in a northern Florida hammock community. *Ecology* 68, 297–309.

Skirvin, R.T. (1962). The underground course of the Santa Fe River near High Springs, Florida. M.S. Thesis, Univ. of Florida, Gainesville.

Skoog, P.J., and Harris, L.D. (1981). Utilization of pine plantations by white-tailed deer in north Florida. *Univ. Fla. Intensive Manage. Pract. Assess. Cent. (IMPAC) Rep.* No. 6(2).

Sloan, W.C. (1956). The distribution of aquatic insects in two Florida springs. *Ecology* 37, 81–98.

Sloey, W.E., Spangler, F.L., and Fetter, C.W., Jr. (1978). Management of freshwater wetlands for nutrient assimilation. *In* "Freshwater Wetlands, Ecological Processes and Management Potential" (R.E. Good, D.F. Whigham, and R.L. Simpson, eds.), pp. 321–340. Academic Press, New York.

Smajstrla, A.G., Clark, G.A., Shih, S.F., Zazueta, F.Z., and Harrison, D.S. (1985). "Potential evapotranspiration probabilities and distributions in Florida." *Fla. Ext. Serv. Bull.* No. 205.

Small, J.K. (1904). Report upon further exploration of southern Florida. *J. N.Y. Bot. Gard.* 5, 157–164.

Small, J.K. (1916). Royal Palm Hammock. *J. N.Y. Bot. Gard.* 16, 165–172.

Small, J.K. (1917). The tree cacti of the Florida Keys. *J. N.Y. Bot. Gard.* 18, 199–203.

Small, J.K. (1918). "Ferns of Royal Palm Hammock." J.K. Small, New York.

Small, J.K. (1920a). Of grottos and ancient dunes. A record of exploration in Florida in December 1918. *J. N.Y. Bot. Gard.* 21, 45–54.

Small, J.K. (1920b). A journey to the fern grottos. *J. N.Y. Bot. Gard.* 21, 25–38.

Small, J.K. (1920c). The land of ferns. The habitats and distribution of the fernworts of Florida. *J. Elisha Mitchell Soc.* 23, 92–104.

Small, J.K. (1921a). Historic trails by land and by water. *J. N.Y. Bot. Gard.* 22, 193–222.

Small, J.K. (1921b). Old trails and new discoveries. A record of exploration in Florida in the spring of 1919. *J. N.Y. Bot. Gard.* 22, 25–40; 49–64.

Small, J.K. (1923a). Green deserts and dead gardens. A record of exploration in Florida in the spring of 1921. *J. N.Y. Bot. Gard.* 24, 193–247.

Small, J.K. (1923b). Land of the question mark. Report on exploration in Florida in December, 1920. *J. N.Y. Bot. Gard.* 24, 1–23; 25–43; 62–70.

Small, J.K. (1924a). The land where spring meets autumn. *J. N.Y. Bot. Gard.* 25, 53–94.

Small, J.K. (1924b). Whence came our orchids? *J. N.Y. Bot. Gard.* 25, 261–266.

Small, J.K. (1927). Among floral aborigines. *J. N.Y. Bot. Gard.* 27, 1–20; 25–40.

Small, J.K. (1929). "From Eden to Sahara, Florida's Tragedy." Science Press, Lancaster, Pennsylvania.

Small, J.K. (1931). "Ferns of Florida." Science Press, New York.

Small, J.K. (1933). "Manual of the Southeastern Flora." Univ. of North Carolina Press, Chapel Hill.

Small, J.K. (1938). "Ferns of the Southeastern United States." Science Press, Lancaster, Pennsylvania.

Smardon, R.C., ed. (1983). "The Future of Wetlands: Assessing Visual-Cultural Values." Allanheld, Osmun, Totowa, New Jersey.

Smart, R.M., and Barko, J.W. (1978). Influence of sediment salinity and nutrients on the physiological ecology of selected salt marsh plants. *Estuarine Coastal Mar. Sci.* 7, 487–495.

Smart, R.M., and Barko, J.W. (1980). Nitrogen nutrition and salinity tolerance of *Distichlis spicata* and *Spartina alterniflora. Ecology* 61, 620–638.

Smith, A.P. (1973). Stratification of temperate and tropical forests. *Am. Nat.* 107, 671–683.

Smith, C.L., and Tyler, J.C. (1975). Succession and stability in fish communities of dome-shaped patch reefs in the West Indies. *Am. Mus. Novit.* No. 2572, 1–18.

Smith, E.A. (1884). Report on the cotton production of the State of Florida, with an account of the general agricultural features of the state. *Census U.S., 10th* 6, 175–257.

Smith, F.B., Leighty, R.G., Caldwell, R.E., Carlisle, V.W., Thompson, L.G., Jr., and Mathews, T.C. (1967). Principle soil areas of Florida: a supplement to the general soils map. *Fla. Agric. Exp. Stn. Bull.* No. 717.

Smith, G. (1976). Ecology and distribution of eastern Gulf of Mexico reef fishes. *Fla. Mar. Res. Publ.* 19, 1–78.

Smith, G., and Ogren, L. (1974). Comments on the nature of the Florida Middle Ground reef ichthyofauna. *In* "Marine Environmental Implications of Offshore Drilling in the Eastern Gulf of Mexico," pp. 229–232. Inst. Oceangr., State Univ. Syst. Florida, St. Petersburg.

Smith, H. (1897). Florida commercial sponges. *Bull. U.S. Fish Comm.* No. 17, pp. 225–240.

Smith, P.W., Robertson, W.B., Jr., and Stevenson, H.M. (1988). West Indian cave Swallow nesting in Florida, with comments on the taxonomy of *Hirundo fulva*." *Fla. Field Naturalist* 16, 86–90.

Smith, S.V., Kimmerer, W.J., Laws, E.A., Brock, R.E., and Walsh, T.W. (1981). Kaneohe Bay sewage diversion experiment: perspectives on ecosystem responses to nutritional perturbation. *Pac. Sci.* 35, 279–395.

Smith, T.J., III (1987a). Effects of light and intertidal position on seedling survival and growth in tropical tidal forests. *J. Exp. Mar. Biol. Ecol.* 110, 133–146.

Smith, T.J., III (1987b). Effects of seed predators and light level on the distribution of *Avicennia marina* in tropical, tidal forests. *Estuarine Coastal Shelf Sci.* 25, 43–51.

Smith, T.J., III (1987c). Seed predation in relation to tree dominance and distribution in mangrove forests. *Ecology* 68, 266–273.

Smith, T.J., III, Chan, H.T., McIvor, C.C., and Robblee, M.B. (1989). Comparisons of seed predation in tropical tidal forests from different continents. *Ecology* 70, 146–151.

Smith, W.G. (1968). Sedimentary environments and environmental change in the peat forming area of south Florida. Ph.D. Thesis, Pennsylvania State Univ., University Park.

Smol, J.P., Battarbee, R.W., Davis, R.B., and Meriläinen, J., eds. (1986). Diatoms and lake acidity. Reconstructing pH from siliceous algal remains in lake sediments. *Dev. Hydrobiol.* 29. Junk, Boston.

Snedaker, S.C. (1963). Some aspects of the ecology of the Florida sandhills. M.S. Thesis, Univ. of Florida, Gainesville.

Snedaker, S.C. (1989). Overview of ecology of mangroves and information needs for Florida Bay. *Bull. Mar. Sci.* 44, 341–347.

Snedaker, S.C., and Lugo, A.E., eds. (1972). "Ecology of the Ocala National Forest." U.S. For. Serv., Southeast Reg., Atlanta, Georgia.

Snedaker, S.C., and Lugo, A.E. (1973). "The Role of Mangrove Ecosystems in the Maintenance of Environmental Quality and a High Productivity of Desirable Fisheries." Final Rep. on Contract 14-16-008-606 to U.S. Bur. Sport Fish. Wildl., Washington, D.C.

Snelson, F.F. (1983). Ichthyofauna of the northern part of the Indian River Lagoon system, Florida. *Fla. Sci.* 46, 187–206.

Snyder, G.H., Burdine, H.W., Crockett, J.R., Gascho, G.J., Harrison, D.S., Kidder, G., Mishoe, J.W., Myhre, D.L., Pate, F.M., and Shih, S.F. (1978). Water table management for organic soil conservation and crop production in the Florida Everglades. *Fla. Agric. Exp. Stn. Inst. Food Agric. Sci. Bull.* No. 801.

Snyder, J.R. (1986). The impact of wet season and dry season prescribed fires on Miami Rock Ridge pineland, Everglades National Park. *Everglades Natl. Park South Fla. Res. Cent. Rep.* No. SFRC-86/06.

Snyder, J.R., and Ward, G. (1987). Effect of season of burning on the flowering response of subtropical prairie plants. *Bull. Ecol. Soc. Am.* 68, 419.

Soil Conservation Service (1954). Soil survey (detailed-reconnaissance) of Collier County, FL. *U.S. Dep. Agric. Soil Conserv. Serv., Ser. 1942* No. 8.

Soil Conservation Service (1958). Soil survey (detailed-reconnaissance) of Dade County, FL. *U.S. Dep. Agric. Soil Conserv. Serv., Ser. 1947* No. 4.

Soil Management Support Services (1984). "Keys to Soil Taxonomy." USDA Soil Conserv. Serv. and Agency Int. Dev. Dep. Agron., Cornell Univ., Ithaca, New York.

Soil Survey Staff (1975). "Soil Taxonomy: a Basic System of Classification for Making and Interpreting Soil Surveys." USDA Soil Conserv. Serv. Agric. Handb. No. 436. U.S. Gov. Print. Off., Washington, D.C.

Sournia, A. (1977). Primary production in coral reefs: a review of organisms, rates and budget. *Ann. Inst. Oceanogr. (Paris)* 53, 47–74.

Sousa, W.P. (1984). The role of disturbance in natural communities. *Annu. Rev. Ecol. Syst.* 15, 353–391.

Southwest Regional Research Institute (1981). "Ecological Investigations of Petroleum Production Platforms in the Central Gulf of Mexico. Vol. II: The Artificial

Reefs." U.S. Dep. Commer. NTIS Rep. No. 167826. Washington, D.C.

Spackman, W., Dolson, C.P., and Riegel, W. (1966). Phytogenic organic sediments and sedimentary environments in the Everglades-Mangrove complex. Part I: Evidence of a transgressing sea and its effect on environments of the Shark River area of southwestern Florida. *Palaeontographica* B117, 135–152.

Spangler, D.P. (1984). Geologic variability among six cypress domes in north-central Florida. *In* "Cypress Swamps" (K.C. Ewel and H.T. Odum, eds.), pp. 60–66. Univ. Presses of Florida, Gainesville.

Spellman, C.W. (1948). The agriculture of the early north Florida Indians. *Fla. Anthropol.* 1, 37–48.

Sprunt, A., Jr. (1954). "Florida's Bird Life." Coward McCann and Natl. Audubon Soc., New York.

Squillace, A.E. (1966). Geographic variation in slash pine. *For. Sci. Monogr.* 10.

Squillace, A.E., Dorman, K.W., and McNees, R.E. (1972). Breeding slash pine in Florida; a success story. *Agric. Sci. Rev.* 10, 25–32.

Squires, D. (1964). Biological results of the Chatham Island 1954 expedition: Scleractinia. *N.Z. Oceanogr. Inst. Mem.* No. 29.

Stalter, R. (1971). Age of a mature pine (*Pinus taeda*) stand in South Carolina. *Ecology* 52, 532–533.

Stalter, R. (1974). Vegetation in the coastal dunes of South Carolina. *Castanea* 39, 95–103.

Stalter, R. (1976). Factors affecting vegetational zonation on coastal dunes, Georgetown County, South Carolina. *3rd Proc. Annu. Conf. Restoring Coastal Veg. Fla.*, (R.R. Lewis and D.P. Cole, eds.). Hillsborough Community Coll., Tampa, Florida.

Stalter, R., and Dial, S. (1984a). Environmental status of the stinking cedar, *Torreya taxifolia*. *Bartonia* 50, 40–42.

Stalter, R., and Dial, S.C. (1984b). Hammock vegetation of Little Talbot Island State Park, Florida. *Bull. Torrey Bot. Club* 111, 494–497.

Stalter, R., and Dial, S. (1986). Some observations on *Pinus glabra* Walter (Pinaceae). *Sida* 11, 325–328.

Stalter, R., Dial, S., and Laessle, A. (1981). Some ecological observations of the arborescent vegetation in Highlands Hammock State Park, Florida. *Castanea* 46, 30–35.

Stankey, D.L. (1982). "Soil Survey of Pasco County, Florida." U.S. Dep. Agric. Soil Conserv. Serv. in coop. with Univ. Fla., Inst. Food Agric. Sci., Agric. Exp. Stn., Soil Sci. Dep. and Fla. Dep. Agric. Consum. Serv. U.S. Gov. Print. Off., Washington, D.C.

Stapor, F.W., Jr. (1975). Holocene beach ridge plain development, northwest Florida. *In* "Contributions to Coastal Geomorphology" (R.W. Fairbridge, ed.). *Z. Geomorphol. Suppl.* 22.

Stapor, F.W., Jr., and Matthews, T.D. (1980). C-14 chronology of Holocene barrier islands, Lee County, Florida. *In* "Shorelines Past and Present," Proceedings of the 5th Symposium on Coastal Sedimentology (W.F. Tanner, ed.), pp. 47–67. Geol. Dep., Florida State Univ., Tallahassee.

Stark, B.P., and Gaufin, A.R. (1979). The stoneflies (Plecoptera) of Florida. *Trans. Am. Entomol. Soc.* 104, 391–433.

Stearns, S.C., and Crandall, R.E. (1981). Bet-hedging and persistence as adaptations of colonizers. *In* "Evolution Today," Proceedings of the 2nd International Congress of Systematic and Evolutionary Biology (G.G.E. Scudder and J.L. Reveal, eds.), pp. 371–383.

Steinberg, B. (1980). Vegetation of the Atlantic coastal ridge of Broward County, Florida, USA based on 1940 imagery. *Fla. Sci.* 43, 7–12.

Stephens, G. (1962). Uptake of organic material by aquatic invertebrates. I. Uptake of glucose by the solitary coral *Fungia scutaria. Biol. Bull. (Woods Hole, Mass.)* 123, 648–659.

Stephens, J.C. (1984). Subsidence of organic soils in the Florida Everglades—a review and update. *In* "Environments of South Florida: Present and Past II" (P.J. Gleason, ed.), pp. 375–384. Miami Geol. Soc., Coral Gables, Florida.

Stephens, J.C., and Johnson, L. (1951). Subsidence of organic soils in the upper Everglades region of Florida. *Soil Sci. Soc. Fla. Proc.* 11, 191–237.

Stephens, J.C., Allen, L.H., Jr., and Chen, E. (1984). Organic soil subsidence. *Geol. Soc. Am. Rev. Eng. Geol.* IV, 107–122.

Sternberg, L., and Swart, P.K. (1987). Utilization of freshwater and ocean water by coastal plants of southern Florida. *Ecology* 68, 1898–1905.

Stetson, T., Squires, D., and Pratt, R. (1962). Coral banks occurring in deep water on the Blake Plateau. *Am. Mus. Novit.* No. 2114, pp. 1–39.

Stevenson, H.M. (1976). "Vertebrates of Florida." Univ. Presses of Florida, Gainesville.

Steward, K.K. (1974). Physiological, edaphic, and environmental characteristics of Everglades sawgrass communities. *In* "Environments of South Florida: Present and Past" (P.J. Gleason, ed.), Mem. No. 2, pp. 37–45. Miami Geol. Soc., Miami, Florida.

Steward, K.K., and Ornes, W.H. (1975). The autecology of sawgrass in the Florida Everglades. *Ecology* 56, 162–171.

Stewart, J.W. (1980). "Areas of Natural Recharge to the Floridan aquifer in Florida." Bur. of Geol. Map Ser. No. 98. U.S. Geol. Surv. in coop. with Florida Dep. Environ. Regul., Bur. Water Resour. Manage., Tallahassee.

Stoddard, H.L., Sr. (1931). "The Bobwhite Quail, Its Habits, Preservation and Increase." Scribner's, New York.

Stoddard, H.L., Sr. (1962). Use of fire in pine forests and game lands of the deep southeast. *Proc. Tall Timbers Fire Ecol. Conf.* 1, 31–42.

Stoddart, D.R. (1969). Post-hurricane changes on the British Honduras reefs and cays: re-survey of 1965. *Atoll Res. Bull.* No. 131.

Stoddart, D.R., and Fosberg, F.R. (1981). Topographic and floristic change, Dry Tortugas, Florida 1904–1977. *Atoll Res. Bull.* No. 253.

Stokes, F., and Stokes, C. (1980). "Handguide to the Coral Reef Fishes of the Caribbean and Adjacent Tropical Waters Including Florida, Bermuda, and the Bahamas." Lippincott and Crowell, New York.

Stone, E.L., ed. (1983). "The Managed Slash Pine Ecosystem." Proc. Symp., Sch. For. Resour. Conserv., Univ. of Florida, Gainesville.

Stone, P.A. (1978). Floating islands. Biogeomorphic features of Hillsboro Marsh, northeastern Everglades, Florida. M.A. Thesis, Florida Atlantic Univ., Boca Raton.

Stoner, A.W. (1980). The role of seagrass biomass in the organization of benthic macrofaunal assemblages. *Bull. Mar. Sci.* 30, 537–551.

Stout, I.J. (1979). "Terrestrial Community Analysis." Vol. 1 of Final Rep. to NASA J.F.K. Space Cent., Florida: "A Continuation of Baseline Studies for Environmental Monitoring of Space Transportation Systems at JFK Space Center." Contract No. NASA 10-8986.

Stout, J.P. (1984). The ecology of irregularly flooded salt marshes of the northeastern Gulf of Mexico: a community profile. *U.S. Fish Wildl. Sev. Biol. Rep.* No. 85(7.1).

Streng, D.R., and Harcombe, P.A. (1982). Why don't east Texas savannas grow up to forest? *Am. Midl. Nat.* 108, 278–294.

Streng, D.R., Glitzenstein, J.S., and Harcombe, P.A. (1989). Woody seedling dynamics in an east Texas floodplain forest. *Ecol. Monogr.* 59, 177–204.

Stringfield, V.T. (1966). Artesian water in Tertiary limestone in the southeastern states. *U.S. Geol. Surv. Prof. Pap.* No. 517.

Stubbs, J. (1983). Paraquat-induced lightwood in southern pine. *In* "The Managed Slash Pine Ecosystem" (E.L. Stone, ed.), Proc. Symp., pp. 385–393. Sch. For. Resour. Conserv., Univ. of Florida, Gainesville.

Stubbs, S.A. (1940). Solution a dominant factor in the geomorphology of peninsular Florida. *Q. J. Fla. Acad. Sci.* 5, 148–167.

Subrahmanyam, C.B., and Coultas, C.L. (1980). Studies on the animal communities in two north Florida salt marshes. Part III. Seasonal fluctuations of fish and macroinvertebrates. *Bull. Mar. Sci.* 30, 790–818.

Subrahmanyam, C.B., and Drake, S.H. (1975). Studies on the animal communities in two north Florida salt marshes. Part I. Fish communities. *Bull Mar. Sci.* 25, 445–465.

Subrahmanyam, C.B., Kruczynski, W.L., and Drake, S.H. (1976). Studies of the animal communities in two north Florida salt marshes. Part II. Macroinvertebrate communities. *Bull. Mar. Sci.* 26, 172–195.

Sugg, A.L., Pardue, L., and Carrodus, R.L. (1970). "Memorable Hurricanes of the United States since 1873." *U.S. Dep. Commer. NOAA Tech. Memo.* No. NWS SR-56. Fort Worth, Texas.

Sullivan, B., Faulkner, D., and Webb, L. (1983). Siphonodictidine: a metabolite of the burrowing sponge *Siphonodictyon* sp. that inhibits coral growth. *Science* 221, 1175–1176.

Sullivan, J.R. (1985). Systematics of the *Physalis viscosa* complex (Solanaceae). *Syst. Bot.* 10, 426–444.

Sullivan, M.J. (1978). Diatom community structure: taxonomic and statistical analysis of a Mississippi salt marsh. *J. Phycol.* 14, 468–478.

Sweet, H.C. (1976). "Final report of a study of a diverse coastal ecosystem of the Atlantic coast of Florida." Bot. Stud. Merritt Isl. NASA, Cape Canaveral, Florida.

Swift, C.C., Yerger, R.W., and Parrish, P.R. (1977). Distribution and natural history of the fresh and brackish water fishes of the Ochlockonee river, Florida and Georgia. *Tall Timbers Res. Stn. Bull.* No. 20.

Swift, C.C., Gilbert, C.R., Bortone, S.A., Burgess, G.H., and Yerger, R.W. (1986). Zoogeography of the freshwater fishes of the southeastern United States: Savannah River to Lake Pontchartrain. *In* "The Zoogeography of North American Freshwater Fishes" (C.H. Hocutt and E.O. Wiley, eds.), pp. 213–265. Wiley, New York.

Swift, D. (1981). Preliminary investigations of periphyton and water quality relationships in the Everglades Water Conservation Areas. *South Fla. Water Manage. Dist. Tech. Publ.* No. 81-5.

Swift, D.J.P. (1975). Barrier island genesis: evidence from the central Atlantic shelf, eastern USA. *Sediment. Geol.* 14, 1–43.

Swift, M.J., Heal, O.W., and Anderson, J.M. (1979). "Decomposition in Terrestrial Ecosystems." Univ. of California Press, Los Angeles.

Swihart, T., Hand, J., Barker, D., Bell, L., Carnes, J., Cooper, C., Deuerling, R., Hinkley, W., Leins, R., Livingston, E., and York, D. (1984). Water quality. *In* "Water Resources Atlas of Florida" (E.A. Fernald and D.J. Patton, eds.), pp. 68–91. Inst. Sci. Public Aff., Florida State Univ., Tallahassee.

Swindel, B.F., Conde, L.F., and Smith, J.E. (1982). Effects of forest regeneration practices on plant diversity and succession in Florida ecosystems. *Annu. Symp. Proc. Impacts Intensive For. Manage. Pract., 14th,* pp. 5–15. Sch. For. Resour. Conserv., Univ. of Florida, Gainesville.

Swindel, B.F., Marion, W.R., Harris, L.D., Morris, L.A., Pritchett, W.L., Conde, L.F., Riekerk, H., and Sullivan, E.T. (1983). Multi-resource effects of harvest site preparation and planting in pine flatwoods. *South. J. App. For.* 7, 6–15.

Swindell, D.E., Jr. (1949). Plant communities and other factors affecting the deer and turkey populations in Gulf Hammock. M.S. Thesis, Univ. of Florida, Gainesville.

Sykes, P.W., Jr. (1979). Status of the Everglades kite in Florida—1969–78. *Wilson Bull.* 91, 495–511.

Sykes, P.W., Jr. (1983a). Recent population trend of the snail kite in Florida and its relation to water levels. *J. Field Ornithol.* 54, 237–246.

Sykes, P.W., Jr. (1983b). Snail kite use of the freshwater marshes of south Florida. *Fla. Field Nat.* 11, 73–88.

Sykes, P.W., Jr. (1984). The range of the snail kite and its history in Florida. *Bull. Fla. State Mus. Biol. Sci.* 29, 211–264.

Szmant-Froelich, A. (1984). Reef coral reproduction: diversity and community patterns. *Adv. Reef Sci., Abstr. Pap. Jt. Meet. Atl. Reef Comm. Int. Soc. Reef Stud., Univ. Miami,* pp. 122–123.

Szmant-Froelich, A. (1985). The effect of colony size on the reproductive ability of the Caribbean coral *Monastraea annularis* (Ellis and Solander). *Proc. Int. Coral Reef Congr., 5th, Tahiti* 4, 295–300.

Tabb, D.C., Dubrow, D.L., and Manning, R.B. (1962). The ecology of northern Florida Bay and adjacent estuaries. *Fla. Board Conserv Tech. Ser.* 39, 1–81.

Tagatz, M.E. (1967). Fishes of the St. Johns River, Florida. *Q. J. Fla. Acad. Sci.* 30, 25–50.

Tai, C.C., and Rao, D.V. (1982). "Hydrologic Change Due to Floodplain Impoundment and Encroachment by Agricultural Activities." ASCE Irrig. Drain. Div., Spec. Conf. Environ. Sound Water Soil Manage., Orlando, Florida.

Tall Timbers Research Station (1962). Tall Timbers Research Station Fire Ecology Plots. *Tall Timbers Res. Stn. Bull.* No. 2.

Tanner, G.W., Terry, W.S., and Yarlet, L.L. (1982). "Vegetation Dynamics of Three Freshwater Marshes within the Kissimmee River Valley." Rep. to Coord. Counc. Restoration Kissimmee River Valley Taylor Creek–Nubbin Slough Basin.

Tanner, W.F. (1960a). Florida coastal classification. *Trans. Gulf Coast Assoc. Geol. Soc.* 10, 259–266.

Tanner, W.F. (1960b). Perched barrier islands, east Florida Coast. *Southeast. Geol.* 2, 133–135.

Tanner, W.F. (1961). Mainland beach changes due to Hurricane Donna. *J. Geophys. Res.* 66, 2265–2266.

Tanner, W.F. (1975). Historical beach changes: Florida's "Big Bend" coast. *Trans. Gulf Coast Assoc. Geol. Soc.* 25, 379–381.

Tanner, W.F., Evans, R.G., and Holmes, C.W. (1963). Low energy coast near Cape Romano, Florida. *J. Sediment Petrol.* 33, 713–722.

Tarver, D.P., Rodgers, J.A., Mahler, M.J., and Lazor, R.L. (1979). "Aquatic and Wetland Plants of Florida." Florida Dep. Nat. Resour., Tallahassee.

Taylor, A.R. (1974). Ecological aspects of lightning in forests. *Proc. Tall Timbers Fire Ecol. Conf.* 13, 455–482.

Taylor, D., ed. (1977). *Proc. Int. Coral Reef Symp, 3rd, Miami, Fla.* 1–2.

Taylor, D. (1983). The black band disease in Atlantic reef corals. II. Isolation, cultivation, and growth of *Phormidium corallyticum. Mar. Ecol.* 4, 321–328.

Taylor, D.L. (1980). Fire history and man-induced fire problems in subtropical South Florida. *Proc. Fire Hist. Workshop,* pp. 63–68, *U.S. For. Serv. Gen. Tech. Rep.* No. RM-81. Fort Collins, Colorado.

Taylor, D.L. (1981). Fire history and fire records for Everglades National Park, 1948-1979. *Everglades Natl. Park South Fla. Res. Cent. Rep.* No. T-619.

Taylor, D.L., and Rochefort, R. (1981). Fire in the Big Cypress National Preserve. *Fire Manage. Notes* Spring, pp. 15–18.

Taylor, J.L., and Saloman, C.H. (1968). Some effects of hydraulic dredging and coastal development in Boca Ciega Bay, Florida. *Fish. Bull.* 67, 213–241.

Teal, J.M. (1962). Energy flow in the salt marsh ecosystem of Georgia. *Ecology* 43, 614–624.

Teal, J.M., and Teal, M. (1969). "Life and Death of the Salt Marsh." Natl. Audubon Soc. and Ballantine Books, New York.

Teal, J.M., and Wieser, W. (1966). The distribution and ecology of nematodes in a Georgia salt marsh. *Limnol. Oceanogr.* 11, 217–222.

Teas, H. (1977). Ecology and restoration of mangrove shorelines in Florida. *Environ. Conserv.* 4, 51–57.

Teas, H. (1979). Silviculture with saline water. *In* "The Biosaline Concept" (A. Hollaender, ed.), pp. 117–161. Plenum, New York.

Teas, H, and Kelly, J. (1975). Effects of herbicides on mangroves of S. Vietnam and Florida. *Proc. Int. Symp. Biol. Manage. Mangroves* (G. Walsh, S. Snedaker, and H. Teas, eds.), pp. 719–728. Univ. of Florida, Gainesville.

Tebeau, C.W. (1971). "A History of Florida." Univ. of Miami Press, Coral Gables, Florida.

Tebeau, C.W. (1974). Exploration and early description of the Everglades, Lake Okeechobee and the Kissimmee River. *In* "Environments of South Florida: Present and Past" (P.J. Gleason, ed.), Mem. No. 2, pp. 1–7, Miami Geol. Soc., Miami, Florida.

Tebo, M. (1985). The Southeastern piney woods: describers, destroyers, survivors. M.A. Thesis, Florida State Univ., Tallahassee.

Tedford, R.H., and Hunter, M.E. (1984). Miocene marine-nonmarine correlations, Atlantic and Gulf Coastal Plains, North America. *Palaeogeogr. Palaeoclimatol. Palaeoecol.* 47, 129–151.

Teichert, C. (1958). Cold- and deep-water coral banks. *Am. Assoc. Pet. Geol. Bull.* 42, 1064–1082.

Terwilliger, V.J., and Ewel, K.C. (1986). Regeneration and growth after logging in Florida cypress domes. *For. Sci.* 32, 493–506.

Teskey, R.O., and Hinckley, T.M. (1977). "Impact of Water Level Changes on Woody Riparian and Wetland Communities." *U.S. Fish Wildl. Serv. Off. Biol. Serv. [Tech. Rep.]* FWS/OBS 77–58.

Tessman, N. (1969). Fossil sharks of Florida. M.S. Thesis, Univ. of Florida, Gainesville.

Thayer, G.W., Colby, D.C., and Hettler, W.F., Jr. (1987). Utilization of the red mangrove prop root habitat by fishes in South Florida. *Mar. Ecol. Prog. Ser.* 35, 25–38.

Thibodeau, F.R., and Nickerson, N.H. (1986). Differential oxidation of mangrove substrate by *Avicennia germinans* and *Rhizophora mangle. Am. J. Bot.* 73, 512–516.

Thom, B.G. (1967). Mangrove ecology and deltaic geomorphology: Tabasco, Mexico. *J. Ecol.* 55, 301–343.

Thom, B.G. (1975). Mangrove ecology from a geomorphic viewpoint. *Proc. Int. Symp. Biol. Manage. Mangroves* (G. Walsh, S. Snedaker, and H. Teas, eds.), pp. 469–481. Univ. of Florida, Gainesville.

Thom, B.G. (1982). Mangrove ecology—a geomorphological perspective. *In* "Mangrove Ecosystems in Australia" (B.F. Clough, ed.), pp. 3–17. Australian Natl. Univ. Press, Canberra.

Thomas, B.P., Law, L., and Stankey, D.L. (1979). "Soil Survey of Marion County Area, Florida." USDA Soil Conserv. Serv., Washington, D.C.

Thomas, J.L. (1961). The genera of the Cyrillaceae and Clethraceae of the southeastern United States. *J. Arnold Arbor.* 42, 96–106.

Thomas, J.P. (1966). Influence of the Altamaha River on primary production beyond the mouth of the river. M.S. Thesis, Univ. of Georgia, Athens.

Thomas, T.M. (1974). A detailed analysis of climatological and hydrological records of south Florida with reference to man's influence upon ecosystem evolution. *In* "Environments of South Florida: Present and Past" (P.J. Gleason, ed.), Mem. No. 2, pp. 82–122 . Miami Geol. Soc., Miami, Florida.

Thompson, F.G. (1984). "Freshwater Snails of Florida. A Manual for Identification." Univ. of Florida Press, Gainesville.

Thompson, S.K. (1980). Hammock vegetation in the northern Gulf hammock region of Florida. M.S. Thesis, Florida State Univ., Tallahassee.

Thor, E., and Nichols, G.M. (1974). Some effects of fires on litter, soil, and hardwood regeneration. *Proc. Tall Timbers Fire Ecol. Conf.* 13, 317–329.

Thorne, R.F. (1949). Inland plants on the Gulf coastal plain of Georgia. *Castanea* 14, 88–97.

Thorne, R.F. (1954). The vascular plants of southwestern Georgia. *Am. Midl. Nat.* 52, 257–327.

Tiedemann, J.A. (1983). Observations on the West Indian manatee, *Trichechus manatus,* in Turkey Creek, Brevard County, Florida. *Fla. Sci.* 46, 1–8.

Tilmant, J.T. (1975). Habitat utilization by round-tailed muskrats (*Neofiber alleni*) in Everglades National Park. M.S. Thesis, Humboldt State Univ., Arcata, California.

Tilmant, J.T. (1984). Reef fish. *In* "The Ecology of the South Florida Coral Reefs: a Community Profile," pp. 52–63. *U.S. Fish Wildl. Serv. Off. Biol. Serv. [Tech. Rep.]* FWS/OBS 82–08.

Tomlinson, P.B. (1979). Systematics and ecology of the Palmae. *Annu. Rev. Ecol. Syst.* 10, 85–107.

Tomlinson, P.B. (1980). "The Biology of Trees Native to Tropical Florida." Privately published. Printed by the Harvard University Printing Office.

Tomlinson, P.B. (1986). "The Botany of Mangroves." Cambridge Univ. Press, London.

Trewartha, G.T. (1981). "The Earth's Problem Climates." Univ. of Wisconsin Press, Madison.

Trimble, S.W. (1970). Alcovy River swamps: the result of culturally accelerated sedimentation. *Bull. Ga. Acad. Sci.* 28, 131–141.

Trimble, S.W. (1974). "Man-Induced Soil Erosion on the Southern Piedmont, 1700–1970." Soil Conserv. Soc. Am., Ankeny, Iowa.

Triska, F.J. (1984). Role of wood debris in modifying channel geomorphology and riparian areas of a large lowland river under pristine conditions: a historical case study. *Proc. Int. Assoc. Theor. Appl. Limnol.* 22, 1876–1892.

Trost, C.H. (1968). *Ammospiza nigrescens* (Ridgway), Dusky Seaside Sparrow. *In* "Life Histories of North American Cardinals, Grosbeaks, Buntings, Towhees, Finches, Sparrows, and Allies" (A.C. Bent, ed.), pp. 849–859. Dover, New York.

Turner, J.S., and Snelson, F.F., Jr. (1984). Population structure, reproduction and laboratory behavior of the introduced *Belonesox belizanus* (Poeciliidae) in Florida. *Environ. Biol. Fishes* 10, 89–100.

Turner, J.T., and Hopkins, T.L. (1985). The zooplankton of Tampa Bay: a review. *Proc. Symp. Tampa Bay Area Sci. Inf., 1982* (S.F. Treat, J.L. Simon, R.R. Lewis, III, and R.L. Whitman, Jr., eds.), pp. 328–344. Bellwether Press, Tampa, Florida.

Turner, R.E., and Gosselink, J.G. (1975). A note on standing crops of *Spartina alterniflora* in Texas and Florida. *Contrib. Mar. Sci.* 19, 113–118.

Tursch, B. (1982). Chemical protection of a reef fish *Abudefduf leucogaster* by a soft coral *Litophyton viridis*. *J. Chem. Ecol.* 8, 1421–1428.

Twilley, R.R. (1982). Litter dynamics and organic carbon exchange in black mangrove (*Avicennia germinans*) basin forests in a southwest Florida estuary. Ph.D. Thesis, Univ. of Florida, Gainesville.

Twilley, R.R. (1985). The exchange of organic carbon in basin mangrove forests in a southwest Florida estuary. *Estuarine Coastal Shelf Sci.* 20, 543–557.

Twilley, R.R., Lugo, A.E., and Patterson-Zucca, C. (1986). Litter production and turnover in basin mangrove forests in southwest Florida. *Ecology* 67, 670–683.

Tyndall, R.W. (1985). Role of seed burial, salt spray, and soil moisture deficit in plant distribution on the North Carolina Outer Banks. Ph.D. Thesis, Univ. of Maryland, College Park.

Ultsch, G.R. (1973). The effects of water hyacinths (*Eichhornia crassipes*) on the microenvironment of aquatic communities. *Arch. Hydrobiol.* 72, 460–473.

Uman, M.A. (1971). "Understanding Lightning." Bek Technical, Carnegie, Pennsylvania.

Unger, I., and Bolster, E. (1966). Artificial reefs—a review. *Am. Littoral Soc. Spec. Publ.* No. 4.

Upchurch, S.B., and Littlefield, J.R. (1987). Evaluation of data for sinkhole-development risk models. *In* "Karst Hydrogeology: Engineering and Environmental Applications" (B.F. Beck and W.L. Wilson, eds.), pp. 359–364. Balkema, Boston, Massachusetts.

U.S. Department of Commerce (1985). "National Estuarine Inventory Data Atlas, Rockville, MD." U.S. Dep. Comm. Gulf Mex. Coastal Ocean Zones Strategic Assess.: Data Atlas. Rockville, Maryland.

U.S. Fish and Wildlife Service (1958). "A Detailed Report of the Fish and Wildlife Resources in Relation to the Corps of Engineers' Plan of Development, Kissimmee River Basin, Florida." Prepared by Branch of River Basins, U.S. Fish Wildl. Serv., Atlanta. Georgia.

U.S. Fish and Wildlife Service (1984). "Draft Highlights of Reconnaissance Level Mapping and National Trend Analysis: Results for the State of Florida." Reg. Wetlands Coord., U.S. Fish Wildl. Serv., Atlanta, Georgia.

U.S. Fish and Wildlife Service (1985). "Florida Key Deer Recovery Plan." U.S. Fish Wildl. Serv., Atlanta, Georgia.

U.S. Fish and Wildlife Service (1986). "Key Tree-Cactus (*Cereus robinii*) Recovery Plan." U.S. Fish Wildl. Serv., Atlanta, Georgia.

U.S. Soil Conservation Service (1985). "26 Ecological Communities of Florida." USDA–Soil Conserv. Serv., Gainesville, Florida.

Van, T.K., Haller, W.T., Bowes, G., and Garrard, L.A. (1977). Effects of light quality on growth and chlorophyll composition in *Hydrilla. J. Aquat. Plant Manage.* 15, 29–31.

van Andel, T.H., and Poole, D.M. (1960). Sources of recent sediments in the northern Gulf of Mexico. *J. Sediment Petrol.* 30, 91–172.

Van Arman, J., and Goodrick, R. (1979). Effects of fire on a Kissimmee River marsh. *Fla. Sci.* 42, 183–195.

van der Valk, A.G. (1974). Environmental factors controlling distribution of forbs on coastal foredunes in Cape Hatteras National Seashore. *Can J. Bot.* 52, 1057–1073.

van der Valk, A.G. (1981). Succession in wetlands: a Gleasonian approach. *Ecology* 62, 688–696.

Van Dyke, J.M., Leslie, A.J., Jr., and Nall, L.E. (1984). The effects of the grass carp on the aquatic macrophytes of four Florida lakes. *J. Aquat. Plant Manage.* 22, 87–95.

Van Meter-Kasanof, N. (1973). Ecology of the microalgae of the Florida Everglades. Part I. Environment and some aspects of freshwater periphyton, 1959–1963. *Nova Hedwigia* 24, 619–664.

Van Montfrans, J. (1981). Decapod crustaceans associated with worm rock (*Phragmatopoma lapidosa* Kinberg) in southeastern Florida. M.S. Thesis, Florida Atlantic Univ., Boca Raton.

Vaughan, T.W. (1911). Recent Madreporaria of southern Florida. *Carnegie Inst. Wash. Year Book* 8, 135–144.

Vaughan, T.W. (1915). The geological significance of the growth-rate of the Floridian and Bahaman shoal-water corals. *J. Wash. Acad. Sci.* 5, 591–600.

Vaughan, T.W. (1916). Growth rate of the Florida and Bahamian shoal-water corals. *Carnegie Inst. Washington Year Book* 14, 221–231.

Vaughan, T.W. (1918). The temperature of the Florida coral reef tract. *Carnegie Inst. Wash. Publ.* No. 213, pp. 321–339.

Vaughan, T.W., and Wells, J.W. (1943). Revision of the suborders, families, and genera of the Scleractinia. *Geol. Soc. Am. Spec. Pap.* No. 44, pp. 1–363.

Veblen, T.T. (1985). Forest development in tree-fall gaps in the temperate rain forests of Chile. *Natl. Geogr. Res.* 1, 162–183.

Veblen, T.T., Ashton, D.H., and Schlegel, F.M. (1979). Tree regeneration strategies in a lowland *Nothofagus*-dominated forest in south-central Chile. *J. Biogeogr.* 6, 329–340.

Veblen, T.T., Schlegel, F.M., and Escobar, R.B. (1980). Structure and dynamics of old-growth *Nothofagus* forests in the Valdivian Andes, Chile. *J. Ecol.* 68, 1–31.

Veno, P.A. (1976). Successional relationships of five Florida plant communities. *Ecology* 57, 498–508.

Vernon, R.O., and Puri, H.S. (1964). "Geologic Map of Florida." *Div. Geol. Map Ser.* No. 18. U.S. Geol. Surv. in coop. with Florida Board of Conserv., Tallahassee.

Vicente, V. (1978). An ecological evaluation of the west Indian demosponge *Anthosigmella varians* (Hodromerida Spirastellidae). *Bull. Mar. Sci.* 28(4), 771–779.

Vignoles, C.B. (1823). "Observations upon the Floridas." E. Bliss & E. White, New York.

Vince, S.W., Humphrey, S.R., and Simons, R.W. (1989). The ecology of hydric hammocks: a community profile. *U.S. Fish Wildl. Serv. Biol. Rep.* No. 85 (7.26). Washington, D.C.

Visher, F.N., and ughes, G.H. (1975). "The Difference between Rainfall and Potential Evaporation in Florida." *Map Ser.* No. 32, 2nd Ed. Bur. Geol., Florida Dep. Nat. Resour., Tallahassee.

Vitousek, P.M. (1982). Nutrient cycling and nutrient use efficiency. *Am. Nat.* 119, 553–572.

Vitousek, P.M. (1984). Litter fall, nutrient cycling, and nutrient limitation in tropical forests. *Ecology* 65, 285–298.

Vittor, B.A., and Johnson, P.G. (1977). Polychaete abundance, diversity, and trophic role in coral reef communities at Grand Bahama Island and the Florida Middle Ground. *Proc. Int. Coral Symp., 3rd, Miami, Fla.* 1, 163–168.

Vogl, R.J. (1973a). Effects of fire on the plants and animals of a Florida wetland. *Am. Midl. Nat.* 89, 334–347.

Vogl, R.J. (1973b). Fire in the southeastern grasslands. *Proc. Tall Timbers Fire Ecol. Conf.* 12, 175–198.

Vollenweider, R.A. (1968). "Scientific Fundamentals of the Eutrophication of Lakes and Flowing Waters, with Particular Reference to Nitrogen and Phosphorus as Factors in Eutrophication." Rep. No. DAS/CSI/68.27, Organ. Econ. Co-Op. Dev., Paris.

Voss, G.L. (1976). "Seashore Life of Florida and the Caribbean." E.A. Seemann Publ. Co., Miami, Florida.

Voss, G.L. (1983). "An Environmental Assessment of the Key Largo National Marine Sanctuary." Rep. Mar. Sanctuary Program Off., Natl. Ocean. Atmos. Adm., Washington, D.C.

Voss, G.L. (1988). "Coral Reefs of Florida." Pineapple Press, Sarasota, Florida.

Wade, D.D. (1983). Fire management in the slash pine ecosystem. *In* "The Managed Slash Pine Ecosystem," Proc. Symp. (E.L. Stone, ed.), pp. 203–223. Sch. For. Resour. Conserv., Univ. of Florida, Gainesville.

Wade, D., Ewel, J., and Hofstetter, R. (1980). "Fire in South Florida Ecosystems." *U.S. For. Serv. Gen. Tech. Rep.* No. SE-17. Southeast For. Exp. Stn., Asheville, North Carolina.

Wagner, R.H. (1964). The ecology of *Uniola paniculata* L. in the dune-strand habitat of North Carolina. *Ecol. Monogr.* 34, 79–96.

Wahlenberg, W.G. (1946). "Longleaf Pine: Its Use, Ecology, Regeneration, Protection, Growth and Management." Charles Lathrop Pack For. Found., Washington, D.C.

Wahlenberg, W.G., Green, S.W., and Reed, H.R. (1939). Effects of fire and cattle grazing on longleaf pine land as studied at McNeil, Mississippi. *U.S. Dep. Agric. Tech. Bull.* No. 683.

Waisel, Y. (1972). "Biology of Halophytes." Academic Press, New York.

Walkinshaw, L. (1976). *Proc. Int. Crane Workshop, Int. Crane Found., Baraboo, Wis.* (J.C. Lewis, ed.), pp. 1–18. Oklahoma State Univ. Publ. Print. Dep., Stillwater.

Waller, B.G. (1975). Distribution of nitrogen and phosphorus in the conservation areas in south Florida from July 1972 to June 1973. *U.S. Geol. Surv. Water Resour. Invest.* No. 5–75.

Waller, B.G., and Earle, J.E. (1975). Chemical and biological quality of water in part of the Everglades, southeastern Florida. *U.S. Geol. Surv. Water Resour. Invest.* No. 56–75.

Walsh, G.E., Barrett, R., Cook, G.H., and Hollister, T.A. (1973). Effects of herbicides on seedlings of the red mangrove, *Rhizophora mangle* L. *BioScience* 23, 361–364.

Wamer, N.O. (1978). Avian diversity and habitat in Florida: analysis of a peninsular diversity gradient. M.S. Thesis, Florida State Univ., Tallahassee.

Wanless, H. (1974). Mangrove sedimentation in geological perspective. *In* "Environments of South Florida: Present and Past" (P.J. Gleason, ed.), Mem. No. 2, pp. 190–200. Miami Geol. Soc., Miami, Florida.

Wanless, H.R. (1989). The inundation of our coastlines: Past, present and future, with a focus on South Florida. *Sea Frontiers* 35, 264–271.

Ward, D.B. (1963a). Contributions to the flora of Florida. 2. *Pinus* (Pinaceae). *Castanea* 28, 1–10.

Ward, D.B. (1963b). Southeastern limit of *Chamaecyparis thyoides*. *Rhodora* 65, 359–363.

Ward, D.B. (1967). Southeastern limit of *Fagus grandifolia*. *Rhodora* 69, 51–54.

Ward, D.B. (1978). Keys to the flora of Florida 8. *Helianthus* (Compositae). *Phytologia* 41, 55–61.

Ward, D.B., ed. (1979). "Rare and Endangered Biota of Florida. Vol. 5: Plants." Univ. Presses of Florida, Gainesville.

Ware, G.H., and Penfound, W.T. (1949). The vegetation of the lower levels of the floodplain of the south Canadian River in central Oklahoma. *Ecology* 30, 478–484.

Ware, S., Frost, C.C., and Doerr, P. (1989). Southern mixed hardwood forest (the former longleaf pine forest). *In* "Biotic Communities of the Southeastern United States. Vol. 1. Terrestrial Communities" (W.H. Martin, ed.). Wiley, New York.

Watkins, C.E., II, Shireman, J.V., and Haller, W.T. (1983). The influence of aquatic vegetation upon zooplankton and benthic macroinvertebrates in Orange Lake, Florida. *J. Aquat. Plant Manage.* 21, 78–83.

Watson, J.D. (1928). Mangrove forests of the Malay peninsula. *Malay For. Rec.* 6, 1–275.

Watts, F.C., and Stankey, D.L. (1980). "Soil Survey of St. Lucie County Area, Florida." U.S. Dep. Agric. Soil Conserv. Serv., Washington, D.C.

Watts, W.A. (1969). A pollen diagram from Mud Lake, Marion County, north-central Florida. *Geol. Soc. Am. Bull.* 80, 631–642.

Watts, W.A. (1971). Postglacial and interglacial vegetation history of southern Georgia and central Florida. *Ecology* 52, 676–690.

Watts, W.A. (1975). A late Quaternary record of vegetation from Lake Annie, south-central Florida. *Geology* 3, 344–346.

Watts, W.A. (1980). The late Quaternary vegetation history of the southeastern United States. *Annu. Rev. Ecol. Syst.* 11, 387–409.

Watts, W.A. (1983). Vegetational history of the eastern United States 25,000 to 10,000 years ago. *In* "Late Quaternary Environments of the United States" (H.E. Wright, Jr., ed.), Vol. 1, pp. 294–310. Univ. Minnesota Press, Minneapolis.

Watts, W.A., and Hansen, B.C.S. (1988). Environments of Florida in the Late Wisconsin and Holocene. *In* "Wet Site Archaeology" (B.A. Purdy, ed.), pp. 307–323. The Telford Press, Caldwell, N.J.

Watts, W.A., and Stuiver, M. (1980). Late Wisconsin climate of northern Florida and the origin of species-rich deciduous forest. *Science* 210, 325–327.

Weaver, J.E. (1960). Flood plain vegetation of the central Missouri Valley and contacts of woodland with prairie. *Ecol. Monogr.* 30, 37–64.

Weaver, J.E., and Clements, F.E. (1938). "Plant Ecology." 2nd Ed. McGraw-Hill, New York.

Webb, K.L., DuPaul, W.D., Wiebe, W., Sottile, W., and Johannes, R.E. (1975).

Enewetak (Eniwetok) Atoll: aspects of the nitrogen cycle on a coral reef. *Limnol. Oceanogr.* 20, 198–210.

Webb, S.D. (1974). "Pleistocene Mammals of Florida." Univ. Presses of Florida, Gainesville.

Webb, S.D. (1981a). *Kyptoceras amatorum,* new genus and species from the Pliocene of Florida, the last protoceratid Artiodactyl. *J. Vertebr. Paleontol.* 1, 357–365.

Webb, S.D. (1981b). The Thomas Farm fossil vertebrate site. *Plaster Jacket* 37, 1–25.

Webb, S.D. (1984). Ten million years of mammal extinctions in North America. *In* "Quaternary Extinctions" (P. Martin and R. Klein, eds.), pp. 189–210. Univ. of Arizona Press, Tucson.

Webb, S.D. (1985). Late Cenozoic mammal dispersals between the Americas. *In* "The Great American Biotic Interchange" (F.G. Stehli and S.D. Webb, eds.), pp. 357–386. Plenum, New York.

Webb, S.D., and Crissinger, D. (1983). Stratigraphy and vertebrate paleontology of the central and southern phosphates districts of Florida. *Geol. Soc. Am., Southeast. Sect. Meet. Field Trip Guideb.,* pp. 28–72.

Webb, S.D., and Hulbert, R.C., Jr. (1986). Systematics and evolution of *Pseudhipparion* (Mammalia, Equidae) from the late Neogene of the Gulf Coastal Plain and the Great Plains. *Contrib. Geol. Univ. Wyo. Spec. Pap.* 3, 237–272.

Webb, S.D., and Tessman, N. (1968). A Pliocene vertebrate fauna from low elevation in Manatee County, Florida. *Am. J. Sci.* 266, 777–811.

Webb, S.D., and Wilkins, K.T. (1984). Historical biogeography of Florida Pleistocene mammals. *Spec. Publ. Carnegie Mus.* (H. Genoways and M. Dawson, eds.), Vol. 8, pp. 370–383.

Webb, S.D., MacFadden, B.J., and Baskin, J.A. (1981). Geology and paleontology of the Love Bone Bed from the late Miocene of Florida. *Am. J. Sci.* 281, 513–544.

Webb, S.D., Morgan, G.S., Hulbert, R.C., Jr., Jones, D.S., MacFadden, B.J., and Mueller, P.A. (1989). Geochronology of a rich early Pleistocene vertebrate fauna, Leisey Shell Pit, Tampa Bay, Florida. *Quaternary Res.* 32, 96–110.

Webb, T., III (1981). The past 11,000 years of vegetational change in eastern North America. *BioScience* 31, 501–506.

Webber, H.J. (1935). The Florida scrub, a fire-fighting association. *Am. J. Bot.* 22, 344–361.

Webber, T.A., and Post, W. (1983). Breeding seaside sparrows in captivity. *In* "The Seaside Sparrow, Its Biology and Management," Proc. Symp., Raleigh, N.C., 1981 (T.L. Quay, J.B. Funderburg, Jr., D.S. Lee, E.F. Potter, and C.S. Robbins, eds.), Occas. Pap. N.C. Biol. Surv. 1983–1985, pp. 153–162. North Carolina State Mus. Nat. Hist., Raleigh.

Webster, G.L. (1970). A revision of *Phyllanthus* (Euphorbiaceae) in the continental United States. *Brittonia* 22, 44–76.

Weiner, A.H. (1979). "The Hardwood Hammocks of the Florida Keys: An Ecological Study." Natl. Audubon Soc. and Florida Keys Land Trust.

Weiss, M.P., and Goddard, D.A. (1977). Man's impact on coastal reefs—an example from Venezuela. *Am. Assoc. Pet. Geol. Stud. Geol.* 4, 111–124.

Wellington, G. (1980). Reversal of digestive interactions between Pacific reef corals—mediation by sweeper tentacles. *Oecologia* 47, 340–343.

Wells, B.W. (1928). Plant communities of the coastal plain of North Carolina and their successional relations. *Ecology* 9, 230–242.

Wells, B.W. (1932). "The Natural Gardens of North Carolina." Univ. of North Carolina Press, Chapel Hill.

Wells, B.W. (1939). A new forest climax: the salt spray climax of Smith Island, North Carolina. *Bull. Torrey Bot. Club* 66, 629–634.

Wells, B.W. (1942). Ecological problems of the southeastern United States coastal plain. *Bot. Rev.* 8, 533–561.

Wells, B.W., and Shunk, I.V. (1931). The vegetation and habitat factors of the coarser sands of the North Carolina coastal plain. *Ecol. Monogr.* 1, 465–520.

Wells, J.W. (1956). Scleractinia. *In* "Treatise on Invertebrate Paleontology" (R.C. Moore, ed.), pp. F328-F334. Geol. Soc. Am., Univ. of Kansas Press, Lawrence.

Wells, J.W. (1957). Coral reefs. *In* "Treatise on Marine Ecology and Paleoecology. Vol. 1: Ecology" (J.W. Hedgepeth, ed.). *Geol. Soc. Am. Mem.* 67, 609–631.

Wenger, M.A. (1956). Growth of hardwoods after clear-cutting loblolly pine. *Ecology* 37, 735–742.

Wennekens, M.P. (1959). Water mass properties of the Straits of Florida and related waters. *Bull. Mar. Sci. Gulf Caribb.* 9, 1–52.

Werner, E.E., Hall, D.J., and Werner, M.D. (1978). Littoral zone fish communities of two Florida lakes and a comparison with Michigan lakes. *Environ. Biol. Fishes* 3, 163–172.

Werner, H.W., and Woolfenden, G.E. (1983). The Cape Sable sparrow: its habitats, habits, and history. *In* "The Seaside Sparrow, Its Biology and Management" (T.L. Quay et al., eds.), Occas. Pap. N.C. Biol. Surv. 1983–1985, pp. 55–75. North Carolina State Mus. Nat. Hist., Raleigh.

Westcott, P.W. (1970). Ecology and behavior of the Florida scrub jay. Ph.D. Thesis, Univ. of Florida, Gainesville.

Wethey, D., and Porter, J. (1976). Sun and shade differences in productivity of reef corals. *Nature (London)* 262, 281–282.

Whale, C.M. (1980). Detection pursuit and overgrowth of tropical gorgonians by milleporid hydrocorals, Perseus and Medusa revisited. *Science* 209, 689–691.

Wharton, C.H. (1978). "The Natural Environments of Georgia." Georgia Dep. Nat. Resour., Athens.

Wharton, C.H., and Brinson, M.M. (1979). Characteristics of southeastern river systems. *In* "Strategies for Protection and Management of Floodplain Wetlands and Other Riparian Ecosystems." (R.R. Johnson and J.F. McCormick, tech. coords.). *U.S. For. Serv. Gen. Tech. Rep.* No. WO-12, pp. 32–40.

Wharton, C.H., Kitchens, W.M., Pendleton, E.C., and Sipe, T.W. (1982). "The ecology of bottomland hardwood swamps of the Southeast—a community profile." *U.S. Fish Wildl. Serv. Off. Biol. Serv. [Tech. Rep.]* FWS/OBS 81–37. Washington, D.C.

Wharton, C.H., Lambou, V.W., Newsom, J., Winger, P.V., Gaddy, L.L., and Mancke, R. (1981). The fauna of bottomland hardwoods. *In* "Wetlands of Bottomland Hardwood Forest" (J.R. Clark and J. Benforado, eds.), pp. 87–160. Elsevier, New York.

Wharton, C.H., Odum, H.T., Ewel, K., Duever, M., Lugo, A., Boyt, R., Bartholomew, J., DeBellevue, E., Brown, S., Brown, M., and Duever, L. (1977). "Forested Wetlands of Florida—Their Management and Use." Div. State Plann., Tallahassee, Florida.

Wheaton, J.L., and Jaap, W.C. (1988). Corals and other prominent benthic Cnidaria of Looe Key National Marine Sanctuary. *Fla. Mar. Res. Publ.* 43, 25.

Whelan, R.J. (1985). Patterns of recruitment to plant populations after fire in

Western Australia and Florida. *Proc. Ecol. Soc. Aust.* 14, 169–178.

Whelan, R.J. (1986). Seed dispersal in relation to fire. *In* "Seed Dispersal" (D.R. Murray, ed.), pp. 237–271. Academic Press, San Diego, California.

Whigham, D.F., O'Neill, J., and McWethy, M. (1982). Ecological implications of manipulating coastal wetlands for purposes of mosquito control. *In* "Wetlands Ecology and Management" (B. Gopal, R.E. Turner, R.G. Wetzel, and D.F. Whigham, eds.), pp. 459–476. Natl. Inst. Ecol. and Int. Sci. Publ., Jaipur, India.

White, D.A. (1987). An American beech–dominated original growth forest in southeast Louisiana. *Bull. Torrey Bot. Club* 114, 127–133.

White, D.L. (1983). A flora of Gold Head Branch Ravine Park. M.S. Thesis, Univ. of Florida, Gainesville.

White, D.L., and Judd, W.S. (1985). A flora of Gold Head Branch ravine and adjacent uplands, Clay County, Florida. *Castanea,* 50 250–261.

White, E.H., and Harvey, A.W. (1979). Modification of intensive management practices to protect forest nutrient cycles. *Proc. Impact Intensive Harvesting For. Nutr. Cycling Symp.,* Syracuse, N.Y., pp. 264–278.

White, L.D. (1975). Ecosystem analysis of Paynes Prairie. *Univ. Fla. Sch. For. Resour. Conserv. Res. Rep.* No. 24.

White, P.S. (1979). Pattern, process, and natural disturbance in vegetation. *Bot. Rev.* 45, 230–299.

White, W.A. (1970). The geomorphology of the Florida peninsula. *Fla. Dep. Nat. Resour. Geol. Bull.* No. 51.

Whitfield, W.K., Jr., and Beaumariage, D.S. (1977). Shellfish management in Apalachicola Bay: past, present, future. *Proc. Conf. Apalachicola Drain. Syst.* (R.J. Livingston and E.A. Joyce, eds.), Publ. No. 26, pp. 130–140. Florida Dep. Nat. Resour. Mar. Res. Lab., St. Petersburg.

Whitford, L.A. (1956). The communities of algae in the springs and spring streams of Florida. *Ecology* 37, 433–442.

Whitlow, T.H., and Harris, R.W. (1979). "Flood Tolerance in Plants: a State-of-the-Art Review." *Environ. Water Qual. Oper. Stud. Tech. Rep.* E-79-2, Dep. Environ. Hortic., Univ. of California, Davis.

Whitmore, T.C. (1975). "Tropical Rain Forests of the Far East." Oxford Univ. Press (Clarendon), London.

Whitmore, T.C. (1989). Canopy gaps and the two major groups of forest trees. *Ecology* 70, 536–538.

Whitmore, T.J. (1989). Florida diatom assemblages as indicators of trophic state and pH. *Limnol. Oceanogr.* 34, 882–895.

Whitmore, T.J., Brenner, M., Japy, K.E., Rood, B.E., and Dorsey, K.T. (1988). Meromixis in a small north Florida lake. *Annu. Meet. Am. Soc. Limnol. Oceanogr., Boulder, Colo.* Program abstr.

Whitney, M. (1898). The soils of Florida. *U.S. Dep. Agric. Div. Soils Bull.* No. 13, pp. 14–27.

Whittaker, R.H. (1953). A consideration of climax theory; the climax as a population and pattern. *Ecol. Monogr.* 23, 41–78.

Whittaker, R.H. (1975). "Communities and Ecosystems." Macmillan, New York.

Wiegert, R.G. (1979). Ecological processes characteristic of coastal *Spartina* marshes of the south-eastern U.S.A. *In* "Ecological Processes in Coastal Environments" (R.L. Jefferies and A.J. Davy, eds.), pp. 467–490. Blackwell, London.

Wiegert, R.G., and Evans, F.C. (1967). Investigations of secondary productivity in grasslands. *In* "Secondary Productivity of Terrestrial Ecosystems" (K. Petrusewicz, ed.), pp. 499–518. Pol. Acad. Sci., Cracow.

Wiegert, R.G., and Freeman, B.J. (1989). "Salt Marshes of the Southeastern Atlantic Coast: a Community Profile." U.S. Fish Wildl. Serv., *Office of Biol. Serv. Rep.* 85(7) Washington, D.C. In press.

Wiegert, R.G., Pomeroy, L.R., and Wiebe, W.J. (1981). Ecology of salt marshes: an introduction. *In* "The Ecology of a Salt Marsh" (L.R. Pomeroy and R.G. Wiegert, eds.), pp. 3–19. Springer-Verlag, New York.

Wiegert, R.G., Chalmers, A.G., and Randerson, P.F. (1982). Productivity gradients in salt marshes: the response of *Spartina alterniflora* to experimentally manipulated soil water movement. *Oikos* 41, 1–6.

Williams, J.L. (1827). "A View of West Florida." H.S. Tanner & J.L. Williams, Publ., Philadelphia, Pennsylvania.

Williams, J.L. (1837). "The Territory of Florida: or Sketches of the Topography, Civil and Natural History of the Country, the Climate, and the Indian Tribes from the First Discovery to the Present Time." Univ. of Florida, Gainesville, Florida. Facsimile ed., 1962.

Williams, L.E., Jr., and Phillips, R.W. (1972). North Florida sandhill crane populations. *Auk* 89, 541–548.

Williams, R.B. (1962). The ecology of diatom populations in a Georgia salt marsh. Ph.D. Thesis, Harvard Univ., Cambridge, Massachusetts.

Williams, V.P., Canfield, D.E., Jr., Hale, M.M., Johnson, W.E., Kautz, R.S., Krummrich, J.T., Langford, F.H., Langland, K., McKinney, S.P., Powell, D.M., and Shafland, P.L. (1985). Lake habitat and fishery resources of Florida. *In* "Florida Aquatic Habitat and Fishery Resources" (W. Seaman, Jr., ed.), pp. 43–119. Florida Chap. Am. Fish. Soc., Kissimmee.

Williamson, G.B., and Black, E.M. (1981). High temperature of forest fires under pines as a selective advantage over oaks. *Nature (London)* 293, 643–644.

Wilson, J. (1979). "Patch" development of the deep-water coral *Lophelia pertusa* (L) on Rockall Bank. *J. Mar. Biol. Assoc. U.K.* 59, 165–177.

Wilson, L.D., and Porras, L. (1983). "The Ecological Impact of Man on the South Florida Herpetofauna." *Spec. Publ.* No. 9. Mus. Nat. Hist., Univ. of Kansas, Lawrence.

Winchester, B.H. (1986). "Recommendations for the Protection of Ecological Resources on the Ringling-MacArthur Reserve." CH2M Hill Rep. to Cty. of Sarasota, Sarasota, Florida.

Winchester, B.H., Bays, J.S., Higman, J.C., and Knight, R.L. (1985). Physiography and vegetation zonation of shallow emergent marshes in southwestern Florida. *Wetlands* 5, 99–118.

Windhorn, S., and Langley, W. (1974). "Yesterday's Florida Keys." E.A. Seeman, Miami, Florida.

Winker, C.C., and Howard, J.D. (1977). Correlation of tectonically deformed shorelines on the southern Atlantic coastal plain. *Geology* 5, 124–127.

Winsberg, M.D. (1990). Florida Weather. Univ. of Central Florida Press, Orlando.

Wise, S.W., Jr., and van Hinte, J.E. (1987). Mesozoic-Cenozoic depositional environments revealed by deep sea drilling project leg 93 drilling on the continental rise off the eastern United States: cruise, summary. *In* "Initial Reports of the Deep Sea Drilling Project" (J.E. van Hinte, S.W. Wise, et al., eds.), Vol. XCII, pp. 1367–1423. U.S. Gov. Print. Off., Washington, D.C.

Wistendahl, W.A. (1958). The flood plain of the Raritan River, New Jersey. *Ecol. Monogr.* 28, 129–153.

Wolfe, J.A. (1985). Distribution of major vegetation types during the Tertiary. *In* "The Carbon Cycle and Atmospheric CO_2: Natural Variations Archean to Present" (E.T. Sundquist and W.S. Broecker, eds.), *Geophys. Monogr. Am. Geophys. Union* No. 32, pp. 357–375.

Wolfe, J.A. (1986). Tertiary floras and paleoclimates of the northern hemisphere. *Stud. Geol.* No. 15, pp. 182–196. Dep. Geol. Sci., Univ. of Tennessee.

Wolfe, S.H., Reidenauer, J.A., and Means, D.B (1988). An ecological characterization of the Florida Panhandle. *USFWS Biol. Rep.* 88(12): Minerals Management Serv. OCS Study/MMS 88-0063.

Wood, D.A., comp. (1986). "Official Lists of Endangered and Potentially Endangered Fauna and Flora in Florida (2 September 1986)." Florida Game Fresh Water Fish. Comm., Tallahassee.

Wood, E.J.F. (1965). "Marine Microbial Ecology." Reinhold, New York.

Wood, G.W., ed. (1981). "Prescribed Fire and Wildlife in Southern Forests." Belle W. Baruch For. Sci. Inst., Clemson Univ., Georgetown, South Carolina.

Woodall, S.L., and Geary, T.F. (1985). Identity of Florida *Casuarinas. U.S. For. Serv. Southeast. For. Exp. Stn. Res. Note* No. SE-332.

Woodburne, M.O., ed. (1987). "Cenozoic Mammals of North America: Geochronology and Biostratigraphy." Univ. of California Press, Berkeley.

Woods, C.A., Post, W., and Kilpatrick, C.W. (1982). *Microtus pennsylvanicus* (Rodentia: Muridae) in Florida: a Pleistocene relict in a coastal salt marsh. *Bull. Fla. State Mus. Biol. Sci.* 28, 25–52.

Woods, F.W. (1955). Control of woody weeds: some physiological aspects. *U.S. For. Serv. Occas. Pap.* No. SO-143.

Woods, F.W. (1959). Converting scrub oak sandhills to pine forests in Florida. *J. For.* 57, 117–119.

Woods, K.D. (1979). Reciprocal replacement and the maintenance of co-dominance in a beech-maple forest. *Oikos* 33, 31–39.

Woods, K.D. (1984). Patterns of tree replacement: canopy effects on understory pattern in hemlock-northern hardwood forests. *Vegetatio* 56, 87–107.

Woolfenden, G.E., and Fitzpatrick, J.W. (1984). "The Florida Scrub Jay: Demography of a Cooperative-Breeding Bird." *Monogr. Popul. Biol.* No. 20. Princeton Univ. Press, Princeton, New Jersey.

Worth, D. (1983). Preliminary environmental responses to marsh dewatering and reduction in water regulation schedule in Water Conservation Area-2A. *South Fla. Water Manage. Dist. Tech. Publ.* No. 83-6.

Wright, H.E., Jr. (1981). The role of fire in land/water interactions. *In* "Fire Regimes and Ecosystem Properties" (H.A. Mooney, T.M. Bonnickson, N.L. Christensen, J.E. Lotan, and W.A. Reiners, eds.). *U.S. For. Serv. Gen. Tech. Rep.* WO-26, pp. 421–444. Washington, D.C.

Wulff, J. (1984). Sponge-mediated coral reef growth and rejuvenation. *Coral Reefs* 3, 157–163.

Wulff, J., and Buss, L. (1979). Do sponges hold coral reefs together? *Nature (London)* 281, 474–475.

Wunderlin, R.P. (1982). "Guide to the Vascular Plants of Central Florida." Univ. Presses of Florida, Gainesville.

Wyngaard, G.A., Elmore, J.L., and Cowell, B.C. (1982). Dynamics of a subtropical plankton community with emphasis on the copepod *Mesocyclops edax. Hydrobiologia* 89, 39–48.

Yerger, R.W. (1977). Fishes of the Apalachicola River. *Proc. Conf. Apalachicola Drain. Syst., Gainesville, Fla, 1976* (R.J. Livingston and E.A. Joyce, Jr., eds.). Mar. Res. Publ. No. 26, pp. 22–33. Florida Dep. Nat. Resour., Tallahassee.

Yonge, C.M. (1930). Studies on the physiology of corals. I. Feeding mechanisms and food. *Sci. Rep. Great Barrier Reef Exped.* 1, 13–57.

Yonge, C.M. (1963). The biology of coral reefs. *Adv. Mar. Biol.* 1, 209–260.

Young, D.L. (1974). Studies of Florida gulf coast salt marshes receiving thermal discharges. *In* "Thermal Ecology," Proc. Symp., Augusta, Ga., 1973 (J.W. Gibbons and R.R. Sharitz, eds.), pp. 532–550. Tech. Inf. Cent., Off. Inf. Serv., U.S. At. Energy Comm., Oak Ridge, Tennessee.

Young, F.N. (1951). Vanishing and extinct colonies of tree snails, *Liguus fasciatus,* in the vicinity of Miami, Florida. *Univ. Mich. Mus. Zool. Occas. Pap.* No. 531.

Young, F.N. (1954). The water beetles of Florida. *Univ. Fla. Stud. Biol. Sci. Serv.* V, 1–238.

Young, H. (1818). A topographical memoir on east and west Florida with itineraries of General Jackson's army. Reprinted in *Fla. Hist. Soc. Q.* 8, 16–50, 82–104, 129–164 (1934).

Youngbluth, M.J. (1976). Plankton in the Indian River Lagoon. *In* "Indian River Coastal Zone Study," Annu. Rep. 1975–1976, Vol. 1, pp. 40–60. Harbor Branch Found., Fort Pierce, Florida.

Zale, A.V., Montague, C.L., and Percival, H.F. (1987). A synthesis of potential effects of coastal impoundments on the production of estuarine fish and shellfish and some management options. *Waterfowl Wetlands Symp.: Proc. Symp. Waterfowl Wetlands Manage. Coastal Zone Atl. Flyway* (W.R. Whitman and W.H. Meredith, eds.), pp. 424–436. Del. Coastal Manage. Program, Delaware Dep. Nat. Resour. Environ. Control, Dover.

Zeiller, W. (1974). "Tropical Marine Invertebrates of Southern Florida and the Bahama Islands." Wiley, New York.

Zieman, J.C. (1970). The effects of a thermal effluent stress on the seagrasses and macroalgae in the vicinity of Turkey Point, Biscayne Bay, Florida. Ph.D. Thesis, Univ. of Miami, Coral Gables, Florida.

Zieman, J.C. (1972). Origin of circular beds of *Thalassia* (Spermatophyta: Hydrocharitaceae) in South Biscayne Bay, Florida, and their relationship to mangrove hammocks. *Bull. Mar. Sci.* 22, 559–574.

Zieman, J.C. (1982). "The Ecology of the Seagrasses of South Florida: a Community Profile." *U.S. Fish Wildl. Serv. Off. Biol. Serv. [Tech. Rep.] FWS/OBS* 82-25.

Zieman, J.C., and Wetzel, R.G. (1980). Methods and rates of productivity in seagrasses. *In* "Handbook of Seagrass Biology" (R.C. Phillips and C.P. McRoy, eds.), pp. 87–116. Garland STMP Press, New York.

Zieman, J.C., Jr., Macko, S.A., and Mills, A.L. (1984). Role of seagrasses and mangroves in estuarine food webs: temporal and spatial changes in stable isotope composition and amino acid content during decomposition. *Bull Mar. Sci.* 35, 380–392.

Zimmerman, M.S., and Livingston, R.J. (1976a). The effects of kraft mill effluents on benthic macrophyte assemblages in a shallow bay system (Apalachee Bay, North Florida, USA). *Mar. Biol. (Berlin)* 34, 297–312.

Zimmerman, M.S., and Livingston, R.J. (1976b). Seasonality and physico-chemical ranges of benthic macrophytes from a north Florida estuary (Apalachee Bay). *Contrib. Mar. Sci. Univ. Tex.* 20, 34–45.

Zimmerman, M.S., and Livingston, R.J. (1979). Dominance and distribution of benthic macrophyte assemblages in a north Florida estuary (Apalachee Bay, Florida). *Bull. Mar. Sci.* 29, 27–40.

Zlatarski, V., and Estalella, N. (1982). "Les Scleractiniaires de Cuba avec des données sur les organismes associés." Acad. Bulg. Sci., Sofia.

Zona, S., and Judd, W.S. (1986). *Sabal etonia* (Palmae): systematics, ecology, and comparisons to other Florida scrub endemics. *Sida* 11, 417–427.

Zuberer, D.A., and Silver, W.S. (1978). Biological nitrogen fixation (acetylene reduction) associated with Florida mangroves. *Appl. Environ. Microbiol.* 35, 567–575.

General Index

Note: numbers in boldface type denote illustration.

Index of Common Names

Index of Scientific Names

CPSIA information can be obtained
at www.ICGtesting.com
Printed in the USA
BVHW070218100522
636497BV00001B/4

9 780813 010229